M.L. Jhingan is an alumnus of the University of Delhi who after his M.A., worked as Research Assistant on a project of Dr.V.K.R.V. Rao, the then Director, Delhi School of Economics. Dr. Jhingan taught economics to postgraduate classes for over three decades and had been contributing to academic journals.

He is the author and co-author of a number of widely acclaimed textbooks on Economics and Management that sell in India and abroad. His books combine theoretical rigour and lucid exposition of the various concepts and theories of economics.

His most popular and the best selling text, The Economics of Development and Planning, was published 50 years ago in 1966 . Dr.Jhingan also guided Ph.Ds in India and abroad. Prof. Jhingan was Head of Economics Department and Principal, Government Post Graduate Evening College, Bhiwani and retired as Deputy Director, Higher Education, Haryana.

MONETARY ECONOMICS

7th

Revised and Enlarged Edition

M.L. JHINGAN

Retired Deputy Director,
Higher Education, Haryana

Simply the text !

VRINDA PUBLICATIONS (P) LTD.

VRINDA PUBLICATIONS (P) LTD.
B-5, Ashish Complex (opp. Ahlcon Public School),
Mayur Vihar, Phase-I, Delhi-110 091
Tel. : 22755315, 22755316
E-mail—info@vrindaindia.com
http://www.vrindaindia.com

First Edition : 1986 / Reprinted Ten Times
Fourth Revised Edition : 1997/Reprinted Three Times
Fifth Revised & Enlarged Edition : 2001/Reprinted Two Times
Sixth Edition : 2004/Reprinted Six Time
Seventh Edition : 2011/Reprinted Six Time
Reprint: 2025

e Textbook Available

ISBN 978-81-8281-383-0
(MONETARY ECONOMICS : 7TH EDITION)

Typeset by : Kumud Printographics, Delhi
Printed at : Nisha Enterprises,

Preface to the Seventh Edition

The present edition has been substantially revised, rearranged, and presented in a new format. Almost every chapter contains some significant alterations and additions. However, the following chapters have been rewritten :

- Assignment of Policy Instruments to Targets
- Crowding Out Effect and Availability Doctrine
- Business Cycles
- Balance of Payments
- International Liquidity
- European Monetary System and Euro

I hope the present edition will be more useful for Hons. and M.A. students, and those preparing for competitive examinations.

Suggestions for its improvement are welcome.

M.L. JHINGAN

E-mail : vrinda@ndf.vsnl.net.in

Preface to the Seventh Edition

The present edition has been substantially revised, rearranged, and presented in a new format. Almost every chapter contains some significant alterations and additions. However, the following chapters have been rewritten :

- Assignment of Policy Instruments to Targets
- Crowding Out Effect and Availability Doctrine
- Business Cycles
- Balance of Payments
- International Liquidity
- European Monetary System and Euro

I hope the present edition will be more useful for Hons. and M.A. students, and those preparing for competitive examinations.

Suggestions for its improvement are welcome.

M.L. JHINGAN
B.K. JHINGAN

Contents

CHAPTER 1

Evolution and Functions of Money

1. THE BARTER SYSTEM

Before the evolution of money, exchange was done on the basis of direct exchange of goods and services. This is known as barter. Barter involves the *direct exchange of one good for some quantity of another good.* For example, a horse may be exchanged for a cow, or 3 sheep or 4 goats. For a transaction to take place, there must be a *double coincidence of wants.* For instance, if the horse-owner wants a cow, he has to find out a person who not only possesses the cow but wants to exchange it with the horse. In other cases, goods are exchanged for services. A doctor may be paid in kind as payment for his services. For example, he may be paid a cock, or some wheat or rice or fruit. Thus a barter economy is a *moneyless economy.* It is also a *simple economy* where people produce goods either for self-consumption or for exchange with other goods which they want. Bartering was found in *primitive societies.* But it is still practised at places where the use of money has not spread much. Such non-monetised areas are to be found in many rural areas of under-developed countries.

DIFFICULTIES OF BARTER

But the barter system is the most inconvenient method of exchange. It involves loss of much time and effort on the part of people in trying to exchange goods and services. As a method of exchange, the barter system has the following difficulties and disadvantages :

1. *Lack of Double Coincidence of Wants.* The functioning of the barter system requires a double coincidence of wants on the part of those who want to exchange goods or services. It is necessary for a person who wishes to trade his good or service to find some other person who is not only willing to buy his good or service, but also possesses that good which the former wants. For example, suppose a person possesses a horse and wants to exchange it for a cow. In the barter system he has to find out a person who not only possesses a cow but also wants a horse. The existence of such a double coincidence of wants is a remote probability. For, it is a very *laborious and time-consuming* process to find out person who want each other's goods. Often the horse-owner would have to carry through a number of intermediary transactions. He might have to trade his horse for some sheep, sheep for some goats and goats for the cow he wants. To be successful, the barter system involves *multilateral* transactions which are not possible practically. Consequently, if the double coincidence of wants is not matched exactly, no trade is possible under barter. Thus a barter system is time-consuming and is a great hindrance to the development and expansion of trade.

2. *Lack of a Common Measure of Value.* Another difficulty under the barter system relates to the lack of a common unit in which the value of goods and services should be measured. Even if the two persons who want each other's goods meet by coincidence, the problem arises as to the proportion in which the two goods should be exchanged. There being no common measure of value, the rate of exchange will be arbitrarily fixed according to the intensity of demand for each other's goods. Consequently, one party is at a disadvantage in

the terms of trade[1] between the two goods.

Moreover, under the a barter system the value of each good is required to be stated in as many quantities as there are types and qualities of other goods and services. The exchange rate formula given by Prof. Culbertson[2] is $n(n-1)/2$. For example, if there are 100 different types of goods in a barter economy, then there would be 4950 exchange rates for it to function smoothly, i.e. 100(100-1)/2=100x99/2 or 9900/2=4950. This makes accounting an impossibility because a balance sheet would consist of a long physical inventory of the various types and qualities of goods owned and owed. Similarly, it is difficult to draw and interpret the profit and loss accounts of even a small shop. That is why the existence of the barter system is associated with a small primitive society confined to a local market.

3. *Indivisibility of Certain Goods.* The barter system is based on the exchange of goods with other goods. It is difficult to fix exchange rates for certain goods which are indivisible. Such indivisible goods pose a real problem, under barter. A person may desire a horse and the other a sheep and both may be willing to trade. The former may demand more than four sheep for a horse but the other is not prepared to give five sheep and thus there is no exchange. If a sheep had been divisible, a payment of four and a half sheep for a horse might have been mutually satisfactory. Similarly, if the man with the horse wants only two sheep, then how will he exchange his horse for two sheep. As it is not possible to divide his horse, no trade will be possible between the two persons. Thus indivisibility of certain goods makes the barter system inoperative.

4. *Difficulty in Storing Value.* Under the barter system it is difficult to store value. Anyone wanting to save real capital over a long period would be faced with the difficulty that during the intervening period the stored commodity may become obsolete or deteriorate in value. As people trade in cattle, grains, and other such perishable commodities, it is very expensive and often difficult to store and to prevent their deterioration and loss over the long period.

5. *Difficulty in Making Deferred Payments.* In a barter economy, it is difficult to make payments in future. As payments are made in goods and services, debt contracts are not possible due to disagreements on the part of the two parties on the following grounds: "[1]. It would often invite controversy as to the quality of the goods or services to be repaid. [2]. The two parties would often be unable to agree on the specific commodity to be used for repayment. [3]. Both parties would run the risk that the commodity to be repaid would increase or decrease seriously in value over the duration of the contract. For example, wheat might rise markedly in value in terms of other commodities, to the debtor's regret, or decrease markedly in value, to the creditor's regret."[3] Thus it is not possible to make just payments involving future contracts under the barter system.

6. *Lack of Specialisation.* Another difficulty of the barter system is that it is associated with a production system where each person is a jack-of-all trades. In other words, a high degree of specialisation is difficult to achieve under the barter system. Specialisation and interdependence in production is only possible in an expanded market system based on the money economy. Thus no economic progress is possible in a barter economy due to lack of specialisation.

The abovementioned difficulties of barter have led to the evolution of money.

2. THE EVOLUTION OF MONEY

The word "money" is derived from the Latin word "Moneta" which was the surname of the Roman Goddess of Juno in whose temple at Rome, money was coined. The origin of money is lost in antiquity. Even the primitive man had some sort of money. The type of money in every age depended on the nature of its livelihood. In a hunting society, the skins of wild animals were used as money. The pastoral society used livestock, whereas the agricultural society used grains and foodstuffs as money. The Greeks used coins as money.

---

1. The terms of trade refer to the rate at which one good exchange for another good,
2. John M. Culbertson, *Money and Banking,* 1972.
3. L.V. Chandler and S.M. Goldfield, *The Economics of Money and Banking,* 7/e, 1977.

STAGES IN THE EVOLUTION OF MONEY

The evolution of money has passed through the following five stages depending upon the progress of human civilisation at different times and places.

1. *Commodity Money.* Various types of commodities have been used as money from the beginning of human civilisation. Stones, spears, skins, bows and arrows, and axe's were used as money in the hunting society. The pastoral society used cattle as money. The agricultural society used grains as money. The Romans used cattle and salt as money at different times. The Mongolians used squirrel skins as money. Precious stones, tobacco, tea, shells, fishhooks, and many other commodities served as money depending upon time, place and economic standard of the society.

The use of commodities as money had the following defects: (1) All commodities were not uniform in quality, such as cattle, grains, etc. Thus lack of standardisation made pricing difficult. (2) Difficult to store and prevent loss of value in the case of perishable commodities. (3) Supplies of such commodities were uncertain. (4) They lacked in portability and hence were difficult to transfer from one place to another. (5) There was the problem of indivisibility in the case of such commodities as cattle.

2. *Metallic Money.* With the spread of civilisation and trade relations by land and sea, metallic money took the place of commodity money. Many nations started using silver, gold, copper, tin, etc. as money.

But metal was an inconvenient thing to accept, weigh, divide and assess in quality. Accordingly, metal was made into coins of predetermined weight. This innovation is attributed to King Midas of Lydia in the eighth century B.C. But gold coins were in use in India many centuries earlier than in Lydia. Thus coins came to be accepted as convenient method of exchange.

But some ingenious persons started debasing the coins by clipping a thin slice off the edge of coins. This led to the hoarding of full-bodied coins with the result that debased coins were found in circulation. This led to the minting of coins with a rough edge.

As the price of gold began to rise, gold coins were melted in order to earn more by selling them as metal. This led the governments to mix copper or silver in gold coins so that their intrinsic value might be more than their face value. As gold became dearer and scarce, silver coins were used, first in their pure form and lateron mixed with alloy or some other metal.

But metallic money had the following *defects:* (1) It was not possible to change its supply according to the requirements of the nation both for internal and external use. (2) Being heavy, it was not possible to carry large sums of money in the form of coins from one place to another by merchants. (3) It was unsafe and inconvenient to carry precious metals for trade purposes over long distances. (4) Metallic money was very expensive because the use of coins led to their debasement and their minting and exchange at the mint cost a lot to the government.

3. *Paper Money.* The development of paper money started with goldsmiths who kept strong safes to store their gold. As goldsmiths were thought to be honest merchants, people started keeping their gold with them for safe custody. In return, the goldsmiths gave the depositors a receipt promising to return the gold on demand. These receipts of the goldsmiths were given to the sellers of commodities by the buyers. Thus the receipts of the goldsmiths were a substitute for money. Such paper money was backed by gold and was convertible on demand into gold. This ultimately led to the development of bank notes.

The bank notes are issued by the central bank of the country. As the demand for gold and silver increased with the rise in their prices, the convertibility of bank notes into gold and silver was gradually given up during the beginning and after the First World War in all the countries of the world. Since then the bank money has ceased to be representative money and is simply fiat money which is inconvertible and is accepted as money because it is backed by law.

4. *Credit Money.* Another stage in the evolution of money in the modern world is the use of the cheque as money. The cheque is like a bank note in that it performs the same function. It is a means of transferring money or obligations from one person to another. But a cheque is different from a bank note. A cheque is made for a specific sum, and it expires with a single transaction. But a cheque is not money. It is simply a written order to transfer money. However, large transactions are made through cheques these days and bank notes are used only for small transactions.

5. *Near Money.* The final stage in the evolution of money has been the use of bills of exchange, treasury bills, bonds, debentures, savings certificates, etc. They are known as "near money". They are close substitutes for money and are liquid assets. Thus in the final stage of its evolution money has become intangible. Its ownership is now transferable simply by book entry.

Thus the origin of money has been through various stages: from commodity money to metallic money, and to paper money, and from credit money to near money.

3. CLASSIFICATION OF MONEY

Money can be classified on the following different basis: (1) the physical characteristics of the materials of which money is made; or the monetary system criterion, and (2) the nature of the issuer such as a government, central bank, commercial bank, or other, or the acceptability criterion, and (3) the relationship between the value of money as money and the value of money as commodity or what Keynes called Money of Account and Money Proper. We shall follow this classification while explaining the various *kinds of money.*

1. Monetary System Criterion

The monetary system criterion classifies money into : (1) metallic money, (2) paper money, and (3) credit money which we discuss below:

(1) Metallic Money

Money made of any metal such as gold, silver, nickel, copper, etc. is called metallic money. Metallic money is further classified into standard money, token money and subsidiary money.

(i) Standard Money. Standard money "is money whose value as a commodity for non-monetary purposes is as great as its value as money." Such money is made of coins whose face value equals their intrinsic or metallic value. The holder of such coins may use them as metal by melting them or as money, because the value of the metal in the coins is the same as their monetary value. Standard money is, therefore, known *as full-bodied money.* Between 1835-93 the Indian Rupee-coin made of silver was a full-bodied coin. Further, standard money is unlimited legal tender in which any amount of payment can be made.

(ii) Token Money. Token money is representative money whose intrinsic value of the metal is less than its face value. The rupee coin in circulation in India is a token coin. If it is melted, its metal will not be sold worth one rupee.

(iii) Subsidiary Money. Subsidiary money is to assist the token money. All coins of the denominations from 5 paise to 25 paise in India are subsidiary money. Such coins are limited legal tender in which payments can be made only up to Rs. 25 in India.

(2) Paper Money

Paper money refers to notes of different denominations made of paper and issued by the central bank and/or the government of the country. Paper money can be classified into (i) representative paper money, (ii) convertible paper money, (iii) inconvertible paper money and (iv) fiat money.

(i) Representative Paper Money. Representative paper money is "in effect a circulating warehouse receipt for full-bodied coins or their equivalent in bullion." It is also known as representative full-bodied money because it is fully backed by gold coins or gold bullion held by the treasury. They are fully convertible into gold coins or bullion. The gold certificates which circulated in the United States prior to 1933 were representative paper money.

(ii) Convertible Paper Money. Convertible paper money is that which does not have 100 per cent backing in the form of standard coins or bullion. But the holder of paper money can get it converted into bullion or coins on demand. The only difference between representative and convertible paper money is that the former is fully backed by standard coins or bullion while the latter is not fully backed by them. But both types of paper money are convertible.

(iii) Inconvertible Paper Money. The paper money which does not have any backing of standard coins or

bullion and is also not convertible into them is known as inconvertible paper money. Notes issued by central banks of all countries represent inconvertible paper money. They are also known as fiduciary money.

(iv) Fiat Money. Paper money which circulates on the authority (i.e. fiat) of the government is fiat money. Fiat money is created and issued by the State. But it is not convertible by law and is legal tender. Fiat money is thus representative or token money. One rupee note issued by the Ministry of Finance and token coins issued by the Government of India are fiat money. Practically, there is no difference between fiat money and inconvertible paper money these days.

(3) Credit Money

Credit money or bank money is transferred by a commercial bank in the form of a cheque or draft. But a cheque or draft is not money. Demand deposits in a bank is money which is withdrawable by a holder of the deposit through a cheque or draft. Thus it is demand deposit which is credit or bank money that is transferable from one person to another through a cheque or draft. But a cheque or draft is not legal tender and may not be accepted as a means of payment or medium of exchange. However, in advanced countries bank money is as important as the paper notes issued by the government or the central bank of the country.

2. Acceptability Criterion

On the basis of acceptability criterion, money is classified into legal tender money and non-legal tender money.

(1) *Legal Tender Money.* Legal tender money is that which the state and the people accept as the means of payment and in discharge of debts. Since it has the authority of the government such money is accepted compulsorily by the people. All notes and coins issued by the government and the central bank of a country are compulsory legal tender in that country. Legal tender money is further divided into limited and unlimited legal tender money.

(i) Limited Legal Tender Money. Limited legal tender money is that in which payments can be made legally upto a certain limit. All coins of the denominations of 5 paise to 25 paise are limited legal tender in India. Payments in them can be made up to a limit of Rs. 25.

(ii) Unlimited Legal Tender Money. A money is unlimited legal tender when payments can be made in it legally in unlimited quantities. All paper notes and coins of 50 paise and 1 Rupee are unlimited legal tender in India. People have to accept payments in unlimited quantities in notes and these coins.

(2) *Non-Legal Tender or Optional Money.* Money which does not possess any legal authority of the state or the central bank is non-legal tender money. Robertson called it "optional money". Bank money in the form of cheques, drafts, etc. are the forms of non-legal tender money. People are not bound to accept such money because there is no legal sanction behind their issue.

Besides cheques and drafts, there are many other forms of optional money such as time deposits, bonds, securities, debentures, bills of exchange, treasury bills, postal certificates, insurance policies, etc. They are known as "near money" or "money substitutes". They are almost perfect substitutes for money as a store of value. They possess moneyness or liquidity. They also yield income. They economise in the use of currency. But they do not have any legal status.

3 Money of Account and Money Proper

Keynes distinguished between money of account and money proper. According to him, "Money of account is that in which Debts and Prices and General Purchasing Power are expressed." On the other hand, money proper is the actual money in which contracts or debts are settled, such as the Indian Rupee, the British Pound, the American Dollar, the French Franc, the German Mark, the Japanese Yen, the Italian Lira, etc. Usually, there is no difference between money of account and money proper when the accounts in a country are maintained in money proper. But if accounts are kept in some other currency money of account differs from money proper, as happened in Germany after World War I when the money of account was the American Dollar and the money proper was the German Mark. However, the two may differ when the value of money as money and the value of money as commodity are different. For example, value of Indian rupee as money of account has remained the same but the value of Indian rupee as commodity or money proper has been changing overtime, that is, it is an unlimited legal tender. It is a token coin or money whose present intrinsic value is negligible in relation to its face value as compared to 1939.

4. MONEY AND NEAR MONEY

Money consists of currency and bank deposit. Coins and currency notes issued by the central bank of a country and cheques of commercial banks of a country are liquid assets. In fact, cheques and bank drafts are almost perfect substitutes for Money. This is because they perform the medium of exchange function of money, but cheques and drafts can be issued at a short notice only in the case of *demand deposits.* This is not the case with time deposits which can be withdrawn either at the end of the fixed period or by giving a prior notice to the bank and incurring a penalty. Thus time deposits are not 'real' money and for them to become money they must be converted into cash or demand deposits. However, they are near money for they can be converted into real money in a short period without any loss. For example, a time deposit of Rs. 10,000 for three years can always be converted into demand deposit or Rs. 10,000 in cash at any time before the completion of three years. They also fetch a fixed rate of interest which may be reduced if the deposit is converted into cash or demand deposit before the expiry of the fixed period. Thus near money assets serve the store of value function of money temporarily and are convertible into a medium of exchange in a short time without loss in their face value.

Besides time deposits, other near money assets are bonds, securities, debentures, bills of exchange, treasury bills, insurance policies, etc. All these types of assets have a market and are negotiable so that they can be converted into real money within a short time. We discuss how these negotiable instruments are near moneys.

Bonds, securities and debentures fall in the same category. Bonds and securities are issued by the government, while debentures are issued by companies. They are the means to borrow funds for short, medium or long periods and carry a fixed rate of interest. They are near money assets because they are convertible into cash at a short notice in the money market.

A bill of exchange is another form of money. It is an IOU (I owe you). It is drawn by an individual or firm to pay a stated sum of money on a specified date which is never more man 90 days. A bill of exchange is not money by itself but is certainly money on the due date. It is, however, near money if its owner wishes to turn it into cash. It can be easily converted into money at a discount or by receiving less money than its face value.

Treasury bills issued by the government also fall in the category of near money. A treasury bill is a promise by the government to pay a stated sum in the near future usually 30, 60 or 90 days. A treasury bill is also like a bill of exchange which is convertible into money at a discount within a short period.

Life insurance policy is another example of near money. The holder of a life insurance policy can obtain cash in the form of loan on his policy at a short notice. Thus a life insurance policy is a form of liquid asset which can be regarded as near money.

Besides these recognised instruments of near money, some intermediaries have come into existence to provide a market for certain assets. Such intermediaries are financial companies which provide funds on the security of some assets, and brokers who buy and sell property, bonds, debentures, shares, etc. They help in increasing the liquidity of such assets thereby converting them into near money.

Money and near money can now be distinguished. Money is a legal-tender and gives the possessor liquidity in hand. It performs the medium of exchange function. On the other hand, near money assets do not have any legal status. They possess moneyness or liquidity but not ready liquidity like money. They are almost perfect substitutes for money as a store of value. They are superior to money because they yield income. They also economise, in the use of money proper and tend to reduce the quantity of money used by the people as a medium of exchange, as a medium of deferred payments and as a store of value.

Despite the fact that near money assets do not possess ready liquidity, they are preferred by individuals. According to Professor A.G. Hart, near money is preferred to cash by individuals because it serves as a margin of safety motive. Prof. Dean points out that 80 per cent of near money in the USA is held by individuals. The tremendous growth of near money assets in the United States is due to the fact that the yield from them is higher than that from demand deposits and that they are safer than cash. Moreover, savings in the near money assets have been encouraged by such special techniques as pay roll saving plan, and commercial bank plans covering automatic regular transfer of specified sums from the demand to time deposits of the customers.

5. CHARACTERISTICS OF MONEY

Economists have pointed towards the following characteristics or qualities for a thing to be money :

1. *General Acceptability.* For anything to be money, it should be acceptable by everybody. People accept a thing as money which is used by everybody as a medium of exchange. Gold and silver are considered good money materials because they have alternative uses and are generally accepted. Paper notes are accepted as money when they are issued by the central bank and/or the government and are legal tender. Cheques and Bills of Exchange are not accepted generally. Hence they are not money.

2. *Durability.* For a thing to be money, it must possess durability. It should be storable and last long without losing its value over a period-of time. Animals and perishable commodities are not good money materials because they do not possess durability. In this sense, gold, silver, alloy, brass etc. are the best materials which are used as money. Paper notes are less durable than these metals. But they are money because they are legal tender.

3. *Portability.* The material used as money should be easily carried and transferred from one place to another. It should contain large value in small bulk. Gold and silver possess this quality. Hence they are good money materials. But they involve risk in carrying or transferring them from one place to another. Therefore, paper is considered as a better material and is used in the form of notes.

4. *Cognisability.* The material with which money is made should be easily recognised by sight or touch. Coins and currency notes of different denominations in different designs and sizes meet this quality of good money.

5. *Homogeneity.* The material with which money is made should be of the same quality. All coins of one denomination must be of the same metal, weight, shape and size. Similarly, paper notes of one denomination must have the same quality of paper, design and size.

6. *Divisibility.* The money material should be capable of being divided into smaller parts without losing value. Gold, silver, and other such materials possess this quality. Gold has the same value in whatever number of parts it may be divided. The same is the case with paper when notes of small and large denominations are issued which facilitate the operation of small and large transactions.

7. *Stability.* Money should be stable in value because it has to serve as a measure of value. Gold and silver possess this quality because they are not available in abundance. They are neither very scarce because being durable, they can be easily stocked. Their supplies can thus be increased or decreased when required. So they act as a store of value because their value is stable. But governments prefer paper money to gold and silver because it is cheap and easily available. Its value is kept stable by keeping control over its issue. It is another thing that the central bank of a country is seldom able to exercise complete control over its issue which makes paper money unstable in value.

6. NATURE AND DEFINITION OF MONEY

There has been lot of controversy and confusion over the meaning and nature of money. As pointed out by Scitovsky, "Money is a difficult concept to define, partly because it fulfils not one but three functions, each of them providing a criterion of moneyness ... those of (i) a unit of account,(ii) a medium of exchange, and (iii) a store of value."[4] Though Scitovsky points toward the difficulty of defining money due to moneyness[5], yet he gives a wide definition of money. Professor Coulborn defines money as "the means of valuation and of payment; as both the unit of account and the generally acceptable medium of exchange." Coulborn's definition

4. T. Scitovsky, *Money and the Balance of Payments,* 1969.
5. Moneyness means liquidity. All things which possess liquidity have moneyness. For its detailed discussion refer to Sections 1 and 5 of Chapter "The Supply of Money".

is very wide. He includes in it the 'concrete' money such as gold, cheques, coins, currency notes, bank draft, etc. and also abstract money which "is the vehicle of our thoughts of value, price and worth." Such wide definitions have led Sir John Hicks to say that "money is defined by its functions: anything is money which is used as money: 'money is what money does.'[6] These are the functional definitions of money because they define money in terms of the functions it performs.

Some economists define money in legal terms saying that "anything which the state declares as money is money." Such money possesses general acceptability and has the legal power to discharge debts. But people may not accept legal money by refusing to sell goods and services against the payment of legal tender money. On the other hand, they may accept some other things as money which are not legally defined as money in discharge of debts which may circulate freely. Such things are cheques and notes issued by commercial banks. Thus besides legality, there are other determinants which go to make a thing to serve as money.

7. THEORETICAL AND EMPIRICAL DEFINITIONS OF MONEY

There being no unanimity over the definition of money, Prof. Johnson[7] distinguishes four main schools of thought in this regard which are discussed below:

1. *The Traditional Definition of Money.* According to the traditional view, also known as the view of the Currency School, money is defined as currency and demand deposits, and its most important function is to act as a medium of exchange. Keynes in his *General Theory* followed the traditional view and defined money as currency and demand deposits. Hicks in his *Critical Essays in Monetary Theory* points towards a threefold traditional classification of the nature of money: "to act as a unit of account (or measure of value as Wicksell put it), as a means of payment, and as a store of value." The Banking School criticised the traditional definition of money as arbitrary. This view about the meaning of money is very narrow because there are other assets which are equally acceptable as media of exchange. These include time deposits of commercial banks, commercial bills of exchange, etc. By ignoring these assets, the traditional view is not in a position to analyse their influence in increasing their velocity.

2. *Friedman's Definition of Money.* The monetarist (or Chicago) view is associated with Prof. Friedman and his followers at the University of Chicago. By money Friedman means "literally the number of dollars people are carrying around in their pockets, the number of dollars they have to their credit at banks in the form of demand deposits and commercial bank time deposits".[8] Thus he defines money as "the sum of currency plus all adjusted deposits in commercial banks". This is the "working definition" of money which Friedman uses for the empirical study of the monetary trends of the US for selected years 1929, 1935, 1950, 1955 and 1960. This was a narrower definition of money and the adjustment in both demand and time deposits of commercial banks was devised to take into account the increasing financial sophistication of the commercial banks and the community. But he could not establish a single index of this sophistication. Even with this adjustment, cash and deposit monies were not strictly comparable over long periods. He also suggested a broader definition of money as "any asset capable of serving as a temporary abode of purchasing power". So Friedman gives two types of definitions of money. One on theoretical basis and the other on empirical basis. This led to a lot of controversy. However, he takes a broader view in his definition of money which includes bank deposits, non-bank deposits and any other type of assets through which the monetary authority influences the future level of income, prices, employment or any other important macro variable.

3. *The Radcliffe Definition.* The Radcliffe Committee[9] defined money as "note plus bank deposits". It includes as money only those assets which are commonly used as media of exchange. Assets refer to liquid assets by which it means the monetary quantity influencing total effective demand for goods and services. This is interpreted widely to include credit. Thus the whole liquidity position is relevant to spending decisions. Spending is not limited to cash or money in the bank but to the amount of money people think they can get

---

6. John Hicks, *Critical Essay in Monetary Theory,* 1967.
7. H.G. Johnson, "Monetary Theory and Policy", *A.E.R.,* Vol. 52, June 1962.
8. M. Friedman, *Employment, Growth and Price Level,* 1959.
9. *Report of the Committee on the Working of the Monetary System,* 1959.

hold of either by selling an asset or by borrowing or by receipts of income from, say, sales. The Committee did not make use of the concept of velocity of circulation because as a numerical constant, it is devoid of any behavioural content. On the basis of crude empirical tests, the Committee did not find either direct or indirect link between money and economic activity via the interest rate. But it gave a new transmission mechanism based on liquidity. It explained that a movement of interest rates implies significant changes in the capital value of many assets held by financial institutions. A rise in the interest rates makes some less willing to lend because capital values have fallen, and others because their own interest rate structure is sticky. A fall in interest rates, on the other hand, strengthens balance sheets and encourages lenders to seek new business.

4. *The Gurley-Shaw Definition.* Gurley and Shaw[10] regard a substantial volume of liquid assets held by financial intermediaries and the liabilities of non-bank intermediaries as close substitutes for money. Intermediaries provide substitutes for money as a store of value. Money proper which is defined as equal to currency plus demand deposits is only one liquid asset. They have thus formulated a wider definition of money based upon liquidity which includes bonds, insurance reserves, pension funds, savings and loan shares. They believe in the velocity of the money stock which is influenced by non-bank intermediaries. Their views on the definition of money are based on their own and Goldsmith's empirical findings.

8. FUNCTIONS OF MONEY

Money performs a number of primary, secondary, contingent and other functions which not only remove the difficulties of barter but also oils the wheels of trade and industry in the present day world.[11] We discuss these functions one by one.

1. PRIMARY FUNCTIONS

The two primary functions of money are to act as a medium of exchange and as a unit of value.

(i) Money as a Medium of Exchange. This is the primary function of money because it is out of this function that its other functions developed. By serving as a medium of exchange, money removes the need for double coincidence of wants and the inconveniences and difficulties associated with barter. The introduction of money as a medium of exchange decomposes the single transaction of barter into separate transactions of sale and purchase, thereby eliminating the double coincidence of wants.[12] This function of money also separates the tran-sactions in time and place because the sellers and buyers of a commodity are not required to perform the transactions at the same time and place. This is because the seller of a commodity buys some money and money in turn, buys the commodity over time and place.

When money acts as a medium of exchange, it means that it is generally acceptable. It, therefore, affords the freedom of choice. With money, we can buy an assorted bundle of goods and services. At the same time, we can purchase the best and also bargain in the market. Thus money gives us a good deal of economic independence and also perfects the market mechanism by increasing competition and widening the market.

As a medium of exchange, money acts as an intermediary. It facilitates exchange. It helps production indirectly through specialisation and division of labour which, in turn, increase efficiency and output. According to Prof. Walters money, therefore, serves as a 'factor of production,' enabling output to increase and diversify.

In the last analysis money facilitates trade. When acting as the intermediary, it helps one good or service to be traded indirectly for others.

(ii) Money as Unit of Value.[13] The second primary function of money is to act as a unit of value. Under barter one would have to resort to some standard of measurement, such as a length of string or a piece of

10. J.G. Gurley and E.S. Shaw, *Money in a Theory of Finance,* 1960.
11. For the "Static and Dynamic Functions of Money", refer to section 2 of the next Chapter.
12. W.T. Newlyn, *op. cit.,* p. 1.
13. This function is known by various other names such as unit of account, standard of value, common measure of value or common denominator of value.

wood. Since one would have to use a standard to measure the length or height of any object, it is only sensible that one particular standard should be accepted as the standard. Money is the standard for measuring value just as the yard or metre is the standard for measuring length.[14] The monetary unit measures and expresses the values of all goods and services. In fact, the monetary unit expresses the value of each good or service in terms of price. Money is the common denominator which determines the rate of exchange between goods and services which are priced in terms of the monetary unit. There can be no pricing process without a measure of value.

The use of money as a standard of value eliminates the necessity of quoting the price of apples in terms of oranges, the price of oranges in terms of nuts, and so on. Unlike barter, the prices of such commodities are expressed in terms of so many units of dollars, rupees, francs, pounds, etc., depending on the nature of the monetary unit in a country. As a matter of fact, measuring the values of goods and services in the monetary unit facilitates the problem of measuring the exchange value of goods in the market. When values are expressed in terms of money, the number of prices are reduced from $n(n—1)$ in barter economy to (n—1) in monetary economy.

Money as a unit of value also facilitates accounting. "Assets of all kinds, liabilities of all kinds, income of all kinds, and expenses of all kinds can be stated in terms of common monetary units to be added or substracted."[15]

Further, money as a unit of account helps in calculation of economic importance such as the estimation of the costs, and revenues of business firms, the relative costs and profitability of various public enterprises and projects under a planned economy, and the gross national product. As pointed out by Culbertson, "Prices quoted in terms of money become the focus of people's behaviour. Their calculations, plans, expectations, and contracts focus on money prices."[16]

2. Secondary Functions

Money performs three secondary functions: (i) as a standard of deferred payments, (ii) as a store of value, and (iii) as a transfer of value. They are discussed below:

(i) Money as a Standard of Deferred Payments. The third function of money is that it acts as a standard of deferred or postponed payments. All debts are taken in money. It was easy under barter to take loans in goats or grains but difficult to make repayments in such perishable articles in the future. Money has simplified both the taking and repayment of loans because the unit of account is durable. Money links the present values with those of the future. It simplifies credit transactions. It makes possible contracts for the supply of goods in future for an agreed payment of money. It simplifies borrowing by consumers on hire-purchase and from house-building and co-operative societies. Money facilitates borrowing by firms and businessmen from banks and other non-bank financial institutions. The buying and selling of shares, debentures and securities is made possible by money. By acting as a standard of deferred payments, money helps in capital formation both by the government and business enterprises. In fine, this function of money develops financial and capital markets and helps in the growth of the economy.

But there is the danger of changes in the value of money over time which harms or benefits the creditors and debtors. If the value of money increases over time, the creditors gain and debtors lose. On the other hand, a fall in the value of money over time brings losses to creditors and windfalls to debtors. To overcome this difficulty, some of the countries have fixed debt contracts in terms of a price index which measures changes in the value of money. Such a contract over time guarantees the future payment of debt by compensating the loser by the same amount of purchasing power when the contract was entered into.

(ii) Money as a Store of Value. Another important function of money is that it acts as a store of value. "The good chosen as money is always something which can be kept for Jong periods without deterioration or

---

14. A.W. Stonier and D.C. Hague, *A Text book of Economic Theory,* 4/e, 1972.
15. Lester V. Chandler and S.M. Goldfield, *The Economics of Money and Banking, 7/e.* 1977.
16. J.M. Culbertson, *Money and Banking,* 1972.

wastage. It is a form in which wealth can be kept intact from one year to the next. Money is a bridge from the present to the future. It is therefore essential that the money commodity should always be one which can be easily and safely stored."[17] Money as a store of value is meant to meet unforeseen emergencies and to pay debts. Newlyn calls this the asset function of money. "Money is not, of course, the only store of value. This function can be served by any valuable asset. One can store value for the future by holding short-term promissory notes, bonds, mortgages, preferred stocks, household furniture, houses, land, or any other kind of valuable goods. The principal advantages of these other assets as a store of value are that they, unlike money, ordinarily yield an income in the form of interest, profits, rent or usefulness ..., and they sometimes rise in value in terms of money. On the other hand, they have certain disadvantages as a store of value, among which are the following: (1) They sometimes involve storage costs; (2) they may depreciate in terms of money; and (3) they are "illiquid" in varying degrees, for they are not generally acceptable as money and it may be possible to convert them into money quickly only by suffering a loss of value."[18]

Keynes placed much emphasis on this function of money. According to him, to hold money is to keep it as a reserve of liquid assets which can be converted into real goods. It is a matter of comparative indifference whether wealth is in money, money claims, or goods. In fact, money and money claims have certain advantages of security, convenience and adaptability over real goods. But the store of value function of money also suffers from changes in the value of money. This introduces considerable hazard in using money or assets as a store of value.

(iii) Money as a Transfer of Value. Since money is a generally acceptable means of payment and acts as a store of value, it keeps on transferring values from person to person and place to place. A person who holds money in cash or assets can transfer that to any other person. Moreover, he can sell his assets at Delhi and purchase fresh assets at Bangalore. Thus money facilitates transfer of value between persons and places.

3. Contingent Functions

Money also performs certain contingent or incidental functions, according to Prof. David Kinley. They are:

(i) Money as the Most Liquid of all Liquid Assets. Money is the most liquid of all liquid assets in which wealth is held. Individuals and firms may hold wealth in infinitely varied forms. They may, for example, choose between holding wealth in currency, demand deposits, time deposits, savings, bonds, Treasury Bills, short-term government securities, long-term government securities, debentures, preference shares, ordinary shares, stocks of consumer goods, and productive equipment."[19] All these are liquid forms of wealth which can be convened into money, and vice-versa.

(ii) Basis of the Credit System. Money is the basis of credit system. Business transactions are either in cash or on credit. Credit economises the use of money. But money is at the back of all credit. A commercial bank cannot create credit without having sufficient money in reserve. The credit instruments drawn by businessmen have always a cash guarantee supported by their bankers.

(iii) Equaliser of Marginal Utilities and Productivities. Money acts as an equaliser of marginal utilities for the consumer. The main aim of a consumer is to maximise his satisfaction by spending a given sum of money on various goods which he wants to purchase. Since prices of goods indicate their marginal utilities and are expressed in money, money helps in equalising the marginal utilities of various goods. This happens when the ratios of the marginal utilities and prices of the various goods are equal. Similarly, money helps in equalising the marginal productivities of the various factors. The main aim of the producer is to maximise his profits. For this, he equalises the marginal productivity of each factor with its price. The price of each factor is nothing but the money he receives for his work.

(iv) Measurement of National Income. It was not possible to measure the national income under the barter system. Money helps in measuring national income. This is done when the various goods and services produced in a country are assessed in money terms.

17. A.W. Stonier and D.C. Hague, *op. cit.*, p. 406.
18. Loc. cit.
19. Ibid.

(v) Distribution of National Income. Money also helps in the distribution of national income. Rewards of factors of production in the form of wages, rent, interest and profit are determined and paid in terms of money.

4. Other Functions

Money also performs such functions which affect the decisions of consumers and governments :

(i) Helpful in making decisions. Money is a means of store of value and the consumer meets his daily requirements on the basis of money held by him. If the consumer has a scooter and in the near future he needs a car, he can buy a car by selling his scooter and money accumulated by him. In this way, money helps in taking decisions.

(ii) Money as a Basis of Adjustment. To carry on trade in a proper manner, the adjustment between money market and capital market is done through money.

Similarly, adjustments in foreign exchange are also made through money. Further, international payments of various types are also adjusted and made through money.

It is on the basis of these functions that money guarantees the solvency of the payer and provides options to the holder of money to use it any way, he likes.

EXERCISES

1. Discuss the principal difficulties faced by a batter economy.
2. What led to the emergence of money in the modern world?
3. Describe the various stages in the evolution of money.
4. Discuss the nature and functions of money.
5. Define money and discuss its main functions.
6. "Money is what money does." Explain this statement and define money.
7. Distinguish between (a) money proper and money-of-account, *(b)* money and near money.
8. Discuss the theoretical and empirical definitions of money.

CHAPTER 2

Role of Money

1. INTRODUCTION

Money is of vital importance to the operation of the national and international economy. Money plays an important role in the daily life of a person whether he is a consumer, a producer, a businessman, an academician, a politician or an administrator. "An individual need not be an economicst to be actually aware that money play an important role in odern life; he need think only ofhis own experience."[1] We study below the importance of money in a modern economy.

2. SIGNIFICANCE OR ROLE OF MONEY

Money is of vital importance to an economy due to its static and dynamci roles.[2] Its static role emerges from its static or traditional functions. In its dynamic role, money plays an mportant part in the life of every citizen and in the economic system as a whole.

STATIC ROLE OF MONEY

In its static role, the importance of money lies in removing the dificulties of barter in the following ways :

(i) By serving as a medium of exchange, money removes the need for double conicidence of wants and the inconveniences and difficulties associated with barter. The introduction of money as a medium of exchange breaks up the single transactionsof barter into separaate transactions of sales and purchases, thereby eliminating the double coincidence of wants. Instead of exchanging commodities directly with commodities *i.e.* $C \leftrightarrow C$, commodities as $C \rightarrow M \rightarrow C$,where C refers to commodities and M to money.

(ii) By acting asa unit of account, money becomes a commes a common measure of value. The use o money asa standard of value eliminates the necessity of pquoting the price of apples in terms of organes, the price of organes in terms of nuts, and so on. Money is the standard of measuring value and value expressed in money is price. The prices of different commodities are expressed in terms of so many units of dollars, rupees, pounds, etc. depending on the nature of monetary unit in a country. The measurement of the values of goods and services in the monetary unit facilitates the problem of measuring the exchange values of goods in the

1. Lester V.Chandler and S.M. Goldfield, *op. cit.*
2. The explanation in this section also relates to the "Static and Dynamic Functions of Money."

market.

(iii) Money acts as a standard of deferred payments. Under barter, it was easy to take loans in goats or grains but difficult to make repayments in such perishable articles in the future. Money has simplified both taking and repayment of loans because the unit of account is durable. It also overcomes the difficulty of indivisibility of commodities.

(iv) By acting as a store of value, money removes the problem of storing of commodities under barter. Money being the most liquid asset can be kept for long periods without deterioration or wastage.

(v) Under barter, it was difficult to transfer value in the form of animals, grains, etc. from one place to another. Money removes this difficulty of barter by facilitating the transfer of value from one place to another. A person can transfer his money through draft, bill of exchange, etc. and his assets by selling them for cash at one place and buying them at another place.

DYNAMIC ROLE OF MONEY

In its dynamic role, money plays an important part in the daily life of a person whether he is a consumer, a producer, a businessman, an academician, a politician or an administrator. Besides, it influences thee economy in a number of ways.

(1) *To the Consumer.* Money possesses much significance for the consumer. The consumer receives his income in the form of money rather than in goods and services. With money in hands, he can get any commodity and service he likes, in whatever equaliser of marginal utilities for the consumer. The main aim of a consumer is to maximise his satisfaction by spending his limited income on different goods which he wants to purchase. Since prices of goods indicate their marginal utilities and are expressed in money, money helps in equalising the marginal utilities of goods. This is done by substituting goods with higher utilities for others having lower utilities. Thus money enable a consumer to make a rational distribution of his income on various commodities of his choice.

(2) *To the Producer.* Money is of equal importance to the producer. He keeps his account of the values of inputs and outputs in money. The raw materials purchased, the wages paid to workers, the capital borrowed, the rent paid, the expenses on advertisements, etc. are all expenses of production which are entered in his account books. The sale of products in money terms are his sale proceeds. The difference between the two gives him profit. Thus a producer easily calculates not only his costs of production and receipts but also profit with the help of money. Further, money helps in the general flow of goods and services from agricultural, industrial and tertiary sectors of the economy because all these activities are performed in terms of money.

(3) *In Specialisation and Divisions of Labour.* Money plays an important role in large scale specialisation and division of labour in modern production. Money helps the capitalist today wages to a large number of worker engaged in specialised jobs on the basis of division of labour. Each worker is paid money wages in accordance with the nature of work done by him. Thus money facilitates specialisation and division of labour in modern production. These, in turn, help in the growth of industries. It is, in fact, through money that production on a large scale is possible. All inputs like raw materials, labour, machinery, etc. are purchased with money and all output is sold in exchange for money. As rightly pointed out by Prof. Pigou, "In the modern world industry is closely enfolded in a garment of money.".

(4) *As the Basis of Credit.* The entire modern business is based on credit and credit is based on money. All monetary transactions consist of cheques, drafts, bills of exchange etc. These are credit instruments which are not money. It is the bank deposits that are money. Banks issue such credit instruments and create credit. Credit creation, in turn, plays a major role in transferring funds from depositors to investors. Thus credit expands investment on the basis of public saving lying in bank deposits and helps in maintaining a circular flow of income within the economy.

(5) *As a Means to capital Formation.* By transforming savings into investment, money acts as a means to capital formation. Money is a liquid asset which can be stored and storing of money implies savings, and savings are kept in bank deposits to earn interest on them. Banks, in turn, lend these savings to businessmen for investment in capital equipment, buying of raw materials, labour, etc. from different sources and places. This makes capital mobile and leads to capital formation and economic growth.

(6) *As an Index of Economic Growth.* Money is also an index of economic growth. The various indicators of

growth are national income, per capita income and economic welfare. These are calculated and measured in money terms. Changes in the value of money or prices also reflect the growth of an economy. Fall in the value of money (or rise in prices) means that the economy is not progressing in real terms. On he other hand, a continuous rise in the value of money (or fall in prices) reflects retardation of the economy. Somewhat stable prices imply a growing economy. Thus money is an index of economic growth.

(7) *In the Distribution and Calculation of Income.* The rewards to the various factors of production in a modern economy are paid in money. A worker gets his wages, capitalist his interest, a landlord his rent, and an entrepreneur his profit. But all are paid their rewards in money. An organiser is able to calculate the marginal productivity of each factor in terms of money and pay it accordingly. For this, he equalises the marginal productivity of each factor with its price. Its price is, in fact, its marginal productivity expressed in terms of money. As payments are made to various factors of production in money, the calculation of national income becomes easy.

(8) *In National and International Trade.* Money facilitates both national and international trade. The use of money as a medium of exchange, as a store of value and as a transfer of value has made it possible to sell commodities not only within a country but also internationally. To facilitate trade, money has helped in establishing money and capital markets. There are banks, financial institutions, stock exchanges, produce exchanges, international financial institutions, etc. which operate on the basis of the money economy and they help in both national and international trade.

Further, trade relations among different countries have led to international cooperation. As a result, the developed countries have been helping the growth of underdeveloped countries by giving them loans and technical assistance. This has been made possible because the value of foreign aid received and its repayment by the developing countries is measured in money.

(9) *In Solving the Central Problems of an Economy.* Money helps in solving the central problems of an economy; what to produce, for whom to produce, how to produce and in what quantities. This is because on the basis of its functions money facilitates the flow of goods and services among consumers, producers and the government.

(10) *To the Government.* Money is of immense importance to the government. Money facilitates the buying and collection of taxes, fines, fees and prices of services rendered by the government to the people. It simplifies the floating and management of public debt and government expenditure on development and non-developmental activities. It would be impossible for modern governments to carry on their functions without the use of money. Not only this, modern governments are welfare states which aim at improving the standard of living of the people by removing poverty, inequalities and unemployment, and achieving growth with stability. Money helps in achieving these goals of economic policy through its various instruments.

(11) *To the Society.* Money confers many social advantages. It is on the basis of money that the superstructure of credit is built in the society which simplifies consumption, production, exchange and distribution. It promotes national unity when people use the same currency in every nook and corner of the country. It acts as a lubricant for the social life of the people, and oils the wheels of material progress. Money is at the back of social prestige and political power.

Thus money is the pivot round which the whole science of economics clusters.

3. DEFECTS OF MONEY

The Bible says, "The love of money is the root of all evil." Rightly so. Perhaps acting on this saying of the Bible the classical economists did not attach much importance to money. They regarded it as a veil or garment or wrapper for goods and services. According to them, money is simply a tool of convenience to facilitate the exchange of goods and services, but it is not a determinant of the quantities produced. The evils of money are shrouded behind a monetary veil, and what really happens behind the veil is sometimes quite different from what appears to take place on the surface. This extreme view has ben discarded. Now economists regard money not merely as veil but also as an extremely valuable social instrument promoting wealth and welfare.

But money which is a useful servant, often misbehaves when it tries to act like a master. This leads to a number of economic and non-economic defects of money.

Economic Defects

The economic defects are as under :

(1) *Instability in the Value of Money.* The first drawback about money is that its value does not remain stable over time. When the value of money falls, it means rise in the price level or inflation. On the contrary, rise in the value of money means fall in the price levels or deflation. These changes are brought about by increase or decrease in the supply for money. Large changes in the value of money are disastrous and even moderate changes have certain disadvantages.

Inflation or fall in the value of money causes direct and immediate damage to creditors and consumers. On the contrary, deflation or rise in the value of money brings down the level of output, employment and income. Thus instability in the value of money adversely affects consumers, producers and other sections of the society.

(2) *Unequal Distribution of Wealth and Income.* The second defect of money is that changes in the value of money lead to unequal distribution of wealth and income. Inflation or deflation which brings benefits to some and damages to others leads to redistribution of wealth and income not only between social and industrial classes, but between different persons in the same class. Such changes in the structure of the society. Widen the differences between the rich and the poor and lead to class conflict.

(3) *Growth of Monopolies.* Too much of money leas to the concentration of capital in the hands of a few capitalists. This leads to growth of monopolies which exploit both consumers and workers.

(4) *Wastage of Resources.* Money is the basis of credit. When banks create too much of credit, it may be used for productive and unproductive purposes. If much credit is used for production, it leads to over capitalisation and overproduction, and consequently to wastage of resources. Similarly, if liberal credit facilities are given for unproductive uses, they also lead to wastage of resources.

(5) *Black Money.* Money being the store of value lures people to hoard it. The tendency to hoard money and become rich is the root cause of the evil of black money. When people evade taxes and conceal their income and hoard it, it is black money. This leads to a "parallel" economy within the country which encourages conspicuous consumption, black marketing, speculation, etc.

(6) *Cyclical Fluctuations.* Another defect of the institution of money is that it leads to cyclical fluctuations in the economy. When the supply of money increases it leads to a boom and when it contracts there is a slump. In a boom, output, employment and income increase which lead to overproduction. On the contrary, they decline during a depression, thereby leading to under consumption. Such cyclical fluctuations bring untold miseries to the people.

Non-economic Defects

Money has the following non-economic defects :

(1) Besides the above noted economic drawbacks of money the institution of money has brought down the moral, social and political fibre of the society. It leads to corruption, turpitude, political bankruptcy and artificiality in religion based on materialism. In fact, money is "the cause of theft and murder, of deception and betrayal. Money is blamed when the prostitute sells her body and when the bribed judge perverts the law. Significantly enough avarice is called the love of money; all evil is attributed to it."[3]

(2) *Political Instability.* Overissue of money leading to hyper-inflation leads to political instability and downfall of government. This has happened in many Latin American countries.

(3) *Tendency to Exploit.* People who want to amass money and wealth, adopt underhand methods and have tendency to exploit others. Even nations are not far behind in this. As pointed out by Davenport, "Money has enabled strong nations to destroy backward communities to win them on their side with the help of financial aid."

3. L. Von Mises, *The Theory of Money and Credit,* p. 93.

Conclusion

All these defect are not due to money but are the result of the attribute of man towards the use of money. It is of immense importance to every type of society whether it be capitalist or socialist. It is impossible to imagine this world without money. Money is an indispensable lubricant, a tool of convenience, for a continuous and smooth functioning of the economic machine. But its uncontrolled use, instead of solving, creates many complicated problems. It is these complex problems that led Disraeli to remark. "Money has made more people mad than love." So the best way is to keep money under control like a faithful and obedient money is the government which can achieve this by a judicious monetary policy.

4. ROLE OF MONEY IN A CAPITALIST ECONOMY

A capitalist economy is one in which each individual in his capacity as a consumer, producer and resource owner is engaged in economic activity with a large measure of economic freedom. Individual economic actions are governed by the instruction of private property, profit motive, freedom of enterprise and consumers's sovereignty. All factors of production are privately owned and managed by individuals who are at liberty to dispose them of within the prevalent laws. Individuals have the freedom to choose any occupation, and to buy and sell any number of goods and services.

Such an economy is essentially a money economy where money plays an important role in its functioning. Consumers and producers receive income in money. Consumers receive money income in the form of wages, rents, interest an dividends by selling the services of the factors of production which they own in the form of labour, land, and capital respectively. They are free to spend their money income on whichever goods and services they wish to buy. They may partly spend their money income and partly save in the form of money.

Big and small firms, in turn, buy the services of the factors of production for producing commodities. These services are purchased in money terms. The entire productive process ina capitalist economy is determined by the profit motive. Profit is the difference between outlay and receipt. All these—profit, outlay and receipt—are calculated interms of money.

In fact, there is a circular flow of money in such an economy. Allirms demand the services of the factors of production to produce consumer goods. All factors of production are paid for their services in money, who buy consumer goods with it. Thus money flows back to firms which again make monetary payments to consumers for the services rendered by them in the further production of goods of varied types.

Money and the Price Mechanism in a Capitalist Economy

The most significant role of money lies in the functioning of the price mechanism. The price system functions through prices of goods and services. Prices determine the production of innumerable goods and services. They organise production and help in the distribution of goods and services. Since prices are expressed in money, the price mechanism under capitalism cannot function without money.

In a capitalist economy where means of production are owned privately and production is also carried out by private enterprise, money performs the important function of solving the central problems of such an economy. This is done through the price mechanism. The price mechanism operates automatically without any direction and control by the government.

The central problems of a capitalist economy as to what, how much, and how and for whom to produce are solved through the price mechanism. We discuss them as under.

This problem of what, how much and how to produce are solved by the price mechanism on the basis of the profit motive. Profit is the difference between expenditure and receipt of a firm. The size of profit depends upon prices of commodities. The larger the difference between price and costs, the higher is the profit. Again the higher the prices, the greater are the efforts of the producers to produce the different types of commodities in different quantities. On the other hand, prices depend upon consumers' choices of the various commodities. It is also the consumer's choices which determine what to produce, how much to produce, how to produce and for what type of consumers.

It is, it fact, competition between consumers and producers which equalises the demand and supply of both goods and services in a capitalist economy. There being sufficient flexibility under capitalism, prices adjust themselves to changes in demand, in production techniques, and in the supply of factors of production. Changes imprecise, in turn, bring adjustments in production, factor demand and consumer incomes. Money is, therefore, the basis of the price mechanism under capitalism. It is a pivot around which the entire capitalist economy revolves. Since such an economy functions without any government interference, money plays a crucial role in maximising the wants of consumers and profits of producers.

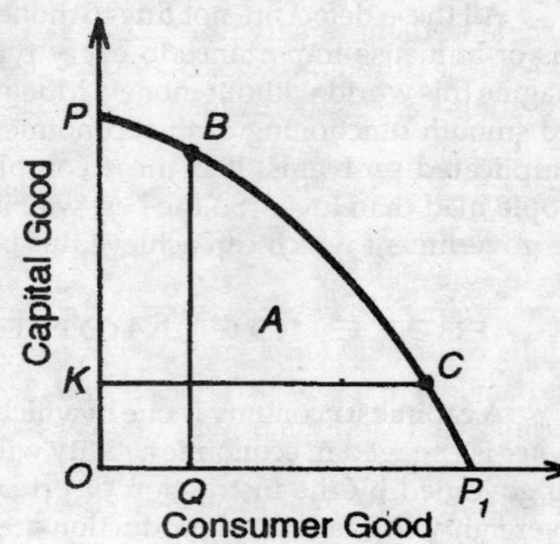

FIG. 1

For the Consumer. Under capitalism, the consumer is the king who buys only those commodities which give him the maximum satisfaction with a given money income. This he does by equalising the marginal utilities of different goods he wishes to buy. When the price of each commodity expressed in money equals its marginal utility, the consumer gets maximum satisfaction. Thus money enables a consumer to make a rational choice out of the various commodities he wants to buy with his given money income. Figure 1 illustrates this argument. Suppose only two commodities are produced in a capitalist economy. They are capital goods and consumer goods taken on the vertical and horizontal axes respectively. The production possibility curve PP_1 represents the area of choice for the consumer. It is for the producer to decide whether to produce capital goods or consumer goods depending on consumer's rational choice. The consumer will choose either combination *B* or *C* which gives him the maximum satisfaction with a given money income. At combination *A* he will be buying lesser quantities of the two goods and will beat a lower level of satisfaction than at any point on the PP_1 curve.

For the Producer. Money is equally important for the producer who buys and sells inputs and outputs in money. His aim being to maximise profits, he calculates the marginal cost and marginal revenue in money. Profits appear when marginal revenue exceeds marginal cost, and they lead to further production. When marginal cost exceeds marginal revenue, losses appear and production is curtailed. But these situations do not continue for long. The price mechanism restores the equilibrium between marginal revenue and marginal cost at prices which do not need further adjustments. Thus producers earn normal profit which they receive in the form of money.

Basis of Capitalist Production

In fact, money is the very basis of the capitalist production. By facilitating the purchase of inputs, and by increasing specialisation and division of labour, money helps in the growth of research in the agricultural, industrial and tertiary sectors of a capitalist economy. Since all these sectors are mutually dependent and are based on mutual exchanges through money, capitalist production tends to increase. In other words, money help in capitalist production through a circular flow of goods and services from these sectors.

Basis of Credit

The entire capitalist system of production is based on credit. Credit instruments are a form of money which are issued by banks to facilitate trade, commerce, agriculture, industry, transport, etc. under capitalism. It is on the basis of credit instruments that banks advance loans to the different sectors of a capitalist economy. The amount of credit is determined by the interest rate which expresses the price of loanable funds, and loans find their expression in money.

Means of Capital Formation

The very basis of capitalism is the capital and money is the most liquid form of capital. The growth of a capitalist economy depends upon the capital accumulation. And capital accumulation is a process whereby people save out of their money incomes, deposit them with banks and other financial institutions which, in turn, lend them to agriculturists, industrialists, transporters and other businessmen for investment in capital assets. The different stages in the process of capital formation under capitalism—receiving income, saving and investing—are all performed in money terms.

Link between the Present and the Future

Money establishes a link between the present and future through the freedom of enterprise and freedom of consumption under capitalism. The freedom of consumption the part of the consumer leads to freedom to save a part of his money income. Saving leads to the production of capital goods via investment and capital goods contribute to the growth of the economy. Thus it is through money that consumers save in the present and saving helps in production in the future. Similarly, freedom of enterprise under capitalism helps the businessman and the trader to make payments in the future for bargains made in the present. This is possible through money when the goods are stored in the present and sold in the future. It is in these way that money helps to establish a link between the present and the future.

Leads to Business Cycles

Besides these apparent merits of money in a capitalist economy, it has one serious defect in that an excess of money leads to inflation and its shortage leads to deflation. These changes in the quantity of money result in cyclical fluctuations with their attendant consequences on the economy. In fact, an excess of money supply creates more demand which, in turn, leads to overproduction, to glut of commodities in the market and finally to depression and mass unemployment. There is thus wastage of resources and loss in productivity when there are business cycles in a capitalist economy. But Schumpeter regarded business cycles as the cost of economic development, a permanent feature of the dynamci path of a capitalist economy which takes it to a higher level of development every time a cycle takes place.

In fine money plays a crucial role in the functioning of a capitalist economy.

5. Role of Money in a Socialist Economy

In a socialist economy, the central authority owns and controls the means of production and distribution All mines, farms, factories, financial institutions, distributing agencies (such as internal and external trade shops, stores, etc.) means of transport and communications, etc., are owned, controlled and regulated by government departments and state corporations. Therefore, the pricing process in a socialist economy does not operate freely but works under the control and regulation of the central planning authority.

Marx believed that money had no role to play in a socialist economy because it led to the exportation of labour at the hands of capitalists. He, therefore, advocated the habilitation of money and exchange by bartering goods measured in terms of labour value.

In keeping with the Marx an ideas, the Bolshevik Government in Russia eliminated money as a medium of exchange in 1917. Money payments for the use of various services and goods were abolished. "But barter transactions proved to be too clumsy. Although some communist writers had prematurely hailed the dying out of money, it became obvious that the socialist economy needed a stable currency nearly as much as a private enterprise economy." Accordingly, market exchanges, money and monetary incentives were reintroduced in the New Economic Policy (1921-27) in the USSR. Since then the Soviet economy has been using money in production, distribution and exchange such that money acts as a medium of exchange, a store of value, and a unit of account.

We have given above a brief description of the role of money in the Soviet economy which is the finest variant of a socialist economy in action.

Theoretically, the role of money in a socialist economy is different from that in a capitalist economy.

Money and Price Mechanism in a Socialist Economy

The price mechanism has little relevance in a socialist economy because it is regarded as a distinguishing feature of a free market economy. In a socialist economy the various elements of the price mechanism—costs, profits and prices—are all planned and calculated by the planning authority in accordance with the objectives and targets of the plan. Thus rational economic calculation or allocation of resources is not possible in a socialist economy. Let us find out how a socialist society solves the central problems of an economy, what, how and for whom to produce.

In a socialist state, it is the central planning authority that performs the functions of the market. Since all the material means of production are owned, controlled and directed by the government, the decisions about *what* to produce are taken within the framework of a central plan. The decisions, as to the nature of goods to be produced and their quantities, depend upon the objectives, targets and priorities laid down by the central planning authority. The prices of the various commodities are also fixed by this authority. Prices reflect the social preferences of the common man. Consumers choice is limited only to the commodities that the planners decide to produce and offer.

The problem of *how* to produce is also decided by the central planning authority. "It establishes the rules for combining factors of production and choosing the scale of output of a plant, for determining the output of an industry, for the allocation of resources, and for the parametric use of prices in accounting." The central planning authority lays down two rules for the guidance of plant managers. *One,* that each manager should combine productive goods and services in such a manner that the average cost of producing a given output is the minimum. *Two,* that each manager should choose that scale of output which equalises marginal cost to price. Since all resources in the economy are owned and regulated by the government, the raw materials, machines and other inputs are also sold at prices which are equal to their marginal cost of production. If the price of a commodity happens to be above its average cost, the plant managers will earn profits, and if it is below the average cost of production, they will incur losses. In the former case, the industry would expand and in the latter case it would cut down production, and ultimately a position of equilibrium will be reached by the *process of trial and error.* The process of trial and error would, however, proceed on the basis of *historically* given prices which would necessitate relatively small adjustments in prices from time to time. Thus "all decisions of the managers of production and of the productive resources in public ownership and also all decisions of individuals as consumers and as suppliers of labour are made on the basis of these prices. As a result of these decisions the quantity demanded and supplied of each commodity is determined. If the quantity demanded of a commodity is not equal to the quantity supplied, the price of that commodity has to be changed. It has to be raised if demand exceeds supply and lowered if the reverse is the case. Thus the central planning board fixes a new set of prices which serves as a basis for new decisions, and which results in a new set of quantities demanded and supplied."

The problem of *for whom to produce* is also solved by the state in a socialist economy. The central planning authority takes this decisions at the time of deciding what and how much to produce in accordance with the overall objectives of the plan. In making this decision, social preferences are given weightage. In other words, higher weightage is given to the production of those goods and services which are needed by the majority of the people over luxury items. They are based on the minimum needs of the people, and are sold at fixed prices through government stores. Since goods are produced in anticipation of demand, an increase in demand brings about shortages and this leads to rationing.

Thus in a socialist society the problem of income distribution is automatically solved because all resources are owned by the state and their rewards are also fixed and paid by the state. Economic surpluses are deliberately created and utilised for capital accumulation and growth.

Capital Accumulation

Besides, capital accumulation is possible through money. It is money that provides liquidity and mobility required for capital accumulation. In a socialist economy the sources of investment funds are basically the same as under a capitalist economy. The turnover tax, planned profits of public enterprises, amortisation quotas and taxation of agricultural produce in kind or in low procurement prices are all expressed in money and help in capital accumulation.

Foreign Trade

Moreover, socialist economies do not enter into foreign trade on bilateral trade relations based on commodity transactions. Rather, being members of the World Bank and the IMF, they make payments in monetary terms in their international trade relations.

Circular Flow of Money

There is also circular flow of money in a socialist economy. The producing units receive funds for investment from the state budget as grants or as loans from the state bank to purchase the necessary inputs and for making payments to workers. The workers spend their wages on consumer goods. The producing units receive revenues from sales, which, in turn, go into tax payments and profit earnings and as repayments of loans to the state bank. These funds again flow from the state budget and the state bank to the producing units. Thus money helps in the circular flow of goods and services in a socialist economy.

To conclude, the role of money in a socialist economy may be less important as compared to a capitalist economy due to state regulation and control. Nevertheless, it helps in fixing prices, wages, incomes and profits. It guides a socialist economy in determining the allocation of its resources equitably, in capital accumulation and flow of resources within and outside the economy.

EXERCISES

1. Define money. What is its social significance?
2. "The institution of money is an extremely valuable social instrument making a large contribution to economic welfare. Money is not merely a veil or a garment or a wrapper." Discuss this statement.
3. "Money is a good servant, but a bad master." Examine this statement.
4. Discuss the role of money in a modern capitalist economy.
5. What role does money play in a socialist economy?
6. Discuss the static and dynamic role of money.

CHAPTER 3

Flow of Funds Accounts

1. INTRODUCTION

The national income accounts do not tell anything about monetary or financial transactions whereby one sector places its savings at the disposal of other sectors of the economy by means of loans, capital transfers, etc. In fact, the national income accounts do not take into consideration the financial dimensions of economic activity and they describe product accounts as if they are operated through barter. The flow of funds accounts are meant to supplement national income and product accounts. The flow of funds accounts were developed by Prof. Morris Copeland[1] in 1952 to overcome the weaknesses of national income accounting.

The flow of funds accounts list the sources of all funds received and the uses to which they are put within the economy. They show the financial transactions among different sectors of the economy and the link between saving and investment aggregates with lending and borrowing by them. The account for each sector reveals all the sources of funds whether from income or borrowing and all the uses to which they are put whether for spending or lending. This way of looking at financial transactions in their entirety has come to be known as the flow of funds approach or of sources and uses of funds.

In the flow of funds accounts, all changes in assets are recorded as uses and all changes in liabilities are recorded as sources. *Uses of funds* are increases in assets if positive or decreases in assets if negative. They refer to capital expenditure or *real investment* spending which involve the purchase of real assets. *Sources of funds* are increases in liabilities or *net worth* or *saving* if positive, and repayment of debt or dissaving if negative. Net worth is equal to a sector's total assets minus its total liabilities. Therefore, a change in net worth equals any change in total assets less any change in total liabilities.

2. FLOW OF FUNDS MATRIX

The flow of funds accounting system is presented in the form of a matrix by placing sources and uses of funds statements of different sectors side by side. It is an interlocking self-contained system that reveals financial relationships among all sectors of the economy. For the economy as a whole, total liabilities must equal total financial assets, although for any one sector its liabilities may not equal its financial assets. The consolidated net worth of an economy is consequently identical to the value of its real assets. This implies that savings must equal investment in an economy. Any single sector may save more than it invests or invests more than it saves. But the economy-wise total of savings must equal investment.

Table 1 presents the flow of funds matrix of an economy. For simplicity, we take the flow of funds accounts matrix of an economy divided into four sectors: households; non-financial corporations, financial institutions, and the government. These institutional sectors are shown in columns and various types of

1. Morris A. Copeland, *A Study of Money Flows in the United States.* 1952.

transactions in rows.

Table 1. Flow of Funds Accounts Matrix

(Rs. Crores)

Sectors → *Transactions* *Category*	*House-holds*		*Non-financial Corpora-tions*		*Financial Institu-tions*		*Govern-ment*		*Saving and Invest-ment*
	U	*S*	*U*	*S*	*U*	*S*	*U*	*S*	
1. Gross saving	–	27	–	17	–	–	–	–4	40
2. Gross investment	12	–	28	–	–	–	–	–	40
3. Net financial investment (4 - 5)	15	–	–11	–	–	–	–4	–	0
4. Financial uses (net) (6+7+8+9+10)	25	–	3	–	6	–	–	–	34
5. Financial sources (net), (6+7+8+9+10)	–	10	–	14	–	6	–	4	34
6. Demand deposits	7	–	–1	–	–	6	–	–	0
7. Government securities	4	–	2	–	2	–	–	–	0
8. Corporate securities	14	–	–	14	–	–	–	–	0
9. Mortgages		10	–	–	8	–	2	–	0
10. Net increase in foreign assets	–	–	2	–	+	–	–2	–	0

Note : 'U* refers lo uses of funds and 'S' to sources of funds,

First take the columns. The household sector includes nonprofit organisations within it. Nonfinancial corporations include savings and loan associations, mutual savings banks, insurance companies, pension funds, mutual funds., etc. The remaining sectors are self-explanatory . The last column showing saving and investment is a measure of domestic saving and investment of all sectors minus the rest of the world.

Row I which relates to gross saving which is a *source* of funds for households (Rs 27 crores) and non-financial corporations (Rs 17 crores), and the minus figure of Rs. 4 crores for the government which indicates a deficit in its budget.

Row 2 relates to gross investment which is a *use* of funds by households (Rs 12 crores) and non-financial corporations (Rs 28 crores). The last column of the table shows that saving and investment are equal to Rs. 40 crores each. The figures of saving and investment are supposed to have been taken from the national income accounts of the economy.

Row 3 shows net financial investment which is the excess of saving over investment or uses over sources of each sector. For instance, the household sector makes positive net investment of Rs. 15 crores (27-12), while the non-financial corporate sector incurs *negative* net investment of Rs. 11 crores because it makes investment in excess of saving (17-28). The same is the case with the government which is shown as minus Rs. 4 crores. (It can also be arrived at by deducting the figure of *S* of row 5 from the *U* figure of row 4 of each sector).

Row 4 shows financial uses (net) of funds. They refer to lending. It equals the sum of the change in each sector's holding of financial assets which include demand deposits, government securities, corporate securities, mortgages and net increase in foreign assets. Thus the net financial uses of the household sector are Rs. 25 crores which include Rs. 7 crores of demand deposits *plus* Rs. 4 crores of government securities *plus* Rs. 14 crores of corporate securities. Similarly for the remaining sectors.

Row 5 Financial sources (net) of funds shows the liability of each sector. They refer to borrowing. For instance, the government sector shows the acquisition of financial assets of Rs. 4 crores by selling securities to the household sector.

Two important points should be noted: *first,* financial uses (net) and financial sources (net) of the economy must equal. They are Rs. 34 crores in our table. *Second,* changes in assets (uses) and liabilities (sources) of each type of funds must total up to zero. This is revealed by the last column of the table in relation to rows 6, 7, 8, 9, and 10. In the case of row 10 we have taken net increase in foreign assets to be zero for the sake of convenience. If it is a positive figure the balance will show surplus in the international current account of the national income accounts, and a negative figure will show a deficit.

3. DIFFERENCE BETWEEN FLOW OF FUNDS ACCOUNTS AND NATIONAL INCOME ACCOUNTS

The flow of funds accounts differ from national income accounts in many ways. *First,* the national income accounts are confined exclusively to non-financial transactions. They neglect the link between saving and investment aggregates with lending and borrowing by different sectors of the economy.

Second, the national income accounts confine all real investment to the business sector with the exception of building construction. Consumers and governments are not allowed to invest in national income accounts. The flow of funds accounts treat consumer purchases of durable goods as real investment: Government enterprises are included in the producing sector of national income . accounts but in the flow of funds accounts they are included in government sector.

Third, the number of sectors in flow of funds accounts are more with larger details than in the national income accounts. They are defined institutionally in flow of funds accounts whereas they are defined functionally in national income accounts.

Fourth, there are fewer imputations in the flow of funds accounts than in national income accounts. For instance, taxes are carried on a cash basis in flow of funds accounts whereas some sectors are shown on an accrual basis in national income accounts.

4. IMPORTANCE OF FLOW OF FUNDS ACCOUNTS

The flow of funds accounts present a comprehensive and systematic analysis of the financial transactions of the economy. As such, they are useful in a number of ways :

1. The flow of funds accounts are superior to the national income accounts. Even though the latter are fairly comprehensive, yet they do not reveal the financial transactions of the economy which the flow of funds accounts do.

2. They provide a useful framework for studying the behaviour of individual financial institutions of the economy.

3. According to Prof. Goldsmith, they bring "the various financial activities of an economy into explicit statistical relationships with one another and with data on the non-financial activities that generate income and production."

4. They trace the financial flows that interact with and influence the real saving-investment process. They record the various financial transactions underlying saving and investment.

5. They are essential raw materials for any comprehensive analysis of capital market behaviour, because they help to identify the role of financial institutions in the generation of income, saving and expenditure, and the influence of economic activity on financial markets.

6. The flow of funds accounts show how the government finances its deficit and surplus budget and acquires financial assets.

7. They also show the results of transactions in government and corporate securities, net increase in deposits and foreign assets in the economy.

8. The flow of funds accounts help in analysing the impact of monetary policies on the economy as to whether they bring stability or instability or economic fluctuations.

5. LIMITATIONS OF FLOW OF FUNDS ACCOUNTS

The flow of funds accounts are beset with a number or problems which are discussed as under:

1. The flow of funds accounts are more complicated than the national income accounts because they involve the aggregation of a large number of sectors with their very detailed financial transactions.

2. There is the problem of valuation of assets. Many assets, claims and obligations have no fixed value. It, therefore, becomes difficult to have their correct valuation.

3. The problem of inclusion of non-reproducible real assets arises in the flow of funds accounts. Economists have not been able to decide as to the type of reproducible assets which may be included in flow of funds accounts.

4. Similarly, economists have failed to decide about the inclusion of human wealth in flow of funds accounts.

Despite these problems, the flow of funds accounts supplement the national income accounts and help in understanding social accounts of an economy.

EXERCISES

1. Explain and illustrate flow of funds accounts. In what respects they are different from national income accounts?
2. Explain fully flow of funds accounts. Discuss their importance and limitations.

C H A P T E R

4

The Circular Flow of Money

1 MEANING

The circular flow of money refers to the process whereby money payments and receipts of an economy flow in a circular manner continuously through time. The various components of money payments and receipts ar saving, investment, taxation, loans, government purchases exports, imports, etc. These are shown on diagrams in the form of currents and cross- currents in such a manner that the total money payments equal the total money receipts in the economy.

2. CIRCULAR FLOW OF MONEY BETWEEN HOUSEHOLD AND BUSINESS SECTORS

We begin with a simple hypothetical economy where there are only two sectors, the household and business. The household sector owns all the factors of production, that is land, labor, capital and enterprise. This sector receives income in the form of rent, wages, interest and profit, by selling the services of these factors to the business sector. The business sector consists of producers who produce commodities and sell them to the household sector. The household sector consists of consumers who buy commodities produced by the business sector

Thus in the first instance, money flows in the form of such income payments as rent, wages, intersest and profits from the business sector to the household sector when the former buys the services of the factors of production to produce good. Money so received is, in turn, spent by the household sector to by goods produced by the business sector. In this way, money flows in a circular manner from the business sector to the household sector and from the household sector to the business sector in the economy.

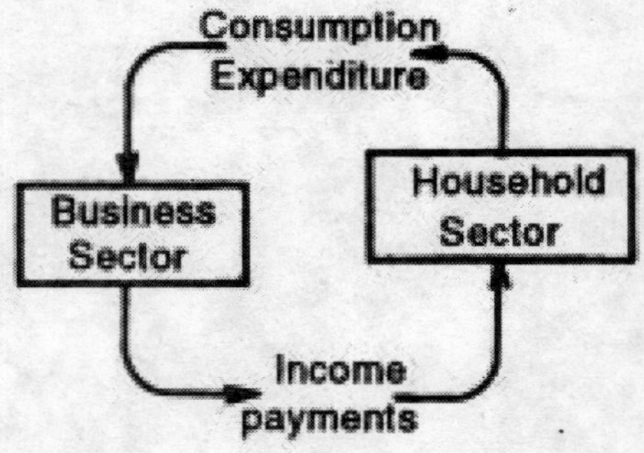

FIG. 1

The circular flow in a two-sector economy is depicted in Figure 1 where the flow of money as income payments from the business sector to the household sector is shown in the form of an arrow in the lower portion of the diagram. On the other hand, the flow of money as consumption expenditure on the purchase of goods and services by the household sector is shown to go to the business sector by an arrow in the upper portion of the diagram. As long as income payments by the business sector for factor services are returned by the household sector to purchase goods, the circular flow of income payments and consumption expenditure tends to continue indefinitely. Production equals sales or supply equals demand, and the economy will continue to operate at this level in a circular flow of money.

Assumptions. The above analysis of the circular flow of money is based on a number of assumptions.

1. It is assumed that the household sector spends the entire income received from the business sector on buying goods and services produced by the latter.

2. The business firms keep their production exactly equal to their sales, and there are no changes in their inventories.

3. The business sector does not keep any undistributed money as reserve. The money it receives by selling goods and services to the household sector is fully spent in making payments as rent, wages, interest and profits to the household sector.

It is these assumptions that keep the flow of money to move in a circular manner in the economy. But these assumptions are unrealistic and do not fit in the actual working of the economy.

The fact is that there are regular withdrawals and injections from the circular flow of money in the economy. A withdrawal or leakage is any income that does not enter into the circular flow of money, and an injection is an addition to the circular flow of money. A leakage occurs in the income flow and an injection in the expenditure flow.

3. CIRCULAR FLOW OF MONEY WITH SAVING AND INVESTMENT

In the circular flow of money, saving is one of the leakages and investment is an injection. In fact, the household and business sectors do not spend their entire money income. The consumers who represent the household sector do not spend their income wholly in purchasing goods and services. Rather, they save a part of their income for a variety of motives. Similarly, business firms do not spend their entire income from the sale of goods. But they keep a part of it in the form of undistributed profit. Such savings of consumers and firms are not hoarded but are invested in bonds, shares, debentures, etc. in the capital market. They flow in to the capital market.

On the other hand, business firms borrow funds from the capital market for making investment. Thus savings which flow into the capital market are taken away by the business sector for investment and the ircular flow of money is maintained in the economy.

Figure 2 shows how the circular flow of money is altered by the inclusion of saving and investment. Expenditure has now two paths: (*i*) directly via consumption from the households to the business sector, and (*ii*) Indirectly via investment expenditure by the business sector.

In the centre of Figure 2, there is the capital (or credit or financial) maarket which shows the inflow of

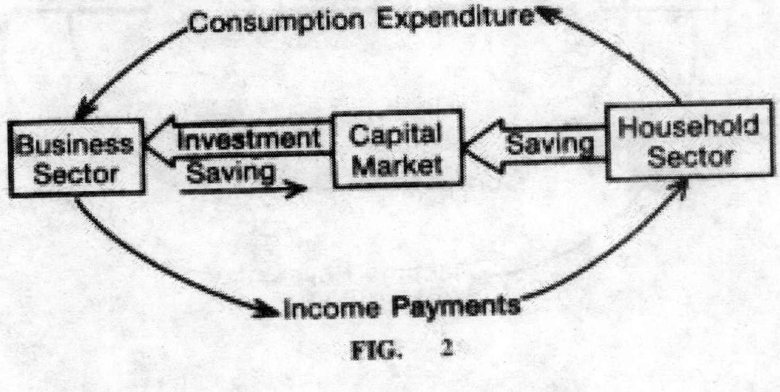

FIG. 2

savings from the household sector and the business sector into the capital market, and the *outflow* of investment into the business sector from the capital market. The capital market coordinates the saving and investment activities of the household and business sector s and maintains the circular flow of money in the economy.

4. CIRCULAR FLOW OF MONEY WITH GOVERNMENT SECTOR

So far we have been working on the circular flow of a two-sector model of an economy. To this we add the government sector so as to make it a three-sector closed model. For this, we add taxation and government purchases (or expenditure) in our presentation. Taxation is a leakage from the circular flow and government purchases are injections into the circular flow of money.

First, take the circular flow between the household sector and the government sector. Taxes in the form of personal income tax and commodity taxes paid by the household sector are outflows or leakages from the circular flow. But the government purchases the services of the households, makes transfer payments in the form of old age pensions, unemployment relief, sickness benefit, etc., and also spends on them to provide certain social services like education, health, housing, water, parks and other facilities. All such expenditures by the government are injections into the circular flow of money.

Next take the circular flow between the business sector and the government sector. All types of taxes paid by the business sector to the government are leakages from the circular flow. On the other hand, the government purchases all its requirements of goods of all types from the business sector, gives subsidies and makes transfer payments to firms in order to encourage their production. These government expenditures are injections into the circular flow of money.

Now we take the household, business and government sectors together to show their inflows and outflows in the circular flow. As already noted, taxation is a leakage from the circular flow. It tends to reduce consumption and saving of the household sector. Reduced consumption, in turn, reduces the sales and incomes of the firms. On the other hand, taxes on business firms tend to reduce their investment and production. The

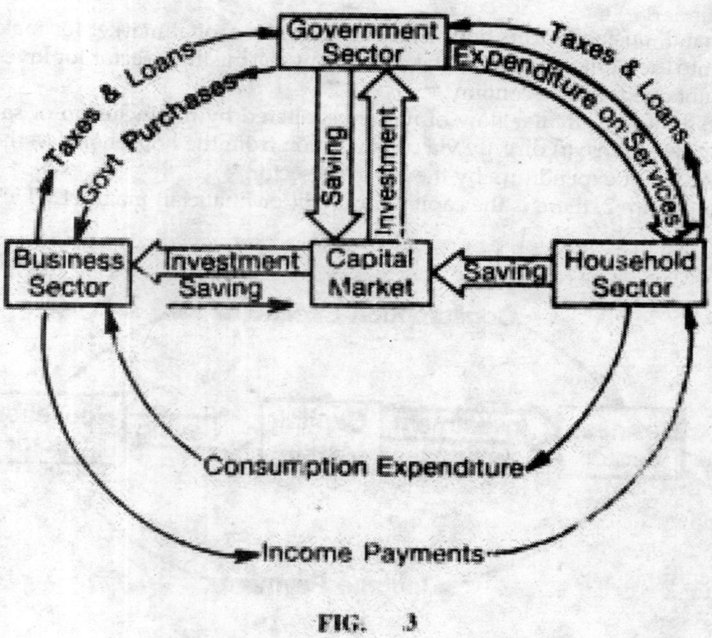

FIG. 3

government offsets these leakages by making purchases from the business sector and buying services of the household sector equal to the amount of taxes. Thus total sales again equal production of firms. In this way, the circular flows of income and expenditure remain in equilibrium.

Figure 3 shows that taxes flow out of the household and business sectors and go to the government. Now the government makes investment and for this purchases goods from the household. Thus government purchases of goods and services are an injection in the circular flow of income and taxes are leakages.

If government purchases exceed net taxes then the government will incur a deficit equal to the difference between the two, i.e., government expenditure and taxes. The government finances its deficit by borrowing from the capital market which receives funds from household sector in the form of saving. On the other hand, if net taxes exceed government purchases the government will have a budget surplus. In this case, the government reduces the public debt and supplies funds to the capital market which are received by the business sector.

5. CIRCULAR FLOW OF MONEY WITH THE FOREIGN SECTOR

So far the circular flow of income and expenditure has been shown in the case of a closed economy. But the actual economy is an open one where foreign trade plays an important role. Exports are an injection or inflows into the economy. They create incomes for the domestic firms. When foreigners buy goods and services produced by domestic firms, they are exports in the circular flow of income. On the other hand, imports are leakages from the circular flow. They are expenditures incurred by the household sector to purchase goods from foreign countries. These exports and imports in the circular flow are shown in Figure 63.4.

Take the inflows and outflows of the household, business and government sectors in relation to the foreign sector. The household sector buys goods imported from abroad and makes payment for them of money. The householder may receive transfer payments from the foreign sector for the services rendered by them in foreign countries.

On the other hand, the business sector exports goods to foreign countries and its receipts are an injection in the circular flow. Similarly, there are many services rendered by business firms to foreign countries such as shipping, insurance, banking, etc. for which they receive payments from abroad. They also receive royalties, interests, dividends, profits, etc. for investments made in foreign countries. On the other hand, the business sector makes payments to the foreign sector for imports of capital goods, machinery, raw materials, consumer goods, and services from abroad. These are the leakages from the circular flow.

Like the business sector, modern governments also export and import goods and services, and lend to and borrow from foreign countries. For all exports of goods, the government receives payments from abroad. Similarly, the government receives payments from foreigners when they visit the country as tourists and for receiving education, etc. and also when the government provides shipping, insurance and banking services to foreigners through the state-owned agencies. It also receives royalities, interest, dividends etc. for investments made abroad. These are injections into the circular flow. On other hand, the leakages are payments made for the purchase of goods and services to foreigners.

Figur 4 shows the circular flow of the four-sector open economy with saving, taxes and imports shown as leakages from the circular flow on the right hand side of the figure, and investment, government purchases and exports as injections into the circular flow on the left side of the figure. Further, imports, exports and transfer payments have been shown to arise from the three domestic sectors—the household, the business and the government. These outflows and inflows pass through the foreign sector which is also called the "Balance of Payments Sector."

Thus Figure 4 shows the circular flow of money where there are inflows and outflows of money, receipts and payments among the business sector, the household sector, the government sector and the foreign sector in currents and cross-currents.

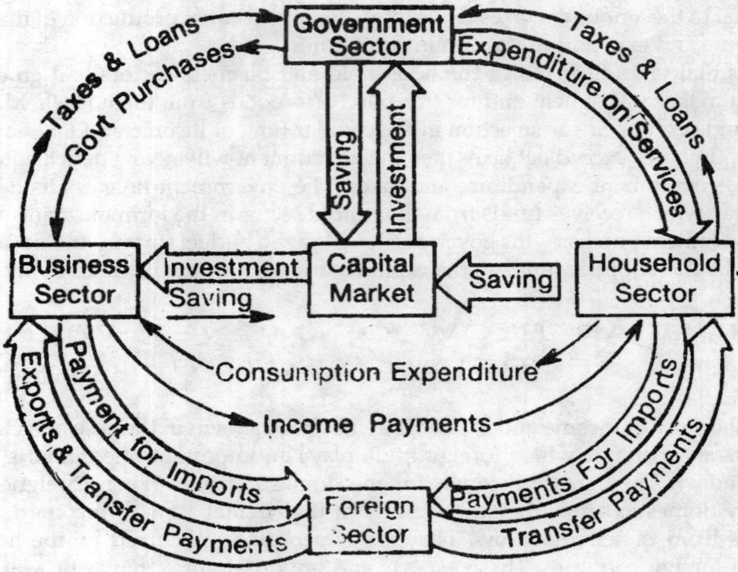

FIG. 4

6. IMPORTANCE OF THE CIRCULAR FLOW OF MONEY

Money being the life blood of a modern economy, its circular flow gives a clear picture of the economy. We can know from its study whether the economy is working smoothly or there is any disturbance in its smooth functioning. As such, the circular flow of money is of immense significance for studying the functioning of the economy and for helping the government in formulating policy measures.

1. *Link between Producers and Consumers*. The circular flow of money establishes a link between producers and consumers. It is through money that producers buy the services of the factors of production with which the latter, in turn, purchase goods from the producers.

2. *Creates a Network of Markets*. As a corollary to the above point, the linking of producers and consumers through the circular flow of money ahs created a network of markets for different goods and services where problems relating to their sale and purchase are automatically solved.

3. *Inflationary and Deflationary Tendencies*. Leakages or injections in the circular flow of money disturb the smooth functioning of the economy. For example, saving is a leakage out of the expenditure stream. If saving increases, this depresses the circular flow of money. Given the supply of money in the economy, this tends to reduce employment, income and prices, thereby leading to a deflationary process in the economy. On the other hand, consumption expenditure and investment are injections in the circular flow of money wihci tend to increase employment, income, output and prices, and thus lead to inflationary tendencies.

4. *Basis of the Multirplier*. Again, if leakages exceed injections in the circular flow of money, the total money supply becomes less than the total output. This leads to a cumulative decline in employment, income, outpur,and prices over time. On the other hand, if injections into the circular flow of money exceed leakages, the money supply is increased in the economy, This leads to a cumulative rise in employment, income, output, and prices over a period of time. In fact, the basis of the Keynesian multiplier is the cumulative movements I the circular flow of money.

5. *Importance of Monetary Policy.* The study of the circular flow of money also highlights the importance of monetary policy in bringing about the equality of saving and investment. Figure 4.2 shows that the equality between saving and investment comes about through the capital market. The capital market is controlled by the government through its monetary policy. When saving exceeds investment or investment exceeds saving, there is deflation or inflation. It is through monetary policy that investment is encouraged or retarded to control deflationary or inflationary situations.

6. *Importance of Fiscal Policy.* The circular flow of money also points towards the importance of fiscal policy. For the circular flow of money to be in equilibrium, saving plus taxes (S+T) must equal investment plus government expenditure (I+G) . S+T represent leakages from the money stream which must be offset by injections of *I+G* into the money stream. So if S+T exceed I+G deflationary tendencies develop in the economy which can be removed by adopting such fiscal measures as reduction in taces and by increase in government expenditure. On the other hand, If $I + G$ exceed $S + T$ there are inflationary tendencies in the economy which can be checked by encouraging saving andincreaing government. revenues through taxation. Thus the circular flow of money highlights the importance of adopting compensatory fiscal policy.

7 *Importance of Trade Policies.* Similarly, imports are leakages in the circular flow of money because they are payments made to a foreign country. To stop it, the government adopts such measures as to increase exports and decrease imports. Thus the circular flow of money points towards the importance of adopting export promotion and import control policies.

8 *Basis of Flow of Funds Accounts .* The circular flow of money helps in calculating national income on the basis of the flow of funds accounts. The flow of funds accounts are concerned with all transactions in the economy that are accomplished by money transfers. They show the financial transactions among different sectors of the economy, and the link between saving and investment, and lending and borrowing by them.

To conclude, the circular flow of money possesses much theoretical and practical significance in an economy.

EXERCISES

1. What do you mean by the circular flow of money? Explain the circular flow of money in an economy. Use diagram to illustrate your answer.
2. What is meant by the circular flow of money? Explain the significance of circular flow of money in an economy.
3. Explain the circular flow of money in an economy including the foreign sector. Use diagrams to illustrate your answer.

CHAPTER 5

Monetary Standards

1. MEANING AND TYPES OF MONETARY STANDARD

Monetary standard refers to the overall set of laws and practices which control the quality and quantity of money in a country. It is, in fact, the standard money of the country which determines and regulates the exchange value of goods and services. Thus the monetary standard of a nation is its standard monetary unit. If, for instance, the standard monetary unit is made of silver, the country is said to be on the silver standard. A monetary standard aims at maintaining stability in the internal as well as external value of the currency.

There have been different types of monetary standards in the evolution of money. But only two types of monetary standards have been popular with nations in the recent past. They are metallic or commodity standard and paper or fiat standard. The metallic standard refers to a monetary system in which the value of the monetary unit is expressed in terms of a fixed quantity of some metal. If the monetary system is related to only one metal, it is known as *monometallism.* Monometallism may refer to the gold standard, if the metal is gold, and to silver standard, if the metal is silver. If the monetary unit is made of two metals, the monetary standard is called *bimetallism.* In the paper standard, paper notes circulate as legal tender money. They may be convertible into the metal, gold or silver, of a fixed weight, or inconvertible.

In this chapter, we shall study the gold standard, bimetallism and paper standard.

2. THE GOLD STANDARD

Meaning. The gold standard is a monometallic standard in which the value of the monetary unit is fixed in terms of a specified weight and purity. As pointed out by Robertson, "Gold standard is a state of affairs in which a country keeps the value of its monetary and the value of a defined weight of gold at an equality with one another."[1] Coulborn's definition is simple. He writes, "The gold standard is an arrangement whereby the chief piece of money of a country is exchangeable with a fixed quantity of gold of a specified quality."[2]

1. D.H. Robertson, *op. cit.,* p. 64.
2. W.A.L. Coulborn. *op. cit.,* p. 117.

TYPES OF THE GOLD STANDARD

The meaning of the gold standard, as given above, relates to its general form. But different countries at different times adopted different types of gold standard which are explained as under.

1. *Gold Currency Standard.* This standard prevailed prior to 1914 in the UK, USA and certain other countries. It was also known as the gold coin standard, gold circulation standard or full or pure gold standard. It had six main features: (i) gold coins of a definite weight and fineness circulated within the country. For instance, in England the sovereign was the gold coin which contained 123.2744 grammes of gold of 11/12th purity. (ii) The gold coin (i.e. sovereign in Britain) was full and unlimited legal tender. (iii) Non-gold metallic coins and paper currency notes also circulated side by side but they were convertible on demand into gold coins at fixed rates, (iv) There was free coinage in gold. Any body could take gold or jewellery to the mint for coinage, (v) Gold coins could be freely minted for other purposes, (vi) Export and import of gold was free and unrestricted.

Since this standard was costly to operate, it was given up after the first world war in favour of the gold bullion standard.

2. *Gold Bullion Standard.* This standard was in operation in the UK between 1925-31 and in India between 1927-31. This monetary system had five distinguishing features: (1) Gold coins did not circulate within the country. The legal tender currency in circulation consisted of paper currency notes and token coins of silver and other metals. (ii) These were convertible at fixed rates into gold bars or bullion. For instance, in England currency notes were convertible into gold bars containing 400 oz. of gold at the fixed price of £3-17s-10d per oz. of ll/12th fineness. When India adopted this system in 1927, rupee was convertible into gold bars containing 40 tolas at the price of Rs. 27, 7 annas 10 pies per tola.[3] (iii) For converting currency into gold, the monetary authority was required to keep gold bars in reserve. (iv) The monetary authority also bought gold from the public at a fixed price. (v) Gold was freely exported and imported.

3. *Gold Exchange Standard.* This system was in operation in India between 1898 to 1913 and in a number of eastern countries which were poor and did not possess sufficient gold. But mostly such countries were under the colonial rule and their currencies were linked with the currency of the ruling country. The principal features of this monetary system were: (i) Gold coins did not circulate within the country. (ii) The currency consisted of paper notes and token coins of silver and other metals. (iii) These were not convertible into gold coins or bullion, (iv) But the local currency was linked with some foreign currency which was on gold currency standard, (v) It was convertible into such foreign currency at a fixed rate. For instance, the Indian rupee coins were convertible into British sterling at the ratio of ls-4d per rupee, (vi) Since the currency was indirectly linked with gold, prices of goods and services were consequently determined by the price of gold, (vii) Gold could not be exported and imported freely. Only the monetary authority was authorised to export or import gold. But actually payments were made in the securities of the two countries. For instance, rupee and sterling securities were bought and sold by England and India respectively at the fixed exchange rate of ls-4d per rupee.

4. *Gold Reserve Standard.* England was the first country to abandon the gold standard in 1931, followed by the USA in 1933 and France in 1936. This led to instability in their exchange rates. To maintain exchange stability, they entered into Tripartite Monetary Agreement in September 1936 and they were joined by the Netherlands, Belgium and Switzerland in the same year. This Agreement came to be known as the Gold Reserve Standard and worked successfully till the outbreak of the Second World War in September 1939. The main features of this system were: *(a)* There were no gold coins within the country, *(b)* The currency consisted of paper notes and token coins of cheap metals, *(c)* This currency was incovertible into bullion, *(d)* Under the Agreement, each country maintained an Exchange Equalisation Fund which kept gold, local currency and foreign exchange. The exchange rate was stabilised by purchase and sale of foreign exchange or gold from the fund, *(e)* There was no free export or import of gold except by the Fund authority for maintaining stability in the exchange rate. Such gold was meant to be kept in the Fund. *(f)* There was strict secrecy about the reserves of gold and foreign exchange kept in the Fund.

5. *Gold Parity Standard.* This system has emerged with the establishment of the International Monetary

3. These weights and currency were prevalent in those times.

Fund in 1944. It does not possess any feature of the various gold standards explained above. Under this system, every country has to declare the par value of its monetary unit in terms of a fixed quantity of gold. So this is not gold standard in the real sense of the term, except that it aims at keeping the exchange rate of the currency stable in terms of gold.

"But whatever form the gold standard may take, its essential characteristic is that the currency is, either directly or at one move, either in volume or in value, linked to gold."[4]

Crowther has distinguished between *domestic and international gold standard.* According to him. "The domestic gold standard is mainly concerned, with the *volume* of money and with its influence on the domestic price level. The international gold standard is concerned with the external *value* of the currency and with problem of maintaining the stability of foreign exchange." All the variants of the gold standard discussed above differ with regard to" the operation of the domestic gold standard in one respect or the other. But they have one feature in common relating to the maintenance of exchange stability under international gold standard. We shall, therefore, be concerned with the discussion of the working of the international gold standard which was abandoned by the countries of the world in 1930s.

Rules of the Gold Standard

The gold standard functioned smoothly before the First World War. In order to study its working, it is essential to analyse the conditions for its success. These conditions have come to be known as the *"rules of the game"*. The Macmillan Committee pointed out in this connection, "It is difficult to define in precise terms what is implied by the rules of the game." The management of an international standard is an art and not a science, and no one would suggest that it is possible to draw up a formal code of action. Much must be left to time and circumstances."[5] But it recommended the following general principles for the successful working of the international gold standard.

1. It should involve a common agreement among nations as to the objectives for which it existed.
2. It should bring stability of prices and guarantee stability of exchange.
3. Individual central banks should avoid such actions which might endanger stability of prices through their effects on the policy of other central banks.

Given these three principles the countries on the gold standard were expected to observe the following rules or conditions for its smooth working.

1. There should be free and unrestricted export and import of gold between countries.
2. The country receiving (importing) gold should expand credit within the country and the gold-exporting country should contract credit.
3. There should be a high degree of price, wages, income and cash flexibility in countries on the gold standard so that these change with gold movements. For instance, when gold flows into the country, money supply should increase which should lead to rise in prices, wages and income, and costs would be adjusted accordingly. The opposite would be the case in the event of the outflow of gold to other countries. It would lead to decrease in money supply, fall in prices, wages, income and costs. Thus the success of the gold standard depends upon flexibility in the economic set-up of the economy.
4. The successful working of the gold standard presupposed the existence of free trade among nations. The gold standard was essentially a laissez-faire standard.
5. The country on the gold standard should strictly adhere to the policy of maintaining exchange stability and other objectives should be subservient to it.
6. There should be no disturbing large capital movements based on speculative activities. In fact, the smooth working of the gold standard depended to a large extent upon the degree to which the movement of short-term funds could be influenced by changes in the bank rate.
7. Another condition was that the gold value of the domestic currency was to be kept stable. It should not be overvalued or undervalued.
8. Last but not the least, the success of the gold standard required normal times. That is why, it broke

---

4. G. Crowther, *op. cit.,* p. 280.
5. *Report of the Committee on Finance and Industry, 1913.*

down during the First World War and the disturbed conditions following the War.

9. The gold standard worked smoothly so long as the countries followed these rules to the letter. As pointed out by Crowther, "The gold standard is a jealous god. It will work provided it is given exclusive devotion."[6] This continued upto 1914 and after that when they started breaking these rules gradually, the gold standard broke down.

Working of the Gold Standard

The question arises: how did the gold standard work or what was the mechanism of the gold standard? The answer to this question is related to the functioning of the gold standard before 1914.

All countries which were on the gold standard in the late 19th and early 20th century were inter-related and inter-dependent. A country having a favourable balance of trade received gold from other country, because it had excess of exports over imports. On the contrary, a country having an unfavourable trade suffered from the loss of gold on account of the excess of imports over exports. This movement of gold affected both the countries, the country with the inflow of gold and that having an outflow of gold.

The monetary reserves of the country with the gold inflow would increase. It would lead to an increase in the internal money supply of the country. The increased money supply was reflected in increased expenditures on goods and services. This led to rise in prices, wages, income, and costs. Consequently, the increase in the cost-price structure of the economy's domestically produced goods became relatively dearer in comparison with foreign goods. This tended to reduce exports and increase imports. Thus a surplus in the balance of payment of a country caused by a favourable balance of trade would be automatically corrected in the country with the gold inflow.

On the other hand, the reverse process would be repeated in the country with the gold outflow. The outflow of gold would lead to decline in its monetary reserves. This would decrease the internal money supply of the country. As a result, prices declined along with wages, income, and costs. This made the domestically produced goods relatively cheaper than foreign goods. So exports increased and imports declined. Thus a deficit in the balance of payments of a country caused by an unfavourable balance of trade was automatically corrected in the country with gold outflow.

Was it Automatic? From the above analysis of the working of the gold standard, it seems that there was some visible hand which helped the attainment of "automatic equilibrium" in the balance of payments of both gold inflow and gold outflow countries. But this is not a correct view about the actual working of the gold standard. In reality, there was a large degree of management in its working even during its hey days before the First World War. Powerful central banks, like the Bank of England managed the internal policies of the government in each country for the gold standard to function the way the economists thought it should function.

One of the principal objectives of the central bank policy was to maintain stable exchange rates for a country on the gold standard. The adjustment in the domestic price level as a result of gold movements was not automatic. Rather, it was modified by the bank rate policy of the central bank.

Moreover, the total currency in a country was connected to gold reserves which increased or decreased with the rise or fall in the latter. It was the total volume of currency which affected the price level in turn. So the central bank operated the bank rate policy to undertake corrective measures within the economy for keeping exchange rates stable with gold outflows or inflows.

When there was an outflow of gold, the gold reserves of the country declined. Consequently, the total volume of currency also declined and prices fell. But in order to protect the monetary reserves of the country, the central bank raised the bank rate. Higher interest rates induced the indigenous capitalists to invest funds internally and also attracted foreign investment to the country. These tendencies led to the reduction of gold outflow and also to an inflow of gold. In either case, the monetary reserves of the country were protected. Similarly, the bank rate was lowered and prices increased when there was an inflow of gold. As a matter of practice, the central bank seldom adopted corrective measures in the event of gold inflow. The increase in the

6. G. Crowther, *op. cit.*, p. 306.

monetary reserves of the country was welcomed. So it was left to the gold losing country to undertake corrective measures.

The Deflationary Bias. Whenever a country lost gold, it experienced falling prices, In fact, it was in the interest of the gold losing country to deflate prices. But it became difficult to bring revival once deflation started. If the country lost much gold during a short period of time, the deflating pressures along with the rise in the bank rate would bring a financial crisis. Since wages are rigid in the downward direction, it would lead to large scale unemployment. Once the economy was in deep depression, it was difficult to bring a revival with the efforts of the central bank. Considering all this, Mrs. Joan Robinson pointed out that the gold standard had an "inherent bias towards deflation".

There were two more reasons for the deflationary bias of the gold standard mechanism. First, trade took place between countries of unequal size. But gold standard presupposed trade relations between homogeneous countries of approximately equal size." Second, for some countries balance of payments were more important relative to their internal economy, while for others balance of payments had less importance. Naturally, countries which depended more on imports having large gold outflows tended to have deflationary bias.

Despite this deflationary bias, the gold standard functioned smoothly prior to 1914. This is because "the gold standard mechanism was ... never put to a really severe test. Major international interruptions were absent, the price-cost structures of the different countries were in conformity with the. exchange rates and internati6nal capital movements served mainly to put sufficient reserves at the disposal of those countries which were, at the moment in need of it."[7]

The Decline and Fall of the Gold Standard

The gold standard could work only if the "rules of the game" were observed which could be observed under normal conditions. But when the First World War broke out in 1914, the belligerent countries went off the gold standard because they had to suspend convertibility of currency into gold. They withdrew gold coins from circulation and replaced them by paper currency. England prohibited the melting of gold coins and the export of gold though it did not stop conversion of notes into gold coins. Some of the countries did make payments to the neutral countries in gold. During the War the belligerent countries suffered from inflation of varying degrees. But they could not be controlled because the countries could not observe the rules of the game. So the gold standard virtually broke down during the War period.

After the War, most countries suffered from inflation of varying degrees which made it difficult to fix gold value of domestic currency at pre-War rates. Prestige led Great Britain to return to the gold standard at the pre-War parity and it was commonly estimated that the pound was overvalued by 10 per cent. This was because the price-level in Britain was higher than in America by this percentage. The actual exchange rate was fixed at $4.866=£1 but the equilibrium rate was $4.38=£1. So England's goods were overpriced and of America's under-priced. This adversely affected British exports and favoured imports from America. But Italy overvalued its Lira and France undervalued its Franc. By 1928 the restoration of the gold standard was complete.

But it was not the same gold standard which existed before the 1914 war. Rather, it was a truncated gold standard with failure of the governments to follow the golden rules of the gold standard game. Consequently, with the beginning of the Great Depression in 1929, the final collapse of the gold standard began. Four South American countries were the first to go off the gold standard by the end of 1930. England, alongwith twenty-two other countries, abandoned the gold standard in 1931. By the end of 1936, practically all countries had left the gold standard.

Causes of the Breakdown of the Gold Standard. Economists have pointed to a number of causes which led to the breakdown of the gold standard. *First,* the monetary authorities in the different countries were no longer exclusively devoted to the aims of the gold standard as they had been before the War. As put by Crowther, "Gold standard is a jealous god. It will work provided it is given exclusive devotion." They were not prepared to follow the rules of the gold standard. After the restoration of the gold standard in 1920s, every country wanted to have price stability. But the primary objective of the gold standard was to have exchange stability.

7. G.N. Halm, *Monetary Theory,* 2/e.

So price stability was not compatible with the maintenance of the gold standard. Hence it broke down for failure to observe this golden rule of the game.

Second, the technical task of maintaining exchange stability was more difficult than before the First World War. Exchange stability could be maintained by making adjustment in the internal price level of countries. But it was difficult to make constant readjustment in prices due to three reasons: (i) The domestic currencies were either overvalued or undervalued; *(ii)* there was downward rigidity in the wage-cost structure in case of downward readjustment of prices; and *(iii)* readjustments were also difficult because the short-term funds of banks could not be influenced by changes in the rate of interest. The short-term funds were affected more by speculation or fear.than by the interest rate.

Third, the imposition of Reparations and the insistence on the repayment of War debts from Germany made it difficult for the foreign market to be controlled by the weapons of the gold standard. To pay Reparations and War Debts, Germany had to buy dollars irrespective of its gold reserve position and the bank rate, and the countries which received such payments could not make adjustments accordingly.

Fourth, almost every country imposed high tariffs. Imposition of high tariffs especially by the creditor countries restricted imports from debtor countries. This was a clear violation of the rule of the gold standard. When a debtor country was losing gold, it was essential for it to lower internal prices in order to expand exports. But high tariffs by the creditor countries prevented the expansion of exports and thus made adjustments in foreign exchange difficult. This led many countries to abandon the gold standard.

Fifth, the central banks failed to observe the golden rule: "expand credit when gold is coming in; contract credit when gold is going out." The United States and France, which were receiving gold did not expand credit sufficiently. On the other hand, Germany and Great Britain which were losing gold tried to make adjustments by borrowing from the gold-receiving countries. This meant the non-observance of the rule of the gold standard. There were, however, some *immediate causes* which led to the breakdown of the gold standard beginning from 1930.

(i) The first cause was the steep fall in the price levels of a number of countries. This brought a fall in the demand for exports and reduced the foreign exchange earnings of exporting countries. These were the countries which depended on exports of raw materials whose prices fell sharply. Their export earnings declined considerably but they could not protect their gold reserves from falling as they continued to make gold payments for their international obligations.

(ii) The second immediate cause of the abandonment of the gold standard was the virtual cessation of international lending from 1929. We saw above that many debtor countries had been borrowing from the United States to meet their international payment and protect their gold reserves during 1920-27. But with the coming in of the Great Depression, such countries stopped borrowings and found it difficult to make repayments of interest and principal because their export earnings were declining.

(iii) The last immediate cause was the presence of large short-term international debts against London and New York financial markets. These were payable on demand at short notice. A wave of fear caused the lenders of these short-term funds or "Hot Money" to ask for their repayments. It all started with the failure of the largest bank in Austria, the Credit Anstalt in May 1931. This led to international banking panic in Germany, France, United States and Great Britain, where there were run on banks by creditors with the result that they stopped payments and froze credits in terms of gold. And the gold standard had finally ended. Hawtrey observes, "The immediate cause of the crisis, it is true, was the withdrawal of foreign money, first from Austria and Germany and then from England, But this was the result of distrust, and the distrust was directly due to the appreciation of gold."

MERITS OF THE GOLD STANDARD

The international gold standard which operated for more than three decades in different forms had certain merits.

1. *Inspired Public Confidence.* The gold standard inspired public confidence because the domestic currency was linked with gold. People knew that gold was an internationally accepted medium of payment, and a standard and a store of value. Therefore, they had full confidence in the paper currency which was convertible into gold bullion or coins or securities.

2. *No Outside Interference.* The international gold standard had the merit of working without any outside interference by any other country or international authority.

3. *Automatic Operation.* The gold standard functioned smoothly provided 'the rules of the game" were observed. These rules were not complex but easy to understand and follow for the countries. Thus the gold standard provided a simple and automatic monetary system to the countries of the world.

4. *Stable Exchange Rates.* Another merit of the gold standard was that it maintained stable exchange rates between countries. The exchange rate of every country was fixed in terms of its mint par or the gold value of its currency. The actual exchange rate between gold export and gold import points which took account of the cost of transporting gold from one country to the other. Thus the exchange rate was stable and fluctuations occurred only between the two gold points.[8]

5. *Stable Internal Prices.* The gold standard secured relative stability of internal prices. When there was an inflow of gold, prices rose. And they fell with gold outflow. But when prices rose, exports diminished and imports increased. On the other hand, fall in prices led to expansion of exports and decline in imports. These opposite tendencies started gold outflow in the former case and gold inflow in the latter case. Ultimately, price stability was maintained in the trading countries.

6. *Check on Inflation.* Under the gold standard the currency of a country was linked with gold and was convertible into it. As the issuing of currency was backed by specified quantity of gold, there was a limit up to which the authorities could issue currency. For every increase in the amount of currency, gold reserves were also required to be increased to a given extent. There was thus an automatic check on the issuing of paper currency by a country. There was also no fear of inflation, because the country could not increase the quantity of money in unlimited quantity. As against this, the present system of managed paper standard, having a fixed gold backing, leads the authorities to issue paper money in unlimited quantities thereby leading to inflation.

7. *Expansion of International Trade.* The gold standard helped in the expansion of international trade. This was made possible by stable exchange rate and stable value of gold in countries. These led to the expansion of international trade and capital movements.

Demerits of the Gold Standard

Despite these merits, the actual working of the gold standard revealed a number of disadvantages which the countries of the world had to experience. Some of them were as under:

1. *Fair Weather Standard.* Critics pointed out that the gold standard acted like a fair weather friend. It worked smoothly in normal or peace times but failed during war or economic crises. Its actual working shows that it had to be suspended during the First World War and finally abandoned during the Great Depression. So it was a fair weather standard.

2. *Not Automatic.* It is a misnomer to say that the gold standard worked automatically. In fact, all varieties of it had to be managed by the.monetary authority or the central bank. The gold standard did not work automatically. The central bank had to change the bank rate in accordance with gold movements in order to affect the price level.

3. *Exchange Stability at the Cost of Economic Stability.* One of the principal objectives of the gold standard was to maintain exchange stability. But this was always attained at the cost of economic stability. When every time there were gold movement, the internal price level had to be adjusted accordingly in order to maintain exchange stability. These price fluctuations led to internal economic instability which ultimately harmed the country. It is for this reason that now-a-days all countries prefer internal price stability to exchange stability.

4. *Anarchy in World Credit Control.* Hawtrey characterised the gold standard as state of anarchy in world credit control.[9] Since the gold standard was a laissezfaire standard and operated only under normal times, it failed miserably in conditions of severe inflation or deflation. During the First World War, inflation spread to all countries of the world. On the other hand, when depression started in 1929 it became a worldwide phenomenon. Thus the gold standard by itself was unable to control either inflation or deflation. Rather, it had

---

8. For the understanding of this mechanism refer- to the Chapter on "Foreign Exchange".
9. R. G. Hawtrey, *The Gold Standard: Theory and Practice,* 5/e, 1947.

to sacrifice itself at the altars of inflation and deflation.

5. *Deflationary Bias.* According to Mrs. Joan Robinson, the gold standard had an inherent bias towards deflation. It was in the interest of the gold losing country to deflate prices, But once deflation started it became very difficult to bring revival even with the best efforts of the central bank. The long drawn depression of 1930s proved this fact without any shadow of doubt.

6. *No Independent Policy. A* country on the gold standard could not follow an independent policy of its own. It had to follow that policy which was adopted by all other countries. Failure to follow a common policy alongwith other countries mean; abandoning the gold standard. This implied breaking of all trade relations with countries on the gold standard which could be harmful for the country.

7. *Costly Standard.* The gold standard was a costly standard because it was based on gold. Every country had to circulate gold coins or keep gold reserves. As against this the paper standard is much cheaper and also economises the use of gold.

8. *Rigid Standard.* The gold standard was a rigid standard because for its success the rules of the game had to be observed in letter and spirit. A country could not increase the money supply to finance a war or development activities or any financial emergency without increasing the gold reserves with its central bank. If it had to export gold to import the necessary equipment, raw materials and other goods it needed for war or development purposes. It was expected to reduce the internal price level by force in keeping with the rules of the gold standard game. Thus it was a highly rigid standard.

9. *Adverse Effects of Interest Rate Changes.* Under one of the rules of the gold standard, the central bank of the country was required to affect changes in the bank rate in keeping with gold movements. When there was an infl6w of gold, the bank rate was lowered, while it was raised with the outflow of gold. Such changes in interest rates were forced upon trade and industry simply to expand or reduce money income within the country. They, therefore, adversely affected trade and industry.

Taking into account the various disadvantages of the gold standard enumerated above, it can be concluded that the gold standard was an unnecessary standard. The managed paper standard can secure on all the advantages enjoyed by the gold standard minus its disadvantages. That is why the gold standard is now a thing of the past and is only of academic interest, never to be restored again.

WHAT LED TO THE NON-RESTORATION OF THE GOLD STANDARD?

After the collapse of the gold standard, no country was willing to restore the gold standard for the following reasons: *First,* the supply of gold could not be increased to meet its increasing demand. So no country was willing to export it to observe the rules of the game. *Secondly,* more so because the majority of gold reserves flowed into the United States. *Thirdly,* no country was willing to bring instability to its economy for the sake of maintaining exchange stability. *Fourthly,* development of nationalism motivated every country to formulate economic policies in keeping with its self-interest. *Lastly,* every country felt that it could manage its monetary affairs in a far better way by adopting a managed paper standard than the gold standard.

3. BIMETALLISM

Bimetallism, also known as bimetallic standard, is a monetary system under which the monetary unit of the country is expressed by law in terms of two metals, usually gold and silver, in a specific ratio. In other words, under bimetallism both silver and gold coins circulate simultaneously within the country. They are unlimited legal tender. They are minted freely and in unlimited quantities free or with some charge. Both metals are imported and exported freely. Both types of coins are exchanged for each other at a fixed mint par ratio.

Bimetallism was in vogue in England throughout the 18th century. The United States adopted it in 1792, when the mint ratio between silver and gold was fixed at 15 :1. France adopted it in 1803 followed by Belgium, Switzerland and Italy in 1865. With the growing popularity of the gold standard, it was abandoned by these European countries in 1874.

Merits of Bimetallism

Bimetallism as monetary system had the following advantages:

1. *Adequate Supply of Currency.* One of the merits of bimetallism was that it ensured an adequate supply of currency within the country. As both gold and silver coins were in circulation and freely minted, there was no likelihood of both becoming short in supply simultaneously.

2. *Price Stability.* It was also argued that flexibility of money supply assured price stability. The internal price level was linked with the prices of gold and silver. And the prices of gold and silver depended upon their supply and demand. If the output of silver rose, that of gold fell and vice versa. It meant that fall in the price of silver was compensated by rise in the price of gold and vice versa. So there was greater stability in the prices of gold and silver taken together than in the case of one metal. It was like two drunken men walking hand in hand steadily than apart.

3. *Stable Price of Silver.* The proponents of bimetallism argued in the last quarter of the 19th century and twenties of the 20th century that bimetallism would stop the fall in the price of silver. In those days, the price of silver was falling and the silver producing countries were at a disadvantage in trading with gold standard countries. It was, therefore, felt that the adoption of bimetallism would increase the demand for silver and raise its price. This would increase the purchasing power of silver-producing countries and also help in overcoming depression in them.

4. *Stable Exchange Rates.* It was further argued that bimetallism helped to maintain stable exchange rates between countries. This was because the ratio of exchange between gold and silver was fixed, being determined by the gold value of silver. Therefore, there was no possibility of the market rate of exchange to deviate from the mint par rate of exchange.

5. *Encouragement to Foreign Trade.* As a corollary to the above, bimetallism encouraged foreign trade in two ways. First, due to exchange stability between countries, and second, a country on bimetallism could have trade relations with any country on bimetallism and on silver or gold standard.

6. *Easy to Keep Cash Reserves.* As both gold and silver coins were unlimited legal tender under bimetallism, it was convenient and easy for commercial banks to keep minimum cash reserves against their liabilities either in gold or silver coins. Similarly, it was also argued that it was more easy for the government to meet its cash requirements with two types of coins than with either silver or gold coins.

7. *Encouragement to Production.* The advocates of bimetallism contended that bimetallism as a monetary system was superior to the silver or gold standard because it encouraged production. As money consisted of gold and silver coins under bimetallism, the total money supply was greater than its demand. As a result, the rate of interest declined which encouraged investment and production.

Demerits of Bimetallism

The opponents of bimetallism give the following arguments against this monetary system.

1. *Inequality of Market Ratio and Mint Ratio.* The success of the bimetallic standard depended upon the maintenance of equality between the market ratio and mint ratio of gold and silver. But it was not possible to maintain this equality because of a strong tendency towards the continuous increase in the supply of one metal. This would bring a fall in its value thereby creating divergence between the two ratios. The metal whose value increased was hoarded by the people. Speculation would start thereby creating confusion within the economy.

2. *Operation ofGresham's Law.* As a corollary to the above, when there was divergence between the mint ratio and the market ratio the Gresham's law would operate and bimetallism would breakdown. According to this law, cheap money drives out dear money, or bad money drives out good money. If silver became cheaper, people used this as medium of exchange and hoarded or melted gold coins with the result that gold coins disappeared from the market. This would happen when the market rate of gold exceeded its mint rate. When Gresham's law operated the country would be on monometallism.

3. *Not Successful Internationally.* It was argued that if bimetallism was adopted by many countries, it would be successful. But this presupposed the adoption of the *same* mint ratio between the gold and silver by all countries. But it was not possible to expect international cooperation on maintaining a uniform ratio in every country. Even if the countries agreed on this question, no government could prevent its citizens to hoard or

melt the costly metal when its price increased within the country.

4. *No Price Stability.* The opponents of bimetallism dispute that flexibility of money led to price stability. According to them, there was no set rule that when the supply of one metal rose that of the other metal would fall. There was every likelihood for the supplies of both metals to fall, as has happened in the case of gold and silver.

Thus on all counts, Bimetallism was never favoured by the nations of the world. For it was a complex and costly standard which could not work smoothly. They found that a constant supply of money could be ensured in a much better way by the managed paper standard. So the study of bimetallism is of historical and academic interest only.

4. GRESHAM'S LAW

During the reign of Queen Elizabeth I it was found that debased coins continued to circulate while full-bodied coins were hoarded or melted for their specie content. The Chancellor of the Exchequer under Elizabeth I, Sir Thomas Gresham enquired about this phenomenon in 1558 and came to the conclusion that "bad money drives out good money." This has come to be known as Gresham's Law. Marshall defined this law more explicitly thus, "whenever the specie value of a certain class of coins exceeds their currency value, the coins will begin to go into the melting pot or be exported." Thus "bad money" refers to debased or clipped or worn out legal tender money such as coins and paper notes.

When full-bodied and debased coins circulate together, people have a tendency to hoard the good and try to pass on the bad ones as medium of exchange. They may even melt the full-bodied coins for bullion in order to export it or use it for jewellery. This actually happened in countries which were on silver or gold standard.

This law also operates under the bimetallic standard when gold and silver coins circulate simultaneously and one metal becomes overvalued relative to the other metal. The metal which is overvalued drives out the undervalued metal out of circulation. Suppose the mint ratio between gold and silver is 1 oz of gold coin= 15 ozs. of silver coin (1: I5). Suppose silver coins become overvalued which means that their money (face) value exceeds their metallic (intrinsic) value. On the other hand, gold coins become undervalued which means their metallic value exceeds their money value. As a result, let us say the market ratio becomes 1:17. People will thus find it profitable to melt gold coins to exchange 1 oz. of gold for 17 ozs. of silver in the market, and thereby gain 2 ozs. of silver. It is in this way that the overvalued (bad) currency drives out the undervalued (good) currency out of circulation under bimetallism.

Further, Gresham's law operates when paper currency notes circulate alongwith gold and or silver coins. In this case paper notes are bad money and gold and or silver coins are good money. This actually happened during the Revolutionary War in the United States of America when the bad paper money drove all gold and silver coins out of circulation between 1775-79.

LIMITATIONS OF THE LAW

There are, however, certain limitations of this law so that it will operate only if the following conditions are fulfilled:

1. If the total money in circulation, including, both good and bad money, exceeds the actual monetary demand of the public.
2. If the public is prepared to accept and circulate bad money.
3. If the good money is full-bodied legal tender whose face value equals its intrinsic value.
4. If the total supply of bad money is sufficient to meet the total monetary demand of the public.

With managed paper standard in circulation alongwith token coins, Gresham's law is only of limited validity in modern times. Still we find the tendency among people to pass on worn out notes and debased coins first. But this is not Gresham's law proper because neither fresh notes nor good coins go out of circulation but their use is suspended for a while.

5. PAPER CURRENCY STANDARD

Paper currency standard consists of paper money which is unlimited legal tender and token coins of cheap metals. Paper money may be either convertible or inconvertible. Convertible paper money is convertible into gold or silver coins or bullion of specified weight on demand. Paper money is not convertible into coins of a precious metal of bullion now-a-days. Therefore, it is inconvertible. People accept it because it is legal tender. Since it has the command of the government, people have to accept it. That is why it is also known as *fiat* money or standard. It is also referred to as managed standard because the issue of paper money and token coins is managed by the central bank of the country.

Merits of the Paper Standard

The paper standard, which is universally used, has a number of merits :

1. *Economical.* The paper standard is cheaper than gold or silver standard. There is no need to waste gold or silver for coinage purposes. Rather precious metals can be used for productive purposes and for making payments to foreign countries. As paper money is not convertible, there is no need to keep gold in the form of reserves. The monetary authorities keep only a fixed quantity of gold in reserve for reasons of security. Thus the paper standard is cheap and economical and even a poor country can easily adopt it.

2. *Elastic.* The paper standard is a highly useful monetary system because it possesses great elasticity. The monetary authority can easily adjust the money supply in accordance with the requirements of the economy. This was not possible under the gold standard. The supply of money can be increased by printing more notes in times of financial emergency, war, and for economic development. It can also be reduced when the economic situation so demands. Thus there is also freedom in the management of the money supply in the economy.

3. *Price Stability.* As a corollary to the above, the paper standard ensures price stability in the country. The monetary authority can stabilise the price level by maintaining equilibrium between demand and supply of money by an appropriate monetary policy.

4. *Free from Cyclical Effects.* The paper standard is free from the effects of business cycles arising in other countries. This merit was not available to other monetary standards, especially the gold standard, where cyclical movements in one country were automatically passed on to other countries through gold movements.

5. *Full Utilisation of Resources.* The gold standard had a deflationary bias whereby the resources of the country remained unutilised. Whenever there was gold outflow prices fell and resources became unemployed. But this is not the case under the paper standard in which the monetary authority can manipulate the monetary policy in order to ensure full utilisation of the country's resources.

6. *Equilibrium in Exchange Rate.* One of the merits of the paper standard is that it immediately restores equilibrium in the exchange rate of a country whenever disequilibrium occurs in the demand and supply of its currency in the foreign exchange market.

7. *Portable.* It is very convenient to carry large sums of paper money from one place to another.

8. *Easy to count.* It is easier to count paper money than metallic money.

9. *Easy to store.* It is easier to store large sums of paper money in a small space.

10. *Cognisable.* It is easy to recognise paper notes of different denominations.

11. *Replaceable.* Paper notes of one type and denomination can be easily replaced by printing notes of different types of the same denomination.

Demerits of the Paper Standard

Despite these merits, the paper standard has certain disadvantages:

1. *Inflationary Bias.* One of the serious defect of the paper standard is that it has an inflationary bias. As paper notes are inconvertible, there is every likelihood of the government printing notes in excess of the requirements. Or, the government may deliberately resort to the printing press to meet a financial emergency or war or even to meet ordinary budget deficits. This leads to excess of money supply and to inflation in the country.

2. *Price Stability a Myth.* It has been pointed out in the merits of the paper standard that it leads to price

stability. In actuality, price stability is a myth as has been the experience of the majority of countries on the paper standard.

3. *Exchange Instability.* Another disadvantage of this system is that it leads to instability in exchange rates whenever there are large fluctuations in external prices as against internal prices. Such wide and violent fluctuations in exchange rates are harmful for the growth of international trade and capital movements among countries. These have led governments to adopt exchange control measures.

4. *Lacks Confidence.* Paper money lacks confidence as it is not backed by gold reserves.

5. *Lacks Durability.* Paper money has less durability than metallic coins. It can be easily destroyed by fire or insects.

6. *Unstable.* Paper money lacks stability because its supply can be changed easily.

7. *Uncertainty.* Instability in the value of paper money leads to uncertainty in the economy which adversely affects business and economic progress.

8. *Token Money.* Paper money is token money and in the event of demonetisation of notes, they have no intrinsic value and are simply like waste paper.

9. *Not Automatic.* The paper currency standard does not operate automatically. It is a highly managed standard which requires much care and caution on the part of the monetary authority. A little carelessness may bring disaster to the economy.

6. STANDARD SYSTEMS OF NOTE ISSUE

Over the years, different countries have evolved various methods of note issue and adopted them from time to time. They are discussed below:

1. *Simple Deposit System.* Under this system, the monetary authority is required to keep 100% of the bullion (gold or silver) for every note issued. That is why it is also known as the Full Reserve System.

This system has certain merits. It is safe and enjoys public confidence because there is full backing of the bullion for every note issued. The monetary authority cannot take any arbitrary decision in issuing notes. So there is no possibility of over issue of notes. There is also the saving of precious metals through debasement because metal coins are not circulated.

However, this system lacks in elasticity *firstly*, because the money supply cannot be increased without the full backing of bullion reserves. This may be harmful during war or emergency or for development. It may also adversely affect trade and currency. *Second,* this system is especially unsuited for poor countries lacking insufficient quantities of gold or silver. *Third,* it is uneconomical for it does not make a profitable use of bullion reserves lying idle with the monetary authority. Thus this system is highly impracticable in modern times. Perhaps this is the reason for its being not put into practice in any country of the world.

2. *Fixed Fiduciary System.* Under this system, a fixed amount of notes is issued by the central bank against reserves of government securities. Such amount is issued on the faith or fiduciary of the central bank and is called the fiduciary limit. The central bank is required to keep 100% gold reserves beyond the fiduciary limit. The fiduciary limit is raised from time to time with the expansion of trade and industry. This system was introduced in England in 1844, in India in 1860, followed by Japan and Norway.

This system ensures security, inspires public confidence, and is without any danger of mismanaging the currency through overissue of notes by the central bank.

But it has also certain disadvantages. *First,* it is a rigid and inelastic system because in times of a financial emergency, notes cannot be issued without keeping cent per cent gold in reserves. *Second,* the system is inconvenient because in the event of a fall in gold reserves, the central bank has to withdraw notes from circulation with the result that the quantity of money is reduced in the country with its adverse effects on prices, trade and industry. Third, this system is uneconomical because gold reserves are blocked up with the central bank. It was, therefore, abandoned by all countries after World War I when they faced these problems.

3. *Maximum Fiduciary System.* Under this system, there is a maximum limit up to which the central bank is authorised to issue notes without any gold reserves. But there has to be full backing of gold reserves beyond this limit. The central bank is, however, authorised to raise or lower the maximum fiduciary limit and to fix the quantity of gold reserves. Thus this system is not rigid but is elastic. It is also economical because the gold

reserves can be kept to the minimum to meet the requirements of trade and industry. In case the central bank fixes the fiduciary limit very high, there may be excess of notes in circulation thereby leading to inflation. This system was in operation in France, Japan, Russia, Norway, Finland and England. This system has one major defect that there is the possibility of inflation through over issue when the maximum limit may be raised by the government.

4. *Proportional Reserve System.* In this system, a certain percentage of the total notes issued by the central bank has to be in gold reserves and the remaining in the form of government securities. This percentage varied between 25 to 40 per cent in countries like Switzerland, Holland, Belgium, USA and India. This system is simple and elastic. The money supply can be changed with changes in the percentage of gold reserves. It provides sufficient security because a certain percentage of note issue is supported by gold.

Still, this system has certain *drawbacks. Firstly,* It is uneconomical because large quantities of gold reserves have to be kept which cannot be issued for productive purposes. *Second,* if the gold reserves fall, the reduction in currency in circulation may be more than in proportion to the fall in reserves. This may lead to deflationary tendencies. The opposite may happen when gold reserves increase.' This system was in vogue in India between 1927 to 1956.

5. *Minimum Reserve System.* Under the minimum reserve system, the central bank is authorised to issue notes up to any extent but it must keep a statutory minimum reserve of gold and foreign securities. India adopted this system of note issue in 1956 after discarding the proportional reserve system. Accordingly, the Reserve Bank of India is required to keep a minimum reserve of Rs 200 crores. Of this, Rs 115 crores must be in gold and Rs 85 crores in foreign securities.

This system is highly useful for developing countries because they can meet their financial requirements by printing more notes. They can also reduce the money supply to check inflation. It is, therefore, an elastic system. Further, it is very economical because only a small and fixed amount of gold is required to be kept in reserve.

Despite these merits, the minimum reserve system is a dangerous tool in the hands of the monetary authority. It can print any number of notes, thereby creating inflationary pressure within the economy. A corrupt and inefficient government can bring disaster to the economy by excessive printing of notes and thus lose confidence of the people. On the other hand, an efficient and honest administration can transform the economy by a judicious use of this system.

Conclusion. It can be concluded from the discussion of the various systems of note issue that an ideal system should fulfil the criteria of elasticity, economy, stability, convenience and safety. Every country tries to adopt that system which is flexible enough to meet its needs of growth and development. On this criterion, the minimum reserve system stands out unique among all the systems of note issue.

EXERCISES

1. When is a country said to be on gold standard? Explain the types of gold standards.
2. Discuss the merits and demerits of the gold standard.
3. What are the main features of gold standard? Distinguish between gold exchange standard and gold currency standard.
4. What were the causes of the failure of the gold standard during the inter-war period? Can the gold standard be restored?
5. Describe the mechanism of the gold standard. Why was the gold standard abandoned in 1930s?
6. What is paper currency standard? Give its merits and demerits.
7. Discuss the standard system of note issue. Which is the present system of note issue in India?

CHAPTER 6

Functions of Commercial Banks

1. MEANING

The word 'bank' is used in the sense of a commercial bank. It is of Germanic origin though some persons trace its origin to the French word 'Banqui' and the Italian word 'Banca'. Chamber's Twentieth Century Dictionary defines a bank as an "institution of the keeping, lending and exchanging, etc. of money." Economists have also defined a bank highlighting its various functions. According to Crowther, "The banker's business is to take the debts of other people to offer his own in exchange, and thereby create money."[1] A similar definition has been given by Kent who defines a bank as "an organisation whose principal operations are concerned with the accumulation of the temporarily idle money of the general public for the purpose of advancing to others for expenditure.[2] Sayers, on the other hand, gives a still more detailed definition of a bank thus: "Ordinary banking business consists of changing cash for bank deposits and bank deposits for cash; transferring bank deposits from one person or corporation (one 'depositor') to another; giving bank deposits in exchange for bills of exchange, government bonds, the secured or unsecured promises of businessmen to repay, etc."[3] Thus a bank is an institution which accepts deposits from the public and in turn advances loans by creating credit. It is different from other financial institutions in that they cannot create credit though they may be accepting deposits and making advances.

2. FUNCTIONS OF COMMERCIAL BANKS

Commercial banks perform a variety of functions which can be divided as : (1) accepting deposits; (2) advancing loans; (3) Credit creation; (4) financing foreign trade; (5) agency services; and (6) miscellaneous services to customers. These functions are discussed as follows :

(1) Accepting Deposits

This is the oldest function of a bank and the banker used to charge a commission for keeping the money in its custody when banking was developing as an institution. Nowadays a bank accepts three kinds of deposits from its customers. The first is the *savings* deposits on which the bank pays small interest to the depositors who are usually small savers. The depositors are allowed to draw their money by cheques up to a

1. G. Crowther, *An Outline of Money,* p. 81.
2. R.P. Kent, *Money and Banking,* p. 76.
3. R.S. Sayers, *Modern Banking,* 7th edn., p. 22.

limited amount during a week or year. Businessmen keep their deposits in current accounts. They can withdraw any amount standing to their credit in current deposits by cheques without notice. The bank does not pay interest on such accounts but instead charges a nominal sum for services rendered to its customers. Current accounts are known as demand deposits. Deposits are also accepted by a bank in *fixed* or *time* deposits. Savers who do not need money for a stipulated period from 6 months to longer periods ranging up to 10 years or more are encouraged to keep it in fixed deposit accounts. The bank pays a higher rate of interest on such deposits. The rate of interest increases with the length of the time period of the fixed deposit. But there is always the maximum limit of the interest rate which can be paid. For instance, the interest rate on fixed deposits over five years is 11 per cent in India.

2. Advancing Loans

One of primary functions of a commercial banks is to advance loans to its customers. A bank lends a certain percentage of the cash lying in deposits on a higher interest rate than it pay on such deposits. This is how it earns profits and carries on its business. The bank advances loans in the following ways:

(a) Cash Credit. The bank advances loan to businessmen against certains specified securities. The amount of the loan is credited to the current account of the borrower. In cash of a new customer a loan account for the sum is opened. The borrower can withdraw money through cheques according to his requirements buy pays interest on the full amount.

(b) Call Loans. These are very short-term loans advanced to the bill brokers for not more than fifteen days. They are advance against first class bill or securities. Such loans can be recalled at a very short notice. In normal times they can also be renewed.

(c) Overdraft. A bank often permits a businessman to draw cheques for a sum greater than the balance lying in his current account. This is done by providing the overdraft facility up to a specific amount to the businessman. But he is charged interest only on the amount by which his current account is actually overdrawn and not by the full amount of the overdraft sanctioned to him by the banks.

(d) Discounting Bills of Exchange. If a creditor holding a bill of exchange wants money immediately, the bank provides him the money by discounting the bill of exchange. It deposits the amount of the bill in the current account of the bill-holder after deducting its rate of interest for the period of the loan which is not more than 90 days. When the bill of exchange matures, the bank gets its payment from the banker of the debater who accepted the bill.

3. Credit Creation

Credit creation is one of the most important functions of the commercial banks. Like other financial institutions, they aim at earning profits. For this purpose, they accept deposits and advance loans by keeping a small cash in reserve for day-to-day transactions. When a bank advances a loan, it opens and account in the name of the customer and does not pay him in cash but allows him to draw the money by cheque according to his needs. By granting a loan, the bank creates credit or deposit.

4. Financing Foreign Trade

A commercial bank finances foreign trade of its customers by accepting foreign bills of exchange and collecting them from foreign banks. It also transacts other foreign exchange business and buys and sells foreign currency.

5. Agency Services

A bank acts as an agent of its customers in collecting and paying cheques, bills of exchange, drafts, dividends, etc. It also buys and sells shares, securities, debentures, etc. for its customers. Further, it pays subscriptions, insurance premia, rent, electric and water bills, and other similar charges on behalf of its clients. It also acts as a trustee and executor of the property and will of its customers. Moreover, the bank acts as an income tax consultant to its clients. For some of these services, the bank charges a normal fee while it renders others free of charge.

6. Miscellaneous Services

Besides the above noted services, the commercial bank performs a number of other services. It acts as the custodian of the valuables of its customers by providing them lockers where they can keep their jewellery and valuable documents. It issues various forms of credit instruments, such as cheques, drafts, travellers' cheques, etc. which facilitate transactions. The bank also issues letter of credit and acts as a referee to its clients. It underwrites shares and debentures of companies and helps in the collection of funds from the public. Some commercial banks also publish journal which provide statistical information about the money market and business trends of the economy.

3. THE BALANCE SHEET OF A COMMERCIAL BANK

The balance sheet of a commercial bank provides a picture of its functioning. It is a statement which shows its assets and liabilities on a particular date at the end of one year. The assets are shown on the right-hand side and the liabilities on the left-hand side of the balance sheet. As in the case of a company, the assets and liabilities of a bank must balance. The balance sheet which every commercial bank in India is required to publish once in a year is shown as under :

TABLE 1. FORM OF BALANCE SHEET

Liabilities	Assets
1. Share Capital	1. Cash
2. Reserve Fund	2. Balances with the Central Bank and other banks.
3. Deposits	3. Money at call and Short-Notice
4. Borrowings from other banks	4. Bills Discounted and Purchased.
5. Bills Payable	5. Investments
6. Bills for collection	6. Loans, Advances, Cash Credits and Overdrafts.
7. Acceptances, Endorsements and other obligations	7. Liabilities of Customer for Acceptances. Endorsements and other Obligations.
8. Contingent Liabilities	8. Property, Furniture, Fixtures less Depreciation
9. Profit and Loss	9. Profit and Loss.

We analyse the distribution of assets and liabilities of a commercial bank on the basis of the division given in the above Table.

The Distribution of Assets

The assets of a bank are those items from which it receives income and profit. The *first* item on the assets side is the cash in liquid form consisting of coins and currency notes lying in reserve with it and in its branches. This is a certain percentage of its total liabilities which it is required to keep by law. Cash reserves do not yield income to the bank but are essential to satisfy the claims of its depositors. The *second* item is in the form of balances with the central bank and other banks. The commercial banks are required to keep a certain percentage of their time and demand deposits with the central bank. They are the assets of the bank because it can withdraw from them in cash in case of emergency or when the seasonal demand for cash is high. The *third* item, money at call and short notice, relates to very short-term loans advanced to bill brokers, discount houses and acceptance houses. They are repayable on demand within fifteen days. The banks charge low rate of interest on these loans. The *fourth* item of assets relates to bills discounted and purchased. The bank earns profit by discounting bills of exchange and treasury bills of 90 days duration. Some bills of exchange are accepted by a commercial bank on behalf of its customers which i ultimately purchases. They are a liability but they are included under assets because the bank can get them rediscounted from the central bank in case of need. The *fifth* item, investments by the bank in government securities, state bonds and industrial shares, yields a fixed income to the banks. The bank can sell its securities when there is need for more cash. The *sixth* item relating to loans and advances is the most profitable source of bank assets as the bank changes interest at a rate higher than the bank rate. The bank makes advances on the basis of cash credits and overdrafts and loans on the basis of recognised securities. In the *seventh* item are included liabilities of the bank's customers which the bank has accepted and endorsed on their behalf. They are the assets of the bank because the liabilities of customers remain in the custody of the bank. The bank charges a nominal commission for all acceptances and endorsements which is a source of income. The *eighth* item relates to the value of permanent assets of the bank in the form of property, furniture, fixtures, etc. They are shown in the balance sheet after allowing for depreciation every year. The *last* item includes profits retained by the bank after paying corporation tax and profits to shareholders.

The Distribution of Liabilities

The liabilities of a commercial banks are claims on it. These are the items which form the sources of its funds. Of the liabilities, the share capital of the bank is the *first* item which is contributed by its shareholders and is a liability to them. The *second* item is the reserve fund. It consists of accumulated resources which are meant to meet contiguencies such as losses in any year. The bank is required to keep a certain percentage of its annual profits in the reserve fund. The reserve fund is also a liability to the shareholders. The *third* item compresses both the time and demand deposits. Deposits are the debts of the bank to its customers. They are the main source from which the bank gets funds for investment and are indirectly the source of its income. By keeping a certain percentage of its time and demand deposits in cash the bank lends the remaining amount on interest. Borrowings from other banks is the *fourth* item. The bank usually borrows secured and unsecured loans from the central bank. Secured loans are on the basis of some recognised securities, and unsecured loans out of its reserve funds lying with the central bank. The *fifth* item bills payable refer to the bills which the bank pays out of its resources. The *sixth* items relates to bills for collection. These are the bills of exchange which the bank collects on behalf of its customers and credits the amount to their accounts. Hence it is a liability to the bank. The *seventh* item is the acceptance and endorsement of bills of exchange by the bank on behalf of its customers. These are the claims on the bank which it has to meet when the bills mature. The *eighth* item contingent liabilities relates to those claims on the bank which are unforeseen such as outstanding forward exchange contracts, claims on acknowledge debts, etc. In the *last* item, profit and loss, are shown profits payable to the shareholders which are a liability on the bank.

The various items of the balance sheet shown in Table 1 are a rough indicator of the assets and liabilities of commercial banks. The balance sheet of a particular bank shown its financial soundness. By studying the balance sheets of the major commercial banks of a country, one can also know the trend of the monetary market. "The bank balance sheet reflects bank credit extension on its asset side in loans and investments, and on the liabilities side reflects the bank's operations as an intermediary in time deposits and its role as an element in the nation's monetary system in demand deposits."

4. ROLE OF COMMERCIAL BANKS INA DEVELOPING COUNTRY

Besides performing the usual commercial banking functions, banks in developing countries play an effective role in their economic development. The majority of people in such countries are poor, unemployed and engaged in traditional agriculture. There is acute shortage of capital. People lack initiative and enterprise. Means of transport are undeveloped. Industry is depressed. The commercial banks help in overcoming these obstacles and promoting economic development. The role of a commercial bank in a developing country is discussed as under.

1. *Mobilising Saving for Capital Formation.* The commercial banks help in mobilising savings through

network of branch banking. People in developing countries have low incomes but the banks induce them to save by introducing variety of deposit schemes to suit the needs of individual depositors. They also mobilise idle savings of the few rich. By mobilising savings, the banks channelise them into productive investments. Thus they help in the capital formation of a developing country.

2. *Financing Industry.* The commercial banks finance the industrial sector in a number of ways. They provide short-term, medium-term and long-term loans to industry. In India they provide short-term loans. Income of the Latin American countries like Guatemala, they advance medium-term loans for one to three years. But in Korea, the commercial banks also advance long-term loans to industry. In India, the commercial banks undertake short-term and medium-term financing of small scale industries, and also provide hire-purchase finance. Besides, they underwrite the shares and debentures of large scale industries. Thus they not only provide finance for industry but also help in developing the capital market which is undeveloped in such countries.

3. *Financing Trade.* The commercial banks help in financing both internal and external trade. The banks provide loans to retailers and wholesalers to stock goods in which they deal. They also help in the movement of goods from one place to another by providing all types of facilities such as discounting and accepting bills of exchange, providing overdraft facilities, issuing drafts, etc. Moreover, they finance both exports and imports of developing countries by providing foreign exchange facilities to importers and exporters of goods.

4. *Financing Agriculture.* The commercial banks help the large agricultural sector in developing countries in a number of ways. They provide loans to traders in agricultural commodities. They open a network of branches in rural areas to provide agricultural credit. They provide finance directly to agriculturists for the marketing of their produce, for the modernisation and mechanisation of their farms, for providing irrigation facilities, for developing land, etc. They also provide financial assistance for animal husbandry, dairy farming, sheep breeding, poultry farming, pisciculture and horticulture. The small and marginal farmers and landless agricultural workers, artisans and petty shopkeepers in rural areas are provided financial assistance through the regional rural banks in India. These regional rural banks operate under a commercial bank. Thus the commercial banks meet the credit requirements of all types of rural people.

5. *Financing Consumer Activities.* People in underdeveloped countries being poor and having low incomes do not possess sufficient financial resources to buy durable consumer goods. The commercial banks advance loans to consumers for the purchase of such items as houses, scooters, fans, refrigerators, etc. In this way, they also help in raising the standard of living of the people in developing countries by providing loans for consumptive activities.

6. *Financing Employment Generating Activities.* The commercial banks finance employment generating activities in developing countries. They provide loans for the education of young persons studying in engineering, medical and other vocational institutes of higher learning. They advance loans to young entrepreneurs, medical and engineering graduates, and other technically trained persons in establishing their own business. Such loan facilities are being provided by a number of commercial banks in India. Thus the banks not only help inhuman capital formation but also in increasing entrepreneurial activities in developing countries.

7. *Help in Monetary Policy.* The commercial banks help the economic development of a country by faithfully following the monetary policy of the central bank. In fact, the central bank depends upon the commercial banks for the success of its policy of monetary management in keeping with requirements of a developing economy.

Thus the commercial banks contribute much to the growth of a developing economy by granting loans to agriculture, trade and industry, by helping in physical and human capital formation and by following the monetary policy of the country.

EXERCISES

1. What is a commercial bank? Discuss the various functions performed by a bank.
2. Draw an imaginary balance sheet of a commercial bank and explain the items mentioned therein.
3. Discuss the role of a commercial bank in promoting economic development.

CHAPTER 7

Organisation and Structure of Commercial Banks

1. INTRODUCTION

Commercial banks differ in their organisation and structure from country to country. The two principal banking systems are the unit banking and the branch banking. The unit banking is peculiar to the USA. Branch banking, on the other hand, is found in the majority of countries such as England, Australia, Canada, New Zealand, etc. Two other important types are the group banking and the chain banking which are also found in the USA. We discuss below these different systems of banking.

2. UNIT BANKING

Unit banks are independent, one-office banks. Their operations are confined in general to a single office. The existence of unit banking in the USA is due to legal restrictions which prevent the growth of monopoly in banking. Some unit banks have grown to large sizes but they operate under severe restrictions which limit or prohibit the establishment of branches. The unit banks operate in small towns and cities and are called country banks and city banks respectively. All unit banks are linked together by a correspondent bank relationship. A country bank has deposits in city banks, and city banks have deposits in branch banks in the same and other big cities like New York and Chicago.

MERITS OF UNIT BANKING

The unit banks, being independent and one-office banks, possess certain advantages :

1. *Efficient Working.* A unit bank works very efficiently and provides prompt service to its customers. For, like a departmental store in a locality, it has competitors in other unit banks.

2. *Personal Relations.* Since its organisers and other staff are generally local people, they have personal relations which help in mobilising larger resources for the bank.

3. *Quick Decisions.* They are able to meet the financial requirements of the people promptly and efficiently. There is always on-the-spot decision-making by the bank management.

4. *Less Irregularities.* There are less chances of fraud and irregularities under the unit banking because of the close supervision and control of the management.

5. *Local Utilisation of Deposits.* Local deposits are utilised by a unit bank on the development of the same locality and they are not to be transferred to other towns as is done under branch banking.

6. *Economies.* The unit banking operations being on a small scale, they are free from the diseconomies

which arise in large scale banking operations.

7. *Prevention of Monopoly.* Unit banking helps in the prevention of monopoly banking.

8. *Enjoy Merits of Branch Banking.* The unit banks also enjoy the advantages of branch banking as they are connected with big banks through correspondent banking system in the USA.

Demerits of Unit Banking

Despite these merits, unit banking suffers from certain disadvantages :

1. *Failure to Spread Risks.* The unit banking system suffers from its failure to spread risks. As the unit banking operations are localised in a particular area, the failure of a big party to repay the loan in time may bring disaster to the bank.

2. *Limited Resources.* Unit bank has another disadvantage that it has limited resources at its disposal. So in the event of a financial or economic crisis, if its depositors start withdrawing their money, the bank fails. This is what actually happened in the USA during the Great Depression of 1930s when 5000 banks failed and an additional 1200 were absorbed by larger banks.

3. *Non-diversified Services.* The unit bank cannot provide diversified banking services to its customers because of its inability to establish branches and higher costs. For example, businessmen may prefer a branch of their city bank in the local business centre to facilitate their business transactions.

4. *No Economies of Large Operations.* The unit banking system cannot have the advantages of a large scale banking in that it cannot recruit more efficient and highly paid staff, and cannot enjoy the economies of large scale and intensive specialisation and division of labour.

5. *Lack of Fund Mobility.* An important argument against the unit banking system is that there is lack of mobility of funds within the country. The unit banks do not attract funds from outside their areas. On the other hand, there is every likelihood of local funds flowing out to the large money markets in pursuit of higher interest rates. This is because the unit banks are unable to pay high interest rates.

6. *Non-Economic Considerations.* A unit bank may not advance loans strictly on economic considerations thereby jeopardising the interests of its depositors. It may be pressurised to give loans to a few local businessmen who may not be creditworthy.

7. *Backward Areas.* Since a unit bank has limited resources at its disposal, it cannot be opened in backward towns. As a result, such areas continue to remain backward.

8. *Unhealthy Competition.* As every company starts a unit bank in a large town, it leads to unhealthy competition among different unit banks with the result that very few survive in the long run.

9. *Remittance of Funds.* As a unit bank has no branches at other towns, it has to depend upon the correspondent banks for remittance of funds. This is very expensive.

These demerits have led to modification of the banking laws in the USA whereby branch banking has been permitted in a number of states, though branch banking across state boundaries is still prohibited.

3. BRANCH BANKING

Branch banking is the most prevalent banking system in the majority of countries. Under this system, a big bank has a number of branches in different parts of the country and even many branches within a cosmopolitan city like Mumbai, Kolkata, Chennai or New Delhi. Small commercial banks also carry on branch banking operations within a state or region. In the USA, branch banking is confined to the states. Accordingly, a number of banks have merged under a holding company to carry on branch banking business efficiently and profitably.

Merits of Branch Banking

The branch banking system has many advantages which make this system superior to the unit banking system.

1. *Spreading of Risks.* The branch banking has the advantage of spreading risks geographically and industrially. If branches in a particular area suffer losses due to recession in industries located there, these losses

can be offset by profits from prosperous areas.

2. *Large Scale Organisation.* The branch banking system has the advantages of large scale organisation because a large bank is able to recruit efficient and trained staff and pay better than the unit banks. It can thus realise the advantages of intensive specialisation and division of labour by carrying out separate banking operations under different staff.

3. *Economy in Reserves.* The branch banking system helps in economising the use of cash reserves. It can move cash reserves from one branch where they are less needed to the other where they are more required in times of necessity.

4. *Advances on Merits.* Under this system, loans are advanced on merits than on personal or local considerations. There are set rules under which loans are advanced to customers.

5. *Diversification of Operations.* Under the branch banking system, there is diversification of banking operations. Big banks can provide banking facilities to trade, industry, businessmen and the common man at cheaper rates and more efficiently than unit banks because they possess larger financial resources.

6. *Equitable Distribution of Funds.* As a corollary to the above, big banks can provide banking facilities throughout the length and breadth of the country, whether it is a small village or a big city, and a backward or a prosperous area. It is in this way that branch banking also helps in the equitable distribution of funds within the country.

7. *Proper Utilization of Funds.* A big bank with large number of bank branches is able to utilise its funds most profitably. It can carry out its banking operations with lower cash reserves in each branch and lend the remaining amount to its customers. In case the need arises for excess cash in one branch, it can be met by transferring funds from some other branch. Thus the commercial banks earn larger profits under branch banking than under unit banking.

8. *Remittance Facilities.* With its network of branches spread in all parts of the country, a big bank can provide cheaper and better remittance facilities to its clients than under the unit banking system having correspondent banking relations.

9. *Large Investments.* Under the branch banking system a big bank with large financial resources is in a better position to choose securities and make large investment in keeping with the principles of safety and liquidity.

10. *Effective Central Bank Control.* The central bank of the country can control the banks more effectively under the branch banking system than under the unit banking. It is easier to control the credit policies of a few large banks than those of numerous unit banks.

Demerits of Branch Banking

The branch banking has its critics who point towards a number of disadvantages of this system. They are discussed as under :

1. *Bureaucratisation.* Under the branch banking system, there is bureaucratisation and the management of all the branches is under the control of the head office, this leads to delay in taking, prompt decisions by the branch managers. They have to refer all cases above a certain limit for advances to the head office.

2. *Do not meet Local Needs.* The branch managers are not able to meet the borrowing needs of the local business community as efficiently and sympathetically as the unit banks. This is because the branch bank managers stay in one locality only temporarily and have to operate under rules set by the head office.

3. *Monopoly Banking.* The branch banking system leads to the establishment of nonopoly banking in the country. When a few big banks open branches in all parts of the country, they limit competition in banking and ultimately lead to the establishment of monopoly in the banking industry. Funds tend to concentrate in a few banks. It may further lead to concentration of economic power in industry and even to. political power by such financially powerful banks.

4. *Lax Supervision.* As big bank has a number of branches spread throughout the country, it is dlfficult to manage and supervise them efficiently. Control becomes lax, the banking services suffer and the clients are hit hard.

5. *Transfer of Funds.* Another disadvantage of branch banking is that deposits of one area may be used for financing business and industry in other areas where the banks expect to earn more by lending. This may

adversely affect the former area if it is already backward.

6. *Fear of Loss.* If branch banking spreads on a large scale, some of the branches may run under losses due to bad debts and low mobilisation of deposits. Such a situation may lead to huge loss to the bank thereby leading to its failure.

7. *Unhealthy Competition.* Branch banking leads to competition among different banks in establishing branches at various places. This tendency leads to unnecessary increase in expenses. The usual practice is for the different commercial banks to open branches in the same locality in big towns and cities. This leads to concentration of branches, thereby resulting in unhealthy competition and rivalry. Sometimes, the banks give inducements in the form of gifts and provide free outstation services to attract customers. Such devices increase bank expenses and lead to wastage of national resources.

Conclusion. Despite demerits, the branch banking system is preferred to the unit banking in developing countries like India. In poor countries, the unit banking cannot be successful. There is need to develop agriculture, industry and trade which is only possible through the branch banking system with its large financial resources. Further, for a balanced regional development, it is through branch banking that funds can be utilised from branches in developed regions to backward regions. However, the disadvantages of the. branch banking can be avoided through their proper regulation by the central bank of the country. If the banks fail to follow the central bank, they can be nationalised by the government. This is what has been done in India and a few other developing countries.

4. GROUP BANKING

Group banking is part of the USA banking system. It is a type of multiple office banking consisting of two or more banks under the control of a holding company, which itself may or may not be a bank. The term "bank holding Company" is based on 25 per cent ownership or control of two or more banks. The holding company is called the parent company and the banks under the parent company are called operating companies. The parent company controls and manages the operating banks under the group but each bank continues to keep its separate entity or name. The parent company may also be an operating bank.

Merits of Group Banking

The group banking system has certain advantages :

1. *Pooling of Resources.* The parent company pools the resources of the group and helps the group banks to provide large loans and advances.

2. *Do not need large Cash Reserves.* The banks in the group need not keep large cash reserves for they can transfer funds to each other when the need arises.

3. *Increase in Efficiency.* The efficiency of the group increases when the parent company provides such specialised services as research, advice on investments, loans and legal matters to all the banks in the group.

4. *Economies of Large Operations.* The group also gains from the economies of large scale banking operations when the parent company advertises, makes bulk purchases, and hires the services of experts on behalf of the banks in the group.

5. *No Mergers.* As already noted above, under the group banking system the operating companies do not merge with the parent company and continue to keep their separate entities but benefit from all the advantages of a large scale organisation.

6. *No Unhealthy Competition.* Group banking avoids unhealthy competition among banks when they are under one holding company.

Demerits of Group Banking

Despite the above merits, the group banking system suffers from certain disadvantages:

1. *Monopoly Banking.* The group banking system is a step towards monopoly banking which is not healthy from the economic view-point.

2. *Inefficient System.* The operating banks may not follow the guidelines and policies laid down by the

parent company from time to time. This may lead to inefficiency.

3. *Chain Reaction.* If the business of one member declines, it may adversely affect the business of other members of the group.

4. *Diversion of Funds.* If the parent company is not an operating banking company, it may divert the funds of the group in furthering its own interests. This may prove harmful for the entire operating group which may be starved of funds and ultimately bring disaster to the group.

5. CHAIN BANKING

Chain banking is also a USA banking system. It is a banking system where the same individual or group of individuals controls two or more banks, as against control by a holding company under group banking. This is done by stock ownership in two or more banks. Stockholders directly or through their nominees exercise control of competing banks. The chain banking system possesses almost the same advantages and disadvantages as that of the group banking discussed above.

6. MIXED BANKING

The mixed banking system is one in which the commercial banks advance both short-term and long-term loans to commerce and industry. Under the British banking system, the commercial banks give short-term loans to commerce and industry. But in other European countries like Germany, the Netherlands, Hungary and Belgium, the mixed banking system operates whereby the commercial banks lend money to meet the short-term and long-term requirements of industry and commerce. Mixed banks perform the usual banking functions and also provide industrial finance.

Merits of Mixed Banking

The mixed banking system has some *advantages* which the British type "pure" banking system lacks. They are as follows :

1. *Provide Initial Capital.* The mixed banks help the establishment of industries by providing them initial capital for long-term.

2. *Underwrite Shares and Debentures.* They undertake to underwrite the equity shares and debentures of industries and thus help them in mobilising public savings for capital formation.

3. *Higher Profits.* The profits of the commercial banks increase when they themselves invest in the long-term securities of industries. For they earn high interest rates on them.

4. *Help in Feasibility Reports.* The industries stand to gain when such banks render expert advice in preparing feasibility reports and in financial matters.

5. *Help in Industrialisation.* The granting of long-term loans to industries by the mixed banks helps in the rapid industrial development of the economy.

6. *Advice to Customers.* Mixed banks help customers by giving valuable advice on investments in shares and debentures of industrial concerns.

Demerits of Mixed Banking

The mixed banking system has the following disadvantages that is why it is not practised in England, the USA and some of the other developed countries :

1. *Against the Liquidity Principle.* It is against the banking principle of liquidity of bank assets. When the bank advances long-term loans to industries, its large funds are locked up which prevent the bank to meet the short-term requirements of trade and commerce.

2. *Heavy Losses.* If there is depression in economy it is not possible for industries to repay the loans. This leads to failure of the banks if they have lent vast sums to industries. This actually happened during the Great Depression of 1930s. Even a recession in industries which have borrowed capital will adversely affect the mixed

banks leading to heavy losses.

3. *Fear of Overinvestment.* During a boom mixed banks overinvest their funds in industries in order to earn more profits. They may also indulge in trade in securities and do speculation. Such operations may lead to huge losses if prices of securities fall suddenly.

Despite many advantages and few disadvantages of mixed banking, many banks failed in America, France, Germany and other European countries because they operated as mixed banks and industries failed to repay the loans.

7. CORRESPONDENT BANKING

Correspondent banking is again an important feature of USA banking system. The USA is geographically a very big country where there are thousands of banks which operate in restricted areas. The various types of banks are able to operate efficiently through a correspondent relationship with one-another. The country banks have deposits with city banks and city banks have deposits in state banks in the same and other cities. The centre of correspondent banking is New York city, followed by Chicago and other regional centres in big American cities. Many banks have deposits fn more than one centre and correspondent banks in one centre have correspondent relations with banks in other centres.

When a small bank maintains its deposits with a big correspondent bank having a network of branches, the latter provides such services to the former as extending large credit facilities, facilitating foreign exchange transactions, cheque clearing and collection, purchase and sale of securities, etc. It also provides a wide range of other services to small banks which include reports on the state of the economy, advice on portfolio management, borrowing from FRS in small lots, sharing computer facilities, etc.

MERITS OF CORRESPONDENT BANKING

This unique American banking system has certain advantages for the country (unit) banks, the city (branch) banks and for the economy. They are as follows :

1. *Rapid Movement of Funds.* Under correspondent banking, cheques of country banks are cleared and collected without much delay. Thus there is a rapid movement of funds from one area to the other. This system facilitates trade and industry.

2. *Help in Dealing in Securities.* Correspondent city banks help the country banks in the buying and selling of securities.

3. *Help in Providing Finance.* Such banks also help the country banks in financing loans and advances by providing them funds.

4. *Help in Transfer of Funds.* They also accept or draw drafts on the country banks and thus help in transferring funds.

5. *Help in Foreign Exchange Transactions.* They facilitate foreign exchange transactions of their correspondent banks.

6. *Increase in Mobility of Credit.* They increase the geographical mobility of credit when business is transacted from one area to the other through these banks.

7. *Render Technical Advice.* City banks also render technical advice to the country banks in installing new machines, providing legal advice, and in making investments in securities and advancing loans.

8. *Provide Information.* They also provide information about the general and economic conditions of the country to the unit banks regularly.

9. *Gain in Deposits and Business.* The correspondent city banks themselves gain in deposits and new business by entering into correspondent relations with the country banks. On the basis of the deposits, the city banks are able to profit more.

10. *Increase in Balances.* Balances in correspondent banks tend to increase manifold which provide liquid assets with the result that they can be utilised as a ready source of funds for all banks engaged in corresponding relations. They can also be used as legal reserves with the Federal Reserve Banks and can be withdrawn in case of need.

11. *Gains to the Economy.* The whole economy benefits from the correspondent banking system. There is no fear of monopoly banking. The general public can easily transfer funds from one part of the country to the other. People can use travellers' cheques issued even by a small unit bank throughout the country. Foreign exchange business can easily be transacted and investments in stocks, shares etc. can be made even from the remotest corner of the vast American mainland through a tiny village bank. Thus the correspondent banking system facilitates ail types of transactions and helps trade and industry.

ITS DEMERIT!

The only *dement* of this system is that the correspondent city banks may .rinke excess advances on the basis of the deposits of their correspondent country banks. They may thus operate against the principles of safety and liquidity and harm not only the country banks but also the entire banking structure in the economy.

EXERCISES

1. Distinguish between unit and branch banking. Which one would you suggest for a country like India? Give reasons.
2. Discuss the relative merits and demerits of unit and branch banking systems.
3. What is the difference between group and chain banking? Give the merits and demerits of group banking.
4. Explain the mixed banking system. Why is it preferred to 'pure' banking system?
5. What is the correspondent banking? Explain its role in the American banking system.

CHAPTER 8

Commercial Bank Policies and Principles

1. INTRODUCTION

The main aim of a commercial bank is to seek profit like any other institution. Its capacity to earn profit depends upon its investment policy. Its investment policy, in turn, depends on the manner in which it manages its investment portfolio. Thus "commercial bank investment policy emerges from a straight froward application of the theory of portfolio management to the particular circumstances of commercial bank." Portfolio management refers to the prudent management of a bank's assets and liabilities in order to seek some optimum combination of income or profit, liquidity, and safety.

When a bank operates, it acquires and disposes of income-earning assets. These assets *plus* the bank's cash make up what is known as it *portfolio. A* bank's *earning assets* consist of (*a*) securities issued by the central and state governments, local bodies and government institutions, and (*b*) financial obligations, such as promissory notes, bills of exchange, etc. issues by firms. There earning assets constitute between one-fourth and one-third of a commercial bank's total assets. Thus a bank's earning assets are an important source of its income. The manner in which banks manage their portfolios, that is acquiring and disposing of their earning assets, can have important affects on the financial markets, on the borrowing and spending practices of households and businesses, and on the economy as a whole.

In this chapter, we study the objective, principles and theories of portfolio management and essentials of a sound banking system.

2. OBJECTIVES OF PORTFOLIO MANAGEMENT

There are three main objectives of potfolio management which a wise bank follows: liquidity, safety and income. The three objectives are opposed to each other. To achieve on the bank will have to sacrifice the other objectives. For example, if the banks seeks high profit, it may have to sacrifice some safety and liquidity. If it seeks more safety and liquidity it may have to give up some income. We analyse these objectives one by one in relation to the other objectives.

1. Liquidity

A commercial bank needs a higher degree of liquidity in its assets. The liquidity of an assets refers to the ease and certainty with which it can be turned into cash. The liabilities of a bank are large in relation to its assets because it holds a small proportion of its assets in cash. But its liabilities are payable on demand at a short notice.

Therefore, the bank must hold a sufficiently large proportion of its assets in the form of cash and liquid assets for the purpose of profitability. If the bank keeps liquidity the uppermost, its profit will below. On the other hands, if it ignores liquidity and aims at earning more, it will be disastrous for it. Thus in managing its investment portfolio a bank must strike a balance between the objectives of liquidity and profitability. The balance must be achieved with a relatively high degree of safety. This is because banks are subject to a number of restrictions that limit the size of earning assets they can acquire.

The nature of conflict between liquidity and profitability is illustrated in Figure 1 where earning assets are taken on the horizontal axis and cash on the vertical axis. *CF* is the *investment possibility line* which shows all combinations of cash and earning assets. For instance, point *A* denotes a combination of *OM* of cash and *OS* of earning assets; and point *B* shows *ON* of cash and *OT* of earning assets. Each bank seeks to obtain its optimum point along the line *CE* which will be a combination of cash and earning assets so as to achieve the highest possible level of earnings consistent with its liquidity and safety.

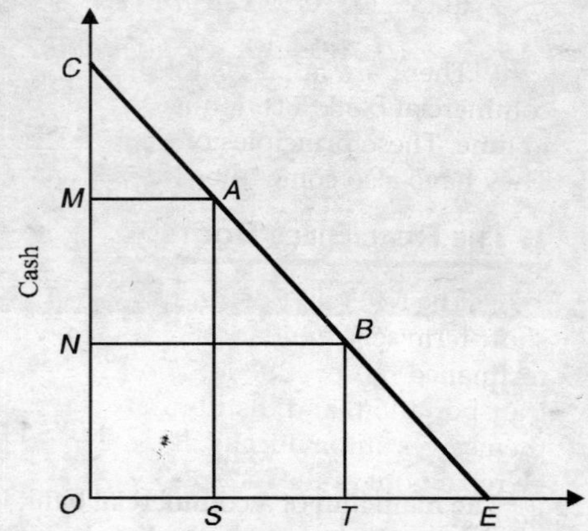

Fig. 1

Many types of assets are available to a commercial bank with varying degrees of liquidity. The most liquid of assets is money in cash. The next most liquid assets are deposits with the central bank, treasury bills and other short-term bills issues by the central and state governments and large firms, and call loans to other banks, firms, dealers and brokers in government securities. The less liquid assets are the various types of loans to customers and investments in long term bonds and mortgages. Thus the principle sources of liquidity of a bank are its borrowings from the other banks and the central bank and from the sales of the assets.

But the amount of liquidity which the bank can have depends on the availability and cost of borrowings. If it can borrow large amounts at any time without difficulty at a low cost (interest rate), it willhod very little liquid assets. But if it is uncertain to borrow funds or the cost of borrowing is high, the bank will keep more liquid assets in its portfolio.

2. Safety

A commercial bank always operates under conditions of uncertainty and risk. It is uncertain about the amount and cost of funds it can acquire and about its income in the future. Moreover, it face two types of risks. The first is the market risk which results from the decline in the prices of debt obligations when the market rate of interest rises. The second is the risk by default where the bank fears that the debtors are not likely to repay the principle and pay the interest in time. "This risk is largely concentrated in customer loans, where banks have a special function to perform, and bank loans to businesses and bank mortgage loans are among the high grade loans of these typs."

In the light of these risks, a commercial bank has to maintain the safety of its assets. It is also prohibited by law to assume large risks because it is required to keep a high ration of its fixed liabilities to its total assets with itself and also with the central bank in the form of cash. But if the bank follows the safety principle strictly by holding only the safest assets it will not be able to create more credit. It will thus lose customers to other banks and its income will also be very low. One the other hand, if the bank takes too much risk, it may be highly harmful for it. Therefore, a commercial bank "must estimate the amount of risks attached to the various types of available assets, compare estimated risk differentials, consider both long-turn and short-run consequences, and strike a balance."

3. Profitability

One of the principle objectives of a bank is to earn more profit. It is essential for the purpose of paying interest to depositors, wage to the staff, dividend to shareholders and meeting other expenses. It cannot afford to hold a large amount of funds in cash for that will mean forgoing income. But the conflict between profitability and liquidity is not very sharp. Liquidity and safety are primary considerations while profitability is subsidiary for the very existence of a bank depends on the first two.

Conclusion. The three conflicting objectives of portfolio management lead to the conclusion that for a bank to earn more profit, it must strike a judicious balance between liquidity and safety.

3. THEORIES OF PORTFOLIO MANAGEMENT

There are apparent conflicts between the objectives of liquidity, safety and profitability relating to a commercial bank. Economists have tried to resolve these conflicts by laying down certain theories from time to time. These principles or theories, in fact, govern the *distribution of assets* keeping in views these objectives. They have also come to be known as the theories of liquidity management which are discussed as under.

1. The Real Bills Doctrine

The real bills doctrine or the commercial loan theory states that a commercial bank should advance only short-term self-liquidating productive loans to business firms. Self-liquidating loans are those which are meant to finance the production, and movement of goods through the successive stages of production, storage, transportation, and distribution. When such goods are ultimately sold, the loans are considered to liquidate themselves automatically. For instance, a loan give by the bank to a businessman to finance inventories would be repaid out of the receipts from the sale of those very inventories, and the loan would be automatically self-liquidated.

The theory states that when commercial banks make only short term self-liquidating productive loans, the central bank, in turn, should only land to the banks on the security of such short-term loans. This principle would ensure the proper degree of liquidity for each bank and the proper money supply for the whole economy. The central bank was expected to increase or diminish bank reserves by rediscounting approved loans. When business expanded and the needs of trade increased, banks were able to acquire additional reserves by rediscounting bills with the central banks. When business fell and the needs of trade declined, the volume of rediscounting of bills would fall, the supply of bank reserves and the amount of bank credit and money would also contract.

Its Merits. Such short-term self-liquidating productive loans possess three advantages. *First,* they possess liquidity that is why they liquidate themselves automatically. *Second,* since they mature in the short run and are for productive purposes, there is no risk of their running to bad debts. *Third,* being productive such loans earn income for the banks.

Its Demerits. Despite these merits, the real bills doctrine suffers from certain defects.

First, if a bank refuses to grant a fresh loan till the old loan is repaid, the disappointed borrower will have to reduce production which will adversely affect business activity. If all the banks follow the same rule, this may lead to reduction in the money supply and price in the community. This may, in turn, make it impossible for existing debtors to repay their loans in time.

Second, the doctrine assumes that loans are self-liquidating under normal economic conditions. If there is depression, production and trade suffer and the debtor will not be able to repay the debt at maturity.

Third, this doctrine neglects the fact that the liquidity of a bank depends on the saleability of its liquid assets and not on real trade bills. If a bank possesses a variety of assets like bills and securities which can be readily should in the money and capital markets, it can ensure safety, liquidity and profitability. Then the bank need not rely on maturitis in time of trouble.

Fourth, the basic defect of the theory is that no loan is in itself automatically self-liquidating. A loan to a retailer to purchase inventor is is not self-liquidating if the inventories are not sold to consumers and remain with the retailer. Thus a loan to be successful involves a third party, the consumers in this case, besides the lender and the borrower.

Fifth, this theory is based on the "needs of trade" which is no longer accepted as an adequate criterion for regulating this type of bank credit. If bank credit and money supply fluctuate on the basis of the needs of trade, the central bank cannot prevent either spiralling recession or inflation.

2. The Shiftability Theory

The shiftability theory of bank liquidity was propounded by H.G. Moulton who asserted that if the commercial banks maintain a substantial amount of assets that can be shifted on to the other banks for cash without material loss in case of necessity, then there is no need to rely on maturities. According to this view, an asset to be perfectly shiftable must be immediately transferable without capital loss when the need for liquidity arises. This is particularly applicable to short term market investments, such as treasury bills and bills of exchange which can be immediately sold whenever it is necessary to raise funds by banks. But in a general crisis when all banks are in need of liquidity, the shiftability theory requires that all banks should possess such assets which can be shifted on to the central bank which is the lender of the last resort.

This theory has certain elements of truth. Banks now accept sound assets which can be shifted on to other banks. Shares and debentures of large companies are accepted as liquid assets along with treasury bills and bills of exchange. This has encouraged term lending by banks.

Its Demerits. But it has its weaknesses. *First,* mere shiftability of assets does not provide liquidity to the banking system. It entirely depends upon the economic circumstances. *Second,* the shiftability theory ignores the fact that in times of acute depression, the shares and debentures cannot be shifted on to others by the banks. In such a situation, there are no buyers and all who possess them want to sell them. *Third,* a single bank may have shiftable assets in sufficient quantities but if it tries to sell them when thee is a run on the bank, it may adversely affect the entire banking system. *fourth,* If all the banks simultaneously start shifting their assets, it would have disastrous effects on both the lenders and borrowers.

3. The Anticipated Income Theory

The anticipated income theory was developed by H.V. Prochanow in 1944 on the basis of the practice of extending term loans by the US commercial banks. According to this theory, regardless of the nature and character of a borrower's business, the bank plans the liquidation of the term-loan from the anticipated income of the borrower. A term-loan is for a period exceeding one year and extending to less than five years. It is granted against the hypothecation of machinery, stock and even immovable property. The bank puts restrictions on the financial activities of the borrower while granting this loan. At the time of granting a loan, the bank takes into consideration not only the security but the anticipated earnings of the borrower. Thus a loan by the bank gets repaid out of the future income of the borrower in instalments, instead of in a lump sum at the maturity of the loan.

Its Merits. This theory is superior to the real bills doctrine and the shiftability theory because it fulfils the three objectives of liquidity, safety and profitability. Liquidity is assured to the bank when the borrower saves and repays the loan regularly in instalments.. It satisfies the safety principle because the bank grants a loan not only on the basis of a good security but also on the ability of the borrower to repay the loan. The bank can utilise its excess reserves in granting term-loan and is assured of a regular income. Lastly, the term-loan is highly beneficial for the business community which gets funds for medium-terms.

Its Demerits. The theory of anticipated income is not free from a few defects.

1. *Analyses Creditworthiness,* It is not a theory but simply a method to analyse a borrower's creditworthiness. It gives the bank criteria for evaluating the potential of a borrower to successfully repay a loan on time.

2. *Fails to Meet Emergency Cash Needs.* Repayment of loans in instalments to the bank no doubt provide a regular stream of liquidity, but they fail to meet emergency cash needs of the lender bank.

4. The Liabilities Management Theory

This theory was developed in the 1960s. According to this theory, there is no need for banks to grant self-liquidating loans and keep liquid assets because they can borrow reserve money in the money market in case of need. A bank can acquire reserves by creating additional liabilities against itself from different sources. These sources include the issuing of time certificates of deposit, borrowing from other commercial banks, borrowing from the central banks, raising of capital funds by issuing shares, and by ploughing back of profits. We discuss these sources of bank funds briefly.

(a) Time Certificates of Deposits. These are the principle source of reserve money for a commercial bank in the USA. Time certificates of deposits are of different maturities ranging from 90 days to less than 12 months. They are negotiable in the money market. So a bank can have access to liquidity by selling them in the money market. But there are two limitations. First, if during a boom, the interest rate structure in the money market is higher than the ceiling rate set by the central bank, time deposit certificates cannot be sold in the market. *Second,* they are not a dependable source of funds for the commercial banks. Bigger commercial banks are at an advantage in selling these certificates because they have large certificates which they can afford to sell at even low interest rates. So the smaller banks are at a disadvantage in this respect.

(b) Borrowing from other Commercial Banks. A bank may create additional liabilities by borrowing from other banks having excess reserves. But such borrowings are only for a very short duration, for a day or week at the most. The interest rate of such borrowings depends upon the prevailing rate in the money market. But borrowings from other banks are only possible during normal economic conditions. In abnormal times, no bank can afford to lend to others.

(c) Borrowing from the Central Bank. Banks also create liabilities on themselves by borrowing form the central bank of the country. They borrow to met their liquidity needs for short term and by discounting bills from the central bank. But such borrowings are relatively costlier than borrowings from other sources.

(d) Raising Capital Funds. Commercial banks acquire funds by issuing fresh shares or debentures. But the availability of funds through this sources depends on the amount of dividend or interest rate which the bank is prepared to pay. Usually the banks are not in a position to pay rates higher than paid by manufacturing and trading companies. So they are not able to get sufficient funds from this sources.

(e) Ploughing Back Profits. Another source of liquid funds for a commercial bank is the ploughing back of its profits. But how much it can get from this source will depend upon its rate of profit and its dividend policy. It is the larger banks that can depend on this source rather than the smaller banks.

4. INVESTMENT POLICY OF A COMMERCIAL BANK

A bank makes investments for the purpose of earning profits. First it keeps primary and secondary reserves to meet its liquidity requirements. This is essential to satisfy the credit needs of the society by granting short-term loans to its customers. Whatever is left with the bank after making advances is invested for long period to improve its earning capacity.

Before discussing the investment policy of a commercial bank, it is instructive to distinguish between a loan and an investment because the usual practice is to regard the two as synonymous. The bank gives a loan to a customer for a short period on condition of repayment. It is the customer who asks for the loan. By advancing a loan, the bank creates credit which is a temporary source of fund for the bank. An investment by the bank, on the other hand, is the outlay of its funds for a long period without creating any credit. A bank makes investments in government securities and in the stocks of large reputed industrial concerns, while in the case of a loan the bank advances money against recognised securities and bills. However, the goal of both is to increase its earnings.

The investment policy of a bank consists of earning high returns on its unloaned resources. But it has to keep in view the safety and liquidity of its resources so as to meet the potential demand of its customers. Since the objective of profitability conflicts with those of safety and liquidity, the wise investment policy is to strike a judicious balance among them. Therefore, a bank should lay down its investment policy in such a manner so as to ensure the safety and liquidity of its funds and at the same time maximise its profits. This requires adherence to certain principles.

PRINCIPLES OF BANK LENDING POLICIES

Banks follow the following principles of lending :

1. Liquidity

Liquidity is an important principle of bank lending. Bank lend for short periods only because they lend public money which can be withdrawn at any time by depositors. They, therefore, advance loans on the security of such assets which are easily marketable and convertible into cash at a short notice.

A bank chooses such securities in its investment portfolio which possess sufficient liquidity. It is essential because if the bank needs cash to meet the urgent requirements of its customers, it should be in a position to sell some of the securities at a very short notice without disturbing their market prices much. There are certain securities such as central, state and local government bonds which are easily saleable without affecting their market prices. The shares and debentures of large industrial concerns also fall in this category. But the shares and debentures of ordinary firms are not easily marketable without bringing down their market prices. So the banks should make investments in government securities and shares and debentures of reputed industrial houses.

2. Safety

The safety of funds lent is another principle of lending. Safety means that the borrower should be able to repay the loan and interest in time at regular intervals without default. The repayment of the loan depends upon the nature of security, the character of the borrower, his capacity to repay and his financial standing.

Like other investments, bank investments involve risk. But the degree of risk varies with the type of security. Securities of the central government are safer than those of the state governments and local bodies. And the securities of state government and local bodies are safer than those of the industrial concerns. This is because the resources of the central government are much higher than the state and local governments and of the latter higher than the industrial concerns. In fact, the share and debentures of industrial concerns are tied to their earnings which may fluctuate with the business activity in the country. The bank should also take into consideration the debt repaying ability of the governments while investing in their securities. Political stability and peace and security are the prerequisites for this. It is very safe to invest in the securities of a government having large tax revenue and high borrowing capacity. The same is the case with the securities of a rich municipality or local body and state government of a prosperous region. So in making investments the bank should choose securities, shares and debentures of such governments, local bodies and industrial concerns which satisfy the principle of safety.

Thus from the bank's viewpoint, the nature of security is the most important consideration while giving a loan. Even then, it has to take into consideration the creditworthiness of the borrower which is governed by his character, capacity to repay, and his financial standing. Above all, the safety of bank funds depends upon the technical feasibility and economic viability of the project for which the loan is advanced.

3. Diversity

In choosing its investment portfolio, a commercial bank should follow the principle of diversity. It should not invest its surplus funds in a particular type of security but in different types of securities. It should choose the shares and debentures of different types of industries situated in different regions of the country. The same principle should be followed in the case of state governments and local bodies. Diversification aims at minimising risk of the investment portfolio of a bank.

The principle of diversity also applies to the advancing of loans to varied types of firms, industries, businesses and trades. A bank should follows the maxim: "Do not keep all eggs in one basket." It should spread it risks by giving loans to various trades and industries in different parts of the country.

4. Stability

Another important principle of a bank's investment policy should be to invest in those stocks and securities which possess a high degree of stability in their prices. The bank cannot afford any loss on the value of its securities. It should, therefore, invest it funds in the shares of reputed companies where the possibility of decline in their prices is remote. Government bonds and debentures of companies carry fixed rates of interest. Their value changes with changes in the market rate of interest. But the bank is forced to liquidate a portion of them to meet its requirements of cash in cash of financial crisis. Otherwise, they run to their full term of 10 years or more and changes in the market rate of interest do not affect them much. Thus bank investments in debentures and bonds are more stable than in the shares of companies.

5. Profitability

This is the cardinal principle for making investment by a bank. It must earn sufficient profits. It should, therefore, invest in such securities which was sure a fair and stable return on the funds invested. The earning capacity of securities and shares depends upon the interest rate and the dividend rate and the tax benefits they carry. It is largely the government securities of the centre, state and local bodies that largely carry the exemption of their interest from taxes. The bank should invest more in such securities rather than in the shares of new companies which also carry tax exemption. This is because shares of new companies are not safe investments.

5. ESSENTIALS OF A SOUND BANKING SYSTEM

The essentials of a sound banking system are usually regarded as liquidity and profitability. As pointed out by Crowther, "The secret of successful banking is to distribute resources between the various forms of assets in such a way as to get a sound balance between liquidity and profitability, so that their is cash (on hand or quickly realizable) to meet every claim, and at the same time enough income for the bank to pay it way and earn profits for its shareholders." But modern bankers also consider a few other essentials which are discussed below.

1. Liquidity

One of the essentials of a sound banking system is to have a higher degree of liquidity. The bank holds a small proportion of its assets in cash. Therefore, its other assets must possess the criterion of liquidity so that they may be turned into such easily. A commercial bank is under an obligation to pay its depositors cash on demand. This is only possible if the bank possesses such securities which can be easily liquidated. Central banks have made it obligatory on the commercial banks to keep a certain proportion of their assets in cash to ensure liquidity.

2. Safety

Another essential of a sound banking system is that it must be safe. Since the bank keeps the deposits of the people, it must ensure the safety of their money. So it should make safe loans and investments and avoid unnecessary risks. If the debtors of the banks donot repay the loans in time and it loses on its investments, the bank shall become insolvent. As a result, its depositors lose money and suffer hardships. Thus the bank must ensure the safety of its deposits.

3. Stability

A sound banking system must be stable. It should operate rationally. There should neither be undue contraction nor expansion of credit. If the bank restricts the creation of credit when trade and industry need it the most, it will harm the interests of the business community. On the other hand, if it expands credit when the economic conditions do not permit, it will lead to boom and inflation. So the banking system should follow a stable lending policy. The central bank of the country can help in achieving stability in the banking operations of the commercial banks by a judicious credit control policy.

4. Elasticity

But the stability of banking operations should not be interpreted as rigidity. Rather, the banking system should have sufficient elasticity in its lending operations. It should be in a position to expand and contract the supply of loanable funds with ease in accordance with the directives of the central bank of the country.

5. Profitability

A sound banking system should be able to earn sufficient profits. Profits are essential for it to be viable. It has to pay the corporation tax like any other company, pay interest to its depositors, dividend to shareholders, salaries to the staff and meet other expenses. So unless the bank earns, it cannot operate soundly. For this purpose, it must adopted judicious loan and investment policies.

6. Reserve Management

Sound banking system must follow the principle of efficient reserve management. A bank keeps some amount of money in reserve for meeting the demand of its customers in case of emergency. Though the money kept in reserve is idle money, yet the bank cannot afford the risk of keeping a small amount in reserve. There are, however, some statutory limits laid down by the central bank in maintaining minimum reserves with itself and with the bank. But how much reserve money should a bank maintain is governed by its own wisdom, experience and the size of the bank. The bank should manage its reserve policy effectively and efficiently without keeping too much or too little cash. It has to balance between profitability and safety.

7. Expansion

A sound banking system must be spread throughout the country. It should not be concentrated only in big towns and cities but in rural areas and backward regions. It is only by widespread expansion of the banking system that the deposits can be mobilised and credit facilities can be made available to trade, industry, agriculture, etc. This is especially the case in a developing country where the banking system must provide these facilities through its expansion in all areas. This is essential for capital formation and economic growth.

EXERCISES

1. Discuss the principles governing the distribution of bank assets.
2. Critically examine the liquidity management theories of commercial banks.
3. Discuss and reconcile the conflicts among the objectives of liquidity, profitability and safety of commercial banks.
4. Explain the main features of an investment policy which a commercial bank should follow.
5. Discuss the essentials of a sound banking system.

CHAPTER 9

Credit Creation by Commercial Banks

1. DO BANKS CREATE CREDIT ?

The creation of credit or deposits is one of the most important functions of commercial banks. Like other corporations, banks aim at earning profits. For this purpose, they accept cash in demand deposits and advance loans on credit to customers. When a bank advances a loan, it does not pay the amount in cash. But it opens a current account in his name and allows him to withdraw the required sum by cheques. In this way, the bank creates credit or deposits.

Demand deposits arise in two ways: *one*, when customers deposit currency with commercial banks, and *two*, when banks advance loans, discount bills, provide overdraft facilities, and make investments through bonds and securities. The first type of demand deposits are called "primary deposits". Banks play a passive role in opening them. The second type of demand deposits are called "derivative deposits". Banks actively create such deposits.

Do banks really create credit or deposits ?

There have been two views on this subject: one held by certain economists like Hartley Withers, and the other held by practical bankers like Walter Leaf.

According to Withers, banks can create credit by opening a deposit, every time they advance a loan. This is because every time a loan is sanctioned, payment is made through cheques by the customers. All such payments are adjusted through the clearing house. So long as a loan is due, a deposit of that amount remains outstanding in the books of the bank. Thus every loan creates a deposit. But this is an exaggerated and extreme view.

Dr Leaf[1] and practical bankers do not agree with this view. They go to the opposite extreme. They hold that banks cannot create money out of thin air. They can lend only what they have in cash. Therefore, they cannot and do not create money.

This view is also wrong becuase it is based on arguments relating to a single bank. As pointed out by Prof Samuelson, "The banking system as a whole can do what each small bank cannot do: it can expand its loans and investments many times the new reserves of cash created for it, even though each small bank is lending out only a fraction of its deposits."[2]

---

1. Water Leaf, *Banking*, 1928, pp. 101-4.
2. Paul A. Samuelson, *Economics*, 10th edn., 1976, p. 301.

In fact, a bank is not a cloak room where one can keep currency notes and claim those very notes when one desires. Banks know by experience that all depositors do not withdraw their money simultaneously. Some withdraw while others deposit on the same day. So by keeping a small cash in reserve for day-to-day transactions, the bank is able to advance loans on the basis of excess reserves. When the bank advances a loan it opens an account in the name of the customer. The bank knows by experience that the customer will withdraw money by cheques which will be deposited by his creditors in this bank or some other bank, where they have their accounts. Settlements of all such cheques are made in the clearing house. The same procedure is followed in other banks. The banks are able to create credit or deposits by keeping a small cash in reserves and lending the remaining amount.

In granting a loan, a bank actively creates a claim against itself in favour of the borrower. "The claims the bank takes from its customers, in exchange for the deposits entered in the books, are the bank's assets. The standard assets of a commercial bank are overdrafts and loans, bills discounted, investments and cash."[3]

The bank provides overdraft facility to a customer on the basis of some security. It enters the amount of the overdraft in the existing account of the customer and allows him to draw cheques for the overdraft amount agreed upon. It thus creates a deposit.

When a bank discounts a bill of exchange, it in fact, buys the bill from the customer for a short period of 90 days or less. The amount of the bill is credited in the account of the customer who withdraws it through a cheque. Or, it pays the sum through a cheque on itself. In both cases, the bank creates a deposit equal to the amount of the bill of exchange less the discount charges.

A commercial bank also creates a deposit by making investments by buying government bonds and securities. The bank pays for the bond through a cheque on itself to the central bank. If it buys a bond from the stock exchange, it credits the amount in the account of the seller, if he happens to be its customer. Otherwise, it pays a cheque on itself which is deposited in some other bank. In any case, a deposit is created either in this bank or some other bank. In all such cases, liabilities and assets in the banking system on the whole are increased. Thus loans by banks create deposits. It is in this sense that credit is created by commercial banks.

2. THE PROCESS OF CREDIT CREATION

Let us explain tha actual process of credit creation. We have seen above that the ability of banks to create credit depends on the fact that banks need only a small percentage of cash to deposits. If banks kept 100 per cent cash against deposits, there would be no credit creation. Modern banks do not keep 100 per cent cash reserves. They are legally required to keep a fixed percentage of their deposits in cash, say 10, 15 or 20 per cent. They lend and/or invest the remaining amount which is called *excess reserves*. A bank can lend equal to its excess reserves. But the entire banking system can lend and create credit (or deposits) upto a multiple of its original excess reserves. The deposit multiplier depends upon the required reserve which is the basis of credit creation. Symbolically, the required reserve ratio:

$$RRr = \frac{RR}{D}$$

or $RR = RRr \times D$

where RR are the required cash reserves with banks, RRr is the required reserve ratio and D is the demand deposits of banks. To show that D depends on RR and RRr, divide both sides of the above equation by RRr:

3. R.S. Sayers, *Modern Banking*, 7th edn,. 1967, pp. 7-8.

$$\frac{RR}{RRr} = \frac{RRr \times D}{RRr}$$

or $$\frac{RR}{RRr} = D$$

or $$\frac{1}{RRr} = \frac{D}{RR}$$

or $$D = \frac{1}{RRr} \times RR$$

where $1/RRr$, the reciprocal of the percentage reserve ratio, is called the *deposit (or credit) expansion multiplier*. It determines the limits of the deposit expansion of a bank. The maximum amount of demand deposits which the banking system can support with any given amount of *RR* is by applying the multiplier to *RR*. Taking the initial change in the volume of deposits (DD) and in cash reserves (D*RR*), it follows from any given percentage of *RRr* that

$$\Delta D = RR \times \frac{1}{RRr}$$

To understand it, suppose the *RRr* for the banks is fixed at 10 per cent and the initial change in cash reserves is Rs 1000. By applying the above formula, the maximum increase in demand deposits will be

$$\Delta D = 1000 \times \frac{1}{0.10} = \text{Rs } 10000.$$

This is the extent to which the banking system can create credit. The above equation can also be expressed as follows:

$DD = RR[1+(1-RRr) + (1-RRr)^2+...+(1-RRr)^n]$

The sum of the geometric progression within brackets gives:

$$\frac{1}{1-(1-RRr)} = \frac{1}{RRr}$$

$$\Delta D = \Delta RR \times \frac{1}{RRr}$$

The deposit expansion multiplier rests on the assumptions that banks lend out all their excess reserves and *RRr* remains constant.

To explain the process of credit creation, we make the following assumptions:

1. There are many banks, say A, B, C, etc. in the banking system.
2. Each bank has to keep 10 per cent of its deposits in reserves. In other words, 10 per cent is the required ratio fixed by law.
3. The first bank has Rs. 1000 as deposits.
4. The loan amount drawn by the customer of one bank is deposited in full in the second bank, and that of the second bank into the third bank, and so on.
5. Each bank starts with the initial deposit which is deposited by the debtor of the other bank.

Given these assumptions suppose that Bank A receives a cash deposits of Rs. 1000 to begin with. This is the cash in hand with the bank which is its asset and this amount is also the liability of the bank by way of deposits it holds. Given the reserve ratio of 10 per cent, the bank keeps Rs. 100 in reserves and lends Rs 900 to one of its customers who, in turn, gives a cheque to some person from whom he borrows or buys something.

The net changes in Bank A' is balance sheet are +Rs 100 in reserves and +Rs 900 in loans on the assets side and Rs 1000 in demand deposits on the liabilities side as shown in Table I. Before these changes Bank A had zero excess reserves.

Table I. Balance Sheet of Bank A

Assets		Liabilities	
Reserves	Rs 1000	Deposits	Rs 1000
	net changes		*net changes*
Reserves	Rs 100	Deposits	Rs 1000
Loans	Rs 900		

This loan of Rs 900 is deposited by the customer in Bank *B* whose balance sheet is shown in Table II Bank *B* starts with a deposit of Rs 900, keeps 10 per cent of it or Rs 90 as cash in reserve. Bank *B* has Rs 810 as excess reserves which it lends thereby creating new deposits.

Table II Balance Sheet of Bank B

Assets		Liabilities	
Reserves	Rs 900	Deposits	Rs 900
net changes		*net changes*	
Reserves	Rs 90	Deposits	Rs 900
Loans	Rs 810		

This loan of Rs 810 is deposited by the customer of Bank *B* into Bank *C*. The balance sheet of Bank C is shown in Table III Bank *C* keeps Rs 81 or 10 per cent of Rs 810 in cash reserves and lends Rs 729.

Table III Balance Sheet of Bank C

Assets		Liabilities	
Reserves	Rs 810	Deposits	Rs 810
net changes		*net changes*	
Reserves	Rs 81	Deposits	Rs 810
Loans	Rs 729		

This process goes on to other banks. Each bank in the sequence gets excess reserves, lends and creates new demand deposits equal to 90% of the preceding bank's. In this way, new deposits are created to the tune of Rs 10000 in the banking system, as shown in Table IV.

Table IV Multiple Credit Creation

Bank	Required Reserves	New Loans	New Deposits
A	Rs 100	Rs 900	Rs 1000
B	Rs 90	Rs 810	Rs 900
C	Rs 81	Rs 729	Rs 810
All other Banks	Rs 729	Rs 6561	Rs 7290
Total for the Banking System	Rs 1000	Rs 9000	Rs 10000

The multiple credit creation shown in the last column of the above table can also be worked out algebraically as:

Rs 1000 [1+(9/10)+(9/10)2+(9/10)3+...+(9/10)"]

=Rs 1000 (1/1-9/10)= Rs 1000 (1/1/10)= Rs 1000´10 = Rs 10000.

3. LIMITATIONS ON THE POWER OF BANKS TO CREATE CREDIT

We have seen above how the banking system as a whole can create credit. But it does not mean that banks have unlimited powers to create credit. In fact, they have to function under certain restrictions. The following are the limitations on the power of commercial banks to create credit.

1. *Amount of Cash.* The credit creation power of banks depends upon the amount of cash they possess. The larger the cash, the larger the amount of credit that can be created by banks. The amount of cash that a bank has in its vaults cannot be determined by it. It depends upon the primary deposits with the bank. The bank's power of creating credit is thus limited by the cash it possesses.

2. *Proper securities.* An important factor that limits the power of a bank to create credit is the availability of adequate securities. A bank advances loans to its customers on the basis of a security, or a bill, or a share, or a stock or a building, or some other type of asset. It turns ill-liquid form of wealth into liquid wealth and thus creates credit. If proper securities are not available with the public, a bank cannot create credit. As pointed out by Crowther, "Thus the bank does not create money out of thin air, it transmutes other forms of wealth into money."

3. *Banking habits of the People.* The banking habits of the people also govern the power of credit creation on the part of banks. If people are not in the habit of using cheques, the grant of loans will lead to the withdrawal of cash from the credit creation stream of the banking system. This reduces the power of banks to create credit to the desired level.

4. *Minimum Legal Reserve Ratio.* The minimum legal reserve ratio of cash to deposits fixed by the central bank is an important factor which determines the power of banks of create credit. The higher this ratio (RRr), the lower the power of banks to create credit; and the lower the ratio, the higher the power of banks to create credit.

5. *Excess Reserves.* The process of credit creation is based on the assumption that banks stick to the required reserve ratio fixed by the central bank. If banks keep more cash in reserves than the legal reserve requirements, their power to create credit is limited to that extent. If Bank A of our example keeps 25 per cent of Rs 1000 instead of 20 per cent, it will lend Rs 750 instead of Rs 800. Consequently, the amount of credit creation will be reduced even if the other banks in the system stick to the legal reserve ratio of 20 per cent.

6. *Leakages.* If there are leakages in the credit creation stream of the banking system, credit expansion will not reach the required level, given the legal reserve ratio. It is possible that some persons who receive cheques do not deposit them in their bank accounts, but withdraw the money in cash for spending or for hoarding at home. The extent to which the amount of cash is withdrawn from the chain of credit expansion, the power of the banking system to create credit is limited.

7. *Cheque Clearances.* The process of credit expansion is based on the assumption that cheques drawn by commercial banks are cleared immediately and reserves of commercial banks expand and contract uniformly by cheque transactions. But it is not possible for banks to receive and draw cheques of exactly equal amount. Often some banks have their reserves increased and otheres reduced through cheque clearances. This expands and contracts credit creation on the part of banks. Accordingly, the credit creation stream is disturbed.

8. *Behaviour of other Banks.* The power of credit creation is further limited by the behaviour of other banks. If some of the banks do not advance loans to the extent required of the banking system, the chain of credit expansion will be broken. Consequently, the banking system will not be "loaned up".

9. *Economic Climate.* Banks cannot continue to create credit limitlessly. Their power to create credit depends upon the economic climate in the country. If there are boom times, there is optimism. Investment opportunities increase and businessmen take more loans from banks. So credit expands. But in depressed times when the business activity is at a low level, banks cannot force the business community to take loans from them. Thus the economic climate in a country determines the power of banks to create credit.

10. *Credit Control Policy of the Central Bank.* The power of commercial banks to create credit is also limited by the credit control policy of the central bank. The central bank influences the amount of cash reserves with banks by open market operations, discount rate policy and varying margin requirements. Accordingly, it affects the credit expansion or contraction by commercial banks.

We may conclude that commercial banks do not possess unlimited powers to create credit.

EXERCISES

1. Explain the statement that "loans create deposits."
2. Explain how "loans make deposits". What are the limitations to such credit creation by banks ?
3. Describe the process of credit creation by commercial banks.
4. How do banks create credit ? What are the limitations on the power of banks to create credit ?

CHAPTER 10

Central Banking : Functions and Credit Control

1. INTRODUCTION

The central bank is the apex bank in a country. It is called by different names in different countries. It is the Reserve Bank of India in India, the Bank of England in England, the Federal Reserve System in America, the Bank of France in France, the Riksbank in Sweden, etc.

2. DIFFERENCE BETWEEN CENTRAL BANK AND COMMERCIAL BANK

A central bank is basically different from a commercial bank in the following ways :

1. The central bank is the apex institution of the monetary and banking structure of the country. The commercial bank is one of the organs of the money market.

2. The central bank is a no-profit institution which implements the economic policies of the government. But the commercial bank is a profit-making institution.

3. The central bank is owned by the government, whereas the commercial bank is owned by shareholders.

4. The central bank is a banker to the government and does not engage itself in ordinary banking activities. The commercial bank is a banker to the general public.

5. The central bank has the monopoly of note issue, while the commercial bank can issue only cheques. The notes are legal tender. But the cheques are in the nature of near-money.

6. The central bank is the banker's bank. As such, it grants accommodation to commercial banks in the form of rediscount facilities, keeps their cash reserves, and clears their balances. On the other hand, the commercial bank advances loans to and accepts deposits from the public.

7. The central bank controls credit in accordance with the needs of business and economy. The commercial bank creates credit to meet the requirements of business.

8. The central bank helps in establishing financial institutions so as to strengthen money and capital markets in a country. On the other hand, the commercial bank helps industry by underwriting shares and debentures, and agriculture by meeting its financial requirements through cooperative or individually.

9. Every country has only one central bank with its offices at important centres of the country. On the other hand, there are many commercial banks with hundreds of branches within and outside the country.

10. The central bank is the custodian of the foreign currency reserves of the country while the commercial bank is the dealer of foreign currencies.

11. The chief executive of the central bank is designated as "Governor", whereas the chief executive of a commercial bank is called 'Chairman'.

3. DEFINITION OF A CENTRAL BANK

A central bank has been defined in terms of its functions. According to Vera Smith, "The primary definition of central banking is a banking system in which a single bank has either complete control or a residuary monopoly of note issue." W.A. Shaw defines a central bank as a bank which control credit. To Hawtrey, a central bank is that which is the lender of the last resort. According to A.C.L. Day, a central bank is "to help control and stabilise the monetary and banking system." According to Sayers, the central bank "is the organ of government that undertakes the major financial operations of the government and by its conduct of these operations and by other means, influences the behaviour of financial institutions so as to support the economic policy of the Government." Sayers refers only to the nature of the central bank as the government's bank. All these definitions are narrow because they refer only to one particular function of a central bank.

On the other hand, Samuelson's definition is wide. According to him, a central bank "is a bank of bankers. Its duty is to control the monetary base.... and through control of this 'high-powered money' to control the community's supply of money." But the broadest definition has been given by De Kock. In his words, a central bank is "a bank which constitutes the apex of the monetary and banking structure of its country and which performs as best as it can in the national economic interest, the following functions: (i) The regulation of currency in accordance with the requirements of business and the general public for which purpose it is granted either the sole right of note issue or at least a partial monopoly thereof. (ii) The performance of general banking and agency for the state. (iii) The custody of the cash reserves of the commercial banks. (iv) The custody and management of the nation's reserves of international currency. (v) The granting of accommodation in the form of re-discounts and collateral advances to commercial banks, bill brokers and dealers, or other financial institutions and the general acceptance of the responsibility of lender of the last resort. (vi) The settlement of clearance balances between the banks. (vii) The control of credit in accordance with the needs of business and with a view to carrying out the broad monetary policy adopted by the state." De Kock's definition is too long to be called a definition. For, a definition must be brief.

4. FUNCTIONS OF A CENTRAL BANK

A central bank performs the following functions, as given by De Kock and accepted by the majority of economists.

1. Regulator of Currency

The central bank is the bank of issue. It has the monopoly of note issue. Notes issued by it circulate as legal tender money. It has its issue department which issues notes and coins to commercial banks. Coins are manufactured in the government mint but they are put into circulation through the central bank.

Central banks have been following different methods of note issue in different countries. The central bank is required by law to keep a certain amount of gold and foreign securities against the issue of notes. In some countries, the amount of gold and foreign securities bears a fixed proportion, between 25 to 40 per cent of the total notes issued. In other countries, a minimum fixed amount of gold and foreign currencies is required to be kept against note issue by the central bank. This system is operative in India whereby the Reserve Bank of India is required to keep Rs 115 crores in gold and Rs 85 crores in foregin securities. There is no limit to the issue of notes after keeping this minimum amount of Rs 200 crores in gold and foreign securities.

The monopoly of issuing notes vested in the central bank ensures uniformity in the notes issued which helps in facilitating exchange and trade within the country. It brings stability in the monetary system and creates confidence among the public. The central bank can restrict or expand the supply of cash according to the requirements of the economy. Thus it provides elasticity to the monetary system. By having a monopoly of note issue, the central bank also controls the banking system by being the ultimate source of cash. Last but not the least, by entrusting the monopoly of note issue to the central bank, the government is able to earn profits from printing notes whose cost is very low as compared with their face value.

2. Banker, Fiscal Agent and Adviser to the Goververnment

Central banks everywhere act as bankers, fiscal agents and advisers to their respective governments. As banker to the government, the central bank keeps the deposits of the central and state governments and makes payments on behalf of governments. But it does not pay interest on governments depostis. It buys and sells foreign currencies on behalf of the government., It keeps the stock of gold of the government. Thus it is the custodian of government money and wealth. As a fiscal agent, the central bank makes short-term loans to the government for a period not exceeding 90 days. It floats loans, pays interest on them, and finally repays them on behalf of the government. Thus it manages the entire public debt. The central bank also advises the government on such economic and money matters as controlling inflation or deflation, devaluetion or revaluation of the currency, deflicit financing, balance of payments, etc. As pointed out by De Kock, "Central banks everywhere operate as bankers to the state not only because it may be more convenient and economical to the state, but also because of the intimate connection between public finance and monetary affairs."

3. Custodian of Cash Reserves of Commercial Banks

Commercial banks are required by law to keep reserves equal to a certain percentage of both time and demand desposits liabilities with the central banks. It is on the basis of these reserves that the central bank transfers funds from one bank to another to facilitate the clearing of cheques. Thus the central bank acts as the custodian of the cash reserves of commercial banks and helps in facilitating their transactions. There are many advantages of keeping the cash reserves of the commercial banks with the central bank, according to De Kock. In the first place, the centralisation of cash reserves in the central bank is a source of great strength to the banking system of a country. *Secondly*, centralised cash reserves can serve as the basis of a large and more elastic credit structure than if the same amount were scattered among the individual banks. *Thirdly*, centralised cash reserves can be utilised fully and most effectively during periods of seasonal strains and in financial crises or emergencies. *Fourthly*, by varying these cash reserves the central bank can control the credit creation by commercial banks. *Lastly*, the central bank can provide additional funds on a temporary and short term basis to commercial banks to overcome their financial difficulties.

4. Custody and Management of Foreign Exchange Reserves

The central bank keeps and manages the foreign exchange reserves of the country. It is an official reservoir of gold and foreign currencies. It sells gold at fixed prices to the monetary authorities of other countries. It also buys and sells foreign currencies at international prices. Further, it fixes the exchange rates of the domestic currency in terms of foreign currencies. It holds these rates within narrow limits in keeping with its obligations as a member of the International Monetary Fund and tries to bring stability in foreign exchange rates. Further, it manages exchange control operations by supplying foreign currencies to importers and persons visiting foreign countries on business, studies, etc. in keeping with the rules laid down by the government.

5. Lender of the Last Resort

De Kock regards this function as a *sine qua non* of central banking. By granting accommodation in the form of re-discounts and collateral advances to commercial banks, bill brokers and dealers, or other financial institutions, the central bank acts as the lender of the last resort. The central bank lends to such institutions in order to help them in times of stress so as to save the financial structure of the country from collapse. It acts as lender of the last resort through discount house on the basis of treasury bills, government securities and bonds at "the front door". The other method is to give temporary accommodation to the commercial banks or discount houses directly through the "back door". The difference between the two methods is that lending at the front door is at the bank rate and in the second case at the market rate. Thus the central bank as lender of the last resort is a big source of cash and also influences prices and market rates.

6. Clearing House for Transfer and Settlement

As bankers' bank, the central bank acts as a clearing house for transfer and settlement of mutual claims of commercial banks. Since the central bank holds reserves of commercial banks, it transfers funds from one bank to other banks to facilitate clearing of cheques. This is done by making transfer entries in their accounts on the principle of book-keeping. To transfer and settle claims of one bank upon others, the central bank operates a seperate department in big cities and trade centres. This department is known as the "clearing house" and it renders the service free to commercial banks.

When the central bank acts as a clearing agency, it is time-saving and convenient for the commercial banks to settle their claims at one place. It also economises the use of money. "It is not only a means of economising cash and capital but is also a means of testing at any time the degree of liquidity which the community is maintaining."[1]

7. Controller of Credit

The most important function of the central bank is to control the credit creation power of commercial bank in order to control inflationary and deflationary pressures within this economy. For this purpose, it adopts quantitative methods and qualitative methods. Quantitative methods aim at controlling the cost and quantity of credit by adopting bank rate policy, open market operations, and by variations in reserve ratios of commercial banks. Qualitative methods control the use and direction of credit. These involve selective credit controls and direct action. By adopting such methods, the central bank tries to influence and control credit creation by commercial banks in order to stabilise economic activity in the country.

Besides the above noted functions, the central banks in a number of developing countries have been entrusted with the responsibility of developing a strong banking system to meet the expanding requirements of agriculture, industry, trade and commerce. Accordingly, the central banks possess some additional powers of supervision and control over the commercial banks. They are the issuing of licences; the regulation of branch expansion; to see that every bank maintains the minimum paid up capital and reserves as provided by law; inspecting or auditing the accounts of banks; to approve the appointment of chairmen and directors of such banks in accordance with the rules and qualifications; to control and recommend merger of weak banks in order to avoid their failures and to protect the interest of depositors; to recommend nationalisation of certain banks to the government in public interest; to publish periodical reports relating to different aspects of monetary and economic policies for the benefit of banks and the public; and to engage in research and train banking personnel etc.

5. CENTRAL BANK AS THE CONTROLLER OF CREDIT

Objectives of Credit Control

Credit control is the means to control the lending policy of commercial banks by the central bank. The central bank controls credit to achieve the following objectives:

1. *To Stabilise the Internal Price Level.* One of the objective of controlling credit is to stabilise the price level in the country. Frequent changes in prices adversely affect the economy. Inflationary or deflationary trends need to be prevented. This can be achieved by adopting a judicious policy of credit control.

2. *To Stabilise the Rate of Foreign Exchange.* With the change in the internal prices level, exports and imports of the country are affected. When prices fall, exports increase and imports decline. Consequently, the demand for domestic currency increases in the foreign market and its exchange rate rises. On the contrary, a rise in domestic prices leads to a decline in exports and an increase in imports. As a result, the demand for foreign currency increases and that of domestic currency falls, thereby lowering the exchange rate of the domestic

1. H.P. Willis, *Theory and Practice of Central Banking*, p. 313.

currency. Since it is the volume of credit money that affects prices, the central bank can stabilise the rate of foreign exchange by controlling bank credit.

3. *To Protect the Outflow of Gold.* The central bank holds the gold reserves of the country in its vaults. Expansion of bank credit leads to rise in prices which reduce exports and increase imports, thereby creating an unfavourable balance of payments. This necessitates the export of gold to other countries. The central bank has to control credit in order to prevent such outflows of gold to other countries.

4. *To Control Business Cycles.* Business cycles are a common phenomenon of capitalist countries which lead to periodic fluctuations in production, employment and prices. They are characterised by alternating periods of prosperity and depression. During prosperity, there is large expansion in the volume of credit, and production, employment and prices rise. During depression, credit contracts, and production, employment and prices fall. The central bank can counteract such cyclical fluctuations through contraction of bank credit during boom periods, and expansion of bank credit during depression.

5. *To Meet Business Needs.* According to Burgess, one of the important objectives of credit control is the "adjustment of the volume of credit to the volume of business." Credit is needed to meet the requirements of trade and industry. As business expands, larger quantity of credit is needed, and when business contracts less credit is needed. Therefore, it is the central bank which can meet the requirements of business by controlling credit.

6. *To Have Growth with Stability.* In recent years, the principal objective of credit control is to have growth with stability. The other objectives, such as price stability, foreign exchange rate stability, etc., are regarded as secondary. The aim of credit control is to help in achieving full employment and accelerated growth with stability in the economy without inflationary pressures and balance of payments deficits.

Methods of Credit Control

The central bank adopts two types of methods of credit control. They are the quantitative and qualitative methods. *Quantitative* methods aim at controlling the cost and quantity of credit by adopting such techniques as variations in the bank rate, open market operations, and variations in the reserve ratios of commercial banks. On the other hand, *qualitative* methods control the use and direction of credit. These involve selective credit controls and direct action.

1. Bank Rate or Discount Rate Policy

The bank rate or the discount rate is the rate fixed by the central bank at which it rediscounts first class bills of exchange and government securities held by the commercial banks. The bank rate is the interest rate charged by the central bank at which it provides rediscount to banks through the *discount window.* The central bank controls credit by making variations in the bank rate. If the need of the economy is to expand credit, the central bank lowers the bank rate. Borrowing from the central bank becomes cheap and easy. So the commercial banks will borrow more. They will, in turn, advance loans to customers at a lower rate. The market rate of interest will be reduced. This encourages business activity, and expansion of credit follows which encourages the rise in prices. The opposite happens when credit is to be contracted in the economy. The central bank raises the bank rate which makes borrowing costly from it. So the banks borrow less. They, in turn, raise their lending rates to customers. The market rate of interest also rises because of the tight money market. This discourages fresh loans and puts pressure on borrowers to pay their past debts. This discourages business activity. There is contraction of credit which depresses the rise in price. Thus lowering the bank rate offsets deflationary tendencies and raising the bank rate controls inflation.

But how do changes in the bank rate affect prices and production ? There are two views which explain this process. One held by R.G. Hawtrey and the other by Keynes.

Hawtrey's View. According to Hawtrey, changes in the bank rate affect changes in the short-term rates of interest which, in turn, affect the behaviour of dealers and producers in holding short of finished and semi-finished goods. Suppose the bank rate rises. It raises the stock-term interest rates. Consequently, the cost of borrowing and of holding stocks of goods increases. The dealers will, therefore, try to reduce their stocks of goods, and place less orders to the producers of goods. The sales of producers will start declining. So they will lower prices to induce dealers to buy more of their goods. Or, they will reduce output. As they curtail output, some of the factors of production become unemployed. Money incomes fall due to unemployment. This further reduces the sale of goods, and the dealers reduce their orders to the producers further who, in turn, reduce their production. So ultimately there will be a fall in prices, production and employment in the economy. The converse will be the case when the bank rate falls which will reduce the short-term interest rates, and encourage prices, production and employment through the encouraging behaviour of traders and producers.

Keynes's View. Keynes in his *Treatise on Money* gives an alternative view based upon changes in the volume of fixed capital following a change in the long-term rate of interest. According to him, when the bank rate changes, the long-term interest rates also change in the same direction and will affect investment, prices and employment in the following manner.

Suppose the bank rate is increased. It will raise the short-term interest rates in the money market, while the long-term interest rates remain unchanged. As a result, short-term securities become more attractive because they carry high rates of interest. But the value of long-term securities declines because they now carry low rates of interest than at which they were purchased in the past. The holders of long-term securities will, therefore, sell their securities and invest in short-term securities. This will adversely affect long-term investments in the economy. Consequently, long-term rates of interest will also rise. With the rise in the long-term interest rates, businessmen and producers will reduce investment on fixed capital assets. Employment falls in the capital goods industries. Money income declines. Expenditure on consumption goods is reduced. This leads to fall in their prices and production. Conversely, a fall in the bank rate will lower the long-term interest rates, investment, employment, income, prices and production.

It is not possible to verify empirically these two views. They presuppose that businessmen and producers are very sensitive to interest rate changes and interest charges form a considerable part of the cost of holding and production of goods. Both the assumptions are unrealistic. *First*, prices and production are not so sensitive to changes in interest rates. *Second*, interest rates form an insignificant part of the total cost of holding and production of goods. Interest rate is only one of the factors which determines the volume of investment in stocks of goods and in fixed capital goods. Further, the two views are neither contrary nor mutually exclusive. Hawtrey lays emphasis on changes in the short-term interest rates and Keynes on the long-term interest rates, as a result of changes in the bank rate. But ultimately both lead to the same results, though the process of causation is a little different in each case. For instance, a change in the bank rate may affect the holdings of stocks of goods as well as the volume of fixed capital goods whether the short-term or the long-term interest rates change.

Views of Radcliffe Committee. The Radcliffe Committee appointed by the British Government in 1959 analysed two effects of the bank rate policy upon business activity. The first is the interest-incentive effect. When the bank rate changes, it brings changes in the market rates of interest, thereby inducing a change in the incentive of investment expenditures of business firms. A rise in the bank rate raises interest rates. The cost of holding capital goods increases which causes a disincentive for investors and business firms to borrow funds. Thus with the increase in the cost of borrowing funds, there will be a disincentive for investors and business firms to borrow from the commercial banks. The opposite will be the case when the bank rate falls. It reduces market interest rates, thereby reducing the cost of borrowing from the banks. This provides an incentive to investors and businessmen to get more advances from the banks. But the Committee ruled out the interest-incentive effect because business decisions are primarily independent of changes in interest rates. Moreover, interest-payments form an insignificant proportion of total costs of business firms.

The Committee analysed a more important effect of the bank rate changes, known as the 'general liquidity effect'. According to the Committee, the interest-incentive effect of a change in the bank rate being small, there may take place a 'valuation effect' or general liquidity effect. Bank rate changes affect the capital values of the assets of business firms, and consequently, their balance sheets and their ability to lend. A rise in the bank rates raises the market rates, thereby reducing the value of capital assets of financial institutions. Thus they are willing to lend less. On the other hand, a fall in the bank rate lowers the market rates, and the value of capital assets increases. It encourages lenders to seek new business. The real force of changes in the bank rate lies in its effects on the liquidity of the various groups of financial institutions through market interest rates which (i.e. liquidity), in turn, affects the liquidity of others. This is the general liquidity effect of changes in the bank rate. While analysing this effect, the Committee takes into view the interrelationship of short, medium and long-term interest rates.

Limitations of Bank Rate Policy

The efficacy of the bank rate policy as an instrument of controlling credit is limited by the following factors:

1. *Market Rates do not change with Bank Rate.* The success of the bank rate policy depends upon the extent to which other market rates of interest change along with the bank rate. The theory of bank rate policy pre-supposes that other rates of interest prevailing in the money market change in the direction of the change in the bank rate. If this condition is not satisfied, the bank rate policy will be totally ineffective as an instrument of credit control.

2. *Wages, Costs and Prices not Elastic.* The success of the bank rate policy requires elasticity not only in interest rates but also in wages, costs and prices. It implies that when suppose the bank rate is raised, wages, costs and prices should automatically adjust themselves to a lower level. But this was possible only under gold standard. Now-a-days the emergence of strong trade unions have made wages rigid during deflationary trends. And they also lag behind when there are inflationary tendencies because it takes time for unions to get a wage rise from employers. So the bank rate policy cannot be a success in a rigid society.

3. *Banks do not approach Central Bank.* The effectiveness of the bank rate policy as a tool of credit control is also limited by the behaviour of the commercial banks. It is only if the commercial banks approach the central bank for rediscounting facilities that this policy can be a success. But the banks keep with them large amounts of liquid assets and do not find it necessary to approach the central bank for financial help.

4. *Bills of Exchange not used.* As a corollary to the above, the effectiveness of the bank rate policy depends on the existence of eligible bills of exchange. In recent years, the bill of exchange as an instrument of financing commerce and trade has fallen into disuse. Businessmen and banks prefer cash credit and overdrafts. This makes the bank rate policy less effective for controlling credit in the country.

5. *Pessimism or Optimism.* The efficacy of the bank rate policy also depends on waves of pessimism or optimism among businessmen. If the bank rate is raised, they will continue to borrow even at a higher rate of interest if there are boom conditions in the economy, and prices are expected to rise further. On the other hand, a reduction in the bank rate will not induce them to borrow during periods of falling prices. Thus businessmen are not very sensitive to changes in interest rates and they are influenced more by business expectations.

6. *Power to Control Deflation Limited.* Another limitation of the bank rate policy is that the power of a central bank to force a reduction in the market rates of interest is limited. For instance, a lowering of bank rate below 3 per cent will not lead to a decline in the market rates of interest below 3 per cent. So the bank rate policy is ineffective in controlling deflation. It may, however, control inflationary tendencies by forcing an increase in the market rates of interest.

7. *Level of Bank Rate in relation to Market Rate.* The efficacy of the discount rate policy as an instrument of credit control depends upon its level in relation to the market rate. If in a boom the bank rate is not raised to such an extent as to make borrowing costly from the central bank, and it is not lowered during a recession so as to make borrowing cheaper from it, it would have a destabilising effect on economic activity.

8. *Non-Discriminatory.* The bank rate policy is non-discriminatory because it does not distinguish between productive and unproductive activities in the country.

9. *Not Successful in Controlling BOP Disequilibrium.* The bank rate policy is not effective in controlling balance of payments disequilibrium in a country because it requires the removal of all restrictions on foreign exchange and movements of international capital.

Conclusion. The above points have led the majority of economists to conclude that the power to alter the bank rate is an extremely weak weapon of monetary management. Friedman even went to the extent of proposing outright elimination of the "discount window" itself.

2. Open Market Operations

Open market operations are another method of quantitative credit control used by a central bank. This method refers to the sale and purchase of securities, bills and bonds of government as well as private financial institutions by the central bank. But in its narrow sense, it simply means dealing only in government securities and bonds.

There are two principal motives of open market operations. *One,* to influence the reserves of commercial banks in order to control their power of credit creation. *Two,* to affect the market rates of interest so as to control the commercial bank credit.

Its method of operation is as follows. Suppose the central bank of a country wants to control expansion of credit by the commercial banks for the purpose of controlling inflationary pressures within the economy. It sells government securities in the money market amounting to, say, Rs 10 crores. The latter give the central bank cheques for this amount drawn against the commercial banks in which the public have their accounts. The central bank reduces this amount in their accounts with it. This applies equally if the commmercial banks have also purchased securities from the central bank. The sale of securities in the open market has thus reduced their cash holdings with the central bank. This tends to reduce the actual cash ratio of the commercial banks by Rs. 10 crores. So the banks are forced to curtail their lending.

Suppose that initially the commercial banks have assets worth Rs 1000 crores and the cash-deposit ratio is 10. This means that Rs 1000 crores are divided between Rs 100 crores cash and Rs 900 crores as deposits or loans. As a result of the sale of securities by the central bank worth Rs 10 crores, the cash is reduced by Rs 100 crores. So the total cash with banks remains Rs 900 crores and loans are also reduced by the same percentage, that is, to Rs 810 crores. This reduction in the cash holding of the commercial banks causes a decrease in the supply of bank money, as shown in Figure 1. In this figure, *S* is the supply curve of bank money which shifts to the left as S_1 showing a decrease in the supply of bank money from *B* to *A*, given the level of interest rate *r*.

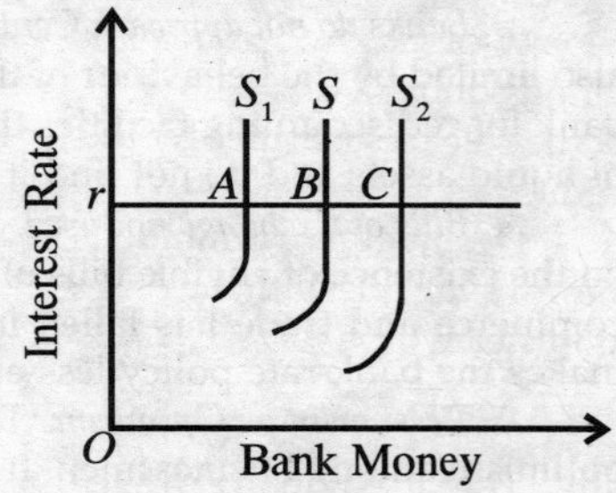

Fig. 1

On the other hand, when the central bank aims at an expansionary policy during a recessionary period, it purchases government securities from the commercial banks and institution dealing with such securities. The central bank pays the sellers its cheques drawn against itself which are deposited into their accounts with the commercial banks. The reserves of the latter increase with the central bank which are just like cash. As a result the supply curve of bank money shifts to the right from *S* to S_2 showing an increase in the supply of bank money from *B* to *C*, as shown in Figure 2. The banks will now lend more at the given rate of interest, *r*.

Another aspect of the open market policy is that when the supply of money changes as a result of open market operations, the market rates of interest also change. A decrease in the supply of bank money through the sale of securities will have the effect of raising the market interest rates. On the other hand, an increase in the supply of bank money through the purchase of securities will reduce the market interest rates. Thus open market operations have a direct influence on the market rates of interest also.

Limitations of Open Market Operations. The effectiveness of open market operations as a method of credit control is dependent upon the existence of a number of conditions, the absence of which limits the full working of this policy.

1. *Lack of Securities Market.* The first condition is the existence of a large and well-organised security market. This condition is very essential for open market operations because without a well developed security market the central bank will not be able to buy and sell securities on a large scale, and thereby influence the reserves of the commercial banks. Further, the central bank must have enough saleable securities with it.

2. *Cash Reserve Ratio not Stable.* The success of open market operations also requires the maintenance of a stable cash-reserve ratio by the commercial bank. It implies that when the central bank sells or buys securities, the reserves of the commercial banks decrease or increase accordingly to maintain the fixed ratio. But usually the banks do not stick to the legal minimum reserve ratio and keep a higher ratio than this. This makes open market operations less effective in controlling the volume of credit.

3. *Penal Bank Rate.* According to Prof. Aschheim, one of the necessary conditions for the success of open market operations is a penal bank rate. If there is no penal discount rate fixed by the central bank, the commercial banks can increase their borrowings from it when the demand for credit is strong on the part of the

latter. In this situation, the scale of securities by the central bank to restrict monetary expansion will be unsuccessful. But if there is a penal rate of discount, which is a rate higher than the market rates of interest, the banks will be reluctant to approach the central bank for additional financial help easily.

4. Banks Act Differently. Open market operations are successful only if the people also act the way the central bank expects them. When the central bank sells securities, it expects the business community and financial institutions to restrict the use of credit. If they simultaneously start dishoarding money, the act of selling securities by the central banks will not be a success in restricting credit. Similarly, the purchase of securities by the central bank will not be effective if people start hoarding money.

5. Pessimistic or Optimistic Attitude. Pessimistic or optimistic attitude of the business community also limits the operation of open market policy. When the central bank purchases securities and increases the supply of bank money, businessmen may be unwilling to take loans during a depression because of the prevailing pessimism among them. As aptly put by Crowther, banks may place plenty of water before the public horse, but the horse cannot be forced to drink, if it is afraid of loss through drinking water. On the other hand, if businessmen are optimistic during a boom, the sale of securities by the central bank to contract the supply of bank money and even the rise in market rates cannot discourage them from getting loans from the banks. On the whole, this policy is more successful in controlling booms than depressions.

6. Velocity of Credit Money not Constant. The success of open market operations depends upon a constant velocity of circulation of bank money. But the velocity of credit money is not constant. It increases during periods of brisk business activity and decreases in periods of falling prices. Thus a policy of contracting credit by the sale of securities by the central bank may not be successful by increased velocity of circulation of bank credit.

Despite these limitations, open market operations are more effective than the other instruments of credit control available with the central bank. This method is being successfully used for controlling credit in developed countries where the securities market is highly developed.

Open Market Operations vs Bank Rate Policy

The question arises whether the bank rate is more effective as an instrument of credit control or open market operations. The bank rate policy influences the cost and supply of commercial bank credit, while open market operations affect the cash reserves of the commercial banks. Changes in the bank rate affect the credit creation power of the commercial bank only if they rediscount their bills with the central bank. If the banks do not feel the necessity of availing rediscounting facilities of the central bank, a rise in the bank rate will have no effect on the commercial banks. On the other hand, the lending power of the commercial banks is directly related to their cash reserves, and open market operations influence their cash reserves directly and immediately thereby affecting their credit creation power.

Further, "from the standpoint of their strategic value to the central bank, open market operations possess a degree of superiority over rediscount policy because of the fact that initiative is in the hands of the monetary authority in the case of the former, whereas bank rate policy is passive in the sense that its effectiveness depends on the responses of commercial banks and their customers to changes in bank rates."[2]

Again, open market operations are flexible with respect to timing and magnitude as compared with the bank rate policy. They are carried on continuously and do not have any destablilising effects on the economy that accompany changes in the bank rate.

It is further argued that since bank rate changes have destabilising effects on the economy, this policy should be used to correct permanent maladjustments in the money market rather than temporary maladjustments. On the other hand, open market policy can be used for correcting both temporary and permanent maladjustments in the money market.

But the experience of developed countries like the USA and the UK tells us that these two policies are not competitive but complementary to each other. If they are supplemented, they can control credit more effectively than individually. For instance, if the central bank raises the discount rate for the purpose of contracting credit, it will not be effective when the commercial bank have large excess reserves with them. They will continue to

2. G.N. Halm, *Monetary Theory*, p.59.

expand credit irrespective of the rise in the bank rate. But if the central bank first draws away to itself the excess reserves of the commercial banks by the sale of securities and then raises the bank rate, it will have the effect of contracting credit. Similarly, the sale of securities alone will not be so effective in contracting credit unless the bank rate is also raised. The sale of securities by the central bank will reduce the cash reserves of commercial banks but if the discount rate is low, the latter will get funds from the "discount window" of the central bank. So for an effective policy credit control, bank rate policy and open market operations should be judiciously supplemented.

3. Variable Reserve Ratio

Variable reserve ratio (or required reserve ratio or legal minimum requirements), as a method of credit control was first suggested by Keynes in his *Treatise on Money* (1930) and was adopted by the Federal Reserve System of the United States in 1935.

Every commercial bank is required by law to maintain a minimum percentage of its deposits with the central bank. The minimum amount of reserve with the central bank may be either a percentage of its time and demand deposits separately or of total deposits. Whatever the amount of money remains with the commercial bank over and above these minimum reserves is known as the excess reserves. It is on the basis of these excess reserves that the commercial bank is able to create credit. The larger the size of the excess reserves, the greater is the power of a bank to create credit, and vice versa. It can also be said that the larger the required reserve ratio, the lower the power of a bank to create credit, and vice versa.

When the central bank raises the reserve ratio of the commercial banks, it means that the latter are required to keep more money with the former. Consequently, the excess reserves with the commercial banks are reduced and they can lend less than before.

This can be explained with the help of the deposit multiplier formula. If a commercial bank has Rs 100 crores as deposits and 10 per cent is the required reserve ratio, then it will have to keep Rs 10 crores with the central bank. Its excess reserves will be Rs 90 crores. It can thus create credit to the extent of Rs 900 crores in this way ER/RRr where ER is the excess reserves, and RRr the required reserve ratio... 90x1/10% = 90 x 100/10 = Rs 900 crores. When the central bank raises the required reserve ratio to 20 per cent, the bank's power to create credit will be reduced to Rs 400 crores = 80 x 100/20.

On the contrary, if the central bank wants to expand credit, it lowers the reserve ratio so as to increase the credit creation power of the commercial banks. Thus by varying the reserve ratio of the commercial banks the central bank influences their power of credit creation and thereby controls credit in the economy.

Limitations of Variable Reserve Ratio. The variable reserve ratio as a method of credit control has a number of limitations.

1. *Excess Reserves.* The commercial banks usually possess large excessive reserves which make the policy of variable reserve ratio ineffective. When the banks keep excessive reserves, an increase in the reserve ratio will not affect their lending operations. They will stick to the legal minimum requirements of cash to deposits and at the same time continue to create credit on the strength of the excessive reserves.

2. *Clumsy Method.* It is a clumsy method of credit control as compared with open market operations. This is because it lacks definiteness in the sense that it is inexact and uncertain as regards changes not only in the amounts of reserves but also the place where these changes can be made effective. It is not possible to tell "how much of active or potential reserve base" has been affected by changes in the reserve ratio. Moreover, the changes in reserves involve far larger sums than in the case of open market operations.[3]

3. *Discriminatory.* It is discriminatory and affects different banks differently. A rise in the required reserve ratio will not affect those banks which have large excess reserves. On the other hand, it will hit hard the banks with little or no excess reserves. This policy is also discriminatory in the sense that non-banking financial intermediaries like co-operative societies, insurance companies, building societies, development banks, etc. are not affected by variations in reserve requirements, though they compete with the commercial banks for lending purposes.

4. *Inflexible.* This policy is inflexible because the minimum reserve ratio fixed by the central banks is

---

3. K. Basu, *A Review of Current Banking Theory and Practice*, 1971.

applicable to banks located in all regions of the country. More credit may be needed in one region where there is monetary stringency, and it may be superfluous in the other region. Raising the reserve ratio for all banks is not justified in the former region though it is appropriate for the latter region.

5. Business Climate. The success of the method of credit control also depends on the business climate in the economy. If the businessmen are pessimistic about the future, as under a depression, even a sizable lowering of the reserve ratio will not encourage them to ask for loan. Similarly, if they are optimistic about profit expectations, a considerable rise in the variable ratio will not prevent them from asking for more loans from the banks.

6. Stability of Reserve Ratio. The effectiveness of this technique depends upon the degree of stability of the reserve ratio. If the commercial banks are authorised to keep widely fluctuating ratio, say between 10 per cent to 17 per cent, and change in the upper or lower limit will have no effect on the credit creation power of the banks.

7. Other Factors. The reserve ratio held by the commercial banks is determined not only by legal requirements but also by how much they want to hold in relation to their deposits in addition to such requirements. This, in turn, will depend upon their expectations about future developments, their competition with other banks, and so on.[4]

8. Depressive Effect. The variable reserve ratio has been criticised for exercising a depressive effect on the securities market. When the central bank suddenly directs the commercial banks to increase their reserve ratios, they may be forced to sell securities to maintain that ratio. This widespread selling of securities will bring down the prices of securities and may even lead to an utter collapse of the bond market.

9. Rigid. It is rigid in its operations because it does not distinguish between desired and undesired credit flows and can affect them equally.

10. Not for Small Changes. This method is more like an axe than a scalpel. It cannot be used for day-to-day and week-to-week adjustments but can be used to bring about large changes in the reserve positions of the commercial banks. Thus it cannot help in 'fine tuning' of the money and credit systems by making small changes.

Conclusion. The variable reserve ratios as a method of credit control is a very delicate and sensitive tool which not only produces a state of uncertainty among the banks but also adversely affects their liquidity and profitability. Therefore, according to De Kock, "it should be used with moderation and discretion and only under obvious abnormal conditions."

Variable Reserve Ratio vs Open Market Operations

There are divergent views about the superiority of variable reserve ratio over open market operations. To those who consider the former as a superior instrument of credit control, it is "a battery of the most improved type that a central bank can add to its armoury." They give the following arguments.

The variable reserve ratio affects the power of credit creation of the commercial banks more directly, immediately, and simultaneously than open market operations. The central bank has simply to make a declaration for changing the reserve requirements of the banks and they have to implement it immediately. But open market operations require sale or purchase of securities which is a time consuming process.

When the central bank sells securities to the banks to control inflation, they are forced to buy them. They are, therefore, prevented from giving more loans to the private credit market. On the other hand, if the reserve ratio is raised, the banks will be required to keep larger balances with the central bank. They will also be faced with reduced earnings. They will, therefore, be induced to sell government securities and give more loans to the private credit market. Thus open market operations are more effective for controlling inflation than the change in reserve ratio.

In another sense, open market operations are more effective as an instrument of credit control than variations in the reserve ratio. In every country there are non-banking financial intermediaries which deal in securities, bonds, etc. and also advance loans and accept deposits from the public. But they are outside the legal

4. H.G. Johnson, 'Recent Development in Monetary Theory', I.E.R., Feb. 1963.

control of the central bank. Since they also deal in government securities, open market sale and purchase of such securities by the central bank also affect their liquidity position. But they are not required to keep any reserves with the central bank, unlike the commercial banks.

Again, variations in the reserve ratio are meant for making major and long-run adjustments in the liquidity position of the commercial banks. They are, therefore, not suited for making short-run adjustments in the volume of available bank reserves, as are done under open market operations.

The effectiveness of open market operations depends upon the existence of a broad and well-organised market for securities. Thus this instrument of credit control cannot be operative in countries which lack such a market. On the other hand, the method of variable reserve ratio does not require any such market for its operation and is applicable equally in developed and underdeveloped markets, and is thus superior to open market operations.

Further, since open market operations involve the sale and purchase of securities on a day-to-day and week-to-week basis, the commercial banks and the central bank which deal in them are likely to incur losses. But variations in the reserve ratio do not involve any losses.

Despite the superiority of variable reserve ratio over open market operations, economists like Prof. Aschheim[5] have argued that open market operations are more effective as a tool in controlling credit than variable reserve ratio. Therefore, changes in the reserve ratio do not have any effect on their lending power. Thus open market operations are superior to variable ratio because they also influence non-banking financial institutions.

Further, as a technique, reserve ratio can only influence the volume of reserves of the commercial banks. On the other hand, open market operations can influence not only the reserves of the commercial banks but also the pattern of the interest rate structure. Thus open market operations are more effective in influencing the reserves and the credit creation power of the banks than variations in reserve ratio.

Last but not the least, the technique of variations in reserve ratio is clumsy, inflexible, and discriminatory whereas that of open market operations is simple, flexible and non-discriminatory in its effects.

It can be concluded from the above discussion of the relative merits and demerits of the two techniques that in order to have the best of the two, they should be used jointly rather than independently. If the central bank raises the reserve ratio, it should simultaneously start purchasing, and not selling, securities in those areas of the country where there is monetary stringency. On the contrary, when the central bank lowers the reserve requirments of the banks, it should also sell securities to those banks which already have excess reserves with them, and have been engaged in excessive lending. The joint application of the two policies will not be contradictory but complementary to each other.

4. Selective Credit Controls

Selective or qualitative methods of credit control are meant to regulate and control the supply of credit among its possible users and uses. They are different from quantitative or general methods which aim at controlling the cost and quantity of credit. Unlike the general instruments, selective instruments do not affect the total amount of credit but the amount that is put to use in a particular sector of the economy. The aim of selective credit control is to channelise the flow of bank credit from speculative and other undesirable purposes to socially desirable and economically useful uses. They also restrict the demand for money by laying down certain conditions for borrowers. They therefore, embody the view that the monopoly of credit should in fact become a discriminating monopoly. Prof. Chandler defines selective credit controls as those measures "that would influence the allocation of credit, at least to the point of decreasing the volume of credit used for selected purposes without the necessity of decreasing the supply and raising the cost of credit for all purposes." We discuss below the main types of selective credit controls generally used by the central banks in different countries.

(A) Regulation of Margin Requirements

This method is employed to prevent excessive use of credit to purchase or carry securities by speculators.

---

5. J. Aschheim, *Theory of Monetary Control*, Ch. 2.

The central bank fixes minimum margin requirements on loans for purchasing or carrying securities. They are, in fact, the percentage of the value of the security that cannot be borrowed or lent. In other words, it is the maximum value of loan which a borrower can have from the banks on the basis of the security (or collateral). For example, if the central bank fixes a 10 per cent margin on the value of a security worth Rs 1,000, then the commercial bank can lend only Rs 900 to the holder of the security and keep Rs 100 with it. If the central bank raises the margin to 25 per cent, the bank can lend only Rs 750 against a security of Rs 1,000. If the central bank wants to curb speculative activities, it will raise the margin requirements. On the other hand, if it wants to expand credit, it reduces the margin requirements.

Its Merits. This method of selective credit control has certain merits which make it unique.

1. It is non-discriminatory because it applies equally to borrowers and lenders. Thus it limits both the supply and demand for credit simultaneously.

2. It is equally applicable to commercial banks and non-banking financial intermediaries.

3. It increases the supply of credit for more productive uses.

4. It is a very effective anti-inflationary device because it controls the expansion of credit in those sectors of the economy which breed inflation.

5. It is simple and easy to administer since this device is meant to regulate the use of credit for specific purposes.

But the success of this technique requires that there are no leakages of bank credit for non-purpose loans to speculators.

Its Weaknesses. However, a number of leakages have appeared in this method over the years.

1. A borrower may not show any intention of purchasing stocks with his borrowed funds and pledge other assets as security for the loan. But it may purchase stocks through some other source.

2. The borrower may purchase stocks with cash which he would normally use to purchase materials and supplies and then borrow money to finance the materials and supplies already purchased, pledging the stocks he already has as security for the loan.

3. Lenders, other than commercial banks and brokers, who are not subject to margin requirements, may increase their security loans when commercial banks and brokers are being controlled by high margin requirements. Further, some of these nonregulated lenders may be getting the funds they lent to finance the purchase of securities from commercial banks themselves.

Despite these weaknesses in practice, margin requirements are a useful device of credit control.

(B) Regulation of Consumer Credit

This is another method of selective credit control which aims at the regulation of consumer instalment credit or hire-purchase finance. The main objective of this instrument is to regulate the demand for durable consumer goods in the interest of economic stability. The central bank regulates the use of bank credit by consumers in order to buy durable consumer goods on instalments and hire-purchase. For this purpose, it employs two devices: minimum down payments, and maximum periods of repayment. Suppose a bicycle costs Rs 500 and credit is available from the commercial bank for its purchase. The central bank may fix the mimimum down payment to 50 per cent of the price, and the maximum period of repayment to 10 months. So Rs 250 will be the minimum which the consumer will have to pay to the bank at the time of purchase of the bicycle and the remaining amount in ten equal instalments of Rs 25 each. This facility will create demand for bicycles. The bicycle industry would expand along with the related industries such as tyres, tubes, spare parts, etc. and thus lead to inflationary situation in this and other sectors of the economy. To control it, the central bank raises the minimum down payment to 70 per cent and the maximum period of repayment to three instalements. So the buyer of a bicycle will have to pay Rs 350 in the beginning and remaining amount in three instalments of Rs 50 each. Thus if the central bank finds slump in particular industries of the economy, it reduces the amount of down payments and increases the maximum periods of repayment. Reducing the down payments tends to increase the demand for credit for particular durable consumer goods on which the central bank regulation is applied. Increasing the maximum period of repayment, which reduces monthly payments, tends to increase the demand for loans, thereby encouraging consumer credit. On the other hand, the central bank raises the amount of down payments and reduces the maximum periods of repayment in boom.

The regulation of consumer credit is more effective in controlling credit in the case of durable consumer goods during both booms and slumps, whereas general credit controls fail in this area. The reason is that the latter operate with a time lag. Moreover, the demand for consumer credit in the case of durable consumer goods is interest inelastic. Consumers are motivated to buy such goods under the influence of the demonstration effect and the rate of interest has little consideration for them.

But this instrument has its *drawbacks*.

It is cumbersome, technically defective and difficult to administer because it has a narrow base. In other words, it is applicable to a particular class of borrowers whose demand for credit forms an insignificant part of the total credit requirements. It, therefore, discriminates between different types of borrowers. This method affects only persons with limited incomes and leaves out higher income groups. Finally, it tends to malallocate resources by shifting them away from industries which are covered by credit regulations and lead to the expansion of other industries which do not have any credit restrictions.

(C) Rationing of Credit

Rationing of credit is another selective method of controlling and regulating the purpose for which credit is granted by the commercial banks. It is generally of four types. The first is the variable portfolio ceiling. According to this method, the central bank fixes a ceiling on the aggregate portfolios of the commercial banks and they cannot advance loans beyond this ceiling. The second method is known as the variable capital assets ratio. This is the ratio which the central bank fixes in relation to the capital of a commercial bank to its total assets. In keeping with the economic exigencies, the central bank may raise or lower the portfolio ceiling, and also vary the capital assets ratio.

Rationing of credit has been used very effectively in Russia and Mexico. It is, therefore, 'a logical concomitant of the intensive and extensive planning adopted in regimented economies.' The technique also involves discrimination against larger banks because it restricts their lending power more than the smaller banks. Lastly, by rationing of credit for selective purposes, the central bank ceases to be the lender of the last resort. Therefore, central banks in mixed economies do not use this technique except under extreme inflationary situations and emergencies.

(D) Direct Action

Central banks in all countries frequently resort to direction action against commercial banks. Direction action is in the form of "directives" issued from time to time to the commercial banks to follow a particular policy which the central bank wants to enforce immediately. This policy may not be used against all banks but against erring banks. For example, the centrl bank refuses rediscounting facilities to certain banks which may be granting too much credit for speculative purposes, or in excess of their capital and reserves, or restrains them from granting advances against the collateral of certain commodities, etc. It may also charge a penal rate of interest from those banks which want to borrow from it beyond the prescribed limit. The central bank may even threaten a commercial bank to be taken over by it in case it fails to follow its policies and instructions.

But this method of credit suffers from several limitations which have been enumerated by De Kock as "the difficulty for both central and commercial bank to make clear-cut distinctions at all times and in all cases between essential and non-essential industries, productive and unproductive activities, investment and speculation, or between legitimate and excessive speculation or consumption; the further difficulty of controlling the ultimate use of credit by second, third or fourth parties; the dangers involved in the division of responsibility between the central bank and commercial bank for the soundness of the lending operations of the latter; and the possibility of forfeiting the whole-hearted and active co-operations of the commercial banks as a result of undue control and intervention."

(E) Moral Suasion

Moral suasion in the method of persuasion, of request, of informal suggestion, and of advice to the commercial bank usually adopted by the central bank. The executive head of the central bank calls a meeting of the heads of the commercial banks wherein he explains them the need for the adoption of a particular monetary policy in the context of the current economic situation, and then appeals to them to follow it. This "jawbone control" or "slaps on the wrist" method has been found to be highly effective as a selective method of credit control in India, New Zealand, Canada and Australia, though it failed in the USA.

Its Limitations. Moral suasion is a method "without any teeth" and hence its effectiveness is limited.

1. Its success depends upon the extent to which the commercial banks accept the central bank as their leader and need accommodation from it.

2. If the banks possess excessive reserves they may not follow the adivce of the central bank, as is the case with the commercial banks in the USA.

3. Further, moral suasion may not be successful during booms and depressions when the economy is passing through waves of optimism and pessimism respectively. The bank may not heed to the advice of the central bank in such a situation.

4. In fact, moral suasion is not a control device at all, as it involves cooperation by the commercial banks rather than their coercion.

It may, however, be a success where the central bank commands prestige on the strength of the wide statutory powers vested in it by the government of the country.

(F) Publicity

The central bank also uses publicity as an instrument of credit control. It publishes weekly or monthly statements of the assets and liabilities of the commercial bank for the information of the public. It also publishes statistical data relating to money supply, prices, production and employment, and of capital and money market, etc. This is another way of exerting moral pressure on the commercial bank. The aim is to make the public aware of the policies being adopted by the commercial bank vis-a-vis the central bank in the light of the prevailing economic conditions in the country.

It cannot be said with definiteness about the success of this method. It presupposes the existence of an educated and knowledgeable public about the monetary phenomena. But even in advanced countries, the percentage of such persons is negligible. It is, therefore, highly doubtful if they can exert any moral pressure on the banks to strictly follow the policies of the central bank. Hence, publicity as an instrument of selective credit control is only of academic interest.

Limitations of Selective Credit Controls. Though regarded superior to quantitative credit controls, yet selective credit controls are not free from certain limitations.

1. *Limited Coverage.* Like general credit controls, selective credit controls have a limited coverage. They are only applicable to the commercial banks but not to non-banking financial institutions. But in the case of the regulation of consumer credit which is applicable both to banking and non-banking institutions, it becomes cumbersome to administer this technique.

2. *No Specificity.* Selective credit controls fail to fulfil the specificity function. There is no guarantee that the bank loans would be used for the specific purpose for which they are sanctioned.

3. *Difficult to distinguish between Essential and Non-essential Factors.* It may be difficult for the central bank to distinguish precisely between essential and non-essential sectors and between speculative and productive investment for the purpose of enforcing selective credit controls. The same reasoning applies to the commercial banks for the purpose of advancing loans unless they are specifically laid down by the central bank.

4. *Require Large Staff.* The commercial banks, for the purpose of earning large profits, may advance loans for purposes other than laid down by the central bank. This is particularly so if the central bank does not have a large staff to check minutely the accounts of the commercial banks. As a matter of fact, no central bank can afford to check their accounts. Hence selective credit controls are liable to be ineffective in the case of unscrupulous banks.

5. *Discriminatory.* Selective controls unnecessarily restrict the freedom of borrowers and lenders. They also discriminate between different types of borrowers and banks. Often small borrowers and small banks are hit harder by selective control than big borrowers and large banks.

6. *Malallocation of Resources.* Selective credit controls also lead to malallocation of resources when they are applied to selected sectors, areas and industries while leaving others to operate freely. They place undue restrictions on the freedom of the former and affect their production.

7. *Not Successful in Unit Banking.* Unit banks being independent one-office banks in the USA operate on

a small scale in small towns and meet the financial needs of the local people. Such banks are not affected by the selective credit controls of the FRS (central bank of the USA) because they are able to finance their activities by borrowing from big banks. So this policy is not effective in unit banking.

Conclusion. From the above discussion, it should not be concluded that selective credit controls are used to the total exclusion of general credit controls. Their demerits primarily arise from this thinking. In fact, they are an adjunct to general quantitative controls. They are meant to supplement the latter and are regarded only as a "second-line instrument". "The vital point is not the question of general vs. selective credit control the assessment of the pros and cons as between the two mehtods, but that of integrating them. Indeed the coordination of selective and general controls appears to have been more effective than the use of any one of them singly and by itself."

6. ROLE OF CENTRAL BANK IN A DEVELOPING ECONOMY

The central bank in a developing economy performs both traditional and non-traditional functions. The principal traditional functions performed by it are the monopoly of note issue, banker to the government, bankers' bank, lender of the last resort, controller of credit and maintaining stable exchange rate.[6] But all these functions are related to the foremost function of helping in the economic development of the country.

ROLE OF CENTRAL BANK IN ECONOMIC DEVELOPMENT

The central bank in a developing country aims at the promotion and maintenance of a rising level of production, employment and real income in the country. The central banks in the majority of underdeveloped countries have been given wide powers to promote the growth of such economies. They, therefore, perform the following functions towards this end.

Creation and Expansion of Financial Institutions. One of the aims of a central bank in an underdeveloped country is to improve its currency and credit system. More banks and financial institutions are requried to be set up to provide larger credit facilities and to divert voluntary savings into productive channels. Financial institutions are localised in big cities in underdeveloped countries and provide credit facilities to estates, plantations, big industrial and commercial houses. In order to remedy this, the central bank should extend branch banking to rural areas to make credit available to peasants, small businessmen and traders. In underdeveloped countries, the commercial banks provide only short-term loans. Credit factilites in rural areas are mostly non-existent. The only source is the village moneylender who charges exorbitant interest rates. The hold of the village moneylender in rural areas can be slackened if new institutional arrangementss are made by the central bank in providing short-term, medium term and long-term credit at lower interest rates to the cultivators. A network of co-operative credit societies with apex banks financed by the central bank can help solve the problem. Similarly, it can help the establishment of lead banks and through them regional rural banks for providing credit facilities to marginal farmers, landless agricultural workers and other weaker sections. With the vast resources at its command, the central bank can also help in establishing industrial banks and financial corporations in order to finance large and small industries.

Proper Adjustment between Demand for and Supply of Money. The central bank plays an important role in bringing about a proper adjustment between demand for and supply of money. An imbalance between the two is reflected in the price level. A shortage of money supply will inhibit growth while an excess of it will lead to inflation. As the economy develops, the demand for money is likely to go up due to gradual monetization of the non-monetized sector and the increase in agricultural and industrial production and prices. The demand for money for transactions and speculative motives will also rise. So the increase in money supply will have to be more than proportionate to the increase in the demand for money in order to avoid inflation. There is, however, the likelihood of increased money supply being used for speculative purposes, thereby inhibiting growth and causing inflation. The central bank controls the uses of money and credit by an appropriate

6. These functions of a central bank in an LDC may be explained briefly.

monetary policy. Thus in an underdeveloped economy, the central bank should control the supply of money in such a way that the price level is prevented from rising without affecting investment and production adversely.

A Suitable Interest Rate Policy. In an underdeveloped country the interest rate structure stands at a very high level. There are also vast disparities between long-term and short-term interest rates and between interest rates in different sectors of the economy. The existence of high interest rates acts as an obstacle to the growth of both private and public investment, in an underdeveloped economy. A low interest rate is, therefore, essential for encouraging private investment in agriculture and industry. Since in an underdeveloped country businessmen have little savings out of undistributed profits, they have to borrow from the banks or from the capital market for purposes of investment and they would borrow only if the interest rate is low. A low interest rate policy is also essential for encouraging public investment. A low interest rate policy is a cheap money policy. It makes public borrowing cheap, keeps the cost of servicing public debt low, and thus helps in financing economic development.

In order to discourage the flow of resources into speculative borrowing and investment, the central bank should follow a policy of discriminatory interest rates, charging *high* rates for non-essential and unproductive loans and *low* rates for productive loans. But this does not imply that savings are interest-elastic in an underdeveloped economy. Since the level of income is low in such economies, a high rate of interest is not likely to raise the propensity to save. In the context of economic growth, as the economy develops, a progressive rise in the price level is inevitable. The value of money falls and the propensity to save declines further. Money conditions become tight and there is a tendency for the rate of interest to rise automatically. This would result in inflation. In such a situation any effort to control inflation by raising the rate of interest would be disastrous. A *stable price* level is, therefore, essential for the success of a low interest rate policy which can be maintained by following a judicious monetary policy by the central benk.

Debt Management. Debt management is one of the important functions of the central bank in an underdeveloped country. It should aim at proper timing and issuing of governnment bonds, stabilizing their prices and minimizing the cost of servicing public debt. It is the central bank which undertakes the selling and buying of government bonds and making timely changes in the structure and composition of public debt. In order to strengthen and stabilize the market for government bonds, the policy of low interest rates is essential. For, a low rate of interest raises the price of government bonds, thereby making them more attractive to the public and giving an impetus to the public borrowing programmes of the government. The maintenance of structure of low interest rates is also called for minimizing the cost of servicing the national debt. Further, it encourages funding of debt by private firms. However, the success of debt management would depend upon the existence of well-developed money and capital markets in which wide range of securities exist both for short and long periods. It is the central bank which can help in the development of these markets.

Credit Control. Central Bank should also aim at controlling credit in order to influence the patterns of investment and production in a developing economy. Its main objective is to control inflationary pressures arising in the process of development. This requires the use of both quantitative and qualitative methods of credit control.

Open market operations are not successful in controlling inflation in underdeveloped countries because the bill market is small and undeveloped. Commercial banks keep an elastic cash-deposit ratio because the central bank's control over them is not complete. They are also reluctant to invest in government securities due to their relatively low interest rates. Moreover, instead of investing in government securities, they prefer to keep their reserves in liquid form such as gold, foreign exchange and cash. Commercial banks are also not in the habit of rediscounting or borrowing from the central bank.

The *bank rate policy* is also not so effective in controlling credit in LDCs due to: (a) the lack of bills of discount; (b) the narrow size of the bill market; (c) a large non-monetised sector where barter transactions take place; (d) the existence of a large unorganised money market; (e) the existence of indigenous banks which do not discount bills with the central baks; and (f) the habit of commercial banks to keep large cash reserves.

The use of *variable reserve ratio* as method of credit control is more effective than open market operations and bank rate policy in LDCs. Since the market for securities is very small, open market operations are not successful. But a rise or fall in the reserve ratio by the central bank reduces or increases the cash available with the commercial banks without affecting adversely the prices of securities. Again, the commercial banks keep large cash reserves which cannot be reduced by a raise in the bank rate or sale of securities by the central bank. But raising the cash-reserve ratio reduces liquidity with the banks. However, the use of variable reserve ratio has certain *limitations* in LDCs. First, the non-banking financial intermediaries do not keep deposits with the central bank so they are not affected by it. Second, banks which do not maintain excess liquidity are not affected than those who maintain it.

The qualitative credit control measures are, however, more effective than the quantitative measures in influencing the allocation of credit, and thereby the pattern of investment. In underdeveloped countries, there is a strong tendency to invest in gold, jewellery, inventories, real estate, etc., instead of in alternative productive channels available in agriculture, mining, plantations and industry. The selective credit controls are more appropriate for controlling and limiting credit facilitates for such unproductive purposes. They are beneficial in controlling speculative activities in foodgrains and raw materials. They prove more useful in controlling 'sectional inflations' in the economy. They curtail the demand for imports by making it obligatory on importers to deposit in advance an amount equal to the value of foreign currency. This has also the effect of reducing the reserves of the banks in so far as their deposits are transferred to the central banks in the process. The selective credit control measures may take the form of changing the margin requirements against certain types of collateral, the regulation of consumer credit and the rationing of credit.

Solving the Balance of Payments Problem. The central bank should also aim at preventing and solving the balance of payments problem in a developing economy. Such economies face serious balance of payments difficulties to fulfil the targets of development plans. An imbalance is created between imports and exports which continues to widen with development. The central bank manages and controls the foreign exchange of the country and also acts as the technical adviser to the government on foreign exchange policy. It is the function of the central bak to avoid fluctuations in the foreign exchange rates and to maintain stability. It does so through exchange controls and variations in the bank rate. For instance, if the value of the national currency continues to fall, it may raise tha bank rate and thus encourage the inflow of foreign currencies.

Conclusion. Thus the central bank plays an important role in achieving economic growth of a developing country through the various measures discussed above. It should promote economic growth with stability, help in attaining full employment of resources, in overcoming balance of payments disequilibrium, and in stabilising exchange rates.

EXERCISES

1. Discuss the essential functions of a central bank.
2. Distinguish between quantitative and qualitative methods of credit control. Which are more effective in an inflationary situation ?
3. Account for the recent shift from conventional quantitative control to qualitative control.
4. Between Bank Rate and Open Market Operations which is more effective as an instrument of credit control ? Give reasons.
5. Explain the significance of selective credit controls. How do they operate and with what success ?
6. Discuss the role of a central bank in promoting economic growth in a developing country.

CHAPTER 11

Index Numbers

1. MEANING OF INDEX NUMBERS

An index number is a statistical derive to measure *changes* in the value of money. It is a number which represents the average price of a group of commodities at a particular time in relation to the average price of the *same* group of commodities at another time. Professor Chandler defines it thus: "An index number of prices is a figure showing the height of average prices at one time relative to their height at some other time that is taken at the base period."[1] To understand the meaning of the term index number, three points are to be noted. *First,* an average figure relates to a single group of commodities. But the various items in the group are expressed in different units. For example, a consumer price index contains such diverse items as food, clothing, fuel and lighting, house rent, and miscellaneous things. Food consists of wheat, ghee, etc. expressed in kgs. cloth is expressed in metres, and lighting in kws. An index number expresses the average of all such diverse items in different units. *Second,* an index number measures the net increase or decrease of the average prices for the group under study. For instance, if the consumer price index has increased from 150 in 1982 as compared to 100 in 1980, it shows a net increase of 50 per cent in the prices of commodities included in the index. *Third,* an index number measures the extent of changes in the value of money (or price level) over a period of time, given a base period. If the base period is the year 1970, we can measure change in the average price level for the preceding and succeeding years.

2. METHODS OF CONSTRUCTION OF INDEX NUMBER

In constructing an index number, the following steps should be noted :

1. *Purpose of the Index Number.* Before constructing an index number, it should be decided the purpose for which it is needed. An index number constructed for one category or purpose cannot be used for others. A cost of living index of working classes cannot be used for farmers because the items entering into their consumption will be different.

2. *Selection of Commodities.* Commodities to be selected depend upon the purpose or objective of the index number to be constructed. But the number of commodities should neither be too large nor too small. Moreover, commodities to be selected must be broadly representative of the group of commodities. They should also be comparable in the sense that standard or graded items should be taken.

3. *Selection of Prices.* The next step is to select the prices of these commodities. For this purpose, care should be taken to select prices from representative persons, places or journals or other sources. But they must be reliable. Prices may be quoted in money terms i.e. Rs. 100 per quantal or in quantity terms. i.e. 2 kg. per

---

1. L.V. Chandler, *op. cit.,* p.10.

rupee. Care should be taken not to mix these prices. Then the problem is to select wholesale or retail prices. This depends on the type of index number. For a consumer price index, wholesale prices are required, while for a cost of living index, retail prices are needed. But different prices should not be mixed up.

4. *Selection of an Average.* Since index numbers are averages, the problem is how to select an appropriate average. The two important averages are the arithmetic mean and geometric mean. The arithmetic mean is the simpler of the two. But geometric mean is more accurate. However, the average prices should be reduced to price relatives (percentages) either on the basis of the fixed base method or the chain base method.

5. *Selection of Weights.* While constructing an index number due weightage or importance should be given to the various commodities. Commodities which are more important in the consumption of consumers should be given higher weightage than other commodities. The weights are determined with reference to the relative amounts of income spent on commodities by consumers. Weights may be given in terms of value or quantity.

6. *Selection of the Base Period.* The selection of the base period is the most important step in the construction of an index number. It is a period against which comparisons are made. The base period should be normal and free from any unusual events such as war, famine, earthquake, drought, boom, etc. It should not be either very recent or remote.

7. *Selection of Formula.* A number of formulas have been devised to construct an index number. But the selection of an appropriate formula depends upon the availability of data and purpose of the index number. No single formula may be used for all types of index numbers.

We give below an example each of the simple price index and the weighted price index.

SIMPLE PRICE INDEX

To construct a simple price index, compute the price relatives and average them. Add the price relatives and divide them by the number of items. Table 1 illustrates the construction of a simple index of wholesale prices.

TABLE 1

Commodity	*Prices in 1970(P_0)*	*Base 1970=100*	*Prices in 1980(P_1) = $P_1/P_0 \times 100$*	*Price Relatives (R)*
A	Rs. 20 per kg	100	Rs. 25	125
B	5 per kg	100	10	200
C	15 per metre	100	30	200
D	25 per kg	100	30	120
E	200 per quantal	100	450	225
N = 5		500		$\Sigma R = 870$

$$\text{Price index in 1980} = \frac{\text{Prices in 1980}}{\text{Prices in 1970}} \times 100 \text{ or } \frac{\Sigma P_1}{\Sigma P_0} \times 100 = \frac{870}{500} \times 100 = 174$$

$$\text{Using arithmetic mean, price index in 1980} = \frac{\Sigma R}{N} = \frac{870}{5} = 174$$

The preceding table shows that 1970 is the base period and 1980 is the year for which the price index has been constructed on the basis of price relatives. The index of wholesale prices in 1980 comes to 174. This means that the price level rose by 74 per cent in 1980 over 1970.

WEIGHTED PRICE INDEX

Taking the example of Table 1 already given, we assign high weights to commodities of greater importance to consumers and low weights to commodities of lesser importance.

TABLE 2

Commodity	*Weight* (W)	*Prices in 1970* Rs	*Base 1970 = 100*	*Prices in 1980* Rs	*Price Relatives* (R)	W×R
A	6	20	100	25	125	750
B	4	5	100	10	200	800
C	2	15	100	30	200	400
D	4	25	100	30	120	480
E	10	200	100	450	225	2250
	Σ24				$\Sigma WR = 4680$	

Using arithmetic mean, the weighted price index in 1980 = $\frac{4680}{24}$ = 195.

The weighted price index is more accurate than the simple price index. In the example given above, the weighted price index shows an increase of 91 per cent in the price level in 1980 over 1970 as against the increase of 74 per cent according to the simple price index.

3. DIFFICULTIES IN THE CONSTRUCTION OF INDEX NUMBERS

There are many difficulties in the construction of index numbers. They are discussed as under :

1. *Difficulties in the Selection of the Base Period.* The first difficulty relates to the selection of the base year. The base year should be normal. But it is difficult to determine a truly normal year. Moreover, what may be the normal year today may become an abnormal year after some period. Therefore, it is not advisable to have the same year as the base period for a number of years. Rather, it should be changed after ten years or so. But there is no fixed rule for this.

2. *Difficulties in the Selection of Commodities.* The selection of representative commodities for the index number is another difficulty. The choice of representative commodities is not an easy matter. They have to be selected from a wide range of commodities which the majority of people consume. Again, what were representative commodities some ten years ago may not be representative today. The consumption pattern of consumers might change and thereby make the index number useless. So the choice of representative commodities presents real difficulties.

3. *Difficulties in the Collection of Prices.* Another difficulty is that of collecting adequate and accurate prices. It is often not possible to get them from the same source or place. Further, the problem of choice between wholesale and retail prices arises. There are much variations in the retail prices. Therefore, index numbers are based on wholesale prices.

4. *Arbitrary Assigning of Weights.* In calculating weighted price index, a number of difficulties arise. The problem is to give different weights to commodities. The selection of higher weight for one commodity and a lower weight for another is simply arbitrary. There is no set rule and it entirely depends on the investigator. Moreover, the same commodity may have different importance for different consumers. The importance of commodities also changes with the change in the tastes and incomes of consumers and also with the passage of time. Therefore, weights are to be revised from time to time and not fixed arbitrarily.

5. *Difficulty of Selecting the Method of Averaging.* Another difficulty is to select an appropriate method of calculating averages. There are a number of methods which can be used for this purpose. But all methods give different results from one another. It is, therefore, difficult to decide which method to choose.

6. *Difficulties Arising from Changes Overtime.* In the present times, changes in the nature of commodities are taking place continuously overtime due to technological changes. As a result, new commodities are introduced and people start consuming them in place of the old ones. Moreover, prices of commodities might

also change with technical changes. They may fall. But new commodities are not entered into the list of commodities in preparing the index numbers. This makes the index numbers based on old commodities unreal.

7. *Not All Purpose.* An index number constructed for a particular purpose cannot be used for some other purpose. For instance, a cost of living index number for industrial workers cannot be used to measure the cost of living of agricultural workers. Thus there are no all purpose index numbers.

8. *International Comparisons not Possible.* International price comparisons are not possible with index numbers. The commodities consumed and included in the construction of an index number differ from country to country. For instance, meat, eggs, cars, and electrical appliance are included in the price index of advanced countries whereas they are not included in that of backward countries. Similarly, weights assigned to commodities are also different. Thus international comparisons of index numbers are not possible.

9. *Comparisons of Different Places not Possible.* Even if different places within a country are taken, it is not possible to apply the same index number to them. This is because of differences in the consumption habits of people. People living in the northern region consume different commodities than those consumed by the people in the south of India. It is, therefore, not right to apply the same index number to both.

10. *Not Applicable to an Individual.* An index number is not applicable to an individual belonging to a group for which it is constructed. If an index number shows a rise in the price level, an individual may not be affected by it. This is because an index number reflects averages.

CONCLUSION

It may be concluded from the difficulties and limitations of index numbers that index numbers are at best approximations to measure changes in the value of money. However, these difficulties become less significant if index numbers are constructed for short intervals. This is because habits, tastes, techniques of production and the qualities of commodities entering into a price index number do not change during the short period.

4. USES OF INDEX NUMBERS

Index numbers possess much practical importance in measuring changes in the cost of living, production trends, trade, income variations, etc. Some of the uses of index numbers are discussed below :

1. *In Measuring Changes in the Value of Money.* Index number are used to measure changes in the value of money. A study of the rise or fall in the value of money is essential for determining the direction of production and employment to facilitate future payments and to know changes in the real income of different groups of people at different places and times. As pointed out by Crowther, "By using the technical device of an index number, it is thus possible to measure changes in different aspects of the value of money, each particular aspect being relevant to a different purpose."[2]

2. *In Cost of Living.* Cost of living index numbers in the case of different groups of workers throw light on the rise or fall in the real income of workers. It is on the basis of the study of the cost of living index that money wages are determined and dearness and other allowances are granted to workers. The cost of living index is also the basis of wage negotiations and wage contracts.

3. *In Analysing Markets for Goods and Services.* Consumer price index numbers are used in analysing markets for particular kinds of goods and services. The weights assigned to different commodities like food, clothing, fuel, and lighting, house rent, etc., govern the market for such goods and services.

4. *In Measuring Changes in Industrial Production.* Index numbers of industrial production measure increase or decrease in industrial production in a given year as compared to the base year. We can know from such as index number the actual condition of different industries, whether production is increasing or decreasing in them, for an industrial index number measures changes in the quantity of production.

5. *In Internal Trade.* The study of indices of the wholesale prices of consumer and industrial goods and of industrial production help commerce and industry in expanding or decreasing internal trade.

---

2. Crowther, *op. cit.*, p. 89.

6. *In External Trade.* The foreign trade position of a country can be assessed on the basis of its export and import indices. These indices reveal whether the external trade of the country is increasing or decreasing.

7. *In Economic Policies.* Index numbers are helpful to the state in formulating and adopting appropriate economic policies. Index numbers measure changes in such magnitudes as prices, incomes, wages, production, employment, products, exports, imports, etc. By comparing the index numbers of these magnitudes for different periods, the government can know the present trend of economic activity and accordingly adopt price policy, foreign trade policy and general economic policies.

8. *In Determining the Foreign Exchange Rate.* Index numbers of wholesale price of two countries are used to determine their rate of foreign exchange. They are the basis of the purchasing power parity theory which determines the exchange rate between two countries on inconvertible paper standard.

CONCLUSION

Thus index numbers are used to measures all types of quantitative changes in the agricultural, industrial, and commercial fields, as also in such economic magnitudes as income, employment, exports, imports, prices, etc. A close study of such changes helps the government to adopt appropriate monetary and fiscal measures in order to achieve growth with stability.

EXERCISES

1. How are changes in the value of money measured? What are the limitations of this measurement?
2. What are index numbers? How are they constructed? Briefly discuss the difficulties faced in constructing them.
3. How would you construct an index number of wholesale prices? What are the uses of the index numbers?

CHAPTER 12

The Quantity Theory of Money and Its Variants

1. MEANING OF VALUE OF MONEY

By value of money is meant the purchasing power of money over goods and services in a country. What a rupee can buy in India represents the value of money of the rupee. Thus the phrase, "value of money" is a relative concept which expresses the relationship between a unit of money and the goods and services which can be purchased with it. This shows that the value of money is related to the price level because goods and services are purchased with a money unit at given prices. But the relation between the value of money and price level is an inverse one. If V presents the value of money and P the price level, then, $V = 1/P$. When the price level rises, the value of money falls, and vice versa. Thus in order to measure the value of money, we have to find out the general price level.

The value of money is of two types: The internal value of money and the external value of money. The internal value of money refers to the purchasing power of money over domestic goods and services. The external value of money refers to the purchasing power of money over foreign goods and services.

2. FISHER'S QUANTITY THEORY OF MONEY: THE CASH TRANSACTIONS APPROACH

The quantity theory of money states that the quantity of money is the main determinant of the price level or the value of money. Any change in the quantity of money produces an exactly proportionate change in the price level. In the words of Irving Fisher, "Other things remaining unchanged, as the quantity of money in circulation increases, the price level also increases in direct proportion and the value of money decreases and vice versa."[1] If the quantity of money is doubled, the price level will also double and the value of money will be one half. On the other hand, if the quantity of money is reduced by one half, the price level will also be reduced by one half and the value of money will be twice.

Fisher has explained his theory in terms of his equation of exchange:

$PT = MV + M'\,V'$

1. Iwing Fisher, *The Purchasing PowerofMoney,* (Revised Ed.), 1926.

where P = price level, or $1/P$ = the value of money;
M = the total quantity of legal tender money;
V = the velocity of circulation of M;
M' = the total quantity of credit money;
V' = the velocity of circulation of M';
T = the total amount of goods and services exchanged for money or transactions performed by money.

This equation equates the demand for money (*PT*) to supply of money (*MV=M'V'*). The total volume of transactions multiplied by the price level (*PT*) represent the demand for money. According to Fisher, *PT* is *SPQ*. In other words, price level (*P*) multiplied by quantity bought (*Q*) by the community (S) gives the total demand for money. This equals the total supply of money in the community consisting of the quantity of actual money *M* and its velocity of circulation *V plus* the total quantity of credit money *M'* and its velocity of circulation *V'*. Thus the total value of purchases (*PT*) in a year is measured by *MV+M'V'*. Thus the equation of exchange is *PT=MV+M'V'*. In order to find out the effect of the quantity of money on the price level or the value of money, we write the equation as

$$P = \frac{MV+M'V'}{T}$$

Fisher points out the price level (*P*) (*M+M'*) provided the volume of tra remain unchanged. The truth of this proposition is evident from the fact that if *M* and *M'* are doubled, while *V*, *V'* and *T* remain constant, *P* is also doubled, but the value of money (1/*P*) is reduced to half.

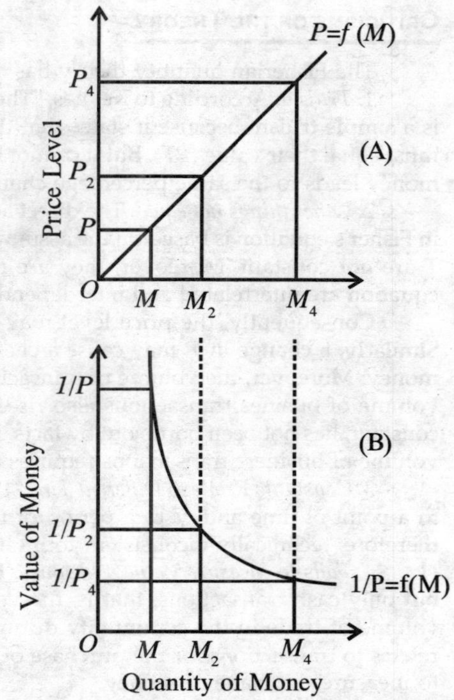

Fig. 1.

Fisher's quantity theory of money is explained with the help of Figure 1. (A) and (B). Panel A of the figure shows the effect of changes in the quantity of money on the price level. To begin with, when the quantity of money is *M*, the price level is *P*.

When the quantity of money is doubled to M_2, the price level is also doubled to P_2. Further, when the quantity of money is increased four-fold to M_4, the price level also increases by four times to P_4. This realtionship is expressed by the curve *P=f (M)* from the origin at 45^0.

In panel B of the figure, the inverse relation between the quantity of money and the value of money is depicted where the value of money is taken on the vertical axis. When the quantity of money is M_1, the value of money is 1/*P*. But with the doubling of the quantity of money to M_2, the value of money becomes one-half of what it was before, $1/P_2$. And with the quantity of money increasing by four-fold to M_4, the value of money is reduced by $1/P_4$. This inverse relationship between the quantity of money and the value of money is shown by downward sloping curve 1/*P=f* (*M*).

ASSUMPTIONS OF THE THEORY

Fisher's theory is based on the following assumptions:
1. *P* is passive factor in the equation of exchange which is affected by the other factors.
2. The proportion of *M'* to *M* remains constant.
3. *V* and *V'* are assumed to be constant and are independent of changes in *M* and *M'*.
4. *T* also remains constant and is independent of other factors such as *M*, *M'*, *V* and *V'*.
5. It is assumed that the demand for money is proportional to the value of transactions.
6. The supply of money is assumed as an exogenously determined constant.
7. The theory is applicable in the long run.
8. It is based on the assumption of the existence of full employment in the economy.

Criticisms of the Theory

The Fisherian quantity theory has been subjected to severe criticisms by economists.

1. *Truism.* According to Keynes, "The quantity theory of money is a truism." Fisher's equation of exchange is a simple truism because it states that the total quantity of money ($MV+M'V'$) paid for goods and services must equal their value (PT). But it cannot be accepted today that a certain percentage change in the quantity of money leads to the same percentage change in the price level.

2. *Other things not equal.* The direct and proportionate relation between quantity of money and price level in Fisher's equation is based on the assumption that "other things remain unchanged". But in real life, V, V' and T are not constant. Moreover, they are not independent of M, M' and P. Rather, all elements in Fisher's equation are interrelated and interdependent. For instance, a change in M may cause a change in V.

Consequently, the price level may change more in proportion to a change in the quantity of money. Similarly, a change in P may cause a change in M. Rise in the price level may necessitate the issue of more money. Moreover, the volume of transactions T is also affected by changes in P. When prices rise or fall, the volume of busines transactions also rises or falls. Further, the assumptions that the proportion M' to M is constant, has not been borne out by facts. Not only this, M and M' are not independent of T. An increase in the volume of business transactions requires an increase in the supply of money (M and M').

3. *Constants Relate to Different Time.* Prof. Halm criticises Fisher for multiplying M and V because M relates to a point ot time and V to a period of time . The former is a static concept and the latter a dynamic. It is therefore, technically inconsistent to multiply two non-comparable factors.[2]

4. *Fails to Measure Value of Money.* Fisher's equation does not measure the purchasing power of money but only cash transactions, that is, the volume of business transactions of all kinds or what Fisher calls the volume of trade in the community during a year. But the purchasing power of money (or value of money) relates to transactions for the purchase of goods and services for consumption. Thus the quantity theory fails to measure the vlaue of money.

5. *Weak Theory.* According to Crowther,[3] the quantity theory is weak in many respects. First, it cannot explain 'why' there are fluctutations in the price level in the short run. Second, it gives undue importance to the price level as if changes in prices were the most critical and important phenomenon of the economic system. Third, it places a misleading emphasis on the quantity of money as the principal cause of changes in the price level during the trade cycle. Prices may not rise despite increase in the quantity of money during depression; and they may not decline with reduction in the quantity of money during boom. Further, low prices during depression are not caused by shortage of quantity of money, and high prices during prosperity are not caused by abundance of quantity of money. Thus, "the quantity theory is at best an imperfect guide to the causes of the trade cycle *in the short period*," according to Crowther.

6. *Neglects Interest Rate.* One of the main weaknesses of Fisher's quantity theory of money is that it neglects the role of the rate of interest as one of the causative factors between money and prices. Fisher's equation of exchange is related to an equilibrium situation in which rate of interest is independent of the quantity of money.

7. *Unrealistic Assumptions.* Keynes in his *General Theory* severely criticised the Fisherian quantity theory of money for its unrealistic assumptions. *Firts*, the quantity theory of money for its unrealistic assumptions. First, the quantity theory of money is unrealistic because it analyses the relation between M and P in the long run. Thus it neglects the short run factors which influence this relationship. Second, Fisher's equation holds good under the assumption of full employment. But Keynes regards full employment as a special situation. The general situation is one of the under-employment equilibrium. Third, Keynes does not believe that the relationship between the quantity of money and the price level is direct and proportional. Rather, it is an indirect one via the rate of interest and the level of output. According to Keynes, "So long as there is unemployment, *output* and employment will change in the same proportion as the quantity of money, and when there is full employment, prices will change in the same proportion as the quantity of money." Thus

---

2. G.N. Halm, *Monetary Theory,* 2/e,p. 22.
3. Crowther, *An Outline of Money, Ch. V,* 1958.

Keynes integrated the theory of output with value theory and monetary theory and criticised Fisher for dividing economics "into two compartments with no doors and windows between *the theory of value and theory of money and prices*."

8. *V not Constant.* Further, Keynes pointed out that when there is underemployment equilibrium, the velocity of circulation of moeny V is highly unstable and would change with changes in the stock of money or money income. Thus it was unrealistic for Fisher to assume V to be constant and independent of M.

9. *Neglects Store of Value Function.* Another weakness of the quantity theory of money is that it concentrates on the supply of money and assumes the demand for money to be constant. In order words, it neglects the store-of-value function of moeny and considers only the medium-of-exchange function of money. Thus the theory is one-sided.

10. *Neglects Real Balance Effect.* Don Patinkin[4] has critcised Fisher for failure to make use of the real balance effect, that is, the real value of cash balances. A fall in the price level raises the real value of cash balances which leads to increased spending and hence to rise in income, output and employment in the economy. According to Patinkin, Fisher gives undue importance to the quantity of money and neglects the role of real money balances.

11. *Static.* Fisher's theory is static in nature because of its such unrealistic assumptions as long run, full employment, etc. It is, therefore, not applicable to a modern dynamic economy.

3. THE CAMBRIDGE EQUATIONS : THE CASH BALANCES APPROACH

As an alternative to Fisher's quantity theory of money, Cambridge economists Marshall, Pigou, Robertson and Keynes formulated the cash balances approach. Like value theory, they regarded the determination of value of money in terms of supply and demand. Robertson wrote in this connection: "Money is only one of the many economic things. Its value, therefore, is primarily determined by exactly nomic things. Its value, therefore, is primarily determined by exactly the same two factors as determine the value of any other thing, namely, the conditions of demand for it, and the quantity of it available."[5]

The supply of money is exogenously determined at a point of time by the banking system. Therefore, the concept of velocity of circulation is altogether discarded in the cash balances approach because it 'obscures the motives and decisions of people behind it'. On the other hand, the concept of demand for money plays the major role in determining the value of money. The demand for money is the demand to hold cash balance for transactions and precautionary motives. Marshall wrote with regard to the demand for money. "To give definiteness to this notion, let us suppose that the inhabitants of a country...find it just worthwhile to keep by them on the average ready purchansing power to the extent of a tenth part of their annual income, together with a fiftieth part of their property, then the aggregate value of the currency of the country will tend to be equal to the sum of these amounts."[6]

Thus the cash balances approach considers the demand for money not as a medium of exchange but as a store of value. Robertson expressed this distinction as money "on the wings" and money "sitting". It is "money sitting" that reflects the demand for money in the Cambridge equations. The Cambridge equations show that given the supply of money at a point of time, the value of money is determined by the demand for cash balances. When the demand for money increases, people will reduce their expenditures on goods and services in order to have larger cash holdings. Reduced demand for goods and services will bring down the price level and raise the value of money. On the contrary, fall in the demand for money will raise the price level and lower the value of money.

The Cambridge cash balances equations of Marshall, Pigou, Robertson and Keynes are discussed as under:

Marshall's Equation. Marshall did not put his theory in equation form and it was for his followers to

---

4. Don Patinkin, *Money Interest andPrices,* 2/e, 1965.
5. Denis H. Robertson, *Money,* 1959.
6. AlfredMarshall, *Money Credit and Commerce,* 1923.

explain it algebraically. Friedman has explained Marshall's views thus: "As a first approximation, we may suppose that the amount one wants to hold bears some relation to one's income, since that determines the volume of purchases and sales in which one is engaged. We then add up the cash balances held by all holders of money in the community and express the total as a fraction of their total income."[7] Thus we can write:

$M = kPY$

where M stands for the exogenously determined supply of money, k is the fraction of the real money income (PY) which people wish to hold in cash and demand deposits, P is the price level, and Y is the aggregeate real income of the community. Thus the price level $P = \frac{M}{kY}$ or the value of money (the reciprocal of price level) is $\frac{1}{P} = \frac{kY}{M}$

Pigou's Equation. Pigou was the first Cambridge economist to express the cash balances approach in the form of an equation:

$$P = \frac{kR}{M}$$

where P is the purchasing power of money or the value of money (the reciprocal of the price level), k is the proportion of total real resources or income (R) which people wish to hold in the form of titles to legal tender, R is the total resources (expressed in terms of wheat), or real income, and M refers to the number of actual units of legal tender money.[9]

The demand for money, according to Pigou, consists not only of legal money or cash but also bank notes and bank balances. In order to include bank notes and bank balances in the demand for money, Pigou modifies his equation as

$$P = \frac{kR}{M}\{c + R(1-c)\}$$

where c is the proportion of total real income actually held by people in legal tender including token coins, (1-c) is the proportion kept in bank notes and bank balances, and h is the proportion of actual legal tender that bankers keep against the notes and balances held by their customers.[10]

Pigou points out that when k and R in the equation $P=kR/M$ and k, R, c and h are taken as constants then the two equations give the demand curve for legal tender as a rectangular hyperbola. This implies that the demand curve for money has a uniform unitary elasticity. This is shown in Figure 2 where DD_1 is the demand curve for money and Q_1M_1, Q_2, M_2, and Q_3M_3 are the supply curves of money drawn on the assumption that the supply of money is fixed at a point of time. The value of money or Pirou's purchasing power of money P is taken on the vertical axis. The figure shows that when the supply of money increases from OM_1 to OM_2, the value of money is reduced from OP_1 to OP_2. The fall in the value of money by P_1 P_2 exactly equals the increase in the supply of money by M_1M_2. If the supply of money increases three times from OM_1 to OM_3, the value of money is reduced by exactly one-third from OP_1 to OP_3. Thus the demand curve for money DD_1 is a rectangular hyperbola because it shows changes in the value of money exactly in reverse proportion to the supply of money.

Robertson's Equation. To determine the value of money or its reciprocal the price level, Robertson

---

7. Miltion Friedman, 'Money : Quantity Theory.' *in International Encyclopedia of the Social Sciences,* 1968.
8. Marshall's equation is also written as *M = kPO or M + kPT or M = kpy or M = KpY or M=kPT.* But all these equations are identical because *k = K, p = P* , and *O = T = y = Y.*
9. In the Februarv 1918 issue of the *QJE.* Pigou issued a modification with regard to *M* that it should be regarded as "the number of titles to units of legal tender."
10. A.C. Pigou 'Value of Money', *QJ.E.* Vol. XXXII, November 1917.

formulated an equation similar to that of Pigou. The only difference between the two being that instead of Pigou's total real resources R, Robertson gave the volume of total transactions T. The Robertsonian equation is $M = PkT$ or

$$P = \frac{M}{kT}$$

where P is the price level, M is the total quantity of money, k is the proportion of the total amount of goods and services (T) which people wish to hold in the form of cash balances, and T is the total volume of goods and services purchased during a year by the community.

If we take P as the value of money instead of the price level as in Pigou's equation, then Robertson's equation exactly resembles Pigou's $P = kT/M$.

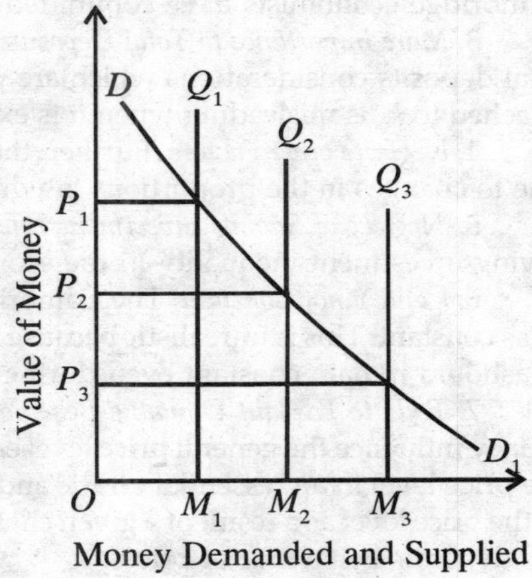

Fig. 2

Keynes's Equation. Keynes in his *A Tract on Monetary Reform* (1923) gave his Real Balances Quantity Equation as an improvement over the other Cambridge equations. According to him, people always want to have some purchasing power to finance their day to day transactions. The amount of purchasing power (or demand for money) depends partly on their tastes and habits, and partly on their wealth. Given the tastes, habits, and wealth of the people, their desire to hold money is given. This demand for money is measured by consumption units. A consumption unit is expressed as a basket of standard articles of consumption or other objects of expenditure.

If k is the number of consumption units in the form of cash, n is the total currency in circulation, and p is the price for consumption unit, then the equation is

$$n = pk$$

If k is constant, a proportionate increase in n (quantity of money) will lead to a proportionate increase in p (price level).

This equation can be expanded by taking into account bank deposits. Let k be the number of consumption units in the form of bank deposits, and r the cash reserve ratio of banks, then the expanded equation is

$$n = p\,(k + rk')$$

Again, if k, k' and r are constant, p will change in exact proportion to the change in n.

Keynes regards his equation superior to other cash balances equations. The other equations fail to point how the price level (p) can be regulated. Since the cash balances (k) held by the people are outside the control of the monetary authority, p can be regulated by controlling n and r. It is also possible to regulate bank deposits k' by appropriate changes in the bank rate. So p can be controlled by making appropriate changes in n, r and k' so as to offset changes in k.

CRITICISMS OF THE CASH BALANCE APPROACH

The cash balances approach to the quantity theory of money has been criticised on the following counts:

1. *Truisms.* Like the transactions equation, the cash balances equations are truisms. Take any Cambridge equation: Marshall's $P=M/kY$ or Pigou's $P=kR/M$ or Robertson's $P=M/kT$ or Keynes's $p=n/k$, it establishes a proportionate relation between quantity of money and price level.[11]

2. *Price Level Does not Measure the Purchasing Power.* Keynes in his *A Treatise on Money* (1930) criticised Pigou's cash balances equation and also his own real balances equation. He pointed out that measuring the price level in wheat, as Piogu did or in terms of consumption units, as Keynes himself did, was a serious defect. The price level in both equations does not measure the purchasing power of money. Measuring the price level in consumption units implies that cash deposits are used only for expenditure on current consumption. But in

11. Here all equations have been changed in terms of the price level.

fact that they are held for "a vast multiplicity of business and personal purposes." By ignoring these aspects the Cambridge economists have committed a serious mistake.

3. *More Importance to Total Deposits.* Another defect of the Cambridge equation "lies in its applying to the total deposits considerations which are primarily relevant only to the income-deposits." And the importance attached to *k* "is misleading when it is extended beyond the income deposits."

4. *Neglects other Factors.* Further, the cash balances equation does not tell about changes in the price level due to changes in the proportions in which deposits are held for income, business and savings purposes.

5. *Neglect of Saving Investment Effect.* Moreover, it fails to analyse variations in the price level due to saving-investment inequality in the economy.

6. *k and Y not Constant.* The Cambridge equation, like the transactions equation, assumes *k* and *Y* (or R or T) as constant. This is unrealistic because it is not essential that the cash balances (*k*) and the income of the people (*Y*) should remain constant even during short period.

7. *Fails to Explain Dynamic Behaviour of Prices.* The theory argues that changes in the total quantity of money influence the general price level equiproportionally. But the fact is that the quantity of money influences the price level in an "essential erratic and unpredictable way." Further, it fails to point out the extent of change in the price level as a result of a given change in the quantity of money in the short period. Thus it fails to explain the dynamic behaviour of prices.

8. *Neglects Interest Rate.* The cash balances approach is also weak in that it ignores other influences, such as the rate of interest which exerts a decisive and significant influence upon the price level. As pointed out by Keynes in his *General Theory*, the relation between quantity of money and price level is not direct but indirect via the rate of interest, investment, output, employment and income. This is what the Cambridge equation ignores and hence fails to integrate monetary theory with the theory of value and output.

9. *Demand for Money not Interest Inelastic.* The neglect of the rate of interest as a causative factor between the quantity of money and the price level led to the assumption that the demand for money is interest inelastic. It means that money performs only the function of medium of exchange and does not possess any utility of its own, such as store of value.

10. *Neglect of Goods Market.* Further, the omission of the influence of the rate of interest in the cash balance approach led to the failure of neoclassical economists to recognise the interdependence between the commodity and money markets. According to Patinkin, they laid an undue concentration on the money market a corresponding neglect of the commodity markets, and a resulting 'dehumanising' of the analysis of the effects of monetary changes."

11. *Neglects Real Balance Effect.* Patinkin has criticised the Cambridge economists for their failure to integrate the goods market and the money market. This is borne out by the dichotomy which they maintain between the two markets. The dichotomisation implies that the absolute price level in the economy is determined by the demand and supply of money, and the relative price level is determined by the demand and supply of goods. The cash balances approach keeps the two markets rigidly apart. For instance, this approach tells that an increase in the quantity of money leads to an increase in the absolute price level but exercises no influence on the market for goods. This is because of the failure of Cambridge economists to recognise "the real balance effect." The real balance effect shows that a change in the absolute price level does influence the demand and supply of goods. The weakness of cash balances approach lies in ignoring this.

12. *Elasticity of Demand for Money not Unity.* The cash balances theory establishes that the elasticity of demand for money is unity which implies that the increase in the demand for money leads to a proportionate decrease in the price level. Patinkin holds that "the Cambridge function does not imply uniform elasticity." According to him, this is because of the failure of Cambridge economists to recognise the full implications of the "real balance effect". Patinkin argues that a change in the price level will cause a real balance effect. For instance, a fall in the price level will increase the real value of cash balances held by the people. So when there is excess demand for money, the demand for goods and services is reduced. In this case, the real balance effect will not cause a proportionate but non-proportionate change in the demand for money. Thus the elasticity of demand for money will not be unity.

13. *Neglects Speculative Demand for Money.* Another serious weakness of cash balances approach is its failure to consider the speculative demand for money. The neglect of the speculative demand for cash balances

makes the demand for money exclusively dependent on money income thereby again neglecting the role of the rate of interest and the store of value function of money.

4. TRANSACTIONS APPROACH VS. CASH BALANCES APPROACH

There are certain points of similarities between Fisher's transaction approach and the Cambridge cash balances approach. These are discussed as under:

1. Similarities

The two approaches have the following similarities:

1. *Same Conclusion.* The Fisherian and Cambridge versions lead to the same conclusion that there is a direct and proportional relationship between the quantity of money and the price level and an inverse proportionate relationship between the quantity of money and the value of money.

2. *Similar Equations.* The two approaches use almost similar equations. Fisher's equation $P = \frac{MV}{T}$ is similar to Robertson's equation $P = \frac{M}{kT}$ However, the only difference is between the two symbols V and k which are reciprocal to each other. Whereas $V = \left|\frac{1}{k}\right|$ $k = \left|\frac{1}{V}\right|$ Here V refers to the rate of spending and k the amount of money which people wish to hold in the form of cash balances or do not want to spend. As these two symbols are reciprocal to each other, the differences in the two equations can be reconciled by substituting $\frac{1}{V}$ for k in Robertson's equation and $\frac{1}{k}$ for V in Fisher's equation.

3. *Money as the Same Phenomenon.* The different symbols given to the total quantity of money in the two approaches refer to the same phenomenon. As such MV+$M'V'$ of Fisher's equation, M of the equations of Pigou and Robertson, and n of Keynes' equation refer to the total quantity of money.

2. Dissimilarities

Despite these similarities the two approaches have many dissimilarities:

1. *Functions of Money.* The two versions emphasize on different functions of money. The Fisherian approach lays emphasis on the medium of exchange function while the Cambridge approach emphasises the store of value of function of money.

2. *Flow and Stock.* In Fisher's approach money is a flow concept while in the Cambridge approach it is a stock concept. The former relates to a period of time and the latter to a point of time.

3. *V and k Different.* The meaning given to the two symbols V and k in the two versions is different. In Fisher's equation V refers to the rate of spending and in Robertson's equation k refers to the cash balances which people wish to hold. The former emphasises the transactions velocity of circulation and the latter the income velocity.

4. *Nature of Price Level.* In Fisher's equation, P refers to the average price level of all goods and services. But in the cambridge equation P refers to the prices of final or consumer goods.

5. *Nature of T.* In Fisher's version, T refers to the total amount of goods and services exchanged for

money, whereas in the Cambridge version, it refers to the final or consumer goods exchanged for money.

6. *Emphasis on Supply and Demand for Money.* Fisher's approach emphasises the supply of money, whereas the Cambridge approach emphasises both the demand for money and the supply of money.

7. *Different in Nature.* The two approaches are different in nature. The Fisherian version is mechanistic because it does not explain how changes in V bring about changes in P. On the other hand, the Cambridge version is realistic because it studies the psychological factors which influence k.

It is on account of these differences that Hansen wrote: "It is not true as is often alleged that the cash balance equation is merely the quantity theory in new algebraic dress."

5. SUPERIORITY OF CASH BALANCES APPROACH OVER TRANSACTIONS APPROACH

The Cambridge cash balances approach to the quantity theory of money is superior to Fisher's transaction approach in many respects. They are discussed as under:

1. *Basis of Liquidity Preference Theory of Interest.* The cash balances approach emphasises the importance of holding cash balances rather than the supply of money which is given at a point of time. It thus led Keynes to propound his theory of liquidity preference and of the rate of interest, and to the integration of monetary theory of value and output.

2. *Complete Theory.* The cash balances version of quantity theory is superior to the transactions version because the former determines the value of money in terms of the demand and supply of money. Thus it is a complete theory. But in the transactions approach, the determination of value of money is artificially divorced from the theory of value.

3. *Discards the Concept of Velocity of Circulation.* The cash balances approach is superior to the transactions approach because it altogether discards the concept of the velocity of circulation of money which 'obscures the motives and decisions of people behind it.'

4. *Related to the Short Period.* Again the cash balances version is more realistic than the transactions version of the quantity theory, because it is related to the short period while the latter is related to the long period. As pointed out by Keynes, "In the long run we may all be dead." So the study of the relationship between quantity of money and price level during the long run is unrealistic.

5. *Simple Equations.* In the cash balances equations, transactions relating to final goods only are included where P refers to the level of final goods. On the other hand, in the transactions equation P includes all types of transactions. This creates difficulties in determining the true price level. Thus the former equations are simpler and realistic than the latter.

6. *New Formulation in the Monetary Theory.* Further, the Cambridge equation regards the cash balances held by the people as a function of the level of income. The introduction of income (Y or R or T or O) in this equation as against V (the velocity of circulation of money) in the transaction equation has made the cash balances equation realistic and led to new formulations in monetary theory. "It points out that changes in the level of money income can come about through changes in the price level, through changes in real output or through both at once."

7. *Explains Trade Cycles.* Hansen[12] regards k in the Cambridge equation superior to V in Fisher's equation for understanding cyclical fluctuations. According to him, "Drastic and sudden shifts in the desire to hold money, reflected in a change in k, may produce large and quickly moving changes in the level of income and prices. Shifts in the public psychology, in expectations must be taken into account not less than changes in the money supply. In the Cambridge analysis, a shift in k may start an upward or downward movement." For instance, when k (the fraction of total real income that people wish to hold in cash balances) increases because of low business expectation, the price level falls, and vice versa.

8. *Study of Subjective Factors.* As a corollary to the above, V in Fisher's equation is mechanistic while k in the Cambridge equation is realistic. The subjective factors behind variations in k have led to the study of such

---

12. A.H. Hansen, *Monetary Theory and Fiscal Policy,* 1949, pp. 49-50, Italics mine.

factors as expectations, uncertainty, motives for liquidity, and the rate of interest in modern monetary theory. In this sense, it can be justifiably said that, "the Cambridge equation moves us on from the tautology represented by the equation of exchange to a study of economic behaviour."

9. *Applicable under All Circumstances.* Fisher's transactions approach holds true only under full employment. But the cash balances approach holds under all circumstances whether there is full employment or less than full employment.

10. *Based on Micro Factors.* The Cambridge version is superior to the Fisherian version because it is based on micro factors like individual decisions and behaviours. On the other hand, the Fisherian version is based on macro factors like *T*, total velocity of circulation, etc.

EXERCISES

1. Critically examine Fisher's Quantity Theory of Money.
2. Discuss the Cambridge Cash Balances Approach to the Quantity Theory of Money. How far is it superior to the Cash Transactions Approach ?
3. Give the similarities and dissimilarities of the Quantity Theory of Money and Cambridge cash balances theory.
4. Write notes on.
   (a) Fisher's Equation of Exchange.
   (b) Keynes' Real Balance Equation.
5. What do you mean by value of money ? What determines value of money, according to Fisher ?

CHAPTER 13

Income and Expenditure Theory*

1. INTRODUCTION

The old quantity theory of money is weak in that it establishes a direct relationship between the money supply and the aggregate demand. According to the quantity theorists, an increase in the money supply leads to an increase in the aggregate demand for goods and services, and vice versa. It is the increase in the quantity of money which by increasing the aggregate demand for goods and services leads to rise in prices, and vice versa. But the experience during the Great Depression has shown that increase in the money supply, failed to increase the aggregate demand.

The income theory was gradually developed by Tooke, Wicksell and Aftalion and finally by Keynes. According to them, it is changes in income rather than in the money supply which cause changes in the aggregate demand. When income increases, aggregate demand for goods and services also increases. People spend more and the price level rises. On the contrary, with the decline in income, the aggregate demand falls. People spend less and the price level falls. Therefore, changes in the price level depend upon the volume of expenditure in the economy which in turn is determined by changes in the level of income, and the level of income depends upon the volume of saving and investment in the economy. Thus changes in the price level or value of money are caused by the income and expenditure of the community or by the volume of saving and investment. Thus income and expenditure, and saving and investment are the two approaches to the income theory which we discuss below.

2. INCOME-EXPENDITURE APPROACH**

The income theory of prices involves on the one side an analysis of income and aggregate demand, and on the other, an analysis of costs and aggregate supply. Prices are determined by money income and real income.

The total *money* income (Y) is the value of goods and services produced in any period of time and expressed in terms of money. It is determined by the remuneration paid in terms of money to the factors of production. Thus it also refers to the sum of total expenditure (E) incurred on goods and services during a period. On the other hand, the 'real' income is the total value of *real* goods and services produced in any period. It is determined by the total money value of goods and services expressed in terms of a general price level of a particular year taken as the base. Thus the money value of real income is the money income which is determined by the prices of goods and services or output. Symbolically,

$$Y = P.O$$

where, Y is money income or money expenditure which produces a flow of income; P is the general level of

* It is also known as the Income Theory or the Saving and Investment Theory of the Value of Money.

** Students should give only that approach which is asked.

prices, and *O* is the physical volume of goods and services produced. It follows that

$P = Y/O$

It means that prices are determined by the ratio of money income to total output. When money income *(Y)* rises more rapidly than output (O) prices *(P)* will tend to increase. If, on the other hand, output *(O)* increases more rapidly than money income *(Y)*, prices *(P)* will tend to fall.

It is clear from the above that total money income equals total expenditure which, in turn, is equal to consumption expenditure (C) plus investment expenditure *(I)*. Therefore, symbolically, $Y=E=C+I$.

According to Keynes, it is the total money income which determines the total expenditure of the community. An increase in the money income means increase in investment expenditure, the propensity to consume being stable in the short run. The increased investment will raise effective demand which will, in turn, raise output and employment. But what about prices? So long as there is unemployment, prices do not rise with increase in output. This is because the supply of factors is perfectly elastic. Therefore, output will change in the same proportion as the quantity of money, and there will be no change in prices. When the supply of factors becomes somewhat inelastic (or factors are in short supply), this may lead to increase in marginal costs and prices. As full employment is reached, the elasticity of supply of output falls to zero (perfectly inelastic), and prices rise in proportion to increase in the quantity of money. Thus the income theory states that the increase in the quantity of money depends upon increase in money income and aggregate expenditure, and prices start rising when the full employment level is being reached. Once the full employment level is reached, prices rise in the same proportion as the increase in money income and aggregate expenditure.

3. SAVING-INVESTMENT APPROACH

INTRODUCTION

An alternative to the Keynesian income-expenditure theory is the saving-investment approach to income theory. In fact the income-expenditure approach *(Y=C+I)* is the same thing as the saving-investment approach. Both saving *(S)* and investment *(I)* are defined as the excess of income over consumption *(Y-C)* so that they are necessarily equal. Symbolically

$S = Y - C$

$I = Y - C$

$S = I$

Keynes also established this equality in another way. He defined income as equal to consumption plus investment *(Y=C+f)*, and saving as the excess of income over consumption *(S-Y-C)*. Thus

$Y = C + I$ or $I = Y - C$

$S = Y - C$

$S = I$

THE THEORY

We have seen above that the equality between saving and investment is brought about by the mechanism of income. On the other hand, income depends upon relation between saving and investment. So long as saving and investment are equal, there will be the equilibrium level of income and the price level will be stable. If saving and investment are disturbed, the price-level also changes via the change in expenditure.

If saving exceeds investment, it means that people reduce their expenditure on goods and services. They are hoarding more money and spending less. This reduces the velocity of circulation of money. This leads to a reduction in the income of the producers of goods and services. Reduced expenditure and income lead to a fall in the price level. As prices fall, investment also declines due to a fall in the marginal efficiency of capital which leads to further fall in income, output, employment, and prices. This process will continue till prices reach the bottom of the depression.

If investment exceeds saving, people increase their expenditure on goods and services. They are spending more and saving less. This causes the velocity of circulation to increase. This increases the income of the producers of goods and services. Increase in expenditure and income lead to a rise in the price level.

This will increase the profit expectations or marginal efficiency of capital. As a result, investment will increase further which will, in turn, raise employment, income, expenditure, output and prices to still higher levels. But the increase in investment leading to an increase in aggregate expenditure, demand, and income do not lead to rise in the price level immediately. So long as the output of goods and services rises proportionately with the increase in the demand for goods and services, there would not be a general rise in the price level. If output does not increase proportionately, increase in investment will increase income and the price level. But increase in output is possible only if there are unemployed resources in the economy. When the economy reaches the full employment level, further increase in income will not raise output to the level of increase in aggregate expenditure. But it will lead to an upward rise in the price level in the same proportion as the increase in income.

To conclude, it is the inequality in saving and investment that brings about changes in the price level, and changes in the price level are due to changes in income rather than in the quantity of money.[1]

Superiority of Income-Expenditure (or Saving-Investment) Theory over the Quantity Theory

The income-expenditure theory of money is considered superior to the quantity theory of money on the following grounds:

1. *Explains Business Cycles.* The quantity theory cannot explain changes in prices during the upswing and downswing of a business cycle. It does not explain why an abundance of money during a depression fails to bring about a revival, and shortage of money stops a boom. The income theory is superior to the quantity theory because it explains them1. According to the saving-investment theory, when investment exceeds saving revival starts from a depression.' Mere increase in the supply of money is not enough to bring about a revival. It is the'rise in business expectations of profit (or the marginal efficiency of capital) that encourage investment and the revival starts. On the other hand, a boom does not stop due to decrease in the money supply alone. Rather it stops because saving exceeds investment due to the fall in the expectations of profit. Thus it is changes in investment due to changes in business expectations of profit that lead to cyclical upswing and downswing. Crowther has aptly said, "The Quantity Theory of Money explains, as it were, the average level of the sea; the Saving and Investment Theory explains the violence of the tides."[2]

2. *Explains Changes in Velocity of Circulation of Money.* The quantity theory of money does not explain the causes of changes in the velocity of circulation of money. The saving-investment theory is superior in that it gives an adequate explanation of such changes. When saving exceeds investment, it means that people are hoarding more money and spending less. This reduces the velocity of circulation of money. On the contrary, when investment exceeds saving, people are spending more which causes the velocity of circulation of money to increase. Thus changes in the velocity of circulation of money are caused by the relationship between saving and investment.

3. *Explains Causal Relationship between Quantity of Money-and Price Level.* The Quantity Theory of Money fails to explain the causal relationship between the quantity of money and the price level. It simply explains that the relationship between the two is direct and proportional. The saving-investment theory is superior in that it shows that the actual relationship between the money supply and price level is neither direct nor proportional. It is disequilibrium between saving and investment that leads to changes in the price level. An increase in the quantity of money is partly saved and partly spent. If investment exceeds saving, income will increase which will raise aggregate expenditure, output, employment and prices. The inverse will be the case when saving exceeds investment. Thus there is no direct relationship between the quantity of money and price level. As pointed out by Crowther, "The effect of a given change in *M {quantity of money) on* the price level is not a simple cause-and-effect relationship as the Quantity Theory supposed, but a most complex chain reaction."[3]

---

1. Students are not expected to give figures of saving and investment as they do not explain changes in the price level when there is inequality between the two.
2. G. Crowther, *op. cit.,* p. 147.
3. *Ibid.*

Moreover, when the quantity of money increases, the price level does not rise proportionately. So long as there are unemployed resources in the economy, an increase in money income will not lead to a rise in the price-level if output increases proportionately to the increase in aggregate demand. It is only when .the resources are fully employed that the price level will increase proportionately to the increase in the quantity of money.

4. *Applicable in the Full Employment and Unemployment.* The quantity theory of money is based on the assumption of full employment that is why it establishes a direct and proportional relationship between the quantity of money and price level. The saving-investment theory is superior to it because it analyses the effect of money on the price level when there is unemployment in the economy.

5. *Explains Short Run Changes.* The saving-investment theory is more realistic than the quantity theory of money because it explains short run changes in the value of money (or price level), whereas the quantity theory of money explains the long run changes. This is unrealistic because in the long run we are all dead.

6. *Considers both Monetary and Real Factors.* Again, the saving-investment theory is superior to the quantity theory of money in that it takes into consideration both the monetary and real factors in determining the value of money. Such factors as saving, investment, aggregate output are taken alongwith the quantity of money and aggregate expenditure. This makes the income theory better than the quantity theory of money.

7. *Policy Implications.* The policy implications of the saving-investment theory are more realistic than the quantity theory of money. The quantity theory of money concentrates exclusively on monetary policy. On the other hand, the saving-investment theory lays more emphasis on expenditure and income that affect economic activity more than the quantity of money. This fact has been proved by the dominance of income (fiscal) policy over the monetary policy since 1950s.

We may conclude with Crowther that the saving-investment theory "goes considerably nearer to the reality of things than the quantity theory. It reveals the fundamental tendencies of which the behaviour of money and prices is merely the surface of the symptom."

EXERCISES

1. Discuss the view that price changes are better explained by Savings and Investment Theory than by the Traditional Quantity Theory of Money.
2. "The value of money, in fact, is a consequence of the total income rather than of the quantity of money." Discuss.
3. What are the shortcomings of the quantity theory of money? How does the income-expenditure approach is an improvement over it?
4. "The saving-investment theory can explain a number of things about the behaviour of money that the quantity theory cannot." Discuss.

CHAPTER 14

The Keynesian Theory of Money and Prices

1. INTRODUCTION

In Chapter 21 of his *General Theory*, Keynes attacked the classical quantity theorists for keeping separate monetary theory and value theory. He then presented a reformulated quantity theory of money which brought about a transition from a monetary theory of prices to a monetary theory of output. In doing this, Keynes made an attempt to intergrate monetary theory with value theory and also linked the theory of interest into monetary theory. But "it is through the theory of output that value theory and monetary theory are brought into just a position with each other."

Keynes does not agree with the older quantity theorists that there is a direct and proportional relationship between quantity of money and prices. According to him, the effect of a change in the quantity of money on prices is indirect and non-proportional.

Keynes complains "that economics has been divided into two compartments with no doors or windows between the theory of value and the theory of money and prices." This dichotomy between the relative price level (as determined by demand and supply of goods) and the *absolute price level* (as determined by demand and supply of money) arises from the failure of the classical monetary economists to integrate value theory with monetary theory. Consequently, changes in the money supply affect only the absolute price level but exercise no influence on the relative price level.

Further, Keynes criticises the classical theory of static equilibrium in which money is regarded as neutral and does not influence the economy's real equilibrium relating to relative prices. According to him, the problems of the real world are related to the theory of shifting equilibrium whereas money enters as a "link between the present and future".

2. KEYNES'S REFORMULATED QUANTITY THEORY OF MONEY

The Keynesian reformulated quantity theory of money is based on the following

ASSUMPTIONS

1. All factors of production are in perfectly elastic supply so long as there is any unemployment.
2. All unemployed factors are homogeneous, perfectly divisible and interchangeable.

3. There are constant returns to scale so that prices do not rise or fall as output increases.

4. Effective demand and quantity of money change in the same proportion so long as there are any unemployed resources.

Given these assumptions, the Keynesian chain of causation between changes in the quantity of money and in prices is an indirect one through the rate of interest. So when the quantity of money is increased, its first impact is on the rate of interest which tends to fall. Given the marginal efficiency of capital, a fall in the rate of interest will increase the volume of investment. The increased investment will raise effective demand through the multiplier effect thereby increasing income, output and employment. Since the supply curve of factors of production is perfectly elastic in a situation of unemployment, wage and non-wage factors are available at constant rate of remuneration. There being constant returns to scale, prices do not rise with the increase in output so long as there is any unemployment. Under the circumstances, output and employment will increase in the same proportion as effective demand, and the effective demand will increase in the same proportion as the quantity of money. But "once full employment is reached, output ceases to respond *at all* to changes in the supply of money and so in effective demand. The elasticity of supply of output in response to changes in the supply, which was infinite as long as there was unemployment falls to zero. The entire effect of changes in the supply of money is exerted on prices, which rise in exact proportion with the increase in effective demand." Thus so long as there is unemployment, output will change in the same proportion as the quantity of money, and there will be no change in prices; and when there is full employment, prices will change in the same proportion as the quantity of money. Therefore, the reformulated quantity theory of money stresses the point that with increase in the quantity of money prices rise only when the level of full employment is reached, and not before this.

This reformulated quantity theory of money is illustrated in Figure 1 (A) and (B)[1] where *OTC* is the output curve relating to the quantity of money and *PRC* is the price curve relating to the quantity of money. Panel A of the figure shows that as the quantity of money increases from *O* to *M*, the level of output also rises along the *OT* portion of the *OTC* curve. As the quantity of money reaches *OM* level, full employment output *OQF* is being produced. But after point *T* the output curve becomes vertical because any further increase in the quantity of money cannot raise output beyond the full employment level OQ_F.

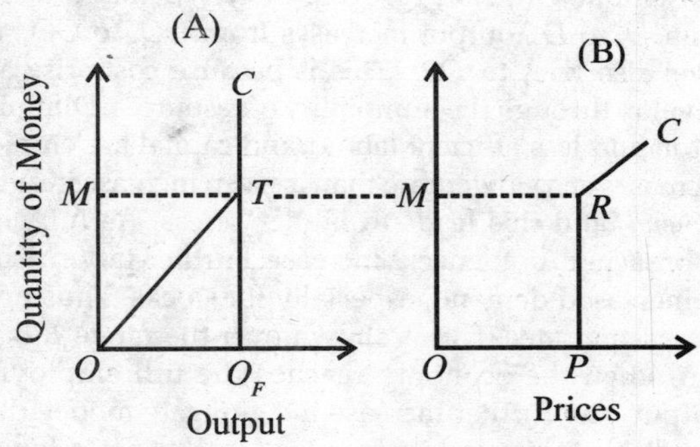

Fig. 1

Panel B of the figure shows the relationship between quantity of money and prices. So long as there is unemployment, prices remain constant whatever the increase in the quantity of money. Prices start rising only after the full employment level is reached. In the figure, the price level *OP* remains constant at the *OM* quantity of money corresponding to the full employment level of output OQ_F. But an increase in the quantity of money above *OM* raises prices in the same proportion as the quantity of money. This is shown by the *RC* portion of the price curve *PRC*.

Keynes himself pointed out that the real world is so complicated that the simplifying assumptions upon which the reformulated quantity theory of money is based, will not hold. According to him, the following possible complications would qualify the statement that so long as there is unemployment, employment will change in the same proportion as the quantity of money, and when there is full employment, *prices* will change in the same proportion as the quantity of money."

(1) "Effective demand will not change in exact proportion to the quantity of money.

(2) Since resources are homogenous, there will be diminishing, and not constant returns as employment gradually increases.

(3) Since resources are not interchangeable, some commodities will reach a condition of inelastic supply

1. Figure adapted from A.W. Stonier and D.C. Hague, *A Text Book of Economic Theory*, 4/e, 1972, p. 561.

while there are still unemployed resources available for the production of other commodities.

(4) The wage-unit will tend to rise, before full employment has been reached.

(5) The remunerations of factors entering into marginal cost will not all change in the same proportion."

Taking into account these complications, it is clear that the reformulated quantity theory of money does not hold. An increase in effective demand will not change in exact proportion to the quantity of money, but it will partly spend itself in increasing output and partly in increasing the price level. So long as there are unemployed resources, the general price level will not rise much as output increases. But a sudden large increase in aggregate demand will encounter bottlenecks when resources are still unemployed. It may be that the supply of some factors becomes inelastic or others may be in short supply and are not interchangeable. This may lead to increase in marginal cost and price. Price would accordingly rise above average unit cost and profits would increase rapidly which, in turn, tend to raise money wages owing to trade union pressures. Diminishing returns may also set in. As full employment is reached, the elasticity of supply of output falls to zero[2] and prices rise in proportion to the increase in the quantity of money.

The complicated model of the Keynesian theory of money and prices is shown diagrammatically in Figure 2 in terms of aggregate supply (S) and aggregate demand (D) curves. The price level is measured on the vertical axis and output on the horizontal axis.

According to Keynes, an increase in the quantity of money increases aggregate money demand on investment as a result of the fall in the rate of interest. This increases output and employment in the beginning but not the price level. In the figure, the increase in the aggregate money demand from D_1 to D_2 raises output from OQ_1 to OQ_2 but the price level remains constant at OP. As aggregate money demand increases further from D_2 to D_3, output increases from OQ_2 to OQ_3, and the price level also rises to OP_3. This is because costs rise as bottlenecks develop through the immobility of resources. Diminishing returns set in and less efficient labour and capital are employed. Output increases at a slower rate than a given increase in aggregate *money demand*, and this leads to higher prices. As full employment is approached, bottlenecks increase. Further-more, rising prices lead to increased demand, especially for stocks. Thus prices rise at an increasing rate." This is shown over the range E_3E_5 in the figure. But when the economy reaches the full employment level of output, any further increase in aggregate money demand brings about a proportionate increase in the price level but output remains unchanged at that level. This is shown in the figure when the demand curve D_5 shifts upward to D_6 and the price level increases from OP_5 to OP_6 while the level of output remains constant at OQ_F.

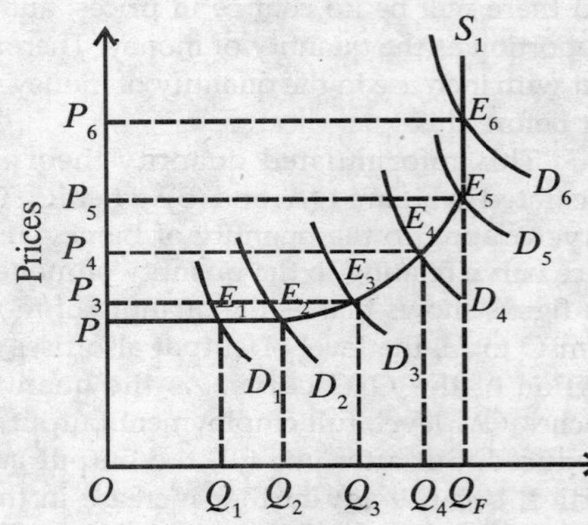

Fig. 2

3. SUPERIORITY OF THE KEYNESIAN THEORY OVER THE TRADITIONAL QUANTITY THEORY OF MONEY

The Keynesian theory of money and prices is surperior to the traditional quantity theory of money for the following reasons.

Keynes's reformulated quantity theory of money is superior to the traditional approach in that he discards the old view that the relationship between the quantity of money and prices is direct and proportional. Instead, he establishes an indirect and non-proportional relationship between quantity of money and prices.

In establishing such a relationship, Keynes brought about a transition from a pure monetary theory of prices to a monetary theory of output and employment. In so doing, he integrates monetary theory with value

2. The elasticity of output with respect to demand $e = DdO/OdD$

theory. He integrates monetary theory with value theroy and also with the theory of output and employment through the rate of interest. In fact, the integration between monetary theory and value theory is done through the theory of output in which the rate of interest plays the crucial role. When the quantity of money increases the rate of interest falls which increases the volume of investment and aggregate demand thereby raising output and employment. In this way, monetary theory is integrated with the theory of output and employment. As output and employment increase they further raise the demand for factors of production. Consequently, certain bottlenecks appear which raise the marginal cost including money wage rates. Thus prices start rising. Monetary theory is integrated with value theory in this way. The Keynesain theory is, therefore, superior to the traditional quantity theory of money because it does not keep the real and monetary sectors of the economy into two separate compartments with 'no doors or windows between the theory of value and the theory of money and prices.'

Again, the traditional quantity theory is based on the unrealistic asumption of full employment of resources. Under this assumption, a given increase in the quantity of money always leads to a proportionate increase in the price level. Keynes, on the other hand, believes that full employment is an exception. Therefore, so long as there is unemployment, output and employment will change in the same proportion as the quantity of money, but there willl be no change in prices; and when there is full employment, prices will change in the same proportion as the quantity of money. Thus the Keynesian analysis is superior to the traditional analysis because it studies the relationship between the quantity of money and prices both under unemployment and full employment situations.

Further, the Keynesian theory is superior to the traditional quantity theory of money in that it emphasises important policy implications. The traditional theory believes that every increase in the quantity of money leads to inflation. Keynes, on the other hand, establishes that so long as there is unemployment, the rise in prices is gradual and there is no danger of inflation. It is only when the economy reaches the level of full employment that the rise in prices is inflationary with every increase in the quantity of money. Thus "this approach has the virtue of emphasising that the objectives of full employment and price stability may be inherently irreconcilable."

4. CRITICISMS OF KEYNES' THEORY OF MONEY AND PRICES

Keynes' views on money and prices have been criticised by the monetarists on the following grounds.

1. *Direct Relation.* Keynes mistakenly took prices as fixed so that the effect of money appears in his analysis in terms of quantity of goods traded rathere than their average prices. That is why Keynes adopted an indirect mechanism through bond prices, interest rates and investment of the effects of monetary changes on economic activity. But the actual effects of monetary changes are direct rather than indirect.

2. *Stable Demand for Money.* Keynes assumed that monetary changes were largely absorbed by changes in the demand for money. But Friedman has shown on the basis of his empirical studies that the demand for money is highly stable.

3. *Nature of Money.* Keynes failed to understand the true nature of money. He believed that money could be exchanged for bonds only. In fact, money can be exchanged for many different types of assets like bonds, securities, physical assets, human wealth, etc.

4. *Effect of Money.* Since Keynes wrote for a depression period, this led him to conclude that money had little effect on income. According to Friedman, it was the contraction of money that precipitated the depression. It was, therefore, wrong on the part of Keynes to argue that money had little effect on income. Money does affect national income.

EXERCISES

1. Show how the Theory of Value has been integrated with the Theory of Money by Keynes.
2. How has Keynes correlated money and rate of interest on the one hand and rate of interest, employment and prices on the other hand ?

CHAPTER

15

Friedman's Restatement of the Quantity Theory of Money

1. INTRODUCTION

Following the publication of Keynes's the *General Theory of Employment, Interest and Money* in 1936, economists discarded the traditional quantity theory of money. But at the University of Chicago "the quantity theory continued to be a central and vigorous part of the oral tradition throughout the 1930s and 1940s." At Chicago, Milton Friedman, Henry Simons, Lloyd Mints, Frank Knight and Jacob Viner taught and developed 'a more subtle and relevant version' of the quantity theory of money in its theoretical form "in which the quantity theory was connected and integrated with general price theory." The foremost exponent of the Chicago version of the quantity theory of money who led to the so-called "Monetarist Revolution" is Professor Friedman. He, in his essay "The Quantity Theory of Money—A Restatement" published in 1956', set down a particular model of quantity theory of money. This is discussed below.

2. FRIEDMAN'S THEORY

In his reformulation of the quantity theory, Friedman asserts that "the quantity theory is in the first instance a theory of the demand for money. It is not a theory of output, or of money income, or of the price level." The demand for money on the part of ultimate wealth holders is formally identical with that of the demand for a consumption service. He regards the amount of real cash balances (M/P) as a commodity which is demanded because it yields services to the person who holds it. Thus money is an asset or capital good. Hence the demand for money forms part of capital or wealth theory.

For ultimate wealth holders, the demand for money, in real terms, may be expected to be a function primarily of the following variables:

1. Total Wealth. The total wealth is the analogue of the budget constraint. It is the total that must be divided among various forms of assets. In practice, estimates of total wealth are seldom available. Instead, income may serve as an index of wealth. Thus, according to Friedman, income is a surrogate of wealth.

2. The Division of Wealth between Human and Non-Human Forms. The major source of wealth is the productive capacity of human beings which is human wealth. But the conversion of human wealth into non-human wealth or the reverse is subject to institutional constraints. This can be done by using current earnings to purchase non-human wealth or by using non-human wealth to finance the acquisition of skills. Thus the fraction of total wealth in the form of non-human wealth is an additional important variable. Friedman calls the

---

1. Milton Friedman (ed.), *Studies in the Quantity Theory of Money*, 1956, pp. 3-21.

ratio of non-human to human wealth or the ratio of wealth to income as *w*.

3. The Expected Rates of Return on Money and Other Assets. These rates of return are the counterparts of the prices of ~~a~~ commodity and its substitutes and complements in the theory of consumer demand. The nominal rate of return may be zero as it generally is on currency, or negative as it sometimes is on demand deposits, subject to net service charges, or positive as it is on demand deposits on which interest is paid, and generally on time deposits. The nominal rate of return on other assets consists of two parts: first, any currently paid yield or cost, such as interest on bonds, dividends on equities, and costs of storage on physical assets, and second, changes in the prices of these assets which become especially important under conditions of inflation or deflation.

4. Other Variables. Variables other than income may affect the utility attached to the services of money which determine liquidity proper. Besides liquidity, variables are the tastes and preferences of wealth holders. Another variable is trading in existing capital goods by ultimate wealth holders. These variable also determine the demand function for money alongwith other forms of wealth. Such variables are noted as *u* by Friedman.

Broadly, total wealth includes all sources of income or consumable services. It is capitalised income. By income, Friedman means "permanent income" which is the average expected yield on wealth during its life time.

Wealth can be held in five different forms: money, bonds, equities, physical goods, and human capital. Each form of wealth has a unique characteristic of its own and a different yield.

1. *Money* is taken in the broadest sense to include currency, demand deposits and time deposits which yield interest on deposits. Thus money is luxury good. It also yields real return in the form of convenience, security, etc. to the holder which is measured in terms of the general price level (*P*).
2. *Bonds* are defined as claim to a time stream of payments that are fixed in *nomianl units*.
3. *Equities* are defined as a claim to a time stream of payments that are fixed in *real* units.
4. *Physical goods or non-human goods* are inventories of producer and consumer durable.
5. *Human capital* is the productive capacity of human beings. Thus each form of wealth has a unique characteristic of its own and a different yield either explicitly in the form of interest, dividends, labour income, etc., or implicitly in the form of services of money measured in terms of *P*, and inventories. The present discounted value of these expected income flows from these five forms of wealth constitutes the current value of wealth which can be expressed as:

$$W = \frac{y}{r}$$

where W is the current value of total wealth, *Y* is the total flow of expected income from the five forms of wealth, and r is the interest rate. This equation shows that wealth is capitalised income. Friedman in his latest empirical study *Monetary Trends in the United States and the United Kingdom* (1982) gives the following demand function for money for an individual wealth holder with slightly different notations from his original study of 1956 as:

$$M/P = f(y, w; R_m, R_b, R_e, g_p, u)$$

where *M* is the total stock of money demanded; *P* is the price level; *y* is the real income; *w* is the fraction of wealth in non-human form: R_m is the expected nominal rate of return on money; R_b is the expected rate of return on bonds, including expected changes in their prices; R_e is the expected nominal rate of return on equities, including expected changes in their prices; $g_p = (1/P)(dP/dt)$ is the expected rate of change of prices of goods and hence the expected nominal rate of return on physical assets; and *u* stands for variables other than income that may affect the utility attached to the services of money.

The demand function for business is roughly similar, although the division of total wealth and human wealth is not very useful since a firm can buy and sell in the market place and hire its human wealth at will. But the othere factors are important.

The aggregate demand function for money is the summation of individual demand functions with *M* and *y* referring to per capita money holdings and per capita real income respectivley, and *w* to the fraction of aggregate wealth in non-human form.

The demand function for money leads to the conclusion that a rise in expected yields on different assets

(R_b, R_e and g_p) reduces the amount of money demanded by a wealth holder, and that an increase in wealth raises the demand for money. The income to which cash balances (M/P) are adjusted is the expected long term level of income rather than current income being received. Empirical evidence suggests that the income elasticity of demand for money is greater than unity which means that income velocity is falling over the long run. This means that the long run demand for money function is stable and is relatively interest inelastic, as shown in fig. 1. where M_D is the emand for money curve. If there is change in the interest rate, the long-run demand for money is neligible.

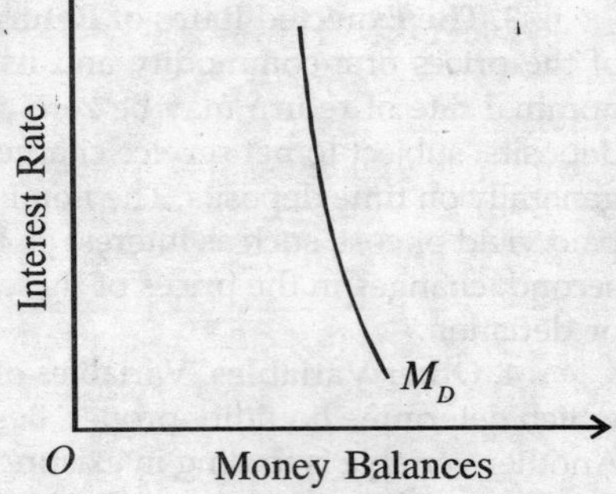

Fig. 1

In Friedman's restatement of the quantity theory of money, the supply of money is independent of the demand for money. The supply of money is unstable due to the actions of monetary authorities. On the other hand, the demand for money is stable. It means that money which people want to hold in cash or bank deposits is related in a fixed way to their permanent income. If the central bank increases the supply of money by purchasing securities, people who sell securities will find their holdings of money have increased in relation to their permanent income. They will, therefore, spend their excess holdings of money partly on assets and partly on consumer goods and services. This spending will reduce their money balances and at the same time raise the nominal income. On the contrary, a reduction in the money supply by selling securities on the part of the central bank will reduce the holdings of money of the buyers of securities in relation to their permanent income. They will, therefore, raise their money holdings partly by selling their assets and partly by reducing their consumption expenditure on goods and services. This will tend to reduce nominal income. Thus, on both counts, the demand for money remains stable. According to Friedman, a change in the supply of money causes a proportionate change in the price level or income or in both. Given the demand for money, it is possible to predict the effects of changes in the supply of money on total expenditure and income. If the economy is operating at less than full employment level, an increase in the supply of money will raise output and employment with a rise in total expenditure. But this is only possible in the short run. Friedman's quantity theory of moeny is explained in terms of Figure 2. where income (Y) is measured on the vertical axis and the demand for the supply of money are measured on the horizontal axis. M_D is the demand for money curve which varies with income. MS is the money supply curve which is perfectly inelalstic to changes in income. The two curves intersect at E and determine the equilibrium inocme OY. If the money supply rise, the MS curve shifts to the right to M_1S_1. As a result, the money supply is greater than the demand for money which raises total expenditure until new equilibrium is established at E_1 between M_D and M_1S_1 cirves. The income rises to OY_1.

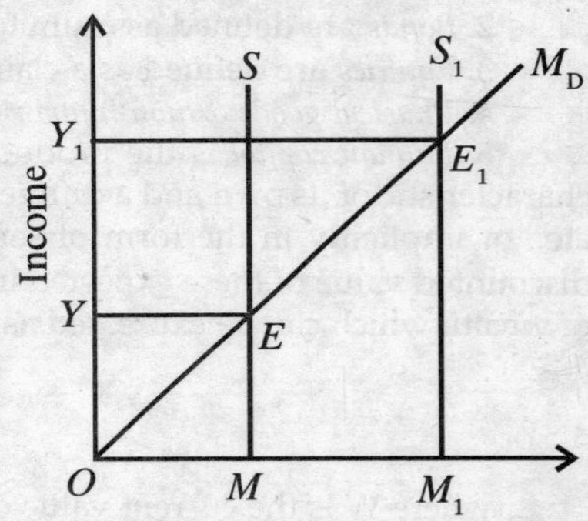

Fig. 2

Thus Friedman presents thw quantity theory as the theory of the demand for money and the demand for money is assumed to depend on asset prices or relative returns and wealth or income. He shows how a theory of the stable demand for money becomes a theory of prices and output. A discrepancy between the nominal quantity of money demanded and the nominal quantity of money supplied will be evident primarily in attempted spending. As the demand for money changes in response to changes in its determinants, it follows that substantial changes in prices or nominal income are almost invariably the result of changes in the nominal supply of money.

Its Criticisms

Friedman's reformulation of the quantity theory of money has evoked much controversy and has led to empirical verification on the part of the Keynesians and the Monetarists. Some of the criticisms levelled against the theory are discussed as under.

1. *Very Broad Definition of Money.* Friedman has been criticised for using the broad definition of money which not only includes currency and demand deposits (M_1) but also time deposits with commercial banks (M_2). This broad definition leads to the obvious conclusion that the interest elasticity of the demand for money is negligible. If the rate of interest increases on time deposits, the demand for them (M_2) rises. But the demand for currency and demand deposits (M_1) falls. So the overall effect of the rate of interest will be negligible on the demand for money. But Friedman's analysis is weak in that he does not make a choice between long-term and short-term interest rates. In fact, if demand deposits (M_1) are used a short-term rate is preferable, while a long-term rate is better with time deposits (M_2). Such an interest rate structure is bound to influence the demand for money.

2. *Money not a Luxury Good.* Friedman regards money as a luxury good because of the inclusion of time deposits in money. This is based on his finding that there is higher trend rate of the money supply than income in the United States. But no such 'luxury effect' has been found in the case of England.

3. *More Importance to Wealth Variables.* In Friedman's demand for money function, wealth variables are preferable to income and the operation of wealth and income variables simultaneously does not seem to be justified. As pointed out by Johnson, income is the return on wealth, and wealth is the present value of income. The presence of the rate of interest and one of these variables in the demand for money function would appear to make the other superfluous.

4. *Money Supply not Exogenous.* Friedman takes the supply of money to be unstable. The supply of money is varied by the monetary authorities in an exogenous manner in Friedman's system. But the fact is that in the United States the money supply consists of bank deposits created by changes in bank lending. Bank lending, in turn, is based upon bank reserves which expand and contract with (a) deposits and withdrawals of currency by non-bank financial intermediaries; (b) borrowings by commercial banks from the Federal Reserve System; (c) inflows and outflows of money from and to abroad: and (d) purchase and sale of securities by the Federal Reserve System. The first three items definitely impart an endogenous element to the money supply. Thus the money supply is not exclusively exogenous, as assumed by Friedman. It is mostly endogenous.

5. *Ignores the Effect of Other Variables on Money Supply.* Friedman also ignores the effect of prices, output or interest rates on the money supply. But there is considerable empirical evidence that the money supply can be expressed as a function of the above variables.

6. *Does not consider Time Factor.* Friedman does not tell about the timing and speed of adjustment or the length of time to which his theory applies.

7. *No Positive Correlation between Money Supply and Money GNP.* Money supply and money GNP have been found to be positively correlated in Friedman's findings. But, according to Kaldor,[2] in Britain the best correlation is to be found between the quarterly variations in the amount of cash held in the form of notes and coins by the public and corresponding variations in personal consumption at market prices, and not between money supply and the GNP.

8. *Conclusion.* Despite these criticisms, "Friedman's application to monetary theory of the basic principle of capital theory—that is the yield on capital, and capital the present value of income—is probably the most important development in monetary theory since Keynes's *General Theory*. Its theoretical significance lies in the conceptual integration of wealth and income as influences on behaviour."

3. FRIEDMAN VS KEYNES

Friedman's demand for money function differs from that of Keynes's in many ways which are discussed as under.

First, Friedman uses a broader definition of money than that of Keynes in order to explain his demand for money function. He treats money as an asset or capital good capable of serving as a temporary abode of purchasing power. It is held for the stream of income or consumable services which it renders. On the other hand, the Keynesian definition of money consists of demand deposits and non-interest bearing debt of the

2. N. Kaldor, 'The New Monetarism,' L.B.R., July 1970

government.

Second, Friedman postulates a demand for money function quite different from that of Keynes. The demand for money on the part of wealth holders is a function of many variables. These are R_m, the yield on money; R_b, the yield on bonds; R_e, the yield on securities; g_p, the yield on physical assets; and u referring to other variables. In the Keynesian theory, the demand for money as an asset is confined to just bonds where interest rates are the relevant cost of holding money.

Third, there is also the difference between the monetary mechanisms of Keynes and Friedman as to how changes in the quantity of money affect economic activity. According to Keynes, monetary changes affect economic activity *indirectly* through bond prices and interest rates. The monetary authorities increase the money supply by purchasing bonds which raises their prices and reduces the yield on them. Lower yield on bonds induces people to put their money elsewhere, such as investment in new productive capital that will increase output and income. On the other hand, in Friedman's theory monetary disturbances will *directly* affect prices and production of all types of goods since people will buy or sell any asset held by them. Friedman emphasises that the market interest rates play only a small part of the total spectrum of rates that are relevant.

Fourth, there is the difference between the two approaches with regard to the motives for holding money balances. Keynes divides money balances into "active" and "idle" categories. The former consist of transactions and precautionary motives, and the latter consist of the speculative motive for holding money. On the other hand, Friedman makes no such division of money balances. According to him, money is held for a variety of different purposes which determine the total volume of assets held such as money, physical assets, total wealth, human wealth, and general preferrences, tastes and anticipations.

Fifth, in his analysis, Friedman introduces permanent income and nominal income to explain his theory. Permanent income is the amount a wealth holder can consume while maintaining his wealth intact. Nominal income is measured in the prevailing units of currency. It depends on both prices and quantities of goods traded. Keynes, on the other hand, does not make such a distinction.

EXERCISES

1. Explain the contribution of Milton Friedman to the Quantity Theory of Money.
2. Critically examine the statement that the revised version of the quantity theory of money is that there exists a stable demand function for real money holdings.
3. Explain Friedman's reformulation of the Quantity Theory of Money. How does if differ from that of Keynes ?
4. Comment on the following statements:
   (a) The Quantity Theory of Money is a Theory of Demand for Money.
   (b) The Quantity Theory of Money is a Theory of Money-Income Determination.

CHAPTER 16

The Supply of Money

1. DEFINITIONS OF MONEY SUPPLY

The supply of money is a stock at a particular point of time, though it conveys the idea of a flow over time. The term 'the supply of money' is synonymous with such terms as 'money stock', 'stock of money', 'money supply' and 'quantity of money'. The supply of money at any moment is the total amount of money in the economy. There are three alternative views regarding the definition or measures of money supply. The most common view is associated with the traditional and Keynesian thinking which stresses the medium of exchange function of money. According to this view, money supply is defined as currency with the public and demand deposits with commercial banks. Demand deposits are savings and current accounts of depositors in a commercial bank. They are the liquid form of money because depositors can draw cheques for any amount lying in their accounts and the bank has to make immediate payment on demand. Demand deposits with commercial banks plus currency with the public are together denoted as M_1, the money supply. This is regarded as a narrower definition of the money supply.

The second definition is broader and is associated with the modern quantity theorists headed by Friedman. Friedman defines the money supply at any moment of time as "literally the number of dollars people are carrying around in their pockets, the number of dollars they have to their credit at banks or dollars they have to their credit at banks in the form of demand deposits, and also commercial bank time deposits." Time deposits are fixed deposits of customers in a commercial bank. Such deposits earn a fixed rate of interest varying with the time period for which the amount is deposited. Money can be withdrawn before the expiry of that period by paying a penal rate of interest to the bank. So time deposits possess liquidity and are included in the money supply by Friedman. Thus this definition includes M_1 plus time deposits of commercial banks in the supply of money. This wider definition is characterised as M_2 in America and M_3 in Britain and India. It stresses the store of value function of money or what Friedman says, 'a temporary abode of purchasing power'.

The third definition is the broadest and is associated with Gurley and Shaw.[1] They include in the supply of money, M_2 plus deposits of savings banks, building societies, loan associations, and deposits of other credit and financial institutions.

The choice between these alternative definitions of the money supply depends on two considerations: *One*, "a particular choice of definition may facilitate or blur the analysis of the various motives for holding cash;"[2] and *two* from the point of view of monetary policy an appropriate definition should include the area over which the monetary authorities can have direct influence. If these two criteria are applied, none of the three definitions is wholly satisfactory.

The first definition of money supply may be analytically better because M_1 is a sure medium of exchange. But M_1 is an inferior store of value because it earns no rate of interest, as is earned by time deposits. Further, the central bank can have control over a narrower area if only demand deposits are included in the money supply.

1. J.G. Gurley and E.S. Shaw, *Money in a Theory of Finance*, 2/e, 1965.
2. R.J. Ball, *Inflation and the Theory of Money*, 1964.

The second definition that includes time deposits (M_2) in the supply of money is less satisfactory analytically because "in a highly developed financial structure, it is important to consider separately the motives for holding means of payment and time deposits." Unlike demand deposits, time deposits are not a perfect liquid form of money. This is because the amount lying in them can be withdrawn immediately by cheques. Normally, it cannot be withdrawn before the due date of expiry of deposit. In case a depositor wants his money earlier, he has to give a notice to the bank which allows the withdrawal after charging a penal interest rate from the depositor. Thus time deposits lack perfect liquidity and cannot be included in the money supply. But this definition is more appropriate from the point of view of monetary policy because the central bank can exercise control over a wider area that includes both demand and time deposits held by commercial banks.

The third definition of money supply that includes M_2 plus deposits of non-bank financial institutions is unsatisfactory on both the criteria. Firstly, they do not serve the medium of exchange function of money. Secondly, they almost remain outside the area of control of the central bank. The only advantage they possess is that they are highly liquid store of value. Despite this merit, deposits of non-bank financial institutions are not included in the definition of money supply.

DETERMINANTS OF MONEY SUPPLY

There are two theories of the determination of the money supply. According to the *first view*, the money supply is determined exogenously by the central bank. The *second view* holds that the money supply is determined endogenously by changes in the economic activity which affect people's desire to hold currency relative to deposits, the rate of interest, etc.

Thus the determinants of money supply are both exogenous and endogenous which can be described broadly as: the minimum cash reserve ratio, the level of bank reserves, and the desire of the people to hold currency relative to deposits. The last two determinants together are called the *monetary base* or *high powered money*.

1. The Required Reserve Ratio

The required reserve ratio (or the minimum cash reserve ratio or the reserve deposit ratio) is an important determinant of the money supply. An increase in the required reserve ratio reduces the supply of money with commercial banks and a decrease in required reserve ratio increases the money supply. The *RRr* is the ratio of cash to current and time deposit liabilities which is determined by law. Every commercial bank is required to keep a certain percentage of these liabilities in the form of deposits with the central bank of the country. But notes or cash held by commercial banks in their tills are not included in the minimum required reserve ratio.

But the short-term assets along with cash are regarded as the liquid assets of a commercial bank. In India the statutory liquidity ratio (SLR) has been fixed by law as an additional measure to determine the money supply. The SLR is called secondary reserve ratio in other countries while the required reserve ratio is referred to as the primary ratio. The raising of the SLR has the effect of reducing the money supply with commercial banks for lending purposes, and the lowering of the SLR tends in increase the money supply with banks for advances.

2. The Level of Bank Reserves

The level of bank reserves is another determinant of the money supply. Commercial bank reserves consist of reserves on deposits with the central bank and currency in their tills or vaults. It is the central bank of the country that influences the reserves of commercial banks in order to determine the supply of money. The central bank requires all commercial banks to hold reserves equal to a fixed percentage of both time and demand deposits. These are legal minimum or required reserves. Required reserves (*RR*) are determined by the required reserve ratio (*RRr*) and the level of deposits (D) of a commercial bank: $RR=RRr \times D$. If deposits amount to Rs 80 lakhs and required reserve ratio is 20 percent, then the required reserves will be 20% × 80=Rs 16 lakhs. If the reserve ratio is reduced to 10 per cent, the required reserves will also be reduced to Rs 8 lakhs. Thus the higher the reserve ratio, the higher the required reserves to be kept by a bank, and vice versa. But it is the excess reserves (*ER*) which are important for the determination of the money supply. Excess reserves are the difference between total reserves (*TR*) and required reserves (*RR*): ER=TR-RR . If total reserves are Rs 80 lakhs and required reserves are Rs 16 lakhs, then the excess reserves are Rs 64 lakhs (Rs 80 – 16 lakhs). When required reserves are reduced to Rs 8 lakhs, the excess reserves increase to Rs 72 lakhs. It is the excess reserves of a commercial bank which influence the size of its deposit liabilities. A commercial bank advances loans equal to its excess reserves which are an important component of the money supply. To determine the supply of money with a commercial bank, the central bank influences its reserves by adopting open market operations and discount rate policy.

Open market operations refer to the purchase and sale of government securities and other types of assets like bills, securities, bonds, etc., both government and private in the open market. When the central bank buys or sells securities in the open market, the level of bank reserves expands or contracts. The purchase of securities by the central bank is paid for with cheques to the holders of securities who, in turn, deposit them in commercial banks thereby increasing the level of bank reserves. The opposite is the case when the central bank sells securities to the public and banks who make payments to the central bank through cash and cheques thereby reducing the level of bank reserves.

The discount rate policy affects the money supply by influencing the cost and supply of bank credit to commercial banks. The discount rate, known as the bank rate in India, is the interest rate at which commercial banks borrow from the central bank. A high discount rate means that commercial banks get less amount by selling securities to the central bank. The commercial banks, in turn, raise their lending rates to the public thereby making advances dearer for them. Thus there will be contraction of credit and the level of commercial bank reserves. Opposite is the case when the bank rate is lowered. It tends to expand credit and consequently bank reserves.

It should be noted that commercial bank reserves are affected significantly only when open market operations and discount rate policy supplement each other. Otherwise, their effectiveness as determinants of bank reserves and consequently of money supply is limited.

3. Public's Desire to Hold Currency and Deposits

People's desire to hold currency (or cash) relative to deposits in commercial banks also determines the money supply. If people are in the habit of keeping less in cash and more in deposits with the commercial banks, the money supply will be large. This is because banks can create more money with larger deposits. On the contrary, if people do not have banking habits and prefer to keep their money holdings in cash, credit creation by banks will be less and the money supply will be at a low level.

4. High-Powered Money

The current practice is to explain the determinants of money supply in terms of the monetary base or high-powered money. High-powered money is the sum of commercial bank reserves and currency (notes and coins) held by the public. High-powered money is the base for the expansion of bank deposits and creation of the money supply. The supply of money varies directly with changes in the monetary base, and inversely with the currency and reserve ratios.

5. Other Factors

Money supply is a function not only of the high-powered money determined by the monetary authorities, but of interest rates, income and other factors. The latter factors change the proportion of money balances that the public holds as cash. Changes in business activity can change the behaviour of banks and the public and thus affect the money supply. Hence the money supply is not only an exogenous controllable item but also an endogenously determined item.

Conclusion. We have discussed above the factors which determine money supply through the creation of bank credit. But money supply and bank credit are indirectly related to each other. When the money supply increases, a part of it is saved in banks depending upon the depositors' propensity to save. These savings become deposits of commercial banks who, in turn, lend after meeting the statutory reserve requirements. Thus with every increase in the money supply, the bank credit goes up. But it may not happen in exactly the same proportion due to the following factors:

(a) The marginal propensity to save does not remain constant. It varies from time to time depending on changes in income levels, prices, and subjective factors.

(b) Banks may also create more or less credit due to the operation of leakages in the credit creation process.

(c) The velocity of circulation of money also affects the money supply. If the velocity of money circulation increases, the bank credit may nor fall even after a decrease in the money supply. The central bank has little control over the velocity of money which may adversely affect bank credit.

HIGH-POWERED MONEY AND THE MONEY MULTIPLIER

The current practice is to explain the determinants of money supply in terms of the monetary base or high-powered money. High -powered money is the sum of commercial bank reserves and currency (notes and coins) held by the public. High-powered money is the base for the expansion of bank deposits and creation of the money supply. The supply of money varies directly with changes in the monetary base, and inversely with the currency and reserve ratios.

The use of high-powered money consists of the demand of commercial banks for the legal limit or required reserves with the central bank and excess reserves and the demand of the public for currency. Thus high-powered money *H=C+RR+ER* where C represents currency, *RR* the required reserves and *ER* the excess reserves.

A commercial bank's required reserves depend upon its deposits. But a bank usually holds reserves in excess of its required reserves. In fact, banks do not advance loans up to the legal limits but precisely less than that. This is to meet unanticipated cash withdrawals or adverse clearing balances. Hence the need arises for maintaining excess reserves by them. The money supply is thus determined by the required reserve ratio and the excess reserve ratio of commercial banks. The required reserve ration (*RRr*) is the ratio of required reserves to to deposits (*RR/D*), and the excess reserve ratio (*ERr*) is the ratio or excess reserves to deposits (*ER/D*).

Currency held by the public is another component of high-powered money. The demand for currency by the public is expressed as a proportion of bank deposits. Thus the currency ratio *Cr=C/D*, where *C* is the currency and *D* deposits. The currency ratio is influenced by such factors as changes in income levels of the people, the use of credit instruments by the public, and uncertainties in economic activity.

The formal relation between money supply and high-powered money can be stated in the form of equations as under:

The money supply (*M*) consists of deposits of commercial banks (*D*) and currency (*C*) held by the public. Thus the supply of money

$$M = D+C \qquad ...(1)$$

High-powered money (*H*) (or monetary base) consists of currency held by the public (*C*) plus required reserves (*RR*) and excess reserves (*ER*) of commercial banks. Thus high-powered money

$$H = C+RR+ER \qquad ...(2)$$

The relation between *M* and *H* can be expressed as the ratio of *M* to *H*. So divide equation (1) by (2):

$$\frac{M}{H} = \frac{D+C}{C+RR+ER} \qquad ...(3)$$

Divide the numerator and denominator of the right hand side of equation (3) by *D*:

$$\frac{M}{H} = \frac{\frac{D}{D}+\frac{C}{D}}{\frac{C}{D}+\frac{RR}{D}+\frac{ER}{D}}$$

or

$$\frac{M}{H} = \frac{1+\frac{C}{D}}{\frac{C}{D}+\frac{RR}{D}+\frac{ER}{D}} \qquad ...(4)$$

By substituting *Cr* for *C/D*, *RRr* for *RR/D* and *ERr* for *ER/D*, equation (4) becomes

$$\frac{M}{H} = \frac{1+Cr}{Cr+RRr+ERr} \qquad ..(5)$$

Thus high-powered money

$$H = \frac{Cr+RRr+ERr}{1+Cr} \times M \qquad ...(6)$$

And money suply

$$M = \frac{1+Cr}{Cr+RRr+ERr} \times H \qquad ..(7)$$

Equation (7) defines money supply in terms of high-powered money. It expresses the money supply in terms of four determinants, *H, Cr, RRr*, and *ERr*. The equation states that the higher the supply of high powered money, the higher the money supply. Further, the lower the currency ratio (*Cr*), the reserve ration (*RRr*), and the excess reserve ratio (*ERr*), the higher the money supply, and vice versa.

The relation between money supply and high-powered money is illustrated in Figure 1. The horizontal curve *Hs* shows the given supply of high-powered money. The curve *Hd* shows the demand for high-powered money associated with each level of money supply and represents equation (6). The slope of the *Hd* curve is equal to the term (*Cr+RRr+ERr*)/(1+*Cr*). Given *Cr, RRr, Err* and the high-powered money Hs, the equilibrium money supply is *OM*. If the money supply is larger than this, say OM_1, there will be excess demand for high-powered money. On the contrary, a less than *OM* money supply will mean less demand for high-powered money.

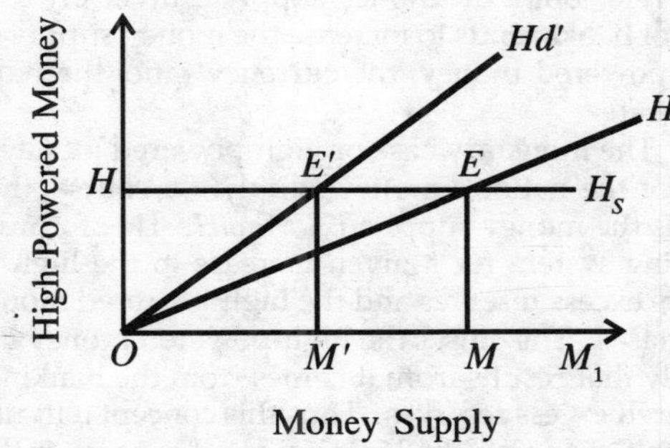

Fig. 1

If there is an increase in any one of the ratios *Cr* or *RRr* or *ERr*, there would be an increase in the demand for high-powered money. This is shown by the *Hd'* curve in Figure 1 where the increase in the demand for high-powered money leads to decline in the money supply to *OM'*. The quotient of equation (7) is the money multiplier *m*. Thus

$$m = \frac{1+Cr}{CR+RRr+ERr} \qquad ...(8)$$

Now the relation between money supply and high-powered money of equation (7) becomes

$$M = mH \qquad ...(9)$$

Equation (9) expresses money supply as a function of m and *H*. In other words, the money supply is determined by high powered money (*H*) and the money multiplier (*m*). The size of the money multiplier is determined by the currency ratio (*Cr*) of the public, the required reserve ratio (*RRr*) at the central bank, and the excess reserve ratio (*ERr*) of commercial banks. The lower these ratios are, the larger the money multiplier is. If *m* is fairly stable, the central bank can manipulate the money supply (*M*) by manipulating *H*. The central bank can do so by open market operations. But the stability of *m* depends upon the stability of the currency ratio and the reserve ratios *RRr* and *ERr*. Or, it depends upon off-setting changes in *RRr* and *ERr* ratios. Since these ratios and currency with the public are liable to change, the money multiplier is quite volatile in the short run.

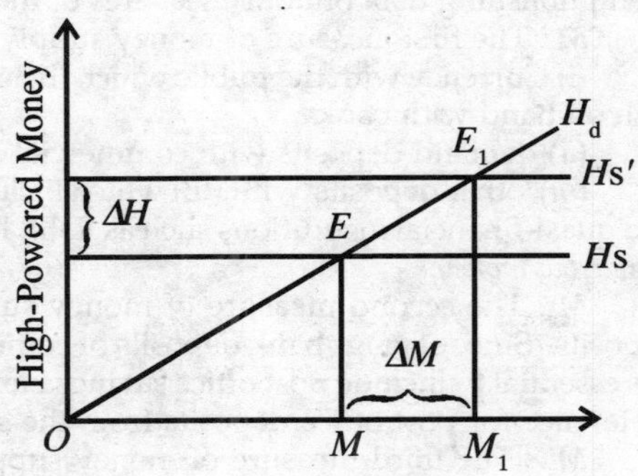

Fig. 2

Given the division of high-powered money between currency held by the public, the required reserves at the central bank, and the excess reserves of commercial banks, the money supply varies inversely with *Cr, RRr* and *ERr*. But the supply of money varies directly with changes in the high-powered money. This is shown in Figure 2. An increase in the supply of high-powered money by ΔH shifts the *Hs* curve upward to *Hs'*. At *E*, the demand and supply of high-powered money are in equilibrium and money supply is *OM*. With the increase in the supply of high-powered money to *Hs'*, the supply of money also increases to OM_1 at the new equilibrium point E_1. Further, Figure 2 reveals the operation of the money multiplier. With the increase in the high-powered money by ΔH, the money supply increases by ΔM. An increase in the high-powered money by Re 1 increases by a multiple of Re 1.

Some economists do not take into consideration excess reserves in determining high-powered money and consequently the money supply. But the monetarists give more importance to excess reserves. According to them, due to uncertainties prevailing in banking operations as in business, banks always keep excess reserves. The amount of excess reserves depends upon the interaction of two types of costs: the cost of holding excess reserves, and the cost generated by deficiency in excess reserves. The first cost is in terms of the market rate of interest at which excess reserves are maintained. The second cost in in terms of the bank rate which is a sort.of penalty to be paid to the central bank for failure to maintain the legal required reserve ratio by the commercial bank. The excess reserve ratio varies inversely with the market rate of interest and direcly with the bank rate. Since the money supply is inversely related to the excess reserve ratio, decline in the excess reserve ratio of banks tends to increase the money supply and vice versa. Thus the money supply is determined by the high-powered money, the currency ratio, the required reserve ratio and the market rate of interest and the bank rate.

The monetary base or high-powered money is directly controllable by the central bank. It is the ultimate base of the nation's money supply. Of course, the money multiplier times the high-powered money always equals the money supply, *i.e.* $M=mH$. This formulation tells us how much new money will be created by the banking system for a given increase in the high-powered money. The monetary policy of the central bank affects excess reserves and the high-powered money identically. Suppose the central bank makes open market purchases. This raises the high-powered money in the form of excess reserves of banks. An increase in money supply that results from it comes from the banking system which creates new money on the baiss of its newly acquired excess reserves. Thus this concept tells us that the monetary authorities can control the money supply through changing the high-powered money or the money multiplier.

MEASURES OF MONEY SUPPLY IN INDIA

There are four measures of money supply in India which are denoted by M_1, M_2, M_3, and M_4. This classification was introduced by the Reserve Bank of India (RBI) in April 1977. Prior to this till March 1968, RBI published only one measure of the money supply, *M* or M_1, defined as currency and demand deposits with the public. This was in keeping with the traditional and Keynesian views of the narrow measure of the money supply. From April 1968, RBI also started publishing another measure of the money supply which it called Aggregate Monetary Resources (AMR). This included M_1 *plus* time deposits of banks held by the public. This was a broad measure of money supply which was in line with Friedman's view. But since April 1977, RBI has been publishing data on four measures of the money supply which are discussed as under:

M_1. The first measure of money supply is M_1 which consists of :

(*i*) Currency with the public which includes notes and coins of all denominations in circulation excluding cash on hand with banks:

(*ii*) demand deposits with commercial and cooperative banks, excluding inter-bank deposits; and

(*iii*) 'other deposits' with RBI which include current deposits of foreign central banks, financial institutions and quasi-financial institutions such as IDBI, IFCI, etc, other than of banks, IMF, IBRD, etc. RBI characterises M_1 as *narrow money*.

M_2. The second measure of money supply is M_2 which consists of M_1 *plus* post office savings bank deposits. Since savings bank deposits of commercial and cooperative banks are included in the money supply, it is essential to include post office savings bank deposits. The majority of people in rural and urban India have preference for post office deposits from the safety viewpoint than bank deposits.

M_3. The third measure of money supply in India is M_3 which consists of M_1 *plus* time deposits with commercial and cooperative banks, excluding inter-bank time deposits. RBI calls M_3 as *broad money*.

M_4. The fourth measure of money supply is M_4 which consists of M_3 *plus* total post office deposits comprising time deposits and demand deposits as well. This is the *broadest* measure of money supply.

Of the four inter-related measures of money supply for which RBI publishes data, it is M_3 which is of special significance. It is M_3 which is taken into account in formulating macroeconomic objectives of the economy every year. Since M_1 is narrow money and includes only demand deposits of banks alongwith currency held by the public, it overlooks the importance of time deposits in policy making. That is why, RBI prefers M_3 which includes total deposits of banks and currency with the public in credit budgeting for its credit policy. It is on the estimates of increase in M_3 that the effects of money supply on prices and growth of national income are estimated. In fact M_3 is an empirical measure of money supply in India, as is the practice in developed countries. The Chakravarty Committee also recommended the use of M_3 for monetary targeting without any reason.

MONEY SUPPLY AND LIQUIDITY

Of the four measures of money supply in India, M_1 which consists of currency with the public and demand deposits with commercial and cooperative banks, is the most liquid form of money. Currency consists of notes, rupee coins, two rupee coins, five rupee coins and small coins, and cash on hand with banks, are the most liquid assets. Demand deposits are savings bank accounts and current accounts in banks from which depositors can withdraw cheques by any amount lying in their accounts. Thus like currency, demand deposits are the most liquid and possess the medium of exchange function of money.

A liquid asset is one which is easily spendable, and transferable at face value anywhere and at any time. It can be turned into the generally acceptable medium of exchange quickly without any risk of loss. The phrase 'without risk of loss' refers to the currency unit (Rs, $ or £) and not to real purchasing power. Government bonds, time deposits (also known as savings deposits which are different from savings bank deposits), shares, real estate, etc. are 'frozen' assets which can be sold or exchanged for money on short notice only. They are thus less liquid than money.

M_2 consists of M_1 *plus* post office savings bank deposits. In India, the majority of people in rural and urban areas prefer to keep their cash in post office savings bank deposits from the safety viewpoint because they think that post offices are government owned and mananged. With the nationalisation of 20 commercial banks and opening of their branches in almost all rural areas of the country, the distinction between post office savings bank deposits and commercial savings bank deposits has disappeared. Still the majority of rual people being illiterate, they prefer post offices to banks even by force of habit.

The inclusion of post office savings bank deposits in M_1 is meant to measure the increase in total money supply which affects the evonomy. But post office savings bank deposits are less liquid than currency and demand deposits because they cannot be easily withdrawn. There are no chequing facilities in post offices, except in metropolitan cities and that too in main post offices. The depositors have to undergo a cumbersome process of cash withdrawals in post offices. M_3 includes M_1 plus time deposits (also known as savings deposits in developed countries) with commercial banks and cooperative banks. This is broad money which stresses the store of value function of money alongwith the medium of exchange function. Time deposits with banks are less liquid than currency and demand deposits because they are held for a fixed time period at a fixed rate of interest. The total money deposited in this account can be withdrawn before the expiry of full period by paying a penal interest rate to the bank. So time deposits do possess liquidity but less than demand deposits.

The fourth measure of money supply is M_4 which includes M_3 *plus* total post office deposits comprising time deposits and savings bank deposits. They tend to increase the money supply in the country manifold. But these total post office deposits are less liquid than total bank deposits for the reasons already given in the case of M_2.

If deposits with non-bank financial institutions such as mutual savings banks, building societies, insurance companies, loan associations and other credit and financial institutions are also included alongwith total post office deposits in M_3, the total money supply would be many times more than what is ordinarily defined as M_1. And if such assets as shares, bonds, government securities, etc. are also included in the supply of money, it would be difficult to measure the money stock in the country.

Taking all such assets vis-a-vis money, they differ in the degree of liquidity. Since *currency* is easily spendable and transferable, and has more stability in value, it possesses the highest degree of liquidity. *Demand deposits* of banks are also as liquid as currency because they are chequing accounts and easily serve as medium of exchange. But demand deposits of post offices do not possess the same degree of liquidity as bank deposits. *Time deposits* of banks, post offices and of other non-bank financial institutions are less liquid than demand deposits because they cannot be easily tranferred to depositors in the form of cash and spent. They serve more as a store of value. So far as *shares* of corporations are concerned, they are also less liquid because they take more time to be sold and transferred. They involve cost in the act of tranferability in the form of brokerage or commission. They cannot be easily converted into cash and spent. Hence they possess less liquidity than demand deposits. *Bonds* of companies also possess less liquidity because they can be converted into cash after the expiry of the bond maturity period. But they are transferable and earn higher interest return. *Government securities* are issued in the name of initial purchasers and, as such, are non-marketable, because they cannot be sold to someone else. So they are not liquid. On the other hand, money market mutual fund shares, post office savings bonds and national savings certificates possess the advantage of being cashable though they are also non-transferable. They can be returned for repayment of principal plus a fixed amount interest after a short waiting period before the actual maturity date. They are thus as liquid as fixed deposits of banks and post offices.

It is on account these reasons that economists prefer M_1 as the measure of money supply because among all the assets, currency and demand deposits possess the highest degree of liquidity. However, for practical purposes in policy formulation and for empirical studies, governments and researchers use M_3 as the measure of money supply which is less liquid than M_2.

But *how does a change in money supply affect liquidity* ? A change in the money supply affects liquidity by bringing changes or readjustments in the portfolio holdings of the assets of the people. This depends on the effect of money supply on aggregate spending. If people decide to spend the increased money supply in purchasing such assets as shares and debentures, there will be less money available in liquid form with the public. If the stock market is bullish, people may convert assets in their portfolios in buying more shares. On the other hand, if there is uncertainty in the stock market , people may hold the increased money supply in bank deposits or invest it in real estate if they expect property prices to rise. But it is the monetary authority that influences money supply in the economy by following "easy" or "tight" monetary policy. It does so by controlling aggregate spending and thereby influencing business activity, output and employment. But the monetary authority is not always successful in controlling spending by increasing or decreasing the money supply and hence liquidity. This is because the central bank has little control over the velocity of circulation of money, non-bank financial intermediaries, business expectations, time lags in monetary policy, etc. It is, therefore, very difficult to predict the effects of changes in money supply on liquidity.

DERIVATION OF MONEY MULTIPLIERS

We have explained above the derivation of the money multiplier and its relation with high-powered money. But the total money supply is usually measured not in terms of M but as M_1, M_2, and M_3. Therefore, the derivation of money multipliers of these three measures M_1, M_2, and M_3 of the total money supply and the relation of each with the high powered money are shown below in the form of equations.

First, Take M_1. In M_1 measure of money supply are included the demand deposits of commercial banks (D) and currency with the public (C). Thus money supply

$$M_1 = D+C \qquad ...(1)$$

In the high-powered money (or monetary base) are included the required reserves of commercial banks (RR) *plus* currency with the public (C). Thus high-powered money

$$H = RR+C \qquad ...(2)$$

By dividing equation (1) by equation (2), the ratio of M_1 to H can be expressed as

$$\frac{M_1}{H} = \frac{D+C}{RR+C}$$

Dividing the right hand side of the above equation by D,

$$\frac{M_1}{H} = \frac{\frac{D}{D}+\frac{C}{D}}{\frac{RR}{D}+\frac{C}{D}}$$

or $$\frac{M_1}{H} = \frac{1+\frac{C}{D}}{\frac{RR}{D}+\frac{C}{D}}$$

By substituting *Cr* for *C/D* and *Rr* for *RR/D*, the equation becomes

$$\frac{M_1}{H} = \frac{1+Cr}{Rr+Cr}$$

$$m_1 = \frac{1+Cr}{Rr+Cr} \times H$$

The higher the value of m_1 multiplier, the lower will be the reserve ratio (*Rr*) and currency-deposit ratio (*Cr*).

Take M_2, defined as M_1 *plus* time deposits (*TD*). Thus

$$M_2 = D + C + TD \qquad ....(3)$$

In high-powered money are included required reserves (*RR*), the excess reserves of commercial banks (*ER*) *plus* currency held by the public (*C*). So

$$H = RR + Er + C \qquad ...(4)$$

In order to find out the ratio of M_2 to *H*, divide equation (3) by equation (4),

$$\frac{M_2}{H} = \frac{D+C+TD}{RR+ER+C}$$

Dividing the right hand side of the above equation by *D*,

$$\frac{M_2}{H} = \frac{\frac{D}{D}+\frac{C}{D}+\frac{TD}{D}}{\frac{RR}{D}+\frac{ER}{D}+\frac{C}{D}}$$

By substituting *Cr* for *C/D*, *Td* for *TD/D*, *RRr* for *RR/D* and *Er* for *ER/D*,

$$\frac{M_2}{H} = \frac{1+Cr+Td}{Rr+Er+Cr}$$

Or $$m_2 = \frac{1+Cr+Td}{Rr+Er+Cr} \times H$$

The value of m_2 multiplier is higher than that of m_1 multiplier because it leads to greater increase in the monetary base (*H*). The higher the value of m_2 multiplier, the lower will be the rates of *Cr*, *Rr* and *Er*.

Take M_3 which includes M_2 *plus* deposits of non-bank financial institutions (*Dn*) and a portion of deposits of these institutions which remains with banks (*Rp*). Thus the deposits of these institutions are taken as *RpDn* which are related to the reserve ratio of commercial banks (*Rr*). Thus

$$M_3 = D + RpDn + Dn + Cr\,(D+Dn) \qquad ...(5)$$

And the monetary base will be determined as :

$$H = Rr\,(D+RpDn) + Cr(D+Dn) \qquad ...(6)$$

$$Rr = RR/D \text{ or } R = Rr\,(D)$$

$$Cr = C/D \text{ or } C = Cr\,(D)$$

To find out the ratio of M_3 and *H*, divide equation (5) by equation (6),

$$\frac{M_3}{H} = \frac{D+RpDn+Dn+Cr(D+Dn)}{Rr(D+RpDn)+Cr(D+Dn)}$$

Or $$\frac{M_3}{H} = \frac{D + Dn(Rp + 1) + Cr(D + Dn)}{Rr(D + RpDn) + Cr(D + Dn)}$$

Dividing the right hand side of the above equation by D.

$$\frac{M_3}{H} = \frac{1 + \frac{Dn}{D}(Rp + 1) + Cr\left(1 + \frac{Dn}{D}\right.}{Rr\left(1 + Rp\frac{Dn}{D}\right. + Cr\left(1 + \frac{Dn}{D}\right.}$$

$$= \frac{1 + \frac{Dn}{D}Rp + \frac{Dn}{D} + Cr + Cr \times \frac{Dn}{D}}{Rr + Rr.Rp.\frac{Dn}{D} + Cr \times \frac{Dn}{D}}$$

$$= \frac{1 + Cr + \frac{Dn}{D}.Rp + \frac{Dn}{D} + Cr \times \frac{Dn}{D}}{Rr + Cr + Rr.Rp.\frac{Dn}{D} + Cr \times \frac{Dn}{D}}$$

$$= \frac{1 + Cr + \frac{Dn}{D}(Rp + 1 + Cr}{Rr + Cr + \frac{Dn}{D}(Rp + 1 + Cr}$$

By substituting d for Dn/D, the equation becomes

$$\frac{M_3}{H} = \frac{1 + Cr + (1 + Rp + Cr)d}{Rr + Cr + (Rr.Rp + Cr)d}$$

Or $$m_3 = \frac{1 + Cr + (1 + Rp + Cr)d}{Rr + Cr + (Rr.Rp + Cr)d} \times \mathrm{H}$$

where m_3 is the money multiplier whose valve is higher than m_2 multiplier.

EXERCISES

1. Explain the various components of the money supply.
2. Discuss the determinants of the money supply. Should time deposits be included under the supply of money ?
3. Discuss the various measures of the money supply adopted by the Reserve Bank of India. How do they differ from those adopted by developed countries?
4. Of the various measures of money supply which possess more liquidity and why?
5. Explain the determinants of high-powered money.
6. Discuss the relation between money supply and high-powered money.
7. Write a note on the money multiplier.

CHAPTER 17

The Demand of Money

INTRODUCTION

The demand for money arises from two important functions of money. The first is that money acts as a medium of exchange and the second is that it is a store of value. Thus individuals and businesses wish to hold money partly in cash and partly in the form of assets.

What explains changes in the demand for money ? There are two views on this issue. The first is the "scale" view which is related to the impact of the income or wealth level upon the demand for money. The demand for money is directly related to the income level. The higher the income level, the greater will be the demand for money. The second is the "substitution" view which is related to relative attractiveness of assets that can be substituted for money. According to this view, when alternative assets like bonds become unattractive due to fall in interest rates, people prefer to keep their assets in cash, and the demand for money increases, and vice versa. The scale and substitution view combined together have been used to explain the nature of the demand for money which has been split into the transactions demand, the precautionary demand and the speculative demand. There are three approaches to the demand for money: the classical, the Keynesian, and the post-Keynesian.[1] We discuss these approaches below.

THE CLASSICAL APPROACH

The classical economists did not explicitly formulate demand for money theory but their views are inherent in the quantity theory of money. They emphasized the transactions demand for money in terms of the velocity of circulation of money. This is because money acts as a medium of exchange and facilitates the exchange of goods and services. In Fisher's "Equation of Exchnage",

$$MV = PT$$

where M is the total quantity of money, V is its velocity of circulation, P is the price level, and T is the total amount of goods and services exchanged for money.

The right hand side of this equation PT represents the demand for money which, in fact, "depends upon the value of the transactions to be undertaken in the economy, and is equal to a constant fraction of those transactions." MV represents the supply of money which is given and in equilibrium equals the demand for money. Thus the equation becomes

$$MV = PT$$

This transactions demand for money, in turn, is determined by the level of full employment income. This is because the classicists believed in Say's Law whereby supply created its own demand, assuming the full employment level of income. Thus the demand for money in Fisher's approach is a constant proportion of the

1. David E.W. Laidler, *The Demand for Money: Theories and Evidence*, 1972, Part Two.

level of transactions, which in turn, bears a constant relationship to the level of national income. Further, the demand for money is linked to the volume of trade going on in an economy at any time. Thus its underlying assumption is that people hold money to buy goods.

But people also hold money for other reasons, such as to earn interest and to provide against unforeseen events. It is, therefore, not possible to say that V will remain constant when M is changed. The most important thing about money in Fisher's theory is that it is transferable. But it does not explain fully why people hold money. It does not clarify whether to include as money such items as time deposits or savings deposits that are not immediately available to pay debts without first being converted into currency.

It was the Cambridge cash balances approach which raised a further question: Why do people actually want to hold their assets in the form of money ? With larger incomes, people want to make larger volumes of transactions and that larger cash balances will, therefore, be demanded.

The Cambridge demand equation for money is

$$Md = kPY$$

where Md is the demand for money which must equal the supply of money (Md=Ms) in equilibrium in the economy. k is the fraction of the real money income (PY) which people wish to hold in cash and demand deposits or the ratio of money stock to income, P is the price level, and Y is the aggregate real income. This equation tells us that "other things being equal, the demand for money in normal terms would be proportional to the nominal level of income for each individual, and hence for the aggregate economy as well."

Its Critical Evaluation

This approach includes time and saving deposits and other convertible funds in the demand for money. It also stresses the importance of factors that make money more or less useful, such as the costs of holding it, uncertainty about the future and so on. But it says little about the nature of the relationship that one expects to prevail between its variables, and it does not say too much about which ones might be important.

One of its major criticisms arises from the neglect of store of value function of money. The classicists emphasized only the medium of exchange function of money which simply acted as a go-between to facilitate buying and selling. For them, money performed a *neutral* role in the economy. It was barren and would not multiply, if stored in the form of wealth. This was an erroneous view because money performed the "asset" function when it is transformed into other forms of assets like bills, equities, debentures, real assets (houses, cars, TVs, and so on), etc. Thus the neglect of the asset function of money was the major weakness of the classical approach to the demand for money which Keynes remedied.

THE KEYNESIAN APPROACH : LIQUIDITY PREFERENCE

Keynes in his *General Theory* used a new term "liquidity preference" for the demand for money. Keynes suggested three motives which led to the demand for money in an economy:(1) the transactions demand, (2) the precautionary demand, and (3) the speculative demand.

The Transactions Demand for Money

The transactions demand for money arises from the medium of exchange function of money in making regular payments for goods and services. According to Keynes, it relates to "the need of cash for the current transactions of personal and business exchange." It is further divided into income and business motives. The *income motive* is meant "to bridge the interval between the receipt of income and its disbursement." Similarly, the *business motive* is meant "to bridge the interval between the time of incurring business costs and that of the receipt of the sale proceeds." If the time between the incurring of expenditure and receipt of income is small, less cash will be held by the people for current transactions, and vice versa. There will, however, be changes in the transactions demand for money depending upon the expectations of income recipients and businessmen. They depend upon the level of income, the interest rate, the business turnover, the normal period between the receipt and disbursement of income, etc.

Given these factors, the transactions demand for money is a *direct proportional* and *positive function* of the level of income, and is expressed as

$$L_T = kY$$

where L_T is the transactions demand for money, k is the proportion of income which is kept for transactions purposes, and Y is the income.

This equation is illustrated in Figure 1 where the line kY represents a linear and proportional relation between transactions demand and the level of income. Assuming $k=1/4$ and income Rs 1000 crores, the demand for transactions balances would be Rs 250 crores, at point A. With the increase in income to Rs 1200 crores, the transactions demand would be Rs 300 crores at point B on the curve kY. If the transactions demand falls due to a change in the institutional and structural conditions of the economy, the value of k is reduced to say, 1/5, and the new transactions demand curve is $k'Y$. It shows that for income of Rs 1000 and 1200 crores, transactions balances would be Rs 200 and 240 crores at points C and D respectively in the figure. "Thus we conclude that the chief determinant of changes in the actual amount of the transactions balances held is changes in income. Changes in the transactions balances are the result of movements along a line like kY rather than changes in the slope of the line. In the equation, changes in transactions balances are the result of changes in Y rather than changes in k."[3]

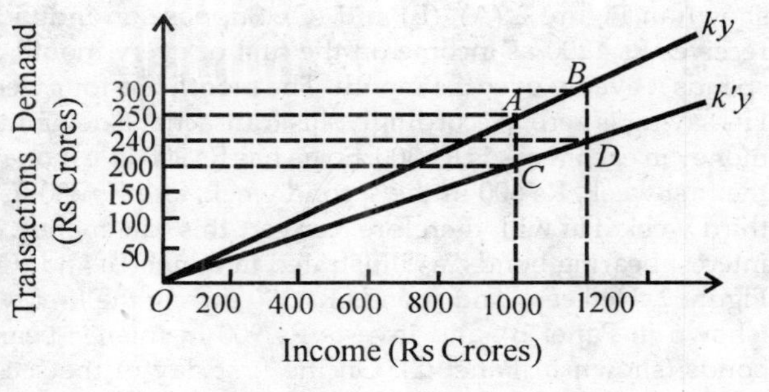

Fig. 1

Interest Rate and Transactions Demand. Regarding the rate of interest as the determinant of the transactions demand for money, Keynes made the L_T function *interest inelastic*. But he pointed out that the "demand for money in the active circulation is also to some extent a function of the rate of interest, since a higher rate of interest may lead to a more economical use of active balances."[4] "However, he did not stress the role of the rate of interest in this part of his analysis, and many of his popularizers ignored it altogether."[5] Two post-Keynesian economists William J. Baumol[6] and James Tobin[7] have shown that the rate of interst is an important determinant of transactions demand for money. The have also pointed out that the relationship between transactions demand for money and income is not linear and proportional. Rather, changes in income lead to proportionately smaller changes in transactions demand.

Transactions balances are held because income received once a month is not spent on the same day. In fact, an individual spreads his expenditure evenly over the month. Thus a portion of money meant for transactions purposes can be spent on short-term interest-yielding securities. It is possible to "put funds to work for a matter of days, weeks, or months in interest-bearing securities such as U.S. Treasury bills or commercial paper and other short-term money market instruments. The problem here is that there is a cost involved in buying and selling. One must weigh the financial cost and inconvenience of frequent entry to and exit from the market for securities against the apparent advantage of holding interest-bearing securities in place of idle transactions balances. Among other things, the cost per purchase and sale, the rate of interest, and the frequency of purchases and sales determine the profitability of switching from ideal transactions balances to earning assets. Nonetheless, with the cost per purchase and sale given, there is clearly some rate of interest at which it becomes profitable to switch what otherwise would be transactions balances into interest-bearing

---

3. Edward Shapiro, *op. cit.*, pp. 367-68.
4. J.M.Keynes in A.D. Gayer (ed.), *The Lessons of Monetary Experience*, 1937, p. 149.
5. David E.W.Laidler, *op. cit.*, p. 52.
6. William J.Baumol, "Transactions Demand for Cash--An Inventory Theoretic Approach", *Quarterly Journal of Economics*, November 1952.
7. James Tobin, "The Interest Elasticity of the Transactions Demand for Cash", *Review of Economics and Statistics*, August 1956.

securities, even if the period for which these funds may be spared from transactions needs is measured only in weeks. The higher the interest rate, the larger will be the fraction of any given amount of transactions balances that can be profitably diverted into securities."[8]

The structure of cash and short-term bond holdings is shown in Figure 2 (A), (B) and (C). Suppose an individual receives Rs 1200 as income on the first of every month and spends it evenly over the month. The month has four weeks. His saving is zero. Accordingly, his transactions demand for money in each week is Rs 300. So he has Rs 900 idle money in the first week, Rs 600 in the second week, and Rs 300 in the third week. He will, therefore, convert this idle money into interest-bearing bonds, as illustrated in Panel (B) and (C) of Figure 2. He keeps and spends Rs 300 during the first week (shown in Panel B), and invests Rs 900 in interest-bearing bonds (shown in Panel C). On the first day of the second week, he sells bonds worth Rs. 300 to cover cash transactions of the second week and his bond holdings are reduced to Rs 600. Similarly, he will sell bonds worth Rs 300 in the beginning of the third week and keep the remaining bonds amounting to Rs 300 which he will sell on the first day of the fourth week to meet his expenses for the last week of the month. The amount of cash held for transactions purposes by the individual during each week is shown in saw-tooth pattern in Panel (B), and the bond holdings in each week are shown in blocks in Panel (C) of Figure 2.

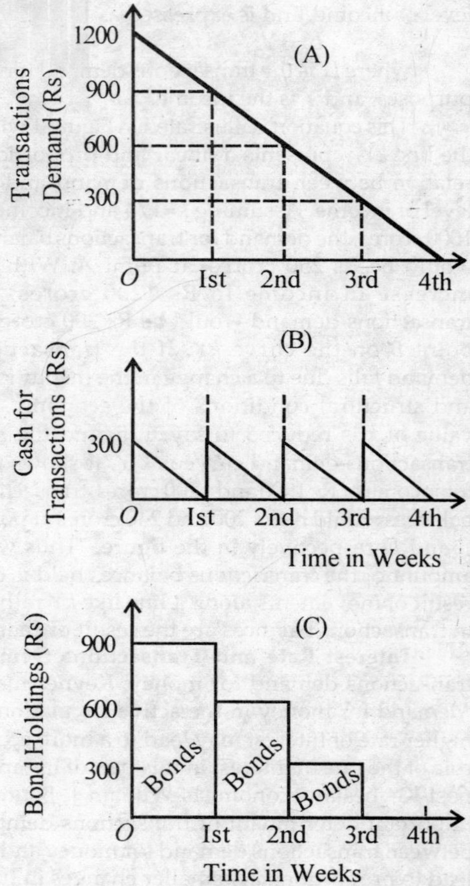

Fig. 2

The modern view is that the transactions demand for money is a function of both income and interest rates which can be expressed as

$$L_T = f(Y, r).$$

This relationship between income and interest rate and the transactions demand for money for the economy as a whole is illustrated in Figure 3. We saw above that $L_T = kY$. If Y=Rs 1200 crores and k=1/4, then L_T=Rs 300 crores.

This is shown as Y_1 curve in Figure 3. If the income level rises to Rs 1600 crores, the transactions demand also increases to Rs 400 crores, given k=1/4. Consequently, the transactions demand curve shifts to Y_2. The transactions demand curves Y_1 and Y_2 are interest-inelastic so long as the rate of interest does not rise above r_8 per cent. As the rate of interest starts rising above r_8, the transactions demand for money becomes interest elastic. It indicates that "given the cost of switching into and out of securities, an interest rate above 8 per cent is sufficiently high to attract some amount of transactions balances into securities." The backward slope of the Y_1 curve shows that at still higher rates, the transaction demand for money declines. Thus when the rate of interest rises to r_{12}, the transactions demand declines to Rs 250 crores with an income level of Rs 1200 crores. Similarly, when the national income is Rs 1600 crores, the transactions demand would decline to Rs 350 crores

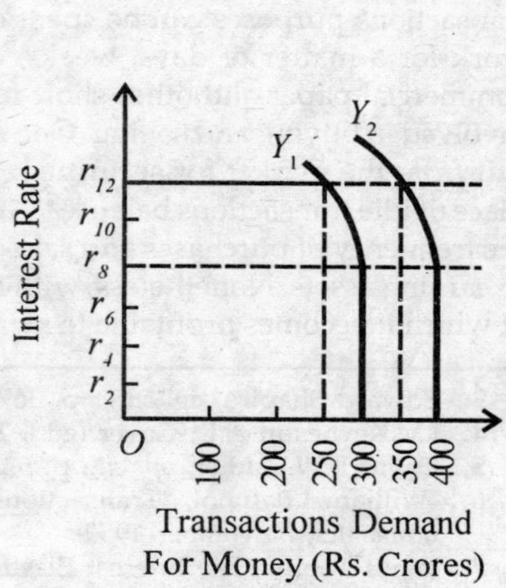

Fig. 3

8. Edward Shapiro, *op, cit.*, pp. 368-69.

at r_{12} interest rate. Thus the transactions demand for money varies *directly* with the level of income and *inversely* with the rate of interest.

The Precautionary Demand for Money

The precautionary motive relates to "the desire to provide for contingencies requiring sudden expenditures and for unforeseen opportunities of advantageous purchases." Both individuals and businessmen keep cash in reserve to meet unexpected needs. Individuals hold some cash to provide for illness, accidents, unemployment and other unforeseen contingencies. Similarly, businessmen keep cash in reserve to tide over unfavourable conditions or to gain from unexpected deals. Therefore, "money held under the precautionary motive is rather like water kept in reserve in a water tank." The precautionary demand for money depends upon the level of income, business activities, opportunities for unexpected profitable deals, availability of cash, the cost of holding liquid assets in bank reserves, etc.

Keynes held that the precautionary demand for money, like transactions demand, was a function of the level of income. But the post-Keynesian economists believe that like transactions demand, it is inversely related to high interest rates. The transactions and precautionary demand for money will be unstable, particularly if the economy is not at full employment level and transactions are, therefore, less than the maximum, and are liable to fluctuate up or down. Since precuationary demand, like transactions demand is a function of income and interest rates, the demand for money for these two purposes is expressed in the single equation $LT = f(Y,r)$.[9] Thus the precautionary demand for money can also be explained diagrammatically in terms of Figures 2 and 3.

The Speculative Demand for Money

The speculative (or asset or liquidity preference) demand for money is "for securing profit from knowing better than the market what the future will bring forth".Individuals and businessmen having funds, after keeping enough for transactions and precautionary purposes, like to make a speculative gain by investing in bonds. Money held for speculative purposes is a liquid store of value which can be invested at an opportune moment in interest-bearing bonds or securities.

Bond prices and the rate of interest are *inversely* related to each other. Low bond prices are indicative of high interest rates, and high bond prices reflect low interest rates. A bond carries a fixed rate of interest. For instance, if a bond of the value of Rs 100 carries 4 per cent interest and the market rate of interest rises to 8 per cent, the value of this bond falls to Rs 50 in the market. If the market rate of interest falls to 2 per cent, the value of the bond will rise to Rs 200 in the market.

This can be worked out with the help of the equation[10]

$$V = \frac{R}{r}$$

where V is the current market value of a bond, R is the annual return on the bond, and r is the rate of return currently earned or the market rate of interest. So a bond worth Rs 100 (V) and carrying a 4 per cent rate of interest (r), gets an annual return (R) of Rs 4, that is, V=Rs 4/0.04=Rs100. When the market rate of interest rises to 8 per cent, then V=Rs 4/0.08=Rs50; when it falls to 2 per cent, then V=Rs 4/0.02=Rs 200.

Thus individuals and businessmen can gain by buying bonds worth Rs 100 each at the market price of Rs 50 each when the rate of interest is high (8 per cent), and sell them again when they are dearer (Rs 200 each when the rate of interest falls (to 2 per cent).

According to Keynes, it is expectations about changes in bond prices or in the current market rate of interest that determine the speculative demand for money. In explaining the speculative demand for money, Keynes had a normal or critical rate of interest (r_c) in mind. If the current rate of interest (r) is above the "critical" rate of interest, businessmen expect it to fall and bond prices to rise. They will, therefore, buy bonds to sell them in future when their prices rise in order to gain thereby. At such times, the speculative demand for money

9. Keynes expressed the amount held under these two motives (M_1) as a function (L_1) of the level of income (Y), M_1=L_1(Y). By making it a function of interest rate (r), it can be written as $M_1 = L_1(Y,r)$.
10. Edward shapiro, *op.cit.*, p. 372

would fall. Conversely, if the current rate of interest happens to be below the critical rate, businessmen expect it to rise and bond prices to fall. They will, therefore, sell bonds in the present if they have any, and the speculative demand for money would increase. Thus when $r>r_c$, an investor holds all his liquid assets in bonds, and when $r<r_c$ his entire holdings go into money. But when $r = r_c$, he becomes indifferent to hold bonds or money.

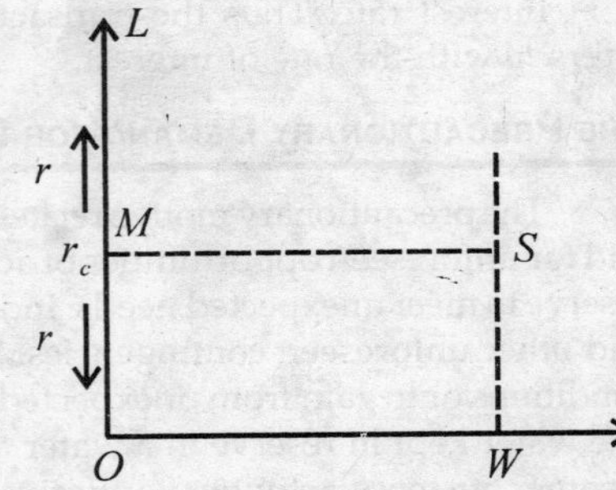

Speculative Demand for Money

Fig. 4

This relationship between an individual's demand for money and the rate of interest is shown in Figure 4 where the horizontal axis shows the individual's demand for money for speculative purposes and the current and critical interest rates on the vertical axis. The figure shows that when r is greater than r_c, the asset holder puts all his cash balances in bonds and his demand for money is zero. This is illustrated by the *LM* portion of the vertical axis. When r falls below r_c, the individual expects more capital losses on bonds as against the interest yield. He, therefore, converts his entire holdings into money, as shown by *OW* in the figure. This relationship between an individual asset holder's demand for money and the current rate of interest gives the discontinuous step demand for money curve *LMSW*.

For the economy as a whole the individual demand curve can be aggregated on this presumption that individual asset-holders differ in their critical rates r_c. It is a smooth curve which slopes downward from left to right, as shown in Figure 5.

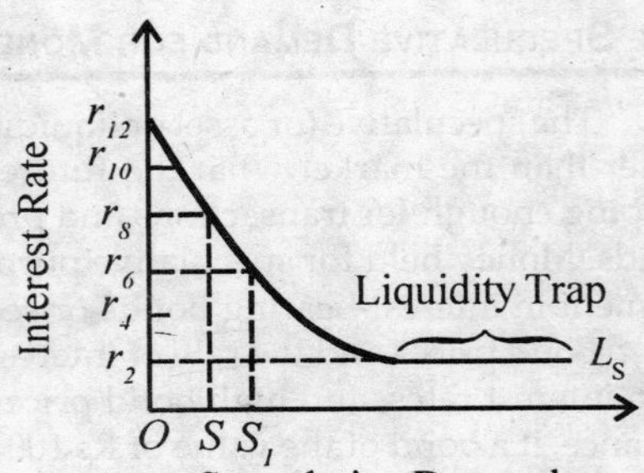

Speculative Demand for Money

Fig. 5

Thus the speculative demand for money is a decreasing function of the rate of interest. The higher the rate of interest, the lower the speculative demand for moeny, and the lower the rate of interest, the higher the speculative demand for money. It can be expressed algebraically as $Ls = f(r)$, where Ls is the speculative demand for money and r is the rate of interest.[11] Geometrically, it is shows in Figure 5. The figure shows that at a very high rate of interest r_{12}, the speculative demand for money is zero and businessmen invest their cash holdings in bonds because they believe that the interest rate cannot rise further. As the rate of interest falls to say, r_8 the speculative demand for money is *OS*. With a further fall in the interest rate to r_6, it rises to OS_1. But at a very low rate of interest r_2, the L_S curve becomes perfectly elastic. This is know as the *liquidity trap* when people prefer to keep money in cash rather than invest in bonds and the speculative demand for money is infinitely elastic. Thus the shape of the *Ls* curve[12] shows that as the interest rate rises, the speculative demand for money declines, and with the fall in the interest rate, it increases. Thus the Keynesian speculative demand for money function is highly volatile, depending upon the behaviour of interest rates.

Liquidity Trap

Keynes visualised conditions in which the speculative demand for money would be highly or even totally elastic so that changes in the quantity of money would be fully absorbed into speculative balances. This is the famous Keynesian *liquidity trap*. In this case, changes in the quantity of money have no effects at all on prices or income. According to Keynes, this is likely to happen when the market interest rate is very low so that yields on bonds, equities and other securities will also be low.

11. Keynes expressed it as $M_2=L_2(r)$
12. This is also known as the liquidity preference curve, *LP*.

At a very low rate of interest, such as r_2, in Figure 5, the *Ls* curve becomes *perfectly elastic* and the speculative demand for money is infinitely elastic. This portion of the *Ls* curve is known as the liquidity trap. At such a low rate, people prefer to keep money in cash rather than invest in bonds because purchasing bonds will mean a definite loss. People will not buy bonds so long as the interest rate remains at the low level and they will be waiting for the rate of interest to return to the "normal" level and bond prices to fall.[13]

According to Keynes, as the rate of interest approaches zero, the risk of loss in holding bonds becomes greater. "When the price of bonds has been bid up so high that the rate of interest is, say, only 2 per cent or less, a very small decline in the price of bonds will wipe out the yield entirely and a slightly further decline would result in loss of the part of the principal." Thus the lower the interest rate, the smaller the earnings from bonds. Therefore, the greater the demand for cash holdings. Consequently, the *Ls* curve will become perfectly elastic.

Further, according to Keynes, "a long-term rate of interest of 2 per cent leaves more to fear than to hope, and offers, at the same time, a running yield which is only sufficient to offset a very small measure of fear." This makes the *Ls* curve "virtually absolute in the sense that almost everybody prefers cash to holding a debt which yields so low a rate of interest."

Prof. Modigliani believes that an infinitely elastic *Ls* curve is possible in a period of great uncertainty when price reductions are anticipated and the tendency to invest in bonds decreases, or if there prevails "a real scarcity of investment outlets that are profitable at rates of interest higher than the institutional minimum."[14]

The phenomenon of liquidity trap possesses certain important implications:

First, the monetary authority cannot influence the rate of interest even by following a cheap money policy. An increase in the quantity of money cannot lead to a further decline in the rate of interest in a liquidity trap situation.

Second, the rate of interest cannot fall to zero.

Third, the policy of a general wage cut cannot be efficacious in the face of a perfectly elastic liquidity preference curve, such as *Ls* in Figure 5. No doubt, a policy of general wage cut would lower wages and prices, and thus release money from transactions to speculative purpose, the rate of interest would remain unaffected because people would hold money due to the prevalent uncertainty in the money market.

Last, if new money is created, it instantly goes into speculative balances and is put into bank vaults or cash boxes instead of being invested. Thus there is no effect on income. Income can change without any change in the quantity of money. Thus monetary changes have a weak effect on economic activity under conditions of absolute liquidity preference.

The Total Demand for Money

According to Keynes, money held for transactions and precautionary purposes is primarily a function of the level of income, $L_T = f(Y)$, and the speculative demand for money is a function of the rate of interest, $Ls = f(r)$. Thus the total demand for money is a function of both income and the interest rate :

$$L_T + L_S = f(Y) + f(r)$$

or

$$L = f(Y) + f(r)$$

or

$$L = f(Y, r)$$

where L represents the total demand for money.[15]

Thus the total demand for money can be derived by the lateral summation of the demand function for transactions and precautionary purposes and the demand function for speculative purposes, as illustrated in Figure 6 (A), (B) and (C)*. Panel (A) of the Figure shows *OT*, the transactions and precautionary demand for money at *Y* level of income and different rates of interest. Panel (B) shows the speculative demand for money at various rates of interest. It is an inverse function of the rate of interest. For instance, at r_6 rate of interest it is *OS* and as the rate of interest falls to r_2, the *Ls* curve becomes perfectly elastic. Panel (C) shows the total demand

13. The remaining portion of this section can be left out safety except for a note on the Liquidity Trap.
14. F. Modigliani, "Liquidity Preference and the Theory of Interest and Money," *Economica* January 1944.
15. In Keynesian terminology, precautionary and transaction demand $M_1 = L_1 (Y)$, and the speculative demand $M_2 = L_2 (r)$, and the total demand for money $M = L (Y, r)$, where $M = M + M$.

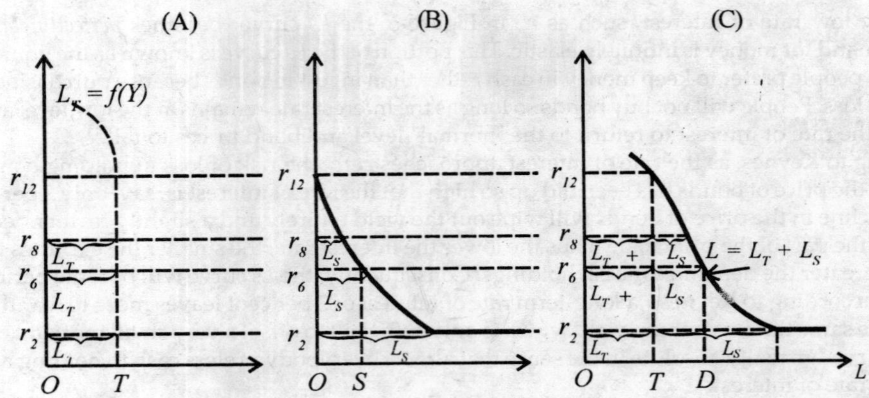

Fig. 6

curve for money L which is a lateral summation of L_T and L_S curves : $L=L_T+L_S$. For example, at r_6 rate of interest, the total demand for money is OD which is the sum of transactions and precautionary demand OT *plus* the speculative demand TD, $OD=OT+TD$, where $TD = OS$. At r_2 interest rate, the total demand for money curve also becomes perfectly elastic, showing the position of liquidity trap.

THE POST-KEYNESIAN APPROACHES

Keynes believed that the transactions demand for money was primarily interest inelastic. Prof. Baumol has analysed the interest elasticity of the transactions demand for money on the basis of his inventory theroretical approach. Further, in the Keynesian analysis the speculative demand for money is analysed in relation to uncertainty in the market. Prof. Tobin has given an alternative theory which explains liquidity preference as behaviour towards risk. The two approaches to the liquidity preference theory are discussed below.

1. Baumol's Inventory Theoretic Approach[16]

William Baumol has made an important addition to the Keynesian transactions demand for money. Keynes regarded transactions demand for money as a function of the level of income, and the relationship between transactions demand and income as linear and proportional. Baumol shows that the relation between transactions demand and income is neither linear nor proportional. Rather, changes in income lead to less than proportionate changes in the transactions demand for money. Further, Keynes considered transactions demand as primarily interest inelastic. But Baumol analyses the interest elasticity of the transactions demand for money.

Its Assumptions

Baumol's theory is based on the following assumptions:

1. The transactions between money and bonds are transparent and occur in a steady stream.
2. The bond market is perfect where there is easy conversion of bonds into cash and vice versa.
3. There is a fixed cost in exchanging bonds for cash and vice versa.
4. The holding of cash involves interest cost and non-interest costs.

* Adapted from Edward Shapiro, *op, cit.*,

16. W.J. Baumol, "Transactions Demand for Cash. An Inventory Theoretic Approach," *Quarterly Journal of Economics*, November, 1952; and James Tobin, "The Interest Elasticity of the Transactions Demand for Cash," *Review of Economic and Statistics*, August 1956. Our analysis follows Baumol.

5. The interest cost (or rate of interest) is constant over the year.
6. The non-interest costs such as brokerage fee, mailing expenses, etc. are also fixed over the year.

The Theory

Given these assumptions, Baumol's analysis is based on the holding of an optimum inventory of money for transactions purposes by a firm or an individual. He writes: "A firm's cash balance can usually be interpreted as an inventory of money which its holder stands ready to exchange against purchase of labour, raw materials, etc." Cash balances are held because income and expenditure do not take place simultaneously. "But it is expensive to tie up large amounts of capital in the form of cash balances. For that money could otherwise be used profitably elsewhere in the firm or it could be invested profitably in securities." Thus the alternative to holding cash balances is bonds which earn interest. A firm would always try to keep minimum transactions balances in order to earn maximum interest from its assets. The higher the interest rate on bonds, the lesser the transactions balances which a firm holds.

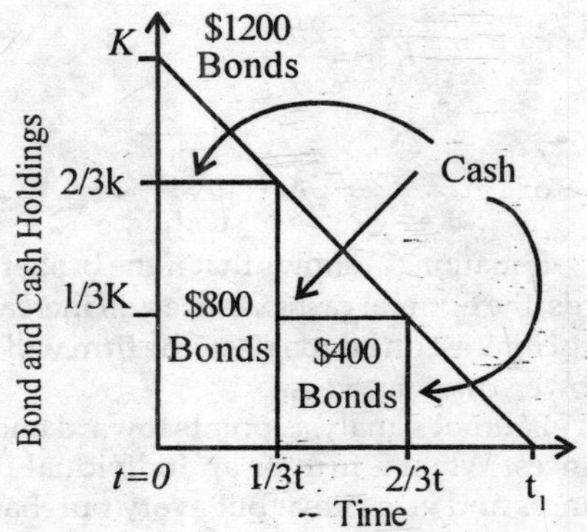

Fig. 7

Baumol assumes that a firm receives Y dollars once per time period, say a year, which are spent at a constant rate over the period. It is, therefore, always profitable for the firm to spend idle funds on buying bonds which can be sold when it needs cash for transactions purposes.

The structure of cash for holdings and bond holdings by a firm is shown in Figure 7. Suppose the firm has $ 1,200 which it has to spend every quarter at a constant rate over the year. Out of this, it keeps $ 400 in cash for transactions purposes and buys bonds with the remaining amount of $800. Half the bonds purchased carry maturity of $1/3t$ (4 months) and the other (half) bonds carry maturity of $2/3t$ (8 months). Further suppose that K is the sum received form the sale of bonds and the firm's average cash holdings equal half the sum ($1/2K$) received from the sale of bonds.

Given these assumptions, the firm buys bonds with $2/3K$ ($800) of its income at time t=0 and keeps $1/3K$ ($400) in cash, as shown in the figure. At time $1/3t$, the first half of the bonds purchased ($400) mature which it sells for cash until time $2/3t$. At time $2/3t$, the remaining bonds mature which the firm sells for transactions purposes until time t_1. At time t_1, when the year is over, the cash balance is zero and the firm is again ready for fresh receipts in the new year.

Now the problem is how to hold assets by a firm, "given that there exist interest-yielding bonds that can be owned as well as cash, and given that there is a fixed cost involved in exchanging bonds for cash."

The solution of this problem requires minimising the cost of holding cash balances over the year. The holding of cash balances consists of interest cost and non-interest costs. Interest cost is in the nature of opportunity cost because when a firm holds cash balances for transactions purposes it forgoes interest income. On the other hand, non-interest costs include such items as brokerage fees, mailing expenses, book-keeping expenses, etc. for converting cash into bonds, and vice versa.

Thus whenever a firm holds money for transactions purposes, it incurs interest costs and brokerage fees (non-interest costs). Let r be the rate of interest which is assumed to be constant over the year and b the brokerage fee which is also assumed to be fixed. Assume that at the beginning of the year, Y is the income of the firm which is equal to the real value of the transactions performed by it, and K is the size of each cash withdrawal at intervals over the year when the bonds are sold. Thus Y/K is the number of withdrawals that occur over the year. The cost on brokerage fees during the year will equal $b(Y/K)$. Since the average cash withdrawal are $K/2$, the interest cost of holding cash balances is $rK/2$. Then the total cost of making transactions, C, may be written in equation form as:

$$C = r\frac{K}{2} + b\frac{Y}{K} \quad ...(1)$$

The optimal value of K is that which minimises the total inventory cost C. By differentiating C with respect to K, setting the derivative dC/dK equal to zero, and solving for C, we obtain

$$\frac{dC}{dK}=\frac{r}{2}+\frac{-bY}{K^2}=0$$

or $$\frac{r}{2}=\frac{bY}{K^2}$$

Multiplying both sides by $2K^2/r$, we obtain

$$K^2=\frac{2bY}{r}$$

or $$K=\sqrt{\frac{2bY}{r}} \qquad ...(2)$$

Equation (2) shows that if the brokerage fee increases, the number of withdrawals will decrease. In other words, the optimal cash balance will increase because the firm will invest less in bonds. On the other hand, if the rate of interest on bonds rises, the firm will find it profitable to invest in bonds and the optimal cash balance will be lower, and vice versa.

Baumol's analysis points toward another important fact about the behaviour of demand for transactions balances. When a firm or an individual purchases large number of bonds, it is left with small transactions balances and vice versa. But every purchase involves non-interest costs in the form of brokerage fee, mailing, etc. which the purchaser has to pay. He has, therefore, to balance the income to be forgone by making fewer bond purchases against the expenses to be incurred by making large bond purchases. This decision depends upon the rate of interest on bonds. The higher the rate of interest, the larger the expenses which a firm can abosrb in making bond purchases. A more important factor which determines this decision is the amount of money involved in transactions because brokerage fees of buying and selling bonds are relatively fixed and do not change much in relation to the former. When the money involved in transactions is larger, the smaller will be the brokerage costs. "On a \$ 1000 bond purchase, minimum brokerage fees can be costly. On a million dollar transaction they are negligible. Hence, the larger the total amounts involved, the less significant will be the brokerage costs, and the more frequent will be optimal withdrawals." This is because of the operation of economies of scale in cash management or use of money.

It implies that at higher levels of income, the average cost of transactions i.e. brokerage fees are lower. As income increases, the transactions demand for money also increases but by less than the increase in income. If income increases fourfold, optimal transactions balances only double. Since Baumol takes the income elasticity of demand for money to be one-half (1/2), the demand for money will not increase in the same proportion as the increase in income. This is because of the economies of scale that encourage larger investment in bonds when the amount of money involved in transactions is larger due to increase in income.

In this inventory theory of the demand for money, Baumol also emphasises that the demand for money is a demand for real balances. Since the value of average cash holdings over the year is $K/2$, the demand for real balances for transactions purposes becomes

$$\frac{M_D}{P}=\frac{K}{2}=\frac{1}{2}\sqrt{\frac{2bY}{r}}$$

$$M_D=\frac{1}{2}\sqrt{\frac{2bY}{r}}.P \qquad ...(3)$$

where M_D is the demand for money and P is the price level.

Equation (3) shows that the demand for real transactions balances "is proportional to the square root of the volume of transactions and inversely proportional to the square root of the rate of interest."

It means that the relationship between changes in the price level and the transactions demand for money is direct and proportional. The pattern of a firm's purchases remaining unchanged, the optimal cash balances (Y) will increase in exactly the same proportion as the price level (P). If the price level doubles, the money value of the firm's transactions will also double. When all prices double, brokerage fee (b) will also double "so that larger cash balances will become desirable in order to avoid investments and withdrawals and the brokerage costs which they incur." Thus the increase in the money value of transactions and in brokerage fees leads to a rise in the optimal demand for money in exactly the same proportion as the change in the price level. Thus Baumol's analysis of the demand for real balances implies that there is no money illusion in the demand for money for transactions purposes.

Its Superiority over the Classical and Keynesian Approaches

Baumol's inventory theoretic approach to the transactions demand for money is an improvement over the classical and Keynesian approaches.

1. The cash balances quantity theory of money assumed the relationship between the transactions demand and the level of income as linear and proportional. Baumol has shown that this relationship is not accurate. No doubt it is true the transactions demand increases with increase in income but it increases less than proportionately because of the economies of scale in cash management.

2. Baumol's theory also has the merit of demonstrating the interest elasticity of the transactions demand for money as against the Keynesian view that it is interest inelastic.

3. Baumol analyses the transactions demand for real balances thereby emphasising the absence of money illusion.

4. Baumol's inventory theoretic approach is superior to both the classical and Keynesian approaches because it integrates the transactions demand for money with the capital-theory approach by taking assets and their interest and non-interest costs into account.

5. Baumol's theory removes the dichotomy between transactions and speculative demand for money of the Keynesian approach.

2. Tobin's Portfolio Selection Model: The Risk Aversion Theory of Liquidity Preference

James Tobin in his famous article "Liquidity Preference as Behaviour Towards Risk,"[17] formulated the risk aversion theory of liquidity preference based on portfolio selection. This theory removes two major defects of the Keynesian theory of liquidity preference. *One*, Keynes's liquidity preference function depends on the inelasticity of expectations of future interest rates; and *two*, individuals hold either money or bonds. Tobin has removed both the defects. His theory does not depend on the inelasticity of expectations of future interest rates but proceeds on the assumption that the expected value of capital gains or losses from holding interest-bearing assets is always zero. Moreover, it explains that an individual's portfolio holds both money and bonds rather than only one at a time.

Tobin starts his portfolio selection model of liquidity preference with this presumption that an individual asset holder has a portfolio of money and bonds. Money neither brings any return nor imposes any risk on him. But bonds yield interest and also bring income. However, income from bonds is uncertain because it involves a risk of capital losses or gains. The greater the investment in bonds, the greater is the risk of capital loss from them. An investor can bear this risk if he is compensated by an adequate return from bonds.

If g is the expected capital gain or loss, it is assumed that the investor bases his actions on his estimate of its probability distribution. It is further assumed that this probability distribution has an expected value of zero and is independent of the level of the current rate of interest, r, on bonds.

His portfolio consists of a proportion M of Money and B of bonds where both M and B add up to 1. They do not have any negative values. The return on portfolio R is

$$R = B\,(r+g) \text{ where } O \leq B \leq 1$$

17. *The Review of Economic Studies*, February 1958. Reprinted in M.G. Mueller (ed), *Readings* in *Macroeconomics*, 2/e, 1971.

Since g is a random variable with expected value zero, the expected return on the portfolio is

$$RE = mR = Br.$$

The risk attached to a portfolio is measured by the standard deviation of R, that is, σR.

Tobin describes three types of investors. The *first* category is of *risk lovers* who enjoy putting all their wealth into bonds to maximise risk. They accept risk of loss in exchange for the income they accept from bonds. They are like gamblers. The *second* category is of *plungers*. They will either put all their wealth into bonds or will keep it in cash. Thus plungers either go all the way, or not at all.

But the majority of investors belong to the *third* category. They are *risk averters* or *diversifiers*. Risk averters prefer to avoid the risk of loss which is associated with holding bonds rather than money. They are prepared to bear some additional risk only if they expect to receive some additional return on bonds, provided every increase in risk borne brings with it greater increase in returns. They will, therefore, diversify their portfolios, and hold both money and bonds. Although money neither brings any return nor any risk, yet it is the most liquid form of assets which can be used for buying bonds any time.

In order to find out risk averter's preference between risk and expected return, Tobin uses indifference curves having positive slopes indicating that the risk averter demands more expected returns in order to take more risk.

This is illustrated in Figure 8 where the horizontal axis measures risk (sR) and the vertical axis the expected returns (sm$R$). The line Or is the budget line of the risk averter. It shows the combinations of risk and expected return on the basis of which he arranges his portfolio of wealth consisting of money and bonds. I_1 and I_2 are indifference curves. An indifference curve shows that he is indifferent between all pairs of expected return and risk that lie on I_1 curve. Points on I_2 curve are preferred to those on I_1 curve. But the risk averter will achieve an equilibrium position between expected return and risk where his budget line is tangent to the indifference curve. It is point T on the budget line O_r and I_1 curve.

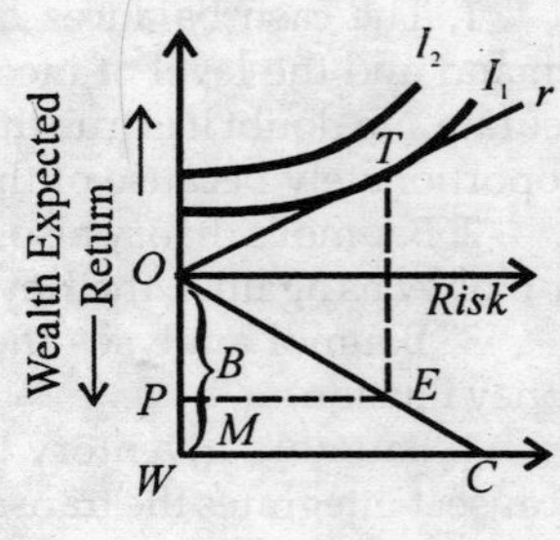

Fig. 8

In the lower portion of the figure, the length of the vertical axis shows the wealth held by the risk averter in his portfolio consisting of money and bonds. The line OC shows risk as proportional to the share of the total portfolio held in bonds. Thus point E on this line drawn as perpendicular from point T determines the portfolio mix of money and bonds. It is OP of bonds shown as B, and PW of money shown as M in the figure.

Thus the risk averter diversifies his total wealth OW by putting partly in bonds and partly keeping in cash. That is why he is called a diversifier. He is not prepared to accept more risk unless he can also expect greater expected return. However, the risk averter possesses an intrinsic preference for liquidity which can be only offset by higher interest rates. The higher the interest rate, the lower the demand for money, and the higher the incentive to hold more bonds. On the contrary, the lower the interest rate, the higher the demand for money, and the lower the willingness to hold bonds. This is illustrated in Figure 9.

The slope of the budget line increases with the increase in the interest rate. This is shown by the budget line r_1 rotating upward to r_2 and r_3. Consequently, returns increase in relation to risk with increase in the interest rate, and the budget line touches higher indifferences curves. In Figure 9, budget lines r_1, r_2 and r_3 are tangents to I_1, I_2 and I_3 curves at points T_1, T_2 and T_3 respectively. These points trace out the optimum portfolio curve, OPC, in the figure which shows that as the tangency points move upward from left to right, both the expected return and risk increase.

These tangency points also determine the portfolio selection of risk averters as shown in the lower portion of Figure 9. When the rate of interest is r_1, they hold OB_1 bonds and B_1W

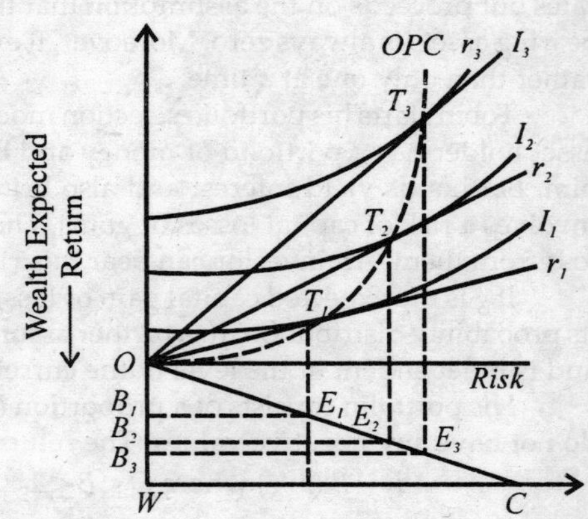

Fig. 9

money. As the rate of interest increases, from r_1 to r_2 and r_3, risk averters hold successively more bonds OB_2 and OB_3 and reduce money to B_2W and B_3W in their portfolios. The figure also shows that as the rate of interest increases by equal increments from r_1, to r_2 to r_3, risk averters hold bonds by decreasing increments, $B_2B_3 < B_2B_1 < OB_1$. This also means that the demand for money falls by smaller amounts, as the rate of interest increases. This is because the total wealth in the portfolio consists of bonds plus money.

The demand for money curve can thus be drawn on the basis of figure 9. This is depicted in Figure 10 as the *Ls* curve. The curve shows that when the rate of interest falls from a higher level, there is a smaller increase in the demand for money. For instance, when the interest rate falls from r_{10} to r_8, the demand for money increases by *AB* which is smaller than *OA*. This is because risk averters prefer to hold more bonds than money. But when the rate of interest falls at a lower level from r_4 to r_2, the increase in the demand for money is much larger. It is *CD* in Figure 10. This demand for money curve relates to the speculative demand for money and not to the aggregate demand for money.

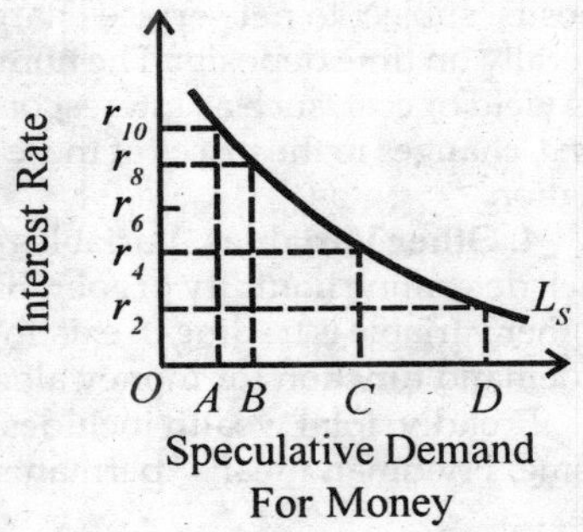

Fig. 10

Its Superiority over Keynesian Theory

Tobins' risk aversion theory of portfolio selection is superior to the Keynesian liquidity preference theory of speculative demand for money on the following counts:

First, Tobin's theory does not depend on inelasticity of expectations of future interest rates, but proceeds from the assumption that the expected value of capital gain or loss from holding interest-bearing assets is always zero. In this respect, Tobin regards his theory as a logically more satisfactory foundation for liquidity preference than the Keynesian theory.

Second, this theory is superior to Keynes's theory in that it explains that individuals hold diversified portfolios of bonds and money rather than either bonds or money.

Third, like Keynes, Tobin regards the demand for money as closely dependent on interest rates and inversely related to interest rates and his theory provides a basis for liquidity preference.

Fourth, Tobin is more realistic than Keynes in not discussing the perfect elasticity of demand for money (the liquidity trap) at very low rates of interest.

Fifth, according to David Laidler, the real importance of the portfolio theory lies in "not what it tells directly about the aggregate economy, but rather it represents an interesting approach to the problem of relating demand for money to the existence of uncertainty, an approach that probably has scope for considerable development in the future."

3. Friedman's Theory of Demand for Money

Friedman's theory of demand for money is a capital or wealth theory, because he regards money as an asset or capital good.

For ultimate wealth holders, the demand for money, in real terms, may be expected to be a function primarily of the following variables:

1. **Total Wealth.** The total wealth is the analogue of the budget constraint. It is the total that must be divided among various forms of assets. In practice, estimates of total wealth are seldom available. Instead, income may serve as an index of wealth. Thus, according to Friedman, income is a surrogate of wealth.

2. **The Division of Wealth between Human and Non-Human Forms.** The major source of wealth is the productive capacity of human beings which is human wealth. But the conversion of human wealth into non-human wealth or the reverse is subject to institutional constraints. This can be done by using current earnings to purchase non-human wealth or by using non-human wealth to finance the acquisition of skills. Thus the fraction of total wealth in the form of non-human wealth is an additional important variable. Friedman calls the ratio of non-human to human wealth or the ratio of wealth to income as w.

3. **The Expected Rates of Return on Money and Other Assets.** These rates of return are the counterparts of the prices of a commodity and its substitutes and complements in the theory of consumer demand. The

nominal rate of return may be *zero* as it generally is on currency, or *negative* as it sometimes is on demand deposits, subject to net service charges, or *positive* as it is on demand deposits on which interest is paid, and generally on time deposits. The nominal rate of return on other assets consists of two parts: *first*, any currently paid yield or cost, such as interest on bonds, dividends on equities, and costs of storage on physical assets, and *second*, changes in the prices of these assets which become especially important under conditions of inflation or deflation.

4. Other Variables. Variables other than income may affect the utility attached to the services of money which determine liquidity proper. Besides liquidity, variables are the tastes and preferences of wealth holders. Another variable is trading in existing capital goods by ultimate wealth holders. These variables also determine the demand function for money alongwith other forms of wealth. Such variables are noted as u by Friedman.

Broadly, total wealth includes all sources of income or consumable services. It is capitalised income. By income, Friedman means "permanent income" which is the average expected yield on wealth during its life time.

Forms of Wealth. Wealth can be held in five different forms: money, bonds, equities, physical goods, and human capital. Each form of wealth has a unique characteristic of its own and a different yield.

1. *Money* is taken in the broadest sense to include currency, demand deposits and time deposits which yield interest on deposits. Thus money is luxury good. It also yields real return in the form of convenience, security, etc. to the holder which is measured in terms of the general price level (P).
2. *Bonds* are defined as claim to a time stream of payments that are fixed in *nominal units.*
3. *Equities* are defined as a claim to a time stream of payments that are fixed in *real* units.
4. *Physical goods or non-human goods* are inventories of producer and consumer durables.
5. *Human capital* is the productive capacity of human beings.

Thus each form of wealth has a unique characteristic of its own and a different yield either explicitly in the form of interest, dividends, labour income, etc., or implicitly in the form of services of money measured in terms of P, and inventories. The present discounted value of these expected income flows from these five forms of wealth constitutes the current value of wealth which can be expressed as:

$$W = \frac{y}{r}$$

where W is the current value of total wealth, y is the total flow of expected income from the five forms of wealth, and r is the interest rate. This equation shows that wealth is capitalised income. Friedman in his latest empirical study *Monetary Trends in the United States and the United Kingdom* (1982) gives the following demand function for money for an individual wealth holder with slightly different notations from his original study of 1956 as:

$$M/P = f(Y, W; R_m, R_b, R_e, g_p, u)$$

where M is the total stock of money demanded; P is the price level; Y is the real income; W is the fraction of wealth in non-human form; R_m is the expected nominal rate of return on money; R_b is the expected rate of return on bonds, including expected changes in their prices; R_e is the expected nominal rate of return on equities, including expected changes in their prices; $g_p = (1/P)(dP/dt)$ is the expected rate of change of prices of goods and hence the expected nominal rate of return on physical assets; and u stands for variables other than income that may affect the utility attached to the services of money.

The demand function for business is roughly similar, although the division of total wealth and human wealth is not very useful since a firm can buy and sell in the market place and hire its human wealth at will. But the other factors are important.

The aggregate demand function for money is the summation of individual demand functions with M and y referring to per capita money holdings and per capita real income respectivley, and w is the fraction of aggregate wealth in non-human form.

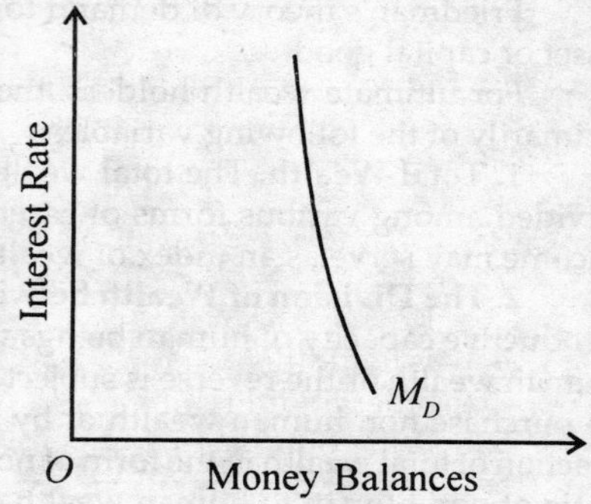

Fig. 11

The demand function for money leads to the conclusion that a rise in expected yields on different assets (R_b, R_e and g_p) reduces the amount of money demanded by a wealth holder, and that an increase in wealth raises the demand for money. The income to which cash balances (M/P) are adjusted is the expected long-term level of income rather than current income being received. Empirical evidence suggests that the income elasticity of demand for money is greater than unity which means that income velocity is falling over the long run. This means that the long-run demand for money function is stable and is relatively interest inelastic, as shown in Fig. 11 where M_D is the demand for money curve. If there is change in the interest rate, the long-run demand for money is negligible.

Its Superiority over Keynesian Theory

Friedman's theory of demand for money is superior to Keynes' Theory in the following ways:

First, Friedman uses a broader definition of money than that of Keynes in order to explain his demand for money function. He treats money as an asset or capital good capable of serving as a temporary abode of purchasing power. It is held for the stream of income or consumable services which it renders. On the other hand, the Keynesian definition of money consists of demand deposits and non-interest bearing debt of the government.

Second, Friedman postulates a demand for money function quite different from that of Keynes. The demand for money on the part of wealth holders is a function of many variables. These are R_m, the yield on money; R_b, the yield on bonds; R_e, the yield on securities; g_p, the yield on physical assets; and u referring to other variables. In the Keynesian theory, the demand for money as an asset is confined to just bonds where interest rates are the relevant cost of holding money.

Third, there is also the difference between the monetary mechanisms of Keynes and Friedman as to how changes in the quantity of money affect economic activity. According to Keynes, monetary changes affect economic activity *indirectly* through bond prices and interest rates. The monetary authorities increase the money supply by purchasing bonds which raises their prices and reduces the yield on them. Lower yield on bonds induces people to put their money elsewhere, such as investment in new productive capital that will increase output and income. On the other hand, in Friedman's theory monetary disturbances will *directly* affect prices and production of all types of goods since people will buy or sell any asset held by them. Friedman emphasises that the market interest rates play only a small part of the total spectrum of rates that are relevant.

Fourth, there is the difference between the two approaches with regard to the motives for holding money balances. Keynes divides money balances into "active" and "idle" categories. The former consist of transactions and precautionary motives, and the latter consist of the speculative motive for holding money. On the other hand, Friedman makes no such division of money balances. According to him, money is held for a variety of different purposes which determine the total volume of assets held such as money, physical assets, total wealth, human wealth, and general preferences, tastes and anticipations.

Fifth, in his analysis, Friedman introduces permanent income and nominal income to explain his theory. Permanent income is the amount a wealth holder can consume while maintaining his wealth intact. Nominal income is measured in the prevailing units of currency. It depends on both prices and quantities of goods traded. Keynes, on the other hand, does not make such a distinction.

EXERCISES

1. What are the motives for holding cash balances according to Keynes ? Give the modifications made by modern economists.
2. Analyse the inventory theory approach to the transactions demand for money. What is its relationship with the rate of interest ?
3. Discuss the portfolio selection approach to the speculative demand for money. How is it superior to Keynes's liquidity preference approach ?
4. Is liquidity preference satisfying the speculative demand for money alone which is interest elastic, or other liquidity preferences also ? Give reasons for your answer.
5. Bring out the relationship between money and interest.
6. Explain Friedman's demand for money theory. How far is it superior to Keynes' theory?

CHAPTER 18

Theories of Interest Rates

1. INTRODUCTION

This chapter discusses some of the important theories of interest rate such as the classical, the loanable funds, the Keynesian, and the modern theory of interest. Besides, certain issues like the natural and market rates of interest are also examined.

Of the theories discussed below, the Keynesian liquidity preference theory that determines the interest rate by the demand for and supply of money is a *stock* theory. It emphasises that the rate of interest is a purely monetary phenomenon. It is a *stock* analysis because it takes the supply of money as given during the short run. and determines the interest rate by liquidity preference or demand for money. On the otter hand, the loanable funds theory is a *flow* theory that determines the interest rate by the demand for and supply of loanable funds. It involves the linking of the interest rate with dissaving, investment and hoarding of funds on the demand side with saving, dishoardings and bank money on the supplyside. These are all flow variables. Hicks and Hansen have reconciled and synthesised these stock and flow theories in a general equilibrium framework and presented a determinate theory of interest rate in terms of the IS-LM formulation.

2. THE CLASSICAL THEORY OF INTEREST

According to the classical theory, rate of interest is determined by the supply of and demand for capital. The supply of capital is governed by the time preference and the demand for capital by the expected productivity of capital. Both time preference and productivity of capital depend upon waiting or saving or thrift. The theory is, therefore, also known as the supply and demand theory of saving.

Demand Side. The demand for capital consists of the demand for productive and consumptive purposes. Ignoring the latter, capital is demanded by the investors because it is productive. But the productivity of capital is subject to the law of variable proportions. Additional units of capital are not as productive as the earlier units. A stage comes, when the employment of an additional unit of capital in the business is just worth while and no more. Suppose, an investor invests Rs.1,00,000 in a factory and expects, a yield of 20%. Another instalment of an equal amount would not be as productive as the first one and might bring him 15%. While a third instalment might yield 10%. If he has borrowed the money at 10%, he will not venture to invest more. For the rate of interest is just equal to the marginal productivity of capital to him. It shows that at a higher rate of interest, the demand for capital is low and it is high at a lower rate of interest. Thus the demand for capital is *inversely* related to the rate of interest, and the demand schedule for capital or investment curve slopes downward from left to right There, are, however, certain other factors which govern the demand for capital, such as the growth of population, technical progress, process of rationalization, the standard of living of the community, etc.

Supply Side. The supply of capital depends upon savings, rather upon the will to save and the power to save of the community. Some people save irrespective of the rate of the interest. They would continue to save even if the rate of interest were zero. There are others who save because the current rate of interest is just enough to induce them to save. They would reduce their savings if the rate of interest fell below this level. Still there are the potential savers who would be induced to save if the rate of interest were raised. To the last two categories of savers, saving involves a sacrifice, abstinence or waiting when they forgo present consumption in order to earn interest. The higher the rate of interest, the larger will be the community savings and the more will be the supply of funds. The supply curve of capital or the saving curve thus moves upward to the right

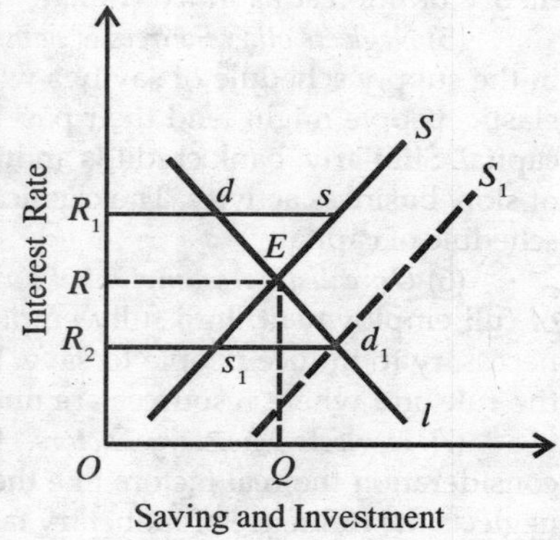

Fig. 1

Determination. Assuming the level of income to be given, the rate of interest is determined by the interaction of the demand curve and the supply curve of saving. This is shown in Figure 1 where *I* and *S* curves intersect at *E* which is the equilibrium point when *OQ* quantity of capital is demanded and supplied at *R* rate of interest. If at any time the rate of interest rises above *R*, the demand for investment funds will fall and the supply of savings will increase. Since the supply of savings is more than the demand ($R_1s > R_1 d$), the rate of interest will come down to the equilibrium level *OR*. The opposite will be the case if the rate of interest falls to R_2. The demand for investment funds is greater than the supply of savings ($R_2d_1 > R_2s_1$) rate of interest will rise to *R*. The ultimate situation is one of equality between saving and investment brought about by the equilibrium or the *natural* rate of interest. If at any time people become thrifty and save more than *OQ*, the rate of interest would fall below *R* because the demand for capital remains the same. This is shown by the downward shift of the saving curve to S_1, where it intersects the *I* curve at d_1 and the rate of interest falls to R_2 At the lower rate of interest, people will save less but the demand for investment funds will increase which will tend to raise the rate of interest to the equilibrium level *R*.

Its Criticisms

The 'pure' or the *real* theory of interest of the classicals, as enunciated by Marshall and Pigou, has been severely criticised by Keynes.

(1) *Income not Constant but Variable.* One of the serious defects of the classical theory is that it assumes the level of income to be given, and regards interest as an equilibrating mechanism between the demand for investible funds and the supply of funds through savings. According to Keynes, income is a variable and not a constant and the equality between saving and investment is brought about by changes in income and not by variations in the rate of interest.

(2) *Saving-Investment Schedules not Independent.* In this theory the two determinants of interest rate, the demand and supply curves of saving are treated as independent of one another. It means that if there is change in demand, the demand curve for savings can shift up or below the *I* curve without causing a change in the supply curve. But according to Keynes, the two curves are not independent of one another. If, for instance, an invention shifts the investment curve upward, income will rise and it will lead to higher savings and thus shift the supply curve too. Similarly, a shift in the supply curve will bring a change in the demand curve.

(3) *Neglects the Effects of Investment on Income.* The classical theory neglects the effect of investment on the level of income. A rise in the rate of interest, for instance, will bring a decline in investment by making it less profitable. This will mean decline in output, employment and income. The latter will, in turn, lead to reduced savings, a fact contrary to the classical assertion that saving is a direct function of the rate of interest. On the other hand, a low rate of interest encourages investment activity, increases output, employment, income and savings. But Keynes does not believe that investment depends on the rate of interest. It depends on the marginal efficiency of capital. Even if the rate of interest were to fall to zero, Keynes argues, investment will not take place if business expectations for profits are at a low level, as is the case in depression.

(4) *Indeterminate Theory.* Since savings depend upon the level of income, it is not possible to know the rate of interest unless the income level is known beforehand. And the income level itself cannot be known without already knowing the rate of interest. A lower rate of interest will increase investment, output, employment, income and savings. So, for each income level a separate saving curve will have to be drawn. This is all circular reasoning and offers no solution to the problem of interest. That is why Keynes characterised the classical

theory of interest as indeterminate.

(5) *Neglects other Sources of Savings.* The propounders of this theory include savings out of current income in the supply schedule of savings which makes it inadequate. Considering the supply of capital to be interst-elastic, people might lend their past savings with the rise in the rate of interest and so increase the supply of capital. Similarly, bank credit is an important source of the supply of capital. Banks lend more during periods of slow business activity. The classical theory remains incomplete when it neglects these factors in the supply schedule of capital.

(6) *Unrealistic Assumption of Full Employment.* The classical theory is based on the unrealistic assumption of full employment. In a fully employed economy interest as a reward for saving, waiting or abstinence is necessary to induce people to save. But according to Keynes, underemployment and not full employment is the rule and where resources are unemployed, interest is not essentially an inducement to savings.

(7} *Neglects Monetary Factors.* The classical theory is a pure or real theory of interest which takes into consideration the real factors like the time preference and the marginal productivity of capital. It completely neglects the influence of monetary factors on the determination of the rate of interest. The classical economists regarded money as a veil, a medium of exchange over goods and services. They failed to consider it as a store of value. Keynes, on the other hand, laid emphasis on explaining the determination of the rate of interest as a monetary phenomenon.

(8) *No Automatic Equality between Equilibrium and Market Rates of Interest.* According to the classical view, the market and the equilibrium (natural) rates of interest are always equal. Any discrepancy between the two is only a temporary phenomenon which would disappear in the long run. Keynes, however, does not regard the discrepancy between the two as accidental and temporary. It can be due to the contraction or expansion of bank credit. An expansion of bank credit by increasing the supply of loanable funds brings about a fall in the market rate of interest below the equilibrium rate and *vice versa.* Thus there is no automatic mechanism for the equality of the market and equilibrium interest rate.

(9) *Difference over the Definition of Interest.* Keynes differs with the classical economists even over the definition and determination of the rate of interest. According to him, it is the reward of not hoarding but the reward of parting with liquidity for a specified period. It is the 'price' which equilibrates demand for money with the available quantity of money. He does not agree that it is determined by the demand for and supply of capital.

Thus, Keynes dismisses the classical theory of interest as absolutely wrong and inadequate.

3. THE LOANABLE FUNDS THEORY OF INTEREST

The neo-classical or the loanable funds theory explains the determination of interest in terms of demand and supply of loanable funds or credit.

According to this theory, the rate of interest is the price of credit, which is determined by the demand and supply for loanable funds. In the words of Prof. Lerner, it is the price which equates the supply of 'credit', or saving *plus* the net increase in the amount of money in a period, to the demand for 'credit', or investment *plus* net hoarding "in the period." Let us analyse the forces behind the demand and supply of loanable funds.

Demand for Loanable Funds. The demand for loanable funds has primarily three sources *i.e.*, government, businessmen and consumers who need them for purposes of investment, hoarding and consumption. The government borrows funds for constructing public works or for war preparations. The businessmen borrow for the purchase of capital goods and for starting investment projects. Such borrowings are interest elastic and depend mostly on the expected rate of profit as compared with the rate of interest. The demand for loanable funds on the part of consumers is for the purchase of durable consumer goods like scooters, houses, etc. Individual borrowings are also interest elastic. The tendency to borrow is more at a lower rate of interest than at a higher rate in order to enjoy their consumption soon. Since this demand for funds is mostly met out of past savings or through *dis-saving,* it is represented by the curve *Ds* in Figure 2. The demand curve for *investment funds,* both for the government and the businessmen is shown as curve *I.* It slopes downward showing that less funds are borrowed at a higher rate and more at a lower rate of interest. *Lastly,* funds are demanded for the purpose of *hoarding* them in liquid form or as idle cash. They are also interest elastic and are shown by the curve

H. The lateral summation of these curves *H, Ds* and *I* gives us the aggregate demand curve for loanable funds *SD*.

Supply of Loanable Funds. The supply of loanable funds comes from savings, dishoardings and bank credit. Private, individual and corporate savings are the main source of savings. Though personal savings depend upon the income level, yet taking the level of income as given they are regarded as interest elastic. The higher the rate of interest, the greater will be the inducement to save and *vice versa.* Corporate savings are the undistributed profits of a firm which also depend on the current rate of interest to some extent. If the interest rate is high, it will act as a deterrent to borrowing and thus encourage savings. *Savings* are indicated as curve *S* in the Figure 2. The second source is the volume of funds coming out of hoards or being added to them. *Dishoarding* may represent not only purchase of old assets or securities from others out of idle cash balances of one's own funds for net investment or for consumption in purchases in excess of net disposable income. Such funds are directly related to the rate of interest. The higher the interest rate the larger the funds that will be coming out of hoards and *vice* versa. These funds are represented by the curve *DH*. Lastly, there is the *bank credit* as an important source of the supply of loanable funds. Bank credit or money is also interest elastic to some extent. More funds are lent at a higher than at a lower rate of interest. Bank credit is shown as the curve *M*. If these curves *DH, M* and *S* are laterally added up, we have the aggregate supply curve *SS* of loanable funds.

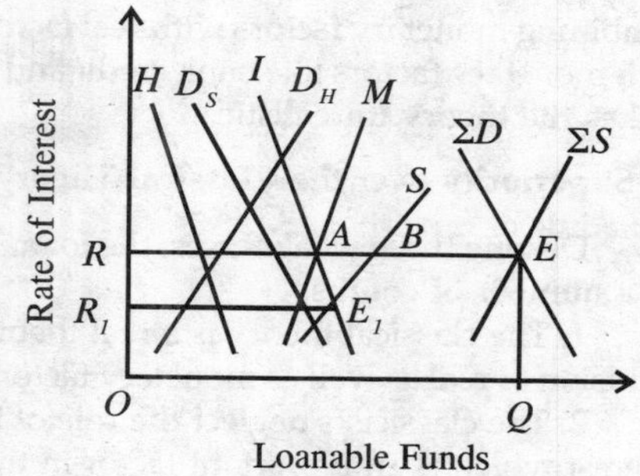

Fig. 2

The total demand curve for loanable funds *SD* and the total supply curve of loanable funds *SS* intersect at *E* and give *OR* rate of interest. At this rate *OQ* amount of funds are borrowed and lent.

Its Criticisms

According to Prof. Robertson, the loanable funds theory is a "commonsense explanation" of the determination of the rate of interest. But this theory is also not free from certain defects.

(1) *Equilibrium Rate reflects Unstable Equilibrium.* The demand and supply schedules for loanable funds determine the equilibrium rate of interest *OR* which does not equate each component on the supply side with the corresponding component on the demand side. Thus the equilibrium rate *OR* reflects unstable equilibrium. For stable equilibrium, it is essential that *ex ante* (planned) investment must equal *ex-ante* savings at the equilibrium rate *OR*. In the figure, *ex-ante* savings *S* exceed *ex-ante* investment *I* by *AB*. They are equal at point E_1 but at a lower rate OR_1 which is the natural rate of interest.

(2) *Indeterminate Theory.* Prof. Hansen asserts that the loanable funds theory like the classical and the Keynesian theories of interest is indeterminate. The supply curve of loanable funds is composed of savings, dishoardings and bank money. But since savings vary with past income and the new money and activated balances with the current income, it follows that the total supply curve of loanable funds also varies with income. Thus the loanable funds theory is indeterminate unless the income level is already known.[1]

(3) *Cash Balances not Elastic.* The loanable funds theory states that the supply of loanable funds can be increased by releasing cash balances of savings and decreased by absorbing cash balances into savings. This implies that the cash balances are fairly elastic. But this does not seem to be a correct view because the total cash balances available with the community are fixed and equal the total supply of money at any time. Whenever there are variations in the cash balances, they are in fact in the velocity of circulation of money rather than in the amount of cash balances with the community.

(4) *Savings not Interest Elastic.* The theory over-emphasises the influence of the rate of interest on savings. It regards savings as interest elastic. Generally speaking, people save not to earn rate of interest but to satisfy precautionary motive. So savings are interest *inelastic.*

1. A. H. Hansen, *A Guide to Keynes,* p. 141.

(5) *Not correct to combine Real and Monetary Factors.* The loanable funds theory has been criticised for combining monetary factors with real factors. It is not correct to combine real factors like saving and investment with monetary factors like bank credit and dishoarding without bringing in changes in the level of income. This makes the theory unrealistic.

Its Superiority over the Classical Theory

Despite these weaknesses, the loanable funds theory is better and more realistic than the classical theory on a number of counts.

1. The classical theory is a real theory of interest and neglects monetary influences on interest. With the inclusion of real as well as monetary factors, the loanable funds theory becomes superior to the classical theory.

2. The classicists neglect the role of bank credit as a constituent of money supply influencing the rate of interest which is an important factor in the loanable funds theory.

3. The classicists also do not consider the role of hoarding. By including the desire to hoard money in the demand for loanable funds, the loanable funds theory becomes more realistic and brings us nearer to Keynes's liquidity preference theory.

4. To the classicists money is merely a 'veil,' a passive factor influencing the rate of interest. The loanable funds theory is superior because it regards money as an active factor in the determination of the interest rate.

4. KEYNES'S LIQUIDITY PREFERENCE THEORY OF INTEREST

Keynes defines the rate of interest as the reward of not hoarding but the reward for parting with liquidity for the specified period. It "is not the 'price' which brings into equilibrium the demand for resources to invest with the readiness to abstain from consumption. It is the 'price' which equilibrates the desire to hold wealth in the form of cash with the available quantity of cash."[2] In other words, the rate of interest, in the Keynesian sense, is determined by the demand for and the supply of money. This theory is, therefore, charaterised as the monetary theory of interest, as distinct from the real theory of the classicals.

Supply of Money. Of the two determinants of the rate of interest, the supply of money refers to the total quantity of money in the country for all purposes at any time. Though the supply of money is a function of the rate of interest to a degree, yet it is considered to be fixed by the monetary authorities, that is, the supply curve of money is taken as perfectly inelastic.

Demand for Money. For the second determinant, the demand for money, Keynes coined a new term "liquidity preference" by which his theory of interest is commonly known. Liquidity preference is the desire to hold cash. The money in cash "lulls our disquietude" and the rate of interest which is demanded in exchange for it is a "measure of the degree of our disquietude." The rate of interest, in Keynes words, is the "premium which has to be offered to induce people to hold the wealth in some form other than hoarded money." The higher the liquidity preference,the higher will be the rate of interest that will have to be paid to the holders of cash to induce them to part with their liquid assets. The lower the liquidity preference, the lower will be the rate of interest that will be paid to the cash-holders.

According to Keynes, there are three motives behind the desire of the people to hold liquid cash: (1) the transaction motive, (2) the precautionary motive, and (3) the speculative motive.

Transactions Motive. The transactions motive relates to "the need of cash for the current transactions of personal and business exchanges." It is further divided into the income and business motives. The *income motive* is meant to bridge the interval between the receipt of income and its disbursement," and similarly, the *business motive* as "the interval between the time of incurring business costs and that of the receipt of the sale proceeds." If the time between the incurring of expenditure and receipt of income is small, less cash will be held by the people for current transactions, and vice versa. There will however be changes in the transactions demand for money depending upon the expectations of the income, of recipients and businessmen. They depend upon the level of income, employment and prices, the business turnover, the normal period between the receipt and disbursement of income, the amount of salary or income, and on the possibility of getting a loan.

2. J.M Keynes, *The General Theory of Employment, Interest and Money, p.* 167.

Precautionary Motive. The precautionary motive relates to "the desire to provide for contingencies requiring sudden expenditures and for unforeseen opportunities of advantageous purchases." Both individuals and businessmen keep cash in reserve to meet unexpected needs. Individuals hold some cash to provide for illness, accidents, unemployment and other unforeseen contingencies. Similarly businessmen keep cash in reserve to tide over unfavourable conditions or to gain from unexpected deals. Money held under the precautionary motive is rather like water kept in reserve in a water tank. The precautionary demand for money depends upon the level of income, and business activity, opportunities for unexpected profitable deals, availability of cash, the cost of holding liquid assets in bank reserves, etc.

Keynes holds that the transactions and precautionary motives are relatively *interest inelastic*, but are highly *income elastic*. The amount of money held under these two motives (M_1) is a function (L_1) of the level of income (Y) and is expressed as $M_1 = L_1(Y)$.

Speculative Motive. Money held under the speculative motive is for "securing profit from knowing better than the market what the future will bring forth." Individuals and businessmen have funds, after keeping enough for transactions and precautionary purposes and like to gain by investing in bonds. Money held for speculative purposes is a liquid store of value which can be invested at an opportune moment in interest-bearing bonds or securities.

Bond prices and the rate of interest are inversely related to each other. Low bond prices are indicative of high interest rates, and high bond prices reflect low interest rates. A bond carries a fixed rate of interest. For instance, if a bond of the value of Rs 100 carries 4% interest and the market rate of interest rises to 8%, the value of this bond falls to Rs 50 in the market. If the market rate of interest falls to 2%, the value of the bond will rise to Rs 200 in the market. Thus individuals and businessmen can gain by buying bonds worth Rs 100 each at the market rate of Rs 50 each when the rate of interest is high (8%), and sell them again when they are dearer (Rs 200 each) when the rate of interest falls (to 2%).,

According to Keynes, it is expectations about changes in bond prices or in the current market rate of interest that determine the speculative demand for money. The speculative demand for money is a decreasing function of the rate of interest. The higher the rate of interest, the lower the speculative demand for money, and lower the rate of interest, the higher the speculative demand for money. Algebraically, Keynes expressed the speculative demand for money as $M_2 = L_2(r)$ where L_2 is the speculative demand for money and r is the rate of interest. Geometrically, it is a smooth curve which slopes downward from left to right, as shown in Figure 3.

But at a very low rate if interest, such as 2% the speculative demand for money becomes perfectly elastic. This portion of the curve is known as the *liquidity trap*. At a very low rate of interest, people prefer to keep money in cash rather than invest in bonds because purchasing bonds will mean a definite loss.

TOTAL DEMAND OF MONEY

If the total liquid money is denoted by M, the transactions plus precautionary motive by M_1 and the speculative motive for holding by M_2, then $M = M_1 + M_2$. Since $M_1 = L_1(Y)$ and $M_2 = L_2(r)$, the total liquidity preference function is expressed as $M = L(Y, r)$. M_1 is circulating or active money and M_2 is idle, or passive money. Though M_1 is a function of income and M_2 of the rate of interest, yet they cannot be held in water-tight compartments. Even M_1 is interest elastic at high interest rates. If there is increased demand for M_1 it can be met by transferring funds from idle balances, M_2. Prof. Haberler distinguishes between liquidity preference in the narrower sense and liquidity preference in the wider sense. The former is the demand for idle balances, M_2 and is called "liquidity preference proper", and the latter is the total liquidity demand (M or $M_1 + M_2$). Given the level of income at high interest rates, liquidity preference refers to the total demand for money ($M_1 + M_2$) and at low interest rates the demand for speculative motive (M_2) alone.

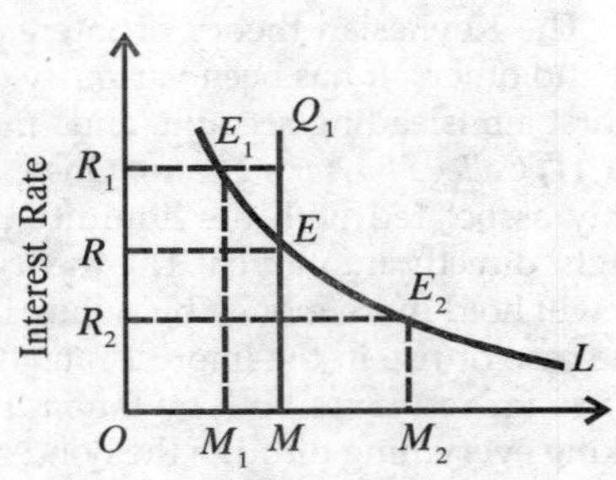

Fig. 3

Determination of the Rate of Interest. We have analysed the factors behind the supply and demand for money. The rate of interest, like the price of any product or service, is determined at a level where the demand for money equals the available supply of money. In Figure 3, the vertical line $Q_1 M$ represents the supply of money and L is the total demand for money curve. Both intersect at E where the *equilibrium rate* of interest R is established. If there is any deviation from this equilibrium position, an adjustment will take place via the rate of interest, and the equilibrium level E is re-established. E_1 is the position of unstable equilibrium where the supply of money OM is greater than the demand for money OM_1. Consequently, the rate of interest will start declining from R_1, till the equilibrium rate of interest R is reached. Similarly at R_2 level of interest rate, the demand for money OM_2 is greater than the supply of money OM. As a result, the rate of interest R_2 will start rising till it reaches the equilibrium rate$R$.

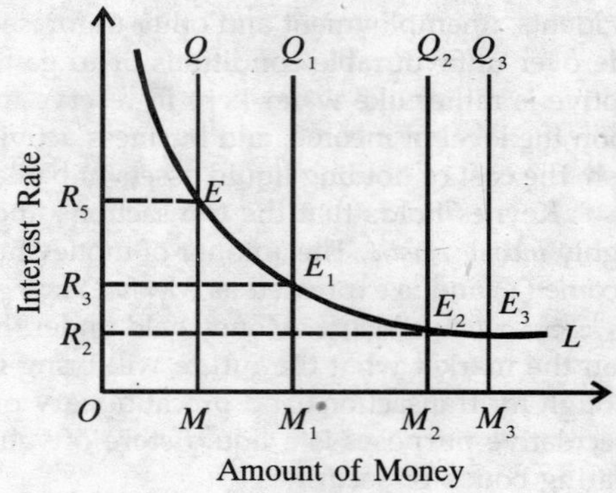

Fig. 4

If the *supply of money* is increased by the monetary authorities, but the liquidity preference curve$L$ remains the same, the rate of interest will fall. This is illustrated in Figure 4. Given the L curve, the supply of money curve being QM, the rate of interest is R_5. With the increase in the supply of money from QM to O_1M_1 and Q_2M_2, the rate of interest falls from R_3 to R_2. But any further increase in the supply of money has no effect on the rate of interest because the liquidity preference curve L is perfectly elastic at R_2 rate of interest. So when the supply of money increases to Q_3M_3, the rate of interest remains stationary at R_2 corresponding to the equilibrium point E_3. This is Keynes "Liquidity Trap".

If the demand for money increases and the liquidity preference carve shifts upward, given the supply of money, the rate of interest rises. This is shown in Figure 5. Given the supply of money curve QM when the L curve shifts upward, the new equilibrium point is E_1 which determines R_6 interest rate. This rate of interest is higher than R_4 interest rate at the equilibrium point E. If with the increase in the liquidity preference, the supply of money also increases in the same proportion to Q_1M_1 there will be no change in the rate of interest R_4, except that the new equilibrium point is E_2. Thus the theory explains that the rate of interest is determined at a point where the liquidity preference curve equals the supply of money curve.

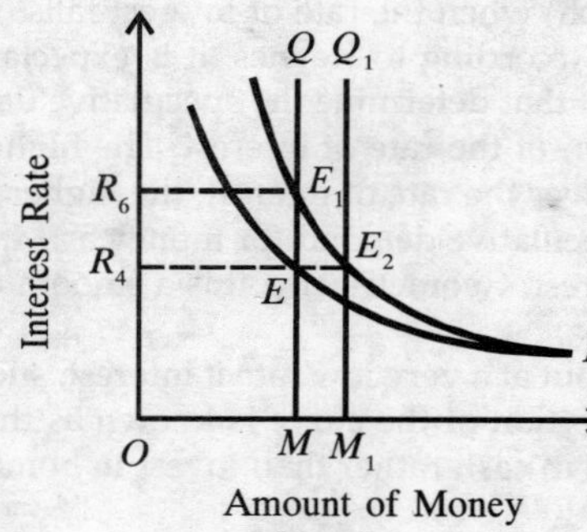

Fig. 5

Its Criticisms

The Keynesian theory of interest has been severely criticised by Hansen, Roberston, Knight, Hazlitt, Hutt and others. It has been variously characterized as "a college bursar's theory", "at best an inadequate and at worst a misleading account, and "preclassical, mercantilist, and man-in-the-street economics."

(1) *College Bursar's Theory.* One of the fallacies of the Keynesian analysis is that the demand for money is mainly associated with the liquidity preference for the speculative motive to which the rate of interest is brought directly into touch. The theory presumes the existence of a number of wealthy and shrewd persons who will hold more money by selling bonds when the rate of interest falls and hold less cash but more bonds in the case of rise in the interest rate. But Robertson does not regard bonds as the only alternative to money, as a use for resources both by the individual and the entrepreneur. And a theory of money which insists on working everything through the bond market is a *College Bursar's theory* and seems to be lacking in realism and comprehensiveness.

(2) *Inadequate and Misleading Theory.* The theory tells us nothing as to what determines the normal rate and therefore, given the degree of divergence, the actual rate of interest. The actual rate of interest cannot be described consistently as measuring the cost of the uncertainty of risk involved in holding bonds rather than

money. If there were no uncertainty at all, the actual rate would simply stand at a certain definite level below the normal rate. It is for these reasons that Robertson regards the liquidity preference theory "is at best an inadequate and at worst a misleading account."

(3) *Falls into Methodological Fallacy.* Just as the rate of interest is explained as the price for parting with liquidity, similarly the price of eggs or any other commodity can be explained by the relative preference for them. But there is a vital difference. A change in the quantity of money would tend to change the price of the good in the same proportion, but not the price of bonds beyond a temporary disturbance. In fact, there is no functional relationship between the price level and any rate of interest while discussing the influence of speculation on the interest rate on loans. As a result, no monetary change has any direct or permanent effect on the rate of interest. Thus the Keynesian theory falls into *"methodological fallacy"* by assuming a definite functional relationship between the quantity of money and the rate of interest.

(4) *Money as a Store of Wealth is Barren.* Keynes holds that only money held for speculative purposes is fruitful for it brings interest as a reward, while money as a store of wealth is barren. This is a mistaken notion. As pointed out by W.H. Hutt, money "is as productive as all other assets, and productive in exactly the same sense. The demand for money assets is a demand for productive resources.

(5) *Inconsistent Theory.* Knight criticised Keynes's theory in view of the facts which are directly contrary to what the theory calls for. Hazlitt also discusses this point without giving credit to Knight. According to the Keynesian theory, the rate of interest should be the highest at the bottom of the depression because the liquidity preference is the strongest at that time due to falling prices. A large reward will have to be paid to induce wealth-holders to part with their cash. But the facts are just the opposite. Short-term interest rates are the lowest in a depression because investment opportunities are temporarily closed and the lenders have no outlets to part with their cash. Contrariwise, the Keynesian short-term interest rates should be lowest during the peak of the boom because people would be investing their money rather than keep it in cash. The liquidity preference being the lowest, a very small reward would be required to partake with it. But in reality, the rate of interest is the highest at the peak of a boom. Thus the theory is inconsistent with facts.

(6) *Saving Essential for Liquidity.* Keynes regards the rate of interest as the reward for parting with liquidity and not a return merely for saving or waiting as such. Saving is necessary for obtaining funds to be invested at interest. In Viner's words "Without saving there can be no liquidity to surrender. The rate of interest is the return for saving without liquidity."

(7) *Liquidity not Essential for Interest Rate.* Even the term liquidity preference is neither helpful nor necessary in explaining the nature of interest. It is more confusing and less illuminating. It is not only vague but is also self-contradictory. For, as pointed out by Hazlitt, "If a man is holding his funds in the form of time deposits or short-term treasury bills, he is being paid interest on them , therefore he is getting interest and "liquidity" too. What becomes, then, of Keynes's theory that interest is the "reward" for parting with liquidity ?"

(8) *Wrong Notion of Liquidity Trap.* Keynes's notion of the "Liquidity Trap" is also wrong. In reality, the liquidity preference schedule may be perfectly *inelastic* rather than elastic at a low rate of interest. We know that during a depression all expectations are extremely pessimistic. It is, therefore, not correct to argue that expectations with regard to the rate of interest will be that it will go up.

(9) *Ignores Real Factors.* The greatest fallacy in Keynes's analysis is that he ignores the influence of real factors in determining the interest rate. He regards the interest rate as a purely monetary phenomenon and thus merely returns "to the pre-classical assumption of the mercantilists and to what has always been the assumption of the man in the street." According to Hazlitt, "Keynes made no new contribution. He merely muddled shallow waters *and* the kind of *interest* theory represented by *him* is pre-classical, mercantilistic and man in the street economics."

(10) *Indeterminate Theory.* The Keynesian theory, like the classical theory of interest, is *indeterminate.* Keynes asserts that the liquidity preference and the quantity of money determine the rate of interest. But this is not correct because a new liquidity preference curve will have to be drawn at each level of income. Therefore, unless the income level is already known, the demand and supply curves of money cannot tell us what the rate of interest will be. Thus, according to Prof. Hansen, "Keynes's criticism of the classical theory applies equally to his own theory."

(11) *Incomplete Theory.* Hicks, Somers, Lerner, Hansen and others opine that the rate of interest alongwith the level of income is determined by four factors: (i) the investment demand function *(MEC), (ii)* The saving function (or the consumption function), *(iii)* the liquidity preference function, and (iv) the quantity of money function. Though all these elements are found in the Keynesian analysis, yet Keynes does not bring them in his interest rate theory. He takes only the last two elements and ignores the first two, thus Keynes fails to provide an integrated and determinate theory of interest.

(12) *Confusion regarding Relation between Interest Rate and Quantity of Money.* There is confusion in Keynes's analysis about the relation between rate of interest and amount of money. On the one hand, he says that the demand for money is inversely dependent on the rate of interest, and on the other, that the equilibrium rate of interest is inversely dependent upon the amount of money. Throughout his analysis, Keynes does not make any distinction between the two propositions and often uses them in an identical manner This is a fundamental error in Keynes's analysis for the former relation holds true for an individual and the latter for the market.

Conclusion. The Keynesian theory of interest is not only indeterminate, but is also an inadequate explanation of the determination of the rate of interest. It treats the interest rate as a purely monetary phenomenon and by neglecting the real factors makes the theory narrow and unrealistic.

Its Superiority over the Loanable Funds Theory

Despite these criticisms of the Keynesian theory, it is considered superior to the loanable funds theory on the following counts:

(1) The Keynesian theory is a *stock* analysis. It is a statement about stocks or quantities of money at a point of time, while the loanable funds theory is a statement about certain *flows* or quantities of money per time period. It is this treatment of stocks and flows of money that leads to a fixed supply of money in the Keynesian analysis, and a variable supply of money in the loanable funds theory. Since the quantity of money is fixed at a point of time, economists prefer the stock approach to the rate of interest. Thus the liquidity preference theory becomes superior to the loanable funds theory.

(2) The liquidity preference theory is more realistic than the loanable funds theory because it is more akin to the behaviour of interest rate in the business world. It clearly spells out the various motives for holding money, and the relation between business, expectations and the rate of interest.

(3) All the variables in the loanable funds theory like saving, investment, hoarding, dishoarding are in terms of partial equilibrium analysis while the demand for and supply of money in the Keynesian system have been treated as a part of the general determinate system. So the loanable funds theory fails to fit in a general determinate system.

(4} In the loanable funds theory, saving and investment are redundant and the rate of interest can be determined by $H+D_S$ and $M+D_H$, whereas in the Keynesian theory savings are interest inelastic and investment funds depend upon the money supply. The Keynesian theory is thus superior to the loanable funds theory of interest.

Despite these apparent differences and the superiority of one over the other, there have been three attempts to prove that the two theories of the interest rate are two ways of looking at the same mechanism. "Like the frugal horse-man who brought only one spur because when one side of the horse went ahead, the other would follow, we could get along with only one of the approaches to the interest rate," as pointed out by a supporter of these views of Hicks, Lerner, Fellner and Somers. Dr. Klein who has critically analysed these attempts at reconciliation of the two theories comes to the conclusion that if only the two theories are explained in terms of stock analysis that they will come to the same thing. Since the loanable funds version is a flow analysis of the interest rate determination, it cannot be reconciled with the liquidity preference theory.[3]

---

3. L..R. Klein, *The Keynesian Revolution, pp.* 118-20.

5. INDETERMINACY OF THE CLASSICAL, THE LOANABLE FUNDS AND THE KEYNESIAN THEORIES OF INTEREST

Keynes criticised the classical theory of interest for being *indeterminate* because it failed to relate the rate of interest with the income level. To Hansen, "Keynes's criticism of the classical theory applies equally to his own theory and to the loanable funds theory." We illustrate the indeterminate nature of these theories.

In the *classical* formulation, since savings depend upon the level of income, it is not possible to know the rate of interest unless the income level is known beforehand. And the income level cannot be known without already knowing the rate of interest. A lower rate of interest will increase investment, output, employment, income and savings. So, for each income level a separate supply curve will have to be drawn.

The same reasoning applies to the *loanable funds* formulation of the rate of interest. The supply schedule of loanable funds is composed of savings, dishoarding and bank money supply. Since savings vary with past income and the new money and activated balances with the current income, it follows that the total supply schedule of loanable funds also varies with income. Thus this theory is *indeterminate* unless the income level is already known.

The indeterminate nature of both the theories is explained with the help of Figure 6. All that the classical formulation gives us is a *family* of saving schedules, and the loanable funds formulation a *family* of investment schedules at various income levels relating them to different interest rates. We take saving and investment (or demand and supply of loanable funds) on the *X*-axis and the rate of interest on the vertical axis. The savings schedules (for both the formulations) are shown as S_1Y_1 and S_2Y_2 and *II* is the investment demand schedule. When income is Y_2, given the investment demand schedule and *II*, and the savings schedule S_2Y_2, savings equal investment at interest rate *r*. Similarly when income is Y_1, the savings schedule S_1Y_1 equals the investment demand schedule *II* at interest r_1. These equilibrium positions tell us about the various levels of income associated with different rates of interest, but not about the rate of interest itself. They show that interest is a function of savings, investment and the level of income. Unless the level of income is known, it is not possible to determine the rate of interest. Hence the classical and the loanable funds theories of interest rate are *indeterminate.*

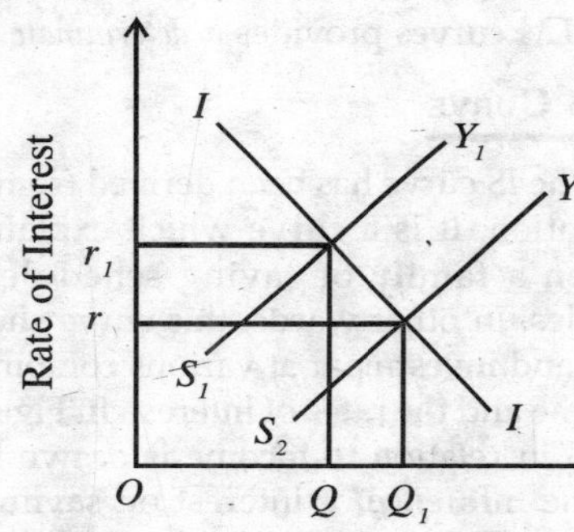

Fig. 6

The *Keynesian* theory of interest rate is also indeterminate because the liquidity preference schedule is not related to the level of income. Unless the income level is known beforehand, the demand and supply curves of money cannot tell us what the rate of interest will be. All that the Keynesian formulation provides us is a *family* of liquidity preference schedules at various income levels relating them to different interest rates. In Figure 7, a *family* of liquidity preference schedules *LY*, L_tY_1 and L_2Y_2 is drawn at various income levels. A perfectly inelastic money supply curve *QM* is drawn on the assumption that the supply of money is fixed by the monetary authority. If Y is the income level, the liquidity preference schedule *LY* equals the money supply schedule *QM* at interest rate *r*. If the income level rises to Y_1, the liquidity preference schedule also shifts upward to L_1M_t and equals the *QM* curve at the interest rate *r*. If income falls to Y_2 level, the liquidity preference curve shifts to L_2Y_2 and equals *QM* curve, at the interest rate r_2. Thus the Kenesian theory simply relates different income levels to various interest rates, but does not show what the rate of interest will be. Hence it is an

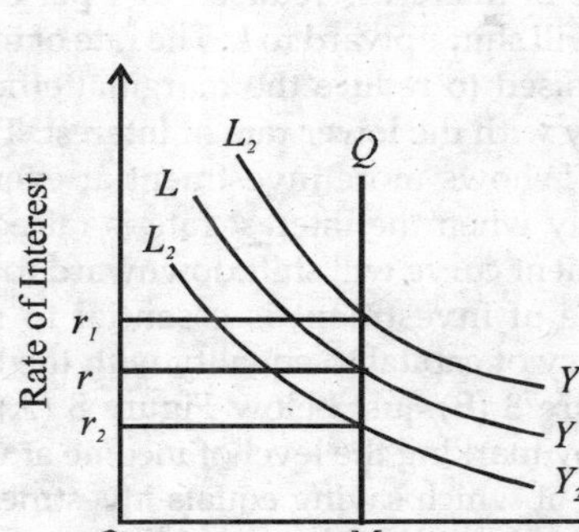

Fig. 7

indeterminate theory.

6. MODERN THEORY OF INTEREST

We have seen above that no single theory of interest rate is adequate and determinate. An adequate theory to be determinate must take into consideration both the real and monetary factors that influence the interest rate. Hicks has utilized the Keynesian tools in a method of presentation which shows that productivity, thrift, liquidity preference and money supply are all necessary elements in a comprehensive and determinate interest theory. According to Hansen, "An equilibrium condition is reached when the desired volume of cash balances equals the quantity of money, when the marginal efficiency of capital is equal to the rate of interest and finally, when the volume of investment is equal to the normal or desired volume of saving. And these factors are inter-related."[4] Thus in the modern theory of interest rate, saving, investment, liquidity preference and the quantity of money are integrated at various levels of income for a synthesis of the loanable funds theory with the liquidity preference theory.

The four variables of the two formulations have been combined to construct two new curves, the *IS* curve representing *flow* variable of the loanable funds formulation (or the real factors of the classical theory) and the *LM* curve representing the *stock* variables of liquidity preference formulation.The equilibrium between *IS* and *LM* curves provides a *determinate* solution.

THE IS CURVE

The *IS* curve has been derived from the loanable funds formulation. It is a curve which explains the relationship between a family of saving schedules and investment schedules. In other wards, this curve shows the equality of saving and investment at various combinations of the levels of income and the rates of interest. In Figure 8 (A), the saving curve *S* in relation to income is drawn in a fixed position, since the influence of interest on saving is assumed to be negligible. The saving curve shows that saving increases as income increases, viz., saving is an *increasing* function of income. Investment, on the other hand, depends on the rate of interest and the level of income. Given a level of interest rates, the level of investment rises with the level of income. At a 5 per cent rate of interest, the investment curve is I_2. If the rate of interest is reduced to 4 per cent, the investment curve will shift upward to I_3. The rate of investment will have to be raised to reduce the marginal efficiency of capital to equality with the lower rate of interest. Thus the investment curve I_3 shows more investment at every level of income. Similarly when the interest rate is raised to 6 per cent, the investment curve will shift downward to l_1. The reduction in the rate of investment is essential to raise the marginal efficiency of capital to equality with the higher interest rate. In Figure 8 (B), just below Figure 8 (A), we derive the *IS* curve by marking the level of income at various interest rates. Each point on this *IS* curve represents a level of income at which saving equals investment at various interest rates. The rate of interest is represented on the vertical axis and the level of income on the horizontal axis. If the rate of interest is 6 per cent, the *S* curve intersects the I_1 curve at E_t which determines OY_1 income. From this income level which equals Rs 100 crores we draw a dashed line downward to intersect the extended line from 6 per cent at point *A*. At interest rate 5 per

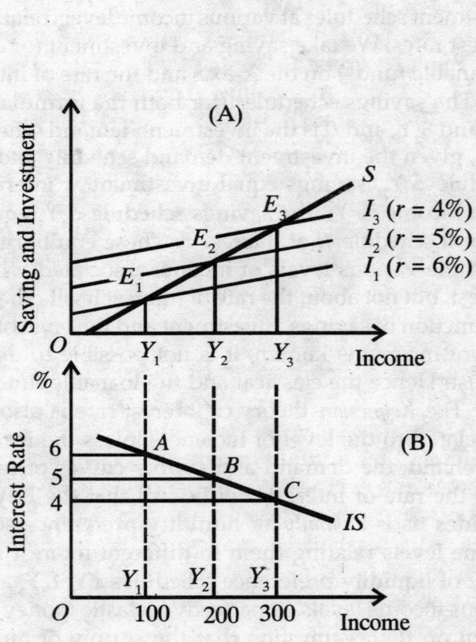

Fig. 8

4. A.H. Hansen, *Monetary Theory and Fiscal Policy*, p. 71

cent, the S curve intersects the I_2 curve at E_2 so as to determine OY_2 income (Rs 200 crores). In the lower Figure 8 (B), the point B corresponds to 5 per cent interest rate and Rs 200 crores income level. Similarly, the point C corresponds to the equilibrium of S and I_3 at 4 per cent interest rate. By connecting these points A, B and C with a line, we get the *IS* curve. The *IS* curve slopes *downward from* left to right because as the interest rate falls, investment increases and so does income.

The LM Curve

The *LM* curve shows all combinations of interest rates and levels of income at which the demand for and supply of money are equal. The *LM* curve is derived from the Keynesian formulation of liquidity preference schedules and the schedule of supply of money. A family of liquidity preference curves L_tY_1, L_2Y_2 and L_3Y_3 is drawn at income levels of Rs 100 crores, Rs 200 crores and Rs 300 crores respectively in Figure 9 (A). These curves together with the perfectly inelastic money supply curve *MQ* give us the *LM* curve. The *LM* curve consists of a series of points, each point representing an *interest-income* level at which the demand for money *(L)* equals the supply of money *(M)*. If the income Level is Y_1 (Rs 100 crores), the demand for money (L_1Y_1) equals the money supply *(QM)* at interest rate OR_1. At the Y_2 (Rs 200 crores.) income level, the L_2Y_2 and the *QM* curves equal at OR_2 interest rate. Similarly at the Y_3 (Rs 300 crores) income level, the L_3Y_3 and *QM* curves equal at OR_3 interest rate. The supply of money, the liquidity preference, the level of income and the rate of interest provide data for the *LM* curve shown in Figure 9 (B). Suppose the level of income is Y_1 (Rs 100 crores), as marked out on the income axis in Figure 9 (B). The income of Rs. 100 crores generates a demand for money represented by the liquidity preference curve L_1Y_1. From the point E_1 where the L_IY_I curve intersects the *MQ* curve, extends a dashed line horizontally to the right so as to meet the line drawn upward from Y_1 at K in Figure 9 (B). Points S and T can also be determined in a similar manner. By connecting these points K, S and T with a line, we get the *LM* curve. This curve relates different income levels to various interest rates, but it does not show what the rate of interest will be.

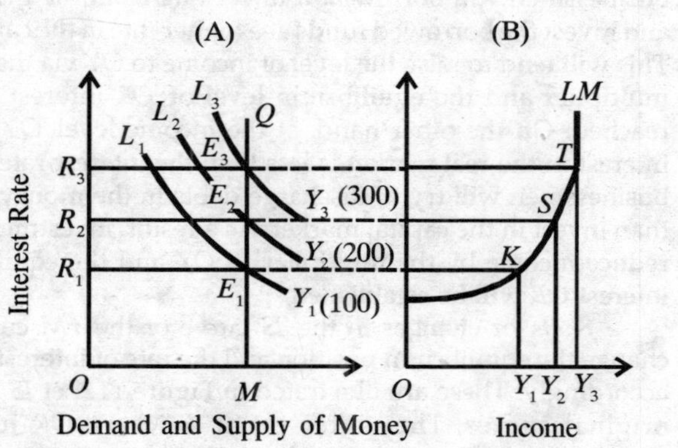

Fig. 9

The *LM* curve slopes *upward* from left to right because given the quantity of money, an increasing preference for liquidity manifests itself in a higher rate of interest. It also becomes gradually *perfectly inelastic* shown as the vertical portion from T above on the *LM* curve in Panel (B) of Figure 9. This is because at higher income levels the demand for transaction and precautionary motives increases so that little is left to satisfy the demand for speculative motive out of a given supply of money. We may also note that at the extreme left the *LM* curve is *perfectly elastic* in relation to the rate of interest. This is shown as the horizontal portion of the *LM* curve which starts from the vertical axis in Panel (B) of Figure 9. With the decline in the level of income, the demand for transactions and precautionary motives also declines. Thus a larger amount is available in the form of idle balances but it does not lead to the lowering of the interest rate because we have reached the limit to which the rate of interest will fall. This lower limit to which the rate of interest will fall is the Keynesian *liquidity trap* already explained above in Keynes's theory of interest.

Determination of the Rate of Interest

The *IS* and *LM* curves relate to income levels and interest rates. Taken by themselves they cannot tell us either about the level of income or the rate of interest. It is only their intersection that determines the rate of interest. This is illustrated in Figure 10 where the *LM* and *IS* curves intersect at point E and *OR* rate of interest is determined corresponding to the income level *OY*. The income level and the interest rate lead to simultaneous equilibrium in the *real* (saving-investment) market and the *money* (demand and supply of money) market. This general equilibrium position persists at a point of time. If there is any deviation from this equilibrium position, certain forces will act and react in such a. manner that the equilibrium will be restored. At the income level OY_t the rate of interest in the real market is Y_1B and it is Y_1A in the money market. When the former rate is higher than the latter rate ($Y_1B > Y_1A$), the businessmen will borrow at a lower rate from the money market and invest the borrowed funds at a higher rate in the capital market. This will tend to raise the level of income to *OY* via the investment multiplier and the equilibrium level of *OR* interest rate will be reached. On the other hand, at the income level OY_2 the rate of interest in the real market is less than the interest rate in the money market ($Y_2C < Y_2D$). In this situation, the businessmen will try to discharge debts in the money market rather than invest in the capital market. As a result, investment will fall and reduce income by the multiplier to *OY* and the equilibrium rate of interest *OR* will be established,

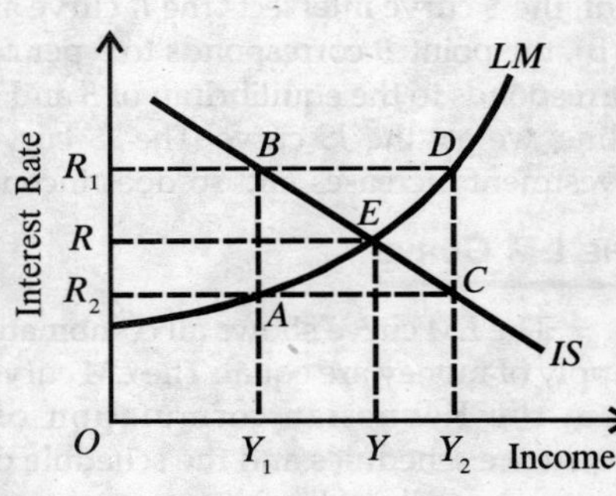

Fig. 10

Shifts or changes in the *IS* curve or the *LM* curve or in both change the equilibrium position and the rate of interest is determined accordingly. These are illustrated in Figure 11. Let *IS* and *LM* be the original curves. They intersect at *E* where *OR* interest rate is determined at *OY* income level. If the investment demand schedule shifts upward, or the saving schedule shifts downward, the curve *IS* would shift to the right as IS_1 curve. Given the *LM* curve, equilibrium will take place at E_1. The rate of interest would be OR_1 and the income level OY_1. If the quantity of money is increased or the liquidity preference cruve is lowered, the *LM* curve would shift to the rights as LM_1. It intersects IS_1 curve at point E_2. The new equilibrium rate of interest is *OR* and the income level is OY_2. *Thus with a given LM curve, when the IS curve shifts to the right income increases and along with it the rate of interest also rises. Given the IS curve, when the LM curve shifts to the right, income increases but the rate of interest falls. The Hicks-Hansen analysis is thus an integrated and determinate theory of interest in which the two determinates, the IS and LM curves, based on productivity, thrift, liquidity preference and the supply of money, all play their parts in the determination of the rate of interest.*

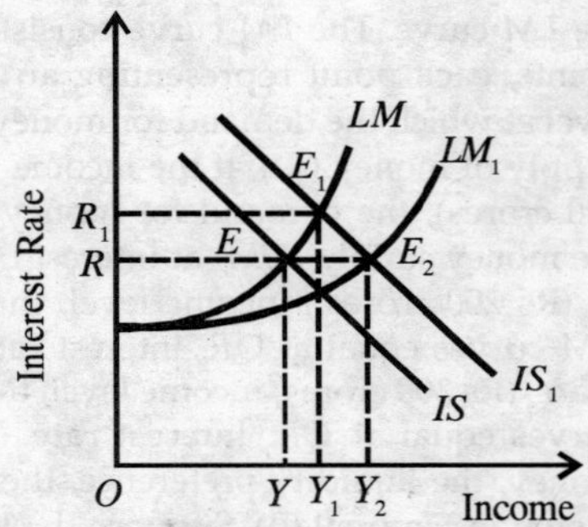

Fig. 11

Its Criticisms

Despite its merits, the Hicks.-Hansen theory of interest rate is not free from certain weaknesses.

1. *Static Theory.* It is a static theory that explains the short-run behaviour of the economy. Thus it fails to explain how the economy behaves in the long run.

2. *Interest Rate not Flexible.* The theory is based on the assumption that the interest rate is flexible and varies with changes in *LM* or/and *IS* curves. But it may not always happen if the interest rate happens to be rigid because the adjustment mechanism will not take place.

3. *Investment not Interest Elastic.* The theory assumes that investment is interest elastic. But if investment is interest inelastic, as is generally the case in practice, then the Hicks-Hansen theory does not hold good.

4. *Highly Artificial.* According to Don Patinkin, the Hicks-Hansen theory is highly artificial and oversimplified because it divides the economy into real and monetary sectors. In reality, the real and monetary sectors of the economy are so interrelated and interdependent that they act and react on each other.

5. *Closed Model.* According to Prof. Rowan, the Hicks-Hansen theory is a closed model which does not take into consideration the effect of international trade. This restricts its usefulness for the study of policy

problems.

6. *Price Level Exogenous Variable.* The price level is treated as an exogenous variable in this model. This is unrealistic because price changes play an important role in the determination of income and interest rates in an economy.

Despite these weaknesses, this theory does not undermine the utility *of* the *IS-LM* technique in explaining the determination of interest rate in an economy.

7. NATURAL AND MARKET RATE OF INTEREST

THE WICKSELL THEORY

Knut Wicksell[5] was the first economist to discuss in detail the relation between natural interest rate and market interest rate. In his book *Interest and Prices,* he uses such phrases as 'ordinary rate', 'the normal rate', and 'the real rate' as synonyms for the natural rate. He defined it in these words: "The rate of interest at which the *demand for loan capital and the supply of savings* exactly agree, and which more or less corresponds to the expected yield on the newly created capital, will then be the normal or natural real rate". It is the rate consistent with a stable money supply and stable prices. On the other hand, the market rate of interest is the money rate prevailing in the loan market. It is the rate of interest charged by banks or lenders. It depends upon the demand and supply of money.

Assumptions

The Wicksell theory is based on. the following assumptions:

1. There is full employment in the economy.
2. Investment is a decreasing function of the rate of interest.
3. Saving is an increasing function of the rate of interest.

Explanation

According to Wicksell, the natural rate is essentially variable. It is partly determined by the demand for loans which, in turn, depends on the expected profitability of new investment. All factors which affect the expected profitability of investment bring changes in the natural rate of interest. They are changes in productive efficiency or technical progress, changes in domestic and foreign demand, changes in the supply of capital, labour and land, etc. But in order to ensure a constant supply of savings, which is the second determinant of the natural rate of interest, the natural rate would have to be the same in all enterprises and in all uses, with the ratio for future land to present land equal to the ratio of future labour to present labour. Any shift in these relationships would change the value of capital and alter the connection between capital goods industries and consumer goods industries.

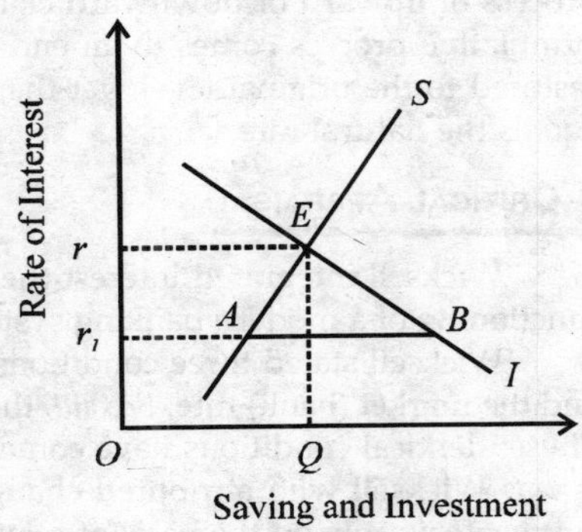

Fig. 12

Wicksell points out that the natural rate is not the same as the market rate. There are disparities between the two rates during the short run which produce changes in the price level. The market rate of interest tends to be sticky and responds slowly to changes in the demand for loanable funds. In the long run, disparities between the two rates automatically generate forces which bring their equality.

According to Wicksell, the natural rate diverges from the market rate when the economy is in disequilibrium. As a result, a cumulative process is created whereby discrepancy emerges between the cost of borrowing capital and expected profitability of new investment. A cumulative process is a disequilibrium situation in which net investment is positive and is constantly increasing from

5. *Knut Wicksell, Interest and Prices: A Study of the Causes Regulating the Value of Money,* 1898; and *Lectures of Political Economy,* Vol. II, 1906 both translated from Swedish, the former by R.F. Kahn, *1936,* and the latter by *E.* Classen, 1935.

period to period. This happens when the market rate is lower than the natural rate. This is shown in Figure 12 where I is the investment demand curve or the demand curve for loans and S is the supply curve of savings or loanable funds. Suppose r is the natural rate of interest and r_1 the market rate of interest. Thus at the market rate of interest r_1, the investment demand (or demand for loans) exceeds the supply of savings by AB. It means that bank loans expand and funds are used to increase the demand for investment goods. As a result, the total demand for money exceeds the available supply of money. In a situation of full employment, this raises the demand for goods and services thereby increasing prices. This increased demand for money, in turn, raises the market rate of interest. With the rise in the market rate of interest, money incomes expand and the transactions demand for money increases which reduces the available supply of money for lending purposes. Assuming no further increase in money supply, the money rate of interest comes into equality with the natural rate of interest at point E in Figure12. On the contrary, if the money rate of interest is higher than the natural rate, the demand for bank loans falls, bringing down the market rate of interest till it equals the natural rate.

According to Wicksell, the cumulative process of disequilibrium may also be caused by increase in the demand for loans due to innovations and technical progress which raise the expected profitability of new investment. This is illustrated in Figure 13. The initial monetary equilibrium is shown by the equality of S and I curves at point E where both the natural and market rates are equal at r interest rate. The increased demand for loans is shown by the shifting of the investment demand curve upward from I to I_1. This causes the natural rate to rise to r_1 when the S and I_1 curves intersect at E_1. If the monetary authority does not raise the market rate r to the level of the natural rate r_1, the banks increase their lendings at the market rate of interest (r). The increased monetary demand will raise prices. As prices rise aggregate demand would increase along the horizontal axis at the market rate r. In terms of Figure 13, at the market rate r, the supply of loans by banks is $OQ(=rE)$ and with the increase in the demand for investment funds to I_1, banks increase the money supply by QQ_1 (=EA). Thus the horizontal line EA is a perfectly elastic supply curve which equals I_1 curve at A and the increased investment demand is met by QQ_1 loans from the banks. With the increase in money supply, the demand for capital goods rises which, in turn, raises the demand for goods and services, and consequently raises their prices. This process of money expansion and inflationary rise in prices will ultimately raise the market rate r to the level of natural rate of interest r_1. In Wicksell's analysis, business fluctuations are traced to the divergence between natural and market rates of interest. Expansion in the economy takes place when the natural rate is above the market rate, and *vice-versa*. In the cumulative process of upward or downward change, expansions and contractions of bank credit play a crucial role. The cumulative process comes to an end when the two rates are brought into equality. But prices would not be restored to the original level, yet there would be a new equilibrium for the economy where the market rate equals the natural rate.

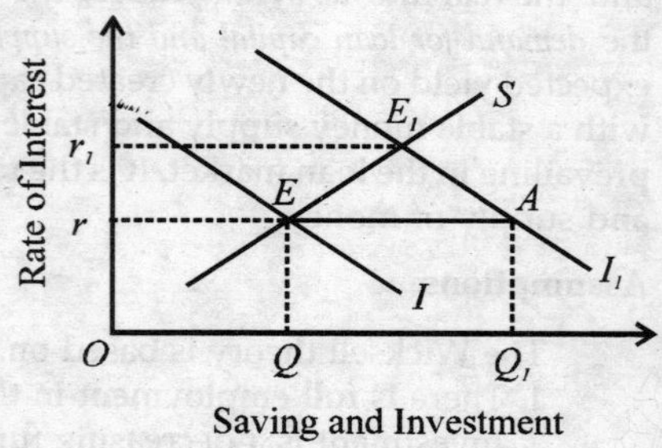

Fig. 13

A Critical Appraisal

Wicksell integrated interest theory, quantity theory, aggregate demand and aggregate supply, and the functioning of a modern banking system. He thus anticipated some of the current notions in monetary theory.

Wicksell stated three conditions in his theory: *First*, the equality between the natural (equilibrium) rate and the market (bank) rate. *Second*, the equality of *ex ante* saving and investment. *Third*, a constant price level. These identical conditions have come to be known as "monetary equilibrium" in modern monetary analysis. It was Wicksell who attributed changes in the price level to discrepancies between aggregate demand and aggregate supply on the basis of relationship between saving and investment. In this way, he formulated an income approach to the problem of money and prices which "contained the embryo of a theory of output as a whole", according to Ohlin.

It was again Wicksell who stressed the importance of the rate of interest in monetary theory. "By concentrating upon the rate of interest", writes Prof. Hansen, "He swept away the narrow foundations of the quantity theory."[6]

Further, Wicksell integrated monetary and non-monetary theories of interest by emphasising the equilibrium of natural interest rate and market interest rate. He thus paved the way for a determinate theory of interest, as developed by Hicks and Hansen, which is regarded as the modern theory of interest.

Again, Wicksell's cumulative process has come to be known as the *Wicksell Effect.* It emphasises the importance of bank credit-creation on the rate of interest. Mrs Robinson regards the Wicksell Effect as "the key to the whole theory of capital accumulation."

Moreover, Wicksell was a quantity theorist who wanted "to arrive at a theory which should be both self-consistent and in full agreement with facts." His analysis of the link between the banking system and short-run inflations during the cumulative process is to be found in the hyper-inflation case studies in Friedman's *Studies in the Quantity Theory of Money.* Similarly the suppressed inflation that followed the post-War years 1945-51 due to the policies adopted by monetary authorities in the USA may also be attributed to the Wicksellian cumulative process. Thus Wicksell was the forerunner of the modern monetary theorists.

Its Defects

But he is not free from critics who have pointed out certain defects in his theory.

1. According to Professor Ackley, "Wicksell's analysis differed from the simple quantity theory only in the *process* by which its results were achieved, not in its results. *In equilibrium,* prices were proportional to the money supply, and both were constant in time. *In equilibrium,* there were no idle balances flowing into the capital market nor additions needing to be made to cash balances in order to finance a larger volume of money transactions."[7]. Thus Wicksell thought of only transactions and precautionary matives neglected the speculative motive to hold money.

2. "Moreover, his work falls short of an adequate theory of income determination. It related to one determinant of income, the investment function," according to Hansen.[8]

3. Hansen further points out that "the multiplier analysis, based on the consumption function was missing. There is, moreover, implicit in much of Wicksell's work an excessively optimistic view with respect to the interest-elasticity of investment. And he saw very dimly the relation of the demand for cash holdings to the rate of interest. He failed to see that in certain situations the investment function may be interest-inelastic while the liquidity preference function may be highly interest-elastic. Wicksell did not clearly understand the conditions under which interest-rate policy becomes futile. Accordingly, he enormously exaggerated the power of the banking system to control, by interest rate manipulations, the flow of aggregate demand and the level of prices:"[9]

Fisher's Analysis

In modern analysis, the *real or natural* rate *of interest refers to the percentage rate paid on borrowed money after making on adjustment for changes in the price level.* On the other hand, *the market or money rate of interest is the percentage* rate paid on *borrowed money.* If a person borrows Rs 10,000 from a bank at 6 per cent, it is the money rate of interest. He will have to return Rs10,600 (Rs 10,000+Rs 600 as interest charges) to the bank after a year. If, however, during this period the price index rises by 1.02, the real rate of interest is reduced. In order to find out the real rate of interest, the sum repaid to the bank is deflated by the price index, i.e. Rs 10,600/1.02=Rs 10,392. It implies that the bank has earned 3.92 per cent as real interest as against the money rate of 6 per cent per annum. If the price index falls, a given money rate of interest will imply a higher real rate of interest.

Following Marshall, Fisher enunciated the proposition that the *money rate of interest is equal to the real rate of interest plus the rate of change in the price level.* Suppose prices are falling at 5 per cent per annum, a zero money

6. A.H Hansen, *Monetary Theory and Fiscal Policy,* p. 71.
7. G. Ackley *op. cit* p. 161.
8. A.H. Hansen *op. cit., p,* 89.
9. *Ibid., p,* 93.

rate of interest in this case implies a real rate of 5 per cent. To quote Marshall, a money rate of 5 per cent per annum corresponds to a *real* rate of 15.5 per cent when prices are falling at 10 per cent per annum, i.e., the purchasing power of \$ 105 at the beginning of the year is equivalent to that of \$ 115.50 at the end of the year. Similarly, a money rate of 5 per cent corresponds to a *negative* real rate of 5.5 per cent when the annual rate at which prices are rising is 10 per cent.

In case the price level is *constant*, the money rate equals the real rate of interest. To take our previous example, let the money rate of interest and the real rate of interest be 6 per cent with a constant price level. Suppose with a rise in the price level by 2 per cent, the real rate of interest falls to 4 per cent equivalent to the rise in the price level. There is, however, no change in the money rate due to "the money illusion or institutional rigidity in the money market." Given the marginal efficiency of investment, a fall in the real rate of interest will encourage investment and *vice-versa*. This is illustrated in Fig 14. Money and real interest rate are taken on the vertical axis along with the marginal efficiency of investment. The amount of investment is shown on the horizontal axis. *MEI* is the curve of marginal efficiency of investment. With a constant price level, *mr* represents money as well as real rate, of interest which is 6 per cent per annum. At this rate, *OI* investment is taking place. With the rise in the price level by 2 per cent, there is an equivalent fall in the real rate, as depicted by the new interest line r_1r_2 at 4 per cent interest rate. Now the *mr* line represents only the money rate of 6 per cent. A fall in the real rate of interest has tended to encourage investment from *OI* to OI_1. Converse is true when the price level falls.

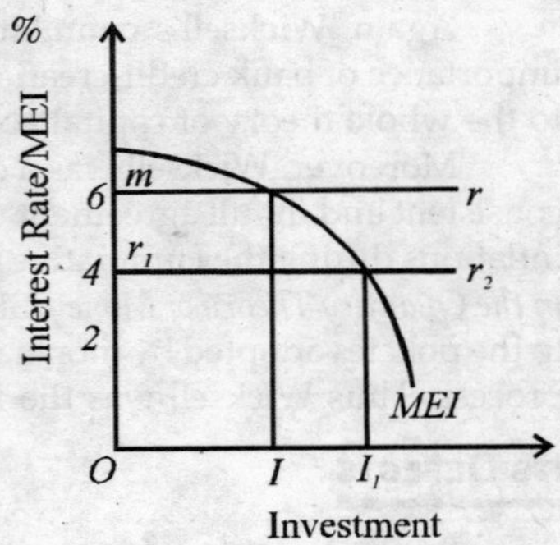

Fig. 14

EXERCISES

1. Discuss the role of the real forces of thrift and productivity in determination of the rate of interest.
2. In what respects is the loanable funds theory of interest an improvement on the classical theory?
3. "Interest theory has been confused by a failure to distinguish clearly between the money rate and the natural rate of interest." Discuss.
4. Critically discuss the Keynesian theory of liquidity preference as an explanation of the determination of the interest rate.
5. Compare the classical and the Keynesian theories of the rate of interest.
6. How are rate of interest and national income determined simultaneously in an economy?
7. Explain the Hicks-Hansen reconciliation of the stock and flow theories of interest rate.
8. Discuss Wicksell's theory of interest rates.
9. Write a note on Fisher's theory of real and market rate of interest.

CHAPTER 19

Term Structure of Interest Rates

MEANING

The term structure of interest rates refers to the relationship between market rates of interest on short-term and long-term securities. It is the interest rate difference on fixed income securities due to differences in time of maturity. It is, therefore, also known as time-structure or maturity-structure of interest rates which explains the relationship between yields and maturities of the same type of security.

If two securities are identical in every respect except maturity, it is likely that they will sell in the market at different prices (or yields or interest rates). Generally, their prices will change in the same direction. If the short-term securities rise in price, the long-term securities will also rise in price. People generally hold both short-term securities and they adjust their holdings of securities depending on the relative yields. Usually the long term securities tend to fluctuate more in price than the short-term securities, even though their yields do not fluctuate as much.

The relationship between yields and terms to maturity is depicted graphically by a yield curve. Figure 1 shows three yield curves. When short-term interest rates are above long-term interest rates, the yield curve slopes downward, as the curve *FF*. When short-term interest rates are below long-term interest rates, the yield curve slopes upward, as the curve *RR*. When the short-term yields equal long-term yields, the yield curve is flat, as the curve *HL*.

FACTORS DETERMINING THE TERM STRUCTURE OF INTEREST RATES

What determines the shape of the yield curve? There are three factors which determine the term structure of interest rates. They are risk preference, supply and demand of securities, and expectations and uncertainty. These factors determine whether short-term interest rates are above or below long-term interest rates. We discuss these factors as under:

1. Risk Preference. Long-term security prices are sensitive to changes in interest rates because the chances to default are higher on long-term securities as compared to short-term securities. Therefore, lenders prefer to lend for short-term, if short-term and long-term securities have identical yields. This would push up short-term prices of securities and bring down their yields. Hence the yield curve slopes upward. On the other hand, borrowers prefer to borrow for long period because they will not have to worry about rising interest rates or to renew their loans frequently. They are, therefore, willing to pay more for long-term securities as compared to short-term securities. This will also cause the yield curve to slope upward. Thus the preferences of both lenders and borrowers lead to low rates on short-term securities and high rates on long-term securities, thereby bringing about an upward sloping yield curve.

2. Supply-Demand Conditions. When the supply of short-term securities falls and that of long-term securities rises, the short-term interest rate comes down and the long-term interest rate is pushed up. The yield curve is upward sloping and vice versa. If the demand for securities is more in the short-run market and the supply is more in the long-run market, this will lead to high short-term and low long-term interest rates, and the yield curve will be downward sloping. The opposite supply-demand conditions will lead to an upward sloping yield curve.

3. Expectations and Uncertainty. Other factors affecting the yield curve are expectations and uncertainty. The expectation of the rise in the long-term interest rate explains that the short-term interest rate remains much below the long-term interest rate for any length of time. This produces an upward sloping yield curve. Further, certain risks and uncertainties may lead to the same results. For instance, if people expect war, social disturbances, political upheavals, uncertainties, inflationary pressures, etc., they will not purchase long-term securities except at a low price or low current yield.

Theories of Term Structure of Interest Rates

Many theories have been put forth by economists to explain differences in the structure of interest rates on short-term and long-term securities. They are discussed as under :

The Expectations Theory

The expectations theory regards future interest rates as the principal determinant of the present structure of interest rates. The theory originated with Irving Fisher, was perfected by Hicks in his *Value and Capital*, and is closely identified with Lutz.[1]

Its Assumptions

The expectations theory is based on the following assumptions:

1. All investors have definite expectations with respect to future short-term interest rates, and these expectations are held with complete confidence.
2. The objective of investors is to maximise expected profits, and they are prepared to transfer funds freely from one maturity to another in order to achieve this objective.
3. There are no costs associated with investment and disinvestment in securities. It means that there are no transaction costs.
4. The short-term and long-term interest rates are adjusted for any differences due to risk and liquidity.
5. 'Safe' securities of various maturities are perfect substitutes in the portfolios of investors.
6. Investors are profit maximisers who hold such financial assets in their portfolios which maixmise return over a period they are held.
7. All investors hold with certainty the same expectations of how future rates are going to behave.

Explanation

Given these assumptions, the theory states that the long-term interest rate at any point in time represents an average of expected short-time interest rates. Suppose a long-term security maturing after three years sells at the short-term interest rate of 2 per cent in the first year, and that the expected short-term interest rates in the second and third years are 3 per cent and 4 per cent respectively. The long-term interest rate on this security will be the average of the short-term interest rates over the three years, that is 3 per cent (=2 per cent + 3 per cent+4 per cent=9 per cent/3). If the interest rate on the short-term security for the first year is expected to decline by 1 per cent the long-term yield on the three-year security will be 2.67 per cent (=1 per cent+3 per cent+4 per cent=8 per cent/3). On the other hand, if the interest rate is expected to increase by 1 per cent on the three-year security, then the long-term yield will be 3.33 per cent (=2 per cent+3 per cent+5 per cent=10 per cent/3).

1. F.A. Lutz, "The Sturcture of Interest Rates", *Q.J.E.*, November 1940, reprinted in W.Fellner and B.F. Hally (Eds.), *Readings in the Theory of Income Distribution*, 1946, Ch. 26.

The expectations theory holds that differences in yields on securities of different maturities are due to the fact that the market expects the interest rates on different securities to be the same over an equal period of time. If this is not the case, the investor will buy security of one maturity by selling security of another maturity that he expects to provide him the highest yield. It is this "arbitrage procedure" (buying security of one maturity and selling of another maturity) which brings the equality of expected yields of different maturities.

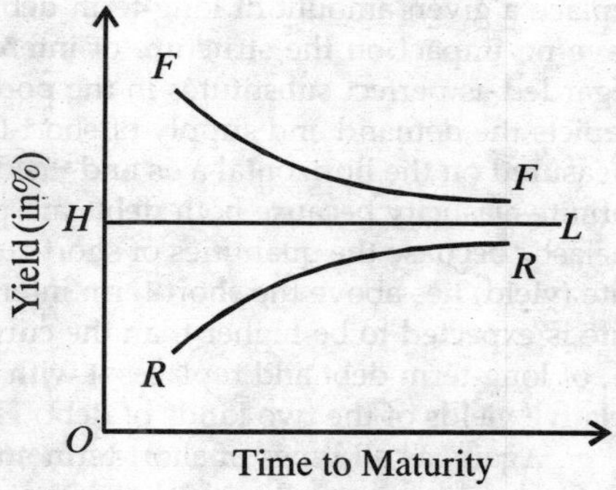

Fig. 1.

According to Warren L. Smith, "Investors generally have *repressive interest rate expectations.* That is to say, at any particular time they have an opinion regarding the level of interest rates they regard as normal, and as short-term rates rise above or fall below this level, they expect them to regress back towards this normal level. Thus, as rates rise above normal, investors expect them to fall; and as rates fall below normal, investors expect them to rise."[2] This relationship implies that "(*a*) when short-term rates are expected to fall, current short-term rates will be above long-term rates and the yield curve will be negatively sloped, and (*b*) when rates are expected to rise, current short-term rates will be below long-term rates and the yield curve will be positively sloped. By the same reasoning, when the short-term rate is at approximately the level judged to be normal and is expected neither to rise nor to fall, rates for all maturities will appoximate a horizontal line."[3]

These relationships between short-term and long-term interest rates are illustrated in Figure 1. where time to maturity, short or long-term, is taken on the horizontal axis, and yield or interest rate is taken on the vertical axis. In the first case, when the current short-term rates are above the long-term rates and are expected to fall, the yield curve *FF* is negatively sloped. In the second case, when the current short-term rates are below the long-term rates, and are expected to rise, the yield curve *RR* is positively sloped. In the third case, when the current short-term rates equal the long-term rates and the short-term rates are expected neither to rise nor to fall, the yield curve *HL* is a horizontal line.

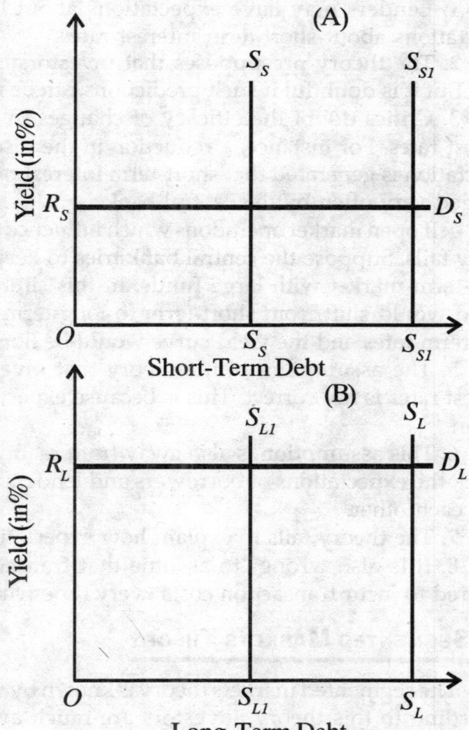

Fig. 2.

Prof. Lutz calls these yield curves as *expectations curves* which represent "the line up of the 'subjective' long rates which correspond to people's expectations after the latter have changed."[4]

The key to the expectations theory is that both short and long-term securities are perfect substitutes for each other in the portfolios of investors. If the supply of long-term securities goes up and that of short-term securities goes down, it makes no difference as far as yields are concerned. Long-term securities will be exchanged for short-term securities with no change in yields as long as expected future short-term rates are unchanged.

Its Policy Implications. The policy implications of this theory are that if the government wishes to

2. *Ibid.*, p. 289
3. Warren L. Smith, *Macroeconomics*, 1970, p. 283.
4. F.A. Lutz, *op. cit.*

replace a given amount of long-term debt with an equivalent amount of short-term debt, such a policy will have no impact on the structure of interest rates. This is because both long-term and short-term debts are regarded as perfect substitutes in the portfolio of investors. This is shown in Figure 2 (A) and (B). Panel (A) depicts the demand and supply of short-term debt and Panel (B) that of long-term debt. Each type of debt is measured on the horizontal axis and yield on the vertical axis. The demand curves D_S and D_L are drawn with infinite elasticity because both debts are perfect substitutes. The supply cuves S_S and S_L are drawn perfectly inelastic becuase the quantities of short-run and long-term debts are fixed. Assume that the long-term interest rate (yield) lies above the short-term interest rate, ie., $OR_L > OR_S$. This is because the future short-run interest rate is expected to be higher than the current short-run rate. If the government wishes to redeem (retire) S_L–S_{L1} of long-term debt and replaces it with S_S–S_{S1} of short-term debt, this is possible without any change in the relative yields of the two kinds of debt. These remain the same at OR_L and OR_S repectively.

Again, as all types of short-term and long-term bonds (securities) are perfect substitutes, therefore the central bank cannot influence the term structure of interest rates as long as it does not affect the expectations of borrowers and lenders.

Its Criticisms

However, the expectations theory has been criticised on several points:

1. Lenders may have expectations about long-term interest rates that may be independent of their expectations about short-term interest rates.

2. The theory presupposes that investors can make long-term expectations about short-term interest rates. But it is doubtful if such predictions can be made accurately.

3. Critics doubt the efficacy of changes in the central bank discount rates to influence the long-term interest rates. For instance, a reduction in the discount rate can bring a fall in the long-term rates only if the expectation is generated that short-term interest rate will remain low. This will prevent the discount rate being changed very often by the central bank.

4. If open market operations which influence the slope of the yield curve are not successful, the expectations theory fails. Suppose the central bank tries to keep long-term rates higher than short-term rates by supplying short-term market with large funds. In this situation, investors expecting that they will gain over the long period would shift from short-term to long-term securities. This would tend to equalise the short-term and long-term rates and the yield curve would be horizontal like *HL*, rather than like *RR* in Figure 1.

5. The assumption of the theory that investors hold with certainty expectations of future short-run interest rates is not correct. This is because expectations of people for short-run interest rates are occasionally certain.

6. This assumption is also away from reality that the expectations of borrowers and lenders are similar. In fact, the expectations of borrowers and lenders regarding short-term and long-term rates are quite different from each other.

7. The theory fails to explain how expectations relating to future short-term interest rates are formed.

8. It is also wrong to assume that transaction costs are zero. In reality, borrowers and lenders are required to incur transaction costs every time when they buy and sell securities.

The Segmented Markets Theory

The segmented markets theory is known by various names such as institutional, hedging or segmentation. According to this theory, investors are much averse to risk. So they hedge against risks by matching the maturity of their assets with that of their liabilities. If the maturity of an investor's assets is longer than that of his liabilities, he incurs a capital loss when he is forced to sell his assets before they are due for redemption. On the other hand, if the maturity of an investor's assets is shorter than that of his liabilities, he runs the risk of income loss. In order to avoid the two kinds of risks, investors match the maturities of their assets and liabilities.

Its Assumptions

This theory is based on the following assumptions:

1. Assets of different maturities are imperfect substitutes with each other.
2. Markets for assets of different maturities are divided into separate markets.
3. Interest rates for one type of asset in every market are determined by their demand and supply which, in turn, affect the yield to maturity.
4. There is uncertainty about the behaviour of interest rates in future.

The Theory

The segmented markets theory holds that short-term and long-term interest rates are determined in several separated or segmented markets. Some investors prefer short-term securities, while other investors, such as insurance companies, prefer long-term securities. Thus securities of different maturities are imperfect substitues for buyers and sellers of securities in the market.

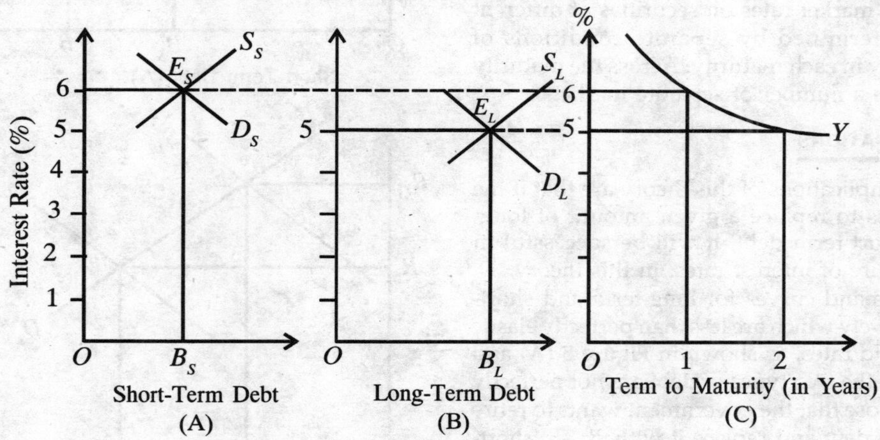

Fig. 3.

Consequently, the yield curve is the result of several demand and supply curves for securities of different maturities. Given the demand for securities, if the supply of short-term securities is less than the demand for long-term securities, the short-term interest rate will be higher than the long-term interest rate. In this situation, the yield curve will slope downward to the right, as shown by the curve Y in Fig. 3 (C). In Panel (A) of the figure, D_S and S_S are the demand and supply curves of short-term debts respectively which are in equilibrium at point E_S. Thus they determine 6% equilibrium interest rate on short-term securities. In Panel (B), D_L and D_S are the demand and supply curves respectively of long-term debts which determine 5% equilibrium interest rate at point E_L on long-term securities. These interest rates provide the downward sloping yield curve Y in Panel (C).

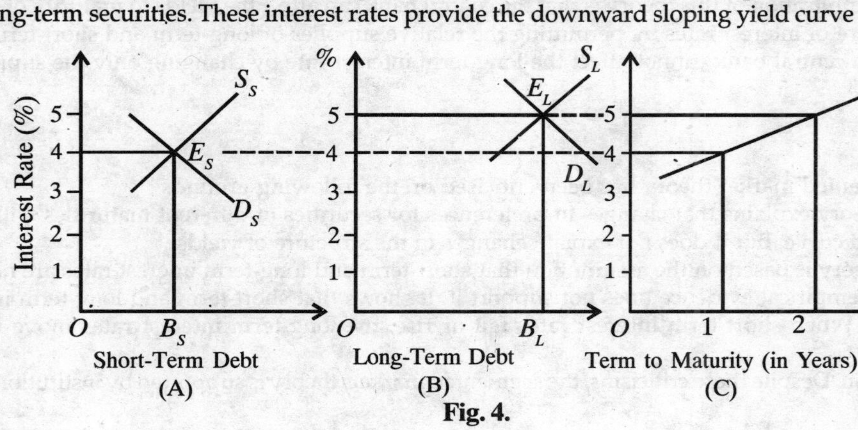

Fig. 4.

On the contrary, given the demand for securities, when the supply of short-term securities is greater than the demand for them, the short-term interest rates will be lower than the long-term interest rates. In such a situation, the yield curve will slope upward to the right, as shown in Fig. 4 (C). In Panel (A) of the figure , D_S and S_S curves determine 4% short-term equilibrium interest rate at point E_S on short-term assets. Similarly in Panel (B), D_L and S_L curves determine 5% long-term equilibrium interest rate at point E_L. These interest rates provide the upward sloping yield curve Y in Panel (C). Thus, according to the segmented market theory, the market rates on securities of different maturities are determined by separate conditions of demand and supply in each maturity. Across the maturity spectrum, there are a number of separate markets.

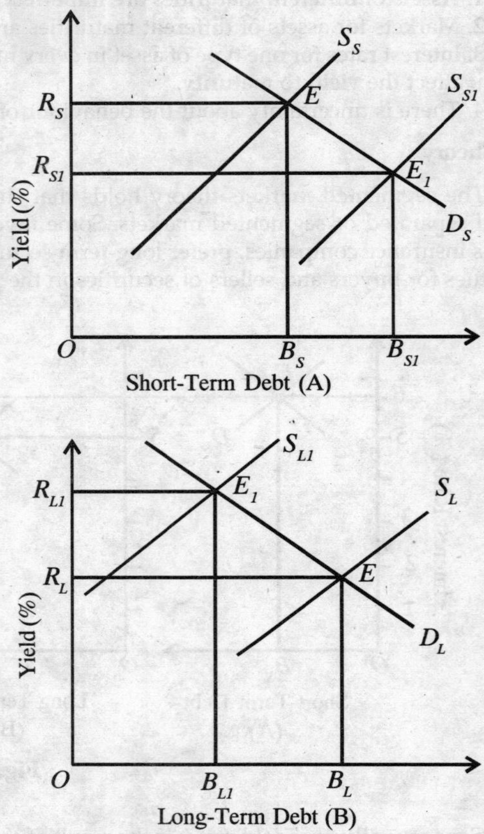

Fig. 5.

Its Policy Implications

The policy implications of this theory are that if the government wishes to replace a given amount of long-term debt by a short-term debt, it will be successful in twisting the structure of interest rates. In this theory, D_S and D_L are the demand curves for long-term and short-term debts respectively which are less than perfectly elastic with respect to yield rates, as shown in Figure 5 (A) and (B). This is because the two types of debt are not perfectly substitutable. Suppose that the government wants to retire $B_L–B_{L1}$ of long-term debt and replace it with $B_{S1}–B_S$ short-term debt. Notice that the spread between the rates has been reduced. When the government substitutes long-term debt by short-term debt, the supply of long-term debt is reduced from S_L to S_{L1} and the long-term interest rate rises from R_L to R_{L1}, as shown in Panel (B) of the figure. On the other hand, the supply of short-term debt increases from S_S to S_{S1} which brings a fall in the short-term interest rate from R_S to R_{S1}, as shown in Panel (A) of the figure. Notice that the fall in the short-term interest rate is less than the rise in the long-term interest rate : $R_S–R_{S1} < R_L–R_{L1}$.

Another implication of this theory is that the central bank can affect the yields to maturity of securities or the term structure of interest rates by permitting the relative supplies of long-term and short-term securities.

Again, the central bank cannot affect the long-term interest rate by changing only the supply of short-term securities.

Its Criticisms

The segmented market theory has been criticised on the following grounds :

1. This theory explains that changes in preferences for securities of different maturities will alter in the form of the yield curve. But it does not explain changes in the structure of yields.

2. This theory is based on the assumption that short-term and long-term interest rates are not related to each other. But empirical evidence does not support it. It shows that short-term and long-term interest rates move together. When short-term interest rates fall or rise, the long-term interest rates move in the same direction.

Conclusion. Despite these criticisms, the segmented markets theory is supported by institutional practices.

Accordingly, commercial banks which place emphasis on liquidity, deal in short-term securities, and insurance companies with long-term securities. Similarly, inventories are financed with short-term loans, and purchases of houses with long-term mortgages.

ITS SUPERIORITY OVER EXPECTATIONS THEORY

The segmented market theory is superior to the expectations theory on the following counts :

1. The segmented market theory is superior to the expectations theory because it does not assume the unrealistic assumption of the expectations theory that short-term and long-term securities are perfect substitutes. The risks in short-term securities are less than those in long-term securities. If a person sells his security before its maturity and the interest rate is more than expected, the price of the long-term security will be less as compared with the short-term security. Thus, short-term and long-term securities are not perfect substitutes.

2. The segmented market theory is also superior to the expectations theory because it rejects the assumption of the latter that the future interest rates are known with certainty. In reality, they are uncertain. Due to large price-changes of long-term securities, there is much uncertainty in holding them. On the other hand, there is great uncertainty of future yields in holding short-term securities.

3. Another reason of the superiority of segmented market theory over the expectations theory is that it does not explain the term structure of interest rates on the basis of the average of expected short-term interest rates. Rather, the segmented market theory determines both the short-term and long-term interest rates in the form of demand and supply of a particular security, as happens in reality in a financial market.

4. As against the expectations theory, the segmented market theory does not explain a unique relation between short-term and long-term interest rates. In reality, the behaviour of short-term and long-term interest rates depends on the relation between money market and bond market. Short-term and long-term interest rates in both markets are determined by the demand and supply of each type of security.

5. The segmented market theory is also superior to the expectations theory because it is supported by institutional practices. Accordingly, commercial banks which place emphasis on liquidity deal in short-term securities, and insurance companies with long-term securities. Similarly, inventories are financed with short-term debts and purchases of houses with long-term mortgages.

THE SUBSTITUTABILITY THEORY

The substitutability theory holds that short-term and long-term securities are substitutes for borrowers and lenders. When buyers and sellers of securities are engaged in arbitrage and switching operations, they tend to eliminate discrepancies between long-term and short-term interest rates in the short run. For such operations, the theory assumes optimising behaviour on the part of buyers and sellers, and relatively free and unrestricted markets.

Given these assumptions, prices of short-term securities move in the same direction as the long-term securities. For instance, a fall in the price of short-term securities (or a rise in the short-term interest rates) will be followed by a fall in the prices of long-term securities (or a rise in the long-term interest rates), and vice versa.

The forces which lead to such parallel moments between short-term and long-term interest rates are (*a*) the substitutability of alternative investment opportunities on the part of lenders and the alternative means of financing on the part of borrowers, and (*b*) by tendency for changes in credit and monetary conditions to have a simultaneous impact on the financial market.

The substitutability theory is important for conducting monetary policy when by arbitrage and switching operations, changes are transmitted from one sector of the financial market to the other by the central bank.

However, it is doubtful if investors will readily switch over from short-term to long-term securities. Therefore, the perfect substitutability assumed between the two types of securities breaks down.

THE KEYNESIAN THEORY

There are two theories associated with Keynes. The *first* is known as the *fluidity theory* which Keynes put forth in his *Treatise on Money*, and the *second* is called the *psychological theory* which he propounded in his *General Theory*. The fluidity theory holds that there is correspondence, both in direction and timing, of movement in interest rates with short-term interest rates moving proportiontely more than long-term interest rates. Further, any action on the part of the central bank to influence short-term interest rates is readily transmitted to long-term interest rates. But Keynes himself admitted that during a slump in security prices, the central bank's action to influence short-term securities through open market operation may not help in reducing yield on long-term securities.

The psychological theory holds that the long-term interest rate is a highly psychological phenomenon dominated by short-run expectations about its future level. The long-term interest rates are sticky in the downward direction even when short-term interest rates decline substantially. This is due to the psychology of investors. If they believe that the long-term interest rates have reached the "irreducible conventional minimum" and the next change would be in the upward direction, they will not deal in long-term securities for fear of capital loss. This happens during a depression when liquidity preference is perfectly interest elastic. All efforts on the part of the central bank to purchase short-term securities in the open market will fail to persuade investors to buy long-term securities.

These Keynesian theories of term-structure of interest rates have been neglected and attention has focussed on the expectational theory and the segmented markets theory which have been empirically tested.

The Liquidity or Risk Premium Theory

A variant of the Expectations Theory and the Keynesian Fluidity Theory is called the Liquidity or Risk Premium Theory. The theory rejects the view that short-term and long-term securities are comparable except for maturity. But it accepts the view that yields on various maturities are related to each other by the expectations of long-run and short-run rates. Thus it adds to the expectations theory that lenders and borrowers differ in their attitudes to short-term and long-term securities. Lenders prefer to lend for short-term and borrowers prefer to borrow for long-term. This is because the return on short-term securities is certain but that on long-term securities is uncertain on account of uncertainties of future interest rates. The uncertainty is greater, the longer the maturity of securities. Thus risks associated with long-term securities are greater. Under the circumstances, lenders prefer the safer short-term securities. To induce the market to hold the long-term securities supplied by long-term borrowers, the expected return on them must exceed that on short-term securities by a premium which is called an *expected risk or liquidity premium*. Thus long-term securities being more risky would command larger liquidity premiums.

As long-term securities carry higher risk premium, it follows that interest rates increase as one moves from short-term to long-term securities. The higher interest rates on longer-term securities are determined by two components: (a) the expectations component, and (b) the liquid premium component. The *liquidity premium* component will always lead to higher interest rates on long-term securities than on short-term securities. This tendency has been called by Hicks the "constitutional weakness" or the "congenital market weakness" by some other supporters of the theory. This tendency of higher interest rates may be counteracted partially or even fully by the *expectations component* which is assumed as given.

Prof. Newelyn in his *Theory of Money* has modified this theory by dropping the expectations component and introducing the concepts of encashment and requirement periods. The concept of *encashment period* is associated with the *lender*. The lender calculates the period for which he is prepared to lend his funds and at the end of which he will encash them. This is the encashment period. If he lends his funds for a period shorter than the encashment period, he is not certain about his interest income which he may be able to get for the remaining period. A part of the interest income will depend on the future behaviour of interest rates. Thus the lender runs an "income risk", accoding to Newelyn, which the lender can avoid if the duration of the loan is equal to the encashment period. On the other hand, if the loan is longer than the encashment period, he runs a capital risk. This may be due to differences in the market price of a loan from its face value. It follows that the lender can avoid both the risks if he lends his funds exactly for the encashment period. So long as the duration of the loan does not exceed the encashment period, the lender is not to be paid any liquidity premium to induce him to part with his funds.

The concept of the *requirement period* is related to the *borrower* who calculates the period for which he requires the loan and at the end of which he will repay it. If the borrower borrows for a period equal to his requirement period, the interest cost of the loan is predetermined and there is no uncertainty about this. When the borrower borrows for the duration of the requirement period, he avoids the income risk which is the interest risk cost. If he borrows for a shorter period than the requirement period and thinks of borrowing for the remaining period later on, he runs the risk of incurring a different interest cost, and thereby incurs an income risk. If he borrows for a longer period than the requirement period, he may pay a price different from the face value of the debt for the excess period. In this case, he runs the capital risk. The borrower can avoid both the risks if he borrows exactly equal to the requirement period.

We find that both the lender and the borrower can avoid the income and capital risks if the maturity of the loan coincides with the encashment and the requirement period repectively. Newelyn's analysis is based on the presumption that the average requirement period of the borrowers exceeds the average encashment period of the lenders. This lures the lenders to lend for a period longer than the encashment period and thereby run the capital risk. As a result, longer maturity loans would be carrying a premium against the capital risk. The premium would be larger as we move from shorter to longer maturities which would move the interest rates upward. Thus long-term interest rates tend to be higher than short-term interest rates and the market demands a premium called *liquidity premium* to hold long-term securities. According to Newelyn, "This can be done by relating the maturity of existing assets to the maturity which would be required if all assets were to mature at the date at which the holders anticipate that ancashment be required."

This is explained in Figure 6. The encashment curve *E* shows the cumulative total funds measured on the horizontal axis increasing to *F* as the period within which encashment is expected to increase to time *T*. Similarly, the maturity curve *M* shows the cumulative total assets increasing to *F* as the period within which their maturity increases to time *T*. The curve *M* rises from a positive value of *M* at zero life to maturity, indicating the existence of money and quasi-money (*M*). Both the curves represent the same total amount of funds (*F*), reflecting that the total funds must be distributed among the existing stock of assets. But they explain the different distributions of two characteristics of this total of funds: (i) the encashment period of the funds and the length of life to maturity of the assets in which the funds must be held; and (ii) the time period *T* is assumed to be sufficiently long to include all bonds and the maximum encashment period.

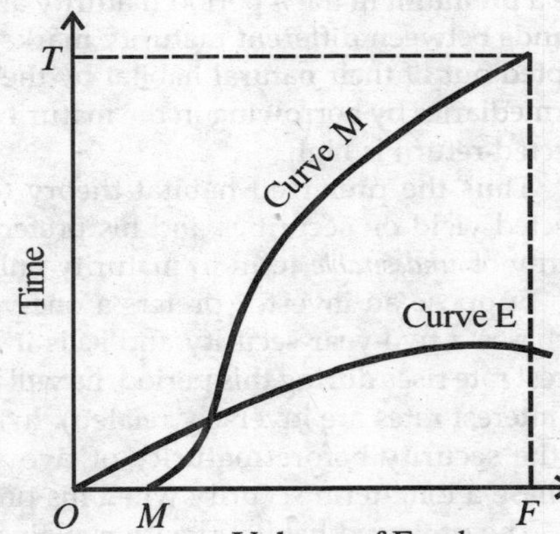

Fig. 6.

The area under the maturity curve *M* will change inversely with changes in the degree of maturity of the existing stock of assets. On the other hand, the area under the encashment curve *E* will change inversely with changes in the degree of maturity consistent with zero capital risk for the investor. Therefore, the general level of interest rates will be a function of the difference between the two areas because this difference measures the extent to which investors must be induced to accept the risk of capital loss if the demand for maturity is to be equated with the given supply of funds.

Conclusion. This theory is more realistic than the expectations theory because it takes into consideration the risk involved by investors of securities of different maturities. Rather, it is an improvement over the other term structure theories and is the most acceptable among the majority of economists.

THE PREFERRED HABITAT THEORY

Modigliani and Sutch[5] have propounded the *Preferred Habitat Theory* of the term structure of interest rates. It combines the main features of both the expectations and segmented market theories. According to this

5. F. Modigliani and R. Sutch, "Innovations in Interest Rate Policy", *A.E.R.*, May 1966.

theory, investors have a preference for securities of a given term and they want to choose them according to their expected yield. But they will be willing to purchase securities of some other term by substituting them for securities of a preferred term. They will do so if they are compensated by the term premium. The term premium is a compensation or an additional yield which induces investors to purchase securities with a different term to maturity than their preferred term.

According to this theory, different investors have different habitats.* Suppose an investor has *n* period habitat which means that he has funds which he does not need for *n* periods and keeps them invested in securities for *n* periods. He knows exactly the result of investment as measured by terminal value of his wealth. If he invests for a short-period, his outcome is uncertain, as it will depend on the future course of the short-term rates. Moreover, he will have to incur greater transaction costs. Thus, if he has risk aversion, he will prefer to hold long-period securities. On the contrary, if the average short-term rates exceed the long-term rate by an amount sufficient to cover extra transaction costs and to compensate him of the extra risk of holding short-period securities, he will stay short. But risk aversion should not lead him to prefer to stay short.

If the investor invests in maturities longer than *n* period habitat, he would face uncertainty as to the price he can get for his unmatured securities. Thus risk aversion should lead him to hedge against risks by continuing to remain in the same maturity habitat unless other longer or shorter maturities offer an expected premium sufficient to compensate for the risk and cost of moving out of his habitat. Similar considerations apply to the borrowers in the market.

Under this theory, if the *n* period demand for funds exceeds the funds with *n* period habitat, there will arise a premium in the *n* period maturity and vice versa. Such premiums have a tendency to bring about shifts in funds between different maturity markets in two ways: *first*, through the speculation of investors who are tempted out of their natural habitat by the lure of higher expected returns, and *second*, through arbitrage by intermediaries by borrowing in the maturity range where the expected return is low, and by lending where the expected return is high.

Thus the preferred habitat theory tells that an investor chooses securities on the basis of both the expected yield on securities and his preference for securities with a particular maturity. He will purchase a security of *undesirable* term to maturity only if he receives a term premium.

Suppose an investor prefers a one-year security because he needs funds at the end of the year. If he purchases a two-year security and sells it at the end of one year before its maturity, he incurs a risk. If the interest rate rises during this period, he will be forced to sell the security at a lower price (because security prices and interest rates are inversely related). In addition, he will have to pay commission to the broker in order to sell the security before maturity of two years. Therefore, the investor must recieve a term premium to pruchase a long-term security when his preference is for a short-term security.

The preferred habitat theory explains the *shapes* of the *yield curve* in a better way than the expectations hypothesis and the segmented market hypothesis. It explains not only upward sloping yield curves but also

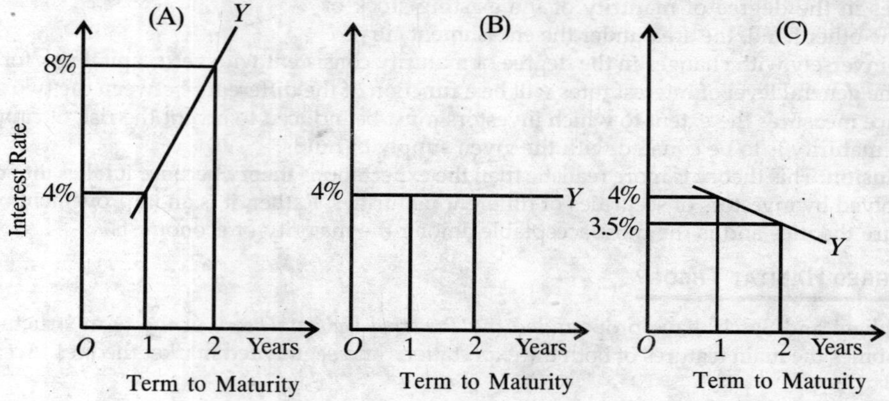

Fig. 7.

* In this theory, 'habitat' refers to short-term security (habitat) or long-term security (habitat)

horizontal and downward sloping yield curves. It also explains why the yield curves are usually upward sloping rather than downward sloping. When the term premium is positive and there are expectations of short-term interest rates to *rise* by a *large amount*, the yield curve will be upward sloping, as shown in Fig. 7 (A). Again, when the term premium is positive and the short-term interest rates are expected to *rise by a small amount*, the yield curve will be relatively horizontal (flat), as shown in Panel (B). If the term premium is positive and the short-term interest rates are expected to *fall* considerably, the yield curve will be downward sloping, as shown in Panel (C). If, however, the short-term interest rates are expected to remain constant or fall a little, the yield curve will slope upward on account of the term-premium on long-term securities.

Conclusion. The preferred habitat theory points out that expecations, risk premium and market segmentation all play a part in determining the term structure of interest rates. If lenders and borrowers in the capital market are not rigidly tied to market segments, but simply have preferred habitats, then expectations play their part in determining interest rates which are not completely independent. Other things being equal, lender's preference for liquidity will have a tendency for long-term rates to be above short-term rates.

In reality, the expectations and segmented market theories are the exptreme versions of the preferred habitat theory. In the expectations theory there is no term premium, that is, it is zero. It is simply the average of expected rates during the term of the long-term security. Investors do not require any premium to hold securities of different maturities. But in the segmented market theory, the term premium is *infinite*. There is no term interest rate which can be offered to an investor to induce him to purchase a security whose maturity does not match his preferences.

Empirical evidence on the habitat theory suggests that the link between expected short-term rates and long-term rates is quite strong, thus justifying the expectations theory. Further, the expected return from long-term securities tends to exceed the short rate by a positive premium. The existence of such a positive premium would indicate a systematic tendency for the primary supply of funds to exeed the primary demand for them in the short period market, and to fall short of the primary demand in the long period market. Under these conditions, the size of the premium on long-term securities would depend on the facilities for effective arbitrage operations.

EXERCISES

1. What do you understand by the term structure of interest rates? Explain the factors which determine short-term and long-term interest rates.
2. What do you mean by the structure of interest rates? Discuss the relationship between short-term and long-term rates of interest.
3. What do you mean by the term structure of interest rates? How do you explain the relationship between interest rates of different maturities in a given time structure?
4. Critically discuss the expectations and the segmented markets theories of term structure of interest rates.
5. Write notes on: (i) Risk Premium Theory, (ii) Preferred Habitat Theory.
6. Explain the pereferred habitat theory. How is it superior to the expectations and segmented market theories of term structure of interest rates.

CHAPTER 20

Inflation and Deflation

INTRODUCTION

Inflation is a highly controversial term which has undergone modification since it was first defined by the neo-classical economists. They meant by it a galloping rise in prices as a result of the excessive increase in the quantity of money. They regarded inflation "as a destroying disease born out of lack of monetary control whose results undermined the rules of business, creating havoc in markets and financial ruin of even the prudent."[1]

But Keynes in his *General Theory* allayed all such fears. He did not believe like the neo-classicists that there was always full employment in the economy which resulted in hyper-inflation with increases in the quantity of money. According to him, there being underemployment in the economy, an increase in the money supply leads to increase in aggregate demand, output and employment. Starting from a depression, as the money supply increases, output at first rises proportionately. But as aggregate demand, output and employment rise further, diminishing returns start and certain bottlenecks appear and prices start rising. This process continues till the full employment level is reached. The rise in the price level during this period is known as *bottleneck inflation* or "semi-inflation". If the money supply increases beyond the full employment level, output ceases to rise and prices rise in proportion with the money supply. This is true inflation, according to Keynes.

Keynes's analysis is subjected to two main drawbacks. *First*, it lays emphasis on demand as the cause of inflation, and neglects the cost side of inflation. *Second*, it ignores the possibility that a price rise may lead to further increase in aggregate demand which may, in trun, lead to further rise in prices.

However, the types of inflation during the Second World War, in the immediate post-war period, till the middle of the 1950s were on the Keynesian model based on his theory of excess demand. "In the latter 1950s, in the United States, unemployment was higher than it had been in the immediate post-war period, and yet prices still seemed to be rising, at the same time, the war time fears of postwar recession had belatedly been replaced by serious concern about the problem of inflation. The result was a prolonged debate...On the one side of the debate was the 'cost-push' school of thought, which maintained that there was no excess demand...On the other side was the "demand-pull" school...Later, in the United States, there developed a third school of thought, associated with the name of Charles Schultz, which advanced the sectoral 'demand-shift theory' of inflation...While the debate over cost-push versus demand-pull was raging in the United States, a new and very interesting approach to the problem of inflation and anit-inflationary policy was developed by A.W. Phillips."[2]

In the present chapter, we shall study all theories mentiond here, besides Keynes's thoery of the inflationary gap. But before we analyse them, it is instructive to know about the meaning of inflation.

---

1. R.J. Ball and Peter Doyle (ed.) *Inflation, 1967*, p. 7
2. Harry G. Johnson, *Essays in Monetary Economics*.

MEANING OF INFLATION

To the neo-classicals and their followers at the University of Chicago, inflation is fundamentally a monetary phenomenon. In the words of Friedman, *"Inflation is always and everywhere a monetary phenomenon...and can be produced only by a more rapid increase in the quantity of money than output."*[3] But economists do not agree that money supply alone is the cause of inflation. As pointed out by Hicks, "Our present troubles are not of a monetary character." Economists, therefore, define inflation in terms of a continuous rise in prices. Johnson defines "inflation as a sustained rise"[4] in prices. Brooman defines it as "a continuing increase in the general price level."[5] Shapiro also defines inflation in a similar vein *"as a persistent and appreciable rise in the general level of prices."*[6] Dernberg and McDougall are more explicit when they write that "the term usually refers to a continuing rise in prices as measured by an index such as the consumer price index (CPI) or by the implicit price deflator for gross national product."[7]

However, it is essential to understand that a sustained rise in prices may be of various magnitudes. Accordingly, different names have been given to inflation depending upon the rate of rise in prices.

1. *Creeping Inflation.* When the rise in prices is very slow like that of a snail or creeper, it is called creeping inflation. In terms of speed, a sustained rise in prices of annual increase of less than 3 per cent per annum is characterised as creeping inflation. Such an increase in prices is regarded safe and essential for economic growth.

2. *Walking or Trotting Inflation.* When prices rise moderately and the annual inflation rate is a single digit. In other words, the rate of rise in prices is in the intermediate range of 3 to 7 per cent annum or less than 10 per cent. Inflation at this rate is a warning signal for the government to control it before it turns into running inflation.

3. *Running Inflation.* When prices rise rapidly like the running of a horse at a rate of speed of 10 to 20 per cent per annum, it is called running inflation. Such an Inflation affects the poor and middle classes adversely. Its control requires strong monetary and fiscal measures, otherwise it leads to hyperinflation.

4. *Hyperinflation.* When prices rise very fast at double or triple digit rates from more than 20 to 100 per cent per annum or more, it is usually called *runaway* or *galloping* inflation. It is also characterised as hyperinflation by certain economists. In reality, hyperinflation is a situation when the rate of inflation becomes immeasurable and absolutely uncontrollable. Prices rise many times every day. Such a situation brings a total collapse of monetary system because of the continuous fall in the purchasing power of money.

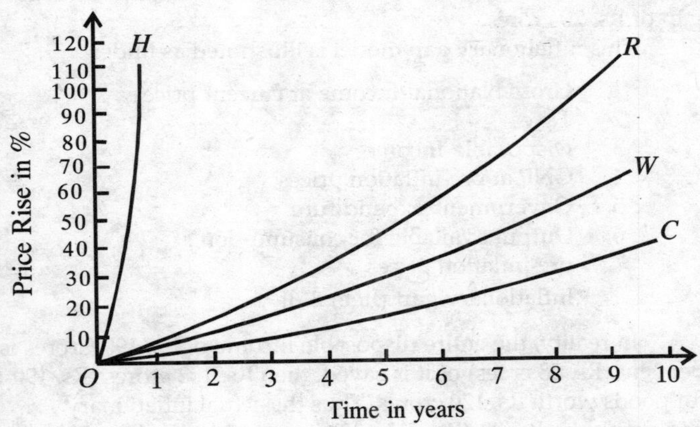

Fig. 1.

The speed with which prices tend to rise is illustrated in Figure 1. The curve C shows creeping inflation when within a period of ten years the price level has been shown to have risen by about 30 per cent. The curve W depicts walking inflation when the price rose by more than 50 per cent during ten years. The curve *R*

---

3. *The Counter Revolution in Monetary Theory*, 1970.
4. Harry W. Johnson *op. cit*, p. 104.
5. F. S. Brooman, *op. cit.*, p. 285.
6. Edward Shapiro, *op. cit.*, p. 142.
7. *Macroeconomics,*, pp. 288.

illustrates running inflation showing a rise of about 100 per cent in ten years. The steep curve *H* shows the path of hpyerinflation when prices rose by more than 120 per cent in less than one year.

THE INFLATIONARY GAP

In his pamphlet *How to Pay for the War* published in 1940, Keynes explained the concept of the inflationary gap. It differs from his views on inflation given in the *General Theory*. In the *General Theory,* he started with underemployment equilibrium. But in *How to Pay for the War,* he began with a situation of full employment in the economy. He defind an inflationary gap as an excess of planned expenditure over the available output at pre-inflation or base prices. According to Lipsey, "The inflationary gap is the amount by which aggregate expenditure would exceed aggregate output at the full employment level of income." The classical economists explained inflation as mainly due to increase in the quantity of money, given the level of full employment. Keynes, on the other hand, ascribed it to the excess of expenditure over income at the full employment level. The larger the aggregate expenditure, the larger the gap and the more rapid the inflation. Given a constant average propensity to save, rising money incomes at full employment level would lead to an excess of demand over supply and to a consequent inflationary gap. Thus Keynes used the concept of the inflationary gap to show the main determinants that cause an inflationary rise of prices.

The inflationary gap is explained with the help of the following example:

Suppose the gross national product at pre-inflation prices is Rs. 200 crores.Of this Rs. 80 crores is spent by the Government. Thus Rs. 120 (Rs. 200-80) crores worth of output is available to the public for consumption at pre-inflation prices. But the gross national income at current prices at full employment level is Rs. 250 crores. Suppose the government taxes away Rs. 60 crores, leaving Rs. 190 crores as disposable income. Thus Rs. 190 crores is the amount to be spent on the available output worth Rs. 120 crores. thereby creating an inflationary gap of Rs. 70 crores.

This inflationary gap model is illustrated as under :

1.	Gross National Income at current prices	=	Rs. 250 Cr.
2.	Taxes	=	Rs. 60 Cr.
3.	Disposable Income	=	Rs. 190 Cr.
4.	GNP at pre-inflation prices	=	Rs. 200 Cr.
5.	Government expenditure	=	Rs. 80 Cr.
6.	Output available for consumption at pre-inflation prices	=	Rs. 120 Cr.
	Inflationary gap (Item 3-6)	=	Rs. 70 Cr.

In reality, the entire disposable income of Rs. 190 Crores is not spent and a part of it is saved. If, say, 20 per cent (Rs. 38 croes) of it is saved, then Rs. 152 crores (Rs. 190-Rs. 38 crores) would be left to create demand for goods worth Rs. 120 crores. Thus the actual inflationary gap would be Rs. 32 (Rs. 152-120) crores instead of Rs. 70 crores.

The inflationary gap is shown diagrammatically in Figure 2 where Y_F is the full employment level of income, 45^0 line represents aggregate supply *AS* and *C+1+G* line the desired level of consumption, investment and government expenditure (or aggregate demand curve). The economy's aggregate demand curve (*C+1+G*) = *AD* intersects the 45 per cent line (A_S) at point *E* at the income level OY_1 which is greater than the full employment income level OY_F. The amount by which aggregate demand (Y_FA) exceeds the aggregate supply (Y_FB) at the full employment income level is the inflationary gap. This is *AB* in the figure. The excess volume of total pending when resources are fully employed

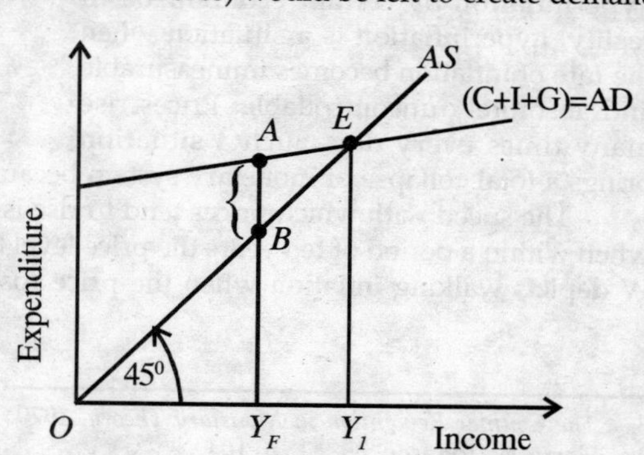

Fig. 2.

creates inflationary pressures. Thus the inflationary gap leads to inflationary pressures. in the economy which are the result of excess aggregate demand.

How can the inflationary gap be wiped out ?

The inflationary gap can be wiped out by increase in savings so that the aggregate demand is reduced. But this may lead to deflationary tendencies.

Another solution is a raise the value of available output to match the disposable income. As aggregate demand increases, businessmen hire more labour to expand output. But there being full employment at the current money wage, they offer higher money wages to induce more workers to work for them. As there is already full employment, the increase in money wages leads to proportionate rise in prices. Moreover, output cannot be increased during the short run because factors are already fully employed. So the inflationary gap can he closed by increasing taxes and reducing expenditure. Monetary policy can also be used to decrease the money stock. But Keynes was not in favour of monetary measures to control inflationary pressures within the economy.

Its Criticisms

The concept of inflationary gap has been criticised by Friedman[8], Koopmans[9], Salant[10], and other economists.

1. The analysis of inflationary gap is based on the assumption that full employment prices are flexible upward. In other words, they respond to excess demand in the market for goods. It also assumes that money wages are sticky when prices are rising., but the share of profits in GNP increases. So this concept is related to excess-demand inflation in which there is profit inflation. This has led to the mixing up of demand and cost inflations.

2. Bent Hansen criticises Keynes for confining the inflationary gap to the goods market only and neglecting the role of the factor market. According to him, an inflationary gap is the result of excess demand in the goods market as well as in the factor market.[11]

3. The inflationary gap is a static analysis. But the inflationary phenomena are dynamic. To make them dynamic, Keynes himself suggested the intorduction of time lags concerning receipts and expenditures of income. Koopmans has developed relationships between eggs and the rate of price increase per unit of time. He has shown with the help of spending lags and wage-adjustment lags that the speed of inflation becomes smaller, that is the inflationary gap is narrowed.

4. Holzman has criticised Keynes for applying the multiplier technique to a full employment situation. According to him, the multiplier technique is not adequate in periods of full employment and inflation. It abstracts from changes in the distribution of income. In a full employment situation, the share of one group in the national output can only be increased at the expense of another.[12]

5. Another weakness of the inflationary-gap analysis is that it is related to flow concepts, such as current income, expenditure, consumption, and saving. In fact, the increase in prices at the full employment level is not confined to prices of current goods alone. But they also affect the prices of goods already produced. Further, the disposable income which is the difference between current income and taxes, may include idle balances from the income of previous periods.

Its Importance

Despite these criticisms the concept of inflationary gap has proved to be of much importance in explaining rising prices at full employment level and policy measures in controlling inflation.

---

8. M. Friedman, "Discussion of the Inflation of the Gap", *A.E.R.*, Vol. 32, 1942.
9. T. Koopmans, "The Dynamics of Inflation", *R.E.S.*, Vol. 24, 1942.
10. W. Salant, "The Inflationary Gap, Meaning and Significance for Policy Making", *A.E.R.* Vol. 32, 1942.
11. Bent Hansen, A Study in the Theory of Inflation, 1951.
12. F. D. Holzman, "Income Determination in Open Inflation", *R.E.S.*, Vol.32, 1950.

It tells that the rise in prices, once the level of full employment is attained, is due to excess demand generated by increased expenditures. But the output cannot be increased because all resources are fully employed in the economy. This leads to inflation. The larger the expenditure, the larger the gap and more rapid the inflation.

As a policy measure, it suggests reduction in aggregate demand to control inflation. For this, the best course is to have a surplus budget by raising taxes. It also favours saving incentives to reduce consumption expenditure. "The analysis of the inflationary gap in terms of such aggregate as national income, investment outlays and consumption expenditures clearly reveals what determines public policy with respect to taxes, public expenditures, savings campaigns, credit control, wage adjustment—in short, all the conceivable anti-inflationary measures affecting the propensities to consume, to save and to invest which together determine the general price level."[13]

DEMAND-PULL OR MONETARY THEORIES OF INFLATION

Demand-pull inflation or excess demand inflation is the traditional and most common type of inflation. It takes place when aggregate demand is rising while the available supply of goods is becoming less. Goods may be in short supply either because resources are fully utilised or production cannot be increased rapidly to meet the increasing demand. As a result, prices begin to rise in response to a situation often decribed as "too much money chasing too few goods."

There are two principal theories about the demand-pull inflation that of the monetarists and the Keynesians. We shall also discuss a third one propounded by the Danish economist, Bent Hansen.*

1. Monetarist View or Monetary Theory of Inflation

The monetarists emphasise the role of money as the principal cause of demand-pull inflation. They contend that inflation is always a monetary phenomenon. Its earliest explanation is to be found in the simple quantity theory of money. The monetarists employ the familiar indentity of Fisher's Equation of Exchange.

$MV = PQ$

where M is the money supply, V is the velocity of money, P is the price level, and Q is the level of real output.

Assuming V and Q as constant, the price level (P) varies proportionately with the supply of money (M). With flexible wages, the economy was believed to operate at full employment level. The labour force, the capital stock, and technology also changed only slowly over time. Consequently, the amount of money spent did not affect the level of real output so that a doubling of the quantity of money would result simply in doubling the price level. Until prices had risen by this proportion, individuals and firms would have excess cash which they would spend, leading to rise in prices. So inflation proceeds at the same rate at which the money supply expands. In this analysis the aggregate supply is assumed to be fixed and there is always full employment in the economy. Naturally, when the money supply increases it creates more demand for goods but the supply of goods cannot be increased due to the full employment of resources. This leads to rise in prices. But it is a continuous and prolonged rise in the money supply that will lead to true inflation.

Friedman's View

Modern quantity theorists led by Friedman hold that "inflation is always and everywhere a monetary phenomenon that arises from a more rapid expansion in the quantity of money than in total output." He argues that changes in the quantity of money will work through to cause changes in nominal income. Inflation everywhere is based on an increased demand for goods and services as people try to spend their cash balances. Since the demand for money is fairly stable, this excess spending is the outcome of a rise in the nominal quantity of money supplied to the economy. So inflation is always a monetary phenomenon.

13. K.K. Kurihara, *Monetary Theory and Public Policy,* p. 45.

* B. Hansen's Monetary Theory of Inflation is not to be given unless asked for.

Next Friedman discusses whether an increase in money supply will go first into output or prices. Initially, when there is monetary expansion, the nominal income of the people increases. Its immediate effect will be to increase the demand for labour. Workers will settle for higher wages. Input costs and prices will rise. Profit margins will be reduced and the prices of products will increase. In the begining, people do not expect prices to continue rising. They regard the price rise as temporary and expect prices to fall later on. Consequently, they tend to increase their money holdings and the price rise is less than the rise in nominal money supply. Gradually people tend to readjust their money holdings. Price then rise more than in proportion to the money supply. The precise rate at which prices rise for a given rate of increase in the money supply depends on such factors as past price behaviour, current changes in the structure of labour, product markets and fiscal policy. Thus, according to Friedman, the monetary expansion works through output before inflation starts.

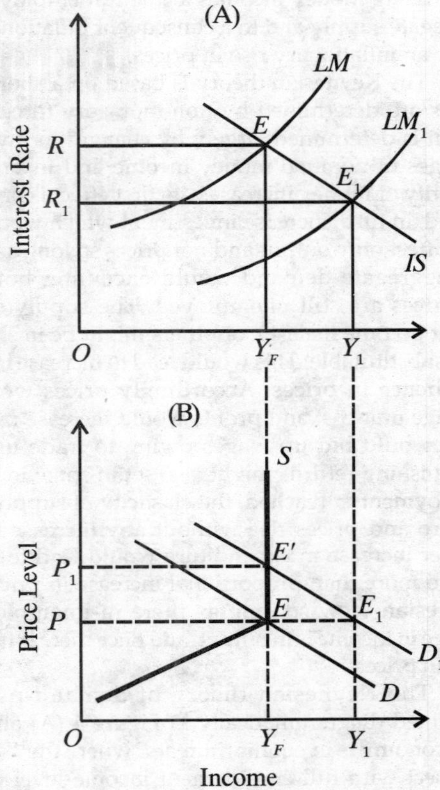

Fig. 3.

The quantity theory version of the demand-pull inflation is illustrated diagrammatically in Figure 3 (A) & (B). Suppose the money supply is increased at a given price level *P* as determined by *D* and *S* curves in Panel (B) of the figure. The initial full employment situation at this price level is shown by the intersection of IS and *LM* curves at *E* in Panel (A) of the figure where *R* is the interest rate and Y_F is the full employment level of income. Now with the increase in the quantity of money, the *LM* curve shifts rightward to LM_1 and intersects the *IS* curve at E_1 such that the equilibrium level of income rises to Y_1 and the rate of interest is lowered to R_1. As the aggregate supply is assumed fixed, there is no change in the position of the *IS* curve.

Consequently, the aggregate demand rises which shifts the *D* curve to the right to D_1 and thus excess demand is created equivalent to EE_1 ($=Y_FY_1$) in Panel (B) of the figure. This raises the price level, the aggregate supply being fixed, as shown by the vertical portion of the supply curve *S*. The rise in the price level reduces the real value of the money supply so that the LM_1 curve shifts to the left to *LM*. Excess demand will not be eliminated until aggregate demand curve D_1 cuts the aggregate supply curve *S* at *E'*. This means a higher price level P_1 in Panel (B) and return to the original equilibrium position *E* in the upper Panel of the figure where the *IS* curve cuts the *LM* curve. The "result, then is self-limiting, and the price level rises in exact proportion to the real value of the money supply to its original value."[14]

2. Keynes' Theory of Demand-Pull Inflation

Keynes and his followers emphasise the incease in aggregate demand as the source of demand-pull inflation. There may be more than one source of demand. Consumers want more goods and services for consumption purposes. Businessmen want more inputs for investment. Government demands more goods and services to meet civil and military requirements of the country. Thus the aggregate demand comprises consumption, investment and government expenditures. When the value of aggregate demand exceeds the value of aggregate supply at the full employment level, the inflationary gap arises. The larger the gap between aggregate demand and aggregate supply, the more rapid the inflation. Given a constant average propensity to

14. T. F. Dernberg and D.M. McDougall, op.cit., p. 291.

save, rising money incomes at the full employment level would lead to an excess of aggregate demand over aggregate supply and to a consequent inflationary gap. Thus Keynes used the notion of the inflationary gap to show an inflationary rise in prices.

The Keynesian theory is based on a short-run analysis in which prices are assumed to be fixed. In fact, prices are determined by non-monetary forces. On the other hand, output is assumed to be more variable which is determined largely by changes in investment spending. The Keynesian chain of causation between changes in nominal money income and in prices is an indirect one through the rate of interest. When the quantity of money increases, its first effect is on the rate of interest which tends to fall. A fall in the interest rate would, in turn, increase investment which would raise aggregate demand. A rise in aggregate demand would first affect only output and not prices so long as there are unemployed resoures. But a sudden large increase in the aggregate demand would encounter bottlenecks when resources are still unemployed. The supply of some factors might become inelastic or others might be in short supply and non-substitutable. This would lead to increase in marginal costs and hence in prices. Accordingly prices would rise above average unit cost and profits would increase rapidly which, in turn, would bid up wages owing to trade union pressures. Diminishing returns might also set in some industries. As full employment in reached, the elasticity of supply of output falls to zero and prices rise without any increase in output. Any further increase in expenditure would lead to excess demand and to more than proportional increase in prices. Thus, in the Keynesian view so long as there in unemployment, all the change in income is in output, and once there is full employment, all is in prices.

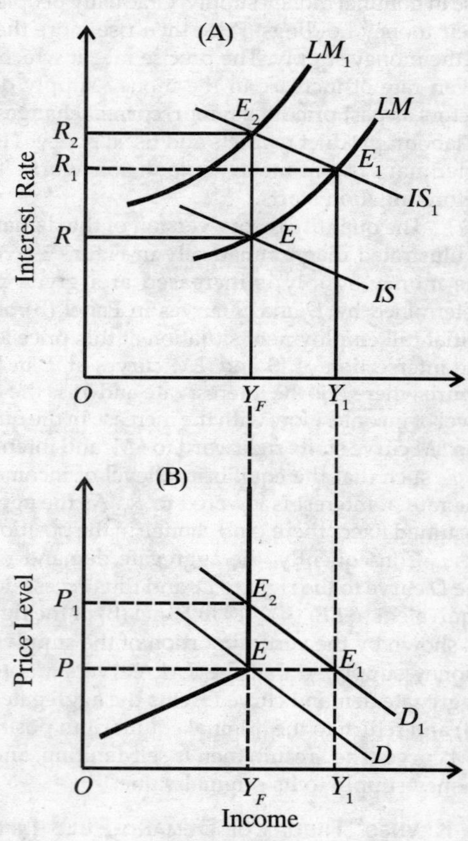

Fig. 4.

The Keynesian theory of demand-pull inflation is explained diagrammatically in Figure 4 (A) and (B). Suppose the economy is in equilibrium at *E* where the *IS* and *LM* curves intersect with full employment income level Y_F and interest rate *R*, as shown in Panel (A) of the figure. Corresponding to this situation, the price level is *P* in Panel (B). Now the government increases its expenditure. This shifts the *IS* curve rightward to IS_1 and intersects the *LM* curve at E_1 when the level of income and the interest rate rise to Y_1 and R_1 respectively. The increase in government expenditure implies an increase in aggregate demand which is shown by the upward shift of the *D* curve to D_1 in the lower Panel (B) of the figure. This creates excess demand to the extent of EE_1 ($=Y_FY_1$) at the initial price level *P*. Excess demand tends to raise the price level, as aggregate supply of output cannot be increased after the full employment level. As the price level rises, the real value of money supply falls. This shifts the *LM* curve to the left to LM_1 such that it cuts the IS_1 curve at E_2 where equilibrium is established at the full employment level of income Y_F, but at a higher interest rate R_2 (in Panel A) and a higher price level P_1 (in Panel B).

Thus the excess demand caused by the rise in government expenditure eliminates itself by changes in the real value of money.

3. Bent Hansen's Excess Demand Model

The Danish economist Bent Hansen[15] has presented an explicit dynamic excess demand model of inflation which incorporates two separate price levels, one for the goods market and other for the factor (labour) market.

Its Assumptions

His dynamic model for demand inflation is based on the following assumptions:

1. There is perfect competition in both the goods market and the factor market.
2. Price at the moment will persist in the future.
3. Only one commodity is produced with the help of only one variable factor, labour services.
4. The quantity of labour services per unit of time is a given magnitude.
5. There is a fixed actual level of employment and consequently of output which is full employment.

The Model

Given these assumptions, the model is explained in terms of Figure 6. The vertical axis measures the price-wage ratio *P/W* (inverse of the real wage). The aggregate real income or output is measured along the horizontal axis. *S* is the supply curve of planned production, *S=F (P/W)*. It varies positively with *P/W* such that the higher the price is relative to the wage rate, the less is the demand for consumer goods, *D=F(P/W)*. *D* is the demand curve of planned demand which has an inverse relationship with *P/W* such that the higher price is relative to the wage rate the larger is the planned production. The vertical line *Q* is the full employment output level Q_F and Q=constant.

The horizontal difference between the curve *D* and *Q* is the "quantitative inflationary gap in the goods markets". Such a gap exists at all price-wage ratios below (*P/W*) in the figure. The horizontal difference between the curves *S* and *Q* is the index for the factor-gap." *Thus (D–Q) is the goods gap and (S–Q) is the factor gap.*

Suppose the two curves *D* and *S* intersect to the right of the full employment level of output at point *E*. This happens if there is monetary pressure of inflation because otherwise it would not be possible with given *P/W* to have a positive inflationary gap in the goods markets and positive factor-gap simultaneously. A monetary pressure of inflation exists only when *P/W* is between P/W_1 and P/W_4. When $P/W > P/W_1$, the inflationary gap in the goods-market is greater than zero; and when $P/W < P/W_4$ both the index for the factor-gap and the factor-gap are negative.

Next Hansen introduces two dynamical equations :

$$dp/dt = f(D-Q) \qquad ...(1)$$
$$dw/dt = F(S-Q) \qquad ...(2)$$

where *dp/dt* is the speed of the rise in the price level, and *dw/dt* is the speed of the rise in the wage rate.

When (*D–Q*) is zero, *dp/dt* = 0; and when (*S–Q*) is zero, *dw/dt* = O. This is a static equilibrium system. When the two gaps are positive, the rates of price and wage changes are also positive.

It follows that when both the excess demand for goods (*D–Q*) and the excess demand for factors (*S–Q*) are positive, both price and wage-rate will rise. Each will be a quasi-equilibrium position which is stable in the sense that whatever price-wage relation is started, there will be forces at work which tend to bring the system back to the quasi-equilibrium position.

The quasi-equilibrium system is given by

Q = Constant $\quad S = F(P/W) \quad D = f(P/W)$

and $$P/W = \frac{f(D-Q)}{F(S-Q)}$$

Let us take the figure where the curves *S* and *D* intersect at point *E*, to the right of the full employment level of output Q_F. Since point *E* cannot be achieved, an initial unstable equilibrium occurs at point *A* where the

15. Bent Hansen, *A study in the theory of Inflation*, 1951, Ch. 7.

price-wage ratio is (P/W_1). In this situation, there is no goods gap and goods prices do not rise because planned demand (D) equals full employment output (Q_F) at A. But there is a large factor gap at point T so that wages rise rapidly. This is because planned production Q_1 exceeds the full employment output Q_F at (P/W_1). But this is not possible because Q_1 output is more than the full employment output Q_F. Consequently, there is excess demand for labour which leads to labour shortages and to rise in the wage rate. Thus P/W falls. When the price-wage ratio falls, an excess demand for goods (goods gap) begins to appear and that for factors (factor gap) simultaneously decreases. Suppose P/W_1 falls to P/W_2. At P/W_2, the goods gap FG is smaller than the factor gap FH which means that the small goods gap produces a slow rise in prices and the larger factor gap produces a higher rise in wage rate. This will lead to a further fall in wage-price ratio to P/W_3. At P/W_3, the factor gap is reduced to KL and the goods gap is raised to KM, thereby leading to a slower rise in wage rate and more rapid rise in prices respectively. This retards the fall in the wage-price ratio. In this way, the price-wage ratio will fall, increasing slowly to a level where the goods gap corresponds to the factor gap. This means that the precentage rise of wage rate per unit time is equal to the percentage rise of the price per unit time. Similar reasoning will apply if we start from P/W_4 where the large goods gap BN and zero factor gap would raise prices and hence the wage-price ratio. A key determinant of the level of price-wage ratio is the flexibility of wage-rate and prices relative to each other. The more flexible are prices relative to wages, the closer is the value of price-wage ratio to P/W_1.

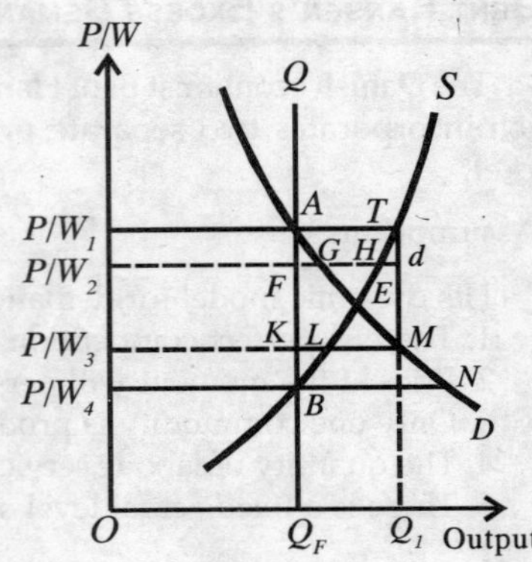

Fig. 5.

Between P/W_1 and P/W_4, there is some quasi-equilibrium at which both prices and wage-rates move together. The quasi-equilibrium is not a static equilibrium but a dynamic one, since both prices and wage rates rise without interruption and the relevant gaps are not zero. "The actual speed of the inflation to quasi-equilibrium will depend on the absolute sensitivity of wage and price change to the size of the relevant gaps. If both are relatively volatile, inflation will be rapid; if both are relatively sluggish, inflation will be slower." The more rigid prices are relative to wages, the closer is the value of price-wage ratio to P/W_4.

To conclude, Hensen's excess demand model of inflation points toward the sources of inflationary pressures and the actual process of inflation in the economy. But, according to Ackley, it fails to specify the rate at which inflation will occur. It is an elegant but perhaps rather empty analysis of demand inflation.

COST-PUSH INFLATION

Cost-push inflation is caused by wage increases enforced by unions and profit increases by employers. The type of inflation has not been a new phenomenon and was found even during the medieval period.[16] But it was revived in the 1950s and again in the 1970s as the principal cause of inflation. It also came to be known as the "*New Inflation.*"[17] Cost-push inflation is caused by wage-push and profit-push to prices.

The basic cause of cost-push inflation is the rise in money wages more rapidly than the productivity of labour. In advanced countries, trade unions are very powerful. They press employers to grant wage increases considerably in excess of increases in the productivity of labour, thereby raising the cost of production of commodities. Employers, in turn, raise prices of their products. Higher wages enable workers to buy as much as before, in spite of higher prices. On the other hand, the increase in prices induces unions to demand still higher wages. In this way, the wage-cost spiral continues, thereby leading to cost-push or wage-push inflation.

Cost-push inflation may be further aggravated by upward adjustment of wages to compensate for rise in the cost of living index. This is usually done in either of the two ways. *First*, unions include an "escalator clause" in contracts with employers, whereby money wage rates are adjusted upward each time the cost of living index increases by some specified number of percentage points. *Second*, in case where union contracts do

16. For a brief survey of post-War developments in inflation theories see M. Bronfenbrenner and F.D. Holzman, "Survey of Inflation Theory," *AER*, Sept. 1963.
17. It is the title of a book by W.L. Thorpe and R.E. Quandt, 1959.

not have an escalator clause, the cost of living index is used as the basis for negotiating larger wage increases at the time of fresh contract settlements.

Again, a few sectors of the economy may be affected by money wage increases and prices of their products may be rising. In many cases, their products are used as inputs for the production of commodities in other sectors. As a result, production costs of other sectors will rise and thereby push up the prices of their products. Thus wage-push inflation in a few sectors of the economy may soon lead to inflationary rise in prices in the entire economy.

Further, an increase in the price of domestically produced or imported raw materials may lead to cost-push inflation. Since raw materials are used as inputs by the manufacturers of finished goods, they enter into the cost of production of the latter. Thus a continuous rise in the prices of raw materials tends to set off a cost-price-wage spiral.

Another cause of cost-push inflation is *proft-push inflation*. Oligopolist and monopolist firms raise the prices of their products to offset the rise in labour and production costs so as to earn higher profits. There being imperfect competition in the case of such firms, they are able to "administer prices" of their products. "In an economy in which so called administered prices abound, there is at least the possibility that these prices may be administered upward faster than costs in an attempt to earn greater profits. To the extent such a process is widespread profit-push inflation will result."[18] Profit-push inflation is, therefore, also called *administered-price theory of inflation* or *price-push inflation* or *sellers' inflation* or *market-power inflation.*

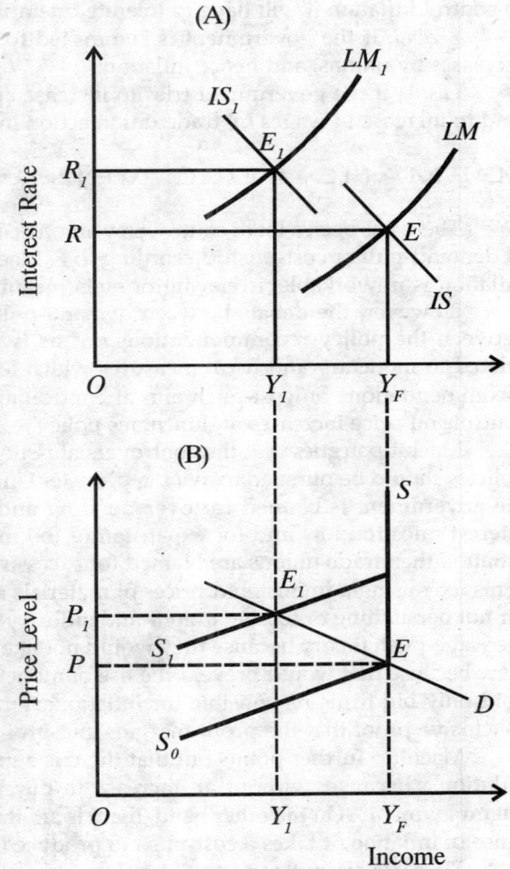

Fig. 6.

But there are certain limitations on the power of firms to raise their profits. They cannot raise their selling prices to increase their profit-margins if the demand for their products is stable. Moreover, firms are reluctant to increase their profits every time unions are successful in raising wages. This is beause profits of a firm depend not only on price but on sales and unit costs as well, and the latter depend in part on prices charged. So firms cannot raise their profits becuase their motives are different from unions. *Lastly*, profits form only a small fraction of the price of the product and a once-for-all increase in profits is not likely to have much impact on prices. Economists, therefore, do not give much importance to profit-push inflation as an explanation of cost-push inflation.

Cost-push inflation is illustrated in Figure 6 (A) and (B). First consider Panel (B) of the figure where the supply curves S_OS and S_1S are shown as increasing functions of the price level up to full employment level of income Y_F. Given the demand conditions as represented by the demand curve D, the supply curve S_O is shown to shift to S_1 in response to cost-increasing pressures of oligopolies, unions, etc. as a result of rise in money wages. Consequently, the equilibrium position shifts from E to E_1 reflecting rise in the price level from P to P_1 and fall in output, employment and income from Y_F to Y_1 level.

Now consider the upper Panel (A) of the figure. As the price level rises, the LM curve shifts to the left to LM_1 because with the increase in the price level to P_1 the real value of the money supply falls. Similarly, the IS

18. Edward Shapiro, *op. cit.*, p. 522.

curve shifts to the left to IS_1 because with the increase in the price level, the demand for consumer goods falls due to the Pigou effect. Accordingly, the equilibrium position of the economy shifts from E to E_1 where the interest rate increases from R to R_1 and the output, employment and income levels fall from the full employment level of Y_F to Y_1.

Its Criticisms

The cost-push theory has been criticised on three issues.

First, cost-push inflation is associated with unemployment. So the monetary authority is in a fix because to control inflation it will have to tolerate unemployment.

Second, if the government is committed to a policy of full employment, it will have to tolerate wage increases by unions, and hence inflation.

Lastly, if the government tries to increase aggregate demand during periods of unemployment, it may lead to increase in wages by trade union action instead of raising output and employment.

DEMAND-PULL VERSUS COST-PUSH INFLATION

There has been a lot of controversy among economists over the issue whether inflation is the consequence of demand-pull or cost-push. According to F. Machlup, "The distinction between cost-push and demand-pull inflation is unworkable, irrelevant or even meaningless."[19]

However, the debate between demand-pull and cost-push inflation arises mainly from the difference between the policy recommendations on the two views. Recommendations on demand-pull inflation are related to monetary and fiscal measures which lead to a higher level of unemployment. On the other hand, recommendations on cost-push aim at controlling inflation without unemployment through administrative controls on price increases and incomes policy.

Machlup argues that the controversial issue is partly who is to be blamed for inflation and partly what policies should be pursued to aviod a persistent increase in prices. If demand-pull is the cause of inflation then the government is blamed for overspending and taxing little, and the central bank is blamed for keeping interest rates too low and for expansion of too much credit. On the other hand, if cost-push is the cause of inflation then trade unions are blamed for excessive wage increases, industry is blamed for granting them, big firms for raising administered prices of materials and goods to earn higher profits and government is blamed for not persuading or forcing unions and industry from raising their wages and profits. But trade unions reject the wage-push theory because they would not like to be blamed for inflation. They also reject the demand-pull view because that would prevent the use of monetary and fiscal measures to increase employment. Thus they hold only big firms responsible for inflationary rise in prices through administered prices. But there is no conclusive proof that the profit margins and profit rates of firms have been increasing year after year.

Machlup further points out that there is a group of economists who holds that cost-push is no cause of inflation, "because, without an increase in purchasing power and demand, cost increases would lead to unemployment." On the other hand, there is another group of economists who believes that demand-pull is no cause of inflation, it takes a cost-push to produce it.

Thus it is difficult to distinguish demand-pull from cost-push inflation in practice and it is easy to say that inflation has been caused by cost-push when, in fact, demand-pull may be the cause. As pointed out by Samuelson and Solow, "The trouble is that we have no normal initial standard from which to measure, no price level which has always existed to which every one has adjusted."[20] It is also suggested that identification of demand-pull or cost-push inflation can be made with reference to timing. If prices increase first, it is a demand-pull inflation, and if wages increase follow, it is a cost-push inflation.

Like Machlup, Johnson regards the issue of demand-pull versus cost-push as "largely a spurious one." He assigns three reasons for this, *First,* the proponents of the two theories fail to investigate the monetary assumptions on which the theories are based. Neither the demand-pull nor the cost-push theory can generate a sustained inflation unless monetary policy followed by the monetary theory is taken into consideration under varying circumstances. The two theories are, therefore, not independent and self-contained. The *second*

19. F. Machlup, "Another View of Cost-Push and Demand-Pull Inflation," *R.E.S.* Vol. 42, May 1960
20. "Analytical Aspects of Anti-Inflationary Policy." *A.E.R.*, Vol. 50, 1960.

reason is based on differences between the two theories about their definitions of full employment. If full employment is defined as a situation when the demand for goods is just sufficient to prevent from rising or falling, then it is a case of demand-pull inflation which is associated with excess demand for goods and labour. Full employment here means overfull employment. On the other hand, if full employment is defined as the level of unemployment at which the percentage of the unemployment just equals the number of persons seeking jobs, then inflation is caused by forces other than excess demand. Such forces cause cost-push inflation. In the *third* place, it is extremely difficult to devise a test capable of determining whether a particular inflation is of the demand-pull or cost-push type.[21]

We may conclude with Lipsey :"Debate continues on the balance between demand and cost as forces causing inflation in the contermporary inflationary climate. The debate is important because the policy implications of different causes of inflation are different, and different target variables need to be controlled, according to the cause. Until the causes of inflation are fully understood, there will be debate about policies."[22]

MIXED DEMAND-PULL COST-PUSH INFLATION

Some economists do not accept this dichotomy that inflation is either demand-pull or cost-push. They hold that the actual inflationary process contains some elements of both. In fact, excess demand and cost-push forces operate simultaneously and interdependently in an inflationary process. Thus inflation is mixed demand-pull and cost-push when price level changes reflect upward shifts in both aggregate demand and supply functions.

But it does not mean that both demand-pull and cost-push inflations may start simultaneously. In fact, an inflationary process may begin with either excess demand or wage-push. The timing in each case may be different. In demand-pull inflation, price increases may precede wage increases, while it may be the other way round in the case of cost-push inflation. So price increases may start with either of the two forces, but the inflationary process cannot be sustained in the absence of the other forces.

Suppose an inflationary process begins with excess demand with no cost-push forces at work. Excess demand will raise prices which will in due course pull up money wages. But the rise in money wages is not the result of cost-push forces. Such a mixed inflation will lead to sustained rise in prices. This is illustrated in Figure 7. The initial equilibrium is at Y_F level of full employment income determined by aggregate demand D_0 and aggregate supply S_0S curves at A. The price level is P_0 with increase in aggregate demand from D_0 to D_1 and D_2 given the vertical portion of the supply curve S_0S, prices rise from P_0 to P_2 to P_5, the inflationary path being A, B and C. This sustained increase in prices has also been the result of the increase in money wage rates due to increase in aggregate demand at the full employment level. When prices rise, producers are encouraged to increase output as their profits rise with increased aggregate demand. They, therefore, raise the demand for labour thereby increasing money wages which further lead to increase in demand for goods and services. So long as the demand for output continues to raise money incomes, inflationary pressures will continue.

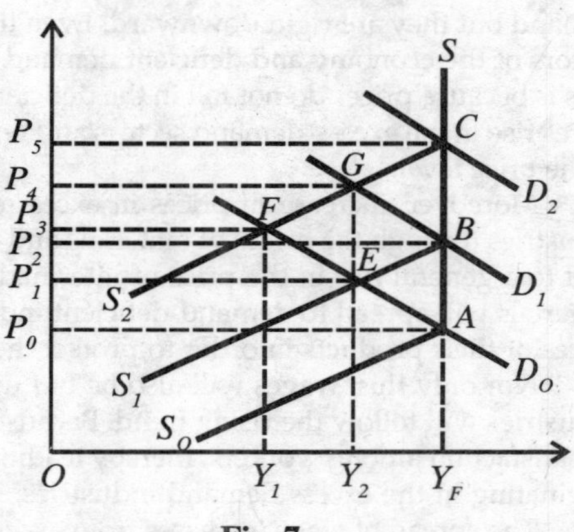

Fig. 7

Consider an inflationary process that may begin from the supply side due to increase in money wage rates. This will raise prices every time there is a wage-push. But the rise in prices will not be sustained if there is no increase in demand. This is illustrated in Fig. 7 where given the aggregate demand curve D_o, a wage-push shifts the supply curve S_o to S_1. The new equilibrium is at *E*. This raises the price level from P_o to P_1 and lowers

21. H. G. Johnson, *Op, cit*, pp. 128-30.
22. Richard G. Lipsey, *Introduction to Positive Economics*, 8/e, 1995

output and employment to Y_2 below the full employment level Y_F. A further wage-push will again shift the supply curve to S_2, and the new equilibrium will be at F, given the demand curve D_o thereby raising the price level further to P_3 and also reducing output and employment to Y_1. In the absence of increase in aggregate demand, this cost-push inflationary process will not be a sustained one and will sooner or later come to an end.

The cost-push inflationary process will be self-sustaining only if every wage-push is accompanied by a corresponding increase in aggregate demand. Since every cost-push is accompained by a fall in output and employment along with a price increase, it is likely that the government will adopt expansionary monetary and fiscal policies in order to check the fall in output and employment. In this way, cost-push will lead to a sustained inflationary process because the government will try to achieve full employment by raising aggregate demand which will, in turn, lead to further wage-push and so on. Such a situation is again explained with the help of Figure 8. Suppose there is a wage-push at E which shifts the supply curve from S_1 to S_2 and equilibrium is established at F with the demand curve D_o. The price level rises to P_3 and the level to employment is reduced to Y_1. When due to an expansionary monetary and fiscal policy, aggregate demand increases to D_1, the new equilibrium position is at G where the price level rises to P_4 and the level of employment rises to Y_2. A further increase in demand shifts the aggregate demand curve upward to D_2, such that equilibrium is attained at point C where the price level rises to P_5 and the economy attains the full employment level Y_F. Thus a wage-push accompanied by an increase in aggregate demand through expansionary monetary and fiscal policies traces out a ratchet-like inflationary parth from A to E to F to G and to C.

SECTORAL OR DEMAND-SHIFT INFLATION

Sectoral or demand-shift inflation is associated with the name of Charles Schulz[23] who in a paper, pointed out that the price increases from 1955-57 were caused by neither demand-pull nor cost-push but by sectoral shifts in demand. Schultz advanced his thesis with reference to the American economy but it has now been generalised in the case of modern industrial economies.

Schultz begins his theory by pointing out that prices and wages are flexible upward in response to excess demand but they are rigid downward. Even if the aggregate demand is not excessive, excess demand in some sectors of the economy and deficient demand in other sectors will still lead to a rise in the general price level. This is because prices do not fall in the deficient-demand sectors, there being downward rigidity of prices. But prices rise in the excess-demand sectors and remain constant in the other sectors. The net effect is an overall rise in the price level.

Moreover, increase in prices in excess-demand industries (or sectors) can spread to deficient-demand industries through the prices of materials and the wages of labour. Excess demand in particular industries will lead to a general rise in the price of intermediate materials, supplies and components. These rising prices of materials will spread to demand-deficient industries which use them as inputs. They will, therefore, raise the prices of their products in order to protect their profit margins.

Not only this, wages will also be bid up in excess demand industries, and wages in demand-deficient industries will follow the rising trend. Because if wages in the latter industries are not raised, they will lead to dissatisfaction among workers, thereby leading to inefficiency and fall in productivity. Thus rising wage rates, originating in the excess demand industries, spread throughout the economy.

The spread of wage increases from excess demand industries to other parts of the economy increases the rise in the price of semi-manufactured materials and components. Other things remaining the same, the influence of increasing costs will be larger at the final stages of production. Thus producers of finished goods will face a general rise in the level of costs, thereby leading to rising prices. This may happen even in case of those industries which do not have excess demand for the products.

Another reason for demand-shift inflation in modern industrial economies is increase in the relative importance of *overhead costs*. This increase is due to two factors. *First*, there is an increase in overhead staff at the expense of production workers. According to Schultz, automation of production methods, instrumentation of control functions, mechanisation of office and accounting procedures, self-regulating materials, handling

---

23. C.L. Shultz, "Recent Inflation in the United States", in *Employment, Growth and Price Level*, Study Paper 1, Joint Economic Committee, U.S. Congress, 1959.

equipments, etc. lead to the growth of professional and semi-professional personnel in supervising, operating and maintenance roles. Similarly, the growth of formal research and development (R&D) as a separate function not only alters the production processes but also the composition of the labour force required to service them. These developments lead to the decline in the ratio of production workers to technical and supervisory staff in industries.

The *second* reason for the rise in overhead costs is that the ratio of relatively short-lived equipment to long-lived plant rises substantially. As a result, depreciation as a proportion of total cost increases. The ultimate effect of an increasing proportion of overhead costs in the total cost is to make average costs more sensitive to variations in output. The distinguishing characteristic of the demand-shift inflation is a continued investment boom in the face of stable aggregate output. All industries expand their capacity and their employment of overhead personnel yet only a few enjoy a concomitant rise in sales. So producers facing shrinking profit margins try to recover a part of their rising costs in higher prices.

Thus demand-shift inflationary process "arises initially out of excess demand in particular industries. But it results in a general price rise only because of the downward rigidities and cost-oriented nature of prices and wages. It is not characterized by an autonomous upward push of costs nor by an aggregate excess demand. Indeed its basic nature is that it cannot be understood in terms of aggregates alone. Such inflation is the necessary result of sharp changes in the composition of demand, given the structure of prices and wages in the economy."

This theory was evolved by Schultz to examine the nature of the gradual inflation to which the American economy had been subjected during the period 1955-57. It has since been generalised in the case of modren industrial economies.

Its Criticisms

Johnson has criticised this theory for two reasons.

First, empirical evidence has failed to confirm Schultz's proposition that sectoral price increases are explained by upward shifts of demand.

Second, it suffers from the same defects as the two rival theories of demand-pull and cost-push, it seeks to challenge. That is, its "failure to investigate the monetary preconditions for inflation, and imprecision respecting the definitions of full employment and general excess demand."

STRUCTURAL INFLATION

The structuralist school of South America stresses structural rigidities as the principal cause of inflation in such developing countries as Argentina, Brazil, and Chile, Of course, this type of inflation is also to be found in other developing countries.

The structuralists hold the view that inflation is necessary with growth. According to this view, as the economy develops, rigidities arise which lead to structural inflation. In the initial phase, there are increases in non-agricultural incomes accompanied by high growth rate of population that tend to increase the demand for goods. In fact, the pressure of population growth and rising urban incomes would tend to raise through a chain reaction mechanism, *first* the prices of agricultural goods, *second*, the general price level, and *third*, wages. Let us analyse them.

1. *Agricultural Goods.* As the demand for agricultural goods rises, their domestic supply being inelastic, the prices of agricultural goods rise. The output of these goods does not increase when their prices rise because their production is inelasitc due to a defective system of land tenure and other rigidities in the form of lack of irrigation, finance, storage and marketing facilities, and bad harvests. To prevent the continuous rise in agricultural products, especially foods products, they can be imported. But it is not possible to import them in large quantities due to foreign exchange constraint. Moreover, the prices of imported products are relatively higher than their domestic prices. This tends to raise the price level further within the economy.

2. *Wage Increases.* When the prices of food products rise, wage earners press for increase in wage rates to compensate for the fall in their real incomes. But wages and/or D.A. are linked to the cost of living index. They

are, therefore, raised whenever the cost of living index rises above an agreed point which further increases the demand for goods and a further rise in their prices.

The effect of increase in the wage rates on prices in illustrated in Figure 8. When wage rates rise, the aggregate demand for goods increases from D_1 to D_2. But the aggregate supply falls due to increase in labour costs which results in the shifting of aggregate supply curve from S_1S to S_2S. Since the production of goods is inelastic due to structural rigidities after a point, the supply curve is shown as vertical from point E_1 onward. The initial equilibrium is at E_1 where the curves D_1 and S_1 intersect at the output level OY_1 and the price level is OP_1. When supply falls due to increase in labour costs, the supply curve shifts from S_1 to S_2 and it intersects the demand curve D_2 at E_2 and production falls from OY_1 to OY_2 and the price level rises from OP_1 to OP_2.

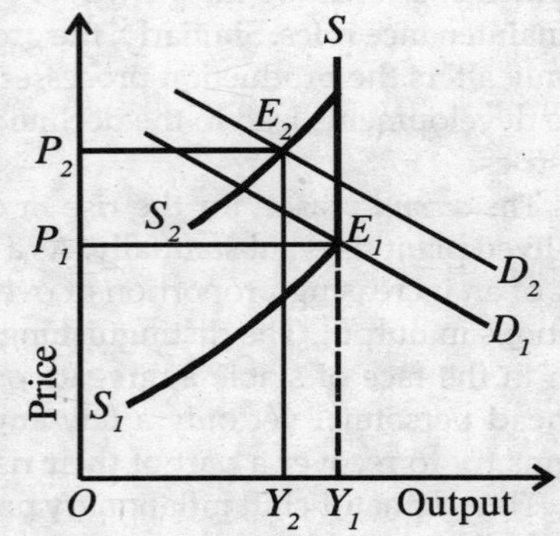

Fig. 8

3. *Import Substitution.* Another cause of structural inflation is that the rate of export growth in a developing economy is slow and unstable which is inadequate to support the required growth rate of the economy. The sluggish growth rate of exports and the foreign exchange constraint lead to the adoption of the policy of industrialisation based on import substitution. Such a policy necessitates the use of protective measures which, in turn, tend to raise the prices of industrial products, and incomes in the non-agricultrural sectors, thereby leading to further rise in prices. Moreover, this policy leads to a cost-push rise in prices because of the rise in prices of imported materials and equipment, and protective measures. The policy of import substitution also tends to be inflationary because of the relative inefficiency of the new industries during the "learning" period. The secular deterioration in the terms of trade of primary products of developing countries further limits the growth of income from exports which often leads to the exchange rate devaluation.

4. *Tax System.* The nature of the tax systems and budgetary processes also help in accentuating the inflationary trends in such economies. The tax system has low inflation elasticities which means that when prices rise, the real vlaue of taxes falls. Often taxes are fixed in money terms or they are raised slowly to adjust for price rises. Moreover, it often takes long time to collect taxes with the result that by the time they are paid by assessees, their real value is less to the exchequer. On the other hand, planned expenditures on projects are often not incurred on schedule due to various supply bottlenecks with the result that when prices rise, the money value of expenditures rises proportionately. As a result of fall in the real value of tax collections and rise in money value of expenditures, governments have to adopt larger fiscal deficits which further accentuate inflationary pressures.

5. *Money Supply.* So far as the money supply is concerned, it automatically expands when prices rise in a developing country. As prices rise, firms need larger funds from banks. And the government needs more money to finance larger deficits in order to meet its expanding expenditure and wages of its employees. For this, it borrows from the central bank which leads to monetary expansion and to a further rise in the rate of inflation.

Thus structural inflation may result from supply inelasticities leading to rise in agricultural prices, costs of import substitutes, deterioration of the terms of trade and exchange rate devaluation.

Its Criticisms

The basic weaknesses in the structural arguments have been :

First, no separation is made between autonomous structural rigidities and induced rigidities resulting from price and exchange controls or mismanagement of government intervention.

Second, the sluggishness in the export growth is not really structural but the result of failure to exploit export opportunities because of overvalued exchange rates.

MARKUP INFLATION

The theory of markup inflation is mainly associated with Prof. Ackley, though formal models have also been presented by Holzman and Duesenberry independently of each other.[24] We analyse below Ackley's simplified version of the markup inflation.

The analysis is based on the assumption that both wages and prices are "administered" and are settled by workers and business firms. Firms fix administrative prices for their goods by adding to their direct material and labour costs, and some standard markup which covers profit.* Labour also seeks wages on the basis of a fixed markup over its cost of living.

This model of inflation can lead to either a stable, a rising, or a falling price level depending on the markups which firms and workers respectively use. If either or both use a percentage markup, the inflation will progress faster than if either or both fix the markups in money terms. If each participant fixes prices on the basis of prices he pays, the inflation will be high and of long duration. If one firm raises its prices in order to maintain its desired markup, the costs of other firms are raised which, in turn, raise their prices and this process of raising costs and prices will spread to other firms in an endless chain. When consumers buy such goods whose prices are rising, their cost of living rises. This causes wage costs to rise, thereby increasing the inflationary spiral. However, the inflationary spiral may come to a halt, if there is a gradual improvement in the efficiency and productivity of labour. A rise in efficiency and productivity means that there is a rise in wage rates or prices of materials leading to a smaller rise in labour and material costs. But stability in prices may not come if firms and workers appropriate the gains of rising productivity by increasing their markups. If each participant increases its markup by 100 per cent of the gains of productivity increase, the inflationary spiral might continue indefinitely.

According to Ackley, the markup can be based on either historical experience or expectations of future costs and prices. Moreover, the size of the markup applied by firms and workers is a function of the pressure of demand felt in the economy. When the demand is moderate, the markups may by applied to historically experienced costs and prices, and the price rise may be slow. But when demand is intense, the markups are based on anticipations of future costs, and prices rise rapidly. Thus there can be no inflation without some change in the size of the markup.

This theory can also be applied to cost-push and demand-pull models of inflation. If firms and workers believe that their markups are lower than the required costs and prices, regardless of the state of aggregate demand, they will increase the size of their markups. Under such a situation, costs and prices rise in an inflationary spiral. This is similar to the cost-push inflation. On the other hand, if firms and workers raise the markups due to increase in demand, markup pricing is related to demand-pull inflation.

To conclude with Ackley, "Inflation might start from an initial autonomous increase either in business and labour markups. Or it might start from an increase in aggregate demand and which first and most directly affected some of the flexible market-determined prices. But however it starts, the process involves the interaction of demand and market elements."

The markup inflation can be controlled by the usual monetary and fiscal tools in order to restrict the demand for goods and increase productivity. Ackley also suggests wage-and-price guidelines or an incomes policy to be administered by a national wage-and-price commission.

Its Criticisms

Ackley's theory suffers from two weaknesses:

First, the theory gives a very limited explanation of the cause of inflation, especially the motives which compel workers and firms to fix higher markups in the absence of demand conditions.

Second, it suffers from the implication that once inflation starts, it is likely to continue indefinitely when costs and prices rise in a spiral.

24. G. Ackley, "A Third Approach to the Analysis and Control of Inflation", in *The Relationship of Prices to Economic Stability and Growth*, Joint Economic Committee, 1958; F.D. Holzman, "Income Determination in Open Inflation," and J. Duesenberry, "The Mechanics of Inflation," *R.E.S.*, May 1959.

* Markup covers both overhead costs and profit.

OPEN AND SUPPRESSED INFLATION

Inflation is often open and suppressed.

Inflation is open when "markets for goods or factors of production are allowed to function freely, setting prices of goods and factors without normal interference by the authorities." Thus open inflation is the result of the uninterrupted operation of the market mechanism. There are no checks or controls on the distribution of commodities by the government. Increase in demand and shortage of supplies persists which tend to lead to open inflation. Unchecked open inflation ultimately leads to hyper-inflation.

Suppressed Inflation. On the contrary when the government imposes physical and monetary controls to check open inflation, it is known as repressed or suppressed inflation. The market mechanism is not allowed to function normally by the use of licensing, price controls and rationing in order to suppress extensive rise in prices. According to Friedman, governments themselves are often producers and sellers of wide range of commodities and they want to keep their own prices low by price restrictions and controls. This leads to the breakdown of the free price system.

Further, suppressed inflation also results when efforts are made to increase domestic production and reduce import demand by tariffs, import restrictions, limits on foreign loans, voluntary import agreements, etc. So long as such controls exist, the present demand is postponed and there is diversion of demand from controlled to uncontrolled commodities. But as soon as these controls are removed, there is open inflation.

Its Effects

Suppressed inflation adversely affects the economy.

(1) When the distribution of commodities is controlled, the prices of uncontrolled commodities rise very high.

(2) Suppressed inflation reduces the incentive to work because people do not get the commodities which they want to have.

(3) Controlled distribution of goods also leads to malallocation of resources. This results in the diversion of productive resources from essential to non-essential industries.

(4) Frictions increase in the labour market when high inflation is associated with higher unemployment.

(5) Suppressed inflation leads to black marketing, corruption, hoarding and profiteering. It invites extra-legal powers of control.

(6) It reduces the prospect of anti-inflationary policy being tried at all.

THE PHILLIPS CURVE : THE RELATION BETWEEN UNEMPLOYMENT AND INFLATION

The Phillips curve examines the relationship between the rate of unemployment and the rate of money wage changes. Known after the British economist A.W. Phillips[25] who first identified it, it expresses an inverse relationship between the rate of unemployment and the rate of increase in money wages. Basing his analysis on data for the United Kingdom, Phillips derived the empirical relationship that when unemployment is high, the rate of increase in money wage rates is low. This is because "workers are reluctant to offer their services at less than the prevailing rates when the demand for labour is low and unemployment is high so that wage rates fall very slowly." On the other hand, when unemployment is low, the rate of increase in money wage rates is high. This is because, "when the demand for labour is high and there are very few unemployed we should expect employers to bid wage rates up quite rapidly."

The second factor which influences this inverse relationship between money wage rate and unemployment is the nature of business activity. In a period of rising business activity when unemployment falls with increasing demand for labour, the employers will bid up wages. Conversely in a period of falling business activity when demand for labour is decreasing and unemployment is rising, employers will be reluctant to grant wage

25. A. W. Phillips, "The Relation between Unemployment and the Rate of Change in Money Wage Rates in the United Kingdowm 1862-1956", *Economica*, November, 1958.

increases. Rather, they will reduce wages. But workers and unions will be reluctant to accept wage cuts during such periods. Consequently, employers are forced to dismiss workers, thereby leading to high rate of unemployment. Thus when the labour market is depressed, a small reduction in wages would lead to large increase in unemployment. Phillips concluded on the basis of the above arguments that the relation between rates of unemployment and a change of money wages would be highly non-linear when shown on a diagram. Such a curve is called the Phillips curve.

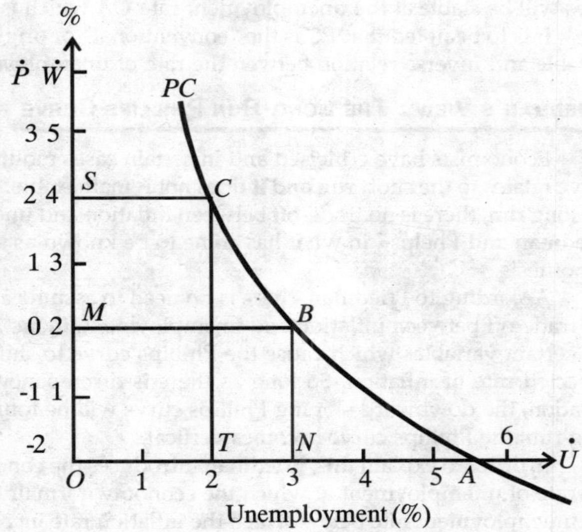

Fig. 9

The *PC* curve in Figure 9 is the Phillips curve which relates precentage change in money wage rate (*W*) on the vertical axis with the rate of unemployment (*U*) on the horizontal axis. The curve is convex to the origin which shows that the percentage change in money wages rises with decrease in the employment rate. In the figure, when the money wage rate is 2 per cent, the unemployment rate is 3 per cent. But when the wage rate is high at 4 per cent, the unemployment rate is low at 2 per cent. Thus there is a trade-off between the rate of change in money wage and the rate of unemployment. This means that when the wage rate is high the unemployment rate is low and vice versa.

The original Phillips curve was an observed statistical relation which was explained theoretically by Lipsey as resulting from the behaviour of labour market in disequilibrium through excess demand.[26]

Several economists have extended the Phillips curve analysis to the trade-off between the rate of unemployment and the rate of change in the level of prices or inflation rate by assuming that prices would change whenever wages rose more rapidly than labour productivity. If the rate of increase in money wage rates is higher than the growth rate of labour productivity, prices will rise and vice versa. But prices do not rise if labour productivity increases at the same rate as money wage rates rise.

This trade-off between the inflation rate and unemployment rate is explained in Figure 10 where the inflation rate (*P.*) is taken alongwith the rate of change in money wages (*W.*). Suppose labour productivity rises by 2 per cent per year and if money wages also increase by 2 per cent, the price level would remain constant. Thus point B on the *PC* curve corresponding to percentage change in money wages (*M*) and unemployment rate of 3 per cent (*N*) equals zero (*O*) per cent inflation rate (*P.*) on the vertical axis.* Now assume that the economy is operating at point B. If now, aggregate demand is increased, this lowers the unemployment rate to *OT* (2%) and raises the wage rate to *OS* (4%) per year. If labour productivity continues to grow at 2 per cent per annum, the price level will also rise at the rate of 2 per cent per annum at *OS* in the figure. The economy operates at point C. With the movement of the economy from *B* to *C*, unemployment falls to *T* (2%). If points *B* and *C* are connected, they trace out a Phillips curve *PC*.

Thus a money wage rate increase which is in excess of labour productivity leads to inflation. To keep wage increase to the level of labour productivity (*OM*) in order to avoid inflation. *ON* rate of unemployment will have to be tolerated.

The shape of the *PC* curve further suggests that when the unemployment rate is less than 5 per cent (that is, to the left of point *A*), the demand for labour is more than the supply and this tends to increase money wage rates. On the other hand, when the unemployment rate is more than 5½ per cent (to the right of point *A*), the

26. R.G. Lipsey, "The Relationship between Unemployment and the Rate of change of money wage rates in the U.K. 1862-1957: A further analysis," *Economica*, Vol. 27, 1960.

* The difference between money wage rate and the rate of labour productivity is the inflation rate.

supply of labour is more than the demand which tends to lower wage rates. The implication is that the wage rates will be stable at the unemployment rate *OA* which is equal to 5½ per cent per annum.

It is to be noted that *PC* is the "conventional" or original downward sloping Phillips curve which shows a stable and inverse relation betwen the rate of unemployment and the rate of change in wages.

FRIEDMAN'S VIEW : THE LONG-RUN PHILLIPS CURVE

Economists have criticised and in certain cases modified the Phillips curve. They argue that the Phillips curve relates to the short run and it does not remain stable. It shifts with changes in expectations of inflation. In the long run, there is no trade-off between inflation and unemployment. These views have been expounded by Friedman and Phelps[27] in what has come to be known as the "accelerationist" or the "adaptive expectations" hypothesis.

According to Friedman, there is no need to assume a stable downward sloping Phillips curve to explain the trade-off between inflation and unemployment. In fact, this relation is a short-run phenomenon. But there are certain variables which cause the Phillips curve to shift over time and the most important of them is the expected rate of inflation. So long as there is discrepancy between the expected rate and the actual rate of inflation, the downward sloping Phillips curve will be found. But when this discrepancy is removed over the long run, the Phillips curve becomes vertical.

In order to explain this, Friedman introduces the concept of the *natural rate of unemployment*. In represents the rate of unemployment at which the economy normally settles because of its structural imperfections. It is the unemployment rate below which the inflation rate increases, and above which the inflation rate decreases. At this rate, there is neither a tendency for the inflation rate to increase or decrease. Thus the natural rate of unemployment is defined as the rate of unemployment at which the actual rate of inflation equals the expected rate of inflation. It is thus an *equilibrium* rate of unemployment toward which the economy moves in the long run. In the long run, the Phillips curve is a vertical line at the natural rate of unemployment.

This natural or equilibrium unemployment rate is not fixed for all times. Rather, it is determined by a number of structural characteristics of the labour and commodity markets within the economy. These may be minimum wage laws, inadequate employment information, deficiencies in manpower training, costs of labour mobility, and other market imperfections.But what causes the Phillips curve to shift over time is the expected rate of inflation. This refers to the extent the labour correctly forecasts inflation and can adjust wages to the forecast. Suppose the economy is experiencing a mild rate of inflation of 2 per cent and a natural rate of unemployment (*N*) of 3 per cent. At point *A* on the short-run Phillips curve SPC_1 in Figure 11, people expect this rate of inflation to continue in the future. Now assume that the government adopts a monetary-fiscal programme to raise aggregate demand in order to lower unemployment from 3 to 2 per cent. The increase in aggregate demand will raise the rate of inflation to 4 per cent consistent with the unemployment rate of 2 per cent. When the actual inflation rate (4 per cent) is greater than the expected inflation rate (2 per cent), the economy moves from point A to B along the SPC_1 curve and the unemployment rate temporarily falls to 2 per cent. This is achieved because the labour has been deceived. It expected the inflation rate of 2 per cent and based their wage demands on this rate. But the workers eventually begin to realise that the actual rate of inflation is 4 per cent which now becomes their expected rate of inflation. Once this happens the short-run Phillips curve SPC_1 shifts to the right to SPC_2. Now workers demand increase in money wages to meet the higher expected rate of inflation of 4 per cent. They demand higher wages because they consider the present money wages to be inadequate in real terms. In other words, they want to keep up with higher prices and to eliminate fall in real wages. As a result, real labour costs will rise, firms will discharge workers and unemployment will rise from *B* (2%) to *C* (3%) with the shifting of the SPC_1 curve to SPC_2. At point *C*, the natural rate of unemployment is re-established at a higher rate of both the actual and expected inflation (4%).

If the government is determined to maintain the level of unemployment at 2 per cent, it can do so only at the cost of higher rates of inflation. From point *C*, unemployment once again can be reduced to 2 per cent via increase in aggregate demand along the SPC_2 curve until we arrive at point *D*. With 2 per cent unemployment

27. M. Friedman, "The Role of Monetary Policy," *A.E.R.*, March 1958 and E.S. Phelps, *Inflation Policy and Unemployment Theory*, 1973.

and 6 per cent inflation at point *D*, the expected rate of inflation for workers is 4 per cent. As soon as they adjust their expectations to the new situation of 6 per cent inflation, the short-run Phillips curve shifts up again to SPC_3, and the unemployment will rise back to its natural level of 3 per cent at point *E*. If points A, C and *E* are connected, they trace out a vertical long-run Phillips curve *LPC* at the natural rate of unemployment. On this curve, there is no trade-off between unemployment and inflation. Rather, any one of several rates of inflation at points *A*, *C* and *E* is compatible with the natural unemployment rate of 3 per cent. Any reduction in unemployment rate below its natural rate will be associated with an accelerating and ultimately explosive inflation. But this is only possible temporarily so long as workers overestimate or underestimate the inflation rate. In the long-run, the economy is bound to establish at the natural unemployment rate.

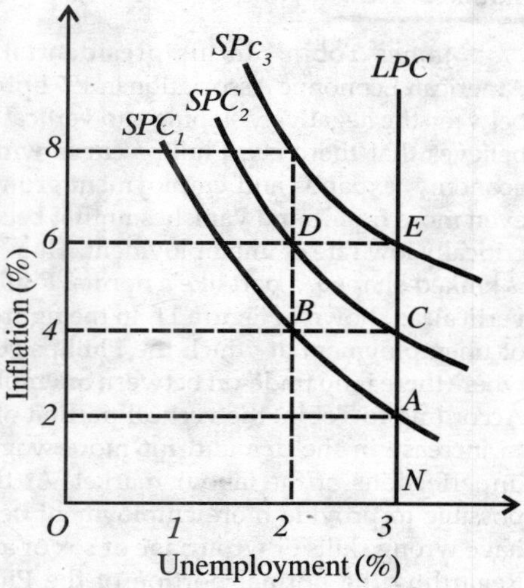

Fig. 10

There is, therefore, no trade-off between unemployment and inflation except in the short run. This is because inflationary expectations are revised according to what has happened to inflation in the past. So when the actual rate of inflation, say, rises to 4 per cent in Figure 10, workers continue to expect 2 per cent inflation for a while and only in the long run they revise their expectations upward to 4 per cent. Since they adapt themselves to the expectations, it is called the *adaptive expections hypothesis*. According to this hypothesis, the expected rate of inflation always lags behind the actual rate. But if the actual rate remains constant, the expected rate would ultimately become equal to it. This leads to the conclusion that a short-run trade off exists between unemployment and inflation, but there is no long run trade-off between the two unless a continuously rising inflation rate is tolerated.

Its Criticisms

The accelerationist hypothesis of Friedman has been criticised on the following grounds :

1. The vertical long-run Phillips curve relates to steady rate of inflation. But this is not a correct view because the economy is always passing through a series of disequilibrium positions with little tendency to approach a steady state. In such a situation, expectations may be disappointed year after year.

2. Friedman does not give a new theory of how expectations are formed that would be free from theoretical and statistical bias. This makes his position unclear.

3. The vertical long-run Phillips curve implies that all expectations are satisfied and that people correctly anticipate the future inflation rates. Critics point out that people do not anticipate inflation rates correctly, particularly when some prices are almost certain to rise faster than others. There are bound to be disequilibria between supply and demand caused by uncertainty about the future and that is bound to increase the rate of unemployment. Far from curing unemployment, a dose of inflation is likely to make it worse.

4. In one of his writings Friedman himself accepts the possibility that the long-run Phillips curve might not just be vertical, but could be positively sloped with increasing doses of inflation leading to increasing unemployment.

5. Some economists have argued that wage rates have not increased at a high rate of unemployment.

6. It is believed that workers have a money illusion. They are more concerned with the increase in their money wage rates than real wage rates.

7. Some economists regard the natural rate of unemployment as a mere abstraction because Friedman has not tried to define it in concrete terms.

8. Saul Hyman has estimated that the long-run Phillips curve is not vertical but is negatively sloped. According to Hyman, the unemployment rate can be permanently reduced if we are prepared to accept an increase in inflation rate.

TOBIN'S VIEW

James Tobin[28] in his presidential address before the American Economic Association in 1971 proposed a compromise between the negatively sloping and vertical Phillips curves. Tobin believes that there is a Phillips curve within limits. But as the economy expands and employment grows, the curve becomes even more fragile and vanishes until it becomes vertical at some critically low rate of unemployment. Thus Tobin's Phillips curve is kinked-shaped, a part like a normal Phillips curve and the rest vertical, as shown in Figure 11. In the figure *Uc* is the critical rate of unemployment at which the Phillips curve becomes vertical where there is no trade-off between unemployment and inflation. According to Tobin, the vertical portion of the curve is not due to increase in the demand for more wages but emerges from imperfections of the labour market. At the *Uc* level, it is not possible to provide more employment because the job seekers have wrong skills or wrong age or sex or are in the wrong place. Regarding the normal portion of the Phillips curve which is negatively sloping, wages are sticky downward because labourers resist a decline in their relative wages. For Tobin, there is a wage-change floor in excess supply situations. In the range of relatively high unemployment to the right of *Uc* in the figure, as aggregate demand and inflation increase and involuntary unemployment is reduced, wage-floor markets gradually diminish. When all sectors of the labour market are above the wage floor, the level of critically low rate of unemployment Uc is reached.

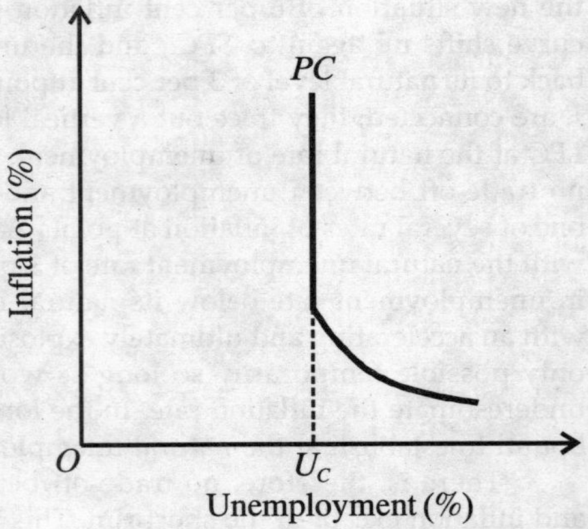

Fig. 11

SOLOW'S VIEW

Like Tobin, Robert Solow[29] does not believe that the Phillips curve is vertical at all rates of inflation. According to him, the curve is vertical at positive rates of inflation and is horizontal at negative rates of inflation, as shown in Figure 12. The basis of the Phillips curve *LPC* of the figure is that wages are sticky downward even in the face of heavy unemployment or deflation. But at a particular level of unemployment when the demand for labour increases, wages rise in the face of expected inflation. But since the Phillips curve *LPC* becomes vertical at that minimum level of unemployment, there is no trade-off between unemployment and inflation.

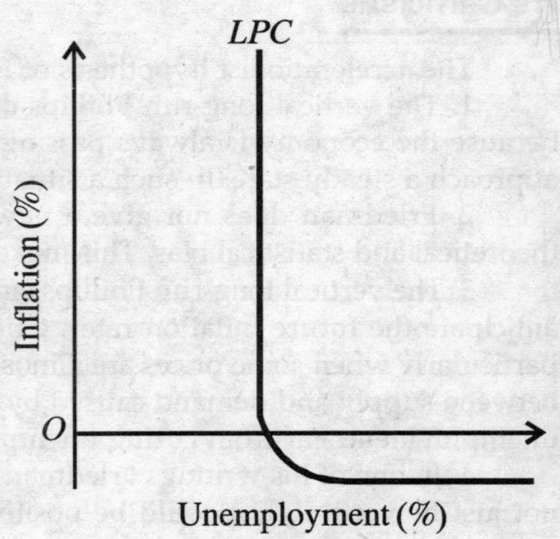

Fig. 12

Conclusion. The vertical Phillips curve has been accepted by the majority of economists. They agree that at unemployment rate of about 4 per cent, the Phillips curve becomes vertical and the trade-off between unemployment and inflation disappears. It is impossible to reduce unemployment below this level because of market imperfections.

28. "Inflation and Unemployment," *A.E.R.,* March 1972.
29. "Down the Phillips Curve with Gun and Camera," in D.A. Belsley *et al.*, (eds), *Inflation, Trade and Taxes*, 1946.

RATIONAL EXPECTATIONS AND LONG-RUN PHILLIPS CURVE

In the Friedman-Phelps acceleration hypothesis of the Phillips curve, there is a short-run trade-off between unemployment and inflation but no long-run trade-off exists. The reason is that inflationary expectations are based on past behaviour of inflation which cannot be predicted accurately. Therefore, there is always an observed error so that the expected rate of inflation always lags behind the actual rate. But the expected rate of inflation is revised in accordance with the first period's experience of inflation by adding on some proportion of the observed error in the previous period so that the expected rate of inflation adjusts toward the actual rate.

Economists belonging to the rational expectations (Ratex) school have denied the possibility of any trade-off between inflation and unemployment even during the long run. According to them, the assumption implicit in Friedman's version that price expectations are formed mainly on the basis of the experience of past inflation is unrealistic. When people base their price expectations on this assumption, they are irrational. If they think like this during a period of rising prices, they will find that they were wrong. But rational people will not commit this mistake. Rather, they will use all available information to forecast future inflation more accurately.

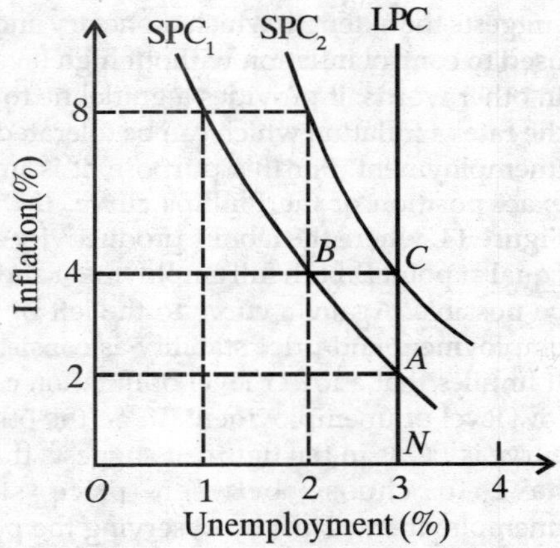

Fig. 13

The rational expectations idea is explained in Figure 13 in relation to the Phillips curve. Suppose the unemployment rate is 3 per cent in the economy and the inflation rate is 2 per cent. We start at point *A* on the SPC_1 curve. In order to reduce unemployment, the government increases the rate of money supply so as to stimulate the economy. Prices start rising. According to the Ratex hypothesis, firms have better information about prices in their own industry than about the general level of prices. They mistakenly think that the increase in prices is due to the increase in the demand for their products. As a result, they employ more workers in order to increase output. In this way, they reduce unemployment. The workers also mistake the rise in prices as related to their own industry. But wages rise as the demand for labour increases and workers think that the increase in money wages is an increase in real wages. Thus the economy moves upward on the short-run Phillips curve SPC_1 from point *A* to *B*. But soon workers and firms find that the increase in prices and wages is prevalent in most industries. Firms find that their costs have increased. Workers realise that their real wages have fallen due to the rise in the inflation rate to 4 per cent and they press for increase in wages. Thus the economy finds itself at the higher inflation rate due to government's monetary policy. As a result, it moves from point *B* to point *C* on the SPC_2 curve where the unemployment rate is 3 per cent which is the same before the government adopted an expansionary monetary policy.

When the government again tries to reduce unemployment by increasing the money supply, it cannot fool workers and firms who will now watch the movements of prices and costs in the economy. If firms expect higher costs with higher prices for their products, they are not likely to increase their production, as happened in the case of the SPC_1 curve. So far as workers are concerned, labour unions will demand higher wages to keep pace with prices moving up in the economy. When the government continues an expansionary monetary (or fiscal) policy, firms and workers get accustomed to it.They build their experience into their expectations. So when the government again adopts such a policy, firms raise prices of their products to nullify the expected inflation so that there is no effect on production and employment. Similarly, workers demand higher wages in expectation of inflation and firms do not offer more jobs. In other words, firms and workers build expectations into their price policies and wage agreements so that there is no possibility for the actual rate of unempolyment to differ from the natural rate even during the short run.

Its Policy Implications

The Ratex hypothesis assumes that people have all the relevant information of the economic variables. Any discrepancy between the actual rate of inflation andthe expected rate is only in the nature of a random error. When people act rationally, they know that past increases inprices and the rate of change in prices have invariably been accompanied by equal proportional changes in the quantity of money. When people act on this knowledge, it leads to the conclusion that there is no trade-off between inflation and unemployment either in the short-run. It implies that monetary (or fiscal) policy is unable to change the difference between the actual and natural rate of unemployment. This means that the economy can only be to the left or right of point *N* of the long-run Phillips curve *LPC* (in Figure 18.12(A)) in a random manner. Thus the implication is that stabilisation policy is ineffective and should be abandoned.

POLICY IMPLICATIONS OF THE PHILLIPS CURVE

The Phillips curve has important policy implications. It suggests the extent to which monetary and fiscal policies can be used to control inflation without high levels of unemployment. In other words, it provides a guideline to the authorities about the rate of inflation which can be tolerated with a given level of unemployment. For this purpose, it is important to know the exact position of the Phillips curve. If the curve is PC_1 as in Figure 14, where the labour productivity and the wage rate are equal at point *E*, both full employment and price stability would be possible. Again, a curve to the left of point *E* suggests full employment and price stability as consistent policy objectives. It implies that a lower level of inflation can be traded-off for a low level of unemployment. If, on the other hand, the Phillips curve is *PC* as in the figure, it suggests that the authorities will have to choose between price stability and more unemployment. Thus by observing the position of the Phillips curve, the authorities can decide about the nature of monetary and fiscal policies to be adopted. For instance, if the authorities find that the inflation rate P_2 is incompatible with the unemployment rate U_1 of Figure 14, they would adopt such monetary and fiscal policies as to shift the Phillips curve *PC* to the left in the position of PC_1 curve. This will give a better trade-off between a lower inflation rate P_1 with the small level of unemployment U_1.

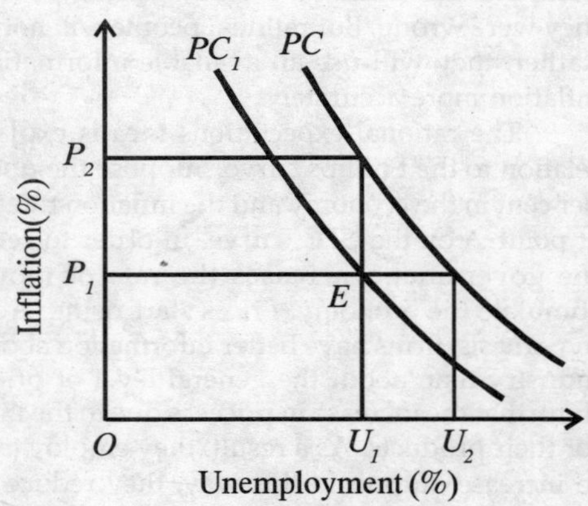

Fig. 14

While explaining the natural rate of unemployment, Friedman pointed out that the only scope of public policy in influencing the level of unemployment lies in the short run in keeping with the position of the Phillips curve. He ruled out the possibility of influencing the long-run rate of unemployment because of the vertical Phillips curve.

According to him, the trade-off between unemployment and inflation does not exist and has never existed. However rapid the inflation might be, unemployment always tends to fall back to its natural rate which is not some irreducible minimum of unemployment. It can be lowered by removing obstacles in the labour market by reducing frictions. Therefore, public policy should improve the institutional structure to make the labour market responsive to changing patterns of demand. Moreover, some level of unemployment must be accepted as natural because of the existence of large number of part-time workers, unemployment compensation and other institutional factors.

Another implication is that unemployment is not a fitting aim for monetary expansion, according to Friedman. Therefore, employment above the natural rate can be reached at the cost of accelerating inflation, if monetary policy is adopted. In his words, "A little inflation will provide a boost at first—like a small dose of a drug for a new addict—but then it takes more and more inflation to provide the boost, just it takes a bigger and bigger dose of a drug to give a hardened addict a high." Thus if the government wants to have a genuine full employment level at the natural rate, it must not use monetary policy to remove institutional restraints, restrictive practices, barriers to mobility, trade union coercion and similar obstacles to both the workers and the employers.

But economists do not agree with Friedman. They suggest that it is possible to reduce the natural rate of unemployment through labour market policies, whereby labour market can be made more efficient. So the natural rate of unemployment can be reduced by shifting the long-run vertical Phillips curve to the left.

But the policy implications of the Phillips curve are not so simple as they appear. The authorities are faced with certain constraints concerning the decision with regard to the rate of inflation that may be compatible with a particular rate of unemployment. Thus the problem of trade-off between inflation and unemployment is one of choice under constraints. This is illustrated in Figure 15. The constraints are a given Phillips curve *PC* and the indifference curves $I_1 I_1$, $I_2 I_2$, $I_3 I_3$ and $I''I''$ representing the choice of authorities between unemployment and inflation. The indifference curves are concave to the origin because if the authorities want to reduce unemployment, they must have higher inflation and vice-versa. So they represent nagative utility. But the cuve I_2I_2 represents a higher level of public welfare than the curve I_1I_1, and the curve I_3I_3 still higher welfare than I_2I_2 curve. This is because any point on the lower curve represents a lower rate of unemployment and inflation than on a higher curve. The optimum trade-off point is *E* where the indifference curve I_1I_1 is tangent to the Phillips curve *PC* and where the trade-off is between *OA* rate of inflation and *OB* rate of unemployment. If, however, the public authorities adopt such monetary and fiscal policies whereby they want to have less inflation and more unemployment, the indifference curve becomes *1'1'*. This curve *I'I'* is tangent to the Phillips curve *PC* at *F* and the trade-off becomes *OC* of inflation and *OD* of unemployment.

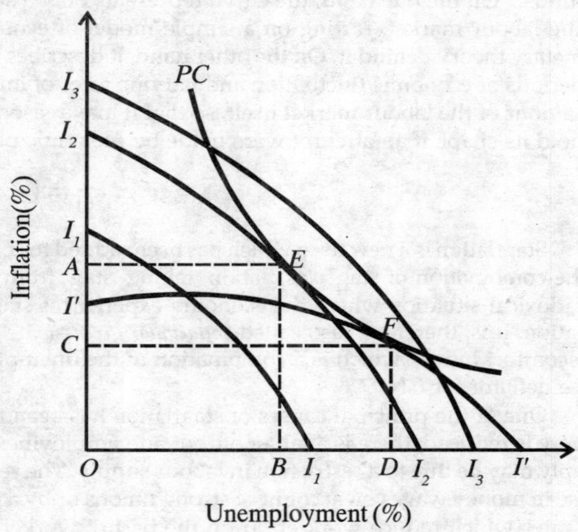

Fig. 15

It has been suggested by certain economists that there is a loop or orbit about the Phillips curve based on observed values of inflation and unemployment. This is illustrated in Figure 16. In the early expansion phase of the business cycle, the unemployment-inflation loop involves rising output with reduced inflation. This is due to demand-pull following an expansionary monetary or fiscal policy. In this phase of the cycle, the nomal relationship between inflation and unemployment suggested by the Phillips curve is maintained. It is shown by the movement of arrows at point *C* from below the *PC* curve when the rate of unemployment falls and the rate of inflation increases. If aggregate demand continues to increase, inflationary pressures gain momentum, and the dotted loop crosses the Phillips curve at point A. A tight monetary or fiscal policy will reduce aggregate demand. But the expectations of increase in prices will

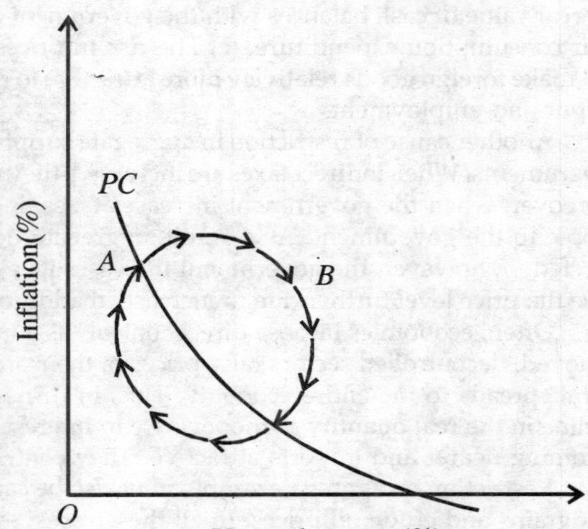

Fig. 16

bring wage increases and inflation will be maintained at the previous rate. So unemployment will increase with no reduction in prices. This is revealed by the upper portion of the loop to the right of the Phillips curve. However, when excess demand is controlled and output increases, the rate of inflation starts falling from point B along with fall in the rate of unemployment. Thus we find that the conclusion of the Phillips curve holds in the early phase of the business cycle due to an expansionary monetary or fiscal policy. But in the downward phase the trade-off between inflation and unemployment goes contrary to the Phillips curve.

Johnson doubts about the applicability of the Phillips curve to the formulation of economic policy on two grounds. "On the one hand, the curve represents only a statistical description of the mechanics of adjustment in the labour market, resting on a simple model of economic dynamics with little general and well-tested monetary theory behind it. On the other hand, it describes the behaviour of the labour market in a combination of periods of economic fluctuation and varying rates of inflation, conditions which presumably influenced the behaviour of the labour market itself, so that it may reasonably be doubted whether the curve would continue to hold its shape if an attempt were made by economic policy to pin the economy down to a point on it."[30]

STAGFLATION

Stagflation is a new term which has been added to economic literature in the 1970s. The word "stagflation" is the combination of stag *plus* flation, taking 'stag' from stagnation and 'flation' from inflation. Thus it is a paradoxical situation where the economy experiences stagnation or unemployment alongwith a high rate of inflation. It is, therefore, also called *inflationary recession*. The level of stagflation is measured in the US by the "discomfort index" which is a combination of the unemployment rate and the inflation rate measured by the price deflator for GNP.

One of the principal causes of stagflation has been restriction in the aggregate supply. When aggregate supply is reduced, there is a fall in output and employment and the price level rises. A reduction in aggregate supply may be due to a restriction in labour supply. The restriction in labour supply, in turn, may be caused by a rise in money wages on account of strong unions or by a rise in the legal minimum wage rate, or by increased tax rates which reduce work-effort on the part of workers.

When wages rise, firms are forced to reduce production and employment. Consequently, there is fall in real income and consumer expenditure. Since the decline in consumption will be less than the fall in real income, there will be excess demand in the commodity market which will push up the price level. The rise in the price level, in turn, reduces output and employment in the following three ways: (a) It reduces the real quantity of money, raises interest rates and brings a fall in investment expenditure. (b) The rise in the price level reduces the real value of cash balances with the government and the private sector via the Pigou effect which reduces their consumption expenditure. (c) The rise in prices of domestic goods makes exports dearer for foreigners and make foreign goods relatively more attractive to domestic consumers, thereby adversely affecting domestic output and employment.

Another cause of restriction in aggregate supply is the increase in indirect taxes by central, state and local governments. When indirect taxes are increased, they raise costs and prices and reduce output and employment. Moreover, when the government increases taxes, it leads to the transfer of real purchasing power from the people to the government. As a result, aggregate demand falls, and output and employment are adversely affected. If, however, the government increases its expenditure equal to the increase in tax revenue, it would raise the price level further due to increase in additional demand.

Often, economies impose direct controls as a means of controlling inflation. But when such controls are removed, decontrolled sectors raise prices of their products with the result that wages rise and the wage-price spiral spreads to the entire economy. This, in turn, advesely affects production and employment through a decline in the real quantity of money, rise in interest rates, fall in investment via the Pigou effect, and exports becoming dearer and imports attractive. They contribute to stagflation.

Restriction on aggregate supply may also be caused by external factors such as rise in the world prices of foodgrains and crude oil prices. In all these cases, the domestic price level is raised by outside forces. When

30. *Op. cit.*, pp.132-3.

international prices of foodgrains and crude oil rise, they lead to the outflow of purchasing power away from domestic consumers. They accentuate inflation, raise wages and prices. As a result, the real quantity of money declines, interest rates rise and investment declines via the Pigou effect, making exports dearer and imports attractive, and domestic output and employment decline. They lead to stagflation.

The phenomenon of stagflation is illustrated in Fig. 17 where employment is measured on the horizontal axis and the price level on the vertical axis. The initial equilibrium is at *E* where the demand curve *D* intersects the supply curve S and the price level is *OP* and the employment level is *ON*. When the aggregate supply is reduced due to any of the factors mentioned above, the supply curve *S* shifts to the left at S_1. The new equilibrium is at E_1 where S_1 intersects the *D* curve. Now the price level rises from *OP* to OP_1 and the level of employment declines from *ON* to ON_1.

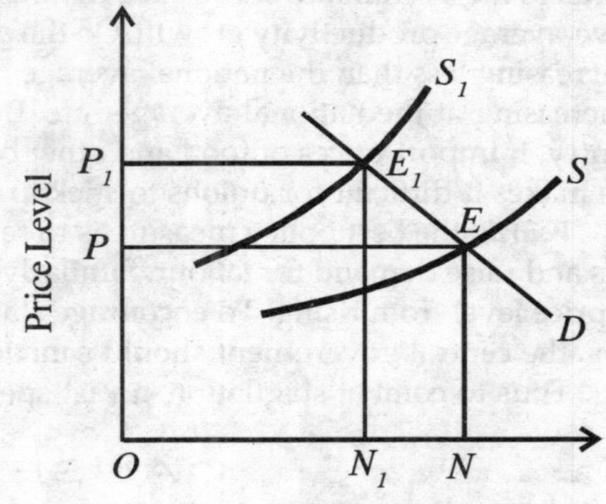

Fig. 17

MEASURES TO CONTROL STAGFLATION

We have observed above that it is inflation that leads to stagflation. The US experience shows that if stagflation is controlled either by restrictive or expansionary measures, it will increase. Suppose restrictive demand managed monetary and fiscal measures are adopted, they tend to lower aggregate demand so that the new demand curve D_1 cuts the supply curve S_1 at point *E'* at the old price level *OP* in Fig 18. This policy reduces the level of employment further to *ON'* and at the same time lowers the price level from OP_1 to *OP*. Thus such a policy tends to increase unemployment by N_1N' and reduces inflation by P_1P. Thus it fails to control stagflation. On the other hand, if expansionary demand managed monetary and fiscal policies are adopted, they will raise the aggregate demand so that the new demand curve D_2 cuts the supply curve S_1 at E_2 at the old employment level *ON*. This raises employment from ON_1 to *ON* but increases the price level to OP_2. Thus such a policy also fails to control stagflation because it generates more inflation combined with higher employment. Economists, therefore, suggest other measures which slow inflation and maintain higher employment.

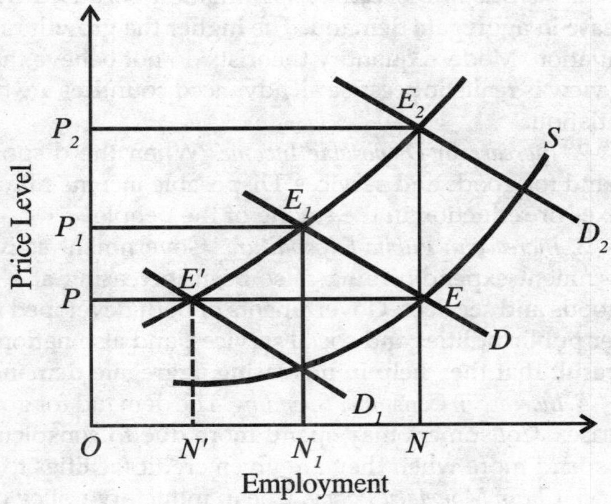

Fig. 18

First, minimum wages should not be raised at all.

Second, *tax-based income* policies should be started. These policies are different for individual and business firms. In the case of individuals, target rates of wage and price inflation are based on some reasonable economic forecast of inflation. Persons who accept wage increases below the target rates are rewarded with tax credits. Those who insist on wage increases above the target rates are levied a penalty tax. Similar is the case with business firms. Firms which keep wages down to the target rates are rewarded with a reduction in their business income tax. On the other hand, those who permit wage increases above the target rates are charged a penalty tax in addition to business income tax.

Third, there is need to introduce *income policies*. One of the important planks of the income policies is to link the increase of money wages to productivity increase. Thus the rate of increase of money wages should be limited to the overall rate of productivity increase. Further, prices should be reduced in those industries having above-average productivity growth. On the other hand, prices should be raised in industries where productivity is increasing less than the national average rate. Prices should be kept stable in industries where productivity is increasing at the national average rate. But such policies are difficult to implement in the case of an open country. If import prices of food and other consumer products rise, they tend to raise the domestic price level. This makes it difficult for unions to stick to wage agreements.

Fourth, the best policy measure is to reduce *personal and business taxes* because they tend to reduce labour costs and raise demand for labour. Similarly, sales tax and excise duties should be reduced in order to prevent the price level from rising. To encourage state and local government to reduce state and local sales and excise taxes, the central government should sanction additional grants-in-aid to them.

Thus to combat stagflation, a vast spectrum of policy measures is needed.

CAUSES OF INFLATION

Inflation is caused when aggregate demand exceeds aggregate supply of goods and services. We analyse the factors which lead to increase in demand and shortage of supply.

FACTORS AFFECTING DEMAND

Both Keynesians and monetarists believe that inflation is caused by increase in aggregate demand. They point toward the following factors which raise it.

1. *Increase in Money Supply.* Inflation is caused by an increase in the supply of money which leads to increase in aggregate demand. The higher the growth rate of the nominal money supply, the higher is the rate of inflation. Modern quantity theorists do not believe that true inflation starts after the full employment level. This view is realistic because all advanced countries are faced with high levels of unemployment and high rates of inflation.

2. *Increase in Disposable Income.* When the disposable income of the people increases, it raises their demand for goods and services. Disposable income may increase with the rise in national income or reduction in taxes or reduction in the saving of the people.

3. *Increase in Public Expenditure.* Government activities have been expanding much with the result that government expenditure has also been increasing at a phenomenal rate, thereby raising aggregate demand for goods and services. Governments of both developed and developing countries are providing more facilities under public utilities and social services, and also nationalising industries and starting public enterprises with the result that they help in increasing aggregate demand.

4. *Increase in Consumer Spending.* The demand for goods and services increases when consumer expenditure increases. Consumers may spend more due to conspicuous consumption or demonstration effect. They may also spend more when they are given credit facilities to buy goods on hire-purchase and instalment basis.

5. *Cheap Monetary Policy.* Cheap monetary policy or the policy of credit expansion also leads to increase in the money supply which raises the demand for goods and services in the economy. When credit expands, it raises the money income of the borrowers which, in turn, raises aggregate demand relative to supply, thereby leading to inflation. This is also known as *credit-induced inflation.*

6. *Deficit Financing.* In order to meet its mounting expenses, the government resorts to deficit financing by borrowing from the public and even by printing more notes. This raises aggregate demand in relation to aggregate supply, thereby leading to inflationary rise in prices. This is also known as *deficit-induced* inflation.

7. *Expansion of the Private Sector.* The expansion of the private sector also tends to raise the aggregate demand. For huge investments increase employment and income, thereby creating more demand for goods and services. But it takes time for the output to enter the market. This leads to rise in prices.

8. *Black Money.* The existence of black money in all countries due to corruption, tax evasion etc. increases the aggregate demand. People spend such unearned money extravagantly, thereby creating unnecessary demand for commodities. This tends to raise the price level further.

9. *Repayment of Public Debt.* Whenever the government repays its past internal debt to the public, it leads

to increase in the money supply with the public. This tends to raise the aggregate demand for goods and services and to rise in prices.

10. *Increase in Exports.* When the demand for domestically produced goods increases in foreign countries, this raises the earnings of industries producing export commodities. These, in turn, create more demand for goods and services within the economy, thereby leading to rise in the price level.

Factors Affecting Supply

There are also certain factors which operate on the opposite side and tend to reduce the aggregate supply. Some of the factors are as follows :

1. *Shortage of Factors of Production.* One of the important causes affecting the supplies of goods is the shortage of such factors as labour, raw materials, power supply, capital, etc. They lead to excess capacity and reduction in industrial production, thereby raising prices.

2. *Industrial Disputes.* In countries where trade unions are powerful, they also help in curtailing production. Trade unions resort to strikes and if they happen to be unreasonable from the employers' viewpoint and are prolonged, they force the employers to declare lock-outs. In both cases. industiral production falls, thereby reducing supplies of goods. If the unions succeed in raising money wages of their members to a very high level than the productivity of labour, this also tends to reduce production and supplies of goods. Thus they tend to raise prices.

3. *Natural Calamities.* Drought or floods is a factor which adversely affects the supplies of agricultural products. The latter, in turn, create shortages of food products and raw materials, thereby helping inflationary pressures.

4. *Artificial Scarcities.* Artificial scarcities are created by hoarders and speculators who indulge in black marketing. Thus they are instrumental in reducing supplies of goods and raising their prices.

5. *Increase in Exports.* When the country produces more goods for export than for domestic consumption, this creates shortages of goods in the domestic market. This leads to inflation in the economy.

6. *Lop-sided Production.* If the stress is on the production of comfort, luxury, or basic products to the neglect of essential consumer goods in the country, this creates shortages or consumer goods. This again causes inflation.

7. *Law of Diminishing Returns.* If industries in the country are using old machines and outmoded methods of production, the law of diminishing returns operates. This raises cost per unit of production, thereby raising the prices of products.

8. *International Factors.* In modern times, inflation is a worldwide phenomenon. When prices rise in major industrial countries, their effects spread to almost all countries with which they have trade relations. Often the rise in the price of a basic raw material like petrol in the international market leads to rise in the prices of all related commodities in a country.

MEASURES TO CONTROL INFLATION

We have studied above that inflation is caused by the failure of aggregate supply to equal the increase in aggregate demand. Inflation can, therefore, be controlled by increasing the supplies of goods and services and reducing money incomes in order to control aggregate demand. The various methods are usually grouped under three heads: monetary meausres, fiscal measures and other measures.

Monetary Measures

Monetary measures aim at reducing money incomes.

(a) Credit Control. One of the important monetary measures is *monetary policy*. The central bank of the country adopts a number of methods to control the quantity and quality of credit. For this purpose, it raises the bank rates, sells securities in the open market, raises the reserve ratio, and adopts a number of selective credit control measures, such as raising margin requirements and regulating consumer credit.

Monetary policy may not be effective in controlling inflation, if inflation is due to cost-push factors.

Monetary policy can only be helpful in controlling inflation due to demand-pull factors.

(b) Demonetisation of Currency. However, one of the monetary measures is to demonetise currency of higher denominations. Such a measures is usually adopted when there is abundance of black money in the country.

(c) Issue of New Currency. The most extreme monetary measure is the issue of new currency in place of the old currency. Under this system, one new note is exchanged for a number of notes of the old currency. The value of bank deposits is also fixed accordingly. Such a measure is adopted when there is an excessive issue of notes and there is hyperinflation in the country. It is a very effective measure. But is inequitable for its hurts the small depositors the most.

Fiscal Measures

Monetary policy alone is incapable of controlling inflation. It should, therefore, be supplemented by fiscal measures. Fiscal measures are highly effective for controlling government expenditure, personal consumption expenditure, and private and public investment. The principal fiscal measures are the following :

(a) Reduction in Unnecessary Expenditure. The government should reduce unnecessary expenditure on non-development activities in order to curb inflation. This will also put a check on private expenditure which is dependent upon government demand for goods and services. But it is not easy to cut government expenditure. Though this measure is always welcome but it becomes difficult to distinguish between essential and non-essential expenditure. Therefore, this measure should be supplemented by taxation.

(b) Increase in Taxes. To cut personal consumption expenditure, the rates of personal, corporate and commodity taxes should be raised and even new taxes should be levied, but the rates of taxes should not be so high as to discourage saving, investment and production. Rather, the tax system should provide larger incentives to those who save, invest and produce more. Further, to bring more revenue into the tax-net, the government should penalise the tax evaders by imposing heavy fines. Such measures are bound to be effective in controlling inflation. To increase the supply of goods within the country, the government should reduce import duties and increase export duties.

(c) Increase in Savings. Another measure is to increase savings on the part of the people. This will tend to reduce disposable income with the people, and hence personal consumption expenditure. But due to the rising cost of living, people are not in a position to save much voluntarily. Keynes, therefore, advocated compulsory savings or what he called 'deferred payment' where the saver gets his money back after some years. For this purpose, the government should float public loans carrying high rates of interest, start saving schemes with prize money, or lottery for long periods, etc. It should also introduce compulsory provident fund, provident fund-cum-pension schemes, etc. All such measures increase savings and are likely to be effective in controlling inflation.

(d) Surplus Budgets. An important measure is to adopt anti-inflationary budgetary policy. For this purpose, the government should give up deficit financing and instead have surplus budgets. It means collecting more in revenues and spending less.

(e) Public Debt. At the same time, it should stop repayment of public debt and postpone it to some future date till inflationary pressures are controlled within the economy. Instead, the government should borrow more to reduce money supply with the public.

Like monetary measures, fiscal measures alone cannot help in controlling inflation. They should be supplemented by monetary, non-monetary and non-fiscal measures.

Other Measures

The other types of measures are those which aim at increasing aggregate supply and reducing aggregate demand directly.

(a) To Increase Production. The following measures should be adopted to increase production: (i) One of the foremost measures to control inflation is to increase the production of essential consumer goods like food, clothing, kerosene oil, sugar, vegetable oils, etc. (ii) If there is need, raw materials for such products may be

imported on preferential basis to increase the production of essential commodities. (iii) Efforts should also be made to increase productivity. For this purpose, industrial peace should be maintained through agreements with trade unions, binding them not to resort to strikes for some time. (iv) The policy of rationalisation of industries should be adopted as a long-term measure. Rationalisation increases productivity and production of industries through the use of brain, brawn and bullion. (v) All possible help in the form of latest technology, raw materials, financial help, subsidies, etc. shold be provided to different consumer goods sectors to increase production.

(b) Rational Wage Policy. Another important measure is to adopt a rational wage and income policy. Under hyperinflation, there is a wage-price spiral. To control this, the government should freeze wages, incomes, profits, dividends, bonus, etc. But such a drastic measure can only be adopted for a short period as it is likely to antagonise both workers and industrialists. Therefore, the best course is to link increase in wages to increase in productivity. This will have a dual effect. It will control wages and at the same time increase productivity, and hence raise production of goods in the economy.

(c) Price Control. Price control and rationing is another measure of direct control to check inflation. Price control means fixing an upper limit for the prices of essential consumer goods. They are the maximum prices fixed by law and anybody charging more than these prices is punished by law. But it is difficult to administer price control.

(d) Rationing. Rationing aims at distributing consumption of scarce goods so as to make them available to a large number of consumers. It is applied to essential consumer goods such as wheat, rice, sugar, kerosene oil, etc. It is meant to stabilise the prices of necessaries and assure distributive justice. But it is very inconvenient for consumers because it leads to queues, artificial shortages, corruption and black marketing. Keynes did not favour rationing for it "involves a great deal of waste, both of resources and of employment."

Conclusion. From the various monetary, fiscal and other measures discussed above, it becomes clear that to control inflation, the government should adopt all measures simultaneously. Inflation is like a hydra-headed monster which should be fought by using all the weapons at the command of the government.

EFFECTS OF INFLATION*

Inflation affects different people differently. This is because of the fall in the value of money. When price rises or the value of money falls, some groups of the society gain, some lose and some stand in-between. Broadly speaking. there are two economic groups in every society, the fixed income group and the flexible income group. People belonging to the first group lose and those belonging to the second group gain. The reason is that the price movements in the case of different goods, services, assets, etc. are not uniform. When there is inflation, most prices are rising, but the rates of increase of individual prices differ much. Prices of some goods and services rise faster, of others slowly and of still others remain unchanged. We discuss below the effects of inflation on redistribution of income and wealth, production, and on the society as a whole.

1. Effects on Redistribution of Income and Wealth

There are two ways to measure the effects of inflation on the redistribution of income and wealth in a society. *First*, on the basis of the change in the real value of such factor incomes as wages, salaries, rents, interest, dividends and profits. *Second*, on the basis of the size distribution of income over time as a result of inflation. i.e. whether the incomes of the rich have increased and that of the middle and poor classes have declined with inflation. Inflation brings about shifts in the distribution of real income from those whose money incomes are relatively inflexible to those whose money incomes are relatively flexible.

The poor and middle classes suffer because their wages and salaries are more or less fixed but the prices of commodities continue to rise. They become more impoverished. On the other hand, businessmen, industrialists, traders, real estate holders, speculators, and others with variable incomes gain during rising prices. The latter category of persons become rich at the cost of the former group. There is unjustified transfer

* It is also known as effects of changes in the value of money.

of income and wealth from the poor to the rich. As a result, the rich roll in wealth and indulge in conspicuous consumption, while the poor and middle classes live in abject misery and poverty.

But which income group of society gains or loses from inflation depends on who anticipates inflation and who does not. Those who correctly anticipate inflation, they can adjust their present earnings, buying, borrowing, and lending activities against the loss of income and wealth due to inflation. They, therefore, do nor get hurt by the inflation. Failure to anticipate inflation correctly leads to redistribution of income and wealth. In practice, all persons are unable to anticipate and predict the rate of inflation correctly so that they cannot adjust their economic behaviour accordingly. As a result, some persons gain while others lose. The net result is redistibution of income and wealth. The effects of inflation on different groups of society are discussed below.

(1) *Debtors and Creditors.* During periods of rising prices, debtors gain and creditors lose. When prices rise, the value of money falls. Though debtors return the same amount of money, but they pay less in terms of goods and services. This is because the value of money is less than when they borrowed the money. Thus the burden of the debt is reduced and debtors gain. On the other hand, creditors lose. Although they get back the same amount of money which they lent, they receive less in real terms because the value of money falls. Thus inflation brings about a redistribution of real wealth in favour of debtors at the cost of creditors.

(2) *Salaried Persons.* Salaried workers such as clerks, teachers, and other white collar persons lose when there is inflation. The reason is that their salaries are slow to adjust when prices are rising.

(3) *Wage Earners.* Wage earners may gain or lose depending upon the speed with which their wages adjust to rising prices. If their unions are strong, they may get their wages linked to the cost of living index. In this way, they may be able to protect themselves from the bad effects of inflation. But the problem is that there is often a time lag between the raising of wages by employees and the rise in prices. So workers lose because by the time wages are raised, the cost of living index may have increased further. But where the unions have entered into contractual wages for a fixed period, the workers lose when prices continue to rise during the period of contract. On the whole, the wage earners are in the same position as the white collar persons.

(4) *Fixed Income Group.* The recipients of transfer payments such as pensions, unemployment insurance, social security, etc. and recipients of interest and rent live on fixed incomes. Pensioners get fixed pensions. Similarly the rentier class consisting of interest and rent receivers get fixed payments. The same is the case with the holders of fixed interest bearing securities, debentures and deposits. All such persons lose because they receive fixed payments, while the value of money continues to fall with rising prices. Among these groups, the recipients of transfer payments belong to the lower income group and the rentier class to the upper income group. Inflation redistributes income from these two groups toward the middle income group comprising traders and businessmen.

(5) *Equity Holders or Investors.* Persons who hold shares or stocks of companies gain during inflation. For when prices are rising, business activities expand which increase profits of companies. As profits increase, dividends on equities also increase at a faster rate than prices. But those who invest in debentures, securities, bonds, etc. which carry a fixed interest rate lose during inflation because they receive a fixed sum while the purchasing power is falling.

(6) *Businessmen.* Businessmen of all types, such as producers, traders and real estate holders gain during periods of rising prices. Take producers first. When prices are rising, the value of their inventories (goods in stock) rise in the same proportion. So they profit more when they sell their stored commodities. The same is the case with traders in the short run. But producers profit more in another way. Their costs do not rise to the extent of the rise in the prices of their goods. This is because prices of raw materials and other inputs and wages do not rise immediately to the level of the price rise. The holders of real estates also profit during inflation because the prices of landed property increase much faster than the general price level.

(7) *Agriculturists.* Agriculturists are of three types, landlords, peasant proprietors, and landless agricultural workers. Landlords lose during rising prices becaused they get fixed rents. But peasant proprietors who own and cultivate their farms gain. Prices of farm products increase more than the cost of production. For prices of inputs and land revenue do not rise to the same extent as the rise in the prices of farm products. On the other hand, the landless agricultural workers are hit hard by rising prices. Their wages are not raised by the farm owners, because trade unionism is absent among them. But the prices of consumer goods rise rapidly. So landless agricultural workers are losers.

(8) *Government.* The government as a debtor gains at the expense of households who are its prinicipal creditors. This is because interest rates on government bonds are fixed and are not raised to offset expected rise in prices. The government, in turn, levies less taxes to service and retire its debt. With inflation, even the real value of taxes is reduced. Thus redistribution of wealth in favour of the government accrues as a benefit to the tax-payers. Since the tax-payers of the government are high-income groups, they are also the creditors of the government because it is they who hold government bonds. As creditors, the real value of their assets decline and as tax-payers, the real value of their liabilities also declines during inflation. The extent to which they will be gainers or losers on the whole is a very complicated calculation.

Conclusion. Thus inflation redistributes income from wage earners and fixed income groups to profit recipients, and from creditors to debtors. So far as wealth redistibutions are concerned, the very poor and the very rich are more likely to lose than middle income groups. This is because the poor hold what little wealth they have in monetary form and have few debts, whereas the very rich hold a substantial part of their wealth in bonds and have relatively few debts. On the other hand, the middle income groups are likely to be heavily in debt and hold some wealth in common stocks as well as in real assets.

2. Effects on Production

When prices start rising production is encouraged. Producers earn wind-fall profits in the future. They invest more in anticipation of higher profits in the future. This tends to increase employment, production and income. But this is only possible up to the full employment level. Further increase in investment beyond this level will lead to severe inflationary pressures within the economy because prices rise more than production as the resources are fully employed. So inflation adversely affects production after the level of full employment. The adverse effects of inflation on production are discussed below.

(1) *Misallocation of Resources.* Inflation causes misallocation of resources when producers divert resources from the production of essential to non-essential goods from which they expect higher profits.

(2) *Changes in the System of Transactions.* Inflation leads to changes in transactions pattern of producers. They hold a smaller stock of real money holdings against unexpected contingencies than before. They devote more time and attention to converting money into inventories or other financial or real assets. It means that time and energy are diverted from the production of goods and services and some resources are used wastefully.

(3) *Reduction in Production.* Inflation adversely affects the volume of production because the expectation of rising prices alongwith rising costs of inputs bring uncertainty. This reduces production.

(4) *Fall in Quality.* Continuous rise in prices creates a seller's market. In such a situation, producers produce and sell sub-standard commodities in order to earn higher profits. They also indulge in adulteration of commodities.

(5) *Hoarding and Blackmarketing.* To profit more from rising prices, producers hoard stocks of their commodities. Consequently, an artificial scarcity of commodities is created in the market. Then the producers sell their products in the black market which increases inflationary pressures.

(6) *Reduction in Saving.* When prices rise rapidly, the propensity to save declines because more money is needed to buy goods and services than before. Reduced saving adversely affects investment and capital formation. As a result, production is hindered.

(7) *Hinders Foreign Capital.* Inflation hinders the inflow of foreign capital because the rising costs of materials and other inputs make foreign investment less profitable.

(8) *Encourages Speculation.* Rapidly rising prices create uncertainty among producers who indulge in speculative activities in order to make quick profits. Instead of engaging themselves in productive activities, they speculate in various types of raw materials required in production.

3. Other Effects

Inflation leads to a number of other effects which are discussed as under:

(1) *Government.* Inflation affects the government in various ways. It helps the government in financing its activities through inflationary finance. As the money incomes of the people increase, government collects that in the form of taxes on incomes and commodities. So the revenues of the government increase during rising

prices. Moreover, the real burden of the public debt decreases when prices are rising. But the government expenses also increase with rising production costs of public projects and enterprises and increase in administrative expenses as prices and wages rise. On the whole, the government gains under inflation because rising wages and profits spread an illusion of prosperity within the country.

(2) *Balance of Payments.* Inflation involves the sacrificing of the advantages of international specialisation and division of labour. It affects adversely the balance of payments of a country. When prices rise more rapidly in the home country than in foreign countries, domestic products become costlier compared to foreign products. This tends to increase imports and reduce exports, thereby making the balance of payments unfavourable for the country. This happens only when the country follows a fixed exchange rate policy. But there is no adverse impact on the balance of payments if the country is on the flexible exchange rate system.

(3) *Exchange Rate.* When prices rise more rapidly in the home country than in foreign countries, it lowers the exchange rate in relation to foreign currencies.

(4) *Collapse of the Monetary System.* If hyperinflation persists and the value of money countinues to fall many times in a day, it ultimately leads to the collapse of the monetary system, as happened in Germany after World War 1.

(5) *Social.* Inflation is socially harmful. By widening the gulf between the rich and the poor, rising prices create discontentment among the masses. Pressed by the rising cost of living, workers resort to strikes which lead to loss in production. Lured by profits, people resort to hoarding, blackmarketing, adulteration, manufacture of substandard commodities, speculation, etc. Corruption spreads in every walk of life. All this reduces the efficiency of the economy.

(6) *Political.* Rising prices also encourage agitations and protests by political parties opposed to the government. And if they gather momentum and become unhandy they may bring the downfall of the government. Many governments have been sacrificed at the alter of inflation.

Inflation as a Tax

Inflation operates like a tax when redistribution results in goods and services being transferred to the government from the poeple. If falls heavily on those least able to pay. When the government issues more money to finance its budget deficit, to repay its past debt and to meet its rising demand for goods and services during inflation, it acts as a tax on the people and it transfers purchasing power to the govenment. High inflation rates decrease the purchasing power of money with the poeple and discourage them from holding money. The rate of inflation is the rate of inflation tax. The inflation tax is defined as the decline in purchasing power of money due to inflation. It is calculated as :

$$M \times \frac{i}{(1+i)}$$

Where M is the average money at year-ending and year-beginnning and i is the decimal inflation rate measured by the change in consumer price index (*CPI*). The formula tells that the period for which prices rise by i, each money unit loses $i/(1+i)$ of its purchasing power.

Inflation as a tax on holding real money balances is explained in terms of Figure 19, where the level of real money balances is measured on the horizontal axis and the interest rate on the vertical axis. Suppose the government issues money to finance its budget deficit which will raise the price level and cause the real money stock to fall. Assuming that the initial price level is stable, and the level of real income is constant, the money interest rate (i) is equal to the real interest rate (r). We begin the analysis by further assuming zero expected rate of inflation which is equal to the money interest rate (i). In such as economy, the demand for real money balances as a function of the money interest rate is shown by

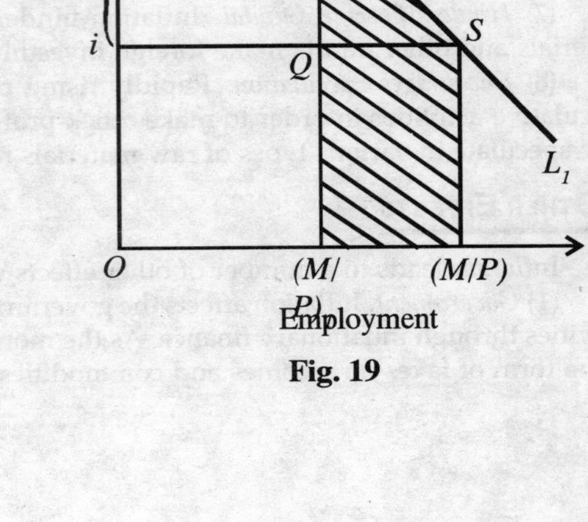

Fig. 19

the curve LL_1. If the money interest rate consistent with the stable price level is i, the amount of real money balances people wish to hold is (M/P). If the expected rate of inflation is $E\%$, the interest rate rises to r_1 and the level of real cash balances falls from (M/P) to $(M/P)_1$. This means that as soon as the government announces the expected rate of inflation to be $E\%$ $(i-r_1)$, everybody desiring to reduce his real cash balances will purchase physical assets and stocks of consumer and other goods, and the price level will rise in the proportion $(M/P)/(M/P)_1$. The proceeds of the tax in real terms are equal to the rectangle r_1 PQ i which is the inflation tax revenue to the government. The tax base is the amount of real money held by the public which is $(M/P)_1$ $(= iQ)$, and the tax rate is the inflation rate $(i–r_1)$

As a result of high inflation rate, the asset holders pay the inflation tax by losing purchasing power on their money holdings. The government as the issuer of money collects the tax in the form of a reduction in the real value of its liabilities. When the government pays interest on these liabilities, it returns some of the tax to holders of money. In practice, central banks do not pay so much interest as to offset the tax on the money issued by them. They pay no interest on currency and usually pay an interest rate on reserves below the market rate.

COSTS OF INFLATION

The costs of inflation may be economic or social loss arising from the effects of inflation. Assuming that people hold only non-interest bearing money in the form of currency issued by the government and demand deposits of banks, the costs of inflation refer to the loss in real money balances held by individuals and businesses. Since money does not bear a rate of interest, the opportunity cost of holding money rises with the inflation rate which, in turn, reduces the demand for real money balances.

Individuals and business enterprises hold cash balances because they yield utility to them. At a higher rate of inflation, they find the purchasing power of the money balances diminishing. In other words, they find that they require more real money balances than before when there is inflation. The costs of inflation arise when they try to change their existing system of transactions or payments to adjust to a smaller stock of real cash holdings. Individuals or households visit the markets more frequently to buy goods. Business enterprises visit banks more often, increase the frequency of ordering inventories, devote more time and attention in converting money into inventories or financial and real assets. Thus the change in the transactions or payments patterns of individuals and business enterprises require more time and energy then before. It leads to the diversion of resources from productive to unproductive uses when they are required to visit markets and banks more frequently, maintain excessive inventories of consumer and producer goods, etc. When the real money balances with the people are reduced due to higher expected rate of inflation, their peace of mind is also disturbed. Thus "the ultimate social cost of anticipated inflation is the wasteful use of resources to economise holdings of currency and other non-interest bearing means of payment."

Another social cost of inflation is in terms of the Phillips curve analysis. When inflation starts and is expected to continue, any attmept to reduce its rate of increase will lead to more unemployment. Increase in unemployment is a loss to the economy in terms of the goods and services which cannot be produced because people available for employment are not used.

The majority of economists also regard the redistributive effects of inflation as the cost of inflation.*

The social cost of inflation can be measured in terms of Figure 20. The curve LL_1 is the demand curve for real cash balances which can be interpreted as the *MP* (utility) curve of real cash balances. When the rate of inflation is zero, the real interest rate is equal to the money interest rate at i. The demand for real cash balanaces is (M/P). The area under the demand curve LL_1 over a given segment of the horizontal axis measures the flow of productivity (utility) from the indicated quantity of real money balances. When inflation increases at the expected rate of $E\%$ $(i–r_1)$ the interest rate rises from i to r_1 and the demand for real cash balances falls to $(M/P)_1$. This reduction in real cash balances by $(M/P)–(M/P)_1$ is the social cost of inflation which is measured by the shaded area $(M/P)_1$ PS (M/P). This area "measures the aggregate loss of productivity (utility) resulting from the destruction of real cash balances which occurs when prices rise initially at the announcement that there will

* May be discussed briefly from the previous section.

be an inflation. The further rise of prices representing the inflation itself is merely sufficient to keep real balances at their new low level and so guarantee that this loss of productivity (utility) will continue as long as the inflation does."

DEFLATION

The opposite of inflation is deflation. It is "a state in which the value of money is rising i.e. prices are falling." It is usually associated with falling activity and employment. As pointed out by Coulborn, "Involuntary unemployment is the hall-mark of deflation." Deflation is caused when prices are falling more than proportionately to the output of goods and services in the economy as a result of decrease in the money supply.

Sometimes, deflation is confused with *disinflation*. Deflation is a situation when prices fall along with reduction in output and employment. Disinflation, on the other hand, is a situation when prices are reduced deliberately but output and employment remain unaffected. According to Coulborn, "A lowering of prices, income, and expenditures, when they would be beneficial, would be disinflation."

EFFECTS OF DEFLATION

The effects of deflation are the reverse of inflaton.** Deflation affects different groups differently. Persons with fixed incomes such as workers, white collar salaried workers, pensioners, the rentier class, etc. gain because the value of money rises with falling prices. On the other hand, all types of producers such as industrialists and farmers lose with falling prices. Traders and equity holders also lose. Thus deflation affects adversely the distribution of income and wealth. When prices are falling, the purchasing power is increasing. So the lower, middle, and other classes with low incomes gain. On the other hand, businessmen, industrialists, traders, real estate holders, and others with variable incomes are hit hard and their profits decline with deflation. But this does not mean that there is improvement in income distribution. Rather, the low income groups suffer more because of the fall in employment and income. So both the better off and the worse off feel discontented under deflation.

Deflation also affects production adversely. With falling prices, production falls because income and employment are also declining and the aggregate demand is on the decline. Commodities start accumulating. Profits fall. Small firms close down. Unemployment spreads. This vicious cricle of fall in demand, production, employment, income and aggregate demand leads to a depression.

The government also suffer under deflation. Revenues from direct and indirect taxes decline. The real burden of public debt increases. Development of the economy suffers because the government is unable to increase public expenditure.

COMPARISON BETWEN INFLATION AND DEFLATION

Of the two—inflation and deflation—which is better than the other. Of course, both are equally bad in their effects on the society. But inflation is the lesser evil. As pointed out by Keynes, "Inflation is unjust, deflation is inexpedient. Of the two deflation is worse. Inflation brings about rising prices and redistribution of income in favour of the better-off classes. On the other hand, deflation leads to fall in output, employment and income. Of all the evils in a capitalist society, unemployment leading to poverty is the worst. We discuss below why Keynes regarded inflation as unjust and deflation inexpedient.

Inflation is unjust because it widens the gulf between the rich and the poor. It makes the rich richer at the cost of the poor. On the other hand, the poor are made poorer. The poor and low income classes suffer because their wages and salaries do not rise to the extent prices rise. It becomes difficult for them to make both ends meet with rising prices of consumer goods. On the other hand, businessmen, traders, industrialists, real estate holders, speculators, etc. gain because their profits and incomes increase much more than the rise in prices. So

---

** For a detailed account write just on the basis of arguments opposite to that given under "Effects of Inflation".

they are not affected by the fall in purchasing power when prices are rising. Thus it leads to inequalities of income and wealth.

When the government resorts to deficit financing to meet its rising expenditure during inflationary pressures, it increases the demand for goods and services. This deprives the people of the use of essential goods, thereby creating shortages and hardships for the common man.

Again, inflation is unjust because persons who save are losers in the long run. When prices are rising, the value of money is falling. Since savers are mostly the low and middle income groups who save for a varietyof reasons, they are the losers. Their savings lying in deposits are reduced automatically in real terms as inflationary pressures increase.

Inflation is unjust because it is socially harmful. People are lured to amass wealth by unscrupulous means. They, therefore, resort to hoarding, black-marketing, adulteration, manufature of sub-standard commodities, speculation, etc. Corruption spreads in every walk of life. All this reduces the efficiency of the economy.

Deflation, on the other hand, is *inexpedient* because it reduces national income, output and employment. While inflation takes away half the bread of the poor, deflation impoverishes them by taking away the whole of it.

Deflation leads to mass unemployment because fall in production, prices and profits force producers and businessmen to close down their enterprises.

Deflation is also inexpedient because falling prices lead to depression. All economic activities are stagnant. Factories are locked out. Trade and business are at a standstill. There is glut of commodities in all types of markets for goods and services. Even a bumper agricultural crop brings poverty to the peasantry. It is a situation of poverty in the midst of plenty.

Again, once the downward movement of prices begins, the economy plunges into a depression. But the downward movement of the economy is much faster as compared to the upward movement in a cycle. This makes depression of a much longer period. Consequently, people suffer a lot and the economy also remains in a state of stagnation for long.

It is on these grounds that inflation is unjust and deflation is inexpedient. Keynes pointed out that, "it is not necessary that we weigh one evil against the other. It is easier to agree that both are evils to be shunned." Still he preferred inflation as the lesser of the two evils. This is because inflation increases national output, employment and income, whereas deflation reduces national income and brings the economy backward to a state of depression. Again inflation is better than deflation because when it occurs the economy is already in a situation of full employment. On the other hand, there is always unemployment under deflation. And unemployment leading to poverty are the two scourges of mankind. Again inflation is a lesser evil than deflation. It redistibutes income and wealth in favour of the rich. But deflation is a greater evil. Though it redistributes income in favour of the low income groups, yet it fails to benefit them because they are unemployed and have little income during deflation. In fact, they are reduced to paupers. It is also easier to control inflation than deflation through appropriate monetary, fiscal, and direct control measures. But to control deflation is a very difficult thing because of the presence of pessimism among producers and businessmen. So far as the increase in inequalities of income and wealth under inflation is concerned, it can be reduced by larger expenditure on social services by the government. The government is in a better position to improve the conditions of the masses under inflation than under deflation due to its larger spending capacity. Moreover, so long as inflation is mild, it helps the economy to grow. It is only when inflation takes the shape of hyperinflation that it is dangerous. Still its effects on the economy may not be so injurious as under deflation.

CONTROL OF DEFLATION

Deflation can be controlled by adopting monetary and fiscal measures in just the opposite manner to control inflation. However, we discuss these measures in brief.

Monetary Policy

To control deflation, the central bank can increase the reserves of commercial banks through a cheap money policy. They can do so by buying securities and reducing the interest rate. As a result, their ability to extend credit facilities to borrowers increases. But the experience of the Great Depression tells us that in a serious depression when there is pessimism among businessmen, the success of such a policy is practically nil. In such a situation, banks are helpless in bringing about a revival. Since business activity is almost at a stand still, businessmen do not have any inclination to borrow to build up inventories even when the rate of interest is very low. Rather, they want to reduce their inventories by repaying loans already drawn from the banks. Moreover, the question of borrowing for long-term capital needs does not arise during deflation when the business activity is already at a very low level. The same is the case with consumers who faced with unemployment and reduced incomes do not like to purchase any durable goods through bank loans. Thus all that the banks can do is to make credit available but they cannot force businessmen and consumers to accept it. In the 1930s, very low interest rates and the piling up of unused reserves with the banks did not have any significant impact on the depressed economies of the world. Thus the success of monetary policy in controlling deflation is severely limited.

Fiscal Policy

Fiscal policy through increase in public expenditure and reduction in taxes tends to raise national income, employment, output, and prices. An increase in public expenditure during deflation increases the aggregate demand for goods and services and leads to a large increase in income via the multiplier process, while a reduction in taxes has the effect of raising disposable income thereby increasing consumption and investment expenditures of the poeple. The government should increase its expenditure through deficit budgeting and reduction in taxes. The public expenditure includes expenditure on such public works as roads, canals, dams, parks, schools, hospitals and other buildings, etc. and on such relief measures as unemployment insurance, pensions, etc. Expenditure on public works creates demand for the products of private construction industries and helps in reviving them while expenditure on relief measures stimulates the demand for consumer goods industries. Reduction in such taxes as corporate profits tax, income tax, and excise taxes tends to leave more income for spending and investment. Borrowing by the government to finance budget deficits utilises idle money lying with banks and financial institutions for investment purposes. But the effectiveness of public expenditure primarily depends upon the public works programme, its importance in the economic system, the volume and nature of public works and their planning and timing.

EXERCISES

1. Give a critical asessment of any one theory of inflation and give reasons for selecting this particular theory.
2. What is inflationary-gap? Examine the usefulness of this concept of analysing a process of inflation.
3. Distinguish between demand-pull and cost-push inflation. How have these two views on inflation beeen reconciled?
4. "The distinciton between cost-push and demand-pull inflation is unworkable, irrelevant and even meaningless." Do you agree with this view. Give reasons in support of your answer.
5. Discuss the theory of structural inflation.
6. Is inflation a purely monetary or purely non-monetary or an institutional phenomenon? Write in the context of a developed country.
7. Discuss the theory of the Phillips curve and bring out its apparent policy implications.
8. How does the Phillips curve expalin the trade-off between unemployment and inflation? Discuss its policy implications.
9. Explain the phenomenon of stagflation. Suggest measures to control it.
10. "Inflation is unjust and deflation is inexpedient." Discuss.
11. What is inflation? Explain its economic effects on different people.
12. Discuss the causes of inflation.How can it be controlled?
13. Explain Bent Hansen's Excess Demand Inflation Theory.
14. Write notes on : Open and Suppressed Inflation, Markup Inflation, Stagflation, Sectoral Inflation, Inflation as a Tax, Costs of Inflation.

CHAPTER

21

FINANCIAL MARKETS

1. MEANING

Financial market is an institution or arrangement which facilitates the exchange of financial assets such as deposits and loans, stocks and bonds, government securities, cheques, bills, etc. Financial markets operate through brokers, banks, non-banking financial institutions, merchant banks, mutual funds, discount houses, central bank, etc.

2. TYPES OR CLASSIFICATION OF FINANCIAL MARKETS

Financial markets can be classified in a number of ways.

1. *Money and Capital Market.* One method is related to the type of assets traded, i.e., short-term or long-term assets. The market in which short-term financial instruments are traded is called *money market* whereas the market in which long-term financial instruments are traded is called *capital market.* This is also called functional classification of financial markets.1

2. *Primary and Secondary Markets.* Financial markets are also classified in to primary and secondary markets. In a primary market, new issues of financial assets are bought and sold, whereas existing financial assets are bought and sold in a secondary market. When a new company issues its shares or an existing company sells its new shares that have not been bought by anyone earlier, they are bought and sold in the primary market. On the other hand, when a person sells his already purchased shares of a company, they will be bought in the secondary market.

Financial markets are further classified on the basis of traded instruments. This classification consists of debt, equity and financial service markets.

3. *Debt Markets.* In the debt market, lenders provide funds to the borrowers for a certain period. In return for the funds, the borrower agrees to pay to the lender the principal amount of the loan and a certain rate of interest. People borrow new cars, houses, etc. from debt markets. Companies borrow from investors for working capital and new equipments by issuing bonds. Central, state, and local governments obtain funds from debt markets to finance various public projects. The purchase of new bonds issued by companies and governments takes place in primary debt market and the purchase and sale of bonds is done in the secondary debt market. Further, debt markets are classified as short-term, medium-term and long-term markets according to the period of bonds. For instance, the period of one year or less refers to short-term, that between 1 and 10 years is called medium-term and of more than 10 years is called long-term. As discussed above, the equity market is classified as primary market and secondary market in which sale and purchase of shares takes place

1. Detailed study of instruments and institutions of money and capital markets has been given in Ch. 14.

through brokers and stock centres.

Equity Markets. Shares of corporates are bought and sold in an equity market. Equity market is further divided into primary and secondary market. New shares are sold in the primary market and existing shares are traded in the secondary market.

Financial Service Markets. Individuals and firms use financial service markets through banks and brokers that enhance the operations of debt and equity markets. Besides providing bank deposit and withdrawal facilities, some offer financial services. They participate in debt markets by providing loans and also purchase bonds and shares on behalf of their customers. Banks charge some fee for these services. However, banks participate only in the primary market. Therefore, there is no secondary market in financial service market. The second financial service is provided by brokers. They help in selling and purchasing of an individual's shares, bonds and debentures, etc. They charge commission for these services.

3. INSTITUTIONS OR COMPOSITION OF FINANCIAL MARKETS

There are two types of institutions in financial markets : *first,* depository i.e., keeping deposits, and *second,* non-depository.

Depository Institutions

Depository institutions are those which accept deposits from individuals and , firms and use these funds for advancing loans in the debt market or purchasing other debt instruments such as Treasury Bills. The main depository institutions are as follows:

1. *Commercial Banks.* They are the largest and most important depository institutions which keep deposits of individuals and firms in various types of accounts in the form of cash and assets, and use them for advancing loans.

2. *Saving and Loan Associations.* They are operated by individuals by collecting their savings in mutual association. They convert their saving funds into mortgage loans.

3. *Mutual Savings Banks.* They operate like savings and loan associations. The only difference is that they are established on the basis of co-operation by employees of some company, trade union or other institutions.

4. *Co-operative Credit Societies.* The members of credit societies purchase shares of co-operative societies, deposit their savings with them and borrow from them.

Non-depository Institutions

Non-depository institutions operate in financial markets as financial intermediaries and provide insurance against financial risks. The major non-depository institutions are as follows :

1. *Mutual Funds.* Mutual funds sell their shares to individuals and firms and invest the proceeds in various types of assets. Some mutual funds, known as money market mutual funds, invest in short-term safe assets such as Treasury Bills, certificates of deposit of banks, etc.

2. *Insurance Companies.* Insurance companies protect individuals and firms against risks. The premium they receive from individuals by insuring their lives, they invest the same in advancing loans for long-term assets, mortgages, construction of houses, etc. On the other hand, the premium received by them for insurancing against loss from fire, theft, accident, etc. of trucks, cars, buildings, etc. is invested in short-term assets.

3. *Pension Funds.* Private and government corporates, and central, state and local governments deposit some amount in pension funds by deducting a certain amount from the salaries of their employees. Pension fund institutions or corporates invest these funds in long-term assets.

4. *Brokerage Firms.* Brokerage firms link buyers and sellers of financial assets. As such, they function as intermediaries and earn a fee for each transaction, known as brokerage. They operate only in the secondary debt market and equity market.

4. EFFICIENCY OF FINANCIAL MARKETS

A financial market is efficient when security prices fully reflect all available information. It is a perfect market which achieves efficiency. An efficient financial market has the following characteristics :

1. Information is available to all buyers and sellers of securities.
2. Transactions must be executed without significant price changes.
3. Security prices are independent of individual buyers and sellers.
4. There are no transaction costs. In other words, there are no brokerage fees, transfer charges or taxes, etc. when securities are bought and sold.
5. Prices of securities are promptly adjusted to equalise their yields. In other words, risk adjusted expected returns on all investments are equalised. If, for example, a bond earns a higher risk-adjusted expected rate of return in comparison with any other bond, the investor will try to buy that bond immediately. This will increase its price and its expected return (yield) will be lower. Thus the returns from bonds of equal risk are equalised.
6. The efficient-market resources are used in a non-wasteful manner.
7. Its resources are allocated to the socially most productive uses.

The concept of efficient financial markets is closely related to rational expectations hypothesis. According to it, expectations should be based on relevant information in an efficient market. The present price of bond portfolios in an efficient market will provide the relevant information. People who make rational expectations about the future price of bond on the basis of information will purchase the bond when its price falls and will sell it when its price rises. Given the available information, the price of bond will rise or fall from the equilibrium level to reflect the relative demand for and supply of bond. Thus risk-adjusted expected returns on various bonds would be equal in equilibrium. If there is any temporary disequilibrium, the market pressurers will correct it. For example, when people forecast in the expectation that inflation will rise, they will try to sell their bond portfolio immediately. This will increase the interest rate quickly and this information will lead to a fall in bond prices.

The efficiency of a financial market can be judged from the following :

1. *Proper Valuation.* There should be proper valuation of financial assets in an efficient market. This requires that the market price of a financial asset must equal its intrinsic value. Its intrinsic value is the present value of its future stream of cash flows from investment made in it. Its present value is calculated by discounting its future cash flows at an appropriate rate of discount.* The equality between the market price and intrinsic value of an asset is possible in a perfectly competitive financial market.
2. *Operationally Efficient.* An efficient market should be operationally efficient. This requires : (i) minimisation of administrative and transaction costs; (ii) providing maximum convenience to lenders and borrowers while transmitting resources; and (iii) providing a fair return to financial intermediaries for these services.
3. *Allocationally Efficient.* An efficient market should be allocationally-efficient. For this, it should channelise its financial resources into such investment projects and uses where the marginal efficiency of capital, after adjusting for risk differences, is the highest.
4. *Insurance against Risk.* A market to be efficient must hedge and reduce risks against possible future contingencies.
5. *Information Arbitrage.* Market efficiency depends on information arbitrage. If a person gains much on the basis of commonly available information, the financial market is not efficient. It is only under perfect competition that a market is efficient where prices of financial assets reflect fully all relevant and available information and possibilities of such a gain are very rare.

---

* If the present amount invested at some interest on an asset is PV, its future value (FV) j in t years is $FV = PV \times (1 + r)^t$

$$\text{or} \quad PV = \frac{FV}{(1+r)^t}$$

It shows the present value (PV) of an amount (FV) of an asset received t years in the future at r% interest rate per year.

5. TYPES OF EFFICIENT MARKETS

There are three types of efficient markets. They represent the levels of efficiency.

1. *Weak Form of Efficient Market.* In the weak form of efficient market, the best forecasting of bond price of the next period is the price of this period. Any past information on bond price cannot improve this forecasting. It is very difficult to forecast returns to bonds on the basis of past data on bonds prices.

2. *Semi-strong Form of Efficient Market.* In the semi-strong form of efficient market, the current price of bonds does better forecasting of future prices. However, any available information will not be helpful in forecasting of future prices or returns to bonds or assets. Such information consists of past prices of assets, rates of interest, profit, etc. But a broker of any stock may earn profit in future by selling or purchasing bonds on the basis of internal information of the company.

3. *Strong Form of Efficient Market.* In the strong form of efficient market, any available current information cannot improve forecasting of future value of the assest by using recently known value of that asset price. In other words, any internal information may not be helpful in forecasting stock price movements. In reality, the strong form of efficient market is not possible because nobody can forecast future stock prices according to internal information. This is because the weak and semi-strong forms of efficient markets are mostly seen in financial markets.

6. FUNCTIONS OF FINANCIAL MARKETS

Financial markets are the transmission mechanism between ultimate lenders and ultimate borrowers. Funds flow from ultimate lenders to ultimate borrowers through financial market institutions. In other words, financial markets are conduits through which ultimate lenders lend their surplus funds to ultimate borrowers. Financial markets mobilise the savings of surplus units (ultimate lenders) and channel them in the hands of deficit units (ultimate borrowers) through a wide variety of financial techniques, instruments and institutions.

Surplus units gain by earning dividend or interest on their funds lent to deficit units. On the other hand, deficit units benefit by getting funds from surplus units to finance their investment plans which otherwise would not be available to them. In the absence of financial markets, surplus units would simply hoard their excess funds and deficit units would borrow internally. But financial markets provide additional options to both the ultimate lenders and ultimate borrowers. Ultimate lenders can acquire financial assets, i.e., buy securities or repay debts by selling them through financial markets, Similarly, ultimate borrowers can sell their financial assets like securities in financial markets to finance their investment plans.

Ultimate lenders are households, business firms, central, state and local government bodies and financial institutions.1 The financial market in which transactions take place between the surplus and deficit units deals in central, state and local body bonds, corporate bonds and equities, mortgages, bills, etc. But the financial institutions act as financial intermediaries (FIs) between ultimate lenders and borrowers in the financial market. They transfer funds from ultimate lenders to borrowers and purchase *primary securities* issued by ultimate borrowers and transfer them to ultimate lenders. They acquire the savings or surplus units and offer, in return, claims on themselves. They also purchase primary securities from non-financial spending units by the creation of claims on themselves through indirect or *secondary securities.* Thus FIs issue secondary securities. FIs are, therefore, dealers in securities. They purchase primary securities and sell their secondary securities in financial markets. Thus FIs function as dealers by buying funds from ultimate lenders in exchange for their own secondary securities and selling funds to ultimate borrowers in exchange for the latter's primary securities. The purchase of primary securities by surplus units is called *direct finance* and by financial intermediaries as *indirect finance.* Both primary and secondary securities are referred to as *financial assets* in the financial markets.

---

1. Financial institutions are commercial banks, co-operative credit societies and banks, mutual savings funds, mutual funds, savings and loans associations, building and housing loans societies, insurance companies, merchant banks, unit trusts and other financial institutions. They are divided into commercial banks and non-banking financial institutions.

Fig. 1. illustrates the flow of funds from ultimate lenders to ultimate borrowers through financial markets. Ultimate lenders are shown on the left side and ultimate borrowers on the right side of the figure. Funds flow from ultimate lenders in the left to ultimate borrowers in the right either directly or indirectly through financial institutions or intermediaries. On the other hand, primary securities issued by ultimate borrowers and purchased by ultimate lenders and financial institutions are shown to flow in the opposite or reverse direction. They

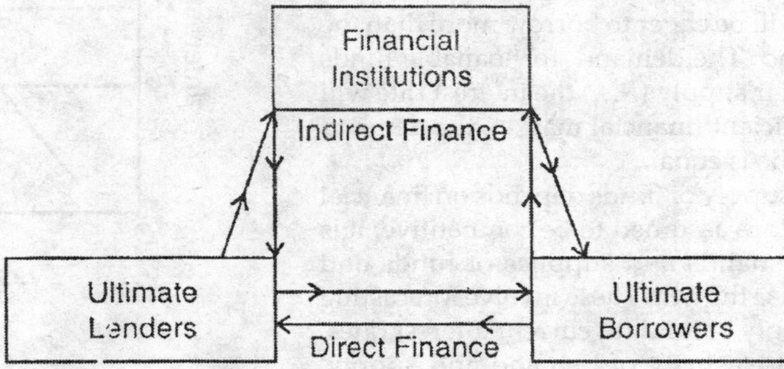

Flow of Funds in Financial Market

Fig. 1

flow from ultimate lenders in the left either directly or indirectly through financial institutions in the financial market.

For smooth flow of funds from ultimate lenders to ultimate borrowers and *vice-versa*, the financial market must be fully developed, perfect and easily accessible to all the participants, as is the case in developed countries. But financial markets in under-developed countries are under-developed, imperfect and inaccessible to both ultimate lenders and ultimate borrowers. But the market participants lack adequate information and knowledge about lending and borrowing channels, opportunities, sources and institutions. Consequently, the flow of funds does not take place adequately, properly and smoothly. The need is to develop money and capital market instruments and institutions for smooth and healthy functioning of financial markets through which funds should flow to meet the financial needs of a developing economy.

7. WORKING OF FINANCIAL MARKET

Financial market deals in financial assets whose prices are expressed in terms of an interest rate. The interest rate is the price of credit or of loanable funds. The fall or rise in the rate of interest depends on the relative demand and supply of loanable funds in the financial market.

The demand for loanable funds is in the form of mortgages, corporate bonds, central government securities, bonds of state governments and local bodies, business loans for working capital and capital equipment, government loans for services, investment in infrastructure, etc., consumer loans and so on. These groups are the *primary* demanders of loanable funds. The demand for loanable funds depends on interest rates on alternative source of funds, business expectations; expectation of inflation rate; business profitability; shift in consumers tastes; tax deduction of interest payments (if interest payments are not taxable, demand for funds will be more); cost and availability of funds; actual and derived capital stock, etc.

The supply of loanable funds comes from commercial banks, savings and loan associations, mutual funds, savings banks, insurance companies, pension funds, credit unions, non-bank financial companies, individuals and so on. The supply of loanable funds depends on interest rate on alternative *uses* of funds; expected inflation rate; tax rate on interest income; wealth of lenders; liquidity and risk investment; level of individual income; distribution of income; corporate and personal tax rates and so on.

Given these factors an efficient financial market is in equilibrium when the demand for and supply of loanable funds is equal. In Fig. 2, D is the demand curve for loanable funds and *S* is the supply curve of loanable funds. They intersect at equilibrium point E and OQ quantity of funds is demanded and supplied at OR interest rate. If the interest rate is OR_1 higher than the equilibrium rate OR lenders of funds are anxious to lend more but borrowers of funds are not willing to borrow. The supply of loanable funds (R_1s) being more than the demand (R_1d) for them ($R_1s > R_1d$), the interest rate will fall to OR. On the contrary, if the interest is OR_2, lower than OR, the borrowers will be eager to borrow more than the lenders are willing to lend. The demand, for loanable funds (R_2d_1) being more than their supply (R_2s_1) the interest rate will rise to OR. Thus in an efficient financial market, the demand for and the supply of funds is equal.

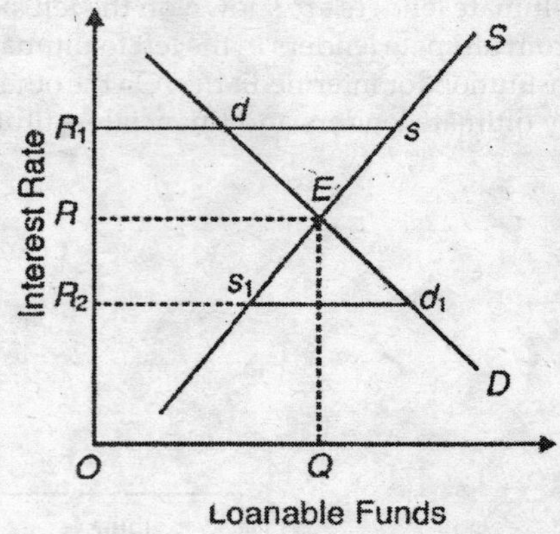

Fig. 2

Since demand and supply of funds depends on financial market conditions which are assumed to be competitive, it is successive changes in demands and supplies of funds and interest rates which equalise the two. These involve forecasting of likely demand and supply of funds at current interest rates. This depends on interest-elasticity of demand and supply. Suppose in Fig. 3(A), the interest rate is OR_1. If both demand and supply are *interest elastic*, a *small* rise in interest rate to OR will reduce the demand (R_1d) for loanable funds and increase the supply (R_1s) of funds to bring the two to equality at point E.

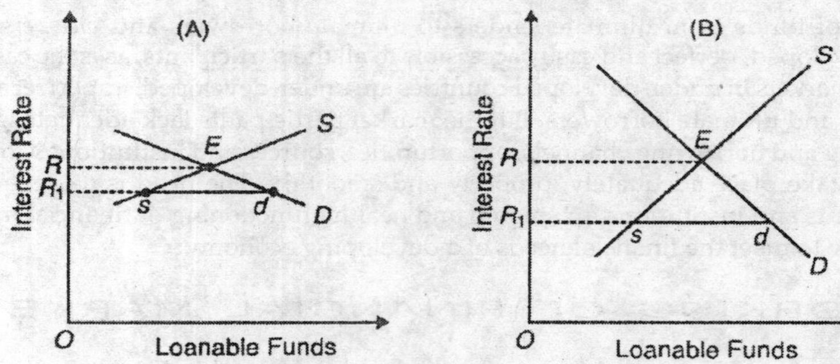

Fig. 3

8. ROLE OF FINANCIAL MARKETS IN ECONOMIC DEVELOPMENT

Financial markets play a special role in economic development.

1. *Capital Formation.* Economic development depends upon capital formation for which saving is essential. For capital formation only saving is not enough, their accumulation is also necessary. This is done by financial institutions which operate in financial markets. Mere accumulation of savings does not lead to capital formation. Savings by different groups of society are required to be channelised in productive investments. Financial markets help in the three processes—to save, to accumulate and to invest—of capital formation which lead to rapid economic development.

Financial markets are unorganised and undeveloped in developing countries. The majority of people are poor and they cannot save. Those who save, invest their savings in real estate, speculation, foreign exchange and conspicuous consumption. Under the circumstances, financial markets undertake the task of encouraging the flow of personal savings for unproductive to productive uses. They encourage households to hold financial assets instead of physical assets. The extent to which households switch from the purchase of physical assets to financial assets by saving more, the more resources are released for development purposes. Thus financial markets reduce cash hoardings of people kept in their homes and encourage their habits of saving and investment which are very helpful for capital formation and economic development.

2. *Non-financial Business Sector*. Financial markets help the non-financial business sector by facilitating the sale and purchase of shares, bonds, debentures, etc. Financial institutions like commercial banks, mutual funds, savings and loan associations, insurance companies, merchant banks, unit trusts, etc. operate in the financial markets and transfer funds from savers to business by lending their surplus funds. Savers earn interest and/ or dividend which they again reinvest in shares, bonds, etc. On the other hand, businessmen also borrow from financial institutions to carry out their investment plans. In this way, they also help in capital formation and economic development.

3. *Help to Governments*. Financial markets help state governments, local bodies and central government financially by buying and selling their bonds and securities through which they invest in various local, state level and central projects to accelerate economic development.

4. *Create New Assets and Liabilities*. Financial markets create new assets and liabilities which provide financial help to business, trade and industry that tend to raise the level of economic development. For instance, banks create credit by buying primary securities which they sell to businesses, traders and industry. They create liabilities by the multiplicity of primary securities they hold. According to Prof. Ackley, FIs in the financial market through intermediation between ultimate savers and direct investors add greatly to the stock of financial assets available to savers. For every extra asset, they create an equal new financial liability. Since FIs also own each others' liabilities, they create increments of assets and liabilities. Ackley concludes that although the increment of assets and liabilities does not increase real wealth or income, even then by financially helping the different categories of the economy they increase economic welfare and promote economic development.

5. *Provide Liquidity*. Financial markets provide liquidity to the economy which is very essential for the economic development of the country. When FIs in the financial markets convert an asset into cash easily and quickly without loss in its money value, they provide liquidity in the economy. When FIs, especially banks, issue claims against themselves and supply funds, they always try to maintain their liquidity. Banks do so by following two rules :

(a) They make short-term loans and by issuing claims against themselves for longer periods provide financial help to business, traders, industries, etc.

(b) They give loans to various types of borrowers according to their needs.

Economic development depends upon capital formation in which investment is an important means, and investment depends on the interest rate. The lower the interest rate, the higher will be the investment. When there is competition for funds, securities, etc. in the financial market, their prices rise and the interest rate declines. With the fall in interest rate, investment is encouraged. Consequently, there is increase in the rate of capital formation and of income for economic development.

6. *Help Central Bank*. Financial markets through their proper working help the central bank of the country in executing its monetary and credit policies and hence in promoting its economic development. When FIs create large financial assets and liabilities by transferring funds from savers to users, they provide the financial markets with money and near-money assets. Since financial markets govern the working of the economy, the monetary and credit policies of the central bank are changed in such a manner from time to time that the financial markets function smoothly in the country.

In brief, the economic development of a country depends upon the proper functioning of the financial markets which leads to rapid capital formation and to the speeding up of the rate of economic growth. -

EXERCISES

1. Briefly explain the working of the financial market. What do you understand by the efficiency of financial market? Explain.
2. Explain the functions of a financial market. Discuss the role of financial markets in the economic development of a country.
3. Explain the concept of efficiency of financial markets. What are the various levels of an efficient market?
4. What is an efficient market? Explain the criteria for judging the efficiency of a financial market.

CHAPTER 22

Money and Capital Markets

The study of money and capital markets in all their facets is so exhaustive that it is not possible to discuss them in one chapter. We shall, therefore, confine our analysis to the nature and scope of money and capital markets. The Indian money market and capital market are studies separately in the last part of the book.

1. THE MONEY MARKET

MEANING AND FEATURES

The money market is a market for short-term instruments that are close substitutes for money. The short term instruments are highly liquid, easily marketable, with little change of loss. It provides for the quick and dependable transfer of short term debt instruments maturing in one year or less, which are used to finance the needs of consumers, business agriculture and the government. The money market is not one market but is "a collective name given to the various form and institutions that deal with the various grades of near-money." In other words, "it is a network of market that are grouped together because they deal in financial instruments that have a similar function in the economy and are to some degree substitutes from the point of view of holders."[1] Thus the money market consists of call and notice market, commercial bills market, commercial paper market, treasury bills market, inter-bank market and certificates of deposit market. All these markets are closely interrelated so as to make the money market. It is a wholesale market where large number of financial assets or instruments are traded.

The money market is divided into direct, negotiated, or customers' money market and the open or impersonal money market. In the former, banks and financial firms supply funds to local customers and also to larger centres such as London for direct lending. In the open money market, idle funds drawn from all-over the country are transferred through intermediaries to the New York City market or the London market. These intermediaries comprise the Federal Reserve Banks in the USA or the Bank of England in England, commercial banks, insurance companies, business corporations, brokerage houses, finance companies, state and local government securities' dealers.[2] The money market is a dynamic market in which new money market instruments are evolved and traded and more participants are permitted to deal in the money market.

INSTITUTIONS OF THE MONEY MARKET

The various financial institutions which deal in short term loans in the money market are its members. They comprise the following types of institutions :

1. J.M. Culbertson, *Money and Banking,* 1972.
2. In underdeveloped Countries, the money market is divided into organised and unoganised categories. These are discusses in the chapter "The Indian Money Market". Also refer to the chapter on "Financial Dualism".

1. *Central Bank.* The central bank of the country is the pivot around which the entire money market revolves. It acts as the guardian of the money market and increases or decreases the supply of money and credit in the interest of stability of the economy. It does not itself enter into direct transactions. But controls the money market through variations in the bank rate and open market operations.

2. *Commercial Banks.* Commercial banks also deal in short-term loans which they lend to business and trade. They discount bills of exchange and treasury bills, and lend against promissory notes and through advances and overdrafts.

3. *Non-bank Financial Intermediaries.* Besides the commercial banks, there are non-bank financial intermediaries which lend short-term funds to borrowers in the money market. Such financial intermediaries are savings banks, investment houses, insurance companies, provident funds, and other financial corporations.

4. *Discount Houses and Bill Brokers.* In developed money markets, private companies operate discount houses. The primary function of discount houses is to discount bills on behalf of other. They, in turn, form the commercial banks and acceptance houses. Alongwith discount houses, there are bill brokers in the money market who act as intermediaries between borrowers and lenders by discounting bills of exchange at a nominal commission. In underdeveloped money markets, only bill brokers operate.

5. *Acceptance Houses.* The institution of acceptance houses developed from the merchange bankers who transferred their headquarters to the London Money Market in the 19th and the early 20 the century. They act as agents between exporters and importers and between lender and borrower traders. They accept bills drawn on merchants whose financial standing is not known in order to make the bills negotiable in the London Money Market. By accepting a trade bill they guarantee the payment of bill at maturity. However, their importance has declined because the commercial banks have undertaken the acceptance business.

All these institutions which comprise the money market do not work in isolation but are interdependent and interrelated with each other.

INSTRUMENTS OF THE MONEY MARKET

The money market operates through a number of instruments.

1. *Promissory Note.* The promissory note is the earliest types of bill. It is a written promise on the part of a businessman today to another a certain sum of money at an agreed future data. Usually, a promissory note falls due for payment after 90 days with three days of grace. A promissory note is drawn by the debtor and has to be accepted by the bank in which the debtor has his account, to be valid. The creditor can get it discounted from his bank till the date of recovery. Promissory notes are rarely used in business these days, except in the USA.

2. *Bill of Exchange or Commercial Bills.* Another instrument of the money, market is the bill of exchange which is similar to the promissory note, except in that it is drawn by the creditor and is accepted by the bank of the debater. The creditor can discount the bill of exchange either with a broker or a bank. There is also the foreign bill of exchange which becomes due for payment from the date of acceptance. The rest of the procedure is the same as for the internal bill of exchange. Promissory notes and bills of exchange are known as trade bills.

3. *Treasury Bill.* But the major instrument of the money markets is the treasury bill which is issued for varying periods of less than one year. They are issued by the Secretary to the Treasury in England and are payable at the Bank of England. There are also the short-term government securities in the USA which are traded by commercial banks and dealers in securities. In India, the treasury bills are issued by the Government of India at a discount generally between 91 days and 364 days. There are three types of treasury bills in India—91 days, 182 days and 364 days.

4. *Call and Notice Money.* There is the call money market in which funds are borrowed and lent for one day. In the notice market, they are borrowed and lent upto 14 days without any collateral security. But deposit receipt is issued to the lender by the borrower who repays the borrowed amount with interest on call. In India, commercial banks and cooperative banks borrow and lend funds in this market but mutual funds and all-India financial institutions participate only as lenders of funds.

5. *Inter-bank Term Market.* This market is exclusively for commercial and cooperative banks in India, which borrow and lend funds for a period of over 14 days and upto 90 days without any collateral security at

market-determined rates.

6. *Certificates of Deposits (CD).* Certificates of deposits are issued by commercial banks at a discount on face value. The discount rate is determined by the market. In India the minimum size of the issue is Rs. 25 lakhs with the minimum subscription of Rs. 5 lakhs. The maturity period is between 3 months and 12 months.

7. *Commercial Paper (CP). Commercial* papers are issued by highly rate companies to raise short-term working capital requirements directly from the market instead of borrowing from the banks. CP is a promise by the borrowing company to repay the load at a specified date, normally for a period of 3 months to 6 months. This instrument is very popular in the USA, UK, Japan, Astrialia and a number of other countries. It has been introduced in India in January 1990.

Working of the Money Market

The money market consisting of commercial banks, discount houses, bill brokers, acceptance houses, non-bank financial houses and the central bank operates through the bills, securities, treasury bills, government securities and call loans of various types. As the money market consists of varied types of institutions dealing in different types of instruments, it operates through a number of sub-markets.

First, the money market operates through the call loan market. It has been defined as "a market for marginal funds, for temporarily unemployed or unemployable funds." In this market the commercial banks use their unsued funds to lend for very short periods to bill brokers and dealers in stock exchange. In developed countries, even big corporations lend their dividends before distribution to earn interest for a very short period. The central bank also lends to commercial bank is for very short periods. Such loans are mostly for a week even for a day or a night and can be recalled at a very short notice. That is why a short period loan is known as call loan or call money market. Bill brokers and stock brokers who borrow such funds use them to discount or purchase bills or stocks. Such funds are borrowed at the "call rate" which is generally one per cent below the bank rate. But this rate varies with the volume of funds lent by the bank. If the brokers are asked to pay off loans immediately, then they are forced to get funds from large corporations and even from the central bank at high interest rate.

Second, the money market also operates through the bill market. The bill market is the short-period loan market. In this market, loans are made available to businessmen and the government by the commercial banks, discount houses and brokers. The instruments of credit are the promissory notes. Internal bills of exchange and treasury bills. The commercial banks discount bills o exchange, lend against promissory notes or through advances or overdrafts to the business community. Similarly, the discount houses and bills brokers lend to businessmen by discounting their bills of exchange before they mature within 90 days. On the other hand, government borrows through the treasury bills from the commercial banks and non-bank financial institutions. Third, the money market operater through the collateral loan market fora short period. The commercial banks lend to brokers and discount houses against collateral bonds, stock, securities, etc. In case of need, commercial banks themselves borrower from the large banks and the central bank on the basis of collateral securities.

Finally, the other important sub-market through which the money market operates is the acceptance market. The merchant bankers accept bills drawn on domestic and foreign traders whose financial standing is not known. When they accept a domestic or foreign trade bill, they guarantee its payment at maturity. In recent years, the commercial banks have also stared the acceptance business.

Functions of a Money Market*

A money market performs a number of functions in an economy.

1. *Provides Funds.* It provides short-term funds to the public and private institutions needing such financing for their working capital requirements. It is done by discounting trade bills through commercial banks, discount houses, brokers and acceptance houses. Thus the money market helps the development of commerce, industry and trade within and outside the country.

* This also relates to the importance of money market.

2. *Use of Surplus Funds.* It provides and opportunity to banks and other institutions to use their surplus funds profitably for a short period. These institutions include not only commercial banks and other financial institutions but also large non-financial business corporations, states and local governments.

3. *No Need to Borrow from Banks.* The existence of a developed money market removes the necessity of borrowing by the commercial banks from the central bank. If the former find their reserves short of cash requirements they can call in some of their loans from the money market. The commercial banks prefer to recall their loans rather than borrow from the central banks at a higher rate of interests.

4. *Helps Government.* The money market helps the government in borrowing short-term funds at low interest rates on the basis of treasury bills. On the other hand, if the government were to issue paper money or borrow from the central bank. It would lead to inflationary pressures in the economy.

5. *Helps in Monetary Policy.* A well developed money market helps in the successful implementation of the monetary policies of the central bank. It is through the money market that the central banks is in a position to control the banking system and thereby influence commerce and industry.

6. *Helps in Financial Mobility. By* facilitating the transfer for funds from one sector to another, the money market helps in financial mobility. Mobility in the flow of funds is essential for the development of commerce and industry in an economy.

7. *Promotes Liquidity and Safety.* One of the important functions of the money market is that it promotes liquidity and safety of financial assets. It thus encourages savings and investments.

8. *Equilibrium between Demand and Supply of Funds.* The money market brings equilibrium between the demand and supply of loanable funds. This it does by allocating saving into investment channels. In this way, it also helps in rational allocation of resources.

9. *Economy in Use of Cash.* As the money market deals in near-money assets and not money proper, it helps in economising the use of cash. It thus provides a convenient and safe way of transferring funds from one place to another, thereby immensely helping commerce and industry.

Characteristics of an Undeveloped Money Market

The money markets in the majority of underdeveloped countries are mostly undeveloped or unorganised. In fact, they are dualistics, both developed and undeveloped money markets exist side by side. The developed money market consists of the central bank, the commercial banks, bill broker; discount houses, acceptance houses, etc. On the other hand, the undeveloped money market consists of the moneylenders, the indigenous bankers, traders, merchants, landlords, pawnbrokers, etc. Since the majority of the people in underdeveloped countries live in rural areas and are poor, the undeveloped market controls a major portion of the money market. The main characteristics of such a market are :

1. *Personal Touch.* The lenders have a personal touch with the borrowers. The lender knows every borrower personally in the village because the latter sides there.

2. *Flexibility in Loans.* There is no rigidity in loan transactions. The borrower can have more or less amount of loan according to his requirements depending upon the nature of security or his goodwill with the moneylender.

3. *Multiplicity of Lending Activities.* Mostly people do not specialise is moneylending alone. They combine moneylending with other economic activities. A merchant may supply goods on loan instead or money in cash.

4. *Varied Interest Rates.* There is multiplicity of interest rates. Interest rates are much higher than rates in the developed sector of the money market. The interest rate are not even uniform. The rate depends on the need of the borrower, the amount of loan, the time for which it is required and the nature of security. The greater the urgency, the higher will be the interest rate.

5. *Defective System of Accounting.* In the unorganised sector of the money market, the system of maintaining accounts is highly defecate. Proper accounts are never maintained. Formal receipts are not issued for interest and the principal repaid by the borrowers. Besides, there is utmost secrecy in maintaining accounts and lending procedures in the undeveloped money market. The accounts of the moneylenders are not liable to checking by any higher authority.

6. *Absence of Link with the Developed Money Market.* The undeveloped sector is not linked with the developed

sector of the money market in such countries. The former works independently of the latter and is also not under the control of the developed market. This has the effect of reducing the volume of monetary transactions and savings, and prevent their use in productive investments.

CHARACTERISTICS OF A DEVELOPMENT MONEY MARKET

The developed money market is a well organised market which has the following main features :

1. *A Central Bank. A* developed money market has a central banks at the top which is the most powerful authority in monetary and banking matter. I controls, regulates and guides the entire money market. It provides liquidity to the money market, as it is the lender of the last resort to the various constituents of the money market.

2. *Organised Banking System.* An organised and integrated banking system is the second feature of a developed money market. In fact, it is the pivot around which the whole money market revolves. It is the commercial banks which supply short-term loans, and discount bills of exchange. They form an important link between the borrowers, brokers, discount houses and acceptance houses and the central bank in the money market.

3. *Specialised Sub-Markets.* A developed money market consists of a number of specialised sub-markets dealing in various types of credit instruments. There is the call loan market, the bill market, the treasury bill market, the collateral loan market and the acceptance market, and the foreign exchange market. The larger the number of sub-markets, the more developed is the money market. But the mere number of sub-markets is not enough. What is required is that the various sub-markets should have a number of dealers in each market and the sub-markets should be properly integrated with each other.

4. *Existence of Large Near-Money Assets.* A developed money market has a large number of near-money assets of various types such a bills of exchange, promissory notes, treasury bills, securities, bonds, etc. The larger the number of near-money assets, the more developed is the money market.

5. *Integrated Interest-Rate Structure.* Another important characteristic of a developed money market is that it has an integrated interest-rate structure. The interest rates prevailing in the various sub-markets are integrated to each other. A change in the bank rate leads to proportional changes in the interest rate prevailing in the sub-markets.

6. *Adequate Financial Resources.* A developed money market has easy access to financial sources from both within and outside the country. In fact, such a market attracts adequate funds from both sources, as is the case with the London Money Market.

7. *Remittance Facilities.* A developed money market provides cash and cheap emittance facilities for transferring funds from one market to the other. The London Money Market provides such remittance facilities throughout the world.

8. *Miscellaneous Factors.* Besides the above noted features, a developed money market is highly influenced by such factors as restrictions on international transactions, crisis, boom, depression, war, political instability, etc.

2. THE CAPITAL MARKET

MEANING AND FEATURES

The capital market is a market which deals in long-term loans. It supplies industry with fixed and working capital and finances medium-term and long-term borrowings of the central, state and local governments. The capital market deals in ordinary stock is, shares and debentures of corporations, and bonds and securities of governments.

The funds which flow into the capital market come from individuals who have savings to invest, the merchant banks, the commercial banks and non-bank financial intermediaries, such as insurance companies, finance houses, unit trusts, investment trusts, venture capital, leasing finance, mutual funds, building societies, etc. Further, there are the issuing houses which do not provide capital but underwrite the shares and debentures of companies and help in selling their new issues of shares and debentures. The demand for funds comes from joint stock companies for working and fixed capital assets and inventories and from local, state and central governments, improvement trusts, port trusts, etc. to finance a variety of expenditures and assets.

The capital market functions through the stock exchange market. A stock exchange is a market which facilitates buying and selling of shares, stocks, bonds, securities and debentures. It is not only a market for old securities and shares but also for new issues shares and securities. In fact, the capital market is related to the supply and demand for new capital, and the stock exchange facilitates such transactions. Thus the capital market comprises the complex of institutions and mechanisms through which medium-term funds and long-term funds are pooled and made available to individuals, business and governments. It also encompasses the process by which securities already outstanding are transferred.[3]

Importance or Functions of Capital Market

The capital market plays an important role immobilising saving and channel is in them into productive investments for the development of commerce and industry. As such, the capital market helps in capital formation and economic growth of the country. We discuss below the importance of capital market.

The capital market acts as an important link between savers and investors. The savers are lenders of funds while investors are borrowers of funds. The savers who do not spend all their income are called. "Surplus units" and the borrowers are known as "deficit units". The capital market is the transmission mechanism between surplus units and deficit units. It is a conduit through which surplus units lend their surplus funds to deficit units. Funds flow into the capital market from individuals and financial intermediaries which are absorbed by commerce, industry and government. It thus facilitates the movement of stream of capital to be used more productively and profitability to increases the national income. Surplus units buy securities with their surplus funds and deficit units sells securities to raise the funds they need. Funds flow from lenders to borrowers either directly or indirectly through financial institutions such as banks, unit trusts, mutual funds, etc. The borrowers issue primary securities which are purchased by lenders either directly or indirectly through financial institutions.

The capital market prides incentives to savers in the form of interest or dividend and transfers funds to investors. Thus it leads to capital formation. In fact, the capital market provides a market mechanism for those who have savings and to those who need funds for productive investments. It diverts resources from wasteful and unproductive channels such as gold, jewellery, real estate, conspicuous consumption, etc. to productive investments.

A well-developed capital market comprising expert banking and non-banking intermediaries brings stability in the value of stocks and securities. It does so by providing capital to the needy at reasonable interest rates and helps in minimising speculative activities.

The capital market encourages economic growth. The various institutions which operate in the capital market give quantities and qualitative direction to the flow of funds and bring rational allocation of resources. They do so by converting financial assets into productive physical assets. This leads to the development of commerce and industry through the private and public sector, thereby inducing economic growth.

In an underdeveloped country where capital is scarce, the absence of a developed capital market is a greater hindrance to capital formation and economic growth. Even though the people are poor, yet they do not have any inducements to save. Others who save, they invest their savings in wasteful and unproductive channels, such as gold, jewellery, real estate, conspicuous consumption, etc. Such countries can induce people to save more by establishing banking and non-banking financial institutions for the existence of a developed capital market. Such a market can go a long way in providing a link between savers and investors, thereby leading to capital formation and economic growth.

3. For a detailed study of the features of the Capital Market refer to the chapter "Indian Capital Market."

3. DISTINCTION BETWEEN MONEY AND CAPITAL MARKETS

The money market differs from the capital market on several grounds.

1. The money market deals in short-term funds which are used for financing current business operations and short-term needs of the government. On the other hand, the capital market deals in long-term funds required by industry and government.

2. Short-term funds in the money market refer to a period of less than a year, while in the capital market long-term funds refer to a period up to 25 years.

3. The money market uses such instruments as promissory notes, bills of exchange, treasury bills, certificates of deposits, commercial papers, etc. On the other hand, the capital market uses long-term securities such as shares, debentures and bonds of industrial concerns, and bonds and securities of the government.

4. The institutions operating in the money market and the capital market also differ from each other. The central bank, commercial banks, non bank financial intermediaries and bill brokers deal in money market instruments. On the other hand, stock exchanges, mutual funds, leasing companies, investment banks, investment trusts, insurance companies, etc. dealing capital market instrument.

4. INTERRELATIONS BETWEEN MONEY AND CAPITAL MARKETS

The money market and capital market are closely interrelated because most corporations and financial institutions are active in both. Firms may borrow funds from the money market for a short period or for a loan period from the capital market. A number of factors may prompt borrowers and lenders to resort to either the money market or the capital market which reflect the interdependence of the two markets. They are discussed below.

1. Lenders may choose to direct their funds to either or both markets depending on the availability of funds, the rates of return, and their investment policies.

2. Borrowers may obtain their funds from either or both markets according to their requirements. A firm may borrow short-term funds by selling commercial paper or it may float additional shares or bonds.

3. Some corporations and financial institutions serve both markets by buying and selling short-term and long-term securities.

4. All long-term securities become short-term instruments at the time of maturity. So some capital market instruments also become money market instruments.

5. Funds flow back and forth between the two market s whenever the treasury finances maturing bills with treasury securities or whenever a bank lends the proceeds of a maturing loan to a firm on a short-term basis.

6. Yields in the money market are related to those of the capital market. A fall in the short-term interest rates in the money market shows a condition of essay credit which is likely to be followed or accompanied by a more moderate fall in the long-term interest rates in the capital market. However, money market interest rates are more sensitive than are long-term interest rates in the capital market.

EXERCISES

1. What is a money market? Describe the working of a money market.
2. Describe the working of money market. Why is the money market important?
3. Define money market. Explain its functions.
4. What do you understand by the capital market? Explain its importance.
5. Distinguish between money and capital markets. How are they interrelated?

CHAPTER 23

Financial Dualism

1. MEANING

Professor Myint[1] has developed the theory of financial dualism. Financial dualism means the coexistence of organised and unorganised money market in the LDCs. The organised money market consists of the central bank, the commercial banks, the cooperative societies and banks, the foreign banks, and other financial institutions like agricultural finance corporation (as NABARD in India), industrial finance corporation (like the IFCI in India), the insurance companies (such as LIC, GIC, etc. in India), and the development banks (like IDBI, SIDBI, etc. in India). The unorganised money market includes indigenous bankers, moneylenders, both professional and non-professional, traders, merchants, landlords, friends and relatives, pawnbrokers, nidhis and chit funds.

The unorganised money market is characterised by: *(i)* personal touch between the moneylenders and borrowers; *(ii)* informality in dealing with borrowers by the moneylenders; *(iii)* flexibility in loan transactions; *(iv)* multiplicity of lending activities, i.e. combining moneylending with other economic activities such as trading; (*v*) multiplicity of interest rates — the interest rate varying with the need of the borrower, the amount of loan, the time for which it is needed, and the nature of security; *(vi)* defective system of maintaining accounts — receipts are not issued for interest charged and the principal repaid; and *(vii)* utmost secrecy in maintaining accounts and lending procedures.

2. EFFECTS OF FINANCIAL DUALISM

The existence of such financial dualism in the money market of an LDC affects its economy in the following ways:

"*Interest Rate Differences.* Financial dualism leads to the existence of different interest rates in the organised and unorganised money markets in such economies. The rate of interest in the organised money market in the traditional sector is much higher than that in the organised money market in the modern sector. The unorganised money market consisting of the non-institutional lenders, such as the village moneylenders, landlords, shopkeepers, traders or the combination of some of them, charge very high interest rates on loans. The main reason is that there is a real shortage of savings in the traditional sector as substantial amount of savings is hoarded in gold and jewellery. Even though risks and costs of lending money to a large number of small borrowers are very high, yet there are other contributory factors arising from imperfections in this unorganised money market. The village shopkeepers, landlords, moneylenders and traders occupy strategic positions in the village economy and create monopoly powers over the peasants. These arise because of personal and informal dealings with borrowers, flexibility in loan transactions, and blending of money-lending with other types of activities such as selling of goods. "The high rates of interest which the peasants have to pay are not

1 H. Myint, *Economic Theory and Underdeveloped Countries,* 1971, and *The Economics of Developing Countries,* 5/e, 1980.

only formal interest charges but also in considerable part concealed charges obtained through manipulating the prices of the commodities which the peasants buy or sell. Concealed charges may take the form of very high prices for goods on credit terms at the local shop or the obligation to repay the landlord the loans advanced with a specified amount of the crop at harvest."

On the other hand, in the organised money market of the LDCs, the interest rates are low and credit facilities are abundant. The organised money market consists of the commercial banks and other financial institutions which lend short-term credit at low interest rates to the modern business sector consisting of the big foreign-owned enterprises in the export industries, the government and the large-scale modern manufacturing enterprises.

Inflation and Balance of Payments Pressures. The LDCs are faced with chronic domestic inflation and balance of payments difficulties. As a result, small business units such as peasants, small traders, handicraft producers, etc. in the traditional sector have to face not only high interest rates but also inaccessibility to foreign exchange and imports. The LDCs have attained monetary independence with the establishment of their own central banks. They have introduced foreign exchange controls and have restricted profit remittances and transfer of funds by foreign commercial banks. As a result, the organised money market of the LDCs has been separated from the world capital market. Coupled with this, they have been following cheap money policy. This has led to the paradoxical situation in which the central banks in the capital-scarce LDCs are maintaining low interest rates than those prevailing in the capital-rich developed countries thereby overvaluing their exchange rates. They fear that devaluation will lead to repeated devaluation of their currencies and to inflationary pressures. Thus the LDCs are faced with inflationary pressures, declining foreign exchange reserves and balance of payments pressures. Thus there is a chronic excess demand for foreign exchange at the overvalued exchange rates.

To overcome this, they have concentrated on foreign exchange and import control and on monetary and fiscal measures and direct controls.

Adverse Effects of Fiscal and Monetary Policies. Financial dualism has led to aggravation of the economic dualism between the traditional sector and the modern industrial sector. These fiscal and monetary policies have tended to favour the modern industrial sector as against the traditional sector. The cheap money policy by maintaining an artificially low interest rates has made credit available to large industrial concerns at favourable terms. The low interest rates have discouraged the flow of capital funds from abroad and savings from within the country, but have created an excess demand for loans. Thus the bulk of domestic savings at low interest rates have flowed to the modern industrial sector. This has reduced the supply of capital to the traditional small industries and the agricultural sector which have to get it at higher interest rates. Consequently, the size of monetary transactions has been reduced and non-monetary transactions have continued to increase.

Adverse Effects of Controls. Further, the imposition of controls on foreign exchange and imports to correct the adverse balance of payments have benefited the modern industrial sector as against the traditional sector. The modern sector is usually allocated the major portion of the available foreign exchange and the manufacturing industries are encouraged to adopt highly capital-intensive methods of production because the imported capital goods are obtained cheaply at the overvalued exchange rates. Thus there is a strong incentive to substitute cheaper imported capital goods for domestic labour.

The agricultural and small-scale sectors suffer from the foreign exchange and import controls on two counts: *first*, they get imported consumer goods at high prices, and *second*, they fail to obtain the foreign exchange and import permits easily because of red-tapism and corruption prevailing in tne LDCs.

Government control over the scarce supply of capital have also retarded the growth of financial intermediaries in the LDCs. These controls favour the large manufacturing units and banks. They discriminate against the small borrowers and the moneylenders who provide credit to the small borrowers. The government believes that capital funds invested only in durable capital goods and modern machinery are productive, while those invested in financing agriculture and trading activities are unproductive.

Inimical Public Policies. The traditional sector also suffers because the government expenditure on public services favours the urban centres as against the rural areas. Public services like transport, communications and electric power are available more readily and at favourable terms to the modern iniustrial sector than to the traditional sector.

The governments in some of the LDCs have tried to improve credit facilities in the traditional sector by establishing agricultural banks and cooperative credit societies and by passing usury laws. But these tend to take the form of supplying a limited amount of subsidised loans through the cooperative societies to some highly favoured 'model villages'. These seemingly impressive 'show pieces' however have no effect on lowering the high rates of interest which prevail in the rest of the traditional sector. It has restricted the growth of banks in rural areas and, in turn, the use of bank credit.

According to Myint, the efforts made to control the activities of the moneylenders and to provide cheap and easy credit in the traditional sector through commercial banks and cooperative credit societies have failed due to *(a)* the high overhead cost and salaries of the officials of the commercial banks in rural areas; *(b)* the red-tapism in dealing with small borrowers according to the rigid rules of creditworthiness; (c) the lack of coordination between the head office and branches; and *(d)* the supply of limited amounts of subsidised loans through cooperative credit societies to some favoured parts of the rural sector.

Retards the Growth of Capital Market. All this has led to malallocation of resources between the modern and the traditional sectors and to the obstruction of the development of an integrated domestic capital market in the LDCs. With the multiplicity of government controls, the free market for credit has developed into the black market. Domestic inflation alongwith overvalued exchange rates have led to speculative flight of capital abroad. In countries which have tried to stop this, the capital funds have been channelised into the purchase of gold, jewellery, real estate and into speculative activities. This is because of the cheap money policy which offers low interest rates to the holders of funds for investment purposes. This stands in the way of the growth of an effective capital market.

Further, credit discrimination against trading activities also stands in the way of the development of an integrated capital market in the LDCs. Due to the non-availability of sufficient capital funds and high costs of holding stocks, the traders have to hold a much lower level of stock of commodities and circulating capital. As a result, the wholesale and retail prices are widened.

3. SUGGESTIONS TO REDUCE FINANCIAL DUALISM

In order to reduce financial dualism in LDCs, a number of measures can be suggested :

1. *Integration of Organised and Unorganised Money Markets.* The organised and unorganised money markets should be properly integrated. For this, the commercial banks should be encouraged to open branches in rural areas, as has been done in India by establishing Regional Rural Banks and Lead Banks.

2. *Strengthening of Co-operatives.* Co-operative societies and cooperative banks should be strengthened so as to enable them to compete more effectively with moneylenders and indigenous bankers.

3. *Multi-agency Approach.* A multi-agency approach should be adopted in the unorganised rural sector where farmers should be advanced loans, seeds, fertilisers, instruments, cattle, etc. and should be helped in providing marketing and trading facilities.

4. *Raising Official Interest Rates.* Prof. Myint suggests that such countries should raise official interest rates in their organised credit markets high enough to reflect their existing shortage of capital funds. This would encourage the growth of an integrated domestic capital market which can effectively attract savings from within the country and from abroad. It would also help to equate the available supply of savings to the demand for loans including the demand for funds by the moneylenders to be re-lent to the unorganised credit market.

5. *Creation of an Integrated Capital Market.* Prof. Myint further suggests the creation of a more integrated domestic capital market so that free access on equal terms to capital funds could be provided both to the modern and traditional sectors. This would also reduce the malallocation of resources between the two sectors. The interest rates in the traditional sector should be reduced by providing unlimited access to credit funds on equal terms both to the cooperatives and the moneylenders so that they can compete to lower the interest rates for the small borrowers.

EXERCISES

1. What do you mean by financial dualism? What are its effects on an underdeveloped economy?
2. How financial dualism adversely affects an underdeveloped economy? How can they be overcome?

CHAPTER 24

Financial Intermediaries

1. MEANING

Financial intermediaries (FIs) are financial institutions that intermediate between ultimate lenders and ultimate borrowers. Funds flow from ultimate lenders to ultimate borrowers either directly or indirectly through financial institutions. FIs are commercial banks, cooperative credit societies and banks, mutual savings banks, mutual funds, savings and loan associations, building societies and housing loan associations, insurance companies, merchant banks, unit trusts, and other financial institutions. Thus FIs are divided into: (a) commercial banks; and *(b)* non-bank financial intermediaries (NBFIs).

The essential function of FIs is to satisfy simultaneously the portfolio preferences of two types of individuals or firms. On the one side are borrowers who are non-financial (deficit) spending units. Their principal function is to produce and purchase current output and not to buy one type of security by issuing another, according to Gurley and Shaw.[1] They wish to expand their holdings of real assets like inventories, real estate, plant and equipment, etc. They finance these by issuing what Gurley and Shaw term *primary securities* which they define as "all liabilities and outstanding equities of non-financial spending units." They are bonds, corporate equities, debts of individuals and businesses, mortgages, bills, etc. These are their liabilities. On the other side are lenders (surplus income units or savers) whose assets are in the form of bank deposits, insurance policies, pensions, etc.

FIs transfer funds from ultimate lenders to ultimate borrowers. They acquire the savings of surplus income units and offer in return claims on themselves. They also purchase primary securities from non-financial spending units by the creation of claims on themselves through indirect or *secondary securities.* Thus FIs issue secondary securities. They are currency issued by the central bank, demand and time deposits of commercial banks, and savings deposits, insurance and pension funds of nonmonetary intermediaries. FIs are, therefore dealers in securities. They purchase primary securities and sell their secondary securities. Thus FIs function as dealers by buying funds from ultimate lenders in exchange for their own secondary securities and selling funds to ultimate borrowers in exchange for the latter's primary securities. The purchase of primary securities by surplus income units is called *direct finance* and by financial intermediaries as *indirect finance.* Both primary and secondary securities are referred to as *financial assets.*

2. PROCESS OF INTERMEDIATION

When the distribution of income among the spending units is exactly the same, all units have balanced budgets on income and product account. When income and spending distributions differ, some spending units have surpluses while others have an equivalent amount of deficits. Surplus units (ultimate lenders) supply options on current output equal to their surpluses and, in return, acquire an equal amount of net financial asset

1. J. Gurley and E. Shaw, *Money in a Theory of Finance,* 1960.

i.e. financial assets less debt increased and equities issued. Deficit units (ultimate borrowers) take up and exercise these options paying for them by increasing their net debt and equity. These budget imbalances normally lead to net issues of primary securities and net accommodation of financial assets.

First we take intermediation by the commercial banks or the monetary system. When the commercial banks intermediate, the ultimate borrowers sell them their primary securities and receive money in demand deposits of banks. These demand deposits are then spent by the borrowers for current output. The ultimate lenders acquire financial assets which represent the options on current output they have realised from the borrowers through bank deposits. In this process of intermediation, ultimate borrowers have created primary securities, the banks have created money by purchasing them, and ultimate lenders have acquired financial assets as a reward for not spending. Unspent incomes have been transferred from surplus to deficit units through bank intermediation.

Now take intermediation by NBFIs. When the ultimate lenders having demand deposits with banks, write cheques and present them to NBFIs, they, in return, receive claims on these intermediaries. NBFIs endorse the cheques and send them to the banks having demand deposits. They use these deposits to purchase primary securities from ultimate borrowers. The latter now have the demand deposits which they spend for current output, and are eventually received by ultimate lenders. The ultimate lenders end up with the same amount of demand deposits that they started with but now they have more of financial assets which represent unspent income they have transferred to the ultimate borrowers.

In this intermediation process, the borrowers have again created primary securities, NBFIs have created secondary securities, and the lenders have acquired financial assets. The nominal size of the monetary system measured by assets or liabilities has not changed. The bank deposits have been transferred from ultimate lenders to NBFIs, then to ultimate borrowers, and finally back to the ultimate lenders. There has been no intermediation by the banking system, its role has been that of administering the payment mechanism of transferring demand deposits on to its ledgers.

Thus both commercial banks and NBFIs intermediate in the transfer of unspent income from surplus to deficit units.

3. ROLE OF FINANCIAL INTERMEDIARIES*

Financial intermediaries play an important role in the modern financial system and benefit the economy as a whole.

They have the following *economic effects.*

Reduce Hoarding. By bringing the ultimate lenders (or savers) and ultimate borrowers together, FIs reduce hoarding of cash by the people under the "mattress", as is commonly said.

Help the Household Sector. The household sector relies on FIs for making profitable use of its surplus funds and also to provide consumer credit loans, mortgage loans, etc. Thus they promote saving and investment habits among the ordinary people.

Help the Business Sector. FIs also help the non-financial business sector by financing it through loan's, mortgages, purchase of bonds, shares, etc. Thus they facilitate investment in plant, equipment and inventories.

Help the State and Local Government. FIs help the state and local bodies financially by purchasing their bonds.

Help the Central Government. Similarly, they buy and sell central government securities and thus they help the central government.

Lenders and FIs both Earn. When savers deposit their funds with FIs, they earn interest. When FIs lend to ultimate borrowers, they earn profits. In fact, the ' reward of intermediation arises from the difference between the rate of return on primary securities held by FIs and the interest or dividend rate they pay on their indirect debt.

Spread of Risks. FIs possess greater resources than individuals to bear and spread risks among different borrowers. This is because of their large size, diversification of their portfolios and economies of scale in portfolio management. They can employ skilled portfolio managers and other financial experts. They also

* This also relates to the functions of FIs.

benerit by exploiting economies of scale in lending and borrowing. On the lending side, they can invest and manage investments in primary securities at unit costs far below the experience of most individual lenders. The large size of their portfolio permits a significant reduction in risks through diversification. The maturity of primary securities can be phased in such a manner that liquidity crises are minimised. Similarly, on the borrowing side, since the number of depositors is very large, FIs can spread the repayment schedule over a longer time period and can reduce the illiquidity of their portfolios.

There are also external economies associated with FIs. External economies are particularly evident in the case of the monetary system. An efficient monetary system is an essential condition for the real growth in the economy. External economies are also important in the case of social and private insurance, and of mortgage and consumer finance.

Creation of New Assets and Liabilities. All FIs create financial assets. The banks create money when they purchase primary securities. Other intermediaries create various forms of non-monetary indirect assets when they deposit money. Non-financial spending units create primary securities. In each case, the financial asset is created by the purchase of another financial asset or by the purchase of tangible assets.

Banks purchase various types of primary securities. They create money in an amount which is the multiple of primary securities they hold. NBFIs initially purchase currency and demand deposits when they create indirect securities. In the same way, these intermediaries create liabilities by some multiple of either their currency or deposit balance. Since they can sell money for primary securities, they can create liability by some multiple of any type of asset they hold.

Prof. Gardner Ackley has shown that in intermediation between ultimate savers and direct investors, FIs add greatly to the stock of financial assets available to savers. For every extra asset, they also create an equal new financial liability. Since FIs also own each others' liabilities, they create increments of assets and liabilities. Still, intermediation does not affect total net worth. He concludes that although the increment of assets and liabilities does not increase total wealth or income, we can assume that it increases welfare.

Provide Liquidity. FIs provide liquidity when they convert an asset into cash easily and quickly without loss of value in terms of money. When FIs issue claims against themselves and supply funds they, especially banks, always try to maintain their liquidity. This they do by following two rules: first, they make short-term loans and finance them by issuing claims against themselves for longer periods; and second, they diversify loans among different types of borrowers.

Help in Lowering Interest Rates. Competition among FIs leads to the lowering of interest rates. FIs prefer to keep their savings with FIs rather than in cash. The FIs, in turn, invest them in primary securities. Consequently, prices of securities are bid up and interest rates fall. Moreover, when people keep their cash holdings with FIs which are safe and liquid, the demand for money falls thereby lowering interest rates. This can be illustrated diagrammatically in Fig. 1. The supply of money is given, as shown by the vertial curve *MS*. The demand for money is shown by the curve *MD*. When FIs shrink the demand for money, the curve *MD* shifts to M_1D_1 and consequently the interest rate falls from r to r_1.

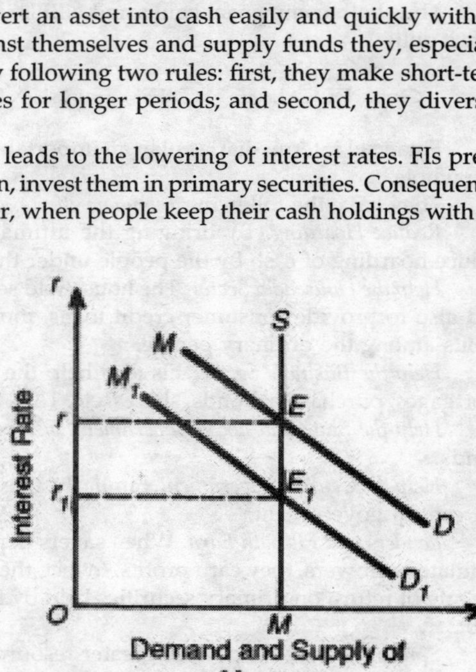

FIG. 1

Patikin has shown in his *Money, Interest and Prices* (1965) that when the interest rate is influenced by FIs, it, in turn, affects the price level of the economy. The greater this effect is, the smaller will be the effect of FIs on the interest rate.

Low Interest Rates Benefit both Savers and Investors. When interest rates decline, both savers and investors benefit. First, the real costs of lending to borrowers are reduced. These, in turn, tend to reduce costs and prices of goods and services. With reduction in interest rates, the return on time deposits is also reduced which induces savers to deposit their funds with FIs even though the latter pay lower interest rates. Still the savers benefit because FIs provide greater safety, convenience and other related services to them thereby increasing the savers' real return and income.

Bring Stability in the Capital Market. FIs deal in a variety of assets and liabilities which are mostly traded in the capital market. If there were no FIs, there would be frequent changes in the demand and supply of financial assets and their relative yields, thereby bringing instability in the capital market. As FIs function within a legal framework and set rules, they provide stability to the capital market and benefit savers and firms through diversified financial services. In fact, the extensive regulation under which FIs operate in advanced countries like the United States has reduced the threat of stock scam, as it occurred in India.

Benefit to the Economy. FIs are of immense help in the working of financial markets, in executing monetary and credit policies of the central bank and hence in promoting the growth of an economy. By transferring funds from surplus to deficit units, FIs create large financial assets and liabilities. They provide the economy with money supply and with near money assets. Thus they help in the working of financial markets. Since the financial markets govern the working of the economy, the monetary and credit policies of the central bank are changed in such a manner from time to time that the financial markets function smoothly in the country. In fact, the growth of the economy is dependent upon the proper functioning of the financial system which, in turn, depends to a large extent upon the FIs.

4. ROLE OF FINANCIAL INTERMEDIARIES IN ECONOMIC GROWTH

Financial intermediaries which consist of commercial banks, cooperative credit societies, mutual savings funds, mutual funds, saving and loan associations, insurance companies, and other financial institutions, help in the growth process of the economy. They intermediate between ultimate lenders who are savers and ultimate borrowers who are investors. By performing this function they discourage hoarding by the people, mobilise their savings and lend them to investors.

Investors can borrow funds internally by using their own savings or/and externally by using the savings of others. FIs provide external finance. Savers who are ultimate lenders deposit their savings with FIs, and FIs, in turn, lend these funds to ultimate borrowers. The difference between lending and borrowing rates are the profits of FIs. FIs lend to borrowers by purchasing primary securities issued by the latter. These are bonds, equities, mortgages, bills, etc. FIs buy them with the funds kept by the savers with them. They are, therefore, able to profit by this transformation process by exploiting the economies of scale in lending and borrowing. On the lending side, the intermediaries can invest and manage investments in primary securities at unit cost far below the experience of most individual lenders. The large size of their portfolios permits a significant reduction in risks through diversification. They can schedule maturities of primary securities in such a manner that chances of liquidity crises are minimised. They are favoured with tax benefits that are not available to individual savers. On the borrowing side, with a large number of depositors they can normally rely on a predictable schedule of claims for repayment. Thus FIs encourage saving and investment which are essential for promoting economic growth.

Savings are essential for capital formation without which economic growth is not possible. Mere savings are not enough for capital formation. They are required to be mobilised which is done by FIs. Even mobilisation of savings does not lead to capital formation. They must be channelised into productive investments. By lending to ultimate borrowers, FIs promote investment. Thus the role of FIs in the growth process is partly that of buying securities of one kind from borrowers and selling securities of another kind to lenders, and thereby contribute to an increase in the willingness to save and the inducement to invest. More importantly they try to find out better investment opportunities and facilitate their exploitation by helping industry.

Among other factors, investment depends upon the rate of interest. The lower the interest rate, the higher is the investment. Competition among FIs for primary securities raises their prices and lowers the interest rate. Moreover, when savers keep their cash holdings with FIs which involve less risk, and are safe and liquid, the demand for money falls which further lowers the interest rate. The fall in interest rate encourages investment which increase the rate of capital formation and hence promotes economic growth. Goldsmith's study[2] has shown that the growth of FIs has been responsible for the economic growth of developed countries in a significant way.

5. FINANCIAL INTERMEDIARIES AND UNDER-DEVELOPED COUNTRIES

Financial intermediaries play a special role in under-developed countries. In such countries the capital market is unorganised and undeveloped. The majority of the people are poor and they cannot save. Those who save, invest their savings in gold, jewellery, real estate, speculation, foreign exchange, and conspicuous consumption. Under these circumstances, FIs undertake the task of encouraging the flow of personal savings from unproductive to productive uses. They encourage households to hold financial assets instead of physical assets. To the extent households are willing to switch from the purchase of physical assets to financial assets to serve as their instruments of saving, resources are released for development purposes.

Further, as the economy develops, the non-monetized sector is gradually transformed into the monetized sector. With the increase in the rate of monetization of the economy, the banking habits of the people also grow. In such a situation, the commercial banks alone are not sufficient to mobilise savings and put them into productive channels. So the role of FIs becomes all the more important in mobilising and investing these savings for capital formation and economic development. In UDCs, there is the absence of an environment for entrepreneurship because of the lack of effective lending institutions. FIs help small firms to a greater degree than the large firms. They find investment opportunities and facilitate their exploitation by helping small, and new enterprises in UDCs.

The growth of FIs in the course of development in such countries helps in economising the use of money. As these financial institutions grow, they sell indirect securities to savers. These securities are close substitutes for money. So the savers buy securities instead of keeping money in cash. It is in this way that these financial intermediaries help in economising the use of money which, in turn, controls the money supply and the demand for goods and services from increasing. Thus FIs help in controlling inflation indirectly in underdeveloped countries.

6. FINANCIAL INTERMEDIARIES IN THE SAVING-INVESTMENT PROCESS

Financial intermediaries transmute funds between savers who lend and investors who borrow. They mobilise savings and channel them into the hands of investors who need more funds than they have on hand. In other words, they are conduits through which savers can lend their excess funds to investors.

Fls are commercial banks, cooperative societies and banks, mutual savings banks, mutual funds, savings and loan associations, insurance companies, merchant banks, unit trusts, and other types of financial institutions. They act as middlemen by transferring funds from savers to investors. By lending their surplus funds, savers stand to gain because they earn interest or dividend on their funds. On the other hand, investors stand to benefit when they borrow to carry out their investment plans. Without financial intermediaries, savers would hoard their surplus funds, and investors (borrowers) would not carry out their investment plans except those who can finance internally.

The essential function of Fls is to satisfy simultaneously the portfolio preference of both savers and investors. Savers are ultimate lenders whose assets are bank deposits, insurance policies, pensions, etc. Investors are ultimate borrowers or non-financial units who wish to expand their holdings of such real assets as inventories, real estate, plant and equipment, etc. They finance these by issuing primary securities which are bonds, corporate equities, debts of individuals and businesses, mortgages, bills, etc. These are their liabilities.

Fls issue indirect or secondary securities. They are currency, demand and time deposits of commercial banks, and saving deposits, insurance and pension funds of nonfinancial intermediaries. Fls intermediate between original savers and ultimate borrowers or investors. Savers deposit funds with Fls instead of directly

2. Raymond W. Goldsmith, *'Financial Intermediaries in the American Economy Since 1900,'* 1958.

purchasing bonds, mortgages or equities, and FIs, in turn, lend funds to ultimate borrowers. FIs acquire *primary securities* issued by ultimate borrowers, and in turn, issue their own *secondary securities* for the portfolio of ultimate lenders (savers). In other words, investors sell securities to banks and receive newly created demand deposits in return in banks. These deposits are then spent on current output and ultimately accrue to the savers in the community as financial assets. Investors also sell securities to non-bank financial intermediaries. These, in turn, sell claim on themselves to the savers. Thus the non-bank financial intermediaries are able to supply debt instruments particularly suitable to the needs of the borrowers independent of the type of assets that the lenders want. Similarly, they offer financial assets to the lenders independent of the type of debt instrument the borrowers are prepared to issue.

Besides bringing savers and lenders together, FIs transmute the primary securities issued by the nonfinancial units (borrowers) into secondary securities (issued by FIs themselves) possessing greater liquidity, convenience, lower risk, etc. in order to attract wealth holders (savers). Thus FIs turn primary securities into secondary securities for the portfolio of ultimate lenders. They give lenders a wide variety of financial assets particularly suited to their needs. They also make it less necessary for borrowers to issue those types of securities which are ill-adapted to their own businesses. Thus FIs by liquifying and diversifying the securities issued by the lenders encourage saving or discourage dissaving.

Further, the techniques of intermediation get primary securities distributed efficiently from ultimate borrowers to ultimate lenders and from one lender to another through dealers and security exchanges. They tend to raise the level of saving and investment by increasing the marginal utility of last dealer's worth of financial assets to the lender and reducing the marginal disutility of the last dealer's worth of debt to the borrower. They also tend to increase the efficiency of resource allocation by placing more investment projects against one another for lenders to examine. Thus FIs are able to improve the efficiency of distributive techniques of intermediation in many ways. Their role in the saving-investment process is quite similar to that of distributive techniques, lotteries or land sales. They enable investors to spend more efficiently.

EXERCISES

1. What are financial intermediaries? Describe their role in a country.
2. Explain the functions performed by financial intermediaries.
3. Discuss the role and importance of financial intermediaries in the saving-investment process.
4. Explain the role of financial intermediaries in the growth process. How do they help in the development of underdeveloped countries?

CHAPTER

25

Non-Bank Financial Intermediaries (NBFIs)

1. MEANING

Non-bank financial intermediaries are such institutions as savings and loan associations, life insurance companies, mutual savings banks, common trust funds, pension funds, and government lending agencies. These intermediaries pool funds from net savers and lend them to finance expenditures of business firms and local bodies. To obtain funds from net savers, the intermediaries issue and sell indirect securities such as time deposits, common fund stocks, saving and loan shares, and insurance policies. They purchase primary securities to lend funds to ultimate borrowers. Primary securities include government securities; mortgages, common and preferred stocks, and consumer and other short-term debts. Thus, NBFIs are financial firms that buy one kind of financial asset and sell another. For instance, savings and loan associations and mutual savings banks mainly buy mortgages and sell savings deposits; insurance companies buy mainly bonds and sell insurance policies; and finance companies buy instalment loans and sell commercial papers.

2. ROLE OF NON-BANK FINANCIAL INTERMEDIARIES*

Non-bank financial intermediaries have been playing an important role in the following directions :

Reduce Hoarding. By bringing the ultimate lenders (or savers) and ultimate borrowers together, NBFIs reduce hoarding of cash by the people under the "mattress", as is commonly said.

Help the Household Sector. The household sector relies on NBFIs for making profitable use of its surplus funds and also to provide consumer credit loans, mortgage loans, etc. Thus they promote saving and investment habits among the ordinary people.

Help the Business Sector. NBFIs also help the nonfinancial business sector by Financing it through loans, mortgages, purchase of bonds, shares, etc. Thus they facilitate investment in plant, equipment and inventories.

Help the State and Local Government. NBFIs help the state and local bodies financially by purchasing their bonds.

Help the Central Government. Similarly, they buy and sell central government securities and thus they help the central government.

Lenders and NBFIs both Earn. When savers deposit their funds with NBFIs, they earn interest. When NBFIs lend to ultimate borrowers, they earn profits. In fact, the reward of intermediation arises from the

---

* This section also relates to the functions of NBFIs.

difference between the rate of return on primary securities held by NBFIs and the interest or dividend rate they pay on their indirect debt.

Provide Liquidity. NBFIs provide liquidity when they convert an asset into cash easily and quickly without loss of value in terms of money. When NBFIs issue claims against themselves and supply funds they, especially banks, always try to maintain their liquidity. This they do by following two rules: *first*, they make short-term loans and finance them by issuing claims against themselves for longer periods; and *second*, they diversify loans among different types of borrowers.

Help in Lowering Interest Rate. Competition among NBFIs leads to the lowering of interest rates. NBFIs prefer to keep their saving with NBFIs rather than in cash. The NBFIs, in turn, invest them in primary securities. Consequently, prices of securities are bid up and interest rates fall. Moreover, when people keep their cash holdings with NBFIs which are safe and liquid, the demand for money falls thereby lowering interest rates.

Low Interest Rates Benefit both Savers and Investors. When interest rates decline, both savers and investors benefit. First, the real costs of lending to borrowers are reduced. These, in turn, tend to reduce costs and prices of goods and services. With reduction in interest rates, the return on time deposits is also' reduced which induces savers to deposit their funds with NBFIs even though the latter pay lower interest rates. Still the savers benefit because NBFIs provide greater safety, convenience and other related services to them thereby increasing the savers' real return and income.

Brokers of Loanable Funds. NBFIs play an important role as brokers of loanable funds. They act as intermediaries between the ultimate saver and the ultimate investor. They sell indirect securities to savers and purchase primary securities from investors. Indirect securities are the short-term liabilities of financial intermediaries. On the other hand, primary securities are their earning assets but they are the debts of the borrowers. Thus NBFIs act as brokers of loanable funds by changing debt into credit.

Reduce Risks. When the non-bank financial intermediaries convert debt into credit, they reduce the risk to the ultimate lender. First, they create liabilities on themselves by selling indirect securities to the lenders. Then they buy primary securities from borrowers of funds. So by acting as intermediaries between the lenders and borrowers of funds, NBFIs take the risk on themselves and reduce it on the ultimate lenders. Moreover, by holding varied types of financial assets, they decrease their own risks. Low returns on some assets can be offset by high returns on others.

Mobilising Savings. NBFIs raise funds in the capital market and supply credit to investors. Expert financial services provided by them have been attracting larger share of public savings. Such services include easy liquidity, safety of principal, and ready divisibility of savings into direct securities of different values. They have been able to mobilise more funds due to the development of two types of non-bank financial intermediaries. The first are the depository intermediaries which include savings and loan associations, credit unions, and mutual savings banks. There is high liquidity of savings in such institutions which attract small savers. Moreover, they issue fixed price assets whose value does not change like the market price of other types of assets. The second are the contractual intermediaries which enter into contract with savers and provide them various types of benefits over the long run. Such institutions are pension funds, life insurance companies and public provident funds. These two types of financial intermediaries in particular help in mobilising public savings.

Investment of Funds. NBFIs exist because they want to earn profit by investing the mobilised savings. Different financial intermediaries follow different investment policies. For instance, savings and loan associations and mutual savings banks invest in mortgages, and insurance companies invest in bonds and securities. Thus intermediaries mobilise public savings, invest them and thereby help in capital formation and economic growth.

Create New Assets and Liabilities. Gardner Ackley has shown that in intermediating between ultimate lenders and direct investors, NBFIs add greatly to the stock of financial assets available to savers and for every extra asset, they also create an equal new financial liability. But intermediation does not affect total net worth. He concludes that although intermediation does not increase total wealth or income, it can be assumed that it increases welfare.

Economies of Scale. NBFIs reap a number of economies of specialisation and scale in mobilising savings and making investments. It would be costly and cumbersome for individual savers to lend their funds to individual borrowers. NBFIs make larger transactions with ultimate lenders and borrowers. They specialise in trading large financial assets and thus have lower costs in buying and selling securities. They employ expert staff and efficient machinery and equipment, thereby increasing productivity in the transfer of funds.

Bring Stability in the Capital Market. NBFIs deal in a variety of assets and liabilities which are mostly traded in the capital market. If there were no NBFIs, there would be frequent changes in the demand and supply of financial assets and their relative yields, thereby bringing instability in the capital market. As NBFIs function within a legal framework and set rules, they provide stability to the capital market and benefit savers and firms through diversified financial services.

Benefit to the Economy. NBFIs are of immense help in the working of financial markets, in executing monetary and credit policies of the central bank and hence in promoting the growth of an economy. By transferring funds from surplus to deficit units. NBFIs create large financial assets and liabilities. They provide the economy with money supply and with near money assets. Thus they help in the working of financial markets. Since the financial markets govern the working of the economy, the monetary and credit policies of the central bank are changed in such a manner from time to time that the financial markets function smoothly in the country. In fact, the growth of the economy is dependent upon the proper functioning of the financial system which, in turn, depends to a large extent upon the NBFIs.

In Economic Growth. NBFIs help in the growth process of the economy. They intermediate between ultimate lenders who are savers and ultimate borrowers who are investors. By performing this function, they discourage hoarding by the people, mobilise their savings and lend them to investors. Thus NBFIs encourage saving and investment which are essential for promoting economic growth. Goldsmith's study has shown that the growth of NBFIs has been responsible for the economic growth of developed countries in a significant way.

We may conclude that NBFIs provide liquidity and safety to financial assets and help in transferring funds from ultimate lenders to ultimate borrowers for productive purposes. They increase capital formation and consequently lead to economic growth.

3. NON-BANK FINANCIAL INTERMEDIARIES AND MONETARY POLICY: THE GURLEY-SHAW THESIS

There has been considerable discussion from the mid-1950s about the role of financial intermediaries in influencing monetary policy. The Radcliffe Committee in Britain studied the growth of financial intermediaries since World War II and came to the conclusion that they adversely affected the power of Bank of England to control credit. Gurley and Shaw also came to the same conclusion.

According to Gurley and Shaw, NBFIs perform the intermediary role of purchasing primary securities such as government securities, mortgages, common and preferred stocks, consumer and other short-term debt. On the other hand, they issue and sell indirect securities such as time deposits, common funds stocks, saving and loan-shares, and insurance policies to the ultimate lenders. By buying primary securities from the ultimate borrowers and selling indirect securities to the ultimate lenders, the intermediaries influence the availability of credit and the structure and level of interest rates. They create credit different from commercial banks. But they create new assets and liabilities which tend to influence the supply of money and thus hinder the operation of an effective monetary policy.

According to them, the savings deposits of NBFIs resemble the demand deposits of commercial banks because it is not difficult for NBFIs to convert their savings deposits into cash. These savings deposits, whether of commercial banks or of NBFIs, are for all practical purposes as liquid as demand deposits. Such savings deposits held by NBFIs are known as near-monies. Since the demand deopsits are not controlled by the central bank, it follows that the savings deposits held by NBFIs will hinder the successful operation of a successtui monetary policy.

If the central bank wishes to control excess liquidity in the economy only through the reduction in money supply, it will not be successful because the savings deposits of NBFIs can be converted into cash. Similarly, if the central bank tries to control lending by commercial banks, it will not be successful if the lending of all other NBFIs are not under its control, as is the case. According to Gurley and Shaw, this problem arises especially when the central bank adopts an anti-inflationary monetary policy. Suppose the central bank reduces the money supply in order to control inflation. Among other effects, the interest rates on market securities rise. In anticipation of higher yields and profits, NBFIs will raise the interest rates on their savings deposits to attract more funds in order to invest them in higher yielding securities.

Persons already holding securities find that their prices have fallen because of the rise in interest rates on present securities. They will, therefore, sell them and deposit their funds with intermediaries in order to earn higher interest rates on savings deposits. In the meantime, attracted by higher interest rate, others holding idle cash balances will also deposit them with intermediaries. So when NBFIs raise the interest rates on their savings deposits, the public reduces its demand for money which, in turn, reduces the market rate of interest. Thus NBFIs make tight monetary policy less successful or effective. This is explained in Fig. 1 where the demand and supply of money are taken on the horizontal axis and the rate of interest on the vertical axis. MS is the money supply curve and *MD* the money demand curve. Both intersect at *E* where *r*, rate of interest is determined. Suppose there is an inflationary situation and the central bank reduces the money supply by a certain amount to control it. The reduction in money supply is shown by the shifting of the *MS* curve to the left as MS_1 so that the new equilibrium point is established at E_1 and the rate of interest rises to r_2. The NBFIs also raise the interest rate on their deposits which, in turn, reduces the demand for money by the public. The *MD* curve shifts to the left to M_1D_1 and intersects the M_1S_1 curve at E_2. The interest rate is now reduced from r_2 to r_1. Thus the NBFIs are able to counteract tight money policy.

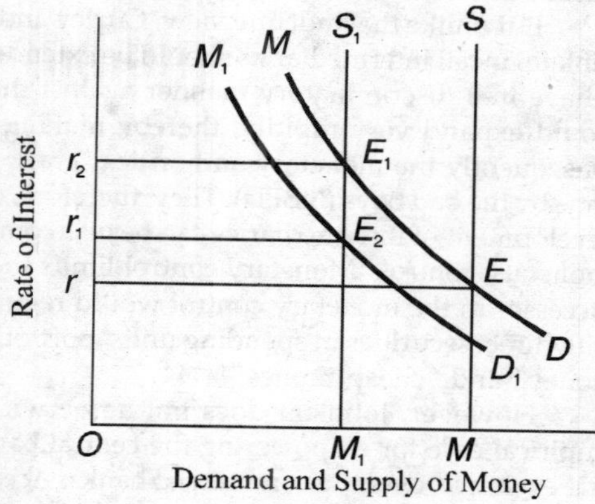

Fig. 1

Credit Creation. NBFIs make monetary policy ineffective even when the central bank adopts a restrictive monetary policy by selling securities in the open market and raising requirements of commercial banks. As a result, money supply with the bank is reduced and interest rates tend to rise. Non-bank financial intermediaries also find arise in the interest rates of their primary securities. They, therefore, raise the interest rate on indirect securities in order to attract more funds from individual savers. This increase in interest rates, in turn, encourages savers to shift their savings from commercial bank demand deposits into time deposits, saving and loan shares, and other indirect securities of non-bank financial intermediaries. This tends to increase funds with the intermediaries for lending purposes and they are able to purchase more primary securities. Thus the supply of available credit is increased in the economy even though the money supply remains unchanged. "When this happens, the intermediary, in effect, acts as an agent facilitating the process of dishoarding cash balances."[1] Ultimately, the purchase of primary securities by intermediaries causes money to flow back into the commercial banks which end up with the same amount of deposits which they had before the operation of intermediaries. Thus when money supply is reduced by a restrictive monetary policy, the non-bank financial intermediaries are able to increase velocity of money and total spending by turning primary securities into indirect securities for the portfolios of ultimate lenders.

Similarly, non-bank financial intermediaries can make an expansionary monetary policy ineffective by reducing the velocity of money.

The question arises as to what extent non-bank financial intermediaries have actually been instrumental in offsetting the monetary policy. If they have been doing so on a large scale, then it is advisable to extend the controls of the central bank over them.

There has been a hot controversy over the issue. But the consensus is that the role played by intermediaries in under-cutting monetary policy is minimal. As the United States Commission on Money and Credit noted: "The evidence, for either the cyclical or the secular periods, does not support a case for an extension of the direct monetary controls over non-bank financial intermediaries. Their contribution to cyclical changes in velocity appears to be too small to warrant such an extension."

The Radcliffe Committee of Britain rejected the idea of controlling the intermediaries because it was not politically feasible in England. It further observed: "Such a prospect would be unwelcome except as a last resort, not mainly because of its administrative burdens, but because the further growth of new financial

1. Warren L. Smith, *Staff Report on Employment, Growth, and Price Level*, 1959.

institutions would allow the situation continually to slip from under the grip of the authorities."

But unlike the Radcliffe view, Gurley and Shaw have argued that the central bank's control over the non-bank financial intermediaries should be extended. In the absence of control over NBFIs, the central bank would behave in a discriminatory manner against the commercial banks. If NBFIs remain outside its control, they would expand very rapidly, thereby making monetary policy less effective. Gurley and Shaw opine that consequently the monetary authorities "crack down" on the good boys (commercial banks) for the mischief done by the bad boys (NBFIs). They, therefore, opine: "The lag of regulatory techniques behind the institutional development of intermediaries can be overcome when it is appreciated that 'financial control' should supplant 'monetary control.' Monetary control limits the supply of one financial asset money. Financial control, as the successor to the monetary control would regulate creation of financial assets in all forms that are competitive with direct securities in spending units' portfolios. "Tight finance" and "cheap finance" are the sequels of "tight money" and "cheap money".

However, Johnson does not agree with Gurley and Shaw. He observes that there seems to be no empirical case for empowering the central bank to extend its control over financial intermediaries similar to that exercised over the commercial banks. According to him, there is little reason for believing that the central bank's control is weakened by the presence of financial intermediaries. Moreover, so long as the public does not switch easily from bank deposits into indirect securities of intermediaries, the presence of intermediaries may increase the leverage of the central bank on economic activity. It implies that it is not possible for the interest rates to settle back at their old levels even by the operation of non-bank financial intermediaries. Rather, interest rates would tend to rise further. The money supply will remain tight and its influence on spending would be restrictive.

4. DISTINCTION BETWEEN BANKS AND NON-BANK FINANCIAL INTERMEDIARIES

Before we discuss how far commercial banks differ from NBFIs, let us study their similarities.

Similarities between Banks and NBFIs. From a functional viewpoint the operations of commercial banks are similar to those of NBFIs on the following counts:

1. Like NBFIs, commercial banks acquire the primary securities of borrowers, loans and deposits, and in turn, they provide their own indirect securities and demand deposits to the lenders. Commercial banks resemble NBFIs in that both create secondary securities in their role as borrowers.

2. Commercial banks create demand deposits when they borrow from the central bank, and NBFIs create various forms of indirect debt when they borrow from commercial banks.

3. Both commercial banks and NBFIs act as intermediaries in bringing ultimate borrowers and ultimate lenders together and facilitate the transfer of currency balances from non-financial lenders to non-financial borrowers for the purpose of earning profits.

4. Both commercial banks and NBFIs provide liquid funds. The bank deposits and other assets of commercial banks and the assets provided by NBFIs are liquid assets. Of course, the degree of liquidity varies in accordance with the nature and the activity of the concerned financial intermediaries.

5. Both banks and NBFIs are important creators of loanable funds. The commercial banks by net creation of money and the NBFIs by mobilising existing money balance in exchange for their own newly issued financial liabilities.

HOW ARE COMMERCIAL BANKS DIFFERENT FROM NBFIS?

Commercial banks are different from NBFIs in the following respects:

1. *Credit Creation.* Prof. J. Tobin[2] has shown that the existence of NBFIs significantly modifies the conventional view of commercial banks as creators of money because they can directly issue their own new liabilities to acquire other assets. On the other hand, NBFIs do not create money.

2. J. Tobin, Commercial Banks as Creators of "Money", in D. Carson (Ed.) *Banking and Monetary Studies,* 1963.

Like all other financial intermediaries (FIs), commercial banks lend to borrowers only currency deposited with them and make profit by charging borrowers a high rate than they pay to lenders. But both differ in the effects of their operations so far as secondary securities are concerned. The two main financial assets that serve as money are currency, known as high powered money, and demand deposits of commercial banks. Demand deposits are the secondary securities issued by commercial banks which are substitutes for currency. They represent a promise to pay currency on demand and are transferred direct by cheque without encashment in settlement of debt. Banks offer convenient safe-keeping, book-keeping and a large number of other services to depositors that are not available by holding currency. Consequently, depositors who lend their currency to commercial banks receive in return a secondary security that itself serves as a medium of payment. Loans made or deposits created by any bank through the issue of cheques will ultimately be deposited by the borrowers or by other persons to whom they made cheque payments in the commercial banking system. Thus cheques help in creating credit by the bank credit multiplier. Money lent by an individual bank is retained as cash reserve by the banking system minus only a small leakage in money used by the borrower. The bank credit multiplier implies that banks if uncontrolled would have an unlimited power to expand deposits, since the latter are determined only by the amount of primary securities that the banking system purchases. "Bank money, once created in the process of bank lending, lives on as a virtually permanent part of the money supply. Thus, banks do manufacture money; and once manufactured, it is relatively immortal." It is in this sense that commercial banks are unique among FIs in their ability to create money. But in the case of NBFIs, the amount of primary securities they can buy is limited by the amount of indirect securities they can sell to lenders. Since they do not possess the bank credit multiplier power of commercial banks, they perform the brokerage function of simply transferring to borrowers the funds entrusted to them by lenders. Moreover, government regulations prevent NBFIs from offering chequing facilities on their liabilities and convertibility into currency on demand. But a number of secondary securities, such as commercial bank time and demand deposits and deposits in some thrift institutions while directly not transferable by cheque can be turned into cash quickly, easily, conveniently and without cost. Therefore, they are a close substitute of money than other assets, are called near money assets. Thus NBFIs can create liquidity and not money. Since the majority of NBFIs are small, the banking system multiplier does not operate fully in their case because of the leakages to banks of the money lent. Suppose a small non-banking financial institution lends and issues a cheque on its bank as payment. This will lead to a drain on its resources unless an equal amount is redeposited by some other borrower. In the case of small NBFIs, the redeposit ratio is low which makes it difficult for them to continue in business unless they have sufficient assets. But a commercial bank faces no problem of this type and can create money as well as liquidity to meet its lending requirements.

2. *Cash Reserve Requirements.* Commercial banks, like other FIs, have to earn a higher rate on their total assets than they pay on their total liabilities. They have to keep cash reserves. But cash reserves do not earn income. So banks wish to maintain their cash reserves as low as possible. But, unlike NBFIs, they are legally required to maintain a minimum cash reserve ratio (CRR). This ratio is always more than what the banks would wish to maintain. As a result, banks do not normally hold cash reserves in excess of those legally required and invest all excess cash in earning assets. With a reduction of required cash reserve ratio, the volume of bank intermediation would expand, and vice versa.

As deposits are preferred to currency, an increase in the stock of high powered money results in an increase in the public's demand for bank deposits. This leads to increase in deposits with the banking system. So long as the average cost of providing and servicing demand deposits is low relative to the interest rate earned on primary securities, banks have a profit incentive to lend all excess cash by buying securities and granting loans. Consequently, the volume of bank intermediation expands. This process will continue until bank assets and deposits have risen to a level where the required cash reserves and actual reserves are equal.

It should, however, be noted that the foreign exchange liabilities of commercial banks are not required to meet cash reserve requirements. So this part of the bank business can be regarded like an NBFI.

On the other hand, NBFIs are not subject to any such restrictions. They are thus in an advantageous position over the banks. But this regulatory distinction between banks and NBFIs does not apply now in almost all the developed and developing countries of the world because reserve requirements have been enforced in one form or another on NBFIs with the exception of insurance companies, pension funds, and investment and unit trusts.

3. *Portfolio Structure.* Commercial banks differ from NBFIs in their portfolio structure. Bank liabilities are very liquid. The liabilities of a bank are large in relation to its assets, because it holds a small proportion of its assets in cash. But its liabilities are payable on demand at a short notice. Many types of assets are available to a bank with varying degree of liquidity. The most liquid is cash. The next most liquid assets are deposits with the central bank, treasury bills and other short-term bills issued by the centre and state governments and large firms, and call loans to other banks, firms, dealers and brokers in government securities. The less liquid assets are the various types of loans to customers and investment in longer-term bonds and mortgages. Thus banks have a large and varied portfolio on the basis of which they create liquidity.

NBFIs also create liquidity but in the form of savings and time deposits which are not used as a means of payment. They are limited in the choice of their assets and are also prohibited from holding certain assets. Thus the size of their portfolio is very small as compared with banks. They generally issue claims against themselves that are fixed in money terms and have maturities shorter than the direct securities they hold. They borrow for short period, and lend for long period. This is because of the small size of their portfolio and they hold less liquid assets than banks.

4. *Risk.* Banks have to follow certain norms at the time of advancing loans. There are detailed appraisals of projects and hence delays in sanctioning loans. On the other hand, NBFIs do not enter into detailed appraisals of projects, they have to follow less stringent rules for advances. There are no time delays in granting loans. Thus NBFIs are able to take greater risk and lesser supervision as compared to banks.

5. *Security.* NBFIs insist on greater security than banks before lending. Normally, it is in the form of shares and post-dated cheques. This is to ensure that if one project goes bad, they can recover from the others.

6. *Recovery.* NBFIs are very innovative in their methods of recovery and calculation of interest rates. They combine a good security with other factors such as upfront fee, and higher lending rates.

Consequently, their recovery rates are good and the percentage of bad debts to their assets is very low. Banks, on the other hand have to follow specific norms in making loans. Their prime lending rates are much lower than the NBFIs. Since banks advance huge loans to corporates, the rate of default is very high in their case.

Conclusion. The entire discussion can be summarised as follows: *(a)* The distinction between commercial banks and NBFIs has been too sharply drawn. The differences are of degree rather than of kind, *(b)* The differences which do exist have little intrinsically to do with the monetary nature of bank liabilities, (c) The differences are more importantly related to the special reserve requirements. If NBFIs are subject to the same kind of regulations they would behave in much the same way. *(d)* Commercial banks do not possess a 'widow's cruse' which means that any expansion of assets will generate a corresponding expansion of deposit liabilities. Despite these differences, commercial banks are unique among financial intermediaries.

EXERCISES

1. "Non-bank financial intermediaries are said to reduce the effectiveness of monetary policy." Examine the statement.
2. What are non-bank financial intermediaries? How do they differ from banks?
3. Explain the main functions of non-bank financial intermediaries. How do they create credit?

CHAPTER 26

Inside Money and Outside Money

1. MEANING

Gurley and Shaw (G-S) have divided the total quantity of money in the economy into two parts: inside money and outside money. They define inside money as money "based on the debt of endogenous economic units".[1] It is money created within the private sector against some private debt. It consists of financial claims by one class of individuals and firms on others within the economy. When banks create deposits through loans and advances, these return to them as secondary deposits. Deposits and loans represent assets and liabilities of the private sector. On the other hand, outside money comes from outside the private sector. It is defined as money "based on the debt of a unit (the government) exogenous to the system." Thus it is currency issued by the government, gold, foreign and government securities. It is the liability of the government as a debtor and claim of the private sector as a creditor.

2. IMPORTANCE

The distinction between inside money and outside money is important from many viewpoints :

First, we study the importance of the distinction between the two in a period of rising or falling prices. When there's inflation or deflation, a change in the purchasing power of money in the case of *inside money* leads to an equal change in the real values of both assets and liabilities of the private sector. Thus a change in the price level does not affect the behaviour of depositors and borrowers possessing inside money. The monetary system also does not gain or lose in real terms by such changes in the real amount of its debt because there is an equal change in the real value of its claims against firms. Given the nominal amount of inside money, its real value varies inversely with the price level. In other words, a change in the price level does not lead to a wealth transfer between the private sector and the government. Instead it results only in a wealth transfer between consumers and firms, the former gaining and the latter losing when the price level falls, and *vice versa*. This transfer is a distribution effect of instability in price level. But such a change in the price level, when money is of the inside variety, does not affect government behaviour and has no net effect on total wealth in the private sector.

G-S have shown that in this system the price level is determinate. A departure from the initial equilibrium price level sets in motion forces which tend to restore the initial level or a new equilibrium price level. For instance, when the price level rises, it disturbs the portfolio equilibrium of the private sector by decreasing its real money holdings relative to its bond holdings. At the new price level there will be excess real demand for money, excess real supply of bonds and goods, so that the system reverts back to the initial price level and the initial stock of nominal bonds. This will induce sales in the bond market to raise the interest rate and expenditure

1. J.G. Gurley and E.S. Shaw, *Money in a Theory of Finance,* 1960.

in the commodity market to raise the price level. The increase in the interest rate would have a depressing effect through commodity market, thereby bringing back the initial price level, and vice versa in case of deflation.

In the case of *outside money* when prices rise, the real value of cash held by exogenous economic units falls. On the contrary, when prices fall, the real value of cash held by economic units rises. Thus a change in the price level affects the behaviour of economic units possessing outside money. Thus given the nominal amount of outside money, its real value varies inversely with the price level, and each change in its real value leads to a wealth transfer between the private sector and the government. This wealth transfer affects private demands for money, goods and labour but not the government demand.

When money is of outside variety, its impact is neutral on the real variables of the economy. A monetary change causes an equi-proportionate change in prices. As a result, relative prices and interest rate would remain unchanged. An expansion in the nominal stock of outside money causes excess supply in the money market and excess demand in the commodity market. This leads to rise in price level above its initial level. The price rise reduces the aggregate real wealth of the private sector and a decline in the real value of government debt. This brings down the real demands in all markets which restore the initial price level. In this process, there is a wealth transfer between the private sector and the government which has a *net* effect on aggregate demands for money, goods and labour.

Inside and Outside Money Combined. If nominal money is composed of a combination of inside and outside money, monetary policy ceases to be neutral and some nominal stock of money is uniquely right for each state of general equilibrium. Suppose in a stationary state, the supply of inside money is doubled by the central bank through the open market purchase of the existing real bonds in the private sector. At the initial price level, the open market operation leads to a real transfer of bonds from the private sector to the monetary system (i.e. central bank). It thus changes the portfolio composition of the private sector whose stock of real bonds is reduced. This brings adjustments in the various markets. There is excess money supply and excess demand in the bond market. There is also excess demand in the commodity market leading to a rise in the price level. Thus increase in the money supply leads to an increase in the price level and a decline in interest rate. The ultimate equilibrium also involves a larger stock of capital, a higher level of real income, and a price level that is higher but proportionately less than the increase in the nominal money. Money has ceased to be neutral. Open market buying by the monetary system leads to growth in the real wealth and income accompanied by inflation. On the contrary, open market selling by the monetary system reduces real wealth and income with accompanying deflation. According to Patinkin, the commodity market in this case can be in equilibrium at an infinite number of combinations of interest rate and price level. Hence the equilibrium condition in this market does not uniquely determine the interest rate, so that there is room for changes in the interest rate from changes arising in the bond or money markets. In particular, the increase in outside money will raise the interest rate, while an increase in inside money will lower it. A proportionate increase in both inside and outside money will cause a proportionate increase in the price level and leave the interest rate unchanged.

Similar conclusions regarding the neutrality or non-neutrality of money apply when the economy operates under *conditions of growth*. Suppose balanced growth occurs at some rate n in all the real and nominal stocks and flows of money. The relative prices and absolute price level are assumed to be constant. The stock of money consists of both inside and outside varieties and is increasing at the rate n. The monetary expansion in the context of real growth leads to three different results:

(a) If the monetary system doubles the rate of expansion of both inside and outside money, the only effect is doubling of other nominal variables including the price level. Money is neutral in its impact on real variables of the economy.

(b) If the monetary system doubles the rate of expansion of the inside money supply alone, there are real effects. It leads to transfer of a larger share of real bonds to the monetary system, leaving a smaller share for private investors. This causes excess supply in the money market and excess demand in the bond market. It leads to a rise in the price level and fall in the interest rate. The adjustment in the private portfolios requires some decline in the interest rate, some increase in the growth rate of capital and income. The increase in the price level is proportionately smaller than the rise in the monetary expansion. Money is non-neutral in its effects on the real variables of the economy.

(c) If the monetary system doubles the rate of expansion of the outside money alone, there are again real effects. There is excess stock of real bonds because it remains relatively unchanged with the private sector. This leads to excess supply in the money market which induces excess demand in the commodity market. This raises the price level which operates on the bond market. The interest rate and the price level both rise above their initial equilibrium levels. Thus the real effects begin with a rise in the bond rate and restraints on real growth.

Real Balance Effect. The distinction between inside and outside money has an important bearing in understanding the real balance effect. The real balance is not related to inside money because changes in the price level do not affect the behaviour of individuals and firms possessing inside money. Inside money possessed by them represents indebtedness of one set of individuals and firms to another. It does not represent real wealth and is simply an indirect means of holding wealth. Thus the real balance effect is not related to inside money and the monetary system cannot influence the level of investment and the rate of capital accumulation through it.

On the other hand, it is on outside money that the operation of the real balance effect consists of government money (notes and coins) in circulation, and the outstanding government bonds which are outside money. When prices rise (or fall), the real value of government money and bonds held by individuals and firms is reduced (or increased).

According to Pesek and Saving[2], the quantity of money relevant for the real balance effect should include both inside money and outside money. In other words, it should include demand deposits of banks as well as money issued by the government. They have argued for the inclusion of interest-bearing government securities in the inside money category. By so doing, the potency of monetary policy is enhanced in the economy. Patinkin[3] observes in this connection that what really matters from the viewpoint of real balance effect is not whether the issuer of the money is the government or the private banking sector, but whether assets are involved in maintaining constant the money stock. Money is wealth from the viewpoint of the real balance effect only to the extent that there is a difference between the value of money stock and the present value of the costs of maintaining that stock constant. Therefore, from the viewpoint of real balance effect, the really relevant distinction is not between inside and outside money but between money which has no cost of production. More generally, it is between money whose marginal cost of production is less than its marginal value and money whose marginal cost of production equals its marginal value. The former represents real balance effect because it leads to positive net wealth and the latter does not.

3. GROSS MONEY AND NET MONEY DOCTRINE

Gurley and Shaw have made a distinction between Gross Money Doctrine (GMD) and Net Money Doctrine (NMD) for monetary analysis. In their "modified second model", they divide the economy into three sectors: consumers, business firms and government. In the financial market, there are deficit spending nonfinancial units, surplus income units, and financial intermediaries. They deal in primary and secondary securities which are called financial assets. Financial assets are further divided into inside financial assets and outside financial assets. Inside financial assets consist of financial claims by one class of individuals and firms on others within the economy. When banks create deposits through loans and advances to individuals and firms, these return to them as secondary deposits. Inside financial assets are called inside money which is based on domestic primary securities. Outside financial assets come from outside the private sector. They consist of money issued by the government, gold, and foreign and government securities. It is called outside money which is based on the debt of a unit (the government) exogenous to the economic system.

G-S explain the relationships among the three sectors of the economy for monetary analysis in the framework of sectoral balance sheets. The first framework relates to NMD in which money is entirely of the inside variety. NMD is that which nets out all private domestic claims (i.e. financial assets) against counterclaims (financial liabilities). It, in turn, means that the net financial assets of the private sector are zero. The regard

2. B.P. Pesek and T.R. Saving, *Money, Wealth and Economic Theory,* 1967..
3. Don Patinkin, "Money and Wealth", *Journal of Economic Literature,* Dec., 1969.

NMD as inappropriate for monetary analysis because it includes money held by the business and consumer sectors and excludes that held by the government and monetary sector. On the other hand, GMD includes both inside and outside financial assets. Therefore, this doctrine is relevant for monetary analysis.

These two doctrines help in estimating the supply of money for monetary analysis. The aggregate stock of money in an economy consists of currency issued by the monetary system plus demand deposits. Here currency is outside money and demand deposits are inside money. Under GMD, the gross money supply equals the sum of inside and outside money. The aggregate stock of money supply is equal to the amount of inside securities held by the monetary system. The aggregate stock of outside money is equal to the assets held by the monetary system in the form of gold, foreign and government securities. Thus a given stock of *outside money,* according to GMD, is the aggregate money stock *minus* inside money. But, according to NMD, it is the sum of the value of gold, foreign securities and government bonds. This is because under it the net value of inside money is zero. That is why G-S favour GMD for monetary analysis.

Next, G-S discuss the determinants of the demand for real balances in the context of these two doctrines. In NMD, the total stock of real wealth is the sum of the real value of the currency and foreign securities and government bonds. In other words, it is the sum of outside money and bonds. Thus the determinants of the demand for money for real balances are the stock of real wealth, yield on real wealth, interest rate on bonds and real income. The real value of private sector securities is excluded from independent variables. On the other hand, the total stock of real wealth in GMD includes the real value of both outside and inside assets. The determinants of demand for real balances are the physical stock of real wealth, real income, real interest rate and nominal rate of interest.

According to G-S, an economy with only inside money is "money-less and bond-less", so that its price level is indeterminate. Patinkin[4] does not agree with G-S that the price level is indeterminate. According to him, an increase in the price level will not affect any demand functions in such an economy. It will be decreasing M/P, create an excess demand for money and an excess supply of bonds. This will increase the interest rate, thereby creating an excess supply of commodities and bringing down the price level again. He, therefore, finds no basis for G-S's contention that NMD leads to indeterminacy and that "the net money doctrine overlooks the bearing of portfolio balance on real bahaviour". So far as the portfolio balance is concerned, the increased price level disturbs the portfolio equilibrium of the private sector by decreasing its real money holdings relative to its bond holdings, and the attempt of the private sector to reestablish equilibrium will cause the system to return to its original position.

Patinkin also contradicts another argument of G-S that the net money doctrine implies that the "management of inside money cannot come to grips with the rate of interest." G-S argue that open market purchases will not affect the rate of interest when money is of inside variety. This is because under the assumption of full employment there is only one rate of interest at which the commodity market is in equilibrium. Hence any change in the bond or money markets alone cannot affect the equilibrium rate of interest. Patinkin does not agree with this reasoning. According to him, the open market purchases of private bonds create an excess demand for bonds and an excess supply of money, thereby bringing down the rate of interest.

Patinkin thus gives equal importance to the net money doctrine alongwith gross money doctrine for monetary analysis.

EXERCISES

1. Distinguish between inside money and outside money. Explain their relative importance in monetary analysis.
2. Distinguish between: (i) inside money and outside money; and (ii) gross money doctrine and net money doctrine.
3. Clearly distinguish between Gross Money Doctrine and Net Money Doctrine. How are they useful in explaining monetary analysis?

4. Don Patinkin, "Financial Intermediaries and the Logical Structure of Monetary Theory", *A.E.R., Vol. LI.,*, 1961.

CHAPTER 27

Neutrality and Non-Neutrality of Money

1. MEANING

Neutrality of money means that money is neutral in its effect on the economy. A change in the money stock can have no long-run influences on the level of real output, employment, rate of interest, or the composition of final output. The only lasting impact of a change in the money stock is to alter the general price level. Patinkin explains the neutrality of money as a situation when "a uniformly introduced increase in the quantity of money causes a proportionate increase in the equilibrium price of commodities and leaves the equilibrium rate of interest unaffected." provided there is absence of money illusion and distribution effects.[1] According to Gurley and Shaw, money is neutral if money is either entirely of the "outside" variety, or entirely of the "inside" variety.[2] They define neutrality of money as the "inability of changes in the nominal stock of money to affect the rate of interest, output and wealth, and other variables."

In other words, money is neutral if it does not affect relative prices and leaves the interest rate unaffected. All prices move equiproportionally. If this happens without a time lag, the neutrality of money is instantaneous. If there is a time lag, there is long-run neutrality. There are changes in absolute (money) prices, but individual economic units are unresponsive to them. The quantity of money determines only absolute prices and their level does not affect the level of income, interest, rate of capital formation and employment. It is in this sense that money is neutral in its effects on the working of the economy.

2. NEUTRALITY OF MONEY IN THE CLASSICAL SYSTEM

In the classical system, money is neutral in its effect on the economy. It plays no role in the determination of employment, income and output. Rather, they are determined by labour, capital stock, state of technology, availability of natural resources, saving habits of the people, and so on. In the classical system, the main function of money is to act as a medium of exchange. It is to determine the general level of prices at which goods and services will be exchanged. The quantity theory of money states that price level is a function of the supply of money. Algebraically, $MV = PT$, where M, V, P and T are the supply of money, velocity of money, price level, and the volume of transactions (or total output) respectively. The equation tells that the total money

1. D. Patinkin. *Money, Interest and Prices*, 2/e, 1965, p. 74.
2. J.G. Gurley and E.S. Shaw, *Money in a Theory of Finance*, 2/e, 1965.

supply, MV, equals the total value of output, *PT*, in the economy. Assuming *V* and *T* to be constant, a change in *M* causes a proportionate change in *P*. Thus money is neutral whose main function is to determine the general price level at which goods and services exchange.

The notion of neutrality of money in the classical system is explained in terms of Fig. 1. where we start with an initial full employment equilibrium position with N_0, Q_0, W/P_0, M_0, P_0, and W_0, as illustrated in Panels (A), (B), (C) and (D) of the Figure. The initial equilibrium is disturbed when the quantity of money is increased from M_0 to M_1. This leads to a rise in effective demand from MV_0 to MV_1 as shown in Panel (C). This raises commodity prices in proportion to the rise in *M*, since real output, Q_0, is fixed. In other words, the rise in *P* by $P_0P_1 = M_0M_1$ the rise in *M*. With the increase in the price level, the money wage rate will rise as rapidly as prices to W_1-P_1 (Panel D) in order to keep the real wage rate W/P_0 unchanged (Panel B). But with increase in the price level, the real wage rate tends to decrease from W/P_0 to W/P_1 as shown in Panel B of the figure. This increases the demand for labour by more than the supply of labour which is shown by the distance *sd* in Panel B. The competitive bidding for labour will ultimately lead to rise in the real wage rate to W/P_0, whereby the labour market equilibrium is restored at point *E*. Thus the result of an increase in money is to raise money wages and prices in equal proportion, leaving output, employment and the real wage rate unaffected. It is in this sense that money is neutral in the long run in the classical system.

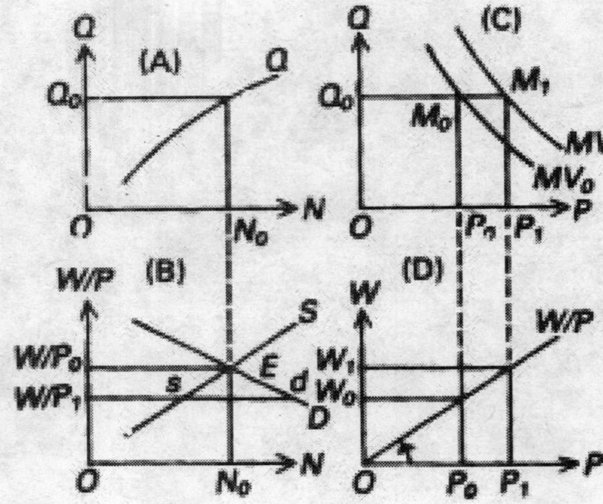

FIG. 1

Conditions for Neutrality of Money

Patinkin and Gurley and Shaw have pointed towards certain conditions or *assumptions* which must be met to establish the neutrality of money.

1. *Wage and Price Flexibility.* There must be wage and price flexibility. If prices and wages are rigid, it is possible that changes in the real wage rate and the level of real output might occur. As pointed out by Gurley and Shaw, "Price flexibility is the unseen hand that may maintain monetary equilibrium with a given nominal stock of money. Price rigidity shackles the unseen hand."

2. *Absence of Money Illusion.* People must be free of money illusion. It means that the behaviour of the people in the economic system must depend on the real and not the nominal value of such variables as output, wages etc.

3. *Absence of Distribution Effects.* Changes in the money supply must not change the distribution of income in the economic system. "Since the society consists of individuals whose tastes are different and for whom the relative attractiveness of saving versus consumption is different, income redistributions can lead to shift in saving schedule and alter the composition of real output, that is, change in relative prices."

4. *Inelastic Expectations.* It is assumed that any equilibrium price level is the permanent price level so that the spending units have inelastic price expectations. According to Patinkin, static expectations are a necessary assumption for the neutrality of money.

5. *Absence of Government Debt or Open Market Operations.* According to Metzler, the neutrality of money requires that there must be absence of government debt or open market operations in the money market.

6. *Absence of a Combination of Inside and Outside Money.* For the establishment of neutrality of money, it is essential that economy contains only "outside" or only "inside" money. According to Gurley and Shaw, "Even within a strict neo-classical framework, however, monetary policy may not be neutral on real variables when there exists a combination of inside and outside money."

7. *Perfect Information.* People must have perfect information about the conditions of demand and supply in various markets. If such information is imperfect, changes in the money supply which affect the price level can also influence such real magnitudes as saving, investment, supply and demand for labour, etc. This will lead to non-neutrality of money.

3. NEUTRALITY OF MONEY IN KEYNESIAN SYSTEM

In the entire Keynesian system, there are two situations in which money is neutral. The first is the situation of full employment when any increase in the quantity of money brings about a proportionate increase in the price level but output remains unchanged at that level. The second is the special case of liquidity trap. When the economy is in the liquidity trap, there cannot be a further fall in the- rate of interest even if the money supply is increased by monetary authorities. This implies that there will be no effect on such real variables as investment and income, and all changes in the money supply are added to idle balances. In this situation, money is neutral. However, money is non-neutral in the intermediate situation between these two extreme cases in the Keynesian system.

4. NON-NEUTRALITY OF MONEY IN KEYNESIAN & POST-KEYNESIAN THEORIES

In the Keynesian system so long as there is unemployment, changes in the money supply produce permanent non-neutral effects on the rate of interest, the level of employment, income and output, the rate of capital formation, and so on. Thus Keynes emphasized non-neutral money and for this he invoked the monetary theory of interest. He wrote: "As soon as we pass to the problem of what determines output and employment as a whole, we require the complete theory of a Monetary Economy."

The post-Keynesians, particularly Friedman,[3] Burner and Metzler have shown that money is non-neutral in the short-run. According to Friedman, interest rates cannot be used as a guide to monetary policy and that an acceleration in the rate of growth of the money supply produces not lower interest rates but higher ones, if the entire cycle of events is considered. Thus monetary policy cannot peg interest rates except for limited period. Any attempt to do so will only produce sustained inflation, just as would a similar attempt to use monetary policy to hold unemployment below its natural rate."

Besides, Friedman also believes that money may be non-neutral in the long-run. If there is a permanent acceleration in the growth rate of the money supply, say from 3 per cent to 8 per cent, it will permanently change the level of real income. This implies non-neutrality of money. This view presupposes that (i) real money balances are a productive factor to business and provider of utility to the wealthholder, and (ii) inflation reduces the real balances with business and wealth-holder.

Metzler[4] has developed a non-neutrality money model under open market operations. According to him, when the central bank's open market operations bring a change in the quantity of money, it will affect the public's holdings of assets. Thus the equilibrium rate of interest will be determined by monetary forces and money will be non-neutral. This is illustrated in Fig. 2. where the initial full employment equilibrium is at E_0, where, the IS_0 and LM_0 curves intersect so that the full employment real income is Y_0 and the corresponding equilibrium interest rate is Or_0. Suppose the central bank increases the money supply by purchasing privately held bonds through open market operations. This shifts the LM_0 curve to the right to LM_1 which intersects the IS_0 curve at E_1 so that the interest rate is reduced to Or_1 and the income rises to OY_1. This leads to an inflationary gap, over the full employment income level equal to YY_1. This inflationary process leads to real-balance effect

3. M. Friedman, *The Optimum Quantity Theory of Money and Other Essays,* 1970.
4. Lloyd A. Metzler. "Wealth, Savings and the Rate of Interest", *J.P.E.*. April, 1951.

which starts shifting the LM_1 curve backward towards its original position, as a result of decline in real balances. At the same time, the IS curve also starts shifting downwards to the left on account of a reduction in consumption as a consequence of the decline in real balances. We find that the real balance effect leads to the shifting of the LM_1, curve to the position of LM_2, curve and of the IS_0 curve to IS_1 curve in the figure. Full employment equilibrium income OY_0 is thus restored at point E_2 where the IS_1 curve intersects the LM_2 curve. But the rate of interest has now fallen from Or_0 to Or_1. This means that money is non-neutral in its effect because the equilibrium rate of interest has been permanently lowered through open market operations.

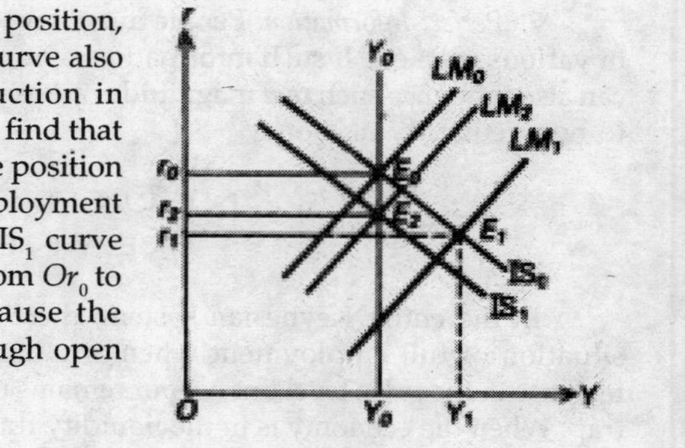

FIG. 2

EXERCISES

1. What do you mean by neutrality of money? How did the classical economists establish the neutrality of money?
2. Explain the concept of neutrality of money. What factors lead to the neutrality of money?
3. Explain how is money non-neutral?

CHAPTER 28

The Real Balance Effect

1. PATINKIN'S INTEGRATION OF MONETARY THEORY AND VALUE THEORY

Don Patinkin in his monumental work *Money, Interest and Prices*[1] criticises the Cambridge economists for the homogeneity postulate and the dichotomisation of goods and money markets and then reconciles the two markets through the real balance effect.

The homogeneity postulate states that the demand and supply of goods are affected only by relative prices. It means that a doubling of money prices will have no effect on the demand and supply of goods. Mathematically, the demand and supply function for goods are homogeneous of degree zero in prices alone. Thus this homogeneity postulate precludes the price level from affecting the goods market as well as the money market. Patinkin criticises this postulate for its failure to have any determinate theory of money and prices.

Another closely related assumption which Patinkin criticises is the dichotomisation of the goods and money markets in the neo-classical analysis. This dichotomisation means that the relative price level is determined by the demand and supply of goods, and the absolute price level is determined by the demand and supply of money. Like the homogeneity postulate, this assumption also implies that the price level has absolutely no effect on the monetary sector of the economy, and the level of monetary prices, in turn, has no effect on the real sector of the economy.

After condemning the neo-classical assumptions outlined above, Patinkin integrates the money market and the goods market of the economy which depend not only on relative prices but also on real balances. Real balances mean the real purchasing power of the stock of cash holdings of the people.

When the price level changes, it affects the purchasing power of people's cash holdings which, in turn, affects the demand and supply of goods. This is the *real balance effect.* Patinkin denies the existence of the homogeneity postulate and the dichotomisation assumption through this effect. For this, Patinkin introduces the stock of real balances *(M/P)* held by community as an influence on their demand for goods. Thus the demand for a commodity depends upon real balance as well as relative prices. Now if the price level rises, this will reduce the real balances (purchasing power) of the people who will spend less than before. This implies a fall in the demand for goods and the consequent fall in prices and wages. The price decline increases the value of money balances held by the people which, in turn, increases the demand for goods directly. The initial decrease in commodity demand creates a state of involuntary unemployment. But unemployment will not last indefinitely because as wages and prices fall, the real balance effect tends to increase commodity demand directly and indirectly through the interest rate. With sufficiently large fall in wages and prices, the full

1. D. Palinkins : Money, Interest & Price 2/e, 1965.

employment level of output and income will be restored. Finally, even if there is the "liquidity trap", the expansion of the money supply will increase money balances and full employment can be restored through the operation of the real balance effect. According to Patinkin, "This is the crucial point. The dynamic grouping of the absolute price-level towards its equilibrium value will—through the real balance effect—react on the commodity markets and hence on relative prices." Thus absolute prices play a crucial role not only in the money market but also in the real sector of the economy. Patinkin further points out that "once the real and monetary data of an economy with outside money are specified, the equilibrium values of relative prices, the rate of interest, and the absolute price level are simultaneously determined by all the markets of the economy." In this way, Patinkin also introduces the real balance effect in the general equilibrium analysis.

Besides removing the classical dichotomy and the homogeneity postulate and integrating the monetary and value theory through the real balance effect, Patinkin also validates the quantity theory conclusion. According to Patinkin, the real balance effect implies that people do not suffer from 'money illusion'. They are interested only in the real value of their cash holdings. In other words, they hold money for 'what it will buy'. This means that a doubling of the quantity of money will lead to a doubling of the price level, but relative prices and the real balances will remain constant and the equilibrium of the economy will not be changed.

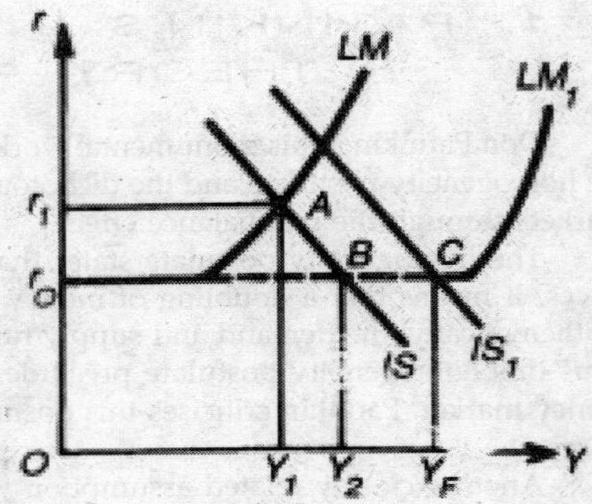

FIG. 1

The real balance effect is illustrated, diagrammatically in Fig. 1 by using the *IS* and *LM* technique because the *IS* curve represents the goods market and the *LM* curve the money market. To begin with, we take a situation when the economy is in equilibrium at OY_1 level of income when the *IS* and *LM* curves intersect at point *A* where the interest rate is Or_1. Assuming OY_F as the full employment level, the pressure of unemployment-is measured by Y_1-Y_1 which causes wages and prices to fall simultaneously. This results in an increase in the real value of people's money holdings which shifts the *LM* curve to the right to LM_1. It intersects the *IS* curve at point *B* the income level OY_2 with the result that the interest rate falls to Or_0, which stimulates investment, discourages savings and increases consumption. Even when the interest rate falls to its minimum level Or_0, the level of demand in the commodity market as represented by the *IS* curve is not high enough to lead the economy to the full employment level OY_F. Rather, unemployment measured by Y_2-Y_1 remains in the economy. This much unemployment leads to a further fall in wages and prices, and to the increase in demand for consumption goods which shifts the *IS* curve to the right to IS_1 so that it intersects the LM_1, curve at point C at the full employment level OY_F.

Thus under conditions of wage and price flexibility when the *IS* and *LM* curves shift rightwards, the real balance effect ultimately leads the economy to full employment level, even in the liquidity trap situation as shown above when investment is interest inelastic.

Conclusion. Thus the real balance effect demonstrates three theoretical points: *first,* it eliminates the classical dichotomy between value and monetary theory; *second,* it validates the conclusions of the quantity theory that in equilibrium, money is neutral and the interest rate is independent of the quantity of money through the real balance effect; and *third,* the wage-price flexibility leads to full employment in the long-run and that the Keynesian underemployment equilibrium is a disequilibrium situation.

ITS CRITICISMS

Patinkin's analysis of the real balance effect has been severely criticised by Johnson, Archibald, Lipsey, Lloyd and other economists.

1. *Not Applicable in Equilibrium Situations.* Johnson[2] points out that there is no need for the real balance effect so long as the real analysis is confined to equilibrium situations. The real balance is needed only to ensure

2. Harry G. Johnson, *Essays in Monetary Theory, 2/e,* 1969

the stability of the price level and not to determine the real equilibrium of the system.

2. *Conceptually Inadequate.* Archibald and Lipsey[3] regard Patinkin's analysis of the real balance effect as conceptually inadequate. According to them, Patinkin traces the real balance analysis as a short-run phenomenon and does not work it out through the long-run.

3. *Price Stability Without Real Balance Effect.* Cliff Lloyd[4] has criticised Patinkin for holding the classical view that people do not suffer from 'money illusion', and that their behaviour is influenced by the real balance effect. He has shown that the stability of the price level can be had without taking the real balance effect. According to him, by assuming that money is available in fixed quantity and people want to hold it, will bring price stability. But 'money illusion' will not be absent.

4. *Failure to Explain Increase in Monetary Wealth.* Shaw[5] has criticised Patinkin for his failure to analyse the manner in which the increase in monetary wealth comes about. According to him, Patinkin simply assumes a doubling of money balances and analyses only the resultant effects. In practice, money stock does not change in this manner. "Nor, in most cases, do people experience the happy variations of helicopters carrying a surfeit of bank notes. . ."

Conclusion. Despite these criticisms, "the introduction of the real balance effect disposes of the classical dichotomy, that is, it makes it impossible to talk about relative prices without introducing money; but it nevertheless preserves the classical proposition that the real equilibrium of the system will not be affected by the amount of money, all that will be affected will be the level of prices."

2. THE PIGOU EFFECT

The Pigou effect, also known as the *wealth effect,* was propounded by A.C. Pigou in 1943 to counter Keynes' argument that wage-price deflation cannot lead to automatic full employment.

Pigou fully recognised that interest-rate effect of Keynes that wage-price deflation raises investment and income through a reduction in the interest rate. But he did not agree that the real income cannot be raised to the level of full employment due to liquidity trap. According to Pigou, a wage-price deflation will generate automatic full employment via an increase in the level of consumption. He argued that when money wages are cut, prices fall and the value of money rises. The rise in the value of money means a rise in the real value of assets such as stocks, shares, bank deposits, government securities, bonds, etc. For example, if prices fall by 50 per cent, the real value of each rupee will be doubled because it will purchase twice as much as it did before. The increase in the real value of fixed assets will make their owners feel richer than before. They will, therefore, save less out of their current income and spend more on consumption. This will increase aggregate demand and output, and will generate automatic full employment in the economy. As a result of the Pigou effect, the consumption function will shift upward (or the saving function will shift downward). In terms of the *IS* function, it means a rightward shift of the *IS* curve.

The important point in Pigou effect is that it is based on the assumptions of flexible wage and price levels, and a constant stock of money. Therefore, it is only the *IS* curve that shifts to the right with increase in consumption or reduction in saving when the real value of fixed assets increases. The *LM* curve is assumed to be given because of the assumption of a constant stock of money. This is because the analysis of Pigou effect runs strictly in terms of static analysis.

Another important point is that this analysis is based upon the flexibility of absolute prices. Patinkin summarises the Pigou effect in the following theorem: "There always exists a sufficiently low price level such that, if expected to continue indefinitely, it will generate full employment." Algebraically, if the money supply which is assumed to be constant is M_0 and the price level is $P_{,1}$ then the saving function (or consumption function) will be $S=f\ [RY\ (M_0/P)]$. Thus saving depends upon the interest rate (R), income (Y) and the ratio of given money supply to absolute prices $\{M_0/P)$. When prices fall the real value of a given stock of money rises

3. G.C. Archibald and R.G Lipsey, 'Monetary and Value Theory: A Critique of Lange and Patinkin', *R.S.E.,* XXXI, (1) No. 69, OCTOBER 1958.
4. The Real Balance Effect: *Sine Que* What? *O.E.P..* XIV No. 3, October, 1962.
5. G K Shaw, *An Introduction to the Theory of Macro-economic Policy,* 1971.

and people reduce their saving or increase consumption, thereby increasing aggregate demand. This process will automatically lead the economy to the level of full employment when decline in wages and prices stops. In the Pigou effect, interest elasticities and positions of the saving and investment functions are irrelevant.

The Pigou effect is illustrated in Fig. 2 (A) and (B). To begin with Panel (A) of the figure, suppose the economy is at Y_1 level of income as determined by IS_1 and LM_0 functions at E_1. Now wage-price deflation starts which raises the consumption function such that the IS_1 function shifts rightwards to IS_3. Given the LM_0 function, the IS_3 function intersects the LM_0 function at E_3 thereby raising the income level from OY_1 to OY_P, the full employment level. Panel (B) of the figure shows that as the price level falls from P_3 to P_1 with reduction in money wages, income increases from OY_1 to the full employment level OY_F through increase in aggregate demand via the Pigou effect. This is shown by the downward sloping aggregate demand curve AD.

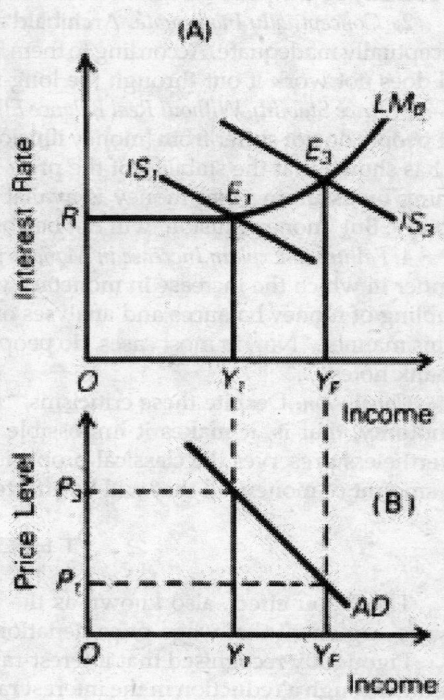

FIG. 2

ITS CRITICISMS

The Pigou effect led to a sort of warfare among the neo-classicals and the neo-Keynesians. It appeared that the former had scored a victory over the latter by providing theoretically that if wage-price deflation is incorporated in the Keynesian model, it will automatically lead to full employment of the economy. But the neo-Keynesian resistance to the Pigou effect has been so strong that economists have pointed out a number of defects in Pigou's analysis of wage price deflation as a means to automatic full employment. The following arguments are advanced against the Pigou analysis :

1. *Ignores Distributional Effects.* The Pigou effect assumes that the depressing effect of a reduction in the price level is offset by its stimulating effect on creditors. Therefore, the private sector being a creditor to the government is stimulated by a reduction in the price level. But there are debtors other than the government. So a price decline will have different reactions on debtors and creditors. Creditors are encouraged to increase their expenditures while debtors are discouraged. But if the debtors are discouraged more than the creditors are encouraged, the price decline will not have encouraging effects on expenditures. Thus Pigou overlooked the possibility of micro-economic "distributional effects."

2. *Neglects the Effect of Wage-Price Deflation on Firms.* The Pigou effect considers only the effects of a change in real balances on consumption or saving of the household sector. It neglects the influence of real balances on firms. This is a serious defect in the Pigou analysis because the motivations of households and firms are different. Investment decisions of firms are favourably influenced when their real balances increase. But if firms are debtors and a price decline continues to persist, it will cause bankruptcies of firms. When debtors become bankrupt, creditors also lose. This will have a depressing effect on the economy. Thus a price decline will not lead to increase in aggregate demand and to automatic full employment in the economy.

3. *Effect on Savings Uncertain.* Another defect of the Pigou analysis is that it assumes a definite knowledge about the effect on saving (or consumption) of an increase in the real balances. As a matter of fact, little is known about this. Moreover, only a small proportion of the lower income groups which form the majority of the population in a country, possess appreciable quantity of assets. Thus very few people save and those who save do not increase their consumption expenditures with the increase in the real value of their assets, following a price decline. Rather, they like to save more as their assets increase.

4. *Wage-Price Deflation not Once-for-all.* The Pigou analysis is based on the assumption of once-for-all wage-price decline. It, therefore, regards a price decline as a temporary phenomenon which is likely to be

reversed when recovery starts. In practice, once-for-all price decline is not obtained. Even if it exists it is not reasonable to suppose that people will feel richer and increase their consumption expenditures at a single price decline.

5. *Difficult to Measure Quantitatively.* The Pigou effect is difficult to weigh quantitatively, that is, how much consumer expenditure will increase for any given decline in the price level. "In the face of a certain amount of unemployment, it is one thing if a 10 per cent decline in the price level and accompanying increase in the real value of the stock of currency and government securities is sufficient to raise consumption spending by the amount needed to restore full employment; it is quite another if the Pigou effect is so weak that the same result can be achieved with an 80 per cent decline in the price level. If a major deflation is required, this in itself rules out reliance on the Pigou effect as a practical means of restoring an economy to full employment.[6] According to Shapiro, "A hyperdeflation may satisfy the purely theoretical requirements of the Pigou effect, but in practice it might also produce economic distress leading to riots and even revolution."

6. *Neglects Price Expectations.* Another weakness of the Pigou effect is that it neglects the role of price expectations. It is not that the price level declines only once in practice. Rather, once there is a wage-price deflation, it creates expectations of a further decline in prices. This is because of the generation of pessimism among businessmen and consumers who have a tendency to reduce their expenditures in the expectation of further decline in prices. Under the circumstances, the Pigou analysis is not likely to lead to automatic full employment.

7. *Pigou Effect Disappears in the Lower Turning Point of a Trade Cycle.* Taking the Pigou analysis in relation to the trade cycle, a once-for-all wage-price reduction will not lead to complete recovery and to full employment. Suppose the wage-price deflation has been completed and the consequent rise in real balances and in the consumption function takes the economy to the level of recovery. But as recovery continues, prices will begin to rise and the real balances with the public will start declining. So the Pigou effect will disappear once the lower turning point of a trade cycle is reached. According to Hansen "it applies to a situation like that of 1936-40 in the United States, when prices *had* fallen and become established *at a lower level.*"[7]

8. *Static in Nature.* The Pigou effect is in terms of static analysis which assumes a constant stock of money. But the real world is dynamic where wage-price deflation with a constant stock of money will lead to full employment only after a long period, or it might even lead to a deflationary spiral with continuous unemployment.

Thus the Pigou analysis leading to automatic full employment is unrealistic and impracticable. As he himself wrote, "The puzzles we have been considering ...are academic exercises, of some slight use perhaps for clarifying thought, but with very little chance of ever being posed on the chequer board of actual life."[8]

3. DIFFERENCE BETWEEN PIGOU EFFECT AND REAL BALANCE EFFECT

Both the terms *"Pigou effect"* and *"real balance effect"* have been coined by Patinkin, but they are not the same, rather, they are quite different. The Pigou effect is a static analysis which consists of the effect of a wage-price deflation on consumption, given the constant stock of money or what Gurley and Shaw call *"outside money"* which includes gold, government securities and fiat paper money. It shows that when consumption increases as a result of wage-price deflation, the *IS* curve shifts to the right such that it intersects a given *LM* function and automatic full employment is attained in the economy.

The real balance effect is a modified version of the Pigou effect given by Patinkin. It is a dynamic analysis which comprises both the Pigou effect and the Keynes effect. The Keynes effect shows that as a result of wage-price deflation when the real value of money increases, smaller transactions, balances are needed which create more demand for securities. Consequently the prices of securities rise and the rate of interest falls at each level of income so that the *LM* curve shifts to the right.

---

6. Edward Shapiro, *op. cit..* p. 419.
7. *Op. cit.,* p.180
8. Economic Progress in a Stable Environment," *Economica,* Vol. XIV, 1947.

Thus the operation of the Keynes effect shifts only the *LM* function to the right and that of the Pigou effect only the *IS* function to the right. But in the real balance effect both the *LM* and *IS* functions are shifted to the right till they intersect at the level of full employment. In the real balance effect, elasticities of the *IS* and *LM* functions are irrelevant. The *LM* curve may be perfectly elastic i.e. in the Keynesian liquidity trap region, or the *IS* curve may be perfectly inelastic, the level of full employment is automatically attained.

EXERCISES

1. Examine Patinkin's contribution to the analysis of the relationship between money supply, interest rate and price level.
2. Explain how Don Patinkin's Real Balance Effect is an improvement over the classical version of the Quantity Theory.
3. Explain the Real Balance Effect. How does it differ from the Pigou Effect and Keynes Effect'.?
4. Explain the Pigou Effect. In what way Patinkin has improved over it in his Real Balance Effect?
5. Examine Pigou's view that price-wage flexibility leads to full employment in the economy.

CHAPTER 29

Patinkin's General Equilibrium Model

1. INTRODUCTION

Keynes was critical of the neo-classical dichotomy between value and monetary theory which was established on the basis of Say's Law and concentrated on the equilibrium system. It was Keynes and his successors who through the liquidity trap, money illusion and rigid prices and wages explained a "general theory" of the determination of interest and prices in which money played a secondary role. Patinkin in his *Money, Interest and Prices* (1965) pointed towards the *invariance* of the real equilibrium of the economy which implies that monetary changes cause an equiproportionate change in the absolute price level and leaves relative prices unchanged. According to him, this was not a major problem which could be eliminated. "by making the demand and supply functions depend on real cash balances as well as relative prices. While this would eliminate the dichotomy, it would preserve the basic features of the classical monetary theory and particularly the invariance of the real equilibrium of the economy (relative prices and rate of interest) with respect to changes in the quantity of money".

2. THE PATINKIN MODEL

Patinkin has developed a neo-classical general equilibrium model in which money is neutral which is called the invariance of the real equilibrium of the economy.

Its Assumptions. The model is based on the following assumptions:

1. There is wage-price flexibility.
2. There is no money illusion.
3. The price of money is unity.
4. Money is purely outside money.
5. There is perfect certainty as to future prices and interest rates.
6. There are spot transactions for all goods.
7. There is absence of distribution effects.
8. Bonds are homogeneous.
9. There is absence of government debt.
10. There are no open market operations.

Given these assumptions, the Patinkin general-equilibrium model has four markets: (1) The market for labour, (2) the market for commodities, (3) the market for bonds, and (4) the market for money. For each market, there are three equations: a demand equation, a supply equation, and an equilibrium equation, which specifies the conditions of equilibrium in a market. For each market, there are also three variables: the amount demanded, the amount supplied, and the price of the goods in question. By virtue of the Walras Law, if equilibrium exists in any three of these markets, it must also exist in the fourth. Therefore, to understand the whole economy, it is sufficient to concentrate on any three markets. The Patinkin general equilibrium relates to the short run because the long-run equilibrium would require the same short-run solution to prevail week after week, according to Patinkin.

1. The Market for Labour Services

In the market for labour services, both the amount demanded of labour *(Nd)* and the amount supplied of labour *(Ns)* depend on the real wage rate *(w/p)* where *w* is the money wage rate and *p* is the general price level of commodities. The equations for this market equilibrium are:

$$N_d = Q\left(\frac{w}{p}, K_o\right) \qquad ...(1)$$

This equation represents the demand curve for labour which is negatively sloped with respect to increase in the real wage rate on the assumption that the law of diminishing marginal productivity holds. In this equation *Ko* represents the total fixed capital equipment of the economy.

The supply curve of labour is represented by the equation:

$$N_s = R\left(\frac{w}{p}\right) \qquad ...(2)$$

The supply of labour depends on the real wage rate and is an increasing function of *(w/p)* so that the supply curve of labour slopes positively.

For this market to be in equilibrium, the following condition, must be satisfied:

$$N_d = N_s \qquad ...(3)$$

This implies that the amount demanded and supplied of labour must equal at an equilibrium wage rate.

The equilibrium of this market is presented diagrammatically in Fig. 1. The curves N_d and N_s intersect at point *E* where the equilibrium wage rate is $(w/p)_o$ which corresponds to N_o amount of labour. If the real wage rate were above this equilibrium level, there would be an excess supply of labour and money wages would fall. On the other hand, if it were below, there would be an excess demand for labour and money wages would rise.

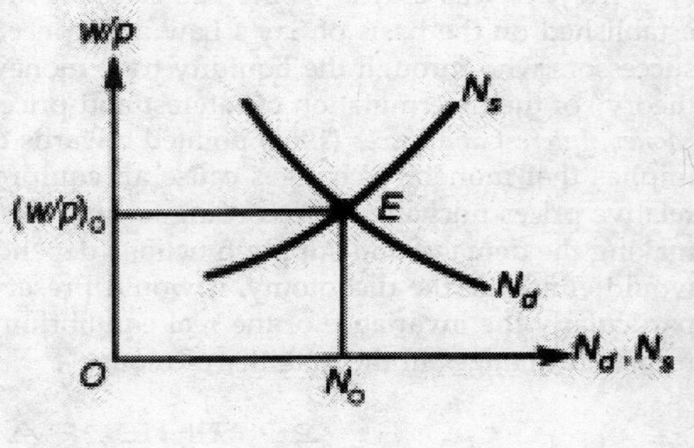

FIG. 1

2. The Market for Commodities

The aggregate demand function *(E)* for commodities is the sum of consumption, investment, and government demands. It is written as

$$E = F\left(Y, r\frac{M_0}{p}\right) \qquad ...(4)$$

where *Y* is the gross national income *r* is the rate of interest; and *M/p* the real value of cash balances in the economy, and *r=ro* and *p=po* so that the equation becomes $E = F(Y, r_o, M_o/p_o)$

" The aggregate demand function in Fig. 2 shows the total amount demanded of commodities at varying levels of real income, assuming the interest rate and price level remaining constant. Further, the relation between the aggregate demand function (*E*) and the real value of cash balances (M_o/p_o) is direct. An increase in the price level above P_o causes an increase in M_o/p and a consequent downward shift in E which causes the amount of commodities demanded to decrease, and vice versa. Thus the. aggregate demand function reflects the absence of money illusion. It implies that any change which affects neither real income and the interest rate nor the real cash balances does not affect economic behaviour. The aggregate supply function (Y) for the economy is dependent on the real wage rate $(w/p)_o$, and on its fixed amount of capital (K_o). This function is expressed as

$$Y = S\left(\frac{w}{p}_o, K_o\right) \quad \text{...(5)}$$

For any given real wage rate, the aggregate supply for commodities is a vertical line drawn at the level of gross national product for that specified wage rate.

The equilibrium condition for the commodity market is

$$E = Y \quad \text{... (6)}$$

The market equilibrium for commodities is illustrated in Fig. 2 when the demand curve E and the supply curve Y intersect on the 45° line at point A. Suppose the interest rate remains r_o but the price and wage levels fall in the same proportion below p_o and w_o respectively. Thus the real wage rate remains unaffected. So the supply curve is not affected. But, due to the real balance effect, the demand function rises and shifts to E_1. The new equilibrium level becomes point B. But the real output level remains fixed at the full employment level Y_o. At point B, there is an excess of commodities demanded over supplied equal to BA. This gap drives the price level upwards, thereby reducing the value of cash balances. This shifts the E_1 curve downwards to E. Again, beginning from point A, if the price level rises due to a fall in the real value of cash balances, the demand function falls and it shifts to E_2. The new equilibrium is at C where there is excess of commodities supplied over demanded equal to AC. This leads to the accumulation of inventories and the price level falls, thereby raising the value of real cash balances. This shifts the E_2 curve upwards to E. Thus equilibrium in the commodity market can exist only when the demand curve intersects the supply curve at point A.

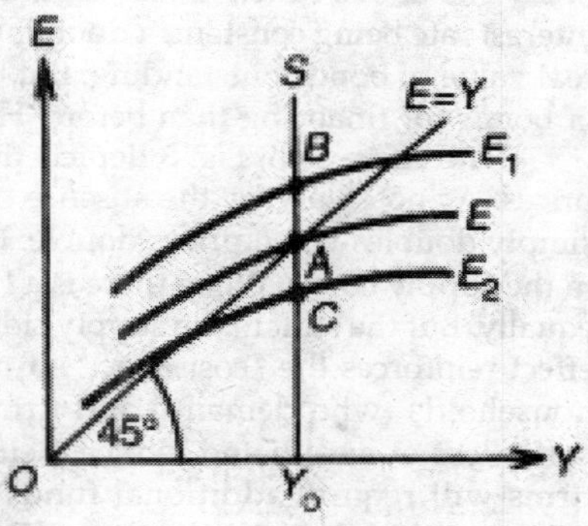

FIG. 2

3. The Market for Bonds

It is assumed in the bond market that only households demand bonds and firms supply bonds. The demand for bonds is expressed by the equation:

$$\frac{B_d}{Y_p} = H\left(Y, \frac{1}{r}, \frac{M_o^H}{p}\right) \quad \text{... (7)}$$

where B_d represents the number of bonds demanded; Y, the real national income; r, the interest rate; $1/r$ the per unit price of bonds (in dollars); and M_0^H, the initial nominal money holdings of households.

The above function in equation (6) describes that the real valm of bond holdings demanded depends on real income, interest rate and the reai value of cash balances held by households. It assumes that there is absence of money illusion. It implies that real income and interest rate being constant, a doubling of prices and initial household holdings $\{M_o^H/p)$ does not affect the amount demanded of real bond holdings (B_d/rp). It only causes the doubling of amount demanded of nominal bond holdings (B_d). The demand curve for bonds at a fixed level of real income and prices is represented by the curve B_d in Fig. 3.

The supply of bonds is represented by the equation:

$$\frac{B_d}{Y_p} = J^f\left(Y, \frac{1}{r}, \frac{M_o^F}{p}\right) \quad \text{... (8)}$$

where, *B* represents the supply of bonds which remains outstanding with firms under various conditions.

What happens to the supply of bonds if these conditions change? It is assumed that an increase in gross real national product increases the amount of bonds supplied. The greater the volume of production, the greater are the requirements of firms for loan capital to finance the necessary plant, equipment and inventories. On the other hand, an increase in real cash balances decreases the amount supplied. Further, an increase in interest rate decreases the amount of real bonds supplied. For the firms will reduce their cash balances when the interest rate rises and use the proceeds to repay their debt. Moreover, with high interest rate, the demand for investment goods will be less and fewer projects will have to be financed. Thus the real value of bonds outstanding *(B_s/rp)* decreases. But the number of bonds outstanding *(B_s)* may decrease, because the rise in interest rate lowers the price of bonds and so may increase the number of bonds required to finance the expenditures of firms on investment goods even though these expenditures have decreased.

The above function also assumes the absence of money illusion. It again implies that real income and interest rate being constant, a doubling of prices, wages, and initial money holdings of firms does not affect the real value of bonds outstanding. But due to increase in prices and costs, they require twice the nominal value of bonds for financing than before. Hence the number of bonds outstanding *(B_s)* doubles.

The curve B_s in Fig. 3 depicts the supply function of bonds at a fixed level of real national product and prices. As noted above, the absence of money illusion means that the nominal demand and supply of bonds simply doubles when prices double. But the shift in the demand curve for bonds is assumed not equal to that in the supply curve. When there is a Price rise, both the demand and supply curves for bonds shift to the right equally. But the shift in the supply side is more than proportionate to the increase in Prices. For the real balance effect reinforces the "cost effect". It means that though both households (who demand) and firms (suppliers) of bonds suffer loss of wealth and reduce their holdings of bonds, yet firms will require additional funds to replenish their real balances which have been reduced. For this, they issue bonds. The condition for equilibrium in the bond market is:

$$B_d = B_s \quad \text{... (8)}$$

which is shown in Fig. 3. The equilibrium will exist only at point *E* where the curves B_d and B_s intersect at the interest rate $1/r_o$. If the interest rate were less than this, there would be an excess supply of bonds thereby lowering the price of bonds and *ipso facto* raising the interest rate and reestablishing equilibrium. If the interest rate were higher than the equilibrium rate, there would be an excess demand for bonds, thereby driving the interest rate down to the equilibrium level.

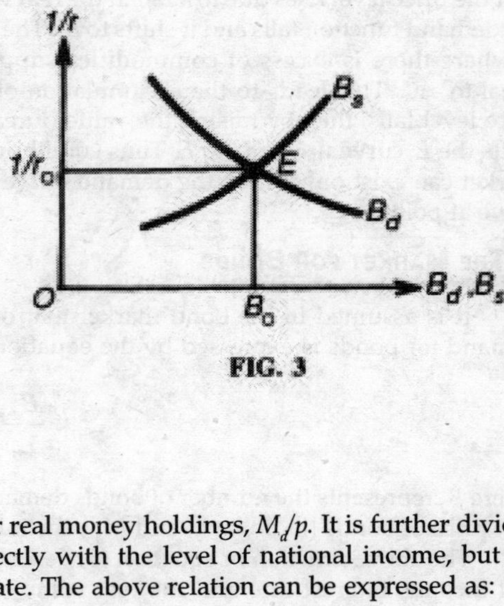

FIG. 3

4. The Market for Money

It is assumed that the demand function for money is for real money holdings, M_d/p. It is further divided into transactions and precautionary demand. Both vary directly with the level of national income, but the speculative motive has an inverse relation with the interest rate. The above relation can be expressed as:

$$\frac{M_d}{P} = L_1(Y) + L_2(r)$$

or

$$M_d = pL_1(Y) + pL_2(r)$$

where $L_1(Y)$ relates to the transactions and precautionary demand and $L_2(r)$ to be speculative demand for money.

The demand function for real money balances can be expressed as:

$$M_d = pL\left(Y, r, \frac{m_0}{p}\right) \qquad ...(9)$$

By assuming the price level and real income constant, the demand curve for money depends on the interest rate which is sloping downwards. It reflects the joint operation of the transactions plus precautionary and speculative motives. A fall in the interest rate increases the demand for money, and vice versa. On the other hand, an increase in either real income *(Y)* or initial money balances *(M_o/p)*, causes a rightwards shift in the demand for money curve. At the same rate, the money demanded is more than before.

Let us assume that the nominal amount of money is fixed at the constant level M_o so that the supply function is

$$M_s = M_o \qquad ... (10)$$

The equilibrium condition for the money market is

$$M_d = M_s \qquad ...(11)$$

which is illustrated in Fig. 4 when the M_d and M_s curves intersect at point *E* and produce the interest rate r_o. If the interest rate were above r_o, there would be a fall in the demand for money. This implies a fall in the price of bonds and a decline in their supply. This would bring down the interest rate to the equilibrium level r_o. On the contrary, if the interest rate were below r_o, then there would be an increase in the demand for money. This implies an increase in the price of bonds leading to their excess supply. This would raise the interest rate to the equilibrium level r_o.

Let us now investigate the effects of a doubling of the quantity of money. This shifts the supply curve rightwards to M_2S_2. It creates an excess supply of money at the equilibrium interest rate r_o which is equal to *EF* (ignore the curve Md_2 for the present). Assuming prices to be constant, the equilibrium can be reestablished in this market only at an interest rate lower than r_0. For it is only by such a reduction that individuals can be induced to hold the additional money now available. But prices cannot remain constant. This is because an excess money supply *(EF)* leads to an excess demand in the commodity market which raises the price level and, in turn, increases the demand for money and shifts the demand curve rightwards to Md_2 In other words, at a higher price level individuals hold larger money balances in order to meet their various needs.

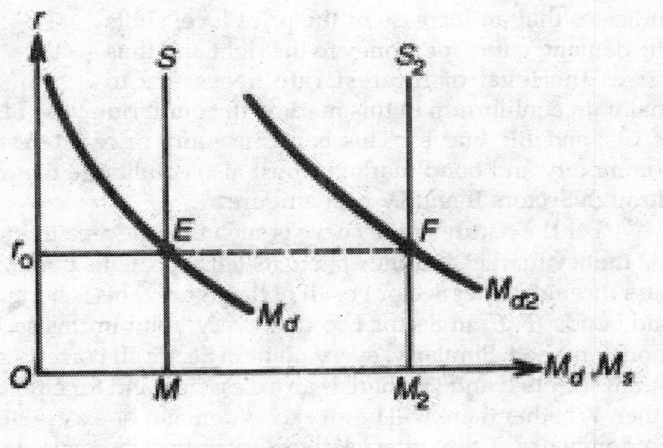

FIG. 4

Hence when the price level doubles, the amount demanded will also double at any given interest rate. That is why, the curve Md_2 intersects the new supply curve M_2S_2 at the same interest rate r_o at point *F*. Patinkin concludes that "the dependence of demand on the absolute price level (as implied by the absence of money illusion) ensures that the transactions, precautionary, and speculative demand for money can together ultimately absorb all of the additional supply — even at an unchanged rate of interest".

5. THE FULL GENERAL EQUILIBRIUM

Having studied the equilibrium of commodity, factor and money markets respectively, let us analyse the simultaneous equilibrium of all the three markets of the model. This is explained in terms of Fig. 5. Consider first the general equilibrium condition of the commodity market where for every interest rate there exists a price level with a corresponding real balance effect just exactly large enough to maintain the state of equilibrium in this market. Let the curve CC_1 be the locus of all such pairs of equilibrium values of the interest rate and price level. The negative slope of the curve reveals that any point to the right of the CC_1 curve reflects a state of excess supply which drives the price level downwards. Contrariwise, any point to the left of the CC_1 curve indicates a state of excess demand which drives the price level upwards.

Similarly, a curve BB_1 can be constructed which is a locus of all pairs of interest rates and price level for which the bond market is in equilibrium. This curve has a positive slope. Any point above the BB_1 curve indicates a state of excess demand which drives the interest rate downwards. Conversely, any point below it reflects a state of excess supply which drives the interest rate upwards.

The curve LL_1 is the locus of all pairs of equilibrium values of the interest rate and the price level for which the demand for and supply of money are equal. Its slope is positive which indicates that an increase in the price level shifts the demand curve for money to the right and thus raises the level of interest rate necessary to maintain equilibrium in this market. In equilibrium, the LL_1 curve must pass through point G, the intersection of CC_1 and BB_1 curves. This is because any price-interest combination, which brings equality between the commodity and bond markets, must also equilibrate the money market. In addition, the curve LL_1 must pass through Sectors II and IV of the figure.

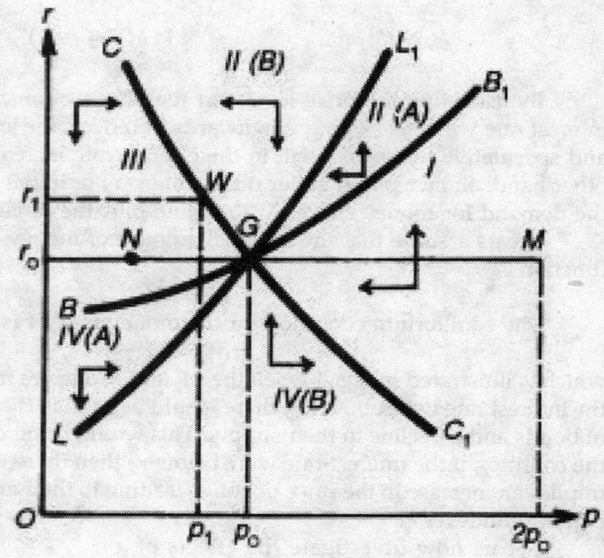

FIG. 5

For the nature of the curve is such that the area to its right represents a state of excess demand *(L >O)* in the money market and the area to its left represents points of excess supply (L<*0*). Hence the curve LL_1 cannot pass through either Sector I or III of the figure. This is because there is excess supply of both commodities *(C<0)* and bonds *(B<0)* in Sector I so that every point in this sector corresponds to a state of excess demand in the money market. Similarly, every point in Sector III corresponds to a state of excess supply in the money market. But in sectors II and IV, there is an excess demand for either commodities or bonds, and an excess supply of the other. Whether there will be an excess demand or excess supply for money depends on which of the two forces predominates. These interrelationship among the markets are shown in Table 1.

Table 1: Inter-relationship among the Markets

Sector or Curve	*Commodities*		*Market Bonds*	*Money*
I	excess supply		excess supply	excess demand
II(A)	excess supply	>	excess demand	excess demand
LL_1	excess supply	=	excess demand	equilibrium
II(B)	excess supply	<	excess demand	excess supply
III	excess demand		excess demand	excess supply
IV(A)	excess demand	>	excess supply	excess supply
LL_1	excess demand	=	excess supply	equilibrium
IV(B)	excess demand	<	excess supply	excess demand

Let us see what happens to these curves when the factors affecting each one of them change. Suppose the quantity of money is doubled. It will shift all the three curves twice as far as to the right so that they intersect at point *M*. Similarly, a neutral increase in liquidity preference will shift all three to the left so that they intersect at *N*. An increase in liquidity preference is only at the expense of bonds so that the curve CC_1 remains unaffected and the curves BB_1 and LL_1 shift to the left so as to intersect at point *W* on the curve CC_1. It means a higher interest rate r_1 and a lower price level p_1 than the equilibrium level *G*. In short, it can be said that any change in the liquidity preference depends on the strength of the real balance effect in the commodity market.

3. DEFECTS OF THE PATINKIN MODEL

The Patinkin model explains the general equilibrium of the economy by taking into consideration the real balance effect. However, Brunner and Metzler, and a few other economists have pointed out certain defects which affect its efficient operation. They are as follows:

1. The assumption of full employment makes the analysis unrealistic.
2. The interest rate is the only relative price in the model so that the analysis of substitution effects necessary to understand the adjustment mechanisms in the economy is not possible.
3. The real balance effect is neither necessary nor a sufficient condition for a positive response of output to changes in money.
4. In fact, the possibility of substitution between money and other assets raises the possibility that the real balance effect can be negative.

But these weaknesses do not undermine the usefulness of the model for analytical purposes.

EXERCISES

1. Explain Patinkin's General Equilibrium Model.
2. Explain briefly Patinkin's General Equilibrium Model when money is neutral. What are its limitations?

CHAPTER 30

IS and LM Functions : General Equilibrium of Product and Money Markets

1. INTRODUCTION

This chapter integrates money, interest and income into a general equilibrium model of product and money markets in the Hicks-Hansen[1] diagrammatic framework, known as the *IS-LM* model. The term *IS* is the shorthand expression of the equality of investment and saving which represents the product market equilibrium. On the other hand, the term *LM* is the shorthand expression of the equality of money demand (*L*) and money supply (*M*) and represents the money market equilibrium.

In order to analyse the general equilibrium of product and money markets, it is instructive to study the derivation of the IS and LM functions and their slopes for the understanding of the effectiveness of monetary and fiscal policies.

2. THE PRODUCT MARKET EQUILIBRIUM

The product market is in equilibrium when desired saving and investment are equal. Saving is a direct function of the level of income,

$$S = f(Y) \qquad ...(1)$$

Investment is a decreasing function of the interest rate,

$$I = f(r) \qquad ...(2)$$

From (1) and (2), we have $S=I$.

The *IS* schedule reflects the equilibrium of the product market. It shows the combinations of interest rate and income levels where saving-investment equality takes place so that the product market of the economy is in equilibrium. It is also known as the "*real sector*" equilibrium.

DERIVING THE IS CURVE

The derivation of the *IS* curve is shown in Figure 1. In Panel (A) of this figure, the saving curve *S* in relation to income is drawn in a fixed position on the Keynesian assumption that the rate of interest has little effect on saving. The saving curve shows that saving increases as income increases, viz., saving is an *increasing*

1. J.R. Hicks, "Mr Keynes and the Classics: A Suggested Interpretation," *Econometrica*, April 1937, reprinted in M.G. Mueller (ed), *Readings in Macroeconomic*, pp. 137-147, and A.H. Hansen, *Monetary Theory and Fiscal Policy*, Ch. 5.

function of income. Investment, on the other hand, depends on the rate of interest and the level of income. Given a level of interest rate, the level of investment rises with the level of income. At a 5 per cent rate of interest, the investment curve is I_2. If the rate of interest is reduced to 4 per cent, the investment curve will shift upward to I_3. The rate of investment will have to be raised to reduce the marginal efficiency of capital to equality with the lower rate of interest. Thus the investment curve I_3 shows more invesment at every level of income. Similarly when the rate of interest is raised to 6 per cent, the investment curve will shift downward to I_1. The reduction in the rate of investment is essential to raise the marginal efficiency of capital to equal the higher interest rate. In Panel (B) we drive the *IS* curve by marking the level of income at various interest rates. Each point on this *IS* curve represents a level of income at which saving equals investment at various interest rates. The rate of interest is represented on the vertical axis and the level of income on the horizontal axis. If the rate of interest is 6 per cent, the *S* curve intersects the I_1 curve at E_1 in Panel (A) which determines OY_1 income. From this income level which equals Rs 100 crores we draw a dashed line downward to intersect the extended line from 6 per cent at point *A* in Panel (B). At interest rate 5 per cent, the S curve intersects the I_2 curve at E_2 so as to determine OY_2 income (Rs 200 crores). In the lower figure, the point *B* corresponds to 5 per cent interest rate and Rs 200 crores income level. Similarly, the point *C* corresponds to the equilibrium of *S* and I_3 at 4 per cent interest rate. By connecting these points *A*, *B* and *C* with a line, we get the *IS* curve. The *IS* curve in Figure 1(B) slopes *downward* from left to right because as the interest rate falls, investment increases and so do income and saving. In other words, there is a negative relationship between income and interest rate in the real sector of the economy.

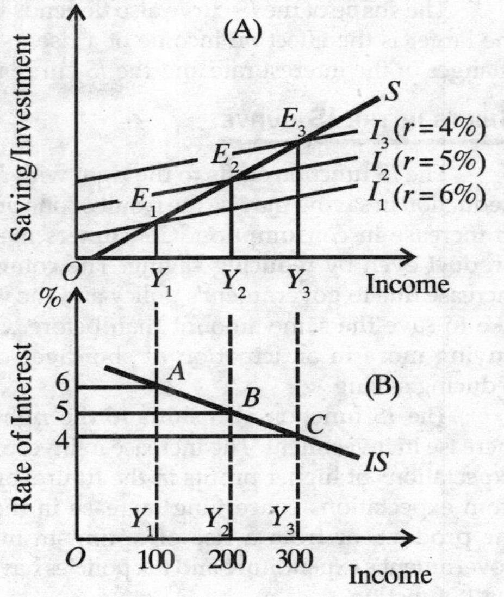

Fig. 1

The Slope of the IS Curve

This negative slope of the *IS* curve reflects the increase in investment and income as the rate of interest falls. The slope of the *IS* curve depends on two factors: *first*, the sensitiveness (elasticity) of investment and saving to changes in the interest rate, and *second*, on the size of the multiplier.

If investment is very sensitive to the rate of interest, the *IS* curve is very *flat*. This is shown by the segment *AB* of the *IS* curve in Figure 2 where a small fall in the rate of interest from R_1 to R_2 leads to a large increase in investment and consequently in saving via proportionately large rise in income from Y_1 to Y_2. The *IS* curve is *interest elastic* in the *AB* segment of the *IS* curve.

On the other hand, if investment is not very sensitive to the rate of interest, the *IS* curve is relatively *steep*. In terms of Figure 2, when the rate of interest falls more from R_2 to R_3, the increase in investment is small and so do saving and income increase by a relatively smaller amount Y_2Y_3. The *BC* segment of the *IS* curve is *less interest elastic.*

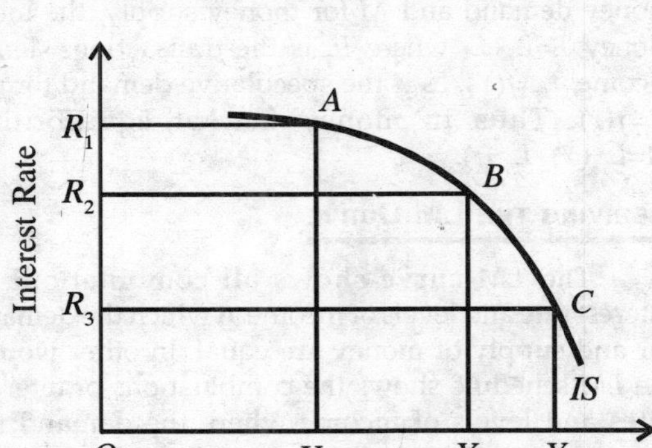

Fig. 2

Any further fall in the rate of interest from R_3 will lead to no change in income because the *IS* curve is vertical in that range. It is *interest inelastic.*

The shape of the *IS* curve also depends upon the size of the multiplier. If the size of the multiplier is large, the larger is the effect on income of a rise in investment and fall in saving. Thus income is more sensitive to changes in the interest rate and the *IS* curve is flatter.

SHIFTS IN THE IS CURVE

The *IS* function shifts to the right with a reduction in saving. Reduction in saving may be the result of one or more factors leading to increase in consumption. Consumers may like to buy a new product even by reducing saving. The community's wealth may increase due to government's policy and the wealth holders do not like to save the same amount than before. Consumers may start buying more in anticipation of shortages or price rise thereby reducing saving.

The *IS* function also shifts to the right by an autonomous increase in investment. The increase in investment may result from expectations of higher profits in the future, or from innovation, or from expectations concerning increase in the future demand for the product, or from a rise of optimism in general. Moreover, government's expenditure and tax policies have the effect of shifting the *IS* function.

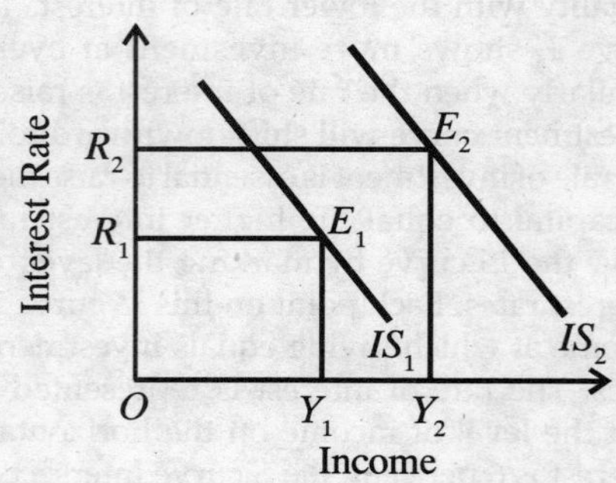

Fig. 3

In all these cases, the *IS* function will shift to the right, equal to the decrease in the supply of saving *times* the multiplier or the increase in the investment *times* the multiplier. With the increase in the autonomous investment (or reduction in saving), the *IS* curve shifts from IS_1 to IS_2 and the new equilibrium is established at point E_2 which indicates a higher level of income Y_2 at a higher interest rate R_2, as shown in Figure 3.

In the opposite case when investment falls or saving increases, the *IS* function will shift to the left and the equilibrium will be established at a lower level of income and interest rate. This situation can be explained by assuming IS_2, as the original curve.

3. THE MONEY MARKET EQUILIBRIUM

The money market is in equilibrium when the demand and supply of money are equal. Denoting *L* for money demand and *M* for money supply, the money market is in equilibrium when $L=M$. The demand for money $L=L_T+L_S$ where L_T is the transactions demand for money which is a direct function of the level of income, $L_T=f(Y)$. *Ls* is the speculative demand for money which is a decreasing function of the rate of interest, $L_S=f(r)$. Thus in money market equilibrium, $M=L_T(Y)+L_S(r)$.

DERIVING THE LM CURVE

The *LM* curve shows all combinations of interest rate and levels of income at which the demand for and supply of money are equal. In other words, the *LM* schedule shows the combinations of interest rates and levels of income where the demand for money (*L*) and the supply of money (*M*) are equal such that the money market is in equilibrium.

The *LM* curve is derived from the Keynesian formulation of liquidity preference schedules and the schedule of supply of money. A family of liquidity preference curves L_1Y_1, L_2Y_2 and L_3Y_3 is drawn at

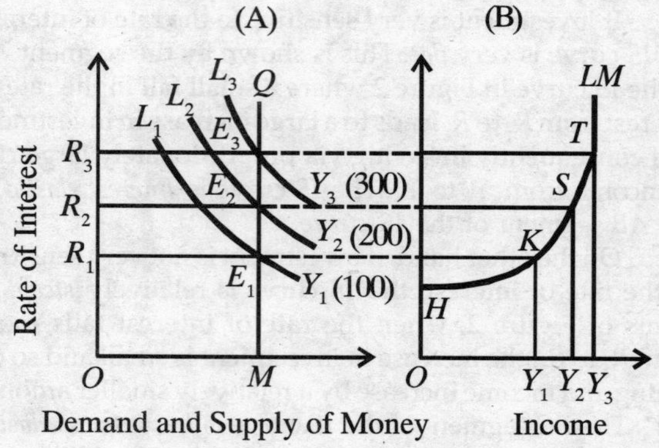

Fig. 4

income levels of Rs 100 crores, Rs 200 crores and Rs 300 crores respectively in Figure 4 (A). These curves together with the perfectly inelastic money supply curve *MQ* give us the *LM* curve. The *LM* curve consists of a series of points, each point representing an interest-income level at which the demand for money (*L*) equals the supply of money (*M*). If the income level is Y_1 (Rs 100 crores), the demand for money (L_1Y_1) equals the money supply (*QM*) at interest rate R_1. At the Y_2 (Rs 200 crores) income level, the L_2Y_2 and the *QM* curves equal at R_2 interest rate. Similarly at the Y_3 (Rs 300 crores) income level, the L_3Y_3 and *QM* curves at R_3 interest rate. The supply of money, the liquidity preference, the level of income and the rate of interest provide data for the *LM* curve shown in Figure4(B).

Suppose the level of income is Y_1 as marked out on the income axis in Figure 4(B). The income of Rs 100 crores generates a demand for money represented by the liquidity preference curve L_1Y_1. From the point E_1 where the L_1Y_1 curve intersects the *MQ* curve, extend a dashed line horizontally to the right so as to meet the line drawn upward from Y_1 and *K* in Figure 4(B). Points *S* and *T* can also be determined in similar manner. By connecting these points *K*, *S* and *T*, we get the *LM* curve. This curve relates different income levels to various interest rates.

The Slope of the LM Curve

The *LM* curve slopes upward from left to right because given the supply of money, an increase in the level of income increases the demand for money which leads to higher rate of interest. This, in turn, reduces the demand for money and thus keeps the demand for money equal to the supply of money. The smaller the responsiveness of the demand for money to income, and the *larger the responsiveness* of the demand for money to the rate of interest, the *flatter* will be the *LM* curve. This means that a given change in income has a smaller effect on the interest rate.

The *LM* curve is steeper, if a given change in income has a larger effect on the rate of interest. In this situation, the responsiveness of the demand for money to income is larger and is smaller for the interest rate. If the demand for money is *insensitive* to the interest rate, the *LM* curve is *vertical* that is, it is *perfectly inelastic*. This is shown in Panel (B) of Figure 4 as the portion from *T* above on the *LM* curve. In this case, a large change in the interest rate is accompanied by almost no change in the level of income to maintain money market equilibrium. If the demand for money is *very sensitive* to the rate of interest, the *LM* curve is *horizontal*. This is shown by the portion of *LM* curve which starts from *H* on the vertical axis in Panel (B) of Figure 4. The *LM* curve is *perfectly elastic* in relation to the rate of interest. In other words, a small change in the interest rate is accompanied by a large change in the level of income to maintain the money market equilibrium. This portion of the *LM* curve at the extreme left is equivalent to the Keynesian liquidity trap, already explained in the Keynes's theory of interest.

Shifts in the LM Curve

The *LM* function shifts to the right with the increase in the money supply, given the demand for money, or due to the decrease in the demand for money, given the supply of money. If the central bank follows an expansionary monetary policy, it will buy securities in the open market. As a result, the money supply with the public increases for both transactions and speculative purposes. This shifts the *LM* curve to the right.

A decrease in the demand for money means a reduction in the quantity of balances demanded at each level of income and interest rate. Such a decrease in the demand for money balances creates an excess of the money supplied over the money demanded. This is equivalent to an increase in money supply in the economy which has the effect of shifting the *LM* curve to the right.

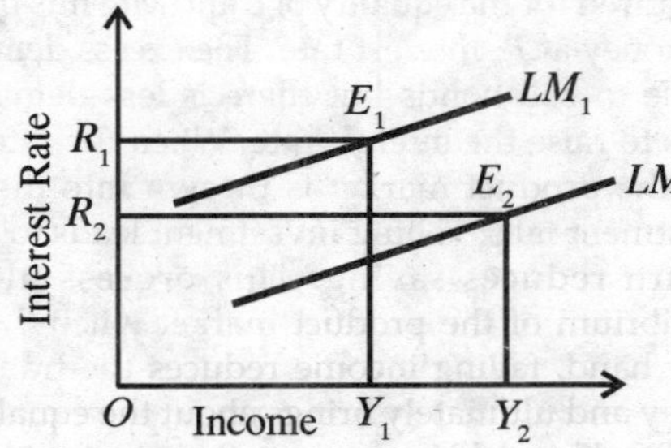

Fig. 5

This is depicted in Figure 5. With the increase in the money supply, the LM_1 curve shifts to the right as LM_2 which moves the economy to a new equilibrium point E_2. The increase in the money supply brings down the interest rate to R_2 in the money market. This, in turn, increases investment thereby raising the level of income to Y_2.

Contrariwise, a decrease in the money supply, or an increase in the demand for money will shift the *LM* function to the left such that a new equilibrium is established at a higher interest rate and lower income level. This case can be explained by assuming LM_2 as the original curve.

4. GENERAL EQUILIBRIUM OF PRODUCT AND MONEY MARKET

So far we have analysed the conditions that have to be satisfied for the general equilibrium of the product and money markets in terms of the *IS* and *LM* functions. Now we study how these markets are brought into simultaneous equilibrium. It is only when the equilibrium pairs of interest rate and income of the *IS* curve equal the equilibrium pairs of interest rate and income of the *LM* curve that the general equilibrium is established. In other words, when there is a single pair of interest rate and income level in the product and money markets that the two markets are in equilibrium.

Such an equilibrium position is shown in Figure 6 where the *IS* and *LM* curves intersect each other at point *E* relating *Y* level of income to *R* interest rate. This pair of income level and interest rate leads to simultaneous equilibrium in the real or goods (saving-investment) market and the money (demand and supply of money) market. This general equilibrium position persists at a point of time, given the price level. If there is any deviation from this equilibrium position, certain forces will act and react in such a manner that the equilibrium will be restored.

Consider point *A* on the *LM* curve where the money market is in equilibrium at Y_1 income level and R_2 interest rate. But the product market is not in equilibrium. In the product market, the interest rate R_2 is lower. The product market can be in equilibrium at Y_1 income level only at a higher interest rate R_1 corresponding to point *B* on the *IS* curve. Consequently at point *A*, there is excess of investment over saving since point *A* lies to the left of the *IS* curve. The excess of *I* over *S* indicates excess demand for goods which raises the level of income. As the level of income rises, the need for transactions purposes increases. In order to have more money for transactions purposes, people sell bonds. This tends to raise the interest rate. This moves the *LM* curve from point *A* upward to point *E* where a combination of higher interest rate *R* and higher income level *Y* exists. On the other hand, rising interest rate reduces investment and an increasing income raises saving. This helps to bring about the equality of *I* and *S* at point *E* where the general equilibrium is re-established by the equality of *IS* and *LM*.

Now consider point *C* on the *IS* curve in Figure 6 where the product market is in equilibrium at R_2 interest rate and Y_2 income level. The money market is not in equilibrium. It can be in equilibrium at Y_2 income level only at a higher interest rate R_1 corresponding to point *D* on the *LM* curve. At point *C*, the demand for money (*L*) is greater than the supply of money (*M*) because point *C* reflects lower rate of interest R_2 than is required for the equality of *L* and *M*. Thus there is excess demand for money at R_2 interest rate. The excess demand for money leads people to sell bonds but there is less demand for bonds which tends to raise the interest rate. When the rate of interest begins to rise, the product market is thrown into disequilibrium because investment falls. Falling investment leads to falling income which in turn reduces saving. This process ultimately brings the equilibrium of the product market when *I=S* at point *E*. On the other hand, falling income reduces the transactions demand for money and ultimately brings about the equality of *LM* at point *E* where the equilibrium is re-established by the equality *IS* and *LM* curves, at *R* interest rate and *Y* income level.

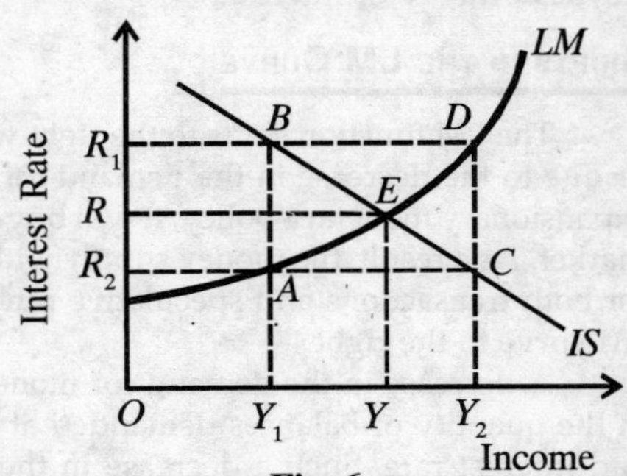

Fig. 6

5. CHANGES IN GENERAL EQUILIBRIUM

The general equilibrium of the product and money markets discussed above is based on the static equilibrium analysis. It started from a point of disequilibrium and again reached the equilibrium point of the equality of *IS* and *LM* functions. But the general equilibrium combination of *Y* income level and *R* rate of interest may change either due to a shift in the *IS* function or the *LM* function, or by both the functions shifting simultaneously. The *IS* function may shift due to changes in the saving function or the investment function. The shifts in the *LM* function may be caused by changes in the money supply or liquidity preference.

The shifting of the *IS* curve to the right and the consequent equilibrium with the given *LM* curve is illustrated in Figure 7. With the increase in the autonomous investment (or reduction in saving), the *IS* curve moves from *IS* to IS_1 and the new equilibrium is established at point E_1 which indicates a higher level of income Y_1 at a higher interest rate R_1. If the interest rate had not increased but remained at *R* level, the increse in investment would have raised income from *Y* to Y_2 level. But this much increase in income would not take place. This is because with the increase in income, the demand for money for transactions purposes will raise the interest rate to R_1 level where the *IS* and *LM* functions intersect at point E_1. Thus the expansionary effect of increase in investment is dampened by the rise in the interest rate and the income rises by less than the full multiplier.

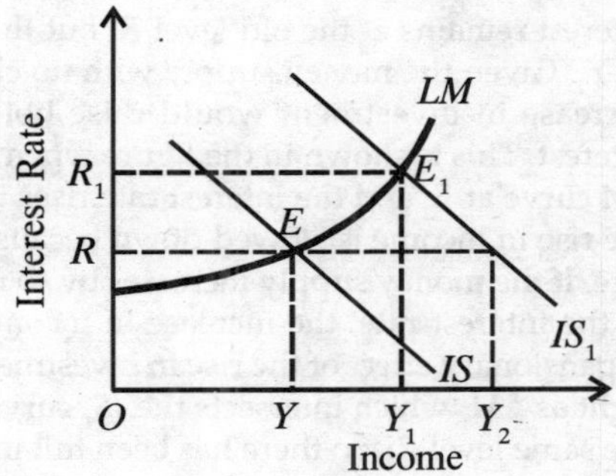

Fig. 7

In the opposite case when investment falls or saving increases, the *IS* function will shift to the left and the equilibrium will be established at a lower level of income and interest rate. This situation has not been depicted in Figure7.

With the increase in the money supply, the *LM* curve shifts to the right as LM_1 which moves the economy to a new equilibrium point E_1 where the *IS* curve intersects the *LM* curve in Figure 8. The increase in the money supply brings down the interest rate R_1 in the money market. This, in turn, increases investment thereby raising the level of income to Y_1. Thus the effect of the increase in money supply is to shift the *LM* function to the right and a new equilibrium is established at a lower interest rate and higher income level. But how much income will rise as a result of an increase in the money supply depends on (1) how much the interest rate falls which in turn depends on the elasticity of speculative demand for money, and (2) how much investment rises as a result of any given fall in the interest rate which in turn depends on the interest-elasticity of investment demand function.

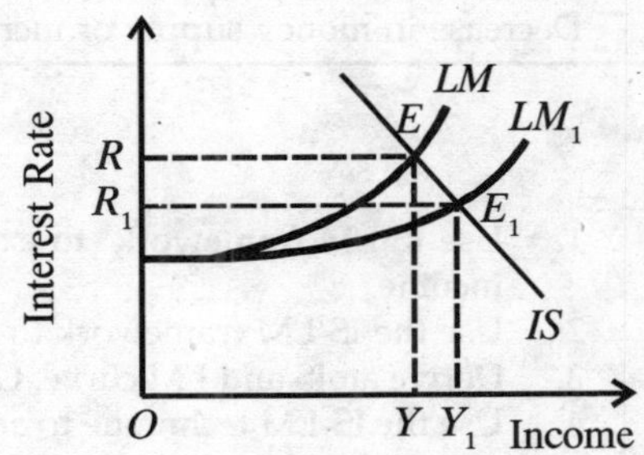

Fig. 8

Contrariwise, a decrease in the money supply or an increase in the demand for money will shift the *LM* function to the left such that a new equilibrium is established at a higher interest rate and lower income level. This case has not been depicted in Figure 8.

SIMULTANEOUS SHIFTS IN THE *IS* AND *LM* FUNCTIONS

We have seen above that with the increase in investment when the *IS* curve shifts to the right, both the rate of interest and the level of the income tend to rise, given the *LM* curve. On the other hand, when an increase in money supply shifts the *LM* curve to the right, it lowers the rate of interest and raises the income level, given the *IS* curve.

Now suppose both the *IS* and *LM* curves shift to the right simultaneously as a result of the increase in investment and money supply respectively. How will these *expansionary fiscal and monetary policies* affect the level of income and the rate of interest ? This is illustrated in Figure 9 where the increase in investment shifts the *IS* curve to IS_1 and the increase in the money supply shifts the *LM* curve to LM_1. Consequently, the new equilibrium position is E_1 where the IS_1 and LM_1 curves intersect. The rate of interest remains at the old level R_1 but the income increases from *Y* to Y_2. Given the money supply with no change in the *LM* curve, an increase in investment would raise both income and the rate of interest. This is shown in the figure when the IS_1 curve intersects the *LM* curve at E_2 and the interest rate rises to R_2 and income to Y_1. But the rise in income is slowed down because of the rise in the interest rate. If the money supply increases by so much as to prevent the rise in the interest rate, the increase in income will be equal to the full expansionary effect of the rise in investment. This is depicted in the figure by the shifting of the *LM* curve to the right as LM_1 which intersects the IS_1 curve at E_1. The income increases to Y_2 but the rate of interest remains at the same level R_1. So there has been full income-expansionary effect of the increase in investment as a result of the simultaneous increase in money supply by just the amount necessary to prevent the rise in the interest rate.

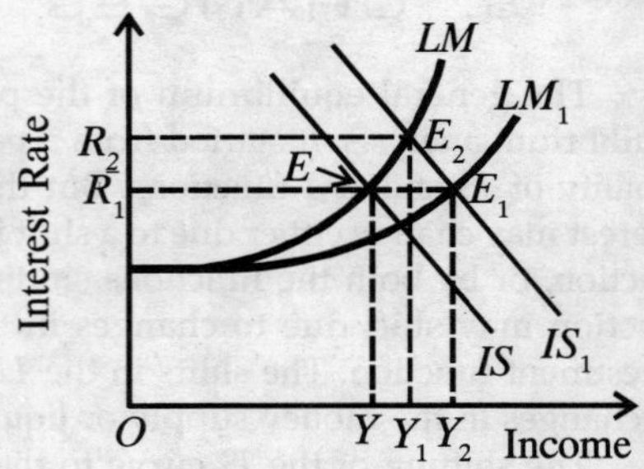

Fig. 9

Table I summarises the causes and directions of shifts in the *IS* and *LM* curves.

Table I : Causes and Directions of Shifts in IS and LM curves

Cause	Curve	Direction
Increase in investment or consumption	*IS*	Right
Decrease in investment or increase in savings	*IS*	left
Increase in money supply or decrease in money demand	*LM*	left
Decrease in money supply or increase in money demand	*LM*	right

EXERCISES

1. Use IS-LM framework to explain the joint determination of the rate of interest and the level of income.
2. Use the IS-LM framework to analyse the effects of an autonomous increase in investment.
3. Derive an IS and LM curve. Give their properties. [Hint: Explain their slopes and shifts.]
4. Use the IS-LM technique to analyse the effects of simultaneous increase in autonomous investment and money supply.

CHAPTER 31

Monetary Policy : Objectives, Targets and Indicators

1. INTRODUCTION

Of late, the discussion on monetary policy has centered around its objectives, targets, indicators and instruments. Jan Tinbergen was the first economist to lay down certain instruments to achieve policy objectives. Economists have extended the discussion to include the targets and indicators of economic policy. These have also been applied to monetary policy. The principal targets, indicators and instruments as applied to monetary policy are as follows:

Targets. The usual targets of monetary policy are: (1) money supply; (2) availability of credit; and (3) interest rates.

Indicators. The monetary targets are also employed as indicators of monetary policy. So they are: (1) money supply; (2) bank credit; and (3) interest rates.

Instruments. The instruments of monetary policy are: (1) bank rate; (2) open market operations; (3) changes in reserve ratios; and (4) selective credit controls.

We discuss the goals, targets and indicators of monetary policy in this chapter, and instruments of monetary policy in the next chapter.

2. MEANING

Monetary policy refers to the credit control measures adopted by the central bank of a country. Johnson defines monetary policy "a policy employing central bank's control of the supply of money as an instrument for achieving the objectives of general economic policy."[1] G.K. Shaw defines it as "any conscious action undertaken by the monetary authorities to change the quantity, availability or cost ... of money."[2]

3. OBJECTIVES / GOALS OF MONETARY POLICY

The following are the principal objectives of monetary policy :

The objectives of monetary policy are: (1) full employment; (2) price stability which also includes controlling economic fluctuations (though some writers mention the latter separately); (3) economic growth; and (4) maintaining balance of payments equilibrium.

---

1. H. G. Johnson, *op. cit.*, p. 53.
2. G. K. Shaw, *An Introduction to the Theory of Macro-economic Policy*, p. 65.

1. Full Employment

Full employment has been ranked among the foremost objectives of monetary policy. It is an important goal not only because unemployment leads to wastage of potential output, but also because of the loss of social standing and self-respect. Moreover, it breeds poverty.

According to Keynes, full employment means the absence of involuntary unemployment. In other words, full employment is a situation in which everybody who wants to work, gets work. Full employment so defined is consistent with frictional and voluntary unemployment. To achieve full employment, Keynes advocated increase in effective demand to bring about reduction in real wages. Thus the problem of full employment is one of maintaining adequate effective demand. Keynes gave an alternative definition of full employment at another place in his *General Theory* thus: "It is a situation in which aggregate employment is inelastic in response to an increase in which aggregate employment is inelastic in response to an increase in the effective demand for its output." It means that the test of full employment is when any further increase in effective demand is not accompanied by any increase in output. Since the supply of output becomes inelastic at the full employment level, any further increase in effective demand will lead to inflation in the economy. Thus the Keynesian concept of full employment involves three conditions: (*i*) reduction in the real wage rate; *(ii)* increase in effective demand; and *(iii)* inelastic supply of output at the level of full employment.

According to Prof. W.W. Hart, attempting to define full employment raises many people's blood pressure. Rightly so, because there is hardly any economist who does not define it in his own way. Lord Beveridge in his book *Full Employment in a Free Society* defined it as a situation where there were more vacant jobs than unemployed men so that the normal lag between losing one job and finding another will be very short. By full employment he does not mean zero unemployment which means that full employment is not always full. There is always a certain amount of frictional unemployment in the economy even when there is full employment. He estimated frictional unemployment of 3% in a full employment situation for England. But his pleading for more vacant jobs than the unemployed cannot be accepted as the full employment level.

According to the American Economic Association Committee, "Full employment is a situation where all qualified persons, who want jobs at current wage rate, find full time jobs.'' It does not mean unemployment is zero. Here again, like Beveridge, the Committee considered full employment to be consistent with some amount of unemployment.

Individual economists may, however, continue to differ over the definition of full employment, but the majority has veered round the view expressed by the U.N. Experts on *National and International Measures for Full Employment* that "full employment may be considered as a situation in which employment cannot be increased by an increase in effective demand and unemployment does not exceed the minimum allowances that must be made for the effects of frictional and seasonal factors." This definition is in keeping with the Keynesian and Beveridgian views on full employment. It is now agreed that full employment stands for 96 to 97 per cent employment, with 3 to 4 per cent unemployment existing in the economy due to frictional factors. Full employment can be achieved in an economy by following an expansionary monetary policy.

2. Price Stability

One of the policy objectives of monetary policy is to stabilise the price level. Both economists and laymen favour this policy because fluctuations in prices bring uncertainty and instability to the economy. Rising and falling prices are both bad because they bring unnecessary loss to some and undue advantage to others. Again, they are associated with business cycles. So a policy of price stability keeps the value of money stable, eliminates cyclical fluctuations, brings economic stability, helps in reducing inequalities of income and wealth, secures social justice and promotes economic welfare.

However, there are certain difficulties in pursuing a policy of stable price level. The *first* problem relates to the type of price level to be stabilised. Should the relative or general price level be stabilised, the wholesale or retail, of consumer goods or producer goods? There is no specific criteria with regard to the choice of a price level. Halm suggests, "The compromise solution would be to try to stabilise a price level which would include consumers' goods prices as well as wages." But this will necessitate increase in the quantity of money but not

3. G.N. Halm, *op. cit.*

by as much as is implied in the stabilisation of consumers goods price.[3] *Second*, innovations may reduce the cost of production but a policy of stable prices may bring larger profits to producers at the cost of consumers and wage earners. Again, in an open economy which imports raw materials and other intermediate products at high prices, the cost of production of domestic goods will rise. But a policy of stable prices will reduce profits and retard further investment. Under the circumstances, a policy of stable prices is not only inequitable but also conflicts with economic progress.

Despite these drawbacks, the majority of economists favour a policy of stable prices. But the problem is one of defining price stability. Price stability does not mean that prices remain unchanged indefinitely. "Comparative prices will change as fluctuating tastes alter the composition of demand, as new products are developed and as cost reducing technologies are introduced. Differential price changes are essential for allocating resources in the market economy. Since modern economies tend to exhibit fairly rigid downward inflexibility of prices, differential price changes can only be attained by gradual increases in the aggregate price level over the long-run. Further, prices may have to be changed if costs of imported goods increase or if taxation policy leads to rise in the domestic cost of production. As pointed out by Dasgupta and Hagger, price stability means *"stability of some appropriate price index in the sense that we can detect no definite upward trend in the index after making proper allowance for the upward bias inherent in all price indexes."*[4]

Price stability can be maintained by following a counter-cyclical monetary policy, that is easy monetary policy during a recession and dear monetary policy during a boom.

3. Economic Growth

One of the most important objectives of monetary policy in recent years has been the rapid economic growth of an economy. Economic growth is defined as *"the process whereby the real per capita income of a country increases over a long period of time."*[5] Economic growth is measured by increase in the quantity of goods and services produced in a country. A growing economy produces more goods and services in each successive time period. Thus, growth occurs when an economy's productive capacity increases which, in turn, is used to produce more goods and services. In its wider aspect, economic growth implies raising the standard of living of the people, and reducing inequalities of income distribution. All agree that economic growth is a desirable goal for a country. But there is no agreement over "the magic number," viz., the annual growth rate which an economy should attain.

Generally, economists believe in the possibility of continual growth. This belief is based on the presumption that innovations tend to increase productive technologies of both capital and labour over time. But there is very likelihood that an economy might not grow despite technological innovations. Production might not increase further due to lack of demand which may retard the growth of the productive capacity of the economy. The economy may not grow further if there is no improvement in the quality of labour in keeping with the new technologies.

However, policy makers do not take into consideration the cost of growth. Growth is not limitless because resources are scarce in every economy. All factors have opportunity cost. To produce more of one particular product will mean reduction in that of the other. New technologies lead to the replacement of old machines which become obsolete. Workers are also displaced because they cannot be fitted in the new technological set up immediately. Moreover, rapid growth leads to urbanisation and industrialisation with their adverse effects on the pattern of living and environment. People have to live in squalor and slums. The environment becomes polluted. Social tensions develop. "But growth has other more basic effect on our environment, and, today, people are not so sure that unrestricted growth is worth all its costs, since the price in terms of change in, deterioration of, or even destruction of the environment is not yet fully known. What does seem clear, however, is that growth is not going to be halted because of environmental problems and that mankind must learn to cope with the problem or face the consequences."

The main problem is to what extent monetary policy can lead to the growth of the economy? It is difficult

4. A K. Dasgupta and A.J. Hagger, *The Objectives of Macro-economic Policy*, 1971.
5. G.M. Meier. *Leading Issues in Development Economics*, p. 20.

to say anything definite on this issue. The monetary authority may influence growth by controlling the real interest rate through its effect on the level of investment. By following an easy credit policy and lowering interest rates, the level of investment can be raised which promotes economic growth. Monetary policy may also contribute towards growth by helping to maintain stability of income and prices. By moderating economic fluctuations and avoiding deep depressions, monetary policy helps in achieving the growth objective. Since rapid and variable rates of inflation discourage investment and adversely affect growth, monetary policy helps in controlling hyper-inflation. Similarly, by a judicious monetary policy which encourages investment, growth can be promoted. For example, tight monetary policy affects small firms more than large firms, and higher interest rates have a greater impact on small investments than on large industrial investments. So monetary policy should be such that encourages investment and at the same time controls hyperinflation so as to promote growth and control economic fluctuations.*

4. Balance of Payments

Another objective of monetary policy since the 1950s has been to maintain equilibrium in the balance of payments. The achievement of this goal has been necessitated by the phenomenal growth in the world trade as against the growth of international liquidity. It is also recognised that deficit in the balance of payments will retard the attainment of other objectives. This is because a deficit in the balance of payments leads to a sizeable outflow of gold. But "it is not clear what constitutes a satisfactory balance of payments position. Clearly a country with a net debt must be at a surplus to repay the debt over a reasonably short period of time. Once any debt has been repaid and an adequate reserve attained, a zero balance maintained over time would meet the policy objective. But how is this satisfactory balance to be achieved on the trading account or on the capital account? ... The capital account must be looked upon as fulfilling merely a short-term emergency role in times of crises."[6]

Again, another problem relates to the question: What is the balance of payments target of a country? It is where imports equal exports. But, in practice, a country whose current reserves of foreign exchange are inadequate will have a mild export surplus as its balance of payments target. But when its reserves become satisfactory, it will aim at the equality of imports and exports. This is because an export surplus means that the country is accumulating foreign exchange and it is producing more than it is consuming: This will lead to low standard of living of the people. But this cannot last long because some other country must be having import surplus and in order to avoid it, it would impose trade restrictions on the export surplus country. So the attainment of a balance of payments equilibrium becomes an imperative goal of monetary policy in a country. How can monetary policy achieve it? A balance of payments deficit is defined as equal to the excess of money supply through domestic credit creation over extra money demand based on increased demand for cash balances. Thus a balance of payments deficit reflects excessive money supply in the economy. As a result, people exchange their excess money holdings for foreign goods and securities. Under a system of fixed exchange rates, the central bank will have to sell foreign exchange reserves and buy the domestic currency for eliminating excess supply of domestic currency. This is how equilibrium will be restored in the balance of payments.

On the other hand, if the money supply is below the existing demand for money at the given exchange rate, there will be a surplus in the balance of payments. Consequently, people acquire the domestic currency by selling goods and securities to foreigners. They will also seek to acquire additional money balances by restricting their expenditure relatively to their income. The central bank, on its part will buy excess foreign currency in exchange for domestic currency in order to eliminate the shortage of domestic currency.

4. TRADE-OFF IN MONETARY GOALS

The four objectives of monetary policy discussed above are not complementary to each other. Rather, they conflict with one another. If a government tries to fulfil one goal, some other goal moves away. It has to

* Other objectives may also be discussed on similar lines.
6. G.K. Shaw, *op. cit., p. 9.*

sacrifice one in order to attain the other. It is, therefore, not possible to fulfil all these objectives simultaneously. We discuss below conflicts or trade-offs between different objectives.

Full Employment and Economic Growth

The majority of economists hold the view that there is no inherent conflict between full employment and economic growth. Full employment is consistent with 4 per cent unemployment in the economy. So the relationship between full employment and economic growth boils down to a trade-off between unemployment and growth. Periods of high growth are associated with low level of unemployment, and periods of low growth with rising unemployment.

In 1961, Aurther Okun[7] established a relationship between real GNP and changes in the unemployment rate. This relationship has come to be known as Okun's Law. This law states that *for every three percentage points growth inreal GNP, unemployment rate declines by one percentage point every year.* This is illustrated in Fig. 1 where the curve *U* represents unemployment and curve *G* the real growth of an economy for a few years. To begin with, the economy is growing at 3 per cent with an unemployment rate of 4 per cent. During the year 1970, when the real GNP increases by 4.5 per cent (from 3 per cert to 7.5 per cent), the unemployment rate falls by 1.5 per cent (from 4 per cent to 2.5 per cent). In the next year 1971, the growth rate of the economy falls to zero and the unemployment rate rises to 5 per cent. In the subsequent year 1972, the real growth rate increases to 3 per cent and the unemployment rate declines to 4 per cent.

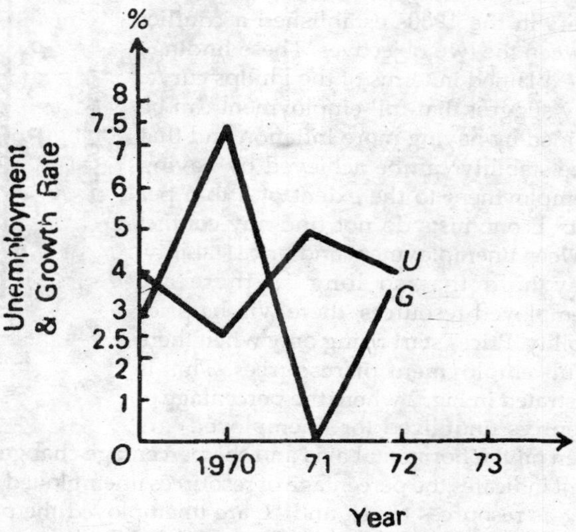

FIG. 1

However, certain economists argue that the unemployment rate increases as the growth rate rises. Economic growth leads to reallocation of resources in the economy whereby there is change in the type and quantity of labour demanded. There is shift in the demand for labour from one sector of the economy to the other. As workers are trained for specific jobs, they are displaced when the demand for the products of a particular industries falls. This creates unemployment. This is particularly so when growth is the result of technological innovations which are labour-saving and require more qualified and skilled workers. Thus unskilled workers are the worst sufferers because they are thrown out of jobs with automation. Employment can, however, increase with growth if demand is increasing at 3 per cent per annum and the productivity is increasing at 4 per cent per year, the output will expand but employment will decline. Under the circumstances, the government should adopt such monetary policy which should increase the overall demand in the economy.

Economic Growth and Price Stability

There is conflict between the goals of economic growth and price stability. The rise in prices is inherent in the growth process. The demand for goods and services rises as a result of stepping up of investments on a large scale and consequent increase in income. This leads to inflationary rise in prices,, especially when the level of full employment is reached. In the long run, when new resources are developed and growth leads to the production of more commodities, the inflationary rise in prices will be checked. But the rise in prices will be there with the growth of the economy and it will be moderate and gradual.

7. A.M. Okun, "Potential GNP: Its Measurement and Significance," in W.L. Smith and R.L. Teigen (eds.), *op. cit.*

Full Employment and Price Stability

One of the objectives of monetary policy in the 1950s was to have full employment with price stability. But the studies of Philips, Samuelson, Solow and others in the 1960s established a conflict between the two objectives. These findings are explained in terms of the Phillps curve. They suggest that full employment can be attained by having more inflation and that price stability can be achieved by having unemployment to the extent of 5 to 6 per cent.[8] Economists do not find any conflict between unemployment and price stability. They hold that so long as there are unemployed resources, there will be price stability. Prices start rising only when there is full employment of resources. This is illustrated in Fig. 2 where the percentage of resources unutilized (or unemployed) are taken on the horizontal axis and the percentage change in price level is taken on the vertical axis. Thus each point indicates the percentage of resources unemployed along with the price level. According to this theory, so long as resources U_1, U_2 and U_3 are unemployed the price level remains constant at P_o. It is only when the economy reaches the full employment level F, prices rise from P_o to P_1 to P_2 to P_3 with successive increases in demand. Thus there is no conflict between unemployment and stable prices, as shown by the shaded area of the figure. However, the policy implications of such a relationship are that there can be no conflict between full employment and price stability so long as the economy is in the shaded area. This is because when there is full employment, resources are not in excess supply and if the government controls the excess demand through appropriate monetary policy, there will be stability of the price level. But if the economy happens to be at point P, which may be taken to be a point on the Phillips curve, there will be conflict between the objectives of full employment and price stability.

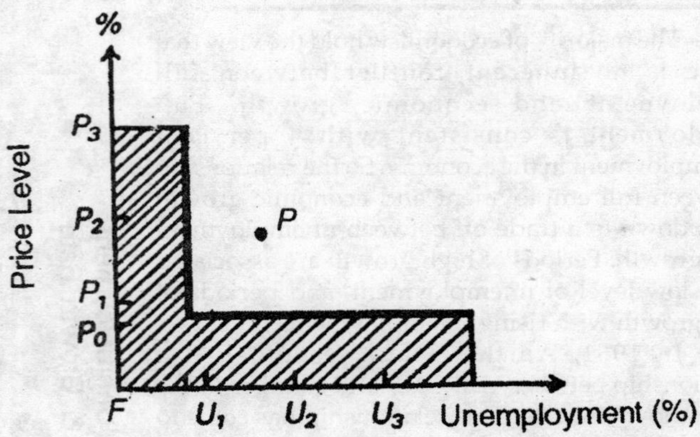

FIG. 2

Full Employment and Balance of Payments

There is a major policy conflict between full employment and balance of payments. Full employment is always related to balance of payments deficit. In fact, the problem is one of maintaining either internal balance or external balance. If there is a balance of payments deficit, then a policy of reducing expenditure will reduce imports but it will lead to increase in unemployment in the country. If the government raises aggregate expenditure in order to increase employment, it will increase the demand for imports thereby creating disequilibrium in the balance of payments. It is only when the government adopts expenditure-switching policies such as devaluation that this conflict can be avoided but that too temporarily.

Price Stability and Balance of Payments

There appears to be no conflict between the objectives of price stability and balance of payments in a country. Monetary policy aims at controlling inflation to discourage imports and encourage exports and thus it helps in attaining balance of payments equilibrium. However, if the government tries to remove unemployment and allows some inflation within the economy, there appears a conflict between these two objectives. For a rise in the price level will discourage exports and encourage imports, thereby leading to disequilibrium in the balance of payments. But this may not happen if prices also rise by the same rate in other

8. P.A. Samuelson and R.M. Solow, "Analytical Aspects of Anti-inflation Policy," *A.E.R.*, May, 1960.

countries of the world.

5. TARGETS OF MONETARY POLICY

The choice of a target for monetary policy is determined by the mechanism through which money effects growth, employment and prices. Since none of the monetary authority's policy tools works directly on these policy variables, the policy makers rely on intermediate targets that they feel they can control tolerably well with the instruments at their disposal, and that are closely linked through transmission mechanism to the ultimate targets of production, employment and price level.

There are three target variables for monetary policy. They are the money supply, availability of credit, and interest rates.

1. *Money Supply.* So far as money supply is concerned, the central bank cannot directly control output and prices. So it selects the growth rate of money supply as an intermediate target. If fact, it selects an "operating target" which it considers to be closely linked to its "intermediate target". Friedman suggests that the money supply should be allowed to grow steadily at the rate of 3 to 4 per cent per year for a smooth growth of the economy and to avoid inflationary and recessionary tendencies.

2. *Availability of Credit and Interest Rates.* Availability of credit and interest rates are the other two target variables of monetary policy. Economists call them as "money market conditions" which refer to short-term interest rates and the banking system's "free reserves" (i.e. excess reserves minus borrowed reserves). The monetary authority can influence the short-term interest rates. It can change credit conditions and affect economic activity by rationing of credit or other means. The monetary authority influences economic activity by following an easy or expansionary monetary policy through low and/or falling short-term interest rates and a tight or contractionary monetary policy through high and/or rising short-term interest rates.

Its Limitations. The use of interest rates and credit availability as target variables are beset with a number of difficulties :

1. No doubt interest rates and the supply of credit influence spending, but it cannot be predicted with definiteness about the size and timing of the effects of any change in them.

2. So far as interest rates are concerned, it is the real interest rate that matters and not the nominal interest rate. It is possible to control and observe the movements in the nominal interest rate and not in the real interest rate because it is difficult to measure the expected rate of price inflation. When the monetary authority raises the nominal interest rate, the real interest rate will also rise, other things being equal. But this does not happen always because when money interest rates are raised, the expectations of price inflation are growing. Under such circumstances, a rise in the nominal interest rate may be associated with a fall in the expected real rate. Thus the nominal interest rate is not a good target of monetary policy.

3. The use of credit availability as a monetary target is not helpful in monetary policy. Suppose there is a reduction in the availability of credit, it may be offset by credit flows through NBFIs. Moreover, it is difficult to predict the amount of reduction/increase in the availability of credit.

Intermediate Targets. Money supply and interest rate are intermediate targets of monetary policy. In fact, they are competing targets. The central bank can either aim at a certain rate of increase in the money supply or at a certain level of interest rate. It cannot adopt both the targets at the same time. The money supply target means loss of control over the interest rate, while the interest rate target means loss of control over the money supply. Let us assume in Fig. 3 that the target money supply fixed by the central bank is *MS* and the demand for money function is M_D. They intersect at *E* and determine the interest rate *R*. With the increase in the demand for money, the M_D curve shifts upwards to M_{D1} which intersects the *MS* curve at E_1, and determines the higher interest rate R_1. On the contrary, a fall in the demand for money

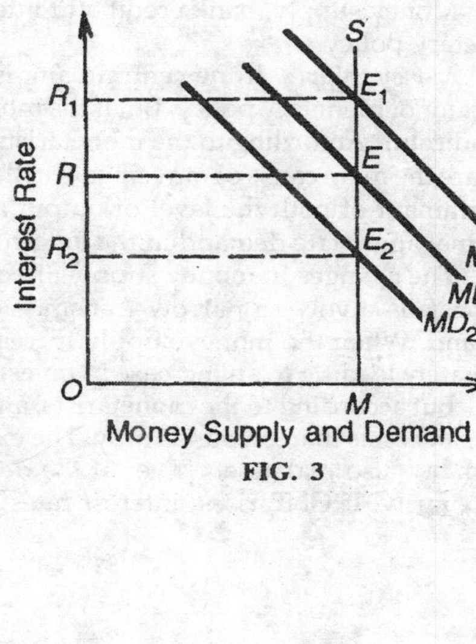

FIG. 3

shifts the curve downwards to M_{D2} so as to reduce the interest rate to R_2. Thus with the money supply fixed by the central bank, the interest rate changes with fluctuations in the demand for money between R_1 and R_2.

Now assume in Fig. 4 that R is the target interest rate when MS and M_D are the original money supply and money demand curves. If the demand for money shifts upwards from M_D to M_{D1}, the central bank will have to increase the money supply from MS to M_1S_1 to match the money demand to maintain the target interest rate R. Contrariwise, it will have to decrease the money supply to M_2S_2, in case of a fall in the demand for money M_{D2} so that the interest rate is stabilised at R. Therefore, to maintain the target interest rate, the central bank has to relinquish control over the money supply.

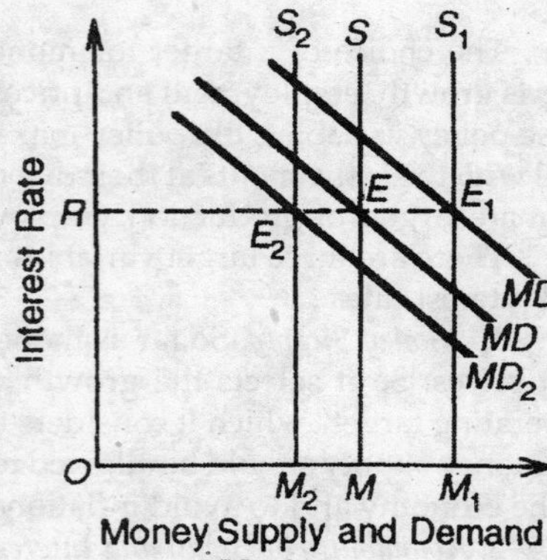

FIG. 4

Of the two targets relating to money supply and interest rate, the monetarists prefer a monetary target for various reasons. *First*, the money supply is measurable, while there are a variety of interest rates. It is, therefore, difficult to adjust nominal interest rates to real interest rates. *Second*, the money supply linkage with nominal GNP is more direct and predictable than the interest linkage with nominal GNP.

3. *Market Yield on Equity*. Tobin suggests the market yield on equity as a target variable for monetary policy. According to him, the monetary authority should try to equate this yield with the real return expected from investment in physical capital. When the real rate of return on equity rises, the value of existing capital equipment falls which discourages the purchase of new capital equipment. Contrariwise, investment is encouraged when the cost of production of new capital is less than its market value. Thus the valuation of investment goods relative to their cost is the proper target of monetary policy. This target is superior to other targets because the market value of equity capital can be observed easily and an index of market value can be compared with a price index of investment goods.

Despite this, it is difficult to compare the value of existing assets with those of newly produced assets. Moreover, it is not possible to link investments with changes in stock market prices. So it is not advisable to adopt market yield on equity as the sole target of monetary policy.

Conclusion. Of the various targets of monetary policy, it is advisable for the monetary authority not to rely on any single target. It should select the targets according to the prevailing economic and financial conditions. The interest rate is more suitable during the short run. But in the long run, the credit availability and the money supply should be relied upon by the monetary authority. The target of market yield on equity is unacceptable by economists.

6. INDICATORS OF MONETARY POLICY

Money supply, bank credit and interest rate which serve as targets are also employed as indicators of monetary policy.

Money Supply. If the central bank is solely responsible for changes in the money supply, it is a good indicator of monetary policy. But if the money supply changes regardless of the central bank policy, it is hardly an indicator. According to the monetarists, it is open market operations and changes in reserve requirements that are the main cause of movements in the money supply. It is the money supply which is the most important determinant of both the level of output and the price level in the short run and of the price level and the nominal aggregate demand in the long run.

The changes in money supply affect aggregate demand through effects on a wide range of assets. The Keynesians involve a narrow transmission mechanism between money supply and changes in aggregate demand. When the money supply increases it will be spent on bonds, thereby lowering interest rates and ultimately leading to an increase in investment.

But according to the monetarists, an increase in money supply will lead to spending on a much broader range of assets than on bonds only. The excess money supply balances will be used to bring not only financial assets but also real assets. Even if the demand for financial assets expands, interest rates will fall but only temporarily. If GNP rises, interest rates will also rise because there is a greater need for day-to-day cash transactions to carry out the expanding business activity. Firms will, therefore, borrow to raise more cash and interest rates will rise. Interest rates will also rise when an expansionary monetary policy generates inflationary expectations. Thus interest rates may be either lower or higher after an expansionary monetary policy, depending on the speed and strength of the change in GNP and on the expectations regarding prices. Similarly, interest rates may either be higher or lower after a contractionary monetary policy begins, depending on the same factors.

Bank Credit and Interest Rate. So far as interest rate as an indicator of monetary policy is concerned, there are vast differences in the views of the Keynesians and the monetarists. The monetarists downgrade interest rate as indicator of monetary policy because it is not under the firm control of the central bank. The same view is held by the Keynesians. But the differences arise in the transmission mechanisms. According to the Keynesians, the increase in money supply reduces the interest rate provided the demand for money does not become perfectly elastic (the liquidity trap case). *Second,* the reduction in the interest rate increases investment provided it is not inelastic to the interest rate. Interest rates will stay down so long as the money supply continues to increase.

The monetarists do not agree with this view. To them, the increase in money supply affects interest rate in the following manner. Suppose the money supply increases through open market purchases of securities by the central bank. This will bring down interest rate by increasing the reserves of commercial banks which will expand their loans. This is the *liquidity effect* which causes a short-run reduction in interest rate. The low interest rate will encourage investment in new capital formation, inventories, construction activities, etc. As a result, prices of investment goods will rise and the demand for financial and real assets will increase and raise their prices. The rise in production and demand for money will bid up the interest rate. This is the *output effect.* Finally, there is the *price expectation effect* because lenders expect prices to rise and they buy interest-bearing securities and other goods. Thus after the initial fall, interest rate will rise again and settle at a new rate. The new rate will depend on the rate of inflation generated by the increase in money supply. So interest rate as an indicator of monetary policy shows that when increase in the money supply leads to increase in interest rate, this will be like an expansionary easy money policy. Friedman, therefore, argues that the monetary authority should concentrate on controlling the money supply rather than manipulating the interest rate.

Conclusion. Economists do not agree over the use of money supply, bank credit and interest rate as indicators of monetary policy. Brunner and Metzler are of the view that both the money supply and interest rate would have identical effects on the economy. It is changes in the real interest rate that affect economic activity. But in reality, it is only changes in nominal interest rate that are measured. The measurement of real interest rate depends on expected price changes. This is both conceptually and empirically a difficult process and subject to errors. Thus to evaluate monetary policy during inflation or deflation by looking at nominal interest rate is misleading. But this problem does not arise in the case of the money supply because it is nominal value of money which influence nominal value of economic activity. Therefore, interest rate is not a reliable and predictable indicator of monetary policy whereas the money supply is.

To select an appropriate indicator of monetary policy requires certain issues which are to be tackled. The first issue concerns the nature of money supply and its control. Friedman includes M_2, that is currency, and demand and time deposits in the money supply. But the problem is to what extent the money supply will respond to changes in a predictable manner. The *second* issue concerns the extent to which the money supply affects economic activity. *Third,* there is the important issue of "the proposed indicator's exogeneity with respect to the economic variables that policy makers are attempting to influence".

EXERCISES

1. Discuss the principal objectives of monetary policy.
2. Is there any conflict between the monetary policy objectives of full employment and price stability? If so, how will you reconcile them?
3. What are the goals of monetary policy? Explain in particular the trade-off in these objectives.
4. Discuss the various targets of monetary policy.
5. Explain the indicators of monetary policy.

CHAPTER 32

Monetary Policy : Instruments and Types

This chapter analyses the various instruments of monetary policy and the controversy over rules and discretion in monetary policy.

1. INSTRUMENTS OF MONETARY POLICY

The instruments of monetary policy are of two types: *first,* quantitative, general or indirect; and *second,* qualitative, selective or direct. The affect the level of aggregate demand through the supply of money, cost of money and availability of credit. Of the two types of instruments, the first category includes bank rate variations, open market operations and changing reserve requirements. They are meant to regulate the overall level of credit in the economy through commercial banks. The selective credit controls aim at controlling specific types of credit. They include changing margin requirements and regulation of consumer credit. We discuss them as under.[1]

Bank Rate Policy. The bank rate is the minimum lending rate of the central bank at which it rediscounts first class bills of exchange and government securities held by the commercial banks. When the central bank finds that inflationary pressures have started emerging within the economy, it raises the bank rate. Borrowing from the central bank becomes costly and commercial banks borrow less from it. The commercial banks, in turn, raise their lending rates to the business community and borrowers borrow less from the commercial banks. There is contraction of credit and prices are checked from rising further. On the contrary, when prices are depressed, the central bank lower the bank rate. It is cheap to borrow from the central bank on the part of commercial banks. The latter also lowers their lending rates. Businessmen are encouraged to borrow more. Investment is encouraged. Output, employment, income and demand start rising and the downward movement of prices is checked.

Open Market Operations. Open market operations refer to sale and purchase of securities in the money market by the central bank. When prices are rising and there is need to control them, the central bank sells securities. The reserves of commercial banks are reduced and they are not in a position to lend more to the business community. Further investment is discouraged and the rise in prices is checked. Contrariwise, when recessionary forces start in the economy, the central bank buys securities. The reserves of commercial banks are raised. They lend more. Investment, output, employment, income and demand rise, and fall in price is checked.

Changes in Reserve Ratios. This weapon was suggested by Keynes in his *Treatise on Money* and the USA was the first to adopt it as a monetary device. Every bank is required by law to keep a certain percentage of its

---

1. For a detailed study of these instruments of monetary policy, refer to chapter on 'Credit Control'.

total deposits in the form of a reserve fund in its vaults and also a certain percentage with the central bank. When prices are rising, the central bank raises the reserve ratio. Banks are required to keep more with the central bank. Their reserves are reduced and they lend less. The volume of investment, output and employment are adversely affected. In the opposite case, when the reserve ratio is lowered, the reserves of commercial banks are raised. They lend more and the economic activity is favourably affected.

Selective Credit Controls. Selective credit controls are used to influence specific types of credit for particular purposes. They usually take the form of changing margin requirements to control speculative activities within the economy. When there is brisk speculative activity in the economy or in particular sectors in certain commodities, and prices start rising, the central bank raises the margin requirement on them. The result is that the borrowers are given less money in loans against specified securities. For instance, raising the margin requirement to 60% means that the pledger of securities of the value of Rs. 10,000 will be given 40% of their value, i.e. Rs 4,000 as loan. In case of recession in' a particular sector, the central bank encourages borrowing by lowering margin requirements.

Conclusion. For an effective anticyclical monetary policy, bank rate, open market operations, reserve ratio and selective control measures are required to be adopted simultaneously. But it has been accepted by all monetary theorists that (i) the success of monetary policy is nil in a depression when business confidence is at its lowest ebb; and (ii) it is successful against inflation. The monetarists contend that as against fiscal policy, monetary policy possesses greater flexibility and it can be implemented rapidly.[2]

2. EXPANSIONARY MONETARY POLICY*

An expansionary (or easy) monetary policy is used to overcome a recession or a depression or a deflationary gap. When there is a fall in consumer demand for goods and services, and in business demand for investment goods, a deflationary gap emerges. The central bank starts an expansionary monetary policy that eases the credit market conditions and leads to an upward shift in aggregate demand. For this purpose, the central bank purchases government securities in the open market, lowers the reserve requirements of member banks, lowers the discount rate and encourages consumer and business credit through selective credit measures. By such measures, it decreases the cost and availability of credit in the money market, and improves the economy.

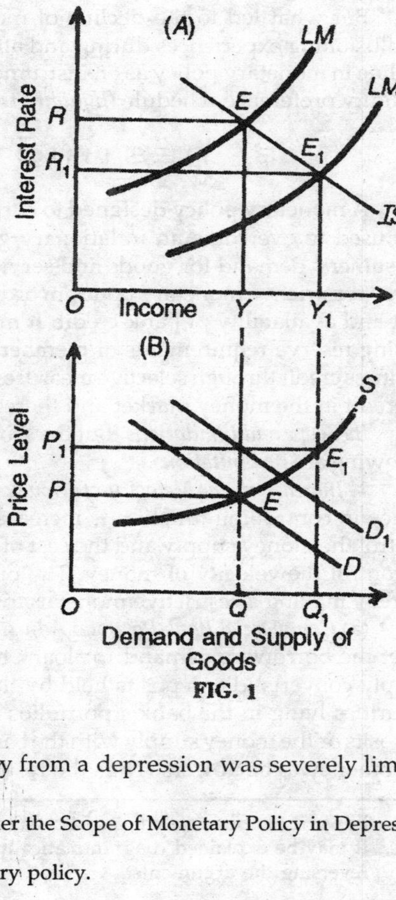

FIG. 1

The expansionary monetary policy is explained in terms of Fig. 1 (A) and (B) where the initial recession equilibrium is at *R*, *Y*, *P* and *Q*. At the interest rate *R* in Panel (A) of the figure, there is already an excess money supply in the economy. Suppose the central bank credit policy results in an increase in the money supply in the economy. This leads to a rightward shift of the *LM* curve to LM_1. This increases income from *OY* to OY_1, and aggregate demand expands and the demand curve *D* shifts upwards to D_1 in Panel (B). With increase in the demand for goods and services, output increases from *OQ* to OQ_1 at a higher price level P_1. If the expansionary monetary policy operates smoothly, the equilibrium at E_1 can be at the full employment level. But this is not likely to be attained because of the following limitations :

Its Scope and Limitations. During the 1930s and 1940s, it was believed that the success of monetary policy in stimulating recovery from a depression was severely limited

2. For limitations of Monetary Policy, refer to the limitations given under the Scope of Monetary Policy in Depression and Inflation discussed below.

* This and the next section also relate to the effectiveness of monetary policy.

than in controlling a boom and inflation. This view emerged from the experiences of the Great Depression and the appearance of Keynes's *General Theory*.

The monetarists hold that during a depression the central bank can increase the reserves of commercial banks through a cheap money policy. They can do so by buying securities and reducing the interest rate. As a result, their ability to extend credit facilities to borrowers increases. But the experience of the Great Depression tells us that in a serious depression when there is pessimism among businessmen, the success of such a policy is practically nil. In such a situation, banks are helpless in bringing about a revival. Since business activity is almost at a standstill, businessmen do not have any inclination to borrow to build up inventories even when the rate of interest is very low. Rather, they want to reduce their inventories by "repaying loans already drawn from the banks. Moreover, the question of borrowing for long-term capital needs does not arise in a depression when the business activity is already at a very low level. The same is the case with consumers who faced with unemployment and reduced incomes do not like to purchase any durable goods through bank loan. Thus all that the banks can do is to make credit available but they cannot force businessmen and consumers to accept it. In the 1930s, very low interest rates and the piling up of unused reserves with the banks did not have any significant impact on the depressed economies of the world.

"This is not to say that an easy monetary policy in times of severe contraction will be without beneficial effect, its effect will be largely that of preventing a bad situation from getting worse. *But* a restrictive monetary policy combined with a business downturn would surely aggravate the downturn—the classical example of this was the monetary policy in 1931 that contributed to the deepening of the Great Depression. . . On the other hand, if credit is readily available on favourable terms, it clearly has a stabilising effect. By meeting the liquidity requirements of business, it can slow and perhaps reduce the extent of the downturn."[3]

But what led to the decline of monetary policy in the 1930s and 1940s? In addition to the sad and disillusioning experiences during and after the Great Depression, it was Keynes's *General Theory* that led to a decline in monetary policy as an instrument of economic stabilisation. Keynes pointed out that a highly elastic liquidity preference schedule *(liquidity trap)* renders monetary policy impotent in time of severe depression.

3. RESTRICTIVE MONETARY POLICY

A monetary policy designed to curtail aggregate demand is called restrictive (or dear) monetary policy. It.is used to overcome an inflationary gap. The economy experiences inflationary pressures due to rising consumers' demand for goods and services and there is also boom in business investment. The central bank starts a restrictive monetary policy in order to lower aggregate consumption and investment by increasing the cost and availability of bank credit. It might do so by selling government securities in the open market, by raising reserve requirements of member banks, by raising the discount rate, and controlling consumer and business credit through selective measures. By such measures, the central bank increases the cost and availability of credit in the money market and thereby controls inflationary pressures.[4]

Its Scope and Limitations. But the scope of monetary policy is severely limited in controlling inflation. The following are its *limitations.*

1. *Increase in the Velocity of Money.* One of the important limitations on the effectiveness of monetary policy in controlling inflation is increase in the velocity of money held by the public. The central bank can control the money supply and the cost of money by a tight monetary policy but it does not possess any power to control the velocity of money. The public can make an effective use of the money supply held by them thereby making a restrictive monetary policy ineffective. This can be done in a number of ways.

(a) *Commercial Bank Portfolio Adjustments.* In the face of a restrictive monetary policy, commercial banks meet the borrowers demand for loans by seiling government securities to the central bank. Such a policy simply converts idle deposits held by the banks in the form of securities into active deposits. Government securities lying in the bank's portfolios are substituted for loans. But there is no change in either the total deposits or the money supply with the banks. However, this leads to increase in total spending when the banks lend money to borrowers. Thus the restrictive monetary policy of the central bank becomes ineffective.

---

3. Edward Shapiro, *op. cit.*, p. 541. Italics mine.
4. It may be explained diagrammatically by starting with the initial equilibrium at R_1 ,Y_1 ,Q_1 and P_1 in Fig. 1 and reversing the arguments.

Moreover, when the banks sell government securities to the central bank, their prices fall and the interest on them rises in the market. This will raise the general interest rate structure in the market. But the fall in the prices of securities brings capital losses to the banks and they may be reluctant to bear them. This depends upon whether they expect the fall in security prices (or rise in interest rate) to be short-lived or continue overtime. If the fall in security prices is expected to be short-lived, the banks will prefer to keep securities rather than sell them at a capital loss. On the other hand, if they expect it to continue for sometime, they will sell securities for giving loans to customers at higher interest rates, thereby recouping the capital loss on the sale of securities through higher interest rates on loans. But once the demand for loans subsides, the banks can buy back government securities now at prices lower than at which they sold, and again gain in the transaction. Thus the commercial banks' policy of portfolio adjustment raises the velocity of total money supply even in the face of a tight monetary policy thereby making the latter ineffective.

(b) The Role of Non-Bank Financial Intermediaries. NBFIs act as a restraint on the effectiveness of monetary policy to restrict the money supply in two ways. *First,* they sell securities for advancing loans, and thus increase velocity in the same manner as commercial banks do, as explained above. *Second,* as interest rates on securities rise in a tight monetary policy, financial intermediaries raise the interest rates on deposits with them to attract more funds from savers. This induces savers to shift more idle money to the intermediaries which increases their lending power further. In this way, they are able to raise the velocity of money thereby making tight restrictive monetary policy ineffective.

(c) *Methods to Make Better Use of Available Money Supply.* The private sector has evolved many ways to make better use of available supply of money which make a restrictive monetary policy ineffective. Some of the methods are the evolvement of improved methods of collecting funds by sales finance companies, borrowing funds by companies from the public at higher rates than offered by commercial banks, etc. By getting funds from sources other than the commercial banks, such institutions are able to increase the velocity of the available supply of money even under restrictive monetary policy.

2. *Discriminatory.* A restrictive monetary policy is discriminatory in its effects on particular sectors of the economy. It is argued that firms that depend upon internal sources of financing are not affected by a restrictive monetary policy. On the other hand, only those firms are affected that depend for funds on the banking system. In particular, a tight monetary policy *"is thought to work against small businessmen, because they are poorer credit risks, and against residential construction and some types of state and local government spending, because they are most sensitive to changes in credit cost."* It may slow down or even halt spending by them.

3. *Threat to Credit Market.* If the central bank rigorously tightens the credit market and investors expect continued increase in interest rates, this may lead to drying up of loanable funds to the credit market. As a result, securities may not be sold and the credit market may cease to function.

4. *Threatens Solvency of NBFIs.* A vigorous restrictive monetary policy by swiftly raising interest rates may threaten the solvency of such NBFIs as savings banks, and savings and loan associations. This is because unlike the commercial banks, they are not in a position to adjust themselves to rapidly increasing interest rates.

5. *Alter Expectations of Borrowers and Lenders.* A very tight monetary policy may alter the expectations of borrowers and lenders. So they bring irreversible changes in credit market conditions. A rapid rise in interest rates may so change expectations that even when this policy is abandoned and an expansionary policy is started, lenders may be reluctant to make long-term loans in anticipation of rise in interest rates again. On the other hand, borrowers may borrow long-term funds even if they do not need them immediately in anticipation of rise in interest rates in the future.

6. *Time Lags.* Another important limitation of a tight monetary policy is the existence of time lags which are related to the need of action, its recognition, and the decision and operation of actions in time. As the monetary authority is not able to adopt restrictive monetary measures in time due to these time lags, monetary policy works very slowly and hence it is not very effective in controlling inflation.

4. ROLE OF MONETARY POLICY IN A DEVELOPING ECONOMY

Monetary policy in an underdeveloped country plays an important role in increasing the growth rate of the economy by influencing the cost and availability of credit, by controlling inflation and maintaining equilibrium in the balance of payments. So the principal objectives of monetary policy in such a country are to control credit for controlling inflation and to stabilise the price level, to stabilise the exchange rate, to achieve equilibrium in the balance of payments and to promote economic development.

To Control Inflationary Pressure. To control inflationary pressure arising in the process of development, monetary policy requires the use of both quantitative and qualitative methods of credit control. Of the instruments of monetary policy, the *open market operations* are not successful in controlling inflation in underdeveloped countries because the bill market is small and undeveloped. Commercial banks keep an elastic cash-deposit ratio because the central bank's control over them is not complete. They are also reluctant to invest in government securities due to their relatively low interest rates. Moreover, instead of investing in government securities, they prefer to keep their reserves in liquid form such as gold, foreign exchange and cash. Commercial banks are also not in the habit of rediscounting or borrowing from the central bank.

The *bank rate policy* is also not so effective in such countries due to : *(i)* lack of bills of discount; *(ii)* narrow size of the bill market; *(iii)* a large non-monetised sector where barter transactions take place; *(iv)* existence of indigenous banks which do not discount bills with the central bank; *(v)* the habit of the commercial banks to keep large cash reserves; and *(vi)* the existence of a large unorganised money market.

The use of *variable reserve ratio* as an instrument of monetary policy is more effective than open market operations and bank rate policy in LDCs. Since the market for securities is very small, open market operations are not successful. But a rise or fall in the variable reserve ratio by the Central bank reduces or increases the cash available with the commercial banks without affecting adversely the prices of securities. Again, the commercial banks keep large cash reserves which cannot be reduced by an increase in bank rate or sale of securities by the central bank. But raising the cash reserve ratio reduces liquidity with the banks. The use of variable reserve ratio has certain *limitations* in LDCs. The non-banking financial intermediaries do not keep deposits with the central bank so they are not affected by it. *Second,* banks which do not maintain excess liquidity are more affected than those who maintain it.

The *qualitative credit control* measures are, however, more effective than the quantitative measures in influencing the allocation of credit, and thereby the pattern of investment. In LDCs, there is a strong tendency to invest in gold, jewellery, inventories, real estate, etc., instead of in alternative productive channels available in agriculture, mining, plantations and industry. The selective credit controls are more appropriate for controlling and limiting credit facilities for such unproductive purposes. They are beneficial in controlling speculative activities in foodgrains and raw materials. They prove more useful in controlling 'sectional inflations in the economy. They curtail the demand for imports by making it obligatory on importers to deposit in advance an amount equal to the value of foreign currency. This has also the effect of reducing the reserves of the banks in so far as their deposits are transferred to the Central bank in the process. The selective credit control measures may take the form of changing the margin requirements against certain types of collateral, the regulation of consumer credit and the rationing of credit.

To Achieve Price Stability. Monetary policy is an important instrument for achieving price stability. It brings a proper adjustment between the demand for and supply of money. An imbalance between the two will be reflected in the price level. A shortage of money supply will retard growth while an excess of it will lead to inflation. As the economy develops, the demand for money increases due to gradual monetization of the non-monetized sector, and increase in agricultural and industrial production. These will lead to increase in the demand for transactions and speculative motives. So the monetary authority will have to raise the money supply more than proportionate to the demand for money in order to avoid inflation.

To bridge BOP Deficit. Monetary policy in the form of interest rate policy plays an important role in bridging the balance of payments deficit. Underdeveloped countries develop serious balance of payments difficulties to fulfil the planned targets of development. To establish infrastructure like power, irrigation, transport, etc. and directly productive activities like iron and steel, chemicals, electricals, fertilisers, etc., underdeveloped countries have to import capital equipment, machinery, raw materials, spares and components thereby raising their imports. But exports are almost stagnant. They are high-priced due to inflation. As a result, an imbalance is created between imports and exports which leads to disequilibrium in the balance of payments. Monetary policy can help in narrowing the balance of payments deficit through high rate of interest. A high interest rate attracts the inflow of foreign investments and helps in bridging the balance of payments gap.

Interest Rate Policy. A policy of high interest rate in an underdeveloped country also acts as an incentive to higher savings, develops banking habits and speeds up the monetization of the economy which are essential for capital formation and economic growth. A high interest rate policy is also anti-inflationary in nature, for it discourages borrowing and investment for speculative purposes, and in foreign currencies. Further, it promotes the allocation of scarce capital resources in more productive channels. Certain economists favour a low interest rate policy in such countries because high interest rates discourage investment. But empirical evidence suggests that investment in business and industry is interest-inelastic in underdeveloped countries because interest forms a very low proportion of the total cost of investment. Despite these opposite views, it is advisable for the monetary authority to follow a policy of discriminatory interest rate—charging high interest rates for non-essential and unproductive uses and low interest rates for productive uses.

To Create Banking and Financial Institutions. One of the objectives of monetary policy in an underdeveloped country is to create and develop banking and financial institutions in order to encourage, mobilise and channelise savings for capital formation. The monetary authority should encourage the establishment of branch banking in rural and urban areas. Such a policy will help in monetizing the non-monetized sector and encourage saving and investment for capital formation. It should also organise and develop money and capital market. These are essential for the success of a development-oriented monetary policy which also includes debt management.

Debt Management. Debt management is one of the important functions of monetary policy in an underdeveloped country. It aims at proper timing and issuing of government bonds, stabilising their prices and minimising the cost of servicing the public debt. The primary aim of debt management is to create conditions in which public borrowing can increase from year to year. Public borrowing is essential in such countries in order to finance development programmes and to control the money supply. But public borrowing must be at cheap rates. Low interest rates raise the price of government bonds and make them more attractive to the public. They also keep the burden of the debt low.

Thus an appropriate monetary policy, as outlined above, helps in controlling inflation, bridging balance of payments gap, encouraging capital formation and promoting economic growth.

LIMITATIONS OF MONETARY POLICY IN LDCs

The experience of underdeveloped countries reveals that monetary policy plays a limited role in such countries. The following arguments are given in support of this view.

1. *Large Non-monetized Sector.* There is a large non-monetized sector which hinders the success of monetary policy in such countries. People mostly live in rural areas where barter is practised. Consequently, monetary policy fails to influence this large segment of the economy.

2. *Undeveloped Money and Capital Markets.* The money and capital markets are undeveloped. These markets lack in bills, stocks and shares which limit the success of monetary policy.

3. *Large Number of NBFIs.* Non-bank financial intermediaries like the indigenous bankers operate on a large scale in such countries but they are not under the control of the monetary authority. This factor limits the effectiveness of monetary policy in such countries.

4. *High Liquidity.* The majority of commercial banks possess high liquidity so that they are not influenced by the credit policy of the central bank. This also makes monetary policy less effective.

5. *Foreign Banks.* In almost every underdeveloped country foreign owned commercial banks exist. They also render monetary policy less effective by selling foreign assets and drawing money from their head offices when the Central bank of the country is following a tight monetary policy.

6. *Small Bank Money.* Monetary policy is also not successful in such countries because bank money comprises a small proportion of the total money supply in the country. As a result, the Central bank is not in a position to control credit effectively.

7. *Money not Deposited with Banks.* The well-to-do people do not deposit money with banks but use it in buying jewellery, gold, real estate, in speculation, in conspicuous consumption, etc. Such activities encourage inflationary pressures because they lie outside the control of the monetary authority.

On account of these limitations of monetary policy in an under-developed country, economists advocate the use of fiscal policy alongwith it.

5. RULES VS DISCRETION IN MONETARY POLICY

A controversy has arisen over the issue whether the central bank should conduct policy in accordance with a set of fixed rules or it should follow a discretionary monetary policy.

Friedman argues that the lag between the initiation of a monetary policy and the time at which the policy is effective is so long and variable that discretionary countercyclical policy aimed at economic stabilisation may be destabilising. When a discretionary monetary policy is adopted, the central bank follows an easy monetary policy in a recession and a tight monetary policy in a boom. Given the long length of the lags and their variability, the effect of an easy monetary policy in order to control a recession may lead to inflationary pressures. Similarly, a tight monetary policy to control a boom may lead to recessionary conditions on account of time lags and delayed effects. Due to unpredictability in forecasting booms and recessions and the length, variability and uncertainty of the time lags, countercyclical discretionary monetary policy is destabilising rather than stabilising. Friedman, therefore, calls for an end to discretionary monetary policy.

Instead of leaving monetary policy to the judgement of the monetary authority, Friedman proposes that it should follow a fixed long-run rule that the money supply should grow at a constant rate year after year. There should be no deviation from this rule under any circumstances. Suppose the rule is 3 per cent growth rate of money supply which closely approximates the economy's past average annual growth rate in real output. Such a stable growth rate of money supply will keep prices stable and allow the aggregate demand to grow with the growth in productive capacity of the economy. It will thus increase employment and income. Any inflationary situation will be temporary because it will not receive an impetus by any increase in the money supply. Similarly, any recessionary tendency will be short-lived because the liquidity provided by the constant money supply will cause aggregate demand to expand. Thus the fixed rule for monetary policy suggested by Friedman would remove the uncertainties associated with discretionary countercyclical monetary policy.

Another variant of the rule is that suppose the money supply grows at 2 per cent per year for every 1 per cent unemployment in excess of, say, 5 per cent. Algebraically such a rule would be expressed as

$$\frac{\Delta M}{M} = 3.0 + 2(U - 4.0)$$

where, $\Delta M / M$ is the annual percentage growth rate of money and U is the percentage unemployment rate. This is illustrated in Fig. 2 where the unemployment rate is shown on the horizontal axis and the growth rate of money supply on the vertical axis. At 4 per cent unemployment, the growth rate of money supply is 3 per cent. If the unemployment rate rises above 4 per cent, the growth rate of the money supply is increased automatically. Thus with 5 per cent unemployment, the growth rate of money supply would be 5 per cent = 3.0 +2(5 – 4). Conversely, if unemployment dropped below 4 per cent, the growth of money supply would be lowered below 3 per cent. By linking the growth of money supply to the unemployment rate, countercyclical monetary policy is achieved without any discretion. This is called the *activist monetary rule* because it expands money supply when unemployment is high and reduces it when it is low. It does not allow any policy discretion and is thus a rule.

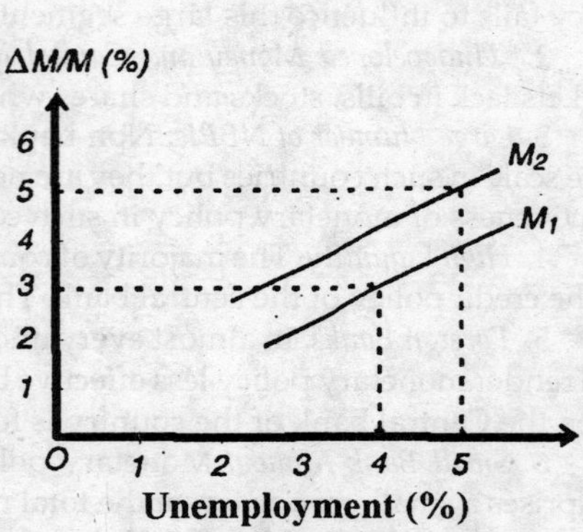

FIG. 2

Many economists do not agree with Friedman and also object to the 'activist monetary rule'. According to them, rules lead to rigidity upon the behaviour of instrument variables, thereby destabilising target variables. As a matter of fact, there should be flexibility of instruments for maintaining stability of targets. Money supply is an instrument that affects such targets of monetary policy as prices, output, income and employment.

Suppose the monetary authority has the fixed interest rate target and follows the fixed money supply rule. Their effects on income are explained in terms of Fig. 3 where the national income is measured along the horizontal axis and the interest rate on the vertical axis. OY_F is the initial full employment equilibrium at R interest rate. When, say, due to fall in business expectations, liquidity preference rises, this causes the *LM* curve to shift to the left to LM_1. As the monetary authority follows the fixed money supply rule, it will take no action so that the national income falls to OY_1 when the LM_1 curve intersects the *IS* curve at E_1. Thus the fixed money supply rule is a bad rule for the monetary authority to follow when it follows the fixed interest rate target.

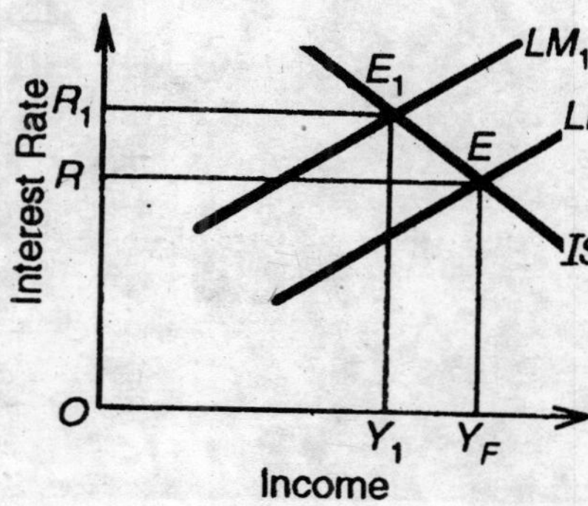

FIG. 3

In general, rules directed at such targets as the rate of interest or the money supply are "second best", and may even destabilise the economy. Therefore, no rule is a substitute for appropriate monetary policy designed to maintain full employment in the economy.

EXERCISES

1. Explain the principal instruments of monetary policy. What are their limitations?
2. Critically discuss the effectiveness of monetary policy in controlling inflation.
3. Discuss the role of monetary policy in a developing economy.
4. Discuss the controversy over Rules and Discretion of monetary policy.
5. Distinguish between cheap and dear monetary policy. Explain their relative effectiveness.

CHAPTER 33

Time Lags in Monetary Policy

1. MEANING AND TYPES

One of the limitations of monetary policy in countercyclical manner is the existence of time lags. It takes time for the monetary authority to realise the need for action and its recognition, and the taking of action and the effect of the action on economic activity. Friedman defines "lag" as the timing relation between the resulting monetary series and resulting series of effects of monetary actions. According to him, monetary actions affect economic conditions only after a lag that is "both long and variable". Friedman distinguishes among three basic lags: the recognition lag, the administrative lag, and the operation lag.

These lags are explained as under:

1. *The Recognition Lag.* It refers to the time between the development of a need for action and the recognition of that need by the monetary authority. It is difficult to know the occurrence of a turning point in a business cycle and recognise the need for action by the monetary authority. Empirical evidence in the U.S. suggests that in the past the Federal Reserve Bank recognised the need for monetary action only three months after the trough in a business cycle and about six months after a boom had started. Thus the recognition has been longer at the peaks than at the troughs.

2. *The Administrative Lag.* This relates to the period of time that occurs when the monetary authority recognises the need for action and the data on which action is actually taken. The length of the administrative lag (or decision or action lag) varies with the type of monetary policy being considered and the decision-making process of the monetary authority. Usually, this lag is very short. The administrative lag and the recognition lag taken together are termed as *inside lags* because they fall within the jurisdiction of monetary authority. Sometimes, it is difficult to distinguish between the two because the time between recognition of the need for action and the taking of action is so short that the administrative lag becomes the recognition lag.

3. *The Operation Lag.* The operation lag (or the effects lag) refers to the period of time between the adoption of monetary policy and the final effect of that policy on the economic activity. For analytical convenience, this lag is divided into the intermediate lag and the outside lag.

(a) The intermediate lag relates to the moment at which action is taken by the monetary authority and the moment at which the economy is faced with changes in interest rates and the money supply through monetary action.

(b) The outside lag refers to the time involved between changes in interest rates, total reserves, credit rationing, etc., and their effects on aggregate spending, income and output of the economy.

The three lags are explained in Fig. 1 where the time lags are taken on the horizontal axis and aggregate income and output on the vertical axis. Starting from time T on the upper turning point of the business cycle, the period R shows the recognition lag, A the administrative lag and E the effect lag. In the effects lag, two alternative effect paths EP and EP_1 are shown alongwith changes in national income as a result of changes in monetary policy. The curve Y represents the movements in national income before the policy changes. When the effects lag EP operates with an expansionary monetary policy to control a downward movement of the business cycle, the curve Y_1 represents the resultant movement in income and output. If the restrictive policy with the effects lag EP_1 is undertaken to control a boom, the resultant path of income is the curve Y_2.

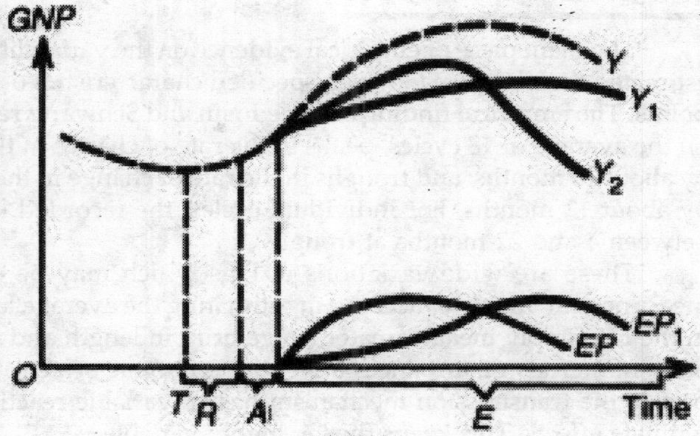

FIG. 1

2. NATURE OF THE LAG

According to Friedman, a lag is both long and variable which describes the timing relation between the money stock and economic activity. Strictly speaking, there are several lags in the effects of monetary action rather than the lag. If the effect on national income of a single monetary change could be isolated, it would begin immediately, rise to a peak, then decline gradually, and not disappear fully for an indefinite time. Such effects of the change are distributed over a long period of time. Friedman calls this *distribution lag* rather than lag proper. This is because monetary changes are never single and instantaneous. They consist of time sequence of changes whose effects accumulate and which are themselves in part the accumulated effect of other changes in the economy. Thus the concept of the lag is very complex, according to Friedman. On the basis of empirical evidence, Friedman comes to the conclusion that peaks in the rate of the money stock precede reference cycles (economic activity series) by 16 months on the average; peaks in the deviation of the money stock from its long term trend precede reference cycle peaks by 5 months on the average; such peaks in the absolute level of the money stock precede reference peaks by less than 5 months and may even lag behind; peaks in the rate of change of income precede peaks in the stock of money, and probably follow peaks in the rate of change of the money stock.

WHY IS THE LAG LONG?

Friedman gives answer to this by explaining the transmission process from changes in the money stock to economic activity in which delays occur between the timing of action and the resultant effects. Suppose the central bank increases the stock of money by purchasing securities in the open market. Its first effect is to change the balance sheet or assets and liabilities structure of the community. It tends to increase cash with people who will seek to purchase other types of financial assets. Consequently, the prices of such assets will rise. Sooner or later, the increased demand for assets will spread to equities, houses, durable producers goods, etc. In the process, the price rise will be reduced in magnitude as the demand spreads over a wide range of assets. This transmission process will not be instantaneous. Rather, it will have a long time lag. *First,* the initial monetary action and its effects will take a long time to reach the whole range of assets. *Second,* the increased demand for assets will encourage producers to create more assets which will also take a long time. With the increase in asset prices, people will consume more services such as renting a house instead of purchasing it. This will raise prices of services and interest rates. All this will raise expenditures in all directions. This process.will entail a very long period of time. Friedman concludes that the lag between monetary change and its impact on the flow of income is expected to be very much longer than between monetary change and financial markets.

WHY IS THE LAG VARIABLE?

The main piece of empirical evidence on the variability of the lag is the variation from cycle to cycle in the estimated time interval between specified characteristics of the money stock series and reference cycle turning points. The empirical findings of Friedman and Schwartz reveal that the lag is highly variable. They found that on the average of 18 cycles, peaks in the rate of change in the money stock precede peaks in economic activity by about 16 months; and troughs in the rate of change in the money stock precede troughs in economic activity by about 12 months. For individual cycles, the recorded lag varied between 6 and 29 months at peaks and between 4 and 22 months at troughs.

These are wide variations in lags which may be due to errors of measurement. But the errors of measurement largely cancel out in estimating the average lag. Given a particular length of lag, large variability in the lag simply means greater irregularity in length and timing of the resulting business cycles. At any one time, numerous disturbances affect the economic system through a variety of reaction mechanisms. If each part of the transmission mechanism has a "variable reaction time", their combined effect would spread the ultimate effects. This keeps the lag highly variable.

3. CRITICISMS

Prof. Culbertson does not agree with Friedman that a lag is both long and variable. He argues that there has been moderateness in economic fluctuations in the past which is a direct testimony against a long and variable lag. But Friedman has refuted his argument. According to him, neither the length nor the variability of the average time interval between a disturbance and its effects is connected with the amplitude of the economic fluctuations produced by a given set of disturbances.

Some critics have pointed out that factors, other than monetary changes, also play an important role in explaining economic fluctuations. Fiscal policy in the form of tax rates and government expenditure influence business cycles and affect greatly on the length and variability of the lag.

4. POLICY IMPLICATIONS

The existence of long and variable lags in the effects of monetary changes has led Friedman to conclude that discretionary countercyclical policy aimed at economic stabilisation may be destabilising. These lags can intensify rather than mitigate cyclical fluctuations. Let us explain Friedman's view in detail.

Countercyclical monetary policy means "leaning against the prevailing economic winds". It implies that the central bank follows an easy money policy in a recession and a tight money policy in a boom. Given the long length of the lags and their variability, the effects of an easy monetary policy to control a recession may lead to inflationary pressures. Similarly, a tight monetary policy to control a boom may lead to recessionary conditions due to time lags and their delayed effects. According to Friedman, "We seldom in fact know which way the economic wind is blowing until several months after the event." Due to unpredictability in forecasting of booms and recessions, and the length, variability and uncertainty of the time lags, a countercyclical monetary policy is destabilising rather than stabilising. Since the implementation and effects of anticyclical monetary policy do not occur at the right time, they will add to the amplitude of the cycle and destabilise the economy. Friedman, therefore, favours an "automatic framework" of monetary policy in which the money supply increases at a steady and inflexible rate. He gives two reasons in support of the automatic framework as against the discretionary monetary action. *First,* discretionary anticyclical monetary policy is often dominated by goals other than, and even contradictory to stabilisation, when the monetary authority adopts such measures as pegging bond yields, halting gold outflows, etc. But the automatic framework cannot be easily exploited for other purposes. *Second,* the automatic framework would be free from inertia and political considerations that inhibit the reversal of discretionary policies when they turn out to be in the wrong direction.

Friedman, therefore, calls for an end to discretion in monetary policy. In place of the judgement of monetary authority, he proposes that it should follow a fixed long-run rule: To increase the money supply at an annual fixed percentage rate regardless of current economic conditions. Set the money supply at a fixed rate and leave it to grow at that rate automatically. Of course, such an automatic framework would not eliminate economic fluctuations, but it would at least prevent the economy from the perverse effects of delayed discretionary monetary action. Friedman is not rigid about any exact rate of increase in the money supply. He suggests a rate in the neighbourhood of 3 to 4 per cent per year which closely approximates the economys past average annual rate of growth in real output. Such a stable growth rate of money supply will keep prices stable and allow the aggregate demand to grow with the growth in productive capacity of the economy. It will thus increase employment and income. Any inflationary situation will be temporary because it will not receive an impetus by any increase in the money supply. Similarly, any recessionary tendency will be short-lived because the liquidity provided by the constant money supply will cause aggregate demand to expand. Thus the automatic framework suggested by Friedman would remove uncertainties of forecasting economic fluctuations and the problems of time lags associated with discretionary countercyclical monetary policy. Fig. 2 illustrates the nature of business cycles in the case of two types of policies. The dotted curve shows the fluctuations in economic activity when countercyclical monetary policy is adopted. The smooth curve shows mild fluctuations in economic activity under the automatic framework.

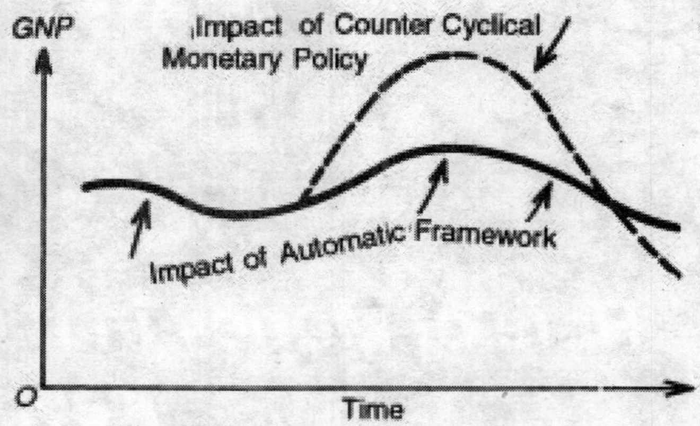

FIG. 2

CRITICISMS OF POLICY IMPLICATIONS

Culbertson does not agree with Friedman's automatic policy framework to eliminate unpredictability and lag problems of a discretionary monetary policy. He opines that "the broad record of experience supports the view that anticyclical monetary debt management and fiscal .adjustments can be counted on to have their prominent direct effects within three to six months, soon enough that if they are undertaken moderately early in a cyclical phase they will not be destabilising".

The Keynesians also do not concur with Friedman's policy prescription to avoid the lag problems. They favour the use of monetary policy to control a boom, and supplementing monetary policy with fiscal policy to control a recession.

Whichever policy is adopted, the lag problems and economic fluctuations cannot be completely eliminated.

EXERCISES

1. Explain the effects of lags in monetary policy.
2. What do you mean by lags in monetary policy? How do they affect monetary policy?
3. Discuss the nature of lags in monetary policy.
4. Explain the statement that "a lag is both long and variable."
5. Discuss the policy implications of effects in lags of monetary policy.

CHAPTER 34

Role of Money in the Classical and Keynesian Theories

1. INTRODUCTION

In the classical theory, money is neutral in its effect on the economy. It is argued that monetary forces do not affect real income, output, and employment in the economy. On the other hand, the Keynesian theory assigns a key role to money. It contends that a change in the supply of money affects the level of income, output and employment via changes in the rate of interest. We discuss below these views in detail.

2. THE CLASSICAL VIEW

In the classical system, *money is.neutral* in its effects on the economy. It plays no role in the determination of employment, income and output. Rather, they are determined by labour, capital stock, state of technology, availability of natural resources, saving habits of the people, and so on. In the classical system, the main function of money is to act as a medium of exchange. It is to determine the general level of prices at which goods and services will be exchanged. The quantity theory of money states that the price level is a function of the supply of money. Algebraically, $MV=PT$, where, M, V, P and T are the supply of money, velocity of money, price level, and the volume of transactions (or total output) respectively. The equation tells that the total money supply, MV, equals the total value of output, PT, in the economy. Assuming V and T to be constant, a change in M causes a proportionate change in P. Thus money is neutral. It is simply a 'veil' whose main function is to determine the general price level at which goods and services exchange.

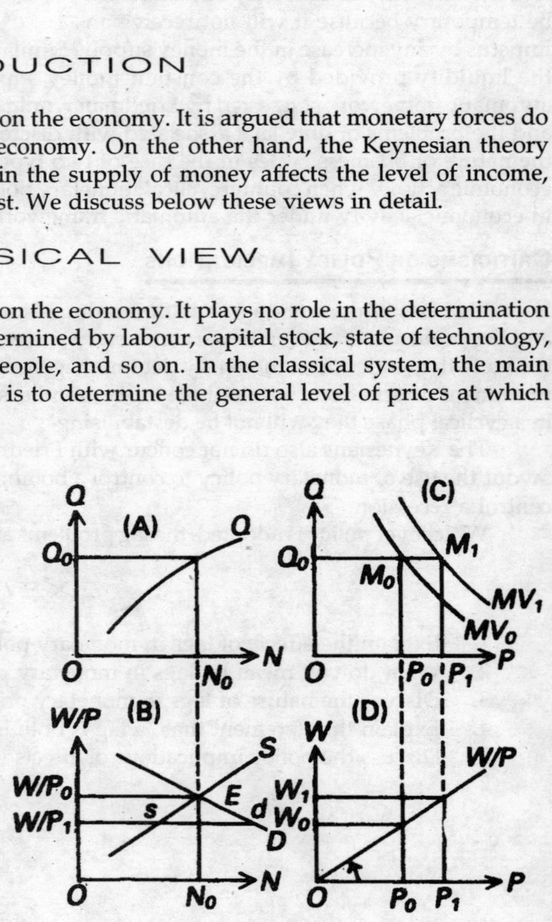

FIG. 1

The notion of neutrality of money in the classical system is explained in terms of Fig. 1. Where we start with an initial full employment equilibrium position with N_o, Q_o, W/P_o, M_o, P_o, and W_o as illustrated in Panels (A), (B), (C) and (D) of Fig. 1. The initial equilibrium is disturbed when the quantity of money is increased from M_o to M_1. This leads to a rise in effective demand from MV_o to MV_1, and shown in Panel (C). This raises commodity prices in proportion to the rise in *M*, since real output *O* is fixed. In other words, the rise in the price level is exactly proportional to the rise in the quantity of money, i.e. $P_oP_1=M_oM_1$. With increase in the price level, the money wage rate will rise as rapidly as prices to W_1-P_1 (Panel *D)* in order to keep the real wage rate W/P_o unchanged (Panel B). But with increase in the price level, the real wage rate tends to decrease from W/P_o to W/P_1, as shown in Panel B of the figure. This increases the demand for labour by more than the supply of labour which is shown by the distance *sd* in Panel B. The competitive bidding for labour will ultimately lead to rise in the real wage rate to W/P_0 whereby the labour market equilibrium is restored at point *E*. Thus the result of an increase in money is to raise money wages and prices in equal proportion, leaving output, employment and the real wage rate unaffected. It is in this sense that money is a veil or neutral in the classical system.

3. THE KEYNESIAN VIEW: MONETARY EQUILIBRIUM

The Keynesian theory assigns a key role to money. It contends that a change in the money supply can permanently change such real variables as the interest rate, the levels of employment, output and income. Keynes believed in the existence of unemployment equilibrium in the economy.

The existence of unemployment equilibrium implies that an increase in money supply can bring about permanent increases in the level of output. The ultimate influence of money supply on the price level depends upon its influence on aggregate demand and the elasticity of the supply of aggregate output. The Keynesian chain of causation between changes in the quantity of money and in prices is an indirect one through the rate of interest. So when the quantity of money is increased, its first impact is on the rate of interest which tends to fall. Given the marginal efficiency of capital, a fall in the rate of interest will increase the volume of investment. The increased investment will raise effective demand through the multiplier effect thereby increasing income, output and employment. Since the supply curve of factors of production is perfectly elastic in a situation of unemployment, wage and non-wage factors are available at constant rate of remuneration. There being constant returns to scale, prices do not rise with the increase in output so long as there is any unemployment. Under the circumstances, output and employment will increase in the same proportion as effective demand, and the effective demand will increase in the same proportion as the quantity of money. But "once full employment is reached, output ceases to respond *at all* to changes in the supply of money and so in effective demand. The elasticity of supply of output in response to changes in the supply, which was infinite as long as there was unemployment falls to zero. The entire effect of changes in the supply of money is exerted on prices, which rise in exact proportion with the increase in effective demand". Thus, so long as there is unemployment, output will change in the same proportion as the quantity of money, and there will be no change in prices; and when there is full employment, prices will change in the same proportion as the quantity of money. Therefore, Keynes stresses the point that with increase in the quantity of money, prices rise only when the level of full employment is reached, and not before this.

This is illustrated in Fig. 2, Panels (A) and (B) where *OTC* is the output curve relating to the quantity of money and *PRC* is the price curve relating to the quantity of money. Panel A of the figure shows that as the quantity of money increases from O to M, the level of output also rises along the *OT* portion of the *OTC* curve. As the quantity of money reaches *OM* level, full employment output OQ_F is being produced. But after point *T* the output curve becomes vertical because any further increase in the quantity of money cannot raise output and the full employment level OQ_F.

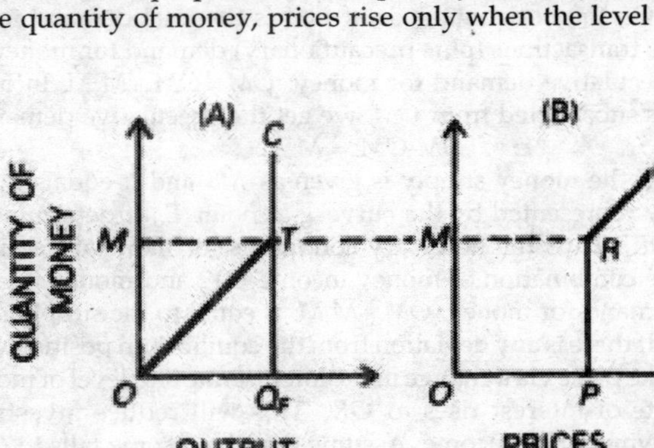

FIG. 2

Panel B of the figure shows the relationship between quantity of money and prices. So long as there is unemployment, prices remain constant whatever increase in the quantity of money. Prices start rising only after the full employment level is reached. In the figure, the price level *OP* remains constant at the *OM* quantity of money corresponding to the full employment level of output OQ_F . But an increase in the quantity of money above *OM* raises prices in the same proportion as the quantity of money. This is shown by the *RC* portion of the price curve *PRC*.

Monetary Equilibrium. So far as the rate of interest is concerned, it is a monetary phenomenon in the Keynesian theory. It is determined by the demand for and supply of money. The theory is thus characterised as the monetary theory of interest. The supply of money is considered to be fixed in the short run by monetary authorities. The demand for money, also called the liquidity preference, is the desire to hold cash. There are three motives on the part of the people to hold cash: (a) transaction demand for money, (b) precautionary demand for money, and (c) speculative demand for money. Money held for transactions and precautionary motives is a function of the level of income. $L_T = f(Y)$. It varies directly with the level of income and inversely with the interest rate.

According to Keynes, it is expectations about changes in bond prices or in the market rate of interest that determine the speculative demand for money, $Ls=f(r)$. The speculative demand for money is a decreasing function of the rate of interest. The higher the rate of interest, the lower the speculative demand for money, and vice-versa. But at a very low interest rate, the speculative demand for money becomes perfectly elastic. This is the "liquidity trap" portion of the demand for money curve. In this range, people prefer to keep money in cash rather than invest in bonds because purchasing bonds will lead to loss.

Thus the total demand for money is a function of both income and the interest rate:

$$L_T+L_S = f(Y)+f(r)$$

Or $L = f(Y)+f(r)$

Or $L = f(Y, r)$

where *L* represents the total demand for money.

The necessary conditions for monetary equilibrium in the Keynesian theory are the equality of the money supply (M) and the demand for money (L) which determines the interest rate,

$$M_s=L(=L_T+L_S)$$

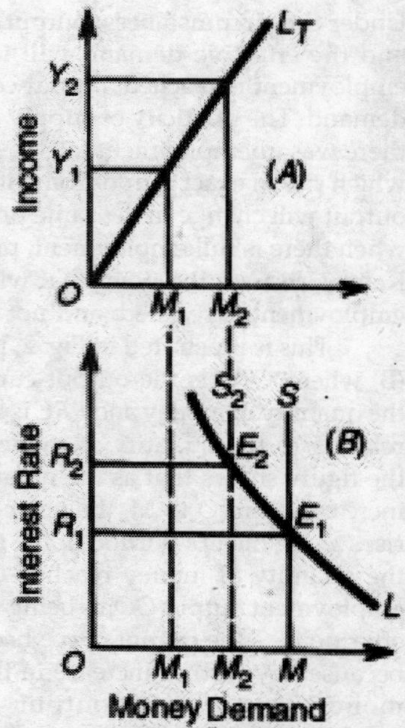

FIG. 3

This is illustrated in Fig. 3 (A) and (B). The transactions (plus precautionary) demand for money is given by the curve L_T at OY_1 and OY_2 levels in Panel (A) of the figure. At OY_1 income level, it is given by OM_1 and at OY_2 level of income by OM_2. In Panel (B), the curve *L* represents the total demand for money consisting of transactions, precautionary and speculative demand, $L_T + L_s$.

On the horizontal axis, if *OM* is the total demand for money, and OM_2 is transactions (plus precautionary) demand for money, then M_2M is the speculative demand for money: $OM = OM_2+M_2M$. In other words, if OM_2 is substracted from *OM*, we get the speculative demand for money:

$$OM-OM_2 = M_2M.$$

If the money supply is given as *MS* and it equals the demand for money represented by the curve *L* at point E_1, it determines the interest rate OR_1. Thus the necessary conditions for monetary equilibrium at E_1 are the combination of money income OY_2 and money interest rate OR_1, the demand for money, OM_2+M_2M, is equal to the supply of money, M_s .

If there is any deviation from the equilibrium position, an adjustment will take place via a change in the interest rate and level of income. Suppose the rate of interest rises to OR_2. This will reduce investment, output, employment and income. Assume that the income falls to OY_1, as shown in Panel (A) of the figure. In Panel (B) of the figure with rise in the interest rate to OR_2, the total demand for money falls to OM_2 which now consists of OM_1 of transactions (plus precautionary) demand and M_1M_2 of speculative demand. If the monetary authority reduces the money supply to M_2S_2 equal to the fall in money demand, the new monetary equilibrium will be set at point E_2 where the L curve intersects it. The opposite will be the case if the rate of interest falls below OR_1 and continues to fall, the economy may be in the "liquidity trap".

In the Keynesian monetary equilibrium, when the economy is in the 'liquidity trap,' there cannot be a further fall in the rate of interest even if the money supply is increased by the monetary authority. This implies that there will not be any effect on investment and income. In this situation, money is *neutral* and monetary policy has no effect on the economy. Given an interest-inelastic investment function, monetary policy will be ineffective.[1]

Money is also neutral and plays no role in the Keynesian system in the full employment situation when an increase in the quantity of money brings about a proportionate increase in the price level, and employment, output and income remain unchanged. But money influences the macro variables of the economy in an important way between these two extreme cases of the liquidity trap and full employment in the Keynesian system.

To conclude, money plays a significant causal role in the Keynesian theory. "The degree of money's importance depends upon its ability to alter money interest rates and upon the degree to which expenditure categories (consumption, investment, government outlays, and so forth) are sensitive to changes in the interest rate. To the extent that a given change in the money supply can induce large changes in the interest rate and that expenditures are highly sensitive to those changes, money matters very much in the Keynesian system."

EXERCISES

1. What role money plays in the Classical and Keynesian theories?
2. Discuss monetary equilibrium in the Keynesian system.
3. What role money plays in the Keynesian theory? When is money neutral in the Keynesian system?

1. Diagram of "liquidity trap" should be explained here

CHAPTER 35

Classical, Keynesian and Modern Views on Monetary Policy

1. THE CLASSICAL VIEW

Money, according to the classicists, is a veil. It is neutral in its effects on the economy. It simply affects the price level, but nothing else. An increase in the money supply leads to an increase in the price level, but the real income, the rate of interest and the level of real economic activity remain unaffected.

In the classical system, the main function of money is to act as a medium of exchange. It is to determine the general level of prices at which 'goods and services will be exchanged. This relationship between money and the price level is explained in terms of the quantity theory of money. The classical quantity theory of money states that the price level is a function of the supply of money. Algebraically, $MV=PT$ where M, V, P, and T are the supply of money, velocity of money, price level and the volume of transactions (or real total output). The equation tells that the total money supply MV equals the total value of output PT in the economy. Assuming V (the velocity of money) and T (the total output) to be constant, a change in the supply of money (M) causes a proportional change in the price level (P).

The classicists believed that there was always full employment in the economy. At the same time, they recognised the existence of unemployment in the event of downward rigidity of money wages. Such a situation could be corrected by an expansionary monetary policy. The process involved is as follows. Suppose the monetary authority increases the money supply, given the velocity of money and the level of real output. With increase in the money supply, liquidity rises with the people who increase the demand for goods and services. This, in turn, raises the price level. The rise in price level reduces the real wage which provides incentive for employers to expand employment and output towards the full employment level. Thus an expansionary monetary policy is effective in restoring full employment in the classical system.

Keynes did not agree with the classical view that the supply of money influences the price level directly and that the economy always stays at the full employment level. Moreover the classical analysis was related to the long-run where market forces worked the economy towards full employment.

2. THE KEYNESIAN VIEW

In the Keynesian analysis, monetary policy plays a crucial role in affecting economic activity. It contends that a change in the supply of money can permanently change such variables as the rate of interest, the aggregate demand, and the level of employment, output and income.

Keynes believed in the existence of unemployment equilibrium. This implies that an increase in money supply can bring about permanent increases in the level of output. The ultimate influence of money supply on the price level depends upon its influence on aggregate demand and the elasticity of the supply of aggregate output.

In a situation of unemployment, Keynes advocated cheap money policy. So when the supply of money is increased, its first effect is on the rate of interest which tends to fall. Given the marginal efficiency of capital, a fall in the rate of interest will increase investment. The increased investment will raise effective demand through the multiplier effect thereby increasing income, output and employment. Since the supply curve of factors of production is perfectly elastic in a situation of unemployment, wage and non-wage factors are available at a constant rate of remuneration. There being constant returns to scale, prices do not rise with the increase in output so long as there is unemployment. Under the circumstances, output and employment will increase in the same proportion as effective demand, and the effective demand will increase in the same proportion as the supply of money. But once full employment is reached, output ceases to respond at all to changes in the supply of money and so in effective demand. An increase in the supply of money beyond the level of full employment would raise the price level in the classical fashion.

What causes the rate of interest to change in the Keynesian monetary policy? In the Keynesian analysis, the rate of interest is determined by the demand for and supply of money. If either the demand for money or the supply of money changes, the equilibrium rate of interest would change. The supply of money is determined by the monetary authority which is normally fixed in the short-run. In other words, the money supply curve is perfectly inelastic. The demand for money is the desire to hold cash for transactions, precautionary and speculative purposes. Money held for transactions and precautionary motives depends upon the level of income. The speculative demand for money depends upon the rate of interest or bond prices.

It is, in fact, expectations about changes in bond prices or in the market rate of interest that determine the speculative demand for money. Keynes considered only two types of assets in his analysis, money and bonds. Money does not yield anything explicitly and bonds pay an explicit rate of interest. Therefore, people wish to hold bonds rather than liquid money because interest is paid to bondholders. Keynes held that the demand for money is a decreasing function of the rate of interest. The higher the rate of interest, the lower the demand for money, and *vice versa.* This negative relationship between the demand for money and the rate of interest provides a link between changes in the supply of money and the level of economic activity.

Keynes himself proceeded to question the efficacy of his monetary policy under certain conditions. He argued that at a very low interest rate, the demand for money curve becomes perfectly elastic. This is the *liquidity trap* portion of the demand for money curve which is completely flat. This means that further increase in the supply of money by the monetary authority cannot reduce the rate of interest. This implies that there will be no effect on investment and income, and monetary policy does not influence economic activity. Given an interest-inelastic investment function, monetary policy will be ineffective in the Keynesian analysis.

Thus Keynes believed on the basis of his experience that monetary policy operated under certain limitations. He wrote, "If we are tempted to assert that money is the drink which stimulates the system of activity, we must remind ourselves that there may be several steps between the cup and the.lip." The effectiveness of monetary policy depends on *first,* if the increase in the supply of money reduces the rate of interest provided the demand for money does not become infinite (i.e. perfectly elastic), and *second,* the reduction in the rate of interest increases investment demand provided it is not inelastic to the rate of interest. These limitations become more serious during depression and thus monetary policy becomes ineffective. That is why, Keynes favoured investment on public projects during depression. He wrote, "I am now somewhat sceptical of the success of a merely monetary policy directed towards influencing the rate of interest." In fact, he advocated supplementing monetary policy with fiscal policy during depression. Recent researches have shown that Keynes was misrepresented by his followers in attributing that he was not a votary of monetary policy.

3. THE MODERN VIEW

The modern monetary economists[1] reject the Keynesian view that the link between the supply of money and output is the rate of interest. The Keynesian analysis considered only two types of assets: bonds and speculative cash balances, and their allocation depended on the rate of interest which, in turn, resulted in changes in output.

The modern monetary policy is based on the portfolio adjustment process. When the central bank purchases securities in open market, it sets in motion substitution and wealth effects, as the public portfolio consists of a wide variety of assets such as bonds, equities, savings, mortgages, etc. These effects will ultimately increase aggregate money demand and expand output. The transmission mechanism is explained under substitution effects and wealth effects.

---

1. For a detailed discussion of the monetarist view refer to chapter *The Monetarist Revolution.*

Substitution Effects

The neo-Keynesians widened considerably the portfolio of assets to include not only government securities but also industrial bonds, equities, savings, mortgages, etc. Given this type of portfolio, suppose the central bank engages in open market operation and purchases securities. This will increase the prices of securities, thereby reducing the yield on them. In other words, the holders of securities sell them to the central bank because they get high prices for them. They now hold more money than they desire. As a result, they try to readjust the structure of their portfolios so as to reduce their money holdings. Suppose they substitute bonds for their excess money balances. The increase in the demand for bonds results in an increase in their market price, thereby reducing their current yield, as interest rate falls. Consequently, the demand for other assets such as equities, consumer durables etc. increases. When people having surplus money balances purchase equities (shares), their prices rise. As a result, the value of capital of such firms rises above the supply price of such new capital. Such firms are, therefore, induced to increase their demand for more capital equipment, thereby raising output in the capital goods industries. This will, in turn, spread to the rest of the economy via the multiplier effect. Thus the "neo-Keynesians contend that financial assets are the closest substitutes for money, and that, consequently, increases in the supply of money will have their effect eventually on the level of economic activity by bringing about increases in the output of capital goods industries."

The monetarists led by Friedman are of the view that excess money balances will be used to purchase not only financial assets but also real assets such as houses, land, consumer durables, etc. So when the Central bank purchases securities and their prices increase and yields fall, the demand for financial and real assets increases. With the increase in their demand, their prices rise. But the rise in the prices of real assets leads to some additional effects. When the prices of real assets rise, their production is encouraged which, in turn, raises the demand for resources used in their production. Moreover, there is also increase in the demand for services as a result of increase in the prices of real assets. To illustrate, suppose the holders of surplus money balances demand more consumer durables, say cars. This will raise the prices of existing cars relative to the prices of new cars. Since the new cars are relatively cheaper, their demand will increase which will raise their output, income and employment in the car industry. With the overall increase in the demand for cars, the demand for their services will also increase. Thus an expansionary monetary policy leads to increase in demand, prices and expenditures for financial and real assets and for services through substitution effect.

The transmission mechanism operates through initial change in interest rates on securities and relative prices of both financial and reaf assets. These changes lead to the substitution of asset holdings which imply changes in the demand for real assets and services.

Wealth Effects

There is a lot of controversy between the neo-Keynesians and the Friedmanians regarding the wealth effect. According to the neo-Keynesians when the central bank engages in open market purchasing of securities, it leads to decline in market interest rates. This produces a wealth effect which results from the fact that at a lower rate of interest the present or the capitalised value of the expected income stream of financial or real capital assets increases. As people feel wealthier, they buy more of all assets in their portfolios, and consequently increase their demand for consumer non-durables.

According to Friedmanians, an open market operation which exchanges money for bonds increases the nominal wealth of society. This is a *direct* wealth effect. A fall in the rate of interest increases the market value of the existing capital stock, thereby raising the nominal wealth of society. This is the *interest-induced* wealth effect. Both these wealth effects lead to an increase in net wealth. As a result, individuals buy financial and real assets including consumer durables.

In fact, the extent to which "the combined wealth effects bring up the price of the existing stock of assets relative to the price of new production, they also serve to increase the rate of flow of output of new producer and consumer durables. In addition, the wealth effect may serve directly to stimulate the purchase of consumer non-durable goods."

EXERCISES

1. Discuss the Classical and Keynesian views on monetary policy.
2. Explain the modern view on monetary policy.

CHAPTER 36

The Liquidity Theory of Money

1. INTRODUCTION

The liquidity theory is a new approach to monetary policy which has been propounded by the Radcliffe Report and Gurley and Shaw. This theory highlights the role of liquid assets in influencing aggregate demand and economic activity. According to this theory, it is non-bank financial intermediaries (NBFIs) which provide a link between liquidity and monetary policy.

Broadly speaking, liquidity means *moneyness.* Liquidity is characterised by the ease of converting an asset into money at little cost. A liquid asset is one which is easily spendable, marketable (transferable) and has capital certainty.

Depending on these properties, different assets differ in the degree of liquidity. Money is the most important liquid asset which consists of coins, currency and bank deposits. This is because they perform the medium of exchange function of money. In the case of bank deposits only *demand deposits* are money because cheques can be issued on their basis. Thus cheques are perfect substitutes for money. But time deposits are *not real* money but are *near money* because they cannot be *withdrawn before* the expiry of a fixed period.

Besides time deposits, other near money assets are bonds, securities, debentures, bills of exchange, treasury bills, insurance policies, etc. All these types of assets are *less* liquid because they involve cost for converting them into real money.

Liquidity is created by the central bank by issuing coins and notes and by commercial banks by creating demand deposits. A change in the supply of money by the central bank affects liquidity by bringing changes or readjustments in the portfolio assets of the people. This depends on the effect of money supply on aggregate spending. For instance, if people decide to spend the increased money supply in purchasing such assets as shares and debentures, there will be less money available in liquid form with the public. If the stock market is bullish, people may buy shares and the liquidity is reduced. On the other hand, if there is uncertainty in the stock market, people may hold the increased money supply in bank deposits or invest in property if they expect property prices to rise. But it is the central bank that influences money supply in the economy by following "easy" or "tight" monetary policy. It does so by controlling aggregate spending and thereby influencing business activity, output and employment. But it is not always successful in controlling spending by increasing or decreasing the money supply and hence liquidity. This is because the central bank has little control over the velocity of circulation of money, non-bank financial intermediaries, business expectations, time lags in monetary policy, etc. It is, therefore, very difficult to predict the effects of changes in money supply on liquidity.

The Radcliffe Report and Gurley and Shaw have shown separately that the existence of NBFIs weaken the effect of monetary policy in increasing the money supply in the economy because they control a large portion of liquidity in the economy. Therefore, the role of NBFIs in increasing liquidity is equally important. We explain their views as under.

2. THE RADCLIFFE COMMITTEE VIEW : RADCLIFFE - SAYERS THESIS

The Radcliffe Committee in its report did not accept the monetarist view that there was any direct link between money supply and national income. This is because money is a close substitute for other financial assets, particularly those issued by non-bank financial institutions. If the central bank wanted to follow a contractional monetary policy by selling securities in the open market, non-bank financial intermediaries would be able to release idle demand deposits and currency. In this way, they would offset the restriction of money supply, and leave aggregate demand unchanged. Thus it held the view that "changes in rates of interest only very exceptionally have direct effects on the level of demand." It also did not find any indirect relation between money supply and national income.

According to the Radcliffe Committee, it is liquidity that influences total effective demand for goods and services rather than the supply of money The Committee pointed out that the "decisions to spend on goods and services, the decisions that determine the level of total demand, are influenced by the liquidity of the spenders. The spending is not limited by the amount of money in existence; but it is related to the amount of money people think they can get hold of, whether by receipt of income (for instance, from sales), by disposal of capital assets or by borrowing". Thus liquidity consists of the amount of money people can get hold of from income, sales, disposal of capital assets or borrowing. Suppose if liquidity is reduced, expenditures would decline to the extent they exceed current income and vice versa.

The second element by which the monetary authority can influence the level of overall liquidity and hence the level of aggregate expenditures is the *interest rate*. It is by manipulating the structure of interest rates which affects the overall liquidity structure. A movement of interest rates means significant changes in the capital values of many assets held by individuals and financial institutions. When interest rates rise, they reduce liquidity because they reduce the capital value of assets held by the latter. Financial institutions, in turn, reduce the supply of loanable funds. Since individuals and businesses cannot procure funds, they reduce their expenditures. On the other hand, a fall in the interest rate "strengthens balance sheets and encourages lenders to seek new business". In this monetary mechanism, the commercial banks hold a special position in the Committee's view, because they are the most convenient institutional source of funds for most borrowers for short-term purposes.

On the basis of this transmission mechanism, the Committee concluded that monetary policy performed a "background function". It thought that business investment was insensitive to changes in short-term interest rates. But it was influenced by long-term interest rates. Therefore, it was undesirable to cause long-term interest rates to fluctuate sharply because sharp fluctuations would undermine the strength and stability of financial institutions. In fact, financial institutions are accustomed to stable interest rates and they plan their lending policies accordingly. The monetary authority should, therefore, try to hold long-term interest rates at the level which maintained approximate balance between saving and investment in the economy.

The Committee did not favour reliance on *monetary policy* alone in severe deflationary or severe inflationary conditions. Apart from the removal of credit control and a possible effect of lower long-term interest rates on house-building activity during a slump, monetary policy was thought to be of not much help. Rather, the use of monetary measures to raise the economy from a slump carried the danger of flooding the financial system with liquidity. It would be difficult to control it later on when business activity expanded during the upswing. Thus in the Committee's view, "in general, the potentialities of monetary policy alone in the face of a severe slump are well represented by the proverb that you can take a horse to water but you cannot make him drink." Similarly, it was against any restriction on the money supply during severe inflation. It advocated measures to strike directly and rapidly at the liquidity of spenders through control of capital issues, bank advances and consumer credit. But it did not favour control over the lending power of the non-bank financial intermediaries because it entailed additional administrative burdens. More so because new financial institutions would be coming up which would make it difficult for the monetary authority to control the situation. Thus the Radcliffe Committee suggested "liquidity controls" through changes in long-term interest rates. According to it, "monetary measures cannot alone be relied upon to keep in nice balance an economy subject to major strains from without and within. Monetary measures can help but that is all". It, therefore, recommended reliance on fiscal policy in normal times which should be supplemented with monetary policy during severe inflations.

Its Criticisms

The views of the Radcliffe Committee have been severely criticised on the following grounds:

1. Economists have criticised it for advocating the control of overall liquidity of the economy rather than the money supply.

2. It did not precisely define liquidity or liquid assets. This makes the whole approach to liquidity as haphazard.

3. Prof. Gurley in his review of the Radcliffe Report found "confusion every where in the role of money supply, in the concept of liquidity, and in money to satisfy the liquidity desire of the public."

4. Other economists characterised the Report as "an utterly muddled one, indicating a stock-flow muddle, a liquidity muddle, and an interest rate muddle."

3. THE GURLEY-SHAW VIEW

According to Gurley and Shaw, it is the NBFIs that provide liquidity and safety to financial assets and help in transferring funds from ultimate lenders to ultimate borrowers for productive purposes. They increase capital formation and consequently lead to economic growth.

By buying primary securities from the ultimate borrowers and selling indirect securities to the ultimate lenders, the intermediaries influence the availability of credit and the structure and level of interest rates. They create credit different from commercial banks. But they create new assets and liabilities which tend to influence the supply of money and thus hinder the operation of an effective monetary policy.

According to them, the savings deposits of NBFIs resemble the demand deposits of commercial banks because it is not difficult for NBFIs to convert their savings deposits into cash. These savings deposits, whether of commercial banks or of NBFIs, are for all practical purposes as liquid as demand deposits. Such savings deposits held by NBFIs are known as near moneys. Since the demand deposits are not controlled by the central bank, it follows that the savings deposits held by NBFIs will hinder the successful operation of a successful monetary policy.

If the central bank wishes to control excess liquidity in the economy only through the reduction in money supply, it will not be successful because the savings deposits of NBFIs can be converted into cash. Similarly, if the central bank tries to control lending by commercial banks, it will not be successful if the lending of all other FIs are not under its control, as is the case. According to Gurley and Shaw, this problem arises especially when the central bank adopts an anti-inflationary monetary policy. Suppose the central bank reduces the money supply in order to control inflation. Among other effects, the interest rates on market securities rise in anticipation of higher yields and profits. NBFIs will raise the interest rates on their savings deposits to attract more funds in order to invest them in higher yielding securities.

Persons already holding securities find that their prices have fallen because of the rise in interest rates on present securities. They will, therefore, sell them and deposit their funds with intermediaries in order to earn higher interest rates on savings deposits. In the meantime, attracted by higher interest rates, others holding idle cash balances will also deposit them with intermediaries. So when NBFIs raise the interest rates on their savings deposits, the public reduces its demand for money which, in turn, reduces the market rate of interest. Thus NBFIs make tight monetary policy less successful or effective. Similarly, NBFIs can make an expansionary monetary policy ineffective by reducing liquidity.

But unlike the Radcliffe Report, Gurley and Shaw argue that the central bank's control over NBFIs should be extended for an effective monetary policy. This is because the NBFIs create more near-money assets and thereby affect the overall liquidity which, in turn, influences aggregate demand and economic activity.

Its Criticisms

The view of Gurley and Shaw has been criticised on the following grounds:

1. Prof. Johnson does not agree with Gurley and Shaw. He observes that there seems to be no empirical case for empowering the central bank to extend its control over financial intermediaries similar to that exercised over the commercial banks. According to him, there is little reason for believing that the central bank's control is weakened by the presence of financial intermediaries. Moreover, so long as the public does not switch easily from bank deposits into indirect securities of intermediaries, the presence of intermediaries may increase the leverage of the central bank on economic activity. It implies that it is not possible for the interest rates to settle back at their old levels even by the operation of non-bank financial intermediaries. Rather, interest rates would tend to rise further. The money supply will remain tight and its influence on spending would be restrictive.

2. Further, the rapid growth of NBFIs has helped to strengthen the effectiveness of monetary policy rather than weaken it where the NBFIs have been controlled. But Gurley and Shaw do not elaborate how they should be controlled.

Conclusion

Despite the weaknesses of both Radcliffe Report and Gurley-Shaw views, they highlight the role of NBFIs in creating liquidity which affects aggregate demand and economic activity. They emphasise that the success of monetary policy depends not in controlling the money supply but general liquidity. Thus the liquidity theory of money provides a new and realistic dimension to monetary policy.

EXERCISES

1. Explain briefly the liquidity theory of money.
2. What do you mean by liquidity? Explain the Radcliffe-Sayers view about the liquidity theory of money.
3. Explain the Gurley-Shaw view about the liquidity theory of money.
4. Explain the liquidity approach to monetary policy.

CHAPTER 37

The Monetarist Revolution

1. MEANING

The "monetarist revolution" refers to the new and important contributions made to monetary theory and policy by Prof. Friedman and his colleagues at the University of Chicago. It was a sort of revolution against the views of Keynesians who held the view that "money does not matter." The Keynesians regarded the money supply as a passive factor in the economic system whose economic effects were highly unpredictable. On the other hand, in the monetarist revolution "only money matters" for three reasons: *one,* because the quantity of money is capable of being controlled fairly accurately by deliberate policy; *two,* because changes in the quantity of money can produce substantial changes in the flow of income, prices and other important variables; and *three,* because the" relationships between stock of money and other assets are relatively stable and dependable."[1]

2. MAIN FEATURES

The monetarist revolution possesses the following characteristics:

1. *The money supply is the crucial determinant of economic activity in the short-run.* It is the money supply that determines total spending, and therefore, output, employment and the price level. Thus there is a direct link between the money supply and the national income. That link is the constant velocity of money. The constant velocity is expressed as Y/M. As a result of the stability of monetary velocity, a change in the money supply will change total spending and national income by a predictable amount. The demand for money is a stable function of income. The demand for money is the transactions demand for money which is determined by the level of income. If the central bank increases the money supply by purchasing securities, people who sell securities find that their holdings of money have increased. They will, therefore, spend their excess holding of money partly on assets and partly on consumer goods and services. This spending will reduce their money balances and at the same time raise the national income. On the contrary, a reduction in the money supply by selling securities on the part of the central bank will reduce money holdings of the buyers of securities. They will, therefore, increase their money holdings partly by selling their assets and partly by reducing their consumption expenditure on goods and services. This will reduce the national income. Thus, on both counts, the demand for money remains stable.

According to Friedman, a change in the money supply causes a proportionate change in the price level or income or both. Given the demand for money, if the economy is operating at less than full employment level, an increase in the money supply will raise output and employment with a rise in total expenditure in the short-run. An increase in the money supply causes national income to rise because with excess money supply,

1. M. Friedman and D. Meiselman, in *Stabilisation Policies,* 1963.

people start spending more until the demand and supply of money are equal. Thus an increase in the money supply in the short run raises output, employment and income. But a rise in the money supply in the long-run, with further increase in demand, prices and wages will increase. In the expectation of inflation, price-wage spiral will rise further. Thus there will be inflation due to inappropriate increase in money supply. That is why the monetarists regard inflation as a purely monetary phenomenon.

The monetarists regard their viewpoint as revolutionary as against the Keynesians because the rate of interest plays no part in influencing either the demand for money or the supply of money. Moreover, changes in the money supply influence economic activity directly and not indirectly through changes in the interest rate like the Keynesians.

2. *The transmission mechanism of monetary influences on economic activity involves reshuffling of both financial and real assets in the portfolios of economic units.* Keynes considered only two types of assets, bonds and speculative cash balances, in his transmission mechanism. According to the monetarists, when the central bank increases the money supply by purchasing securities in the open market, their prices rise but yields fall due to a fall in the market rate of interest.

People will, therefore, sell securities, and their holdings of money will increase. This raises the demand for financial and real assets. This will lead to the substitution of excess money balances for financial assets and durable consumer goods. The increase in aggregate expenditure on assets and goods will tend to raise the national income. This is the substitution effect of the portfolio adjustment process.

Further, when money is converted into securities with their purchase in the open market, the nominal wealth of the community increases. This is the *direct wealth effect.* Again, with the fall in the market rate of interest, the market value of current capital stock increases which also raises the nominal wealth of the society. This is the *interest induced effect* of wealth effect. But these effects increase the net wealth. Consequently, people buy financial and real assets which lead to the production of new producer and consumer durables goods and encourage the purchase of consumer non-durable products.

In the monetarist system, a central bank cannot influence interest rates through changes in the supply of money. If it tries to reduce the interest rate by releasing large quantity of money, this will only cause inflation since the economy is already at near-full employment level. In fact, this will reduce the real money supply and increase interest rates.

3. *In the long-run the level of real national income is determined by the forces of demand and supply.* This is based on the assumptions that prices and wages in all markets are inherently flexible. They rise in response to excess demand and fall in response to excess supply. If some prices are inflexible, the burden of their adjustments would fall on other products. Thus the economy is usually at or near the full employment level where there is no involuntary unemployment. Friedman refers to this as the *natural rate of unemployment.* This view is in marked contrast to the Keynesian view that there is always underemployment equilibrium in the economy and unemployment is involuntary.

4. *The monetarists hold that the economy is stable.* They do not believe like the Keynesians that it is subject to wide or sudden fluctuations due to changes in the propensities to consume and invest. According to them, instability exists in the economy on account of monetary and fiscal policies adopted by the government. These policies destabilise rather than stabilise the economy. Friedman does not favour even contracyclical monetary policy. According to him, monetary policy might do more harm than good because of the operation lag. On average, it takes a long time for a change in the money supply to affect national income. The time lag involved is so large that contracyclical monetary policy might actually have a destabilising effect on the economy. Fiscal policy has no place in the monetarist system. It does not affect the economy unless it is accompanied by changes in the money supply. So there is no need for fiscal policy as the same results can be achieved by monetary policy.

However, to stabilise the economy and avoid inflation, Friedman advocates a steady and inflexible growth in the rate of money supply. When the money supply increases at the same rate as output, the national income grows without inflation.

5. *Expectations play an important role in the monetarist's view.* Every person whether he is a businessman, consumer or worker is capable of correctly anticipating the effects of his own and other persons' actions. The monetarists hold that expectations are rational. "Decisions taken on the basis of such expectations will cause the

anticipated future results to occur even more quickly, if not at once. Thus intelligent expectations are self-reinforcing and stabilising, so long as the government does not create false signals by erratic and irrational intervention." They have revolutionised economic thinking through the rational expectations hypothesis. *e.g.*, the rational expectationists deny the possibility of any inflation-unemployment trade-off even in the short run.

Economists regard the above views of the monetarists as revolutionary.[2]

3. CRITICISMS

Prof. Kaldor does not regard the above views of the monetarists as revolutionary. He characterises them as a "counter-reformation—the reaction against the new economics of the 1930s and return to 19th century orthodoxies."[3] He and many Keynesians have criticised the monetarist tenets on the following grounds:

1. *Money Supply Endogenous.* The supply of money is varied by the monetary authorities in an exogenous manner in Friedman's system. But the fact is that in the United States the money supply consists of bank deposits created by changes in bank lending. Bank lending, in turn, is based upon bank reserves which expand and contract with *(a)* deposits and withdrawals of currency by non-bank financial intermediaries; *(b)* borrowings by commercial banks from the Federal Reserve System; (c) inflows and outflows of money from and to abroad; and *(d)* purchase and sale of securities by the Federal Reserve System.

The first three items definitely impart an endogenous element to the money supply. Thus the money supply is not exclusively exogenous, as assumed by Friedman. It is mostly endogenous.

1. Demand for Money not Stable. Regarding the stability of the demand for money, Prof. Kaldor found that the demand for money as a proportion of income is neither stable between countries nor stable over time except in some countries.

3. *Money Supply and GNP not Positively Correlated.* Money supply and money GNP have been found to be positively correlated in Friedman's findings. But Kaldor found his evidence to be largely irrelevant. For example, he found that in Switzerland, Italy and Japan, the money supply on the broad definition, M_3 had been rising for over twenty years in relation to incomes, while it had been falling in the US and the UK. Even on the narrow definition, M_1, the money supply in Switzerland was nearly three times as great as in the UK or the US as a proportion of the GNP. From this, he concludes that "yet no one would regard Switzerland as an 'inflation prone' country (let alone more inflation prone) than the US cr the UK."[4]

4. *Neglects the Role of NBFIs.* The transmission mechanism explained by the monetarists has also been questioned. The Radcliffe Committee and Gurley and Shaw criticise the monetarist transmission mechanism for neglecting the role played by the non-bank financial intermediaries and their effects on real and financial assets.

5. *Real World does not approximate to a General Equilibrium System.* The monetarist view that prices in all markets are completely flexible, is based on the Walrasian general equilibrium model of the economy. This implies that the economy is at the full employment level. Critics point out that wages and prices do not adjust themselves simultaneously in the Walrasian sense. In fact, trade unions are engaged in wage bargains with the rise in prices in the past. Similarly, entrepreneurs try to adjust their reduced profit margins which have been eroded by inflation. This further increases inflation. As pointed out by Kaldor, the monetarists failed to recognise the all-important difference between a demand inflation and cost-inflation. Thus the real world does not approximate to a general equilibrium system.

6. *Economy not inherently stable.* The monetarists contend that the economy is inherently stable and it is interference in the form of monetary policy that brings instability. This view has not been accepted by the Keynesians who argue that there are frequent wild and erratic shocks in the economy due to variations in investment and consumption spendings that produce business cycle. This necessitates appropriate contracyclical monetary and fiscal policies.

---

2. For a detailed analysis of the monetarist policy, measures, refer to the last section of Chapter *Monetarism vs Keynesianism.*
3. Nicholas Kaldor, *Failure of Monetarism,* C.D. Deshmukh Memorial Lecture, RBI, 18 January, 1984.
4. Nicholos Kaldor, *The Scourge of Monetarism,* 1982.

7. *Money Supply fails to grow at a Smooth and Steady Rate.* Further, to stabilise the economy and avoid inflation, the monetarists favour a steady growth in the rate of money supply, and the rate of interest finds no place in their policy-frame. But the experience of both the US and the UK tells a different story where the monetarist monetary policy was put into operation in 1979-80. "The money supply failed to grow at a smooth and steady rate; its behaviour exhibited a series of wriggles. The rate of interest and the rate of inflation, though both were very high at the start, soared to unprecedented heights in a very short time."

Thus on the basis of above criticisms, it can be concluded that the monetarist viewpoint was not a revolution but a sort of reformation of the Keynesian economics and the revival of the orthodox monetarism.

EXERCISES

1. What is monetarist revolution? How has it affected our views about inflation and monetary policy?
2. What is meant by monetarist revolution? Explain its main features.
3. Critically examine the main features of the monetarist revolution.
4. "The views of monetarists are a counter-reformation rather than revolutionary." Examine the statement.

CHAPTER 38

Monetary Transmission Mechanism

1. INTRODUCTION

The transmission mechanism refers to the channels through which changes in the money supply affect aggregate expenditure (or aggregate demand), prices, income and other real variables of the economy. We shall discuss below the monetary mechanism in the classical, Keynesian, monetarist, and neo-Keynesian theories.

2. TRANSMISSION MECHANISM IN THE CLASSICAL THEORY

In the classical monetary transmission mechanism, a change in the money supply does not affect the real variables like output, employment and income. Money is neutral in its effects on the economy. This analysis is based on a direct and mechanical relationship between money and prices. If the quantity of money is raised, the price level will also rise in the same proportion, and *vice versa*. Such a relationship is based on the Quantity Theory Equation

$$MV=PT \text{ or } M/P = VT$$

where, M is the total quantity of money, P is the price level of commodities traded, V is the velocity of circulation of M, and T is the volume of transactions of goods.

The equation shows that the supply of real cash balances (M/P) must equal the demand for real cash balances (VT).

Thus money plays a causal role in the classical theory which means that changes in the money supply cause changes in the absolute price level, and in normal income. To explain it, the classicists specified two channels through which monetary changes are transmitted to the real sector of the economy. They are the direct mechanism and the indirect mechanism which are discussed below.

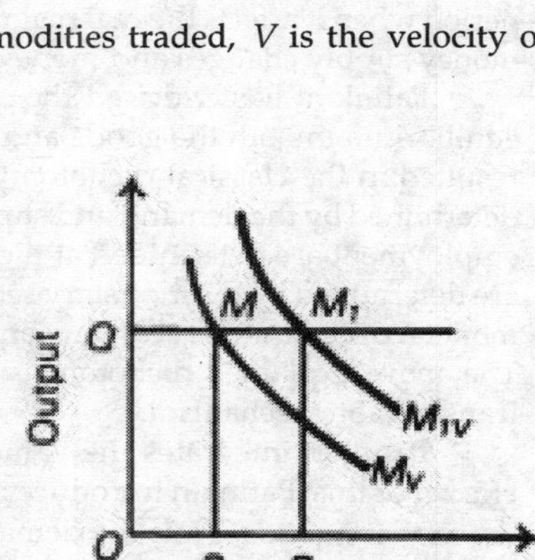

FIG. 1

The Direct Mechanism. The direct mechanism is based on the long run equilibrium of the demand for and supply of money. Suppose the money supply is increased. This leads to increase in the supply of actual money balances (M/P) of the public which now exceed the demand for them. Now the actual money holdings are more than those desired by the people relative to their expenditure and wealth. They have a tendency to spend their excess money holdings by buying consumer durable goods, and financial assets. These, in turn, increase the demand for goods and services. As a result, the price level rises which reduces the supply of real cash balances (M/P) until the actual money balances are equal to those people desire to hold. In this way, the equilibrium is restored in the money market. The direct mechanism is explained in terms of Fig. 1 where the price level is taken on the horizontal axis and the total output (or income) on the vertical axis. *MV* is the money supply curve which is a rectangular hyperbola. This is because the equation $MV=PT$ holds on all points of this curve. Given the output level *OQ*, there would be only one price level *OP* consistent with the quantity of money as shown by point *M* on the *MV*curve. When people spend their excess money balances on goods and assets, the *MV* curve will shift to M_1V. As a result, the price level would rise from *OP* to OP_1, given the same level of output *OQ*. This rise in price level is exactly proportional to the rise in the quantity of money, *i.e.* $PP_1=MM_1$.

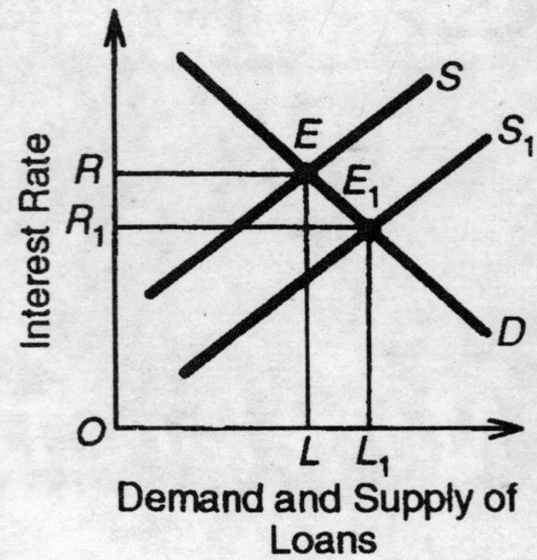

FIG. 2

Indirect Mechanism. The indirect mechanism operates through the money rate of interest and involves the commercial banking system. Suppose the central bank makes open market purchases of government securities which increase the reserves of commercial banks. With excess reserves, the banks lend more which lowers the money rate of interest. This is illustrated in Fig. 2 where the curves *D* and *S* represent the demand and supply of loanable funds respectively. The equilibrium interest *OR* is determined at point *E* where the two curves intersect each other. With increase in the reserves of banks, the supply of loanable funds increases which shifts the *S* curve to the right to S_1. Now the banks lend LL_1 more of funds and the interest rate falls to OR_1. The reduction in the market rate relative to the real rate creates a disparity between the actual and desired stock of real capital. This encourages businessmen to invest more in new capital assets.- This, in turn, raises the aggregate demand for money which is financed by new money creation. This expands *MV* to M_1V, as shown in Fig. 1. Given the full employment level *OQ* in the economy, the increase in the money supply raises the price level proportionately so that $MM_1= PP_1$

Its Criticisms

The classical monetary transmission mechanism shows that money is neutral in equilibrium and it does not affect real aggregate demand, output, employment and income. But it is non-neutral in the transition period when it affects the real magnitudes. But in the long run only nominal magnitudes are affected when the money supply changes and money is neutral.

Patinkin[1] has criticised the classical transmission mechanism for its failure to analyse the stability of equilibrium in both the goods and money markets through the operation of the real balance effect. This has resulted in the classical dichotomy between the real sector and monetary sector. The relative price level is determined by the demand and supply of goods in the real sector m which all real magnitudes like income and employment are determined at the full employment level. The absolute price level and nominal magnitudes are determined by the monetary sector. This dichotomy implies that the relative price level has no effect on the monetary sector of the economy and absolute price level has no effect on the real magnitudes of the economy. The above explained dichotomy of the real and monetary sectors leads to an inconsistency in the classical transmission mechanism.

Patinkin integrates the value theory (real sector) and the monetary theory through the real balance effect. For this, Patinkin introduces the stock of real balances *(M/P)* held by community as an influence on their demand for goods. Thus the demand for a commodity depends upon real balance as well as relative prices. Now if the price level rises, this will reduce the real balances (purchasing power) with the people who will spend less than before. This implies a fall in the demand for goods and the consequent fall in the price level. Contrariwise, a fall in the price level increases the real balances thereby increasing the demand for goods and

---

1. Don Patinkin, *Money, Interest and Prices*, 2/e, 1965.

the price level. In Patinkin's words: "This is the crucial point. The dynamic grouping of the absolute price level towards its equilibrium value will—through the real balance effect—react on the commodity markets and hence on relative prices." Thus absolute prices play a crucial role not only in the money market but also in the real sector of the economy.

Besides removing the classical dichotomy and integrating the monetary and value theory through the real balance effect, Patinkin also validates the quantity theory conclusion. According to Patinkin, the real balance implies that people do not suffer from 'money illusion'. They are interested only in the real value of their cash holdings. In other words, they hold money for 'what it will buy'. This means that a doubling of the quantity of money will lead to a doubling of the price level, but relative prices and the real balances will remain constant and the equilibrium of the economy will not be changed.

3. TRANSMISSION MECHANISM IN THE KEYNESIAN THEORY

The transmission mechanism in the Keynesian theory is *indirect* via the interest rate. It is based on the existence of unemployment equilibrium in the economy and on the assumption of short run. In the Keynesian analysis, there are three motives for holding money: precautionary, transactions and speculative. The demand for money for speculative motive is determined by the interest rate, while the demand for precautionary and transactions motives is determined primarily by the level of income. Given the level of national income, the demand for money is a decreasing function of the rate of interest. The higher the interest rate, the lower the demand for money and vice versa. This negative relationship between the interest rate and the demand for money provides a link between changes in the money supply and the aggregate variables of the economy.

The Keynesians further believe that money and financial assets (bonds) are good substitutes. They are highly liquid and yield interest. So even small changes in interest rates lead to substitution between money and financial assets. A fall in the interest rate will mean a rise in the price of bonds (or securities) which will induce people to sell bonds and hold more money for speculative purposes. Given these main elements of the Keynesian theory, its transmission mechanism is explained below.

The Transmission Mechanism

In the Keynesian transmission mechanism, changes in the money supply affect aggregate expenditure, output, employment and income *indirectly* through changes in the interest rate. Suppose the Central bank increases the money supply by open market purchase of government bonds, it lowers the interest rate which, in turn, increases investment and expenditure, thereby raising the national income.

The mechanism by which changes in the money supply are transmitted into the income level is the *asset effect.* With income level unchanged, when the money supply is increased, it causes people to spend their excess holdings of money on bonds. This means an increase in the demand for bonds and a rise in their prices. A rise in the prices of bonds brings down the money interest rate. This, in turn, increases the speculative demand for money. People prefer to keep money in cash rather than lend it at a low interest rate. This, is called the *liquidity effect.* This is the first stage in the Keynesian transmission mechanism.

In the next stage, the fall in the interest rate and an increase in the speculative demand for money stimulates investment. Businessmen prefer to invest in capital goods rather than hold money in cash for speculative purposes.

In the final stage of the transmission mechanism, the increase in investment raises the level of income through the multiplier process. The increased income generates additional savings equal to the increase in investment and equilibrium will prevail in the commodity market. On the other hand, the rise in real income or output brings diminishing returns to labour, thereby raising per unit labour cost and the price level.

The Keynesian transmission mechanism consisting of three stages is called *the cost of capital channel* and is summarised thus: Money ⟶ Interest Rate ⟶ Investment ⟶ Income, where with increase in the money supply, interest rate falls and investment and income rise. The rise in price level raises nominal income that leads to an increase in the transactions and precautionary demand for money, thereby bringing a "feedback effect" on the economy. The increase in transactions and precautionary balances, in turn, reduces the speculative balances. The latter raise the interest rate, and bring a fall in investment and income, and lead to a further feedback effect. Friedman calls the feedback effect the *income effect*.

The Keynesian transmission mechanism is explained in Fig. 3. Given OI_1 level of investment in Panel (B) of the figure, income is OY_1 at which savings OS_1 equal investment OI_1 in Panel (A). Panel (C) shows that the interest rate OR_1 is determined by the equality of money demanded M_1, and money supplied *Ms* at point E_1. It is this rate of interest rate which calls forth the level of investment OI_1 with which we started. Now the rise in the money supply to Ms_1 brings a fall in the interest rate to OR_1, a rise in investment to OI_2 and a rise in income to OY_2. Thus equilibrium is restored in the circular flow. The feedback process is not shown in the figure to keep the analysis simple. This is how the effects of an increase in the money supply are transmitted to the real variables of the economy under the Keynesian transmission mechanism.

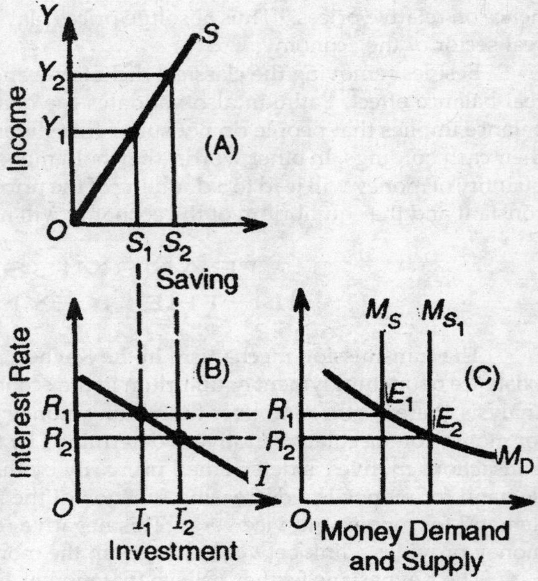

FIG. 3

ITS WEAKNESSES

The transmission mechanism explained above is neither smooth nor reliable because the velocity of money is not assumed as stable in the Keynesian theory. For example, when the money supply is increased by the monetary authority, this increases liquidity with the public. People may want to hold it rather than spend it. In such a situation, when the money supply increases, the interest rate falls. But the demand for money is

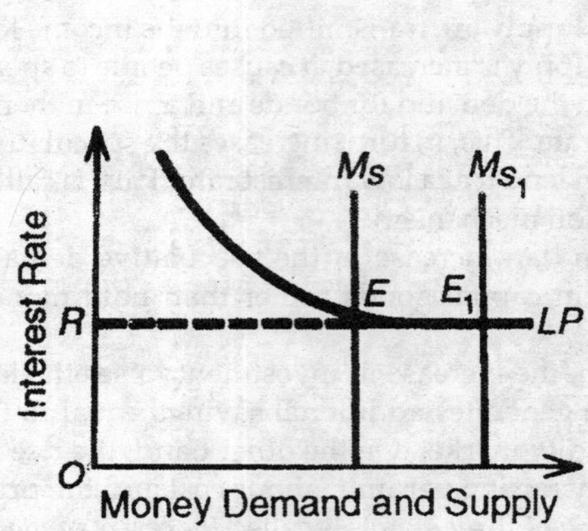

FIG. 4

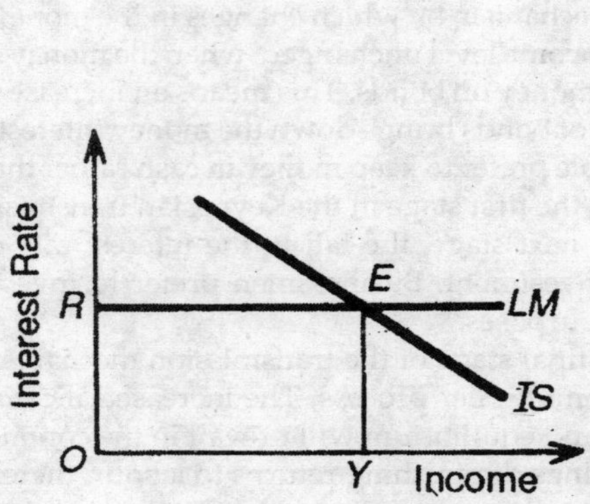

FIG. 5

insensitive to the change in interest rate. The investment and income remain unaffected. The velocity of circulation of money falls. This is the Keynesian liquidity trap at a very low interest rate, people prefer to keep money in cash even with an increase in the money supply rather than invest it. As a result, the money supply does not affect national income. Fig. 4 and 5 depict these cases. Fig. 4 shows that with a liquidity trap when the money supply increases from *Ms* to Ms_1 at the interest rate *OR*, the EE_1 portion of the *LP* curve is perfectly elastic. Again, when the money supply increases from *Ms* to Ms_1, it is held by the people and not spent. As a result, the *LP* curve is horizontal and the *IS* curve intersects it at point *E* in Fig. 5. There is no change in equilibrium income *OY* and interest rate *OR*. Keynes himself accepts the weakness of his transmission mechanism when he explains the liquidity trap.

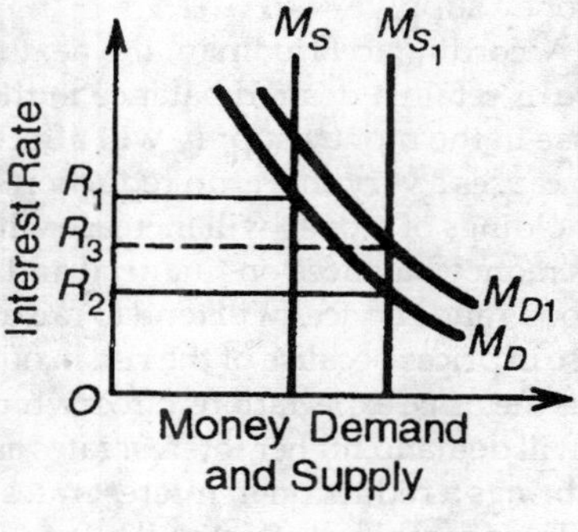

FIG. 6

The transmission mechanism also does not operate smoothly by the expectations of moneyholders over future interest rates. These are highly volatile. The demand for money curve shifts with changes in expectations. This is illustrated in Fig. 6 which extends the explanation of Panel *(C)* of Fig. 3. The increase in the money supply to Ms_1 brings a fall in the interest rate from OR_1 to OR_2, given the demand for money M_{D_1}. But a rise in future expectations shifts the M_D curve to the right to M_{D_1} due to increase in the speculative demand for money. This raises the interest rate to OR_3 with increase in the money supply to Ms_1.

Another factor which inhibits the smooth operation of the Keynesian transmission mechanism is the interest rate elasticity of investment. The less elastic is the investment curve, the less is the increase in investment as a result of a fall in the interest rate, and vice versa. This is illustrated in Fig. 7 where the ID_1 curve in Panel (A) is less elastic. When the interest rate falls from OR_1 to OR_2 investment increases by I_1I_2 which is less than increase in investment I_3I_4 when the investment curve I_{D_2} is elastic in Panel (B).

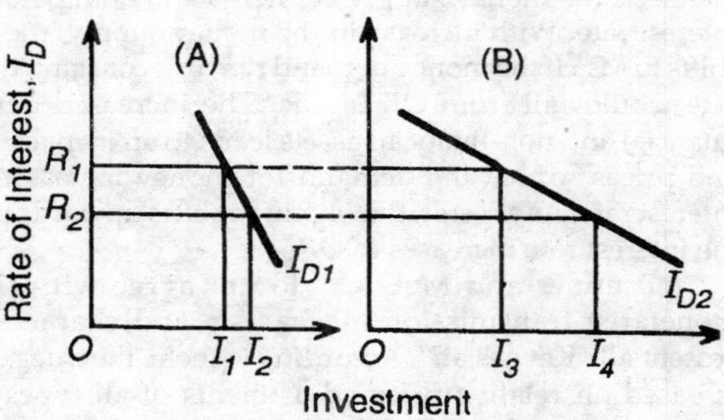

FIG. 7

4. TRANSMISSION MECHANISM IN THE MONETARIST THEORY

The monetarists hold that the transmission mechanism by which changes in the money supply cause changes in aggregate demand (or expenditure), prices, interest rates and other economic variables is essentially a *portfolio adjustment process.* The economy is composed of individuals, households and firms who hold their wealth in the form of portfolios of assets. These assets are both financial and non-financial which include money, securities, durable and semi-durable goods, and services etc. Any change in the money supply causes disequilibrium between the public's actual and desired real cash balances of assets in their portfolios. Suppose the money supply is increased, this increases the cash balances with the public. People will reduce their excess cash balances by spending on a wide range of financial and non-financial assets like shares, bonds, goods and services, etc.

The portfolio holders are always shifting their holdings of wealth among different assets in order to obtain satisfactory relative rates of return on their entire portfolios of financial and non-financial assets. If they find that the returns in the securities market are relatively higher than returns in the real estate market, they will shift some of their portfolio holdings of land and buildings into shares and bonds. Thus the relative prices of assets are always changing in response to shifts in the spending patterns of the people caused by changes in the money supply.

According to Friedman, the next step in the transmission process is the attempt of holders of money to restore or retain a desired balance in their portfolios after an unexpected increase in the money supply. The increase in the money supply will affect interest rates in three different ways. *First,* there is the *liquidity effect* which causes a very short run reduction in interest rates. As a result, the portfolio holders will sell securities and their holdings of money will increase which means rise in liquid money with them. *Second,* they will spend their excess money balances on financial and non-financial assets. This increase in aggregate expenditure on assets and goods and services will tend to raise output, employment and income. This is the *output effect.* This will lead to a rise in prices because of the rise in output and demand for money resulting from the liquidity effect. Finally, there is the price expectations effect which occurs due to the expectations of lenders that inflation will continue. They will demand higher interest rates as a premium on the expected inflation rate. Thus the short-run liquidity effect brings a reduction in interest rates and both the output and price expectation effects increase the interest rates. Their combined effect will be an increase in interest rates. These will, in turn, discourage investment and reduce output and employment. Thus the channel of monetarists' mechanism is: Money → Prices → Interest Rates.

This is illustrated in Fig. 8 where the initial equilibrium is at point *E*, where the money demand curve M_D intersects the money supply curve *Ms* and both determine *OR* interest rate. With increase in the money supply, the *Ms* curve shifts to Ms_1. If the money demand remains constant, the interest rate would fall from *OR* to OR_1. The increased demand for financial and non-financial assets leads to an increase in output and prices so that the demand for money increases at every interest rate. As a result, the M_D curve shifts upwards to M_{D1} and the interest rate increases to OR_2.

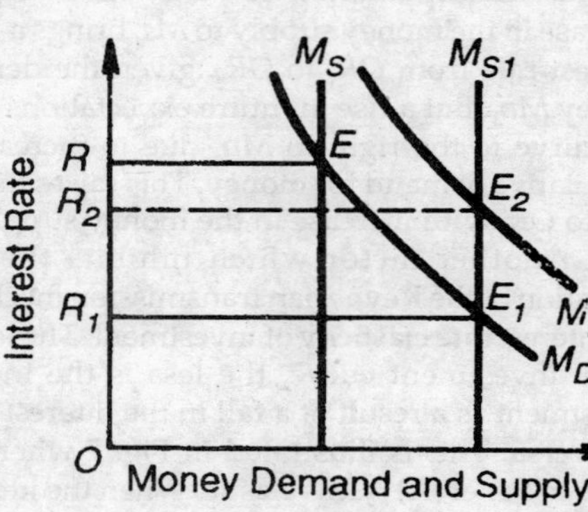

FIG. 8

Brunner and Metzler[2] do not agree with the above monetarist transmission mechanism and characterise it as "essentially Keynesian". According to them, the true mechanism is based on relative price adjustments of all types of assets including capital goods. The increase in the money supply by reducing the rate of interest on financial assets switches the demand to consumption and capital goods. This increases the size of the optimal capital stock which will bring adjustments in the actual capital stock until equilibrium is restored in the economy. All these effects will ultimately lead to an increase in output and prices. As a result, the market rate of interest rises which discourages investment, thereby reducing output and employment.

Modern monetarists also argue that a change in the money supply influences the real variables such as output and employment in the short run, while the nominal variables such as nominal national income, interest rates and prices are influenced in the long run by the monetarist transmission mechanism.

Its Criticisms

The post-Keynesians have criticised the monetarist transmission mechanism on several counts :

1. The monetarists have not clearly specified the channels of monetary influence in a structural way. They have done little to specify exactly how and through what channels money influences nominal income, price level and output. How a million dollar increase in the money supply will have the same effects on nominal

2. K. Brunner and D.A. Metzler, "Friedman's Monetary Theory", *J.P.E.*, Sep.-Oct., 1972.

national income when there are changes in technology and in consumer and investor psychology? The transmission mechanism fails to clarify these doubts.

2. The post-Keynesians do not agree with the monetarist proposition that the money supply basically determines the national income. The money supply and national income can also move in a reverse manner because changes in national income lead to changes in the money supply.

3. The monetarist transmission mechanism is weak in that it fails to determine as to what proportion of an increase in the money supply affects the price level and what proportion the output level.

5. TRANSMISSION MECHANISM IN THE NEO-KEYNESIAN THEORY

The Keynesian analysis considered only two types of assets: speculative cash balances and bonds. Their allocation depended on the rate of interest which, in turn, led to changes in the real sectors of the economy with a change in the money supply. The neo-Keynesians discuss the monetary transmission mechanism through the portfolio adjustment process. When the supply of money changes, it sets in motion wealth effect, substitution effects, and availability effects, These channels of monetary mechanism are discussed as under.

WEALTH EFFECT

In the Keynesian analysis, no direct wealth effect is involved when the central bank engages in open market purchases of bonds or securities. It simply involves the transfer of money for bonds. But in the neo-Keynesian analysis, changes in the money supply affect the economy through wealth effect channels. The increase in the money supply through open market purchase of securities by the central bank increases consumer wealth which, in turn, leads to a rise in consumer spending. The increased money supply lowers the interest rate and produces a wealth effect. As a result, the expected value of real capital assets increases and the asset holders feel wealthier. They buy more of all assets in their portfolios and thus increase their demand for capital non-durable goods which ultimately lead to increase in output, employment and income in the economy.

SUBSTITUTION EFFECTS

The neo-Keynesians widened considerably the portfolio of assets to include not only government securities but also industrial bonds, equities, savings, mortgages, etc. Given this type of portfolio, suppose the Central bank engages in open market purchases of securities. This will increase the prices of securities, thereby reducing the yield on them. In other words, the holders of securities sell them to the central bank because they get high prices for them. They now hold more money than they desire. As a result, they try to readjust the structure of their portfolios so as to reduce their money holdings. Suppose they substitute bonds for their excess money balances. The increase in the demand for bonds results in an increase in their market price, thereby reducing their current yield, as interest rate falls. Consequently, the demand for other assets such as equities, consumer durables, etc. increases. When people having surplus money balances purchase-equities (shares), their prices rise. As a result, the value of capital of such firms rises above the supply price of such new capital. Such firms are, therefore, induced to increase their demand for more capital equipment, thereby raising output in the capital goods industries. This will, in turn, spread to the rest of the economy via the multiplier effect Thus the "neo-Keynesians contend that financial assets are the closest substitutes for money, and that, consequently, increases in the supply of money will have their effect eventually on the level of economic activity by bringing about increase in the output of capital goods industries."

CREDIT AVAILABILITY EFFECTS

The credit availability effects relate to the transmission mechanism following effects of changes in the interest rate on banks and financial institutions. Banks and other financial institutions which advance loans to private borrowers generally charge a standard interest rate and resort to non-price credit rationing depending on the status, credit worthiness and wealth of borrowers. The non-price rationing of credit is also due to the absence of a market clearing interest rate. Non-price credit rationing leads to "lock-in" effect. Both these are called credit availability effects.[3]

Suppose the central bank increases the money supply by purchasing government securities. This increases the money supply with the banks. Consequently, the reserves of banks increase and there is increase in bank credit. This leads to a fall in interest rates. The banks will reduce credit rationing and make more credit available to their customers. At the same time, they will not "lock-in" securities in their portfolios because the prices of securities rise in the market with a fall in interest rates. They will, therefore, prefer to sell them to have more capital gain. Thus they use these additional funds for advancing more loans. If, however, the interest rate charged on bank loans is very low in relation to ihe interest rate earned by the banks on other assets in their portfolios, the banks may continue with credit rationing. If there is free competition among financial and non-financial lending institutions, credit rationing will be a temporary phenomenon. Further, if the funds are being advanced by non-bank financial institutions such as a building society, the banks may continue credit rationing due to the absence of market clearing interest rate. Interest rates may also be slow to adjust or they may continue to be administered by the non-bank financial institutions. In all such cases, banks may resort to credit rationing.

CONCLUSION

When the wealth effect, substitution effects and credit availability effects operate through an increase in the money supply, their initial impacts lead to additional income which, in turn, will expand the demand for consumer non-durable and durable goods and services and ultimately to increase in output and employment. The opposite will happen when the money supply is decreased.

EXERCISES

1. Explain critically the Transmission mechanism of the classical theory?
2. Describe the transmission mechanism in the Keynesian system. What are its weaknesses?
3. Explain the transmission mechanism of the monetarists. How differs from the Keynesian transmission mechanism?
4. In what ways the neo-Keynesian transmission mechanism is an improvement over the Keynesian transmission mechanism?

3. For an understanding of these concepts refer to Ch.

CHAPTER 39

Monetarism versus Keynesianism

1. INTRODUCTION

Monetarism refers to the followers of Milton Friedman who hold that *"only money matters"*, and as such monetary policy is a more potent instrument than fiscal policy in economic stabilisation. On the other hand, Keynesianism refers to the followers of Keynes who believe that *"money does not matter,"* and for economic stabilisation fiscal policy is a more powerful tool than monetary policy. The adherents of monetarism are known as the monetarists and of Keynesianism as the fiscalists. We discuss below the views of the monetarists and fiscalists about the causes of changes in national income and the roles of monetary and fiscal policies in economic stabilisation.

2. THEORETICAL DIFFERENCES

The monetarists emphasise the role of money in explaining short-term changes in national income. They argue that the role of money has been neglected by Keynesians, if not by Keynes himself. Friedman and Schwartz[1] have shown that changes in the money supply cause changes in national income. The monetarists believe that all recessions and depressions are caused by severe contraction of money and credit, and booms and inflations by excessive increases in the money supply. The Keynesians reject the monetarists view that changes in national income are caused solely by changes in the money supply. Rather they hold that changes in national income cause changes in the supply of money. The moderate Keynesians still believe like monetarists that hyper-inflations are caused by excessive money supply. On the other hand, the extreme Keynesians hold that non-monetary factors like investment cause depressions and booms.

The Monetarist View

According to the monetarists, the money supply is the "dominant, though not exclusive" determinant of both the level of output and prices in the short run and of the level of prices in the long run. The long-run level of output is not influenced by the money supply. It is dependent on such real factors as technology and the quantity and quality of productive resources. Although factors other than the money supply affect the level of output, employment and prices in the short run, yet their effects are subordinate to that of^the money supply. A change in the money supply will inevitably affect the price level and output in the short run. But in the long run, the effect of change in the money supply will be entirely on the price level. Because the economy is near full employment in the long run and the increase in national income will consist mainly of higher prices. Thus

1. M. Friedman and Anna Schwartz, *A Monetary History of the United States, 1957-60,* 1963

changes in the money supply affect national income directly. This is due to the assumption that the velocity of circulation of money is stable.

The Keynesians, on the other hand, maintain that changes in the money supply work *indirectly* on the level of aggregate expenditure and income through changes in the interest rates. The main difference between the monetarists and Keynesians rests on the influence of interest rates on the demand for and supply of money and aggregate expenditure.

The monetarists hold that the rate of interest plays no part in determining the demand for money. The demand for money is the transactions demand for money which is determined by the level of income. The monetarists believe that the money supply is also not influenced by interest rates. This insensitiveness of both demand for and supply of money is based on the quantity theory of money. The simplest quantity equation is $MV=PQ$, where M is the quantity of money, V is its velocity, Q is the number of physical transactions, and P is the price level. Taking $PQ=Y$, where Y is the national income, the quantity equation becomes $MV=Y$. As V remains constant, changes in M cause changes in Y.

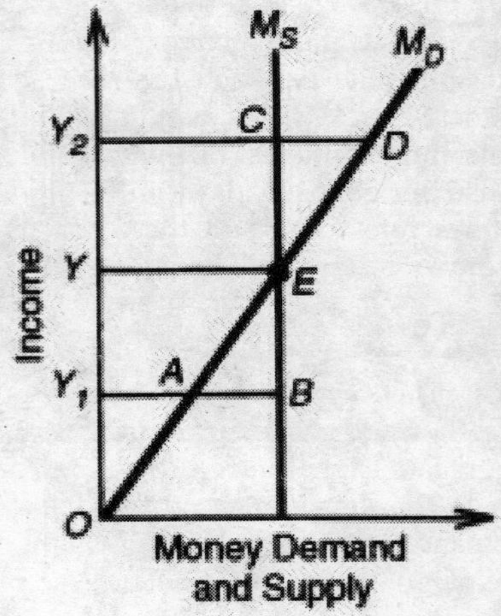

FIG. 1

Fig. 1 explains the monetarist view graphically. The demand for and supply of money are taken on the horizontal axis and income on the vertical axis. The demand curve M_D is drawn from the origin which shows the amount of money people want to hold for transaction purposes at various levels of income. M_S is the money supply curve which is drawn vertical to show a given supply of money. OY is the equilibrium level of income where the money demanded and supplied equal at E. If people have more money than they want equal to AB at OY_1 income level, they will start spending it till income increases to the equilibrium level OY. If they have less money than they want equal to CD at OY_2 income level, they will start reducing their spending till it reaches the equilibrium level OY.

The changes in the money supply affect aggregate demand and income through effects on a wide range of assets than "the bonds only" model of the Keynesians. This view of the monetarists is based on the belief that money is a good substitute for all types of assets such as securities, houses, durable consumer goods, etc. Friedman's historical findings show a *"stable money demand function"* which implies that the demand for money is a stable function of peoples' income. In other words, the amount of money people want to hold is related in a fixed way to their income. If the central bank increases the money supply, it affects interest rates in three different ways. *First*, there is the *liquidity effect* which causes a very short-run reduction in interest rates. As a result, people will sell securities and their holdings of money will increase. They will, therefore, spend their excess money balances on financial assets and on durable consumer goods, houses, etc. This increase in aggregate expenditure on assets and goods will tend to raise output, employment and income. This is the *output effect*. This will lead to a rise in interest rates because of the rise in output and demand for money resulting from the liquidity effect. *Finally*, there is the *price expectations effect* which occurs due to the expectations of lenders that inflation will continue. They will demand higher interest rates in order to cover the expected inflation rate. Thus with the short-run liquidity effect bringing a downward pressure on interest rates and both the output and price expectations effects

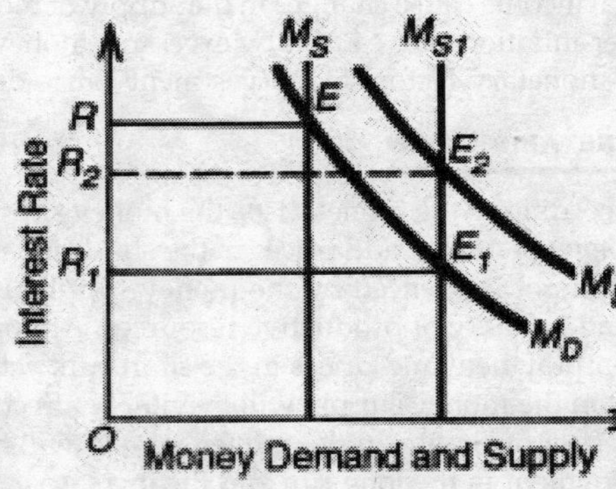

FIG. 2

bringing an upward pressure on them, the combined effect will be an increase in interest rates. These will, in turn, discourage investment, and reduce output and employment. This is illustrated in Fig. 2.

The demand for and supply of money are taken on the horizontal axis and the interest rate on the vertical axis. M_D is the demand curve for money and *Ms* the money supply curve. Both intersect at *E* and determine *OR* interest rate. With increase in the money supply the *Ms* curve shifts to Ms_1 . If the money demand remains constant, the interest rate would fall from *OR* to OR_1. The increased demand for financial assets and durable consumer goods leads to an increase in output and prices so that the demand for money increases at every interest rate. As a result, the M_D curve shifts upwards to M_{D1} and the interest rate increases to OR_2. The M_D curve is drawn steeply which reflects the monetarist view that the demand for money is interest elastic.

The Keynesian View

The Keynesians hold just the opposite views to monetarists about the demand for and supply of money and the aggregate expenditure. Both the demand for and supply of money are highly interest elastic while the aggregate expenditure is not.

The Keynesians consider the supply of money to be fixed in the short run by monetary authorities. The demand for money, also called the liquidity preference, is the desire to hold cash. There are three motives on the part of the people to hold cash transactions, precautionary and speculative demand for money. Money held for transactions and precautionary motives is a function of the level of income, and for the speculative motive, it is a function of the interest rate.

To the Keynesians, it is expectations about changes in bond prices or in the market rate of interest that determine the speculative demand for money. The speculative demand for money is a decreasing function of the rate of interest. The higher the rate of interest, the lower the speculative demand for money, and vice-versa. But at a very low interest rate, the speculative demand for money becomes perfectly elastic. This is the "liquidity trap" portion of the demand for money curve. In this range, people prefer to keep money in cash rather than invest in bonds because purchasing bonds will lead to loss.

On the whole, given the level of national income, the demand for money is a decreasing function of the interest rate. The Keynesians believe money and financial assets to be good substitutes for each other. They are highly liquid and yield interest. So even small changes in interest rates lead to substitution between money and financial assets. A small fall in the interest rate will mean a rise in the price of securities, which will induce people to sell securities and hold more money. The reverse will be the case in the event of a small rise in the' rate of interest. Thus the demand for money is highly interest-elastic under Keynesianism.

The Keynesians believe in the existence of unemployment equilibrium. This implies that an increase in money supply can bring about permanent increases in the level of output. The ultimate influence of money supply on the price level depends upon its influence on aggregate demand and the elasticity of the supply of aggregate output.

The Keynesian chain of causation between changes in the quantity of money and in prices is an indirect one through the rate of interest.[2] So when the quantity of money is increased, its first impact is on the rate of interest which tends to fall. Given the marginal efficiency of capital, a fall in the rate of interest wili increase the volume of investment. The increased investment will raise effective demand through the multiplier effect thereby increasing income, output and employment. Since the supply curve of factors of production is perfectly elastic in a situation of unemployment, wage and non-wage factors are available at constant rate of remuneration. There being constant returns to scale, prices do not rise with the increase in output so long as there is any unemployment. Under the circumstances, output and employment will increase in the same proportion as effective demand, and the effective demand will increase in the same proportion as the quantity of money. But "once full employment is reached, output ceases to respond *at all* to changes in the supply of money and so in effective demand. The elasticity of supply of output in response to changes in the supply, which was infinite as long as there was unemployment, falls to zero. The entire effect of changes in the supply of money is exerted on prices, which rise in exact proportion with the increase in effective demand". Thus so long as there is

2. For its diagrammatic representation, see Fig. 1 of Ch. 14.

unemployment, output will change in the same proportion as the quantity of money, and there will be no change in prices; and when there is full employment, prices will change in the same proportion as the quantity of money.

In the Keynesian transmission mechanism, changes in the money supply affect aggregate expenditure and national income *indirectly* by changes in interest rates. Suppose the money supply is increased, it lowers the interest rate which, in turn, increases investment and expenditure thereby raising the national income. The mechanism by which changes in the money supply are transmitted into the level of income is the asset effect. For example, an increase in the money supply causes people to spend their excess holdings of money on financial assets. This means an increase in the demand for such assets and a rise in their prices. Rise in the prices of assets (securities), brings down the interest rates which, in turn, increase aggregate expenditure, investment and hence income. Thus, according to the Keynesian view, a change in the money supply can only affect aggregate spending and national income first through changes in interest rates, and then only if the aggregate spending is sensitive to interest rate changes.[3]

3. POLICY DIFFERENCES

Another point of difference between the monetarists and the Keynesians is over the policy prescriptions. According to the monetarists, monetary policy has a greater influence on economic activity than fiscal policy, and fiscal policy is important only in making changes in the money supply. On the other hand, the Keynesians emphasise the importance of both fiscal and monetary policy in influencing the economy but they attach more importance to the former than to the latter. First, we study the monetarist view on monetary and fiscal policy and then the Keynesian view.

THE MONETARIST VIEW

As already analysed above, the monetarists hold that changes in the money supply have a direct influence on aggregate expenditure and thus on income. Let us analyse an expansionary monetary policy followed by monetarists. To begin, suppose the central bank purchased securities in the open market. It raises the price of securities and lowers the rate of interest. People will, therefore, start selling securities and hold more money. People spend their excess money balances on financial assets and durable consumer goods. Others attracted by low interest rates borrow from banks for expenditure on houses, durable consumer goods, plants and

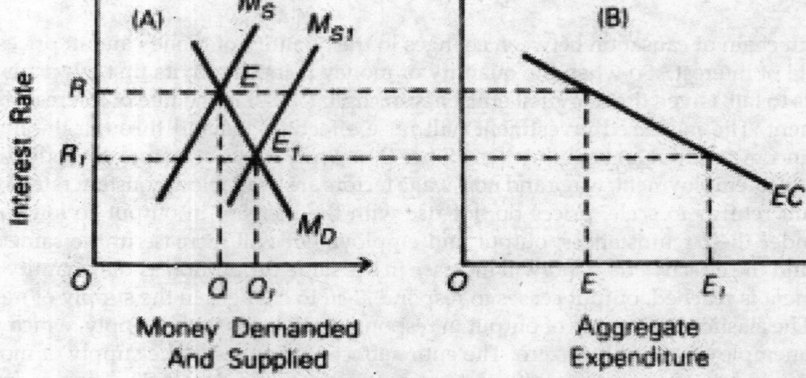

FIG. 3

3. For more details refer to Ch. 38.

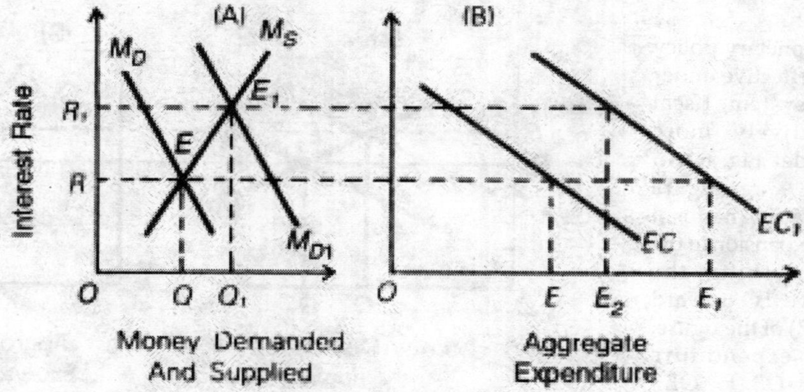

FIG. 4

equipments, etc. These forces tend to increase aggregate expenditure and income. This is illustrated in Fig. 3. M_D is the demand for money curve and M_s the money supply curve. Both the curves are interest inelastic. Initially both are in equilibrium at *OR* interest rate. The increase in money supply to M_{s1} reduces the interest rate from *OR* to OR_1. The demand for money being relatively insensitive to the interest rate, it increases from *OQ* to OQ_1. But the aggregate expenditure is very sensitive to this fall in interest rate so that it increases from *OE* to OE_1 in Panel (B) of the figure where *EC* represents the expenditure curve. Thus an expansionary monetary policy is highly successful in increasing aggregate expenditure and income. Now consider the fiscal policy in Fig. 4 (A) and (B). An increase in aggregate expenditure leads to expansion in the economy which shifts the expenditure curve upward from *EC* to EC_1 in Panel (B) of the figure. As aggregate expenditure increases from *OE* to OE_1 national income also rises. This leads to greater demand for money for transactions purposes. In order to meet this increased demand for money, households and firms sell securities which they have and also borrow from banks and other financial institutions. These tendencies have the effect of raising the interest rate. As the demand for money is relatively insensitive to interest rate changes, a very high rate of interest is required to equate the supply of money to the demand for money. This is shown in Panel (A) of Fig. 4 where the increased demand for money is shown by the MD_1 curve and the rise in the interest rate by RR_1. But such a large increase in interest rate has the effect of reducing private expenditure from OE_1 to *OE*, so the net effect on aggregate expenditure of an expansionary fiscal policy is only EE_2. Thus according to the monetarists, an increase in government expenditure as a result of an expansionary fiscal policy leads to an increase in government expenditure and income which leads to a large rise in the rate of interest that, in turn, reduces private expenditure almost equal to the increase in government expenditure.

The Keynesian View

In contrast to the monetarists, the Keynesians regard monetary policy relatively less effective because of the relative interest inelasticity of aggregate expenditure. To illustrate, consider an expansionary monetary policy. Suppose the central bank purchases securities in the open market. As a result, the price of securities rises and the interest rate falls. People will, therefore, start selling securities in order to hold more money. As the demand for money is highly interest elastic in the Keynesian system, even a small fall in the rate of interest will induce people to sell securities and hold more money. This is illustrated in Fig. 5. Panel (A) of the figure shows that in the initial situation, *OR* is the interest rate and *OQ* the money demanded and supplied. Now the money supply increases due to the central bank's action. This is shown by the M_{s1} curve. When the money supply rises to OQ_1 the interest rate falls from *OR* to OR_1. This small fall in the interest rate by RR_1 increases aggregate expenditure by only EE_1, as shown in Panel (B) of the figure. Thus an expansionary policy is not successful in raising aggregate expenditure and income much.

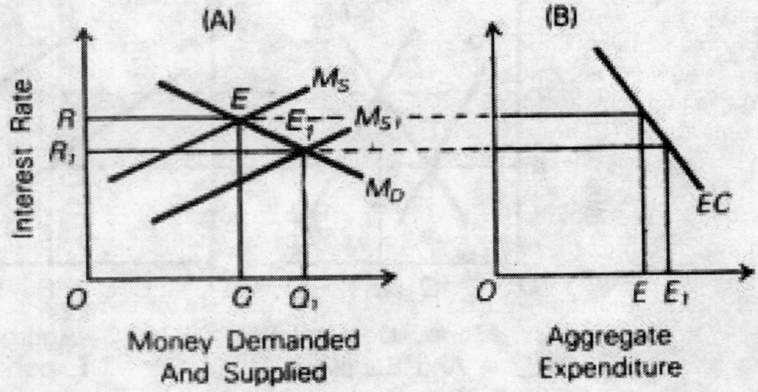

FIG. 5

Though monetary policy is relatively less effective under the Keynesian system, fiscal policy is relatively more effective. Consider Fig. 6. An increase in aggregate expenditure for raising national income leads to expansion in the economy. This shifts the expenditure curve *EC* upward to EC_1 in Panel (B) of the figure. As aggregate expenditure increases from *OE* to OE_1, national income rises. This leads to greater demand for money by the people for transactions purposes. To meet this increased demand for money, householders and firms sell securities they possess, and also borrow funds from the banks and other financial institutions. These moves tend to raise the rate of interest. Higher interest rates and the demand for more loans induce commercial banks to reduce their excess reserves, thereby increasing the supply of money from *OQ* to OQ_1 in Panel (A) of the figure. Further, high interest rates induce bond holders to reduce the amount of money held for speculative purposes because high interest rates mean fall in the price of bonds. As the demand for money is highly interest elastic only a small rise in the interest rate from *OR* to OR_1 is required to equate the money supply curve M_s with the new money demand curve M_{D1} at E_1, in Panel (A) of Fig. 6. But this small increase in interest rate by RR_1, has a very small effect in reducing private expenditure from OE_1 to OE_2, as shown in Panel (B) of the figure. This is because aggregate expenditure is relatively - interest inelastic in the Keynesian system. Thus the effect of an expansionary fiscal policy is that there is a net increase in aggregate expenditure by EE_2 and only a small amount of private expenditure is reduced by E_1E_2 due to a rise in the rate of interest by RR_1. Thus the Keynesians regard fiscal policy more effective than monetary policy.

4. CONCLUSION

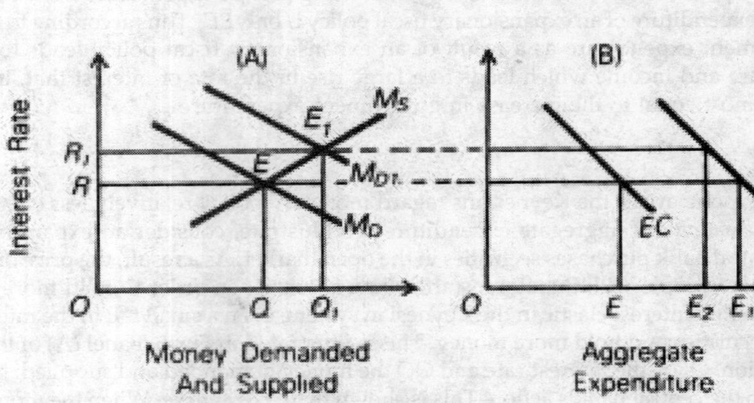

FIG. 6

The above analysis about monetarism and Keynesianism reveals that both hold almost the opposite views. The monetarists argue that only money matters, and that economic recessions and expansions are caused by decreases and increases of the money supply. They, therefore, advocate control of the money supply to stabilise cyclical fluctuations. They emphasise that the growth rate of money is the principal determinant of the behaviour of national income. This view is based on a number of historical studies carried out by Friedman and Schwartz, Friedman and Meiselman,[4] and Anderson and Jordan[5] of the Federal Reserve Bank of St. Louis. These studies reveal that there is a very close relation between money supply and national income than between national income and any of the Keynesian variables like aggregate expenditure.

Though the monetarists have tried to enforce their position on the basis of empirical studies yet they are themselves skeptical about the success of monetary policy in contrast to fiscal policy. They agree that as economic stabiliser, monetary policy may do more harm than good because of the operation lag. The operation lag refers to the time elapsing between the taking of action and the effective impact of that action on the economic situation. On an average, it takes a long time for a change in the money supply to affect national income, so the operation lag is long. Friedman himself admits that the time lag involved is so large that contracyclical monetary policy might actually have a destabilising effect on the economy. The monetarists, therefore, hold that the economy is basically stable and when disturbed by some change in basic conditions, will quickly revert to its long-run growth path. That is why, they advocate an annual fixed percentage growth in the money supply and an end to discretion in monetary policy. Friedman, therefore, believes that fiscal policy does not have any potent influence on the economy except that it affects the behaviour of money.

On the other hand, the Keynesians are not diehards like the monetarists. They take a more realistic view of monetary and fiscal policy in contrast to the latter. They do not regard the two as competitive but complementary to each other. They do not deny that money does matter, for they believe that monetary policy does influence national income but via changes in the interest rate. But they find monetary policy ineffective in controlling severe depressions and therefore depend upon fiscal policy for this. On the other hand, they combine monetary policy with fiscal policy for controlling booms and inflations. In this connection, the views of Walter Heller merit consideration: *"The 'new economies'*. . . assigns an important role to both fiscal and monetary policy. Indeed, the appropriate mix of policies has been the cornerstone of the argument ... To anyone who fears that the 'new economics' is all fiscal policy, the record offers evidence, and the new economics assurance, that money *does* matter."[6]

EXERCISES

1. Discuss the views of monetarists and Keynesians on monetary policy.
2. Examine Monetarist and Keynesian controversy about monetary and fiscal policy.
3. Explain the main points of difference between the monetarists and the Keynesian about monetary and fiscal policy.

---

4. M. Friedman and David Meiselman, "The Relative Stability of Monetary Velocity and the Investment Multiplier in the United States, 1897-1958," *Stabilization Policies,* 1963.
5. L.C. Anderson and J.L. Jordan, "Monetary and Fiscal Actions: A Test of their Relative Importance in Economic Stabilisation," *Federal Reserve Bank of St. Louis Review,* November, 1968.
6. Walter W. Heller, *New Dimensions of Political Economy,* 1966

CHAPTER 40

Fiscal Policy and Debt Management

1. FISCAL POLICY

MEANING

Fiscal policy is a powerful instrument of stabilisation. "By fiscal policy we refer to government actions affecting its receipts and expenditures which we ordinarily take as measured by the government's net receipts, its surplus or deficit."[1] The government may offset undesirable variations in private consumption and investment by anticyclical variations of public expenditures and taxes. Arthur Smithies defines fiscal policy as "a policy under which the government uses its expenditure and revenue programmes to produce desirable effects and avoid undesirable effects on the national income, production and employment." Though the ultimate aim of fiscal policy is the long-run stabilisation of the economy, yet it can be only achieved by moderating short-run economic fluctuations. In this context Otto Eckstein defines fiscal policy as "changes in taxes and expenditures which aim at short-run goals of full employment and price-level stability".[2]

INSTRUMENTS OF FISCAL POLICY

Fiscal policy, through variations in government expenditure and taxation, profoundly affects national income, employment, output and prices. An increase in public expenditure during depression adds to the aggregate demand for goods and services and leads to a large increase in income via the multiplier process; while a reduction in taxes has the effect of raising disposable income thereby increasing consumption and investment expenditures of the people. On the other hand, a reduction of public expenditure during inflation reduces aggregate demand, national income, employment, output and prices; while an increase in taxes tends to reduce disposable income thereby reducing consumption and investment expenditures. Thus the government can control deflationary and inflationary pressures in the economy by a judicious combination of expenditure and taxation programmes. We discuss below the various *instruments* of fiscal policy.

1. BUDGETARY POLICY—CONTRACYCLICAL FISCAL POLICY

The budget is the principal instrument of fiscal policy. Budgetary policy exercises control over size and relationship of government receipts and expenditures. We discuss below the common budget policies that can be adopted for stabilising the economy.

(1) *Budget Deficit—Fiscal Policy During Depression.* Deficit budgeting is an important method of overcoming depression. When government expenditures exceed receipts, larger amounts are put into the stream of national income than they are withdrawn. The deficit represents the net expenditure of the government which increases

---

1. J.M. Culberston, *Macroeconomic Theory and Stabilisation Policy,* 1968.
2. O. Eckstein, *Public Finance,* (2nd ed.), 1967.

national income by the multiplier times the increase in net expenditure. If the *MPC* is 2/3, the multiplier will be 3; and if the net increase in government expenditure is Rs. 100 crores it will increase national income to Rs. 300 crores (= 100 x 3). Thus the budget deficit has an expansionary effect on aggregate demand whether the fiscal process leaves marginal propensities unchanged or whether a redistribution of disposable receipts occurs. The expansionary effect of a budget deficit is shown diagrammatically in Fig. 1. *C* is the consumption function. *C+I+G* represents consumption, investment and government expenditure (the total spendings function) before that budget is introduced. Suppose government expenditure of ΔG is injected into the economy. As a result, the total spendings function shifts upward to *C+I+G′*. Income increases from *OY* to OY_1 when the equilibrium position moves from *E* to E_1. The increase in income YY_1 (= $EA = E_1A$) is greater than the increase in government expenditure $E_1B(=\Delta G)$. $BA(E_1A-E_1B)$ represents increase in consumption. Thus the budget deficit is always expansionary, the rise in national income being (YY_1) greater than the actual amount of government spending ($\Delta G=E_1B$). In this method of budget deficit taxes are kept intact.

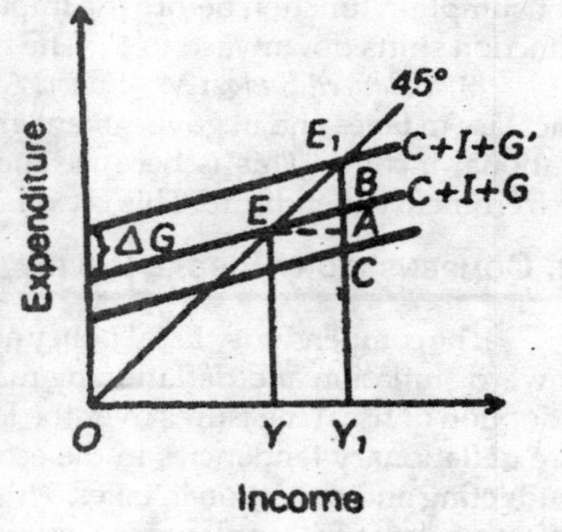

FIG. 1

Budget deficit may also be secured by reduction in taxes and without government spending. Reduction in taxes tends to leave larger disposable income in the hands of the people and thus stimulates increased consumption expenditure. This, in turn, would lead to increase in aggregate demand, output, income and employment. This is illustrated in Fig. 2, where *C* is the original consumption function. Suppose tax is reduced by *ET*, it will shift the consumption upward to C′. Income will increases from *OY* to OY_1.

However, reduction in taxes is not so expansionary via increased consumption expenditure because the tax relief may be saved and not spent on consumption. Businessmen may not also invest more if the business expectations are low. Therefore, to safeguard against such eventualities the government should follow the policy of reduction in taxes with increased government spending and its multiplier effect will be much higher in case we also assume that some consumption and investment expenditures increase due to tax relief.

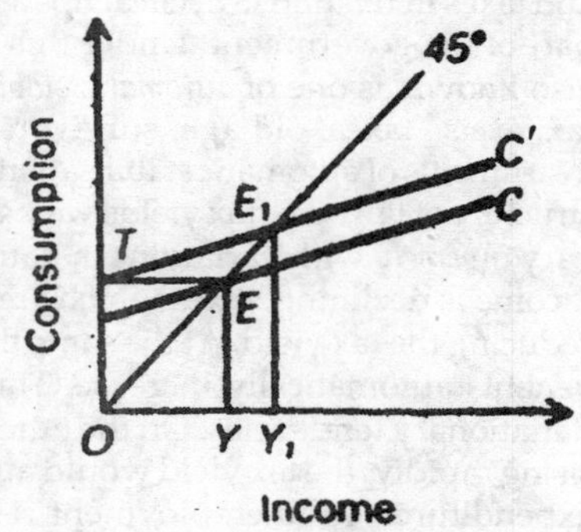

FIG. 2

(2) *Surplus Budget—Fiscal Policy during Boom.* Surplus in the budget occurs when the government revenues exceed expenditures. The policy of surplus budget is followed to control inflationary pressures within the economy. It may be through *increase in taxation or reduction in government expenditure or both.* This will tend to reduce income and aggregate demand by the multiplier times the reduction in government or/and private consumption expenditure (as a result of increased taxes). This is explained with the aid of Fig. 1, where the economy is at the initial equilibrium position E_1. Suppose the government expenditure is reduced by ΔG so that the total spending function *C+I+G′* shifts downward to *C+I+G*. Now *E* is the new equilibrium position which shows that the income has declined to *OY* from OY_1 as a result of reduction in government expenditure by E_1B. The fall in income Y_1Y ($=AE$)$>E_1B$, the reduction in expenditure because consumption has also been reduced by *BA*.

There may be budget surplus without government spending when taxes are raised. Enhanced taxes reduce the disposable income with the people and encourage reduction in consumption expenditure.

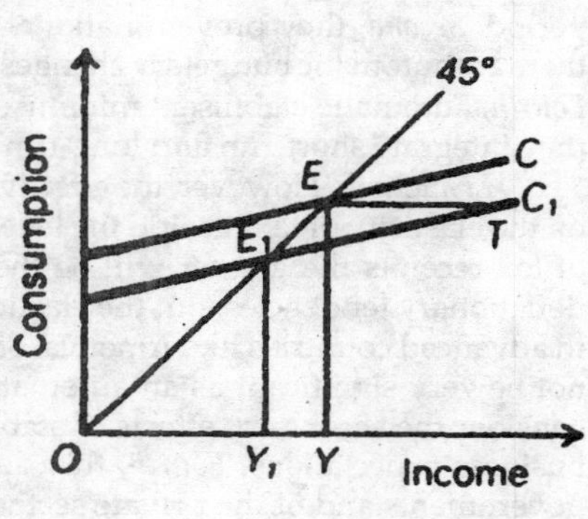

FIG. 3

The result is fall in aggregate demand, output, income and employment. This is illustrated in Fig. 3. C is the consumption function before the imposition of tax. Suppose a tax equal to ET is introduced. The consumption function shifts downward to C_1. The new equilibrium position is E_1. As a result, income falls from OY to OY_1.

(3) *Balanced Budget Multiplier.* Another *expansionist* fiscal policy is the balanced budget. In this policy, the increase in taxes and in government expenditures are of an equal amount. This has the impact of increasing net national income. This is because the *reduction* in consumption resulting from the tax is not equal to the government expenditure. This is explained in terms of what is known as the *balanced budget theorem or multiplier.*

2. Compensatory Fiscal Policy

The compensatory fiscal policy aims at continuously compensating the economy against chronic tendencies towards inflation and deflation by manipulating public expenditures and taxes. It, therefore, necessitates the adoption of fiscal measures over the long-run rather than once-for-all measures at a point of time. When there are deflationary tendencies in the economy, the government should increase its expenditure through deficit budgeting and reduction in taxes. This is essential to compensate for the lack in private investment and to raise effective demand, employment, output and income within the economy. On the other hand, when there are inflationary tendencies, the government should reduce its expenditure by having a surplus budget and raising taxes in order to stabilise the economy at the full employment level. The compensatory fiscal policy has two approaches: (i) built-in stabilisers and (ii) discretionary fiscal policy.

(i) Built-in Stabilisers

The technique of built-in flexibility or stabilisers involves the automatic adjustment of the expenditures and taxes in relation to cyclical upswings and downswings within the economy without deliberate action on the part of the government. Under this system, changes in the budget are automatic and hence this technique is also known as one of *automatic stabilisers.* The various automatic stabilisers are corporate profits tax, income tax, excise taxes, old age, survivors and unemployment insurance and unemployment relief payments. As instruments of automatic stabilisation, taxes and expenditures are related to national income. Given an unchanged structure of tax rates, tax yields vary *directly* with movements in national income, while government expenditures vary *inversely* with variations in national income. In the downward phase of the business cycle when national income is declining, taxes which are based on a percentage of national income automatically decline, thereby reducing the tax yield. At the same time, government expenditures on unemployment relief and social security benefits automatically increase. Thus there would be an automatic budget deficit which would counteract deflationary tendencies. On the other hand, in the upward phase of the business cycle when national income is rising rapidly, the tax yield would automatically increase with the rise in tax rates. Simultaneously, government expenditures on unemployment relief and social security benefits automatically decline. These two forces would automatically create a budget surplus and thus inflationary tendencies would be controlled automatically.

Merits. Built-in stabilisers have certain *advantages* as a fiscal device. *First,* the built-in stabilisers serve as a cushion for private purchasing power when it falls and lessen the hardships on the people during deflationary period. *Second,* they prevent national income and consumption spending from falling at a low level. *Third,* there are automatic budgetary changes in this device and the delay in aking administrative decisions is avoided. *Fourth,* automatic stabilisers minimise the errors of wrong forecasting and timing of fiscal measures. *Lastly,* they integrate short-run and long-run fiscal policy.

Limitations. However, the effectiveness of built-in stabilisers as an automatic compensatory device depends on the elasticity of tax receipt, the level of taxes and flexibility of public expenditure. The greater the elasticity of tax receipts the greater will be the effectiveness of automatic stabilisers in controlling inflationary and deflationary tendencies. But the elasticity of tax receipts is not so high as to act as an automatic stabiliser even in advanced countries like America. *Second,* with low level of taxes even a high elasticity of tax receipts would not be very significant as an automatic stabiliser during a downswing. *Third,* the built-in stabilisers do not consider the secondary effects of stabilisers on after-tax business incomes and of consumption spending on business expectations. *Fourth,* this device keeps silent about the stabilising influence of local bodies, state governments and of the private sector economy. *Fifth,* they cannot eliminate the business cycle. At the most, they can reduce its severity. *Sixth,* their effects during recovery from recession are unfavourable. Economists, therefore, suggest that built-in stabilisers should be supplemented by discretionary fiscal policy.

(ii) Discretionary Fiscal Policy

Discretionary fiscal policy requires deliberate changes in the budget by such actions as changing tax rates or government expenditures or both. It may generally take three forms: *(i)* changing taxes with government expenditure constant, *(ii)* changing government expenditure with taxes constant, and *(iii)* variations in both expenditures and taxes simultaneously.

First, when taxes are reduced, while keeping government expenditure unchanged, they increase the disposable income of households and businesses. This increases private spending. But the amount of increase will depend on whose taxes are cut, to what extent, and on whether the taxpayers regard the cut temporary or permanent. If the beneficiaries of tax cut are in the higher middle income group, the aggregate demand will increase much. If they belong to the lower income group, the aggregate demand will not increase much. If they are businessmen with little incentive to invest, tax reductions will not induce them to invest. Lastly, if the taxpayers regard tax reductions as temporary, this policy will again be less effective. So this policy is more effective in controlling inflation by raising taxes because high rates of taxation will reduce disposable income of individuals and businesses thereby curtailing aggregate demand.

The *second* method is more useful in controlling deflationary tendencies. When the government increases its expenditure on goods and services, keeping taxes constant, aggregate demand goes up by the full amount of the increase in government spending. On the other hand, reducing government expenditure during inflation is not so effective because of high business expectations in the economy which are not likely to reduce aggregate demand.

The *third* method is more effective and superior to the other two methods in controlling inflationary and deflationary tendencies. To control inflation, taxes may be increased and government expenditure reduced. On the other hand, taxes may be reduced and government expenditure be raised to fight depression.

Limitations. The discretionary fiscal policy depends upon *proper timing* and *accurate forecasting. First,* accurate forecasting is essential to judge the stage of cycle through which the economy is passing. It is only then that appropriate fiscal action can be taken. Wrong forecasting may accentuate rather than moderate the cyclical swings. Economics is not an exact science in correct forecasting. As a result, fiscal action always follows after the turning points in the business cycles. *Second,* there are delays in proper timing of public spending. In fact, discretionary fiscal policy is subject to two time lags. First, there is the "decision lag," the time required in studying the problem and taking the decision. The lag involved in this process may be too long. Second, once the decision is taken, there is an "execution lag." It involves expenditure which is to be allocated for the execution of the programme. In a country like the USA, it may take two years and less than a year in the UK. *Third,* certain public works projects are so cumbersome that it is not possible to accelerate or slow them down for the purpose of raising or reducing public spending on them.

Conclusion. Despite the higher multiplier effect of government spending as against changes in tax rates, the latter can be operated more promptly than the former. Emphasis has thus shifted to taxation as the best fiscal device for controlling cyclical fluctuations. Thus when the turning point of a business cycle is already underway, discretionary fiscal action tends to strengthen the built-in stabilisers, as has been the experience of developed countries like the USA.

2. DEBT MANAGEMENT

Meaning

Debt management is often referred to the amount, composition and refunding of the national debt. But, in actuality, it is related to the *composition* (the types of securities sold) and the *refunding* of the debt held by the public within a country. So far as the number of new securities sold by the government is concerned, it falls within the jurisdiction of fiscal policy. The number of securities bought and sold by the Central bank is a monetary policy decision. Thus debt management is defined as "all actions of the government, including both the treasury and central bank, which affect the composition and retirement of the public-held debt".

Objectives of Debt Management

The main objectives of debt management are :

1. To minimise the interest cost of servicing the debt to the taxpayer.

2. To employ it contracyclically as a stabilisation weapon to supplement monetary and fiscal policy.

There are potential conflicts between these two objectives because they often entail opposite policy actions. Minimising the interest cost means that during a recession, interest rates are low. The government should exchange its maturing securities with hew long-term securities carrying low interest rates so that their interest cost is less in the future. On the other hand, when interest rates are high during a boom, the government should exchange its maturing securities with short-term securities which carry low interest rates so that it has not to pay high rates when the interest rates fall to normal levels.

The stabilisation objective requires opposite policies. During a recession, the government should sell short-term securities which should lower interest rates and increase investment spending. On the other hand, during a boom, it should sell long-term securities which would raise iong-term interest rates. This would reduce investment spending.

Techniques of Debt Management

Many techniques have been suggested by economists to achieve the objectives of debt management. We discuss below a few practical and important techniques :

1. *Lowering the Interest Cost.* The most important objective of debt management is that the interest cost of the public debt to the government should be low so that the burden of servicing the debt should be the minimum to the taxpayers. The government repays the debt by raising revenues from taxation. The higher the cost of servicing the debt, the higher would be the level of taxation and the greater the burden on taxpayers. The government should so work out the pattern of interest rates that it conforms to the preference pattern of security holders. The lower the interest rates on government securities, the smaller will be the transference of resources from the taxpayers to bond holders.

In practice, most governments keep very low interest rates on short-term securities and gradually increase the interest rates as the maturity period of the debt lengthens. This method gives rise to wide spreads between the short-term and long-term interest rates. This induces bond holders to switch over from short-term to long-term securities thereby increasing the debt burden of the government and imposing a higher tax burden on the taxpayers.

2. *Changing the Maturity Structure.* One of the techniques of debt management is to change the maturity structure of the debt as a device for economic stabilisation. This is done by "swapping operations" by the central bank. During boom period, the central bank sells more long-term government securities in the open market and purchases a corresponding amount of short-term government securities with the same amount of money. This lengthens the average maturity structure of the existing public debt which tends to raise the interest rate. Since long-term securities are not good substitute for money, they increase the liquidity preference. As a result, the liquidity preference curve will shift to the left from *LM* to LM_1. This raises the equilibrium interest rate from *OR* to OR_1 and reduces the equilibrium income from *OY to* OY_1, as shown in Fig. 4. The rise in the long-term interest rate would curb private spending by reducing availability of credit. The value of outstanding assets of financial institutions is also reduced with the increase in interest rate. They, therefore, tend to hold more liquid short-term government securities. This is likely to cause a rise in the short-term interest rate. If the short-term interest rate rises slightly, financial institutions will tend to hold more short-term government securities rather than cash. Thus reduction in the availability of credit and holding of more short-term securities will have a tendency to control a boom.

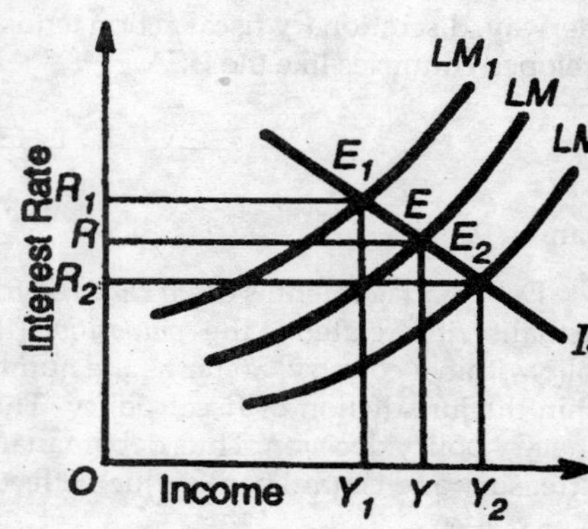

FIG. 4

On the other hand, debt management requires the shortening of the average maturity structure of the outstanding public debt through the sale of short-term government securities to replace them by purchasing long-term government securities during a recession. This would tend to bring a sharp fall in the long-term interest rate accompanied with a mild fall in the short-term interest rate. Since short-term securities are a close substitute for money, the asset holders tend to substitute them for money.

This will reduce the liquidity preference and shift the *LM* curve to the right from *LM* to LM_2 with a lower equilibrium level of interest rate OR_2 and a higher income level OY_2, as shown in Fig. 4. Thus debt management requires the manipulation of the term structure of the debt to bring about economic stability.

3. *Advance Refunding*. Another method of lengthening the public debt is to advance refunding of securities. The central bank offers the holders of a particular long-term government security, which still has some years to mature, to exchange their securities for a new security with a longer maturity. The new security carries a little higher yield and the holders of the old security do not realise any capital loss or gain. This technique has the advantage over the other techniques described above in that the central bank is not required to resort to open market operations for managing the public debt.

CONCLUSION

Debt management leads to a number of problems which should be tackled in co-ordination with monetary and fiscal policy. A large size of public debt is likely to siphon off funds from the capital market. This reduces the availability of credit in the capital market and raises the interest rate. This is likely to increase the burden of public debt to the government and makes investors feel that they would suffer a capital loss. Moreover, any holding of public debt by the central bank correspondingly increases the cash holdings of commercial banks. The banks, in turn, make a multiple expansion of their deposit liabilities which leads to inflationary pressures in the economy. Further, fluctuations in the demand, supply and prices of government securities during booms and recessions tend to increase the severity and longevity of booms and recessions. For this, the central bank should be ready to purchase or sell government securities in the open market in order to bring upward or downward pressure on interest rates for economic stabilisation and to minimise the interest cost of the debt to the government.

Similarly, the government should resort to fiscal policy so as to manage the public debt effectively. A budget surplus is used as a fiscal device during boom periods. A surplus budget acts in a deflationary manner upon the money supply and bank reserves. A budget surplus means that the government revenue is more than its expenditure. It involves reduction of money in the hands of taxpayers who are levied heavy taxes. This leads to a reduction in the deposits of the public with the commercial banks which, in turn, reduces the reserves of commercial banks. As a result, their reserves with the central bank are reduced. This leads to the reduction in the spendable money with the government. This makes the retirement of public debt held by the central bank difficult. This goes against the commonly held view that a budget surplus can be used for the retirement of public debt held by the central bank.

Despite this, coordination between monetary and fiscal policies is essential on a regular basis because of the frequent debt refunding operations of the central bank. When government securities mature, it is the central bank which is required to refund them on behalf of the government. At the same time, the government has to follow a surplus budgetary policy to retire the public debt. But this policy is deflationary in nature and requires to be controlled by an appropriate anti-deflationary monetary policy. If the government adopts a deficit budgetary policy for debt retirement, it would be inflationary in nature which is again required to be controlled by an appropriate anti-inflationary monetary policy. Thus for an effective debt management, there should be a close coordination between monetary, fiscal and debt management policies.

EXERCISES

1. What do you mean by fiscal policy? Distinguish clearly between the three main types of discretionary fiscal policy?
2. How do automatic stabilisers affect the economy? What are their limitations?
3. Explain compensatory fiscal policy.
4. What do you mean by debt management? How is the public debt managed?
5. Explain and evaluate debt management as a stabilisation weapon.

CHAPTER 41

Effectiveness of Monetary and Fiscal Policy

1. INTRODUCTION

The relative effectiveness of monetary and fiscal policy has been the subject of controversy among economists. The monetarists regard monetary policy more effective than fiscal policy for economic stabilisation. On the other hand, the Keynesians hold the opposite view. In between these two extreme views are the synthesists who advocate the middle path. Before we discuss them, we study the effectiveness of monetary and fiscal policy in terms of shape of the *IS* curve and the *LM* curve. The *IS* curve represents fiscal policy and the *LM* curve monetary policy.

2. MONETARY POLICY

The government influences investment, employment, output and income through monetary policy. This is done by increasing or decreasing the money supply by the monetary authority. When the money supply is increased, it is an expansionary monetary policy. This is shown by shifting the *LM* curve to the right. When the money supply is decreased, it is a contractionary monetary policy. This is shown by shifting the *LM* curve to the left.

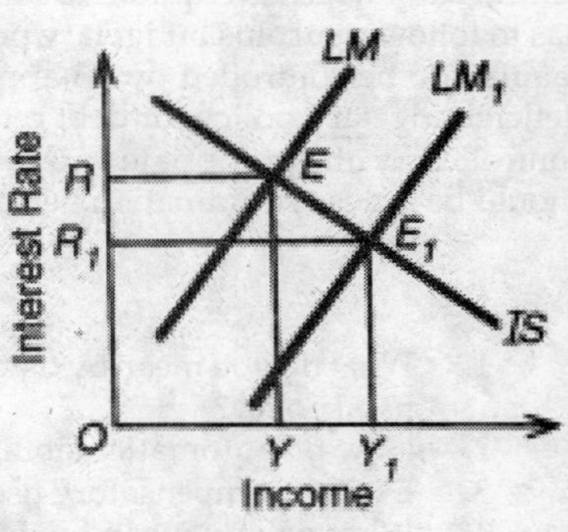

FIG. 1

Fig. 1 illustrates an expansionary monetary policy with given *LM* and *IS* curves. Suppose the economy is in equilibrium at point *E* with *OY* income and *OR* interest rate. An increase in the money supply by the monetary authority shifts the *LM* curve to the right to LM_1, given the *IS* curve. This reduces the interest rate from *OR* to OR_1, thereby increasing investment and national income. Thus the national income rises from *OY* to OY_1.

But the relative effectiveness of monetary policy depends on the shape of the *LM* curve and the *IS* curve. *Monetary policy is more effective if the LM curve is steeper.* A steeper *LM* curve means that the demand for money is less interest elastic. The less interest elastic is the demand for money, the larger is the fall in interest rate when the money supply is increased. This is because when the demand for money is less elastic to a change in interest rate, an increase in money supply is more powerful in bringing about a large fall in interest rate. A large fall in the interest rate leads to a higher increase in investment and in national income. This is depicted in Fig. 2 where *E* is the original equilibrium position of the economy with *OR* interest rate and *OY* income. When the *steep* LM_1 curve shifts to the right to *LMs,* the new equilibrium is set at E_2 .As a result, the interest rate falls from *OR* to OR_2 and income rises from *OY* to OY_2.On the other hand, *the flatter is the LM curve, the less effective is monetary policy.* A flatter *LM* curve means that the demand for money is more interest elastic. The more interest elastic is the demand for money, the smaller is the fall in interest rate when the money supply is increased. A small fall in the interest rate leads to a smaller increase in investment and income. In Fig. 2, *E* is the original equilibrium position with *OR* interest rate and *OY* income. When the flatter LM_2 curve shifts to the right to LM_F the new equilibrium is established at E_1 which produces OR_1 interest rate and OY_1 income level. In this case, the fall in interest rate to OR_1 is less than OR_2 of the steeper *LMs* curve and the increase in income OY_1 is also less than OY_2 of the steeper curve. This shows that monetary policy is less effective in the case of the flatter *LM* curve and more effective in the case of the steeper curve.

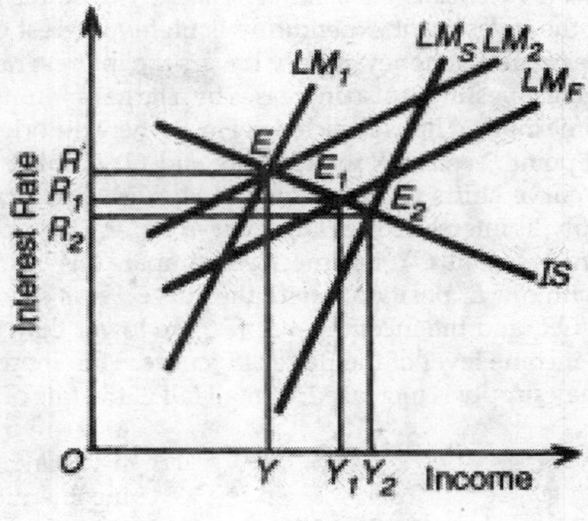

FIG. 2

If *the LM curve is horizontal, monetary policy is completely ineffective* because the demand for money is

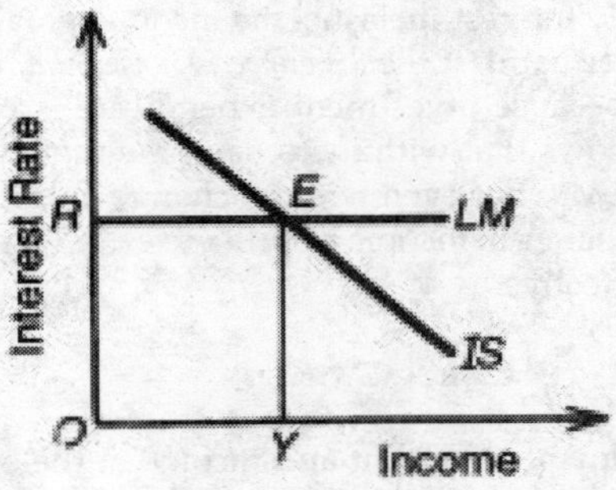

FIG. 3

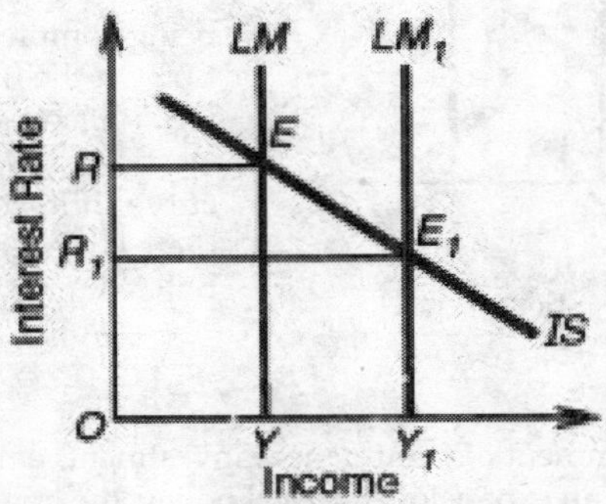

FIG. 4

perfectly interest-elastic. This is the case of "liquidity trap" shown in Fig. 3 where the increase in the money supply has no effect on the interest rate *OR* and the income level *OY*. On the other hand, if *the LM curve is vertical, monetary policy is highly effective* because the demand for money is perfectly interest-inelastic. Fig. 4 shows that when the vertical *LM* curve shifts to the right to LM_1 with increase in the money supply, the interest rate falls from *OR* to OR_1 which has no effect on the demand for money and the entire increase in the money supply has the effect of raising the income level from OY_1 to OY_2.

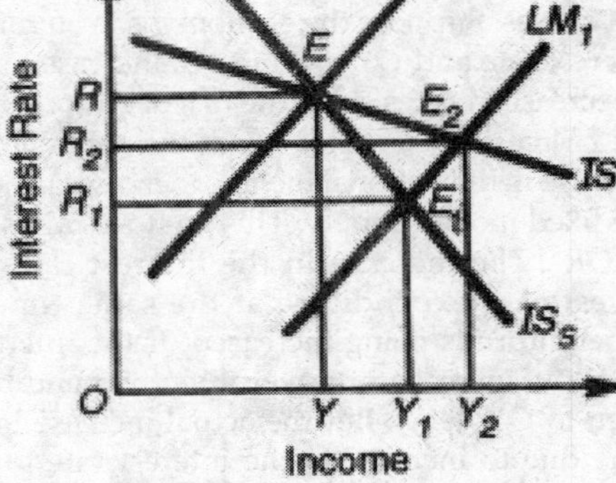

FIG. 5

Now take the slope of the *IS* curve. *The flatter is the IS curve, the more effective is the monetary policy.* The flatter *IS* curve means that the investment expenditure is highly interest elastic. When an increase in the money supply lowers the interest rate even slightly, private investment also increases by a large amount, thereby raising income much. This is depicted in Fig. 5 where the original equilibrium is at point *E* with *OR* interest rate and *OY* income level. When the *LM* curve shifts to the right to LM_1 with the increase in money supply, it intersects the flatter curve IS_F at E_2 which produces OR_2 interest rate and OY_2 income. If we compare this equilibrium position E_2 with the E_1 position where the curve *ISs* is steeper, the interest rate OR_1 and the income level OY_1 are lower than the interest rate and income level of the flatter IS_F curve. This shows that when the money supply is increased, a small fall in the rate of interest leads to a large rise in private investment which raises income more (by YY_2) with the flatter *IS* curve as compared to the steep *IS* curve (by YY_1) thus making monetary policy more effective.

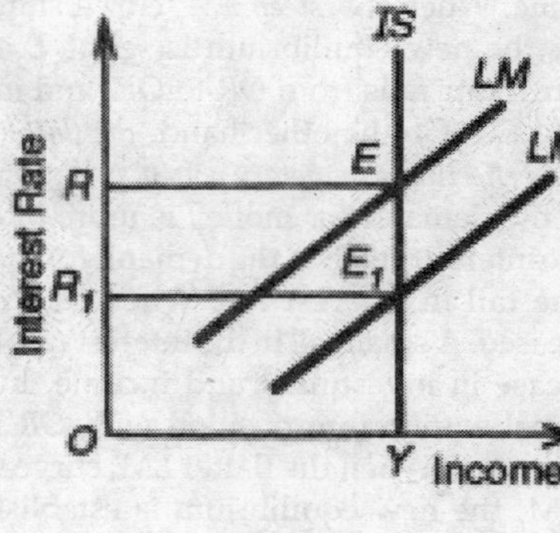

FIG. 6

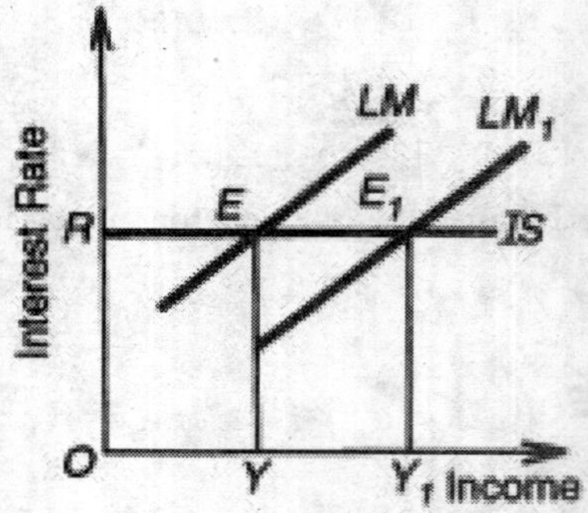

FIG. 7

If the *IS curve is vertical, monetary policy is completely ineffective* because investment expenditure is completely interest-inelastic. With the increase in the money supply the *LM* curve shifts to the right to LM_1 in Fig. 6, the interest rate falls from *OR* to OR_1 but investment being completely interest-inelastic, the income remains unchanged at *OY*. On the other hand, if the *IS curve is horizontal, monetary policy is highly effective* because investment expenditure is perfectly interest-elastic. Fig. 7 shows that with increase in the money supply, the *LM* curve shifts to LM_1, but even with no change in the interest rate *OR*, there is a large change in income from *OY* to OY_1. This makes monetary policy highly effective.

3. FISCAL POLICY

The government also influences investment, employment, output and income in the economy through fiscal policy. For an expansionary fiscal policy, the government increases its expenditure or/and reduces taxes. This shifts the *IS* curve to the left. It follows a contractionary fiscal policy by reducing its expenditure or/and increasing taxes. This shifts the *IS* curve to the right.

Fig. 8 illustrates an expansionary fiscal policy with given *IS* and *LM* curves. Suppose the economy is in equilibrium ai pornt *E* with *OR* interest rate and *OY* income. An increase in government spending or a decrease in taxes shifts the *IS* curve upwards to IS_1, which intersects the *LM* curve at E_1. This raises the national income from *OY* to OY_1. The rise in the national income increases the demand for money, given the fixed money supply. This, in turn, raises the interest rate from *OR* to OR_1. The increase in the interest rate tends to reduce private investment expenditure at the same time when the government expenditure is being increased. If the interest rate had not changed with the increase in government expenditure, income would have risen to OY_2 level. But the actual increase in income has been *less* by Y_2Y_1 due to increase in the interest rate to OR_1 which has reduced private investment expenditure.

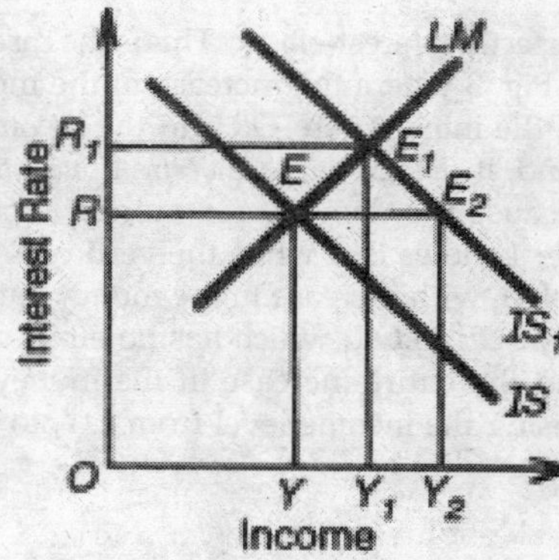

FIG. 8

The relative effectiveness of fiscal policy depends on the *slope* of the *LM* curve and the *IS* curve. *Fiscal policy is more effective, the flatter is the LM curve, and is less effective when the LM curve is steeper.* When the *IS* curve shifts upwards to IS_1 with the increase in government expenditure, its impact on national income is more with the flatter *LM* curve than with the steeper *LM* curve. This is shown in Fig. 9 where the IS_1 curve intersects the flatter LM_F curve at point E_2 which produces OY_2 income and OR_2 interest rate. On the other hand, it intersects the steeper *LMs* curve at E_1 which determines OY_1 income and OR_1 interest rate. In the case of the steeper curve *LMs,* the increase in income to OY_1 leads to a large rise in the demand for money which raises the interest rate to a very high level OR_1. The large increase in the interest rate reduces private investment despite increase in government expenditure which ultimately brings a small rise in income OY_1. But in the case of the flatter curve LM_F, the rise in the interest rate to OR_2 is relatively small. Consequently, it reduces private investment to a lesser degree and its net effect on national income is relatively large. Thus increase in national income with the flatter curve LM_F is more $(YY_2 > YY_1)$ as compared with the steeper curve *LMs.*

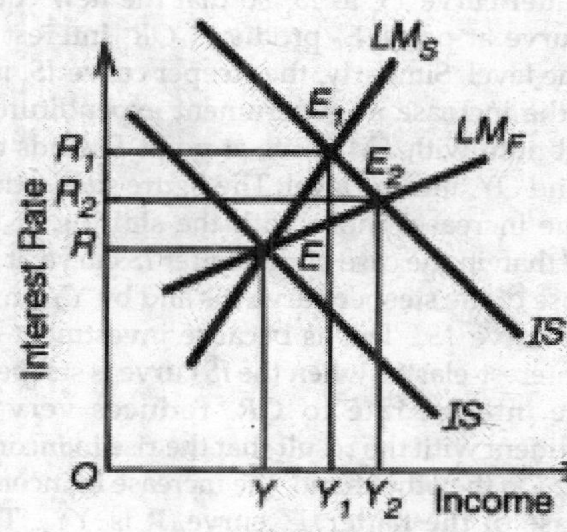

FIG. 9

Fiscal policy is completely ineffective, if the LM curve is vertical. It means that the demand for money is perfectly interest-inelastic. This is shown in Fig. 10 where the level of income remains unchanged. When the *IS*

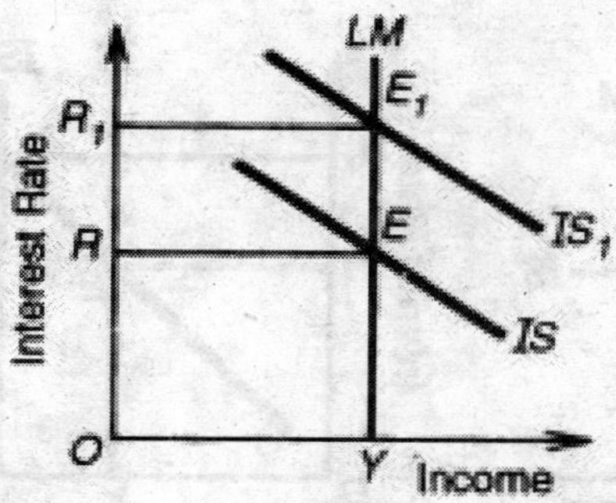

FIG. 10

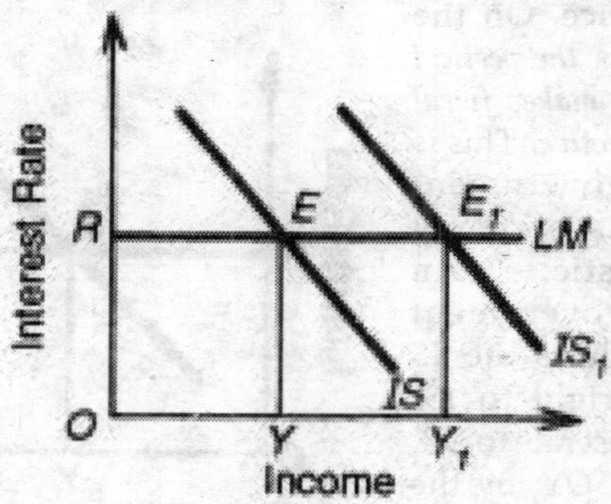

FIG. 11

curve shifts upwards to IS_1, only the interest rate rises from *OR* to OR_1 and increase in government expenditure does not affect national income at all. It remains constant at *OY*. At the other extreme is the *perfectly horizontal LM curve* where *fiscal policy is fully effective.* This situation implies that the demand for money is perfectly interest-elastic. This is shown in Fig. 11 where the horizontal *LM* curve is intersected by the *IS* curve at *E* which produces *OR* interest raie and *OY* income. When the *IS* curve shifts to the right to IS_1, income rises by the full multiplier of the increase in government expenditure. It rises to OY_1 but there is no change in interest rate.

Now take the *slope* of the *IS* curve. *The steeper is the IS curve the more effective is fiscal policy. The flatter is the IS curve, the less effective is the fiscal policy.* These two cases are illustrated in Fig. 12 where *E* is the original equilibrium point with *OR* interest rate and *OY* income level. The increase in government expenditure shifts the flatter curve IS_1 to IS_F so that the new equilibrium with *LM* curve at point E_1 produces OR_1 interest rate and OY_1 income level. Similarly, the steeper curve IS_2 is shifted to *ISs* with the increase in government expenditure and the new equilibrium with *LM* curve at point E_2 leads to OR_2 interest rate and OY_2 income level. The figure shows that the national income increases more with the shifting of the steeper *IS* curve than in the case of the flatter *IS* curve. It rises by YY_2 in the case of the steeper curve *ISs* and by YY_1 in the case of the flatter curve IS_F. This is because investment expenditure is less interest-elastic, when the *IS* curve is steeper. The increase in the interest rate to OR_2 reduces very little private investment with the result that the rise in income is greater. It is YY_2. On the other hand, the increase in income is smaller in the case of the flatter *IS* curve. It is YY_1. This is because investment expenditure is more interest-elastic. The increase in the interest rate to OR_1 reduces large private investment so that the rise in income is smaller. Thus fiscal policy is more effective, the steeper is the *IS* curve and is less effective in the case of the flatter *IS* curve.

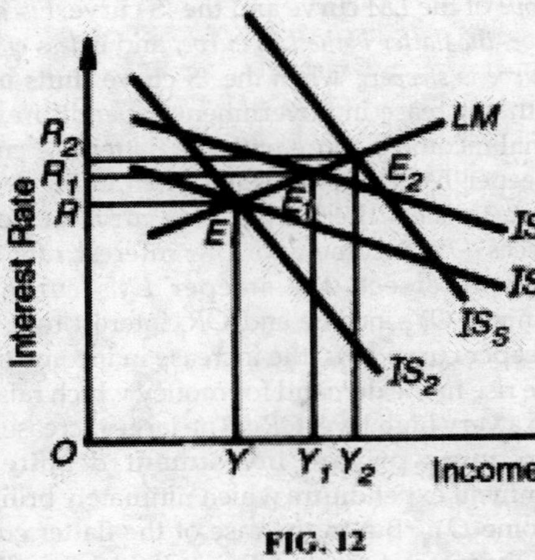

FIG. 12

Fiscal policy is completely ineffective, if the IS curve is horizontal. An horizontal *IS* curve means that investment expenditure is perfectly interest-elastic. This is depicted in Fig. 13 where *LM* curve intersects the *IS* curve at *E*. An increase in government expenditure has no effect on the interest rate *OR* and hence on the income level *OY*. Such a situation is not likely to be in practice. On the other extreme is *the vertical IS curve which makes fiscal policy highly effective.* This is because government expenditure is perfectly interest-inelastic. An increase in government expenditure shifts the *IS* curve to the right to IS_1 raises the interest rate to OR_1 and income to OY_1 by the full multiplier of the increase in government expenditure, as shown in Fig. 14. This makes fiscal policy highly effective.

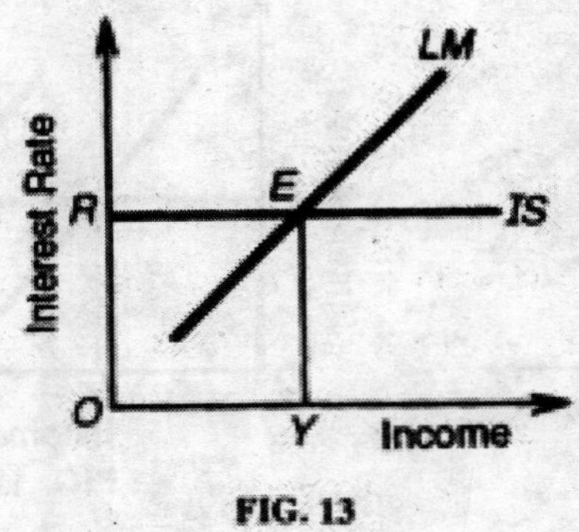

FIG. 13

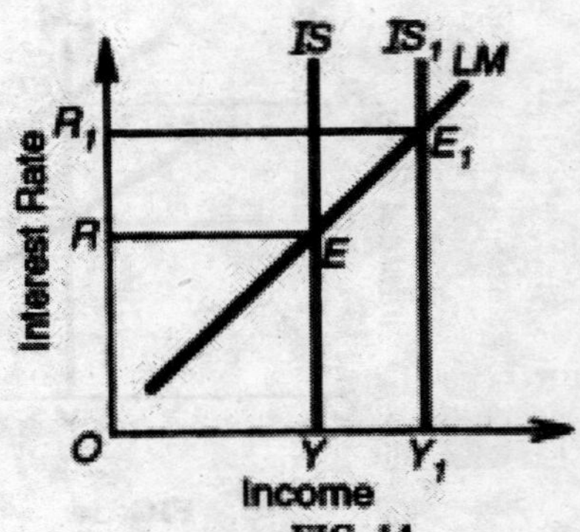

FIG. 14

4. THE SYNTHESIST VIEW : THREE RANGE ANALYSIS

Economists have explained the effectiveness of monetary and fiscal policies in three ranges in order to reconcile the *extremes* of the Keynesian and monetarist (or classical) views. The *LM* curve slopes upward to the right and has three segments, as shown in Fig. 15. Starting from the left it is perfectly elastic. This segment is known as *"the Keynesian range,"* reflecting the "liquidity trap". At the other extreme to the right, the *LM* curve is perfectly inelastic. This segment of the curve is known as *"the classical range"* because the classicals believed that money is held only for transactions purposes and nothing is held for speculative purposes. In between these two segments of the curve is *"the intermediate range"*. The Keynesian range represents the fiscalist or Keynesian view, the classical range the monetarist view, and the intermediate range the synthesist view.

We take expansionary monetary and fiscal policies in order to explain their effectiveness which depend upon the extent to which they affect the level of income and the rate of interest in the Keynesian, the classical and the intermediate ranges. They, in turn, are determined by the responsiveness of the demand for money to changes in the interest rate.

MONETARY POLICY

Monetary policy is explained in Fig. 15 where the three-range *LM* curves LM_1 and LM_2 are shown with three *IS* curves. The LM_2 curve emerges after an increase in the money supply.

The Keynesian Range

First, consider the Keynesian range where the *LM* curve is perfectly elastic. This is the Keynesian liquidity-trap situation in which the *LM* curve is horizontal, and the interest rate cannot fall below OR_1. An increase in the money supply shifts the *LM* curve from LM_1 to LM_2. This shift in the curve has no effect on the rate of interest. Consequently, investment is not affected at all so that the level of income remains unchanged at OY_1. This is because at a very low rate of interest such as OR_1, people prefer to keep money in cash rather than in bonds (or securities) in the hope of converting it into bonds when the interest rate rises. Thus under the Keynesian assumption of the liquidity trap, the horizontal portion of the *LM* curve is not affected by an increase in the money supply. The *IS* curve intersects the *LM* curve in the flat range at *A* with little effect on the interest rate, and consequently on investment and income. Monetary policy is, therefore, totally ineffective in the Keynesian range.

The Classical or Monetarist Range

Consider the classical range where *LM* curve is perfectly inelastic. In the classical range, the system is in equilibrium at *D* where the IS_3 curve intersects the LM_1 curve and the interest rate is OR_5 and income level OY_4. Suppose the central bank adopts an expansionary monetary policy whereby it increases the money supply by open market operations. The increase in money supply shifts the LM_1 curve to the right to LM_2 position. As a result, the income level increases from OY_4 to OY_5, and the interest rate falls from OR_5 to OR_4 when the IS_3 curve crosses the LM_2 curve at *E*.

The increase in the income level and fall in the interest rate as a result of the increase in the money supply is based on the classical assumption that money is primarily a medium of exchange. When the central bank buys securities in the market, the security prices are bid up and the rate of interest falls. The wealth holders then find other assets more attractive than securities. They, therefore, invest the increased cash holdings in new or existing capital investments which, in turn, raise the level of income. But as long as wealth holders possess more money balances than are required for transactions purposes,

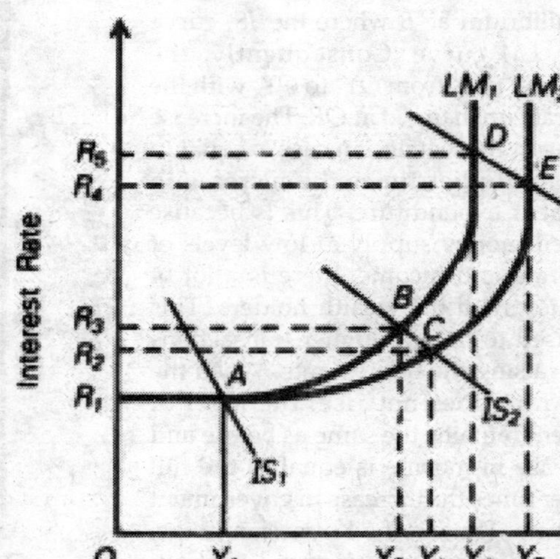

FIG. 15

they will continue to compete for earning assets. Consequently, the interest rate will continue to fall and investment will continue to rise until the excess money balances are absorbed in such transactions. Ultimately, the equilibrium level of income rises by the full amount of the increase in the money supply. Thus the monetary policy is highly effective in the classical range when the economy is at high levels of income and interest rate and utilises the entire increase in the money supply for transactions purposes thereby raising national income by the full increase in the money supply.

The Intermediate Range

Now consider the intermediate range when the initial equilibrium is at *B* where the IS_2 curve intersects the LM_1 curve, and the income level is OY_2 and the interest rate is OR_3. The increase in the money supply shifts the LM_1 curve to LM_2 position. As a result, the new equilibrium is established at point *C* where the IS_2 curve crosses the LM_2 curve. It shows that with the increase in the money supply the rate of interest falls from OR_3 to OR_2 and the income level rises from OY_2 to OY_3. In the intermediate range, the increase in income by Y_2 to Y_3 is less than that in the range Y_4 to Y_5. This is because in classical case the entire increase in the money supply is absorbed for transactions purposes. But in the intermediate case, the increased money supply is partly absorbed for speculative purposes and partly for transactions purposes. That which is held for speculative purposes is not invested by wealth holders and remains with them in the form of idle balances. This has the effect of raising the income level by less than the increase in the money supply. Thus in the intermediate range monetary policy is less effective than in the classical range.

FISCAL POLICY

Fiscal poiicy is explained in Fig. 16 in which the three range *LM* curve is taken along with six *IS* curves that arise after increase in government expenditure in the case of the Keynesian, intermediate and classical ranges.

The Keynesian Range

Consider first the Keynesian range when the initial equilibrium is at *A* where the IS_1 curve intersects the *LM* curve. Suppose the government expenditure is increased. This brings about new equilibrium at *B* where the IS_2 curve cuts the *LM* curve. Consequently, the income level rises from OY_1 to OY_2 with the interest rate unchanged at *OR*. The increase in income in the Keynesian case is equal to the full multiplier times the increase in government expenditure. This is because with fixed money supply at low levels of interest rate and income, there is a lot of idle money with the wealth holders. This can be used to finance higher transactions without raising the interest rate. When the interest rate does not rise, the level of investment remains the same as before and the increase in income is equal to the full multiplier times the increase in government expenditure. Thus in the Keynesian range, the fiscal policy is very effective.

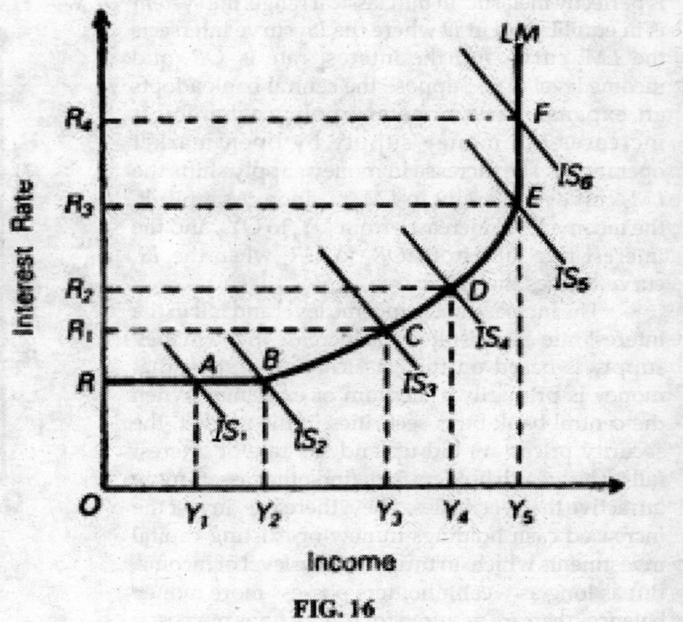

FIG. 16

The Classical or Monetarist Range

In the classical range, the *LM* curve is perfectly inelastic and the IS_5 curve intersects it at *E* so that the interest rate is OR_3 and the income level is OY_5. When the government expenditure increases for an expansionary fiscal policy, the IS_5 curve shifts upwards to IS_6. As a result, the IS_6 curve crosses the *LM* curve at *F* and the interest rate rises to OR_4 with income remaining unchanged at OY_5. This is because the classical case relates to a fully employed economy where the increase in government expenditure has the effect of raising the interest rate which reduces private investment. Since the increase in government expenditure exactly equals the reduction in the private investment, there is no effect on the level of income which remains constant at OY_5. Thus fiscal policy is not at all effective in the classical range.

The Intermediate Range

In the intermediate range, the initial equilibrium is at C where the IS_3 curve intersects the *LM* curve. Here OR_1 is the interest rate with OY_3 the level of income. With increase in the government expenditure, the IS_1 curve shifts upward to the right from IS_3 to IS_4 and the new equilibrium between IS_4 and *LM* curves is established at point *D*. As a result, the increase in government expenditure raises the income level from OY_3 to OY_4 and the interest rate from OR_1 to OR_2. The increase in both the income level and the interest rate in the intermediate range is due to two reasons. *First,* the increase in income resulting from a rise in government expenditure occurs because additional money balances are available for transaction purposes. *Second,* given a fixed money supply, a part of available transactions are held as idle balances by wealth holders which raise the interest rate. As a result of the rise in the interest rate, investment falls and the fiscal policy is not so effective as in the Keynesian range. In general, fiscal policy "will be more effective the closer equilibrium is to the Keynesian range and less effective the closer equilibrium is to the classical range."

Effects of Elasticities of IS Curve on Monetary and Fiscal Policies

The elasticities of the *IS* curve affect monetary and fiscal policies in a slightly different way. This is explained in terms of Fig. 17. In the *Keynesian range, monetary* policy is *ineffective* whether the *IS* curve is elastic (*ISF*) or inelastic (IS_F). On the other hand, fiscal policy is only *effective* when the *IS* curve is elastic or inelastic. The elastic curve IS_F shifts to IS_{F1} and income rises from OY_1 to OY_2 in Fig. 17. The same result follows in the case of the shifting of an inelastic *IS* curve (not shown in the figure).

In the *classical range, fiscal* policy is *ineffective* whether the *IS* curve is elastic (IS_{F2}) or inelastic (IS_{S2}). But monetary policy is *effective* under both the elastic and inelastic curves. Income rises from OY_1 to OY_6, as shown in Fig. 17.

In the *intermediate* range, *monetary* policy is *less* effective when the *ISs* curve is inelastic because the rise in income in this case is Y_2Y_3 whereas in the case of the elastic curve IS_{F1}, it is more effective, the rise in income being Y_2Y_5 ($>Y_2Y_3$). But fiscal policy is more effective, whether the *IS* curve is elastic or inelastic. The shifting of the inelastic curve IS_{S1} to IS_{S0} in Fig. 17 shows the increase in income from OY_2 to OY_3. The same result follows with the shifting of the elastic curve (IS_{F1}) upwards (not shown in the figure).

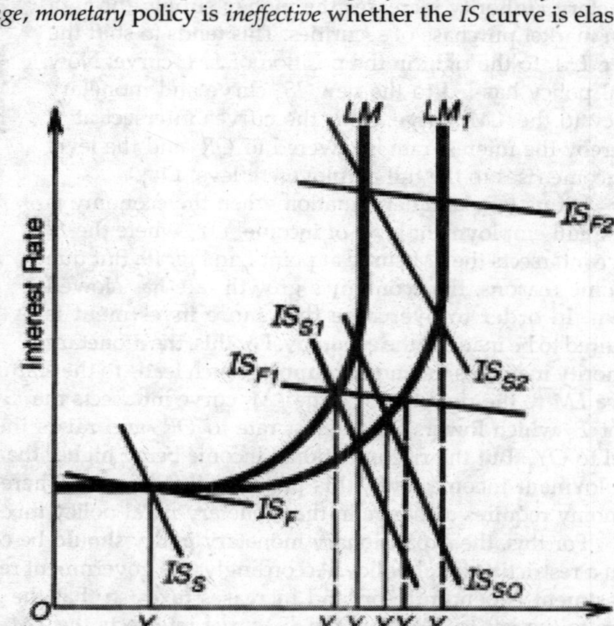

FIG. 17

CONCLUSION

The relative effectiveness of monetary and fiscal policy depends upon the shape of the *IS* and *LM* curves and the economy's initial position. If the economy is in the Keynesian range, monetary policy is ineffective and fiscal policy is highly effective. On the other hand, in the classical range, monetary policy is effective and fiscal policy is ineffective. But in the intermediate range both monetary and fiscal policies are effective. This case bridges the gap between the Keynesian and classical views. In this range, the elasticities of the *IS* and *LM* curves are neither highly interest elastic nor highly interest inelastic. In fact, in the intermediare range, the effectiveness of monetary and fiscal policies depends largely on the elasticities of the *IS* curve. If the *IS* curve is inelastic, fiscal policy is more effective than monetary policy. On the other hand, if the *IS* curve is elastic, monetary policy is more effective than fiscal policy. Thus for a complete effectiveness of both monetary and fiscal policies the best course is to have a monetary-fiscal mix.

5. MONETARY-FISCAL MIX

Consider a situation where an expansionary mix of monetary-fiscal policies is adopted to achieve full employment in the economy. This is illustrated in Fig. 18 where the economy is in the initial situation at *A* on the basis of the interaction of IS_1 and LM_1 curves. This situation depicts OR_2 interest rate and OY_1 income level. Now an expansionary fiscal policy is adopted in the form of increase in government expenditure or decrease in taxes. This shifts the curve IS_1 to IS_2. This will have the effect of raising the interest rate further to OR_3 if an expansionary monetary policy is not adopted simultaneously. So in order to reduce the interest rate and encourage investment for achieving full employment, the monetary authority increases the money supply through open market purchase of securities. This tends to shift the curve LM_1 to the right in the position of LM_2 curve. Now fiscal policy has led to the new IS_2 curve and monetary policy to the LM_2 curve. Both the curves intersect at *B* whereby the interest rate is lowered to OR_1 and the level of income rises to the full employment level OY_F.

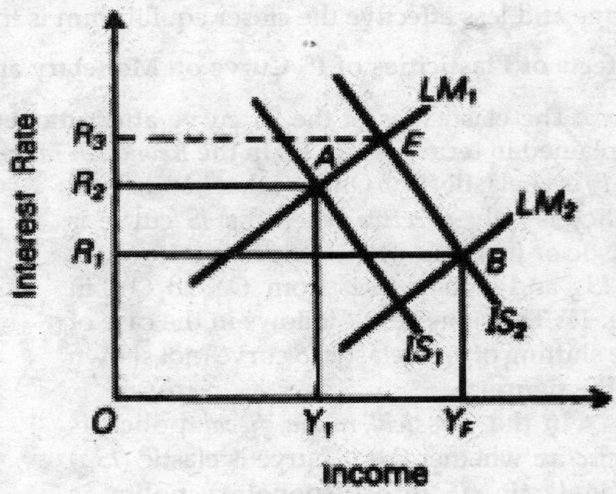

FIG. 18

Let us take another situation when the economy is at the full employment level of income, OY_F where the *IS* curve intersects the *LM* curve at point *E* in Fig. 19. But due to some reasons, the economy's growth rate has slowed down. In order to overcome this, more investment is required to be made in the economy. For this, the monetary authority increases the money supply which leads to the shifting of the curve *LM* to the right to LM_1. The LM_1 curve intersects the *IS* curve at point E_1 which lowers the interest rate to OR_1 and raises the income level to OY_1. But the rise in national income being higher than the full employment income level, this policy is inflationary. Therefore, the economy requires a change in the monetary-fiscal policy mix.

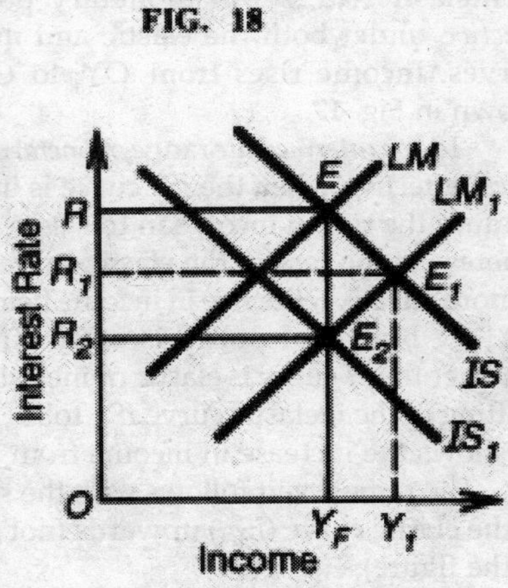

FIG. 19

For this, the expansionary monetary policy should be combined with a restrictive fiscal policy. Accordingly, the government reduces its investment expenditure or/and increases taxes so that the *IS* curve shifts to the left to IS_1. Now the IS_1 curve intersects the LM_1 curve at point E_2 so that the new equilibrium is established at a lower interest rate OR_2 and income OY_F which is the full employment income level. This level can be maintained by the present monetary-fiscal policy mix because the lower interest rate would keep large investment spending in the economy and reduced government expenditure or high taxes would control inflation.

EXERCISES

1. Examine the effectiveness of monetary and fiscal policies in terms of the *IS* and *LM* functions.
2. Examine the extent of effectiveness of monetary and fiscal policies in counteracting recessionary forces.
3. How would you reconcile the extremes of the Keynesian and classical views on the effectiveness of monetary and fiscal policies?
4. Explain the monetary-fiscal mix to achieve and maintain full employment.

CHAPTER 42

Assignment of Policy Instruments to Targets

1. INTRODUCTION

There are certain goals of monetary-fiscal policies which are required to be achieved through the use of policy instruments. They are full employment, economic growth, price stability and balance of payments equilibrium. These goals often conflict with each other. Macro-economic policy studies the nature of these conflicts and the appropriate means of resolving or coordinating between them. The discussion on these problems has primarily centered around the twin objectives of internal and external balance. Internal balance refers to income and full employment and external balance refers to the balance of payments equilibrium.

2. THE ASSIGNMENT PROBLEM

The theory of economic policy has concentrated on two distinct problems. *First*, the relation between the number of policy objectives and the number of policy instruments; and *second*, the assignment of policy instruments to the realisation of targets.

Jan Tinbergen[1] was the first economist to lay down that the number of policy instruments must be equal to the number of objectives. If there are more objectives than policy instruments it means that there are not enough tools to achieve the policy objectives. The system is undetermined. On the other hand, if the number of policy instruments are more than the number of objectives, then there is not one combination of tools and objectives that will solve the problem, but any number. The system is over-determined. Thus the number of policy tools must equal the number of targets for economic policy to be successful. This has come to be known as the *Tinbergen Principle* or the fixed targets approach.

In order to achieve given objectives with the same number of policy instruments, the second problem of the assignment of instruments to targets arises. The formulation of the assignment problem will eventually lead to equilibrium values of the objectives, despite lack of coordination between them.

CONFLICTS BETWEEN INTERNAL AND EXTERNAL BALANCE

Meade[2] was the first economist to discuss the potential conflicts between policies for internal and external balance with only one policy instrument, financial or demand management, and with repercussions on a trading partner country. If there are two countries *A* and *B*, deflation of domestic expenditure in *A* will reduce

1. *On the Theory of Economic Policy.* 1952.
2. J. E. Meade. *The Theory of International Economic Policy,* Vol I, 1951.

employment and income in *A*. This will reduce *A's* imports which will improve its balance of payments. Since *B'* s exports are reduced, B's income and employment will fall and make its balance of payments unfavourable. If *B* does not adopt any policy measure, *A* faces no policy conflict because if it expands its demand, it will raise employment and income in *A* and reduce its surplus balance of payments. But if A does nothing, *B* faces a policy conflict. If *B* adopts a policy of increasing its domestic expenditure to overcome internal depression, and a policy of deflation of domestic expenditure to restrict the demand for imports in *B*, there is a sharp conflict of policy. It is inflationary policy to stabilise employment and income, and deflationary policy to bring balance of payments equilibrium. Meade examines all possible types of disequilibrium in the two countries and shows that when each country adopts a policy which requires action in the same direction for both internal and external balance, very few conflicting situations arise. But if one or the other country does not take appropriate policy action in the same direction, the number of conflicting situations increase.

When there are conflicts between two goals, two instruments are required, instead of one, which are discussed as under.

Policies for Internal and External Balance

It was Johnson[3] who pointed towards the range of policy instruments for bringing about both internal and external balance. He called them expenditure-reducing or internal policies, and expenditure-switching or external policies.

A deficit in the balance of payments implies an excess of expenditure over income. To correct it, expenditure and income should be brought into equality. Expenditure-reducing policies aim at reducing aggregate demand through higher taxes and interest rates thereby reducing expenditure and output. The reduction in expenditure and output, in turn, reduces the domestic price level. This gives rise to switching of expenditure from foreign to domestic goods. Consequently, the country's imports are reduced. Expenditure-switching policies aim at increasing the demand for domestic goods and to change expenditure from imported goods to domestic goods. Such expenditure-switching increases domestic output. So long as the marginal propensity to spend is less than unity, it will improve the country's balance of payments

To achieve both objectives of internal and external balance simultaneously, a judicious combination of expenditure-reducing and expenditure-switching instruments is needed. For instance, if the economy is already at the full employment level, a policy of devaluation may cause inflation within the economy. So expenditure-switching policy of devaluation must be accompanied by expenditure-reducing policies of tighter fiscal and monetary controls to maintain full employment and balance of payments equilibrium.

In order to attain simultaneously the two targets of internal and external balance, the relationship between policy instruments are discussed in terms of Trevor Swan's model explained in Fig. 1.

The Swan Model

Swan explains the appropriate combinations of expenditure-switching and expenditure-reducing policies to attain internal and external balance.

Assumptions. The model is based on the assumptions that (1) there are no trade restrictions; (2) there are no capital movements; and (3) productivity, terms of trade and other financial transfers are given.

In Fig. 1 the horizontal axis measures real domestic expenditure, and the vertical axis measures the cost ratio which is an index of relative costs measuring the competitiveness of the economy. A movement to the left (towards *O)* on the horizontal axis means the use of expenditure-reducing policy, and a movement upwards along the vertical axis means the use of expenditure-switching policy. *FF* is the internal balance curve which represents a situation of full employment. It represents the various combinations of cost ratio and real domestic expenditure. A given level of employment can be achieved by *either* a highly favourable cost ratio and a relatively low level of domestic expenditure *or* by a less favourable cost ratio and a relatively higher level of expenditure. Thus the *FF* curve slopes downward to the right. Obviously, points to the right (above) the *FF* curve relate to inflation or over full employment, and points to the left (below) of the curve refer to recession

3. "Long-Run Problems of Balance of Payments." in R.E. Caves and H. G. Johnson.

or unemployment.

The *XX* curve represents the external balance where exports equal imports, in the absence of capital movements. So external balance occurs when net exports equal zero. This curve slopes upwards from left to right which shows that for the economy to remain in external balance, devaluation must be balanced by an increase in domestic expenditure. (Devaluation will improve the country's trade balance by encouraging exports and discouraging imports, and the increase in real domestic expenditure will increase the country's imports sufficiently.) Obviously, points above the *XX* curve refer to a surplus and points below the curve relate to a deficit in the balance of payments.

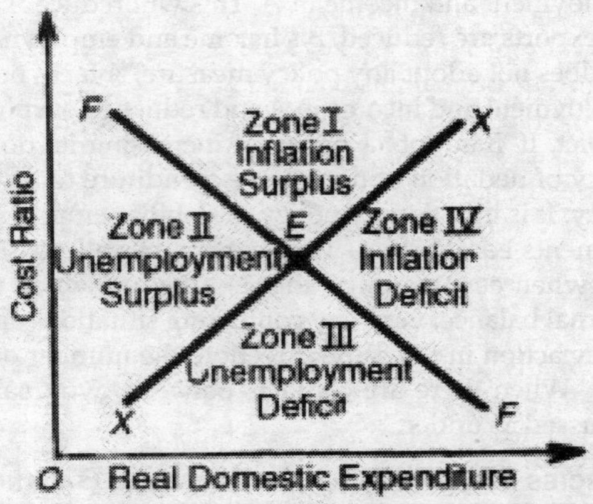

FIG. 1

The point where the FF curve intersects the *XX* curve represents the point of "bliss", where the economy is simultaneously in internal and external balance. *E* is such a point in Fig. 1 where the exchange rate and real domestic expenditure are in equilibrium. If the economy is not at point *E*, it is in disequilibrium. According to Swan, "The two curves of internal balance and external balance divide existence into four zones of economic unhappiness." The four zones of disequilibrium are:

Zone I : Inflation and balance of payments surplus
Zone II : Unemployment and balance of payments surplus.
Zone HI : Unemployment and balance of payments deficit.
Zone IV : Inflation and balance of payments deficit.

Policy Measures

In order to explain the type of policy measures which may be required to achieve internal and external balance simultaneously, we take eight possible cases of disequilibrium in Fig. 2. These cases require different combinations of policy measures.

A country at point *A* has equilibrium in the balance of payments and unemployment (or recession). Such a situation requires expansion of the domestic economy through increase in domestic expenditure. This will reduce net exports. In order to counteract this tendency, devaluation should be combined with increase in domestic expenditure.

If unemployment and a deficit in the balance of payment exist simultaneously, as at point *K* in zone III, there should be increase in domestic expenditure. A policy that raises internal demand through expansionary measures also increases domestic employment, but this policy widens the deficit in the balance of payments. This is described as the "dilemma zone", because instead of an expansionary policy, devaluation is the preferable policy.

If the economy combines full employment with a deficit in the balance of payments, as at point *D*, devaluation is the remedy. This will create a large export surplus and excess foreign demand will lead to inflation in the domestic economy. To counteract these tendencies, a smaller devaluation will have to be combined with a cut in domestic expenditure.

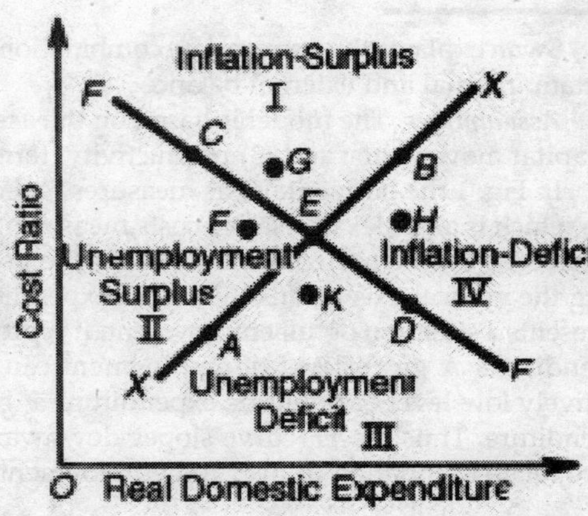

FIG. 2

Take point *H* in Zone IV where domestic inflation is combined with a deficit in the balance of payments. Inflation should be combated with reduction in domestic expenditure which would also reduce the deficit in the balance of payments, and ultimately move the economy towards the equilibrium position *E*.

If the country has balance of payments equilibrium and inflation as at point *B*, it should appreciate its exchange rate and reduce domestic expenditure.

Take point *G* in Zone I where a surplus in the balance of payments is combined with inflation. In this situation, the exchange rate should be appreciated to correct the surplus and expenditure be reduced to combat inflation. But reduction in expenditure would increase the surplus. This again represents the "dilemma zone".

If the country has full employment and a surplus in the balance of payments, as at point *C*, it should appreciate its exchange rate. But appreciation would create unemployment. To avoid it, it should increase domestic expenditure.

Finally, move to point *F* in Zone II where a surplus in the balance of payments is combined with unemployment. Here increase in domestic expenditure would be appropriate for both internal and external balances. Such a policy will raise employment and also induce an increase in imports to reduce the size of the surplus.

The above discussion reveals that if the economy is on neither the *FF* (internal balance) curve nor the *XX* (external balance) curve, it is in one of the four zones. When the economy follows only one policy or both expenditure-switching and domestic expenditure policies simultaneously to achieve one target (say, internal balance), it moves away from the other target (say, external balance). This problem arises not only in the "dilemma zones" I and III but also in the "simple zones" II and IV. For instance, if we take point *F* in Zone II where a surplus in the balance of payments is combined with unemployment an expansionary policy will reduce unemployment and reduce the surplus. But to move the economy to full equilibrium point *E*, appreciation or depreciation of the exchange rate will have to be adopted which will move the economy away from one target or the other.

FISCAL-MONETARY POLICY FOR INTERNAL AND EXTERNAL BATANCE: THE MUNDELLIAN MODEL[4]

Mundell discusses the case of relationship between two tools and two objectives. The two instruments are monetary policy represented by interest rate and fiscal policy represented by government expenditure. The two objectives are full employment (internal balance) and balance of payments equilibrium (external balance). The assignment rule is to assign monetary policy to the objective of external balance and fiscal policy to internal balance. The assignment of these instruments to the objectives is illustrated in Fig. 3.

In the figure, the horizontal axis measures interest rate (monetary policy) and the vertical axis budget surplus (fiscal policy). *FF* is the internal balance line and *XX* the external balance line. The *FF* line represents full employment. It is negatively sloped because a reduction in budget surplus* must be balanced by an increase in interest rate** in order to maintain full employment. There is inflation below this line *FF* (zone III and IV), and recession above it (zone I and II). On the other hand, line *XX* gives all points of equilibrium in the balance of payments. It is also negatively sloped because a reduction in the budget surplus increases imports which must be counteracted by an improvement on capital account through an increase in interest rate. There is deficit in the balance of payments below this line (zone I and IV), and surplus above this line (zone II and III). The *XX* line is steeper than the *FF* line because an increase in interest rate in order to balance an expansionary fiscal policy (increase in budget deficit or reduction in budget surplus) induces a short-term capital inflow for an external balance. The more responsive capital movements are to interest rate changes, the steeper is the *XX* line relative to the *FF* line. This makes monetary policy relatively more effective for maintaining external balance.

4. R.A. Mundell, "The Appropriate Use of Fiscal and Monetary Policy for Internal and External Stability," *I.M.F. Staff Papers*, 1962.

* Reduction in budget surplus means increase in government expenditure.

** Increase in interest rate implies reduction in the money supply.

Fig. 3 illustrates external and internal balance and the role played by monetary and fiscal policy in maintaining equilibrium between the two. Suppose the economy is at point *A* in zone I where there is full employment within the economy and deficit in the balance of payments. To remove balance of payments deficit, the monetary authority acts first by increasing the interest rate by *AB* in order to reduce the money supply. The reduction in money supply will reduce demand for goods and this will, in turn, decrease imports, and restore equilibrium in the balance of payments at *B*. But here the economy is having recession and unemployment. To correct these and to have internal balance, budget surplus will have to be reduced by *BC*. But at C, there is again deficit in the balance of payments which necessitates further increase in interest rate by *CD* for reducing the money supply. At *D* the internal balance is again disturbed leading to a further reduction in budget surplus. This process of reduction in money supply followed by reduction in budget surplus will ultimately lead the economy to the equilibrium point *E* where there is simultaneous internal and external balance.

On the other hand, if budget surplus is used to remedy the deficit in balance of payments and monetary policy to correct recession and unemployment, there would be neither external balance nor internal balance. Starting from point *A*, an increase in budget surplus would move the economy to *K* where the external balance is achieved but there is recession and unemployment in the economy. To remedy it, the interest rate is reduced by *KL* for increasing the money supply. But at *L* the deficit in the balance of payments rises over its previous level. This will require a still greater budget surplus by *LM*. This will necessitate still larger reduction in interest rate to remove recession and unemployment. In this way, the economy would move further and further away from point *E* and there would not be simultaneous internal and external balance. In this case, the assignment rule leads to explosive instability because the two policies are badly coordinated.

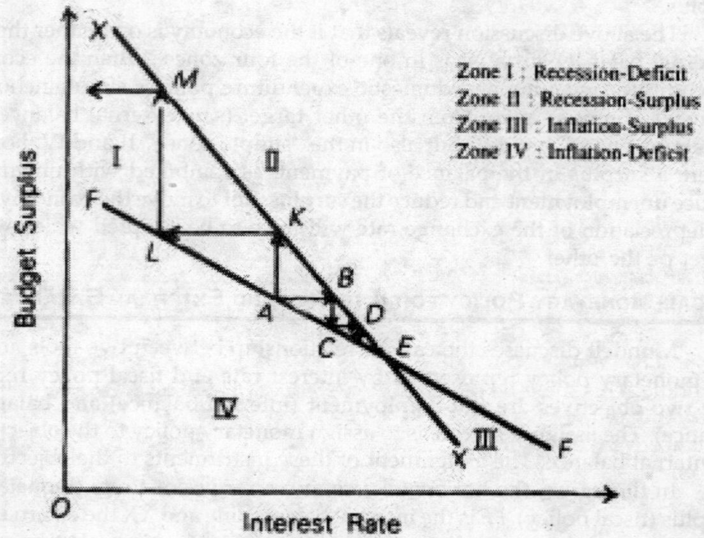

FIG. 3

Thus monetary policy should be assigned to the objective of external balance and fiscal policy to that of internal balance. However, the assignment rule can work only if monetary and fiscal policy can be adjusted smoothly and continuously without long lags before their effects are visible. This is Mundell's principle of effective use of monetary and fiscal policy for internal and external stability, according to which an instrument should be matched with the target on which it exerts the greatest relative influence. He calls it the *Principle of Effective Market Classification.*

In fact, Mundell argues for a judicious monetary and fiscal-policy mix. In zones II and IV, there is no inconsistency in jointly using both monetary and fiscal policies. In Zone II both policies should be restrictive, and in Zone IV both policies should be expansionary. In the remaining two zones monetary and fiscal policies must be mixed in order to realise both objectives simultaneously. Both objectives will be realised, according to Mundell, when monetary policy is paired with the objective of external balance and fiscal policy with the objective of internal balance.

CRITICISMS OF MUNDELL'S MODEL

There are, however, several shortcomings of this analysis. *First,* this model assumes that the authorities know the extent to which the economy is away from both internal and external balance so that appropriate monetary and fiscal policy can be applied. It also presupposes that they know the quantitative results which are expected from the application of each policy. Both these assumptions are away from reality because it is not possible to estimate the degree of disequilibrium correctly. Accordingly, the policy changes may not be appropriate to the type of disequilibrium.

Second, this analysis overlooks the situation of unemployment and inflation. This is unrealistic because this phenomenon, known as stagflation, is found in almost all developed countries.

Third, this analysis considers only differences in interest rates as the cause of capital movements and neglects other factors such as exchange rate variations. Moreover, it is not possible that a persistent deficit may be financed by means of capital movements.

Fourth, monetary and fiscal policies operate under certain practical constraints. Due to political reasons, some governments are unable to follow a restrictive fiscal policy and a monetary policy of high interest rates. Even if such policies can be started, they may not be successful because capital flows may not be interest-sensitive.

Fifth, the prescribed policy mix may be unable to correct a current account deficit. Since the policy mix affects both the capital flows and imports, it can only ensure that a negative trade balance is offset by a positive capital flow, and vice versa.

Sixth, the monetary-fiscal mix is not a true adjustment mechanism. It is just a palliative. It does not adjust the balance of payments but simply stabilises it. Capital flows only fill the gap between autonomous demand and supply of foreign exchange, leaving prices and incomes unchanged.

Seventh, this analysis does not take into account the debt-servicing requirements that a continuous capital inflow would have on the current account of the balance of payments when the domestic interest rate is raised.

Eighth, when the interest rate is raised through monetary policy, it will lead to a decrease in investment at home. This must be accompanied either by increase in government expenditure or by tax reductions or by a combination of both. Such a monetary-fiscal mix wastes the economy's savings by diverting them into debts financed government expenditure which retards capital formation. According to Johnson, this raises the problem of "inefficiency versus efficiency in the use of domestic saving potential."

Ninth, there is the possibility of conflicts between the prescribed policy mixes among governments of different .countries. As pointed out by Johnson, "Arriving at the right combination of fiscal and monetary policies in all countries simultaneously, especially if the adjustment of policies takes place by sequential trial and error, will be a complicated process and may in some circumstances lead away from rather than towards equilibrium."

EXERCISES

1. Indicate the way and the extent to which monetary and fiscal instruments could be successfully used to bring about internal and external balance.
2. What policy instruments would you suggest for maintaining both internal and external equilibrium?
3. "Fiscal policy should always be directed toward the achievement of internal balance." This is most obviously true when a policy 'conflict' arises." Discuss.
4. Explain the conflicts between internal and external balance in terms of the Swan model.
5. Discuss the monetary fiscal mix for internal and external balance.

C H A P T E R

43

Crowding Out Effect and Availability Doctrine

1. CROWDING OUT EFFECT

MEANING

The term "crowding out" refers to the reduction in private expenditures on consumption and investment caused by an increase in government expenditure which increases aggregate demand and hence interest rates. The amount by which private expenditures fall with a given increase in government expenditure is called the *crowding out effect.* When government expenditure displaces or crowds out an equal amount of private expenditure, the crowding out effect is said to be *complete* or *total.* On the contrary, the government expenditure may reduce private expenditure by less than the increase in government expenditure, then the crowding out effect is *partial* or *incomplete.* If private expenditures do not fall at all with increase in government expenditure, the crowding out effect is zero.

TYPES OF CROWDING OUT

Crowding out is of three types: physical, fiscal and financial. We discuss them as under :

1. **Physical Crowding Out.** Physical crowding out occurs when the government demand for factors and inputs increases in the event of their inelastic supply. This raises their prices and makes private investment schemes unviable and unprofitable thereby reducing private expenditure. Thus physical crowding out results from a shortage of real productive resources. For example, the government increases direct public sector expenditure by starting new industries. It pays higher wages to attract technical experts from private sector industries and increases the demand for other resources, thereby reducing private investment. If the economy is at full employment level, any rise in government expenditure will inevitably crowd out an equal amount of private expenditure. Such a situation is depicted in Fig. 1 in terms of the *IS-LM* model. The original full employment equilibrium is at Y_F. The increase in public sector investment shifts the *IS* curve to the right to IS_1. This increases the demand for labour and other resources which are in inelastic supply. As a result, their prices rise which require larger transactions

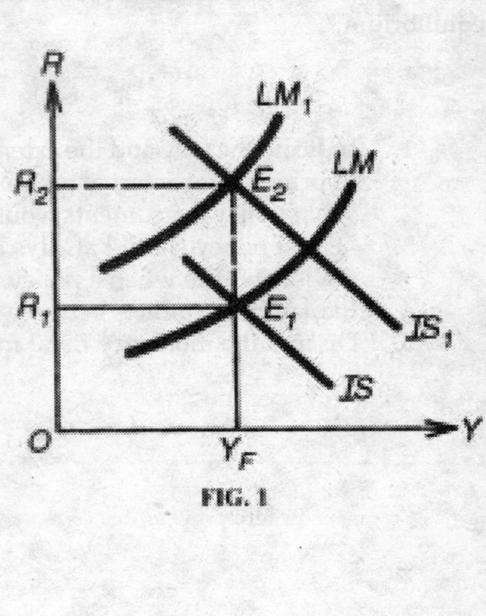

FIG. 1

balances. The rise in prices will continue till the *LM* curve shifts to the left as LM_1 and intersects the *IS* curve at E_2. Thus the interest rate is raised to R_2 which crowds out private investment.

Physical crowding out is a temporary and short run phenomenon. In the long run, there is the possibility of increasing real resources. The government can also stimulate private investment by selective industrial subsidies and adopting appropriate fiscal and monetary measures.

2. **Fiscal Crowding Out.** Fiscal crowding out occurs when a rise in government expenditure from a budget deficit raises aggregate demand. Given a constant money supply, the interest rate rises. The stimulative effect of government deficit (or expenditure) will crowd out in greater or lesser degree a certain amount of private investment. The fiscal crowding out is usually explained in terms of the Keynesian analysis. The mechanism is that the rise in government expenditure raises the aggregate demand. This sets in motion the multiplier process which raises nominal income. The rise in nominal income requires more money for transaction purposes. Further as investment increases, the demand for labour also rises which increases wages and prices. The degree to which prices rise depends on the extent of the unemployment prevailing in the economy. The nearer is the economy to the level of full employment level, the higher will be the price level. When the economy is in full employment, the price level rises in proportion to the increase in government expenditure. The rise in the price level leads to the rise in nominal income which, in turn, diverts money balances for transactions purposes and decreases the quantity of money available for speculative purposes. As the money supply is fixed, the residual money supply contracts and interest rates rise. The rise in interest rates causes a fiscal crowding out of private investment with the increase in government expenditure. In a full employment situation, the fiscal crowding out is complete because government expenditure equals private expenditure which it displaces. If there is liquidity trap, there is no crowding out.

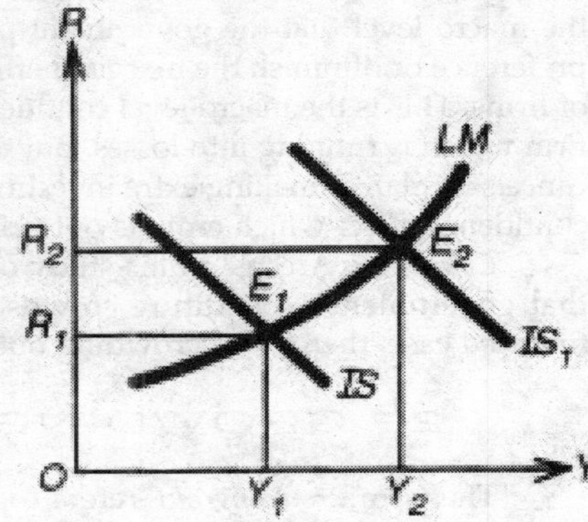

FIG. 2

The fiscal crowding out is explained diagrammatically in Figure 2 where the rise in government expenditure is shown by the shifting of the *IS* curve to the right to IS_1 when this curve intersects the rising *LM* curve at E_2. Since the money supply is constant, the equilibrium level of the economy rises from E_1 to E_2.The multiplier process raises the income level from OY_1 to OY_2 and the interest rate from R_1 to R_2. Higher interest rate crowds out a certain amount of private investment.*

3. **Financial Crowding Out.** Financial crowding out occurs when the government increases its expenditure and finances it by selling new bonds in the money market. When the government sells bonds, the prices of securities fall and interest rates rise. As a result, the private sector postpones or curtails some schemes because obtaining funds has become dearer. Thus the government expenditure crowds out private investment spending. Total financial crowding out occurs when the bond-financed government expenditure equals the same amount of displaced private investment.

Financial crowding out may occur in the following ways :

(1) *Purchase of Gilt-edged Securities by Banks.* Private investment may be crowded out when banks buy gilt-edged securities and reduce the sanction of new loans to the private sector. Banks are attracted by such securities because the government offers higher returns in order to sell them.

(2) *Competition with Private Sector Bonds.* When government bonds are sold in the market to finance government expenditure, they compete with bonds being sold to finance private investment. This leads to a rise in interest rates. Higher interest rates are assumed to have no effect in reducing the planned increase in government spending. It is only the financing of private investment which is crowded out.

* If the money supply is not influenced by market (money) interest rates, the LM curve is vertical. If it depends on market interest rates, the *LM* curve has a positive slope.

(3) *Wealth Effect.* When the government sells bonds, their buyers feel wealthier than before because they expect to have more resources available for consumption in future. But the incomes of these purchasers of bonds is reduced which lead to the curtailment of their present consumption expenditures which adversely affect private investment.

(4) *Cut in Taxes.* There is another way for interest rates to rise and crowd out private investment. The government may cut taxes in order to create a budget deficit or to increase the size of the existing budget. The tax cut raises the consumption schedule which raises total output and income. People will like to hold more money in order to maintain the normal ratio of money to income. They will try to increase their money stocks by selling securities which will raise interest rates. Higher interest rates will crowd out private investment.

(5) *Confidence Effects.* Private expenditure may also be crowded out by what are now called "confidence effects". The confidence effects may be macro or micro. It was Keynes who suggested in his *General Theory* at the macro level that the government programme may through its effect on "confidence", increase liquidity preference or diminish the marginal efficiency of capital, which again may retard other investment on the part of firms. This is the macro level confidence effect. Suppose a firm expects to benefit from the closure of a rival firm which is running into losses. But the government gives subsidy to the loss-making firm. So the first firm cancels its plan of making extra investment to cater to expected expansion of the market. This is the micro level confidence effect which crowds out private investment.

Conclusion. Arestis[1] in his study of the crowding out effect on the UK economy came to the conclusion that government expenditure crowds out private expenditure only if it is tax-financed. But in the bond-financed case, there is no crowding out of private investment.

2. CROWDING OUT AND FISCAL POLICY

The term *crowding out* refers to the reduction in private expenditure (or investment) caused by an increase in government expenditure through deficit budget via a tax cut or increased money supply or bond issue. An increase in government expenditure raises aggregate demand, national income and interest rates thereby reducing private investment. This is called the *crowding effect* of fiscal policy.

The Keynesian and monetarists differ on the effects of budget deficit on the crowding out effect. The main difference between the two arises from the fact that the Keynesians emphasise on "first-round" (short-run) effects which show "once-for-all-shift" of the IS curve, whereas the monetarists emphasise the "ultimate (long-run) effects".

The Keynesian crowding out theory states that when the government resorts to deficit financing by issuing new bonds, its spending increases. National income rises. If the money supply is held constant people will need more money for business which will raise the rate of interest. A higher rate of interest will crowd out (reduce) private investment spending. These are the first-round effects which are explained in Fig. 3 where E_1 is the initial equilibrium position. The rise in government expenditure financed by issuing bonds shifts the IS_1 curve rightward to IS_2 on a "once-for-all" basis and it cuts the LM curve at point E_2. Since the money supply is constant, E_2 is the new equilibrium level of the economy. The multiplier process raises the income level from Y_1 to Y_2 and the interest rate from R_1 to R_2. Higher interest rate crowds out a certain amount of private investment.

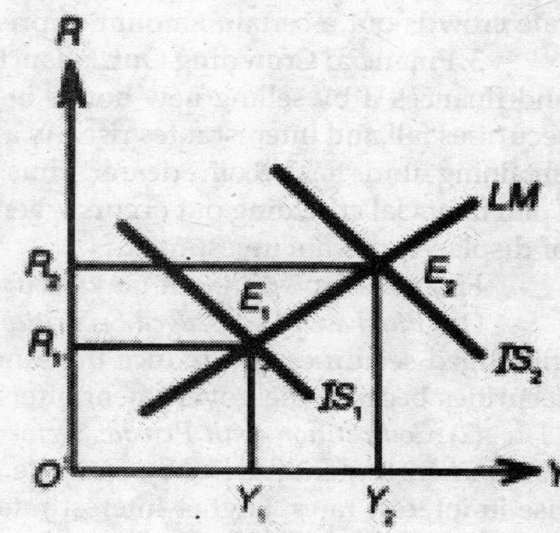

FIG. 3

The Keynesians hold that a deficit financed by printing notes (money creation) is more expansionary than bond-financed. But they do not believe that the reduction in private expenditure caused

1. A.P. Arestis, "The Crowding Out of Private Investment Expenditure by Fiscal Actions: An Empirical Investigation," *Public Finance,* Vol. 34, 1979.

by a higher interest will completely offset the increased government expenditure. In other words, the crowding out of private investment will not be full. The reason for this is that a high interest rate has dual effects. *First*, it reduces private spending. *Second*, a high interest rate leads people to economise on cash balances. They, therefore, divert idle cash holdings for transactions purposes. That is why crowding out of private investment is only partial. On the other hand, Friedman emphasises the *ultimate effects* of a budget deficit (whether bond-financed or money financed) by taking account of the *wealth effect*. When the government increases its expenditure by selling bonds in the market, their buyers feel themselves wealthier than before. The reason is that they expect to have more resources available for consumption and other purposes in future. As a result, they tend to increase the demand for money which shifts the *LM* curve *leftward*. This analysis assumes that bonds issued by the government are considered as wealth. Further, both the demand for money and expenditure on consumption are positively related to wealth.

Suppose the government increases its expenditure with bond-financed budget deficit. As a result, the public expenditure on buying bonds also increases. The rise in public expenditure shifts the IS_1 curve rightward to IS_2 in Fig. 4 on a "once-for-all basis". This "first-round" effect raises the level of national income from Y_1 to Y_2, given the *LM* schedule. The increase in national income, in turn, raises the demand for money and the purchase of government bonds by the public further raises the demand for money due to the wealth effect. As the LM_1 curve shifts leftward to LM_2 and the IS_2 curve shifts rightward to IS_3 so that the ultimate equilibrium is established at the initial level of income Y_1. According to Friedman, the rise in interest rate to R_3 reduces private investment so that bond-financed government expenditure crowds out private investment. But the total expenditure remains unchanged and fiscal policy has no expansionary effect on national income.

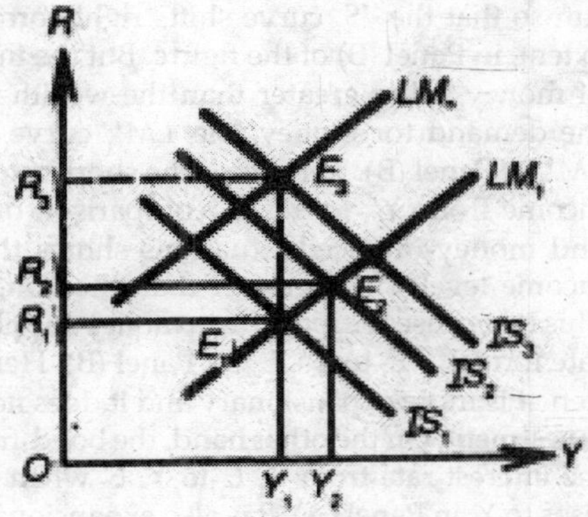

FIG. 4

If the budget deficit is *money-financed*, it will have an expansionary effect. This is because increase in money supply is greater than the wealth effect on the demand for money. In this case, the LM_1 curve shifts rightward to LM_2, as shown in Fig. 5. The increase in government expenditure shifts the IS_1 curve rightward to IS_2. The first-round effect raises the level of income from Y_1 to Y_2. According to Friedman, in a money-financed deficit, the money stock continues to grow and the *LM* curve continues to shift to the right causing falling interest rates. In this case, the *LM* schedule exerts a dominant influence on subsequent changes in income than the *IS* schedule. The ultimate (long-run) equilibrium is shown with the shifting of the IS_2 curve rightward to IS_4 and also of the LM_2 curve rightward to LM_4 so that Y_4 equilibrium income level is established. The rate of interest has fallen from Y_2E_2 to Y_4E_4. Thus money-financed deficit is expansionary and it does not crowd out private investment.

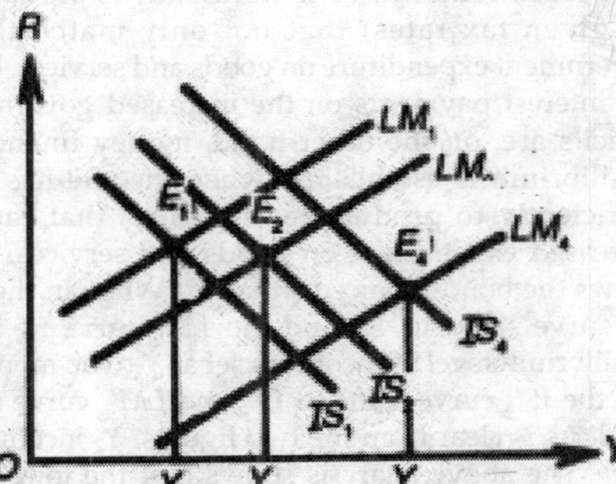

FIG. 5

Blinder and Solow have criticised Friedman's crowding out model of debt-financed deficit for ignoring interest payments on outstanding debt. They point out that the government has not only to finance the budget deficit but also interest payments on outstanding debt. They have shown that if private expenditure and demand for money are subject to wealth effects, then the *IS* and *LM* curves will be shifting from period to period and the short-run equilibrium will differ from the long-run equilibrium depending upon whether the budget is bond-financed or money-financed.

The short-run and long-run equilibrium situations in the case of *bond-financed* budget deficit are shown in Figure 6 (A). The rise in government expenditure as a result of bond-financed deficit shifts the IS_1 curve *rightward* to IS_2. This shift is due to both the increase in government expenditure and rise in private expenditure following the wealth effect of bonds. The LM_1 curve shifts leftward to LM_2 as a result of wealth effect which increases the demand for money. This raises the short-run equilibrium level of income from Y_1 to Y_2.

If the budget deficit is *money financed* creation, the increase in government expenditure is once-for-all increase in the short-run so that the IS_1 curve shifts rightward to IS_2 by the same extent, in Panel (B) of the figure. But the increase in the supply of money being greater than the wealth-induced increase in the demand for money, the LM'_1 curve shifts rightward to LM'_2 in Panel (B). This raises the short-run equilibrium level of income from Y'_1 to Y'_2. A comparison of the bond-financed and money-financed situations shows that money-financed income level Y'_2 is greater than the bond-financed level Y_2. This is because the increase in money supply lowers the interest rate form $Y'_1 E_1$ to $Y'_2 E_2$, in Panel (B). Hence money-financed deficit is more expansionary and it does not crowd out private investment. On the other hand, the bond-financed deficit raises the interest rate from $Y_1 E_1$ to $Y_2 E_2$ when the national income rises to Y_2 in Panel (A). It is also expansionary but it crowds out a part of private investment.

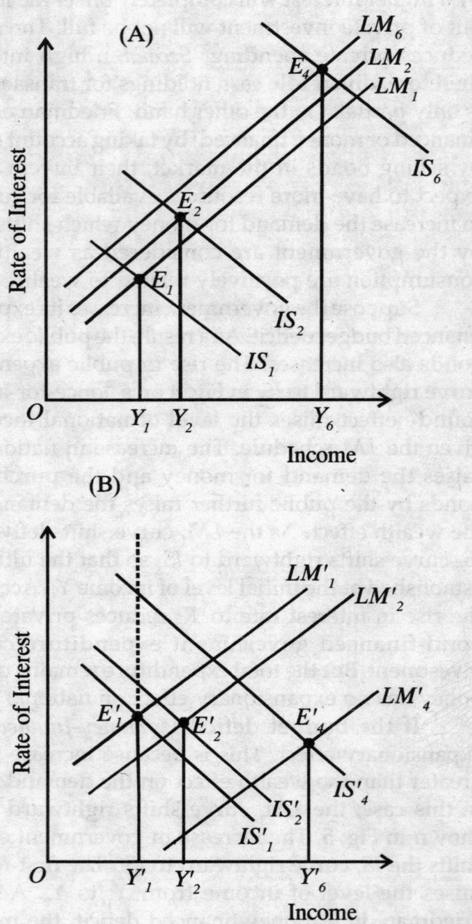

Fig. 6

In the long-run, bond-financing is more expansionary than money-financing. This is because when "deficits are bond-financed, income must rise sufficiently to produce tax receipts (at given tax rates) that not only match the increased government expenditure on goods and services, but also cover the interest payments on the increased government debt. If deficits are, on the other hand, money financed, long-run equilibrium is established when income has merely risen sufficiently to produce tax revenues that each match the increased expenditure on goods and services." Figure 6 (A) shows the bond-financed situation. When in the long-run the IS_2 curve shifts to IS_6 and the LM_2 curve to LM_6, the new equilibrium level of income is set at Y_6. The money-financed situation is shown in Panel (B) where in the long-run the IS'_2 curve shifts to IS'_4 and LM'_2 curve to LM'_4 and the new equilibrium is established at Y'_4 income level. As is clear from the two figures, Y_6 income level is greater than Y'_4 level.

The above analysis shows that the long-run effect of increased bond-financed government deficit is more expansionary but it crowds out private investment because the rate of interest rises sufficiently high. But the money-financed deficit though less expansionary than the former, it does not crowd out private investment through wealth effects.

3. CREDIT AVAILABILITY DOCTRINE OR ROOSA EFFECT

1. Introduction

The credit availability doctrine is associated with R.V. Roosa, a former official of both the Federal Reserve System and the US Treasury who in 1951 emphasised on the effect of a tight monetary policy on lenders rather than on borrowers in the money market. This is also called the Roosa Effect.[2]

The availability thesis was put forward by Roosa primarily against two policies: (i) that investment demand is interest-inelastic; and (ii) that tight monetary policy works only by raising the interest rate.

2. The Availability Thesis

The availability doctrine explains how tight monetary policy achieves its objectives even though investors are unresponsive to increases in interest rates. This is possible when tight monetary policy induces *lenders (i.e.* banks) to cut back the availability of credit to borrowers. Thus the Roosa effect operates not on the demand for credit but on its supply so that monetary policy affects lenders rather than borrowers. The level of interest rates is assumed to govern the credit availability.

There are two main components of the credit availability doctrine: non-price credit rationing, and lock-in effect.

(1) *Credit Rationing.* It is argued that banks prefer to keep interest rates relatively at low levels during tight monetary policy, and ration the amount of lending to certain customers via non-price devices. When the central bank follows a tight monetary policy, the resources of commercial banks are cut which reduce their lending capacity. But banks in effect ration credit so that the level of interest rates does not rise to a market-clearing level. They generally charge a standard interest rate from private borrowers. They deny credit to prospective borrowers who are willing to pay the going market interest rate. The decision to lend by banks depends not only on the interest rate but also on the status, creditworthiness and wealth of the borrowers or favouritism to old, valued customers.

What leads banks to embark upon credit rationing? When the central bank sells government securities in the open market, it increases their supply on the open market which lowers their price. These changes affect the banks in two ways: *First,* they introduce uncertainties and expectations into the money market as a result of increases in bond yields.* *Second,* the increase in yields of government securities make banks *unwilling* to sell government securities in order to obtain funds for advancing loans. That is why they resort to credit rationing.

(2) *Lock-in Effect.* There is another reason for the unwillingness of banks to sell government securities which is called the "lock-in effect". When the central bank sells government securities to implement its tight monetary policy, it increases their supply on the market. This lowers their price in the bank portfolios. It means that banks which want to obtain funds for advancing loans by selling government securities do so at a capital loss. Since banks would be reluctant to realise capital losses, they would be "locked-in" to some of their holdings of government securities by their portfolio balancing behaviour. In other words, capital losses on the sale of government securities to the public to get more funds for advancing loans, make banks unwilling to sell government securities. Thus under the locking-in effect banks keep government securities in their asset portfolios which leads them to credit rationing and prevents them from advancing business loans.

---

2. Robert V. Roosa, "Interest Rates and the Central Bank", *Money, Trade and Economic Growth: Essays in Honour of John H. Williams,* 1951

* Bond yields are interest earned on them. When the price of bonds is lowered, their yields increase.

The credit availability thesis is explained in Fig. 7. Suppose the economy is in equilibrium at point *E* where the supply curve of loanable funds *S* intersects the demand curve for loanable funds *D*. At this point, *OL* loans are supplied and demanded at the *OR* interest rate. When the money supply is increased by the Central bank through the open market purchase of securities, the supply curve shifts leftwards to S_1.

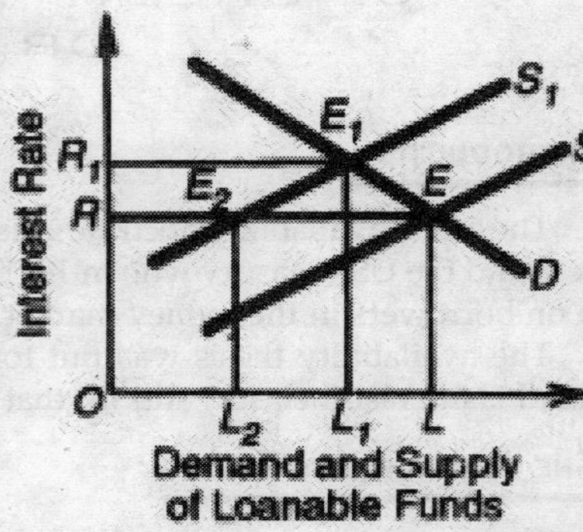

FIG. 7

But the banks are reluctant to raise the interest rate to their depositors and resort to non-price credit rationing. If they charge the same interest rate *OR*, they will ration L_2L credit. If they charge the higher interest rate OR_1 the amount of credit made available would still decline to OL_1 from *OL*.

So far as the *lock-in effect* is concerned, it is equal to the distance E_2E at the interest rate *OR*. It shows unfilled demand for loanable funds equal to L_2L when banks keep government securities in their portfolios in order to avoid capital losses.

3. Its Criticisms

The credit availability doctrine has been criticised both on theoretical and empirical grounds :

1. It is based on the existence of different imperfections in the money market. So it is not possible to generalise the Behaviour of banks with regard to the holding of government securities and advancing of loans.

2. It is also assumed that when the central bank follows a tight monetary policy through open market sale of securities, it introduces uncertainties in the money market and in bank behaviour. But there is no clear evidence regarding market structure and bank behaviour.

3. This doctrine expects a bank to adjust its lending rate to changes in the market interest rate, but this adjustment involves time lag about which it is silent. In none of the versions of the credit availability, the time lag has not been precisely measured.

4. The credit availability thesis is incomplete because it includes only commercial banks and leaves out other financial intermediaries from the analysis.

5. So far as the "locking-in effect" is concerned, economists doubt its effectiveness because data on the behaviour of banks in the US during tight money periods in the 1960s and 1970s do not prove its operation.

Conclusion. Despite these criticisms, the non-price credit rationing argument has been formalised and shown to be empirically relevant. This doctrine has thus popularised the view that tight monetary policy wields its effect through the availability of credit. To conclude with Prof. Johnson, "The availability doctrine has left its mark on the field, in as much as the majority of monetary economists would probably explain how monetary policy influences the economy by reference to its effects on the availability of and cost of credit, with the stress on availability."

EXERCISES

1. What is meant by "Crowding Out"? Explain the process of crowding out.
2. Discuss the various types of crowding out effect.
3. Define crowding out. How financial crowding out takes place?
4. Critically discuss the availability doctrine.
5. Examine the Rooza Effect. Why do banks resort to credit rationing and locking-in?
6. Write notes on: Financial Crowding Out; Credit Availability Effects.
7. Explain the views of monetarists and Keynesians on the crowding out effect.

CHAPTER 44

The Rational Expectations Hypothesis

INTRODUCTION

In the 1930s when Keynes wrote his *General Theory,* unemployment was the major problem in the world. During the Second World War, inflation emerged as the main economic problem. In the postwar years till the late 1960s, unemployment again became a major economic issue. From the late 1960s to 1970s, a new phenomenon appeared in the form of both high unemployment and inflation, known as *stagflation*. This phenomenon of stagflation posed a serious challenge to economists and policy makers because the Keynesian theory was silent about it. Out of this crisis emerged a new macroeconomic theory which is called the Rational Expectations Hypothesis (Ratex).

ADAPTIVE EXPECTATIONS

Before we discuss the Ratex hypothesis, it is essential to understand the meaning of adaptive expectations used in macroeconomics before the Ratex theory was developed.

Expectations are forecasts or predictions by an economic agent regarding the uncertain economic variables which are relevant to his decision. They are based on post trends as well as current information and experience. The main body of economic theory is based on the assumption of rational behaviour of economic agents (i.e., consumers, producers, etc.) in forming their expectations. But till recently economists have not been able to incorporate the role of expectations in measuring human behaviour. Keynes discussed the *importance* of expectations but he was silent as to how they are formed.

In recent years, economists have mostly used the adaptive expectations hypothesis in model building. The pioneering work was done by Cagan[1] in 1956 and Nerlove[2] in 1957. According to the adaptive expectations hypothesis, economic agents expect the future to be essentially a continuation of the past. They expect the future values of economic variables like prices, incomes, etc. to be an *average* of past values and to change very slowly. The economic agents make the expected values of these variables equal to a *weighted* average of their present and past values. They revise their expectations in accordance with the last forecasting error. Errors resulting from past behaviour represent an important source of information for forming expectations. But such expectations are based on the assumption that the economic agents expect them to change very little. This often leads to absurd forecasts when there is change in economic policy.

---

1. P. Cagan, "The Monetary Dynamics of Hyperinflation," in M. Friedman (ed.), *Studies in the Quantity Theory of Money*, 1956.
2. M. Nerlove, "Adaptive Expectations and Cobweb Phenomena," *Q.J.E.*, May 1958.

For instance, according to the adaptive expectations hypothesis, economic agents form expectations of future inflation rates from a weighted average of experienced average past inflation rates and they periodically revise those expectations if actual inflation turns out to be different than expected. This implies irrational behaviour on the part of economic agents. Friedman's analysis of the long-run Phillips curve is based on the adaptive expectations hypothesis. The assumption implicit in Friedman's *acceleration* hypothesis that price expectations are based mainly on the basis of the experience of past inflation is unrealistic. When economic agents base their price expectations on this assumption, they are irrational. If they think like this in a period of rising prices, they will find that they were wrong. This is because expectations are formed from direct forecasts of the future as from mere projections of the past. People base their expectations as much on current information about a variety of factors as on past price changes. Thus rational people will use all available information to forecast future inflation more accurately.

RATIONAL EXPECTATIONS

The idea of rational expectations was first put forth by Johy Muth[3] in 1961 who borrowed the concept from engineering literature. His model dealt mainly with modelling price movements in markets. By assuming that economic agents optimise and use information efficiently when forming expectations, he was able to construct a theory of expectations in which consumers' and producers' responses to *expected* price changes depended on their responses to *actual* price changes. Muth pointed out that certain *expectations are rational in the sense that expectations and events differ only by a random forecast error.*

Muth's notion of rational expectations related to microeconomics. It did not convince many economists and lay dormant for ten years. It was in early 1970s that Robert Lucas, Thomas Sargent and Neil Wallace applied the idea to problems of macroeconomic policy.

BASIC PROPOSITIONS OF THE RATIONAL EXPECTATIONS HYPOTHESIS

The Ratex hypothesis holds that economic agents form expectations of the future values of economic variables like prices, incomes, etc. by using all the economic information available to them. This information includes the relationships governing economic variables, particularly monetary and fiscal policies of the government. Thus the rational expectationists assume that economic agents have full and accurate information about future economic events. According to Muth, information should be considered like any other available resource which is scarce. Further, rational economic agents should use their knowledge of the structure of the economic system in forming their expectations. Thus the Ratex hypothesis "presumes that individual economic agents use all available and relevant information in forming expectations and that they process this information in an intelligent fashion. It is important to recognise that this does not imply that consumers or firms have "perfect foresight" or that their expectations are always "correct". What it does suggest is that agents reflect upon past errors and, if necessary, revise their expectational behaviour so as to eliminate regularities in these errors. Indeed the hypothesis suggests that agents *succeed* in eliminating regularities involving expectational errors, so that the errors will on the average be unrelated to available information."

The Ratex hypothesis has been applied to economic (monetary, fiscal and income) policies. The rational expectationists have shown the short-run ineffectiveness of stabilisation policies. According to them, no one knows much about what happens to the economy when economic (monetary or fiscal) policy is changed. Specifically, it means that macroeconomic policies designed to control recession by cutting taxes, increasing government spending, increasing the money supply or the budget deficit may be curbed. They argue that the public has learnt from the past experience that the government will follow such a policy. Therefore, the government cannot fool the people by adopting its effects and mere signs of such a policy in the economy create expectations of countercyclical action on the part of the public. Thus, according to the Ratex hypothesis, people form expectations about government monetary and fiscal policies and then refer to them in making

3. John F. Muth, "Rational Expectations and the Theory of Price Movements" *Econometrica,* July 1961.

economic decisions. As a result, by the time signs of government policies appear, the public has already acted upon them, thereby offsetting their effects. In other words, the Ratex hypothesis holds that the only policy moves that cause changes in people's economic behaviour are those that are not expected, the surprise moves by the government. Once the public acquires knowledge about a policy and expects it, it cannot change people's economic behaviour. We discuss some of the policy changes in the light of the Ratex hypothesis below.

RATIONAL EXPECTATIONS AND THE PHILLIPS CURVE

In the Friedman-Phelps acceleration hypothesis of the Phillips curve, there is a short-run trade-off between unemployment and inflation but no long-run trade-off exists. The reason is that inflationary expectations are based on past behaviour of inflation which cannot be predicted accurately. Therefore, there is always an observed error so that the expected rate of inflation always lags behind the actual rate. But the expected rate of inflation is revised in accordance with the first period's experience of inflation by adding on some proportion of the observed error in the previous period so that the expected rate of inflation adjusts toward the actual rate.

Economists belonging to the rational expectations school have denied the possibility of any trade-off between inflation and unemployment even during the long run. According to them, the assumption implicit in Friedman's version that price expectations are formed mainly on the basis of the experience of past inflation is unrealistic. When people base their price expectations on this assumption, they are irrational. If they think like this during a period of rising prices, they will find that they were wrong. But rational people will not commit this mistake. Rather, they will use all available information to forecast future inflation more accurately.

The rational expectations idea is explained diagrammatically in Figure 1 in relation to the Phillips curve. Suppose the unemployment rate is 3 per cent in the economy and the inflation rate is 2 per cent. We start at point A on the SPC_1 curve. In order to reduce unemployment, the government increases the rate of money supply so as to stimulate the economy. Prices start rising. According to the Ratex hypothesis, firms have better information about prices in their own industry than about the general level of prices. They mistakenly think that the increase in prices is due to the increase in the demand for their products. As a result, they employ more workers in order to increase output. In this way, they reduce unemployment. The workers also mistake the rise in prices as related to their own industry. But wages rise as the demand for labour increases and workers think that the increase in money wages is an increase in real wages. Thus the economy moves upward on the short-run Phillips curve SPC_1 from point *A* to *B*. But soon workers and firms find that the increase in prices and wages is prevalent in most industries. Firms find that their costs have increased. Workers realise that their real wages have fallen due to the rise in the inflation rate to 4 per cent and they press for increase in wages. Thus the economy finds itself at the higher inflation rate due to government's monetary policy. As a result, it moves from point *B* to point C on the SPC_2 curve where the unemployment rate is 3 per cent which is the same before the government adopted an expansionary monetary policy

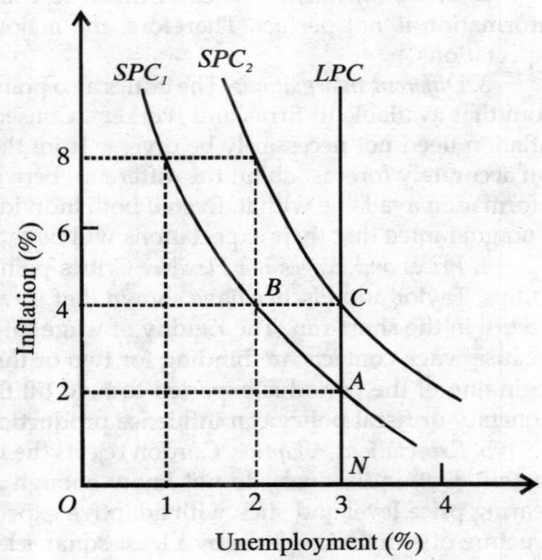

Fig. 1

When the government again tries to reduce unemployment by again increasing the money supply, it cannot fool workers and firms who will now watch the movements of prices and costs in the economy. If firms expect higher costs with higher prices for their products, they are not likely to increase their production, as happened in the case of the SPC_1 curve. So far as workers are concerned, labour unions will demand higher wages to keep pace with prices moving up in the economy. When the government continues an expansionary monetary (or fiscal) policy, firms and workers get accustomed to it. They build their experience into their expectations. So when the government again adopts such a policy, firms raise prices of their products to nullify the expected inflation so that there is no effect on production and employment. Similarly, workers demand higher wages in expectation of inflation and firms do not offer more jobs. In other words, firms and workers build expectations into their price policies and wage agreements so that there is no possibility for the actual rate of unemployment to differ from the natural rate, *N*, even during the short run.

Its Policy Implications

The Ratex hypothesis assumes that people have all the relevant information of the economic variables. Any discrepancy between the actual rate of inflation and the expected rate is only in the nature of a random crror. When people act rationally, they know that past increases in prices and the rate of change in prices have invariably been accompanied by equal proportional changes in the quantity of money. When people act on this knowledge, it leads to the conclusion that there is no trade-off between inflation and unemployment even in the short-run. It implies that monetary (or fiscal) policy is unable to change the difference between the actual and natural rate of unemployment. This means that the economy can only be to the left or right of point N of the long-run Phillips curve *LPC* (in Figure 1) in a random manner. Thus the implication is that stabilisation policy is ineffective and should be abandoned.

Its Criticisms

The Ratex hypothesis has been criticised by economists on the following grounds.

1. *Unrealistic Assumption.*The assumption of rational expectations is unrealistic. The critics argue that large firms may be able to forecast accurately, but a small firm or the average worker will not be able to do so.

2. *Costly Information.* It costs much to collect, distill and disseminate information. So the market for information is not perfect. Therefore, the majority of economic agents cannot act on the basis of rational expectations.

3. *Different Informations.* The critics also point out that the information available to the government differs from that available to firms and workers. Consequently, expectations of the latter about the expected rate of inflation need not necessarily be diverse from the actual rate only by the random error. But the government can accurately forecast about the difference between the expected inflation rate and actual rate on the basis of information available with it. Even if both individuals and government have equal access to information, there is no guarantee that their expectations will be rational.

4. *Prices and Wages not Flexible.* Critics point out that prices and wages are not flexible. Economists like Philips, Taylor and Fischer have shown that if wages and prices are rigid, monetary or fiscal policy becomes *effective* in the short-run. The rigidity of wage rates implies that they adjust to market forces relatively slowly because wage contacts are binding for two or three years at a time. Similarly, the expected price level at the beginning of the period is expected to hold till the end of the period. Thus even if expectations are rational, monetary or fiscal policy can influence production and unemployment in the short-run.

5. *Expectations Adaptive.* Gordon rejects the logic of the Ratex hypothesis entirely. He assigns two reasons for this: *first*, individuals do not know enough about the structure of the economy to estimate the market clearing price level and stick with adaptive expectations; and *second*, if individuals gradually learn about the structure of economic system by a least-squares learning method, rational expectations closely approximate to adaptive expectations.

6. *Government not Impotent.* It is generally said that according to the Ratex hypothesis, the government is impotent in the economic sphere. But the Ratex economists do not claim this. Rather, they believe that the government has a tremendous influence on economic policies.

STABILISATION POLICY AND RATEX HYPOTHESIS

According to the Ratex hypothesis, monetary and fiscal (stabilisation) policies are ineffective even in the short-run because it is not possible to anticipate accurately how expectations are formed during the short-run. This is called "policy impotence." The Ratex hypothesis is based on the assumption that consumers and firms have accurate information about future economic events. Their expectations are rational because they take into account all available information, especially about expected government actions. If the government is following any consistent monetary or fiscal policy, people know about it and adjust their plans accordingly. So when the government adopts the expected policy measure, it will not be effective because it has been anticipated by the people who have already adjusted their plans. This means that government policy is *ineffective*. Another important assumption is that all markets are fully competitive and prices and wages are completely flexible.

Let us first take *fiscal policy*. The Keynesians advocate an "activist" fiscal policy to reduce unemployment. But, according to the Ratex hypothesis, a tax cut and/or increase in government spending will reduce unemployment only if its short-run effects on the economy are *unexpected* (or unanticipated) by people. In other words, an expansionary fiscal policy may have short-term effects on reducing unemployment provided people do not anticipate that prices will rise. But when the government persists will such a policy, people expect the rate of inflation to rise. So the workers will press for higher wages in anticipation of more inflation in the future and firms will raise the prices of their products in anticipation of the rise in future costs. As a result, fiscal policy will become ineffective in the short-run. It may cause more unemployment and inflation in the long-run when the government tries to control inflation.

Similarly, if the government adopts an expansionary *monetary policy* by increasing the money supply to reduce unemployment, it is also ineffective in the short-run. Such a policy may reduce unemployment, in the short-run provided its effects on the economy are unanticipated. But when the government persists with such an expansionary monetary policy, people expect the inflation rate to rise. Firms raise the prices of their products to overcome the anticipated inflation so that there is no effect on production. Similarly, workers press for higher wages in anticipation of inflation and firms do not employ more workers. So there is no effect on employment.

Thus the Ratex hypothesis suggests that expansionary fiscal and monetary policies will have a temporary effect on unemployment and if continued may cause more inflation and unemployment. For such policies to be successful, they must be unanticipated by the people. Once people anticipate these policies and make adjustments towards them, the economy reverts back to the natural rate of unemployment. Thus for expansionary fiscal and monetary policies to have an impact on unemployment in the short-run, the government must be able to fool the people. But it is unlikely to happen all the time. If the government continues to persist with such policies, they become ineffective because people cannot be fooled for long and they anticipate their effects on production and unemployment. Thus fiscal-monetary policies become ineffective in the short-run. According to the advocates of the Ratex hypothesis, inflation can be controlled without causing widespread unemployment, if the government announces fiscal and monetary measures and convinces the people about it and do not take them be surprise.

EXERCISES

1. State the basic propositions of the rational expectations hypothesis.
2. What is the rational expectationists' position on inflation-unemployment trade-off ? What is the implication of this position for stabilisation policy ?
3. Write a note on adaptive expectations.

CHAPTER 45

Business Cycles

1. MEANING

Business cycle or trade cycle is a part of the capitalist system. It refers to the phenomenon of cyclical booms and depressions. In a business cycle, there are wave-like fluctuations in aggregate employment, income, output and price level. The term business cycle has been defined in various ways by different economists. Prof. Haberler's definition is very simple: "The business cycle in the general sense may be defined as an alternation of periods of prosperity and depression of good and bad trade." Keynes' definition in his *Treatise of Money* is more explicit : "A trade cycle is composed of periods of good trade characterised by rising prices and low unemployment percentage, altering with periods of bad trade characterised by falling prices and high unemployment percentages." Gordon's definition is precise: "Business cycles consist of recurring alternation of expansion and contraction in aggregate economic activity; the alternating movements in each direction being self-reinforcing and prevading virtually, all parts of the economy." The most acceptable definition is by Estey: "Cyclical fluctuations are characterised by alternating waves of expansion and contraction. They do not have a fixed rhythm, but they are cycles in that the phases of contraction and expansion recur frequently and in fairly similar patterns."[1]

2. CHARACTERISTICS OF BUSINESS CYCLES

Business cycles possess the following characteristics :

1. Cyclical fluctuations are wave-like movements.

2. Fluctuations are recurrent in nature.

3. They are non-periodic or irregular. In other words, the peaks and troughs do not occur at regular intervals.

4. They occur in such aggregate variables as output, income, employment and prices.

5. These variables move at about the same time in the same direction but at different rates.

6. The durable goods industries experience relatively wide fluctuations in output and employment but relatively small fluctuations in prices. On the other hand, nondurable goods industries experience relatively wide fluctuations in prices but relatively small fluctuations in output and employment.

7. Business cycles are not seasonal fluctuations such as upswings in retail trade during Diwali or Christmas.

8. They are not secular trends such as long-run growth or decline in economic activity.

9. Upswings and downswings are cumulative in their effects.

Thus business cycles are recurrent fluctuations in aggregate employment, income, output and price level.

---

1. J.A. Estey, *Business Cycles,* 1956.

3. PHASES OF A BUSINESS CYCLE

A typical cycle is generally divided into four phases : (1) expansion or prosperity or the upswing; (2) recession or upper-turning point; (3) contraction or depression or downswing; and (4) revival or recovery or lower-turning point. These phases are recurrent and uniform in the case of different cycles. But no phase has definite periodicity or time interval. As pointed out by Pigou, cycles may not be twins but they are of the same family. Like families they have *common* characteristics that are capable of description. Starting at the trough or low point, a cycle passes through a recovery and prosperity phase, rises to a peak, declines through a recession and depression phase and reaches a trough. This is shown in Figure 1 where *E* is the equilibrium position. We describe below these characteristics of a business cycle.

RECOVERY

We start from a situation when depression has lasted for some time and the revival phase or the lower-turning point starts. The "originating forces" or "starters" may be exogenous or endogenous forces. Suppose the semi-durable goods wear out which necessitate their replacement in the economy. It leads to increased demand. To meet this increased demand, investment and employment increase. Industry begins to revive. Revival also starts in related capital goods industries. Once begun, the process of revival becomes cumulative. As a result, the levels of employment, income and output rise steadily in the economy. In the early stages of the revival phase, there is considerable *excess* or *idle* capacity in the economy so that output increases without a proportionate increase in total costs. But as time goes on, output becomes less elastic; bottlenecks appear with rising costs, deliveries are more difficult and plants may have to be expanded. Under these conditions, prices rise. Profits increase. Business expectations improve. Optimism prevails. Investment is encouraged which tends to raise the demand for bank loans. It leads to credit expansion. Thus the cumulative process of increase in investment, employment, output, income and prices feeds upon itself and becomes self-reinforcing. Ultimately, revival enters the prosperity phase.

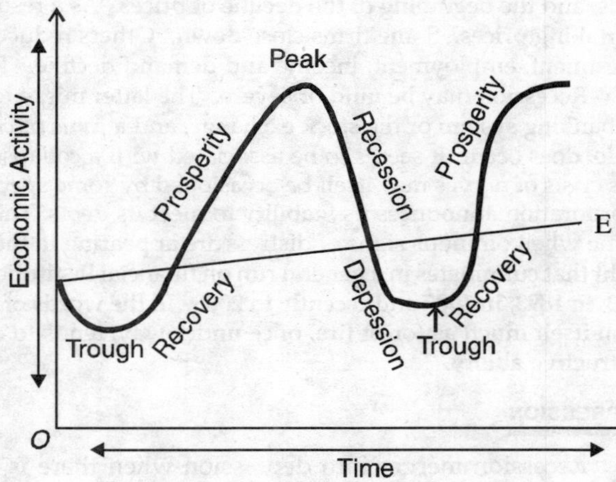

Fig. 1

PROSPERITY

In the prosperity phase, demand, output, employment and income are at a high level. They tend to raise prices. But wages, salaries, interest rates, rentals and taxes do not rise in proportion to the rise in prices. The gap between prices and costs increases the margin of profit. The increase of profit and the prospect of its continuance commonly cause a rapid rise in stock market values. The economy is engulfed in waves of optimism. Larger profit expectations further increase investment which is helped by liberal bank credit. Such investments are mostly in fixed capital, plant, equipment and machinery. They lead to considerable expansion in economic activity by increasing the demand for consumer goods and further raising the price level. This encourages retailers, wholesalers and manufacturers to add to inventories. In this way, the expansionary process becomes cumulative and self-reinforcing until the economy reaches a very high level of production, known as the *peak* or *boom*.

The peak or prosperity may lead the economy to over full employment and to inflationary rise in prices. It is a symptom of the end of the prosperity phase and the beginning of the recession. The seeds of recession are contained in the boom in the form of strains in the economic structure which act as brakes to the expansionary path. They are : (*i*) scarcities of labour, raw materials, etc. leading to rise in costs relative to prices; (*ii*) rise in the rate of interest due to scarcity of capital; and (*iii*) failure of consumption to rise due to rising prices and stable propensity to consume when incomes increase. The first factor brings a decline in profit margins. The second makes investments costly and along with the first, lowers business expectations. The third factor leads to the piling up of inventories indicating that sales (or consumption) lag behind production. These forces become cumulative and self-reinforcing. Entrepreneurs, businessmen and traders become over cautious and over optimism gives way to pessimism. This is the beginning of the upper turning point.

Recession

Recession starts when there is a downward descend from the 'peak' which is of a short duration. It marks the turning period during which the forces that make for contraction finally win over the forces of expansion. Its outward signs are liquidation in the stock market, strain in the banking system and some liquidation of bank loans, and the beginning of the decline of prices. As a result, profit margins decline further because costs start overtaking prices. Some firms close down. Others reduce production and try to sell out accumulated stocks. Investment, employment, income and demand decline. This process becomes cumulative.

Recession may be mild or severe. The latter might lead to a sudden explosive situation emanating from the banking system or the stock exchange, and a *panic* or *crisis* occurs. "When a crisis, and more particularly a panic, does occur, it seems to be associated with a collapse of confidence and sudden demands for liquidity. This crisis of nerves may itself be occasioned by some spectacular and unexpected failure. A firm or a bank, or a corporation announces its inability to meet its debts. This announcement weakens other firms and banks at a time when ominous signs of distress are appearing in the economic structure; moreover, it sets off a wave of fright that culminates in a general run on financial institutions"...Such was the experience of the United States in 1873, in 1893, in 1907 and recently in 2008. In the words of M.W. Lee, "A recession, once started, tends to build upon itself much as forest fire, once under way, tends to create its own draft and give internal impetus to its destructive ability."[2]

Depression

Recession merges into depression when there is a general decline in economic activity. There is considerable reduction in the production of goods and services, employment, income, demand and prices. The general decline in economic activity leads to a fall in bank deposits. Credit expansion stops because the business community is not willing to borrow. Bank rate falls considerably. According to Professor Estey, "This fall in active purchasing power is the fundamental background of the fall in prices, that despite the general reduction of output, characterises the depression." Thus a depression is characterised by mass unemployment; general fall in prices, profits, wages, interest rate, consumption, expenditure, investment, bank deposits and loans; factories close down; and construction of all types of capital goods, buildings, etc. comes to a standstill. These forces are cumulative and self-reinforcing and the economy is at the *trough*.

The trough or depression may be short-lived or it may continue at the bottom for considerable time. But sooner or later limiting forces are set in motion which ultimately tend to bring the contraction phase to end and pave the way for the revival. A cycle is thus complete.

4. CAUSES OF BUSINESS CYCLES

During the last several hundred years, philosophers, economists, stock brokers and men in the street have tried to give various causes of business cycles. Some attribute them to monetary and non-monetary factors while others to psychological factors. Samuelson attributes business cycles to external and internal factors which we explain below.

2. M.W. Lee, *Economic Fluctuations*, 1955.

EXTERNAL FACTORS

The external factors emphasise the causes of business cycles in the fluctuations of something outside the economic system. Such external factors are sunspots, wars, revolutions, political events, gold discoveries, growth rate of population, migrations, discoveries and innovations. These outside factors change the level of national income by affecting either the investment or consumption component of aggregate demand. For example, a drought that destroys many crops due to sunspots may reduce the quantity of goods produced in the country and adversely affect both consumption and investment. An innovation by opening the door to new markets, raw materials, products and production processes encourages new investments in plant and equipment. Inventions of railroads, electricity, telephone, automobiles, TVs, computers, etc. have led to the burst of investments in both capital and consumer goods from time to time. Discoveries of gold, oil and natural resources have led to large scale investments. Similarly, population expansion and migrations are the causes of huge investments in both housing and other infrastructure and consumer durables. All the above noted external factors have been responsible for booms in business cycles from time to time.

INTERNAL FACTORS

The internal factors relate to "mechanisms within the economic system itself which will give rise to self-generating business cycles, so that every expansion will breed recession and contraction, and every contraction will in turn breed revival and expansion, in a quasi-regular, repeating, never-ending chain."[3] Haberler divides the internal factors into monetary and non-monetary which we briefly explain.

1. *Bank Credit.* Hawtrey, Friedman and other monetarists regard business cycles as "a purely monetary phenomenon". According to Hawtrey, cyclical fluctuations are caused by expansion and contraction of bank credit. These in, turn, lead to changes in the demand for money on the part of producers and traders. Bank credit is the principal means of payment. Credit is expanded or reduced by the banks by lowering or raising the rate of interest or by purchasing and selling of securities to traders. This increases or decreases the supply of money in the economy. An increase in the money supply brings about prosperity and a decrease in the money supply leads to depression.

2. *Over-Saving or Under-Consumption.* According to economists like Hobson, Foster and Douglas, business cycles are caused by oversaving or under-consumption. They argue that wide disparities of income and wealth lead to depression in the country. The rich people are not able to spend their entire income. So they save more and invest more in producing consumer goods. On the other hand, the poor people have low incomes or wages. As a result, their demand for consumer goods is low which means that there is under-consumption. According to Hobson, oversaving leads to production of consumer goods in large quantities and to a boom. But under-consumption on the part of the workers due to low wages brings a fall in the demand for consumer goods. Stocks pile up at the current level of prices. These, in turn, lead to a fall in the prices of consumer goods and in the income of the producers. As a result, depression sets in.

3. *Over-Investment.* Hayek, Spiethoff, Cassel and Robertson find the root cause of business cycles in over-investment. According to Hayek, it is bank loans which lead to over-investment in capital goods industries relative to consumer goods industries that ultimately brings depression in the economy. When the total money supply exceeds the amount of voluntary savings, it leads to increase in the investment activity and ultimately to a boom. But banks cannot continue to give credit for long due to the shortage of voluntary savings. As a result, production will decline which will bring about a depression. Thus it is over-investment in the capital goods industries which is the cause of a boom and a depression.

4. *Competition.* According to Chapman, the main cause of business cycles is the existence of competition in an economy which leads to over-production and ultimately to a crisis (depression). Under competitive conditions, firms produce in anticipation of demand. The profit motive attracts new firms. Production increases and boom starts. Competition and profits lead to overproduction and glut of commodities in the market and to fall in prices. On the other hand, the race to produce more and profit more on the part of producers increases

3. P.A. Samuelson, *Economics*, p. 293

the demand for factors of production. Competition among producers to hire more factors raises their prices. Thus costs rise which raise the prices of products. Demand falls and there is glut of commodities which eventually leads to fall in prices and to a depression.

5. *Psychological Causes.* According to Pigou, the alternating waves of "over optimism" and "over pessimism" are the sole causes of the industrial fluctuations. He traces cyclical fluctuations to the tendency of businessmen to react excessively to the changing conditions of the economy. It is this tendency that causes alternating periods of over-production and under-production. Errors of optimism and pessimism are interacting forces. As soon as the business community discovers that it has made an error of optimism, it tries to correct it by making errors of pessimism. Each phase of the cycle produces a state of psychology which produces forces that bring about reversal of that psychology and in turn another reversal. These alternating waves of over-optimism (over-production) and over-pessimism (under-production), as a result of these reversals, are the main causes of business cycles.

6. *Innovations.* According to Schumpeter, innovations in the structure of an economy are the source of economic fluctuations. To him, "the cause of depression is prosperity." The boom consists in the carrying out of innovations in the industrial and commercial fields. The cyclical upswing is set in motion when an innovator starts making investment in his innovation of a new product. This enables him to make profit. Soon other enrepreneurs adopt this new product in "swarm-like clusters". Innovations in one field induce innovations in related fields. There is large increase in the output of new products. Consequently, money incomes and prices rise and help to create a cumulative expansion in the economy. Overoptimism adds further to the boom. When there is glut of new products in the market, their prices fall, and profit margins of entrepreneurs are reduced. Banks ask for repayment of loans. The quantity of money is reduced and prices fall further. Some entrepreneurs cut down production and others are forced into liquidation. Thus the economy enters into depression.

7. *Marginal Efficiency of Capital (MEC).* According to Keynes, the cycle consists primarily of fluctuations in the rate of investment. And fluctuations in the rate of investment are caused mainly by fluctuations in the MEC. The MEC depends on the supply price of capital assets and their prospective yield. The supply price of capital assets being stable in the short-run, the MEC is determined by the prospective yield of capital assets. The prospective yield, in turn, depends on business expectations. Fluctuations in the rate of investment are also caused by fluctuations in the rate of interest. But it is fluctuations in the MEC which are the principal cause of cyclical fluctuations.

Conclusion. To conclude with Samuelson, business cycles are caused both by external and internal factors. The economic system responds to fluctuations in external factors according to its internal factors, and vice versa.

5. EFFECTS OF BUSINESS CYCLES

Business cycles have both good and bad effects depending upon whether the economy is passing through a phase of prosperity or depression.

In the *prosperity* phase, "the real income consumed, real income produced and the level of employment are high or rising and there are no idle or unemployed workers or very few of either." There is general increase in economic activity : aggregate output, demand, employment and income are at a high level. Prices are rising. Profits are increasing. Stock markets are rapidly reaching new heights. Investments are increasing with liberal bank credit. This entire process is cumulative and self-reinforcing.

But different sections of the society are affected differently during the prosperity phase. The landless, factory and agricultural workers and middle classes suffer because their wages and salaries are more or less fixed but the prices of commodities rise continuously. They become more poor. On the other hand, businessmen, traders, industrialists, real estate holders, speculators, landlords, shareholders and others with variable incomes gain. Thus the rich become richer and the poor poorer.

The social effects are also bad. Lured by profit, there is hoarding, black-marketing, adulteration, production of substandard goods, speculation, etc. Corruption spreads in every walk of life.

When the economy is nearing the *full employment level* of resources, the ill-effects on production start appearing. Rising prices of raw materials and increase in wages raise costs of production. As a result, profit margins decline. There is rise in interest rates due to scarcity of capital which makes investment costly. These two factors lower business expectations. Lastly, the demand for consumer goods does not rise due to inflationary rise in prices. This leads to piling up of inventories (stocks) with producers and traders. Thus sales lag behind production. There is decline is prices. Producers, businessmen and traders become pessimists and the recession starts.

During *recession*, profit margins decline further because costs start rising more than prices. Some firms close down. Others reduce production and try to sell accumulated stocks. Investment, output, employment, income, demand and prices decline further. This process becomes cumulative and recession merges into depression.

During a *depression*, there is mass unemployment. Prices, profits and wages are at their lowest levels. Demand for goods and services is the minimum. Investment, bank deposits and bank loans are negligible. Construction of all types of capital goods, buidlings, etc. is at a standstill. There is mass unemployment in the economy. The government revenues from direct and indirect taxes decline. The real burden of the debt increases. The economic development of the country suffers.

6. THEORIES OF BUSINESS CYCLES

In fact, the causes of business cycles given above are based on the theories of business cycles propounded by economists from time to time. We discuss some of the important theories as under.

1. Hawtrey's Monetary Theory

According to Prof. R.G. Hawtrey,[4] "The trade cycle is a purely monetary phenomenon." It is changes in the flow of monetary demand on the part of businessmen that lead to prosperity and depression in the economy. He opines that non-monetary factors like strikes, floods, earthquakes, droughts, wars, etc. may at best cause a partial depression, but not a general depression. In actuality, cyclical fluctuations are caused by expansion and contraction of bank credit which, in turn, lead to variations in the flow of monetary demand on the part of producers and traders. Bank credit is the principal means of payment in the present times. Credit is expanded or reduced by the banking system by lowering or raising the rate of interest or by purchasing or selling securities to merchants. This increases or decreases the flow of money in the economy and thus brings about prosperity or depression.

The *expansion phase* of the trade cycle starts when banks increase credit facilities. They are provided by reducing the lending rate of interest and by purchasing securities. These encourage borrowings on the part of merchants and producers. This is because they are very sensitive to changes in the rate of interest. So when credit becomes cheap, they borrow from banks in order to increase their stocks or inventories. For this, they place larger orders with producers who, in turn, employ more factors of production to meet the increasing demand. Consequently, money incomes of the owners of factors of production increase, thereby increasing expenditure on goods. The merchants find their stocks being exhausted. They place more orders with producers. This leads to further increase in productive activity, income, outlay, and demand, and a further depletion of stocks of merchants. According to Hawtrey, "Increased activity means increased demand, and increased demand means increased activity. A vicious circle is set up, a cumulative expansion of productive activity."

As the cumulative process of expansion continues, producers quote higher and higher prices. Higher prices induce traders to borrow more in order to hold still larger stocks of goods so as to earn more profits. Thus optimism encourages borrowing, borrowing increases sales, and sales raise optimism.

According to Hawtrey, prosperity cannot continue limitlessly. It comes to an end when banks stop credit expansion. Banks refuse to lend further because their cash funds are depleted and the money in circulation is absorbed in the form of cash holdings by consumers. Another factor is the export of gold to other countries when imports exceed exports as a result of high prices of domestic goods. These factors force the banks to raise

4. R.G. Hawtrey, *Trade and Credit*, 1928

interest rates and refuse to lend. Rather, they ask the business community to repay their loans. This starts the recessionary phase.

In order to repay bank loans, businessmen start selling their stocks. This sets the process of falling prices. They also cancel orders with producers. The latter curtail their productive activities due to fall in demand. These, in turn, lead to reduction in the demand for factors of production. There is unemployment. Incomes fall. Falling demand, prices and incomes are the signals for depression. Unable to repay bank loans, some firms go into liquidation, thus forcing banks to contract credit further. Thus the entire process becomes cumulative and the economy is forced into depression.

According to Hawtrey, the *process of recovery* is very slow and halting. As *depression* continues, traders repay bank loans by selling their stocks at whatever prices they can. As a result, money flows into the reserves of banks and funds increase with banks. Even though the bank rate is very low, there is "credit deadlock" which prevents businessmen to borrow from banks due to pessimism in economic activity. This deadlock can be broken by following a cheap money policy by the central bank which will ultimately bring about recovery in the economy.

Its Criticisms

Monetarists like Friedman have supported Hawtrey's theory. But the majority of economists have criticised him for over-emphasising monetary factors to the neglect of non-monetary factors in explaining cyclical fluctuations. Some of the points of criticism are discussed below.

(1) *Credit not the Cause of Cycle.* None can deny that expansion of credit leads to the expansion of business activity. But Hawtrey believes that an expansion of credit leads to a boom. This is not correct because the former is not the cause of the latter. As pointed out by Pigou, "Variations in the bank money supply is a part of the business cycle, it is not the cause of it." At the bottom of the depression, credit is easily available. Even then, it fails to bring a revival. Similarly, contraction of credit cannot bring about a depression. At best, it can create conditions for that. Thus expansion or contraction of credit cannot originate either boom or depression in the economy.

(2) *Money Supply cannot Continue a Boom or Delay a Depression.* Haberler has criticised Hawtrey for "his contention that the reason for the breakdown of the boom is always a monetary one and that prosperity could be prolonged and depression stayed off indefinitely if the money suply were inexhaustible."[5] But the fact is that even if the supply of money is inexhaustible in the country, neither prosperity can be continued indefinitely nor depression can be delayed idefinitely.

(3) *Traders do not Depend Only on Bank Credit.* Hamberg[6] has criticised Hawtrey for the role assigned to wholesalers in his analysis. The kingpin in Hawtrey's theory is the trader or the wholesaler who gets credit from banks and starts the upturn or vice-versa. In actuality, traders do not depend exclusively on bank credit but they finance business through their own accumulated funds and borrowing from private sources.

(4) *Traders do not React to changes in Interest Rates.* Further, Hamberg also does not agree with Hawtrey that traders react to changes in interest rates. According to Hamberg, traders are likely to react favourably to a reduction in the interest rate only if they think that the reduction is permanent. But they do not react favourably during the depression phase because traders expect a further reduction every time the interest rate is reduced. On the other hand, if traders finance their stocks with their own funds, interest rate changes will have little effect on their purchases.

(5) *Factors other than Interest Rate More Important.* It is an exaggeration to say that the decisions of traders regarding accumulation or depletion of stocks are solely governed by changes in interest rate. As a matter of fact, factors other than the rate of interest are more important in influencing such decisions. They are business expectations, price changes, cost of storage, etc.

(6) *Inventory Investments do not Produce True Cycles.* Hamberg further points out that in Hawtrey's theory cumulative movements in economic activity are the result of changes in stocks of goods. But fluctuations in inventroy investment can at best produce minor cycles which are not cycles in the true sense of the term.

5. G. Haberler, *Business Cycles*, pp. 27-28.
6. D. Hamberg, *Business Cycles*, 1937.

(7) *Does not Explain Periodicity of Cycle.* The theory also fails to explain the periodicity of the cyle.

(8) *Ignores Non-Monetary Factors.* Hawtrey's theory is incomplete because it emphasises only monetary factors and totally ignores such non-monetary factors as innovations, capital stock, multiplier-accelerator interaction, etc.

2. Hayek's Monetary Over-Investment Theory

F.A. Hayek formulated his monetary over-investment theory of trade cycle. He explained his theory on the basis of Wicksell's distinction between the natural interest rate and the market interest rate. The natural rate of interest is that rate at which the demand for loanable funds equals the supply of voluntary savings. On the other hand, the market rate of interest is the money rate which prevails in the market and is determined by the demand and supply of money. According to Hayek, so long as the natural rate of interest equals the market rate of interest, the economy remains in the state of equilibrium and full employment . Trade cycles in the economy are caused by inequality between market and natural interest rates. When the market interest rate is less than the nautral rate, there is prosperity in the economy. On the contrary, when the market interest rate is more than the natural rate, the economy is in depression.

According to this thoery, prosperity begins when the market rate of interest is less than the natural rate of interest. In such a situation, the demand for investment funds is more than the supply of available savings. The demand for investment funds is met by the increase in the supply of money. As a result, the interest rate falls. Low interest rate induces producers to get more loans from banks. The producers get more loans to invest for the production of more capital goods. They adopt capital-intensive methods for producing more of capital goods. As a result, production costs fall and profits increase. The production process becomes very lengthy with the adoption of capital-intensive methods. This has the effect of increasing the prices of capital goods in comparison to consumer goods. There being full employment in the economy, they transfer factors of the production from consumer goods sector to capital goods sector. Consequently, the production of consumer goods falls, their prices increase and their consumption decreases. Forced savings increase with the fall in consumption which are invested for the production of capital goods. This leads to increase in their production. On the other hand, with increase in the prices of consumer goods, their producers earn more profits. Induced by high profits, they try to produce more. For this, they pay higher remuneration to factors of production in comparison with the producers of capital goods. There being competition between the two sectors, prices of factors and prices in the economy continue to rise. This leads to the atmosphere of prosperity in the country and monetary over-investment on factors spreads the boom.

According to Hayek, when the prices of factors are rising continously, the rise in production costs bring fall in profits of producers. The producers of capital goods invest less in the expectation of loss in the future. Consequently, the natural interest rate falls. Simultaneously, banks impose restrictions on giving loans to them. With low profits and reduction in loans, producers reduce the production of capital goods and adopt labour-intensive production processes. There is less investment in capital goods. Production process being small and labour-intensive, the demand for money is reduced, which increases the market interest rate which is more than the natural interest rate. Producers transfer the factors from the production of capital goods to that of consumer goods. But more factors cannot be used in the consumer goods sector as compared to the capital goods sector. This leads to fall in the prices of factors and resources become unemployed. Thus, with the continuous reduction in the prices of goods and factors in the economy, a long period of depression and unemployment begins.

According to Hayek, when the fall in prices comes to an end during depression, banks begin to raise the supply of money which reduces the market interest rate below the natural interest rate. This encourages investment and the process of revival begins in the economy.

Its Criticisms

The monetary over-investment theory of Hayek has been criticised on the following counts:

(1) *Narrow Assumption of Full Employment.* This theory is based on the assumption of full employment according to which capital goods are produced by reducing consumer goods. In reality, there is no full employment of resources. If resources remain unutilised, the expansion of both the capital goods sector and

consumer goods sector may occur simultaneously. In such a situation, there is no need of transferring resources from one sector to the other.

(2) *Unrealistic Assumption of Equilibrium.* The assumption of this theory that in the beginning savings and investment are in equilibrium in the economy and the banking system destroys this equilibrium is unrealistic. This is because the equilibrium may deviate due to both internal and external reasons.

(3) *Interest Rate not the only Determinant.* Hayek assumes changes in the rate of interest as the cause of fluctuations in the economy. This is not correct because besides changes in the rate of interest, the expectations of profit, innovation, invention, etc. also affect trade cycles.

(4) *Undue Importance to Forced Savings.* Prof. Strigl has criticised this theory for giving undue importance to forced savings. According to him, when people with fixed incomes reduce their consumption with the increase in prices and the high income groups also reduce their consumption to the same extent, savings will not be forced but voluntary.

(5) *Investment does not fall with Increase in Consumer Goods.* Hayek argues that with the production of consumer goods and the increase in profits from them, investment falls in capital goods. This is not correct. According to Keynes, the marginal productivity of capital increases with the increase in profits of consumer goods. As a result, investment in capital goods also increases and does not fall.

(6) *Incomplete Theory.* Hayek's theory is incomplete because it does not explain the various phases of trade cycle.

3. Schumpeter's Innovations Theory

The innovations theory of trade cycles is associated with the name of Joseph Schumpeter.[7] According to Schumpeter, innovations in the structure of an economy are the source of economic fluctuations. Trade cycles are the outcome of economic development in a capitalist society. Schumpeter accepts Juglar's statement that "the cause of depression is prosperity," and then gives his own view about the originating cause of the cycle.

Schumpeter's approach involves the development of his model into two stages. The first stage deals with the initial impact of innovation and the second stage follows through reactions to the original impact of innovation.

The first approximation starts with the economic system in equilibrium with every factor fully employed. Every firm is in equilibrium and producing efficiently with its costs equal to its receipts. Product prices are equal to both average and marginal costs. Profits and interest rates are zero. There are no savings and investments. This equilibrium is characterised by Schumpeter as the "circular flow" which continues to repeat itself in the same manner year after year, similar to the circulation of the blood in an animal organism. In the circular flow, the same products are produced every year in the same manner.

Schumpeter's theory starts with the breaking up of the circular flow by an innovation in the form of a new product by an entrepreneur for earning profit.

By innovation Schumpeter means "such changes in the production of goods as cannot be affected by infinitesimal steps or variations on the margin." An innovation may consist of : (1) the introduction of a new product; (2) the introduction of a new method of production; (3) the opening up of a new market; (4) the conquest of a new source of raw materials or semi-manufactured goods; and (5) the carrying out of the new organisations of an industry. Innovations are not inventions. According to Schumpeter, there is nothing that can explain that inventions occur in a cyclical manner. It is the introduction of a new product and the continual improvements in the existing ones that are the principal causes of business cycles.

Schumpeter assigns the role of an innovator not to the capitalist but to an entrepreneur. The entrepreneur is not a man of ordinary ability but one who introduces something entirely new. He does not provide funds but directs their use.

To perform his economic function, the entrepreneur requires two things: first, the existence of technical knowledge in order to produce new products, and second, the power of disposal over the factors of production in the form of bank credit. According to Schumpeter, a reservoir of untapped technical knowledge exists in a capitalist society which he can make use of. Therefore, credit is essential for breaking the circular flow.

7. J.A. Schumpeter, *Business Cycles*, 1939.

The innovating entrepreneur is financed by expansion of bank credit. Since investment in an innovation is risky, he must pay interest on it. With his newly acquired funds, the innovator starts bidding away resources from other industries. Money incomes increase. Prices begin to rise, thereby stimulating further investment. The new innovation starts producing goods and there is an increased flow of goods in the economy. Consequently, supply exceeds demand. Prices and cost of production of goods start declining until recession sets in. Because of the low prices of goods, producers are not willing to expand production. During this period of recession, credit, prices and interest rate decline but total output is likely to average larger than in the preceding prosperity.

Thus Schumpeter's first approximation consists of a two-phase cycle. The economy starts at the equilibrium state, rises to a peak and then starts downward into a recession and continues till the new equilibrium is reached. This new equilibrium will be at a higher level of income than the initial equilibrium because of the innovation which started the cycle. This is shown as the "Primary Wave" in Figure 2.

The second approximation of Schumpeter follows through the reaction of the impact of original innovation. Once the original innovation becomes successful and profitable, other entrepreneurs follow it in "swarm-like clusters." Innovation in one field induces innovations in related fields. Consequently, money incomes and prices rise and help to create a cumulative expansion throughout the economy. With the increase in the purchasing power of consumers, the demand for the products of old industries increases in relation to supply. Prices rise further. Profits increase and old industries expand by borrowing from the banks. It induces a *secondary* wave of credit inflation which is superimposed on the primary wave of innovation. Overoptimism and speculation add further to the boom. After a period of gestation, the new products start appearing in the market displacing the old products and enforcing a process of liquidation, readjustment and absorption.

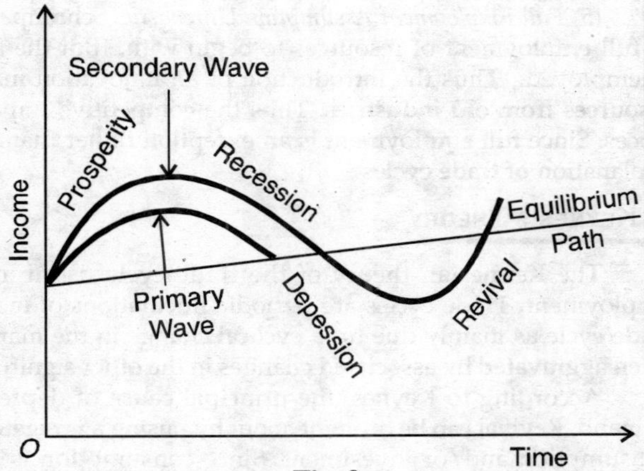

Fig. 2

The demand for the old products is decreased. Their prices fall. The old firms contract output and some are even forced to run into liquidation. As the innovators start repaying bank loans out of profits, the quantity of money is decreased and prices tend to fall. Profits decline. Uncertainty and risks increase. The impulse for innovation is reduced and eventually comes to an end. Depression sets in, and the painful process of readjustment to the "point of previous neighbourhood of equilibrium" begins. Ultimately, the natural forces of recovery bring about a revival.

Schumpeter believes in the existence of Kondratieff long wave of upswings and downswings in economic activity. Each long wave upswing is brought about by an innovation which leads to abundance of goods for the masses. Once the upswing ends, the long wave downswing begins.

Thus the second approximation of Schumpeter's theory of trade cycle develops into a four phase cycle with the recession which was the second phase in the first approximation continuing downward to give the depression phase. This extension of cycle is followed by a period of revival which continues till the equilibrium level is reached. This is shown as the "Secondary Wave" in Figure 2.

Its Criticisms

Schumpeter's treatment of the different phases and turning points of the cycle is novel and different from all other economists. But it is not free from certain criticisms.

(1) *Innovator not Necessary for Innovations.* Schumpeter's analysis is based on the innovator. Such persons were to be found in the 18th and 19th centuries who made innovations. But now all innovations form part of

the functions of joint stock companies. Innovations are regarded as the routine of industrial concerns and do not require an innovator as such.

(2) *Innovations not the Only Cause of Cycles.* Schumpeter's contention that cyclical fluctuations are due to innovations is not correct. As a matter of fact, trade cycles may be due to psychological, natural or financial causes.

(3) *Bank Credit not the Only Source of Funds.* Schumpeter gives too much importance to bank credit in his theory. Bank credit may be important in the short run when industrial concerns get credit facilities from banks. But in the long run when the need for capital funds is much greater, bank credit is insufficient. For this, business houses have to float fresh shares and debentures in the capital market. Schumpeter's theory is weak in that it does not take these factors into consideration.

(4) *Innovation financed through Voluntary Savings does not produce a Cycle.* Critics point out that if an innovation is financed through voluntary savings or internal funds, there will not be an inflationary rise in prices. Consequently, in an underemployed economy an innovation financed through voluntary savings might not generate a cycle.

(5) *Full Employment Assumption Unrealistic.* Schumpeter's analysis is based on the unrealistic assumption of full employment of resources to begin with. But the fact is that at the time of revival, the resources are unemployed. Thus the introduction of an innovation may not lead to the withdrawal of labour and other resources from old industries. Thus the competitive impact of an innovation would not increase costs and prices. Since full employment is an exception rather than the rule. Thus Schumpeter's theory is not a correct explanation of trade cycles.

4. Keynes's Theory

The Keynesian theory of the trade cycle[8] is an integral part of his theory of income, output and employment. Trade cycles are periodic fluctuations of income, output and employment. Keynes regards the trade cycle as mainly due to "a cyclical change in the marginal efficiency of capital, though complicated and often aggravated by associated changes in the other significant short-period variables of the economic system."

According to Keynes, the principal cause of depression and unemployment is the lack of aggregate demand. Revival can be brought about by raising aggregate demand which, in turn, can be raised by increasing consumption and/or investment. Since consumption is stable during the short-run, revival is possible by increasing investment. Similarly, the main cause of the downturn is reduction in investment. Thus in the Keynesian explanation of the trade cycle, "the cycle consists primarily of fluctuations in the rate of investment. And fluctuations in the rate of investment are caused mainly by fluctuations in the marginal efficiency of capital."[9] The *MEC* (marginal efficiency of capital) depends on the supply price of capital assets and their prospective yield. Since the supply price of capital assets is stable in the short-run, the MEC is determined by the prospective yield of capital assets, which, in turn, depends on business expectations. Fluctuations in the rate of investment are also caused by fluctuations in the rate of interest. But Keynes gives more importance to fluctuations in the MEC as the principal cause of cyclical fluctuations.

To explain the course of the Keynesian cycle, we start with the *expansion phase*. During the expansion phase, the MEC is high. Businessmen are optimistic. There is rapid increase in the rate of investment. Consequently, output, employment and income increase. Every increase in investment leads to a multiple increase in income via the multiplier effect. This cumulative process of rising investment, income and employment continues till the boom is reached.

As the *boom* progresses, there is a tendency for the MEC to fall due to two reasons. *First*, as more capital goods are being produced steadily, the current yield on them declines. *Second*, at the same time the current costs of new capital goods rise due to shortages and bottlenecks of materials and labour.

During the *downturn*, investment falls due to a fall in the MEC and rise in the rate of interest. This leads to a cumulative decline in employment and income via the reverse operation of the multiplier. Further, the fall in the MEC may shift the consumption function downward thereby hastening the depression. Keynes attaches

8. J.M. Keynes, *op. cit.*, Ch. 22.
9. A.H. Hansen, *A Guide to Keynes*, 1953.

more importance to the sudden collapse of the MEC than to a rise in the rate of interest as an explanation of the downturn of the cycle leading to the crisis and the depression.

Unlike the sudden collapse of the economic system, the *revival* takes time. It depends on factors which bring about the recovery of the MEC. "The time which must elapse before recovery begins, depends partly upon the magnitude of the *normal rate of growth of the economy* and partly upon *the length of life of capital goods*. The shorter the length of life of durable assets, the shorter the depression. And also, the more rapid the *rate of growth*, the shorter the depression." Another factor which governs the duration of depression is the "carrying costs of surplus stocks." According to Keynes, the carrying cost of surplus stocks during the depression is seldom less than 10 per cent per annum. So for a few years, disinvestment in stocks will continue till the surplus stocks are exhausted. Optimism takes the place of pessimism. The MEC increases. Fresh investment starts taking place. Revival has started.

Its Criticisms

Keynes's theory of the trade cycle is superior to the earlier theories because "it is more than a theory of the business cycle in the sense that it offers a general explanation of the level of employment, quite independently of the cyclical nature of changes in employment."[10] However, critics are not lacking in pointing out its weakness.

(1) *Overemphasis on the Role of Expectations.* Keynes has been criticised for his analysis of business cycle based on expectations. In fact, he overemphasised the role of expectations in influencing the MEC. According to Hart, Keynes relied on "convention" for forecasting changes in business expectations. The reliance on the conventional hypothesis makes Keynes' concept of expectations superfluous and unrealistic.

(2) *Psychological Theory.* Keynes considers the trade cycle as mainly due to fluctations in the MEC. The MEC, in turn, determines the rate of investment. And investment decisions, depend upon the psychology of businessmen or producers. Thus Keynes' theory is not much different from Pigou's psychological theory of the trade cycle.

(3) *Explanation of Crisis Wrong.* Keynes attributes the downturn to the sudden collapse in the MEC. Accroding to Hazlitt, the term MEC being vague and ambiguous, "Keynes' explanation of the crisis of the marginal efficiency of capital is either a useless truism or an obvious error."

(4) *Incomplete Theory.* Another weakness of Keynes' theory of the trade cycle is that some of its variables such as expectations, MEC and investment cannot explain the different phases of the cycle. In the words of Dillard, "It is less than a complete theory of the business cycle because it makes no attempt to give a detailed account of the various phases of the cycle."

(5) *Not Based on Empirical Data.* Saulnier criticises Keynes's for lacking in factual proof. According to him, Keynes makes no attempt to test any of his deductions with facts. Dillard also points toward this defect when he writes that Keynes "does not examine closely the empirical data of cyclical fluctuations."

(6) *One-Sided Theory.* One of the serious omissions of Keynes's theory of the trade cycle is the acceleration principle. This made his theory one-sided because his explanation centres round the principle of multiplier. As pointed out by Sir John Hicks, "The theory of acceleration and the theory of multiplier are two sides of the theory of fluctuations, just as the theory of demand and the theory of supply are the two sides of the theory of value."

. FRIEDMAN'S THEORY OF BUSINESS CYCLES*

Friedman and Schwartz[11] have argued on the basis of US historical data that business cycles are mostly monetary in origin. It is the money stock itself that shows a consistent cyclical behaviour which is closely related to the cyclical movements in economic activity at large. About the causal relation between the money stock and economic activity, they make the following generalisations: (i) changes in economic activity have always been accompanied by changes in the money stock; (ii) there have not been major changes in the money

10. Dudley Dillard, *op.cit.*, p. 267.

* This theory is also known as *Money and Business Cycles.*

11. M. Friedman and A.W. Schwartz, Money and Business Cycles, R.ES., (Supplement), 1963.

stock that have not been accompanied by changes in economic activity; and (iii) changes in the stock of money have been attributed to a specific variety of exogenous factors rather than to changes in economic activity. Thus changes in the money stock are a consequence as well as independent cause of changes in economic activity. But once they occur, they will, in turn, produce still further effects on economic activity. There is also much evidence that during business cycles the money stock plays largely an independent role.

In one of his earlier writings, Friedman emphasises that the concept of lag is related to the business cycle. These cycles are mostly monetary in origin. A monetary change effects different economic magnitudes, some of which adjust faster than others which cause distortions in economis activity, thereby giving rise to the business cycles. Thus it can be said in Fisher's words that the cycle is largely a "dance of the dollar".

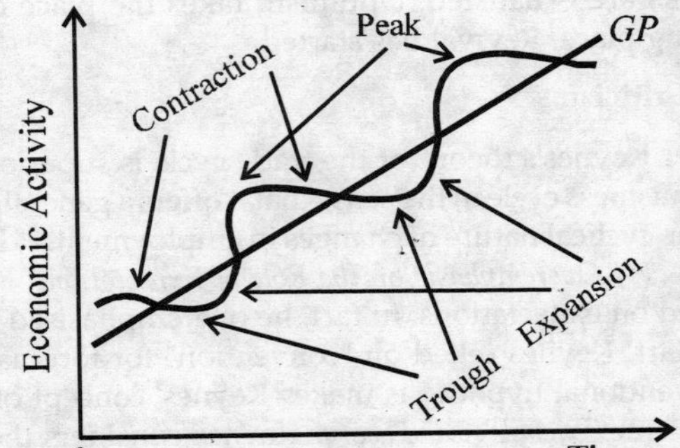

Fig. 3

Major US historical economic fluctuations include inflationary and deep depression cycles. According to Friedman and Schwartz, the empirical evidence justifies the generalisations noted above. These show that the stock of money has displayed a systematic cyclical pattern over the decades. The money stock generally reaches its peak before the 'reference' peak of the cycles. Similarly, it reaches its trough before the 'reference' trough. One of their estimates of the lag between turning points in the growth of the money stock and in the level of economic activity reveals that during the seven cycles between 1927 and 1970, peaks in the rate of change in the money stock precede reference cycle peaks (in economic activity series) before downturns by 20 months on an average, and troughs in the rate of change of the money stock precede reference troughs by about 11 months on an average before upturns. The lag of economic activity appears to be greater for peaks than for troughs. There has been strong secular changes in the money stock over these decades. On the other hand, in deep depression cycles, there has been a greater fall in money stock. But in mild depressions, there has been a reduction in the growth rate of the money stock rather than any actual fall.

The usual cycle consists of a contraction phase in which economic activity declines to trough of the cycle, followed by expansion and reaching the peak of the cycle. These cycles are superimposed over a long run secular growth path, *GP*, as shown in Figure 3.

On the basis of the above analysis, Friedman and Schwartz point toward two propositions: *First*, appreciable changes in the growth rate of the money stock are necessary and sufficient conditions for appreciable changes in growth rate of economic activity or money income. *Second*, this is true both for long secular changes and also for changes over periods roughly the length of business cycles.

They further observe that a *secular change* in the gowth rate of the money stock leading to longer period changes in money income are reflected mainly in different price behaviour rather than in different growth rates of output. On the other hand, a short period change in the growth rate of money stock also exerts a substantial influence on the growth rate of *output*. The greater stability of the "money multiplier" in contrast to the Keynesian investment multiplier has led Friedman and Schwartz to come to the above conclusion. According to them, substantial expansions in the quantity of money over short periods have been a major proximate source of the accompanying inflation of prices. Substantial contractions in the quantity of money over shorter periods have been a major factor in producing severe economic contractions. Cyclical variations in the quantity of money may well be an important element in the ordinary mild business cycle.

Next, Friedman and Schwartz explain the *mechanism* which brings about monetary changes leading to the business cycles. They begin their explanation of the transmission mechnaism with a state of moving equilibrium in which real per capita income, the stock of money, and the price level are changing at constant annual rates. Suppose the central bank increases the stock of money in the market by open market operations by purchasing securities. The non-bank sellers and commercial banks will try to readjust their portfolios. The commercial banks will create more money with increase in their reserves, thereby transmitting the increase i high-powered stock of money. On the other hand, the non-bank holders of cash will seek to purchase other categories of securities such as high-risk fixed coupons, equities, real property, etc. This will bid up prices of such assets. As the process continues, the initial impacts will spread throughout the economy. The increased demand for assets will spread sooner or later affecting equities, houses, durable producer goods, durable consumer goods, etc. All these will bid up the prices of assets and of both producer and consumer goods. People will tend to consume more services, such as renting houses rather than purchasing them. This will tend to raise service prices. These effects will raise interest rates on the whole range of assets. Ultimately, expenditures rise on all directions without any change in interest rates at all. "Interest rates and asset prices may simply be conduit through which monetary change is transmitted to expenditures without being altered at all, just as a greater inflow into a tank may, after an interval, simply increase the rate of outflow without altering the level of the tank itself." All these forces operate simultaneously and there are cyclical fluctuations.

This explanation of the transmission mechanism fits with the empirical observations of business cycles. Initially, the rise in the growth rate of the money stock occurs early in the contraction phase. Its first impact is on the financial markets where first bonds, then equities and only later on payments for real resources will be affected. The financial markets tend to revive well before the trough. This is what has happened historically.

The dynamic process of transition from one equilibrium path to another involves a cyclical adjustment process. *Exogenous fluctuations* in the money stock will lead to fluctuations in the demand for goods and services. In addition, there may be an endogenous cycle. A rise in demand raises prices. If there is a lag in the adjustment of real money balances to the new price level, the initial portfolio adjustment will tend to overshoot. The initial rise in demand will thus be followed by a fall in demand. The result will be a damped cycle.

According to Friedman, the *lag* plays an important role in business cycles. The amplitude of economic fluctuations depends: *First*, on the amplitude, time pattern, number and independence of the disturbances affecting the economic system. *Second*, on the reaction mechanism of the economic system to the disturbances. The lag may be long because the effects of monetary disturbances are distributed over an extended period. A long lag may mean a larger damping of disturbances than a short lag. Hence there is a smaller amplitude of resulting fluctuations. The lags in economic activity behind peaks and troughs in the rate of change of the money stock are not uniform. Friedman concludes on the basis of empirical evidence that lags involving changes in the rate of the money stock that affect the level of economic activity are both long and variable.

Its Criticisms

Economists have criticised Friedman's theory of money and business cycles on the following grounds:

(1) *Monetary Changes not the Only Cause of Changes in Economic Activity.* Friedman argues that it is monetary changes that cause changes in economic activity. But critics point out that the direction of causation is just the opposite of it. It is changes in the level of business activity which cause changes in the growth rate of the money stock.

(2) *Monetary Changes not the Main Cause of Business Cycles.* According to this theory, monetary changes are the main cause of business cycles. But in reality, business cycles are the result of the other exogenous factors like innovations. Monetary changes may be one among other factors, and not the only factor.

(3) *Time Lag of Peaks and Troughs not Long and Variable.* According to Friedman, the time lag of peaks and troughs in the rate of change of the money stock relative to economic changes in business cycles is both long and variable. Prof. Culbertson regards this evidence as faulty for two reasons: *First*, it relates turning points in one series in the money stock to turning points in economic activity. *Second*, it implies that monetary change has been an exogenous variable and that causation runs only from monetary change to economic change. In fact, causation also has run in other direction.

Despite these criticisms, it cannot be denied that one of the important causes of business cycles is "a dance of the dollar."

6. Samuelson's Model of Business Cycle*

Prof. Samuelson[12] constructed a multiplier-accelerator model assuming one period lag and different values for the *MPC* (a) and the accelerator (b) that result in changes in the level of income pertaining to five different types of fluctuations.

The Samuelson model is

$$Y_t = G_t + C_t + I_t \qquad ...(1)$$

where Y_t is national income *Y* at time t which is the sum of government expenditure G_t, consumption expenditure C_t and induced investment I_t.

$$C_t = aY_{t-1} \qquad ...(2)^{**}$$

$$I_t = b(C_t - C_{t-1}) \qquad ...(3)$$

Substituting equation (2) in (3) we have,

$$I_t = b(aY_{t-1} - aY_{t-2})$$

$$I_t = baYt\text{-}1 - baY_{t-2} \qquad ...(4)$$

$$G_t = 1 \qquad ...(5)$$

Substituting equations (2), (4) and (5) in (1) we have

$$Y_t = 1 + aY_{t-1} + baY_{t-1} - baY_{t-2} \qquad ...(6)$$

$$= 1 + a(Y_{t-1} + bY_{t-1}) - baY_{t-2}$$

$$= 1 + a(1+b)\,Y_{t-1} - baY_{t-2} \qquad ...(7)$$

According to Samuelson, "If we know the national income for two periods, the national income for the following period can be simply derived by taking a weighted sum. The weights depend, of course, upon the values chosen for the marginal propensity to consume and for the *relation* (i.e.accelerator)". Assuming the value of the marginal propensity to consume to be greater than zero and less than one (0< a <1) and of the accelerator greater than zero (b > 0), Samuelson explains five types of cyclical fluctuations which are summarised in the Table 1.

Table 1. Samuelson's Interaction Model

Case	Values	Behaviour of the Cycle
1	a = .5, b = 0	Cycleless Path
2	a = .5, b = 1	Damped Fluctuations
3	a = .5, b = 2	Fluctuations of Constant Amplitude
4	a = .5, b = 3	Explosive Cycles
5	a = .5, b = 4	Cycleless Explosive Path

Case 1 : Samuelson's case 1 shows a cycleless path because it is based only on the multiplier effect, the accelerator playing no part in it. This is shown in Fig. 4 (A).

Case 2 shows a damped cyclical path fluctuating around the static multiplier level and gradually subsiding to that level, as shown in Fig. 4 (B).

Case 3 depicts cycles of constant amplitude repeating themselves around the multiplier level. This case is depicted in Fig. 4 (C).

Case 4 reveals anti-damped or explosive cycles, see Fig. 4 (D).

Case 5 relates to a cycleless explosive upward path eventually approaching a compound interest rate of growth, as shown in Fig. 4 (E).

Of the five cases explained above, only three cases 2, 3 and 4 are cyclical in nature. But they can be reduced to two because case 3 pertaining to cycles of constant amplitude has not been experienced. So far as

* For its understanding students should read 'Use ofMultiplier-Accelerator Interaction'.

12. Paul A. Samuelson, "Interactions between the Multiplier Analysis and Principle of Acceleration," *R.E.S.*, May 1939, reprinted in *Readings in Macroeconomics,* (ed.) M.G. Mueller.

** Consumption in period t is regarded as a function of the previous period (t–1).

case 2 of damped cycles is concerned these cycles have been occurring irregularly in a milder form over last half century. Generally, cycles in the post-World War II period have been relatively damped compared to those in the inter-World War II period. They are the result of "such disturbances—which may be called erratic shocks—arising from exogenous factors, such as wars, changes in crops, inventions and so on 'which' might be expected to come alongwith fair persistence." But it is not possible to measure their magnitude.

Case 4 of explosive cycles has not been found in the past, its absence being the result of endogenous economic factors that limit the swings. Hicks has, however, built a model of the trade cycle assuming values that would make for explosive cycles kept in check by ceilings and floors.

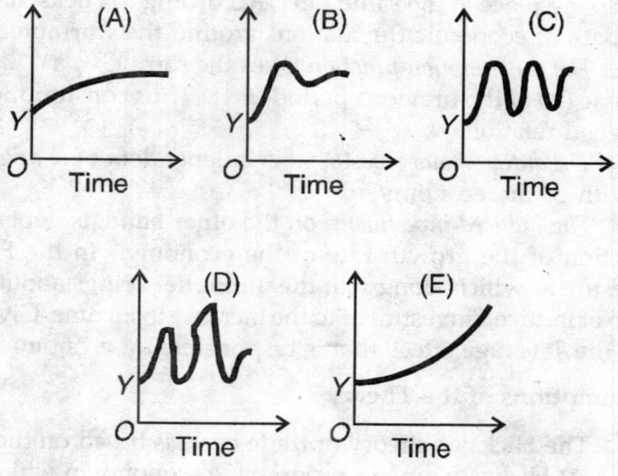

Fig. 4

Critical Appraisal of the Model

The interaction of the multiplier and the accelerator has the merit of raising national income at a much faster rate than by either the multiplier or the accelerator alone. It serves as a useful tool not only for explaining business cycles but also as a guide to stabilisation policy. As pointed out by Prof. Kurihara, "It is in conjunction with the multiplier analysis based on the concept of marginal propensity to consume (being less than one) that the acceleration principle serves as a useful tool of business cycle analysis and a helpful guide to business cycle policy." The multiplier and the accelerator combined together produce cyclical fluctuations. The greater the value of the accelerator (b), the greater is the chance of an explosive cycle. The greater the value of the multiplier, the greater the chance of a cycleless path.

Limitations

Despite these apparent uses of the multiplier-accelerator interaction, this analysis has its limitations:

(1) Samuelson is silent about the length of the period in the different cycles explained by him.

(2) This model assumes that the marginal propensity to consume (a) and the accelerator (b) are constants, but in reality they change with the level of income so that this is applicable only to the study of small fluctuations.

(3) The cycles explained in this model oscillate about a stationary level in a trendless economy. This is not realistic because an economy is not trendless but it is in a process of growth. This has led Hicks to formulate his theory of the trade cycle in a growing economy.

(4) According to Duesenberry, it presents a mechanical explanation of the trade cycle because it is based on the multiplier-accelerator interaction in rigid form.

(5) It ignores the effects of monetary changes upon business cycles.

7. Hicks's Theory of Business Cycle

J.R. Hicks in his book *A Contribution to the Theory of the Trade Cycle* builds his theory of business cycle around the principle of the multiplier-accelerator interaction. To him, "the theory of the acceleration and the theory of the multiplier are the two sides of the theory of fluctuations." Unlike Samuelson's model, it is concerned with the problem of *growth* and of a moving equilibrium.

Ingredients of the Theory

The ingredients of Hicks's theory of trade cycle are warranted rate of growth, consumption function, autonomous investment, an induced investment function, and multiplier-accelerator relation.

The warranted rate of growth is the rate which will sustain itself. It is consistent with saving-investment equilibrium. The economy is said to be growing at the warranted rate when real investment and real saving are taking place at the same rate. According to Hicks, it is the multiplier-accelerator interaction which weaves the path of economic fluctuations around the warranted growth rate.

The consumption function takes the form $C_t = aY_{t-1}$. Consumption in period *t* is regarded as a function of income (Y) of the previous period (*t*–1). Thus consumption lags behind income, and the multiplier is treated as a lagged relation.

The autonomous investment is independent of changes in the level of output. Hence it is not related to the growth of the economy.

The induced investment, on the other hand, is dependent on changes in the level of output. Hence it is a function of the growth rate of the economy. In the Hicksian theory, the accelerator is based on induced investment which alongwith the multiplier brings about an *upturn*. The accelerator is defined by Hicks as the ratio of induced investment to the increase in income. Given *constant* values of the multiplier and the accelerator, it is the 'leverage effect' that is responsible for economic fluctuations.

Assumptions of the Theory

The Hicksian theory of trade cycle is based on the following assumptions:

(1) Hicks assumes a progressive economy in which autonomous investment increases at a constant rate so that the system remains in a moving equilibrium.

(2) The saving and investment coefficients are disturbed overtime in such a way that an upward displacement from equilibrium path leads to a lagged movement away from equilibrium.

(3) Hicks assumes *constant* values for the multiplier and the accelerator.

(4) The economy cannot expand beyond the full employment level of output. Thus "the full employment ceiling" acts as a direct restraint on the upward expansion of the economy.

(5) The working of the accelerator in the downswing provides an *indirect* restraint on the downward movement of the economy. The rate of decrease in the accelerator is limited by the rate of depreciation in the downswing.

(6) The relation between the multiplier and accelerator is treated in a lagged manner, since consumption and induced investment are assumed to operate with a time lag.

(7) It is assumed that the average capital-output ratio (v) is greater than unity and that gross investment does not fall below zero. Thus the cycles are inherently explosive but are contained by ceilings and floors of the economy.

The Hicksian Theory

Hicks explains his theory of the trade cycle in terms of Fig. 5. Line *AA* shows the path of *autonomous* investment growing at a constant rate. *EE* is the equilibrium level of output which depends on *AA* and is deduced from it by the application of the multiplier accelerator interaction to it. Line *FF* is the full employment ceiling level above the equilibrium path *EE* and is growing at the constant rate of autonomous investment. *LL* is the lower equilibrium path of output representing the floor or 'slump equilibrium line'.

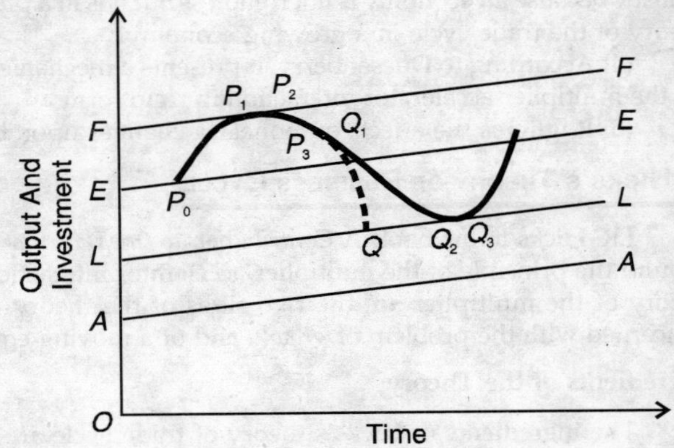

Fig. 5

Hicks begins from a cycleless situation P_o on the equilibrium path *EE* when an increase in the rate of autonomous investment leads to an upward movement in income. As a result, the growth of output and income propelled by the combined operation of the multiplier and accelerator moves the economy on to the upward expansion path from P_o to P_1. According to Hicks, this *upswing* phase relates to the *standard* cycle which will lead to an *explosive* situation because of the given values of the multiplier and the accelerator. But this does not happen because of the upper limit or ceiling set by the full employment level *FF*. Hicks writes in this connection: "I shall follow Keynes in assuming that there is some point at which output becomes inelastic in response to an increase in effective demand." Thus certain bottlenecks of supply emerge which prevent output from reaching the peak and instead encounter the ceiling at P_1.

When the economy hits the full employment ceiling at P_1, it will creep along the ceiling for a period of time to P_2 and the downward swing will not start immediately. The economy will move along the ceiling from P_1 to P_2 depending upon the time period of the investment lag. The greater the investment lag, the more the economy will move along the ceiling path. Since income at this level is decreasing relative to the previous stage of the cycle, there is a decreased amount of investment. This much of investment is insufficient to keep the economy at the ceiling level, and then the downturn starts.

During the *downswing*, "the multiplier-accelerator mechanism sets in reverse, falling investment reducing income, reduced income reducing investment, and so on, progressively. If the accelerator worked continuously, output would plunge downward below the equilibrium level *EE*, and because of explosive tendencies, to a greater extent than it rose above it." The fall in output in this case might be a steep one, as shown by $P_2 P_3 Q$. But in the downswing, the accelerator does not work so swiftly as in the upswing. If the slump is severe, induced investment will quickly fall to zero and the value of the accelerator becomes zero. The rate of decrease in investment is limited by the rate of depreciation. Thus the total amount of investment in the economy is equal to autonomous investment *minus* the constant rate of depreciation. Since autonomous investment is taking place, the fall in output is much gradual and the slump much longer than the boom, as indicated by Q_1Q_2. At Q_2, the slump reaches the bottom or floor provided by the *LL* line. The economy does not turn upward immediately from Q_2 but will move along the slump equilibrium line to Q_3 because of the existence of excess capacity in the economy. Finally, when all excess capacity is exhausted, autonomous investment will cause income to rise which will in turn lead to an increase in induced investment so that the accelerator is triggered off which alongwith the multiplier moves the economy toward the ceiling again. It is in this way that the cyclical process will be repeated in the economy.

Its Criticisms

The Hicksian theory of the business cycle has been severely criticised by Duesenberry, Smithies and others on the following grounds:

1. *Value of Multiplier not Constant.* Hicks's model assumes that the value of the multiplier remains constant during the different phases of the trade cycle. This is based on the Keynesian stable consumption function. But this is not a realistic assumption, as Friedman has proved on the basis of empirical evidence that the marginal propensity to consume does not remain stable in relation to cyclical changes in income. Thus the value of the multiplier changes with different phases of the cycle.

2. *Value of Accelerator not Constant.* Hicks has also been criticised for assuming a constant value of the accelerator during the different phases of the cycle. The constancy of the accelerator presupposes a constant capital-output ratio. These are unrealistic assumptions because the capital-output ratio is itself subject to change due to technological factors, the nature and composition of investment, the gestation period of capital goods, etc. Lundberg, therefore, suggests that the assumption of constancy in accelerator should be abandoned for a realistic approach to the understanding of trade cycles.[13]

3. *Autonomous Investment not Continuous.* Hicks assumes that autonomous investment continues throughout the different phases of the cycle at a steady pace. This is unrealistic because financial crisis in a slump may reduce autonomous investment below its normal level. Further, it is also possible, as pointed out by Schumpeter, that autonomous investment may itself be subject to fluctuations due to a technological innovation.

4. *Growth not Dependent only on changes in Autonomous Investment.* Another weakness of the Hicksian model is that growth is made dependent upon changes in autonomous investment. It is a burst of autonomous investment from the equilibrium path that leads to growth. According to Prof. Smithies,[14] the source of

13. E. Lunberg, "*The Stability Growth*," *J.E.P.*, No. 8, 1958.
14. A Smithies, "Economic Fluctuations and Growth" *Econometrica*, Jan. 1957.

growth should lie within the system. In imputing growth to an unexplained extraneous factor, Hicks has failed to provide a complete explanation of the cycle.

5. *Distinction Between Autonomous and Induced Investment not Feasible.* Critics like Duesenberry[15] and Lundberg point out that Hicks's distinction between autonomous and induced investment is not feasible in practice. As pointed out by Lundberg, every investment is autonomous in the short run and a major amount of autonomous investment becomes induced in the long run. It is also possible that part of a particular investment may be autonomous and a part induced, as in the case of machinery. Hence this distinction between autonomous and induced investment is of doubtful validity in practice.

6. *Ceiling Fails to Explain adequately the onset of Depression.* Hicks has been criticised for his explanation of the ceiling or the upper limit of the cycle. According to Duesenberry, the ceilling fails to explain adequately the onset of depression. It may at best check growth and not cause a depression. Shortage of resources cannot bring a sudden decline in investment and thus cause a depression. The recession of 1953-54 in America was not caused by shortage of resources. Further, as admitted by Hicks himself, depression may start even before reaching the full employment ceiling due to monetary factors.

7. *Explanation of Floor and Lower Turning Point not Convincing.* Hicks's explanation of the floor and of the lower turning point is not convincing. According to Hicks, it is autonomous investment that brings a gradual movement towards the floor and it is again increase in autonomous investment at the bottom that leads to the lower turning point. Harrod doubts the contention that autonomous investment would be increasing at the bottom of the depression. Depression may retard rather than encourage autonomous investment. Further, Hicks's contention that revival would start with the exhaustion of excess capacity has not been proved by empirical evidence. Rendings Fels's study of the American business cycles in the 19th century has revealed that the revival was not due to the exhaustion of excess capacity. Rather in certain cases, revival started even when there was excess capacity.[16]

8. *Full Employment level not Independent of Output Path.* Another criticism levelled against Hicks's model is that the full employment ceiling. As defined by Hicks, it is independent of the path of output. According to Dernburg and McDougall, the full employment level depends on the magnitude of the resources that are available to the country. The capital stock is one of the resources. When the capital stock is increasing during any period, the ceiling is raised. "Since the rate at which output increases determines the rate at which capital stock changes, the ceiling level of output will differ depending on the time path of output. One cannot therefore separate the long-run full employment trend from what happens during a cycle."[17]

9. *Explosive Cycle not Realistic.* Hicks assumes in his model that the average capital-output ratio (v) is greater than unity for a time lag of one year or less. Thus explosive cycles are inherent in his model. But empirical evidence shows that the response of investment to a change in output (v) is spread over many periods. As a result, there have been damped cycles rather than explosive cycles.

10. *Mechanical Explanation of Trade Cycle.* Another serious limitation of the theory is that it presents a mechanical explanation of the trade cycle. This is because the theory is based on the multiplier-accelerator interaction in rigid form, according to Kaldor and Duesenberry. Thus it is a mechanical sort of explanation in which human judgement, business expectations and decisions play little or no part. Investment plays a leading role based on formula rather than on judgement.

11. *Contraction Phase not Longer than Expansion Phase.* Hicks has been criticised for asserting that the contraction phase is longer than expansion phase of trade cycle. But the actual behaviour of the postwar cycles has shown that the expansionary phase of the business cycle is much longer than the contractionary phase.

Conclusion. Despite these apparent weaknesses of the Hicksian model, it is superior to all the earlier theories in satisfactorily explaining the turning points of the business cycle. To conclude with Dernburg and McDougall, "The Hicks's model serves as a useful framework of analysis which, with modification, yields a fairly good picture of cyclical fluctuation within a framework of growth. It serves especially to emphasise that

15. J.B. Duesenberry, *Business Cycles and Economic Growth*, 1958.
16. QDuoted in E. Lundbert, *op. cit.*
17. T.F. Demburg and D.M. McDougall, *op. cit.*, p. 323.

in a capitalist economy characterised by substantial amounts of durable equipment, a period of contraction inevitably follows expansion. Hicks's model also pinpoints the fact that in the absence of technical progress and other powerful growth factors, the economy will tend to languish in depression for long periods of time."[18] The model is at best suggestive.

8. Kaldor's Model of the Trade Cycle

Nicholas Kaldor[19] built a model of the trade cycle based on the Keynesian terminology of saving and investment. He showed that the cycle is the result of pressures that push the economy toward the equality of ex-ante (anticipated, expected or planned) saving and investment. In fact, it is the difference between ex-ante saving and investment that leads to a cycle.

Kaldor shows the stability and instability conditions in the form of linear diagrams, though the cycle is only possible when I and S are non-linear. Take Figure 6 (A) and (B) where I and S are equal at the equilibrium level of income Y_0. But in each case there is a single equilibrium position. In Panel (A) of the figure where $I>S$ there is an unstable equilibrium position beyond Y_0 because such a situation will lead to limitless expansion, to full employment and hyper-inflation. On the other hand, if $S>I$, it means a downward movement to the left of Y_0 which will lead to zero output and employment and to collapse of the economy as shown in Panel (B) of the figure. Kaldor discards linear saving and investment functions because they fail to produce a cycle. Instead, be adopts non-linear saving and investment functions.

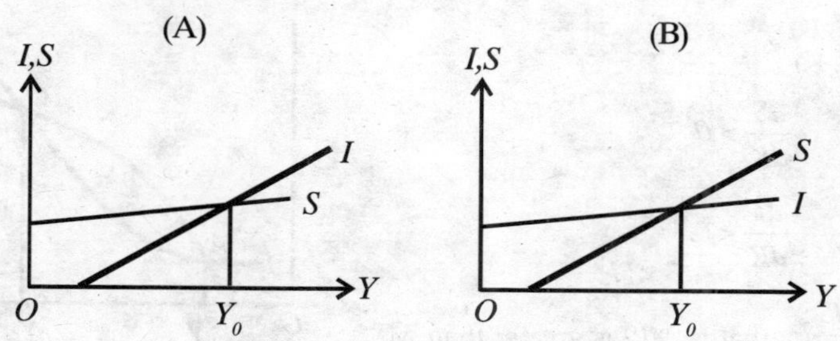

Fig. 6 (A) and (B)

A non-linear investment function I is shown in Figure 7. As the economy moves into the expansion phase, shown by the movement from the left along the I curve, the curve is almost flat. It means that there is excess capacity at a low level of income and the net investment is zero. But "when expansion gets under way, the negative effect of accumulated capital is a more powerful influence for investment decisions than the higher levels of output and profit. In the opposite case of a high level of income when the economy moves into the contraction phase, the I curve is again flat and the net investment is small "because rising costs of construction, increasing costs and increasing difficulty of borrowing will dissuade entrepreneurs from expanding still faster." This slows down the rate of increase in output. It means that the existing capital stock and the capacity are more than the current output. This leads to decline in further investment. Thus income falls and the cumulative effect is that the economy moves

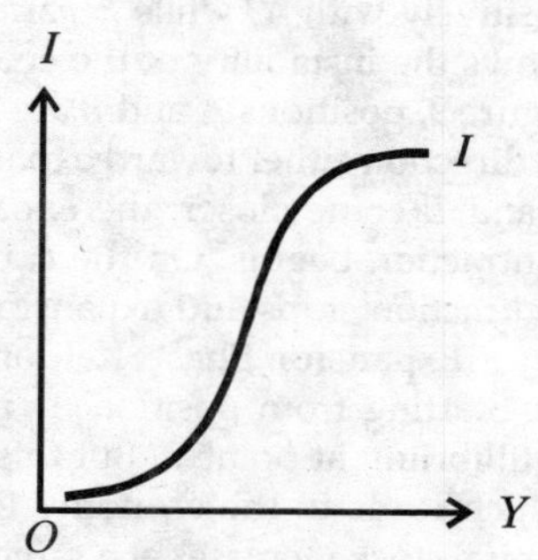

Fig. 7

18. *Ibid.*, p. 322.
19. "A Model of the Trade Cycle", *E.J.*, March, 1940.

into the contraction phase.

Similarly, a non-linear saving function is shown in Figure 8. At very low levels of income, saving is much reduced and may even be negative. So during the expansion phase, the *MPS* is large. At normal levels of income, saving will increase at a smaller rate. This is shown by the middle range of the *S* curve. But at very high income levels, saving will be absolutely large and people will save a large proportion of their income.

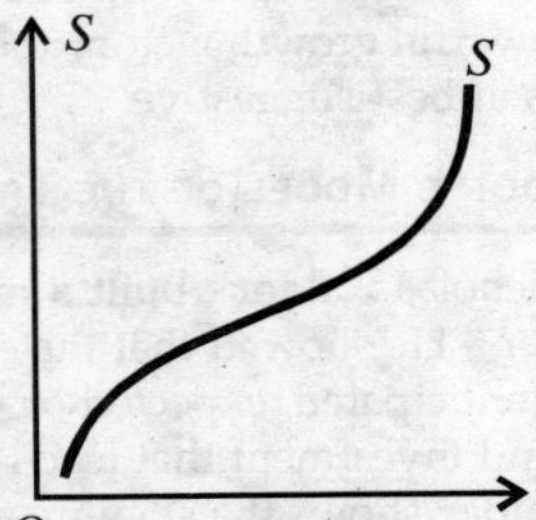

Fig. 8

The cycle is visible when the non-linear saving and investment curves are brought together, as in Figure 14. The figure shows multiple equilibria at positions *A*, *B* and *C*. Of these, *A* and *B* are stable positions and *C* an unstable position. Between positions *C* and *B* and below position *A*, *I* is greater than *S*. This will lead to the rise in income level. Between positions *A* and *C* and above *B* position, *S* is greater than *I*. This will lead to the fall in income.

But *A* and *B* are stable positions only in the short run. It is only in the long run that they become unstable and the path of the cycle is visible. For this, Kaldor introduces the capital stock as another variable that affects the relationship between saving and investment. He takes both saving and investment as functions of income and capital stock so that

$$S = f(Y, K)$$
$$I = f(Y, K)$$

and $\frac{dS}{dY} > 0$, $\frac{dS}{dK} > 0$

$\frac{dI}{dY} > 0$, $\frac{dI}{dK} < 0$

and $\frac{dI}{dY} > \frac{dS}{dY}$, that is *MPI* is greater than *MPS*

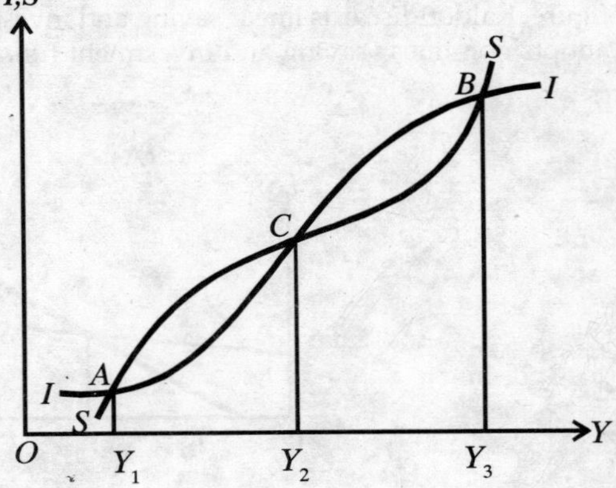

Fig. 9

over the expansion or contraction phase of the cycle.

The above relationships show that both *S* and *I* vary positively with *Y*; while *S* varies directly with *K*, and *I* varies inversely with *K*. The relationship *MPI* > *MPS* shows the instability of the economy which will move it either toward expansion or contraction. In terms of Figure 9, positions *A* and *B* are *"switch points"* in the long run. They are the points at which the economy alters its direction either toward expansion or contraction. Point C is unstable in both directions. It is only when points C and B come closer, the expansion phase of the cycle starts. When they are joined, expansion stops and contraction begins. On the contrary, when *C* and *A* come closer contraction starts. When they are joined, contraction stops and expansion begins.

Expansion Phase. Kaldor shows the expansion phase of his trade cycle in three stages, as shown in Figure 10. Starting from position Y_0 in figure stage 1 (which is the same as Figure 8), suppose the economy is in equilibrium at point C. But this is the point of unstable equilibrium. An upward displacement shows that *I*>*S* which leads to the economy towards the expansion path. As the rate of invesment is high, the economy's capital stock increases at a rapid rate. But as the capital stock increases, the MEC declines and investment curve shifts downward At the same time as the economy's capital stock increases, it raises the income of the economy thereby raising its saving. Thus the saving curve shifts upward. So a downward shift of the investment curve *I* and upward shift of the saving curve *S* bring the point *C* nearer to *B*, as shown in figure stage 2. This process of the downward shifting of the *I* curve and upward shifting of the *S* curve continues till the two curves are tangential and points C and *B* coincide, as shown in figure stage 3. But at this position *S*>*I* in both directions. So this is an unstable equilibrium position in the downward direction. This leads to the downward movement of

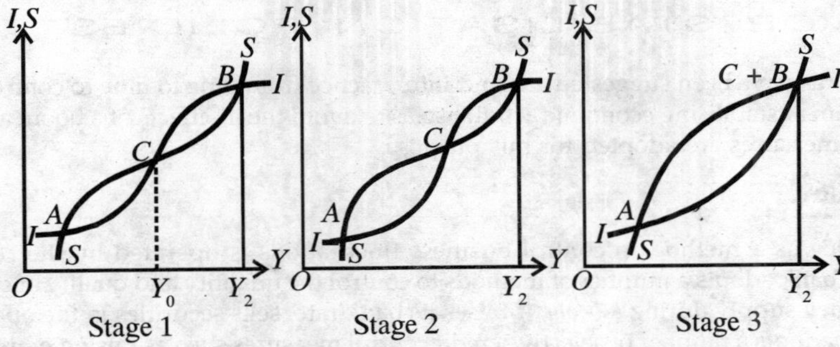

Fig. 10

the economy till point *A* is reached in stage 3.

Contraction Phase. The contraction of the trade cycle is also shown in three stages, as in Figure 16. We start from position Y_1 corresponding to point *A* in stage 4 of the figure. It is the point of short-run stable equilibrium but at a very low income level. But over the long run at such a low level of income, the capital stock decreases due to excess capacity and the investment curve *I* shifts upward. Simultaneously, saving falls which shifts the saving curve downward. Thus the shifting of the *I* curve upward and of the *S* curve downward bring positions *A* and *C* nearer, as shown in stage 5. This process will continue gradually till *I* and *S* curves arc tangential and positions *A* and *C* coincide, as in stage *6* figure. But this *A+C* position at Y_1 income level is unstable in the upward direction because $I>S$. This will lead to an expansionary process till the economy reaches the higher level of income Y_2 at point *B*. From *B*, the *I* and *S* curves gradually reach the positions shown in stage 1 of Figure 11, and again the cyclical process starts. Thus Kaldor's cyclical process is self-generating.

According to Kaldor, the forces which bring about the lower turning point are not so certain at the higher level. "A boom left to itself, is certain to come to an end; but the depression might get into a position of stationariness, and remain there until external changes (the discovery of new inventions or of the opening up of new markets) come to the rescue."

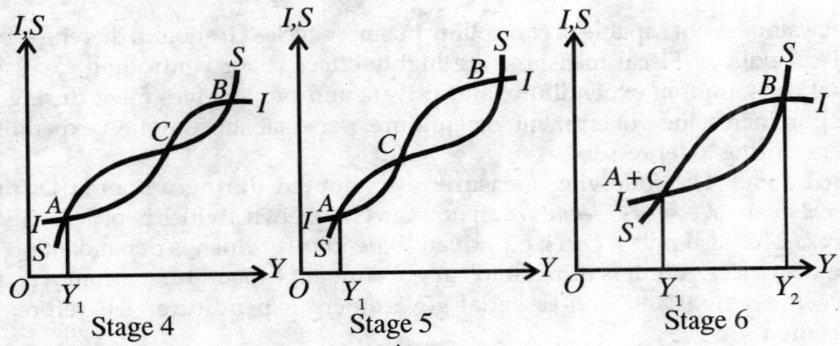

Fig. 11

Further, cycles in the Kaldor model are not necessarily of the same length and duration. Neither are expansions and contractions necessarily symmetrical. In fact, these depend upon the slopes of the *I* and *S* curves and the rate at which they shift in each phase of the cycle.

Kaldor neither uses the acceleration principle nor the monetary factors in explaining his theory of the trade cycle. At the same time, he demonstrates how a cycle could exist in the absence of any growth factor.

7. MEASURES TO CONTROL BUSINESS CYCLES OR STABILISATION POLICIES

Various measures have been suggested and put into practice from time to time to control fluctuations in an economy. They aim at stabilising economic activity so as to avoid the ill-effects of a boom and a depression. The following three measures are adopted for this purpose.

1. Monetary Policy

Monetary policy as a method to control business fluctuations is operated by the central bank of a country. The central bank adopts a number of methods to control the quantity and quality of credit. To control the expansion of money supply during a *boom,* it raises its bank rate, sells securities in the open market, raises the reserve ratio, and adopts a number of selective credit control measures such as raising margin requirements and regulating consumer credit. Thus the central bank adopts a *dear money policy*. Borrowings by business and trade become dearer, difficult and selective. Efforts are made to control excess money supply in the economy.

To control a *recession or depression*, the central bank follows an *easy* or *cheap* monetary policy by increasing the reserves of commercial banks. It reduces the bank rate and interest rates of banks. It buys securities in the open market. It lowers margin requirements on loans and encourages banks to lend more to consumers, businessmen, traders, etc.

Limitations of Monetary Policy

But monetary policy is not so effective as to control a boom and a depression. If the boom is due to cost-push factors, it may not be effective in controlling inflation, aggregate demand, output, income and employment. So far as depression is concerned, the experience of the Great Depression of 1930s tells us that when there is pessimism among businessmen, the success of monetary policy is practically nil. In such a situation, they do not have any inclination to borrow even when the interest rate is very low. Similarly, consumers who are faced with reduced incomes and unemployment cut down their consumption expenditure. Neither the central bank nor the commercial banks are able to induce businessmen and consumers to raise the aggregate demand. Thus the success of monetary policy to control economic fluctuations is severely limited.

2. Fiscal Policy

Monetary policy alone is not capable of controlling business cycles. It should, therefore, be supplemented by compensatory fiscal policy. Fiscal measures are highly effective for controlling excessive government expenditure, personal consumption expenditure, and private and public investment during a boom. On the other hand, they help in increasing government expenditure, personal consumption expenditure and private and public investment during a depression.

Policy during Boom. The following measures are adopted during a boom. During a boom, the government tries to *reduce unnecessary expenditure* on non-development activities in order to reduce its demand for goods and services. This also puts a check on private expenditure which is dependent on the government demand for goods and services. But it is difficult to cut government expenditure. Moreover, it is not possible to distinguish between essential and non-essential government expenditure. Therefore, this measure is supplemented by taxation.

To cut personal expenditure, the government *raises* the *rates* of personal, corporate and commodity taxes.

The government also follows the policy of having a *surplus budget* when the government revenues exceed expenditures. This is done by increasing the tax rates or reduction in government expenditure or both. This tends to reduce income and aggregate demand through the reverse operation of the multiplier.

Another fiscal measure which is usually adopted is to *borrow* more from the public which has the effect of reducing the money supply with the public. Further, the repayment of public debt should be stopped and postponed to some future date when the economy stabilises.

Policy during Depression. During a depression, the government increases public expenditure, reduces taxes and adopts a budget deficit policy. These measures tend to raise aggregate demand, output, income, employment and prices. An increase in public expenditure increases the aggregate demand for goods and services and leads to increase in income via the multiplier. The public expenditure is made on such public works as roads, canals, dams, parks, schools, hospitals and other construction works. They create demand for labour and the products of private construction industries and helps in reviving them. The government also increases its expenditure on such relief measures as unemployment insurance, and other social security measures in order to stimulate the demand for consumer goods industries. Borrowing by the government to finance budget deficits utilises idle money lying with the banks and financial institutions for investment purposes.

Conclusion. The effectiveness of anti-cyclical fiscal policy depends upon proper timing of policy action and the nature and volume of public works and their planning.

3. Direct Controls

The aim of direct controls is to ensure proper allocation of resources for the purpose of price stability. They are meant to affect strategic points of the economy. They affect particular consumers and producers. They are in the form of rationing, licensing, price and wage controls, export duties, exchange controls, quotas, monopoly control, etc. They are more effective in overcoming bottlenecks and shortages arising from inflationary pressures. Their success depends on the existence of an efficient and honest administration. Otherwise, they lead to black marketing, corruption, long queues, speculation, etc. Therefore, they should be resorted to only in emergencies like war, crop failures and hyper-inflation.

Conclusions

Of the various instruments of stabilisation policy, no single method is sufficient to control cyclical fluctuations. Therefore, all methods should be used simultaneously. This is because monetary policy is easy to apply but less effective while fiscal measures and direct controls are difficult to operate but are more effective. Since cyclical fluctuations are inherent in the capitalist system, they cannot be eliminated completely. Some fluctuations may be beneficial for economic growth and others may be undesirable. Stabilisation policy should, therefore, control undesirable fluctuations. We conclude with Keynes, "The right remedy for the trade cycles is not to be found in abolishing booms and thus keeping us permanently in a semi-slump; but in abolishing slumps and thus keeping us permanently in a quasi-boom."

EXERCISES

1. What do you mean by a business cycle ? Explain its various phases.
2. What is a business cycle? Explain the main causes and effects of business cycles.
3. "The trade cycle is a purely monetary phenomenon." Discuss.
4. Now monetary changes affect business cylces? Explain with references to empricial evidence provided by Friedman.
5. Discuss critically Samuelson's model of trade cycles.
6. Critically discuss the Hicksian theory of the trade cycle.
7. Explain Kaldor's model of the trade cycle.

CHAPTER 46

Balance of Payments : Meaning and Components

1. MEANING

The balance of payments of a country is a systematic record of all its economic transactions with the outside world in a given year. It is a statistical record of the character and dimensions of the country's economic relationships with the rest of the world. According to Bo Sodersten, "The balance of payments is merely a way of listing receipts and payments in international transactions for a country."[1] B. J. Cohen says, "It shows the country's trading position, changes in its net position as foreign lender or borrower, and changes in its official reserve holding."[2]

2. STRUCTURE OF BALANCE OF PAYMENTS ACCOUNTS

The balance of payments account of a country is constructed on the principle of double-entry book-keeping. Each transaction is entered on the credit and debit side of the balance sheet. But balance of payments accounting differs from business accounting in one respect. In business accounting, debits (–) are shown on the left side and credits (+) on the right side of the balance sheet. But in balance of payments accounting, the practice is to show credits on the left side and debits on the right side of the balance sheet.

When a payment is received from a foreign country, it is a credit transaction while payment to a foreign country is a debit transaction. The principal items shown on the credit side (+) are exports of goods and services, unrequited (or transfer) receipts in the form of gifts, grants, etc. from foreigners, borrowings from abroad, investments by foreigners in the country, and official *sale* of reserve assets including gold to foreign countries and international agencies. The principal items on the *Debit* side (–) include imports of goods and services, transfer (or unrequited) payments to foreigners as gifts, grants, etc., lending to foreign countries, investments by residents to foreign countries, and official *purchase* of reserve assets or gold from foreign countries and international agencies.

These credit and debit items are shown vertically in the balance of payments account of a country

1. Bo Sodersen, *International Economics*, 2/e, 1980.
2. B.J. Cohen, *Balance of Payment Policy*, 1969.

according to the principle of double-entry book-keeping. Horizontally, they are divided into three categories : the current account, the capital account, and the official settlements account or the official reserve assets account.

The balance of payments account of a country is constructed in Table 1.

Table 1. Balance of Payments Account

Credits (+) (*Receipts*)	*Debits* (–) (*Payments*)
1. Current Account	
Exports	Imports
(*a*) Goods	(*a*) Goods
(*b*) Services	(*b*) Services
(*c*) Transfer Payments	(*c*) Transfer Payments
2. Capital Account	
(*a*) Borrowings from Foreign Countries	(*a*) Lending to Foreign Countries
(*b*) Direct Investments by Foreign Countries	(*b*) Direct Investments in Foreign Countries
3. Official Settlements Account	
(*a*) Increase in Foreign Official Holdings	(*a*) Increase in Official Reserve of Gold and Foreign Currencies
Errors and Omissions	

1. Current Account. The current account of a country consists of all transactions relating to trade in goods and services and unilateral (or unrequited) transfers. Service transactions include costs of travel and transportation, insurance, income and payments of foreign investments, etc. Transfer payments relate to gifts, foreign aid, pensions, private remittances, charitable donations etc. received from foreign individuals and governments to foreigners.

In the current account, merchandise exports and imports are the most important items. Exports are shown as a positive item and are calculated f.o.b. (free on board) which means that costs of transportation, insurance, etc. are excluded. On the other side, imports are shown as a negative item and are calculated c.i.f. which means that costs, insurance and freight are included. The difference between exports and imports of a country is its *balance of visible trade* or merchandise trade or simply *balance of trade*. If visible exports exceed visible imports, the balance of trade is favourable. In the opposite case when imports exceed exports, it is unfavourable.

It is, however, services and transfer payments or invisible items of the current account that reflect the true picture of the balance of payments account. The balance of exports and imports of services and transfer payments is called the *balance of invisible trade*. The invisible items alongwith the visible items determine the actual current account position. If exports of goods and services exceed imports of goods and services, the balance of payments is said to be *favourable*. In the opposite case, it is unfavourable.

In the current account, the exports of goods and services and the receipts of transfer payments (unrequited receipts) are entered as credits (+) because they represent receipts from foreigners. On the other hand, the imports of goods and services and grant of transfer payments to foreigners are entered as debits (–) because they represent payments to foreigners. The net value of these visible and invisible trade balances is the balance on current account.

2. Capital Account. The capital account of a country consists of its transactions in financial assets in the form of short-term and long-term lendings and borrowings, and private and official investments. In other words, the capital account shows international flow of loans and investments, and represents a change in the country's foreign assets and liabilities. Long-term capital transactions relate to international capital movements with maturity of one year or more and include direct investments like building of a foreign plant, portfolio investment like the purchase of foreign bonds and stocks, and international loans. On the other hand, short-term international capital transactions are for a period ranging between three months and less than one year.

There are two types of transactions in the capital account—private and government. Private transactions include all types of investment : direct, portfolio and short-term. Government transactions consist of loans to and from foreign official agencies.

In the capital account, borrowings from foreign countries and direct investment by foreign countries represent capital inflows. They are positive items or credits because these are receipts from foreigners. On the other hand, lending to foreign countries and direct investments in foreign countries represent capital outflows. They are negative items or debits because they are payments to foreigners. The net value of the balances of short-term and long-term direct and portfolio investments is the *balance on capital account.*

Sodersten and Reed refer to the *external wealth account* of a country which shows the stocks of foreign assets held by the country (positive item) and of domestic assets held by foreign investors (liabilities or negative item). The net value of a country's assets and liabilities is its balance of indebtedness. If its assets are more than its liabilities, then it is a *net creditor.* If its liabilities are more than its assets, then it is a net debtor.[3]

Basic Balance. The sum of current account and capital account is known as the basic balance.

3. The Official Settlements Account. The official settlements account or official reserve assets account is, in fact, a part of the capital account. But the U.K. and U.S. balance of payments accounts show it as a separate account. "The official settlements account measures the change in nation's liquidity and non-liquid liabilities to foreign official holders and the change in a nation's official reserve assets during the year. The official reserve assets of a country include its gold stock, holdings of its convertible foreign currencies and SDRs, and its net position in the IMF." It shows transactions in a country's net official reserve assets.

Errors and Omissions. Errors and ommissions is a balancing item so that total credits and debits of the three accounts must equal in accordance with the principles of double entry book-keeping so that the balance of payments of a country always balances in the accounting sense.

3. IS BALANCE OF PAYMENTS ALWAYS IN EQUILIBRIUM ?

Balance of payments always balances means that the algebraic sum of the net credit and debit balances of current account, capital account and official settlements account must equal zero. Balance of payments is written as

$$B = R_f - P_f$$

where, B represents balance of payments,

R_f receipts from foreigners,

P_f payments made to foreigners.

When $B = R_f - P_f = 0$, the balance of payments is in equilibrium.

When $R_f - P_f > 0$, it implies receipts from foreigners exceed payments made to foreigners and there is *surplus* in the balance of payments. On the other hand, when $R_f - P_f < 0$ or $R_f < P_f$ there is *deficit* in the balance of payments as the payments made to foreigners exceed receipts from foreigners.

If net foreign lending and investment abroad are taken, a flexible exchange rate creates an excess of exports over imports. The domestic currency depreciates in terms of other currencies. The exports become cheaper relatively to imports. It can be shown in equation form :

$$X + B = M + I_f$$

Where X represents exports, M imports, I_f foreign investment, B foreign borrowing

or $$X - M = I_f - B$$

or $$(X - M) - (I_f - B) = 0$$

The equation shows the balance of payments in equilibrium. Any positive balance in its current account

---

3. *Bo Sodersten and Geoffery Reed, Internationael Economics,* 3/e, 1994.

is exactly offset by negative balance on its capital account and vice versa. In the accounting sense, the balance of payments always balances. This can be shown with the help of the following equation :

$$C + S + T = C + I + G + (X - M)$$

or

$$Y = C + I + G + (X - M) \qquad [Y = C + S + T]$$

where *C* represents consumption exepnditure, *S* domestic saving, *T* tax receipts, *I* investment expenditures, *G* government expenditures, *X* exports of goods and services, and *M* imports of goods and services.

In the above equation

$C + S + T$ is *GNI* or national income (*Y*), and

$C + I + G = A$,

where *A* is called 'absorption'.

In the accounting sense, total domestic expenditures $(C + I + G)$ must equal current income $(C + S + T)$ that is $A = Y$. Moreover, domestic saving (S_d) must equal domestic investment (I_d). Similarly, an export surplus on current account $(X > M)$ must be offset by an excess of domestic savings over investment $(S_d > I_d)$. Thus the balance of payments always balances in the accounting sense, according to the basic principle of accounting. In the accounting system, the inflow and outflow of a transaction are recorded on the credit and debit sides respectively. Therefore, credit and debit sides always balance. If there is a deficit in the current account, it is offset by a matching surplus in the capital account by borrowings from abroad or/and withdrawing out of its gold and foreign exchange reserves, and vice versa. Thus, the balance of payments always balances in this sense also.

4. MEASURING DEFICIT OR SURPLUS IN BALANCE OF PAYMENTS

If the balance of payments always balances, then why does a deficit or surplus arise in the balance of payment of a country? It is only when all items in the balance of payments are included that there is no possibility of a deficit or surplus. But if some items are excluded from a country's balance of payments and then a balance is struck, it may show a deficit or surplus.

There are three ways of measuring deficit or surplus in the balance of payments.

First, there is the *basic balance* which includes the current account balance and the long-term capital account balance.

Second, there is the *net liquidity balance* which includes the basic balance and the short-term private non-liquid capital balance, allocation of SDRs, and errors and ommissions.

Third, there is the *official settlements balance* which includes the total net liquid balance and short-term private liquid capital balance.

If the total debits are more than total credits in the current and capital accounts, including errors and omissions, the net *debit balance* measures the *deficit* in the balance of payments of a country. This deficit can be settled with an equal amount of *net credit balance* in the official settlements account. On the contrary, if total credits are more than total debits in the current and capital accounts, including errors and omissions, the *net debit* balance measures the *surplus* in the balance of payments of a country. This surplus can be settled with an equal amount of *net debit* balance in the official settlements account.

The relationship between these balances is summarised in Table 2 below.

Table 2

Trade balance	*a*	
Transfer payments balance	*b*	Autonomous
Current Account Balance	*c* (= *a* + *b*)	Items
Long-term capital balance	*d*	
Basic Balance	*e* (= *c* + *d*)	
Short-term private non-liquid capital balance	*f*	

Allocation of SDRs	g	Accommodating
Errors and omissions	h	Items
Net Liquidity Balance	$i\ (= e + f + g + h)$	
Short-term private liquid capital balance	j	
Official Settlements Balance	$k\ (= i + j)$	

AUTONOMOUS AND ACCOMMODATING ITEMS

Each balance would give different figure of the deficit. The items that are included in a particular balance are placed 'above the line' and those excluded are put 'below the line'. Items that are put above the line are called *autonomous items*. Items that are placed below the line are called *settlement or accommodating or compensatory* or *induced items*. All transactions in the current and capital accounts are autonomous items because they are underaken for business or profit motives and are independent of balance of payments considerations. According to Sodersten and Reed, "Transactions are said to be autonomous if their value is determined independently of the balance of payments". Whether there is *BOP* deficit or surplus depends on the balance of autonomous items. If autonomous receipts are less than autonomous payments, *BOP* is in deficit and vice versa.

"Accommodating items on the other hand are determined by the net consequences of the autonomous items", according to Sodersten and Reed. They are in the official reserve account. They are compensating (induced or accommodating) short-term capital transactions which are meant to correct a disequilibrium in the autonomous items of balance of payments.

But it is difficult to determine which item is compensatory and which is autonomous. For instance, in the table given above, the main difference in the three balances is their treatment of short-term capital movements which are responsible for deficit in the balance of payments. The basic balance places short-term private non-liquid capital movements below the line while the net liquid balance puts them above the line. Similarly, the net liquid balance places short-term private liquid capital movements below the line and the official settlements balance puts them above the line. Thus, as pointed out by Sodersten and Reed, "Essentially the distinction between autonomous and accommodating items lies in the motives underlying a transaction, which are almost impossible to determine"[4].

Conclusion. The above analysis is based on the assumption of fixed exchange rates. Thus a deficit (or surplus in the balance of payments is possible under a system of fixed exchange rates. But under freely floating exchange rates, there can in principle be no deficit (or surplus) in the balance of payments. The country can prevent a deficit or (surplus) by depreciating (or appreciating) its currency. Further, balance of payments always balances in an ex-post accounting sense, according to the basic principle of accounting. Lastly, such balance of payments can be in equilibrium only if there are no compensating transactions.

5. BALANCE OF TRADE AND BALANCE OF PAYMENTS

The *balance of payments* of a country is a systematic record of its receipts and payments in international transactions in a given year. Each transaction is entered on the credit and debit side of the balance sheet (see Table 1). The principal items on the credit side are : (1) Visible exports which relate to the goods exported for which the country receives payments. (2) Invisible exports which refer to the services rendered by the country to other countries. Such services consist of banking, insurance, shipping, and other services rendered in the form of technical know-how, etc., money spent by tourists and students visiting the country for travel and education, etc. (3) Transfer receipts in the form of gifts received from foreigners. (4) Borrowings from abroad and investments by foreigners in the country. (5) The official sale of reserve assets including gold to foreign countries and international institutions.

---

4. Bo Sodersten and G. Reed, *International Economics*, 3/e, 1994, Italics added.

The principal items on the debit side are : (1) Visible imports relating to goods imported for which the country makes payments to foreign countries. (2) Invisible imports in the form of payments made by the home country for services rendered by foreign countries. These include all items referred to under (2) in the above para. (3) Transfer payments to foreigners in the form of gifts, etc. (4) Loans to foreign countries, investments by residents in foreign countries, and debt repayments to foreign countries. (5) Official purchase of reserve assets or gold from foreign countries and international institutions.

If the total receipts from foreigners on the credit side exceed the total payments to foreigners on the debit side, the balance of payments is said to be *favourable*. On the other hand, if the total payments to foreigners exceed the total receipts from foreigners, the balance of payments is *unfavourable*.

The *balance of trade* is the difference between the value of goods and services exported and imported. In contains the first two items of the balance of payments account on the credit and the debit side. This is known as "balance of payment on current account." Some writers define the balance of trade as the difference between the value of merchandise exports and imports. Prof. Meade regards this way of defining the balance of trade as wrong and of minor economic significance from the point of view of the national income of the country. In equation form, the balance of payments of $Y = C + I + G + (X - M)$ which includes all transactions which give rise to or exhaust national income. In the equation, Y refers to national income, C to consumption expenditure, I to investment expenditure, G to government expenditure, X to exports of goods and services and M to imports of goods and services. The expression $(X - M)$ denotes the balance of trade. If the difference between X and M is zero, the balance of trade balances. If X is greater than M, the balance of trade is *favourable*, or there is *surplus* balance of trade. On the other hand, if X is less than M, the balance of trade is in *deficit* or is *unfavourable*.

6. DISEQUILIBRIUM IN BALANCE OF PAYMENTS

A disequilibrium in the *BOP* of a country may be either a deficit or a surplus. A deficit or surplus in *BOP* of a country appears when its autonomous receipts (credits) do not match its autonomous payments (debits). If autonomous credit receipts exceed autonomous debit payments, there is a surplus in the *BOP* and the disequilibrium is said to be *favourable*. On the other hand, if autonomous debit payments exceed autonomous credit receipts, there is a *deficit* in the *BOP* and the disequilibrium is said to be unfavourable or adverse.[5]

Causes of Disequilibrium

There are many factors that may lead to a BOP deficit or surplus:

1. *Temporary Changes (or Disequilibrium).* There may be a temporary disequilibrium caused by random variations in trade, seasonal fluctuations, the effects of weather on agricultural production, etc. Deficits or surpluses arising from such temporary causes are expected to correct themselves within a short time.

2. *Fundamental Disequilibrium.* Fundamental disequilibrium refers to a persistent and long-run *BOP* disequilibrium of a country. It is a chronic *BOP* deficit, according to *IMF*. It is caused by such dynamic factors as : (1) Changes in consumer tastes within the country or abroad which reduce the country's exports and increase its imports. (2) Continuous fall in the country's foreign exchange reserves due to supply inelasticities of exports and excessive demand for foreign goods and services. (3) Excessive capital outflows due to massive imports of capital goods, raw materials, essential consumer goods, technology and external indebedness. (4) Low competitive strength in world markets which adversly affects exports. (5) Inflationary pressures within the economy which make exports dearer.

3. *Structural Changes (or Disequilibrium).* Structural changes bring about disequilibrium in BOP over the long run. They may result from the following factors: (*a*) Technological changes in methods of production of products in domestic industries or in the industries of other countries. They lead to changes in costs, prices and

---

5. The distinction between deficit and disequilibrium in *BOP* should be clearly understood. The former refers to unfavourable or adverse *BOP* as explained above whereas disequilibrium refers to a deficit or surplus in *BOP*.

quality of products. (*b*) Import restrictions of all kinds bring about disequilibrium in *BOP*. (*c*) Deficit in *BOP* also arises when a country suffers from deficiency of resources which it is required to import from other countries. (*d*) Disequilibrium in *BOP* may also be caused by changes in the supply or direction of long-term capital flows. More and regular flow of long-term capital may lead to *BOP* surplus, while an irregular and short supply of capital brings *BOP* deficit.

4. *Changes in Exchange Rates.* Changes in foreign exchange rate in the form of overvaluation or undervaluation of foreign currency lead to *BOP* disequilibrium. When the value of currency is higher in relation to other currencies, it is said to be overvalued. Opposite is the case of an undervalued currency. Overvaluation of the domestic currency makes foreign goods cheaper and exports dearer in foreign countries. As a result, the country imports more and exports less of goods. There is also outflow of capital. This leads to unfavourable *BOP*. On the contrary, undervaluation of the currency makes *BOP* favourable for the country by encouraging exports and inflow of capital and reducing imports.

5. *Cyclical Fluctuations (or Disequilibrium).* Cyclical fluctuations in business activity also lead to *BOP* disequilibrium. When there is depression in a country, volumes of both exports and imports fall drastically in relation to other countries. But the fall in exports may be more than that of imports due to decline in domestic production. Therefore, there is an adverse *BOP* situation. On the other hand, when there is boom in a country in relation to other countries, both exports and imports may increase. But there can be either a surplus or deficit in *BOP* situation depending upon whether the country exports more than imports or imports more than exports. In both the cases, there will be disequilibrium in *BOP*.

6. *Changes in National Income.* Another cause is the change in the country's national income. If the national income of a country increases, it will lead to an increase in imports thereby creating a deficit in its balance of payments, other things remaining the same. If the country is already at full employment level, an increase in income will lead to inflationary rise in prices which may increase its imports and thus bring disequilibrium in the balance of payments.

7. *Price Changes.* Inflation or deflation is another cause of disequilibrium in the balance of payments. If there is inflation in the country, prices of exports increase. As a result, exports fall. At the same time, the demand for imports increase. Thus increase in export prices leading to decline in exports and rise in imports results in adverse balance of payments.

8. *Stage of Economic Development.* A country's balance of payments also depends on its stage of economic development. If a country is developing, it will have a deficit in its balance of payments because it imports raw materials, machinery, capital equipment, and services associated with the development process and exports primary products. The country has to pay more for costly imports and gets less for its cheap exports. This leads to disequilibrium in its balance of payments.

9. *Capital Movements.* Borrowings and lendings or movements of capital by countries also result in disequilibrium in *BOP*. A country which gives loans and grants on a large scale to other countries has a deficit in its *BOP* on capital account. If it is also importing more, as is the case with the USA, it will have chronic deficit. On the other hand, a developing country brorrowing large funds from other countries and international institutions may have a favourable *BOP*. But such a possibility is remote because these countries usually import huge quanties of food, raw materials, capital goods, etc. and export primary products. Such borrowings simply help in reducing *BOP* deficit.

10. *Political Conditions.* Political condition of a country is another cause of disequilibrium in *BOP*. Political instability in a country creates uncertainty among foreign investors which leads to the outflow of capital and retards its inflow. This causes disequilibrium in *BOP* of the country. Disequilibrium in *BOP* also occurs in the event of war or fear of war with some other country.

IMPLICATIONS OF DISEQUILIBRIUM

A disequilibrium in the balance of payments whether a deficit or surplus has important implications for a country.

A deficit in the combined current and capital accounts is regarded as undesirable for the country. This is because such a deficit has to be covered by borrowing from abroad or attracting foreign exchange or capital from abroad. This may require paying high interest rates. There is also the danger of withdrawing money by foreigners, as happened in the case of the Asian crisis in the late 1990s. An alternative may be to draw on the reserves of the country which may also lead to a financial crises. Moreover, the reserves of a country being limited, they can be used to pay for *BOP* deficit upto a limit.

But the above analysis of a combined current and capital account deficit is not correct in practice. The reason being that a current account deficit is the same thing as a capital account surplus. However, it is beneficial for a country to have a current account deficit even if it equals capital account surplus in *BOP*. In the short-run, the country may benefit from a higher level of consumption through import of goods and consequently a higher standard of living. But the excess of imports over exports may be financed by foreign investments in the country. These may lead to increased production, employment and income in the country. In the long-run, foreign investors may purchase large assets in the country and thus adversely affect domestic industry as is the case with *MNCs* (multinational corporations).

The current account deficit in *BOP* of a country may have either good or bad effects depending on the nature of an economy.

Take a country where domestic industries are rapidly growing and it has current account *BOP* deficit. These industries offer a high rate of return on their investment. This would, in return, attract foreign investments. As a result, the country would have a capital account surplus due to the inflow of capital and a current account deficit. This current account deficit is good for the economy. No doubt, the external debt of the country increases, but this debt is being utilised to finance the rapid growth of the economy. The real burden of this debt will be very low because it can be repaid out of higher income in the future.

On the contrary, a country having an inefficient and unproductive domestic industry will be adversely affected by its current account *BOP* deficit. The country borrows from abroad to finance the excess of spending over consumption. To attract foreign borrowings, the country will have to pay high interest rates. These will increase the money burden of the debt. The real burden of the debt will also increase because of the low productive capacity of domestic industries. If the current consumption is being financed by foreign borrowings, the wealth of the economy will decline. This, in turn, will lead to either a reduction in domestic expenditure or a change in government policy so as to control the rising debt.

On the other hand, if foreign borrowings are being used to finance real investment, the current account *BOP* deficit will be beneficial for the economy. A higher rate of return on real investment than the interest on foreign borrowings would increase the country's wealth over time through rise in its national income. Thus a current account *BOP* deficit is not always undesirable for a country.

7. MEASURES TO CORRECT DEFICIT IN BALANCE OF PAYMENTS[6]

When there is a deficit in the balance of payments of a country, adjustment is brought about automatically through price and income changes or by adopting certain policy measures like export promotion, monetary and fiscal policies, devaluation and direct controls. We study these as follows:

1. Adjustment through Exchange Depreciation (Price Effect)

Under flexible exchange rates, the disequilibrium in the balance of payments is automatically solved by the forces of demand and supply for foreign exchange. An exchange rate is the price of a currency which is determined, like any other commodity, by demand and supply. "The exchange rate varies with varying supply and demand conditions, but it is always possible to find an equilibrium exchange rate which clears the foreign exchange market and creates external equilibrium."[7] This is automatically achieved by depreciation of a country's currency in case of deficit in its balance of payments. Depreciation of a currency means that its relative value

6. If the question relates to disequilibrium in *BOP*, then measures opposite to whatever are given in the paras should also be explained relating to *BOP* surplus, such as appreciation, revaluation, etc. The best answer would be to write at the end of each para : The opposite measures would be adopted in case of *BOP* surplus. Mention the measures in the dotted portion.
7. Bo Sodersten, *International Economics*, p. 215.

decreases. Depreciation has the effect of encouraging exports and discouraging imports. When exchange depreciation takes place, foreign prices are translated into domestic prices. Suppose the dollar depreciates in relation to the pound. It means, that the price of dollar falls in relation to the pound in the foreign exchange market. This leads to the lowering of the prices of U.S. exports in Britain and raising of the prices of British imports in the U.S. When import prices are higher in the U.S., the Americans will purchase less goods from the Britishers. On the other hand, lower prices of U.S. exports will increase exports and diminish imports, thereby bringing equilibrium in the balance of payments.

2. Devaluation or Expenditure-Switching Policy

Devaluation raises the domestic price of imports and reduces the foreign price of exports of a country devaluing its currency in relation to the currency of another country. Devaluation is referred to as expenditure switching policy because it switches expenditure from imported to domestic goods and services. When a country devalues its currency, the price of foreign currency increases which makes imports dearer and exports cheaper. This causes expenditures to be switched from foreign to domestic goods as the country's exports rise and the country produces more to meet the domestic and foreign demand for goods with reduction in imports. Consequently, the balance of payments deficit is eliminated.

3. Direct Controls

To correct disequilibrium in the balance of payments, government also adopts direct controls which aim at limiting the volume of imports.The government restricts the import of undesirable or unimportant items by levying heavy import duties, fixation of quotas, etc. At the same time, it may allow imports of essential goods duty free or at lower import duties, or fix liberal import quotas for them. For instance, the government may allow free entry of capital goods, but impose heavy import duties on luxuries. Import quotas are also fixed and the importers are required to take licenses from the authorities in order to import certain essential commodities in fixed quantities. In these ways, imports are reduced in order to correct an adverse balance of payments. The government also imposes exchange controls. Exchange controls have a dual purpose. They restrict imports and also control and regulate the foreign exchange. With reduction in imports and control of foreign exchange, visible and invisible imports are reduced. Consequently, an adverse balance of payment is corrected.

4. Adjustment through Capital Movements

A country can use capital imports to correct a deficit in its balance of payments. A deficit can be financed by capital inflows.When capital is perfectly mobile within countries, a small rise in the domestic rate of interest brings a large inflow of capital. The balance of payments is said to be in equilibrium when the domestic interest rate equals the world rate. If the domestic interest rate is higher than the world rate, there will be capital inflows and the balance of payments deficit is corrected.

5. Adjustment through Income Changes

Given the foreign exchange rate and prices in a country, an increase in the value of exports, causes an increase in the incomes of all persons associated with the export industries. These, in turn, create demand for other goods and services within the country. This will raise the incomes of persons engaged in the latter industries and services. This process will continue and the national income increases by the value of the multiplier.

6. Stimulation of Exports and Import Substitutes

A deficit in the balance of payments can also be corrected by encouraging exports. Exports can be encouraged by producing quality products, by increasing exports through increased production and productivity, and by better marketing. They can also be increased by a policy of import substitution. It means that the country produces those goods which it imports. In the beginning, imports are reduced but in the long run exports of such goods start. An increase in exports cause the national income to rise by many times through the operation of the foreign trade multiplier. The foreign trade multiplier expresses the change in income caused by a change in exports. Ultimately, the deficit in the balance of payments is removed when exports rise faster than imports.

7. Expenditure-Reducing Policies

A deficit in the balance of payments implies an excess of expenditure over income. To correct it, expenditure and income should be brought into equality. For this expenditure reducing monetary and fiscal policies are used. A contractionary or tight monetary policy relates to increase in interest rates to reduce money supply and a contractionary fiscal policy relates to reduction in government expenditure and or increase in taxes. Thus expenditure reducing policies reduce aggregate demand through higher taxes and interest rates, thereby reducing expenditure and output. The reduction in expenditure and output, in turn, reduces the domestic price level. This gives rise to switching of expenditure from foreign to domestic goods. Consequently, the country's imports are reduced and the balance of payments deficit is corrected.

EXERCISES

1. Enumerate the principle items in the balance of payments of a country. How can a deficit in the balance of payments be corrected?
2. "Balance of Payments always balances." Elucidate. But how do you explain disequilibrium in balance of payments.
3. Distinguish between balance of payments and balance of trade. How can an unfavourable balance of payments be corrected?
4. What are the causes of an adverse balance of payments? Give suggestions to remove an unfavourable balance of payments?
5. Distinguish between : (*a*) Balance of Current Account and Balance of Capital Account; (*b*) Autonomous Balance and Overall Balance; (*c*) Autonomous Transactions and Accommodating Transactions; (*d*) Deficit and Disequilibrium in Balance of Payments.

CHAPTER 47

Adjustment Mechanisms of Balance of Payments

1. INTRODUCTION

When there is a deficit or surplus in *BOP* of a country, it is adjusted through the following mechanisms :

1. Automatic adjustment through price and income changes. Price changes are studied under flexible or floating exchange rates and under the Gold Standard. Income changes are explained in terms of the foreign trade multiplier in the next chapter.

2. Adjustment policies are induced changes to correct disequilibrium in *BOP* by the government of a country. They include expenditure changing and expenditure switching policies, maintaining external and internal balance, direct controls, etc. They are discussed in a separate chapter.

3. There are also approaches to balance of payments which form part of policy measures but are usually discussed separately as Elasticity, Absorption, and Monetary Approaches. They are explained below.

2. AUTOMATIC PRICE ADJUSTMENT UNDER GOLD STANDARD

Under the international gold standard which operated between 1880-1914, the currency in use was made of gold or was convertible into gold at a fixed rate. The central bank of the country was always ready to buy and sell gold at the specified price. The rate at which the standard money of the country was convertible into gold was called the *mint price* of gold. This rate was called the *mint parity* or *mint par of exchange* because it was based on the mint price of gold. But the actual rate of exchange could vary above and below the mint parity by the cost of shipping gold between the two countries. To illustrate this, suppose the US had a deficit in its balance of payments with Britain. The difference between the value of imports and exports would have to be paid in gold by US importers because the demand for pounds exceeded the supply of pounds. But the transhipment of gold involved transportation cost and other handling charges, insurance, etc. Suppose the shipping cost of gold from the US to Britain was 3 cents. So the US importers would have to spend \$ 6.03 (\$ 6 + .03c) for getting £ 1. This could be the exchange rate which was the US *gold export point* or *upper specie point*. No US importer would pay more than \$ 6.03 to obtain £ 1 because he could buy \$ 6 worth of gold from the US treasury and ship it to Britain at a cost of 3 cents per ounce. Similarly, the exchange rate of the pound could not fall below \$ 5.97 in the case of a surplus in the US balance of payments. Thus the exchange rate of \$ 5.97to a pound was the US *gold import point* or *lower specie point*. The exchange rate under the gold standard was determined by the forces of demand and supply between the gold points and was prevented from moving outside the gold points by shipments of gold. The main objective was to keep *BOP* in equilibrium. A deficit or surplus in *BOP* under the gold standard was automatically adjusted by the price-specie-flow mechanism. For instance, a *BOP* deficit of a country meant a fall in its foreign exchange reserves due to an outflow of its gold to a surplus country. This reduced the country's money supply thereby bringing a fall in the general price level. This, in turn, would increase its exports and reduce its imports. This adjustment process in *BOP* was supplemented by a rise in interest rates as a result of reduction in money supply. This led to the inflow of short-term capital from the surplus country. Thus the inflow of short-term capital from the surplus to the deficit country helped in restoring *BOP* equilibrium.[1]

3. AUTOMATIC PRICE ADJUSTMENT UNDER FLEXIBLE EXCHANGE RATES (PRICE EFFECT)

Under flexible (or floating) exchange rates, the disequilibrium in the balance of payments is automatically solved by the forces of demand and supply for foreign exchange. An exchange rate is the price of a currency which is determined, like any other commodity, by demand and supply. "The exchange rate varies with varying supply and demand conditions, but it is always possible to find an equilibrium exchange rate which clears the foreign exchange market and creates external equilibrium."[2] This is automatically achieved by a depreciation (or appreciation) of a country's currency in case of a deficit (or surplus) in its balance of payments. Depreciation (or appreciation) of a currency means that its relative value decreases (or increases). Depreciation has the effect of encouraging exports and discouraging imports. When exchange depreciation takes place, foreign prices are translated into domestic prices. Suppose the dollar depreciates in relation to the pound. It means, that the price of dollar falls in relation to the pound in the foreign exchange market. This leads to the lowering of the prices of U.S. exports in Britain and raising of the prices of British imports in the U.S. When import prices are higher in the U.S., the Americans will purchase less goods from the Britishers. On the other hand, lower prices of U.S. exports will increase their sales to Britain. Thus the U.S. exports will increase and imports diminish, thereby bringing equilibrium in the balance of payments.

Its Assumptions

This analysis is based on the following assumptions :

1. There are two countries Britain and U.S.
2. Both are on flexible exchange rate system.
3. *BOP* disequilibrium is automatically adjusted by changes in exchange rates.
4. Prices are flexible in both the countries.
5. There is free trade between the two countries.

Explanation

Given these assumptions, the adjustment process is explained in terms of Figure 1 where *D* is the U.S. demand curve of foreign exchange representing its demand for British imports, and *S* is the U.S. supply curve of foreign exchange representing its exports to Britain. At *P* the demand and supply of the U.S. foreign exchange is in equilibrium where the rate of exchange between U.S. dollar and British pound is *OE* and the quantity of exchange is *OQ*.

Suppose disequilibrium develops in the balance of payments of the U.S. in relation to Britain. This is shown by a shift in the demand curve from *D* to D_1 and the incipient deficit equals PP_2. This means an increase in the U.S. demand for British imports which leads to an increase in the demand for pound. This implies depreciation of the U.S. dollar and appreciation of the British pound. As a result, import prices of British goods rise in the U.S. and the prices of U.S. exports fall. This

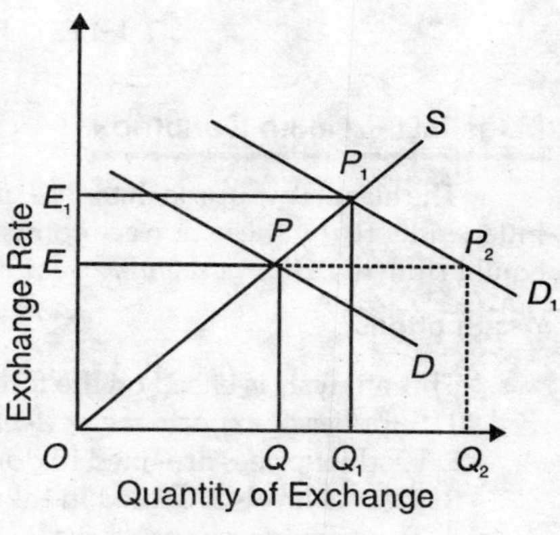

FIG. 1

1. For assumptions and criticisms refer to the Mint Parity Theory in the chapter "Foreign Exchange Rate.'
2. Bo Sodersten, *International Economics*, p. 215.

tends to bring about a new equilibrium at P_1 and a new exchange rate at OE_1 whereby the deficit in the balance of payments is eliminated. The demand for foreign exchange equals the supply of foreign exchange at OQ_1 and the balance of payments is in equilibrium.

When the exchange rate rises to OE_1, U.S. goods become cheaper in Britain and British goods become expensive in U.S. in terms of dollar. As a result of changes in *relative prices,* the lower prices of U.S. goods increase the demand for them in Britain, shown by the new demand curve D_1 . This tends to raise the U.S. exports to Britain which is shown as the movement from P to P_1 along the supply curve S. At the same time, the higher price of British goods in terms of dollars tends to reduce demand for British goods and to switch demand to domestic goods in the U.S. This leads to the movement from P_2 to P_1 along the new demand curve D_1. Thus the *incipient* deficit PP_2 in *BOP* is removed by increase in the foreign exchange supplied by QQ_1 and decrease in the foreign exchange demanded by Q_2Q_1 so that *BOP* equilibrium is achieved at the exchange rate OE_1 whereby OQ_1 foreign exchange is supplied and demanded.

The above analysis is based on the assumption of *relative elasticities* of demand and supply of foreign exchange. However, in order to measure the full effect of depreciation on relative prices in the two countries, it is not sufficient for demand and supply conditions to be relatively elastic. What is important is *low elasticities* of demand and supply of foreign exchange. This is illustrated in Figure 2 where the original *less elastic* demand and supply curves of foreign exchange are D and S respectively which intersect at P and the equilibrium exchange rate is OE. Now a deficit in the balance of payments develops equals to PP_2. Since the *elasticities* of demand and supply of foreign exchange are very low (inelastic), it requires a very large amount of depreciation of the dollar and the appreciation of the pound for the restoration of the equilibrium. The equilibrium will be established through relative price movements in the two countries, as explained above, at P_1 with a very high rate of foreign exchange OE_1. But such a high rate of depreciation would lead to very high price changes in the two countries thereby tending to disrupt their economies.

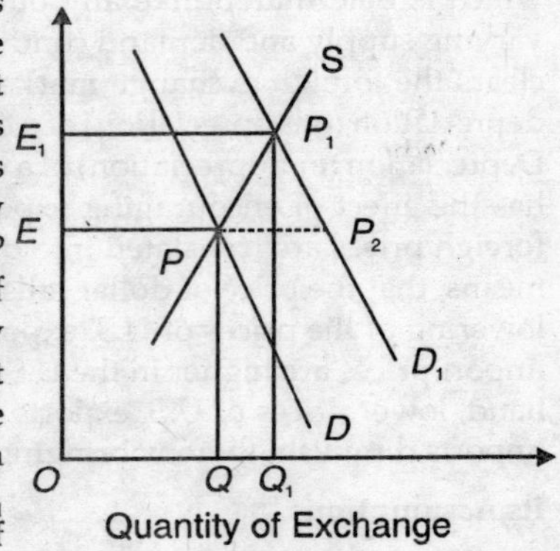

FIG. 2

Its Criticism. The practical use of flexible exchange rates is severely limited. *Depreciation* and *appreciation* lead to fall and rise in prices in the countries adopting them. They lead to severe depressions and inflations respectively. Further, they create insecurity and uncertainty. This is more due to speculation in foreign exchange which destabilises the economies of countries adopting flexible exchange rates. Governments, therefore, favour fixed exchange rates which require adjustments in the balance of payments by adopting policy measures.

4. THE ELASTICITY APPROACH

MARSHALL-LERNER CONDITION

The elasticity approach to *BOP* is associated with the Marshall-Lerner condition which was worked out independently by these two economists. It studies the conditions under which exchange rate changes restore equilibrium in *BOP* by *devaluing* a country's currency. This approach is related to the price effect of devaluation.

Assumptions

This analysis is based on the following assumptions :

1. Supplies of exports are perfectly elastic.
2. Product prices are fixed in domestic currency.
3. Income levels are fixed in the devaluing country.
4. The supply of imparts are large.
5. The price elasticities of demand for exports and imports are *arc* elasticities.
6. Price elasticities refer to absolute values.

7. The country's current account balance equals its trade balance.

The Theory

Given these assumptions, when a country devalues its currency, the domestic prices of its imports are raised and the foreign prices of its exports are reduced. Thus devaluation helps to improve *BOP* deficit of a country by increasing its exports and reducing its imports. But the extent to which it will succeed depends on the country's price elasticities of domestic demand for imports and foreign demand for exports. This is what the Marshall-Lerner condition states: *when the sum of price elasticities of demand for exports and imports in absolute terms is greater than unity, devaluation will improve the country's balance of payments, i.e.*

$$e_x + e_m > 1$$

where e_x is the demand elasticity of exports and E_m is the demand elasticity for imports. On the contrary, if the sum of price elasticities of demand for exports and imports, in absolute terms, is less unity, $e_x + e_m < 1$, devaluation will *worsen* (increase the deficit) the *BOP*. If the sum of these elasticities in absolute terms is equal to unity, $e_x + e_m = 1$, devaluation has no effect on the *BOP* situation which will remain unchanged.[3]

The following is the *process* through which the Marshall-Lerner condition operates in removing *BOP* deficit of a devaluing country.

Devaluation reduces the domestic prices of exports in terms of the foreign currency. With low prices, exports increase. The extent to which they increase depends on the demand elasticity for exports. It also depends on the nature of goods exported and the market conditions. If the country is the sole supplier and exports raw materials or perishable goods, the demand elasticity for its exports will be low. If it exports machinery, tools and industrial products in competition with other countries, the elasticity of demand for its products will be high, and devaluation will be successful in correcting a deficit.

Devaluation has also the effect of increasing the domestic price of imports which will reduce the import of goods. By how much the volume of imports will decline depends on the demand elasticity of imports. The demand elasticity of imports, in turn, depends on the nature of goods imported by the devaluing country. If it imports consumer goods, raw materials and inputs for industries, its elasticity of demand for imports will be low. It is only when the import elasticity of demand for products is high that devaluation will help in correcting a deficit in the balance of payments.

Thus it is only when the sum of the elasticity of demand for exports and the elasticity of demand for imports is greater than one that devaluation will improve the balance of payments of a country devaluing its currency.

The J-Curve Effect. Empirical evidence shows that the Marshall-Lerner condition is satisfied in the majority of advanced countries. But there is a general consensus among economists that both demand-supply elasticities will be greater in the long run than in the short run. The effects of devaluation on domestic prices and demand for exports and imports will take time for consumers and producers to adjust themselves to the new situation. The short-run price elasticities of demand for exports and imports are lower and they do not satisfy the Marshall-Lerner condition. Therefore, to begin with, devaluation makes the *BOP* worse in the short-run and then improves it in the long-run. This traces a J-shaped curve through time. This is known as the *J-curve effect* of devaluation. This is illustrated in Fig. 3 where time is taken on the horizontal axis and deficit-surplus on the vertical axis. Suppose devaluation takes place at time *T*. In the beginning, the curve *J* has a big loop which shows increase in *BOP* deficit beyond *D*. It is only after time T_1 that it starts sloping upwards and the deficit begins to reduce. At time T_2 there is equilibrium in *BOP* and

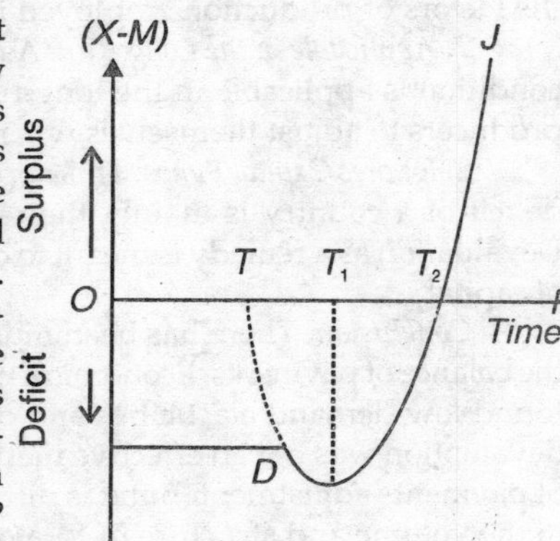

FIG. 3

3. For the derivation of the Marshall-Lerner condition interested students may refer to C.P. Kindleberger, *op. cit.*, Appendix H.

then the surplus arises from T_2 to J. If the Marshall-Lerner condition is not satisfied, in the long run the J-curve will flatten out to F from T_2.

However, in case the country is on a flexible exchange rate, *BOP* will get worse when there is devaluation of its currency. Due to devaluation, there is excess supply of currency in the foreign exchange market which may go on depreciating the currency. Thus the foreign exchange market becomes unstable and the exchange rate may overshoot its long-run value.

Its Criticisms

The elasticity approach based on the Marshall-Lerner condition has the following defects.

1. *Misleading*. The elasticity approach which applies the Marshallian concept of elasticity to solve *BOP* deficit is misleading. This is because it has relevance only to incremental change along a demand or supply curve and to problems dealing with shifts in these curves. Moreover, it assumes constant purchasing power of money which is not relevant to devaluation of the country's currency.

2. *Partial Elasticities*. The elasticity approach has been criticised by Alexander because it uses partial elasticities which exclude all factors except relative prices and quantities of exports and imports. This is applicable only to single-commodity trade rather than to a multi-commodity trade. It makes this approach unrealistic.

3. *Supplies not Perfectly Elastic*. The Marshall-Lerner condition assumes perfectly elastic supplies of exports and imports. But this assumption is unrealistic because the country may not be in a position to increase the supply of its exports when they become cheap with devaluation of its currency.

4. *Partial Equilibrium Analysis*. The elasticity approach assumes domestic price and income levels to be stable within the devaluing country. It, further, assumes that there are no restrictions in using additional resources into production for exports. These assumptions show that this analysis is based on the partial equilibrium analysis. It, therefore, ignores the feedback effects of a price change in one product on incomes, and consequently on the demand for goods. This is a serious defect of the elasticity approach because the effects of devaluation always spread to the entire economy.

5. *Inflationary*. Devaluation can lead to inflation in the economy. Even if it succeeds in improving the balance of payments, it is likely to increase domestic incomes in export and import-competing industries. But these increased incomes will affect the *BOP* directly by increasing the demand for imports, and indirectly by increasing the overall demand and thus raising the prices within the country.

6. *Ignores Income Distribution*. The elasticity approach ignores the effects of devaluation on income distribution. Devaluation leads to the reallocation of resources. It takes away resources from the sector producing non-traded goods to export and import-competing industries sector. This will tend to increase the incomes of the factors of production employed in the latter sector and reduce that of the former sector.

7. *Applicable in the Long Run*. As discussed above in the J-curve effect of devaluation, the Marshall-Lerner condition is applicable in the long-run and not in the short. This is because it takes time for consumers and producers to adjust themselves when there is devaluation of the domestic currency.

8. *Ignores Capital Flows*. This approach is applicable to *BOP* on current account or balance of trade. But *BOP* deficit of a country is mainly the result of the outflow of capital. It thus ignores *BOP* on capital account. Devaluation as a remedy is meant to cut imports and the outflow of capital and increase exports and the inflow of capital.

Conclusion. There has been much controversy over the Marshall-Lerner condition for improvements in the balance of payments. Economists tried to measure demand elasticities in international trade. Some economists found low demand elasticities and others high demand elasticities. Accordingly, the former suggested that devaluation was not an effective method while the latter suggested that it was a potent mechanism of balance of payments adjustment. But it is difficult to generalise due to these diverse findings on account of differences in the volume and structure of foreign trade.

5. THE ABSORPTION APPROACH

The absorption approach to balance of payments is general equilibrium in nature and is based on the Keynesian national income relationships. It is, therefore, also known as the Keynesian approach. It runs through the *income effect of devaluation* as against the price effect to the elasticity approach. The theory states that if a country has a deficit in its balance of payments, it means that people are 'absorbing' more than they produce. Domestic expenditure on consumption and investment is greater than national income. If they have a surplus in the balance of payments, they are absorbing less. Expenditure on consumption and investment is less than national income. Here the *BOP* is defined as the difference between national income and domestic expenditure.

This approach was developed by Sydney Alexander.[4] The analysis can be explained in the following form

$$Y = C + I_d + G + X - M \quad ...(1)$$

where Y is national income, C is consumption expenditure, I_d total domestic investment, G is autonomous government expenditure, X represents exports and M imports.

The sum of $(C + I_d + G)$ is the total absorption designated as A, and the balance of payments $(X - M)$ is designated as B. Thus Equation (1) becomes

$$Y = A + B$$

or

$$B = Y - A \quad ...(2)$$

which means that *BOP* on current account is the difference between national income (Y) and total absorption (A). *BOP* can be improved by either increasing domestic income or reducing the absorption. For this purpose, Alexander advocates devaluation because it acts both ways. *First*, devaluation increases exports and reduces imports, thereby increasing the national income. The additional income so generated will further increase income via the multiplier effect. This will lead to an increase in domestic consumption. Thus the net effect of the increase in national income on the balance of payments is the difference between the total increase in income and the induced increase in absorption, i.e.,

$$DB = DY - DA \quad ...(3)$$

Total absorption (DA) depends on the marginal propensity to absorb[5] when there is devaluation. This is expressed as a. Devaluation also directly affects absorption through the change in income which we write as D. Thus

$$DA = aDY + DD \quad ...(4)$$

Substituting equation (4) in (3), we get

$$DB = DY - aDY - DD$$

or

$$DB = (1 - a)\, DY - DD \quad ...(5)$$

The equation points toward three factors which explain the effects of devaluation on *BOP*. They are : (*i*) the marginal propensity to absorb (a), (*ii*) change in income (DY), and (*iii*) change in direct absorption (DD). It may be noted that since a is the marginal propensity (*MP*) to absorb, $(1 - a)$ is the propensity to hoard or save. These factors, in turn, are influenced by the existence of unemployed or idle resources and fully employed resources in the devaluing country.

Effects of Devaluation on BOP

1. *MP to Absorb.* To take the *MP* to absorb, it it is less than unity ($a < 1$), with idle resources in the country, devaluation will increase exports and reduce imports. Output and income will rise and *BOP* on current account will improve. If, on the other hand, $a > 1$, there will be an adverse effect of devaluation on *BOP*. It means that people are absorbing more or spending more on consumption and investing more. In other words, they are spending more than the country is producing. In such a situation, devaluation will not increase exports and reduce imports, and *BOP* situation will worsen.

Under conditions of full employment if $a > 1$, the government will have to follow expenditure reducing policy measures along with devaluation whereby the resources of the economy are so reallocated as to increase exports and reduce imports. Ultimately, *BOP* situation will improve.

2. *Income Effects.* Let us take the income effects of devaluation. If there are idle resources, devaluation

4. S. Alexander "Effects of Devaluation on a Trade Balance," *I.M.F. Staff Papers*, April 1952. But it was R.F. Harrod who was the first economist to apply the Keynesian analysis to *BOP* in his *International Trade.*
5. The marginal propensity to absorb (a) is the sum of the marginal propensity to consume and marginal propensity to invest. G has no role as it is autonomous government expenditure.

increases exports and reduces imports of the devaluing country. With the expansion of export and import-competing industries, income increases. The additional income so generated in the economy will further increase income via the multiplier effect. This will lead to improvement in *BOP* situation. If resources are fully employed in the economy, devaluation cannot correct an adverse *BOP* because national income cannot rise. Rather, prices may increase thereby reducing exports and increasing imports, thereby worsening the *BOP* situation.

3. *Terms of Trade Effect.* The effect of devaluation on national income is also through its effects on the terms of trade. The conditions under which devaluation *worsens* the terms of trade, national income will be *adversely* affected, and *vice versa*. Generally, devaluation worsens the terms of trade because the devaluing country has to export more goods in order to import the same quantity as before. Consequently, the trade balance deteriorates and national income declines. If prices are fixed in buyer's (other country's) currency after devaluation, the terms of trade improve because exports increase and imports decline. The importing country pays more for increased exports of the devaluing country than it receives from its imports. Thus the trade balance of the devaluing country improves and its national income rises.

4. *Direct Absorption.* Devaluation affects direct absorption in a number of ways. It the devaluing country has idle resources, an expansionary process will start with exports increasing and imports declining. Consequently, income will rise and so will absorption. If the increase in absorption in less than the rise in income, *BOP* will improve. Generally, the effect of devaluation on direct absorption is not significant in a country with idle resources.

If the economy is fully employed and has also a *BOP* deficit, national income cannot be increased by devaluing the currency. So an improvement in *BOP* can be brought about by reduction in direct absorption. Domestic absorption can fall automatically as a result of devaluation due to real cash balance effect, money illusion and income redistribution.

5. *Real Cash Balance Effect.* When a country devalues its currency, its domestic prices rise. If the money supply remains constant, the real value of cash balances held by the people falls. To replenish their cash balances, people start saving more. This can be possible only by reducing their expenditure or absorption. This is the real cash balance effect of devaluation.

If people hold assets and when devaluation reduces their real cash balances, they sell them. This reduces the prices of assets and increases the interest rate. This, in turn, will reduce investment and consumption, given the constant money supply. As a result, absorption will be reduced. This is the *asset effect* of real cash balance effect of devaluation.

6. *Money Illusion Effect.* The presence of money illusion also tends to reduce direct absorption. When prices rise due to devaluation, consumers think their real incomes have fallen, even though their money incomes have risen. They have the money illusion under whose influence they reduce their consumption expenditure or direct absorption.

7. *Income Re-distribution Effect.* Direct absorption falls automatically if devaluation redistributes income in favour of people with high marginal propensity to save and against thosee with high marginal propensity to consume. If the marginal propensity to consume of workers is higher than those of profit-earners, absorption will be reduced. Further, when money incomes of lower income groups increase with devaluation, they enter the income tax bracket. When they start paying income tax, they reduce their consumption as compared with higher income groups which are already paying the tax. This leads to reduction in absorption in case of the former.

Income redistribution also takes place between *production sectors* after devaluation. Those sectors whose prices rise more than their costs of production earn more profits than the other sectors whose costs rise more than their prices. Thus the effect of devaluation will be to redistribute income in favour of the former sectors.

Devaluation will also redistribute income in favour of sectors producing and selling *traded goods* and against *non-traded goods* sectors. Prices of traded goods rise more than that of non-traded goods. As a result, profits of producers and traders and wages of workers producing traded goods rise more as compared to those engaged in non-traded goods.

8. *Expenditure-Reducing Policies.* Direct absorption is also reduced if the government adopts expenditure-reducing monetary-fiscal policies which are deflationary. They will make devaluation successful in reducing

BOP deficit. But they will create unemployment in the country.

Its Criticisms

The absorption approach to *BOP* deficit has been criticised on the following grounds :

1. *Neglects Price Effects.* This approach neglects the price effects of devaluation which are very important.

2. *Calculation Difficult.* Analytically, it appears to be superior to the elasticity approach but propensities to consume, save and invest cannot be accurately calculated.

3. *Ignores Effects on Other Countries.* The absorption approach is weak in that it relies too much on policies designed to influence domestic absorption. It does not study the effects of a devaluation on the absorption of other countries.

4. *Not Operative in a Fixed Exchange Rate System.* The absorption approach fails as a corrective measure of *BOP* deficit under a fixed exchange rate system. When prices rise with devaluation, people reduce their consumption expenditure. With money supply remaining costant, interest rate rises which brings a fall in output alongwith absorption. Thus devaluation will have little effect on *BOP* deficit.

5. *More Emphasis on Consumption.* This approach places more emphasis on the level of domestic consumption than on relative prices. A mere reduction in the level of domestic consumption for reducing absorption does not mean that resources so released will be redirected for improving *BOP* deficit.

6. THE MONETARY APPROACH

The monetary approach to the balance of payments is an explanation of the overall balance of payments. It explains changes in balance of payments in terms of the demand for and supply of money. According to this approach, "a balance of payments deficit is always and everywhere a monetary phenomenon." Therefore, it can only be corrected by monetary measures.

Its Assumptions

This approach is based on the following assumptions:

1. The 'law of one price' holds for identical goods sold in different countries, after allowing for transport costs.

2. There is perfect substitution in consumption in both the product and capital markets which ensures one price for each commodity and a single interest rate across countries.

3. The level of output of a country is assumed exogenously.

4. All countries are assumed to be fully employed where wage price flexibility fixes output at full employment.

5. It is assumed that under fixed exchange rates the sterilisation of currency flows is not possible on account of the law of one price globally.

6. The demand for money is a stock demand and is a stable function of income, prices, wealth and interest rate.

7. The supply of money is a multiple of monetary base which includes domestic credit and the country's foreign exchange reserves.

8. The demand for nominal money balances is a positive function of nominal income.

The Theory

Given these assumptions, the monetary approach can be expressed in the form of the following relationship between the demand for and supply of money :

The demand for money (M_D) is a stable function of income (Y), prices (P) and rate of interest (i)

$$M_D = f(Y, P, i) \qquad \text{...(1)}$$

The money supply (M_S) is a multiple of monetary base (m) which consists of domestic money (credit) (D) and country's foreign exchange reserves (R). Ignoring m for simplicity which is a constant,

$$M_S = D + R \qquad \text{...(2)}$$

Since in equilibrium the demand for money equals the money supply,

$$M_D = M_S \qquad \text{...(3)}$$

or $$M_D = D + R \quad [M_S = D + R] \quad ...(4$$

A balance of payments deficit or surplus is represented by changes in the country's foreign exchang reserves. Thus

$$\Delta R = DM_D - DD \quad ...(5$$

or $$\Delta R = B \quad ...(6$$

where *B* represents balance of payments which is equal to the difference between change in the demand for money (DM_D) and change in domestic credit (DD).

A balance of payments deficit means a *negative B* which reduces *R* and the money supply. On the othe hand, a surplus means a positive *B* which increases *R* and the money supply. When *B* = *O*, it means *BOP* equilibrium or no disequilibrium of *BOP*.

The automatic adjustment mechanism in the monetary approaches is explained under both the fixed and flexible exchange rate systems.

Under the *fixed exchange rate system*, assume that $M_D = M_S$ so that *BOP* (or *B*) is zero. Now suppose the monetary authority increases domestic money supply, with no change in the demand for money. As a result $M_S > M_D$ and there is a *BOP* deficit. People who have larger cash balances increase their purchases to buy mor foreign goods and securities. This tends to raise their prices and increase imports of goods and foreign assets This leads to increase in expenditure on both current and capital accounts in *BOP*, thereby creating a *BOP* defici To maintain a fixed exchange rate, the monetary authority will have to sell foreign exchange reserves and bu domestic currency. Thus the outflow of foreign exchange reserves means a fall in *R* and in domestic mone supply. This process will continue until $M_S = M_D$ and there will again be *BOP* equilibrium.

On the other hand, if $M_S < M_D$ at the given exchange rate, there will be a *BOP* surplus. Consequently people acquire the domestic currency by selling goods and securities to foreigners. They will also seek t acquire additional money balances by restricting their expenditure relatively to their income. The monetar authority on its part, will buy excess foreign currency in exchange for domestic currency. There will be inflow of foreign exchange reserves and increase in domestic money supply. This process will continue until $M_S = M$ and *BOP* equilibrium will again be restored. Thus a *BOP* deficit or surplus is a temporary phenomenon and i self-correcting (or automatic) in the long-run.

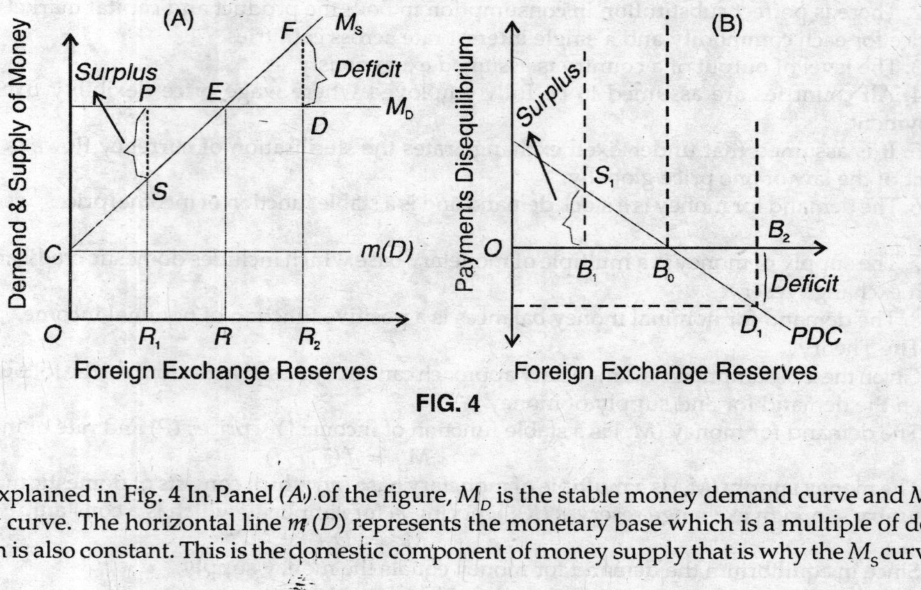

FIG. 4

This is explained in Fig. 4 In Panel *(A)* of the figure, M_D is the stable money demand curve and M_S is th money supply curve. The horizontal line *m* (*D*) represents the monetary base which is a multiple of domest credit, *D* which is also constant. This is the domestic component of money supply that is why the M_S curve star from point *C*.

M_S and M_D curves intersect at point *E* where the country's balance of payments is in equilibrium and i oreign exchange reserves are *OR*. In Panel (*B*) of the figure, *PDC* is the payments disequilibrium curve which s drawn as the vertical difference between M_S and M_D curves of Panel (*A*). As such, point B_0 in Panel (*B*) orresponds to point *E* in Panel (*A*) where there is no disequilibrium of balance of payments.

If $M_S < M_D$ there is *BOP* surplus of *SP* in Panel (*A*). It leads to the inflow of foreign exchange reserves vhich rise from OR_1 to *OR* and increase the money supply so as to bring *BOP* equilibrium at point *E*. On the ther hand, if $M_S > M_D$, there is deficit in *BOP* equal to *DF*. There is outflow of foreign exchange reserves which ecline from OR_2 to *OR* and reduce the money supply so as to reestablish *BOP* equilibrium at point *E*. The same rocess is illustrated in Panel (*B*) of the figure where *BOP* disequilibrium is self-correcting or automatic when $_1S_1$ surplus and B_2D_1 deficit are equal.

Under a system of *flexible* (or *floating*) *exchange rates*, when *B* = *O*, there is no change in foreign exchange eserves (*R*). But when there is a *BOP* deficit or surplus, changes in the demand for money and exchange rate lay a major role in the adjustment process without any inflow or outflow of foreign exchange reserves. uppose the monetary authority increases the money supply ($M_S > M_D$) and there is a *BOP* deficit. People aving additional cash balances buy more goods thereby raising prices of domestic and imported goods. There s depreciation of the domestic currency and a rise in the exchange rate. The rise in prices, in turn, increases the emand for money thereby bringing the equality of M_D and M_S without any outflow of foriegn exchange eserves. The opposite will happen when $M_D > M_S$, there is fall in prices and appreciation of the domestic urrency which automatically eliminates the excess demand for money. The exchange rate falls until $M_D = M_S$ nd *BOP* is in equilibrium without any inflow of foreign exchange reserves.

ts Criticisms

The monetary approach to the balance of payments has been criticised on a number of counts:

1. *Demand for Money not Stable.* Critics do not agree with the assumption of stable demand for money. The emand for money is stable in the long run but not in the short run when it shows less stability.
2. *Full Employment not Possible.* Similarly, the assumption of full employment is not acceptable because ere exists involuntary unemployment in countries.
3. *One Price Law Invalid.* Frankel and Johnson[6] are of the view that the law of one price holds for identical oods sold is invalid. This is because when factors of production are drawn into sectors producing non-trading oods, the excess demand for non-traded goods will spill over into reduced supplies of traded goods. This will ad to higher imports, and disturb the law of one price for all traded goods.
4. *Market Imperfections.* There are also market imperfections which prevent the law of one price from orking properly in many markets for traded goods. There may be price differentials due to the lack of formation about overseas prices and trade regulations faced by traders.
5. *Sterilisation not Possible.* The assumption that the sterilisation of currency flows is not possible under xed exchanged rates, has not been accepted by critics. They argue that "the sterilisation of currency flows is ntirely possible if the private sector is willing to adjust the composition of its wealth portfolio with regard to e relative importance of bonds and money balances, or if the public sector is prepared to run a higher budget eficit whenever it has a balance of payments deficit with which to contend."
6. *Link between BOP and Money Supply not Valid.* The monetary approach is based upon direct link etween *BOP* of a country and its total money supply. This has been questioned by economists. The link etween the two depends upon the ability of the monetary authority to neutralise the inflows and outflows of reign exchange reserves when there is *BOP* deficit and surplus. This requires some degree of sterilisation of ternal flows. But this is not possible due to globalisation of financial markets.
7. *Neglects Short Run.* The monetary approach is related to the self correcting long-run equilibrium in OP. This is unrealistic because it fails to describe the short time through which the economy passes to reach the w equilibrium. As pointed out by Prof. Krause, the monetary approach's "concentration on the long-run sumes away all of the problems that make the balance of payments a problem."
8. *Neglects Other Factors.* This approach neglects all real and structural factors which lead to disequilibrium

---

6. L.A. Frankel and H.G. Johnson (eds.), *The Monetary Approach to the Balance of Payments*, 1976.

in *BOP* and concentrates only on domestic credit.

9. *Neglects Economic Policy.* This approach emphasises the role of domestic credit in bringing *BOP* equilibrium and neglects economic policy measures. According to Prof. Currie, the balance of payments equilibrium can also be "achieved by expenditure-switching policies working through real flows and government budget."

Conclusion. Despite these criticisms, the monetary approach is realistic in that it takes into consideration both domestic money and foreign money. Emphasis is not on relative price changes, but on the extent to which the demand for real money balances will be satisfied from internal sources, through credit creation or from external sources through surplus or deficit in the balance of payments. A balance of payments deficit or surplus can be corrected through changes in money supply and their consequent effects on income and expenditure, or more generally on production and consumption of goods.

EXERCISES

1. Critically discuss the monetary approach to the balance of payments problem.
2. Discuss the alternative automatic adjustment mechanisms for balance of payments. What are their assumptions?
3. Discuss the elasticity approach to the effect of devaluation on balance of payments.
4. Discuss the process of adjustment in the balance of payments through the variations in prices. Explain its limitations.
5. Discuss the role of devaluation in reducing deficits in the balance of payments of a country. State its limitations.
6. Discuss the Marshall-Lerner Condition for effective devaluation.
7. Discuss the mechanism of the absorption approach to the balance of payments adjustment. What are its assumptions and limitations?

CHAPTER 48

The International Monetary Fund

1. ORIGIN OF IMF

The International Monetary Fund (IMF), also called the Fund, is an international monetary institution established by 44 nations under the Bretton Woods Agreement of July 1944. The principal aim was to avoid the economic mistakes of the 1920s and 1930s. The attempts of many countries to return to the old gold system after the First World War failed miserably. The World Depression of the thirties forced every country to abandon the gold standard. This led to the adoption of purely nationalistic policies whereby almost every country imposed trade restrictions, exchange controls and resorted to exchange depreciation in order to encourage its exports. This, further, brought a marked decline in world trade and extension of depression. It was against this background that 44 nations assembled at the United Nations Monetary and Financial Conference at Bretton Woods, New Hampshire (USA) from July 1 to July 22, 1944. Thus the IMF was established to promote economic and financial co-operation among its members in order to facilitate the expansion and balanced growth of world trade. It started functioning from March 1, 1947. In June 1996, the Fund had 181 members.

OBJECTIVES OF THE FUND

The fundamental purposes and objectives of the Fund had been laid down in Article 1 of the original Articles of Agreement and they have been upheld in the two amendments that were made in 1969 and 1978 to its basic Charter. They provide the framework within which the Fund functions. They are as under :

1. To promote international monetary co-operation through a permanent institution which provides the machinery for consumption and collaboration in international monetary problems.
2. To facilitate the expansion and balanced growth of international trade and to contribute thereby to the promotion and maintenance of high levels of employment and real income and to the development of the productive resources of all members as primary objectives of economic policy.
3. To promote exchange stability, to maintain orderly exchange arrangements among members, and to avoid competitive exchange depreciation.
4. To assist in the establishment of a multilateral system of payments in respect of current transactions between member and in the elimination of foreign exchange restrictions which hamper the growth in the world trade.
5. To lend confidence to members by making the Fund's resources available to them under adequate safeguards, thus providing them with opportunity to correct maladjustments in their balance of payments without resorting to measures destructive of national or international prosperity.
6. In accordance with the above, to shorten the duration and lessen the degree of disequilibrium in the international balance of payments of members.

Ogranisation and Structure of the Fund

The Second Amendment of the Articles of Agreement made important changes in the organisation and structure of the Fund. As such, the structure of the Fund consists of a Board of Governors, an Executive Board, a Managing Director, a Council and a staff with its headquarters in Washington, U.S.A. There are ad hoc and standing committees appointed by the Board of Governors and the Executive Board. There is also an Interim Committee (now the International Monetary and Financial Committee—IMFC) appointed by the Board of Governors. The Board of Governors and the Executive Board are decision-making organs of the Fund. They exercise powers and take decisions that are binding on members and the Fund. The Board of Governors is at the top in the structure of the Fund. It is composed of one Governor and one alternate Governor appointed by each member. Normally, a member appoints its minister of finance or the Governor of its central bank as its Governor. The alternate Governor can participate in the meetings of the Board but has the power to vote only in the absence of the Governor.

The Board of Governors which has now 24 members, meets annually in which details of the Fund activities for the previous year are presented. The annual meeting also takes a few decisions with regard to the policies of the Fund. Special meetings can be convened by any of the five members having 25 per cent of the total voting rights. As a matter of practice, the majority of decision-making powers of the Board of Governors have been delegated to the Board of Executive Directors such a decisions on access by the members of the Fund's resources, decisions on charges and remuneration and the review of consultations between the Fund and its members.

The Executive Board has 21 members at present. Five Executive Directors are appointed by the five members (USA, UK, W. Germany, France and Japan) having the largest quotas. Saudi Arabia has appointed a sixth Executive Director by being one of the two largest contributors to the Fund. 15 Executive Directors are elected at intervals of two years by the remaining members according to the constituencies on a roughly geographical basis.

There is a *Managing Director* of the Fund who is elected by the Executive Directors. He is usually a politician or an important international official. He is the non-voting Chairman of the Executive Board. Besides acting as the Chairman of the Executive Board, the Managing Director is the head of the Fund staff and is responsible for its organisation, appointment and dismissal.

The *Executive Board* is the most powerful organ of the Fund and exercises vast powers conferred on it by the Articles of Agreement and delegated to it by the Board of Governors. So its powers relate to all Fund activities, including its regulatory, supervisory and financial activities. Any major change in the IMF procedure requires 85 per cent majority in the Executive Board. Hence the discretion lies with the US and EEC as they have 22 per cent and 27 per cent of the voting strength respectively. The Executive Board is in the continuous session and meets several times a week.

The Interim Committee (now IMFC) was established in October 1974 to advise the Board of Governors on supervising the management and adaptation of the international monetary system in order to avoid disturbances that might threaten it. It currently has 22 members.

The Development Committee was also established in October 1974 and consists of 22 members. It advises and reports to the Board of Governors on all aspects of the transfer of real resources to developing countries and makes suggestions for their implementation.

Quotas and their Fixation

The Fund has General Account based on quotas allocated to its members. When a country joins the Fund, it is assigned a quota that governs the size of its subscription, its voting power, and its drawing rights. At the time of the formation of the IMF, each member was required to pay 25 per cent of its quota in gold or 10 per cent of its net official holdings of gold and US dollars whichever was less. Under the Second Amendment effective 1 April 1978, 25 per cent of a member's quota payable in gold was substituted by SDRs or usable currencies. The remaining 75 per cent of quota was to be furnished in the country's own currency. But it was kept in the country's central bank. The practice of keeping gold reserves with the Fund was discontinued from

April 1978 and the Fund has been delinked from the gold since then. Now a member country is allowed to maintain the value of its currency and quota in terms of the Special Drawing Rights (SDRs).

In order to meet the financial requirements of the Fund, the quotas are reviewed every five years and are raised from time to time. But quotas can only be raised by a resolution of the majority of 85 per cent of the total voting power of the Fund's members. When the Fund started operation in March 1947, the total quotas were 7.6 billion dollars which had been increased to SDR 146 billion in April, 1994 with the Tenth General Review of Quotas. This increase was 50% of members quotas. With the Eleventh Review of Quotas effective March 1998, the quotas were raised by 45% to SDR 212 billion.

Thus a member country's quota determines its subscription to the Fund, its relative voting power, allocation of SDRs and access to Fund's resources. A member's voting power is based on one vote for each SDR 100,000 of quota in addition to the basic votes of 250 for each member. When a country becomes the member of the Fund, it is allocated a quota which raises the total resources of the IMF.

Functions of the Fund

The IMF operates in such a way as to fulfil its objectives as laid down in the Bretton Woods Articles of Agreements. It is the Fund's duty to see that these provisions are observed by member countries. Some of the provisions of the original Articles such as relating to exchange rates have become obsolete due to international monetary events. Accordingly the Fund has amended its Articles of Agreement to make appropriate adjustments.

The Fund is regarded "as the guardian of good conduct" in the sphere of balance of payments. It aims at reducing tariffs and other trade restrictions by the member countries. Articles VII of the Charter provides that no member shall, without the approval of the Fund, impose restrictions on the making of payments or engage in discriminatory currency arrangements or multiple currency practices. It is the functions of the Fund to have a surveillance of the policies being adopted by the member countries.

The Fund also renders technical advice to its members on monetary and fiscal policies. It conducts research studies and publishes them. It provides technical experts to member countries having BOP difficulties. It also conducts short training courses on fiscal, monetary and balance of payments for personnel from member nations through its Central Banking Service Development, the Fiscal Affairs Department, the Bureau of Statistics and the IMF Institute.

Exchange Rates

The original Fund Agreement provided that the par value of each member country was to be expressed in terms of gold of certain weight and fineness or US dollars. The underlying idea was to create a system of stable exchange rates with orderly cross rates. But the Fund was obliged to agree to changes in exchange rates which did not exceed ± 1 per cent of the initial par value. A further change of ± 1 per cent required the permission of the Fund. Since 1971, these provisions have been changed and the international monetary system has moved from fixed exhcange rates to flexible exchange rates. Under the new system, the member countries are not expected to maintain and establish par values with gold or dollar. The Fund has no control over the exchange rate adjustment policies of the member countries.

But under Article IV of the Second Amendment, effective April 1978, the Fund has laid down principles for the guidance of exchange rate policies of its members : (*a*) to avoid manipulation of exchange rates in order to gain an unfair competitive advantage over other members; (*b*) to intervene in the exchange market to counter disorderly conditions; and (*c*) to take into account in their intervention policies the interests of other members.

Fund Borrowings

Besides performing regulatory and consultative functions, the Fund is an important financial institution. The bulk of its financial resources comes from quota subscriptions of member countries. Besides, it increases its funds by selling gold to members. Further, it borrows from government, central banks or private institutions of industrialised countries, the Bank for International Settlements, and even from OPEC counties, like Saudi Arabia.

General Arrangements to Borrow (GAB)

The Fund also borrows under the General Arrangements to Borrow from its eleven industrialised members in order to forestall or cope with an impairment of the international monetary system. The GAB remained in force from October 1962 to December 1998, when its total borrowings was SDR 17 billion. Under the *New Arrangements to Borrow*, the developed countries have sanctioned $ 25 billion.

Fund Lending

The Fund has a variety of facilities for lending its resources to member countries. Lending by the Fund is linked to temporary assistance to members in financing disequilibrium in their balance of payments on current account. If a member has less currency with the Fund than its quota, the difference is called *reserve tranche*. It can draw up to 25 per cent on its reserve tranche automatically upon representation to the Fund for its balance needs. It is not charged any interest on such drawings, but is required to repay within a period of three to five years.

Credit Tranches

A member can draw further annually from balance quota in 4 instalments upto 100% of its quota from credit tranches. Drawings from credit tranches are conditional because the members have to satisfy the Fund of adopting a viable programme to ensure financial stability. To meet the severe BOP problems, the Fund has been gradually raising the limit of borrowings by its members over the years under the credit tranche. Now members can draw up to the equivalent of 300 per cent of their new quotas on the total net use of the Fund's resources. The limits exclude drawings under CCFF, BSAF, SAF, STF and ESAF. Purchases by members are made under stand-by arrangement rather than directly. Borrowings up to this limit are allowed if a member country is making particularly strong efforts to correct its balance of payment disequilibrium and adjust its economy. Since the 1960s, the Fund has created several new credit facilities for its members. Loans from these facilities are separate from tranches and are available for a longer period. These are :

Buffer Stock Financing Facility (BSFF). It was created in 1969 for financing commodity buffer stock by member countries. The facility is equivalent to 30 per cent of the borrowing member's quota. Repurchases are made in 3¼ to 5 years. But the member is expected to cooperate with the Fund in establishing commodity prices within the country.

The Extended Fund Facility (EFF). It is another specialised facility which was created in 1974. Under EFF, the Fund provides credit to member countries to meet their balance of payments deficits for longer periods, and in amounts larger than their quotas under normal credit facilities. EFF provides credit upto a period of 10 years and loans upto 300 per cent of a member's quota are allowed. It is based on performance criteria and drawings instalments. It is availed of by developing countries.

Supplementary Financing Facility (SFF). It was established in 1977 to provide supplementary financing under extended or stand-by arrangements to member countries to meet serious balance of payments deficits that are large in relation to their economies and their quotas. The facility has been extended to low-income developing member countries of the Fund. To reduce the cost of borrowing under SFF to such countries, the Fund established Subsidy Account in 1980 through which it makes subsidy payments to borrower countries.

Structural Adjustment Facility (SAF). The Fund set up SAF in March 1986 to provide concessional adjustment to the poorer developing countries. Under it, loans are granted to them to solve balance of payments problems and to carry out medium term macro-economic and structural adjustment programmes. The SAF was created with SDR 2.7 billion of resources which come mainly from repayments on loans from the Trust Fund. Resources are made available to the poorer countries on highly concessional terms of .5 to 1 per cent interest with the principal repayable over 5½ to 10 years with a five-year grace period. Disbursements are made annually and are linked to the approval of annual arrangements with members receiving equivalent of 15 per cent of quota under the first annual arrangement, 20 per cent under the second and 15 per cent under the third.

Enhanced Structural Adjustment Facility (ESAF). The ESAF was created in December 1987 with SDR 6 billion of resources for the medium term financing needs of low income countries. The objectives, eligibility and basic programme features of this facility are similar to those of the SAF. But eligible members can receive a great deal more assistance under the ESAF than under the SAF upto 100 per cent of quota over a three-year programme period, with provision for upto 250 per cent in exceptional circumstances. Disbursements under the ESAF are semi-annual instead of annual.

Compensatory and Contingency Financing Facility (CCFF). The CCFF was created in August 1988 to provide timely compensation for temporary shortfalls or excesses in cereal import costs due to factors beyond the control of the member and contingency financing to help a member to maintain the momentum of Fund-supported adjustment programmes in the face of external shocks on account of factors beyond its control. In 1990, the Fund introduced an import element into CCFF for a temporary period upto the end of 1991 to help members overcome the Gulf War Crisis. This was within 95 per cent of quota for CCFF. The Fund also decided to expand the coverage of CCFF. Besides workers' remittances and travel receipts, shortfalls in other services such as receipts from pipelines, canals, shipping, transportation, construction and insurance have been included in the calculation of export shortfalls under compensatory financing.

Systematic Transformation Facility (STF). In April, 1993, the IMF established STF with $6 billion to help Russia and other Central Asian Republics to face balance of payments crisis.

Emergency Structural Adjustment Loans (ESAL). The Fund eastblished ESAL facility in early 1999 to help the Asian and Latin American countries inflicted with the financial crisis. Under it, such countries are given shot-term loans 3% to 5% above the Fund's normal interest rate which are to be repaid in a short period.

Contingency Credit Line (CCL). The CCL was created in April 1999 to protect fundamentally sound countries from the contagion of financial crisis occurring in other countries, rather than from domestic policy weaknesses. Only countries that over the medium term can finance BOP comfortably and enjoy healthy financial sectors and strong debtor-creditor relations are considered for CCL. So far no country has drawn from it.

Critical Appraisal of the Fund's Working

The IMF advises its member countries on various problems concerning their BOP and exchange rate problems and on monetary and fiscal issues. It sends specialists and experts to help solve BOP and exchange rate problems of member countries. They confer with local officials and suggest monetary, fiscal and other measures in their reports. The Fund has set up three departments to solve banking and fiscal problems of member countries. *First*, there is the Central Banking Service Department which helps member countries with the services of its experts to run and manage their central banks and to formulate banking legislation. Such services are especially provided to developing countries to reform their banking system. *Second*, the Fiscal Affairs Department renders advice to member countries concerning their fiscal matters. *Third*, The IMF Institute conducts short-term training courses for the officers of member countries relating to monetary, fiscal, banking, and BOP policies. Besides, the Fund's research department publishes many reports in a year containing material relating to different policy measures. These publications include IMF Annual Report and IMF Staff Papers, Finance and Development Journal, etc.

The IMF has been severely criticised in recent years for mishandling global finanacial crises in East Asia and Latin America, aggravating poverty in developing countries, encouraging bad policies by governments and financial investors and favouring the developed countries. We discuss below some points of criticism.

1. Fund Conditionalities. The Fund has developed conditionalities over the last five decades or so which a country has to fulfil for getting a loan from the Fund. Prior to the 1970s, the Fund laid stress on *expenditure reduction* for meeting disequilibrium in the balance of payments of a country. In the 1970s, the Fund conditionality included the need to take into account the *causes of balance of payments difficulties* of members requesting for Fund resources, their *economic priorities and their social and political* requirement. On March 2, 1979, a *new set of guidelines* was laid down for the use of Fund resources, besides the previous conditionality practices. These include periodic assessment of the experience of the member country with adjustment programmes financed by Fund resources. The new emphasis is on policies to increase productivity and to improve resource allocation in the programmes supported by Fund resources. They also include stringent Fund conditionalities or performance criteria such as controlling deficits, reforming the banking system, even closing down non-viable units, altering systems of administration and laws which give rise to corruption. The release of every installment requires their review.

The Fund has laid down some more conditionalities after the 1995 Mexican and the Asian financial crises. (1) to liberalise trade by removing exchange and import controls; (2) to eliminate all subsidies so that the exporters are not in an advantageous position in relation to the other trading countries; and (3) to treat foreign lenders on an equal footing with domestic lenders. Besides, the Fund insists on good governance. Thus the Fund exercises surveillance ever the exchange rates monetary, fiscal and related policies of the borrowing countries which makes a mockery of its policy of non-interfering in their internal economic affairs.

2. *High Interest Rates.* Besides, these hard conditionalities, the Fund charges high interest rates on loans of different types. They are a great burden on the borrowing countries. This is the reason that developing countries like India are so heavily burdened with the debt service charge that fresh borrowings are negative.

3. *Secondary Role.* The Fund has been playing only a secondary role rather than the central role in international monetary relations. It does not provide facilities for short-term credit arrangements. This has resulted in "swap" arrangements among the central banks of the Group of Ten of the leading developed countries. Under these arrangements, these countries exchange each other's currencies and also provide short-term credit to tide over temporary disequilibria in their balance of payments. Such swap arrangements have led to the growth of Euro-currency Market. All this has reduced the importance of the Fund.

4. *Lack of Resources.* The IMF has not enough resources for immediate future. But these are not sufficient to meet the future needs of its members. The need is to raise the resources of the Fund to safeguard the international financial system which is dominated by volatile capital flows. The developed countries are not willing to increase the quota of the Fund.

5. *Failure to Maintain Exchange Rate Stability.* The Fund has failed in its objective of promoting exchange stability and to maintain orderly exchange arrangements among members. Under the original Fund agreements, the exchange rate was permitted to fluctuate within a range of 1 per cent above to 1 per cent below the official price. This was known as the "adjustable peg" system. The exchange rate of every member country was fixed in terms of the "golden dollar". Over the years US gold stock continued to decline, the US balance of payments continued to deteriorate. Consequently, the Bretton Woods system collapsed on 15 August, 1971 when President Nixon announced that United States would no longer convert dollars into gold and that it would not intervene in foreign exchange markets to maintain exchange rate stability. Since then there has been a mixture of exchange rate systems of nationally managed floating, joint floating, and pegged exchange rates. According to Prof. Schwartz, the IMF has lost its objective.

6. *Failure to Eliminate Foreign Exchange Restrictions.* One of the objectives of the Fund has been to eliminate foreign exchange restrictions which hamper the growth in world trade. The Fund has not been successful in achieving this objective. The world trade is restricted by a variety of exchange controls and multiple exchange practices.

7. *Discriminatory Politics.* The Fund has been criticised for its discriminatory policies against the developing countries and in favour of the developed countries. It is, therefore, characterised as "Rich Countries Club". Although the majority of its members are the developing countries of Asia, Africa and Latin America, yet it is dominated by the rich countries especially the United States. The latter often adopts a rigid attitude in matters concerning increasing the Fund resources and granting loans to developing countries.

8. *Responsible for Asian Crisis.* The sudden and unexpected East-Asian crisis in Phillipines, South Korea, Thailand, Indonesia and Malaysia put a question mark on the working of the Fund. Friedman has put the blame on the IMF for global crisis because it has been the result of government's intervention in the market, both internationally via loans, subsidies or taxes, and externally via the IMF. With the collapse of the Bretton-Woods system in 1971 when the member countries adopted the floating exchange rate policy, the Funds role of regulating the exchange rate ended. Prior to the 1995 Mexican crisis, the objective of the Fund was to provide advice, information and loans to its members. But when it helped Mexico in a bail out package in its crisis of

1995, it acted the international lender of last resort. Under it, the Fund laid emphasis on close financial relations among banks, corporations and governments and to increase the operations of stock and bond markets so that there is greater competition between domestic and global financial institutions. This very policy led to the Asian and global financial crisis when there was successive decline in shares, bonds and currencies of these countries. The real beneficiaries of this policy were not the borrowing countries but the foreign banks and financial institutions who lend to these countries which failed to repay the loans. When due to declining exchange rates, they started withdrawing their funds, there was a crisis in the borrowing countries. A Michael Musa, the IMF Chief Economist, admitted in August 2000 that the recent financial crisis was due to high openness to international capital flows, especially short-run credit flows of countries with fragile financial systems. According to Schwartz, since the Fund lacks in high powered base money, it failed to act as an international lender of last resort. Thus the IMF has been weak in controlling financial crisis. Schwartz, therefore, suggests that it should be shut down. According to Friedman, it should be abolished as it did more harm than good.

Despite these criticisms, the IMF has shown sufficient flexibility to mould itself in keeping with the changing international economic conditions. The original Articles of Agreement were amended in 1978 to legalise flexible exchange rates, raise quotas to increase the Fund's resources and to dethrone the gold in Fund transactions. To solve the problem of international liquidity, it has created deficits, the Fund has been successively raising the limit of their borrowings which stands at 450 per cent of their quotas. The Fund has been helping the developing countries in their balance of payments and other problems through such facilities as CFF, BSFF, EFF, SFF, SAF, ESAF, CCFF, etc. Finally, the usefulness and success of the Fund lies in that its membership has risen from 44 in 1947 to 182.

2. THE ROLE OF GOLD IN THE IMF

The Fund Agreement fixed the par values of currencies of its members in terms of gold. This led economists like Williams and Halm to suggest that the Fund's gold provisions were "not just window dressing". Rather, they essentially related to a gold standard plan. On the other hand, Keynes held that the IMF had "dethroned" gold and its proposals were "the exact opposite of the gold standard". Let us analyse these views one by one.

According to the first view, the Fund incorporates all the features of the international gold standard minus its disadvantages. The par values of the currencies of its members are fixed in terms of gold. Therefore, the exchange rates of member countries are fixed in the same manner as under the gold standard. Further, gold is expressed as a common denominator for international transactions, they are like short-term capital movements under the gold standard. Member countries may buy and sell gold at the international price fixed by the Fund. The Fund may also buy gold from members at the same price. Again, the Fund mechanism has the same monetary and price effects as under the gold standard, affecting central bank reserves of member countries in precisely the same manner as the movement of gold under the gold standard. For example, when a deficit country buys foreign exchange from the Fund, the volume of international currency with its central bank is reduced which in turn reduces the reserve position of its commercial banks. They are forced to contract credit and deflation starts. In the opposite case, the volume of international currency increases in surplus country. As a result, the reserves of its commercial banks increase. They expand credit and there is inflation. Thus the Fund mechanism resembles the gold standard mechanism.

The Fund scheme differs from the gold standard in the following ways : *First*, under the gold standard all countries must adopt gold standard within their countries. Under the Fund scheme, the member countries are not required to adopt the gold standard. *Second*, the exchange rates are rigidly fixed under the gold standard. But they are flexible under the Fund scheme. They can be changed to correct fundamental disequilibrium by a member country. *Third*, the gold standard requires automatic adjustment of international prices and incomes in order to maintain rigid exchange rates. But the Fund requires adjustments in exchange rates in keeping with the internal price and income structure of the country. *Fourth*, under the Fund Charter, there is not provision for a deficit country to adopt deflationary policies. Rather, it aims at removing deflationary tendencies in member countries. *Fifth*, the supply of gold influences the value of national currency under the gold standard.

But the Fund makes international currencies available to members independent of the international currencies in the "Fund pool" and loans them to deficit member countries. *Sixth,* the Fund allows temporary exchange restrictions by its member to correct their fundamental disequilibria, whereas such restrictions are not allowed under the gold standard. *Seventh,* according to Ellsworth, since the Fund Agreement "did not prescribe gold as the sole form in which reserves could be held it did not usher in a true gold standard". Thus the Fund mechanism differs fundamentally from the gold mechanism in so many way, that led Keynes to remark that it is "the exact opposite of the gold standard".

Although the Fund "dethroned" the gold standard, yet gold continued to play an important role in the Fund till the Second Amendment to the IMF Charter. The par values of currencies of member countries were expressed in terms of gold or US dollar, one dollar being equivalent to 0.888671 gram or $35 an ounce of gold. When the US devalued the dollar in May 1972, the weight of gold behind dollar was reduced to 0.818513 gram or $ 38 an ounce for gold. With the Second Amendment, a new international currency, SDR, has been introduced for all Fund transactions with member countries. This currency is no longer linked to gold but to a basket of five major currencies viz. the US Dollar, German Mark, French Franc, Japanese Yen, and British Pound. There is no official price of gold and members are required to make payments in gold to the Fund. Part of Fund's gold holdings have been sold in the market for the benefit of developing member countries. At the time of the Second Amendment, the Fund's gold holdings were equal to more than 150 million ounces or 4710 tons. It was decided to sell 50 million ounces. Accordingly, the Fund held 45 auctions from June 1976 to May 1980 amounting to 47 million ounces at gold prices prevailing in the London Market. The Fund's present gold holdings amount to 130 million ounces which can only be sold if a majority of 85 per cent in the Fund's financial transactions except that the Fund continues to value its holdings at SDR $ 35 an ounce. According to Prof. Bernstein, "All that now remains of the historic monetary role of gold is its function as reserve asset."

3. INDIA AND THE IMF

India is one of the founder members of the IMF. It signed the Fund Agreement on 27 December, 1945. Till 1970 India's quota in the Fund was the fifth and it had the power to appoint a permanent Executive Director. With the increase in the Fund quota after May 1970, the quotas of Japan, Canada and Italy increased more than that of India. Accordingly, India ceased to hold a permanent position as Executive Director of the Fund. With the Eleventh Review of Quotas, India's quota in the IMF declined from 2.09 per cent to 1.96 per cent. As a result, India's position in the Fund quota came down to 13th. However, in absolute terms, India's quota increased from SDR 3.56 billion to 4.16 billion.

The par value of the Indian rupee was fixed at 0.26801 gram of gold or 30.225 US cents when India became its member. When the rupee was devalued on September 18, 1949, its par value was reduced to 0.186621 gram of gold or 21 US cents. It was further reduced to 0.118489 gram of gold or 13.33 US cents on June 6, 1966 when the rupee was again devalued. Since the devaluation of the dollar in May 1972, its par value fell further. But with the Second Amendment of the Fund Agreement, the exchange rate of the rupee has been floating like other currencies and is linked to SDR.

India has been one of the major beneficiaries of the Fund assistance. It has been getting aid from the various Fund agencies from time to time and has been regularly repaying its debt. Between 1947 to 1955, India borrowed $100 million twice to tide over its balance of payments difficulties. India borrowed eight times between 1957 to 1975 a total sum of $1764 million. It also received loan disburse-ments at concessional terms to overcome balance of payments difficulties amounting to SDR $529 million from July 1, 1978 to February 21, 1981 under the IMF Trust Fund.

In 1979, India entered into agreement with the IMF for a loan of $5.6 billion or Rs. 5,220 crores under the EFF. It started receiving the loan in instalments for a three-year period beginning from November 9, 1981. Till April 1984, it had drawn $ 3.9 billion and intimated the Fund that it would not be drawing the remaining amount at all. After April 1984, India did not take any recourse under its modified Compensatory and Contingency Financing Facility (CCFF). In January 1991, it received $ 0.79 billion as the first credit tranche of a stand-by arrangement for three months. At the same time, India got the first credit of $ 1.09 billion under CCFF, followed by the second loan of $ 220 million in July 1991 and the third loan of $ 635 million in September

1991. On 31 October, the IMF approved a stand-by credit of $ 2.2 billion to be disbursed to India in 8 tranches over a 20-month period from November 1991 to June 1993. Normally, member countries get only 50 to 60 per cent of their quotas in loans. But India received more than 100 per cent of its quota. India's quota in the Fund was $ 3.01 billion (or SDR 2.2 billion) and its gross drawings from the Fund from January 1991 to June 1993 were $ 3.5 billion. This speaks of the Fund's confidence in the Indian economy.

Besides receiving loans to meet deficit in its balance of payments, India has benefitted in certain other respects from the membership of the Fund. By virtue of being a member of the Fund, India is also a member of the IBRD (World Bank) from which it has been receiving financial aid for its various development projects. It has been getting advisory help from the Fund under the Fund surveilance conditionality. A Fund team of four or five economists often visits India. These economists exchange views with Indian officials on India's balance of payments and exchange rate problems and suggest monetary, fiscal, and other measures to solve them. The Fund has also been providing short-term training courses to Indian personnel on monetary, fiscal, banking, exchange, and balance of payments policies through its Central Banking Service Department, the Fiscal Affairs Department, and the IMF Institute. Thus India has gained much as a member of the Fund.

4. SPECIAL DRAWING RIGHTS (SDRS)

MEANING

Special Drawing Rights (SDRs), also known as the *paper gold*, are a form of international reserves created by the IMF in 1969 to solve the problem of international liquidity. They are not paper notes or currency. They are international units of account in which the official accounts of the IMF are kept. They are allocated to the IMF members in proportion to their Fund quotas and are used to settle balance of payments deficits between them.

ORIGIN OF SDRs

SDRs were created through the First Amendment to the Fund Articles of Agreement in 1969 following persistent US deficits in balance of payments to solve the problem of international liquidity. Until December 1971, an SDR was linked to 0.88867 gram of gold and was equivalent to US $1. With the breakdown of the fixed parity system after 1973 when the US dollar and other major currencies were allowed to float, it was decided to stabilise the exchange value of the SDR. Accordingly, the value of the SDR was calculated each day on the basis of a basket of 16 most widely used currencies of the member countries of the Fund. Each country was given a weight in the basket in accordance with its importance in international trade and financial markets. After the Second Amendment to the Fund Articles of Agreement in 1978, the SDR became an international unit of account. To facilitate its valuation, the number of currencies in the "basket" were reduced to five in January 1981. They include the US dollars, the German Deutsche Mark, the British Pound, the French Franc and the Japanese Yen. The present currency composition and weighting pattern of the SDR is revised every five years beginning January 1, 1986. The revision of weights is based on both the values of the exports of goods and services and the balances of their currencies held by other members. In 1977, they were US dollar (39%), German DM (21%), UK pound and French franc (11% each) and Japanese yen (18%). The value of one SDR was equal to US $ 1.35610 on October 1, 1997.

USES OF SDRs

SDR is an international unit of account which is held in the Fund's Special Drawing Account. The quotas of all currencies in the Fund General Account are also valued in terms of the SDR. As the international monetary asset, the SDR is held in the international reserves of central banks and governments to finance their deficits or surpluses of balance of payments. All transactions by the Fund in the form of loans and their repayments, its liquid reserves, its capital, etc., are expressed in the SDR.

SDRs are used as a means of payment by Fund members to meet balance of payments deficits and their total reserve position with the Fund. They cannot be used for any other purpose. Thus SDRs act both as an international unit of account and a means of payment.

There are *three* principal uses of SDRs.

1. *Transactions with Designation.* Under it, Fund designates a participant in the SDR scheme who has a strong balance of payments and reserve position to provide currency in exchange for SDRs to another participant needing its currency. The currency to be exchanged for SDRs may belong to the designated participated or/and to other participants. Participants are allowed to accept SDRs in this way as long as their holdings are less than three times their total allocations.

2. *Transactions with General Account.* SDRs are used in all transactions with the General Account of the Fund. Participants pay charges in SDRs to the General Account for the use of the Fund resources and also to repurchase their own currency from it.

3. *Transactions by Agreement.* The Fund allows sales of SDRs for currency by agreement with another participant.

In order to further widen the uses of SDRs, the Second Amendment empowered the Fund to lay down uses of SDRs not otherwise specified. Accordingly, the following additional uses of SDRs are : (*i*) in swap arrangements, (*ii*) in forward operations, (*iii*) in loans, (*iv*) in the settlement of financial objections, (*v*) as security for the performance of financial obligations, and (*vi*) in donations or grants.

The Fund also empowers certain institutions as "other holder" of SDRs. Besides the World Bank and its associates, some of the other holders of SDRs are the Bank for International Settlements, the African Development Bank. These 'other holders' acquire and use SDRs in transactions and operations by agreement under the same terms and conditions as applicable to the participants. Efforts are being made by the Fund to have a greater use of the SDR as a unit of account in private transactions and in financial markets of the world.

The Fund pays interest on all holdings of SDRs kept in the Special Drawing Account and charges interest at the same rate on allocations to participants.

Allocation of SDRs

The Fund allocates SDRs to participants in proportion to their quotas for various uses mentioned above. Initially, the Fund created SDR $ 9.3 billion over the three years 1970-72. The total holdings of SDR $ 9.3 billion continued till 1978. In 1978, the Fund decided to raise them by SDR $ 4 billion in each of the years 1979, 1980 and 1981. As a result, the total holdings of SDRs were SDR $ 13.1 billion in 1979, SDR 17.3 $ billion in 1980 and SDR $ 21.4 billion in 1981. Since 1981 no further allocation of SDRs has been made by the Fund. The quantity of SDRs is determined by members of the Fund. It can only be increased if 85% votes of its members favour their increase. The basis of allocation of SDRs among the members of IMF is their quota subscriptions. At present, about 70% of SDRs are distributed to 26 rich countries and the remaining 30% to developing countries.

Merits of SDRs

Despite these weaknesses, the SDRs scheme possesses the following merits:

1. SDRs are a new form of international monetary reserves which have been created to free the international monetary system from its exclusive dependence on the US dollar.
2. They have rid the world of its dependence on the supply of gold and fluctuations in gold prices.
3. They cannot be demonetised like gold or become scarce when the demand for dollar increases in the world.
4. Unlike gold, SDRs are costless to produce because production of gold requires resources to mine, refine, transport and guard it.
5. SDRs have been created to improve international liquidity so as to correct fundamental disequilibria in balance of payments of Fund members. Under this scheme, the participants receive SDRs under *transactions with designation and transaction by agreement* unconditionally.
6. Fund members are not required to change their domestic economic policies as they are expected under the Fund aid programmes.
7. The payment and repayment of SDRs out of the Special Drawing Account is easier and more flexible than under the Fund schemes.

8. Last but not the least, SDRs act both as a unit of account and a means of payment of international monetary system.

Criticisms of SDRs

Despite these merits, the SDR scheme has been criticised on the following grounds:

1. *Inequitable Distribution.* It is an inequitable scheme which has tended to make unfair distribution of international liquidity. The allocation of SDRs to participating countries is proportional to their quotas. In this sense, the allocation of SDRs to developing countries is too low as compared to their needs. Low allocation of SDRs reduces the borrowing capacity of such countries.

2. *Not Linked with Development Finance.* SDR scheme does not link the creation of international reserves in the form of SDRs with the need for development finance on the part of developing countries. The need for liquidity on the part of developing countries is great "because of their higher costs of adjustment, limited access to private banking and higher capital markets, greater variability of exchange earnings, and opportunity cost of holding foreign exchange reserves". Under these circumstances, there is need to create more SDRs with fair distribution so that more unconditional liquidity is made available for the greater needs of developing countries.

3. *High Interest Rate.* The interest rate originally payable on net use of SDRs is 1.5 per cent. This has been gradually raised through time in order to make a more acceptable asset to hold. Now both users of SDRs pay and holders of SDRs receive, a market rate of interest based on interest rates prevailing in US, Britain, France, Germany and Japan which are quite high for developing countries.

4. *Failure to Distribute Social Saving.* Williamson and others have criticised the SDR scheme for its failure to distribute social saving of SDRs to the developing countries. The present rules for allocation distribute the social saving to a participant country in proportion to his contribution or its demand for SDRs. If the supply of SDRs equals the demand for it, there will no redistribution of resources between countries. But this is not so in the case of developing countries whose holdings of SDRs are very low as compared to the 26 developed countries. Thus the present scheme of SDRs fails to transfer social savings to the developing countries.

5. *Failure to meet International Liquidity Requirements.* Unfortunately, due to the rigid attitude of the United States and some other developed countries, the Fund has not been able to resume allocation of SDRs from January 1982, despite the repeated pleas of the developing countries over these years. So the Fund has failed in its objective of increasing international liquidity through SDRs. Consequently, faced with a recession, an inadequate flow of concessional aid and falling prices of commodities and raw materials, developing countries have been facing severe balance of payments and debt problems. Thus SDRs have failed to solve the problem of international liquidity.

EXERCISES

1. What were the main objectives behind the establishment of the IMF? How far the Fund has been successful in achiving these objectives?
2. Explain the objectives and functions of the IMF. Critically examine its achievements.
3. Discuss the role of gold in the scheme of the IMF.
4. Outline the objectives and functions of the IMF and explain the benefits which have flowed to India for being its member.
5. Discuss the nature and uses of Special Drawing Rights (SDRs) by the member countries of the IMF. Has their creation solved the problem of international liquidity?

CHAPTER

49

The World Bank

The International Bank for Reconstruction and Development (IBRD) or the World Bank was established in 1945 under the Bretton Woods Agreement of 1944 to assist in bringing about a smooth transition from a war-time to peace-time economy. It is a sister institution of the International Monetary Fund.

1. FUNCTIONS

The IBRD, also called the World Bank, performs the following functions :

1. To assist in the reconstruction and development of territories of its members by facilitating the investment of capital for productive purpose, and the encouragement of the development of productive facilities and resources in less development countries.

2. To promote private foreign investment by means of guarantees on particpation in loans and other investment made by private investors, and when capital is not available on reasonable terms, to supplement private investment by providing finance for productive purpose out of its own resources or from borrowed funds.

3. To promote the long-range balanced growth of international trade and the maintenance of equilibrium in the balance of payments of member countries by encouraging international investment for the development of their productive resources, thereby assisting in raising productivity, the standard of living and conditions of workers in their territories.

4. To arrange the loans made or guaranteed by it in relation to international loans through other channels so that more useful and urgent small and large projects are dealt with first.

2. MEMBERSHIP

The members of the International Monetary Fund are the members of the IBRD. It had 182 members in 2000. If a country resigns its membership, it is required to pay back all loans with interest on due dates. If the Bank incurs a financial loss in the years in which a member resigns, it is required to pay its share of the loss on demand.

3. ORGANISATION

Like the IMF, the IBRD has a three-tier structure with a President, Executive Directors and Board of Governors. The President of the World Bank Group (IBRD, IDA and IFC) is elected by the Bank's Executive Directors whose number is 21. Of these, 5 are appointed by the five largest shareholders of the World Bank. They are the US, UK, Germany, France and Japan. The remaining 16 are elected by the Board of Governors. There are also Alternate Directors. The first five belong to the same permanent member countries to which the Executive Directors belong. But the remaining Alternate Directors are elected from among the group of countries who cast their votes to choose the 16 Executive Directors belonging to their regions.

The President of the World Bank presides over the meetings of the Board of Executive Directors regularly once a month. The Executive Directors decide about policy within the framework of the Articles of Agreement. They consider and decide on the loan and credit proposal made by the President. They also present to the Board of Governors at its annual meetings audited accounts, an administrative budget, and the Annual Report on the operations and policies of the Bank. The President has a staff of more than 6,000 persons who carry on the working of the World Bank. He is assisted by a number of Senior Vice-Presidents and Directors of various departments and regions. The Board of Governors is the supreme body. Every member country appoints one Governor and an Alternate Governor for a period of five years. The voting power of each Governor is related to the financial contribution of its government.

4. CAPITAL STRUCTURE

The IBRD started with an authorised capital of $ 10 billion divided into 1,00,000 shares of $ 1,00,000. Of this, $ 9,400 million was actually subscribed. On June 30, 1985 the authorised capital stock of the IBRD comprised 7,16,500 authorised shares of the par value of SDR 1,00,000 each. In July 1992, the total authorised Bank capital was $ 184.1 billion with a capital increase of $ 9.3 billion or 77,159 shares provided to the republics of the former Soviet Union.

5. FUNDING STRATEGY

The IBRD's funding strategy has the following four basic objectives :

The *first* is to ensure the *availability of funds* to the Bank. For this purpose, the IBRD seeks to maintain unutilised access to funds in the markets in which it borrows.

The *second* objective is to *minimise the effective cost* of those funds to its borrowers. This is done through the currency mix of its borrowings and the time of borrowings. In the former case, it tends to maximise borrowings in currencies with low nominal interest rates. The time of borrowings is manipulated in two ways : (*a*) when interest rates are expected to rise, the Bank seeks to increase its borrowigs, and (*b*) when interest rates are expected to fall, it seeks to defer borrowings.

The *third* objective is to *control volatility in net income and overall loan charges.* For this purpose, the Bank started in July 1982 a pool-based variable lending rate system that uniformly adjusts interest charges applicable to the outstanding balance on all loans made under it. The existing loans were not affected by this lending system. When the majority of loans and borrowings are incorporated into the new lending rate system in future, the volatility of interest rates will be much reduced.

The *fourth* objective of the funding strategy is to provide an appropriate degree of *maturity transformation* between its borrowing and lending. Maturity transformation refers to the Bank's capacity to lend at longer maturities than it borrows. At the same time, it provides its borrowers with a modest degree of maturity transformation.

6. BORROWING AND LENDING ACTIVITIES

The Bank borrows from the following sources :

The IBRD is a corporate institution whose capital is subscribed by its members. It finances its lending operations primarily from its own medium and long-term borrowings in the international capital markets, and currency swap agreements (CSA). Under the CSA proceeds of a borrowing country are converted into a different currency, and simultaneously, a forward exchange agreement is exectuted providing for a schedule of future exhcanges of the two currencies in order to recover the currency converted. The effect of currency swaps is to transform the cost of original borrowing to a cost which reflects the market yield of the currency obtained in the conversion.

The Bank also borrows under the Discount-Note Programme. *First,* it places bonds and notes directly with its member governments, government agencies and central banks. *Second,* it offers issues to investors and in the public markets through investing banking firms, merchant banks and commercial banks.

The IBRD has evolved two new borrowing instruments. *First*, Central Bank Facility (CBF) is a one-year, Us dollar dominated facility for borrowing from official sources, particularly central banks. It is designed to reverse the declining trend in the IBRD's borrowings from such sources since the 1970s. In 1984, the Executive Directors authorised the Bank to borrow under the Facility upto $ 750 million with a one-year maturity plus funds maturity within a month under the Facility. *Second*, borrowings in Floating Rate Notes (FRNs) is meant to help the IBRD to meet some of the objectives of its funding strategy. The FRN market enables the Bank to gain access to a set of investors like commercial banks and certain other financial institutions which have not traditionally bought IBRD notes. The FRNs carry a medium/long-term maturity. A substantial amount of its resources also comes from its retained earnings and the flow of payments on its loans.

The Bank lends to member countries in any of the following ways :

(*i*) by marketing or participating in loans out of its own funds; (*ii*) by making or participating in direct loans out of funds raised in the market of a member or otherwise borrowed by the Bank; (*iii*) by guaranteeing in whole or in part loans made by private investors through the usual investment channels.

The total amount outstanding of participating in loans, direct loans and guarantees should not exceed 100 per cent of its unimpaired subscribed capital, reserves and surplus. It guarantees, participates in or makes loans to its members on the following conditions :

(*i*) If it is satisfied that in the prevailing market conditions the borrower would be unable to obtain the loan under conditions which in the opinion of the Bank are reasonable to the borrower.

(*ii*) Loans are for specific projects of reconstruction or development, except in special circumstances.

(*iii*) If the member in whose territory the project is located is not itself the borrower, the member or its central bank fully guarantees the repayment of the principal, the payment of interest and other charges on the loan.

(*iv*) The project for which the loan is required has been recommended by a competent committee in the form of a written report after a carefully study of the proposal.

(*v*) The borrower or the guarantor is in a position to meet its obligations under the loan.

In 1991, the Executive Board of the Bank approved modification in IBRD repayment terms which include shifting repayment of new loans for low income countries to annuity, extension of grace period through fiscal year 1991 on new loans to middle income countries from 3 to 5 years and review of repayment terms for middle income countries within 3 years.

Development credits carry a service charge of 0.75% and generally have 35-40 year final maturities with a 10-year grace period for principal payments.

The bank provides the following facilities to member countries :

Structural Adjustment Facility (SAF). Since 1985, the IBRD has introduced SAF to borrowing countries in order to reduce their balance of payments deficits while maintaining or regaining their economic growth. SAF funds are used to finance general imports with a few agreed exceptions such as luxury and military imports. SAFs are released in two parts and are based on stiffer conditions laid down by the Bank. The Bank aims at providing support to programmes running from 5 to 7 years through a series of up to five SAFs to a borrowing country.

Enhanced Structural Adjustment Facility (ESAF). In December 1987, the Bank has set up the ESAF to increase the availability of concessional resources to low-income member countries. It provides new concessional resources totalling SDR 6 billion which will be financed by special loans and contributions from developed and OPEC countries. Like the SAF, ESAF is meant to help the borrowing countries reduce their balance of payments deficits and encourage growth. Its financial terms are similar to the SAF. The interest rate is 0.5 per cent with repayments in ten semi-annual instalments beginning after 5½ years of disbursements.

The Bank makes medium and long-term loans unusually running up to the completion of the project. Loans generally have a grace period of 5 years and repayable over 20 years or less. The interest rate charged on loans by the Bank is calculated in accordance with a guideline related to its cost of borrowing. So loans are at variable interest rates. It charges an annual commitment charge of 0.75 per cent on undistributed balance and a one-time front-end on the amount of loan.

The Bank's lending operations for two decades since its inception were concentrated heavily upon capital infrastructural projects such as power generation and distribution, railway and roads, ports, telecommunications, major irrigation works, etc. Since the 1970s, loans for infrastructural investments have come down. Instead, it has begun to finance changes in the educational system in the developing countries, to establish institutions for the financing of industrial investments and provision of technical assistance in the selection and appraisal of industrial projects, and to help in the preparation of agricultural projects. Its present development strategy lays more emphasis on investments that can directly affect the welfare of the poor people of the developing countries by increasing their productivity and standard of living. Towards this end, it has been financing projects for agriculture and rural development, education, family planning, nutrition, low-cost housing, drinking water and sewerage. The distribution of IBRD funds is made by the country-income group and by the sector to the developing countries.

Special Action Programme (SAP). The Special Action Programme (SAP) has been started in 1983 to strengthen the IBRD's ability to assist member countries in adjusting to the current economic environment. It has four major elements: (1) An expansion in lending for high-priority operations that support structural adjustment, policy changes, production for export, fuller use of existing capacity, and the maintenance of crucial infrastructure. (2) Accelerated disbursements under existing and new investment commitments to ensure timely implementation of high priority projects. (3) Expanded advisory services on the design and implementation of appropriate policies. These include reviews of state enterprises studies to strengthen development-orientation and project-implementation capabilities, studies to increase the mobilisation of domestic resources, reviews of incentives for export diversification, and exploration of ways to stengthen debt-management capabilities. (4) Enlisting familiar efforts by other donors for fast disbursing assistance in support of programmes of the Bank and IMF.

Conditionalities for Lending

The World Bank conditionalities for lending are : (1) an unflinching commitment towards economic stability so as to reduce inflation and deficits; (2) an efficient regulatory mechanism ensuring transparent policies and depoliticised environment; (3) adequate risk management; (4) provision for long-term finance; and (5) increase in the share of the private sector in the country's GDP. In the Bank meeting of 1996, the Bank President declared that countries plagued by corruption would not be liable to receive Bank assistance in future.

7. Other Activities

The other activities of the IBRD include training, technical assistance, inter-organisational cooperation, economic research and studies, operations evaluation, and settlement of investment disputes of its members.

Training. The Bank set up a staff college in 1956, known as the Economic Development Institute (EDI) for training senior officials of the member developing countries. It helps them to improve the management of their economies and to increase the efficiency of their investment programmes. Its training material ranges from macro-economic planning, pricing, and development policies to the management of agricultural research, rural health care, industrial policy, energy policy, railway management, etc. The EDI also organizes seminars in Washington and in different regions of the world in cooperation with regional institutes.

Technical Assistance. Technical assistance has been an integral part of the Bank operation since its inception. It consists of two broad categories : (*i*) engineering-related, such as feasibility studies, engineering design, and construction supervision; and (*ii*) institution-related, such as dignostic policy and institutional studies, management support and training. The primary way of providing technical assistance is through loans made for specific sectors and in components of loans made for capital infrastructures. Such technical assistance includes funds for supervision, implementation and engineering services, energy, power, transportation, water supply, industry, etc. To meet gaps in project preparation and for institution building, the bank advances funds to prospective buyers through Project Preparation Facility (PPF) created in 1975. The Bank also serves as executing agency for project financed by the United Nations Development Programme (UNDP). Further, it provides such technical assistance as short-term training, appointment of advisers for technology service on evaluation and monitoring panels, and demographic, economic advice on project preparation.

Inter-Organisational Cooperation. The IBRD is also engaged in inter-organisational cooperation. Cooperation between the IBRD and other international organisations is based on formal agreements such as the Co-operative Programmes between it and the FAO, the UNESCO, the WHO, the GATT, the UNCTAD, the United Nations Environment Programmes (UNEP), the UNDP, the United Nations Industrial Development Organisation (UNIDO), the International Fund for Agricultural Development (IFAD), the ILO, the African Development Bank, the Asian Development Bank, etc.

Economic and Social Research. The Bank devotes roughly 3 per cent of its administrative budget to economic and social research. In 1983, the Bank established a Research Policy Council (RPC) to provide leadership in the guidance, co-ordination, and evaluation of all bank research. A Bank Research Advisory group has been set up to advise the RPC. A small and more technically oriented Research Projects Approval Committee has been created. Research activities are undertaken by the Bank's own research staff and also in collaboration with outside researchers. The results of completed research projects appear in articles in international economic journals, books, in World Bank Staff Working Papers, and its own journal, *Finanace and Development.* It also publishes World Development Report every year. Research projects in progress are described in an annual publication, *World Bank Research Programme : Abstracts of Current Studies.* The Bank also helps strengthen indigenous research capacity in member developing countries.

Operations Evaluation. The Bank helps borrowers in the post-evaluation of their Bank assisted projects. It has set up the Operations Evaluation Department (OED) for this purpose. Projects reviewed are also subject to performance audit by the OED staff. Members of borrowers' staff visit this Department for seeking help in the preparation of project completion report. The EDI also includes a course devoted to monitoring and evaluation by borrowers which is conducted by it in collaboration with EDI staff.

Settlement of Investment Disputes. The Bank has set up the International Centre of Settlement of Investment Disputes (ICSID) between States and Nationals of other States. All members of the Bank have signed and deposited their instrument of ratification pertaining to this. The Bank has successfully mediated in solving many international investment disputes such as the River Water Dispute between the India and Pakistan, and of the Suez Canal between Egypt and the UK.

CONCLUSION

The Bank's overall performance must be judged not just on its lending but on its success in providing advice and technical assistance. The Bank is laying greater emphasis on developing human resources such as education, population, health and nutrition, and on environment. The Bank also provides assistance to the private sector in such areas as financial, power, telecommunications, information technology, oil and gas, and industry and mining.

In the fiscal year 2000, the World Bank disbursements totalled $ 18.5 billion.

8. CRITICAL APPRAISAL

The IBRD has been quite successful in achieving its principal objective of reconstruction and development. It helped in the reconstruction of Europe after its destruction in the Second World War. It has also been helping the developed and developing countries alike in the process of growth. Since the 1970s, it has been lending more to developing countries not only for infrastructural investment but also for raising the productivity and standard of living of the poor people. Of the total IBRD loans of $ 18.5 billion in the fiscal year 2000, member countries in Latin America and Carribean received 22 per cent, in Europe and Central Asia 16 per cent, in East Asia and Pacific 16 per cent, in Africa 12 per cent, in South Asia 11 per cent and in Middle East and North Africa 5 per cent and in others 18 per cent. Still critics are not lacking in pointing out certain criticisms of its lending policies. Some of them are discussed as under:

1. *High Interest Rate.* It is argued that the bank charges a very high rate of interest on loans, as also an annual commitment charge on undistributed balances and a front-end fee. Recently the Bank has adopted a new procedure related to the cost of borrowing for calculating the interest rate and front-end fee. So they are no longer fixed arbitrarily at a high level. Still the interest rate continues to be high. It is 7.6 per cent now.

2. *Less Aid to Developing Countries.* The Bank has also been criticised for its failure to meet the financial needs of the developing countries fully. Its loans have just touched the fringes of the total capital requirements for their economic and social uplift. In order to increase the Bank funds to such countries, it established the International Development Association (IDA) in 1960. Despite this, the Bank has not been successful in raising

the productivity and standard of living of their people. Its lending operations account for only a small proportion of the total net aid to developing countries. The poorest countries hardly receive 3.5 per cent of the total loans.

3. *Faulty Lending Procedure.* The Bank's lending procedure is faulty because it lays emphasis on the repaying capacity of the borrowing country before granting any loan. Such a condition is very harsh and discriminatory for developing countries which are poor and need financial help on a large scale. In fact, the repaying capacity of a poor country follows the utilisation of a loan. As the project is completed with the loan assistance, the repaying capacity of the borrower increases gradually.

4. *Discriminatory.* The Bank has been criticised for being discriminatory in its purpose-wise and region-wise assistance to its members. It is from the fiscal year 1990 that the lending policy of the Bank has been directed more towards the developing countries and for the development of agriculture and rural development, energy, transportation, communications, water supply, sewrage, human resources development, environment, etc.

5. *Hard Conditionalities.* The introduction of SAF and ESAF has made IBRD loans terms tighter. The borrowing country is required to follow an action programme set out in a letter of development policies such as open trade, reform in public budgeting and debt management, revision of price policies, better planning of public investment and management of public enterprises, etc. The second instalment of SAF is only released after a review of the reform programmes that are date-bound.

9. INDIA AND THE WORLD BANK

India is one of the founder members of the Bank and held a permanent seat on its Board of Executive Directors for a number of years. The Bank has been assisting India in its planned economic development by granting loans, conducting field surveys, rendering expert advice, sending missions, study teams, and training Indian personnel at the EDI. There is also a Chief of Mission of the Bank at New Delhi who represents it for monitoring and consultations on its aided projects in India. India has been the largest receiver of the World Bank assistance since August 1949. The Bank's disbursement to India during fiscal year 2000 amounted to \$ 1.8 billion. The total sanctioned loans received by India till June 2000 were \$ 11,071 million. Of these, outstanding loans stood at \$ 7,508 million. The World Bank has been assisting India in such projects as development of ports, oil exploration including the Bombay High and gas power projects, aircrafts, coal, iron, aluminium, fertilizers, railway modernisation, technical assistance, industrial development finance corporations, etc.

The Aid India Consortium of twelve developed countries which was giving aid to India for its development plans at the instance of the World Bank has been replaced by India Development Forum since 1995. The Bank also helped India to solve amicably its river water dispute with Pakistan.

India has, thus, gained much from being the member of the World Bank for the development of agriculture, industry, energy and transport. But with reduced availability from the IDA. India will have to borrow more from the Bank in future. This will entail a heavy burden on India's resources for the terms of world Bank loans are much harder than those of the IDA credits.

EXERCISES

1. Explain the functions and activities of the International Bank for Reconstruction and Development. How far has it been successful in achieving them?
2. Explain briefly the working of the World Bank. What contributions has it made for the economic development of India?

CHAPTER 50

The World Bank Group

The World Bank has, at present, three affiliates : the International Development Association, the International Finance Corporation, and the Multilateral Investment Guarantee Agency. These are discussed below.

1. THE INTERNATIONAL DEVELOPMENT ASSOCIATION (IDA)

The International Development Association (IDA) is the "soft loan window" of the IBRD which was established in September 1960. It is an affiliate of the World Bank. The President of the World Bank is its head.

ITS OBJECTIVES

The main objectives of the IDA are two-fold.

1. To provide assistance for poverty alleviation to the world's poorest countries.

2. To provide concessional financial assistance and macroeconomic management services to the poorest countries so as to raise their standard of living. These relate to human resource development, including population control, development of health, nutrition and education for the overall objective of removing poverty.

ITS MEMBERSHIP

The membership of the IDA is open to all members of the World Bank. In June 2001, it had 182 members. If a country ceases to be a member of the World Bank, its membership of the IDA automatically ends. As per the Articles of Association of the IDA, its members are divided into two parts. In Part I are the developed countries which include among others Iceland, Japan, South Africa, the Russian Federation, Kuwait and UAE. It is known as G-24. Part II includes all the developing countries.

ITS ORGANISATION

The organisation of the IDA is that of the World Bank. With the exception of a few separate sections, the staff of the World Bank operates this Association. Right from the President, all the senior officers of the World Bank are its officers. Its Annual Report forms part of the World Bank Report and is submitted simultaneously.

ITS FINANCIAL RESOURCES

The resources of the IDA include the initial subscriptions from members, general replenishments from its more industrialised members, transfers from the net earnings of the World Bank, Special Funds contributions and adjustments and accumulated surpluses. The initial capital subscription from member countries at the time of its formation in 1960 was $ 757 million. A Special Fund was created in October 1982 with contributions from member countries. But its major source of funds has been the IDA replenishments for a period of three years. The IDA had 32 donor countries who provided $ 15.5 billion for the three-year IDA-9 which ended on June 30, 1993. The IDA-10 beginning July 1, 1993 had been fixed at $ 18 billion. The IDA-11 replenishment beginning July 1, 1996 had been fixed at $ 22 billion over the next three years. All contributions to capital subscription, replenishments and Special Fund are paid in convertible currencies by Part I member countries. The developing member countries of Part II make their contributions of 10 per cent in convertible currencies or gold and 90 per cent in their own currencies.

IDA Credits

The IDA loans are known as "credits" which are made to governments only. At present, countries with per capita income of less than $ 695 at 1990 prices can borrow from it. These are given for such projects for which no assistance is provided by the World Bank. Before approving a credit, the Special Committee of the IDA considers three criteria :

(a) Poverty Criterion. A country where population pressure is high and productivity is low, thereby leading to a low standard of living of the people.

(b) Performance Criterion. It relates to the past performance of the country in terms of loans received whether from the IDA or the World Bank. It must have been pursuing macroeconomic policies and executing projects satisfactorily.

(c) Project Criterion. The projects for which credits are to be utilised must yield financial and economic returns to justify them.

On the basis of these criteria, the IDA sanctions credits to LDCs for agriculture, education, health, nutrition, water supply, sewerage, etc. Such credits which are known as "soft loans", are given on the following terms :

(*i*) They are repayable over a period of 35-40 years; (*ii*) they have a 10-year grace period; (*iii*) the commitment fee (interest rate) which was charged from 0 to 0.5 per cent has now been waived; and (*iv*) a small administrative fee of 0.75 per cent is charged on the dibursed amount.

The gross disbursements by the IDA during the fiscal year 2000 were $ 6.8 billion.

India and IDA

Upto 1979-80, India had been the single largest beneficiary of the IDA assistance which was 40 per cent of the total credits committed to LDCs. With China becoming a member of the IDA in 1980, India's share in IDA's credits has been continuously on the decline. Between 1981-85, India received 30.5 per cent of the total assistance. From 1985 onwards, it has ranged between 15 to 20 per cent every year. During 2000, India received $ 1.2 billion interest-free IDA loan for elementary education, health, nutrition, food safety, social safety programme, environment security and supervision, etc.

Evaluation of IDA's Working

Since its inception in 1960 as the "soft window" of the World Bank, the IDA has been helping the poorest countries of the world in order to remove their poverty and raise their living standards. As a result of its assistance, the infant mortality rate in the LDCs, has been reduced to half of what it was earlier. The average life expectancy has increased by 13 per cent, and the adult literacy rate has risen to 60 per cent.

Despite these achievements, the IDA has not been able to render development assistance for the complete removal of poverty in LDCs due to lack of resources. The developed countries, especially the USA, have been the stumbling blocks in increasing the IDA replenishments. Consequently, the IDA assistance to the poorest countries had fallen from 100 per cent in 1988 to 85 per cent in 2000. According to a recent World Bank assessment, out of 350 IDA-supported projects in developing countries, only 59 per cent performed satisfactorily due to the efforts of governments of developing countries. Still, it has been successful in acting as a catalyst for their development.

2. THE INTERNATIONAL FINANCE CORPORATION (IFC)

The International Finance Corporation (IFC) is the private sector arm of the World Bank family which was established in July 1956. It is the major multilateral agency promoting productive private investment in developing countries. It helps finance private sector projects to mobilise finance for them in the international financial markets, and provides advice and technical assistance to business and governments.

Its Membership

The Articles of Agreement of the IFC are similar to that of the World Bank. A country has to be a member of the World Bank in order to join the IFC. In June 2001, it had 182 members.

Its Financial Resources

In the beginning, the authorised capital of the IFC was $ 100 million which was divided into 1,00,000 shares of $ 1000 each. At present, its authorised capital is $ 1300 million. The IFC can borrow from theWorld Bank four times its subscribed capital and surpluses. It can also borrow from the International money market.

Its Objectives

The objectives for which the IFC was set up, have been laid down in Article 1 of its Article of Agreement as under :

"The purpose of the Corporation is to further economic development by encouraging the growth of productive private enterprise in member countries, particularly in the less development areas, thus supplementing the activities of the International Bank for Reconstruction and Development. In carrying out this purpose, the Corporation shall :

(*i*) in association with private investors, assist in financing the establish-ment, improvement and expansion of productive private enterprise which would contribute to the development of its member countries by making investments, without guarantee of repayment by the member Government concerned, in cases where sufficient private investment is not available on reasonable terms;

(*ii*) seek to bring together investment opportunities, domestic and foreign private capital, and experienced management; and

(*iii*) seek to stimulate, and to help create conditions conducive to the flow of private capital, domestic and foreign, into productive investment in member countries."

Its Organisation

The IFC is an affiliate of the World Bank but it is separate from the World Bank, except for the fact that only a member of the World Bank can be its member. It has its own staff but draws upon the Bank for administrative services. Its organisational structure regarding the President, the Chairman, the Board of Governors, and Executive Directors is on the pattern of the World Bank. The World Bank President is the ex-officio Chairman of the Board of Directors of the IFC. But all the administrative powers of the IFC are vested in the Vice President of the IFC. The corporation has eight departments. Of these four relate to investment which function on geographical basis. The remaining four deparments relate to capital markets, finance and management, legal matters, and engineering which operate on functional basis.

Types of Assistance

The IFC renders assistance to a wide variety of sectors relating to large, medium and small industries which include financial services, mining, petro-chemicals, power, oil and gas exploration, telecommunications, tourism, general manufacturing and agro-based industries. The assistance to private enterprise in developing countries is in three ways : (*i*) by direct investment both in the form of loans and equity participation; (*ii*) by securing foreign and local capital; and (*iii*) by providing technical assistance.

(1) *Direct Investment.* It invests in partnership with private investors from the capital exporting country and/or from the country in which the enterprise is located. But its investments will not be more than half of the capital requirements of the enterprise. The minimum investment by the Corporation in an enterprise is $ 1 million, but there is no upper limit. The enterprise seeking loans from the IFC should be industrial, located in a developing country, and should satisfy the criteria of both economic development and reasonable commercial return. The Corporations assistance is not tied to expenditure in any particular country, but must be spent in the member countries. It is used to buy machines and other equipment and to meet foreign exchange, local costs, working capital and any other legitimate business expenses. It does not seek or accept any type of government guarantee for making investments and repayments of loans, except when it is required by law in a country. Loans and risk capital are provided at commercial rates with maturity of 7 to 12 years.

(2) *Foreign and Local Capital.* The IFC participates in promoting productive private investment in developing countries by way of equity and/or loan investment. It underwrites equity capital and helps in sponsoring and bringing together investors for new enterprises. Thus it secures the co-operation of both foreign and local enterprises. It helps them in making feasibility studies of the proposed projects.

(3) *Technical Assistance.* The IFC provides project sponsors with the necessary technical assistance so that their enterprises are potentially productive and financially sound. For this prupose, it undertakes financial studies and analysis. It also provides policy assistance to member governments so that they may develop the necessary investment climate to attract foreign and local private enterprise.

(4) *Capital Markets Development.* The Corporation has a Capital Markets Department which provides specialised resources for studying the problems and needs of the financial markets of developing countries. It provides financial support and advice for the development of financial institutions and helps in developing a legal, financial, and institutional framework which may encourage local and foreign capital in developing countries. The Corporation has been instrumental in the promotion of financial institutions, development finance companies, leasinig and venture capital companies, mutual funds, etc. by giving technical assistance to developing countries.

(5) *Help to Small Scale Industries.* The IFC also renders help to small scale industries in the form of advice for the preparation of project reports and technical assistance. It has established four such facilities for developing countries of different regions. They are the South Pacific Project Facility, the Africa Project Development Facility, the Business Advisory Service for the Caribbean and Central America, and the Polish Business Advisory Service. It has also established the African Management Services Company which provides skilled and experienced managers to small enterprises in the African region to improve their working. The IFC has a Technical Advisory Service in its Engineering Wing which gives expert advice to government institutes and small enterprises in preparing market and feasibility studies, for technical restructuring and for strategic planning. For all these services it charges a nominal fee. Finally, as in the case of medium and large scale industries, the IFC helps the small scale sector in raising funds.

In the fiscal year ending June 30, 2000, the IFC approved $ 2.6 billion in financing 264 projects in various sectors in 65 developing countries.

India and IFC

India is a founder member of the IFC. She has been receiving assistance in a variety of areas from the IFC since its inception. These include automobiles, shipping, electricity, cement, fertilisers, oil and gas, petro-chemicals, iron and steel, general manufacturing, and the financial sector. India is the second major client of IFC assistance. It has been giving about 10 per cent of total loans and equity to developing countries. The IFC invested $ 48.1 million in India, composed of loans of $ 25.4 million and an equity of $ 22.7 million, covering 11 projects which included the expansion of manufacturing facilities in computer diskettes, polyster and textiles, agribusiness exports. etc.

Its Evaluation

Over the year, the IFC has played a catalytic role in promoting productive private investment in developing countries by providing loans and equity capital, by rendering technical advice in the promotion of money and capital markets, by bringing local and foreign enterprises to co-operate in joint ventures, in starting new industrial projects in large, medium and small sectors. But its development assistance has gone more to developing countries and very little to the least developing economies.

3. THE MULTINATIONAL INVESTMENT GUARANTEE AGENCY (MIGA)

The multinational Investment Guarantee Agency (MIGA) is the newest affiliate of the World Bank family which was established in April 1988. It has been created to supplement the World Bank and the IFC to assist where the Bank and the IFC do not reach. It is joint venture with the International Finance Corporation. The MIGA has an authorised capital of $ 1.08 billion.

Its Objectives

The MIGA has the following objectives :

1. Its primary objective is to encourage the flow of direct foreign investment into developing member countries.
2. It provides insurance cover to investors against political risks.
3. The MIGA's guarantee programme protects investors against four types of non-commercial risks. They are : any danger involved in currency transfer, expropriation, war and civil disturbance, and breach of contract by governments.
4. It insures only new investments, including the expansion of existing investments, privatisation and financial restructuring.
5. It provides promotional and advisory services to the governments of developing countries to enable them to increase the attractiveness of their investment climate.
6. Another objective of the MIGA is to establish credibility among investors, and higher credit rating among global banking and financial markets of its members.

Its Working

In order to become a full-fledged member of the MIGA, a country has to ratify the convention and pay its capital subscription. By June 30, 2000, 160 countries had signed the MIGA convention. Of these, 136 countries had become its full-fledged members.

Before the investments are made, projects are to be registered with the MIGA. 90 per cent of the investment amount can be insured by the MIGA subject to a limit of $ 50 million per project. Among its eligible investments are included equity loans made or guaranteed by equity holders, and certain other types of direct investments. It covers insurance for projects for fifteen years which may be extended to 20 years in exceptional cases. It also insures eligible investments in cooperation with national insurance agencies and private insurers. All projects insured by the MIGA have to support the environmental and development objectives of the World Bank.

The MIGA provides promotional and advisory services to its developing member countries to help them attract more foreign direct investments. These services include the organisation of investment-promotion conferences, executive development programmes, foreign-investment policy, round-table conferences, and specialised advisory assistance to governments of developing member countries. It operates the Foreign Investment Advisory Service in Policy, institutional and legal matters relating to direct foreign investment. It also gives advice on such policies and programmes which promote backward linkages between foreign investors and local investors.

Its Progress

The MIGA had signed a total or 226 contracts of guarantee for investments in 52 developing countries and its outstanding contingent liabilities were $ 2.8 billion in fiscal year 2000. It issued 68 investment guarantee contracts worth $ 862 million and the amount of insured projects of foreign investment was $ 8.4 billion. It assisted private firms from 17 different countries in making investments in 27 host countries. It launched and actively promoted "IPA-Net"—a global, Internet-based information in exchange, communications network and market-place—which facilitates the exchange of information among members of the international investment community. Thus MIGA's guarantees serve as a catalyst for multinational investments.

INDIA AND MIGA

India became the 113th country when she signed the MIGA convention on April 13, 1992. By becoming a member of the MIGA, India has entered into a commitment to provide against non-commercial risks to direct foreign investments. With the on-going process of structural adjustments and liberalisation of the Indian economy, the insurance guarantee of the MIGA to direct foreign investments and the help rendered by its advisory services, are bound to benefit its programmes for industrial development.

EXERCIESES

1. What are the objectives of the International Development Association? To what extent it has been successful in helping the developing countries?
2. Examine the working of the International Finance Corporation.
3. What is Multinational Investment Guarantee Agency (MIGA)? Explain its objectives and working.

CHAPTER 51

International Liquidity

1. MEANING

International liquidity is defined as the aggregate stock of internally acceptable assets held by the central bank to settle a deficit in a country's balance of payments. In other words, international liquidity provides a measure of a country's ability to finance its deficit in balance of payments without resorting to adjustment measures. Shortage of liquidity hampers the expansion of global trade and its surplus leads to global inflationary pressures.

International liquidity is generally used as a synonym for international reserves. Such reserves include a country's official gold stock holdings, its convertible foreign currencies, SDRs, and its net reserve position in the IMF. Economists like Heller and McKinnon use a broader definition of international liquidity to include international borrowings, commercial credit operations, and the international financial structure in a country's reserves. This definition implies international availability of liquidity and the possibility of obtaining credit from financial institutions operating in international financial markets. Thus, in the broader sense, international liquidity includes private as well as official holdings of international liquidity assets.

In the literature on international liquidity distinction is made between owned and borrowed reserves, and between conditional and unconditional reserves. Foreign exchange surplus, after meeting all current and capital account obligations of the country with the rest of the world, are *"owned" reserves*. Similarly, the official gold stock of a country constitutes its owned reserves. Capital imports in the form of borrowings from abroad and direct investments by foreign countries constitute *borrowed reserves*. Both owned and borrowed reserves are the source of international liquidity.

Unconditional international liquidity consists of a country's official gold stock, holdings of its foreign currencies and SDRs, its net position in the IMF, and private holding of international assets. In all such cases, liquidity assets are available to the country without any conditions or restrictions on their use. But in the case of borrowed reserves, the lender country may impose conditions or restrictions on the use of liquid assets by the borrowing country. Many international financial institutions provide funds on conditional basis for specific projects and on specified repayment provisions. All these are cases of *conditional liquidity*. This is done to avoid the misue of liquidity by the borrowing country.

2. NEED AND PROBLEM OF INTERNATIONAL LIQUIDITY

The (need or) problem of international liquidity arises because the demand for internatonal liquidity is rising more than its supply, thereby implying shortage of international liquidity. The principal causes for the shortatge of international liquidity are the following:

1. *BOP Deficits.* There have been increasing BOP deficits of the majority of countries in the world. In

particular, after the opening of LDCs to world markets, these countries have been facing persistent BOP deficits. Too much dependence on exports has exposed these economies to international fluctuations in the demand for and prices of their products. They have become unstable due to international cyclical instability. On the other hand, their import requirements have been on the increase in order to develop. As a result, they are faced with foreign exchange constraints. This has necessitated larger inflow of aid and foreign investment. Consequently, debt serving and interest on debt have risen and payments of dividends, profits and royalties on private direct foreign investment have grown, thereby leading to decline in the net inflow of foreign capital. All these have led to further shortage of foreign exchange reserves.

2. *High Tariff Barriers.* The exports of LDCs to developed countries have not been increasing, thereby adversely affecting their export earnings. One of the reasons for the non-expansion of their exports has been high tariff barriers imposed by the developed countries on their exports, especially by their regional groups like the EEC. At the same time, the LDCs are trying to cut down their essential imports from the developed countries by means of exchange controls, high tariffs, import quotas and similar protectionist devices in order to conserve foreign exchange. This has adversely affected their development process.

3. *Attitude of Developed Countries.* The majority of developed countries have surplus in their balance of payments. They are creditors of LDCs and do not take any interest in getting rid of their surplus so as to increase international liquidity.

4. *Unequal Distribution of International Reserves.* The distribution of international reserves is biased and favours the developed countries. It is primarily based on the their quotas in the IMF. Whenever the IMF quotas are revised, the larger share goes to the developed countries. It is the developing countries whose need for international liquidity is far greater which suffer from its shortage.

Measures to Solve the Problem of International Liquidity

The following measures have been suggested to solve the problem of international liquidity.

1. *Promoting Export Expansion.* Developing countries should reduce BOP deficit by promoting export expansion. The choice lies in concentrating the expansion of primary or secondary products or both. The expansion of secondary products requires import substitution for export expansion. These policies will earn them foreign exchange.

2. *Limiting Exports.* They should ban non-essential consumer goods, and limit imports of specific goods by selective tariffs, physical quotas, etc. This policy will enable them to conserve foreign exchange.

3. *Changing Official Echange Rate.* A developing country can change its official exchange rate by devaluing its currency so that its export prices are lowered and import prices are increased. This will help in earning foreign exchange.

4. *Restrictive Monetary-Fiscal Policies.* By following restrictive monetary and fiscal policies, a developing country can reduce domestic demand for products which will lower import prices, reduce inflationary pressures and BOP deficit.

5. *Reduction in BOP Surplus.* The majority of developed countries have BOP surplus which they should reduce by (*a*) accepting the national currencies of developing countries for payments; (*b*) removal of trade barriers to the products of developing countries; and (*c*) accepting products of developing countries in exchange for their products, as was done by the earstwhile USSR.

6. *Expanding International Reserves.* The IMF should expand international reserves by fresh allocation of larger quotas to member countries. In particular, all new issues of SDRs should be distributed to developing countries so that they may pay then to developed countries to solve their foreign exchange problem.

3. INTERNATIONAL RESERVES

The main features of international reserves or international liquidity have been :

1. Gold reserves of the countries of the world increased from $ 33.9 billion in 1951 to SDR 224.1 billion in 1997.
2. Marked increase in the share of foreign exchange reserves from $13.7 billion in 1951 to SDR 1078.2 billion in 1997.

3. Increase in reserve position in the IMF from $ 1.7 billion in 1951 to SDR 36.2 billion in 1997.
4. Emergence of SDRs since 1972 which increased from SDR 8.7 billion to SDR 18.7 billion in 1997.

Thus the total international reserves comprising the above four items increased from $ 49.3 billion to SDR 1357.2 billion in 1997.

No doubt, international reserves have been on the increase but they have not been rising as much as the increase in the volume and value of world trade. More so in the case of LDCs whose needs are greater and more urgent than that of developed countries.

4. IMF AND INTERNATIONAL LIQUIDITY*

There was no problem of international liquidity prior to 1970. This was because under the Bretton Woods Agreement the exchange rates of countries were fixed in terms of gold or the US dollar at $ 35 per ounce of gold. Member countries were forbidden to impose restrictions on payments and trade, except for a transitional period. They were allowed to hold their monetary reserves partly gold and partly in dollars and sterling. These reserves were meant to incur temporary deficits by member countries while keeping their exchange rates stable. The IMF insisted on expenditure reducing policies and devaluation to correct deficit in balance of payments. "Therefore, apart from ad hoc loans made by the IMF, the growth in liquidity needed to finance the expansion of world trade had to be found in liquidity needed to finance the expansion of world trade had to be found in the expansion of gold and the supply of dollar and sterling. But the physical supply of gold is virtually limited to the output of the mines in South Africa and the Soviet Union." Since the dollar acted as a medium of exchange, a unit of account and a store of value of the IMF system, every country wanted to increase its reserves of dollar which led to dollar holdings to a greater extent than needed. Consequently, the US gold stock continued to decline and the US balance of payments continued to deteriorate. Robert Triffin warned in 1959 that the demand for world liquidity was growing faster than the supply because the incremental supply of gold was increasing little. Since the dollar was convertible into gold, the supply of US dollars would be inadequate in relation to the liquidity needs of countries. This might introduce trade barriers by countries in order to have balance of payments surpluses and build up reserves. Thus, according to Triffin, a growing liquidity shortage would generate strong contractionary forces that would threaten the expansion of the world economy and lead to a world recession of the 1931 type.

A crisis of confidence had already erupted. The pound had been devalued in November 1967. There was no control over the world gold market with the appearance of a spearate price in the open market. On 15 August, 1970, the United States suspended the conversion of dollars into gold and refused to intervene in the foreign exchange markets to maintain exchange rate stability. The 'Group of Ten' industrial countries met at the Smithsonian Institute in Washington in December 1971 and agreed to the realignment of major currencies by devaluing the dollar by 10 per cent and revaluing their currencies. The Smithsonian Agreement broke down following the US dollar devaluation of February 1973 again and in March 1973 a number of countries had floating exchange rates and the EEC countries had a "joint float" of their currencies. The Jamaica Agreement of January 1976 formalised the regime of floating exchange rates. By the Second Amendment of the IMF Charter in 1978, the member countries are not expected to maintain and establish par values with gold or dollar. The Fund has no control over the exchange rate adjustment policies of the member countries. The system of flexible exchange rates has tended to reduce the need for more reserves.

5. ROLE OF THE IMF IN INCREASING WORLD LIQUIDITY

The IMF is an international monetary institution which is the principal source of supply of world liquidity to its 182 members. Over the years, it has adopted the following measures to increase international liquidity.

SDRs. In early 1970, it introduced a scheme for the creation and issue of Special Drawing Rights (SDRs) as unconditional reserve assets to influence the level of world reserves and to solve the problem of international liquidity. There are SDR 146 billion in the Fund's General Account. The Fund also creates SDRs and allocates them to members in proportion of their quotas. For this purpose, the Fund has established the Special Drawing

Account. As the international monetary asset, SDRs are held in the international reserves of central banks and governments to finance improve international liquidity so as to correct fundamental disequilibria in the balance of payments of Fund members. The participants in the SDR scheme receive SDRs under "transactions with designation" and "transactions by agreement" unconditionally. The IMF acts as a clearing house in these transactions. Since 1981 there are 21.4 billion SDRs in the Fund.

Quotas. The bulk of Fund's financial resources comes from quota subscriptions of member countries. To meet the global demand for liquidity, it has been increasing quotas of members every four years under the General Review of Quotas. As a result, it increased the member quotas from 7.6 billion in 1947 to SDR 212 billion in 1998.

Selling Gold. It increases its funds by selling gold to members.

Borrowings. It borrows from governments, central banks or private institutions of industrialised countries, the Bank for International Settlements, and even from OPEC countries, like Saudi Arabia.

Reserve Tranche. The Fund has a variety of facilities for lending its resources to member countries. Lending by the Fund is linked to temporary assistance to member in financing disequilibrium in their balance of payments on current account. If a member has less currency with the Fund than its quota, the difference is called gold or reserve tranche. It can draw upto 25 per cent on its reserve tranche automatically upon representation to the Fund for its balance of payments needs. It is not charged any interest on such drawings, but is required to repay within a period of three to five years.

Credit Tranche. A member can draw further from balance quota in 4 instal-ments upon 100 per cent of its quota from credit tranche annually. Drawings from credit tranche are conditional because the members have to satisfy the Fund of adopting a viable programme to ensure financial stability. To meet the severe balance of payments problems, the Fund has been gradually raising the limit of borrowings by its members over the years under the credit tranche. Now members can draw upto the equivalent of 300 per cent of their new quotas on the total net use of the Fund's resources. The limits exclude drawings from CCFF, BSAF, SAF, STF and ESAF. The purchases are made under *stand-by arrangements* rather than directly.

New Credit Facilities. Since the 1960s, the Fund has created several new credit facilities for its members. Loans from these facilities are separate from tranches and are available for a longer period. These are : BSFF (Buffer Stock Financing Facility), EFF (Extended Fund Facility), SFF (Supplementary Financing Facility), SAF (Structural Adjustment Facility), ESAF (Enhanced Structural Adjustment Facility), CCFF (Compensatory and Contingency Financing Facility), STF (Systematic Transformation Facility), ESAL (Emergency Structural Adjustment Loans) and CCL (Contingency Credit Line).[1] These facilities provide for members annual access to Fund resources up to 150% of their quotas or up to 450% over a three year period.

IDA Replenishments. Another important source for increasing world liquidity is the IDA Replenishments to the poor developing countries for three years by the developing countries. In recent years, IDA-9 Replenishment gave $ 15.55 billion in 1990, IDA-10 gave $ 18 billion in 1993, and IDA-11 gave 22 billion in 1996 for three years.

6. ITS CRITICISMS

The various Fund schemes for increasing global liquidity have been criticised for favouring the developed countries. They are inequitable which have tended to mark unfair distribution of international liquidity. For instance, the allocation of SDRs to participating countries is proportional to their quotas. In this sense, the allocation of SDRs to developing countries is too low as compared to their needs. Low allocation of SDRs reduces the borrowing capacity of such countries.

Moreover, the SDR scheme does not link the creation of international reserves in the form of SDRs with the need for development finance on the part of developing countries. The need for liquidity on the part of developing country is great. Therefore, there is need to create more SDRs with fair distribution so that more unconditional liquidity is made available for the greater needs of developing countries.

Unfortunately, due to the rigid attitude of the United States and some other developed countries, the Fund has not been able to resume allocation of SDRs from January 1982, despite the repeated pleas of the developing countries over these years. So the Fund has failed in its objective of increasing international liquidity through SDRs. Consequently, faced with a recession, an inadequate flow of concessional aid and falling prices of commodities and raw materials, developing countries have been facing severe balance of payments and debt problems. To solve this problem, there is urgent need for fresh allocation of SDRs which should be distributed only to developing countries.

EXERCISES

1. What is meant by international liquidity? Comment upon the efforts made by the International Monetary Fund to solve this problem.
2. Write an essay on the problems and solution of international liquidity.
3. What do you mean by international liquidity? Discuss the causes and measures adopted to solve this problem.

CHAPTER 52

International Monetary System

1. MEANING

International monetary system refers to the system prevailing in world foreign exchange markets through which international trade and capital movements are financed and exchange rates are determined. We discuss below the international monetary system since the end of the World War II.

2. THE BRETTON WOODS SYSTEM

During the period preceding World War I almost all the major national currencies were on a system of fixed exchange rates under the international gold standard. This system had to be abandoned during World War I. There were fluctuating exchange rates from the end of the War to 1925. Efforts were made to return to the gold standard from 1925. But it collapsed with the coming of the Great Depression. Many countries resorted to protectionism and competitive devaluations—with the result that world trade was reduced to almost half. But depression completely disappeared during World War II.

In July 1944, the allied countries met at Bretton Woods in the USA to avoid the rigidity of the gold standard and the chaos of the 1930s in international trade and finance and to encourage free trade. The new system was the present International Monetary Fund (IMF) which worked out an *adjustable peg system*.

Under the Bretton Woods system exchange rates between countries were set or pegged in terms of gold or the US dollar at $ 35 per ounce of gold. This related to a fixed exchange rate regime with changes in the exchange within a band or range from 1 per cent above to 1 per cent below the par value. But these adjustments were not available to US which had to maintain the gold value of dollar. If the exchange rate hit either of the bands, the monetary authorities were obliged to buy or sell dollars against their currencies. Large adjustments could be made where there were "fundamental disequilibrium" (i.e. persistent and large deficits or surpluses) in BOP with the approval of the IMF and other countries. Member countries were forbidden to impose restrictions on payments and trade, except for a transitional period. They were allowed to hold foreign reserves partly in gold and partly in dollars. These reserves were meant to incur temporary deficits or surpluses by member countries, while keeping their exchange rates stable. In case of a BOP deficit, there was a *reserve outflow* by selling dollar and *reserve inflow* in case of a BOP surplus.

Reserve outflows were a matter of concern under the Bretton Woods system. So the IMF insisted on expenditure reducing policies and devaluation to correct BOP deficit. Temporary BOP deficits were also met by borrowing from the Fund for a period of 3 to 5 years. A country could borrow from the Fund on the basis of the size of its quota with it. The loans made by the IMF were in convertible currencies.

The first 25 per cent of its quota was in *gold tranche* which was automatic and the remaining under the *credit tranches* which carried high interest rates. To provide long-term loans the World Bank (or IBRD) was set up in 1946 and subsequently its two affiliates, the International Finance Corporation (IFC) in 1956 and International Development Association (IDA), in 1960. For the removal of trade restrictions, the *General*

Agreement on Tariffs and Trade (GATT) came into force from January 1948. To supplement its resources, the Fund started borrowing from the ten industrialised countries in order to meet the requirements of the international monetary system under General Agreements to Borrow (GAB) from October 1962. Further, it created special Drawing Rights (SDRs) is January 1970 to supplement international reserves to meet the liquidity requirements of its members. The Bretton Woods system worked smoothly from 1950s to mid 1960s. During this period world output increased and with the reduction of tariffs under the GATT, world trade also rose.

3. THE BREAKDOWN OF THE BRETTON WOODS SYSTEM

The following are the principal causes and sequences of the breakdown of the Bretton Woods system.

1. *Built-in Instability.* The Bretton Woods System had a built-in instability that ultimately led to its breakdown. It was an adjustable peg system within plus or minus 1 per cent of the par value of $ 35. In case of fundamental disequilibrium, a country could devalue its currency with the approval of the IMF. But countries were reluctant to devalue their currencies because they had to export more goods in order to pay for dearer imports from other countries. This led countries to rely on deflation in order to cure BOP deficits through expenditure-reducing monetary-fiscal policies. The UK often restored to deflation such as in 1949, 1957 and 1967.

2. *The Triffin Dilemma.* Since the dollar acted as a medium of exchange, a unit of account and a store of value of the IMF system, every country wanted to increase its reserves of dollar which led to dollar holdings to a greater extent than needed. Consequently, the US gold stock continued to decline and the US balance of payments continued to deteriorate. Robert Triffin warned in 1960 that the demand for world liquidity was growing faster than the supply because the incremental supply of gold was increasing little. Since the dollar was convertible into gold, the supply of US dollars would be inadequate in relation to the liquidity needs of countries. This would force the US to abandon its commitment to convert dollars into gold. This is the Triffin Dilemma which actually led to the collapse of the Bretton Woods System in August 1971.

3. *Lack of International Liquidity.* There was a growing lack of international liquidity due to increasing demand for the dollar in world monetary markets. With the expansion of world trade, BOP deficits (and surpluses) of countries increased. This necessitated the supply of gold and of the dollar. But the production of gold in Africa was increasing very little. This led to larger demand and holdings of the dollar. Countries also wanted to have more dollar holdings because they earned interest. As the supply of dollars was inadequate in relation to the liquidity needs of countries, the US printed more dollars to pay for its deficits which other countries accepted as reserves.

4. *Mistakes in US Policies.* The BOP deficits of the US became steadily worse in the 1960s. To overcome them, the policies adopted by the US government ultimately led to the world crises. Rising US government expenditure in the Vietnam War, the financing of US space programme and the establishment of the "Great Society" (social welfare) programme in the 1960s led to large outflow of dollar from the US. But the US monetary authority (FED) did not devalue the dollar. Rather, it adopted monetary and fiscal measures to cut its BOP deficit.

5. *Destabilising Speculation.* Since countries with "fundamental disequilibrium" in BOP were reluctant to devalue their currencies and also took time to get the approval of the IMF, it provided speculators an opportunity to resort to speculation in dollars. When devaluations were actually made, there were large doses of devaluation than originally anticipated. This was due to destabilising speculation which made controls over capital flows even through monetary-fiscal measures ineffective. This was the immediate reason for the UK to devalue the pound in 1967.

6. *Crisis of Confidence and Collapse.* The immediate cause of the collapse of the Bretton Woods System was the eruption of a crisis of confidence in the US dollar. The pound had been devalued in November 1967. There was no control over the world gold market with the appearance of a separate price in the open market. The immediate cause for the collapse of the Bretton Woods System was the rumour in March 1971 that the US would devalue the dollar. This led to a huge outflow of capital from the US. On 15 August 1971, the US

suspended the conversion of dollars into gold when some small European central banks wanted to convert their dollar reserves into gold at the US. It refused to intervene in the foreign exchange markets to maintain exchange rate stability and imposed a 10% import surcharge. Thus the main cause of breakdown of the Bretton Woods System was the problems of liquidity, adjustment and confidence. The increase in liquidity (international reserves) was in the form of dollars arising from BOP deficits of the US. But as the US was unable to adjust its deficits and excessive dollars accumulated in foreign countries, there was a *crisis* of *confidence* in the dollar and the Bretton Woods System brokedown.

Between 15 August 1971 and the Smithsonian Agreement of 18 December 1971, 48 countries including the United States, Japan and a large number of European countries abandoned fixed exchange rates. The 'Group of Ten' industrial countries met at the Smithsonian Institution in Washington on 18-19 December, 1971 and agreed to a new system of stable exchange rate with *wider bands.* As a first step towards realignment of major currencies, the US, devalued the dollar by 8 per cent, the Japanese revalued the yen by 17 per cent and the Germans their mark by 14 per cent. *The Smithsonian Agreement* widened the margin of fluctuations of the exchange rates to 2.25 per cent above or below the new parities of central rates. It officially devalued the dollar against gold from $ 35 to $ 38 per ounce. In 1973, the band was widened to 4.5 per cent. The Smithsonian Agreement broke down following the devaluation of the US dollar by 10% in February, 1973.

Another development took place in Europe when the EEC countries decided to limit the fluctuation of their currencies relative to each other to a smaller band. This came to be known as "*the snake in the tunnel*". Under this arrangement, the EEC currencies were tied together and could fluctuate within narrow limits in relation to one another but could fluctuate in relation to other currencies within the limits set by the band proposals.

4. THE PRESENT INTERNATIONAL MONETARY SYSTEM

At the beginning of March 1973 India, Canada, Japan, Switzerland, the UK and several smaller countries had floating exchange rates. However, the *"joint float"* of the EEC countries continued even after March 1973 and was now called the "*snake in the lake*", as there was no band within which the EEC currencies could fluctuate relative to other currencies. In March, 1979 the European Monetary System (EMS) was formed which created the European Currency Unit (ECU) which is a "basket" currency of a unit of account consisting of the major European currencies. The EMS limits the internal exchange rate movement of the member countries to not more than 2.25 per cent from the "central rates" with the exception of Italy whose lira can fluctuate up to 6 per cent.

In the meantime, the *Jamaica Agreement* of January 1976 (ratified in April 1978) formalised the regime of floating exchange rates under the auspices of the IMF. A number of factors forced the majority of member countries of the IMF to float their currencies. There were large short-term capital movements and central banks failed to stop speculation in currencies during the regime of adjustable pegs. The oil crisis in 1973 and the increase in oil prices in 1974 led to the great recession of 1974-75 in the industrial countries of the world. As a result "the dollar went into a rapid decline, which, by late 1978, had such alarming proportions that the United States government finally decided on a policy of massive intervention in order to prevent a further fall in the value of the dollar". At last, the system of managed floating exchange rates had come to stay by 1978. By the *Second Amendment of the IMF Charter* in 1978, the member countries are not expected to maintain and establish par values with gold or dollar. The Fund has no control over the exchange rate adjustment policies of the member countries. But it exercises international "surveillance" of exchange rate policies of its members.

The Second Amendment has reduced the position of gold in the global monetary system in the following ways by : (*a*) abolishing the official price of gold; (*b*) delinking it with the dollar in exchange arrangements; (*c*) eliminating the obligations of the Fund and its members to transfer or receive gold; and (*d*) selling a part of Fund's gold holdings.

The Second Amendment has also made SDRs as the chief reserve assets of the global monetary system whose value is expressed in currencies and not gold. It is now a unit of account, a currency peg and medium of transactions.

The present international monetary system of floating exchange rates is not one of free flexible exchange rates but of "managed floating". It has rarely operated without government intervention. Periodic intervention by governments has led the system to be called a "managed" or "dirty" floating system. In 1977, when the intervention was very heavy, it was characterised as a "filthy" float. When Governments do not intervene, it is a "clean" float. But the possibilities of a clean float are very remote. Thus a system of managed floating exchange rates is evolving where the central banks are trying to control fluctuations of exchange rates around some "normal" rates even though the Second Amendment of the Fund makes no mention of normal rates.

"The present international monetary system has also evolved in a number of important ways, including new allocation of SDRs, increased nations' quota in the IMF, renewal of the General Agreements to Borrow (GAB), the abolishment of the official gold price, and the formation of the European Monetary System (EMS) and the Euro Currency."[1]

The US is the major country which has been influencing the global monetary system. It has permitted the dollar to float in realtion to other currencies with occasional interventions when the dollar has reached extreme highs or lows. When the dollar was extremely high (appreciating), the G-5 (US, UK, Germany, Japan and France) agreed to intervene to bring the dollar down by the *Plaza Accord* in September 1985. Subsequently, the dollar depreciated substantially i.e. by more than 50% relative to the yen. By early 1987, the dollar had become undervalued and by the *Louvre Accord,* the G-7 countries (G-5 plus Canada and Italy) agreed to cooperate in keeping their exchange rates around their current levels at that time. "The Louvre Accord was successful in stabilising exchange rates for the rest of the year. Since then there seems to have been a consensus that exchange rates should be broadly stabilised, but there is little overt cooperation *among countries."*

Its Problems

The present international monetary system is faced with excessive fluctuations and large disequilibria in exchange rates. Often countries, both developed and developing, have been faced with either excessive appreciation or depreciation of their currencies in relation to the dollar which continues to dominate the world monetary system.

Reforms in International Monetary System

Economists have suggested a number of measures in order to avoid the excessive fluctuations and large disequilibria in exchange rates for reforming the international monetary system.

1. *Coordination and Cooperation of Policies.* A few economists, and McKinnon in particular, suggested international co-operation and co-ordination of policies among the leading developed countries for exchange rate stability. According to McKinnon[2], the US, Germany and Japan should have the optimal degree of exchange rate stability by fixing the exchange rates among their currencies at the equilibrium level based on the purchasing power parity. Thus they would co-ordinate their monetary policies for exchange rate stability.

2. *Improving Global Liquidity.* The reform package of the present world monetary system should improve global liquidity. As a *first* step, both developed and developing countries having BOP deficit and surplus should take steps to reduce a persistent imbalance through exchange rate changes via internal policy measures. *Second,* they should also cooperate in curbing large flows of "hot money" that destabilise their currencies. *Third,* they should be willing to settle their BOP imbalances through SDRs rather than through gold or dollar as reserve assets. *Fourth,* there should be increasing flow of resources to the developing countries.

3. *Leaning Against the Wind.* To reduce the fluctuations in exchange rates, the IMF *Guidelines for the Management of Floating Exchange Rates,* 1974 suggested the idea of leaning against the wind. It means that the central banks of developed and developing countries should intervene to reduce short-term fluctuations in exchange rates but leave the long-term fluctuations to be adjusted by the market forces.

4. Richard Cooper suggests a global central bank with a global currency which should be a global lender of the last resort to developing countries.

5. Jaffrey Sachs proposes the creation of an international bankruptcy court for developing countries which should deal with countries having large external debt.

6. George Soros opines that the IMF should set ceilings for external finance for each developing country

beyond which access to private capital need not be insured. But there should be mandatory insurance by an international credit insurance corporation.

7. Economists also suggest the establishment of a fund by developed countries which should provide guarantee to private loans by corporations and banks for lending to developing countries.

8. The developed countries should adopt appropriate measures to overcome price fluctuations in the primary products of developing countries through the creation of international buffer stocks, commodity agreements, compensatory financing, etc. These are necessary to control fluctuations in their exchange rates.

9. Paul Krugman suggests reintroduction of capital controls as a "least bad response" to an international crisis which developed in the Asian Tigers' Countries.

10. *Objective Indicators.* To iron out exchange rate fluctuations, the IMF *Interim Committee* suggested the adoption of such objective indicators as inflation-unemployment, growth of money supply, growth of GNP, fiscal balance, balance of trade and international reserves. The variations in these indicators require the adoption of restrictive monetary-fiscal measures to bring stability in exchange rates by both developed and developing countries.

Conclusion

The various suggestions to reform the present monetary system are closely inter-linked. But there is lack of unanimity over the various proposals among the nations. Given the differences of opinion between the developing and developed countries and among the developed countries themselves, there is no hope that any concrete proposal to reform the global monetary system would be acceptable to nations. So the present system of managed floating exchange rate is likely to stay on.

EXERCISES

1. Explain briefly the working of the Bretton Woods System. What led to its breakdown?
2. What were the causes for the collapse of Bretton Woods System? Explain briefly the present international monetary system.
3. What are the main problems of the present international monetary system. Give suggestions to remove these problems.

CHAPTER 53

The Euro-Currency Market

1. MEANING

Euro-currency is a currency held by individuals and institutions in a European country other than its country of origin. It is accumulated in European banks that deal in other currencies such as American dollar, Japanese Yen, Swiss Francs, etc. This market is the largest market in the international monetary system. It has been playing a central role in short and medium term international borrowing and lending by large corporations and banks and for financing international trade.

2. ORIGIN AND GROWTH

The origin of the Euro-currency market can be traced back to the 1920s when the US dollars were deposited in the European banks which converted them into their local currencies for lending purposes. But the real growth of the Euro-currency market began after the Second World War. The following factors led to its growth:

1. *Flow of US Aid.* The United States emerged as the most powerful nation in the post-war period which spent huge sums of money on the rehabilitation of Europe both in terms of economic and military aid. This led to the transfer of a large number of dollars in Eurobanks.

2. *Cold War.* The cold war which started in the 1950s led the Soviet Union and the East European government to transfer their dollar deposits from America to Eurobanks for fear that they might be blocked by the American Government.

3. *Decline in the Importance of Sterling.* In the post-war period Britain emerged as a debtor country. Consequently, the British sterling which had dominated the international financial market in the pre-war era gave place to the dollar in the post-war period. The importance of sterling further fell when the British Government placed severe restrictions on the grant of sterling to central banks outside the sterling area under the British Exchange Control Act in the early post-war period.

4. *Regulation-Q.* Regulation-Q of the US Federal Reserve System had been a major factor which gave rise to the Euro-currency market in the late 1960s. Under Regulation-Q, a ceiling was imposed on the interest rate payable on time deposits with the US banks and it prohibited the payment of any interest at all on deposits upto 30 days. This encouraged the US banks to open branches in Europe and attract dollar deposits to be used for financing international trade. In particular, this happened in 1968 and 1969 and again from 1979 onwards when the Regulation-Q ceiling kept low interest rates on time deposits. Consequently, both the US citizens and foreigners having dollars in excess of their transactions requirements transferred them in Eurobanks because they paid higher interest rate than the US banks. This also encouraged European lenders and borrowers to

---

1. The Euro-currency market is different from the Euro. The Euro is the name given to the combined currency of the 11-member states of the European Union.

trade in dollars and their currencies in London and other European financial markets rather than in New York.

5. *Other US Measures.* There were some other measures which hampered the capacity of US banks to compete for international business including curbs on the release of taxes on profits earned by foreigners in the United States, the introduction of the Interest Equalisation Tax in 1964, controls over the US direct investment abroad, and tight monetary policy to control inflationary pressures. These led to heavy borrowing by US banks from the Euro-currency market to meet the demand for dollars in the US.

6. *BOP Deficits in US.* There have been large and persistent BOP deficits in the US thereby leading to the outflow of the US dollars to the Eurobanks in countries having surplus with it.

7. *Petro-dollars.* The increase in the oil prices since 1973 has resulted in the tremendous increase in the incomes of the oil producing countries of the world which are known as petro-dollars. These are deposited in Eurobanks. These have further expanded the Euro-currency market.

8. *Innovative Banking.* Because of special circumstances that were present in the 1950s, there came into being a banking system distinct from but supplementary to the banking system of Europe. Like any other banking system, its elements consisted of reserves, deposits and loans, in US dollars and other currencies and recorded in Eurobanks. Consequently, the Euro-currency market has grown rapidly, in which deposits are received and loans made in currencies other than that of the country in which the market is situated. Now the Eurocurrency market dominates international transactions and traditional foreign banking accounts of international banking.

3. FEATURES OF EURO-CURRENCY MARKET

The Euro-currency market has the following features :

1. *International Market.* The Euro-currency market is an international market which accepts deposits and gives credit in currencies from throughout the world.

2. *Independent Market.* It is a free and independent market which does not function under the control of any monetary authority.

3. *Wholesale Market.* It is a wholesale market in which different currencies are bought and sold usually above $ 1 million.

4. *Competitive Market.* It is a highly competitive market in which the supply and demand for currencies depends on interest rate changes of Eurobanks.

5. *Short-Term Market.* It is a short-term money market in which deposits in different currencies are usually accepted for a period ranging from a few days to a year and interest is paid on them.

6. *Inter-Bank Market.* It is an inter-bank market in which the Eurobanks borrow and lend dollars and other Euro-currencies from each other.

4. HOW DOES IT FUNCTION?

The Euro-currency market is very extensive and complex. It is a means of transferring short-term and medium-term funds from one country to another. Euro-currency deposits and loans expand whenever funds flow into the Eurobanks as deposits from (*i*) commercial banks or residents of the United States; (*ii*) transfers by commercial banks or residents of other countries; and (*iii*) central banks, either directly or through the Bank for International Settlements. The first type of flow from the United States can be caused by one or more of the following factors : (1) a fall in US interest rates relative to Euro-currency rates; (2) an increased desire for asset diversification; (3) a fall in covered yield of foreign assets; or (4) an expected appreciation of the US dollar.

The flow of Euro-currency from commercial banks or residents outside Europe involve a portfolio shift out of domestic currency assets into Euro-currency. Moreover, many central banks also redeposit a substantial proportion of their reserve gains in the Euromarket.

The Euromarket is connected closely to the foreign exchange market because banks are able to manage their foreign currency positions in two ways : (1) They can buy and sell currencies outright in the spot and forward exchange markets. (2) They can borrow and lend currencies in the interbank market. However, many Euro-currency loans are made to non-bank borrowers also. Let us analyse the functioning of the Euromarket.

Suppose that a bank in London acquires dollar-deposits on a New York bank. If the London bank simply keeps these deposits, no Euro-dollars are created. But if this bank lends these dollars to some individual at interest rate, it creates dollar deposit claims against itself. These claims are Euro-dollars which the bank in London has created in excess of what it holds on a New York bank. Thus the ultimate increase in Euromarket aggregates will not be identical to initial deposit inflows because there are always subsequent flows induced by interest differentials and portfolio adjustments.

The above process of credit creation in the Euromarket has led economists to use the credit-multiplier analysis to explain its behaviour. Given the initial levels of US and foreign interest rates, this multiplier is always less than 1. This is because an initial deposit inflow of, say, $ 100 will encourage dollar rates to fall relative to foreign rates. This will, in turn, lead to a leakage in the original inflow. Moreover, the Euromarket is very vast and unregulated. Therefore, it does not operate like the ordinary banking system. Last but not the least, the multiplier analysis is essentially a tool for examining a credit creation in a closed economy, whereas the Euromarket is an open market. This fact severely limits the usefulness of the credit multiplier as a method for expanding the growth of the Euro-currency market.

5. ROLE IN INTERNATIONAL FINANCIAL SYSTEM*

The Euro-currency market has been playing an important role in international financial system. Investing and borrowing US dollars is the core function of the Euro-currency market. It transfers short and medium terms funds throughout the world, thereby increasing international capital mobility. It not only enables individual banks to improve their portfolio allocation, but also provides important services to the non-bank private sector. The Euro-currency market attracts funds because it offers higher interest rates, greater flexibility of maturities, and a wider range of investment qualities than other short-term capital markets. It attracts borrowers because it lends funds at relatively low interest rates. It is competitive in the interest rates it charges and receives, both because of the economies of scale afforded by concentrating on wholesale transactions, and because the Eurobanks are not subject to the regulations which tend to raise costs in domestic banking. Commercial banks, central banks, government treasuries, international banks like the Bank of International Settlement, and multinational corporations are the borrowers and lenders in the Euro-currency market.

Positive Effects. The following have been the economic consequences of the Euro-currency market :

1. The expansion of the Euro-currency market has greatly increased international capital mobility and has helped in easing the global liquidity problem.

2. It has helped in integrating international capital markets.

3. It has played an effective role in recycling funds from countries having surplus balance of payments to those having deficit balance of payments.

4. International flows of Euro-currencies have improved economic efficiency by reducing interest differential among nations.

5. The Euro-currency market has also resolved the problems of countries whose policy objectives aim at controlling international capital movements by transferring their currencies from and to Eurobanks.

6. It has helped in financing BOP deficits and surpluses of countries through lending and borrowing their currencies in exchange for other currencies from the Euro-currency market.

Adverse Effects. However, these flows of Euro-currencies have three adverse effects :

First, when the monetary authority of a country is trying to curb inflation through a restrictive monetary policy, an inflow of short-term capital defeats such a policy. Again when there is an outflow of capital and the country is following an easy monetary policy to combat unemployment, such a policy again becomes ineffective. This is because the Euro-currency market does not operate under the regulations of any authority.

Second, Euro-currencies provide an enoromous fund of liquid resources which are used for speculative capital movements. These expose the economies of the concerned countries to severe strains of sudden and large withdrawals of credits. Such financial upheavals and disturbances also affect the international monetary

* This also relates to the economic consequences (or effects) of the Euro-currency market.

system as a whole, especially when the countries involved are not protected by exchange controls or trade barriers.

Third, according to Milton Friedman, "The Euro-currency market has almost surely raised the world's nominal money supply (expressed in dollar equivalents) and has thus made the world price level (expressed in dollar equivalents) higher than otherwise it would be."

Its Role in Developing Countries

The developing countries have also benefitted from the Euro-currency market. They have been borrowing from the Eurobanks in terms of medium-term syndicated loans. Euro-currency and Eurobonds are important sources of finance for the developing countries. They have helped in meeting BOP deficits, particularly of such developing countries as India, Brazil, Mexico, Chile, etc. It is not only the governments but also business corporations of developing countries that are receiving European funds through the Eurobanks. However, the least developing countries have not been able to borrow much from this market. Despite this, speculative capital movements in the Euro-currency market have been adversely affecting the developing countries more than the developed countries. This is because the former are more dependent on the international financial centres and capital markets like the Euromarket and London Stock Exchange.

EXERCISES

1. What is Euro-currency market? How does it function? What role does it play in the international financial system?
2. What is Euro-currency market? Explain its working and economic consequences.

CHAPTER 54

The European Monetary System and Euro

1. INTRODUCTION

This chapter analyses the formation and functioning of the European Monetary System (EMS) which ultimately led to the establishment of the European Monetary Union (EMU) and the adoption of the Euro as the common currency unit by the European Union (EU).

2. THE EUROPEAN MONETARY SYSTEM

ORIGIN

The dollar crises which led to the breakdown of the Bretton Woods System prompted the EU countries to establish the *"Snake in the tunnel"* in 1972. Under this *arrangement,* the EU currencies were tied together and could fluctuate within narrow limits in relation to one another "(snake in the tunnel")[1] but jointly floating against other currencies of the world ("the snake out of the tunnel"). But this arrangement was brief and sporadic because countries moved into or out of the arrangement with changing circumstances. After 1973, the "snake" was left to float against the dollar and the tunnel vanished. In the end, the "snake" became a German Mark currency area, with Germany the only large country of the EU. However, the "snake" was the forerunner of the more comprehensive European Monetary system.

At the initiative of France and Germany, by the *Bremen Declaration* of July 1978, the European Council decided to establish the European Monetary System (EMS). The EMS was formed in 1979 to coordinate or integrate monetary and fiscal policies and exchange rates among EU members.

WORKING

The main elements in the EMU were :

(i) The exchange Rate Mechanism (ERM),

(ii) The European Currency Unit (ECU),

(iii) the European Monetary Cooperation Fund (EMCF), and

(iv) Financing facilities.

Their working is explained as under :

(i) The Exchange Rate Mechanism (ERM). The ERM was established by the EU to replace the currency

---

1. Germany, the Netherlands, Belgium, Luxemberg, France, Italy and Britain joined this arrangement.

"snake" for the control of exchange rates. It was meant to keep the exchange rates of member countries within specified bands in relation to each other. Most exchange rates fixed by the EMS until August 1993 could fluctuate up or down between + 2.25 percent against any currency. To begin with, this applied to France, Germany, Belgium, Denmark, Luxembourg, the Netherlands, Italy and Ireland. Spain joined in 1989, Britain in 1990 and Portugal in 1992 with 6 percent band. For some years' the ERM seemed to be working well. The bands had to be adjusted a numbers of times to stabilise exchange rates and control inflation in member countries. But after the unification of Germany in 1990, the ERM began to collapse when member were forced to follow different monetary policies. In September 1992, Britain and Italy left it. In August 1993, all bands were widened to + 15 percent under speculative pressures, except for the German mark and the Dutch guilder. However, Austria joined the system in 1995, followed by Finland and Italy at 15 percent in 1996.

(ii) The European Currency Unit (ECU). The ECU was introduced as a unit of account by the EU on the formation of EMS in 1979. Its value was equal to a weighted average of the currencies of member countries. The weight given to each currency was according to the relative size of a country's GDP and its intra-community trade. By 1981, it had replaced all other units of accounts being used in the EU. However, it was used very little by other financial markets. Despite this the ECU was a success. It was not only embraced by the member countries but also by the private sector which issued bonds and did bank transactions on a large scale in ECUs.

(iii) The European Monetary Cooperation Fund (EMCF). The EMCF was an important part of the EMS. It acted as the clearing house for the central banks of the EMS. But, in practice, routine working of the system was carried out by the Bank for International Settlements. The central banks of the EMS were required to deposit 20% of their gold and foreign exchange reserves with the Fund on a short-term basis in exchange for ECUs.

On the basis of the above elements, the Working of the EMS was not smooth. During the early years of its operation, some members imposed exchange controls to reduce the possibility of speculation in their currencies by directly limiting the sale of domestic currencies for foreign currencies.

There were also periodic currency alignments in relation to the "bands." There were eleven currency realighments between March 1979 and January 1987. Exchange controls helped the members to protect their foreign exchange reserves from speculators. From January 1987 to the end of 1992, exchange controls were removed by a number of EU countries. But the EMS continued with its fixed exchange rates. The unification of Germany in 1990 led to differences in macro-economic policies of member countries which weakened the EMS. There was boom and high inflation in Germany which the Bundesbank (central bank) of Germany tried to control through high interest rates. But major EMS countries like France, Britain and Italy were not prepared to raise interest rates so as to keep their currencies fixed against Germany. This policy conflict led to a crisis in the EMS exchange bunks which ended only when the bands were widened to + 15 percent for most countries by August 1993. These remained inforce until the introduction of the Euro in 1999.

(iv) Financing Facilities. The members of the EMS had access to credit facilities which aimed at helping countries with public deficit to manage their transitory problems and defend their exchange rate parities. These facilities covered their very short-term, short-term and medium term requirements and were operated by their central banks.

CONCLUSION

On the whole, the EMS worked well in bringing monetary cooperation among member countries. The success of the EMS encouraged the EU countries to have a single currency which led to the Maastricht Treaty.

3. THE EUROPEAN MONETARY UNION : THE EURO

The early up and downs in the working of the EMS which were characterised by currency realighments and strict exchange controls set the EU members to think about having a monetary union. In 1989, the *Delors Committee* recommended a three-stage transition for the formation of a European Monetary Union (EMU).

In the *first stage,* all EU members were to join the Exchange rate Mechanism (ERM) of the European Monetary System (EMS). In the *second stage,* exchange rate bands were to be narrowed and certain macroeconomic policy decisions placed under EU control. In *stage three,* the national currencies of EU countries were to be replaced by a single European currency and all monetary policy decisions were to be vested in a European Central Bank.

The Maastricht Treaty

On 10 December, 1991, the leaders of the EU countries met at *Maastricht* in the Netherlands and agreed to establish a single European currency which is called the Euro. In February 1992, the 15-member countries signed the *Maastricht Treaty* for the European Monetary Union (EMU). It called upon the members to start stage two of the Delors Plan on 1 January, 1994 and stage three not later than 1 January, 1999.

Its Main Features

The Maastricht Treaty lays down that EU countries must satisfy four macroeconomic *convergence criteria* before they can be admitted to the EMU. They are :

(1) The rate of inflation in the country must not be more than 1.5% above the average of the three EU member countries with the lowest inflation rate.

(2) The country must have maintained a stable exchange rate under the Exchange Rate Management System without devaluation.

(3) The country must not have a public deficit higher than 3% of its GDP, except temporarily and in exceptional circumstances.

(4) The country's public debt must be below or near 60% of its GDP.

The Treaty provides for a regular monitoring of criteria (3) and (4) by the European Commission and for imposing penalties on countries that violate these two criteria and fail to correct excessive deficits and debts.

Post-Maastrict Developments

Besides this Treaty, the EU members signed the *Stability and Growth Pact* (SGP) in 1997 which further tightens the fiscal measures by laying down the medium-term budgetary objective of being near to balance or surplus. It also sets out a timetable for levying penhalities on countries that fail to correct excessive deficits and debts.

By May 1998, eleven EU countries had satisfied the convergence criteria and became founder members of the EMU. Britain and Denmark had ratified the treaty but they did not join it and retained their national currencies. Sweden and Greece failed to qualify in terms of criteria to be members. Greece subsequently joined in 2001.

The time table for the implementation of EMU and adoption of the Euro was divided into three stages :

In the *first stage,* the European Central Bank (ECB) was established on 30 June, 1998 at Frankfurt (Germany) for a smooth change-over of the currencies of member nations to the Euro. The main functions of the Bank till the circulation of Euro coins and bank notes from 1 January, 2002 were to control inflation and create confidence of the global financial markets in the Euro.

In the *second stage,* beginning 1 January, 1999, the central banks of EU countries adopted the Euro as a single monetary unit.

In the *third stage* beginning January, 2002 more than 14 billion Euro bank notes and 50 billion Euro coins replaced national currencies and bank notes and coins of members. They were made available at all banks, and post offices. Till 31 December, 2002, banknotes of each Euro area country could be exchanged at banks in the country concerned. At least until the end of 2012, national central banks will exchange free of charge their old national banknotes against the Euro. In most countries, the redemption periods are longer or even indefinite.

The EMU currency consists of Euros of 100 cents. The Euro banknotes have seven denominations of 5,10,20,50,100, 200 and 500 Euro. The Euro coins have eight denominations of 1, 2, 5, 10, 20, 50 cent and 1 and 2 Euro. Euro coins have a European side and a national side on which national symbol of the issuing country appears. But Euro banknotes do not have national symbols. They are uniform throughout the EU. Countries like Britain which have their own currencies in circulation have fixed exchange rates with the Euro and it circulates in such countries.

The *European Central Bank* (ECB) and national central banks (NCBs) of 15 EU countries form the *European System of Central Banks* (ESCB). The NCBs of the EU countries who have not joined the Eurozone are members with special status. They conduct their respective national policies but do not take part in decision making of the EMU and the implementation of its policies. All heads of NCBs sit on the ECB general council which conducts monetary policy for the entire Eurozone. Besides this, (i) the ECB conducts foreign exchange operations, (ii) holds and manages the official foreign exchange reserves; (iii) promotes the smooth operation of the payment system; and (iv) supports the policies of its member banks.

CONCLUSION

The Euro, as the international currency of the European Monetary Union, was weak against the dollar in the beginning. To begin with, it opened at 1 EUR = $ 1.16 in 1999. But when the Euro actually started operating in January 2002, it fell to 1 EUR = $ 0.89. With the U.S. budget and current account deficits widening and the U.S. Federal Reserve (central Bank) reducing the bank rate to as low as 1%, the Euro rose 46% against the dollar in the past two years. It surged to a record high of $ 1.29 in February 2004.

ADVANTAGES OF THE EURO

The following have been the advantages of adoption of the Euro:

1. The Euro has brought a greater degree of European market integration.
2. It has removed the threat of currency realighnments.
3. It has eliminated the costs and inconveniences of traders to convert one currency to another of the EU countries.
4. There is no longer any risk of fluctuations between currencies.
5. Rates of interest and inflation rates are much lower now.
6. Exchange rates are permanently fixed,
7. There is freedom of capital movements.
8. People now buy, sell and borrow within a larger and more competitive market.
9. Prices are displayed in the same currency throughout the EU. They are easier to compare and help the buyers to make the right choice.
10. Travelling in Europe has become more convenient because a traveller has to change money only once in the Euro. This saves both time and money.
11. The European Central Bank has put an end to the hegemony of the German Bundesbank in the management of EMU monetary policy. All NCBs participate and follow monetary policy decisions taken by the ECB's general council.

EXERCISES

1. Explain the origin and working of the European Monetary System.
2. Trace the origin of the Euro in Europe. What has been its advantages?
3. What led to the Maastricht Treaty? Explain its main features and post-Maastricht developments in the European Monetary System.
4. Explain the formation of the European Monetary Union. What has been its merits?

CHAPTER 55

The Asian Development Bank

1. ORIGIN

During the 1950s, it was strongly felt that there should be a bank for Asia like the World Bank to meet the development needs of this region. This view was suggested for the first time at the Ministerial Conference on Asian Cooperation held at Manila in December 1963. The Conference constituted a working group of experts which submitted its report to the UN Economic Commission for Asia and Far East (ECAFE) at its session held at Wellington in March 1965. It was on the basis of this report that an Agreement Eastablishing the Asian Development Bank was drafted and adopted at the Second Ministerial Conference on Asian Economic Cooperation at Manila in November-December 1965. By January 1966, 33 countries had signed its Charter and the Asian Development Bank was set up on December 19, 1966 with its headquarters at Manila in the Philippines.

2. ITS OBJECTIVES

The aim for the establishment of ADB was to supplement the work of the World Bank in Asia. Its objectives are :

1. To promote public and private investment for economic development in the ECAFE region.

2. To utilise the available resources for financing of economic development. To achieve this, it gives priority to those regional and sub-regional and national projects and programmes which contribute more effectively to the harmonious growth of the entire region, especially of the smaller and less developed members of the region.

3. To help the regional members in the coordination of their plans and policies for economic development to enable them to achieve a better utilisation of their resources.

4. To provide technical assistance for the preparation, financing and implementation of projects and programmes for economic development, including the formulation of specific projects.

5. To co-operate with the United Nations and its organs and subsidiaries, including, in particular, the ECAFE and other international institutions and organisations and national entities in the investment of development funds in the region.

6. To undertake all such activities and provide such services which may fulfil the above objectives.

3. ITS MEMBERSHIP

The membership of ADB is open to the following : (1) Members of the ECAFE; (2) associate members of ECAFE; (3) other countries of the ECAFE region which are the members of the United Nations or any of its specialised agencies; and (4) developed countries outside the ECAFE region which are the members of the UN or any of its specialised agencies. It has a membership of 56 countries at present. Any country can become its member when two-third members of the Board of Governors cast their vote in its favour.

4. ITS MANAGEMENT

The ADB is manged by a President, Vice-President, and a Board of Governors alongwith an administrative staff. The President is the administrative head of the Bank. The Vice-President performs the duties of the President in his absence. Each member country nominates a Governor and an Alternate Governor to the Board of Governors. Atleast one meeting of the Board of Governors is held every year. The Board of Governors has delegated its executive powers to the Board of Directors. The Board of Directors consists of ten members of whom seven belong to regional countries and three to non-regional countries. The Board of Directors takes all decisions relating to the Bank, passes its annual budget and presents the accounts of the Bank to the Board of Governors for approval. There are certain functions which only the Board of Governors has to perform. They are : (*a*) entry of new members; (*b*) change in the authorised capital of the Bank; (*c*) election of the President and administrators; and (*d*) amendment in the Charter of the bank.

5. ITS FINANCIAL RESOURCES

The Bank started its operations with an authorised capital of $ 2.9 billion which was raised to $ 25 billion in 1992. Out of this, 50 per cent had been contributed by Japan and the remaining by member countries. To increase its resources, the Bank issues debentures and accepts deposits from its special funds. To augment its resources further, the Bank borrows from the capital markets of the world.

6. ITS FUNCTIONS

The ADB performs the following functions :

Financial Assistance

The Bank provides financial assistance in the form of grants and loans. It gives three types of loans : project loans, sector loans, and programme loans. Project loans are tied to specific projects. Sector loans are given to a number of related projects in a given sector. Programme loans cover more than one sector and relate to the implementation of a policy or programme for bringing about certain changes.

The Bank advances loans out of its Ordinary Funds Reserve and Special Funds Reserve. The Ordinary Funds Reserve refers to the Bank's ordinary capital resources OCRs out of which direct loans are given for development projects or specific projects. These consist of the financing of foreign exchange or local currency component of the cost of specific projects. The Bank also lends to development banks of member countries for relending to specific projects. All direct loans are "hard loans" for a period of 20 years repayable with in 15 years with a five-year grace period. The interest rate is determined in accordance with ADB's poolbased variable lending rate system for US dollar loans.

For sector lending, the Bank has established Special Funds such as the Asian Development Fund, Multipurpose Special Funds and Agriculture Special Fund. Loans out of these funds are given for projects of high development priority for longer periods and at lower rates of interest than for ordinary loans. These are called "soft loans". The Special Funds are different from the Bank's ordinary capital resources. The Bank contributes 10 per cent of its paid-in capital to these funds and the remaining amount comes as donations from its members countries such as America, Britain, Germany, Canada, Switzerland, Denmark, India, Pakistan, China, etc. For lending out of Special Funds, the sanction by two-thirds of the total number of Governors of the Bank is required.

In short, the ADB sanctions for the following types of loans : (1) To development finance institutions on the guarantee of the government : (2) to small and medium enterprises on the government's guarantee; (3) to private enterprises in the form of equity and loans without government guarantee; (4) to strengthen financial institutions and capital market; and (5) to public sector enterprises for privatisation without government guarantee.

The ADB grants loans on the basis of certain *criteria*. At the time of evaluating projects that it proposes to finance, the Bank considers their economic, technical and financial feasibility, their effects on the general activity of the concerned country, their contributions to the removal of economic bottlenecks, and their capacity to repay the loans. In granting loans to the various types of projects, the ADB Charter does not impose any restrictions. Even the minimum and maximum limits of loans are left open to be decided by the Bank on merits and viability of the projects. Since July 1990, it charges 6.53% interest rate annually on dollar loans.

Technial Assistance

The ADB also provides technical assistance to member countries out of the Technical Assistance Special Fund. The technical assistance is provided to the members in ECAFE region through their governments, agencies, regional institutions and private firms. It may be in the form of grants or loans or both. The Bank's technical assistance has two main objectives : *first*, to prepare and finance and implement specific national and/or regional development plans and projects; and *second*, to help in the working of existing institutions and/or the creation of new institutions on a national or regional basis in such areas as agriculture, industry, public administration, etc. The Bank also provides advisory services under its technical assistance programme. It sends its own experts and even hires consultants from other institutions on short and long missions for setting up or reorganising institutions for project implementation in member countries.

Surveys and Research

One of the functions of ADB is to conduct surveys and research in order to formulate policies for the future and to promote regional economic integration. It brings out an annual report in which it highlights the achievements, prospects and failures relating to the economic development of the member countries of the ECAFE region and also suggests measures to solve their problems.

Poverty Reduction

Since the 1990s, Bank's greater emphasis has been to promote employment and reduce poverty through improved efficiency, sustainable pro-poor economic growth and better development opportunities for the poor. In promoting economic growth, the Bank stresses the importance of increasing productivity. Productivity improvement depends on new investments, the efficiency with which new and existing capital are used and incorporation of technological changes. The Bank encourages domestic resource mobilisation to finance new investments, private sector development and public sector reform to improve efficiency. The Bank targets resources where private sector provision is inadequate and seeks to involve the private sector in services formerly left to the public sector. The ADB now pays more attention to human resource development, poverty reduction, social infrastructure development, urban environmental improvement and development, comprehensive economic and structural reforms, etc.

7. ITS PROGRESS

The ADB was set up in 1966. For the first time, it sanctioned loans amounting to $ 41.6 million in 1968. The Bank has been providing assistance in the fields of agriculture and agro-based industries, energy, industry and non-fuel minerals, development banking, transport and communications, water supply, urban development, education, health and population planning.

The ADB commenced lending to India in 1986, though it has been a founder member of the Bank. In the earlier period, loans to India were mainly for infrastructure sectors such as power, roads, ports, etc. In recent years, the emphasis has shifted to public resource management programme, urban environmental improvement and development, health and nutrition, and housing finance to reduce poverty. Since 1966, India had received 65 loans amounting to $ 5.8 billion at the end of 2000 for infrastructure, energy and financial sectors.

9. ITS EVALUATION

The ADB has been playing an important role in providing finance in the form of loans and grants to its member developing countries for their development. There have been two factors for the increase in the Bank's lending operations. *First*, at the time of its establishment, India had agreed not to get loans from the Bank so that smaller developing member countries might be given larger aid. But when China became its member and started getting assistance from the Bank, India followed it. This has led to increase in the Bank's lending operations. The *second* factor has been the introduction of non-project loans through the Bank's concessional window, the Asian Development Fund (ADF). China and India do not receive 'soft' loans from it which carry a nominal rate of interest.

Some Weaknesses

Even though the bank has made long strides in providing assistance for the economic development of its ECAFE member countries, yet it is dogged by a number of problems : (1) its financial resources are limited because the regional member countries are mostly poor. Developed member countries which include Japan, Britain, America and others are not prepared to contribute much. (2) There have been negative transfer to the Bank during the last few years from such countries as Fiji, Malaysia and Philippines. (3) No doubt, loan sanctions have increased from the Asian Development Fund, but their disbursements have been less. The Bank should undertake such measures whereby the loan-absorption capacity of the recipients may increase. (4) It provides assistance for mega projects and does not consider cheap community-based alternative projects.

Despite these weaknesses, the ADB's contribution to the economic development of the developing member countries of the region has been creditable.

EXERCISES

1. Discuss the working and achievements of the Asian Development Bank.
2. Discuss the functions of the Asian Development Bank. What has been its contribution to the regional development of Asia?

CHAPTER

56

Present Monetary System of India

1. INTRODUCTION

This chapter studies the present monetary system of India and narrates a brief history of the Indian currency in the pre-independence and post-independence periods.

2. INDIA'S PRESENT MONETARY SYSTEM

The monetary system is related to the control and regulation of the supply of money in a country. According to Prof. Shapiro, "The monetary system of a nation involves the overall set of laws and practices that control the quantity and quality of money in an economy." Every country has its own monetary system which consists of the country's unit of money (Rupee in the case of India), the types of coins and notes in circulation, the system of note issue, the monetary standard and the relation of the country's currency with other countries. As such, the monetary system of a country is divided into two parts: internal and external. The internal aspect consists of the internal problems of the monetary system such as the nature of money, system of issue, monetary standard and money supply. The external aspect consists of the relation of the country's currency with foreign currencies, foreign exchange, exchange control etc.

We study below the internal and external features of India's present monetary (or currency) system.

A. INTERNAL FEATURES OF INDIA'S PRESENT MONETARY SYSTEM

The following are the features of present monetary system of India:

1. **Unit of Money.** The unit of money in India is the rupee, it is not only a medium of exchange but also a unit of value which facilitates accounting. As a unit of account, the rupee helps in the estimation of costs and prices and revenues of firms and projects, and the gross national product.

2. **Monetary Standard.** The present monetary standard of India is *the managed paper currency standard.* According to this, the paper currency is in circulation which is non-convertible into gold. It is managed paper standard because the issue of notes and coins is managed by the Reserve Bank of India.

3. **Types of Coins and Notes (or Currency).** The following types of coins and notes are included in India's present monetary system:

(i) *Coins.* The Rupee-coin in India is a standard token coin whose intrinsic value of the metal is less than its face value. If the Rupee-coin is melted, its metal will not be sold worth one rupee. The Rupee-coin is an unlimited legal tender in which payment of any amount can be made. There are also 2-Rupee coin and 5-Rupee coins in circulation since 1990.

(ii) *Subsidiary Coins.* There are also subsidiary coins in India to assist the token money. At present, coins of the denominations of 1 paisa and 3, 5, 10, 20, 25 and 50 paisa are in circulation. The 50-paise coin like the

Indian rupee-coin is unlimited legal tender. But all coins from 1 paisa to 25 paise are limited legal tender for which payment can be made only up to Rs. 25 . The minting of 1, 3, 5,9 and 10 paisa coins has been stopped since 1996 but they will remain in circulation till their transactions are stopped by the public themselves.

(iii) *Notes or Paper Currency.* Paper currency in India consists of notes of various denominations which are issued by the Reserve Bank of India and the Government of India. The *one-rupee note* is issued by the Ministry of Finance of the Government of India and bears the signature of the Secretary. It is inconvertible paper money which is also known as fiat money or representative or token money. But it is unlimited legal tender. The other notes of the denominations of Rs. 2, 5, 10, 20, 50, 100 and 500 are issued by the Reserve Bank of India.[1] They are inconvertible into gold but are unlimited legal tender. They are convertible into coins and notes. They are *fiduciary* money.

(iv) *System of Note Issue.* The present system of note issue in India is the *Minimum Reserve System.* Under this system, the RBI is authorised to issue notes up to any extent but it must keep a statutory minimum reserve of gold and foreign securities. Accordingly, the RBI is required to keep a minimum reserve cf Rs. 200 crores. Of this, Rs. 115 crores must be in gold and Rs. 85 crores in foreign securities.

4. Money Supply. In India, the money supply consists .of both narrow money (M_1) and broad money (M_3). M_1 consists of currency notes and coins with the public, demand deposits with commercial and co-operative banks and other deposits with RBI. M_3 consists of M_1 plus time deposits with banks and is also known as aggregate monetary resources. As on 31 March, 2003, the total M(in India was Rs. 4,72,827 crores and M_3 was Rs 17,25,222 crores.

B. External Features of India's Monetary System

The external features of India's present monetary system are the following:

1. **Foreign Exchange Rate.** Since January 1976 with the signing of Jamaica Agreement, India is following the policy of floating exchange rates. According to this, the external value of Indian rupee is linked to a 'basket' of currencies of those countries with which India has large trade. This is the Nominal Effective Exchange Rate (NEER) of the rupee which is a weighted average of exchange rates vis-a-vis the currencies of India's major trading partners. Upto February 1993, India followed a *dual* exchange rate regime. According to it, the RBI fixed the exchange rates in terms of the various currencies such as dollar, pound, mark, yen, franc, rouble, etc. from time to time and all legal exchange transactions took place at the announced official rates. In March 1993, India moved to a single market-determined exchange rate system. Under it, there is no officially fixed exchange rate of the rupee. Instead, the exchange rate is determined by the demand and supply conditions in the foreign exchange market. But the RBI intervenes only to maintain orderly market conditions and to curb excessive speculation.

2. **Exchange Control.** In order to conserve foreign exchange, the RBI controls all foreign receipts and payments in the form of foreign currencies. It has an Exchange Control Department for this purpose. Foreign currencies coming into India are required to be sold and exchanged for the rupee either direct to the RBI or to its authorised dealers (ADs). Its authorised dealers include certain commercial banks, hotels, firms, shops, etc. which deal in foreign currencies and foreign travellers' cheques. They are also authorised to lend and borrow foreign currency among themselves in the inter-bank market locally. The actual lending limit for etch AD is fixed by the RBI depending upon the size of its operations and other relevant factors.

In March 1992, the RBI introduced the *partial* convertibility of the rupee in 60:40 ratio. This was the Liberalised Exchange Rate Management System (LERMS). Under this system, all foreign exchange receipts on current account transactions (i.e. exports, remittances, etc.) were required to be surrendered to the authorised dealers (ADs) in full. The rate of exchange for these transactions was the free market rate quoted by the ADs. The ADs, in turn, surrendered to the RBI 40 per cent of their purchase of foreign currencies at the exchange rate announced by the RBI. They were free to sell the balance of 60 per cent of foreign exchange in the free market. All importers of goods and services and persons travelling abroad bought foreign exchange at market-determined rates from the ADs subject to liberalised exchange control rules.

In March 1994, *full convertibility* of the rupee on the entire current account transactions was introduced. Consequently, the RBI announced further relaxations in the exchange control regulations upto a specified limit relating to: (a) exchange earners foreign currency accounts; (b) basic travel quota; (c) studies abroad; (d) gift

1. Printing of Rs 1, 2 and 5 notes has been stopped and Rs. 1000 note started.

remittances; (e) donations; (f) 100% export oriented units; and (g) payments of certain services rendered by foreign parties. Further relaxations in them are made from time to time in keeping with the foreign exchange position of the country.

3. **Foreign Exchange Reserves.** Foreign exchange reserves with the RBI show the quantity of foreign currencies which can be utilised by the country for trade and other foreign transactions. The variations in foreign exchange reserves also show the balance of payments position of the country. India's foreign exchange reserves comprising foreign currency assets of the RBI, gold held by it, and SDR balances held by the Government stood at Rs. 3,58,280 crores at the end of March 2003.

3. BRIEF HISTORY OF INDIAN CURRENCY SYSTEM

Prior to the Indian Currency Act of 1835 about 994 multiple types of gold and silver coins were in circulation in India. This Act brought uniformity in the Indian currency system by issuing silver coins of 180 grains. Thus one-rupee silver coin was legal tender and the country was on the Silver Standard.

With increase in the supply of silver in 1871, its value in terms of gold decreased considerably. This adversely affected India's foreign trade. This led to the appointment of the Herchell Committee, on whose recommendations the silver standard was given up in 1893. With the Indian Currency Act of 1893, paper notes and gold coins were put into circulation and the Indian currency was related to the British pound. The exchange rate of rupee was fixed' at 1 shilling 4 pence. Free coinage of silver was also stopped. On the recommendations of the Fowler Committee, the Indian Currency Act of 1899 was passed which led to the establishment of the Gold Exchange Standard. The circulation of gold coins was stopped. The currency consisted of paper notes and token coins of silver and other metals. These were not convertible into gold coins or bullion. The rupee coins were converted into gold at the fixed exchange rate of ls-4d per rupee only to make payments to Britain. On the recommendations of the Babington Committee in 1920, the rupee was revalued to 2s-10d.

The recommendations of the Hilton Young Commission led to the passing of the Indian Currency Act of 1929 which devalued the rupee to ls-6d. The Gold Exchange Standard was replaced by the Gold Bullion Standard. According to this rupee notes were convertible into gold bars of 40 tolas at the rate of Rs 27-7 annas - 10 pies per tola. (These weights and currency were prevalent in those times). But a purchaser was required to buy 1065 tolas of gold at a time. Gold was freely exported and imported.

The Great Depression of 1929 and some other factors led to the abandonment of the gold standard by England on 21 September, 1932. The rupee was delinked from gold and linked with pound at the rate of ls-6d under the Sterling Exchange Standard. According to it, rupee was inconvertible into bullion and currency consisted of paper notes and metallic coins. With the establishment of the Reserve Bank of India in 1935, it was given the sole right to issue notes. It issued notes on the basis of the Proportional Reserve System, whereby it was required to keep 40 per cent of the total value of notes issued in the form of gold.

The Sterling Exchange Standard continued during the 2nd World War (1939 to 1948), when India adopted the Gold Parity Standard after the establishment of the International Monetary Fund (IMF). In this standard, the rupee was linked with gold or US dollar at $ 35 per ounce of gold. In January 1976, the IMF gave up the Gold Parity Standard and allowed the Managed Floating Exchange System. Under this system which is in operation at present, India is not expected to maintain and establish par values with gold or dollar. The rupee is allowed to adjust itself to the different currencies on the basis of their demand and supply in the market. But the system of floating exchange rates is not one of *free* flexible exchange rates but of *managed* floating. In case the exchange rate changes beyond a certain level, the Reserve Bank of India often intervenes to bring stability in the exchange rate.

EXERCISES

1. Discuss the present monetary system of India.
2. Discuss the present currency system of Indian.
3. Give a brief history of the Indian Currency System.

CHAPTER 57

Indian Capital Market

The capital market comprises the various institutions and mechanisms through which medium-term and long-term funds are pooled and lent to individuals, businesses and the governments. It includes various types of securities which are bought and sold to serve the requirements of investors and borrowers of funds.

1. FEATURES OF INDIAN CAPITAL MARKET

The capital market in India consists of unorganised and organised markets. The unorganised sector, also known as the informal sector, comprises indigenous bankers, moneylenders, etc. who operate in the small industry sector, in trade and agriculture. A large part of private savings are invested by people in their own businesses. Many people invest in the enterprises of their relatives and friends. Large chunks of black money and wealth flow freely between the unorganised and organised sectors. Thus the unorganised capital market in India is unsystematic with no uniform policy relating to interest rate charged, maturity of financial assets, etc. It is free from any regulation and control though efforts have been made towards this direction by the Government of India and the Reserve Bank. On the other hand, the organised capital market comprises a variety of financial institutions which mobilise private savings in various ways and provide long-term funds to the capital market. They are: UTI, IFCI, ICICI, IDBI, IRBI, LIC, GIC, SIDBI, State Financial Corporations, State Industrial Development Corporations, commercial banks, merchant bankers, leasing companies, venture capital companies, mutual funds, housing finance banks, Stock Holding Corporation of India, and Discount and Finance House of India. The organised sector of the Indian capital market is regulated by the Securities and Exchange Board of India (SEBI).

Capital Market Instruments

The Indian capital market deals in a variety of securities or instruments to serve the requirements of borrowers and investors of funds. These differ in nature, maturity, interest rate, dividend, liability, ownership, voting right, etc. The various capital market instruments are the following:

(1) Corporate securities which include preference, bonus and rights issue shares, stocks, bonds, convertible and nonconvertible debentures, etc., and PSULs (public sector undertaking) bonds.

(2) Shares issued by mutual funds under their income, growth and tax planning schemes such as UTI Master Shares, UTI Master Growth, Canshare, Cangrowth, SBI Magnums, GIC Growth Plus, Goldshare, Starshare, etc.

(3) Government bonds and securities issued by the Central and State Governments and local bodies. They are also known as gilt-edged securities. Recently, a variety of innovative and hybrid instruments have been introduced to attract more investors for new issues like warrants attached to convertible and non-convertible debentures, secured premium notes attached with warrants, deep discount bonds, accident insurance attached with warrants and non-convertible debentures.with sale of *khokhas* to banks, zero-coupon bonds, zero-interest bonds, etc.

Security Market

On the basis of instruments or securities, the capital market in India is divided into the gilt-edged market and industrial security market.

(1) **Gilt-edged Market.** It is the market for Government securities. Central and State Governments and local bodies sell long-term bonds or securities to the public, banks and financial institutions. These bonds are backed by the Reserve Bank. They carry lower interest rates than bonds issued by companies. But they attract more investors because they carry a variety of tax incentives and rebates on income tax and wealth tax. They are less risky, more safer and more liquid than industrial securities.

(2) **Industrial Security Market.** This market deals in a variety of new and old shares and debentures of commercial, financial and industrial concerns. It is divided into the primary market and the secondary market.

(a) *The Primary or New Issues Market.* The primary capital market is for new issues by public limited companies in the form of new capital issues directly to the public in the form of shares, fully convertible debentures, non-convertible debentures, preferential issues of shares and debentures, and rights issues at par or at a premium. Capital is also raised by companies in the primary market by private placement whereby shares are sold to specific group of investors such as relatives, friends, and holders of shares of the same industrial group or house. Merchant bankers, mutual funds, commercial banks and other financial institutions operate as underwriters and lead managers. They help in mobilising the savings of the public in new issues market and channelising them into productive uses by trade and industry.

(b) The Secondary Market. It is the market which deals in shares and debentures at the stock exchanges. Such a market is also known as the stock market where various types of shares and debentures are actively traded by brokers, mutual funds and NBFIs like the UTI, GCI, etc. Presently, there are 22 recognised stock exchanges operating in the secondary market in India.

2. WORKING OF INDIAN CAPITAL MARKET

Introduction

India is one of the few countries among the developing nations where the Bombay Stock Exchange began to function as early as in 1874, where the Government securities and bonds issued by Port Trust Municipal Corporation, etc. were traded. At the time of partition in 1947, there were nine stock exchanges on the Indian side at Mumbai, Kolkata, Chennai, Ahmedabad, Delhi, Kanpur, Hyderabad and Bangalore. They traded in ordinary and preference shares of the British Managing Agency houses and of Indian companies such as the Tata Iron and Steel Company, in addition to Government securities.

In the early 1950s, the capital market in India helped to mobilise financial resources for the corporate sector. But with the nationalisation of insurance companies in 1956, the State Bank of India in 1955, the establishment of development banks like IDBI, ICICI, IFCI, etc., and the nationalisation of 14 commercial banks in 1969, the capital market suffered a setback, because subsidised credit was available to trade and industry from these institutions. Consequently, companies had to issue equities at a discount substantially below market value.

With the amendment of the Foreign Exchange Regulation Act (FERA), the expansion of foreign owned and controlled companies was limited. Accordingly, the FERA companies were required to dilute their capital by issuing new capital either at par or at an approved premium to the Indian shareholders. This led to the issue of 40 per cent of their shares at low prices to Indians. The capital market continued to grow substantially during the 1980s as various measures were taken to stimulate both demand and supply in the capital market. The Government gave a number of incentives to equity and debenture issues such as reducing the corporate tax rate for listed companies and allowing higher interest rate for debentures above that for fixed deposits but below that for bank loans. Besides, the companies were authorised to use cumulative and convertible preference shares and equity-linked debentures, and investors were given tax incentives in new issues. Thus the Indian capital market was undeveloped till the 1970s. For instance, during the Fifth Plan (1974-79), Rs. 551 crores were raised from the primary market. The secondary market was also very small with only 8 stock exchanges, 1203 listed companies, Rs. 2600 crores of market capitalisation which was 7.6 per cent of GDP and with less than one million investors. Since the 1980s both the primary and secondary capital markets have been showing remarkable growth. In 1995-96, 1704 companies raised Rs. 22,918 crores from the primary market. The secondary market had a phenomenal growth. At present there are 22 stock exchanges in India with over 6,500 listed companies, thus putting India a little behind the United States. There are 15 million shareholders, the second largest in the world after the United States. The total market capitalisation of the Indian stock market is $ 138.6 billion. The Indian capital market has thus emerged as one of the important markets in the world. It has been identified as the primary source of finance for the private and public sectors in the Eighth Five-Year Plan, in which it was estimated to raise Rs 50,000 crores.

Despite the rapid growth of the capital market in the 1980s, a number of abuses existed such as insider trading, price rigging, inadequate, vague and misleading prospectuses of companies, delays in share allocation and in issuing refund orders and manipulation of prices in stock exchanges. The capital market was less liquid and lacked in transparency thereby providing little protection to investors.

Capital Market Reforms

On the recommendations of the Narasimham Committee and other committees and groups appointed by the Government of India from time to time, a number of measures have been taken up to reform the Indian capital market. These are listed below :

(A) Securities and Exchange Board of India (SEBI). On 31 March, 1992, the Securities and Exchange Board of India was established as an autonomous and statutory body. With the repeal of the Capital Issues Control Act, 1947 in May 1992, the office of the Controller of Issues was abolished from 29 May, 1992. The SEBI is the regulatory authority to oversee the new issues, protect the interests of investors, promote the development of the capital market and to regulate the working of stock exchanges. It has initiated a number of measures in these directions such as registration of intermediaries, strict disclosure norms, regulations on insider trading and inspection of the functioning of the stock exchanges and mutual funds, etc.

These and other measures explained below are likely to impart confidence in investors.

(B) Primary Market Reforms. The following measures have been taken up to reform the primary or new issues capital market in order to remove the inadequacies and deficiencies in the issue procedures.

(1) The control over price and premium of shares has been removed. Companies are now free to fix the price and premia of shares and debentures after clearance from the SEBI. Vetting of offer documents is not done by the SEBI.

(2) Companies issuing shares and debentures in the primary market are required to disclose all material facts and specific risk factors associated with their projects. They are also required to disclose the basis of calculation of premium on equity issues.

(3) The minimum percentage of securities to be issued to the public has been fixed at 25 per cent.

(4) Minimum subscription for public issue has been fixed at Rs. 2000 in the case of an individual w.e.f. 1.11.1996.

(5) The SEBI has ensured through an advertisement code that advertisements do not contain such statements which may mislead the investors.

(6) The allotment procedure requires that shares are allotted on a pro-rata basis and mutual funds and foreign institutional investors (FIIs) are allowed firm allotment in public issues.

(7) A SEBI representative supervises the allotment process in the case of oversubscribed public issues.

(8) Bonds of Public Sector Undertakings (PSUs) have been brought under the regulatory authority of the SEBI.

(9) NRIs and overseas companies are free to invest in the Indian capital market without the prior approval of the RBI.

(10) FIIs have been allowed to invest in the capital market on registration with the SEBI and foreign brokers are allowed to assist them on the same condition.

(11) The stock exchanges have been directed by the SEBI to collect from companies making public issues

a deposit of one per cent of the issue amount which is liable to forfeiture in case the companies do not comply with the listing agreement, and do not despatch the refund orders and share certificates by registered post within 3 months of allotment.

(12) The company is required to complete the allotment of shares within 30 days of the closure of the issue. Thereafter it is required to pay interest at the rate of 15 per cent per annum.

(13) Banks have been permitted to operate in the secondary market since November 1996.

(C) Secondary Market Reforms. The SEBI has also introduced a number of regulatory and supervisory measures for intermediaries in the secondary market. Specific rules and regulations have been laid down for intermediaries in the secondary market. They are the merchant bankers, portfolio managers, underwriters, registrars, brokers and sub-brokers, and share transfer agents. They are required to adhere to specific capital adequacy norms, meet certain eligibility criteria and follow a code of conduct towards investors. They also provide for action by the SEBI in case of default. Some of these are as under:

(1) All brokers are required to register themselves with the stock exchange in which they wish to operate.

(2) The capital adequacy norms laid down by the SEBI for stock brokers are: 3 per cent for individual brokers and 6 per cent for corporate members.

(3) Stock Exchanges have been directed to ensure that contract notes are issued by brokers to clients within 24 hours of dealings. Time limit has been laid down for payment of sale proceeds and deliveries by brokers and payment of margins by clients to brokers. Penalties have been provided for default.

(4) To control rigging of prices and other malpractices in the stock exchanges, the SEBI has introduced such measures as penal margin on net undelivered portion at the end of the settlement, special margin for buyers in case of rise in share prices, joint suspension of trading by stock exchanges in case of price stipulation, etc.

(5) To bring greater transparency in transactions, Brokers are required to maintain separate accounts for clients and for themselves. The contract notes issued to clients must contain the transaction price and brokerage separately.

(6) Share jobbers have been introduced in the stock exchanges who simultaneously display buying-selling rates of scrips in which they are doing jobbing.

(7) Stock brokers are required to have their books audited, and audit reports are required to be filed with the SEBI every year.

(8) The SEBI has broad-based the governing boards of the stock exchanges and has changed the composition of their arbitration, default and disciplinary committees.

(9) The SEBI has started the inspection of the working of stock exchanges.

(10) The trading in the stock exchanges has been fixed for three hours instead of the earlier two-and-a-half hours.

(11) Failure to comply with the instructions issued by the SEBI on the working of stock exchanges, will invite penalties including fines and suspension from trading.

(12) Screen-based on-line trading has been introduced by NSE, OTCEI, and major stock exchanges like Mumbai, Delhi, etc.

(13) Efforts are being made to revamp the operations of stock exchanges in India. The lead has been given by the Bombay Stock Exchange which has introduced several changes to revamp its operations such as making the BOLT system operational for all the scrips, regrouping of shares, and introduction of weekly settlements for *A* and *B* group shares, dealing in odd lot shares, etc.

(D) Institutional and Market Development. Besides the establishment of SEBI, the Government has initiated the following steps for institutional and market development.

(i) *Market Makers.* Steps have been taken to promote the emergence of market makers. Since in the stock exchanges not more than 20 per cent of the scrips are actively traded, the holders of ihe majority of other scrips do not find sufficient liquidity. The institution of market makers is meant to rectify this lacuna. The market maker is required to make a market for a minimum of, say, five scrips (equity shares) which are not included in group A traded shares at a stock exchange. Market makers are required to offer two-way quotes for a minimum period of 18 months from the date on which the securities (shares) are admitted for dealing. The minimum quantity offered or bid for at any price has to be three times the market lot (either 50 or 100). Moreover, the bid-ask spread (difference between quotations for sale and purchase) cannot exceed 10 per cent. Unlisted companies planning public issues below Rs 5 crores are required to appoint market makers on all stock exchanges where the share is proposed to be listed. To ensure that market makers are able to impart liquidity to scrips and reduce volatile movements in share prices, the RBI issued guidelines on 5 August, 1993 regarding bank financing of their operations. Market makers require financial support from banks like other traders. Banks have been permitted by the RBI to exercise their commercial judgement in determining the working capital requirements of market makers which are different from those laid down for traders. Market makers are approved by the SEBI on the recommendations of the stock exchanges.

(ii) Foreign Institutional Investors (FIIs). FIIs such as pension funds, mutual funds, asset management companies, investment trusts, nominee companies, and incorporated or institutional portfolio managers have been allowed to operate in the Indian capital market. The SEBI has simplified the common application forms for registration with it by FIIs. Foreign brokers have also been allowed to assist FIIs and operate on their behalf to buy and sell scrips in the Indian stock exchanges. They have been permitted to open bank and custodial accounts. Foreign firms have also been allowed to set up joint ventures in the financial sector. Portfolio investments by FIIs are subject to a ceiling of 24 per cent of issued share capital for the total holdings of all registered FIIs in one company. To attract FIIs to participate in the Indian capital market, a number of concessions have been provided to them. They have the right of repatriation of capital, capital gains, dividends, and income received by way of interest. They have been given tax concessions at a flat rate of 20 per cent on dividend and tax rate of 10 per cent on capital gains. The cumulative net FII investment was more than 47 billion on 31 March, 2003

(iii) Selling in Global Markets. There has been globalisation of Indian equity with the selling of scrips by Indian companies in the international capital markets. During 2002-03, Indian companies had raised Rs. $ 600 million by issuing foreign currency convertible bonds and shares through the global depository receipts (GDRs) mechanism. The selling of scrips in global markets and the entry of FIIs in the Indian capital market reflect the confidence of international business community in India's sound financial system.

(iv) *Over-the-Counter Exchange of India* (OTCEI). Over-the-counter exchange of India has been promoted jointly by ICICI, UTI, IDBI, IFCI, GIC, L1C, SB1 Capital Markets, and Canbank Financial Services. It has been registered as a stock exchange with the SEBI and has commenced its operations from 6 October, 1992. Its main aim is to provide small and medium companies an access to capital market in order to raise capital in a cost effective manner. It is also meant to provide a convenient and efficient avenue for investors in the capital market. OTCEI is a ringless, electronic and national exchange which trades in selected scrips and debt instruments. It is a regulatory body which supervises, monitors and controls the trading activity at OTC (over-the-counter). It is a national stock exchange in the sense that all the scrips listed with the OTCEI are traded over its counter throughout the country. No separate listing at different places is needed unlike the regular stock exchange. Companies can make public offer in two ways. In the case of a new issue, a company can offer its shares directly to the public through a sponsor. But in the case of a secondary issue, the company may first offer its shares to the sponsor who can make a public offer later on at a convenient time. This is the "indirect offer" where the pricing of the shares is done by the sponsor as per SEBI guidelines. The OTCEI listed share-issue application forms are similar to the normal public issue forms of companies. But it has the name of the sponsor who is solely responsible for appraising the company, to its listing and to trading. In the event of under-subscription, he is responsible for putting in the required money. The OTCEI approves the allotment of shares with the Registrar to the issue and takes it for listing with itself. All refund/allotment letters are issued to subscribers within 28 days of the closing of the issue. All share certificates remain with the Registrar and are not sent to the shareholders. The shareholders are issued Counter Receipt (CR) which is a tradeable document. The shareholder wanting to sell his shares has to give the CR and the transfer deed at the OTC. He receives in exchange a sales confirmation slip. After verification from the Registrar, the seller receives the sale note and the cheque from the OTC. The OTCEI operates at Bombay with regional windows at other metropolitai cities and representative offices in a few major cities. The OTC scan screens display selling and buying prices of OTCEI listed shares and debentures at which market makers are willing to buy and sell. The exact transaction price is displayed at the OTC computer. The Infrastructure Leasing and Financial Services (ILFS) is the compulsory market maker for debt instruments in which the OTCEI deals in. For scrips, there are separate market makers appointed by it.

(v) *National Stock Exchange of India* (NSEI). The NSEI has been jointly promoted by IDBI, ICICI, IFCI, GIC, LIC, SBI Capital Markets, SHCIL (Stock Holding Corporation of India Limited) and ILFS as a limited company. It has been recognised by the Government of India from 26 April, 1993. Its main objective is to have a comprehensive nationwide trading facility in scrips, debentures and PSUs bonds to investors through electronic screen-based trading, post-trade clearing and settlement. It is an order-driven system where there are neither jobbers nor market makers. It operates in two segments: in wholesale debt instruments and in capital market instruments. In the first segment are included such instruments as Government securities, PSUs bonds. Units 64 of UTI, CDs, CPs by banks, institutions and brokerage houses, etc. The second segment includes equity and corporate debt instruments traded by the financial companies and individuals. The capital market segment follows a weekly settlement cycle with all settlements completed within seven days of the last trading day of the cycle. The NSEI is an on-line, screen-based and scripless trading exchange which enables buyers and sellers to operate from anywhere in India. In its effort to further improve the settlement system and minimise risks associated therein, the NSEI has set up a subsidiary, the National Securities Clearing Corporation (NSCC). It guarantees settlement of trades executed and settled through it.

(vi) *National Securities Depository Ltd.* (NSDL). On 8 November, 1996, India's first depository, the National Securities Depository Ltd. (NSDL) was started. It has been jointly promoted by the IDBI, UTI and NSEI. Initially, it will start dematerialising the shares of ten companies. They are ACC, BPCL, Cnsil, LML. HDFC, ICICI, L&T, RIL, TISCO and Siemens. The depository participants of the NSDL are SCHIL, NSCC, IDBI, ILFS, Global Trust Bank, HDFC Bank, IIT Trust Corporate Services, Citibank, Morgan Stanley Custodial, SBI, and Standard Chartered Bank.

A depository is a bank for share certificates. The investor operates his account in the depository in the same way as a bank account. Shareholders have the choice of continuing with the share certificates or opt for the depository mode. Those opting for the latter will send the share certificates through the "participants" which will be "dematerialised" and the names of the owners would be registered in the electronically operated registers of the depository or participants. The NSDL will enable investors to settle "paperless" transactions through electronic book entry adjustment. It will, thus provide an alternative to the paper-based system of settling of shares. It will do away with risks associated with paper-based settlements such as delays in transfers, loss or theft of shares in transit and fear of certificates tearing or catching fire. The transfer of ownership of shares through the depository will be exempt from payment of stamp duty. The companies, investors, transfer agents and brokers will be able to save on space in the depository system because there will be no need to store share certificates. It will take 15 days for the registrar to dematerialise the shares before they can be sold whereas it takes 40 days at present. The Depository will charge a.nominal custodial fee for holding the share certificates. Thus in the paperless depository system, settlement problems will be simplified, trading costs will be reduced, and the volume of trade and returns will improve. Morevoer, it will encourage FIIs to participate more in the Indian capital market.

3. DEFECTS OF INDIAN CAPITAL MARKET

Despite these reforms, there are many defects in the working of the Indian capital market which are discussed as under :

1. *Poor Liquidity.* The Indian capital market does not possess sufficient liquidity. A recent study shows that only 20 per cent of the scrips are traded everyday arid that too of Group "A". Another 20 per cent are traded 2 to 3 times a week and 10 per cent once in a fortnight. Thus 50 per cent scrips listed on the Bombay Stock Exchange, the biggest in the country, have very poor liquidity. At other stock exchanges two-thirds of the scrips listed are not traded at all.

2. *Delay in Delivery.* There is unusual delay in the delivery of scrips and settlement or payment of transactions. The delivery of scrips usually takes 3 to 4 months and payments range between 2 to 3 months. Bad deliveries mainly due to the verification of signatures of sellers further lengthen the period and complicate the problem. There are also delays in payments which usually range between 1 to 2 months. Often delays in payments and deliveries lead to suspension of stock exchange operations.

3. *Insider Trading.* The Indian capital market has been plagued with fluctuations due to insider trading. Persons working inside a company often buy or sell shares on the basis of the expected profitability or losses of the company. This brings about price fluctuations in the scrips of the company thereby adversely affecting the interests of the small investors. Some big industrial houses alsc resort to transactions in the shares of group companies thereby accentuating this problem of insider trading to the detriment of ordinary shareholders.

4. *Inadequate Market Instruments.* The capital market instruments in India are confined primarily to shares and debentures which are inadequate for the proper functioning of a capital market. The newly introduced warrants, zero-coupon bonds, etc. are not yet popular with the investors.

5. *Inefficient Banking and Postal Services.* Banking and postal services are inefficient which add to the woes of the small investors. Refunds, dividend warrants and interest payments are sent by companies to the small clients by ordinary post which often do not reach them. Some dishonest postal and bank employees often collaborate and pocket such cheques through fraudulent means and dupe the small investors.

6. *Stockinvest not Popular.* The stockinvest instrument has been virtually cornered by big investors. The non-availability of stockinvests of small denominations, procedural difficulties and high bank charges have kept the small investors away from this instrument.

7. *Existence of Grey Market.* The unofficial unregulated market before the listing of shares, called the grey market, attracts and misleads gullible investors. They are also led to invest in new shares by financial analysts who are neither fair nor objective in their analysis. They often mislead investors at the instance of companies. Consequently, the small investors suffer the most.

8. *Vague Prospectus.* Despite SEBI's guidelines, the prospectuses issued by individual companies do not contain all the information and are vague. Free pricing norms laid down by the SEBI are not strictly followed. Premium fixing is also not fair. As a result, many companies dupe the investors outright and close down without any trace.

9. *Stock Broking System Defective.* The system of stock broking continues to be defective. The brokers have their sub-brokers and sub-brokers, in turn, have their own sub-sub-brokers who manipulate prices and cheat the sellers and buyers of shares and debentures in the secondary market.

10. *Lacks Transparency.* Trading transactions in stock exchanges still lack transparency. Buyers and sellers of scrips are at the mercy of brokers and sub-brokers who often quote the lowest traded rate of a scrip to the sellers and the highest to the buyers. Thus they pocket the maximum fraudulent gain on both the transactions besides their brokerage. There is also no uniformity in charging brokerage from clients by them. They do not maintain proper accounts and manipulate them.

11. *Inadequate Protection to Investors.* The protection given to clients in case of default by brokers and sub-brokers is inadequate. The protection given to an individual shareholder under the Consumers' Protection Fund set up at each stock exchange is limited to Rs. 40,000 in case of a defaulting broker. This limit is very low because it may be the cost of one lot of a high priced share.

12. *Odd Lot Shares Problem.* Despite SEBI's instructions regarding the non-issuing of odd lot shares by the companies, bonus shares and rights issue shares are being allotted in odd lots. Nothing has also been done for small investors who already hold odd lot shares issued prior to the instructions of the SEBI. The holders of odd lots have to pay brokerage upto 15 per cent while buying and selling odd lot shares. The efforts of the BSE, UTI and GIC to buy and sell odd lots at fair brokerage are limited only to selective and good scrips.

13. *Defective Operations of Stock Exchanges.* The stock exchanges in India continue to be defective in their operations. They do not have proper infrastructure. They lack adequate space for the stock brokers to operate efficiently. They do not possess adequate telecommunication and computerisation facilities. Old trading practices are still followed. All these defects deter trading of listed shares in the majority of stock exchanges in India. This has led to great rush at the Bombay Stock Exchange with its consequent delays in transactions, deliveries and payments.

14. *Inadequate Stock Exchanges.* With the phenomenal increase in the number of companies being listed every month and in the number of shareholders, the existing stock exchanges numbering 22 with Mumbai having three, are inadequate. This has resulted in the mushrooming of unauthorised and unregistered private stock exchanges all over the South. These share trading "houses" and "associations" indulge in speculative transactions.

15. *Fragmented Market.* The secondary capital market is fragmented into the *ring operated* stock exchanges and *ringless* OTCEI. It has further fragmented with the operation of the on-line, screen-based and scripless NSEI. All this has confused the ordinary buyers and sellers of scrips with the multiplicity of brokers and sub-brokers already duping them. This has the effect of reducing liquidity.

4. SOME SUGGESTIONS FOR IMPROVEMENT

In the light of the defects noted above and the reform measures already adopted by the Government to streamline the working of stock exchanges and to rectify the defects of the Indian capital market, the following suggestions are made to improve upon them :

1. *Improving Liquidity.* The distinction between Group A and Group B shares should be removed in order to enhance liquidity in the capital market. There should be limited carry-forward of shares and all sales should be for delivery.

2. *Streamlining the Working of Stock Exchanges.* For removing delays in transactions, delivery of scrips and transfer of shares, to increase liquidity further, and to improve the working of stock exchanges, a number of suggestions have been made. *First,* there should be computerisation at all stock exchanges so that trading becomes automatic and transparent. This step will also help in removing other defects of stock exchanges and streamlining their operations. *Second,* the transfer of scrips and debentures should be done through book entry without the movement of share/debenture certificates. *Third,* the shareholders should be issued Counter Receipts (CR) in lieu of share certificates, as has been done by the OTCEI. The share certificates should remain with the Registrars. *Fourth,* to eliminate trading by illegal trading houses, registration of spot transactions should be made compulsory.

3. *Controlling Insider Trading.* To control insider trading and manipulation of prices, strict regulatory and punitive measures should be adopted by the SEBI and stock exchanges. Companies and brokers engaged in unlawful activities should be severely punished by fines and legal actions.

4. *Devising New Market Instruments.* New market instruments should be devised to mobilise larger capital resources. They should have liquidity, safety and fair return. They should attract rural investors, be of small lots, be able to buy goods and services, and banks and post offices should deal in them. Besides, such instruments as convertible cumulative preference shares, non-voting shares for NRIs, risk-free instruments by banks and merchant bankers, etc. should be introduced. The recently introduced new instruments like warrants of a variety of types, deep discount bonds, zero-interest bonds, etc. should be made popular for investors by highlighting their merits in comparison to traditional instruments.

5. *Banning Grey Market Operations.* To stop operations in the unofficial and unregulated grey market, the publication of unofficial quotations in newspapers and magazines should be declared illegal and the sale of shares before acquisition by buyers should be banned. The SEBI should also lay down guidelines and a code of conduct for financial analysts.

6. *Transparency in Prospectus.* Companies which do not follow the guidelines in supplying the required information in their prospectuses at the time of public issue should be penalised through legal action against them. There should be full transparency in the prospectus for the benefit of investors before the SEBI gives *its* permission for the public issue.

7. *Streamlining the Stock Broking System.* 'The system of appointing sub-brokers should be dispensed with. But this is not possible till the offices of brokers and stock exchanges are fully computerised and automatic trading is introduced, till then, the activities of sub-brokers should also be regulated by the SEBI and the stock exchanges should be authorised to deal with them as in the case of brokers. The operation of illegal trading houses should be declared illegal.

8. *Protecting Investors and Brokers.* To protect the interests of small investors from the fraudulent devices of some dishonest postal and bank employees, the SEBI has already instructed the companies to ask for the bank account numbers of the share/debenture holders to be indicated on the refund orders, dividends and interest warrants. The companies should be instructed to strictly adhere to them. The best course would be for the companies to direct the Registrars to deposit the amount direct into the bank accounts of investors under intimation to them. This will also discourage benami or bogus deals. The maximum limit of Rs. 40,000 to be paid

to an individual client in the case of a defaulting broker out of the Customers' Protection Fund at the stock exchanges should be raised to Rs. 1 lakh. A similar fund should be created for the brokers when some clients default by not making payments for deals to brokers.

9. *Disposal of Odd Lots.* A separate trust should be formed to dispose off odd lots held by millions of shareholders in India. It should purchase odd lot shares from holders, get them converted into marketable lots from the companies and then sell them in the market at a profit. To solve the problem of odd lots permanently, companies should be instructed by the SEBI not to issue rights and bonus shares to small shareholders in odd lots but compensate them by offering cash incentives.

10. *Opening More Stock Exchanges.* Keeping in view of the large number of listed shares and listing of fresh shares every month at the stock exchanges, their number should be increased in the country. This is essential to deal with a large number of operators in stock trading and to enhance liquidity in the capital market. This will also eliminate to some extent the mushroom growth of illegal trading houses.

11. *Regulating the Activities of Intermediaries.* For the proper functioning of the secondary capital market, the operations of such intermediaries as sub-brokers, underwriters, registrars, transfer agents, portfolio managers, merchant bankers and other intermediaries should be regulated by the SEBI. It should lay down rules for their proper functioning in the capital market.

12. *Coordinating the Activities of Stock Exchanges.* To avoid confusion among the investors, there should be proper coordination among the three types of stock exchanges in India, viz. the traditional stock exchanges, the OTCEI and the NSEI. There should not be any overlapping in their areas of operations.

13. *Giving Tax Concessions.* To encourage the market, more tax concessions shculd be given to investors by abolishing double tax on dividends and by increasing the minimum tax-free levels of dividends and capital gains.

CONCLUSION

Thus the SEBI should address itself to such reforms as paperless settlement, futures and options markets, free issuing pricing and more transparency and greater competition.

EXERCISES

1. What is meant by capital market? Describe the main features of the Indian capital market.
2. Explain the working of the Indian capital market.
3. Explain the main defects in the capital market. Describe the measures that have been adopted in recent years to rectify them.
4. Explain the weaknesses of the Indian capital market. Suggest measures for its improvement.
5. Write notes on:
   New Issues Market; Secondary Capital Market; Over-the-Counter Exchange of India; National Stock Exchange of India; National Securities Depository.

CHAPTER 58

Indian Money Market

1. MEANING

The money market is not a market in the usual sense of the term. It does not mean a single trading place or trading organisation dealing in money. But "it is a collective name given to the various forms and institutions that deal with the various grades of near money".[1] It is a market in short-term funds in which the lenders of money meet the borrowers of money. The lenders of money are the Reserve Bank of India, all scheduled commercial banks, co-operative banks, financial institutions like the LIC, UTI, GIC, foreign exchange banks, and indigenous bankers, moneylenders, etc. The borrowers of money are the Central Government, State Governments, local bodies, traders, merchants, businessmen, exporters, importers, companies, farmers, and the public. Thus the money market is a market for monetary assets in which the short-term requirements of the borrowers are met in order to provide liquidity or cash to the lenders.

2. NATURE OF INDIAN MONEY MARKET

The structure of money market in India comprises of both organised and unorganised markets.

The organised money market consists of the Reserve Bank of India, all scheduled commercial banks, cooperative banks, and financial institutions like Life Insurance Corporation, General Insurance Corporation and Unit Trust of India and foreign exchange banks, and DFHI.

The unorganised money market includes indigenous bankers, moneylenders, both professional and non-professional traders, merchants, landlords, pawn brokers, nidhis, and chit funds. Nidhis are mutual loan associations and chit funds are voluntary loan associations for mobilising savings.

CHARACTERISTICS OF THE UNORGANISED MONEY MARKET IN INDIA

The main characteristics of the unorganised money market in India are:

1. *Personal Touch.* The moneylenders have a personal touch with the borrowers. The moneylender knows every borrower personally in the village because the latter resides there.

2. *Informality.* The moneylenders have considerable amount of informality in dealing with their borrowers.

3. *Flexibility in Loans.* There is no rigidity in loan transactions. The borrower can have more or less amount of loan according to his requirements depending upon the nature of security or his goodwill with the moneylender.

4. *Multiplicity of Lending Activities.* Mostly peopie do not specialise in moneylending alone. They combine moneylending with other economic activities. A moneylender may supply goods on loan instead of money in cash.

---

1. G. Crowther, *op. cit.,* p 66.

5. *Varied Interest Rates.* There is multiplicity of interest rates. Interest rates are much higher than rates in the developed sector of the money market. The interest rates are not even uniform. The rate depends on the need of the borrower, the amount of loan, the time for which it is required and the nature of security. The greater the urgency, the higher will be the interest rate.

6. *Defective System of Accounting.* In the unorganised sector of the money market, the system of maintaining accounts is highly defective. Proper accounts are never maintained. Formal receipts are not issued for the interest charged and the principal repaid by the borrowers. Besides, there is utmost secrecy in maintaining accounts and lending procedures. The accounts of the moneylenders are not liable to checking by any higher authority.

7. *Absence of Link with the Developed Money Market.* The undeveloped sector is not linked with the developed sector of the money market. The former works independently of the latter and is also not under the control of the developed market. This has the effect of reducing the volume of monetary transactions and savings, and prevents their use in productive investments.

3. FUNCTIONS OF INDIAN MONEY MARKET*

The money market performs a number of functions in the Indian economy.

1. It provides short-term funds to public and private institutions needing such financing for their working capital requirements. It is done by discounting trade bills through commercial banks, discount houses, brokers and acceptance houses. Thus the money market helps the development of commerce, industry and trade within and outside the country.

2. It provides an opportunity to banks and other institutions to use their surplus funds profitably for a short period. These institutions include not only commercial banks and other financial institutions but also large non-financial business corporations, states and local governments.

3. The money market removes the necessity of borrowing by the commercial banks from the Reserve Bank of India. If the former find their reserves short of cash requirements they can call in some of their loans from the money market.

The commercial banks prefer to recall their loans rather than borrow from the central bank at a higher rate of interest.

4. The money market helps the government in borrowing short-term funds at low interest rate on the basis of treasury bills. On the other hand, if the government were to issue paper money or borrow from the Reserve Bank of India, it would lead to inflationary pressures in the economy.

5. The money market helps in the successful implementation of the monetary policies of the central bank. It is through the money market that the Reserve Bank of India is in a position to control the banking system and thereby influence commerce and industry.

6. By facilitating the transfer of funds from one sector to another, the money market helps in financial mobility. Mobility in the flow of funds is essential for the development of commerce and industry in an economy.

7. One of the important functions of the money market, is thai it promotes liquidity and safety of financial assets. It thus encourages savings and investment.

8. The money market brings equilibrium between the demand and supply of loanable funds. This it does by allocating savings into investment channels. In this way, it also helps in rational allocation of resources.

9. As the money market deals in near-money assets and not money proper it helps in economising the use of cash. It thus provides a convenient and safe way of transferring funds, from one place to another, thereby immensely helping commerce and industry.

---

* This also relates to the Importance of Money Market.

4. CONSTITUENTS OF INDIAN MONEY MARKET

The constituents of the organised sector of the Indian money market consist of DFHI, STCI, call money market, treasury bills, commercial bills, intercorporate funds, certificates of deposits, commercial paper and Repos. We explain these constituents (or *instruments*) of the Indian money market as under :

1. Call Money Market

The call money market or the inter-bank call money market is an important constitutent of the organised money market and it functions as an immediate source of short-term funds. The major suppliers of the funds in the call money market are SBI, LIC, GIC, UTI, IDBI and NABARD and the major borrowers are the scheduled commercial banks. As the participants are mostly banks, it is called inter-bank call money market. The commercial banks use their unused or surplus cash to lend for very short periods to bill brokers. The bill brokers, in turn, use them to discount or purchase bills. Such funds are borrowed at the "call-rate" which varies with the volume of funds lent by the banks. When the brokers are asked to pay off loans immediately, then they borrow from SBI, LIC, GIC, UTI, etc.

Of the total market for short-term funds, the public sector banks account for about 80 per cent of the borrowings. The foreign banks and private sector banks account for the remaining 20 per cent. While some banks operate both as lenders and borrowers, others are either only borrowers or lenders in this market. Non-bank financial institutions such as IDBI, LIC, GIC, etc., participate only as lenders. DFHI and STCI operate as borrowers and lenders in this market. All call money transactions have a maturity of one day to a fortnight.

The call money rate is determined by demand and supply of short-term funds in the call money market The variations in it depend upon busy and slack seasons and the credit policy of the RBI. When the demand for credit increases in the money market and the RBI does not take any action, the call money rates rise. On the contrary, if the RBI influences the money market by reducing CRR or/and Bank Rate or/and through additional money supply, the call money rates decline.

2. Commercial Bills Market

The commercial bills market in India is under-developed. There is nc proper market for bills of exchange. The Reserve Bank of India introduced the bill market scheme in 1952. Its aim was to provide finance against bills of exchange and promissory notes for 90 days. The scheduled commercial banks were allowed to convert a part of their advances, loans, cash credits or overdrafts into usance promissory notes for 90 days for lodging as collateral (security) for advances from the RBI. Since this scheme was primarily meant to accommodate banks, it did not help in developing a bill market.

On the recommendations of the Narsimham Committee, the RBI introduced the Bill Rediscounting Scheme on November 1, 1970. Under this scheme, all licensed scheduled commercial banks are eligible to rediscount with RBI genuine trade bills arising out of sale or despatch of goods. Apart from scheduled commercial banks, certain other financial institutions like LIC, GIC, UTI, IDBI, ICICI, IRBI, IFCI, ECGC, NABARD, NHB, EXIMBANK, SCICI, Tourism Development Finance Corporation, SBI and CANBANK Mutual Funds and select urban cooperative banks are included in the scheme. The DFHI participates actively in this market and provides bid rates on daily basis. With the introduction in October 1988 of the usance promissory note for the purposes of rediscounting of bills, banks could draw a derivative usance promissory note for suitable sums with maturity period upto 90 days on the basis of bonafide commercial or trade bills discounted at their branches. In August 1989, the Government remitted the stamp duty on usance bills and thereby removed a major administrative constraint in the use of bill system.

3. Inter-Bank Participation (IBP)

The Reserve Bank of India has introduced a new instrument called Inter-Bank Participations with a view to facilitate the adjustment of short-term liquidity within the banking system. These participations are of two types—one on risk sharing basis and the other without risk sharing. IBPs on risk sharing basis can be for 91-

180 days at an interest rate to be determined between the issuing bank and the participating bank. IBP without risk taking can have a tenure not exceeding 90 days at an interest rate to be determined between the concerned banks. IBPs without risk taking are treated as a part of the demand and time liabilities of the borrowing bank and subject to reserve requirements.

4. Certificates of Deposit (CD)

In March 1989, the Reserve Bank of India introduced the certificates of deposit in order to widen the range of money market instruments and give investors greater flexibility in the deployment of their short-term surplus funds. The minimum size of the issue of CDs to a single investor is Rs. 5 lakh in multiple of Rs. 1 lakh at present. There is no bank-wise limit for issue of CDs and banks are free to issue CDs depending upon their requirements. The CD can be issued at a discount on face value and the discount rate can be freely determined. The maturity period of CDs is between 3 months and one year. The CDs can be freely transferable by endorsement and delivery but only after 15 days from the date of issue. CDs are subject to the reserve requirements. Banks are also required to maintain CRR and SLR on the issue price of CDs. The DFHI also operates in the secondary market for CDs. Six all India financial institutions, viz., IDBI, ICICI, IFCI, IRBI, SIDBI and EXIM Bank have also been permitted to issue CDs with maturity of more than one year and upto 3 years. The interest rates on CDs with a maturity of 3 months have been less than that for one year and more upto 3 years, as is the case with term deposits.

5. Commercial Paper (CP)

The commercial paper is a short-term money market instrument. It is in the nature of an unsecured promissory note. It can be either sold directly by the issuer to the investors or placed by an intermediary bank or securities dealer. It is not tied to any specific transaction. It attracts stamp duty. It does not carry any collateral security. In brief, the aim of CP is to enable high-rated corporate borrowers to diversify their sources of short-term borrowings and to provide an additional instrument to investors to deploy their short-term surplus funds.

The RBI issued detailed guidelines for the issue of CP on 4 January, 1990. As amended, they are as under : (1) The tangible network of a company should be at least Rs. 5 crores. (2) It should enjoy a fund-based working capital limit of Rs. 5 crores and above. (3) If should obtain a P2 + rating from the Credit Rating and Information Services of India Ltd. (CRISIL) which should not be more than 2 months old at the time of issue. (4) It should have Health Code No. 1 rating from the company's bankers. (5) Its shares should be listed on at least one stock exchange. (6) The minimum size of a CP issue is Rs. 50 lakhs and the face value of each CP should be Rs 10 lakhs. (7) The maturity period of each CP is 3 months to 1 year without any grace period. (8) The company has to get the permission of RBI every time it issues CP and the RBI will operate a queue system to regulate the CP market. (9) Non-resident Indians can invest in CP only on a non-repatriable basis and such CP will also be non-transferable. (10) Now closely held companies are also permitted to issue CPs even though their shares are not listed on a stock exchange. (11) CP cannot be purchased by any individual, firm or corporate body. The DFHI is the- market maker for this instrument and provides daily bid rates. When short-term surplus funds shrink with banks and interest rates are rising, there is a decline in the outstanding amount of CP and *vice versa.* Commercial banks are significant holders of CPs.

6. Treasury Bills Market

The treasury bills are short-term monetary instruments issued by the Government of India at a discount and for a fixed period. There are treasury bills of varied maturities. There are : 14-day and 28-day Treasury Bills, that are auctioned on a weekly basis. 182-day Treasury Bills are auctioned on a fortnightly basis and 364-day Treasury Bills on a monthly basis. These Treasury Bills provide investors with financial instruments of varying short-term maturities and facilitate the cash management requirements of various segments of the economy.

7. Repurchase Auctions (Repos)

The RBI introduced the Repurchase Agreements Auctions (Repos) in the Central Government- dated securities on 10 December, 1992 to even out interest rates in the call money market. Repos are repurchase agreements for the sale and subsequent repurchase of Government Securities. They allow the holder of the security to raise cash using the security as collateral. Under repos transactions, a part of one kind of asset is liquidated in order to buy it back. In the case of banks, repos result in the substitution of either cash or RBI balance for securities. The RBI indirectly intervenes in the money market through *reverse repo operations* to undo pressure on overnight call money rates. Initially, repos/reverse repo auctions were conducted on a daily basis (Monday through Friday) and with one-day maturity (except on Fridays/days preceding holidays) were introduced. Subsequently, multiple repo/reverse repo auctions with 3-7 days maturity period were introduced in August, 2000. Interest rates in respect of both repo and reverse repos are the cut-off yields which arise from auctions conducted on a uniform price basis. The transactions of repos are conducted through SCL (Subsidiary Central Ledger) of the RBI.

Inter-Bank Repos. The RBI has also allowed repo transactions among banks and in select bonds of public sector undertaking (PSUs) and in private corporate debt securities. These provide liquidity support to the debt market. In July, 1999, non-bank participants in the money market were also permitted to access short-term liquidity through repos on par with banks and PDs (primary dealers), thereby providing them facility to manage their cash.

8. Discount and Finance House of India (DFHI)

The Discount and Finance House of India Limited (DFHI) was set up on 25 April, 1988 with its own resources of Rs. 100 crores and the financial support of RBI. Its aims are (i) to bring into the fold of the Indian money market the entire financial system comprising the scheduled commercial banks, public sector banks, foreign banks and private sector banks, cooperative banks, state cooperative banks, scheduled urban cooperative banks, all-India financial institutions, and non-banks in the public and private sectors, and (ii) to equilibrate short-term surpluses and deficits of these instruments at market related rates through inter-bank transactions in the case of banks, and through money market instruments in the case of banks and others. It deals in call funds (including notice funds), Treasury bills, commercial bills, certificates of deposit, commercial paper, term deposits and Central Government dated securities. The DFHI aims at increasing the liquidity of these money market instruments. It operates both as a borrower and a lender. It aims at stabilising the call money market rates by building up a large turnover, while retaining for itself only a small spread between the borrowing and lending rates. Since June 1996 the RBI has extended liquidity support to DFHI in the form of "reverse repos facility" in Government dated securities to stabiise call money rates. Now the DFHI has also become operational as primary dealer in Government securities.

9. Securities Trading Corporation or India (STCI)

The STCI was set up in May 1994 with a fully issued paid-up capital of Rs 100 crores. It started operating from June 1994. It aims at developing secondary market in Government securities and Treasury Bills. It undertakes ready forward transactions in Treasury Bills and Government dated securities. These transactions take place in Mumbai and are routed through the SGL accounts maintained by the RBI. Like the DFHI, it borrows and lends in the call/notice money market. It receives liquidity support from the RBI in the form of "reverse Repos facility" and in Government dated securities and Treasury Bills. It has also become a primary dealer in Government securities.

10. Primary Dealers (PDs)

Besides the DFHI and the STCI, there are 13 more primary dealers who are operating in Government securities. They are the ICICI Securities, the SBI Gilts Ltd., the PNB Gilts Ltd., the Gilt Securities Trading Corporation Ltd., etc. Like the DFHI and the STCI, they receive liquidity support from the RBI in the form of reverse Repos facility in Government dated securities and Treasury Bills. The RBI pays to PDs commission for underwriting Government of India dated securities and Treasury Bills. PDs are provided advances against the security of their holdings of Government dated securities and Treasury Bills in Subsidiary General Ledger (SGL) Accounts of the RBI.

11. Satellite Dealers (SDs)

The RBI has also set up SDs in Government securities market. They act as second tier in trading and distribution of Government securities. It has registered nine financial institutions and two banks (Bank of America and Bank of Madura) as SDs. They have been provided ready forward transaction facility in Government securities market. They can get loans by issuing short period commercial papers which cannot be of less than Rs. 25 lakh in multiples of Rs. 5 lakh. Like PDs, satellite dealers can get advances from the RBI on the basis of Government dated securities and Treasury Bills.

12. Money Market Mutual Funds (MMMFs)

The RBI allowed scheduled commercial banks and public financial institutions to set up MMMFs in April 1992. They invest their resources mobilised from the public in such money market instruments as Treasury Bills, Government dated securities and rated corporate bonds and debentures with a maturity upto one year, call/notice money, commercial paper, accepted or co-accepted commercial bills by banks, and certificates of deposit. MMMFs have not made any progress in the money market because their number has come down to three from eight.

Conclusion

The foregoing analysis of the constituents of the money market in India shows that there have been significant changes in their structure and growth in recent years which have strengthened it. The setting up of DFHI has imparted greater liquidity to money market instruments and has helped in developing an active secondary market in them.

5. DEFECTS OF INDIAN MONEY MARKET

The Indian money market is not well developed. Compared to the growth in the economy, the growth of the money market has been slow and the influence of the money market in the economy has been quite limited. This can be traced to the following deficiencies in the Indian money market :

1. *Dual Character.* The Indian economy has dichotomic money markets with an organised sector and an unorganised sector. The organised sector consists of specialised banking and financial institutions like the RBI, SBI, commercial banks, cooperative banks, LIC, UTI, GIC, etc. which operate in the money market in accordance with rules laid down. On the other hand, the unorganised sector includes indigenous bankers, moneylenders, traders, merchants, landlords, brokers, nidhis, chit funds, etc. which do not follow any set rules in loan operations. The two sectors do not have any contact with each other and lack coordination or cooperation. In fact, the unorganised sector reduces the effectiveness of monetary policy measures because it does not fall under the jurisdiction of the RBI.

2. *Captive Market.* The Indian money market is captive. It is governed by a few institutions which participate in it. The participants in the organised money market are limited to banks and a few all-India financial institutions like UTI, GIC, LIC, etc., while in the unorganised market the principal participants are moneylenders and indigenous bankers.

3. *Narrow Based.* The Indian money market is narrow based and is functioning with limited number of instruments. The main instruments are inter-bank call money, treasury bills, commercial bills, inter-corporate funds, certificates of deposit and commercial paper. The last two have just been started and others have made little impact on the working of the money market. In fact, only few instruments are being used in practice and others remain only in paper. Moreover, these instruments do not serve those institutions which can deal in the money market whenever they have excess funds or paucity of funds.

4. *Small Geographical Area.* The Indian money market is confined to a small geographical area comprising four capital cities of India, viz., Delhi, Mumbai, Kolkata and Chennai. This inhibits the growth of the money market. A large segment of rural, semi-urban, and urban India is out of the purview of the organised money market.

5. *Slow Rate of Monetisation.* The slow rate of monetisation is another factor which has kept the Indian money market under-developed. There are still large backward areas in rural India in which monetisation is taking place at a very slow pace. They fall in the unorganised sector of the money market and get loans from the merchant-moneylenders.

6. *Shortage of Capital.* There is shortage of capital in the Indian money market which fails to meet the requirements of the trade and industry. The main reasons for the insufficiency of funds are: (i) low saving capacity of the people due to low levels of income; *(ii)* inadequate banking facilities in the rural areas; *(iii)* preferences of savers to invest in physical assets like land, real estate, gold, etc. than in financial savings.

7. *Defects in the Call Money Market.* The Call Money Market is highly skewed with a few predominant lenders and a large number of borrowers. The entry of participants in the market is strictly regulated. Until 1 May, 1989, the interest rate was also regulated. It was 10 per cent. But the banks often violated the guidelines relating to this ceiling rate. From 1 May, 1989 the interest rate has been freed and is determined by market forces with the result that there have been wide variations in the interest rate which fell to as low as 4 per cent and rose to as high as 72 per cent within one year. In fact, such frequent and wide changes in the interest rate affect the profitability of banks and also create conditions inimical to the growth of a healthy money market.

8. *Defects in the Bill Market.* Despite the introduction of the Bill Market Scheme in 1952 and the Bill Rediscounting Scheme in 1970, the bill market in India continues to remain underdeveloped. In fact, bill culture has not been developed properly because preference for cash credit type of financing still continues. The bill rediscounting business constitutes a very small part of the total lending activities of the banks in India. Several factors are responsible for the non-development of the bill market: (i) reluctance of industry and trade, and Government departments and undertakings to move towards bill culture; - (ii) absence of specialised credit information agency; *(iii)* absence of an active secondary market; (iv) lack of first class commercial bills; (v) administrative problems like physical scrutiny of invoices accompanying bills to ensure that they are related to trade, physical presentation of bills for repayment, requirement of physical endorsement, and endorsement of bills at the time of rediscount; (vi) no proper market for bills; and *(vii)* absence of strict discipline on the part of industry, trade and Government departments.

9. *Large Unorganised Sector.* A major defect of the Indian money market is the existence of a large unorganised sector. This sector is dominated by indigenous bankers and money-lenders. They are neither under the control of the RBI nor are they influenced by market rates of interest. There is also no clear demarcating line for short-term and long-term finance in this sector.

10. *No Relation between Organised and Unorganised Sectors.* In India the organised and the unorganised sector of the money market do not have any relation with each other. The moneylenders and indigenous bankers work independently and they fail to get funds from commercial banks except like other customers. Rather, they prefer to borrow from each other because the commercial banks insist on observance of formal rules and procedures.

6. SUGGESTIONS TO IMPROVE THE INDIAN MONEY MARKET

To remove the defects of the Indian money market and to develop it on sound lines, the Reserve Bank of India appointed the Chakravarty Committee and the Veghul Committee which submitted their respective Reports in 1985 and 1987. It was on the basis of their recommendations that the RBI has taken a number of measures to develop the money market. We have already discussed them in detail under the Constituents of Indian Money Market. To recapitulate they are: *(i)* introduction of 182-Days Treasury Bills on an auction basis with flexible interest rates; *(ii)* lowering of the bill discount rate to encourage the bill market; *(iii)* setting up the DFHI; *(iv)* introduction of Inter-Bank participations, Certificates of Deposit, and Commercial Paper; and (v) total freeing of interest rates on call and notice money, inter-bank term money, rediscounting of commercial bills, and on Inter-Bank Participation without risk.

Despite the introduction of the above noted instruments and adoption of new measures, the Indian money market is still not developed properly and continues to suffer from certain serious defects as outlined above.

The following suggestions are made to further improve the Indian money markets :

1. *Control over Indigenous Bankers.* After nationalisation of banks in 1969, banking facilities have considerably expanded in rural India under the branch expansion scheme of commercial banks, lead bank scheme, regional rural banks, cooperative banks, etc. But the hold of the indigenous bankers still continues over the majority of villagers. As recommended by the Banking Commission, 1972, the activities of the indigenous bankers should be controlled through the commercial banks and they should encourage the former to transform themselves into corporate bodies. The RBI should lay down guidelines for commercial banks in dealing with indigenous bankers.

2. *Control over Chit Funds.* To control the activities of chit funds which exploit and cheat their members of their hard-earned savings, the Banking Commission suggested that there should be a uniform legislation for chit funds throughout the country and that only public limited companies with a minimum paid-up capital should be allowed to run chit funds.

3. *Standard Forms of Hundis.* In the unorganised sector of the money market, large transactions are performed by discounting *hundis* by indigenous bankers. But these hundis are not accepted by commercial banks. In order to bring these hundis within the purview of the organised money market, the Banking Commission recommended that standard forms of *Darshni* (sight) and *Muddati* (usance) hundis should be prescribed and the Negotiable Instruments Act be made applicable to these hundis.

4. *Development of Bill Market.* In the organised sector of the money market, a properly developed bill market is essential for the growth of money market in India. For this purpose, the Government should direct departmental undertakings and public sector organisations that payments for all credit purchases should be in the form of bills which should be strictly honoured on due dates. A similar procedure should be adopted in respect of CAS parties. The procedure for rediscounting of bills should be simplified. Further, rediscounting by the institutions should be freely permitted. The need is to develop bill culture in the country.

5. *Growth of Money Market in Other Centres.* The money market is restricted to four major cities in India. To expand the money market in other cities, banking and clearing house facilities should be provided on a larger scale. Discount houses and acceptance houses should be established. Cheap remittance facilities should be extended throughout the country to increase the mobility of funds. These measures will go a long way in the growth of the money market in other cities.

6. *Creation of Secondary Market.* For the smooth functioning and growth of the money market, an active secondary market should be created by establishing new sets of institutions which should impart sufficient liquidity in the Indian money market.

EXERCISES

1. Explain the various constituents of Indian money market.
2. Point out the main defects of the Indian money market. Suggest suitable measures to remove them.
3. Write notes on : Bill Market in India, Inter-Bank Call Money Market, Treasury Bills Market.
4. Explain the nature of Indian money market. What are its functions?
5. Explain the main features of the unorganised money market in India.
6. Write notes on : Discount and Finance House of India, Certificates of Deposit, Commercial Paper.

CHAPTER 59

Moneylenders and Indigenous Bankers

The moneylenders and indigenous bankets ate the two main organs of the unorganised sector of the Indian money market: We discuss below their working and importance.

1. MONEYLENDERS

Moneylenders are those whose primary business is moneylending. They are classified into two categories: (a) professional, and *(b)* non-professional. The professional moneylenders are those whose primary business is moneylending. On the other hand, the non-professional moneylenders are those who are engaged in some other profession but whose side business is moneylending. They include landlords, agriculturists, merchants, traders, rich widows, pensioners, advocates, teachers, or any other person who has got surplus money. The professional and non-professional money lenders operate both in rural and urban areas. But this division is not water-tight because an urban merchant may also lend to a farmer whose produce he buys.

1. Working of Moneylenders

The functions pf moneylenders are:

(1) The main function of moneylenders is to give short-term loans. Loans may be given for consumption purposes, to meet social and religious obligations *or* the needs of farmers for seeds, cattle, fertilisers, etc.

(2) Loans are generally given on the personal security of borrowers. However, grant of loans on the security of costly things in urban areas and against land or crop in rural areas; is also common.

(3) They have personal contacts with the borrowers who approach them directly and informally,

(4) The moneylenders normally lend their own funds.

(5) The non-professional moneylenders prefer to lend in kind.

(6) Since the moneylenders have a personal knowledge about the creditworthines of borrowers they adopt rigid or flexible attitude while lending, charging interest, and recovery of loans.

(7) They charge excessively high rates of interest.

(8) The moneylenders in rural areas are quite influential persons who adopt pressure tactics in the recovery of loans, such as forcible occupation of the cultivator's land, caste disapproval, pressure from panchayats, etc.

(9) The moneylenders also resort to some malpractices in rural areas which are: manipulating accounts, deducting interest in advance, demanding presents, exacting free services from the borrower, demanding donations, obtaining thumb impression of borrower on blank paper, non-issue of receipts for payment of interest and principal, keeping the deed of land or house of the borrower as a security, forcing the borrower-farmer to sell his produce in advance at a price lower than the market, etc.

2. Importance of Moneylenders

The importance of moneylenders is immense in rural India because of the inadequacy of institutional financing agencies like commercial banks and cooperative banks. They meet the short-term monetary requirements of farmers, landless agricultural workers, marginal farmers, rural artisans, and petty shopkeepers and traders. They give loans for consumption needs, for social and religious ceremonies, and for such productive purposes as seeds, fertilisers, cattle etc. The professional moneylender is more useful because he also provides articles of daily requirements. There being personal contact with the moneylender, the borrowers approach him directly and informally. Generally they get loans on personal security. As the moneylender is known to every borrower personally, the former is in a position to get the loan easily. A moneylender is often regarded as the friend, guide, and helper of the people in rural areas.

The importance of moneylenders can be assessed from the All India Rural Credit Survey Committee's findings that in 1950-51 professional and agricultural moneylenders accounted for nearly 70 per cent of the total borrowings of cultivators, and only 7.3 per cent was contributed by the organised institutions like commercial banks and cooperatives. The All India Investment and Rural Debt Survey estimated that in 1960-61 the moneylenders accounted for 49 per cent of the total borrowings by farmers.

During the British rule in India, a number of Provinces passed Acts in 1938 to restrain some of the objectionable practices of moneylenders, such as provisions for registration, licensing, and regulation of their activities. But these Acts remained on paper.

However, after nationalisation of 14 banks and with branch expansion and opening of rural banks, and strengthening of cooperative banks, the hold of moneylenders on rural credit has become weak.

2. INDIGENOUS BANKERS

The indigenous bankers are those who accept deposits and deal in *hundis.* An indigenous banker may also combine banking and business, but banking is his main function. As such, indigenous bankers are of two types: *(a)* Professionals, such as Shroffs of Gujarat, Sahukars of U.P. Chettiars of the South, etc. who function as bankers, and *(b)* non-professionals, such as Marwaris, Multanis, wholesale and retail traders, etc.

1. Functions of Indigenous Bankers

The indigenous bankers perform a number of banking and non-banking functions which are explained as under:

1. *Accepting Deposits.* The indigenous bankers accept deposits from the public which are of current account and for a fixed period. Higher interest rate is paid on fixed account than on current account. Entries relating to deposits received, amount withdrawn and interest paid are made in the pass-books issued to the clients. The indigenous bankers also get funds from the commercial banks, friends, relatives and even from each other.

2. *Advancing Loans.* The indigenous bankers advance loans against security of land, jewellery, crops, goods, etc. Loans are given to known parties on the basis of the promissory notes. Loans given on the security of land and buildings are based on mortgages registered with the Registrar of the area.

3. *Discounting Hundis.* Discounting of hundis is an important function of indigenous bankers. They write, buy and sell hundis which are bills of exchange.

Hundis are of two types:

(a) Darshni or sight hundi which is payable on demand, and

(b) Muddati or time hundi which is payable after the period mentioned on the face of. the hundi.

4. *Remittance Facilities.* The indigenous bankers also provide remittance facilities to their clients. This is done by writing a finance bill to their branches, if they have at other place, or to some other indigenous banker, with whom they have such arrangements.

5. *Financing Inland Trade.* They finance both wholesale and retail traders within the country and thus help in buying, selling, and movement of goods to different trading centres.

6. *Speculative Activities.* They indulge in speculation of food and non-food crops, and other articles of

consumption.

7. *Commission Agents.* They act as commission agents to firms.

8. *Run Firms.* Some of the non-professional indigenous bankers run their own manufacturing, processing or service firms, and on the strength of that they provide expertise and working capital to small industrialists.

9. *Subscribe to Shares and Debentures.* They provide long-term finance by subscribing to the shares and debentures of large companies.

2. Importance of Indigenous Bankers

The indigenous bankers have been playing a significant role in the economic life of India. When commercial banking had not developed, they were the main source of finance for agriculturists, traders, businessmen, small industrialists, etc. After nationalisation of commercial banks and the spread of banking in urban and rural areas, the activities of indigenous bankers have declined, but their importance has not become less because of the difficulties still faced by the borrowers in getting loans from the banks. The borrowers approach them directly and informally and get loans promptly and easily. They do not have any fixed banking hours and do not enter into formalities and procedures followed by commercial banks in advancing loans. That is why they are still popular with traders, businessmen, agriculturists, and ordinary people. They give loans mostly for productive purposes to meet the immediate and short-term needs of the borrowers.

Indigenous bankers provide finance and remittance facilities to traders and small industrialists by advancing loans; writing, buying and selling hundis; writing finance bills and trade bills. Thus they help not only in financing internal trade but also in expanding it. In particular, they help in the movement of agricultural products from rural areas to markets, and of industrial products to different parts of the country.

Those indigenous bankers who combine banking with trading and agriculture help the farmers by lifting their produce from the farms, paying them in cash on the spot, and also giving them loans.

The indigenous bankers act as commission agents when they purchase agricultural products on behalf of firms, mills, and trading houses. In this way, they again help in the development of internal trade.

The importance of indigenous bankers has increased further with the development of capital market in India. They now provide long-term credit to companies by subscribing to their shares and debentures.

3. Defects of Indigenous Banking

The following defects are associated with the majority of indigenous bankers:

(1) They are a *hindrance* in the development of an organised money market in India. The Reserve Bank of India has no control over them.

(2) They follow *old methods of business* which are based on secrecy of accounts and activities. Accounts are mostly maintained in vernacular. They are neither audited nor published.

(3) They also provide loans for *unproductive* purposes.

(4) They combine *banking with other activities* which bring them more profits such as speculation, trading, brokerage, etc.

(5) They charge very *high rates of interest.*

(6) They also indulge in some *undesirable practices,* such as manipulating accounts, deducting interest in advance, non-issue of receipts for payment of interest and principal, etc.

(7) They are *unorganised* except at a few places like Mumbai and Kolkata. This has hindered the mobility of funds.

(8) They do not work in co-operation with the commercial and cooperative banks. This has kept *dichotomy* in the Indian money market.

(9) They are *unable to mobilise savings* because they prefer giving loans than accepting deposits.

(10) Except in big towns, they *have failed to develop the hundi* (bill market) in trade and business. They do business in cash.

(11) They are *not able to meet the financial needs* of borrowers because they operate with insufficient capital.

4. Suggestions to Reform Indigenous Banking

From time to time suggestions have been made to reform the working of indigenous bankers by certain committees, commissions, and organisations, such as the Indian Central Banking Enquiry Committee, 1931, the Banking Commission, 1971, etc. We summarise these suggestions as under:

(1) The indigenous bankers should do only banking business and not any other activity.

(2) They should maintain proper account books in a prescribed and recognised form and get them audited.

(3) They should be registered with the, Reserve Bank o£ India and licence should be issued to them.

(4) For this purpose, every indigenous banker should have a minimum capital requirement.

(5) The indigenous bankers should be linked with commercial banks and their hundis should be discounted by commercial banks like other bills of exchange.

(6) The indigenous bankers registered with the RBI should be provided remittance facilities by all commercial banks.

(7) They should also be allowed to collect cheques, drafts, etc. like other banks.

(8) The indigenous bankers should form an association at all India level and become its members.

(9) They should develop the hundi in a proper format duly approved, by the RBI so that it may be accepted like other bills by the commercial banks.

(10) They should be encouraged to develop the business of bill-broking like the bill-brokers of the London Money Markets.

(11) The benefit of the Bankers' Book Evidence Act should also be extended to the indigenous bankers.

These suggestions have failed to elicit any response from the indigenous bankers who are not prepared to give up their non-banking functions, to publish their audited accounts, and to register themselves with the RBI. The Reserve Bank of India is also not prepared to relax its conditions and provide facilities to them like commercial banks. The best course is to link the indigenous bankers with commercial banks, as suggested by the Banking Commission. The Reserve Bank of India should lay down guidelines for this purpose.

3. DISTINCTION BETWEEN INDIGENOUS BANKERS AND MONEYLENDERS

The indigenous bankers are distinguished from moneylenders in the following ways:

(1) Banking is the main function of an indigenous banker while that of a moneylender is moneylending.

(2) The indigenous bankers accept deposits and deal in hundis but the moneylenders do not perform these functions.

(3) The scale of operations of indigenous bankers is larger than that of moneylenders. They combine banking with trading, speculation, commission agent, etc., while the moneylenders combine moneylending with petty shopkeeping.

(4) The indigenous bankers have larger funds at their disposal than the moneylenders. They accept deposits from the public, borrow from each other and also from commercial banks. On the other hand, the moneylenders operate with small funds of their own and also borrow from their relatives and friends.

(5) The indigenous bankers finance trade, industry and agriculture, while the moneylenders finance the common man, small farmers, landless workers, and petty shopkeepers.

(6) The indigenous bankers give productive loans, while the moneylenders mostly give unproductive loans.

(7) The financial transactions of indigenous bankers are based on hundis, while those of moneylenders are in cash and promissory notes.

(8) The indigenous bankers operate in a business-like manner from properly maintained offices, while the moneylenders operate from their residences or shops.

(9) The indigenous bankers maintain proper accounts and issue receipt against deposits and for payments received from their clients. The moneylenders neither maintain proper accounts nor issue receipts for payments

received from the borrowers.

(10) As the operations of indigenous bankers are more systematic and on a larger scale, they charge lower rates of interest than the moneylenders.

(11) The indigenous bankers work in cooperation with one-another, while the moneylenders function in isolation and compete with each other.

(12) The indigenous bankers have links with the commercial banks from whom they borrow and also keep their deposits. On the other hand, the moneylenders do not have any link with the commercial banks.

4. DISTINCTION BETWEEN INDIGENOUS BANKERS AND COMMERCIAL BANKS

There are marked differences between indigenous banking and commercial banking which are discussed as under:

(1) The indigenous bankers perform banking as well as non-banking functions, such as trading, speculation, etc. while the commercial banks perform only banking functions.

(2) The indigenous bankers work as individual proprietors, while the commercial banks work as joint stock companies with a number of shareholders as their owners.

(3) The financial resources of indigenous bankers are limited whereas those of commercial banks are very vast. The former can get funds from relatives, friends, and even from commercial banks but only in limited quantity, while the latter have their own large resources from the shareholders and also get funds from the Reserve Bank of India.

(4) The indigenous bankers deal in cash, whereas the commercial banks deal both in cash and cheques.

(5) The indigenous bankers operate at one place. Very few indigenous bankers have a branch at some other place. But the commercial banks have a network of branches throughout the country.

(6) The lending policy of the indigenous bankers is very liberal. They advance money even on personal security and bear high risk. But the commercial banks lend money on the basis of a security and under the rules framed by the Reserve Bank of India.

(7) The indigenous bankers give short-term, medium-term and lcng-term loans, whereas the commercial banks give only short-term loans.

(8j The indigenous bankers operate only within the country, whereas the commercial banks also operate outside the country and do foreign exchange business.

(9) The indigenous bankers do not have a proper accounting system. They operate under a veil of secrecy. On the other hand, the commercial banks operate under the modern accounting system by publishing and submitting their balance sheets to the RBI.

(10) The indigenous bankers are not under the jurisdiction of the RBI or any other authority, whereas the commercial banks are under the RBI and operate as per the guidelines issued by the former from time to time.

(11) The indigenous bankers form part of the unorganised sector of the Indian money market. On the other hand, the commercial banks are an important constituent of the organised Indian money market.

EXERCISES

1. Examine the role of indigenous bankers in the Indian economy.
2. What is an indigenous banker? What is his importance in our economy?
3. Give the defects of the working of indigenous bankers. Suggest remedies to improve their working.
4. Distinguish between a moneylender and an indigenous banker.
5. Discuss the working and importance of moneylenders in India.
6. Write notes on: Importance of Moneylenders, Functions of Indigenous Bankers.
7. How do indigenous bankers differ from commercial banks?

CHAPTER 60

Co-operative Banks in India

The organisational set up of the cooperative banking system in India is based on the credit needs of agriculturists. It consists of three tiers for the short-term and medium-term credit: (1) Primary Agricultural Cooperative Credit Societies at the village level; (2) Central Cooperative Banks at the district level; and (3) State Cooperative Banks at the state level. For meeting the long-term credit needs, there are the Land Development Banks. We discuss below the functions, organisational set up, progress and weaknesses of these institutions.

1. PRIMARY AGRICULTURAL CREDIT SOCIETIES (PACSs)

Primary Agricultural Credit Societies, also known as Agricultural Cooperative Societies, are meant to develop the spirit of mutual help and cooperation among their members, besides meeting their credit and other needs. The main features of PACSs are as under:

OBJECTIVES

The main objectives of PACSs are: (i) to provide short-term and medium-term credit; *(ii)* to foster the habit of saving; *(iii)* to distribute fertilisers and seeds; *(iv)* to provide help in milk production, egg production, sugar production or any other product depending upon the resources of the area; and (v) to distribute consumer goods to their members.

MEMBERSHIP

The membership of a PACS is confined to persons belonging to a village or a group of villages where every person is known to other person. Ten or more persons of a locality can form a PACS. Any person can become its member by purchasing a minimum number of shares. The liability of members is unlimited which means that each member is fully responsible for the loss in the event of failure of the society.

MANAGEMENT

The management of PACSs is on democratic lines. Each member has the right to cast only one vote, irrespective of the number of shares held by him. All members form the General Body which, in turn, elects the Managing Committee annually. It consists of the President or Chairman, Secretary and members. Except the Secretary who is paid some remuneration, all others work in a honorary capacity.

FUNDS

The working funds of PACSs consist of share capital, membership fee, reserve fund (which is 25% of profits), deposits of members and non-members, and loan from the Central Cooperative Bank. They also accept grants, gifts and charities.

Loans

The PACSs grant short-term loans for meeting productive as well as unproductive needs of their member only. The medium-term loans are granted up to a certain limit and in special cases. Loans are given against personal security and security of land or crop. The rate of interest charged is lower than the rate in the organised money market. Loans are repayable in instalments.

Progress

In terms of membership, PACSs have spread widely in the country. There were 98,247 PACSs having about 10 crore members as on 31 March, 2002. Their deposits increased from Rs. 4 crores in 1950-51 to Rs. 6,518 crores in 1998-99. Total loans issued in 1998-99 amounted to Rs 16,081 crores as against Rs. 24 crores in 1950-51. Total loans outstanding increased from Rs. 6 crores in 1950-51 to Rs. 34,522 crores in 2000-01.

Drawbacks

The performance of PACSs in the issue of loans has no doubt been commendable, but they suffer from some serious weaknesses. They are: (1) They have failed to mobilise deposits. (2) The recovery of loans advanced has been disappointing. (3) Majority of them are non-viable, and the States of Maharashtra, Gujarat and J & K have not taken steps to reorganise them. (4) PACSs take very long time in granting loans. (5) The share capital of many PACSs is very small. (6) There is lack of properly trained staff. Majority of them do not have full-time paid secretaries. (7) PACSs have failed to meet the credit needs of small farmers and tenants. (8) PACSs do not possess adequate finance.

Measures to Remove Weaknesses

The Agricultural Credit Review Committee (ACRC) of the RBI in its Report (1989) made a number of recommendations to remove the weaknesses of PACSs, and to strengthen them so as to enable them to carry out their functions effectively. They are grouped as under:

(1) *Viability.* The minimum criterion of viability of a PACS can be summed up as its ability to *(i)* appoint a full-time paid secretary; *(ii)* set up a regular office in a building; *(iii)* contribute to statutory and other reserves on the scales considered necessary; and (iv) pay a reasonable dividend. Non-viable PACSs should be reorganised as per the guidelines laid down by the RBI.

(2) *Strengthening of Share Capital.* The share capital of PACSs in many cases needs strengthening. For this: (a) The NABARD should provide the minimum essential requirement of share capital loan to State Governments in the light of the action programme irrespective of overdues level. *(b)* The ratio of share linking at the Central Cooperative Bank level for PACSs should be fixed at 5% so that they are able to retain with them a part of the share capital received from their members, (c) The ratio of share linking in respect of cash credit to PACSs should be reduced from 2.5% to 1%.

(3) *Deposit Mobilisation.* Deposit mobilisation is absolutely vital for the future growth and strength of PACSs. For this: (i) The PACSs should preferably mobilise low cost deposits such as savings bank deposits, *(ii)* They should maintain 15% of deposits with Central Cooperative Banks in a special account. *(iii)* To provide insurance cover to the deposits of PACSs the State Cooperative Banks in coordination with their State Governments should formulate suitable schemes.

(4) *Improving Lending Policies and Procedures for Crop Loans.* Crop loans are granted for a period not exceeding 12 months. The Committee has recommended that: *(a)* The cash credit system should be introduced in areas where perennial irrigation is available and multiple cropping is practised. *(b)* The credit statements for fixing individual crop loans limits by PACSs should be prepared once in three years, instead of every year, except in cases where crop acreages are changed, (c) In areas where fertiliser/pesticide use is well-established, the PACSs should not insist on disbursing the input part of the loan in kind, *(d)* Where due to shortage of resources it becomes necessary to reduce the quantum of crop loans fixed, the larger farmers should be given less and smaller ones their full credit requirements.

(5) *Management.* To improve the quality of management of PACSs, a full-time trained secretary should be provided to every PACS. The Committee suggested a two-part salary structure for the secretary: one, a reasonable fixed salary in a scale of pay; and *two*, a variable payment based on increased performance, such as

recovery, deposits, additional loan, business generated, and additional non-credit business undertaken. It should be in terms of additional remuneration by way of percentage of salary. Further, the Managing Committee of a PACS should be provided training through orientation and educational programmes.

(6) *Office Premises and Godowns.* All PACSs should have proper office premises and godown space to conduct their activities as multipurpose societies.

(7) *Loans for Non-productive Purposes.* PACSs should be allowed to give loans out of their resources for non-productive purposes such as consumption loans, upto certain prescribed limits, but against tangible security only. They may also be allowed to grant loans upto 20% of their deposits against the security of gold and silver ornaments at a rate of interest higher than that on crop loans. This will provide added viability to PACSs.

(8) *Audit.* The audit of PACSs should be done free of cost or at a nominal fee only.

2. CENTRAL CO-OPERATIVE BANKS (CCBs)

The Central Cooperative Banks are federations of primary agricultural credit societies in a particular district. That is why they are also known as District Central Cooperative Banks (DCCBs). They are of two types : *One,* whose membership is confined to PACSs. This type is known as Banking Union and such banking unions exist in Kerala, Orissa, Punjab, Haryana and Rajasthan. *Two,* those having mixed membership, consisting of both PACSs and individuals. Such banks exist in the majority of States in India.

Functions

The CCBs perform the following functions: (1) They give credit to PACSs without any security. (2) They also give credit to individual customers on the security of gold, etc. (3) They foster the habit of thrift and saving among their clients by accepting deposits and paying higher rate of interest than commercial banks. (4) They also provide remittance facilities to their customers. (5) They help in solving the problems of PACSs. (6) They also control and rupervise the working of PACSs especially where the recovery of loans is slow. (7) They help in maintaining a balance among the PACSs under their jurisdiction by transferring funds from a surplus society to a deficit society. (8) They help in the proper utilisation of the reserve fund of PACS lying with them.

Management

The CCBs are managed by a Board of Directors who are elected on the principle of one member one vote. Its members vary between 10 and 20. The Board appoints trained staff like manager, accountant, etc. for proper functioning of the bank.

Funds

The working capital of CCBs consists of : (i) the share capital which they get by selling their shares to individuals and PACSs under their jurisdiction; (ii) reserve fund of PACSs and owned funds; (iii) deposits of members and non-members; (iv) borrowings from the State Cooperative Bank, commercial banks, and the State Government; and (v) deposits of local bodies and even of educational institutions.

Loans

CCBs give loans to their PACSs to meet their financial needs. Short-term loans are provided far agricultural operations for a period not exceeding 12 months. The medium-term loans are given for the purchase of cattle, for installing pumps, and for the repair of wells or sinking of well for a period ranging from 1 to 5 years. Loans arc given to societies on their promissory notes.

Progress

The number of CCBs-decreased from 509 in 1950-51 to 343 in 2003 as a policy of amalgamation of having one CCB for every district. Deposits with them increased from Rs 38 crores in 1950-51 to Rs 72,983 crores in 2002-03, and loans advanced from Rs 106 crores in 1950-51 to Rs 50,482 crores in 2002-03.

Drawbacks

The CCBs suffer from a number of weaknesses: *(i)* There is lack of coordination between PACSs and CCBs. *(it)* There are political considerations in granting loans. *(iii)* They lack efficient and sufficient staff to examine the credit-worthiness of PACSs. (iv) They lack funds, *(v)* There is undue delay in grant of loans, (vi) They hesitate to grant medium-term loans because of the lack of proper planning, *(vii)* They charge very high interest rates, *(viii)* The majority of CCBs have low level of deposits and high level of overdues which adversely affect their working. During 1998-99, the percentage of their overdues to demand was 70%. Consequently, they are week. *(ix)* They are not allowed to lend to individuals and non-cooperative institutions with the result that they are not in a position to earn more by way of interest.

Suggestions

The various committees appointed by the Reserve Bank of India from time to time suggested measures to remove the drawbacks of CCBs and to improve their functioning. Some of them are: (1) They should make efforts to mobilise more deposits from individuals and non-cooperative institutions. (2) They should open more branches in a district. (3) They should provide more banking facilities to the people. (4) As recommended by the Agricultural Credit Review Committee (1989), CCBs should be permitted to lend to non-members whether individuals or institutions, to the extent of not more than 20 per cent of their deposits. (5) The programme of improving the working of weak CCBs was launched by the RBI in 1971. But it has not made any impact and the number of such banks has been on the increase. For this the ACRC recommended a multi-ironged attempt at providing finance adequately to eligible borrowers, intensive deposit mobilisation, recovery of overdues and current dues, strengthening of PACSs etc.

3. STATE CO-OPERATIVE BANKS (SCBs)

The State Cooperative Banks are federations of District Central Cooperative Banks. They are Apex Banks in the three tier cooperative structure in India. Each State has one SCB.

Functions

The SCBs perform the following functions: (1) They coordinate the activities of PACSs and CCBs in the State. (2) They arrange funds for the entire credit structure of the State. (3) They control the activities of the CCBs. (4) They act as an important link between the Indian money market and the cooperative sector. (5) They help in maintaining a balance among the CCBs by transferring funds from surplus CCBs to deficit CCBs within a State. (6) In case there is no CCB in a district, it provides credit facilities direct to PACSs in that district. (7) It also functions as a commercial bank.

Management

A SCB is managed by a General Body which holds its meeting once a year. It is formed by. the representatives of PACs, CCBs and individuals. But it is governed by a Board of Directors whose number varies between 10 and 30 which also appoints the staff.

Funds

The working capital of a SCB consists of: (i) the share capital which it gets by selling its share to PACSs, CCBs, and individuals; *(ii)* reserve fund which comprises 25% of its profits; (iii) deposits from members and non-members; and (iv) borrowings from the Reserve Bank of India, State Government, commercial banks and inter-bank borrowings.

Loans

SCBs lend to CCBs for short-term to meet the needs of PACSs. They do not lend direct to PACSs except in those cases where there is no CCB in a district. Loans are given on the basis of promissory note.

PROGRESS

The number of SCBs increased from 16 in 1950-51 to 29 in 2002-03 with total deposits rising from Rs. 21 crores to Rs 37,439 crores over the period. Total loans advanced by them increased from Rs. 55 crores in 1950-51 to Rs. 38,318 crores in 2002-03 and loans outstanding were 34,864 crores.

DRAWBACKS

There are a number of drawbacks in the working of SCBs, which are: (i) They lack sufficient funds to meet the needs of the farm sector, (ii) They are more involved in commercial banking operations, (iii) There is no proper planning in granting loans to farmers through the DCCBs. (iv) They do not have adequate and trained staff to supervise and help in the efficient working of CCBs. (v) They are influenced by political considerations in sanctioning loans than by the genuine needs of agriculturists, (vi) They have failed to recover overdues. (vi) The Board of Directors is not properly managed, and its members are not experienced.

SUGGESTIONS

The All India Rural Credit Survey Committee and the Agricultural Credit Review Committee made a number of suggestions to improve the working of banks. Some of them are: (I) The membership of SCBs should be restricted only to PACSs and DCCBs. (2) They should try to increase their share capital, mobilise more deposits from the urban sector, and keep.the reserve funds of PACSs and DCCBs with them in order to have larger funds as working capital. (3) They should meet the farm needs of agriculturists rather than function as commercial banks. (4) Not more than 33 per cent of the members should be nominated by the State Government on the Board of Directors and one of them must be the Registrar of Cooperative Societies, (5) Each SCB should set up a technical cell with trained staff to formulate schemes for financing and helping DCCBs in credit planning and project formulation. Besides, expertise should be developed at the SCBs' level to advise DCCBs on better financial management and investment/portfolio management. (6) For an efficient working of SCBs, the staff should be recruited in the same manner as is being done in the case of Regional Rural Banks and commercial banks through Banking Commission of the respective-region. (7) The Government of India along with the State Governments should chalk out a concrete long-term policy to recover overdues and take firm steps in respect of wilful defaulters. (8) The politicisation of agricultural credit system should be stopped, loan 'melas' should be discouraged, and loans should be given to needy farmers.

4. LAND DEVELOPMENT BANKS (LDBs)

The Land Development Banks, which were earlier known as Land Mortgage Banks are meant to meet the long-term credit needs of agriculturists. Their structure is not uniform in the country. It is unitary in some States, while in some others it is federal, and in Himachal Pradesh and West Bengal, it is both unitary and federal. Under the federal structure, there is the Central Land Development Bank at the State level, and the Primary Land Development Banks (PLDBs) at the district level. The Central Land Development Bank lends to agriculturists through the PLDBs. They are now known as State Cooperative Agriculture and Rural Development Banks (SCARDBs).

FUNCTIONS

The LDBs provide long-term loans to agriculturists for a period ranging from 5 to 25 years, for the following purposes: (i) to make improvements on the land; (ii) to repay old debts; *(iii)* to free the mortgaged land; and (iv) to buy new land. In recent years, they have also started lending for non-agricultural purposes such as, to the rural cottage industries and small enterprises in rural areas.

MANAGEMENT

The LDBs are registered under the Cooperative Societies Act. A Land Development Bank is managed by a Board of Directors consisting of 15 to 20 members duly elected by the members of PLDBs, and nominated members by the State Government, and the Registrar of Cooperative Societies.

Funds

The financial resources of LDBs consist of: (i) the share capital contributed by borrowing and non-borrowing members; *(it)* deposits from the public; and (iii) by issuing debentures. Debentures are of three types: *First,* ordinary debentures purchased by institutions and individuals. *Second,* rural debentures issued to farmers at the time of harvesting for 7 years and 15 years. *Third,* special development debentures issued for land development or improvement which are purchased by NABARD, the concerned State Government and the Central Government.

Loans

The LDBs give loans to their members on the security of their lands which are generally limited to 50% of the value of land mortgaged. Loans are given for a maximum period of 25 years. They are meant to meet the long-term needs of the agriculturists such as land development, land reclamation, buying new land, for minor irrigation works like buying pump sets, digging wells and tubewells or tanks, for related agricultural activities like dairy, poultry farming, bee-keeping, sericulture, biogas, etc. LDBs also give credit to non-agriculturists such as village, household and handicraft industries in rural areas.

Progress

The number of LDBs increased from 6 in 1950-51 to 20 in 2002-03. Loans advanced increased from Rs 2.5 crores in 1950-51 to Rs. 2,631 crores in 2002-03. Their loans outstanding rose from Rs. 8 crores to Rs. 13,870 crores.

Drawbacks

The LDBs have been facing a number of problems which hinder their proper functioning. Some of their problems are:

(1) *Overdues.* The LDBs have not been able to recover past loans with the result that their overdues have been rising which affect their smooth working. During 2000-01 the percentage of their overdues was 58 per cent of the demand.

(2) *Restricted Lending Eligibility.* Due to the lack of working capital, the lending eligibility of PLDBs and of the branches of LDBs have restricted lending eligibility. There are hardly one-third of them which have unrestricted lending eligibility.

(3) *Non-viable.* Due to the restricted lending eligibility, 30% of the total PLDBs and the branches of LDBs are not viable.

(4) *Falling Profits.* Due to their non-viability, there is deterioration in their profitability.

(5) *Debentures.* People are reluctant to buy their debentures and the cost of raising even ordinary debentures is very high.

(6) *Delay.* There is delay in the grant of loans.

(7) *High Margin.* The LDBs keep a high margin of 50% of the value of land mortgaged for the grant of loans.

(8) *Discharge of Past Debts.* More loans are granted to repay past debts and less for productive purposes.

(9) *Benefits to Rich Farmers.* Rich farmers are able to get more benefits as they have more land than the other farmers having less land.

(10) *Interference.* There is much external interference and government intervention in the management of LDBs.

(11) *Inefficient Working.* The LDBs are not working properly due to lack of adequate and trained staff. There is no definite policy in regard to recruitment, appointment, promotion and training of staff. The Chief Executives are either IAS or PCS officers or from the cooperative departments.

Suggestions

The various committees appointed by the Reserve Bank of India have made a number of suggestions to remove the defects and improve the working of LDBs in the country. Some of the suggestions made by the

Agricultural Credit Review Committee (1989) are:

(1) Effective steps should be taken by the LDBs to recover overdues in order to make theni viable.

(2) For LDBs to work as viable units, every effort should be made to increase their volume of business with such diversification of activities as may be feasible.

(3) The LDBs should adopt viability criterion in place of eligibility criteria in order to obtain adequate funds from the NABARD.

(4) The NABARD should provide adequate interim finance for issue of loans before debentures are floated at concessional rates.

(5) The State Governments and institutions should support the programme of issuing of ordinary debentures. So far as the flotation of special development debentures is concerned, the NABARD should provide refinance by way of term loans instead of by contribution to special development debentures.

(6) Politicisation of loans should be stopped and loans should be primarily given for productive purposes.

(7) LDBs should have a definite policy for recruitment, appointment, career planning and development of the staff. They should have their own staff and taking of government staff on deputation should be resorted to only in exceptional cases. There should be no government interference in the management of LDBs.

(8) Loans should be granted without unnecessary delay.

(9) The keeping of high margins for the grant of loans should be relaxed for the benefit of farmers.

5. STRENGTHENING THE CO-OPERATIVE STRUCTURE

The Agricultural Credit Review Committee (ACRC) had made comprehensive recommendations-for improving the cooperative credit structure in the country.[1] The Government of India has implemented a number of recommendations which are discussed as under :

1. Reorganisation of PACSs

The process of reorganisation of PACSs has been started on the model laid down by the NABARD. It envisages an area of. operation of 5 km. radius and a potential loan business of Rs. 13.50 lakhs for the reorganised society. Except in Maharashtra and the Kashmir region of J & K, the process of reorganisation of PACSs has been completed. However, the majority of states have not achieved the norms laid down by the NABARD though they have completed the reorganisation work.

2. Business Development Plans (BDPs) for PACSs

In view of the poor financial position of PACSs, the Government of India has launched a business-oriented development programme for PACs. The programme envisages preparation of BDPs for selected PACSs for implementation in a phased manner. Its aim is to develop selected societies in certain States into viable units to serve all socio-economic groups in their areas of operation through economically viable activities. It is expected to cover, in phases, all PACSs in the country.

3. Deposit Insurance Scheme for PACSs

The main thrust of BDPs is on deposit mobilisation by PACSs. But the absence of deposit insurance has been the major constraint in deposit mobilisation at the PACS level. To overcome this, the Government of India has formulated a model deposit insurance scheme for PACSs to create a sense of security in the depositors. The scheme would be applicable only to viable PACSs which are implementing BDPs. The scheme lays down the following conditions: (a) the PACSs covered under the scheme should have deposits of maturity period of more than 6 months; (*b*) such deposits should be at least Rs. 25,000 per society; (c) the accounts of the society should be maintained regularly.

1. These have already been enumerated above under "Suggestions" in different sections.

4. Kisan Credit Card (KCC) Scheme

This scheme was introduced in 1998-99 with a view to facilitating the flow of timely and adequate short-term credit to farmers. The KCC scheme is an on-going scheme which is meant to gradually replace the traditional system and procedures in the short-term crop, loans. Loans disbursed under the scheme have also been brought under the Krishi BimaYojna of the General Insurance Corporation. KCCs are issued to eligible farmers for even amounts below Rs. 5,000 per card by cooperative banks, Regional Rural Banks and commercial banks in rural areas.

5. Institutional Strengthening Programme (ISP)

The ISP aims at making non-solvent banks such as SCBs, DCCBs, State LDBs and PLDBs as viable units within a period of 3 to 5 years. The programme includes investigation of overdues, measures for their recovery, rationalising loans policies and procedures, expansion and diversification of loan portfolio, mobilisation of resources, revitalisation of primary cooperative societies, reduction in management costs, and redeployment of manpower and resources, etc. The programme also requires administrative support and financial assistance from Central and State Governments, RBI and NABARD. The banks which fail to become viable within 3 to 5 years would not be given refinance facility by the NABARD and alternative arrangements would be made to maintain credit flow in these banks.

6. The Model Cooperative Societies Act

The Planning Commission appointed a committee to review the status of cooperative laws which submitted its report on the Model Cooperative Societies Act in May 1991. The main thrust of the Act is to impart a federal character to cooperatives, facilitate self-reliance and to minimise Government control and interference. The State Governments have been asked by the Planning Commission to incorporate the amendments to the Model Act in a phased manner. So far, only Orissa State has accepted it fully and implemented it. Some States have yet to initiate legislative action while others are in the process of taking action.

7.. Integrated Cooperative Development Projects (ICDPs)

The National Cooperative Development Corporation launched a scheme during the Seventh Plan for Integrated Cooperative Development Projects for selected districts. The scheme aims at strengthening and developing cooperative infrastructure in order to cater to the overall needs of the rural community in selected areas of districts.

EXERCISES

1. Describe the organisation, structure, working and progress of Primary Agricultural Credit Societies.
2. Why have Primary Agricultural Credit Societies been not successful? Suggest measures to improve their working.
3. Describe the functions, working and progress of Land Development Banks.
4. Explain the defects found in the agricultural cooperative societies. What measures have been taken to improve them?

CHAPTER 61

Regional Rural Banks and NABARD

1. RURAL BANKS

In India four sets of cooperative credit institutions have been providing farm credit. These have been the Primary Agricultural Societies and other primary level farm credit societies and Land Development Banks which deal directly with the farmer-borrowers. There are also State Cooperative banks and Central Cooperative Banks which extend only indirect finance. Both before and after Independence, these institutions failed to meet the farm credit requirements, and the farmers had to depend primarily on the moneylenders. The involvement of commercial banks in rural banking began with the nationalisation of Imperial Bank of India into the State Bank of India in 1955. The SBI started providing finance to agriculture through cooperative banks, land mortgage banks and cooperative processing and marketing societies in 1956.

With the adoption of the New Agricultural Strategy in 1968, it was felt that the cooperative institutions helped by the SBI would not be able to meet the credit requirements of the expanding farm sector by themselves. Accordingly, the government accepted the principle of Multi-Agency Approach to farm credit with the entry of commercial banks in the sphere of agricultural finance. This led to nationalisation of 14 commercial banks in 1969. It was only after this that commercial banks as a class began to enter the rural sector in a big way. There was remarkable expansion of branches of commercial banks in rural areas. But they failed to meet the credit needs of the farmers except that of the rich farmers and landlords. Instead of supplementing cooperative credit, they weakened cooperative societies by mobilising the savings of rich farmers and channelising them into urban areas for earning profits. Moreover, commercial banks experienced that working in rural areas was very costly and not viable, and secondly, the urban staff was unable to understand the needs and problems of rural finance.

It was against this background that the Banking Commission in its report published in 1972 recommended the establishment of a chain *of Rural Banks* in one of the three ways: (1) Conversion of primary agricultural credit societies into rural cooperative banks providing all the banking services; (2) restructuring sound agricultural credit societies as subsidiaries of commercial banks to be called 'rural subsidiary banks'; and (3) establishing special type of 'rural banks' sponsored by commercial banks with local participation in capital and management; if suitable primary credit societies are not available.

The Banking Commission laid down the following functions for the rural banks to accept deposits; to advance loans to provide ancillary banking services; to supply farmi inputs and equipment to farmers; to help in the marketing of farm output; to maintain godowns; and to help in the overall development of villages in the area of operations. It emphasised that rural banks would meet the farm needs of the marginal, small and medium farmers and rural artisans.

The Banking Cojnmission observed that in a country like India any single type of financial institution was incapable of meeting the credit needs of the rural sector. It, therefore, recommended a multi-pronged programme where cooperative credit societies, commercial banks, SBI, and sponsored rural banks had to play an important role.

But the Government of India did not give any thought to the recommendations of the Banking Commission to start a chain of rural banks in the country till 1975, when five Regional Rural Banks were started in five selected districts in the country.

2. REGIONAL RURAL BANKS (RRBs)

The idea of establishing Regional Rural Banks was mooted in the Twenty Point Economic Programme of July 1975 to cater to the credit needs of rural people. The Government of India appointed Narasimham Committee in July 1975 to set up the new institution in order *(i)* to provide employment to the rural educated youth; and (ii) to bring down the cost of rural banks by recruiting their staff on the same scale of pay and allowances as for the employees of State Government/local bodiss. It was on the recommendations that the first five RRBs were set up on 2 October, 1975 under an Ordinance promulgated on 26 September, 1975 which was replaced by the Regional Rural Banks Act of 1976.

Objectives

The major objectives of the RRBs are to develop the rural economy hy providing credit and other facilities for agriculture, trade, commerce, industry and other productive activities in the rural areas, particularly to the small and marginal farmers, agricultural labourers, artisans and small entrepreneurs.

Organisational Structure of Regional Rural Banks

A Regional Rural Bank is sponsored by a commercial bank. For this purpose, the sponsor bank requests the Central Government, which issues a notification after consulting the concerned State Government. Normally, a RRB covers one district but it is also permitted to open its branches in other districts. So far the maximum coverage has been eight districts, as in the case of Manipur Regional Rural Bank which covers the entire State of Manipur.

The authorised capital of an RRB at present is Rs. 5 crcres. The issued share capital is Rs. 1 crore now and is subscribed by the Central Government, the sponsor bank and the concerned State Government in the ratio of 50:35:15. The Government of India raised the issued share capital of 27 RRBs from Rs. 50 lakh to Rs. 75 lakh and of 42 RRBs from Rs. 75 lakh to Rs. 1 crore during 1994-95. This has raised the number of RRBs having issued capital of Rs. 1 crore to 62 and those having issued capital of Rs. 75 lakh to 122.

The RRB is governed by a Board of Directors who exercises all the powers and discharges all the functions of RRB. It consists of a Chairman appointed by the Central Government for five years, three directors nominated by the Central Government, two directors nominated by the concerned State Government, and three directors nominated by the sponsor bank. Usually the Chairman of the RRB belongs to the sponsor bank, though he is nominated by the Central Government.

The NABARD is vested with powers of inspection of RRBs and to call for any data from them. For opening of new branches, applications are routed through NABARD to Reserve Bank of India for issue of licences. The responsibility of overseeing the overall functioning of RRBs rests on NABARD. NABARD also provides refinance at concessional interest rate to RRBs.

Functions of Regional Rural Banks

The main functions (or objectives) of-the RRBs are:

1. To grant loans and advances to the weaker sections of the rural population, especially to the small and marginal farmers, agricultural labourers, artisans and small entrepreneurs who are engaged in agriculture, trade, commerce, industry and other productive activities.

2. To grant loans and advances to cooperative societies, including marketing societies, agricultural processing societies, cooperative farming societies, primary agricultural credit societies or farmers' service

societies for agricultural purposes.

3. To take banking services to the doorsteps of the rural masses, particularly in hitherto unbanked rural areas.

4. To mobilise rural savings by accepting deposits and channelise them for productive activities in the rural areas.

5. To create a supplementary channel for flow of credit from the urban money market to the rural areas through refinance.

6. To generate employment opportunities in rural areas.

7. To bring down the cost of supplying credit in rural areas.

In recent years, the RRBs have been permitted to extend advances for purchase of durable consumer goods and loans for various purposes against the security of gold ornaments, National Savings Certificates, Indira Vikas Patras to both target and non-target groups up to 10 per cent of their fresh lending within the over ceiling of 60 per cent of fresh loans to non-target group lending.

They have also been allowed to issue guarantees on behalf of their customers without any limition 100 per cent cash margin and upto Rs. 20 lakh on Rs. 40 lakh cash margin plus collateral security of more than 50 per cent.

The limits for purchase of demand drafts and cheque have been raised per customer and per branch to Rs. 25,000 and Rs. 1 lakh respectively. The RRBs can issue travellers' cheques as agents of their sponsor banks and also provide locker facilities.

The RRBs can invest their surpluses in UTI listed schemes, fixed deposits of profit making term lending institutions, bonds of nationalised banks and other public sector undertakings, non-convertible debentures of blue chip companies and in credit portfolios of their sponsor banks-subject to a maximum of 15 per cent of their fresh lending during the year. Effective 8 January, 1997, RRBs have been allowed to invest in corporate shares and debentures and units of mutual funds. But these investments cannot exceed 5 per cent of the RRBs' incremental deposits. They have also been allowed to buy corporate shares and debentures from the secondary market. They are also free to fix their lending and deposit rates.

Achievements (or Progress) of Regional Rural Banks

The RRBs have carried banking to the doorsteps of rural masses. They have opened branches in remote and isolated villages which had no banking facilities. Initially starting with five RRBs at Moradabad and Gorakhpur in Uttar Pradesh, Jaipur in Rajasthan, Bhiwani in Haryana and Malda in West Bengal on 2 October, 1975, the RRBs have achieved a phenomenal growth over the years. As on June 30, 2003, they numbered 196, covering 451 districts, with a network of 14,522 branches.

The aggregate outstanding deposits of 196 RRBs in 2002-03 were Rs. 48,346 crores. Their aggregate direct and indirect outstanding advances stood at Rs.. 15,944 crores in 2002-03. The credit-deposit ratio increased from 43 per cent as at the end of March, 1999 to 45 per cent in March, 2003. Investment-deposit ratio increased from 19.7 per cent in 1998-99 to 25.9 per cent in March 2003.

The loans and advances disbursed by RRBs for agriculture accounted for 46.3 per cent and the share of non-agricultural advances was 53.7 per cent. Out of 196 RRBs, the number of profit making banks stood at 156 in 2002-03 as compared with 170 out of 196 in 2000-01. Their operating profit fell by 7.7 per cent and net profit by -13.7 per cent over the period. The RRBs showed significant improvement in terms of reduction in their NPAs (non-performing assets). The share of NPAs in total assets declined from 18.8 percent to 16.1 per cent in 2002-03.

During 2002-03, the NABARD sanctioned Rs. 1,406 crores as short-term credit limits for seasonal and non-seasonal agricultural operations to RRBs. It sanctioned medium-term loans to RRBs amounting to Rs. 3 crores.

Thus, the RRBs have been highly successful in mobilising rural savings. In advancing loans, they have been concentrating on target groups viz., small and marginal farmers, landless labourers, rural artisans, self-employed persons, etc. They have also been playing a vital role in implementing the IRD Programme. Mostly, they have employed local persons. Clerical staff is recruited from within the area of operation of the RBBs from adjoining districts, whereas the officer staff is from the concerned State.

Problems of Regional Rural Banks

Despite the important role played by RRBs in providing credit to the weaker sections of society in rural areas, they are faced with serious problems which have led critics to question their very existence. The Dantwala Committee (1978), the Kelkar Committee (1986) and the Khusro Committee (1989) have pointed towards some of the weaknesses in the working of RRBs which are as follows:

1. *Haphazard Branch Expansion.* A large network of branches has been opened at a fast pace which has not contributed to substantial increase in business. It has added to overhead costs without contributing to profits.

Moreover, major variations persist among States in the coverage of districts/ branches by the RRBs. In some States, backward areas still remain uncovered by these banks. In many districts, the RRBs do not have link branches at the Taluka/ Block headquarters for meeting the cash requirements and to overcome other operational problems. In some of the places where branches are essential, it is difficult to get suitable accommodation for housing the branches.

2. *Defective Recruitment Policy.* Being rural oriented, the RRBs are expected to recruit staff locally. With the transfer of recruitments in RRBs to the Banking Service Recruitment Boards, the candidates outside the area of operations of RRBs are also made eligible for recruitment into RRBs. This is against the concept of RRBs where the 'local feel and familiarity' of the staff is essential for the successful working of the RRBs.

3. *Rigid Norms.* The norms laid down for the selection of beneficiaries in RRBs are rigid and based on an all India income level. The poverty line available in Haryana is not the poverty line obtained in Andhra Pradesh. The village, its people, their occupations and economic status differ widely in Andhra Pradesh with that of All India average. But to apply the same norms to all the States leave out many persons who are in need of credit from the RRBs.

4. *Weak Capital Base.* The capital base of each RRB is weak. Initially, the issued capital was Rs. 50 lakh which has been raised to Rs. 75 lakh and Rs. 1 crore in the case of selected RRBs. But the State Governments failed to contribute their share. In view of its enormous credit obligation in rural areas, this limit is on the lower side. The working of many RRBs reveals that they have eroded their capital base on account of continuous losses.

5. *Constraints in Deposit Mobilisation.* As the RRBs supply credit only to the weaker sections of the rural population, they have been unable to mobilise sufficient deposits. The weaker sections who are the main beneficiaries are poor and do not save so much as to deposit in the RRBs. The middle classes and the rural elite are not interested to deposit their saving in the RRBs. They deposit them in commercial banks from whom they get credit facilities.

6. *Erosion of Profitability.* The RRBs have not been able to operate on a viable basis. The major factors which have contributed to the erosion of their profitability have been their lending exclusively to the weaker sections, low interest margins and high operating cost involved in handling small loans. During 1999-2000 there were 33 loss making RRBs which incurred a net loss of Rs. 109 crores.

7. *Poor Recoveries.* The recover of loans due has been very poor. The estimate of the Khusro Committee revealed that as on June 1986, the recoverv of RRBs was 49 per cent. During 1999, the recovery level was below 30 per cent. The main factors have been wilful defaults, misuse of loans, lack of follow-up, wrong identification of borrowers, extension of benami loans, staff agitations, etc.

8. *Defective Credit Deployment.* In many districts, the credit deployment has not been proper., The loaning activities are mainly confined to crop loans and the schemes sponsored by the State Governments. The schematic approach towards lending is lacking in many cases. Activities allied to agriculture, cottage and rural industries, rural artisans/craftsmen and other self-employed programmes have not been given due importance in the loaning activities of the RRBs.

9. *High Loan Transaction Cost.* With parity in pay scales between the RRBs and commercial banks, the loan transaction costs in RRBs are many times higher than in rural branches of commercial banks.

Conclusion. Notwithstanding the constraints under which the RRBs are operating, they constitute one of the effective instruments for bringing about faster rural development with social justice.

Suggestions to Improve the Working of RRBs

To improve the working of the RRBs, the Dantawala Committee (1978), the Kelkar Committee (1986) and the Khusro Committee (1989) have made a number of suggestions. Some of these are enumerated below:

1. To improve the *viability* of RRBs, the Khusro Committee recommended that the RRBs should be merged with the commercial banks. The merger would solve the problems of accumulated losses, of insolvency, and of the in-built non-viability of the majority of RRBs. But it is wrong to presume that after merger with sponsor banks, the RRBs will be viable because many branches of commercial banks are incurring huge losses. Therefore, the suggestions made by the Kelkar Committee should be implemented. They are the bifurcation of unwieldy RRBs, and the amalgamation of small RRBs.

2. In order to strengthen the capital structure of RRBs, the Kelkar Committee recommended the raising of issued capital of RRBs from Rs. 25 lakhs to Rs. 100 lakhs and the authorised capital from Rs. 1 crores to Rs. 5 crore.

3. As the very purpose of establishing RRBs is to transfer funds from urban money market to rural centres, the State Governments should permit the Panchayats and other quasi-government bodies functioning in rural areas to keep their funds with the RRB branches functioning within their area of operations.

4. The State Governments should either reorganise agricultural credit societies or establish new Farmers' Service Societies through which RRBs can provide production credit on a large scale and thereby the cost of servicing will be reduced considerably.

5. The sponsor banks should play a more active role in advising and helping their RRBs in managing their funds, in appraising loan schemes, in making proper end-use of credit, and in providing staff for internal audit of RRBs.

6. The sponsor banks should charge a lower interest rate on the refinance to RRBs and involve themselves less in RRBs short-term and non-schematic loans.

7. The sponsor banks should invest the deposits of RRBs in long-term Government securities which are being kept in non-interest earning current accounts.

8. To increase the profit margin, the RRBs should extend credit facilities to non-target groups subject to a ceiling of 25 percent of their total outstanding advances. The State Government should help the RRBs in recovering dues by creating a proper climate for recovery and in taking action against wilful defaulters.

9. The RRBs should have their own recovery system with adequate trained staff and organise recovery camps involving the Government officials, local leaders and branch staff.

10. The business of rural branches of commercial banks should be handed over to RRBs.

11. There should be uniform scales of pay for all the RRBs staff.

12. The RRBs should devise suitable strategies to develop banking habits and practices among the rural folk by imbibing banking education and awareness.

13. The RRBs should widen their sphere of activity. Instead of concentrating mainly on lending, they should provide rural consultancy services, phased credit programmes, create better avenues for employment, and take over the work of farmers' service societies.

14. Since RRB is an area specific and target specific bank, its working hours should be suitably amended to enable the customers to make full use of its facilities. It is inconsistent to have the usual office hours between 10 AM and 5 PM in a village where the customers are busy in the fields at that time., Therefore, the working hours of RRBs should be fixed according to the needs of the area.

15. New RRBs should be opened in areas where SC/ST population predominates.

16. The entire recruitment process in the RRBs should be streamlined. Local people should be preferred and training should be given on the problems of rural life which are peculiar to the RRBs.

Restructuring of RRBs

These suggestions apart, keeping in view that only 29 RRBs were profit making in 1991-92, the Government of India had been considering a number of options which include the merger of RRBs with the sponsor banks as suggested by the RBI or making them rural subsidiaries of sponsor banks as suggested by the Narasimhan Committee or their amalgamation with the proposed National Rural Bank of India. As the RRBs became non-viable, the Government's interest in supporting them financially declined. The budgetary support for RRBs was Rs. 11 crores in 1992-93 which declined to Rs. 5 crores in 1993-94. There was no provision for them in the budget for 1994-95 though it was announced by the Finance Minister that 50 select RRBs would be taken up for revival and restructuring. Accordingly, the Government appointed the Bhandari Committee on Restructuring of RRBs which has since submitted its report. Based on its recommendations, action has been taken on the managerial, operational and organisational restructuring of RRBs including cleansing up their balance sheets and infusing fresh capital. In the first phase, 49 RRBs were taken up for selective restructuring. These RRBs drew up their Development Action Plans in consultation with NABARD and sponsor banks and Mou were entered between them and sponsor banks. The Government of India contributed Rs. 180 crores as its share of 50 per cent during 1994-95. During 1995-96, a sum of Rs. 223.57 crores was further released by the Government for capital restructuring of select RRBs. The Budget for 1996-97 made, a further provision for the same purpose in the second phase.

In June 1995, the Reserve Bank set up an Expert Group under Dr Thingalaya to examine the major policy issues concerning the managerial and financial restructuring of RRBs undertaken during 1994-95 and to monitor their progress on an ongoing basis. Another Committee headed by K. Basu was set up by the NABARD to look into the norms afresh and for revamping the RRBs. It recommended the selection of 68 RRBs for comprehensive restructuring in the second phase.

In order to impart durability to the restructuring process, the RRBs have been advised by the Reserve Bank to adopt income recognition, asset classification and exposure norms from 1995-96 and provisioning norms from 1996-97 onwards. As a result of these restructuring measures the number of profit making RRBs stood at 156 in 2002-03

3. NATIONAL BANK FOR AGRICULTURE AND RURAL DEVELOPMENT (NABARD)

The National Bank for Agriculture and Rural Development (NABARD) was established on 12 July, 1982 by Government of India by merging the Agricultural Credit Department of the RBI, the Agricultural Refinance and Development Corporation, the National Agricultural Credit (Long Term Operations) Fund and the National Agricultural Credit (Stabilisation) Fund of the RBI.

Objectives of NABARD

The NABARD is an apex development bank which provides help for agricultural and rural development. It has been established with the following objectives:

1. To give undivided attention and purposeful direction to integrated rural development.
2. To act as a centre piece for the entire rural credit system at the national level.
3. To act as a provider of supplemental funding to rural credit institutions.
4. To arrange for investment credit to small industries, village and cottage industries, handicrafts and other rural crafts, artisans, and farmers.
5. To improve the credit distribution system by institution building, rehabilitation of credit institutions and training of bank personnel.
6. To provide refinance facilities to SLDBs, SCBs, RRBs and commercial banks for development purposes in rural areas.
7. To coordinate the working of different agencies engaged in development work in rural areas at the regional level, and to have liaison with Government of India, RBI, State Governments and other policy making institutions at the national level.
8. To inspect, monitor and evaluate projects getting refinance from the NABARD.

Functions of NABARD

The functions of NABARD have been divided into three categories: *(a)* Credit Distribution; *(b)* Development, and (c) Regulatory.

These are discussed as under:

(a) Credit Distribution

The NABARD provides refinance of various types to the following institutions :

(1) *Short Term Credit.* It provides short term credit to State Cooperative Banks (SCBs), Regional Rural Banks (RRBs), and other financial institutions approved by the RBI for the following purposes: (i) seasonal agricultural operations; *(it)* marketing of agricultural produce; (iii) marketing and distribution of such inputs as pesticides, fertilisers, etc.; (iv) other activities related to rural/agriculture sector; (v) real commercial trade activities; *(vi)* production and marketing of the following activities: handicrafts, small industries, village and cottage industries, artisans, silk industry, etc. The duration of short term loans for the above purposes is up to 15 months.

(2) *Medium Term Credit.* The NABARD provides medium term credit to SCBs, LDBs, RRBs, and other approved institutions for a period ranging from 18 months to 7 years. The medium term loans are given for investment schemes relating to agriculture and rural sector.

(3) *Long Term Credit.* The NABARD provides long term credit to State Land Development Banks, RRBs, commercial banks, SCBs, and to any approved financial institution. It provides refinance for investment in the following activities: minor irrigation, land development, soil conservation; dairy development, sheep rearing, poultry farming, pig rearing, farm mechanisation, afforestation, fish farming, storage and market yard, agricultural operations through aeroplane, biogas and other alternative sources of energy, silk production, beekeeping, cattle and cattle driven carts, compost equipment, pump set, and other agricultural and related activities. The duration of the loan is for a period of 25 years.

(4) *Facilities for Changes and Rearrangement.* The NABARD provides refinance facilities to SCBs and RRBs in the event of changes and rearrangement of credits when there is drought, famine or other natural calamities, army operations, enemy operations, etc. Such facilities are also provided to loans given to artisans, small industries, etc. The duration of such refinance facilities is not more than 7 years.

(5) *Refinancing of Industries in Rural Areas.* The NABARD provides refinancing facilities to all small, village and cottage industries in rural areas.

(*b*) Developmental Functions

The NABARD performs the following developmental functions: (i) coordinates the rural credit institutions; *(ii)* takes measures towards institution building to improve the capacity of credit delivery system; *(iii)* develops specialisation to solve problems relating to agriculture and villages; (iv) helps the Government, **RBI,** and other institutions in their rural development efforts; (v) acts as an agent of the Government and RBI for monitoring work in agricultural related areas; (vi) provides facilities for research and training to the staff of RRBs, SCBs, LDBs, .etc. and promotes research in agricultural and rural development activities out of its R & D (Research & Development) Fund. To provide training facilities in the fields of rural banking, and agriculture and rural development, the NABARD has the Banker Rural Development Institute -and National Bank Staff Colleges at Lucknow, Bolpur and Manglore, and College of Agriculture Banking (CAB) at Pune; *(vii)* spreads information regarding rural banking and development; *(viii)* helps the State Governments so that they may subscribe to the share capital of State Cooperative Banks; *(ix)* provides direct credit in cases approved by the Central Government connected with agriculture and rural development; and *(x)* maintains an Easy Credit Aid Fund out of its profits so that entrepreneurs getting refinance facilities for village, cottage and very small industries may be provided margin money. This help is given interest-free and is recovered in yearly instalments after the loan is repaid.

(c) Regulatory Functions

The NABARD also performs the following regulatory functions: *(i)* It inspects the working of RRBs and cooperative banks of all types except the primary cooperative banks, *(ii)* It also inspects apex cooperative marketing federations, state handloom weaving societies, etc. which are financed on voluntary basis, (iii) All applications for opening of a branch by the RRB or a cooperative bank, other than a primary cooperative society, are required to be submitted to the RBI through the NABARD. (iv) All RRBs and cooperative banks submitting returns to the RBI are required to furnish a copy of returns to the NABARD. (v) It is empowered to obtain any information or statement from the RRBs and cooperative banks.

(*d*) Recent Additions to Its Functions

For the last few years a number of additions have been made the functions of NABARD relating to farm and non-farm sectors in order to make it more broad-based. They are:

(i) *Farm Sector.* The National Bank has been engaged in reorienting its policies relating to the farm sector in tune with emerging needs. Accordingly, it has taken some major initiatives for promoting agriculture and rural development. These include: (1) refinement and updating of Potential Linked Credit Plans (PLCPs) and their synthesis with Service Area Plans (SAPs); (2) introduction of full refinance scheme in those districts where such synthesis has taken place; (3) rationalization and liberalisation of eligibility criteria for refinance of term credit; (4) introduction of Self Help Groups Scheme for providing institutional credit to weaker sections; (5) rationalisation of interest rate structure for ultimate borrowers; (6) issuance of guidelines to banks on new/ innovative schemes for diversification of lending under agriculture; and (7) creation of a Cooperative Development Fund to promote institutional strengthening activities.

(ii) *Non-Farm Sector.* For accelerating the development of non-farm sector, NABARD has taken the following initiatives: (1) introduction of Small Road Transport Scheme for automatic refinance to all banks for financing transport vehicles to carry farm produce and products of village industries for marketing; (2) project finance for commercial banks for financing non-agro small industry units; (3) assisting Khadi and Village Industries Centres in modifying their schemes so as to conform them to banking norms and bringing them under automatic refinance facility; (4) formation of an Advisory Committee for the* non-farm sector in its office to guide in the formulation of policies to promote non-farm sector and to introduce innovative schemes; (5) appointment of technical experts in non-farm sector at its offices in order to identify, formulate and appraise schemes and conduct surveys for estimating industrial potential; (6) formulation of District Rural Industries Project; and (7) setting up of Agriculture and Rural Enterprises Incubation Fund.

Its Resources

The authorised capital of NABARD has been raised from Rs. 500 crores to Rs. 5,000 crores effective 1 February, 2001 with equal contributions by the RBI and Government of India. Besides share capital contribution, the RBI has been providing the NABARD a General Line of Credit (GLC) I & II to meet the short-term credit requirements of cooperatives and RRBs. Its other resources consist of National Rural Credit Funds, reserves and surplus, deposits and borrowings. In addition, the Union Government provides funds received from the World Bank Group. IFAD, EU and other countries. The aggregate resources mobilised by NABARD through various sources amounted to Rs. 5,786 crores during 2002-03.

Its Organisation

The NABARD is managed by a 15-member Board of Directors consisting of Chairman, Managing Director, two experts of rural economies, three experts from cooperative and commercial banks, three directors from the current directors of the RBI, three directors from the Government of India, and two directors representing the State Governments.

Achievements of NABARD

The NABARD is an apex institution in the organised rural credit structure. It plays an important role in reducing regional disparities and helps small farmers, marginal farmers and the weaker sections of the society. It channelises its refinance facilities for agricultural and rural development in the country through major financial intermediaries like SCBs, SLDBs, RRBs, commercial banks, etc.

1. *Short Term Credit.* During 2002-03, it sanctioned Rs. 8,764 crores as short term credit to SCBs and RRBs for financing seasonal agricultural operations, marketing of crops, purchase and distribution of fertilisers, and working capital requirements of cooperative sugar factories.

2. *Medium Term Credit.* The NABARD sanctioned Rs. 496 crores in 2002-03 as medium term credit to SCBs and RRBs for approved agricultural purposes.

3. *Long Term Credit.* The NABARD provides long term loans not exceeding 20 years to State Governments to enable them to contribute to the share capital of the cooperative credit institutions. In 2002-03 it sanctioned

Rs. 62 crores to State Governments for this purposes.

4. *Schematic Lending.* The NABARD provides refinance facilities relating to minor irrigation, land development, farm mechanisation, plantation, horticulture, poultry, sheep breeding, piggery, fisheries, dairy development, storage, market yards, IRDP, etc.

5. *Assistance to Non-Farm Sector.* The NABARD provides financial assistance to the non-farm sector. The ceiling on individual loans under Composite Loan Scheme is Rs. 50,000 and under Integrated Loan Scheme Rs. 7.5 lakhs to enable the financing banks to meet the credit requirements of entrepreneurs for setting up cottage, tiny, village and small scale industries. Further, State Cooperative Banks have been permitted to get refinance on an automatic basis from the NABARD through CCBs for financing industrial cooperative societies upto Rs. 7.5 lakhs. The Integrated Loan Scheme has also been extended to Land Development Banks for financing non-farm activities upto Rs. 7.5 lakhs. SCBs have been permitted to draw refinance on automatic basis for loans to industrial cooperative Societies for modernisation of existing units upto Rs. 7.5 lakhs. With the introduction of Swarnajayanti Gram Swarozgar Yojna from April 1999 in rural areas, the NABARD provides refinance to commercial banks for loans extended by them under the scheme. A wide spectrum of activities covering agricultural allied activities, industries, services and business that are bankable and viable are eligible for refinance.

6. *Other Types of Assistance.* The NABARD has started the following types of assistance recently:

(a) It undertakes on a modest scale cofinancing/direct financing of hi-tech and other special projects.

(b) Beginning 1995-96, it has started sanctioning a separate Short Term (Seasonal Agricultural Operations) Credit limit to each of the SCBs/RRBs operating in the 114 identified districts in the country.

(c) To step up credit flow to weaker sections including SCs/STs, the NABARD has earmarked a sum of Rs. 150 crores for refinance under the "SC/ST Action Plan" for allocation among commercial and cooperative banks. The level of refinance is 100 per cent.

7. *Institutional Development.* One of its important function is institutional development. In addition to inspection of cooperative banks and RRBs, it helps in their rehabilitation, reorganisation and re-establishment.

8. *Cooperative Development Fund (CDF).* NABARD set up CDF in 1993 for strengthening the cooperative credit institutions in the areas of organisational structure, human resource development, resource mobilisation, recovery position, etc. The assistance is provided to SCBs, CCBs, etc. by way of a grant or a soft loan or both. At the end of March 2003, cumulative loans sanctioned from CDF amounted to Rs.. 65 crores.

9. *Rural Infrastructure Development Fund {RIDF).* KIDF-I was set up in 1995-96 with a corpus of Rs. 2,000 crores for providing funds to State Governments and State owned corporations to enable them to complete various types of rural infrastructure projects. This scheme had been continued in subsequent years as RIDP-II with Rs. 2,500 crores in 1996-97, RIDF-III with Rs. 2,500 crores in 1997-98, RIDF-IV with Rs. 3,000 crores in 1998-99, RIDF-V with Rs. 3,500 crores in 1999-2000, RIDF-VI with Rs. 4,500 crores in 2000-01, RIDf-VII with Rs. 5,000 crores in 2001-02, RIDF-VIII with Rs. 5,500 crores in 2002-03 and RIDF-IX with Rs. 5,500 crores in 2003-04. The amount mobilised under various RIDF schemes amounted to Rs. 16,145 crores as at ending March 2002. The cumulative sanctions of loans under RIDF were Rs. 29,475 crores as at 31 March, 2003.

10. *Memorandum of Understandings (MOUs).* The NABARD signs MOUs with the' Cooperative banks and the concerned State Government for revamping and improving the cooperative credit structure. Similar MOUs exist between tthe RRBs and the sponsor banks.

11. *Research and Development.* It has been providing financial assistance for research and training to the staff of rural banking structure out of its R & D Fund and for strengthening the technical, monitoring, and evaluation cells of RRBs. Its three staff colleges, CAB, and Banker Rural Development Institute have been providing research and training facilities in rural credit and development to the staff of banks.

Despite its manifold achievements, NABARD has yet to become an apex regulator and development bank for farm lending.

Views of the Khusro Committee

The ACRS or Khusro Committee in its Report published in January 1989 pointed out certain weaknesses and made suggestions to improve the working of NABARD. Some of these are as under:

1. NABARD's activities in institutional development are primarily reactive rather than proactive in nature. It should therefore undertake a more effective role in institutional development, particularly with regard to cooperative development. Its role should be one of policy planning and review, besides extension of necessary financial assistance.

2. The inspection function of NABARD is not integrated with refinancing and institutional development function. It should redefine the purpose and objectives of inspections to facilitate such integration.

3. The training of NABARD's staff should be separated from that of client banks.

4. R & D Fund should be used much more aggressively and imaginatively to identify, evaluate, develop and promote new and practical initiatives in rural development.

5. It has to find resources to meet its client banks' demand for investment loans which it will have to provide in an increasing measure in the next 10-12 years. If NABARD has to expand its operations, either its equity base should be strengthened or low cost borrowings should be resorted to at a concessional rate of 5.5 per ceni from GOI/RBI.

6. There is lack of control over NABARD's member institutions. It should be rectified with the help of and in coordination with RBI.

The Khusro Committee observed, "If NABARD has to emerge as a strong development bank of rural regeneration, it has to take certain fresh initiatives. It should concentrate more on building up of the cooperatives, improve its functional capabilities in project identification, preparation, appraisal, and monitoring, forge a better linkage between inspection and function, pay greater attention to-the non-farm sector and staff training and extend its network to the district level. NABARD will have to play its part in open market borrowing also, so that it could meet its refinance commitments."

Conclusion

The Government has not implemented the recommendations of the Khusro Committee, except raising the issued capital of the NABARD to Rs. 5,000 crores. Mere increasing its capital base is not enough. What is important is that it should be allowed to keep its surpluses which are to be transferred to the Central Government and the RBI after 1997.

EXERCISES

1. Describe the objectives and working of Regional Rural Banks.
2. Discuss the working of Regional Rural Banks. Critically examine their achievements.
3. To what extent Regional Rural Banks have achieved their objectives? Suggest measures to improve their operations.
4. Describe the objectives and achievements of NABARD.
5. Explain the functions of NABARD.
6. Discuss the achievements of NABARD. Give suggestions for making improvement in its working.

CHAPTER 62

Exchange Banks

1. FUNCTIONS OF EXCHANGE BANKS

Exchange banks perform the following functions in India:

1. *Financing Exports.* The exchange banks facilitate the payment of goods exported. This is done through Document Against Acceptance (D.A.) Bill which the Indian exporter draws against the importer. This bill is sent to the importer through the exchange bank. The importer returns it to the exporter after acceptance and the latter discounts it from his exchange bank.

2. *Financing Imports.* The exchange banks also facilitate the financing of imports. When an Indian importer imports goods, he receives through the exchange bank on the basis of the Document Against Payment (D.P.) Bill drawn by the foreign exporter.

3. *Financing Internal Trade.* The exchange banks finance the internal trade of the country. They finance the movement of goods from one commercial centre to another. They advance loans to traders and discount their bills of exchange.

4. *General Banking Functions.* The exchange banks perform general banking functions like Indian banks such as accepting deposits, advancing loans, agency services, credit remittance facility, locker facility, stock invest facility, card facility, etc.

5. *Encourage Foreign Investments.* The exchange banks encourage the flow of foreign investments into India. Foreign investors usually rely on their banker's judgement for overseas investment. Exchange banks are an important medium for projecting the country's image abroad. They provide Indian corporations access to foreign collaborators as well as introduce foreign companies to Indian corporations.

6. *Access to International Capital Markets.* The exchange banks help in providing Indian corporations and government agencies access to international capital markets.

7. *Develop Expertise and Innovations.* The exchange banks help in developing expertise and innovations in several areas such as trade, finance, payment systems, currency and interest rate risk management and financial engineering. To the extent these help in improving the efficiency of Indian banks, competitiveness improves.

8. *Mobilising Funds from Non-Resident Indians.* The exchange banks help in mobilising deposits from non-resident Indians (NRI) abroad through their network of branches located in foreign countries.

9. *Canalising Agent.* The exchange banks play the role of canalising agents for foreign currency credits for major projects. For example, Grindlays helped in arranging credits for the HBJ gas pipeline.

10. *Revival of Sick Industries.* The exchange banks help in the revival of Indian sick industries by putting their Indian clients in touch with NRIs who might be willing to invest in the equity of firms in question, and also facilitate the transfer of technology.

11. *Cover the Risks of Exchange Rate.* The exchange banks cover the risks of exchange rate movements by booking forward contracts.

12. *Some Innovative Schemes.* Some exchange banks in India have started a number of new schemes for their clients which are as follows:

(a) General Purpose Loan. Some exchange banks offer the Freedom Finance Scheme whereby the client can avail of loan facility from Rs. 10,000 to 50,000 for expenditure like a marriage, a holiday or even an admission to an institute for higher studies.

(b) Fixed Deposits. The exchange banks have introduced an innovation in fixed deposits which they call under different names to attract customers. The Citibank has Unfixed Deposit, the Grindlays has an Easy Access Deposit and a High Performance Saving Account, and the Hongkong Bank the Smart Money Account. These banks provide the facility of withdrawing up to 75 per cent of the deposit to a depositor while paying 2 per cent interest during the withdrawal period over the overall interest earned for the deposit period.

(c) *Global Banking Systems (GBS).* GBS is the Bank of America's standard computer system which operates worldwide in Europe, Asia and America. GBS enables the BOA to provide its customers speedy and efficient service throughout the world. Banking services like funds transfers or letters of credit involving any of its branches worldwide are automatically transmitted through BOA global network of telecommunication.

(d) Finance Against Securities in Time. The Standard Chartered Bank has started Finance Against Securities in Time (FAST) facility which provides loans to all individuals who have invested in shares and other securities.

(e) Non-Fund Business. The exchange banks undertake non-fund business on a fairly substantial scale. It includes letters of credit for imports, advising of letters of credit to exporters, execution of overseas contracts, syndication of international loans, and public flotation of equities and debentures.

(f) Mutual Funds and Technology Funds. Several exchange banks have opened divisions like mutual funds and technology funds which provide venture capital for new and existing companies to expand, modernise and diversify.

(g) Merchant Banking. They are engaged in merchant banking, equipment leasing, housing finance, car finance, venture capital, factoring, etc.

2. WORKING OF EXCHANGE BANKS IN INDIA

The number of exchange banks, better known as foreign banks, operating in India at present is 36. They have a network of 204 branches. Among the biggest foreign banks in India are: Citi Bank, ANZ Grindlays Bank, Standard Chartered Bank, Hongkong Bank, American Express Bank, Bank of America, British Bank of Mideast, Bank of Tokyo, and Deutsche Bank.

For operating in India, every foreign bank is required to obtain a licence from the RBI. The licence is given with the condition that there should not be any discrimination against any Indian bank operating in that country to which the foreign bank belongs. A foreign bank is required to bring in $ 10 million for the first branch it sets up, $ 10 million for the second and $ 5 million for the third. It is also required to deposit with the RBI either in cash or in the form of unencumbered approved securities or both an amount equal to the amount specified above.

Every foreign bank operating in India is also required to deposit with the RBI at the end of each calendar year 20 per cent of its profits earned in India. Every foreign bank is further required to keep 12 per cent of the total of its time and demand liabilities with the RBI as CRR (Cash Reserve Ratio) which is interest free. In addition to the CRR, it is required to maintain in cash, gold or unencumbered securities, known as Statutory Liquidity Ratio (SLR) upto the level of its outstanding net demand and time liabilities equal to 25 per cent with effect from 13 April, 1996. Every foreign bank is required to maintain its assets equivalent to not less than 85 per cent of its demand and time liabilities in India at the close of business on the last Friday of every quarter.

Foreign banks operating in India are required to comply with the capital adequacy norm of 8 per cent from 1 April, 1993 which they have achieved.

The foreign banks operating in India are required to provide a minimum of 32 per cent of their net outstanding advances to the priority sector in India every year. It is inclusive of the sub-targets of 10 per cent each in respect of credit for exports and small scale industries, the shortfall, if any, in the overall target as well as sub-targets has to be made good by placing deposits with the Small Industries Development Bank of India (SIDBI) at a rate of 8 per cent with effect from March 1995.

For opening a new branch or to change the location of an existing branch, a foreign bank is required to take prior permission of the RBI. With effect from 22 April, 1992, they have been permitted to expand branches on considerations of national advantage from the viewpoint of facilitating exports and investment, with no change in other conditions.

They are also required to submit the various statements of their assets, liabilities, investments and advances, etc. to the RBI as per the RBI guidelines. Besides, the RBI is empowered to inspect their books and accounts whenever it deems essential from time to time.

The performance of 36 foreign banks in India during 2002-03 showed decrease in their income by 7.10 per cent over 2001-02, operating profits by 6.10 per cent, net profits by 22.25 per cent and total assets by 2.72 per cent.

The foreign banks have an edge over Indian banks in the spheres of customer service and technology back-up.[1]

3. DEFECTS IN THE WORKING OF EXCHANGE BANKS

Despite better and efficient working of exchange banks, these banks have certain defects in their working from the Indian viewpoint. These arise from the liberal attitude of the Reserve Bank of India towards them. Some of the defects are :

1. *Vast Funds in Non-Costing Deposits.* The exchange banks hold vast funds in their non-costing current accounts. They are able to invest out of them at prescribed rates of interest so that their margin of profits on these no-cost funds increases. In the case of nationalised banks the share of non-costing current Accounts in total deposits is IS per cent whereas in the case of exchange banks it is 21 per cent. Thus their deposits cost them less as compared to Indian banks. As a result, they earn more profits than Indian banks.

2. *Large Non-Fund Business.* The exchange banks undertake non-fund business on a fairly large scale. The combined average ratio of non-fund income of exchange banks is 13 per cent against 9.0 per cent in the case of nationalised banks, except the State Bank of India. Consequently, they are able to earn more profits than Indian banks. This is because of their monopolistic position in foreign business.

3. *Ignore Term Advances.* The exchange banks ignore such advances as term loans, hypothecation advances and other short term advances, But they engage themselves in bill business for very short periods of 30 to 90 days with the result that their current account funds increase. They are able to invest these funds for short periods in the inter-bank call, money market ancl earn interest

4. *Ignore Priority Sectors.* They are required to lend 32 per cent of net bank credit to priority sectors including 10 per cent for exports. But in 1999-2000, they lent 22.5 per cent for exports and 10.2 per cent to SSIs and ignored all other priority sectors.

5. *Operate Funds Management Schemes.* Due to the liberal policy of RBI, the exchange banks accept funds under the funds management schemes. These funds are not considered deposits. They are treated as non-statutory because the banks are not required to maintain the prescribed Cash Reserve Ratio (CRR) and Statutory Liquidity- Ratio (SLR) on these Funds. These banks are making a profit of about Rs. 200 crores annually from these funds.

6. *Discriminate against Indian Firms.* The exchange banks discriminate against Indian trading firms. They offer D.P. Bills to Indian importers whereby they are required to make full payment in order to get possession of goods. On the other hand, the Indian exporters are required to export goods against D.A. Bills whereby they receive deferred payments.

7. *Encourage Foreign Shipping and Insurance Companies.* These banks generally force Indian exporters and importers to get the services of foreign shipping and insurance companies. This goes against the interests of Indians.

8. *Unhealthy Competition with Indian Banks.* Due to their superior management techniques, larger funds and RBI's liberal policy towards them, the exchange banks have been able to provide better services and higher interest rates to their customers. This has led to unhealthy competition with Indian banks. As a result, their profits have been rising at a much higher rate than those of Indian banks.

9. *Foreign Links.* The exchange banks being foreign banks have links in foreign countries where they have their head offices. Their directors, shareholders and management are entirely foreign. So their main

---

1. We have not studied Indian banks operating abroad as Exchange banks as they operate as foreign banks in other countries. However, for the information of readers, there are 8 nationalised Indian banks and one private scheduled bank with 93 branches and 17 representative offices operating abroad in 25 countries.

interest is to earn higher profits, part of which are taken away.

10. *Hindrance to Bill Market.* They are a hindrance to the development of Indian Bill Market because they discount the export bills in London Bill Market while the import bills are fully paid before the delivery of goods.

11. *Help Transfer Illegal Money.* The exchange banks help transfer the i! illegal money kept abroad into Foreign Currency Non-Resident (FCNR) deposits oi their branches. Thus they encourage black money within the country.

4. SUGGESTIONS FOR IMPROVEMENT

A number of suggestions have been made to improve the working of exchange banks in India so that they may be more helpful to the economy. Some of the suggestions are:

1. *No Preferential Treatment.* The exchange banks operating in India should be treated at par with Indian commercial banks.

2. *Restriction on Branch Expansion.* RBI should not allow exchange banks to open more branches in the country so that their activities are confined to port cities and big commercial centres. RBI has done well in asking the exchange banks to bring in an initial capital of Rs. 15 crore in foreign exchange to open a branch.

3. *Restriction on Non-Costing Deposits.* The exchange banks encourage the opening of current accounts by multinational corporations and big industrial houses because they bring them more profits without payinp interest. They do not welcome small depositors. RBI should direct them to accept small saving deposits and place a limit on non-costing deposits.

4. *Restriction on Funds Management'Schemes.* The exchange banks are earning huge profits by accepting money under the funds management schemes which are not considered deposits. RBI should place restrictions on such schemes by asking these banks to maintain the prescribed Cash Reserve Ratio and the Statutory Liquidity Ratio on these funds as applicable to Indian banks.

5. *Regulation of Lendmg Activities.* The exchange banks are allowed to undertake lending, advancing and investment activities without much restriction. RBI should regulate such activities. They should be directed to give more advances for long term and invest in Indian companies rather in multinationals operating in India.

6. *Participate in Social Banking.* The exchange banks participate less in social banking. RBI should direct them to lend more to small scale industry sector, retail trade, self-employed persons, etc.

7. *Limit on Repatriation of Profits.* As exchange banks in Indian earn huge profits, they also repatriate huge sums to their head offices abroad, even after keeping 20 per cent of their annual profits with RBI. Recently, RBI has asked these banks to keep another 20 per cent of their profits in the Indian books. This is not enough. They should be asked to keep at least 50 per cent of their profits in India.

8. *Removal of Discrimination against Indian Importers.* The exchange banks should remove discrimination against Indian importers by offering them D.A. Bills, as is the practice in advanced countries.

9. *Indians in Management.* All exchange banks operating in India should be directed to have at least one Indian on the Management working in India.

10. *No Mergers.* The exchange banks operating in India should not be allowed to merge their branches without the permission of the Reserve Bank.

11..*No Control over Indian Banks.* The exchange banks should not be allowed to have any type of direct or indirect control over Indian banks. They should not be permitted to acquire the shares of Indian banks.

12. *No Association.* The exchange banks operating in India should not be allowed to form any association without the permission of RBI.

5. PARTICIPATION OF INDIAN BANKS IN FINANCING FOREIGN TRADE

There were 93 branches, including off-share branches and mobile agencies of 8 public sector banks and one Indian private sector bank, operating in foreign countries as on September, 2002. These branches are spread over 25 countries and located in major international centres like London, New York, etc. They specialise in various areas of international banking including financing of foreign trade. Besides these branches, they are having 17 representative offices and also 15 wholly owned subsidiaries and 5 joint ventures in various countries of the world.

The commercial banks help in receiving payments from the overseas importers and to make payments ɔ overseas exporters. But Indian banks mostly finance export trade. They meet the credit needs of the xporters both at the preshiptnent and post-shipment stages. The exporter requires pre-shipment credit in rder to manufacture or assemble the goods meant for export. The exporter can also obtain pre-shipment nance from his bank in two ways: *(i)* By asking the overseas buyer to open in his favour an anticipatory letter f credit; and *(ii)* By applying for an export packing credit to his bank. It is granted by the bank against goods armarked for export by lodging the letter of credit covering the export order to the bank.

The commercial banks in India also grant medium term advances ranging trom 6 months to 5 years gainst the deferred instalments receivable from importers. The exporter furnishes to his bank the promissory ote executed by him or a guarantee from the importer's bank covering the deferred payment receivable.

In November 1992, all scheduled commercial banks were asked to reach an export credit target of 10 per ent of each bank's net bank credit by June 1993. The RBI stated that failure to achieve the stipulated target of xport credit and/or failure to achieve this would invite raising of reserve requirements and withdrawal of finance facilities. In April 1993, the rediscounting of export bills abroad was allowed at rates linked to aternational rates. The RBI also fixes interest rate structure for advances of scheduled commercial banks for xports. It is for pre-shipment credit, post-shipment credit, usance bills and deferred credit for the period eyond 180 days. The interest rates usually range between 13 to 15 per cent. Besides, the RBI provides export edit rupee refinance to scheduled commercial banks to the extent of 60 per cent of increase in outstanding xport credit. The refinance facility provided against post-shipment export credit in US dollars is equivalent to 00 per cent of outstanding credit.

Prior to 1982, the refinance, facility for financing foreign trade was being provided by the Reserve Bank. ut with the establishment of the Export-Import (Exim) Bank of India on 1 January, 1982, the refinance business as also been entrusted to this Bank. The main objective of the bank is to provide financial assistance to xporters and importers, and to function as the principal financial institution for coordinating the working of stitutions engaged in financing export and import of goods and services with a view to promoting the ountry's international trade. Thus the Exim bank extends direct and indirect financial assistance in the short, edium and long-term for the promotion of international trade, and acts as an apex body for coordinating the tivities of institutions engaged in similar business. The Exim Bank is empowered for the purpose of export d import to extend loans and advances to banks or financial institutions, to provide refinance facilities, nder international merchant banking services, extend buyer's credit and lines of credit to parties, including reign governments and financial institutions, outside India, finance Indian joint ventures abroad, deal in reign exchange, and undertake and finance technical consultancy services.

Presently, the Exim Bank refinances only the export trade of India and the financing of imports has been ft entirely to foreign banks, the ICICI (Industrial Credit and Investment Corporation of India), the World ank, etc. The short term requirements of exporters are largely met by the commercial banks. The Exim Bank ncentrates mainly on medium and long term credit for export of goods and services on deferred terms. It fers credit on liberal terms to enable Indian exporters to compete in international markets. It extends ancial assistance to foreign buyers for the purchase of Indian goods. It also gives financial assistance to dian promoters towards their equity participation in joint ventures abroad.

Thus the participation of Indian banks in financing foreign trade is limited only to exports and the ancing of imports is done by exchange banks, the ICICI, the World Bank, etc.

EXERCISES

1. Explain the functions of exchange banks.
2. In what ways the exchange banks are harmful to Indian interest? What measures do you suggest to nove these defects?
3. To what extent Indian banks participate in financing India's foreign trade?
4. Write a note on the participation of Indian banks in financing foreign trade of India.

CHAPTER

63

Commercial Bank in India

The joint stock banks in India are the most important segment of the Indian banking system. They a the major source of institutional credit in India. They are commercial banks registered under the India Companies Act, 1936 and are also governed by the Indian Banking Regulation Act, 1949.

1. CLASSIFICATION OF COMMERCIAL BANKS

Indian joint stock banks or commercial banks are classified on statutory and ownership basis.

On the statutory basis, they are further classified into scheduled banks and non-scheduled banks.

A *scheduled bank* is one which has been included in the second schedule of the Reserve Bank of India A 1934. To be a scheduled bank, it must be financially and economically sound and satisfy the following thr conditions: (i) it must have a paid-up capital and reserves of an aggregate value of not less than Rs 5 lakhs; (its affairs are not being or likely to be conducted in a manner detrimental to the interests of its depositors; (i it must be a joint stock company and not a sole trader or partnership firm. Besides, it is required to keep certain percentage of its cash reserves with the RBI and submit periodical returns to the latter under t Banking Regulation Act, 1949. In return, the scheduled bank receives concessional remittance and borrowi facilities from the RBI or its agents.

On the other hand, a non-scheduled bank is that which has not been included in the second schedule the RBI Act, 1934. But is subject to the statutory cash reserve requirements which it is required to keep wi itself and not with the RBI. It is not entitled to concessional remittance and borrowing facilities from the R There were 95 scheduled commercial banks in India having 5 1.970 branches as on 30 June 2003. Of these were State Bank of India and its associate banks with 13.499 branches: 19 nationalised banks with 32,6 branches; 32 Indian private sector banks (23 old + 9 new) with 5.624 branches; and 36 foreign banks with 2 branches. There are also 196 Regional Rural Bank which are sponsored by scheduled commercial banks B they are considered as rural banks even though they perform as commercial banks also. There is no nc scheduled bank in India.

On the *basis of ownership,* banks are classified into public sector banks and private sector banks. A pub sector bank is a Government of India undertaking and a private sector bank is owned by the shareholde Both types cjf banks perform the same functions, pay and charge the same rates of interest, and also pay t same salary and allowances to their staff, except the non-scheduMJd banks. Hie first public sector bank w established in India on 1 July, 1955 fwith the nationalisation of Imperial Bank of India as State Bank of India lias seven subsidiaries which were nationalised in 1959. These seven associate banks are State Bank of Hyderaba State Bank of Jaipur and Bikaner, State Bank of Travancore, State Bank of Mysore, State Bank of Patiala, St Bank of Indore, and State Bank of Saurashtra.

On 19 July 1969, fourteen major scheduled banks were nationalised. They are: Allahabad Bank-, Bank Baroda, Bank of India, Bank of Maharashtra, Canara Bank, Central Bank of India, Dena Bank, Indian Ba Indian Overseas Bank, Punjab National Bank, Syndicate Bank, Union Bank of India, United Bank of India, a United Commercial Bank. Six more scheduled banks were nationalised on 15 April 1980. They are And ank, Corporation Bank, New Bank of India) Oriental Bank of Commerce, Punjab and Sind Bank and Vijaya ank. New Bank of India was merged with Punjab National Bank with effect from 4 September 1993.

The regional rural banks which have been sponsored by the nationalised banks are also public sector ınks which at present number 196. Thus the total public sector banks in India are 223 comprising State Bank ᶠ India arid its 7 subsidiaries, 19 nationalised banks and 196 regional rural banks.

2. FUNCTIONS OF INDIAN COMMERCIAL BANKS

The Indian joint stock banks are in fact commercial banks which perform a number of functions and nder a variety of ancillary services. The Banking Regulation Act, 1949 lists them as under:

(1) the borrowing, raising or taking of deposits of money;

(2) the lending or advancing of money either with or without security;

(3) the drawing, making, accepting, discounting, buying, selling, collecting and dealing with bills of change, bundis, promissory notes, coupons, drafts, bills of lading, railway receipts, warrants, debentures, rtificates, scrips and other securities whether transferable or negotiable or not;

(4) the granting and issuing of letters of credit, travellers' cheques and circular notes;

(5) the buying, selling and dealing in bullion and species;

(6) the buying and selling of foreign exchange, including foreign bank notes;

(7) the acquiring, holding, issuing on commission, underwriting and dealing in stock, funds, shares, bentures, stock, bonds, obligations, securities and invest" ments of all kinds;

(8) the purchasing and selling of bonds, scrips or other forms of securities on behalf of constituents or ners;

(9) the negotiation of loans and advances;

(10) the receiving of all kinds of bonds, scrips or valuables on deposit or for safe custody or otherwise;

(11) the providing of safe deposit vaults for custody of valuables of customers;

(12) the collecting and transmitting of money and securities;

(13) the acting of agents for any government or local authority or any other person or persons, but not managing agent or secretary and treasury of a company;

(14) the contracting of private and public loans and negotiating and issuing them;

(15) the insuring, guaranteeing, underwriting, participating in managing and carrying out of any issue of ıns or securities made by state, municipality, company, corporation or any other association, and also ıding for the purpose;

(16) the carrying on and transacting every kind of guarantee" and indemnity business;

(17) the managing, selling and realising any property which may come into its possession in satisfaction ıts claims;

(18) the acquiring, holding and dealing with any property or any .right, titie-or interest therein which ms the security for any loans or advances sanctioned;

(19) the undertaking and executing of trusts, as also administering estates as executor, trustee or otherwise;

(20) the establishing and supporting or aiding in the establishment of associations, institutions, funds, sts and conveniences for the benefit of its present and past employees and their dependents, and granting guaranteeing moneys for charitable purposes;

(21) the acquiring, constructing, maintaining and altering of any building or works necessary for its rposes;

(22) the selling, improving, managing, developing, exchanging, leasing, mortgaging, disposing of or erwise dealing with any of its properties and rights;

(23) the taking over and undertaking the whole or any part of (he business of any person or company en such business is of a nature described above;

(24) the doing of all such other things as are incidental or conducive to the promotion and advancement ts business, such as giving an opinion as to its customer's financial standing as a referee; and

(25) the engaging in any other form of business which the Central Government specifies to be lawful.

Besides, the Indian joint stock banks have started performing a number of other functions in recent years, such as issuing credit cards, setting of mutual funds, engaging in merchant banking, giving advances to priority sectors like agriculture, small scale industries, retail trade, small business, professional and self-employed persons, consumption loans, education loans, housing loans, etc.[1]

3. WORKING RESULTS OF SCHEDULED COMMERCIAL BANKS

The total deposits of scheduled commercial banks accounted for 79.8 per cent of their total liabilities and their loans and advances 43.6 per cent of their total assets as on 31 March 2003. The total income of 95 scheduled commercial tanks was 10.1 per cent, total expenditure 9.1 per cent, operating profit 2.4 per cent and net profit 1.0 per cent of their total assets in 2002-03. The credit-deposit ratio of these banks was 59.4 per cent, cash balance-deposit ratio 6.35 per cent and investment-deposit ratio 51.17 per cent during this year. The ratio of net non-performing assets (NPAs) to net advances was 4.4 per cent and to total assets 1.9. per cent as on 31 March 2003.

EXERCISES

1. Give the classification of joint Stock Banks in India.
2. Distinguish between a scheduled bank and non-scheduled bank
3. Describe the functions of Indian scheduled commercial banks.
4. Describe the working of scheduled commercial banks in India. Point out their defects.

1. For their defects, refer to section 5 of the Chapter "Recent Trends in the Indian Banking System".

CHAPTER 64

Banking Legislation in India

Banks deal with the money of a large number of depositors who do not have any say in their working. Banking legislation is enacted to safeguard the interest of the depositors and the shareholders of banks.

The first attempt at banking legislation in India was the passing of the Indian Companies (Amendment) Act, 1936 which contained special provisions relating to banking companies. Prior to that they were governed by the general provisions of the Indian Companies Act, 1913. The Indian Companies (Amendment) Act, 1936 was subsequently amended in 1942 to incorporate a few more provisions concerning banks. But the years following this amendment led to a mushroom growth of banking companies in India which ultimately led the Government alter Independence to pass a comprehensive law exclusively for their regulation and control under the name of Banking Companies Act, 1949 which was renamed as the Banking Regulation Act, 1949.

This Act has been amended a number of times to suit the needs of changing circumstances and to plug the loopholes found in its provisions. Its two important amendments have been: (1) the Banking Companies (Acquisition and Transfer of Undertakings) Act, 1970 whereby the Government nationalised 14 banks, and the Banking Companies (Acquisition and Transfer of Undertakings) Act, 1980 nationalising 6 more scheduled banks; and (2) the Banking Laws (Amendment) Act, 1983 which amended the following banking legislation: Bankers' Book Evidence Act, 1891; Reserve Bank of India Act, 1934; Banking Regulation Act, 1949; State Bank of India Act, 1955; State Bank of India (Subsidiary Banks) Act, 1959; Deposit Insurance and Credit Guarantee Corporation Act, 1961; Banking Companies (Acquisition and Transfer of Undertakings) Act, 1970; Regional Rural Banks Act, 1976; Banking Companies (Transfer and Acquisition of Undertakings) Act, 1980; and Banking Companies (Acquisition and Transfer of Undertakings) Amendment Act, 1994.

Another important banking legislation has been the Banking Laws (Application to Cooperative Societies) Act, 1966 which brought the cooperative societies under the RBI's statutory control by including the State Cooperative Banks in the Second Schedule of the RBI.

1. BANKING REGULATION ACT, 1949

The Banking Regulation Act, 1949 as amended up-to-date contains the following five parts:

Part I: Preliminary (Sections 1 to 5A).

Part II: Business of Banking Companies (Sections 6 to 36A).

Part IIA: Control and Management (Sections 6 to 36A).

Part IIB: Prohibition of Certain Activities in Relation to Banking Companies (Section 36AD).

Part IIC: Acquisition of the Undertakings of Banking Companies in Certain Cases (Sections 36AE to 36AJ).

Part III: Suspension of Business and Winding up of Banking Companies (Sections 36 to 45).

Part IIIA: Special Provision of Speedy Disposal of Winding up Proceedings (Sections 45A to 45X).

Part IIIB: Provisions relating to Certain Operations of Banking Companies (Sections 45Y to 45ZF).

Part IV: Miscellaneous (Sections 46 to 55).

Part V: Main Provisions as Applicable to Cooperative Banks (Section 56).

The above details reveal that the Act contains 56 sections, Parts I, II, IIA, IIB, and IIIB are important because they relate to a banking company as a going concern. The last Section 56 relates to cooperative banks.

We give below some of the important provisions of the Act.

1. *Definition of a Banking Company.* The Act defines the term 'Banking' as "accepting, for the purpose of lending or investment, of deposits of money from the public, repayable on demand or otherwise, and withdrawable by cheque, draft, order, or otherwise". It also defines a banking company as "any company which transacts the business of banking in India". As such, it performs the functions of accepting deposits and lending or investing the same.

2. *Minimum Capital Requirements.* The Act prescribes minimum capital requirement for banking companies. A banking company incorporated *outside* India (i.e. foreign bank) is required to have its paid-up capital and reserves of the aggregate value of not less than Rs. 15 lakhs, but if it has a place or places of business in the city of Mumbai or Kolkata, or both, Rs. 20 lakhs. It is also required to deposit with the RBI either in cash or in the form of unencumbered approved securities or both an amount equal to the minimum capital specified above (i.e. Rs. 15 lakhs or Rs. 20 lakhs). The Act also requires a foreign banking company to deposit with the RBI at the end of each calendar year 20 per cent of its profit earned in India. On the other hand, a banking company incorporated within India is required to have paid-up capital and reserves of an aggregate value of not less than Rs. 5 lakh. If it has business in more than one State, and if any such place is situated in the city of Bombay, or Calcutta, or both, Rs. 10 lakhs. The subscribed capital of a banking company should not be less than *one half* of its authorised capital, and the paid-up capital should not be less than *one half of* the subscribed capital.

3. *Reserve Fund.* Every banking company incorporated *within* India is required to create a Reserve Fund and to transfer to such Fund, before any dividend is declared, 20 per cent of its profit.

4. *Cash Reserve.* Every scheduled bank is required to keep 3 per cent of the total of its time and demand liabilities with the RBI as cash reserve which is interest-free. But a non-scheduled bank is permitted to maintain its cash reserve either (i) with itself; or (ii) in current account opened with the RBI or the State Bank of India, or any other bank notified by the Central Government for the purpose; or *(iii)* partly in cash with itself or partly in such account or accounts. The cash reserve ratio (CRR) can be raised up to 15 per cent. The CRR is 15 per cent with effect from 1 July, 1989.

5. *Maintenance of Liquid Assets.* Maintenance of adequate liquid assets is essential for sound banking. The Act requires every bank to maintain in cash, gold or unencumbered approved securities not less than 25 per cent of the total of its demand and time liabilities in India. The RBI is empowered to step up the Statutory Liquidity Ratio (SLR) to 40 per cent. Since 4 April, 1992, the SLR has been fixed at 30 per cent. The SLR is in addition to the CRR which a bank is required to maintain with the RBI.

6. *Maintenance of Assets in India.* Every bank is required to maintain its assets equivalent to not less than 75 per cent of its demand and time liabilities in India at the close of business on the last Friday of every quarter.

7. *Management of Banking Companies.* The Act has also tried to tone up the administration and management of banks. It lays down that no banking company can employ or be managed by a managing agent, or any person who has been declared an insolvent, or has been convicted by a criminal court of an offence involving moral turpitude, or who takes a commission or a share in the profits of the company, or is a director of any other company, or engaged in any other business or vocation, or has a contract with the company for a period exceeding five years at a time, or whose remuneration is excessive in the opinion of the RBI.

8. *Prohibitions and Restrictions on Banking Companies.* To safeguard the interests of depositors, the Act provides for a number of prohibitions and restrictions on the banking companies. They are as under:

(i) The Act prohibits a banking company from engaging directly or indirectly in trading activities and undertaking trade risks.

(ii) It prohibits a banking company from holding any immovable property, howsoever acquired, except for its own use, for a period exceeding 7 years from its acquisition.

(iii) A banking company cannot form any subsidiary company.

(iv) It cannot hold shares in any company exceeding 30 per cent of the paid-up share capital of that company, or its own capital and reserves, whichever is less.

(v) It cannot grant any loan or advance on the security of its own shares, or on behalf of or to any of its

directors, any firm in which any of its directors is interested as partner, manager, employee or guarantor, or any company in which any of its directors has substantial interest of any kind, or to any individual, in whom any of its directors is a partner or guarantor.

(vi) A banking company cannot create a charge upon its unpaid capital. It cannot create a floating charge on the company or any of its property or any of its parts unless the RBI certifies that the creation of such floating charge shall not be detrimental to the interests of its depositors.

(vii) A banking company is prohibited from payment of dividend until all its capitalised expenses have been completely written off.

(viii) A director of a banking company, other than the chairman or the whole time director, cannot be continued for more than eight years.

(ix) The Act prohibits violent demonstrations by bank employees or by others within the premises of a banking company.

9. *Powers of the Reserve Bank of India.* The Act confers wide powers on the RBI to control and regulate the working of banking companies. Some of these are as under:

(i) No banking company can operate in India without getting a licence from the RBI. The Reserve Bank issues a licence, if it is satisfied that the banking company is or will be in a position to pay its present or future depositors in full; that its operations are not detrimental to the interests of its depositors; that it has adequate capital structure and earning prospect; that public interest will be served by it; and that it would not be prejudicial to the operation and consolidation of the banking system. If the banking company is incorporated *outside* India, then an additional condition for the grant of licence is that there should not be any discrimination against Indian banking companies operating in that country to which the foreign bank belongs.

(ii) The Act requires every banking company, Indian as well as foreign, to take prior permission of the RBI for opening a new branch or to change the location of an existing branch in India.

(iii) Every banking company is required to submit the following return/statements: monthly return of liquid assets and liabilities; quarterly return of assets and liabilities; return of unclaimed deposits; and half-yearly returns regarding the investments of a banking company and the classification of its advances in respect of industry, commerce, and agriculture.

(iv) The RBI is empowered to inspect any banking company and its books and accounts.

(v) The Act confers powers on the RBI to issue directions from time to time to banking companies generally or to any banking company in particular in the public interest or in the interest of banking policy or in the interest of depositors, or to secure the proper management of any banking company.

(vi) The RBI has been given wide powers to issue directions to the banking companies to control advances. The directions may relate to: (a) the purpose for which advances may or may not be made; *(b)* the margins to be maintained in respect of secured advances; (c) the maximum amount of advance to any one company, firm, individual, or association of persons; *(d)* the maximum amount up to which guarantees may be given by the banking company on behalf of any one company, firm etc., and *(e)* the rate of interest and other terms and conditions on which advances or guarantees may be given.

(vii) No bank can remit, without the prior approval of the RBI any debt due to it by any of its directors, or by any firm, company or individual in which any of its directors may be interested.

(viii) It is empowered to inspect a bank thoroughly and without previous notice and to order the bank to rectify actions which it considers unsound, unsafe of antisocial.

(ix) Every bank has to obtain the prior consent of the RBI for all advances of Rs.. 5 crores and over to any one borrower.

(x) The Act requires every banking company to take prior approval of the RBI for the appointment, reappointment or termination of chairman, managing or wholetime director, manager or chief executive officer.

(xi) It empowers the RBI to appoint one or more additional directors of a banking company but not exceeding 5 or one-third of the maximum strength of the Board of Directors, whichever is less.

(xii) The RBI is empowered to acquire the undertaking of any banking company, or to approve its merger with any other bank.

(xiii) The RBI is authorised to publish any information relating to banking companies in such consolidated

form as it thinks fit, and as such brings out many reports and brochures relating to the trend and progress of banking in India.

CONCLUSION

The Banking Regulation Act, 1949 as amended up-to-date is a very comprehensive piece of legislation which has played an important role in establishing the banking system on sound lines throughout the country and providing stability and flexibility to the Indian monetary system in keeping with the overall objective of growth and stability.

2. BANKING AMENDMENT ACT, 1994

The Banking Companies (Acquisition and Transfer of Undertakings) Amendment Act, 1994 amends the Banking Companies Acts of 1970 and 1980 whereby 14 and 6 scheduled commercial banks were nationalised respectively. The present Act provides for partial privatisation of these banks which are 19 at present with the merger of New Bank of India with the Punjab National Bank in 1993. The main features of the amendments are:

(1) The authorised capital of every nationalised bank has been set at Rs. 1,500 crores divided into Rs. 150 crores fully paid up shares of Rs. 10 each.

(2) The Centre may, after consultation with the RBI and by notification in t:ie official gazette, increase or reduce the authorised capital subject of the condition that the authorised capital shall not exceed Rs. 3,000 crores or be less than Rs. 1,500 crores.

(3) The Central Government shall retain 51 per cent of the share in these banks and private individuals and companies, including NRIs shall hold upto 49 per cent of their shares.[1]

(4) However, the holdings of NRIs, including companies not registered in India, shall not be more than 20 per cent of the 49 per cent private shares.

(5) The shares not held by the Central Government shall be freely transferable.

(6) No shareholder other than the Union Government shall be entitled to exercise voting rights in respect of any shares held by them in excess of one per cent of the total voting rights of all shareholders of the bank.

(7) Each bank shall have 15 Directors on the Board, out of which 9 shall be nominated by the Central Government, and the other six shall be non-official nominees. There shall be one Directör from among the workmen of the bank and one from other employees.'

(8) Every bank shall ensure that its total capital equals at least 8 per cent of its risk weighted assets-by 31 March, 1996.

EXERCISES

1. Explain the provisions of the Banking Regulation Act, 1949.
2. Discuss the main powers of the Reserve Bank of India under the Banking Regulation Act, 1949.
3. Discuss the main,provisions of the Banking Regulation Act, 1949 with regard to: (i) Requirement as to minimum paid-up Capital and Reserve, *(it)* Restrictions on Loans and Advances, (iii) Cash and Liquid Asset Reserves.
4. Write a note on Banking Companies (Acquisition and Transfer) Amendment Act of 1994.

---

1. By an amendment to the 1994 Act in 2000 the Government has reduced its minimum shareholding in nationalised banks from 51 to 33 percent.

CHAPTER 65

Nationalisation of Commercial Banks

1. INTRODUCTION

Prior to 1949, commercial banks in India were exclusively owned, controlled and managed by private entrepreneurs and shareholders. The process of nationalisation of banks began when the Reserve Bank of India was nationalised on 1 January, 1949 with the passing of the Reserve Bank (Transfer of Public Ownership) Act, 1948. It was essential to nationalise the RBI as the central bank of the country in order to ensure greater coordination of monetary, economic and fiscal policies in independent India which was to embark itself on the path to planned economic development.

But the first step towards the nationalisation of commercial banks was taken with the nationalisation of the Imperial Bank of India as the State Bank of India on 1 July, 1955. The second step was taken when 7 State-associated banks were nationalised as subsidiaries of the State Bank of India in 1959. These seven associate banks are: the State Bank of Hyderabad, the State Bank of Jaipur and Bikaner, the State Bank of Travancore, the State Bank of Mysore, the State Bank of Patiala, the State Bank of Indore, and the State Bank of Saurashtra.

The third major step was the nationalisation of 14 major commercial banks with deposits exceeding Rs. 50 crores each on 19 July 1969. They are: Allahabad Bank, Bank of Baroda, Bank of India, Bank of Maharashtra, Canara Bank, Central Bank of India, Dena Bank, Indian Bank, Indian Overseas Bank, Punjab National Bank, Syndicate Bank, Union Bank of India, United Bank of India, and United Commercial Bank.

The last step was the nationalisation of 6 more commercial banks on 15 April 1980. They were: Andhra Bank, Corporation Bank, New Bank of India, Oriental Bank of Commerce, Punjab and Sind Bank, and Vijaya Bank. At the time of nationalisation, each one of these had crossed the deposit mark of Rs. 200 crores, though at the time of nationalisation of 14 banks their individual deposits were below Rs. 50 crores.

In June 1996, there were 19 nationalised banks, New Bank of India was merged with Punjab National Bank in 1993.

We discuss below the justification, objectives, achievements and failures of nationalisation of commercial banks in India. As nationalisation of major commercial banks is an established fact now, the case against nationalisation is uncalled for and hence of purely academic interest.

2. JUSTIFICATION FOR NATIONALISATION OF COMMERCIAL BANKS

The nationalisation of the commercial banks in India was a very controversial issue till the nationalisation of 14 major banks in July, 1969. A number of arguments were advanced by economists, political leaders, bankers, workers, and the public in support of nationalisation of banks which are enumerated below:

1. *Neglect of Priority Sectors.* A major charge against banks in India was that they advanced loans to large scale industries, and neglected the priority sectors such as agriculture, small scale industries, etc. The banks advanced 60% of the total bank credit to big industries and 19% to trade in March 1968. On the other hand, the share of agriculture was 2.2%, of small industries 6.9%, and of retail trade less than 2% in the total bank credit. It would be possible to direct bank credit on a large scale through bank nationalisation.

2. *Neglect of Plan Priorities.* Another charge was that commercial banks neglected plan priorities and diverted credit into less important channels. Bank nationalisation would help the Government in directing bank credit in accordance with plan priorities.

3. *High Profits.* It was alleged, that banks earned huge profits which were disproportionate to the capital invested in the banks. The ratio of profits of scheduled banks before tax to the paid-up capital and reserve increased from 12.2% to 42.5% in 1968. In other words, they earned Rs. 42.5 crores annually. On the other hand, their capital base was declining. The ratio of paid-up capital and reserves to deposits fell from 9.7% in 1951 to 2.6% in 1968. This was in contravention of RBI's directives to banks to keep at least 6% of their deposit liabilities in reserve. Whereas the banks earned huge profits and used them for their interests, the shareholders earned almost nothing because they had hardly more than 1% of deposits as share capital. This was one of the arguments advanced by the Government for bank nationalisation.

4. *Funds for Plans.* By nationalising the banks, these huge profits of the banks would be available to the Government for financing plans and achieving the plan objectives.

5. *Concentration of Economic Power.* It was alleged that commercial banks had led to the concentration of wealth and economic power in the hands of a few big business houses and industrialists. For instance, the Central Bank of India Ltd. was being controlled by the Tatas, the Bank of India Ltd. by the Mafatlals, the Punjab National Bank Ltd. by the Dalmias, the United Commercial Bank Ltd. by the Birlas, etc. These big business houses, in turn, controlled a number of industries, thereby enjoying a virtual monopoly in their business.

Moreover, about 90% members of the Board of Directors of banks consisted of industrialists and big businessmen. A single director of a bank was a common director of many other industrial concerns and with his control over the bank he was able to turn the bank for the benefit of his industrial house. This interlocking of directorship in banks led to unusually high amount of credit to big business houses. Bank nationalisation was, therefore, essential to stop the misuse of the resources of the banks for the benefit of directors and their concerns, and to reduce the concentration of economic power and wealth in a few hands.

6. *Socialist Arguments.* It was argued that bank nationalisation,was essential for the attainment of a socialist society in India. Such a step would not only reduce concentration of economic power and wealth but also give the State, control over the resources of the banks to be utilised for the masses.

7. *Regional Imbalances.* It was alleged that commercial banks were increasing regional imbalances. Banking was concentrated in big cities, urban centres and a few States. The Gadgil Study Group of the National Credit Council (1969) vividly brought out the imbalances in banking in the country. It pointed out that till December 1967, out of 5,64,000 villages in India, not even 1% were served by commercial banks. In 13 districts of the country, there was not a single commercial bank office. More than 600 towns did not have commercial banking facilities. There were 63 districts in which per capita credit was less than one rupee, in another 13 districts, credit was not extended even to a single individual, although deposits were mobilised from there. The two metropolitan cities of Mumbai and Kolkata accounted for one-third of total deposits and one-half of total credit disbursed by banks. The ratio of credit to deposits was more than 100% in the metropolitan cities, which means that deposits mobilised in smaller centres were diverted to these cities for financing the activities of big business. It was argued that bank nationalisation would remove these imbalances, ensure even distribution of banking facilities, and spread banking to rural unbanked and under-banked areas.

8. *Ignored RBI Directives.* Big banks with strong financial background often ign6red the Reserve Bank's directives under the Banking Regulation Act, 1949. This, in turn, adversely affected the RBI's monetary policy. By nationalising such banks, the RBI would be in an advantageous position to implement its monetary policy more effectively.

9. *Protection to Depositors.* It was argued that bank nationalisation would remove the fear of bank failures from the mind of public, thereby protecting the interests of depositors. This, in turn, would inculcate banking

habits among the people, especially in the rural non-monetised sector of the economy.

10. *Check of Undesirable Activities.* The commercial banks often indulged in anti-social and undesirable activities. They advanced credit for such activities which encouraged speculation, profiteering, black marketing, etc. which led to accumulation of black money in bank accounts. All such activities would be stopped when banks were nationalised.

11. *Encouraged Inflation.* It was alleged that commercial banks encouraged inflation by increasing the supply of money without due regard to the directives of the RBI. Banks often used their resources to the discretion of their directors for their own interest and that of their business friends. So they did not follow the guidelines issued by the RBI for credit restriction. This led to inflation. Thus nationalisation of banks was considered to be the only remedy.

12. *Increase in Efficiency.* It was argued that bank nationalisation would improve the efficiency of banks and the quality of service to the customers because the employees would have a greater sense of security. The efficiency of banks would also increase due to the standardisation of banking operations throughout the country.

13. *Better Management.* With the nationalisation of banks, the Government would be in a position to develop and provide adequate training and modern managerial techniques to the staff. This would lead to greater efficiency in bank operations.

14. *Better Service Conditions.* It was hoped that bank nationalisation would provide better service conditions for the employees. They would have the satisfaction of being Government employees. This would also improve employer-employee relations and pave the way for a smooth working of the banking system in the country.

15. *Success in Other Countries.* The protagonists of bank nationalisation argued that in a number of developed and developing countries where commercial banking was in the hands of State, it had been highly successful in helping the masses and mobilising resources for development. For example, 90% of commercial banking was in the public sector in Italy, 80% in France and 70% in Germany. Among the developing countries, Egypt, Myanmar, Indonesia, and Srilanka had been successfully operating nationalised banks.

CONCLUSION

Out of the above only a few arguments seemed to have weighed with the Government in nationalising 14 major commercial banks on 19 July, 1969 and 6 more commercial banks on 15 April, 1980. This becomes clear from the objectives of bank nationalisation outlined by the Government in the Parliament.

3. OBJECTIVES OF BANK NATIONALISATION

The Banking Companies (Acquisition and Transfer of Undertakings) Act, 1970 under which 14 banks were nationalised with effect from 19 July, 1969 spelt the main objective as "to serve better the needs of development of the economy in conformity with national policy and objectives and for matters connected therewith or incidental thereto". The specific objectives which the nationalised banks were expected to pursue were outlined by the then Prime Minister Mrs. Indira Gandhi in her statement to the Parliament on 21 July, 1969. These objectives included:

(1) To mobilise the savings of the people to the largest possible extent and to utilise them for productive purposes in accordance with our plans and priorities;

(2) To ensure the operations of the banking system for a larger social purpose and to subject them to close public regulation;

(3) To meet the legitimate credit needs of private sector industry and trade, big or small;

(4) To meet in an increasing manner the needs of productive sectors of the economy and in particular those of farmers, small scale industrialists and self-employed professional groups;

(5) To actively foster the growth of the new and progressive entrepreneurs and credit fresh opportunities for hitherto neglected and backward areas in different parts of the country;

(6) To curb the use of bank credit for speculative and other unproductive purposes;

(7) To develop adequate professional management and modern managerial techniques and practices in

the banking field;

(8) To provide adequate training and reasonable terms of service to bank staff;

(9) To considerably expand the branch network of banks in all parts of the country, and

(10) To reduce regional and sectoral imbalance in banking and through that in economic development.

4. A CRITICAL APPRAISAL OF THE FUNCTIONING OF NATIONALISED BANKS IN INDIA

With study the extent to which bank nationalisation has been able to achieve its objectives.

ACHIEVEMENTS

The nationalisation of 14 commercial banks on 19 July, 1969 was a watershed in the history of Indian banking. Together with the State Bank of India and its 7 associates which were brought under public ownership in the 1950s, the nationalisation of 20 commercial banks thereafter resulted in bringing about 90% of banking business under the direct control, ownership and management of the public sector. We enumerate below some of the achievements of nationalisation:

1. *Branch Expansion.* There has been a sea-change in the banking landscape, both geographically and functionally. The objective of creating an infrastructure for banking activity has, by and large, been achieved. From 6,596 branches and offices in June 1969, their number increased to 32,643 in June 2003.

2. *Deposit Growth.* Besides, there has been functional diversification in the form of growth in bank deposits. The deposits of these banks in June 1969 were Rs.. 3,897 crores which increased to Rs. 6,88,361 crores in March 2003 and grew by 11.47 per cent during 2002-03 over 2001-02.

3. *Credit Expansion.* There has been an impressive record of the nationalised banks in the realm of credit expansion. The amount advanced by them increased from Rs.. 3,035 crores in June 1969 to Rs. 3,60,147 crores in March, 2003 and grew by 14.12 per cent during 2002-03 over 2001-02.

4. *Priority Sector Lending.* These banks have undergone a major transformation from 'wholesale' banking to 'retail' banking. In other words, there has been greater emphasis on disbursing credit to the priority sector comprising agriculture, small scale industry, transport operators, retail trade, professional and self-employed persons, and education. The priority sector lending by the nationalised banks increased from Rs. 441 crores in June 1969 to Rs. 2,03,095 crores in March 2003. As percentage to net bank credit, the same increased from 14.6% to 42.5 during the above period. Agricultural advances increased from 5.4% to 15.3%, the share of credit to SSI units increased from 8.5% to 11.1 and the share of other priority sectors in overall net bank credit increased from 0.7% to 15% during the same period.

5. *Spread of Banking in Rural Areas.* Since nationalisation, the spread of banking has increased considerably in rural areas. As a result of the deliberate policy of opening a large number of branches in rural areas, 63.1 % of the branches of the 19 nationalised banks were operating in rural and semi-urban areas in June 2003 as against 22% on the eve of nationalisation in June 1969.

6. *Reduction in Regional Disparities.* Regional imbalances in the availability of banking facilities have been considerably reduced. The majority of these branches have been opened in unbanked areas. In June 1969, there were 74 bank branches in Assam, 172 in Haryana, 42 in Himachal Pradesh and only 2 in Nagaland. In June, 2003 their number had increased to 1,212; 1,580; 784 and 70 respectively. 35% of branches had been opened in those States where banking facilities were less. Consequently, the average population per bank office declined to 16,000 in June 2003 against 65,000 in June 1969.

7. *Some New Schemes.* Public sector banks have been departing from their traditional role and introducing some new schemes. Besides launching a range of new savings and other innovative schemes, these banks have taken up merchant banking and leasing, and have also been floating mutual funds and venture capital funds.' A number of other steps have been taken up to improve customer service. Courier services have been introduced to expedite collection of outstation credit instruments. Nomination facilities have been extended to the depositors to avoid hardship to the legal heirs of deceased account holders. Customer service centres have

been set up in all major cities. Customer relations programmes are organised periodically. The system of personal hearing of the grievances of customers has been introduced at appropriate levels to serve the customer better. Nine nationalised banks have opened offices in foreign countries thereby opening new vistas in international trade and finance.

FAILURES

Despite the above enumerated achievements, the public sector banks suffer from a number of weaknesses which are discussed as under:

1. *Deterioration in Customer Service.* One of the important drawbacks of nationalisation of banks has been deteriorating customer service. The evils connected with public sector undertakings have crept in these banks thereby resulting in red-tapism, inordinate delays and lack of responsibility. Despite the directives of the RBI for improving the quality of customer service, little has been done to implement it at the branch level. For instance, there are delays in opening of the counters and sometimes counters are closed for short periods on flimsy grounds causing inconvenience to customers. The branch managers are helpless to control the staff due to the spread of unionism. Complaint boxes are not maintained in many branches nor are the addresses of regional/zonal managers displayed to help customers who want to appeal to higher officers. Facilities like automatic credit of outstation cheques of Rs. 5000 and above and crediting of interest at savings bank rate in case of collection of outstation cheques being delayed beyond three weeks are not being extended to customers. Moreover, most bank branches give demand drafts against cash to businessmen towards the end of the day.

2. *Political Interference.* There has been much political interference in granting of loans by public sector banks which has destroyed the sanctity of banking norms. This defeats the very purpose of social banking and leads to malpractices. An important instance is politically organised loan melas.

3. *Social Banking Inadequate.* Social banking in the form of flow of credit to the priority sector is inadequate. It is less than the total advances of public sector banks. Even today these banks mainly cater to the needs of the corporate sector.

4. *Window-dressing of Balance Sheets.* Some of the public sector banks have been resorting to window-dressing of their balance sheets so that their balance sheets do not reveal the actual state of affairs. They artificially step up their deposits in the last week of the fiscal year. This has been possible because auditing in the banks is incomplete and partial.

5. *Large Scale Irregularities.* A number of public sector banks have been resorting to large scale irregularities in their operations. Some of these are:

(i) *Indulging in Share Speculation.* A few banks have started Mutual Funds and subsidiary financial companies and instances have been found of their involvement in share speculation. For instance, Bob Fiscal, a subsidiary of the Bank of Baroda arranged for funds for the Reliance Company in order to corner the shares of Larsen & Toubro. The securities scam involving Harshad Mehta and others revealed the involvement of the SBI and a number of other banks.

(ii) Favouritism in Granting Loans. Some of the banks are guilty of favouring certain companies in granting loans. For instance, Vijaya Bank advanced large loans to a certain big industrial house and its group companies in small tranches so as to avoid clearance under the credit authorisation scheme.

(iii) Bad Quality of Loan Portfolios. Despite the bad quality of loan portfolios, the banks have been advancing loans under extraneous pressures. Some of the banks have been extending letters of credit and guarantee limits as a routine affair without adopting normal commercial procedure in granting loans. The non-performing assets (NPAs) of banks reflect the quality of their loan portfolios. NPAs include sub-standard assets, doubtful assets, loss assets, etc. During 1999-2000, the gross NPAs of public sector banks were Rs. 53,294 crores, constituting 14.0 per cent of their gross advances.

(iv) *Irregularities in Accounts.* Some of the public sector banks have been resorting to large scale irregularities in operating their accounts. In certain cases, .bad accounts have been taken over by one bank from the other without proper scrutiny and judgement.

(v) *Large Bad Debts.* These banks have accumulated large amounts of bad debts. As on 31 December 1999, there were 3,185 cases of frauds involving Rs. 640 crores of public sector banks.

6. *Declining Profitability.* The most important problem of the nationalised banks has been their declining

profitability. Irregularities and corruption in lending operations, misappropriation, fraud, rising operating cost, deterioration in customer services, etc. have led to declining profitability of these banks. The ratio of net profit to total assets was (-) 1.15% in 1993-94 which improved to onlv 0.96 per cent in 2002-03.

7. *Some Banks as Sick Units.* In October 1990, the Reserve Bark of India in a survey found all the nationalised banks in a bad shape and identified eight banks as 'sick'. The 'sick' included: New Bank of India, Punjab and Sind Bank, Bank of India, UCO Bank, Vijaya Bank of India, Syndicate Bank, Bank of Maharashtra, and United Bank of India. Some of these banks had eroded their reserves and paid-up capital and there had been erosion of their deposit base. To this 'sick-list* were added: Central Bank, Indian Overseas Bank, Allahabad Bank, Andhra Bank, and Dena Bank, in 1992.93. New Bank of India became so sick that the Government merged it with Punjab National Bank effective 4 September 1993. During 1999-2000, three nationalised banks had been identified as weak. To adjust the losses of weak banks, the Government had contributed Rs. 20,466 crores towards their recapitalisation by 31 March 1999. But no amount was provided during 1999-2000. However, it provided Rs. 297 crores towards writing down of the investments of Vijaya Bank for adjustment of its losses.

8. *Low Capital Adequacy Ratio.* Every bank is required to achieve minimum capital to risk assets ratio, known as capital adequacy ratio (CAR) of at least 9 percent. Out of 27 public sector banks, two banks had not achieved it during 2002-03.

Conclusion. In a confidential report, the World Bank came out with trenchant criticism of the Indian banking system and called for urgent reforms. Since nationalised banks account for more than 90% of the assets of the entire banking in India. The World Bank's criticisms was directed against the sloppy management of these banks. The Report noted that these "banks were uncompetitive, overstretched, overstaffed and often provide poor service". It suggested a number of urgent reforms like cutting subsidised loans to targeted socially backward areas by half, making rates more flexible and rational, and giving commercial banks a measure of operational autonomy.

The fault also lies with the Government which has placed these banks under the Banking Department of the Ministry of Finance with the result that the RBI cannot regulate the working of these banks independently instead of sharing the responsibility with a parallel controlling authority. This dyarchy must go. There must be a thorough review of the working of these banks. The secrecy clause must be scrapped and the banking business made open and accountable. The defaulters must be identified. The machinery for the grant and recovery of toans should be streamlined and the entire procedure should be closely monitored.

Keeping these in view, the Finance Ministry and RBI took a series of measures to improve the performance and profitability of public sector banks. These included augmentation of capital, higher coupon rates on Government securities and higher return on cash balances. The banks were advised to draw up Action Plans to improve their operational efficiency.[1]

EXERCISES

1. What led the Government of India to nationalise commercial banks in India? What have been the achievements of these banks since 1969?
2. Discuss the achievements and failures of nationalised banks in India.
3. Give a critical appraisal of the functioning of nationalised banks in India.
4. What were the objectives of nationalisation of banks in India? How far these objectives have been achieved?

1. For details refer to the "Recent Bank Reforms" in the Chapter "Recent Trends In the Banking System".

CHAPTER 66

The Reserve Bank of India (RBI)

1. ITS CONSTITUTION

The origin of the Reserve Bank of India in 1935 was the culmination of a long series of efforts. The earliest effort to set up a central bank dates back to January 1773 when Warren Hastings, the Governor of Bengal, recommended the establishment of a "General Bank in Bengal and Bihar". The next attempt was made in 1807-08 when Robert Richards, a member of the Bombay Government submitted a scheme for a "General Bank". But the Governor-General was not impressed. The name of John Maynard Keynes also figures in the events leading to the establishment of the RBI. As a member of the Royal Commission on liidian Finance and Currency of 1931, Keynes submitted a memorandum entitled "Proposals for the Establishment of a State Bank in India". The State Bank proposed by Keynes was to perform both central banking and commercial banking functions. However, the scheme could not be implemented due to the outbreak of the First World War.

The first major step was taken in 1921 when the three Presidency Banks were amalgamated to form the Imperial Bank of India. It was primarily a commercial bank but it also performed certain central banking functions, such as acting as banker to the Government and to some extent as bankers' bank. But the regulation of note issue and management of foreign exchange were the diiect responsibility of the Central Government.

In 1926, the Hilton Young Commission recommended that the dichotomy of functions and division of responsibility should be ended. It suggested the establishment of a central bank to be called the "Reserve Bank of India". Accordingly, the Gold Standard and Reserye Bank of India Bill was introduced in the Legislative Assembly in January 1927 but was dropped on account of sharp differences of opinion on the bank's ownership and the composition of its Board of Directors. The Indian Constitutional Reforms in 1933 made it obligatory that the transfer of responsibility from the British Government in India to Indian hands was dependent on the establishment of a Reserve Bank free from political influence and its successful operation. These events led to the introduction of a fresh bill in the Indian Legislative Assembly on 8 September, 1933; which was passed by it on 22 December, 1933 and by the Council of States on 16 February, 1934. It received the Governor-General's assent on 6 March, 1934. The Reserve Bank of India was constituted in accordance with the provisions of the Act containing 58 Sections and was inaugurated on 1 April, 1935.

The RBI was constituted as a shareholders' bank with a fully paid-up capital of Rs. 5 crores divided into shares of Rs. 100 each . Of these 5 lakh shares, 2200 shares were subscribed by the Directors of the Bank and the remaining by private shareholders.

In view of the need for close integration between the Bank's policies and those of the Government, the question of State ownership of the Bank was raised from time to time. But it was only after Independence that the decision to nationalise the Bank was taken. In terms of the Reserve Bank (Transfer to Public Ownership) Act, 1948, its entire paid-up capital was transferred to the Central Government on 1 January 1949 when it became a State-owned institution.

2. ITS ORGANISATIONAL STRUCTURE AND MANAGEMENT

The organisational structure of the RBI consists of the Central Board and the Local Boards.

The RBI is managed by the Central Board of Directors comprising 20 members. There is one Governor who is the executive head of the Bank. He is assisted by four Deputy Governors. They are appointed by the Government of India for a period of five years. Four Directors are nominated by the Central Government, one each from the four Local Boards situated at "Mumbai, Kolkata, Chennai and Delhi. In addition, the Central Government nominates ten Directors who are experts from various fields. They are appointed for four years. The 20th member of the Board is one Government official who is usually the Secretary, Ministry of Finance nominated by the Central Government. The government official and the four Deputy Governors do not have the right to vote at the meetings of the Board. All powers of the Bank are vested in the Central Board of Directors. It must hold at least six meetings in a year and atleast one in three months. However, the Governor is empowered to call a meeting of the Board whenever he likes. The Governor and Deputy Governors are whole-time paid officers of the Bank while the other Directors are part-time officers who receive T.A. and other allowances prescribed for them when they attend the meetings of the Board.

There are four Local Boards with headquarters at Mumbai, Kolkata, Chennai and Delhi representing the Western, Eastern, Southern and Northern regions respectively. The Central Government nominates five members on each Local Board for a four-year term. The Chairman is elected from among the members and the Manager of the RBI office in a region acts as the ex-officio Secretary of the Local Board.

The RBI is managed by the Central Board of Directors with the Governor as its Chairman. The Governor is the chief executive of the Bank who exercises wide powers of supervision and issues directions on behalf of the Board. He is assisted by four Deputy Governors and four Executive Directors.

The Head Office of the RBI at Mumbai, which has sixteen departments such as the Banking, Issue, Currency Management, Exchange Control, Industrial Credit, Agricultural Credit, etc. The bank has 15 offices and 2 branches in different parts of the country. Where the RBI has no office or branch, the State Bank of India and its 7 associates act as its agents or sub-agents.

3. OBJECTIVES OF RESERVE BANK OF INDIA

The broad objectives of the Reserve Bank of India as spelt out in the preamble to the RBI Act, 1934 are "to regulate the issue of Bank notes and the keeping of reserves with a view to securing monetary stability in India and generally to operate the currency and credit system of the country to its advantage". What was implied in the objectives stated was more concretely stated in the First Five-Year Plan: "It would have to take on a direct and active role, firstly, in creating and helping to create the machinery needed for financing developmental activities all over the country, and secondly, ensuring that the finance available flows in the directions intended". Thus the main objectives of the RBI have been:

1. To promote monetisation and monetary integration of the economy.
2. To manage currency and regulate foreign exchange.
3. To institutionalise savings through promotion of banking habit.
4. To build up a sound and adequate banking and credit structure.
5. To evolve a well-differentiated structure of institutions purveying credit for agriculture and allied activities.
6. To set up or promote several specialised financial institutions at the all-India level and regional levels to widen facilities for term finance to industry.
7. To lend support to planning authorities and governments in their efforts to accelerate the pace of economic development with stability and social justice.

The extent to which the RBI has been able to fulfil these objectives shall be discussed-in the last section of this chapter entitled "A Critical Appraisal of the Functioning of Reserve Bank of India".

4. FUNCTIONS OF RESERVE BANK OF INDIA

The Reserve Bank of India performs all the traditional functions of a central bank. At the same time, it also undertakes active promotional and developmental functions. Thus we divide the functions of the RBI into two parts:

(1) Traditional Functions, and (2) Promotional and Developmental Functions, These are discussed as under:

1. TRADITIONAL FUNCTIONS

The RBI performs the following traditional functions: (1) *Issue of Currency.* The RBI acts as the currency authority. As such, it has the monopoly of issuing currency of all denominations except one rupee notes and coins, and small coins which are issued by the Ministry of Finance of the Government of India. At present, the RBI is issuing notes of the denominations of Rs. 10, 20, 50, 100. and 500.[1] These notes are printed and issued by its Issue Department. Rs. 1,2 and 5 coins, and small coins issued by the Ministry of Finance are also distributed by the Issue Department. For the distribution of notes and coins of all denominations to the public and banks, the Issue Department maintains currency chests at its 15 offices and 2 branches and elsewhere keeps them with the State Bank of India, and its 7 associates, some public sector banks, and State Government treasuries and sub-treasuries. The RBI issues currency on the basis of minimum of Rs. 200 crores of gold and foreign exchange reserves, of which at least Rs. 115 crores worth of gold must be there.

(2) *Banker to Government.* The RBI acts as banker to the Central Government and the State Governments. As such, it renders the following services to them:

(*i*) It maintains and operates the cash balances of the Central and State Governments in the current account deposit on which it pays no interest.

(*ii*) It receives and makes payments on behalf of the Central and State Governments.

(*iii*) It carries out exchange, remittance and other banking operations on behalf of these Governments.

(*iv*) It buys and sells Government securities in the market.

(*v*) It manages the public debt by issuing Government loans and paying interest and principal.

(*vi*) It also sells treasury bills through tender on behalf of the Government.

(*vii*) It makes ways and means advances to the Central and State Governments by purchasing treasury bills from them for a period not exceeding 91 days.

(*viii*) It advises the Governments on all banking and financial matters, such as financing of five year plans and resource mobilisation, balance of payments, etc.

(*ix*) It acts as the agent of the Central and State Governments in their dealings with the International Monetary Fund, the World Bank, International Financial Corporation, IDA, Exim Bank, and other financial institutions.

(3) *Bankers' Bank. Firstly,* The RBI acts as banker to the scheduled commercial banks in India. As such, it keeps a part of the cash reserves of these banks and provides them with remittance facilities. Under the Banking Regulation Act, 1949, every bank is required to keep between 3% to 15% of the total of its time and demand liabilities with the RBI as cash reserve ratio which is interest-free. The CRR which was reduced to 14 per cent effective 15 May, 1993 was again raised to 15 per cent effective 6 August, 1994. Besides, every bank is required to maintain with the RBI between 25% to 40% of its net time and demand liabilities as the Statutory Liquidity Ratio (SLR). It had been reduced from 34.75 per cent to 33.75 per cent effective 16 May 1994. The incremental SLR continues to be 25 per cent. *Secondly,* the RBI supervises, regulates and controls the working of banks in India. These powers relate to issue of licence for opening and branch expansion, calling of returns/statements, inspection of books and accounts, issue of directions concerning terms and conditions of advances, giving approval for the appointment of chairman and directors, and to acquire or approve the merger of any bank. *Thirdly,* the RBI acts as a clearing house for banks. It has clearing houses at its 17 offices/branches and at

1. Printing of Re 1, 2 and 5 notes has been stopped and Rs 1000 note started.

other places the State Bank of India and its associates provide clearing and remittance facilities on its behalf. *Fourthly,* the RBI provides refinance facilities to commercial banks for export credit, against 364-Day Treasury Bills, stand-by refinance limits against the collateral of approved securities (that is for those banks having excess SLR) and discretionary refinance including limits under the facility to draw without prior approval from the RBI.

(4) *Exchange Management and Control.* The RBI manages and controls the country's foreign exchange reserves and external value of the rupee. Under the Foreign Exchange Regulation Act, 1973, the RBI controls the receipts and payments of foreign currencies. Foreign currencies coming into India are required to be sold and exchanged for the rupee either direct to the RBI or to major commercial banks authorised by it. Similarly, foreign currencies are allowed to persons travelling abroad and to importers by the RBI as per rules laid down by it. All such transactions of foreign currencies are made at rates fixed by the RBI fron; time to time.

The RBI determines the external value of the rupee in relation to the weighted basket of India's major trading partners with pound-sterling as the intervention currency. Since the exchange value of these currencies keeps on changing in the international market, the RBI also changes the exchange rate of the rupee in relation to other currencies such as dollar, mark, yen, sterling, etc. Effective 1 March, 1994, the RBI introduced full convertibility of rupee to the entire current account transactions.

(5) *Control of Credit.* The RBI controls the money supply and credit to ensure price stability and meet the varying economic conditions of the country. It estimates the credit needs of the economy in relation to the targets laid down in the five-year plans and ensures the supply of credit to different sectors. For this purpose, it uses various credit control measures such as variations in interest rates, open market operations, changes in CRR and SLR, selective credit controls, etc.

(6) *Collection and Publication of Data and Reports.* The RBI has a Division of Reports, Reviews, and Publications under its Department of Economic Analysis and Policy which collects data on economic matters such as money, credit, finance, agricultural and industrial production, balance of payments, prices, etc. and publishes them in various publications. Some of its important publications are the Reserve Bank of India Bulletin (monthly) and its Weekly Statistical Supplements, Annual Report on Currency and Finance, and Report on Trend and Progress on Banking in India, etc. Besides, it brings out Occasional Papers by its experts, and conducts surveys and publishes reports on them.

(7) *Training Facilities.* The RBI has set up a number of training colleges and centres to provide training to the banking personnel at different levels. They are:

(i) Bankers Training College (BTC). The BTC is located at Mumbai. It provides training to senior officers of the Bank in the areas of application of statistical methods, negotiating skills, counselling, import-export financing. Service Area Approach, etc.

(ii) Reserve Bank Staff College (RBSC). The RBSC is located at Chennai. It conducts training programmes for officers of the Bank on areas of investment and fund management, financial services, housing finance, customer service, etc. Officials of foreign banks also participate.

(iii) College of Agricultural Banking (CAB). The CAB is located at Pune-and it caters to the training needs of personnel of co-operative banks, commercial banks, regional rural banks, NABARD, RBI, Deposit Insurance and Credit Guarantee Corporation, Government officials, and also officials from South Asian and African countries. It conducts training programmes in the field of agricultural finance, rural banking and allied subjects.

(iv) Zonal Training Centres (ZTCs). The ZTCs are situated in Mumbai, Kolkata, Chennai and New Delhi. They provide training to class III and class IV staff of the Bank. These centres also conduct training programmes on computer and customer service. The RBI has also introduced training in commercial banking for the banks' officers at these Zonal centres.

(v) Indira Gandhi Institute of Development Research. This was set up by the RBI in 1987. It conducts research on projects and arranges workshop, conferences and seminars.

(vi) Training in Computer Technology. The RBI set up the Department of Computer Technology in 1995 for efficient and quick use of new technologies. This Department provides incentives to the Bank's staff to acquire qualifications in computer technology.

2. Promotional and Developmental Functions

The RBI has been taking a direct and active role, *first*, in creating or helping to create the machinery needed for financing development activities all over the country, and *secondly*, ensuring that the finance available flows in socially desired directions. In order to achieve these two objectives the RBI has been financing agriculture, industry and exports. It has also been instrumental in the development and regulation of the banking system and the bill market. We refer to these activities of the RBI briefly. They are discussed in detail in subsequent sections.

(1) *Agricultural Finance.* The RBI has been extending advice and financial assistance to the co-operative credit institutions for the development of agriculture and allied rural activities since its inception in 1935. For this purpose it set up an Agricultural Credit Department and separate funds for providing medium-term and long-term finance. Since 1982, the functions of this Department and those of the funds have been passed on to the National Bank for Agriculture and Rural Development (NABARD).

(2) *Industrial Finance.* The RBI set up an Industrial Credit Department in 1957 to advise and help the bank in providing financial assistance to industries and in setting up financial institutions like State Financial Institutions, IFCI, IDBI, ICICI, etc. It also established the National Industrial Credit (Long-Term Operations) Fund in 1964 to provide financial assistance to large scale industries.

(3) *Export Credit.* The RBI provides concessional credit, refinance facilities and guarantee to commercial banks for exporters. It has also set up the Export-Import Bank of India to finance export trade.

(4) *Credit to Priority Sector and Weaker Sections.* Under its Differential Rate of Interest Scheme, the RBI provides concessional finance to priority sectors and weaker sections of the society at 4 per cent interest rate.

(5) *Bill Market Scheme.* The RBI has been instrumental in developing a well-organised bill market scheme in order to provide rediscounting facilities to commercial banks from the Bank and other financial institutions.

(6) *Development and Regulation of Banking System.* The RBI has played an important role in the development and promotion of banking in the country. It has spread banking to the remotest corners of India through its Lead Bank Scheme, SAA, and Regional Rural Banks. It has helped in promoting development banking by establishing such financial institutions as IDBI, IFCI, ICICI, SIDBI, etc. Further, the RBI has strengthened the banking system in India and placed it on a sound footing through a judicious policy of regulation and control of banks.

3. Other Functions

The RBI also performs the following banking functions also :

(a) It issues demand drafts made payable at its own offices or agencies, and makes, issues and circulates bank post-bills.

(b) It can borrow money from a scheduled bank in India or from central banks in other countries.

(c) It is authorised to open an account or make an agency agreement with central banks in other countries and act as their agent and invest funds in their shares.

(d) It purchases and sells gold and bullion.

4. Prohibitory Functions

The RBI Act prohibits the Bank to perform certain functions so that it may not compete with other banks and may keep its assets in liquid form to meet any eventuality. Some of its prohibited functions are: *(a)* It cannot participate in any business, trade or industry, *(b)* It cannot buy its own shares or those of any other banking company or of any corporation. Nor can it give loan on the security of shares, *(c)* It cannot give loans against immovable property, *(d)* It cannot purchase immovable property except for its offices, *(e)* It cannot accept bills not payable on demand. *(f)* It cannot give interest on deposits held by it.

5. RBI and Agricultural Finance

Since its inception in 1935, the Reserve Bank of India has been entrusted with the task of formulating agricultural credit policy, developing an infrastructure for implementing it, giving advice on these matters to the State and Central Governments, and providing credit for agricultural and allied activities. The RBI has been performing these tasks in the following ways:

Agricultural Credit Department (ACD)

Alongwith the RBI, a separate Agricultural Credit Department was set up in 1935 to study the problems of agricultural credit, to develop co-operative credit movement, and to provide necessary advice, guidance and financial assistance. Its main functions were: (a) to maintain an expert staff to study all problems of agricultural credit and provide consultation to the Central and State Governments, State Co-operative Banks, and other banking organisations; and *(b)* to co-ordinate the operations of the RBI relating to agricultural credit with those State Co-operative Banks and other organisations engaged in the supply of agricultural credit. The ACD was engaged in the collection of statistics and research in rural credit. It was only with the beginning of the planning era that this Department became more active and it was entrusted with an additional function: to finance the processing, marketing, and other agricultural operations through State Co-operative Banks and other agencies of rural credit. The ACD has been merged with NABARD effective July, 1982.

All India Rural Credit Survey Committee

The RBI appointed an All India Rural Credit Survey Committee in 1951 which submitted its report in 1954. The Committee observed that the contribution of co-operatives in providing rural finance was only 3 per cent in total rural credit. It, therefore, made a number of recommendations for strengthening co-operative credit movement and to provide more funds for agricultural and allied activities. On the recommendations of the Committee, the Reserve Bank made the following changes to develop co-operative credit movement and to provide agricultural finance:

(1) *Integrated Scheme of Rural Credit.* The RBI Act was amended to implement the integrated scheme of rural credit. The main features of the scheme were: (a) State partnership in co-operative credit institutions between credit societies with marketing and processing activities; and *(b)* administration through adequately trained and efficient personnel responsive to the needs of the rural population. The RBI was required to play an active role in the development of co-operative credit, co-ordinating credit with marketing, processing end ware housing activities, and training of co-operative personnel. As a result of the implementation of this scheme, it was revealed by the All India Rural Debt and Investment Survey conducted by the RBI (1961-62) that the share of co-operatives in rural credit increased from 3.1 per cent in 1951-52 to 25.8 per cent in 1961-62.

(2) *State Bank of India.* It was on the recommendations of the Committee that the Imperial Bank of India was nationalised in 1955 and renamed the State Bank of India. The RBI became its major share holder. The SBI has been entrusted with the task of financing agricultural operations.

(3) *Agricultural Credit Board (ACB).* Though the Committee recommended the formation of a Statutory Agricultural Credit Board, the RBI constituted a Standing Advisory Committee on Agricultural Credit in 1956. Lateron it was changed into the Standing Advisory Committee on Rural and Co-operative Credit. It was again reconstituted in 1970 as the Agricultural Credit Board. It formulated policies relating to agricultural finance and co-ordinated the activities of co-operative credit institutions-, the RBI, and commercial banks in providing refinance facilities. The NABARD has taken over the activities of the Board since July 1982.

(4) *Rural Credit Funds.* On the recommendations of the Committee, the RBI established in February 1956 the National Agricultural Credit (Long-Term Operations) Fund to grant long-term loans to State Governments and Land Development Banks to enable them to subscribe to the share capital of co-operative banks and co-operative societies. The RBI also established the National Agricultural (Stabilisation) Fund in June 1956 for converting short term agricultural loans into medium term loans by the State Co-operative Banks to enable co-operative societies to repay loans in case of default by borrowers as a result of drought, famins or other natural calamities. These funds have been transferred to the NABARD since July 1982 and renamed as National Rural Credit (Long Term Operations) Fund and National Rural Credit (Stabilisation) Fund.

Establishment of Other Organisations

With a view to provide larger credit facilities to the rural sector, the RBI has also been instrumental in the establishment of the following organisations:

(1) *Nationalisation of Banks.* In 1969, 14 scheduled banks were nationalised and 6 more commercial banks were nationalised in 1980 in order to spread a network of their branches in rural areas so as to provide larger credit facilities for agricultural and allied activities.

(2) *Agricultural Refinance and Development Corporation (ARDC).* The RBI set up the Agricultural Refinance Corporation in July, 1963 which was subsequently renamed as Agricultural Refinance and Development Corporation. The main objectives of the Corporation were to provide medium and long term refinance to Central Land Mortgage Banks, State Co-operative Banks and commercial banks; and to subscribe to the debentures of Central Land Mortgage Banks and State Co-operative Banks. Since its inception in 1963 to June 1982, it sanctioned 19,601 schemes and disbursed Rs. 2,808 crores. With the establishment of the NABARD in July 1982, the ARDC was merged with it.

(3) *Regional Rural Banks (RRBs).* The RBI was instrumental in establishing RRBs in 1975. The RBI issues licences to sponsoring commercial banks for opening branches of RRBs which are routed through the NABARD after July 1982. The RBI has vested the work of financing and supervision of the RRBs to the NABARD. The principal objective of the RRBs is to grant loans and advances to the weaker sections of the rural population and to co-operatives.

(4) *National Bank for Agriculture and Rural Development (NABARD).* The NABARD was established in July 1982 as an apex rural development bank by merging ACD of the RBI, ARDC, and the NRC (LTO) Fund and NRC (Stabilisation) Fund of the RBI. The RBI lends to the NABARD.under the General Line of Credit (GLC) for short periods, and also contributes annually to the NRC (LTO) Fund and NRC (Stabilisation) Fund of the NABARD. The National Bank provides credit, refinance and institutional building facilities fo integrated rural development. The RBI sanctioned Rs. 3,750 crores to NAB ARE» in 1992-93 under general line of credit.

(5) *Service Area Approach (SAA).* The RBI introduced the SAA scheme from April 1989 whereby the service area of the branch of a commercial hank, a co-operative bank, and a RRB covers 15 to 25 villages. Every branch in the service area prepares a credit plan relating to agricultural and allied activities for the target groups and for lending to the priority sector categories of borrowers in particular.

HELP TO CO-OPERATIVES

The RBI inspects and audits the accounts of co-operative societies. It provides cheap remittance facilities to them. It renders them advice about making adjustments of their loans and assets. It also runs the College of Agricultural Banking at Pune where it conducts training programmes in the field of agricultural finance, rural banking and allied subjects for the personnel of co-operative and other banks.

FINANCIAL ASSISTANCE

The RBI dos not provide direct finance to agriculturists but through the State Co-operative Banks and NABARD. It provides short-term, medium-term and long-term financial assistance to meet the needs of rural and allied activities.

(1) *Short-Term Advances.* The RBI grants short term loans and advances to State Co-operative Banks for the purpose of general banking business against the pledge of Government and other approved securities. The RBI also lends to NABARD under the GLC for short term lending operations for agricultural and other purposes. The NABARD, in turn, makes short-term advances to State Co-operative Banks for agricultural operations, marketing of crops, purchase and distribution of chemical fertilisers, financing of cottage and small scale industries, working capital requirements of co-operative sugar factories, etc. Short term advances of the RBI/NABARD to the State Co-operative Banks amounted to Rs, 7,358 crores in 2002-03.

(2) *Medium-Term Advances.* Medium term loans and advances are granted by the RBI to the State Co-operative Banks for the purpose of general banking business against the pledge of Government and other approved securities for a period of 15 months to 5 years at an interest rate below the bank rate. The NABARD also gives medium term loans from NRC (Stabilisation) Fund for conversion of short term into medium term loans, and from the NRC (LTO) Fund for approved agricultural purposes and purchase of shares in co-operative processing societies by farmer members of PACs. The medium term loans and advances by RBI/

NABARD to the State Co-operative Banks amounted to Rs. 493 crores in 2002-03.

(3) *Long-Term Advances.* The RBI provides long term advances for agricultural and allied activities to the State Governments to enable them to contribute to the share capital of co-operatives and the NRC (LTO) Fund and NRC (Stabilisation) Fund. During 1990-91, the RBI contributed Rs. 375 crores to the NRC (LTO) Fund and Rs. 10 crores to the NRC (Stabilisation) Fund. The RBI/NABARD sanctioned long-term credit limits amounting to Rs. 61 crores to State Governments for contribution to the share capital of co-operative credit institutions during 2002-03.

Conclusion

The Reserve Bank's role in rural finance is confined to the following areas: advisory, training, supervision, strengthening of rural credit institutions, formulating rural credit policy and providing refinance facilities. The RBI has been successful in creating a number of institutions like the RRBs, NABARD, etc., and strengthening of co-operative banking in rural areas in order to provide credit facilities for agricultural and allied activities.'

6. RBI AND INDUSTRIAL FINANCE

The Reserve Bank has been playing an important role in providing finance indirectly to large, medium and small scale industries. Towards this end, it has been instrumental in setting up a number of financial corporations at the Centre and in the States. The RBI provides long term loans as well as medium/short term credit facilities to these financial institutions.

RBI Assistance to Financial Institutions

To provide credit facilities to industries, the RBI has helped in the establishment of the following financial institutions:

(1) *Industrial Finance Corporation of India (IFCI).* The IFCI was set up in 1948 by the RBI with the objective of providing medium and long-term financial assistance to the industrial sector. The RBI subscribed 40 per cent of the issued capital of the Corporation. It also subscribed to the debentures of the Corporation. In 1964, it was made a subsidiary of the Industrial Development Bank of India. The RBI provides medium/short term credit limits to the IFCI against the security of eligible usance bills rediscounted by it. During 1990-91, the RBI sanctioned Rs. 60 crores as credit limits to the Corporation. No amount had been sanctioned after this.

(2) *National Industrial Credit (Long Term Operations) Fund.* The RBI created the NIC (LTO) Fund in 1964 for providing long term credit limits to the leading financial institutions such as IDBI, IRBI, etc.

(3) *Industrial Development Bank of India (IDBI)* The RBI established in 1964 'the IDBI as the principal financial institution for industrial finance in the country. It is a wholly owned subsidiary of the RBI. It provides direct assistance to medium and large industrial concerns by purchasing/underwriting their shares and debentures. It also provides refinance facilities to other term lending institutions in the large, medium and small scale sectors. During 1992-93, the RBI sanctioned a special refinance facility of Rs. 400 crores to IDBI. It did not sanction any amount after this.

(4) *Industrial Credit and Investment Corporation of India (ICICl).* The ICIC1 was established in 1955 as a public limited company at the initiative of the World Bank. The RBI played an indirect role in its formation. The 1CICI provides assistance for industrial development and investment, by way of rupee and foreign currency loans, underwriting and direct participation to shares, debentures and guarantees. The RBI provides medium/short term credit limits to the ICICI against the security of eligible usance bills rediscounted by it. It sanctioned Rs. 33 crores to the ICICI as credit limits for the year 1990-91. No amount was sanationed after this.

(5) *Industrial Reconstruction Bank of India (IRBI).* The IRBI was established in 1985 after reconstituting the erstwhile Industrial Reconstruction Corporation of India. It is the principal credit and reconstruction agency for rehabilitation of sick and closed industrial units. It assists industrial concerns by grant of term loans and advances, underwriting of stocks, shares, bonds and debentures, and guarantees for loans/deferred payments. During 1990-91, the RBI sanctioned Rs. 35 crores to the IRBI as long-term assistance from the NIC (LTO) Fund. No amount had been sanctioned after this.

(6) *State Financial Corporations (SFCs).* SFCs are the state-level development banks set up under the SFCs

Act, 1951 for the development of medium and small scale industries in their respective States. At present there are 18 SFCs which provide financial assistance to industries by way of term loans, direct subscription to equity/debentures, discounting of bills of exchange and guarantees. Most of the IDBI schemes for assistance to small and medium sectors are operated through SFCs. During 1999-2000, the RBI sanctioned fresh adhoc borrowing limits aggregating to Rs. 152.5 crores to 15 SFCs.

(7) *Small Industries Development Bank of India (SIDBI).* The SIDBI was set up as a wholly-owned subsidiary of IDBI on 2 April, 1990. It aims at ensuring larger flow of financial and non-financial assistance to smill scale industrial sector. Its major activities relate to refinance of loans and advances, discounting and rediscounting of bills, extension of seed capital/soft loans, granting direct assistance and refinancing of loans, providing services like factoring, leasing, etc., and extending financial support to Small Industries Development Corporations. During 1995-96, the RBI sanctioned long-term credit assistance to SIDBI amounting to Rs. 224 crores. It made no sanction after this.

(8) *Export-Import Bank of India (Exim Bank).* The Exim Bank was set up in January 1982 as a statutory corporation of the Central Government. It provides financial assistance to promote Indian exports through direct financial assistance, overseas investment, finance, term finance for export production and export development, pre-shipment credit, buyers' credit, lines of credit, relending facility, export bills rediscounting, refinance to commercial banks, finance for computer software exports, finance for export marketing and bulk import finance to commercial banks. It also extends non-fund facility to Indian exporters in the form of guarantees. The lending programme of the Exim Bank covers various stages of export such as from the developmentof export markets to expansion of production capacity for exports production for exports and post-shipment financing. Its focus is on export of manufactured goods, project exports, exports of technology services, export of manufactured goods and export of computer software. The RBI sanctioned Rs. 120 crores as long-term assistance to the Exim Bank out of NIC (LTO) Fund in 1990-91. It made no sanction after this.

(9) *National Housing Bank (NHB).* The NHB was set up in 1988 to meet the requirements of housing finance. Its paid-up capital of Rs. 250 crores is fully subscribed by the RBI. The bank is providing assistance through Home Loan Account Scheme, liberalised lending by commercial banks and refinance facilities. Refinance is for land development and shelter programmes of public/private agencies and co-operatives. During 1992-93 the RBI sanctioned a loan of Rs. one crore to NHB out of the National Housing Credit (Long-Term Operations) Fund set up by the RBI. No amount was sanctioned after this.

Credit Guarantee Schemes

The RBI established in 1971 the Credit Guarantee Corporation of India in order to encourage greater flow of bank credit to small borrowers. In 1978, this Corporation was merged with the Deposit Insurance Corporation and renamed as Deposit Insurance and Credit Guarantee Corporation (DICGC). This Corporation guarantees support for the entire priority sector advances by banks and other approved financial institutions to small borrowers and small scale industries. At present, the DICGC is operating three credit guarantee schemes. The RBI does not lend to the Corporation and has simply helped in its formation.

Industrial Credit Department

Earlier, the RBI had established the Industrial Credit Department in 1957 to solve the problems of industrial finance. It was this Department which administered the Credit Guarantee Scheme for SSI introduced in July 1960. With the formation of DICGC, this department was wound up by the RBI in 1981.

Credit Monitoring Arrangement (CMA)

The RBI introduced the CMA in place of the Credit Authorisation Scheme (CAS) in October 1988 whereby it delegated authority to banks to sanction credit proposals of large borrowers and thereafter submit the same for post-sanction scrutiny to the RBI. These credit limits relate to working capital (of Rs. 5 crores and above), term finance (of Rs. 2 crores and above), sale of machinery on deferred payments, etc. in case of large scale industries. The CMA has made possible prompt and easy availability of credit to large industries with post-sanction by the RBI.

From 1992-93, the working capital credit limit has been raised from Rs. 5 crores to Rs. 10 crores. The CMA has also been extended to the export sector. The RBI has advised banks to meet the additional credit needs of exporters in full even if sanction of additional credit exceeds maximum permissible bank finance (MPBF), provided exporters have firm orders or confirmed letters of credit. This facility has been extended to exports by small scale industries where the working capital limit from banks is less than Rs. one crore, provided their exports are not less than 25 per cent of their total turnover during the previous accounting year. Further, this facility has been given to companies/organisations engaged in the marketing/trading of the products of village, tiny and small scale industrial units.

Conclusion

The RBI has done a remarkable job in creating a number of financial institutions aiid evolving credit guarantee schemes to help finance large, medium and small industries, and small borrowers. It provides direct long-term assistance from the NIC (LTO) Fund and medium/short-term assistance to financial institutions. It also changes its credit policy from time to time to help the industrial sector to get larger financial assistance from banks.

7. RBI and Bill Market Scheme

The RBI pioneered the development of the bill market scheme for trade and industry in 1952. Its aim was to induce banks to provide finance against bills of exchange and promissory notes for 90 days. The scheduled commercial banks were allowed to convert a part of their advances, loans, cash credits or overdrafts into usance promissory notes for 90 days for lodging as collateral (security) for advances from the RBI. Since this scheme was primarily meant to accommodate the banks, it did not help in developing a bill market.

In November 1970, the RBI introduced the Bill Rediscounting Scheme with several new features. Under this scheme, all licensed scheduled commercial banks were made eligible to rediscount with the RBI genuine trade bills arising out of sale or despatch of goods. But this did not lead to the development of bill culture as preference for cash credit type of financing continued in the country: Several difficulties were cited by trade and industry in developing the bill market: (a) non-availability of stamp paper of required denomination, *(b)* the need to affix stamp on each bill and payment of stamp duty, (c) reluctance of industry, trade and Government Departments to accept bills, *(d)* absence of specialised credit information agencies, *(e)* absence of any active secondary market for bills as rediscounting is permitted only with the apex level financial institutions, and *(f)* administrative work involved in handling invoices/documents of title to goods.

The Committee to Review the working of the Monetary System (1985) and the Working Group on the Money Market (1986) set up by the RBI made a number of recommendations which have sir.ce been accepted and implemented by the RBI as under:

1. The RBI has developed the treasury bills or Government Securities market in 14-day Treasury Bills, 91-day Treasury Bills, 182-day Treasury Bills and 364-day Treasury Bills.

2. In order to augment the facilities for rediscounting and to provide liquidity to the bills, the RBI has been progressively permitting a larger number of financial institutions eligible for rediscounting bills. Apart from all scheduled commercial banks and selected urban co-operative banks, 21 other financial institutions like LIC, UTI, GIC, NABARD, all development banks; all mutual funds, etc., are included in the scheme.

3. The RBI has set up the Discount and Finance House of India (DFHI) as a major financial institution to rediscount commercial bills, treasury bills and Government dated securities which it has been doing since its inception on 15 April 1988.

4. In May 1994, the RBI set up the Securities Trading Corporation of India (STCI) to develop secondary market in Government securities and Treasury bills. The STCI undertakes ready forward transactions in Treasury Bills and Government dated securities. From March 1996, it has become a primary dealer in Government securities.

5. Besides, the DFHI and the STCI, the RBI has granted permission to ICICI Securities, SBI Gilts Ltd., PNB Gilts Ltd. and Gilt Securities Trading Corporation Ltd. to operate as primary dealers in Government securities. The RBI also provides liquidity support to them in the form of reverse Repos in Government dated securities

and 91-Day Treasury Bills.

6. Upto September 1988 under the bill rediscounting procedure, the bills had to be endorsed and lodged with the rediscounting banks or institutions. But preference for cash-credit type of financing continued because certain administrative difficulties, were faced by banks in following this procedure. In October, 1988, the RBI introduced the scheme *of derivative usance promissory note* for the purpose of rediscounting of bills whereby banks could draw a derivative usance promissory note for suitable sums with maturity upto 90 days on the basis of bona-fide commercial or trade bills discounted at their branches. Since August, 1989, the derivative promissory note has been exempted from stamp duty. Thus a major administrative constraint in the use of the bill system has been removed.

7. To encourage the development of bill finance and bill culture, the RBI had fixed a discount rate equivalent to an effective interest rate of 15.5 per cent. Further, to stimulate the supply of funds in the rediscount market, the RBI had fixed the ceiling on rediscount rate at 12.5 per cent. But this rediscount rate was not applicable when banks and financial houses rediscounted bills with DFHI which could fix its own discount rates for bills. With effect from 1 May, 1989, the bill rediscounting rate has been totally freed.

8. The Working Group on the Money Market (1986) made recommendations for developing bill financing in relation to cash credit system and developing the bill culture. In pursuance of the recommendations, the RBT advised banks to fix for the Credit Authorisation Scheme (CAS) now covered by the Credit Monitoring Scheme since October 1988, to attain a ratio of bill acceptance to their inland credit purchases of 25 per cent and a bill discounting limit of the same order.

9. To secure finance from banks against bills accepted by the large scale units for prompt payment to small scale units, the RBI has introduced a Drawee Bill Scheme.

10. The RBI advised commercial banks in July, 1992 that (a) they should be cautious in discounting bills drawn by finance companies set up by large industrial houses on other group companies; *(b)* they should not rediscount the bills discounted by non-bank financial companies and thus desist from providing any rediscount facility to finance companies; and (c) they should ensure that the overall credit limit provided to finance companies and to hire-purchase and equipment leasing companies should not exceed three times the net worth of such companies.

11. Recognising the need to derive the benefit of internationally competitive rates, the RBI decided to allow with effect from 7 April, 1993 authorised dealers in India to rediscount export bills abroad at rates linked to international interest rates.

DEFECTS

Despite these measures, the RBI has failed to develop bill finance and bill culture in the country. Bill financing hardly covers about 4 per cent of the total credit covered by banks today. There are many reasons for this: *(a)* The Government, public sector undertakings, and large industries do not accept bills as a basis for financing business, *(b)* The bill market is primarily confined to derivative usance promissory notes rather than to genuine trade bills, (c) Indigenous bills of exchange, known as *hundis,* which finance a large segment of commerce and trade in India are not recognised by the RBI. For a faster growth of bill financing and bill culture, the RBI should try to remove these drawbacks of the bill market.

8. EXCHANGE CONTROL MANAGEMENT BY RBI

The RBI manages and controls the country's foreign exchange reserves and the external value of the rupee. Foreign exchange is managed and controlled in order to overcome the deficit in balance of payments. The RBI controls and manages the inflow and outflow of foreign currencies under the Foreign Exchange Regulation Act, 1973 and Foreign Exchange Regulation (Amendment) Act, 1993.

Foreign currencies coming into India are required to be sold and exchanged for the rupee either direct to the RBI or to its authorised dealers. Its authorised dealers include certain commercial banks, hotels, firms, shops, etc. which deal in foreign currencies and foreign travellers' cheques. They are also authorised to lend and borrow foreign currency among themselves in the inter-bank market locally. The actual lending limit for each authorised dealer is fixed by the RBI depending upon the size of its operations and other relevant factors. Authorised dealers are permitted to maintain with overseas branches and correspondents, balances in foreign currencies at levels which are commensurate with normal needs of their business, such as payments towards imports or maturing deliveries under forward contracts. They are also permitted to transfer foreign currency funds rendered surplus over normal anticipated needs of their business on a day-to-day basis to special interest bearing accounts.

The blanket foreign exchange permits are issued to exporters in lump sums. Exporters are allowed to receive export proceeds through normal banking channels. The payments for imports against foreign currency loans/credits extended by foreign governments/financial institutions are made either under the Direct Payment Method, also known as Letter of Commitment Method or Reimbursement Method.

Since 1991 significant changes have been made in the exchange rate system by the RBI. In July, 1991, the rupee was devalued by about 20 per cent with respect to US dollar in two stages. Simultaneously, the Exim Scrip Scheme was introduced under which certain imports were permitted only against export entitlement. This was followed by partial convertibility of rupee in 60:40 ratio with effect from 1 March, 1992. This was the Liberalised Exchange Rate Management System (LERMS). Under this system, all foreign exchange receipts on current account transactions (i.e. exports, remittances etc.) were required to be surrendered to the authorised dealers (ADs) in full. The rate of exchange for these transactions was the free market rate quoted by the ADs. The ADs, in turn, surrendered to the RBI 40 per cent of their purchase of foreign currencies at the exchange rate announced by the RBI. They were free to sell the balance of 60 per cent of foreign exchange in the free market. All importers of goods and services and persons travelling abroad bought foreign exchange at market-determined rates from the ADs subject to liberalised exchange control rules.

The RBI issued instructions to authorised dealers to sell foreign exchange without prior approval for business visits overseas sponsored by firms/companies/ organisations, visits by self-employed professionals and by journalists on short-term assignments, for medical treatment abroad, persons proceeding abroad for employment/emigration and on the hospitality of the overseas organisation, to exporters by way of agency commission and settlement of quality claims, for sundry personal and commercial remittances, etc. In all such cases, except exporters, the sale of foreign exchange limit had been raised between $ 100 to $ 500.

Under LERMS, the Reserve Bank provides foreign exchange at the official exchange rate in the following cases: *(a)* For import of crude, diesel and kerosene by the Indian Oil Corporation, *(b)* For import of fertilisers by MMTC. *(c)* For discharge of financing arrangements like payments under Banker's Acceptance Facility and Suppliers' Credit in respect of items *(a)* and *(b)* above by IOC and MMTC respectively, *(d)* For import of goods by Ministries and Departments of Government of India on a certification from the Financial Adviser/Internal Finance Wing of the Ministry concerned that the import of such goods is as per authorisation of the Foreign Exchange Budget of the Department of Economic Affairs, *(e)* For import of Life-saving Drugs and Equipment. *(f)* For meeting 40 per cent of foreign exchange requirements of Advance Licences, Imprest Licence and import for replenishment of raw materials for Gem and Jewellery exports.

With effect from 2 March, 1993, the dual exchange rate system was replaced by the Unified Exchange Rate System (UERS) under which the 60:40 ratio was extended to 100 per cent conversion. The UERS was introduced to rectify the anomally of the LERMS under which exporters and other earners of foreign exchange indirectly subsidised certain imports. Under this system, the exchange rate was fully determined by market forces of relative demand and supply. The RBI had been announcing its buying and selling rates at the ongoing market rates for transactions with ADs. This system permitted 100 per cent conversion of the rupee for all exports and imports of goods. But the official RBI exchange rate continued for the conversion of items not permitted under the UERS. These included more than half-a-dozen invisible items of current account and all capital account payments. Further, various exchange control norms of the RBI remained in operation with a few relaxations.

As a result of the operation of the UERS, the exchange rate remained more or less steady at the level of Rs. 31.37 per dollar. With stability in the exchange rate and the large inflow of resources following liberalisation of foreign investment policy and removal of industrial and trade restrictions, there had been substantial improvement in the current account deficit. This led to the *current account convertibility* of the rupee effective 1 March, 1994. The RBI announced further relaxations in the exchange control regulations on a number of invisible items as part of the *current account* convertibility of the rupee. The final step towards current account convertibility was taken in August 1994 by further liberalisation of invisibles payments and acceptance of the obligations under Article VIII of the IMF. Under it, India is committed to forsake the use of exchange restrictions on current international transactions. There is no officially fixed exchange rate of the rupee. Instead, the rate is determined by the demand and supply conditions in the foreign exchange market. The RBI intervenes to maintain orderly market conditions and to curb excessive speculation in foreign exchange.

Foreign exchange is released by authorised dealers (ADs) for various purposes like foreign travel, medical treatment, gifts, services, studies, etc. Release of foreign exchange by ADs for the above purposes was initially governed by limits laid down by the RBI. Beyond the specified limits foreign exchange could be obtained after seeking prior approval of the RBI. Effective July 1995, the RBI has permitted ADs to provide exchange facilities to their customers for the above mentioned purposes beyond the indicative limit without its prior approval, provided they are satisfied about the bonafides of the application. But, they are required to report such transactions to the RBI.

The process of liberalisation towards current account convertibility has been continued by delegating more powers to ADs. (1) They have been permitted to export their surplus stocks of *foreign currency notes* and coins for realisation of proceeds to private money changers abroad, in addition to their overseas branches and correspondents. (2) They have been permitted to allow EEFC (Exchange Earners Foreign Currency) account holders to utilise funds held in such accounts for making remittances in foreign exchange connected with their trade and business related transactions which are of current account nature. (3) The RBI has set up *Inter-Bank Forex Clearing House* where foreign exchange transactions by ADs are cleared. (4) The RBI has set up a *Market Intelligence Cell* to study and closely monitor the developments in the Indian foreign exchange market. The Cell receives from the ADs on a daily basis information on forex transactions which are critically analysed and followed up.

9. CRITICAL APPRAISAL OF THE FUNCTIONING OF RBI

From a rudimentary beginning in 1935, the Reserve Bank of India has developed into a major central banking institution after it became a state-owned bank in January, 1949. Besides, it has been performing a variety of promotional and development functions.

Its Achievements

Some of the principal achievements of the RBI are as follows: 1. *Regulator of Credit.* The bank has been successfully regulating credit in the economy to meet the requirements of trade, industry and agriculture during periods of recession and inflation. For this purpose, it followed a cheap money policy in the early phase of development planning and after that a policy of controlled monetary expansion to meet the requirements of a growing economy.

2. *Banker to the Government.* As banker to the Government, the RBI has been admirably managing the public debt. It has successfully floated loans on behalf of the Central and State Governments at low interest rates. It has also provided ways and means advances to the State Governments through the sale of treasury bills. It has been rendering advice to the Government on economic matters in general and on financial matters in particular.

3. *Development of Sound Banking System.* Another achievement of the Bank has been that it has developed and promoted sound banking practices in the country. In exercise of the powers vested in it by the Banking Regulation Act, it has been keeping a constant vigil over the banks, trying to remove their defects, and strengthening them. Consequently, this has inspired public confidence in the banking system as a whole.

4. *Institutionalisation of Savings.* The RBI has been successfully promoting the institutionalisation of savings by promoting banking habits, by large scale extension of banking facilities in rural and urban areas, and promoting and establishing new specialised financial agencies.

5. *In the Field of Co-operative Credit.* The RBI has successfully promoted co-operative credit. It has strengthened co-operatives by setting up NRC (LTO) Fund and NRC (Stabilisation) Fund and NABARD which

now administers these Funds. It also finances the State Co-operative Banks. It has been due to the efforts of the RBI that the co-operative movement has been placed on a sound footing.

6. *In the Field of Rural Credit.* The Bank has been admirably engaged in the task of promoting rural credit since its inception. It runs a separate department to render advice to the Government on rural credit. By adopting the multi-agency approach (viz. the commercial banks, the co-operative banks, the RRBs, and NABARD), it has been successful in providing credit for the development of agriculture, trade, commerce, industry, and other productive activities in the rural areas.

7. *In the Sphere of Industrial Finance.* In the sphere of industrial credit, the RBI has played a pioneering role by promoting a wide range of institutions for providing medium and long term credit such as IDBI, IFCI, ICICI, IFC, UTI, etc. It also provides medium/short term credit limits to these institutions by rediscounting their usance bills and long-term assistance from the NIC (LTO) Fund.

8. *In the Field of Export Finance.* Another achievement of the bank has been in providing credit facilities to exporters. It has been providing concessional credit, refinance facilities, and guarantee to commercial banks for exporters. It has been instrumental in establishing the Export-Import Bank to provide credit and other facilities to exporters.

9. *Guardian of Banking System.* As the guardian of banking system, the RBI has been providing deposit insurance and credit guarantee facilities to the banks. For this purpose it has set up the Deposit Insurance and Credit Guarantee Corporation (DICGC).

10. *Promotion of Social Banking.* The RBI has played a vital role in the promotion of social banking in the country. It has progressively directed the banking system since 1969 towards national social economic objectives, including rural development and uplift of the weaker sections of the society. It has converted banks in India as instruments of social uplift instead of simply profit-making institutions.

11. *Change in the Pattern of Lending.* The Reserve Bank has been successful in changing the pattern of bank lending. *Firstly,* banks have been directed to lend 40 per cent of their total advances to the priority sectors. *Secondly,* they have been asked to ensure that 60 per cent of their deposits raised from rural and semi-urban centres are deployed as credit in those very areas. *Thirdly,* under the DRI scheme, the public sector banks have to ensure that one per cent of the previous year's advance is earmarked each year to be lent to certain specified weaker sections at a low rate of interest of 4 per cent.

12. *Development of Bill Market.* The RBI has been successful to a considerable extent in developing bill market in India. For this purpose, it has set up the Discount and Finance House of India (DFHI) and the Securities Trading Corporation of India (STCI) as major financial institutions to rediscount commercial bills. It has introduced a number of schemes such as 364-Day Treasury Bills, primary dealers in securities, etc.

13. *Providing Information and Research.* The Reserve Bank has been doing an excellent job in providing information and data on the different sectors of the economy through its weekly and monthly journals and annual reports. Its Department of Economic Analysis and Policy conducts highly useful surveys and carries on research on economic matters and publishes reports on them.

14. *Clearing House Facilities.* The Bank has been successfully rendering clearing house facilities at its 15 branches and 2 offices and at other places in the country through the SBI and its associates. It has introduced Electronic Clearing System. This has helped in the use of cheques and inter-bank transactions.

15. *Exchange Management and Control.* Another achievement of the RBI has been its admirable management and control of the foreign exchange. It has gradually and successfully led the Indian economy to current account convertibility of the rupee.

16. *Representation at International Fora.* The Bank has been successfully representing the country at the international monetary forum such as the IMF and the World Bank.

17. *Human Resource Development.* One of the principal achievements of the RBI has been the setting up of a number of training centres and colleges to impart training to the staff of co-operative banks, commercial banks, RRBs, NABARD etc. Thus it has played a major role in human resource development in the field of banking.

18. *Computerisation.* To modernise the functioning of the RBI, its Department of Information Technology (DIT) has introduced advanced computer technology for inter-office communication and Internet technology for information collection and sharing. It has also encouraged computerisation of branches of commercial

banks.

Failures of the RBI

Despite the above achievements, there are certain fields in which the RBI has not been able to function successfully. They are as under:

1. *Failure to Control Unorganised Money Market.* The Bank has not been able to control the unorganised sector of the money market. The indigenous bankers function independently of the policies of the RBI. The latter has failed to bring them under its control and supervision.

2. *Multiplicity of Interest Rates.* As there is a large unorganised monetary sector which is not under the RBI, there is no uniformity in the bank rate and other money market rates. Even the money market rates charged by banks and non-bank financial intermediaries differ widely.

3. *Failure to Check Inflationary Pressures.* Despite following the policy of controlled monetary expansion, the RBI has failed to control and contain inflationary pressure within the economy.

4. *Falling ProfitabHity of Banks.* The RBI's policy of credit squeeze has led to the decline in the profitability of banks. With total deposits of banks blocked by reserves upto about 54 per cent, only 46 per cent are left with them for lending. Out of this 40 per cent is required to be given to the priority sector. On the other hand, the deposits of banks are on the decline due to the growing number of alternative saving instruments. All these measures by RBI have led to decline in the profitability of banks.

5. *Failure to Develop Bill Culture.* Despite its best efforts, the RBI has failed to develop an organised bill market to provide rediscounting facilities to banks. In fact, it has not been able to develop bill culture so that commerce, trade and industry may deal in bills of exchange. Further, it has not done anything to systematise and recognise *hundis* as bills of exchange.

6. *Failure to Provide Sufficient Rural Credit.* No doubt, the RBI has done a lot in providing rural credit through multiple agencies, but it is insufficient keeping in view the credit needs of the rural population. Consequently, it has not been able to free the ruralites from the hold of the indigenous bankers and money-lenders.

7. *Failure to Develop Exchange Banks.* The Bank has failed to develop Indian exchange banks with the result that foreign banks operating in the country continue to pocket a major portion of the foreign exchange business. The State Bank of India and a few public sector banks which deal in foreign exchange business and have their offices in foreign countries have not been able to achieve much in this direction because of the lack of clear policy guidelines by the RBI

8. *Deterioration of Customer Service.* Since the nationalisation of 20 banks, the customer service in these banks has deteriorated. The RBI has recently adopted a few measures in this direction, but customer service in public sector still lags behind private and foreign banks.

9. *Failure to Control Black Money.* The RBI has failed to check the growth of black money in the country. In fact, its credit squeeze policy has encouraged black money because traders and businessmen are able to get credit from the black money.

Conclusion

Despite these failures, the RBI has ushered-in a new era of social banking. It has carried banking to the remotest corners of the country. It has created sound credit and monetary policies in keeping with the development efforts of the country. It has brought stability to the banking system. It has been instrumental in providing credit facilities to agriculturists, industrialists, exporters, and to ordinary persons engaged in different vocations. It is thus one of the prime movers in the development process.

EXERCISES

1. Describe the constitution and organisational structure of the Reserve Bank of India.
2. What are the functions of the Reserve Bank of India? How far has it succeeded as the Central Bank of the country?

3. Discuss the achievements and failures of the Reserve Bank of India.
4. What has the Reserve Bank of India done to develop and regulate banking in India?
5. Explain the role of Reserve Bank of India in developing Bill Market.
6. Explain how the Reserve Bank of India manages the exchange control system.
7. What role the Reserve Bank of India has been playing with regard to the financing of agriculture?
8. Discuss the policy of the Reserve Bank of India in financing industries in the country.
9. Give a critical appraisal of the functioning of Reserve Bank of India.
10. Write notes on : Bill Market Scheme; Exchange Control Management, Social Banking, Regulation of Banking in India by the Reserve Bank.

CHAPTER 67

Monetary Policy of Reserve Bank of India*

1. INTRODUCTION

Monetary policy in India is an adjunct of economic policy. As such, the objectives of monetary policy are not different from the objectives of economic policy. The three major objectives of economic policy in India have been growth, social justice, and price stability. The Government of India tries to manipulate its monetary policy through the Reserve Bank of India which is the monetary authority in the country. The monetary (or credit control) policy of the Reserve Bank has been characterised as one of controlled monetary expansion. It aims at controlling inflation by restraining the secondary expansion of credit and regulating the supply of money in order to meet the requirements of different sectors of the economy to accelerate the pace of economic growth.

ITS OBJECTIVES

Broadly speaking, the following are the objectives of monetary policy wrich the Reserve Bank has been trying to achieve:

1. *Price Stability.* The RBI tries to achieve price stability by controlling inflationary pressures in the area of aggregate demand through controlled monetary expansion and by facilitating allocation and effective utilisation of credit in relatively more productive channels.

2. *Reduce Deficit.* It tries to reduce the monetised deficit (net RBI credit to the Government) in order to bring down Government's gross fiscal deficit.

3. *Encourage Exports.* It boosts exports in order to solve the problem of balance of payments deficit.

4. *Growth.* It promotes growth through appropriate credit policy by promoting savings, mobilisation of resources and encouraging the requirements of different sectors of the economy according to plan priorities.

5. *Social Justice.* It supports programmes of social justice (i.e. more equitable distribution of income) by influencing the cost, volume and direction of credit to priority sectors of the economy.

Of these objectives, price stability is the dominant one. It is price stability which provides the appropriate environment in which growth can take place and social justice can be ensured. Price stability is also required to augment our exports and to service our external debt. In the context of economic growth, price stability does not mean no increase in prices. In fact, price stability refers to controlling inflation or keeping the general price level from rising by more than four per cent per year, as suggested by the RBI Chakravarty Committee (1985).

---

1. This also relates to Management of Credit and Currency.

For this the Committee advocated "monetary targeting with feed-back" in order to keep the growth of money supply in step with the demand for it. The monetary target is not fixed but may be revised on a mid-year assessment of the price situation.

2. METHODS OF CREDIT CONTROL

To achieve these objectives, the RBI follows the following methods of credit control:[1]

1. Open Market Operations

Open market operations refer to the sale and purchase of gold related securities and other securities, bills and bonds of Government by the RBI from and to the public and financial institutions. To control inflation and tackle the problem of excess liquidity due to foreign exchange inflows, the RBI sells Government securities. As a result, there is reduction in the cash balances of banks and other deposits of banks held by the RBI. The opposite happens when the RBI purchases securities from the open market. In Government securities, there were adhoc Treasury Bills which were replaced by Ways and Means Advances from April 1997. They are meant to serve as a means of meeting temporary mismatches between the receipts and expenditure of the Central Government rather than a source of financing fiscal deficit. This has provided more flexibility to the RBI in operating its monetary policy. Besides, to control fluctuations in call money market rates repos/reverse repo auctions, first on daily basis then with 3-7 day maturity, were introduced under full-fledged liquidity, Adjustment Facility (LAF) effective August 2000. Besides, weekly auctions of 14-day Treasury Bills and 28-days Treasury Bills; fortnightly auctions of 182-day Treasury Bills; and monthly auctions of 364-day Treasury Bills were started from 1997-98.

The RBI has been resorting to open market operations in order to reduce the lending power of commercial banks because its sale of securities have normally exceeded its purchases. But the effectiveness of open market operations as an instrument of credit control in India is limited by a number of factors. *First,* except for the gilt-edged market in India, there is the absence of other first class securities. *Second,* the market for Government securities is a 'captive' market over which the RBI has almost a monopoly and some institutional investors like LIC, UTI, GIC, and commercial banks, etc. are required to invest in them. *Third,* open market operation: are being used as an instrument of debt-management rather than to influence the cost and availability of credit. As such, open market operations have not been a success in India.

1. Bank Rate Policy

The bank rate is the' rate fixed by the central bank at which it rediscounts first class bills of exchange and government securities held by commercial banks. But in India, the bank rate policy is limited to give advances to commercial banks against first class bills of exchange by the RBI. The latter include Government securities and genuine trade bills. Under the Bill Rediscounting Scheme introduced in November 1970, all licensed scheduled commercial banks are eligible to rediscount with the RBI genuine trade bills arising out of sale or despatch of goods.

The objectives of the RBI's bank rate policy are to influence the availability and cost of credit. The RBI has been unsuccessful in achieving these objectives. From its establishment in 1935 up to 14 November. 1951, the bank rate was stable at 3 per cent. It was cheap monetary policy which led to an unlimited expansion of credit. Consequently, speculative activities received encouragement and the deficit in balance of payments increased. For the first time, the bank rate was raised to 3.5 per cent in November 1951. It was raised to 4 per cent in May 1957, to 4.5 per cent in January, 1963; to 5 per cent in September, 1964; to 6 per cent in January, 1971 and to 7 per cent in May 1973. With an unprecedented rise in prices, the RBI resorted to a policy of dear money in July 1974 and raised the bank rate to 9 per cent in 1977, to 10 per cent in July 1981, to 11 per cent in July 1991 and to 12 per cent in October 1991. To overcome recession in the economy, the RBI started following cheap money policy by reducing the bank rate to 11 per cent in April 1997 and subsequently by stages to 6 per cent on April 29, 2003.

1. We have given a detailed emanation which may be confined to the latest measures without loss in continuity.

Thus the bank rate had not been used as an instrument of credit control till 1973. It is only in the 1980s and 1990s that its proper use has been made in the form of cheap or dear monetary policy.

3. Interest Rate Policy

Interest rate adjustment is a flexible and potent tool of credit policy. It reinforces restrictive/liberal impact of credit policy. In order to supplement the bank rate policy, the RBI has been following the policy of changing the interest rate structure for different sectors of the economy in the light of evolving economic trends.

(i) *Deposit Rates.* Since November 1975, the RBI has been following the policy of administered interest rates. This policy has the twin objectives of mobilising savings and providing funds for productive activities in the priority sectors of the economy at concessional rates of interest The interest rates on all saving instruments including bank deposits are sometimes reduced to prevent banks from getting locked into longer period maturities. At other times, they are raised to assist the banks in deposit mobilisation and to offer a better rate of savings. Upto 21 April, 1992, the term deposit rates of scheduled commercial banks were prescribed in three slabs of maturities and rates. Effective 22 April, 1992, the banks were given freedom to determine the term deposits of three maturity slabs of their chbice, subject to a choice of interest rate 'not exceeding 13 per cent*. With the fall in inflation rate, the ceiling rate was gradually reduced to 'not exceeding 10 per cent' by 2 September 1993. When the inflation rate started rising, the ceiling rate was gradually raised to 'not exceeding 12 per cent' effective 18 April, 1995 for 46 days to 3 years and above.

To augment the resources of banks and to impart greater flexibility to term deposit rate structure, the banks have been allowed freedom to fix their own interest rates on domestic term deposits of all categories. The minimum period of term deposits has been gradually reduced from 46 days to 30 days; and subsequently to 15 days. Effective May 2001, the banks had been permitted to pay higher interest rates to senior citizens on their term deposits by 0.5 to 1.0 per cent.

The savings deposit rate has been lowered from to 4.0 per cent to 3.0 per cent effective March 1,2003.

Term deposit rates on NRE accounts were also rationalised in accordance with the domestic rates. With a view to maintaining the differential between the interest rates on term deposits and NRE Rupee term deposits, banks were permitted to offer differential rates of interest on NRE deposits on size-group basis subject to the overall ceiling rate effective 27 April, 2000. Effective 4 April, 1996, interest rates on NRE term deposits of over two years had been freed for banks.

(ii) *Lending Rates.* The lending rate structure prescribed for banks since their nationalisation in 1969 had been cumbersome and complicated. It was characterised by a multiplicity of rates relating, to numerous criteria, such as size of loan, priority of a sector, location of activity, specific programmes, income of borrowers, etc. In September 1990, the RBI rationalised the lending rate structure of commercial banks. It is linked to the size of loan granted by the commercial banks.

When the inflation rates were high, upward revisions were made in the lending rates of commercial banks. The first upward revision was made on 13 April, 1991, when the minimum rate on advances above Rs. 2 lakh was raised from 16 per cent to 17 per cent effective 13 April, 1991 and gradually to 20 per cent on 9 October, 1991. As the inflation rate declined and the macroeconomic situation improved, the lending rate was reduced gradually from 20 per cent to 14 per cent effective 1 March, 1994. Effective 18 October, 1994, the prescription of a *minimum* lending rate has been abolished and banks have been given freedom to fix the prime lending rate (PLR) for all advances above Rs. 2 lakh. Each bank is required to declare its PLR and made uniformly applicable to all its branches.

In keeping with its policy of rationalisation of the lending rate structure according to the size of credit limit, the RBI reduced the number of categories from six to three by April 1993. The three categories with interest rates effective 18 October, 1994 were: (a) Upto Rs. 25,000 at 12 per cent (fixed); *(b)* Over Rs. 25,000 and upto Rs. 2 lakh at 13 per cent (fixed); and (c) Over Rs. 2 lakh freed.

Under the DIR (Differential Interest Rate) scheme, term loans are provided to small and water transport operators, professionals and self-employeds in the priority sector at the concessional rate of 4 per cent by both the commercial banks and urban co-operative banks. They are required to lend 40 per cent of their total advances to the priority sector.

Alongwith the above measures, interest rates on export credit are reviewed from time to time with a view to providing an incentive to exporters for repatriating the proceeds as well as discouraging them from delaying repatriation of export proceeds. On *pre-shipment* export credit, banks have been allowed to charge 10 per cent interest upto 180 days and 13 per cent beyond 180 days to 270 days since 1 April, 1999. On *post-shipment* export credit upto 90 days, the interest rate has been 10 per cent since 1 April, 1999, beyond 90 days to 6 months, and beyond six months the banks are free to charge interest rates decided by them.

4. Changes in Variable Reserve Ratio

The variable reserve ratio is a very effective instrument of monetary control with the RBI. In India, the variable reserve ratio is of the following types:

(i) Cash Reserve Ratio (CRR). Since the establishment of RBI till 1956, the commercial banks were required to keep 2 per cent of their time deposits and 5 per cent of their demand deposits with the RBI in the form of reserves. Thus this tool of monetary policy was not used for more than 20 years in India. With the RBI Amendment Act, 1956, the RBI was empowered to raise the time deposits of commercial banks from 2 to 8 per cent and the demand deposits from 5 to 20 per cent. By the RBI Amendment Act, 1962 the distinction between time and demand deposits was abolished and the provision was made to keep the CRR between 3 to 15 per cent. After this, the RBI had been making changes in the CRR in keeping with the monetary and economic conditions.

Effective 1 July, 1989, instead of separate ratios for different types of liabilities, there is a uniform CRR of 15 per cent of the entire net demand and time liabilities (NDTL) of banks, including FCNR and NRE accounts. The CRR was reduced to 14 per cent effective 15 May, 1993 and again raised to 15 per cent effective 6 August, 1994. This was to meet monetary pressure arising from large capital inflows. For the same reason, the CRR on FCNR accounts was raised to 15 per cent and on NRNR deposits to 7.5 per cent. When these conditions reversed and money growth slowed, the CRR was reduced from 15 per cent to 14 per cent effective 9 December 1995 and that on FCRR and NRNR deposited removed. To augment the lendable resources of banks, the CRR was further reduced from 14 per cent to 13 per cent effective 11 May, 1996, and to 12 per cent effective 6 July, 1996 and in subsequent years gradually to 8 per cent on l April, 2000 and to7.5 per cent on 14 May, 2001 .The reduction in CRR to 7.5 per cent has been done to enable banks to reduce their PLR and to release more liquidity into the monetary system. As a policy measure, the variations in CRR has been more successful in controlling credit than open market operations and bank rate policy.

(ii) Statutory Liquidity Ratio (SLR). Another important tool of monetary policy with the RBI is the Statutory Liquidity Ratio (SLR) which supplements the CRR. Under the Banking Regulation Act, 1949, the commercial banks are required to keep 20 per cent of their net demand and time liabilities (NDTL) deposits with them in the form of liquidity ratio. In this liquidity ratio are included excess reserves, current account balances of the commercial banks with the RBI and other banks, gold and unencumbered approved securities. But whenever the RBI raised the CRR, the commercial banks would make this unsuccessful by increasing their liquidity power through the sale of government securities. In order to overcome this weakness, the SLR was raised to 25 per cent by the Banking Amendment Act of 1962. But the cash reserves kept with the RBI were not included in this ratio. In order to contain the liquidity growth in the banking system and consequent monetary expansion, the SLR was raised to 30 per cent in November, 1972. Since then it had been revised upward regularly so that with effect from 22 September, 1990 it had been 38.5 per cent. To make more funds available for. commercial bank lending, the *base* SLR on NDTL was reduced gradually and by the end of 1996, it was brought down to 25 per cent as per the recommendations of the Narasimhan Committee. The incremental SLR is 25 per cent. This refers to the ratio, the banks are required to keep if there NDTL increase over the base SLR. The advantages of SLR are that by implementing it along with CRR, it controls the liquidity of banks and thereby limits their power to make advances to trade and industry. Thus the quantitative monetary policy is successful in reducing inflationary pressures. Second, more financial resources are available to the government for its use.

5. Selective Credit Controls

Selective credit controls are meant to regulate and control the supply of credit. They aim at channelising the flow of bank credit from speculative and other undesirable purposes to socially desirable and economically useful uses. Thus they help in curtailing the rise in prices of commodities.

The method of selective credit controls was introduced in India by the RBI in May 1956. Under this: *(i)* it fixes minimum margins for advances against securities for banks. These margins are from 20 to 100 per cent; *(ii)* it fixes ceilings on maximum advances against stocks of certain commodities to traders; *(iii)* it fixes minimum discriminatory rates of interest for certain kinds of advances by banks; *(iv)* it prohibits advances for financing hoarding of certain commodities; and *(v)* prohibits the discounting of bills of exchange relating to the sale of some selected commodities.

Selective credit controls relate to such commodities as cotton, wheat, paddy/ rice, pulses, oilseeds, vegetable oils, sugar, gur and khandsari, man-made fibres and cloth. The rate of interest charged on advances by banks against the security of such commodities is higher than on other securities. If the RBI wants to control speculation on the prices of such commodities, it raises the minimum margins. In case it wants to liberalise credit facilities for them, it lowers the minimum margins. It does so in keeping with changing market conditions.

For instance, to curb inflationary pressures, the RBI had fixed the ceiling of 45 per cent on the incremental net non-food credit deposit ratio for banks from October 1989. Further, restrictions had been placed on loans for purchase of consumer durables and other non-priority sector personal loans. The minimum margin for loans against shares and debentures/bonds was fixed at 75 per cent. When in early 1992, the inflation rate started declining, the banks were advised to support the revival of productive activity. At the same time, effective 22 April, 1992, all restrictions on credit or purchase of consumer durables, other non-priority sector personal loans and stipulation on net non-food credit-deposit ratio were removed. Effective 21 October, 1996, selective credit controls on pulses, coarse grains, oil seeds, vanaspati, sugar, gur, khandsari, cotton, kapas had been abolished, except buffer stocks. Banks were given freedom to fix margins on advances against sensitive commodities, except unreleased stocks of sugar for which 15 per cent margin had been fixed. Effective 2 December, 1996, the banks were granted freedom to advance loans against shares/debentures with the maximum limit of Rs. 10 lakh. It has since been raised to Rs. 20 lakh.

Credit Monitoring Arrangement (CMA). With effect from 10 October 1988, the RBI dispensed with the Credit Authorisation Scheme (CAS) and introduced the Credit Monitoring Arrangement (CMA) for bank lending for working capital purposes. Under the revised scheme effective 30 October, 1996 all sanctions/ renewals of credit limits to borrowers enjoying fund-based working capital limits of Rs. 10 crores and above and term loans in excess of Rs. 5 crores were required to be reported by the banks to the RBI for post-sanction scrutiny. All sanctions/renewals of credit limits were required to be reported to the RBI. In this way, the RBI regulated the sanctioning of loans by banks through CMA. The CMA was discontinued from 8 December, 1997.

In recent years, the Reserve Bank has announced several steps to facilitate the flow of credit to the commercial sector, particularly for exports, information technology, infrastructure, agriculture, small scale industries, etc. The coverage of the priority sector credit has been widened considerably. Bank credit to NBFCs (non-bank financial companies) for on-lending to small road and water transport operators, software industry having credit limit up to Rs. 1 crore, to the food and agro-based sector, to NBFCs and financial institutions for on-lending to the tiny sector, and to both public and private sector undertaking for financing infrastructure projects is now being treated as priority sector lending. Besides, bank lending to sensitive sectors comprising capital market, real estate (housing) and commodities is regulated in keeping with the trends in the economy.

Their Effectiveness. Selective credit controls have been more effective in controlling credit than the quantitative methods. They have been instrumental in channelising the flow of credit from speculative and other undesirable purposes to socially desirable and economically useful purposes. They have helped in restricting the demand for money by laying down certain conditions for borrowers by fixing minimum margin requirements and other limits. Thus they have been successful in regulating credit for different uses in various sectors of the economy according to plan priorities.

Despite all these successes, selective credit controls have failed to control the demand for and supply of money in the country. They have, therefore, failed to control inflationary pressures.

With the introduction of commercial paper by the large organised sector, the RBI's control over credit through the CMA had become less effective. Now large industries can raise money directly from the market at cheaper rates than bank credit.

Moreover, trade and industry can get funds from non-bank financial institutions, mutual fund's, etc. which have made selective credit controls less effective.

Above all, selective credit controls alone are not effective in controlling credit. They must be combined with general (or quantitative) control measures like bank rate, open market operation, CRR, SLR, etc.

6. Direct Action

The Banking Companies Act, 1949 empowers the RBI to caution or prohibit banks generally or any individual bank in particular, from entering into any particular transaction or class of transactions. The RBI has also the power to inspect any bank and its books accounts. On a report from the RBI, the Central Government may prohibit any bank from receiving fresh deposits or direct the RBI to order for the winding up of the bank or its merger with some other bank.

7. Moral Suasion

Besides, the above noted quantitative and qualitative measures of credit control, the RBI also follows the method of moral suasion. By this method of persuasion, suggestion and advice, the RBI asks the banks to follow its declared monetary policy from time to time. By sending circular letters or calling meetings of directors of banks, it persuades them not to give credit for speculative activities and/or to give more credit facilities to priority sectors of the economy. Before the nationalisation of 20 banks in India, the method of moral suasion was not successful but now all banks follow the RBI guidelines. As a matter of fact, the RBI is so powerful that no bank dares to ignore its circulars and suggestions.

3. CRITICAL APPRAISAL OF MONETARY POLICY

The main aim of India's monetary policy which is regulated by the RBI, is to have growth with stability. It is also known as the policy of controlled monetary (or credit) expansion. In pursuance of this policy, the RBI affects the quantity, availability and cost of credit by adopting both the quantitative and qualitative methods of credit control. It increases the quantity of money and credit to meet the growing requirements of the developing economy, and at the same time imposes restrictions on the use of credit for non-essential and unproductive activities. In periods of recession, it follows the policy of easy credit or cheap money, and to control inflationary pressures, it follows the policy of credit squeeze or tight money. It is contributing to the economic development of the economy in an important way by giving cheap and easy credit to the priority sector consisting of marginal and small farmers, artisans, unemployeds, small traders, village and small industries, etc. At the same time, it also provides credit to large industries and to exporters to meet their expanding credit requirements so that production may increase and exports expand.

4. CAUSES OF FAILURE OF MONETARY POLICY

Despite these achievements, the monetary policy of RBI has not been a success in bringing stability to the economy. Some of the reasons are:

(1) *Inflationary Pressures.* During the plans, the average growth rate of money supply has been 15 per cent per annum with the average growth rate of domestic product of 5 per cent per annum. The disproportionate and persistent increase in liquidity has been a significant factor contributing to inflationary pressures in the economy.

(2) *Excessive Government Borrowing and Budgetary Deficits.* Another reason for the failure of monetary policy in India has been the impact of large and growing Government borrowing and budgetary deficits over the plans. The budgetary deficits have been virtually monetised (i.e. financed) by the RBI through the creation of ad hoc treasury bills. Besides, the RBI has been providing support to the Government's market borrowing programmes. Consequently, this has led to the phenomenal increase in reserve money contributed (i.e.

created) by RBI credit to the Government. This has led to inflationary pressure in the economy.

(3) *High CRR and SLR.* In order to contain the inflationary impact of monetisation of the budget deficits, the RBI has been continuously increasing the CRR and SLR. The reserve ratios in India are quite high being 45 per cent of the deposits, leaving 55 per cent for lending. Out of these, 40 per cent go to priority sector advances at low rates of interest. Thus only a small portion of funds is available for deployment in non-food and trading activities at commercial rates of interest. This has tended to reduce the profitability of banks.

(4) *Defective Interest Rate Policy.* The RBI has been following a policy of administered interest rates. The structure of these rates is complex and cumbersome. It conceals an element of arbitrariness. It fails to take into account the risk involved, the maturity period or the liquidity factor on individual instruments of credit: The interest rate structure is also not separate for the captive market and the borrowing public.

(5) *Organised Sector Uninfluenced by Bank Credit.* With the introduction of commercial paper by the large organised sector, industries can raise money directly from the market at cheaper rates than bank credit. This has blunted the edge of monetary policy in controlling the activities of the organised sector.

(6) *Other Sources for Banks.* Besides getting funds from NBFIs, commercial banks are able to maintain enough liquidity with them from the call money market, mutual funds and similar other sources. As a result, the RBI is not in a position to control the lending activities of the banks.

(7) Little Co-ordination between Monetary and Fiscal Policies. There is little co-ordination between monetary and fiscal policies being pursued by the RBI and the Government. There is no co-ordination between the expansion in RBI credit to the Government and Central Government's budgetary deficits. With increasing budgetary deficits from year to year, the RBI has to monetise them. Consequently, its power to regulate the volume of money is limited. This has made monetary policy less effective in India.

(8) *Existence of Parallel Economy.* There is a large sector of unaccounted black money which is beyond the jurisdiction of RBI. The existence of this parallel economy makes a mockery of the credit policy of the RBI because individuals, traders and businessmen borrow, lend and spend money at their will.

(9) *Government Policy.* There are some more weaknesses of monetary policy of the RBI due to Government policies. These are: (i) the government depends more on the public for borrowing outside the captive market, and *(ii)* yields on the Government securities are not fixed independently of the conditions in the capital market.

Conclusion. We have seen above that one of the principal reasons for the failure of monetary policy in controlling inflationary pressures in India has been the growing budgetary deficits. Monetary policy at best can control the secondary effects of excessive budget deficits. It is, therefore, essential that monetary and fiscal policies should move in tandem.

EXERCISES

1. Explain critically monetary policy in India.
2. Explain India's monetary policy. To what extent it has been successful in its objectives?
3. Discuss critically the monetary policy of the Reserve Bank of India.
4. What are the instruments of selective credit control employed by the Reserve Bank of India? Discuss their effectiveness.
5. Explain how the Bank Rale Policy is operated by the Reserve Bank of India.

CHAPTER 68

The State Bank of India (SBI)

1. ITS CONSTITUTION

The original name of the State Bank of India was Imperial Bank of India. The Imperial Bank of India was formed in 1921 by amalgamating the three Presidency banks of Bengal, Bombay and Madras. Prior to Independence, the Imperial Bank was handling the entire business and banking transactions of the Government. Though the Reserve Bank of India had been established in 1935, it was undertaking only central banking functions. Therefore, the Imperial Bank continued to handle Government transactions.

On the recommendations of the All India Rural Credit Survey Committee (1954), the Government of India nationalised the Imperial Bank of India and renamed it as the State Bank of India with effect from 1 July, 1955. Further, eight banks of the former princely States were brought under the SBI as its subsidiaries in 1959. They were State Bank of Bikaner, State Bank of Jaipur, State Bank of Patiala, State Bank of Saurashtra, State Bank of Indore, State Bank of Hyderabad, State Bank of Mysore, and State Bank of Travancore. In 1963, State Bank of Bikaner and State Bank of Jaipur were merged as State Bank of Bikaner and Jaipur.

2. ITS ORGANISATIONAL STRUCTURE

The SBI is not a bank wholly owned by the Government. It is a corporate body with an authorised share capital, of Rs. 1000 crore and paid-up capital of Rs. 526 crores of shares of Rs. 10 each as on 31 March, 1998. The apex body in the organisational structure of the SBI is the Central Board of Directors, which consists of a Chairman, two Managing Directors and 17 Directors appointed/elected under Section 19(1) of the State Bank of India Act, 1955. The Chairman and the Managing Directors are appointed by the Central Government in consultation with the RBI for a period not exceeding five years. Out of 17 Directors 6 are ex-officio representing different organisations, 4 are elected by the shareholders, 6 are nominated by the Central Government and one is nominated by the RBI. To manage the different Departments of the Bank, there is a Central: Management Committee which has ten members consisting of the Chairman, two Managing Directors and seven Deputy Managing Directors. The Chairman is the ex-officio member of the Committee. All the Deputy Managing Directors function under the overall charge of the Managing Directors. During 1995-96, several organisational changes have been carried out in the areas of structure, systems and-strategies of the SB I. Lean and integrated top management now consists of the Chairman, group executives for National Banking Group, Corporate Banking Group, International Banking Group and Associates and Subsidiaries Group and four staff functionaries in charge of financial, credit, human resources and technology management, and inspection and audit.

Three Strategic Business Units (SBUs) have been set up under the Corporate Banking Group to focus attention on very large corporate customers, lease finance and project finance.'They are the Corporate Accounts Group, Leasing Group and Project Finance Group. Each SBU has been given profit responsibility.

A committee approach has been adopted, both at the apex and circle levels for sanctioning large advances.

For this purpose, Central Office Credit Committee and Circle Credit Committees have been set up. They have been delegated higher financial powers to ensure faster decision-making of credit disposals. At the circle level, Commercial and Development and Personal Banking Networks have been created under the charge of General Managers to cater to the client-specific banking needs.

3. ITS OBJECTIVES

The State Bank of India was established with the following specific objectives:

1. To have a strong commercial bank under the control and supervision of the Government.
2. To spread banking facilities in rural, semi-urban and metropolitan areas by opening 400 branches within five years of its establishment. This policy of branch expansion has since been continued.
3. To help spread banking in rural areas for the purpose of encouraging and mobilising savings among the ruralists and to provide credit to them.
4. To subscribe to the debentures of State Land Development Banks and to advance loans on their security.
5. To strengthen co-operative societies, help in the establishment of licensed warehouses arid co-operative marketing societies.
6. To provide financial assistance to small, cottage and village industries.
7. To help other banks and strengthen the banking system.
8. To help the RBI in implementing its monetary and credit policies.

4. ITS FUNCTIONS

The State Bank performs the following functions:

1. *Central Banking Functions.* The SBI performs a number of functions on behalf of the Reserve Bank of India.

(a) It acts as the agent of the RBI where the latter has no branch, *(b)* It receives money on behalf of the Central and State Governments and makes payments on their behalf, (c) It buys and sells securities on behalf of the Government and manages the public debt, *(d)* It receives deposits from commercial banks and state co-operative banks and in turn lends to them, *(e)* It provides remittance facilities to these banks. *(f)* It rediscounts their bills of exchange, *(g)* It acts as a clearing house at places where the RBI has no office.

2. *Accepts Deposits.* The State Bank accepts deposits of all kinds from the Indian public and NRIs in rupees and foreign currencies.

3. *Gives Loans and Advances.* It gives loans and advances against an eligible security including goods, bills of exchange, promissory notes, fully paid shares and debentures or other securities of a civil authority, etc.

4. *Invests and Borrows.* The SBI invests in Government securities and borrows from the Reserve Bank.

5. *Deals in Bills of Exchange.* The State Bank draws, accepts, discounts, buys and sells bills of exchange and deals in letters of credit payable in and outside India.

6. *Deals in Gold and Silver.* The SBI buys and sells gold and silver. In June and July 1991, it sold gold to the Swiss Bank and pledged gold to the Bank of England on behalf of the Reserve Bank.

7. *Deals in Foreign Currencies.* The SBI is an authorised agent for dealing in foreign currencies. As such, it exchanges foreign currencies in Indian rupees and rupees into foreign currencies.

8. *Acts as Agent.* It acts as the agent of any registered co-operative bank.

9. *Business on Commission.* The State Bank transacts pecuniary business on commission.

10. *Underwrites Issues.* It underwrites issues of stocks, shares, debentures and other securities in which it is authorised to invest.

11. *Capital Stock of Banking Company.* It can subscribe to, buy, acquire, hold and sell any shares in the capital stock of any banking company.

12. *Form Subsidiary.* It can form any banking company as its subsidiary or take over any banking company on the direction of the Reserve Bank.

13. *Hire Purchase Companies.* It is authorised to make loans and advances to firms and companies engaged

in the financing of hire-purchase transactions on the security of book debts, etc. subject to the approval of the Central Board.

14. *Housing Schemes.* The State Bank is authorised to act as an agent of the Central Government, a State Government or any corporation in implementing schemes for financing the construction of houses and manage the funds placed at its disposal for this purpose.

15. *Finances Foreign Trade.* The SBI finances the foreign trade of the country.

5. WORKING OR ACHIEVEMENTS OF STATE BANK OF INDIA

The State Bank of India is the biggest commercial bank in the country with the largest number of branches and offices in India and abroad. Since its nationalisation in 1955, its working reveals that it has made tremendous progress in deposits, advances, rural credit, industrial finance, priority sectors, merchant banking, mutual fund, housing finance, factoring etc. We discuss below its role and importance as the leading commercial bank of the country.

A. Banking Trends

1. *Paid-up Capital and Reserves.* There has been a phenomenal growth in the paid-up capital and reserves of the State Bank over the years. From mere Rs. 12 crores in 1955 and Rs. 20 crores in 1969, they had risen to Rs. 9,608 crores as at the end of March 1998.

2. *Deposits Growth.* The SBI has made great efforts towards deposit mobilisation. In absolute terms, they increased from Rs. 226 crores in 1955 to Rs. 131,091 crores in 1998.

3. *Credit Expansion.* The Bank has expanded much its policy of giving loans and advances for food and non-food purposes. The overall amount of advances increased from Rs. 106 crores in 1955 to Rs. 841 crores in 1969 to Rs. 74,237 crores as on March, 1998.

4. *Investments.* Its investments in Government securities also show considerable growth. In absolute amount, they increased from Rs. 117 crores in 1955 to Rs. 350 crores in 1969 and to Rs. 54,982 crores in March, 1998.

5. *Branch Expansion.* Since its nationalisation in 1955, the SBI has been successfully carrying on its policy of branch expansion. Its number of offices including foreign offices increased from 497 in 1955 to 8,979 in June 2003. Alongwith branch expansion, the number of employees also increased from 14,682 to 2,33,000 over the period.

6. *Other Highlights.* Its credit-deposit ratio was 47 per cent in 1995 which increased to 62 per cent in 1996. Its capital adequacy ratio was 13.50 per cent in 2002-03 well above the stipulated 9 per cent.

B. State Bank of India and Agricultural Finance

The State Bank of India is a pioneer in the field of agricultural finance. In fact, it has been a pace setter for other banks in rural banking. It has been helping in providing rural finance in the following ways:

1. *Branch Expansion.* At the time of nationalisation, the State Bank was required to open not less than 400 branches within five years of its inception mainly in rural and semi-urban areas. In fact, it opened 416 branches during the stipulated period. Since then it has kept up the tempo of branch expansion with the result that at the end of June, 2003, it had 4,098 branches in rural areas which formed about 46 per cent of its total branches in the country.

2. *Remittance Facilities.* With the spread of a network of branches in rural areas, the SBI has been providing cheap remittance facilities to State and Central Co-operative Banks, Land Development Banks, farmers and traders.

3. *Help to Co-operative Banks.* The SBI has been of great help to co-operative and land development banks engaged in providing rural credit. It grants short term credit to the State and Central Co-operative Banks against Government securities at a concessional rate. It also grants advances to these banks for financing marketing of agricultural produce, distribution of fertilisers, and procurement of foodgrains.

4. *Help to Land Development Banks.* The State helps the Land Development Banks which provide long term credit to agriculturists in the following ways: The SBI subscribes to the debentures of LDBs and grants them loans and advances on the security of such debentures. It also gives advances to them for a short-term on the guarantee of the State Government, pending flotation of debentures by them.

5. *Credit to Co-operative Marketing and Processing. Societies.* It provides direct credit to co-operative marketing and processing societies for working capital requirements. This help is given when they are unable to get financial assistance from Central/State Co-operative Banks. The marketing societies are given advances against the pledge of their goods/produce to the SBI till they sell the produce in the market. Similarly, the Bank grants loans to co-operative processing societies engaged in the processing of sugar, jute, cotton, etc.

6. *Production Finance.* The SBI provides short term credit to individual farmers for raising of crops.

7. *Finance for Irrigation.* The Bank has been extending assistance by way of term loans to various minor irrigation projects, command area development schemes, dugwell and tubewell sinking projects, etc. Besides, under the Special Project Agriculture sponsored by the Rural Electrification Corporation for energisation of pumpsets. The Bank has also been financing *drip irrigation scheme* which involves application of adequate water to the plant root at definite intervals, thereby ensuring efficient management of limited water resources.

8. *Modernisation of Farm Practices.* The SBI provides finance to farmers from raising agricultural productivity through modernisation of farm practices.

9. *Wasteland Development.* The Bank extends credit facilities to farmers for reclaiming wastelands under social forestry schemes, for raising nurseries and planting trees to meet the raw material requirements of fuel and fodder. It also provides credit for setting up plantations in order to meet the raw material requirements of user industries, joint sector undertaking, companies, co-operatives and individual entrepreneurs.

10. *Financing of Warehouses.* The establishment of warehouses helps in the marketing of agricultural produce by farmers. The SBI has been associated with development of warehouses in a number of States. It also gives advances to farmers against warehouse receipts thereby preventing distress sales on the part of growers and provides a cushion against violent fluctuations in the prices of farm produce. Warehouses help in storing farm products and prevent their wastage.

11. *Financing of Fisheries.* The SBI finances fisheries schemes for increasing fish production to meet the domestic demand and export potential.

12. *Financing of Other Activities.* The SBI also provides financing assistance to special agricultural activities such as animal husbandry, cattle breeding, dairy farming, piggery, poultry farming, horticulture, sericulture, vermi-culture, tissue-culture and mushroom cultivation and high-tech agriculture. During 1995-96, the Bank's advances to agriculture and allied activities amounted to Rs. 6,749 crores.

13. *Service Area Approach.* Under the Service Area Approach introduced from 1 April, 1989, 86 per cent of the Bank's branches had implemented village credit plans in 1,12,064 villages allotted under SAA. The Bank's branches had also to finance 'non-target' group of borrowers in 54,353 villages allotted to branches of Regional Rural Banks sponsored by the RBI, but falling outside the service areas of the branches of the Bank. Under the activity-wise Special Credit Plan, the Bank disbursed Rs. 2,706 crores during 1995-96.

14. *Integrated Area Approach.* Since 1971, the SBI has been laying emphasis on an integrated area approach with developing compact areas where economic growth could be accelerated with the Bank's support, preference being given to areas which are backward and where special schemes of the Government have been taken up. In keeping with this approach, the SBI has started the *Village Adoption Scheme.* Under this scheme, the Bank adopts a village, fixes a target and meets the entire financial needs of the village including its farmers, artisans and others.[1]

15. *ADBs and ABDs.* The State Bank has Agricultural Development Branches (ADBs) and Agricultural Banking Divisions (ABDs) in selective areas particularly included in IRDP, HYVP and IAAP areas. The aim is to finance allround development of agriculture. The Bank works in close co-operation with NABARD.

16. *RRBs.* The Bank also finances rural activities through the Regional Rural Banks. It has sponsored 30 RRBs in 14 States covering 76 districts with a network of 2,385 branches. Under the first phase of restructuring, 8 SBI-sponsored RRBs were covered. In the second phase, 9 RRBs have been covered.

---

1. Assistance to Weaker Sections of Society under Other Achievements of SBI given below should also be mentioned here.

Conclusion. The State Bank has been a pioneer in agricultural finance in the country. It has been providing direct as well as indirect credit facilities to farmers, artisans, marginal farmers, and weaker sections of rural India.

C. State Bank of India and Industrial Finance

The State Bank of India occupies the premier position in providing finance to large/medium, and small scale industries. The type of financial assistance being rendered to them is as under:

1. Financing Large/Medium Scale Industries

The Bank has been financing medium/large scale industries on a selective basis. On the one hand, it has been financing new ventures of industrial groups with a good track record and on the other, new generation entrepreneurs with viable ventures. During 1995-96, the Bank's industrial advances were Rs. 8,298 crores. The Bank has been making loans and advances to such industrial groups as iron and steel, coal, electricity generation, chemicals, cement, petroleum, engineering, cotton textiles, food processing, gem and jewellery, paper products, etc.

Industrial Finance Branches (IFBs). To strengthen infrastructure for catering 'to medium/large industries, it has set up 9 IFBs at important centres.

Monitoring of Credit. The Bank has been making special efforts for monitoring of credit by exposing the officials to different training programmes, including on-the-job training at the apex level.

Industrial Rehabilitation. The SBI set up a separate Department of Industrial Rehabilitation in 1990-91 to deal with sick and financially weak units and to rehabilitate them. Its main thrust towards this direction has been to extend nursing assistance to the sick units, mainly under the aegis of the Board for Industrial and Financial Reconstruction (BIFR). At the same time, speedy disposal of cases which are not amenable to nursing has been achieved through compromises, recoveries, write-offs and mergers with healthy companies. So far, 101 out of the 351 rehabilitation packages drawn up for assisted units under the direction of BIFR have been put in operation, and 51 companies ordered to be wound up during the year.

Infrastructure Development. For financing infrastructure projects, the Bank assisted 9 independent power projects envisaging Rs. 2,276 crores. The Bank also sanctioned Bid Bond guarantees to enable 8 companies bid for Basic and Cellular services during 1995-96.

2. Financing of Small Scale Industries

The State Bank has been meeting the growing needs of the small scale sector by providing credit facilities on liberal terms. Its financial assistance covers all stages of manufacturing, viz. working capital, purchase of raw materials, marketing, entrepreneurial assistance, etc. It also covers expansion and modernisation of plants and equipment. Smaller units predominate the Bank's portfolio of small scale industries and about 66 per cent of the small industrial units financed by the Bank have limits below Rs. 25,000. The Bank's outstanding advances to small scale units stood at Rs. 7,790 crores at the end of March, 1996 and the number of units financed was 10 lakh.

Equity Fund. To provide equity support to small scale units, the Bank operates its Equity Fund Scheme. Under this scheme, it provides interest free loans, repayable over a period of 5-7 years with an initial starting period. Equity support is provided up to Rs. 1 lakh to deserving entrepreneurs setting up new small scale units and upto Rs. 50,000 to professionals and self-employed persons.

Entrepreneur Scheme. Under this scheme, the Bank finances technically qualified persons and experienced craftsmen up to Rs. 10 lakhs for starting new projects. Assistance up to Rs. 2 lakhs is made available free of margin. Where project cost exceeds Rs. 2 lakhs, margins ranging from 5 to 12.5 per cent are required to be contributed by the entrepreneur.

Consultancy Cells. The Bank has Consultancy Cells which provide management consultancy support to small scale units and technical guidance to operating staff. These Cells are also actively engaged in the work relating to technology upgradation. Officials of the Cell are trained to act as nodal points for collecting and making available necessary information relating to the industry, including techno-economic aspects.

Entrepreneurial Development Programme. The Bank conducts entrepreneurial development programmes in the backward districts and its lead districts to motivate first generation entrepreneurs to set up risk-bearing ventures.

Rehabilitation of Sick Units. Under the guidance of its Department of Industrial Rehabilitation, the Bank identifies sick small units and formulates expeditious nursing programmes for the viable units. So far about 90 per cent of the total viable small scale sick units in the Bank's books have been placed under suitable rehabilitation programmes. The Bank has also initiated steps for upgradation of technology of selected groups of small scale industries to make them more competitive.

Technology Upgradation. The Bank has a separate Department of Systems aiid Technology which set up the Industrial Technology Group (known as UPTECH Group) in 1988. This Group directs and guides programmes aimed at facilitating technology upgradation in the small scale industrial sectors. For this purpose, the Bank has set apart Rs. 2 crores to form a Technology Data and Information Services Centre Fund. The UPTECH group has taken up location and industry-specific programmes. Upgradation of products and processes are attempted in these programmes to bring about quality control, increased productivity and efficiency. The Bank offers packages of assistance to units which wish to implement the technological upgradation programmes.

Small Business Finance. The Bank also provides finances to small business enterprises which include retail traders, transport operators, professionals and others. The main objective of the Bank has been to increase opportunities for self-employment in the tertiary sector. The Bank's advances to small business units amounted to Rs. 2,414 crores covering 25 lakh accounts at the end of March 1996.

Conclusion. The above analysis reveals that the State Bank has been playing a vital role in financing large scale industries. But its contribution in supplying loans and advances, in providing equity funds, in modernisation, in helping to supply inputs, in marketing, etc., to small scale industries and small business has been immense. No other commercial bank in the country is in a position to compete with it.

D. Other Achievements of the State Bank of India

Other achievements of the State Bank spread to a wide range of activities which are discussed as under:

1. Assistance to Weaker Sections of Society

The Bank has been carrying out a number of schemes to assist the weaker sections of society so that they are provided gainful employment opportunities and are able to raise their income levels. Some of the schemes are:

Integrated Rural Development Programme. The Bank is actively engaged in alleviating rural poverty under the Government sponsored IRDP. It assists the rural poor in acquiring income-generating assets. Since the inception of the Programme in 1980 the cumulative disbursement of the Bank upto March, 1996 amounted to Rs. 2,195 crores covering 61.55 lakh beneficiaries. .

Differential Rate of Interest (DRI) Scheme. Under this scheme, the Bank has been providing financial assistance at a concessional rate of interest of 4 per cent to persons belonging to the weaker sections of society who are engaged in productive activities. At the end of March, 1996, the Bank's DRI advances stood at Rs. 1,443 crores. Over 60 per cent of the Bank's DRI advances were made to SC/ST and women beneficiaries, exceeding the stipulation of 40 per cent laid down by the Government involving Rs. 248 crores.

Twenty-Point Programme. The Bank has achieved considerable progress under the restructured Twenty-Point Programme which mainly aims at raising agricultural productivity, eradication of rural poverty and ensuring justice to the underprivileged sections of the society. As at the end of March 1996, the Bank's aggregate loans under the Programme stood at Rs. 4,142 crores covering 95 lakh borrowal accounts. The major chunk of Bank's assistance has been in the spheres of attack on poverty, needs of SC/ST borrowers, strategy for rainfed agriculture, better use of irrigation water, bigger harvests, energy for villages, etc.

Scheme for Urban Micro Enterprises. The Scheme which is a component of the Jawahar Rozgar Yojana, was introduced in 1990. The scheme aims at encouraging the unemployed and underemployed urban poor living below the poverty line in metropolitan areas, cities and towns with population exceeding 10,000, to take up self-employment ventures with the help of Bank loans and Government subsidy.

Prime Minister's Rozgar Yojana. The Prime Minister's Rozgar Yojana was launched on 2nd October 1993 to help educated unemployed youth in establishing self-employment ventures. The Bank financed 68,889 beneficiaries to the tune of Rs. 375 crores during 1995-96.

Total Assistance to Weaker Sections. At the end of March 1996, the Bank's total advances to weaker sections such as SC/ST, small and marginal farmers, landless labourers, including beneficiaries under IRDP and DRI Schemes amounted to Rs. 3,886 crores.

2. Community Services Programmes

The Bank has a number of Community Services Programmes which aim at closer identification with various strata of society, especially the weaker ones, such as women, slum-dwellers, physically handicapped, victims of natural calamities, ex-prisoners, orphans, ex-defence personnel etc. Financial assistance is provided under these Programmes for self-employment and rehabilitation of the beneficiaries. As at the end of March 1996, aggregate financial assistance rendered by the Bank under various community services programmes amounted to Rs. 317 crores spread over 11 lakh beneficiaries. Under the 15-Point Programme on minorities welfare, the Bank disbursed Rs. 372 crores to 5 lakh beneficiaries in 41 identified districts.

3. Area Development

The State Bank has been successfully carrying out its responsibility of the development of districts under the Lead Bank Scheme. As on March 1996, the Bank had lead responsibility in 113 districts in different parts of the country where it had been acting as a catalyst agent of banking and rural development. Under the Annual Action Plans for 1995-96, the Bank had extended Rs. 464 crores as credit and under the Annual Action Plans for non-lead districts, the credit extended amounted to Rs. 3,052 crores.

4. Development of Backward Areas

The Bank lays special emphasis on the balanced development of different regions, with greater emphasis on the development of backward districts. More than 46 per cent of the Bank's direct agricultural advances are in backward districts, covering over 51 per cent of the borrow accounts. The Bank has also been assisting in the creation of self-employment opportunities as well as industrial development of backward districts in the country. About 50 per cent of the small scale industrial units and 55 per cent of the transport operators assisted by the Bank are in the backward districts. Of the small business units financed by the Bank, 50 per cent are in backward areas, amounting for 48 per cent of the total quantum of assistance provided to the small business sphere. Out of the 187 Entrepreneurial Development programmes organised by the Bank so far, 118 have been conducted in the backward districts.

5. Export Finance

The Bank has been providing larger credit facilities to exporters and also promotional and development support to them at the national level. The total export credit provided by the Bank amounted to Rs. 6,955 crores as at the end of March, 1996. The share of export credit in Bank's total credit was 12.4 per cent which was higher than the export credit target of 10 per cent laid down for banks by the RBI.

Among the promotional measures taken by the Bank was the creation of an Export Promotion Fund, with an allocation of Rs. 1 crore out of the Bank's profits in 1987. The Bank has been actively associated with a number of Export Promotion Councils relating to different commodities and with the Ministry of Commerce, Government of India in streamlining the procedures and to render speedy and smooth service to exporters. Further, the State Bank is the sole commercial bank nominated by the Government of India for implementing financial transactions under the lines of credit extended by the Government of India to various countries. The Bank also administers Gold and Silver Jewellery Export Promotion Schemes as a canalising agency on behalf of the Government of India.

6. Merchant Banking

The State Bank has been rendering merchant banking services to its customers since 1972. But it was with the setting up of SBI Capital Markets Ltd. in 1986, SBI Mutual Fund in 1987, SBI Home Finance Ltd. and SBI Funds Management Ltd. that its merchant banking activities have spread considerably. These subsidiaries promote merchant banking, equipment leasing, venture capital finance, portfolio management services, hire-purchase activity, housing finance activities, etc. In fact, the Bank is a pioneer in the field of merchant banking and house finance.

7. Development of Debt Market

With a view to further develop the debt market in India, the Bank has set up a subsidiary called the SBI Gilts Ltd., to act as a Primary Dealer in Government securities. During 1995-96, the Bank acquired controlling interest in Discourt and Finance House of India Ltd.

8. Factors and Commercial Services

The Bank launched the SBI Factors and Commercial Services Pvt Ltd. (FACS) on 30 July, 1991 as a new subsidiary. The SBI has 54 per cent share holding in the subsidiary, the Small Industries Development Bank of India 20 per cent, Union Bank of India 10 per cent, State Bank of Indore 6 per cent and State Bank of Saurashtra 10 per cent. The SBI has been allotted the west zone for factoring. The SBI FACS performs the function of discounting the bills of its customers by buying invoices on a continuing basis. The customer prepays upto 80 per cent of the value of the invoices immediately. The SBI FACS maintains the sales ledger and performs the function of realising the invoices purchased. All types of business organisations engaged in either manufacturing or trading are eligible for factoring.

9. Human Resources Development (HRD)

The State Bank has been a pioneer in the field gf HRD. As such,-it has been focusing attention on development of job knowledge, skills and appropriate attitudes of its employees. Manpower Planning, Performance Appraisal System, Career Planning and Development, Organisation Development, and Training and Research are the various tools used in the process of development of human resources.

The Bank lays more emphasis on training its employees at all levels and prepares them to meet the growing needs of the Bank in the context of changing market scenario and environment. For this purpose, the Bank has two training Staff Colleges at Hyderabad and Gurgaon, and the Institute of Rural Development, Hyderabad and 55 Staff Training Centres. In February 1990, it started the Institute of Information and Communication Management in Hyderabad to spread computer education and information, and communication management skills. In addition to the above institutional training system, the Bank also has in-branch training arrangements in the form of visiting faculty and on-site training.

10. Customer Services

It has been the constant endeavour of the Bank to improve its service to the satisfaction of customers. It has Customer Service Committees and Customer Councils at almost all branches in important towns and cities. The 'Speedline' system introduced in 1986 now covers 209 centres. It expedites collection, remittances and transfer of accounts of customers. The Bank operates eight Customer Service Centres in different parts of the country which receive and dispose customer complaints pertaining to all public sector banks at the centres.

Tele-Service has been introduced at select branches to enable customers to obtain information over telephone.

11. New Schemes for Customers

The Bank has been a pace setter in introducing several new schemes for the benefit of its customers. There are a number of schemes for grant of loans to purchase consumer durables such as Big Buy, SCO-OM and Computer Loan. The State Bank Card and the High Value Card Scheme have created a place in the market. There is the Travelcash Scheme for granting loans to individuals for meeting travelling expenses. Under the 'Cash-key' Scheme, individuals making deposits in the form of Term/Special Term Deposits, Cash Certificates, Recurring Deposits with the Bank and in Magnum Certificates of SBICAP can be granted simultaneous overdraft facility for drawing up to 75 per cent of the amount of such deposit. In order to cover investment counselling and portfolio management activities under a 'single window service', Personal Investment Cells have been established in a number of metropolitan and urban branches. On 4 May, 1992, the SBI launched the Stock-invest Scheme. SBINET facility has been extended to all main branches, zonal offices and regional offices of the Bank. 72 branches have been connected by SWIFT. A fast cheque collection scheme has been introduced at major centres. ATM has been installed at Mumbai, New Delhi, Kolkata, Bangalore, Patna and Jamshedpur.

12. Overseas Operations

The SBI is the foremost Indian bank with overseas operations and international network. Its international network comprises 50 offices spread over 34 countries. The Bank has established correspondent relations with several established banks in six republics of CIS to increase trade relations between India and CIS. In December 1992, the Bank set up the SBI Europlan Bank Limited in London to exploit opportunities and meet the challenges arising out of integration of markets in the European Community. This subsidiary is engaged in wholesale banking. The Bank's other branches advance loans to both the private and public corporate sector in order to finance commodity and raw material imports into India. To serve the NRIs better, the Bank has exclusive NRI centres in Flushing (New York) and in Melbourne. The Bank operates the SWIFT network in its ten foreign branches. The Bank is empanelled as a consultant with the World Bank, the Commonwealth Fund for Technical Co-operation, UK, the Food and Agricultural Organisation (FAO) and the European Bank for Reconstruction and Development.

Conclusion. The State Bank has been highly successful in its objectives in opening a network of branches in rural and semi-urban areas. It has established itself as the largest commercial bank of the country. Further, it has helped in developing agriculture, small industry and business, and uplifting the weaker sections and priority sectors through liberal credit facilities. Besides, it operates a number of customer oriented services, engages in export promotion and successfully carries out overseas operations.

EXERCISES

1. Explain the functions, objects and organisational structure of the State Bank of India.
2. Discuss the achievements of the State Bank of India.
3. Give the objectives of the State Bank of India. Has it succeeded in achieving its objectives?
4. Explain the role of the State Bank of India in agricultural finance.
5. Explain the role of the State Bank of India in financing industries.

CHAPTER 69

Recent Trends in the Banking System

1. INTRODUCTION

The Indian banking system after independence has passed through distinct phases of development. During the first phase stretching upto the nationalisation of 14 banks in 1969, Indian banks followed almost traditional banking with small time innovation.;. During the second phase beginning from July 1969, the emphasis had been on the diversification of the banking system in terms of expansion of branches, deposits and advances on the one hand, and on the other hand on social banking. This phase is still continuing. Simultaneously the third phase of innovative banking has started which consists of merchant banking, leasing, mutual funds, venture capital, factoring, housing finance, deposit insurance etc. We will study in this chapter the second and third phase.

2. SOCIAL BANKING

During the post-nationalisation period Indian banks have been assigned the role of catalyst agents for achieving rapid economic growth accompanied by higher income and removal of poverty. The first step towards realisation of this objective was the change in the style of banking operations from "wholesale" or "elitist" banking to "retail" or "mass" banking. The phenomenal expansion of bank branches, lead bank scheme, service area approach, advance to priority sectors, etc. are some of the programmes which try to fulfil the goal of social banking. We will study these programmes in detail.

1. Branch Expansion

In the post-nationalisation period, commercial banks have made tremendous progress in the field of branch expansion. The branch expansion policy of banks has two main objectives: *first*, to narrow down regional imbalances; and *second*, to provide more banking facilities in rural and semi-urban areas. The RBI formulates branch licensing and branch expansion policy for the commercial banks, generally for three years. In June 2003 there were 66,514 bank branches in the country of which 49 per cent were in rural areas as compared with 32.5 per cent in June 1969. As a result of the rapid pace of branch expansion since 1969, the average population served per branch office was 65,000 at the time of bank nationalisation which came down to 16,000 as at end of June 2003. But there are still some inter-State disparities in the spread of banking, particularly in the Eastern, North-Eastern and Central Regions.

2. The Lead Bank Scheme

The Lead Bask Scheme was introduced by the Reserve Bank in December 1969 as an adjunct to the branch expansion programme of commercial banks. Its main objective was to ensure the flow of bank credit to priority sector and to coordinate the activities of the various agencies, such as banks and developmental agencies of Government at various levels. It was the first attempt towards 'Area Approach'.

Initially, a Study Group of the National Credit Council under Prof. D.R. Gadgil recommended in October 1969 the adoption of an Area Approach by commercial banks to identify and study local problems and evolve an integrated credit plan in rural areas of the country's districts. The Nariman Committee appointed by the RBI also recommended in November 1969 that banks should be allotted specific districts where they should take 'the lead' in surveying the potential of banking development, in extending branch expansion and expanding credit facilities. The RBI accepted its recommendations and introduced the Lead Bank Scheme in December 1969.

Under the Scheme, the major public sector banks were allotted all the 388 districts at that time in the country. A particular bank was made responsible for a particular district to develop banking and credit in that district. All other agencies operating in the district were also to be involved. The bank so selected was designated as the Lead Bank for that district. It was expected to act as a consortium leader for coordinating the efforts of all credit institutions in the allotted district for branch expansion and for meeting the credit needs of the rural economy. .

Functions of a Lead Bank. A Lead Bank is expected to perform the following functions:

(1) To survey the resources and potential for banking development in its district

(2) To identify unbanked growth centres for branch opening on the basis of a phased programme.

(3) To survey the number of commercial units and other establishments not having banking accounts or which were dependent primarily on moneylenders.

(4) To examine the facilities for the marketing of agricultural produce and industrial production, storage and warehousing space and the linking of credit with marketing in the district.

(5) To survey the facilities for the stocking of fertilizers and other agricultural inputs and for the repair and servicing of equipment.

(6) To recruit and train staff for offering advice to small borrowers and farmers and for the follow-up and the inspection of end-use loans.

(7) To assist other primary lending agencies.

(8) To maintain contacts and laison residually with Government and semi-Government agencies.

Working of Lead Bank Scheme. The Lead Bank Scheme initially consisted of two phases. The first was the survey of districts to identify institutional and credit gaps, and the second was the preparation and implementation of District Credit Plans (DCPs). Both the phases were completed by July 1978. But there was no uniformity in the DCPs. So the RBI advised the lead banks to terminate them. Instead, it issues fresh guidelines from time to time for the preparation of new DCPs, accompanied by separate Annual Action Plans (AAPs). The DCP is the perspective plan and the AAP is its yearly phasing. The RBI constituted the High Power Committee on Lead Bank Scheme which issues guidelines for the preparation of DCPs for specified periods, the last being for the period January 1988 to December 1990.

The Lead Bank Scheme has been successful in bringing about a phenomenal growth in branch expansion and providing larger credit facilities in rural areas. It extended banking facilities to the under-banked and unbanked rural and semi-urban areas from 5,175 branches in June 1969 to 47,216 in June 2003 and increased the share of public sector banks' priority sector advances from 14.6 per cent to 42.5 per cent over the period. Upto the end of June 2003, it covered 575 districts in the country. Despite these merits, the Lead Bank Scheme suffers from certain weaknesses. *First,* there has been the lack of coordination and cooperation among various agencies such as commercial banks, cooperatives, State Governments and others. *Second,* the designation of a particular bank as the lead bank does not make it a leader automatically. But it dilutes the enthusiasm of other banks for the scheme. The scheme is considered to be the scheme of the lead bank and the other agencies feel like being only spectators. *Third,* the attitude of Government agencies at the block level in the preparation of DCPs has been one of indifference. There has been absence of block-wise monitoring. There has been no awareness of targets and no conscious implementation of these targets. *Fourth,* under broad sectoral heads, agriculture and small industries lag far behind the targets whereas the service sector exceeds the target to a considerable extent. This phenomenon is almost common for all the districts. *Fifth,* the degree of cohesion at the block and village level where the AAPs are implemented, has been much wanting, reflecting the failure to realise the consortium approach. *Sixth,* the scheme is based on the principle of voluntary team work which is lacking, and therefore fails to produce the desired results. This is because the lead bank staff and officers do not take interest.

In order to have a certain uniformity and homogeneity in the operations of commercial banks, the Service Area Approach under the overall lead bank scheme has been started since April 1989.

3. The Service Area Approach (SAA)

The Lead Bank Scheme introduced by the Reserve Bank in December 1969 fulfilled only the quantitative aspects of branch expansion and priority sector advances. But it failed to touch the qualitative aspects like identification of needy people and extension of timely credit to them. To assess the impact of credit from banks on the overall economic development of the rural sector in general and agricultural productivity and production in particular, the RBI asked the Chief Executives of the public sector banks to carry out field visits in rural areas of different districts all over the country. They visited 88 districts in 21 States in November 1987. They discussed the findings of these visits in a seminar convened by the RBI in January 1988 and recommended that the time was opportune to adopt a system in which each bank could concentrate in a specified area to develop productive lending. Therefore, the RBI set up a Committee under the chairmanship of its Deputy Governor, Dr. P.D. Ojha, to examine the operational aspects involved in implementing this approach. The RBI accepted the Ojha Committee recommendations. Subsequently, the 1988-89 Budget announced the 'Service Area Approach'. The RBI instructed all commercial banks including the Regional Rural Banks to start implementation of SAA under the overall Lead Bank Scheme with effect from 1 April, 1989.

The SAA involves five distinct stages in its implementation which are discussed as under:

1. *Allocation of Service Area.* There is the allocation of specific villages to all the rural and semi-urban bank branches including RRB branches for providing credit for all-round development. Each branch on an average is allocated 15 to 25 villages under the area of its operation known as Service Area. There are at least five States, viz., Himachal Pradesh, Arunachal Pradesh, Manipur, Meghalaya, Orissa and one Union Territory Andaman where the average number of villages allocated per branch exceeds 25 villages. Similarly, the average number of kms to be covered by each branch is more than 100 sq kms for at least nine States and one Union Territory.

2. *Survey of Villages.* After fixation of the service area, each branch is to undertake village-wise surveys in respect of their allotted villages and prepare village profiles in a proforma prescribed by the RBI. The village profile has to be updated periodically taking into account the development changes which may have taken place in the intervening period. The branch managers are expected to periodically visit the villages in their service area to have a continuous contact with extension and developmental agencies.

3. *Preparation of Credit Plans.* Each branch is required to prepare an annual credit plan for its service area on an ongoing basis. *First,* the credit plan is prepared for each village and then the village credit plans are aggregated into service area credit plan. The annual credit plan should reflect the potentialities, and needs of the people of the area on the basis of survey reports. The Lead Bank Officer plays a crucial role in this regard and is expected to provide necessary support to all the branch managers in the district. The RRB branches prepare credit plans for the target group only and for the non-target group the designated bank prepares the credit plan.

4. *Coordination.* A Block Level Bankers' Committee (BLBC) has to be formed to coordinate the activity of the banks and Government agencies. The Lead Bank Officer is the convenor-chairman of BLBC and all the bank branch managers located in the block, including cooperative banks, BDO and his extension officers in the block are its members. The officers of the RBI and NABARD can also attend the BLBC meetings. The BLBC finalises the branch credit plans and these plans are aggregated to block credit plans.

5. *Monitoring.* The BLBC holds periodical meetings at least once in a quarter to review the progress of implementation of the branch credit plans and sort out operational problems.

Working of SAA. The SAA was introduced as part of the Lead Bank Scheme for improving the quality of rural lending by commercial banks including RRBs. It came into operation from 1 April, 1989 covering 6,18,216 villages which had been allocated to 42,158 branches of the various banks. The survey of villages and preparation of credit plans had been completed by March 1989. The RBI asked the public sector banks to conduct a second round of field studies in December 1989 with a view to ascertaining the manner of implementation of the SAA in rural branches, the problems encountered in effective implementation and steps needed for improving the operational aspects of the Scheme. Following these studies, it was felt that the Scheme held the promise of improving the productivity of rural credit and efforts should be made towards stabilising it at the earliest. It was also decided that the relaxations already granted to bank branches to lend to their old clients residing in the service area of other bank branches may continue for some time more, so that the credit flow does not get disrupted. Further, cooperative banks were advised to prepare credit plans and their staff would be given training in this direction. The RBI issues fresh guidelines for the preparation of branch credit plans for each year keeping in view the deficiencies observed in the credit plans prepared for the previous years in order to remove their shortcomings. To plan, co-ordinate and effectively monitor the credit plans prepared by bank branches and improve upon them, the NABARD has been setting up district level offices in a phased manner so as to cover all the districts in the country within the next 3 or 4 years. These offices also transmit potential linked credit plans to rural and semi-urban branches of banks to help them prepare their credit plans. The RBI issues revised guidelines on credit planning and monitoring from time to time to make the SAA more effective. The following modifications have been introduced recently: *(i)* SA branches may be grouped block-wise without disturbing their SA identities or their obligation to prepare village level/service area plans so that the borrowers have the flexibility to approach other branches within the block to meet their credit requirement adequately; *(ii)* satellite/mobile offices be opened in Service Areas which are very large and are located in tribal/hilly and inaccessible areas; *(iii)* the area of operations of the specialised branches such as agricultural development branches, agricultural banking division and *gram vikas kendras* may be enlarged to use their infrastructure to the maximum; *(iv)* realigning the sacred service areas; and *(v)* exemptions from the SAA in respect of large projects covering several districts/ States.

Under the SAA, Annual Credit Plan is prepared by the concerned commercial bank under the Lead Bank Scheme. During 1999-2000, the all-India sector-wise targets were : Rs. 39,168 crores for agriculture and allied activities; Rs. 12,773 crores for SSIs and Rs. 12,945 crores for services. These figures reveal that the quality of delivery system in rural lending has definitely improved under the SAA. These figures reveal that the quality of delivery system in rural banking has definitely improved under the SAA.

4. Local Area Banks (LABs)

The Finance Minister in his budget speech for 1996-97 announced the Local Area Banks scheme. The LAB scheme owes its origin to the complaints of many State governments that public sector banks were extorting the rural areas of all their money. States like Punjab, Haryana, Uttar Pradesh, Kerala are much below the national average in their credit-deposit ratios. They have been complaining that the public sector banks are taking away their resources to lend them in other States. These banks are expected to remedy these defects by concentrating their operations in rural areas. Unlike the RRBs, these banks will be set up in the private sector and registered and licensed as scheduled banks. The RBI issued the following guidelines on setting up of the LABs on 24 August, 1996.

Object. The aim is to set up LABs in the private sector in district towns to cater to the credit needs of the local people and to provide efficient and competitive financial intermediation services in their area of operation. These banks will promote rural savings and provide credit to viable economic activities in local areas. They are expected to bridge the gaps in credit availability and enhance the institutional credit framework in rural and semi-urban areas.

Functions. Since the LABs will be located in district towns, their activities will be focussed on the local customers. They will promofe and mobilise savings. They will lend to agriculture and allied activities, SSI, agro-industrial units, trading units and the non-farm sector in their area of operation. These will observe the priority sector lending target of 40 per cent of net bank credit, as applicable to other commercial banks. Within this target, they will lend at least 25 per cent or 10 per cent of net bank credit to the weaker sections.

Capital. The minimum paid-up capital for starting an LAB shall be Rs. 5 crores. The promoters' contribution shall be at least Rs. 2 crores. The promoters may comprise individuals, corporations, trusts or societies.

Area of Operation. The area of operation of such a bank shall be a maximum of three geographically contiguous districts. Its Head/Registered Office will be located at a centre within its area of operation. The Bank shall be allowed to open branches only in its area of operation. In regard to branch licensing, it shall be governed by the existing policy.

Prudential Norms. Such a bank shall be subject to prudential norms, accounting policies and other policies as are laid down by the RBI. The SLR and CRR to these banks will be the same as that for RRBs. So will be the deposit rates and lending rates. The .bank will have to achieve capital adequacy ratio of 8 per cent from the very beginning. Similarly, norms for income recognition, asset classification and provisioning will be applicable from day one.

Critical Appraisal. Academicians and bankers have questioned the wisdom of the Government and RBI in adding another institution to the plethora of financial institutions and agencies for providing credit to the rural areas. If the existing large number of institutions have failed to deliver the goods, the introduction of one more may be a futile exercise. What is ths guarantee that the LABs will be a success, given the attitudes and approaches of the people and the banking staff? However, it is hoped that the LABs will be successful where the RRBs have failed. Presently, eight 'in-principle' approvals have been given for setting up Local Area Banks, of which three have been registered.

5. Financing of Priority Sectors

The concept of 'Priority Sector Advances' was formulated in 1968 with the introduction of social control over banks. The National Credit Council pointed out that those sectors of the economy which did not have adequate access to bank finance but which due to their economic importance deserved due recognition from the banking system should be treated as 'Priority Sectors'. Therefore, there should be a conscious and deliberate effort to ensure that these sectors obtained adequate credit from the banking system. At that time, the priority sectors consisted of agriculture, small scale industry and exports. With the nationalisation of 14 commercial banks in 1969, the term 'Priority Sectors' was enlarged to include 'hitherto neglected sectors' comprising of small road and water transport operators, retail trade including petty shopkeepers and self-employed persons such as artisans, craftsmen, etc. and indigent students receiving education. A Working Group set up by the RBI under the Chairmanship of Dr K.S. Krishnaswamy introduced the concept of 'weaker sections' within the priority sectors. Consequently, at present the priority sector advances as redefined on 13 June 1995 include:

1. Agriculture, both direct and indirect
2. Small scale industries.
3. Other priority sectors which comprise of:
   (*a*) road and water transport operators;
   (*b*) retail trade and small business:
   (c) setting of industrial estate;
   (*d*) professional and self-employed persons;
   (*e*) education;
   (*f*) financial assistance to ex-servicemen; and
   (*g*) SUME—Scheme of Urban Micro Enterprises.
4. Weaker sections consisting of: (i) small and marginal farmers with land holdings upto 5 acres, landless labourers, tenant fanners and share croppers; (*ii*) artisans, village and cottage industries enjoying credit limits upto Rs. 25,000; (*iii*) IRDP beneficiaries; (*iv*) beneficiaries belonging to scheduled castes/scheduled tribes; (*v*) beneficiaries under the DRI and SUME schemes, as also those under the Scheme for Liberation and Rehabilitation of Scavengers (SLRS); and (*vi*) Self Help Groups under NABARD's Pilot Projects.

Both the Government and the RBI have laid down the fallowing targets for lending to priority sectors. The banks are expected to ensure that 40 per cent of the total credit is extended to priority sectors. With the overall target of 40 per cent, the following sub-targets have been laid down: (*i*) 18 per cent of the bank credit to the agricultural sector; (*ii*) 50 per cent of the direct lending to agriculture for small and marginal farmers and agricultural labourers; *(iii)* 12.5 per cent of the total credit advanced to small scale industries reserved for artisans, village craftsmen and cottage industries; (*iv*) advances to the weaker sections to the level of 25 per cent of priority sector advances or 10 per cent of the total bank credit outstandings; and (*v*) 1 per cent of aggregate advances under DRI scheme.

During 1993-94, the RBI made certain changes in the composition of priority sector targets within its overall 40 per cent target for commercial banks. Banks have been allowed to combine direct and indirect advances to agriculture within the 18 per cent target. Their indirect lending to agriculture has been limited to one-fourth of the total agricultural lending. Within the SSI credit limit, 40 per cent has been earmarked for khadi, village, cottage and tiny units. Effective 1 July, 1993, the priority sector target for foreign banks has been raised to 32 per cent. They have been allowed to include credit of 10 per cent for loans to the export sector and SSI units each in the overall target of 32 per cent. If they fail to achieve the targets, they are required to deposit the deficit with the SIDBI. The SIDBI pays the foreign banks 10 per cent interest on the deposited amount.

In the case of other banks, the shortfall in lending to agriculture (18 per cent) is required to be deposited with the NABARD for making funds available to the Rural Infrastructure Development Fund (RIDF) from 1996. These deposits with the NABARD are subject to a maximum of 1.5 per cent of the bank's net credit. The NABARD pays such a bank 0.5 per cent above the ceiling rate of interest on deposits.

Effective 6 July, 1996, the private sector banks which fail to reach the required target of 40 per cent are directed to deposit 50 per cent of the shortfall for one year either with the NABARD or SIDBI. The rate of interest on such deposits is 8 per cent.

The priority sector advances under major categories are discussed briefly as under:

1. Priority sector advances of *public sector banks* increased from 14.6 per cent as at the end of June 1969 to 42.5 per cent as at the end of March 2003. Within the priority sectors, the share of advances to agriculture increased from 5.4 per cent in June 1969 to 15.3 per cent in March 2003. Of this, direct finance to agriculture increased from 1.3 per cent to 10.8 per cent. The share of SSI increased from 8.5 per cent in June 1969 to 11.1 per cent in March 2003, and other priority sector advances increased from 0.7 per cent to 15.0 per cent.

2. The proportion of priority sector advances by *foreign banks* to their net bank credit was well above the target of 32 per cent as at the end of March 2003. It was 33.9 per cent with credit to export constituting 18.7 per cent and SSI 8.7 per cent.

3. Priority sector advances by *private sector* commercial banks were 44.4 per cent as at the end of March 2003 against the target of 40 per cent.

4. The advances to *weaker sections* within the priority Sectors constituted 6.76 per cent of the net bank credit of public sector banks ending March, 2003 as against the target of 10 per cent.

3. INNOVATIVE BANKING

Public sector banks in India in recent years have been engaged in innovative banking. The RBI has given them freedom to innovate in the promotion of a variety of financial services such as merchant banking, leasing, venture capital, mutual funds, factoring, housing, etc. We will explain these services briefly here.

1. Merchant Banking

Merchant banking includes such services as management of public issues, loan syndication, financial and management consultancy, project counselling, mergers and acquisitions, management of non-resident investments, etc. The credit for starting merchant banking in India goes to foreign banks like Grindlays Bank, Citibank, etc. At present, a number of public sector banks are performing merchant banking services which are the subsidiaries of banks. Some of these are SBI Capital Markets Limited, Bank of Baroda Merchant Bank Division, Canbank Financial Services Ltd., Allbank Finance Ltd., Union Bank of India Merchant Bank Division, PNB Capital Services Ltd., BOI Finance Ltd., etc.

2. Leasing

Leasing is an instrument of corporate finance whereby industries enter into a contractual arrangement with a leasing company to use an asset (i.e. plant, equipment, transportation facilities or any other services) in return for rent for an agreed period of time. Leasing companies also provide finance to industries. Equipment leasing and financial leasing in India have been in the hands of private companies since 1973. It is only recently with the establishment of merchant banking subsidiaries that public sector banks have made their entry into the leasing business. As at the end of June 1991, there were nine equipment leasing-cum-merchant banking subsidiaries set up by Indian banks. But they have yet to make a niche for themselves in a very competitive leasing market where about 400 private leasing companies are operating.

3. Venture Capital

Venture capital relates to finance provided to small/medium business units promoted by firms or individuals having sound project ideas. These projects involve new technology or products but the promoter lacks financial resources to promote his project. Venture capital provided by banks or financial institutions imply equity investment in the initial stages of the company. Financial institutions like ICICI, IDBI, UTI and IFCI have been the pioneers in promoting venture capital finance in India. Of the banks, SBI Capital Markets Limited has been in the forefront in providing assistance to industries under its Equity Support and Venture Capital Schemes.

4. Mutual Funds

Mutual funds mobilise savings from the public and invest them in different types of securities in the stock markets and thus help both the investor and the industry. Mutual funds earn interest, dividend and capital gains from such investments and distribute them to small investors as return. Thus they provide safety, liquidity and growth to investors. They provide stability to share prices by buying them when they are falling and selling them when they are rising. They provide safety and income to investors and resources to entrepreneurs for the growth of industry. The UTI was the first mutual fund set up in India in 1964. In recent years a number of public sector banks have set up mutual funds as their subsidiaries. These banks are Indian Bank, Bank of India, SBI, Canara Bank, Bank of Baroda, PNB, etc. The SBI group also launched the India Magnum Fund in 1989, a maiden offshore fund which was privately placed with institutional investors and others primarily in the USA.

5. Factoring

A 'Factor' is a commission agent who besides offering funds to its clients, undertakes management of accounts receivables, collection of debts and safety against risk of default. Factoring agencies ensure smooth of cash flows. The factor undertakes collection of a client's (say a small scale unit) debts and finances it on the basis of accounts receivables. In fact, debts are assigned to the factor which are collected in due course. The factor, in turn, receives the service charge by way of discount or rebate deducted from the bills. In short, factoring is a collection and finance service designed to improve the cash flow of small firms by turning their sales invoices into ready cash.

The Vaghul Committee recommended the introduction of factoring services with a view to undertaking the collection of dues on behalf of suppliers in the small scale sector. The Kalyanasundaram Committee examined the feasibility of factoring services and recommended their introduction in India. The Banking Regulation Act was amended in July 1990 for this purpose and the RBI directed that factoring be done by banks through separate subsidiaries. Accordingly, the State Bank of India launched a new subsidiary called the SBI Factors and Commercial Services Ltd on 30 July, 1991. The aim is to render factoring services to the industrial and commercial units in Western India, covering the States of Maharashtra, Gujarat, Goa, Madhya Pradesh and the Union Territories of Daman, Diu, Dadra and Nagar Haveli. Similarly, the Canara Bank launched its factoring subsidiary, the Canbank Factoring Ltd. on 24 August, 1991 to serve units in Southern India and the Punjab National Bank and Allahabad Bank have come forward to set up factoring agencies in Northern India and Eastern India respectively.

Its Working. Factoring in India involves the following procedure:

The factoring service buys invoices on a continuing basis, prepays upto 80 per cent of the value of the invoices immediately, performs the accounting function of sales ledger maintenance and the collection function of realising invoices purchased. The suppliers invoice their customers in the usual way but only add that the debt due on the invoice must be paid to the Factor. The suppliers offer the assigned invoices to the Factor with a schedule of offer, accompanied by a copy of the receipted delivery of the challan. The Factor provides prepayment up to 80 per cent of the value of each invoice. When the Factor collects the debts, the supplier receives an official notification and personalised statement of accounts from the former. When the supplier settles the invoice, the Factor pays, the supplier the remaining 20 per cent of the invoice value. To keep the supplier informed of the factored invoices, the Factor sends monthly statements of accounts.

The Factor charges discount on the prepayment drawn by its client. The discount rate which is comparable to bank lending rate is collected monthly on actual drawings, in the prepayment account. In addition, there is a service charge (or fee) which varies between one and five per cent depending on the services availed of and the volume of transactions made.

Its Benefits. Factoring benefits the supplier, his banker and his customer. The supplier converts his invoice into instant cash up to 80 per cent of its value, without having to wait for the usual 30 or more credit days. His bank can leave the post-sale finance to the factor and concentrate only on inventory finance. The factor need not accept a bill of exchange. He has just to abide by a notice on the invoice to pay money direct to the Factor.

But it will take some time before full factoring is started in India where the risk is entirely borne by the Factor. For the present, there is recourse factoring where, in case of default, the risk ultimately devolves on the supplier.

6. Housing

Habitat banking is fast catching up in India. For meeting the requirements of housing finance, a National Housing Bank (NHB) was established as an apex institution in 1988. It has been providing assistance through a number of schemes. These include: Home Loan Account Scheme, liberalised lending by commercial banks, and refinance facilities. Besides, the banking sector has been involved substantially in housing finance in recent years. Commercial banks provide finance to low and middle income groups to purchase or construct houses or flats. Interest rates are fixed by the RBI and NHB for the loans advanced by commercial banks and housing finance institutions. Effective 5 June, 1991, banks were allowed to provide housing finance to builders by way of term loans for periods ranging from 3 to 5 years, linked to specific projects for development of plots together with construction of flats/houses under the refinance scheme of the NHB. A number of public sector and private sector banks have promoted housing finance companies such as SBI, Bank of Baroda, Andhra Bank, Central Bank of India, Vijaya Bank etc.

7. New Technology in Banking Mechanisation

Another innovation in Indian banking has been the use of new technology in banking mechanisation. Majority of Indian banks, have provided Electronic Accounting Machines and Advance Ledger Posting Machines in their branches. Banks have taken up the project of total computerisation of operations of their branches. About 260 offices of banks have been hooked through BANKNET, a data communication network for the Reserve Bank and public sector banks at Mumbai, New Delhi, Chennai, Kolkata, Bangalore, Hyderabad and Nagpur. Banks have been asked to introduce Magnetic Ink Character Recognition (MICR) cheques. The RBI is providing MICR-based cheque clearing facilities at Mumbai, Chennai, Kolkata, New Delhi and Nagpur. Several banks are using SWIFT (Society for Worldwide Inter-bank Financial Telecommunications) network and have installed hardware and software required for connecting to SWIFT. With a view to further improving the communication network in regard to speed, dependability and security, a number of banks have installed satellite disk antennae at their offices in many cities. When fully operational, these would form part of the Remote Area Business Message Network (RABMN) and would be used to transmit messages including SWIFT messages, between bank offices in India and abroad. A number of banks have started Electronic Clearing Service which is being used by several corporate bodies to effect dividend/interest to their shareholders/customers.

8. Customer Service

Improvement in the level of customer satisfaction has been another innovation of banking services. To ensure efficient customer service, banks collect feedback on a regular basis through visits of senior officials from controlling offices to their branches. To elicit customer reactions about the quality of service rendered, the system of holding Customer Meets at regular intervals at branches has been evolved. Some banks have formed Customer Service Committees and Customer Councils. Banks have put up 'Complaints and Suggestions' boxes at all branches which are dealt with promptly. Some of the banks have also introduced courier system to expedite collections, remittances and transfer of accounts of customers.

9. Banking Ombudsman

For expeditious and inexpensive settlement of customer complaints against deficiency in banking services, including non-observance of the RBI directives on loans and advances, etc., the Banking Ombudsman has been appointed on a full time basis each at Mumbai, Delhi, Bhopal, Chandigarh, Hyderabad, Patna, Jaipur, etc. The scheme covers all scheduled commercial banks, except RRBs and PCBs.

10. Credit Cards

The credit card is now-a-days an integral part of better customer service. Under the credit scheme, card holders are allowed credit facilities for a specified period of time without obtaining any security from them. The card holders can purchase commodities and pay for services such as hotel bills, railway and airways tickets, etc. without making cash payments. The bank issuing the credit card is able to make increased earnings by way of commission from dealers and interest from card holders. The credit card system has become an aggressive area of business for Indian banks. Major public sector and private sector banks have come out with their credit cards. Some of them have been permitted by the RBI to have tie-up arrangements with other banks in India and abroad. This has facilitated wider use of cards nationally and internationally.

11. Installation of ATMs

Several banks have installed Automated Teller Machines (ATMs) at licensed branches and extension counters where clients can withdraw cash 24 hours a day upto a certain Jrmii.

12. Hire-Purchase Business

On the recommendations of the Reserve Bank, the Government of India notified on 7 September, 1990 hire-purchase as a permissible form of business for banks to engage in. Accordingly, Canara Bank, State Bank of India, Punjab National Bank and Indian Bank have been permitted to engage in hire-purchase business through their respective merchant banking subsidiaries.

13. Consumer Credit

Consumer credit is also developing as a profitable area of business for banks in India. Banks help the middle class customers to purchase durable consumer goods such as motor vehicles, refrigerators, TVs, etc. The banks earn interest on such credits. The consumer goods industry gets a boost in its sales which in turn help in increasing employment opportunities.

4. DEPOSIT INSURANCE CORPORATION

The Deposit Insurance Corporation (DIC) was established on 1 January, 1962 under the Deposit Insurance Corporation Act, 1961 passed by the Parliament. The failure of the Palai Central Bank and the Laxmi Bank in 1960 shook the confidence of the depositors in the banking system. The DIC aimed at providing protection to small depositors by insuring their deposits in banks. In case an insured bank failed, the Corporation was to pay depositors upto a specified limit. Originally the limit was Rs 1,500 per depositor in respect of all deposits held by him in an insured bank. The limit was raised to Rs. 5,000 in 1968, to Rs. 10,000 in 1970, to Rs. 20,000 in 1976 and to Rs. 30,000 in July, 1980. The premium rate paid by the banks to the Corporation quarterly was reduced from 5 paise to 4 paise per Rs. 100 per annum in October, 1971. The DIC has authorised and paid-up capital of Rs 2 crores. It could also borrow from the Reserve Bank upto Rs. 5 crores. It maintained a Deposit Insurance Fund (DIF) in which all premia collected from the registered bankers was deposited and out of which deposit insuranced claims were paid. It also maintained a General Fund made up of its capital, reserves and income from investments by the DIC.

Originally only commercial banks were eligible for insurance cover. But in 1968, the DIC Act was amended to provide insurance cover to cooperative banks having paid-up capital and reserves of Rs 1 lakh and above. But the co-operative banks were eligible for insurance provided the State Government concerned enacted legislation. It was only from 1971 that cooperative banks in a few States were registered with the DIC. Not all State Governments have enacted such a legislation till now.

Credit Guarantee Corporation of India (CGCI)

To examine the problem of insurance of advances of commercial banks and cooperative banks to small borrowers in the priority sector, the Department of Banking of the Government of India appointed a Working Group which submitted its report in November 1969. It recommended a centralized credit guarantee scheme for various segments of priority sector under the DIC. But the Government decided to set up a separate organization to extend guarantee to commercial banks in respect of their advances to small and neglected borrowers. Accordingly the Credit Guarantee Corporation of India came into existence as a Government company in January, 1971. Its main function was to administer the scheme of guarantees in respect of advances granted by the credit institutions and to indemnify them in respect of such advances.

Deposit Insurance and Credit Guarantee Corporation (DICGC)

On 15th July, 1978, the Deposit Insurance Corporation took over the Credit Guarantee Corporation of India and it was named the Deposit Insurance and Credit Guarantee Corporation. The DICGC has a paid-up capital of Rs. 50 crores which is entirely issued and subscribed by the RBI. It has two main functions. *First,* to insure the deposits of the small depositors in banks. For this purpose, it operates the Deposit Insurance Scheme which was earlier operated by the DIC. *Second,* to provide guarantee support to eligible credit institutions for the priority sector advances to small borrowers and small scale industries. The DICGC had been operating six credit guarantee schemes. Out of these, the Corporation terminated three schemes with effect from 1 April, 1992 on account of either nil or negligible guaranteed advances and continued default in payment of guarantee fee, etc. by participating institutions. The three schemes were Small Loans (Financial Corporations) Guarantee Scheme, 1971, Service Cooperative Societies Guarantee Scheme, 1971, and Small Loans (Cooperative Credit Societies) Guarantee Scheme, 1992.

At present, the DICGC provides insurance cover to depositors in banks through its Deposit Insurance Scheme and guarantees coyer to eligible credit institutions through its three credit guarantee schemes—two for small borrowers and one for SSIs.The limit of insurance cover is Rs 1 lakh per bank and the premium payable by insured banks on their assessable deposits is at 5 paise per Rs 100 per annum. To reform the deposit insurance system, the Reserve Bank appointed a Working Group which submitted its Report in October, 1999. It recommended : (i) raising the capital of DICGC to Rs 500 crores; (ii) withdrawing the function of credit guarantee on loans from it; and (iii) risk-based pricing of the deposit-insurance premium in place of the flat rate system. These recommendations are in the process of being implemented.

5. DEFECTS OF INDIAN BANKING SYSTEM

Despite the tremendous progress made by Indian commercial banks during the last two decades, they are still faced with a number of problems which are as under:

1. *Low Profitability.* Banks in India have low profitability. Irregularities and corruption in lending operations, misappropriation, frauds, rising operating costs, etc. have led to decline in their profitability. During 1992-93

and 1993-94, scheduled commercial banks incurred a net loss of R 4,150 crores and Rs 3,625 crores respectively. But in 2002-03 they earned a net profit of Rs 17,077 crores.

2. *Growing Non-performing Assets.* The non-performing assets of Indian commercial banks have been growing rapidly. Non-performing assets consist of *(i)* debts recalled, *(ii)* suit-filed accounts i.e. where legal action or recovery proceedings have been initiated, *(iii)* decreed debts i.e. where suits have been filed and decrees obtained; and (iv) debts classified as bad and doubtful. In the case of public sector banks ending March 2003 non-performing assets accounted for 9.36 per cent of their gross advances.

3. *Low Capital Base.* The capital base of Indian banks in India was very low and not uniform. In the case of 28 public sector banks, the capital base was the same as at the time of their nationalisation. For rivate sector banks, the required capital was linked to their geographical location while foreign banks operating in India were required to have foreign funds equivalent to 3.5 per cent of the deposits deployed in Indian business as at the end of each year. As a measure of capital adequacy, there was no weighted risk-asset ratio system for banks in India till March, 1993. There were 2 commercial banks with a ratio of less than 9% in 2002 - 03.

4. *Window-dressing of Balance Sheets.* Despite compulsory audit of banks, many banks indulge in window-dressing of their balance sheets. They artificially, increase their deposits in the last week of the fiscal year.

5. *Favouritism in Advancing Loans.* Some banks favour certain companies in advancing loans. This is not only in the case of public sector banks. Often such loans turn into bad debts, thereby weakening the financial position of the concerned banks.

6. *Bad Quality of Loan Portfolios.* The quality of loan portfolios of a number of banks is very bad. Often, they advance loans under extraneous (or political) pressures. They extend letters of credit and guarantee limits as a routine affair without adopting commercial procedure in granting loans.

7. *Indulge in Share Speculation.* Many banks indulge in share speculation, thereby misutilising public deposits. A number of public sector banks and their subsidiaries in the form of mutual funds have been found to be involved in share speculation. The recent securities scam involving Harshad Mehta and other brokers revealed the role of a number of public and private sector banks in the entire episode.

8. *Irregularities in Maintaining Accounts.* Many banks resort to large scale irregularities in operating their accounts. Often, bad accounts of one bank have been taken over by the other bank without proper scrutiny.

9. *Banks as Sick Units.* As a corollary to the above, many banks operate as sick units. Consequently, they are amalgamated, dissolved or liquidated. During 1985-91, ten banks were amalgamated. As on 30 June, 1991, three banks were dissolved. New Bank of India became so sick that it was merged with Punjab National Bank in 1993. Even during 1999-2000, three nationalised banks were sick.

10. *Social Banking Inadequate.* Despite the fact that a number of schemes have been in operation to help the weaker sections of Indian society, banks mainly cater to the needs of the corporate sector. For instance, bank credit to medium and large scale industry was 33.7 per cent in 1999-2000 to agriculture 9.5 per cent, to small scale industries 8.7 per cent and to trade 5.7 per cent.

11. *Dual Control.* The Indian banking system suffers from dual control of the Government and Reserve Bank. It is over-regulated and over-administered. The credit decisions in individual cases and matters pertaining to internal management have been subjected to excessive administrative and political pressures and interferences. The investing and lending programmes are directed from above. So are the appointments of chief executives and directors.

Conclusion. All this shows that Indian commercial banks are not operating properly, their management is sloppy, they are uncompetitive, overstretched, overstaffed and provide poor service.

6. SUGGESTIONS TO IMPROVE WORKING: NARASIMHAM COMMITTEE REPORT

From time to time, a number of committees have suggested measures to improve the working of the Indian banking system. However, we give a summary of the recommendations of the Narasimham Committee of 1991.

1. Structure of the banking sector should be revamped so as to have 3 or 4 large banks which could become international in character.

2. Eight to ten national banks with a network of branches throughout the country should be engaged in universal banking.

3. Local bank operations should be confined to a specific region.

4. Rural banks, including RRBs, should operate only in rural areas and their business should be predominantly to engage in financing of agriculture and allied activities, but based on profitability considerations.

5. One or more rural banking subsidiaries by each public sector bank should be set up to take over all its rural branches.

6. RRBs should be allowed to engage in all types of banking business.

7. Abolition of branch licensing and opening or closing of branches should be left to the individual banks.

8. Foreign banks should be permitted to open offices in India as branches or as subsidiaries.

9. Foreign banks should be subject to the same requirements as applicable to Indian banks.

10. Foreign operations of Indian banks should be rationalised.

11. Computerisation of bank operations needs to be stepped up.

12. No need to set up a banking commission.

13. Individual banks should be permitted to recruit officers.

14. Inspection by supervisory staff should be based on the internal audit and internal inspection reports.

15. Duality of control over the banking system between the RBI and the Banking Division of the Ministry of Finance should end, and the RBI should be the primary agency for regulation of the banking system.

16. To perform supervisory function over the banks and other financial institutions, there should be a separate authority to operate as a quasi-autonomous body under the aegis of the Reserve Bank.

17. Appointment of chief executives of the banks and directors should be depoliticised.

18. SLR requirements of banks should be brought down to 25 per cent over a period of five years.

19. CRR should be progressively reduced.

20. Directed credit programmes should be phased out.

21. The priority sector should be redefined.

22. There should be deregulation of interest rate so as to reflect emerging market trends.

23. The commercial banks should achieve a minimum 4 per cent capital adequacy ratio in relation to risk weighted assets by March, 1993.

24. Banks should adopt uniform accounting practices

25. They should impart transparency to balance sheets and make full disclosure in them.

26. Government should set up Special Tribunals to speed up the process of recovery of loans.

27. An Assets Reconstruction Fund (ARF) should be established to take over from basks and financial institutions a portion of their bad and doubtful debts at a discount

The recommendations of the Narasimham Committee would have far reaching implications on the working of the banking system. They have not yet been implemented except in the case of reduction of SLR.*

7. RECENT BANKING REFORMS

Since nationalisation of 14 commercial banks in 1969, the Indian banking system has made tremendous progress both in terms of deposit mobilisation and branch expansion. Aggregate deposits of all banks rose from about 15 per cent in 1969 to 79.8 percent in 2003. The total number of bank branches went up from 8,262 to 66,514 over the period. Of these, about 50 per cent were in rural areas in 2003 as against less man 25 per cent in 1969. Besides performing ordinary banking services, Indian Banks also started innovative banking thereby diversifying their activities in new directions.

Despite all this, they 'failed to provide reliable, efficient and low-cost services. Both productivity and profitability of banks declined and especially, the public sector banks became a burden on the exchequer. To overcome the defects of the Indian banking system, the Narasimham Committee made a number of suggestions. Some of these have been implemented from 1991-92 onwards. They are enumerated as under:

1. *Capital Adequacy Norms.* To avoid risk, the RBI laid down capital adequacy norms in April 1992 to be complied by banks by March, 1996. All banks in India were required to achieve a risk-weighted capital adequacy

* Recommendations relating to the financial system have not been given in the above paras.

ratio of 4 per cent by 31 March 1993 and of 8 per cent by 31 March, 1996. Foreign banks operating in India and Indian banks with branches abroad were to attain 8 percent by March, 1993. This has been raised to 9 per cent from March 2000 for all banks

2. *Recapitalisation.* In order to enable the public sector banks to meet the prescribed capital adequacy ratio, the Government of India has been contributing to the capital of such banks. During 1993-94, the Government provided Rs. 5,700 crores towards recapitalisation of 19 nationalised banks; during 1994-95 Rs. 5,293 crores to 13 banks; Rs. 850 crores to 6 banks; during 1995-96 and Rs. 909 crores to 4 banks during 1996-97; and Rs 297 crores to one bank in 1999-2000.

3. *Partial Privatisation of Public Sector Banks.* But recapitalisation is not a permanent solution of the problem. As the Government resources are limited, banks have been allowed to mobilise equity resources from the public. First, the State Bank of India Act was amended to enable the Bank to have access to the capital market. The RBI shareholding in SBI has been reduced to 67 per cent. Similarly, by the Banking Companies (Acquisition and Transfer of Undertakings) Amendment Act, 1994, the Government's share in the paid-up capital of public sector banks had been reduced to 51 per cent. With another amendment in 2000. it has been reduced to 33 per cent.

4. *Prudential Accounting Norms.* The RBI has introduced prudential accounting norms for banks since 1992-93. A credit facility is required to be treated as non-performing asset (NPA) if interest or instalment of principal are in arrears for *any* two quarters in the accounting year. Provisioning requirement for NPAs with balances of less than Rs 25,000 was increased to 10 per cent of the aggregate amount outstanding for the year ended March, 1995 from 7.5 per cent a year ago. For substandard and" doubtful advances of Rs 25,000 and above, they are required to make 100 per cent provision with regard to loss assets.

5. *Recovery of Debts.* Indian banks suffer from large debt arrears which adversely affect their current cash flow position and reduce profits. To recover bad debts, a new Act known as the "Recovery of Debts due to Banks and Financial Institutions Act, 1993" has been passed to set up Debt Recovery Tribunals. Such tribunals have been set up at major centres.

6. *Freedom about Bank Branches.* Banks have been given freedom to open new branches and upgrade extension counters on attaining capital adequacy norm of 8 per cent, net profits for last 3 consecutive years, NPAs of less than 15 per cent and minimum owned funds of Rs 110 crores. They are also permitted to close non-viable branches except in rural and semi-urban areas.

7. *Entry of Private Sector Banks.*To introduce greater competition in banking so as to improve banking services to customers, private banks have been allowed entry as per RBI guidelines. Approval has been given to a few proposals for setting up new private sector banks. Private banks have been allowed to raise capital from institutional investors upto 20 per cent and from NRIs upto 40 per cent. Ten new private sector banks have been established since 1994. It has also been made clear by the RBI that existing private sector banks will be allowed to expand without fear of nationalisation.

8. *Department of Supervision.* A Department of Supervision has been set up in the RBI with effect from 22 December 1993 to supervise the working of commercial banks. It undertakes inspection, surveillance and special investigations including those connected with frauds, and appointment of statutory auditors.

9. *Board for Financial Supervision (BFS).* The BFS has been set up within the RBI in November, 1994. The Board ensures implementation of regulations in the areas of credit management, asset classification, income recognition, provisioning, capital adequacy and treasury operations.

10. *Disclosure on Defaulting Borrowers.* To enforce payments discipline among borrowers, a scheme for disclosure of information regarding defaulting borrowers of banks with outstandings aggregating to Rs. 1 crore and above as on 31 March and 30 September every year has been in operation since April, 1994.

11. *Banking Ombudsman Scheme.* The Banking Ombudsman Scheme has been started from June, 1995 for speedy and inexpensive settlement of customer complaints about the deficiencies in banking services. Ten Ombudsmen are functioning at important centres in the country.

12. *Central Board of Bank Frauds (CBBF).* The Finance Ministry has set up the CBBF in January, 1997 to advise it on the merits of the cases being pursued by the CBI against bank officials up to the level of the general manager. The Board is to scrutinise banking transactions referred to it and give its opinion within 3 months as to whether there is sufficient basis for proceeding with criminal investigations against the officials.

13. *Consortium Arrangements.* To encourage competition and slow-down disintermediation, lending restrictions on banks have been reduced. Large borrowers above a specified credit limit have been allowed to borrow through a consortium of scheduled commercial banks headed by a lead bank. The threshold limit for such consortium arrangement was raised from Rs 5 crores to Rs 50 crores from October 1993. The number of borrower accounts subject to this procedure had been fixed at 76. Borrowers beyond this limit are permitted to induct new banks into a consortium. Banks have been permitted to leave the consortium after two years of joining it.

14. *Lending Norms Liberalised.* Bank lending norms have been liberalised subject to the observance of prescribed prudential norms and quarterly reporting requirements, as laid down by the RBI. They are free to decide levels of holding of individual items of inventory and receivables to be permitted to borrowers. They are also free to decide about the quantum and period of adhoc credit limits without charging additional interest.

15. *Measures to Streamline Working of Banks.* A number of measures have been adopted by the RBI to improve the quality of performance and management of banks. These include: management information systems and the internal audit and control mechanisms; computerisation of banking operations; prudential norms for income recognition assets, etc.

16. *Liberal Credit Control Measures.* A number of steps have been taken to reduce controls and distortions in the working of banks. Statutory Liquidity Ratio (SLR) on incremental net demand and time liabilities (NDTL) has been reduced to 25 per cent. SLR on total NDTL has been brought down to 25 per cent by 1996. The banks have been allowed freedom to fix their deposit and lending rates. They can invest in corporate shares, debentures and units of mutual funds, not exceeding 5 per cent of their outstanding advances effective March 2001. They can also buy shares and debentures of companies from the secondary market.'

17. *Entry of New Private Banks.* The RBI issued in January 2001 guidelines for the entry of new private sector banks other than 10 previous banks. They are : (i) minimum paid-up capital of Rs. 200 crores to be raised to Rs 300 crores within three years of opening; (ii) promoters' contribution of minimum 40 per cent; (iii) NRI contribution in primary equity 40 per cent; (iv) no large industrial house can promote a new bank but individual companies can contribute up to 10 per cent equity; (v) NBFCs with AAA rating and 12 per cent capital adequacy can become private sector banks; (vi) 10 per cent capital adequacy ratio to be maintained by the new bank; (vii) 40 per cent of net bank credit for priority sector lending, and (viii) 25 per cent branches in rural/semi-urban areas.

18. *Entry of Banks into Insurance.* All banks have been allowed to enter insurance business subject to having a minimum net worth of Rs. 500 crores and satisfying other criteria in regard to capital adequacy, profitability, etc.

EXERCISES

1. Explain briefly recent trends in the Indian Banking System.
2. Write notes on: (i) Lead Bank Scheme, (ii) Service Area Approach, (iii) Financing of Priority Sector, (iv) Factoring, (v) Deposit Insurance and Credit Guarantee Corporation.
3. Explain the main features of Innovative Banking in India.
4. What are the principal defects in the Indian Banking System? Give suggestions to remove them.
5. Give the main recommendations of the Narasimham Committee relating to the Indian Banking System.

CHAPTER 70

Development Banking in India

1. INTRODUCTION

Development banking is a post-World War II financial innovation. However, the first development bank was the Industrial Development Bank of Japan established in 1902. Initially, it provided ship mortgage loans. After 1927, it started financing small scale industries. But it was after the Second World War that it started functioning as a development bank in the modern sense of the term. Development banks were also started in a number of developed countries in the post-war era such as the Industrial Bank of Canada (1944), the Finance Corporation for Industry Ltd. and the Commercial Finance Corporation Ltd. of Great Britain (1945), the Industrial Finance Department of the Commonwealth Bank of Australia (1946), the Dutch Herstel Bank (1949), the Industriekredit Bank of Germany (1949), etc. Development banks were also established in many developing countries like India, Pakistan, Sri Lanka, Iran, Chile, Ghana, Malaysia, Thailand, Nigeria, etc. These banks were mostly sponsored by the World Bank. The World Bank itself had its affiliates like the IFC and IDA. In 1959 was established the Inter-American Development Bank with the participation of 19 Latin American countries. The Asian Development Bank came into existence in 1967. The first development bank in India was the IFC established in 1946.

2. MEANING

Development banks are those financial institutions which provide term finance, promote entrepreneurship, enhance organisational effectiveness and upgrade know-how and do-how. They provide either loan or equity capital or both, as also advisory, promotional and entrepreneurial services. Thus development banks administer a blend of financial and developmental services. Boskey defines a development bank as "a financial intermediary supplying medium and long-term funds to bankable economic development projects and providing related services".

3. FUNCTIONS OF DEVELOPMENT BANKS

Development banks have certain distinct characteristics which distinguish them from commercial banks and other financial institutions. *First,* unlike commercial banks, they do not accept deposits from the public. *Second,* they provide medium and long-term finance, whereas commercial banks provide long term finance. *Third,* they do not perform ordinary banking functions but perform promotional, developmental and innovative functions. *Fourth,* they are motivated by social profit, while commercial banks are motivated by commercial profit.

We enumerate some of the functions of development banks below:

1. They provide risk capital.

2. They grant medium and long-term loans or advances.

3. They subscribe to the issue of stocks, shares, bonds and debentures of industrial concerns.

4. They underwrite the issue of stocks, shares, bonds and debentures of industrial concerns.

5. They guarantee loans raised from within and outside the country.

6. They guarantee deferred payment of loans in connection with the purchase of capital goods or machinery within and outside the country.

7. They develop capital market by trying to broaden ownership and by other devices.

8. They provide assistance for setting up new industrial projects.

9. They provide assistance for the expansion of existing units.

10. They provide assistance for modification, renovation and modernisation of existing plants and machinery.

11. They arrange for general industrial surveys and feasibility studies for specific projects.

12. They formulate specific proposals for new enterprises.

13. They assist in finding technical and entrepreneurial partners for local clients or for foreign investors.

14. They provide consultancy assistance in respect of technical know-how and market information to new entrepreneurs.

15. They provide necessary guidance, training and other facilities like project identification, project formulation, project implementation, etc. to new entrepreneurs.

16. They sponsor programmes for the upgradation of managerial skills and professionalism of management.

17. They help in the dispersal of industries and development of backward areas.

4. IMPORTANCE OF DEVELOPMENT BANKS

Development banks have unique importance in the development process of a country. In fact, they are a catalyst agent for development. We enumerate their role as active engines of growth.

1. *Engines of Development.* Development banks are engines of development. By providing expertise, arranging for feasibility studies and finance, they act as active agents of growth.

2. *Spirit of Development Finance.* The importance of development banks lies in spreading the spirit of development finance whereby entrepreneurs learn to invest in real fixed assets.

3. *Creation and Promotion of Enterprise.* Development banks are the instruments for the creation, promotion and spread of enterprise and initiative.

4. *Promotion of Balanced Regional Development.* Development banks are important in that they help in decentralisation and diversification by financing small, medium and large entrepreneurs in backward regions of the country. They are thus the promoters of balanced regional development.

5. *Increasing Productivity of Investment.* They help increase productivity of investment by bringing professionalism in management and providing consultancy and extension services to the tiny, small and new entrepreneurs.

6. *Upgradation of Skills.* By providing appropriate training and upgradation of managerial skills, they help in skill formation among small entrepreneurs.

7. *Upgradation of Technology.* With their technical, advisory and R & D departments, development banks give advice and training in new technology and also help in the upgradation of indigenous technology.

8. *Research.* Development banks undertake market and investment research and surveys as also technical and economic studies related to development of industries.

9. *Gap-Filling.* They help in filling gaps in the industrial structure of the economy by providing and developing industries.

10. *Coordination.* To avoid haphazard growth of financial institutions, development banks coordinate the working of other financial term lending institutions engaged in financing, promoting and developing industries.

11. *Institution Building.* Development banks are the instruments of institution building. They assist in the creation and promotion of term lending institutions. For instance, the Risk Capital and Technology Finance Corporation has been sponsored by the IFCI.

12. *Assist in Purveying Foreign Capital.* It is development banks which acquire foreign capital and allocate

it to varied industrial sectors in keeping with national priorities. They get finance from the World Bank, IDA, etc. and allocate it to different industrial projects.

5. DEVELOPMENT BANKS IN INDIA

There are three types of development banks in India: *First,* there are development banks for agriculture at local, state and national level. They are Primary Land Development Banks, State/Central Land Development Banks, and NABARD. *Second,* there are development banks for industry at the national and State level. At the national level are included Industrial Development Bank of India (IDBI), Industrial Finance Corporation of India (IFCI), Industrial Credit and Investment Corporation of India (ICICI), Small Industries Development Bank of India (SIDBI), Industrial Reconstruction Bank of India (IRBI), Risk Capital and Technology Finance Corporation (RCTF), Technology Development and Information Company of India (TDICI), Shipping Credit and Investment Corporation of India (SCICI), and Tourism Finance Corporation of India (TFCI). At the same level are State Financial Corporations (SFCs) and State Industrial Development Corporations (SIDCs). *Third,* there is the Export-Import (EXIM) Bank of India for the foreign sector.

We shall confine our study to some of the important financial institutions as development banks.

1. Industrial Finance Corporation of India (IFCI)

The IFCI was the first development bank established in India in 1948. It has been converted into a public limited company with effect from 1 July, 1993. Its main objective is to make medium and long term credit to industrial concerns in the private, public, joint and co-operative sectors in India. It is a subsidiary of the IDBI which holds 50 per cent of its share capital and the remaining 50 per cent is held by banks, insurance companies, and co-operative banks. It augments its resources by borrowing from the Government of India, RBI, IDBI, UTI, LIC and by issuing its bonds and debentures in the market, and by borrowing in foreign currency from the World Bank and other foreign organisations.

Its Functions

The IFCI performs the dual function of a financier and promoter. These functions reveal its multifaceted activities :

(1) As a Financier. As a financier, the IFCI performs the following functions:

(a) It grants loans and advances both in rupee and foreign currencies to individual concerns which are repayable within a period of 25 years.

(b) It subscribes to the issue of shares, bonds and debentures by industrial concerns.

(c) It underwrites the issue of shares, bonds and debentures by industrial concerns which must be disposed by the IFCI within seven years of their acquisition.

(d) It guarantees loans both in rupee and foreign currencies and deferred payments in connection with machinery imported from abroad or purchased within India.

(e) It provides financial assistance for setting up new industrial projects, expansion of existing units, and modernisation, renovation and modification of existing units.

(f) It can convert in full or part its rupee loan into equity capital of the industrial concern assisted by it. But it cannot acquire more than 40 per cent of the share capital except in case of persistent default of repayment of loan when its share holding may go up to 51 per cent or more. But this conversion clause is not applicable to loans sanctioned in foreign currency, to co-operative banks and for modernisation and rehabilitation of sick units, etc.

(g) As part of its financial services, it provides equipment financing, equipment leasing, equipment procurement, suppliers' credit, buyers' credit, merchant banking and hire-purchase services to industrial concerns.

(h) It also provides financial support to other financial concerns.

(i) It has introduced Instalment Credit Scheme in November 1991.

(j) It has entered into a Memorandum of Understanding (MoU) with Housing and Urban Development

Corporation Ltd (HUDCO) for joint financing of infrastructure projects.

(2) *As a Promoter,* (a) The promotional activities of the IFCI cover funds supplied for technical consultancy, risk capital, venture capital, technical development,, tounsm, housing, development of securities market, entrepreneurship development and subsidy support to help entrepreneurs and enterprises in the village and small industries sector.

(b) It sanctions assistance to industrial units in backward areas for balanced regional development.

(c) The IFCI sponsored the *Risk Capital and Technology Finance Corporation* (RCTC) in January 1988 after reconstituting the Risk Capital Foundation set up by it in 1975. The RCTC operates two schemes viz. first, Risk Capital Schene, and second, Technology Finance and Development Scheme. Under these schemes, assistance is available to first generation entrepreneurs, particularly technocrats and professionals who have proposals for technology oriented ventures. Assistance is available for funding innovative technologies, technological upgradation, energy conservation processes, systems, environment protection, infrastructural support for advanced/complex technologies, setting up of pilot plants, etc. Assistance is provided on soft terms by way of conventional loans on predetermined interest rates, grace period, repayment period, etc.

(d) It set up a credit rating agency known as the Investment-Information and Credit Rating Agency of India (IICRA) in January 1991, as a public limited company with an authorised capital of Rs 10 crores.

(e) It established the Merchant Banking and Allied Services Department (MB&AD) in 1986 which handles merchant banking assignments relating to public issue management.

(f) It has recently promoted three subsidiary companies, viz, IFCI Financial Services Ltd., IFCI Investors Services Ltd., and IFCI Custodial Services Ltd.

Its Working

During 2002-03, the IFCI sanctioned financial assistance under its various schemes amounting to Rs 2,031 crores. Component wise, sanctions of rupee loans amounted to Rs 16.38 crores., Sanctions by way of underwriting and direct subscriptions amounted to Rs 394 crores and others nil.

The IFCI is required to achieve 9 per cent capital adequacy norm since 2000 which it has been maintaining on an average of more than 8 per cent.

, Thus the IFCI has helped in industrial development through financial and promotional assistance and through diversification of industries in backward areas and states. The criticisms levelled against it for delay in sanctioning loans, favour shown to big industrial houses and neglect of backward regions and industries are unwarranted.

2. Industrial Development Bank of India (IDBI)

The IDBI was established in July 1964 as a wholly owned subsidiary of the Reserve Bank but was made an autonomous institution in February 1976. At the time of its formation, it took over the Refinance Corporation for Industry which was set up in June 1958. At present, the IFCI, UTI and Small Industries Development Bank of India (SIDBI) are its subsidiaries. Since 1986, the authorised capital of IDBI has been raised to Rs 1,000 crores which can be further increased to Rs. 2,000 crores. It mobilises funds through borrowings from the Government of India, the RBI, by way of bonds/debentures, by selling capital bonds, through investment deposit account scheme, foreign currency borrowings, etc.

Its Functions

The IDBI is an apex institution in the sphere of development banking in India which performs financing, coordination and promotional functions. It renders assistance to small, medium and large scale industries in public, private, joint and co-operative sectors.

(1) As a Financier. As a financier, the IDBI renders direct and indirect assistance to all types of industrial concerns :

(a) Schemes of Direct Assistance. It extends direct assistance to industry under its Project Finance Scheme and the Technical Development Fund Scheme. The Project Finance Scheme also covers assistance under the Textile Modernisation Fund, Venture Capital Fund, Technology Upgradation, Energy Audit Subsidy, and Equipment Finance for Energy Conservation Schemes. The Project Finance Scheme of the IDBI mainly covers

project loans to industries, underwriting and direct subscriptions to shares and bonds or debentures of industrial concerns, guarantees for loans/deferred payments due from industrial concerns, and equipment finance, asset credit, and equipment leasing.

(b) Schemes of Indirect Assistance. The IDBI renders the following types of indirect assistance to industrial concerns.

(i) *Refinance of Industrial Loans.* It renders indirect assistance by refinancing ine term loans extended by SFCs, SIDCs, commercial/cooperative banks and RRBs to industrial concerns.

(ii) *Bills Rediscounting Scheme.* This scheme is meant to help the use of indigenous machinery by industrial concerns. Under this scheme, the purchaser draws the bill in favour of the manufacturer of machinery who discounts it with his banker who in turn gets it rediscounted from the IDBI. This facility is provided mainly to sugar, jute, cotton textiles, cement and engineering industries.

(iii) Seed Capital Scheme. Under this scheme, financial assistance is available to new entrepreneurs for meeting the gap in promoters' contribution as well as equity where no issue of public shares is done.

(*iv*) *Assistance to Leasing Companies.* Financial assistance is also sanctioned to leasing companies for refinancing their hire-purchase and leasing schemes.

(*v*) *Resources Support to Other Institutions.* The IDBI provides resource support to other financial institutions by subscribing to their shares and bonds/debentures such as IFCI, ICICI, SFCs, SIDCs, NSIC, TCOc, etc.

(*vi*) *Merchant Banking.* It carries out merchant banking activities and helps the industry in raising capital from the market and renders advice.

(vii) Commercial Banking. It has set up the IDBI Bank Ltd. since 1995 as a private commercial bank.

(2) **As a Coordinator.** The primary objective of the IDBI is to act as a coordinator. As such, it coordinates the activities and operations of other term lending institutions engaged in financing, promoting or developing industries. Coordination is achieved through the inter-institutional meetings and uniform policies and code of conduct in formulation of policies. This has led to the emergence of consortium financing.

(3) **As a Promoter.** This is an important function of the IDBI which includes planning, promoting and developing industries to fill the gaps in the industrial structure of the country. For this purpose, it provides technical and administiative assistance, undertakes market and investment research and surveys, and also technical and economic studies related to development of industry. We discuss its following promotional activities.

(a) Development of Backward Areas. The IDBI conducts surveys of backward areas for assessing their industrial growth potential and publishes reports. It then identifies projects which can be implemented in specific backward areas. It gives both direct and indirect financial assistance for the implementation of such projects in backward areas. The IDBI also undertakes follow-up of those projects on a selective basis.

(b) Promotion of Institutions for SSI. The IDBI promoted the Small Industries Development Fund (SIDF) and National Equity Fund (NEF) for assistance to the small scale sector. In 1990, the IDBI created the Small Industries Development Bank of India (SIDBI) as its wholly owned subsidiary. From April 1990 the SIDBI took over the operations of the two Funds.

(c) The IDBI has sponsored credit rating agency CARE.

(d) It has entered into corporate trusteeship by accepting assignments as mortgage trustee and trustee to odd-lot shareholders.

(e) It has also started stock broking.

(f) It has set up a mutual fund.

(g) Establishment of Technical Consultancy Organisations (TCOs). The IDBI has set up a network of TCOs in collaboration with Stale level financial and development institutions and commercial banks to provide inexpensive consultancy services to small and new entrepreneurs in the country. The activities of TCOs include preparing project profiles and feasibility studies, undertaking industrial potential surveys, conducting entrepreneurship development programmes and rendering technical and administrate e assistance. They also provide consultancy services for modernisation and rehabilitation of industrial units, transfer of technology, design and engineering services, management and export consultancy, rural industrial development, retainer consultancy services, turnkey assignments, and energy and conservation services.

(h) In association with other all-India financial institutions and the Department of Biotechnology of the

Government of India, it has set up the Bio-tech Consortium India Ltd. to help commercialisation of processes and products in the field of biotechnology developed in the research institutes of the country. It aims at the transfer of technology, product development, feedback from market, minimisation of investment risk, and to supplement the efforts of existing research and development institutes in the field of biotechnology.

Its Working

During 2002-03, the 'IDBI sanctioned financial assistance to industrial concerns amounting to Rs 3,889 crores. Out of this, Rs. 2,924 crores were disbursed. Of the total financial assistance disbursed, rupee loans, foreign currency loans and guarantees amounted to Rs 7,853 crores; underwriting and direct subscriptions Rs. 140 crores; and others Rs. 117 crores. The IDBI is required to achieve 9 per cent capital adequacy norm which it has been maintaining on an average of 11 per cent. The IDBI has been merged with IDBI Bank in 2004.

Critical Appraisal of its Working. The IDBI is an apex development bank in the country. Its performance has been quite impressive in terms of the range and pattern of assistance rendered by it. Despite the fact that it has to work under the prevailing economic policy and environment, it has certain flaws.

1. Its emphasis has been on providing project loans. It has therefore been giving less importance to underwriting of shares and debentures of industrial concerns. It has thus failed to develop the capital market.

2. The IDBI's assistance to industries has been mainly of the financial type. As a result, it has paid less attention to promotional and consultancy services.

3. The major portion of its financial assistance has gone to the large scale industries and hardly 28 per cent of the total assistance has gone to the small scale industries.

4. The major portion of its assistance has gone to the already developed states and that too only to a few states. It has thus failed to foster balanced development of all states.

5. Its financial assistance to backward areas has been hardly 42 per cent and that has also been provided to such areas mostly in developed states. This has not been a healthy trend.

6. The major portion of its financial assistance has gone to the private sector which already has access to a variety of sources. It has, therefore, neglected the other sectors, especially the cooperative.

In fact, there is not much weight in these criticisms[1] because the assistance to be provided by the IDBI to different industries, areas, and purposes depends upon the criteria laid down by it. Therefore, those who meet these criteria are sanctioned assistance.

3. Industrial Credit and Investment Corporation of India (ICICI)

The ICICI was established in January 1955 as a public limited company. It is a private sector development bank in India. The World Bank played a key role in its formation. Its authorised capital is Rs 100 crores. About 11 per cent of its share capital is held by the World Bank and other foreign financial institutions, and the remaining by Indian Banks, UTI, GIC, LIC, etc. During 1990-91 for the first time, ICICI entered the capital market with a public issue and raised Rs 100 crores.

Its Objectives

The ICICI was established to fulfil the following main objectives: *(a)* to finance the foreign exchange component of industrial projects; *(b)* to provide assistance in the creation, expansion and modernisation of industrial enterprises; (c) to encourage and promote industrial development and investment; and *(d)* to expand capital markets in the country.

Its Functions

The ICICI renders both financial and promotional assistance to private, joint, public and cooperative sector industrial concerns.

(1) **Financial Assistance.** The ICICI provides financial assistance of the following types:

(a) Project Finance. Assistance for project finance is by way of rupee and foreign currency loans,

1. 'The points of criticism. " *inter alia* apply to all Development Banks.

underwriting and direct subscriptions to shares and debentures, and guarantees.

(b) Financial Services. Assistance by way of financial services to industry includes assistance under schemes of deferred credit since 1982-83, equipment leasing since 1983-84, venture capital during 1986-87 to 1987-88, instalment sale since 1988-89 and asset credit facility since 1989-90.

(c) Merchant Banking. The ICICI also renders merchant banking services.

(d) Commercial Banking. It has set up the ICICI Banking Corporation as a commercial bank since 1994.

(2) **Promotional Assistance.** The ICICI renders the following promotional assistance to industrial concerns:

(a) Assistance to Backward Areas. It provides project finance assistance on concessional terms to industries in backward areas. It also gives loans on soft terms to suitable rural development schemes sponsored by corporate bodies. It extends financial assistance in the form of seed money/margin money or interest rate subsidy in backward areas.

(b) Project Assistance. The ICICI provides assistance to new projects and to expansion/diversification projects. It renders assistance for modernisation/rehabilitation/balancing equipment projects. Further, it provides supplementary assistance to industrial concerns which includes equipment finance and finance for meeting cost overrun and for various other purposes like energy conservation, pollution control, etc.

(c) Technology Upgradation. The ICICI has promoted a number of institutions for technology upgradation. It has promoted TCQs in a number of states in collaboration with IDBI, IFCI and state level institutions. It provides assistance to Indo-US collaboration projects under the US-aided Programme for the Advancement of Commercial Technology (PACT) for development of innovative products and processes in such areas as informatics, biotechnology, engineering, etc. It also renders assistance for R & D projects under the Programme for Acceleration of Commercial Energy Research (PACER) funded by USAID with a grant of S 20 million. In July 1988, the ICICI established the Technology Development and Information Company of India (TDICI) to finance technology-intensive development activities, including commercial R & D schemes. During 1992-93, the iCICI introduced two new projects with the help of USAID: First, Agricultural Commercialisation and Enterprise (ACE) Project, and *second*. Trade in Environmental Services and Technologies (TEST) Programme with grants of S 20 million and $ 25 million respectively.

(d) Venture Capital. The venture capital operations of the ICICI have been taken over by the TDICI since July 1988. However, in association with UTI ard corporate sector, the ICICI floated a second Venture Capital Fund (VECAUS-II) of Rs. 100 crores in April 1990.

(e) It has promoted a new company for providing share registry and transfer services to investors.

(f) It has promoted a mutual fund.

Its Working

"Financial assistance sanctioned and disbursed by the ICICI during 2001-02 amounted to Rs. 36,229 crores and 25,831 crores respectively. Of the total disbursed amount, rupee loans, foreign currency loans and guarantiees amounted to Rs. 14,475 crores; underwriting and direct subscriptions Rs 3,348 crores; and others Rs 8,009 crores. The ICICI is required to achieve 9 per cent capital adequacy norm which it has been maintaining on an average of 13 per cent. The ICICI has been merged with the ICICI Bank in April 2002.

4. Industrial Investment Bank of India (IIBI)

Earlier the IIBI was known as the Industrial Reconstruction Corporation of India and renamed as Industrial Investment Bank of India from March 27,1997. It is the principal credit and reconstruction institution for rehabilitation of sick and closed industrial units in the public, joint and cooperative sectors and those units in the private sector whose management has been taken over under the Industrial (Development & Regulation) Act. It mobilises funds for its use from: *(a)* external sources which include borrowings from the Government of India, RBI and by way of subscription of bonds and debentures of Industrial concerns; and *(b)* internal sources which include repayments by borrowers, and interest and dividend received. Its total financial assets in 1980-81 were Rs 924 crores which increased to Rs 4,526 crores in 2002-03.

Its Functions

The IIBI Performs the following functions :

1. It grants term loans and advances to sick industrial concerns tor modernisation/rehabilitation/ balancing equipment.

2. It provides supplementary assistance for (a) meeting cost overrun, *(b)* correcting imbalances, and (c) other purposes.

3. It underwrites stocks, shares, bonds and debentures and gives guarantees for loans/deferred payments of such industrial concerns.

4. It provides infrastructural facilities, consultancy, managerial and merchant banking facilities.

5. It makes available machinery and other equipment on lease and hire-purchase basis.

Its Working

Sanctions and disbursements by the IIBI during 2002-03 aggregated to Rs 1,207 crores and Rs 1,045 crores respectively. Of the total sanctioned amount, term loans amounted to Rs 163 crores, underwriting and direct subscriptions Rs 1,043 crores.

The IIBI is required to achieve capital adequacy ratio of 9 per cent per annum since 2,000 which it has been maintaining at a higher level.

5. Small Industries Development Bank of India (SIDBI)

The SIDBI was established in April 1990 as a wholly owned subsidiary of the IDBI. The authorised capital of the Bank is Rs 250 crores which can be increased up to Rs 1,000 crores. The Small Industries Development Fund (SIDF) and National Equity Fund (NEF) were taken over by it. Apart from these funds and its share capital, its other sources of funds comprise loans from the IDBI, short-term and long-term funds from the RBI, loans from the Government of India, etc.

Its Functions

The SIDBI performs the following functions:

(i) It is the principal financial institution for the promotion, financing and development of small scale industries.

(ii) It coordinates the functioning of existing institutions engaged in similar activities.

(iii) It renders assistance to small scale industries through refinance of loans and advances, bills finance, seed capital/soft loans, direct assistance, providing services like factoring, leasing, etc.

(iv) It refinances National Industries Development Corporation, State Industrial Development Corporations, State Small Industries Corporations, scheduled banks, state cooperative banks, etc.

(v) It subscribes or purchases stocks, shares, bonds or debentures of State Financial Corporations, State Industrial Development Corporations, etc.

(vi) It renders assistance to small scale industries by way of resource support to NSIC and SSIDCs for their hire purchase, raw material supply and marketing support schemes.

(vii) It initiates steps for technological upgradation and modernisation of existing units.

(viii) It expands channels for marketing products of SSI sector in domestic and overseas markets.

(ix) It promotes employment-oriented industries, especially in semi-urban areas, to create more employment opportunities and thereby check migration of population to urban and metropolitan areas.

Since 1991-92, the SIDBI has introduced the following new schemes:

(1) a scheme of direct assistance to widen the supply base of small-scale ancillary units;

(2) a scheme to provide resource support to factoring companies against factored debts of SSIs;

(3) a refinance scheme for acquisition of computers including their accessories;

(4) a scheme for refinancing assistance to qualified professionals for setting up their ewn business enterprises;

(5) an equipment financing scheme to assist existing small-scale units;

(6) a refinance scheme to resettle voluntarily retired workers of National Textile Corporation (NTC) and

to help them in purchasing upto four looms at the maximum;

(7) a venture capital fund was created with an initial corpus of Rs 10 crores;

(8) a special Self-Employment Scheme for Ex-servicemen;

(9) Mahila Udyam Nidhi Scheme to help women entrepreneurs;

(10) it is enrolled as member of the Over-The-Counter Exchange of India (OTCEI) to help SSIs to get access to capital market through SIDBI.

(11) Under the Single Window Scheme (SWS) in operation since the inception of SIDBI, the limit of refinance against cash credit sanctioned by banks has been raised to 75 per cent. The limit of term loans under the Automatic Refinance Scheme (ARS) has been raised to Rs. 50 lakh and the limit of refinance to 90 per cent.

(12) During 1993-94, SIDBI took new initiatives such as the extension of foreign currency loans to Export Oriented Units (EOUs) and support to Non-Government Organisations (NGOs) for promoting self-help by the rural poor.

(13) It has signed MoUs with 5 public sector banks for jointly extending direct assistance to SSI units.

(14) The SIDBI has started a venture capital fund with a corpus of Rs 20 crores.

(15) During 1994-95, it introduced new schemes such as direct equity investment in SSIs and financial assistance to enable well-run EOUs to acquire ISO-9000 series certification.

(16) It has set up a Technology Bureau for SSI units in New Delhi in collaboration with Asia Pacific Centre for Transfer of Technology.

Its Working

The SIDBI sanctioned and disbursed Rs 10,904 crores and Rs 6,789 crores respectively during 2002-03. Of the total disbursed amount, term loans amounted to Rs 6,789 crores; underwriting and direct subscriptions; and others nil.

6. Export-Import Bank of India (EXIM)

The Export-Import Bank of India *was* established in January 1982 as a statutory corporation wholly owned by the Government of India.

Its Objectives : The main objectives of the Exim Bank are:

1. To ensure an integrated arid coordinated approach to solve the problems of exporters;
2. To provide special attention to the export of capital goods;
3. To encourage project exports;
4. To finance Indian joint ventures abroad;
5. To undertake and finance the export of technical consultancy services;
6. To deal in foreign exchange;
7. To render international merchant banking services;
8. To provide refinance facilities;
9. To extend buyers credit and lines of credit to parties outside India; and
10. To tap domestic and overseas markets for resources for undertaking developmental and financing activities in the sphere of exports.

Its Functions

The Exim Bank performs the following promotional and developmental functions:

1. To undertake and finance research, surveys, techno-economic or any other study in connection with the promotion and development of international trade;
2. To provide technical, administrative and financial assistance of any kind for export or import;
3. To plan, promote, develop and finance export-oriented concerns; and
4. To collect, compile and disseminate market and credit information in respect of international trade.

Its Resources

The authorised capital of the Exim Bank is Rs. 200 crores which can be raised to Rs 500 crores. Its paid-up capital is Rs 75 crores. The Central Government sanctioned a loan of Rs 20 crores repayable in equal annual instalments, commencing on the expiry of fifteen years from the date of receipt of loan. The Exim Bank can also raise resources by issuing and selling bonds and debentures, borrowing from the Reserve Bank, Government of India, and domestic and international markets.

The Exim Bank maintains three funds: the Export Development Fund (EDF), the General Fund, and the Export Marketing Fund (EMF).

The EDF is a special fund in which the following can be credited: (a) all amounts received by way of loans, gifts, grants, donations from the Government or any other source in or outside India; *(b)* repayments or recoveries in respect of loans, advances or facilities granted the Fund; (c) income or profits from investments made from the Fund; and *(d)* income accruing or arising to the Fund by way of interest or otherwise.

The Fund is used for the grant of loans or advances for its export development activities. All receipts of the Exim Bank, except those which are credited to the EDF, are credited to the General Fund, and all payments, other than those which are debited to the EDF are made out of the General Fund.

The Exim Bank set up the EMF in June 1986. It consists of a component of World Bank loan to India which is managed by the Bank on behalf of the Government of India. This Fund provides grants and loans for the promotion of select group of engineering products for export to developed countries.

Its Working

The Exim Bank provides both funded and non-funded assistance to promote Indian exports. It provides funded assistance in the following forms: direct financial assistance, export credit refinance, buyers' credit, lines of credit, overseas investment finance, finance for export oriented units, finance for computer software exports, agency credit lines, pre-shipment credit, export bills rediscounting, small scale industry export bills rediscounting, bulk import finance, etc. During 1999-2000, sanctions of funded assistance under various programmes amounted to Rs 2831.8 crores.

New Export Promotion Programmes. The Exim Bank has recently introduced a number of programmes and schemes for export promotion. They are: (i) Africa Project Development Facility (APDF) which is meant to promote private sector investment in Africa through financial support for consultancy studies. It has started generating business for Indian consultants in African countries. *(ii)* Project Preparatory Services Overseas Programme (PPSOP) provides finance for feasibility studies in other countries for Indians. *(iii)* Financing Market Entry Costs Programme which provides assistance to Indian exporters to cover the costs of entry into new markets abroad, *(iv)* Pre-shipment Export Credit Scheme Denominated in Foreign Currency which provides exporters access to imports of raw material components, (v) Post-shipment Export Credit Denominated in Foreign Currency Scheme which enables exporters to avail of this scheme and pay interest at rates applicable to foreign currency concerned, *(vi)* Production Equipment Finance Programme which ensures rupee term finance to eligible export-oriented units for acquiring equipment, *(vii)* European Community International Investment Partners (ECIIP) which aims at promoting and financing joint ventures in India with private sector small and medium enterprises in the EC. *(viii)* Forfeiting is meant to provide to Indian exporters facilities for discounting of their medium and long term export receivables with forfeiting international agencies, *(ix)* Business Advisory and Technical Assistance (BATA) programme which provides services of Indian exports to the International Finance Corporation (IFC) sponsored BATA programme for the Caribbean, Central America, South Pacific, and East European countries, *(x)* Export Marketing Finance programme which provides financial assistance to Indian manufacturing companies to undertake strategic export marketing activities with industrialised country markets, *(xi)* Export Vendor Development Finance (EVDF) programme which provides integrated financing packages to manufacturer/exporters and export/trading houses to implement strategic vendor development schemes.

Thus, the Exim Bank's programmes cover various stages of exports from the development of export markets to expansion of production capacity for exports, production for exports, consultancy and feasibility studies for exports and pre-and post-shipment financing.

7. State Financial Corporations (SFCs)

SFCs are the state-level development banks for the development of small and medium scale industries in 18 States of India. They aim at bringing about balanced regional development by wider dispersal of industries, promoting greater investment and generating larger employment opportunities. Besides their paid-up capital, SFCs augment their funds by borrowings from the Governments, RBI, IDBI, banks and by way of bonds/debentures, by accepting deposits and sale of investment in shares and debentures of industrial concerns.

Their Functions

SFCs perform the following functions:

(*i*) They provide financial assistance to industries by way of term loans, direct subscription to equity/debentures, discounting of bills of exchange and guarantees.

(*ii*) They meet the term loan requirements of small and medium scale industries for acquisition of fixed assets like land, building, machinery and equipment.

(*iii*) They provide loans for setting up new industrial units as well as for expansion and modernisation of the existing units.

(*iv*) They also promote the development of medium and small scale industries in backward areas of the country.

(*v*) Under the Special Capital Scheme, SFCs provide equity type support of upto Rs 4 lakhs on soft terms to entrepreneurs for bridging the gap in equity or promoters' contribution. Entrepreneurs with viable projects but lacking adequate own funds are assisted under the scheme.

(*vi*) SFCs operate a number of schemes on behalf of the IDBI. These include composite loan scheme, schemes for women entrepreneurs, modernisation scheme, equipment finance scheme, schemes for hospitals and nursing homes, scheme for ex-servicemen, single window scheme, and special capital and seed capital schemes.

Their Working

SFCSs sanctioned an amount of Rs 2,210 crores in 2001-02 and their disbursements amounted to Rs 1,750 crores. Top four SFCs in terms of annual sanctions were Gujarat, Uttar Pradesh, Maharashtra, and Karnataka. These four SFCs together accounted for about 50 per cent of the totai sanctions by all SFCs up to the end of March 1999. Industry-wise five industries were viz. services, food products, textiles, chemicals and chemical products, and metal products together accounted for more.than 54 per cent of the cumulative sanctions of all SFCs to industries. Cumulative sanctions to backward areas by SFCs accounted for more than 51 per cent of total sanctions. Small scale sector accounted for more than 76 per cent of cumulative sanctions. New projects claimed the bulk of sanctions from SFCs and accounted for about 84 per cent of total sanctions, followed by expansion/diversification, supplementary assistance, and modernisation/rehabilitation/balancing equipment.

8. State Industrial Development Corporations (SIDCs)

SIDCs were set up during the sixties and early seventies as wholiy-owned State Government undertakings for the promotion and development of medium and large scale industries. Their main objective is to act as catalytic agents for the development of industries in their respective States. There are at present 26 SIDCs in the country. Nine of them also function as SFCs and provide assistance to small scale units and act as promotional agencies in their respective areas of operation. Seven SIDCs are also involved in infrastructure development and other extension services for promotion of small sector.

Besides increase in paid-up capital, SIDCs borrow funds from the Government, IDBI, banks and other financial institutions. They also borrow by way of bonds, by accepting deposits, sale of investments in shares and debentures of industrial concerns, and repayments by borrowers.

Their Functions

SIDCs perform the following functions:

(*i*) They provide financial assistance to industrial units by way of term loans, underwriting and direct subscriptions to shares/debentures and guarantees.

(*ii*) They undertake a variety of promotional activities like preparation of feasibility reports, industrial potential surveys, entrepreneurship development programmes and developing industrial areas/estates.

(iii) They are engaged in setting up of medium and large industrial projects in joint sector in collaboration with private entrepreneurs or as wholly-owned subsidiaries.

(iv) Some SIDCs also administer the incentive schemes of Central/State Governments and participate in risk capital.

(v) Some SIDCs extend assistance by way of interest free sales tax/unsecured loans on behalf of respective State Governments.

(vi) SIDCs are agents of IDBI for operating its seed capital scheme. Under the scheme, equity type assistance is provided to deserving first generation entrepreneurs who possess necessary skills but lack adequate resources required towards promoter contribution.

Their Working

Assistance sanctioned by SIDCs (excluding sales tax, loans) amounted to Rs 1,594 crores during 2001-02. Out of this, Rs 1,718 crores were disbursed. Component-wise, term loans accounted for 96.63 per cent of total disbursements of SIDCs during 2001- 02. Assistance by way of underwriting/direct subscriptions, others constituted 3.37 per cent of total disbursements. Cumulatively, seven SIDCs in the States of Uttar Pradesh, Maharashtra, Gujarat, Karnataka, Andhra Pradesh, Punjab and Tamilnadu together constituted nearly 66 per cent of the total sanctions of all SIDCs. In the industrywise cumulative assistance, chemicals and chemical products, textiles, food products, basic metals and services together accounted for 48 per cent of total sanctions by SIDCs. Assistance sanctioned to backward areas accounted for a share of 62 per cent in the cumulative sanctions of SIDCs up to the end of March 1999. Of the sector-wise assistance, private sector accounted for 79.5 per cent of the cumulative sanctions of SIDCs followed by joint sector, public sector and cooperative sector (0.5 per cent). Under the purpose-wise assistance, new projects constituted about 70 per cent of the cumulative sanctions followed by expansion/diversification, modernisation/rehabilitation/balancing equipment and supplementary assistance.

Appraisal of Development Banking in India

The study of various development banks in India reveals that they have been playing a crucial role in setting, promoting and developing industrial units in the small, medium and large scale sectors of the Indian economy. They have helped in the dispersal of industries in backward regions/areas. They have been providing necessary know-how, technical, expertise, machinery and equipment for the modernisation of industrial units. In fact, they have been acting as catalytic agents of industrial growth in India.

Despite these achievements, they suffer from certain weaknesses. *First,* the main sources of funds of development banks are borrowings from the Government of India, RBI, banks and other financial institutions and foreign sources. But they do not raise funds from the public. They do not sell their shares, bonds or debentures in the market. These borrowings by development banks have encouraged high debt-equity ratios and since they borrow at low rate of interest, it has led to high capital intensity in industry because the latter is able to procure term loans at low rates in turn. *Second,* the majority of financial assistance is provided by development banks in the form of term loans to industrial units. This has led to large defaults on loans by companies which have become weak units. *Third,* the development banks do not encourage lending on the basis of loans/debentures of industrial units. They have, therefore, failed to develop a corporate bond market. *Fourth,* these development banks have provided more financial assistance to the private sector than to the public, joint and cooperative sectors. They also provide soft loans to them at concessional rates at the cost of public exchequer with the result that the State's revenue from them is insufficient. It has led to highly capital-intensive technology and has failed to absorb the growing labour force of the country thereby leading to more unemployment. *Fifth,* they have not been successful in achieving balanced regional development of industries. More assistance has flowed to the already developed States and to backward areas of these States. *Sixth,* their role as promotional agencies has been weak. *Seventh,* there are unnecessary delays in sanctioning and disbursing assistance due to red-tapism. *Eighth,* their overdues to industries have been mounting and the problem of industrial sickness is on the increase. *Ninth,* they have failed to develop adequate human resources with the result that their personnel lack in proper managerial, administrative and technical skills which are essential for the rapid growth of industries.

EXERCISES

1. Discuss the importance of development banking in India.
2. What is a development bank? Explain its functions.
3. Discuss the functions and working of Industrial Finance Corporation of India.
4. Discuss critically the functions and working of the Industrial Development Bank of India.
5. Write notes on: (1) Industrial Credit and Investment Corporation of India; (2) Industrial Reconstruction Bank of India; (3) Small Industries Development Bank of India; (4) Exim Bank.
6. Define a development bank. Give its functions. Critically examine development banking in India.

CHAPTER 71

Non-Bank Financial Intermediaries in India

1. INTRODUCTION

In India Non-bank financial intermediaries1 (NBFIs) are of two types: organised and unorganised. Organised NBFIs are all development banks which include IDBI, IFCI, ICICI, SIDBI, SFCs, NABARD, Land Development Banks, etc. They raise funds from various sources and provide medium and long-term advances. Besides these, there are the UTI, GIC and LIC. The UTI is a pure NBFI while the later two are insurance companies which raise funds from the insurance premia and lend to individuals and companies. There are also provident funds and pension funds' which mobilise savings and invest them in Government and other approved securities. Lastly, post offices mobilise small savings of the public which go to the Government for investment purposes. All organised NBFIs are in the public sector. They follow rules and regulations laid down by the Government.

2. NON-BANKING FINANCIAL COMPANIES (NBFCs)

NBFIs in the unorganised sector are called Non-Banking Financial Companies (NBFCs) in India. They are equipment leasing companies, hire-purchase finance companies, loan (or finance) companies, investment companies, mutual benefit financial companies, chit funds, miscellaneous non-banking companies (nidhis), residuary non-banking companies, non-banking non-financial companies, and housing finance companies.

Regulation of NBFCs

NBFCs were registered under the Indian Companies Act and not the Banking Regulation Act. So the RBI had no control over them. In recent years, they have grown in number and volume of business by entering into those areas where banks were not allowed to enter due to regulatory restrictions. In view of their increasing role in the financial intermediation process, the Narasimham Committee recognised the need for integrating them within the mainstream of the financial system. Accordingly, the RBI constituted a Working Group under Dr. A.C. Shah in May 1992 to set out a programme of reform for financial companies.

On the basis of its recommendations, the RBI introduced a scheme of registration of NBFCs on 12 April, 1993. All NBFCs having Net Owned Fund (NOF) of Rs. 50 lakhs and above were required to register with the

1. For a theorietical discussion on the role of NBFIs, refer to Chapter 25.

Reserve Bank. On 13 June, 1994, it issued prudential norms relating to income recognition, accounting standards, assets classification, provisioning for bad and doubtful debts, capital adequacy and concentration of credit/ investments for registered NBFCs. The RBI also specified compulsory credit rating for them in a phased manner. They were required to achieve a minimum capital adequacy norm of 8%. Besides, they were required to get themselves rated by any one of the credit rating agencies atleast once a year. Credit rating provides objective information to depositors and creditors and helps in protecting their interest. The RBI directions brought all public deposits and inter-corporate deposits of NBFCs within the discipline of its regulations. Further, the interest rates payable on deposits by NBFCs were also laid down. They were also required to attain a minimum liquid asset ratio to deposits. These measures had no statutory backing because the RBI Act, 1934 did not confer such'powers to the Reserve Bank.

By the January 9,1997 Ordinance, the RBI has been given greater control over ihe activities of NBFCs. This ordinance was replaced by the RBI (Amendment) Act in March 1997. The conditions under which NBFCs can operate have been laid down by the RBI through several amendments to NBFCs regulations upto 2001.

(1) Entry point norm of Rs. 25 lakhs as minimum NOF which can be raised to Rs. 2 crores;
(2) compulsory registration with the RBI;
(3) maintenance of certain percentage of liquid funds in the form of unencumbered approved securities;
(4) creation of reserve funds in which 20% of the net profit to be transferred every year;
(5) issuing of directions for prudential norms by the RBI;
(6) prohibition of NBFCs from accepting public deposits;
(7) filing of winding-up positions for violation of RBI directions;
(8) empowering the Company Law Board to direct a defaulting NBFC to repay deposits; and
(9) stringent penal provisions in the form of pecuniary penalties for violation of RBI directions.

The various steps taken up by the RBI to consolidate the functioning of NBFCs failed to streamline their working. It, therefore, instituted a new regulatory framework for the operation of NBFCs. Consequently, NBFCs were classified into the following three categories for purposes of regulation:

(a) those accepting public deposits;
(*b*) those not accepting public deposits but engaged in financial business; and
(c) core investment companies holding atleast 90% of their assets as investments in the securities of group/holding/subsidiary companies.

While NBFCs accepting public deposits are subject to all types of regulations, those not accepting public deposits are regulated in a limited manner.

We will discuss each category briefly.

(a) Regulations over NBFCs accepting Public Deposits

These regulations are applicable to equipment leasing/hire purchase (EL/HP) and loan companies/ investment companies (LC/IC).

(1) For old NBFCs, the minimum NOF remains at Rs. 25 lakhs. But those seeking registration with the RBI and commencing business on or after April 21,1999, the minimum NOF is Rs. 2 crores. NBFCs with NOF of below 25 lakhs cannot accept deposits. Companies with Rs. 25 lakhs and above NOF can have public deposits not exceeding 1.5 times of NOF or Rs. 10 crores whichever is less.

(2) The period of deposits should not be less than 12 months but not exceed 60 months.

(3) The rate of interest payable on such deposits should not be more than 16 per cent per annum.

(4) The brokerage fees and other expenses should not exceed 2% and 0.5% of the deposits respectively.

(5) The capital adequacy ratio has been fixed at 12% and above, in accordance with the eligibility criteria for accepting deposits.

(6) An EL/HP finance company accepting deposits is required to disclose in its advertisement and application form that it is an un-rated company having capital adequacy ratio of not less than 15% and within the RBI regulations mentioned above.

(7) Restrictions have been placed on NBFCs to invest in real estate, except for their own use, upto 10% of their NOF for EL/HP finance companies and 20% of NOF for LC/IC companies.

(8) NBFCs which fail to repay matured deposits cannot create assets in any manner, including giving

loans or making investment, until the default is rectified. Depositors can also lodge their complaints to the Company Law Board.

(9) NBFCs are required to maintain liquid assets of not less than 15% of their public deposits effective April 1,1999. In case of default in maintaining approved securities of requisite value, the RBI imposes penalties.

(10) The liquid assets of NBFCs are required to be deposited in scheduled commercial banks appointed by the RBI so that the securities are not utilised otherwise, except for repayment to depositors. They are also permitted to keep their liquid securities with the Stock Holding Corporation of India.

(11) The RBI has introduced certain regulations in respect of opening and closing of branches. For instance, for closing a branch 3 months' public notice prior to the date of closure has to be given in atleast one national newspaper.

(12) The RBI has also instituted a comprehensive supervisory mechanism over NBFCs. This includes on-site inspection, external auditing and off-site surveillance system regarding submission of various returns at quarterly/half-yearly/annual intervals irrespective of the size of their NOF.

(13) An independent Department of Non-Banking Supervision has been opened in the RBI to supervise the operations of NBFCs with its 16 regional offices at different centres of the country.

(14) NBFCs are required to follow a uniform accounting year of March 31 every year effective March 31, 2001.

(15) Any NBFC with NOF of Rs. 2 crores has been permitted to undertake insurance business as agent on fee basis without any risk participation since July 2000. But those NBFCs which have NOF of not less than Rs. 500 crores with good trackrecord in terms of net profits, subsidiaries, net NPA of not less 5%, etc. can set up joint venture company or insurance business with risk participation.

(16) The RBI has also allowed an NBFC to become a private sector bank effective March 31,2001. For this it has laid down: *(a)* The NBFC should have a minimum net worth of Rs. 200 crores as per its' latest balance sheet which would increase to Rs. 300 crores within three years of the date of conversion, *(b)* It should not have been promoted by a large industrial house or by local, state or central public authority, *(c)* It should have a *triple A* credit rating in the previous year, *(d)* It should have capital adequacy of not less than 12% and its net NPA should be below 5%.

(17) Effective April 2001, the RBI has permitted foreign direct investment (FDI) in the NBFC sector. Foreign NBFCs can set up wholly-owned operating subsidiaries subject to bringing in $ 50 million. Joint venture operating NBFCs having 75% or less foreign investment have been allowed to set up subsidiaries, provided they comply with the applicable minimum capital inflow of $ 50 million.

(b) Other NBFCs

Since January 2000, NBFCs engaged in *(a)* micro-financing activities; *(b)* not accepting public deposits; and (c) mutual benefit companies, have been exempted from the purview of registration, maintenance of liquid assets, creation of reserve funds, etc. Similarly, core investment companies, not accepting public deposits have been exempted from all prudential norms except registration and creation of reserve fund.

Operations of NBFCs

Prior to the RBI (Amendment) Act of 1997, there were over 40,000 NBFCs in the organised and unorganised sectors. With the implementation of various regulations by the RBI from time to time, there were 13,849 NBFCs in June 2003. Of these, only 918 NBFCs were registered with the RBI and only 710 NBFCs were accepting public deposits. The total assets of 910 reporting NBFCs as on March 31,2002 were Rs 50,290 crores, with NOFs of Rs 4,383 crores and public deposits amounting to Rs 18,822 crores.

Critical Appraisal

NBFCs have been performing a vital function in economic development by mobilising savings and making investments, advancing loans, providing equipment leasing and hire-purchase facilities. But their operations leave much to be desired. However, the RBI (Amendment) Act, 1997 has empowered the RBI with greater controlling powers over the activities of NBFCs of both the incorporated and unincorporated varieties.

Now there is a compulsory registration for all NBFCs. The RBI is empowered to issue directions to them on such matters as deposits, NOF, recognition, asset classification, capital adequacy, loan and investment, interest payment, credit rating, accounting standards, etc. Giving more statutory powers to the RBI has been felt long ago because the NBFCs have been openly flouting rules. They lack transparency with regard to the sources of income, bad debts and non-recuring income. There has been no provision in the RBI Act to force an NBFC to refund the depositor his amount.

Still, there is dichotomy in control and regulation of NBFCs. The RBI is to control and regulate the activities of NBFCs. The Company Law Board (CLB) is the agency to redress the grievances of depositors.

With the changing national scenario in the financial markets, most of the NBFCs face difficulties in getting lower-cost funds, stiff competition from large NBFCs and subsidiaries of foreign NBFCs and joint venture foreign companies with the result that their business is dwindling. Even though the RBI has opened more avenues in the form of entry into insurance business and private sector banks, they are only for larger NBFCs. The smaller NBFCs are trying to spread to rural and semi-urban areas. A few NBFCs have started new lines of business, such as financing vehicles, working as agents of larger NBFCs and foreign banks, etc.

EXERCISE

1. Explain the working of non-bank financial companies in India. What has been done to control and regulate them? Explain briefly.

CHAPTER

72

Financial Reforms in India

1. INTRODUCTION

Financial reforms in India relate to the banking sector, money market, foreign exchange market, government securities market and capital market reforms. We explain here the reforms undertaken in India's financial sector.

2. BANKING SECTOR REFORMS

The reforms of the banking sector started with the nationalisation of 14 private banks in 1969 and 6 more banks in 1980. The focus of bank nationalisation was on social banking. The emphasis was on branch expansion in rural, semi-urban and urban areas, to mobilise deposits on a massive scale and to lend funds for productive activities, with greater emphasis on the weaker sections of the society. These public sector banks were successful in extending their geographical coverage and increasing their targets of deposit mobilisation and advancing loans. But they were afflicted with low profitability, inefficiency and a high proportion of non-performing assets (NPAs), *i.e.,* bad loans.

One of the serious problems of the banking system was the massive pre-emption of banks' resources to finance Government's budgetary needs. At the beginning of the reforms process in 1991, the statutory pre-emptions under both CRR and SLR on an incremental basis were as high as 63.5%. Of the remaining 36.5%, there were 40% pre-emptions under the priority sector, export credit, food credit and other formal and informal pre-emptions. These pre-emptions along with administered interest rates were referred to as "financial repression". There were restrictions on the use of funds by banks which affected their profitability. Many of the public sector banks had become unprofitable and under-capitalised. To remedy the growing deficiencies of the Indian banking sector, the Government of India set up the Narasimham Committee on Financial System in 1991. It recommended deregulation and liberalisation of the banking sector. This was followed by the recommendations of Narasimham Committee (II) of 1998. Besides, prior to the pre-reform era, there were administered interest rates on term deposits of varied maturities and various categories of loans by banks.

There was no transparency and disclosure in the working of accounting policies of banks. There were no prudential norms relating to banks and risk management techniques like capital adequacy ratio (CAR), capital to risk-weighted assests ratio (CRAR), non-performing assets (NPAs) norms, income ratios, asset-liability management, and risk management guidelines for banks, etc. Due to lack of these norms and guidelines in the Indian banking system, there were bank failures. Therefore, there was an urgent need for adequate regulation and supervision of banks.

Moreover, the banking sector did not have sufficient competition because there were reestrictions on the entry and expansion of domestic and foreign private banks. The branch expansion of banks was rigidly controlled by the RBI. No bank was allowed to open a branch without its permission. Despite reforms, there have been direct administrative controls on the direction of credit allocation and rates at which credit is given,

Last but not the least, the customer service in the public sector banks was at its lowest level due to lack of competition from private and foreign banks.

To remedy all the above noted defects of the Indian banking system, the following policy measures have been adopted.

1. *Reduction of Pre-emption.* The total effective pre-emption has been brought down from the pre-reform level of 65% to less than 35% now. This has been done by reducing the CRR from 15% to 4.5% and SLR from 38.5% to 25%.

2. *De-regulation of Interest Rates.* Phase-wise de-regulation of interest rates on both deposits and advances has been done. At present, only saving deposits and those for less than 15 days and loans upto Rs. 2 lakh are under administered interest rate regime. Banks are free to fix their own Prime Lending Rate (PLR) for advances over Rs. 2 lakh. But foreign currency deposits and advances and export credit rates are being regulated.

3. *Adoption of Prudential Norms and Risk Management.* Prudential norms relating to capital adequacy ratio (8% — 9%), asset classification, income recognition, classification and valuation of investment portfolio, etc. are being introduced gradually to meet international standards.

4. *Promoting Competition.* Competition is being promoted in the banking sector by permitting new private sector banks and by allowing foreign banks to open more branches. Local Area Banks (LABs) are also being encouraged in rural and semi-urban areas to foster competition.

The transparency and disclosure standards of banks have been raised to meet international standards. They relate to disclosure of accounting policies, capital adequacy ratio, percentage of Government shareholding, percentage of non-performing assets (NPAs) to net advances, income ratios, business and profit per employee, etc. As per the recommendations of Narasimham Committee (II), the banks are required, effective March 31,2000, to disclose maturity pattern of loans and advances, investment securities, deposits and borrowings, foreign currency assets and liabilities, movement in NPAs (non-performing assets), etc.

5. *Allowing PSBs to Raise Capital.* To enable public sector banks to meet their additional needs of capital, the Government has allowed the banks to approach the capital market directly to raise funds. They can sell 49% of the share capital to the public. Few banks which have raised capital from the public are State Bank of India, Bank of India, Oriental Bank of Commerce, Bank of Baroda, Indian Overseas Bank, etc.

6. *Supervision.* The RBI has set up an independent Board for Financial Supervision (BFS) which undertakes on-site and off-site supervision of banks and reports to the RBI. The on-site supervision relates to solvency, liquidity, operational soundness and prudent management. The off-site supervision consists of submission of returns by banks on capital adequacy, asset quality, large credit, lending earnings, and currency, liquidity and interest rate risks, etc.

7. *Credit Delivery System.* Loan system for delivery of bank credit for working capital has been introduced to bring greater discipline in credit utilisation and control in credit flows.

8. *Customer Service.* To strengthen customer service, a number of measures have been implemented as recommended by the Jaipuria Committee. To ensure efficient customer service, banks collect feed-back on a regular basis through visits of senior officials from controlling offices to their branches. To elicit customer reactions about the quality of service rendered, the system of holding customer meets at regular intervals at branches has been evolved. Some banks have formed customer service committees and customer councils. Banks have put up 'Complaints and Suggestions Boxes' at all branches which are dealt with promptly. Some of the banks have also introduced courier system to expedite collections, remittances and transfer of accounts of customers.

For expeditious and inexpensive settlement of customer complaints against deficiency in banking services, including non-observance of the RBI directives on loans and advances, etc. the Banking Ombudsman has been appointed on a full time basis each at Mumbai, New Delhi, Bhopal, Chandigarh, Hyderabad, Patna, Jaipur, etc. The scheme covers all scheduled commercial banks, except RRBs and PCBs.

3. MONEY MARKET REFORMS

Prior to the beginning of reforms in early 1990s, the Indian money market was dual in character being divided into organised and unorganised sectors. It had a limited number of participants, limited number of instruments, small geographical areas, shortage of capital, highly skewed call money market, undeveloped bill market, etc.[1] Moreover, it was a highly regulated market lacking in depth. In particular, interest rates on money market instruments were tightly regulated by the Government.

To remove these defects of the Indian money market and to develop it on sound lines, the RBI appointed Chakravarty Committee in 1985 and the Vighul Working Group in 1987. It was on the basis of their recommendations that the following measures have been taken to develop and deepen the money market.

(i) Introduction of Inter-bank Participations, Certificates of Deposits (CDs), Commercial Paper (CP) Repos, Reverse Repos and Inter-bank Repos; *(ii)* setting up the Discount and Finance House of India (DFHI); *(iii)* allowing commercial banks and public financial institutions to set up Money Market Mutual Funds (MMMFs) to provide greater liquidity and depth to the money market; *(iv)* total freeing of interest rates on call and notice money, inter-bank term money, rediscounting of commercial bills and on Inter-bank participation; and *(v)* lowering the bill discount rate to encourage the bill market.[2]

GOVERNMENT SECURITIES MARKET

Before the beginning of the reform era, the Government Securities and Treasury Bills market in India was under-developed and lacked in liquidity and depth. There were only 91-Day Treasury Bills in the Government securities market. They were a permanent source of Government funds. To keep the cost of Government borrowings low, the discount (or coupon) rates on them remained unchanged at 4.6% per annum, whereas the average lending rate had been much higher. Thus the coupon rate on them remained negative in real terms for several years. As a result of low coupon rates offered on Government securities to investors, the securities market did not attract much investment. Further, the RBI had little control over the volume and maturity structure of Government securities and the term structure of interest rates.

To remedy these defects and develop the Government securities market, the following measures have been adopted by the RBI since the middle of 1991.

(1) The maximum coupon rate on Central Government loans is fixed at near market rates at the time of issuing.

(2) A variety of Treasury Bills have been introduced such as 14-Day Treasury Bills, 91-Day Treasury Bills, 182-Day Treasury Bills, and 364-Day Treasury Bills. They are auctioned by DFHI.

(3) Some new instruments like conversion of auction Treasury Bills into term securities, Zero Coupon and Capital Indexed Bonds, Tap Stocks and Partly Paid Stocks have been introduced in the Government securities market.

(4) A system of primary dealers and satellite dealers has been esstablished to deal in Government securities.

(5) The practice of automatic monetisation of Central Government budget deficit through *ad hoc* Treasury Bills has been replaced by a new scheme of Ways and Means Advances.

(6) RBI has introduced a delivery *versus* payment (DVSP) system for transactions in Government securities in Mumbai. This system ensures settlement by simultaneously transfering securities with cash payments. This has reduced risk in settlement of securities transactions and prevention of diversion of funds.

(7) RBI has started providing liquidity support to those mutual funds which exclusively invest in Government securities.

(8) FIIs (foreign institutional investors) with 100% debt funds are allowed to invest in Government securities and Treasury Bills. Other FIIs are permitted to invest up to 30%.

(9) Banks are allowed to have minimum of 75% of their Government securities as current investments

---

1. For details refer to the chapter on Indian Money Market.
2. For details, refer to the section "Constituents of Indian Money Market" in the chapter on Indian Money Market.

effective March 31, 2000 which can be traded on a day-to-day basis.

(10) The interest income from Government securities has been exempted from tax.

(11) The primary subscription of RBI in Government securities has been mainly for carrying out its open market operations.

(12) As a result of the various measures undertaken to build and strengthen the Government Securities and Treasury Bills market, its investor base has expanded on a large scale in favour of short-term and medium-term borrowings. The number of participants in the primary market for Government Securities now include banks, insurance corporations, finance companies, mutual funds, FIIs, financial institutions and corporates.

(13) There is also a secondary market for Government Securities in which transactions take place through Subsidiary General Ledger (SGL) Accounts of the Reserve Bank.

4. CAPITAL MARKET REFORMS[3]

The Indian capital market, both in its primary and secondary segments, suffered from some serious defects prior to the beginning of reforms in 1991. The principal deficiencies in the primary market were vague prospectus containing little and often wrong information about the proposed financial position of the company, unfair pricing and premium fixing, high cost of new issues, etc. There was no regulatory authority to supervise new issues.

The secondary market had more serious problems. There were limited number of stock exchanges in the country. Consequently, there were mushrooming of unauthorised and unregistered stock exchanges which indulged in speculative practices and duped the shareholders. Recognised stock exchanges did not function satisfactorily. They were governed by their internal bye-laws framed by their governing bodies which operated under elected member-brokers. There was unusual delay in the delivery of shares and settlement (or payment) of transactions. There was excessive speculation and price fluctuation due to insider trading which adversely affected ordinary shareholders. The stock broking system was defective. Brokers manipulated prices and cheated the buyers and sellers of shares. There was no transparency in trading operations. Settlement cycles were often uncertain and long which led to frequent payment crisis and suspension of market activity. In post-made settlements, there were delayed settlements, bad deliveries, clubbing of settlements, loss of shares in transit, etc. There was inadequate protection to clients in case of default by sub-brokers and brokers.

Since 1992, the following policy measures have been undertaken to reform both the primary and secondary segments of the Indian capital market :

(1) SEBI was established as an autonomous and statutory body to regulate and oversee the new issues, protect the interests of investors, promote the orderly development of primary and secondary markets and regulate the working of stock exchanges. It has initiated a number of measures in these direction such as registration of intermediaries, strict disclosure norms, regulations on insider trading and inspection of the functioning of stock exchanges, etc.

(2) A company raising issue capital from the market is not required to have the consent of any authority, except following the guidelines of SEBI for disclosure and investor protection.

(3) Restrictions on rights and bonus issues have been removed.

(4) Interest rate on debentures has been freed.

(5) The primary market has been strengthened and diversified with mutual funds, merchants bankers, investment and consultancy agencies, registrar to the issue, etc.

(6) The primary capital market has been widened and deepened by permitting public sector banks, financial institutions and public sector enterprises to raise resources from the market through bonds and equity.

(7) On-line screen-based electronic trading has been started in all 23 stock exchanges of the country.

(8) Trading and settlement cycles have been reduced from 14 days to 7 days in all stock exchanges. All stock exchanges have established clearing houses.

---

3. For more details refers to the chapter on Indian Capital Market.

(9) In order to reduce counter-party risk, major stock exchanges have set up Trade Settlement Guarantee Funds, while the NSE has a separate clearing corporation.

(10) Insider trading has been completely stopped and is a criminal offence.

(11) FIIs (foreign institutional investors) such as mutual funds, pension funds, etc. have been permitted to invest and operate in the indian capital market. They now invest in equity shares, debentures, Government Securities and Treasury Bills.

(12) There has been globalisation of Indian equity by Indian companies through the issue of Global Depository Receipts (GDRs), American Depository Receipts (ADRs), Foreign Currency Convertible Bonds (FCCBs), etc. Shares of Indian companies are being traded at New York and London Stock Exchanges.

(13) To protect the investors and to encourage FIIs to participate in the Indian Capital Market, dematerialisation of shares through depositories and their transfer through electronic book entry have been in progress.

(14) Companies have been permitted to buy back their own shares provided the buy-back does not exceed 25% of the paid-up capital.

(15) All institutions and agencies related to the Indian Capital market such as stock exchanges, stock brokers, sub-brokers, mutual funds, intermediaries, share transfer agents, merchant bankers, portfolio managers, underwriters, debenture trustees, bankers to an issue, custodians of securities, venture capital funds etc. have been brought under SEBI regulations.

EXERCISES

1. Explain briefly the financial reforms undertaken in India since 1990s.
2. Discuss the problems of Indian financial sector. Suggest measures to reform it.
   [**Hint**: Problems have been discussed in the beginning of each sector. For suggestions, refer to suggestions for Improvement at the end of chapters on Indian Money Market and Indian Capital Market.]

CHAPTER 73

Role and Achievements of SEBI

The Securities and Exchange Board of India (SEBI) was established in 1992 as an autonomous and statutory authority for the working of capital market in India. It regulates the issue of new shares, debentures and bonds, protects the interests of investors, promotes the development of the capital market and regulates the working of stock exchanges. It has been trying to develop a modern, efficient, transparent, fair and safe, and investor-friendly capital market[1] in the following ways:

Primary Market Reforms

SEBI has successfully taken up primary market reforms in order to remove the inadequacies and deficiencies in the issue procedures of new shares and debentures. There is now transparency in fixing price and premium of a share. Issuing companies are required to disclose all material facts and risk factors in the prospectus.

Secondary Market Reforms

To bring *efficiency* in the working of the secondary market, SEBI has laid down specific rules and regulations for intermediaries in the secondary market. Such intermediaries are merchant bankers, portfolio managers, underwriters, registrars, brokers and sub-brokers, and share transfer agents. They are required to adhere to specific capital adequacy norms, meet certain eligibility criteria and follow a code of conduct towards investors. They are penalised by SEBI in case of default.

Help in Institutional and Market Development

SEBI has helped in the process of institutional and market development in the secondary market. It approves 'market makers' on the recommendations of stock exchanges. By dealing in scrips, market makers impart liquidity in them and reduce volatile movements in share prices.

SEBI has encouraged the participation of foreign institutional investors (FIIs) in the Indian capital market. It has simplified the procedure for their registration and operation in the stock exchanges. FIIs have been permitted to repatriate capital, capital gains, dividends and interest on shares and debentures.

SEBI issues guidelines to various stock exchanges including the National Stock Exchange of India (NSEI) for their efficient operation in order to improve their working and make them safe and friendly for investors.

Regulating Working of Institutions

SEBI regulates the working of such institutions as mutual funds, money market mutual funds, merchant bankers, portfolio managers, etc. By regulating their working, SEBI has tried to improve the working of

1. For the features and defects of the Indian capital market, refer to the chapter on *The Indian Capital Market.*

primary and secondary capital markets in India,

Modernisation of Stock Exchanges

SEBI has modernised the entire operations of stock exchanges in India. All stock exchanges are computerised. The stock market trading is 100% computerised and is on-line. In many developed countries of the world, including America and Japan, the trading is not fully computerised and a large part of their trade is still on-the-floor. This is a big achievement of SEBI. The introduction of electronic trading in all the 23 stock exchanges has reduced transaction costs.

Dematerialisation of Shares

The Government introduced the depository system in 1996 by establishing the National Securities Depository Ltd. (NSDL) and a number of depository participants. The aim was to start "paperless" transactions in stock exchanges. But its progress had been slow. So SEBI introduced an element of compulsion by. making dematerialisation of shares compulsory for trading. This has been done in phases for shares being traded daily on a large scale. At present more than 50% of the trade in stock exchanges is in the demat form. Dematerialisation of shares has encouraged trading especially by FIIs because it removes the fear of fake or forged shares and bad deliveries. It has also eliminated transfer problems.

Internet Trading

SEBI has allowed internet trading under Order Routing System (ORS) through registered stock brokers on behalf of clients. It has thus facilitated investors to buy and sell shares through the internet on their computers. It is a major advancement in trading shares at stock exchanges in India.

Derivatives Trading

With the introduction of derivatives trading in securities, the secondary market has been modernised. There is the cash market, the forward market and the *badla* system.

Solving Investors' Complaints

SEBI has set up a separate cell where complaints received from the investors are attended to. According to SEBI, more than 2 lakh investors complain against companies every year regarding transfers, non-receipt of share certificates, dividend, interest on debentures, etc. It is able to solve about 90% of them. SEBI hopes to remove such complaints with more shares coming under the demat form.

Safety Measures

SEBI has adopted a number of measures to safeguard the interests of investors. Companies have been directed to call for the bank account number of a share/debenture holder and mention it on the dividend/interest certificate or deposit it direct in his bank account. It has guided stock exchanges in setting up Investor Protection Fund and Trade Guarantee Fund to safeguard the interests of investors. Further, it has set up the Clearing Corporation for Trade Settlements.

Further, it has made it obligatory for the broker to make the payment within 21 days even if there is a bad delivery. Thus an investor cannot lose his money.

Circuit-Breaker System

SEBI has introduced a circuit-breaker system based on the market volatility of individual stocks. According to this system, if market volatility in a stock crosses a certain limit, the trading in this stock is stopped for a few days so that speculators may not take undue advantage. This is a better system than the American circuit-breaker system which is related to the index of stocks. The New York Stock Exchange is closed even for half-an-hour or more whenever the market volatility crosses the index limit. Thus SEBI has developed a better circuit-breaker system whereby there is no need to close the stock exchange.

CONCLUSION

Besides introducing primary market reforms, SEBI has undertaken several measures to promote efficiency and investor protection, increasing investor interest and confidence in the secondary market. Some of these measures include demat, derivatives, insider trading, market making, electronic trading and order matching system, rolling settlement in selected scrips, internet trading, etc. Thus SEBI has introduced new instruments and efficient settlement mechanism, strengthened the institutional infrastructure, widened the participant base, and improved transparency in operations.

EXERCISES

1. Explain the role and achievements of Securities and Exchange Board of India in improving capital market in India.
2. What are the defects of the Indian capital market? How has SEBI removed them?
3. Write a note on SEBI.

CHAPTER 74

Mutual Funds in India

1. ROLE OF MUTUAL FUNDS

Mutual Funds are financial intermediaries which collect the savings of investors and invest them in primary and secondary securities, like money market instruments, corporate and government bonds, and equity shares of joint stock companies. They have emerged as rivals to banks in savings mobilisation because banking services could not show extra-ordinary efforts to employ household savings in remunerative sectors. Individual investors have developed keen interest in the capital market, attaining higher returns and capital gains alongwith fiscal concessions. Since small investors generally do not have sufficient time, knowledge, experience and resources for directly approaching the capital market, they have to rely on an intermediary which undertakes informed investment decisions and provides the benefits of professional expertise. This is what a mutual fund does. Investors achieve important advantages from mutual funds such as expert professional management, reduction in risk, diversified portfolios, liquidity of investment, tax benefits and economies of scale. The interests of the investors are protected by SEBI. Mutual funds are governed by SEBI. SEBI has the authority to issue guidelines and to supervise and regulate the working of mutual funds through Mutual Funds Regulations, 1993 have been amended from time to time. Mutual funds provide stability arid sustainability to the stock market also.

Mutual funds in India provide linkage among various financial institutions operating in the money and capital markets with which the household and corporate sectors are closely linked. They mobilise personal savings and enable small and medium investors to reap benefits of their investments. The corporate sector benefits by investing these investments for its production and growth. Therefore, mutual funds have been playing a crucial role in India's economic growth by mobilising and allocating savings and investments.

2. OBJECTIVES

The main investment objectives of mutual funds are :

1. *Growth.* They aim at large capital gains. Generally, they cover the highest risk.

2. *Growth-Income.* Mutual funds strive for both dividend income and capital gains from common shares and bonds. They cover intermediate risk.

3. *Balanced Income.* They hold a portfolio of diversified and common stocks, preferred stocks and bonds with the objectives of realising capital gains, dividend and interest income. For these, they invest in high interest and high dividend yielding securities which covers the lowest risk.

3. BENEFITS OF MUTUAL FUNDS

Mutual funds have the following merits :

1. *Reduction in Risk.* Mutual funds offer reduced risk and diversified investment. They help small investors

in reducing risk through diversification, economies of scale in transaction cost and professional portfolio management.

2. *Tax Benefits.* Mutual funds, authorised by the SEBI are exempted from tax, under Section 10 (23D) of IT Act, provided they distribute 90% of their profits.

3. *Expert Professional Management.* Small investors generally do not have sufficient time, knowledge and experience for directly approaching the capital market. Mutual funds supply professional expertise in stock selection and timely purchase and sale of securities to investors. In this way, they generate higher returns from them.

4. *Liquidity of Investment.* The units of mutual funds can be converted to cash without any delay. Thus they relieve investors from various rules and regulations.

5. *Economies of Scale.* Investors achieve economies of scale by aggregating their assets through mutual funds.

6. *Diversified Portfolio.* Mutual funds offer the opportunity of diversified investment, thereby reducing risk. They also offer rotating type of investments. Automatic re-investment of dividends and capital gains provide tax relief to the unit holders.

4. SCHEMES OF MUTUAL FUNDS

Mutual funds can float different schemes with the prior approval of SEBI. They are allowed both close-end and open-end schemes.

Close-end Schemes. It has the following characteristics.

(1) The shares of a closed-end scheme cannot be sold after initial offering by the mutual fund.

(2) For obtaining corporate securities they are channelised into the secondary market.

(3) The shares are not redeemable at their Net Asset Value (NAV). Further, these shares are traded in the secondary market on a stock exchange at market prices, that may be higher or lower than their NAV.

(4) The price of close-end shares is determined by demand and supply.

Open-end Scheme. The main features of an open-end scheme are as follows :

(1) The shares of an open-end mutual fund can be sold continuously.

(2) The shares of these funds are redeemable at their NAV.

(3) They sell their shares to the investing public, whenever, they can, at their net asset value per share and become ready to repurchase the same. Hence these funds do not have a fixed capitalisation.

(4) The prices of open-end mutual fund shares are determined by NAV.

In India, mutual funds simultaneously operate close-end and open-end schemes. But in recent years the emphasis has shifted from close-end to open-end schemes based on their NAVs.

The schemes of mutual funds can be further, classified into growth funds, income funds, equity funds, real estate funds, leveraged funds, hedge funds and off-share funds which are listed on the stock exchanges for dealings in the secondary market. Besides, sector funds like information technology funds, Pharmaceuticals funds, fast moving consumer goods funds are operating in India.

5. RETURN FROM MUTUAL FUNDS

Unit holders of mutual funds obtain return in the form of dividends, capital gains and evaluation of the value of NAV. NAV is the market value of one unit of the scheme. Suppose NAV is more than the face value, it means that the unit has appreciated and *vice versa.* Mutual funds sell their units in their various schemes to the public at face value and redeem them at current NAV.

NAV is calculated in the following manner.

$$\text{NAV of MF} = \frac{\text{Total Market Value of All MF Holdings} - \text{All Liabilities}}{\text{Number of Units}}$$

Thus the NAV of a mutual fund scheme is the per unit market value of all the assets of the scheme.

6. GROWTH AND FUNCTIONING OF MUTUAL FUNDS IN INDIA

The first mutual fund in India is the Unit Trust of India which was set up in 1964 under an Act of Parliament. It was to encourage and mobilise small savings of small investors through the sale of 'units' and to channelise them into corporate securities. The first scheme of the UTI was-Unit Scheme 1964 which is known as US-64. In 1986, the Government allowed the State Bank of India and other commercial banks to set up mutual funds. Accordingly, seven new mutual funds were established between 1987-92 by public sector banks and one each by LIC and GIC in 1987.

There being no regulatory framework for mutual funds, these funds were being managed by the respective managements in their own ways. The first guidelines for mutual funds were issued by the Reserve Bank of India (RBI) on 5 July, 1989 and by the Government of India on 28 June, 1990. But these guidelines had no co-ordination.

Since there were no penal provisions in them, they were ineffective in regulating the mutual funds. There was no transparency in the operations of mutual funds, fairness in their dealings and healthy competition among them. Consequently, the Government issued comprehensive guidelines on 14 February, 1992 which superseded all the earlier guidelines. Subsequent investigations on the working of mutual funds by the Securities and Exchange Board of India (SEBI) found serious irregularities. In order to avoid them and to protect the interest of investors, the regulation of mutual funds has been brought under SEBI (Mutual Funds) Regulations, 1993.

Under the SEBI Regulations for Mutual Funds, the mutual funds have been permitted to invest only in transferable securities in the money and capital markets or any privately placed debentures or securities debt. The regulations indicate that investments under an individual scheme do not exceed 5% and investment in all the schemes in the aggregate does not exceed 10% of the total. Investments in all the schemes do not exceed 15% of the funds in the shares and debentures of a single company.

Mutual funds are required to be formed as trusts and managed by saparately formed Asset Management Companies (AMC). The minimum net worth of such AMC is stipulated at Rs. 5 crores of which, the minimum contribution of the sponsor must be 40%. A close-ended scheme should have Rs. 20 crores as minimum amount and for open-ended scheme it should be Rs. 50 crores. Mutual funds have to publish scheme-wise annual reports, furnish six-monthly unaudited accounts, quarterly statements of the movemens of the NAV and quarterly portfolio statements to the SEBI. SEBI is authorised to appoint an auditor to investigate into the books of accounts or the working of mutual funds. It can also suspend the registration of mutual funds when they are found guilty of deliberate manipulation, price rigging or deterioration of the financial position.

Replacing the Regulations of 1993, SEBI announced new mutual fund regulations in December 1996. According to the new regulations mutual funds have been permitted to launch specialized schemes in real estate, property, money market instruments and various debt instruments. SEBI determines some investment valuation norms and accounting practices for the mutual fund schemes. Mutual funds have been made more attractive to investors. Minimum lock-in period has been reduced from 46 days to 30 days. In 1997, SEBI permitted mutual funds to mention indicative returns for regular income schemes with payment capacity. The RBI also allowed SEBI registered mutual funds to invest in the overseas markets initially within an overall limit of US $ 500 million and a ceiling for individual fund at US $ 50 million. They are allowed to invest in rated corporate bonds and debentures with a residual maturity of upto one year.

The SEBI (Mutual Funds) Regulations, 1996 were amended in 1998. The new regulations bar mutual funds from investing in unlisted or privately placed securities by associate or group companies of the sponsors. A limit of 25% of the NAV of the fund has been imposed on their investment in listed securities of the group companies of the sponsers. Mutual funds are required to fully disclose their portfolio in annual reports. Independent trustees are required to constitute two-thirds of the trustee Board. All open-ended schemes, including unit scheme 64 would declare their NAV on a daily basis.

The Government initiated several policy measures for mutual funds in the 1999-2000 Budget. It announced exemption from income-tax of all incomes earned through mutual funds. The Monetary and Credit policy,

1999-2000 allowed mutual funds to offer cheque writing facility to the investors through a commercial bank.

As on March 31, 1999, the total number of mutual funds (excluding UTI) registered with SEBI was 40. Net resource mobilisation by mutual funds from 1981-82 to 1991-92 grew at an average rate of 71%. This was due to buyont secondary market, setting up of new mutual funds, new schemes introduced by them and high rate of return. Net resource mobilisation by MFs in 1992-93 was Rs. 11,275 crores, the highest so far which became Rs. (-) 5, 833 crores in 1995-96, Rs. (-) 2,037 crores in 1996-97, increased to Rs. 4,064 crores in 1997-98 and declined to Rs. 2695 crores in 1998-99. The decline between 1995-97 was due to depressed market conditions while the decline during 1998-99 was the result of redemption faced by UTI relating to US-64. Since then the MF mobilisation had been on the decline. It was Rs 4,520 crores in 2002-03.

7. MONEY MARKET MUTUAL FUNDS—MMMF

After the considerable success of mutual funds in India, RBI announced a scheme for a new type of mutual funds, called Money Market Mutual Funds (MMMF) by scheduled commercial banks and public financial institutions on April 12,1992. MMMF refers to a scheme of mutual funds which has been set up with the objective of investing exclusively in the money market instruments with a maturity of less than a year. They provided additional short-term avenue to investors and bring high-quality money market instruments within the reach of individuals and small orgnisations. They ensure high liquidity, sufficient surety and high returns.

The guidelines regulating MMMFs issued by RBI in April 1992 were subsequently relaxed between November 1995 and July 1996 to make the scheme more flexible and to provide .greater liquidity.

Scheduled commercial banks, public financial institutions or their mutual funds/subsidiaries and private sector mutual funds are permitted to set up MMMF. An MMMF could be set up as a division or department of a bank or as a "Trust". At present, MMMFs have come under the purview of the SEBI regulations and they are allowed to be set up as a separate entity in the form of a 'Trust' only.

The units or shares of MMMFs can be issued only to individuals both resident and non-resident Indians. In the case of the latter, only dividends/income is allowed to be repatriated and not the principal amount.

The minimum lock-in period for units of MMMFs has been reduced from 30 to 15 days effective May 1998. They have been allowed cheque writing facility to provide more liquidity to unit holders under a tie-up arrangement with a bonk. The resources mobilised by MMMFs are invested in such money market instruments as Treasury Bills and dated Government Securities upto 1 year, call and notice money, commercial paper, accepted or co-accepted commercial bills by banks and certificates of deposit. Since October 1997, they have been permitted by RBI to invest in rated corporate bonds and debentures with a residual maturity of one year.

MMMFs have not made any progress in India. Initially, there were 8 MMMFs but currently only three funds are operational. The difference between MMMF and existing mutual funds is with regard to their investment portfolios. MMMFs continuously invest their resources in high quality money market instruments. On the other hand, a mutual fund adequately invests in capital market securities and keeps its surplus funds in money market instruments for short term.

EXERCISES

1. Give a critical account of the growth and functioning of Mutual Funds in India.
2. Write notes on Money Market Mutual Funds, Open-end and Close-end Mutual Funds.
3. What are Mutual Funds? Explain why people invest in them?
4. Briefly explain the growth and functioning of Mutual Funds in India. What is their role in economic development of India?

CHAPTER 75

Merchant Banking in India

1. INTRODUCTION

Merchant banks are different from commercial banks. Commercial banks receive deposits from and make payments to private individuals, companies and other organisations. They advance short-term and long-term loans to the latter. They provide a number of other services to their customers such as trustee and executor facilities, credit transfer, credit card, supply of foreign exchange, agency services, etc. On the other hand, merchant banks (known as investment banks in the U.S.) are secondary banks which specialise in a variety of activities such as financing trade, providing hire purchase, industrial finance, underwriting new issues, advising and arranging finance for mergers and takeovers, managing investments for institutions, management of non-resident investments etc.

The institution of merchant banking started in Britain where the merchant bankers were merchants engaged in financing foreign trade by accepting bill of exchange. They also carried out other banking services relating to foreign trade like dealing in gold, foreign currency and helping foreign borrowers to raise money in the London money market. Since the beginning of the 20th century, they have expanded their functions to include advising firms on mergers, takeovers and other financial matters. They are active in the market for Eurocurrency and deal in hire-purchase and bullion. They also perform the functions of administration, promotion and distribution of securities and guarantee the issuer companies of certain price.

2. GROWTH AND WORKING OF MERCHANT BANKING IN INDIA

In India before the advent of commercial banking, the indigenous bankers were performing the functions of merchant bankers. They provided finance and remittance facilities to traders and small industrialists by advancing loans; writing, buying and selling *hundis;* writing finance bills, and trade bills. They helped in financing internal trade.

Now merchant banking includes such services as management of public issues, loan syndication, financial and management consultancy, project counselling, mergers and acquisitions, management of non-resident investments, etc. The credit for starting merchant banking in India goes to foreign banks like Grindlays Bank, Citibank, etc. At present, a number of public sector banks are performing merchant banking services which are the subsidiaries of banks. There are also private financial service companies, all India financial institutions like ICICI, IDBI, etc., private banking companies, foreign banking companies, and technical consultancy organisations which provide commercial banking services. Some of these are SBI Capital Markets Ltd., Bank of Baroda Merchant Bank Division, Canbank Financial Services Ltd. Allahabad Bank Finance Ltd., BOI Finance Ltd., DSP Financial Consultants, J.M. Financial and Investment Services Ltd., etc.

FUNCTIONS

Merchant banks in India perform the following functions:

1. *Managing Capital Issues.* Merchant banks manage new issues of companies by providing the following services :

(i) working out the capital structure;
(ii) drafting the prospectus;
(iii) obtaining permission of SEBI;
(iv) getting approval of stock exchanges;
(v) arranging participation of institutions in the share capital of the company through private arid market placement;
(vi) arranging underwriting of the issue from brokers, banks and financial institutions;
(vii) selecting managers, brokers, issue houses and bankers to the issue;
(viii) acting as managers to the issue themselves;
(ix) undertaking the publicity of the issue;
(x) receiving applications for shares and debentures, their allotment, collection of money and sending them to subscribers or informing the shareholders and depositories about them.

2. *Advice on New Industrial Units.* They render advice to firms for setting up new industrial units relating to their location, technical collaborations, selecting appropriate technologies, financing, tax planning, obtaining approvals of governments, etc.

3. *Project Formulation.* They help companies in formulating their projects by preparing preinvestment projects, project reports, and making market surveys, etc.

4. *Loan Syndication.* They help companies in loan syndication by arranging finance from banks and financial institutions. For this, merchant banks prepare applications for submission to banks and financial institutions; undertake negotiations for sanction of loan facilities; collaborate with banks for working capital facilities, tie-up for consortium arrangements with financial institutions; and help in completing loan documents.

5. *Trustees.* Merchant banks act as trustees of debenture holders when companies issue secured debentures. They arrange for their rating from the credit rating agencies to protect the interests of the debenture holders.

6. *Restructuring and Mergers.* They render advice, formulate schemes and prepare documents on restructuring, mergers, amalgamations and takeovers of companies. They also help in obtaining approvals of concerned persons and authorities.

7. *Portfolio Management.* Merchant banks manage the portfolios of companies by selling and purchasing their securities. They also provide them market intelligence and advisory services.

8. *Equipment Leasing.* They help companies by procuring equipment and leasing it to companies.

9. *Sick Industrial Units.* They help in rehabilitating sick industrial units. For this, they conduct studies, prepare reports for rehabilitation and arrange financial assistance from banks and financial institutions. As a last resort, they help in preparing a report for submission to the Board for Industrial and Financial Reconstruction (BIFR).

10. *Advice to Non-Resident Indians.* Merchant banks help non-resident Indians (NRIs) who want to set up industrial units in India in the following ways: by rendering advice on projects, locations, investment opportunities, collaborations, managing capital issue, portfolio management, etc.

WORKING

Merchant banks in India are regulated by SEBI (Merchant Bankers) Regulations, 1992. They are required to register with SEBI for doing business. The SEBI regulations relating to merchant bankers were amended in 1996 and 1997 in order to bring structural changes in merchant banking activities. The earlier four-fold categorisation of merchant bankers on the basis of different eligibility criteria was abolished.[1] They have been

1. Upto September 8, 1997 there were minimum four categories : I. with a minimum net worth of Rs. 5 crore; II. of Rs. 50 lakh, III. of Rs. 25 lakh and IV. nil.

replaced by one entity of merchant banker with a minimum net worth of Rs. 5 crore. Only one body corporate is allowed to function as a merchant banker. The merchant banker is permitted to perform underwriting activity but is required to seek separate registration to function as a Portfolio Manager under the SEBI (Portfolio Manager) Rules and Regulations, 1993. At present, merchant bankers are prohibited to carry on fund based activities other than those related exclusively to the capital market. The activities undertaken by NBFCs (Non-Banking Financial Companies) such as accepting deposits, leasing, bill discounting, etc. are not allowed to be undertaken by a merchant banker. Further, NBFCs operating as merchant bankers are required to separate their capital market related activities from their NBFCs activities. Distant relationship has also been introduced between an issue and the registrar to issue.

3. DEFECTS AND REMEDIES OF MERCHANT BANKING

There was a mushroom growth of merchant bankers in India prior to the SEBI (Merchant Bankers) Regulations Amendment, 1997. Merchant bankers were engaged in fraudulent and unfair trade practices. There was no transparency in the public offer document of new issues. They made misleading statements to induce the sale of shares and debentures. They connived with the issuer company in floating bad issues and were involved in price rigging. In fact, they did not have experts to manage new issues.

SEBI has removed all the defects in the working of merchant bankers by amending its regulations in 1997. The disclosure requirements in offer documents have been made more transparent. Every prospectus is submitted to SEBI for approval before the public issue is made. The size of issue, its firm allotment to different categories, means and sources of financing, year-wise break-up of proposed project expenditure, profit/loss statement, management perception of internal and external risk factors, mandatory underwriting by a merchant banker, etc. have been introduced. Thus, SEBI has tried to remove the defects of merchant bankers through strict regulation. As a result, there are a few merchant bankers which are operating successfully in the capital market.

EXERCISES

1. Distinguish between a commercial banker and a merchant banker. Briefly explain the working of merchant bankers in India.
2. What is merchant banking? What functions a merchant banker performs?
3. Explain the growth and working of merchant banking in India.

Bibliography

Ackley, G., *Macroeconomics*, 1978.
Aschheim, J., *Techniques of Monetary Control*, 1961.
Bain, A.D., The *Control of Money Supply*, 1980.
Barro R.J. and Grossman, H.I., *Money, Employment and Inflation*, 1976.
Basu, A.K. and Ghosh, A., *A Review of Current Banking Theory and Practice*, *2/e*, 1974.
———, *Fundamentals of Banking Theory and Practice*, 1982.
Berger, H., *Money, Banking and Public Policy*, 1970.
Bober, S., *The Economics of Cycles and Growth*, 1968.
Brroman, F:S., *Macroeconomics*, *Alt*, 1970.
Burger, A.E., *The Money Supply Process*, 1971.
Burnstein, M.L, *Money*, 1963.
Burrows, P. and Hilris, T., *Macroeconomic Theory*, 1974.
Campbell, C. and Campbell, R., *An Introduction to Money and Banking*, 3/e, 1978.
Caster, H. and Partington, I., *Applied Economics in Banking and Finance*, 1979.
Cary Brown, E., et al. (eds.), *Stabilisation Policies*, 1963.
Carson, D. (ed.), *Banking and Monetary Studies*, 1963.
Chandler, L.V. and Goldfeld, S.M., *The Economics of Money and Banking*, *7/e*, 1977.
———, *Central Banking and Economic Development*, 1962.
Chick, V., *The Theory of Monetary Policy*, 1977.
Clower, R.W. (ed.), *Monetary Theory*, 1969.
Cochran, J.A., *Money, Banking and the Economy*, 3/e, 1975.
Cramp, A.B., *Monetary Management*, 1971.
Croome, I., *Introduction to Money*, 1956.
Crowther, G., *An Outline of Money*, rev. ed., 1958.
Culbertson, J.M., *Money and Banking*, 1972.
Davidson, P., *Money and the Real World*, *lit*, 1978.
Day, A.C.L., *An Outline of Monetary Economics*, 1960.
Dernberg, T.F. and McDougall, D.M., *Macroeconomics*, 5/e, 1977.
DeCock, M.H., *Central Banking*, 3/e, 1956.
Dennis, G.E.C., *Monetary Economics*, 1981.
Dow, A.C., *Monetarism and Inflation*, 1980.
Dow, S.C. and Earl, P.E., *Money Matters*, 1982.

Drake, P.J., *Money, Finance and Development*, 1980.

Fisher, D., *Monetary Policy*, 1976.

———, *Monetary Theory^and the Demand for Money*, 1980.

Frazer, W.J. and William, P.Y., *Analytics and Institutions of Money and Banking*, 1966.

Frenkel, J.A. and Johnson, H.G. (edS.), *The Monetary Approach to the Balance of Payments*, 1976.

Friedman, M., *Employment, Growth and Price Level, 1959.*

———, *Studies in the Quantity Theory of Money*, 1956.

———, *A Monetary History of the United States*, 1870-1960, 1963.

———, *The Counter Revolution in Monetary Theory*, 1970.

———, *The Optimum Quantity Theory of Money and Other Essays*, 1969.

Galbraith, J.K., *Money: Whence it Came, Where it Went*, 1975.

Ghatak, S., *Monetary Economics in Developing Countries*, 1981

Ghosh, A., *Financial Intermediaries and Monetary Policy in a Developing Country*, 1964.

Gibson, W.E. and Kaufman, G.G., *Monetary Economics*, 1971.

Goldsmith, R.W., *Financial Structure and Development*, 1969.

Goodhart, C.A.E., *Money, Information and Uncertainty*, 1975

Gordon, R.J., *Macroeconomics*, 1979.

Gurley, G.J. and Shaw, S.E., *Money in a Theory of Finance*, 1960.

Halm, G.N., *Economics of Money and Banking*, 1965.

———, *Monetary Theory*, 1964.

Hansen, B., *The Theory of Inflation*, 1951.

Hanson, J.L., *Monetary Theory and Practice*, 4/e, 1970

Harris, C.L., *Money and Banking*, 1961

Havrilesky, T., *Money in the Economy*, 1972

Hayek, F.A., *A Tiger by the Tail: The Keynesian Legacy of Inflation*, 1972.

Hicks, J.R., *The Crisis in Keynesian Economics*, 1974.

Hodgman, D.R., *Commercial Bank Loan and Investment Policy*, 1963.

Johnson, H.G., *Essays in Monetary Theory*, 2/e,, 1969.

———, *Inflation and Monetary Controversy*, 1972.

———, *Macroeconomics and Monetary Theory*, 1970.

———, (ed.) *Issues in Monetary Economics*, 1974.

———, *Selected Essays in Monetary Economics*, 1978.

Kent, R.P., *Money and Banking*, 4/e, 1961.

Kessels, R.H., *The Cyclical Behaviour of the Terms Structure of Interest Rates*, 1965.

Keynes, J.M., *A Trade on Monetary Reforms*, 1923.

———, *A Treatise on Money*, 1930.

———, *The General Theory of Employment, Interest and Money*, 1936.

Klise, E.S., *Money and Banking*, 3/e, 1964.

Kurihara, K.K., *Monetary Theory and Public Policy*, 1970.

Laidler, D.E.W., *Essays on Money and Inflation*, 1975.

———, *The Demand for Money*, 1977.

Makinen, G.E., *Money, the Price Level and Interest Rates*, 1977.

Moore, B.J., *An Introduction to the Theory* of Finance, 1978

Mueller, M.G. (ed.), *Readings in Macroeconomics, 2/e*, 1971.

Nadler, P.S., *Commercial Banking in the Economy*, 1979.

Newlyn, W.T. and Bootle, R.P., *Theory of Money, 3/e*, 1978.

Nichans, J., *The Theory of Money*, 1978.

O'hara, J.L., *Money and Banking*, 1948.

Patinkin, Don, *Money, Interest and Prices, 2/e, 1965.*

———, *Studies in Monetary Economics*, 1972.

Pearce, G.D. and Shaw, M.D., *Monetary Economics*, 1977.

Pesk, B.P. and Saving, T.R., *Money, Wealth and Economic Theory*, 1967

———, *The Foundations of Money and Banking*, 1968.

Prather, C.L., *Money and Banking*, 1961.

Radcliffe, *Report of the Committee on the Working of the Monetary System*, 1959.

Ranlett, J.G., *Money and Banking*, 1965.

Ritter, S.L., *Principles of Money, Banking and Financial Markets, 2/e.*, 1977.

———, and Silber, W.L., *Money*, 1970.

Robertson, D.H., *Economic Commentaries*, 1956.

———, *Money*, 1959.

Robinson, R.S., *The Management of Banks Fund*, 2/e, 1962.

Rousseas, S., *Monetary Theory*, 1972.

Sayers, R.S., *Central Banking after Bagehot*, 1957.

———, *Modern Banking, 7/e*, 1967.

Sen, S.N., *Central Banking in Underdeveloped Markets*, 1961.

Shapiro, E., Solomon, E. and White, W.L., *Money and Banking*, 1968.

Smith, P.F., *Economics of Financial Institutions and Markets*, 1971.

Smith, W.L. and Teigen, R.L. (eds.), *Readings in Money, National Income and Stabilisation Policy*, 2/e, 1974.

Surrey, M.J.C., (ed.), *Macroeconomic Themes*, 1976.

Thomas, G., *Our Modern Banking and Monetary System*, 1964.

Thorn, S.R., *Introductions to Money and Banking*, 1976.

Timberlake, R.H., *Money, Banking and Central Banking*, 1965.

Wai, U.T., *Financial Intermediates and National Savings in a Developing Country*, 1972.

Weintraub, R., *Introduction to Monetary Economics*, 1970.

Whittlesey, C.R., *Principles and Practices of Money and Banking*, 1954.

Wrightsman, D., *An Introduction to Monetary Theory and Policy*, 1971.

Indian Banking.
Economic and Political Weekly.
Economic Times.
Financial Express.
Reserve Bank of India Bulletin.
Reserve Bank of India Occasional Papers.
RBI, *Annual Report*, 1991-92 & 1992-93.
RBI, *Report on Trend and Progress of Baulking in India*, 1991-92.
RBI, *Report on Currency and Finance*, 1991-92 & 1992-93.

Index

A

B

G

N

Q

R